Contents

France

Spain

Portugal

Italy

CampingCard ACSI 2018

This year you can take advantage of large discounts at no fewer than
3,330 campsites in 21 countries.

Also of interest:

Find a campsite quickly on:
www.CAMPINGCARD.com.
See page **33**.

You can always have campsite
information to hand, even without an
internet connection, with the
CampingCard ACSI app.
See page **26**.

Book your spot online, directly with the
campsite. See page **22**.

You will find your discount card
in part 2.

19	in	Norway
33	in	Sweden
62	in	Denmark
391	in	The Netherlands
53	in	Belgium
26	in	Luxembourg
332	in	Germany
40	in	Switzerland
90	in	Austria
4	in	Poland
13	in	The Czech Republic
11	in	Hungary
20	in	Slovenia
76	in	Croatia
39	in	Greece
42	in	The United Kingdom
12	in	Ireland
1,464	in	France
271	in	Spain
22	in	Portugal
310	in	Italy

Check
www.CAMPINGCARD.com/modifications
before you leave for the most up to date information.

Validity of CampingCard ACSI

The CampingCard ACSI card is valid for one calendar year and is non-transferable. We ask you therefore to complete the back of the card in full and sign it. A campsite has the right to ask you for additional identification.

The information in this guide applies specifically to 2018. Each year new campsites join, other sites change the period in which the discount card is accepted or their rates. The details in this guide are therefore updated annually. Check www.CAMPINGCARD.com/modifications for the most up to date information. If you use the CampingCard ACSI app, the campsite information in this app is updated multiple times a year.

Take note! Only campsites which appear in this guide display the blue CC logo, and you will only get a discount on your overnight stay with your CampingCard ACSI discount card at these sites. See also 'Only campsites with the CC logo' on page 9.

Please also note that expired discount cards will not be accepted at campsites.

Visit: **www.CAMPINGCARD.com**

VALDERROBRES ★   R 🚢 C7   48   N40°52.429' E000°09.364'   44580

➡️ Calle Elvira Hidalgo. From Arnes follow A-231 east into Valderrobres. Turn left, sp 'Alcañiz', and cross river bridge; the Aire is visible on right. Turn 1st right into Calle Elvira Hidalgo, then 1st right again into riverside car park, signed.

🚐 20; Max 48hrs   🛡️ Custom

ℹ️ Large, open Aire in riverside car park with views of town. Parking shared with cars and HGVs, but suitable for any unit configuration. Popular with Spanish motorhomers at weekends. Town commerce 200m via medieval bridge. Fortified castle, 500m, open Fri-Sun in winter and Tues-Sun in summer; €5pp. http://castillodevalderrobres.com Els Ports nature park adj with numerous walking/cycling trails. A-231 is a pleasant drive. www.valderrobres.es Reinspected 2017.

All The Aires Spain And Portugal entry above. All The Aires France map below.

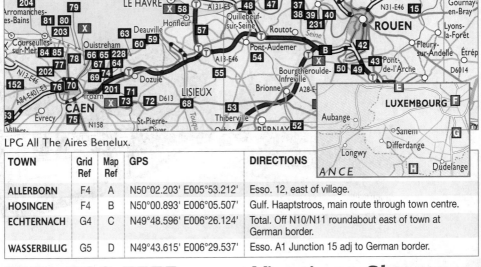

LPG All The Aires Benelux.

TOWN	Grid Ref	Map Ref	GPS	DIRECTIONS
ALLERBORN	F4	A	N50°02.203' E005°53.212'	Esso. 12, east of village.
HOSINGEN	F4	B	N50°00.893' E006°05.507'	Gulf. Haaptstroos, main route through town centre.
ECHTERNACH	G4	C	N49°48.596' E006°26.124'	Total. Off N10/N11 roundabout east of town at German border.
WASSERBILLIG	G5	D	N49°43.615' E006°29.537'	Esso. A1 Junction 15 adj to German border.

0131 208 3333   www.Vicarious-Shop.com

The history of ACSI

No more closed barriers

Teacher Ed van Reine set off with his family in the summer of 1965. The fervent camper steered his car towards the Spanish sun in good spirits. However the journey ended in disappointment as there was no room for the family at the campsite they had so carefully selected. Situations such as this could surely be prevented? Van Reine brainstormed on the spot with two teacher colleagues about a reservation system for popular European campsites. They called it 'Auto Camper Service International'. ACSI had been born and the basis was formed for the familiar green ACSI campsite guides.

The three pioneers selected 55 campsites, collected information and distributed it in a duplicated booklet for the modest price of one Dutch guilder. No more closed barriers; from now on it was possible to contact the campsite in advance to reserve a pitch. In the Sixties when camping was something of a national sport, demand for the guide grew.

The way to the top

By the third year a number of campsites asked if it was possible to supplement their entry in the guide for a fee to include a piece of text and a photo. Inspectors were recruited (then known as selectors) and so was created the first team to travel around Europe to collect campsite details.

Ed van Reine

At the beginning of the Eighties ACSI set its sights high when the company decided to publish the campsite guide itself. The number of campsites increased to 7,500 and in 1985 the first group of Dutch campers went on holiday with ACSI Camping Tours: group tours offering individual freedom. These tours are now also being organised for German and English speaking campers. ACSI officially became a family business from the moment that Ed van Reine introduced his son Ramon, the current director of ACSI. From that moment things developed rapidly.

ACSI diversifies

In the Nineties ACSI was involved with digitisation, product expansion and internationalisation. In 1999 ACSI was the first in Europe to launch a dynamic campsite search engine on the internet. The information on the www.eurocampings.net website could be accessed in four languages (nowadays www.EUROCAMPINGS.eu is available in 14 languages) and the visitor could already filter the inspected amenities.

Various new guides with different interests and themes have appeared and these are also published in multiple languages. The introduction of CampingCard ACSI in 2004 put the campsite specialist on the record for good: the incredibly simple, user-friendly discount system for the low season proved to be immensely popular with campers!

Nowadays 180 permanent employees are occupied in optimising existing products and developing new ones. More than 300 enthusiastic inspectors travel throughout Europe in order to ensure that only campsites with the highest standards of quality appear in the ACSI campsite guides. The extensive and objective information that results from these

annual inspections has for years been ACSI's strength.

Progressive since 1965

ACSI brings campers and campsites together throughout Europe by publishing campsite information, but ACSI does much more. ACSI Club ID members can go on holiday with a camping carnet (an alternative identity document, accepted at almost 9,000 campsites).

ACSI continues to listen to the wishes of both campers and campsites and react to them. The results say it all: over the years, ACSI has grown into the leading campsite specialist receiving over 10 million visitors a year on Eurocampings.eu, it expects two million visits to the CampingCard ACSI app in 2018 and will reach a record distribution of 674,500 campsite guides. You now have one of them. Thanks for your trust! ACSI wishes you lots of enjoyable camping in 2018.

It couldn't be easier. Using your discount card you can enjoy bargain holidays in low season at top-quality campsites throughout Europe. And all that for just one of five fixed rates: 11, 13, 15, 17 or 19 euros per night.

The rates

The fixed rates of 11, 13, 15, 17 and 19 euros are lower than the minimum prices charged by the participating campsites in the low season. You can therefore be certain of big discounts on the overnight price! At least 10% - and in some cases as much as 50%! Some campsites offer an extra discount if you stay for a longer period. Campsites are just as attractive in the low season as in the high season; the owners guarantee the same standards of facilities and service and the main facilities are also available in the low season; you just pay less. You can therefore avoid the busy period and take advantage of your discount in early and late season!

What do you have to do to enjoy your discount?

It couldn't be easier - take the CampingCard ACSI with you and present it to the receptionist when you arrive at one of the participating

campsites and take advantage of our preferential rates! Show your discount card again at the reception when you pay and you will be charged the advantageous CampingCard ACSI rate. You can see what is included in the rate in the 'Rate per overnight stay' section on page 20 of this guide, and you can see any supplementary charges there may be in the 'Not included in the overnight rate' section on page 21.

Payment conditions

CampingCard ACSI may look like a credit or debit card but it is actually a discount card. You show your CampingCard ACSI and you can stay on selected sites at advantageous rates. You don't usually have to pay in advance for a fixed number of nights; just pay when you depart.

However, ultimately the payment method is determined by the rules of the campsite, and that includes when you need to pay or provide a deposit. If for example you announce that you will be staying for just one night or want to reserve, the campsite may ask you to pay in advance or pay a deposit. The campsite reception will inform you of their policy in this matter.

Reservation with CampingCard ACSI

On some campsites you can reserve in advance with CampingCard ACSI. A campsite has then indicated facility 6A 'Reservation with CampingCard ACSI possible' in the campsite's information.

A reservation with your CampingCard ACSI is in fact considered a normal reservation, only the overnight rate is lower. In some cases you will have to pay a reservation charge and a deposit may be required. A reservation made well in advance by a CampingCard holder can cause problems for campsites. In such cases a campsite may have a policy not to accept your reservation. There are also some sites where reservation is never possible.

It is important when making a reservation to mention that you are a CampingCard holder. If you fail to do this there is a chance that you will have to pay the regular rate.

Only campsites with the CC logo

All participating campsites featured in this guide have been individually inspected and approved by ACSI.

Take note: ACSI annually inspects 9,900 campsites in Europe. Of these 9,900 campsites, 3,330 are participating in CampingCard ACSI in 2018.

You only have the right to a CampingCard ACSI discount if a campsite appears in this guide or on www.CAMPINGCARD.com. Also make sure to check whether the discount card will be accepted during the period you wish to stay at the campsite of your choice. CampingCard ACSI sites can be recognised by the blue CC logo that you will see on a sticker at the reception or by a large flag near the reception.

Only campsites with a blue CC logo participate in CampingCard ACSI so you only have the right to a discount at these campsites.

323 inspectors

Inspectors set off every year throughout Europe to visit campsites for the renowned ACSI campsite guides. This is how ACSI has been collecting the most reliable campsite information for the past 53 years. In 2017, 323 inspectors visited the campsites.

They inspect the campsites using a 220 point checklist and also pay attention to details that cannot easily be rated, such as surroundings, recreational facilities and the friendliness of the staff, etc.

The opinion of the campers themselves is of course of the utmost importance, so our inspection teams regularly ask campsite guests for their opinions of the campsite. You can let your opinion count after visiting a CampingCard site. See page 35 for more information.

Probably the biggest advantage of camping in low season…

CampingCard ACSI is first and foremost a discount card for the low season. Money saved by camping in these bargain periods can be used for any number of enjoyable pursuits. Another advantage of camping outside the high season – and for some the biggest reason – is relaxation. You avoid congested roads, the sites are quieter, you rarely need to reserve a pitch and the staff have much more time and attention for you. Additionally, the local sights around your campsite are less busy.

In other words: everything you need for a relaxing and carefree holiday awaits you. We hope you will make the most of it!

How to find a campsite?

This CampingCard ACSI guide consists of two parts. Participating CampingCard ACSI campsites are described one by one in an 'editorial entry', which includes a description of the rate, the acceptance periods and the amenities.

In this guide campsites have been arranged alphabetically by place name per country. An example: Zaton Holiday Resort in Zaton/Nin (Zadar) in Croatia can be found under Z for Zaton/Nin (Zadar).

Exceptions to this are the Netherlands, Germany, France, Spain and Italy. These countries are divided up into regions. Within a region you will find the campsite by place name. In the contents page of this guide and in the accompanying mini-atlas you will also see that the Netherlands, Germany, France, Spain and Italy are divided up into regions.

Using the general maps which precede the country information you will easily be able to find a campsite in your favourite holiday area!

How to find a participating campsite

There are several possibilities:

In this campsite guide:
- Search for a campsite by place. Use the register at the back of the guide or the mini-atlas for this purpose.
- Search the country or region where you want to camp. For this you can use the table of contents in the front of the guide. Or use the mini-atlas. The CampingCard ACSI campsites are indicated by a blue logo, together with a number. The numbers in the

guide go upwards, so you can easily find the corresponding editorial entry and you will find the information for the campsite you are looking for.
- You can also search for a particular amenity. Using the fold-out cover at the front of this book, you can easily see if the campsite offers the facilities that are important to you.
- But of course it's quite possible that by just browsing through the guide, a photograph or a description will catch your attention and make you decide 'That's the place for me!'

On the website:
Website www.CAMPINGCARD.com. See also page 33.

In the app:
The special CampingCard ACSI app. See also page 26.

In the mini-atlas:
Enclosed in this guide you will find a mini-atlas showing all the participating CampingCard ACSI campsites in Europe. In the mini-atlas you will see blue logos showing a number which corresponds to the blue logo and number in the editorial entry for each campsite.

The register in the mini-atlas is composed as follows: campsite number, campsite name, place name in alphabetical order, page number and sub-area on the page. In the Netherlands, Germany, France, Spain and Italy the campsites have been arranged in alphabetical order by region.

1. Place name - Postal code - Region

4. Campsite name and star ratings

5. Address

6. Telephone and fax

7. Opening period

8. E-mail address

Cisano di Bardolino, I-37010 / Lago di Garda

 Cisano/San Vito*****
Via Peschiera 48
+39 045-6229098
FAX +39 045-6229059
17/3 - 8/10
@ cisano@camping-cisano.it

15ha 460**T**(50-110m²) 6-16A CEE

1 ABCDEIJKLMOPQ
2 ADGIJKLRTVWXY
3 BKLMNQRUV**W**Z
4 (B+G 30/4-15/9) JP
(Q+S+T+U+V+Y+Z)
5 **AB**EFGIJKLMNOP**QRST**UV
WXYZ
6 ACEG**J**M(N 0,3km)QRTV

Cisano c...
on Lake Gar...
road wher...
the rest...
under...

9. Facilities
(see fold-out flap)

 Facilities open throughout the campsite's entire opening period

(CC € **17** 17/3-30/6 25/8-...

10. Surface area of the campsite in hectares (1 ha = 1... metres) or approximately 2.5 acres)

11. Number of touring pitches (size of the pitches...

12. Maximum loading available for electrical co...

13. Three pin Euro adaptor required (CEE)

2. 👫 Three children up to and including the age of 5 included

NEW New CampingCard ACSI campsite in 2018

🚫 Dogs not permitted

🧍 Campsite totally suitable for naturists

🧍 Campsite partially suitable for naturists

🎿 Winter sports campsite

♿ Amenities suitable for the disabled

📶 Wifi zone on the campsite

📶 Wifi coverage on at least 80% of the campsite

✿ Recognised by the environmental organisation in that particular country

iD ACSI Club ID accepted as an identity card

3. 3095 Campsite number

1. Place name, postal code and region

The place name and postal code of the campsite and the region in which it is located.

2. Three children up to and including the age of 5 included (possible) 👫

You will find 656 campsites in this guide where (maximum) three children up to and including the age of 5 are included in the CampingCard ACSI rate. The symbol 👫 is shown in the editorial entry for these campsites. Take note: where a campsite displays this symbol they may still require you to pay tourist tax for children, as the campsite has to pay the tourist tax directly to the local authorities. Items such as shower tokens for children are not included.

Dogs not allowed 🚫

The stay of one dog is included in the CampingCard ACSI rate, assuming dogs are allowed on the campsite. If you are bringing more dogs, it is possible that an extra payment will be required. At some campsites there is a limit to the number of dogs per guest and/or

18. Sectional map with the exact position of the campsite

19. GPS coordinates

some breeds are not permitted. You can find the number of dogs you are allowed to bring with you on the campsite on the campsite page on www.CAMPINGCARD.com. If you are in doubt if your dogs are permitted or not, please contact the campsite.

At campsites with the above symbol, dogs are not permitted at all.

Wifi zone and/or wifi 80-100% coverage

If there is a wifi zone on the campsite, then there is a location on the campsite where you can access wireless Internet. In the editorial entry for these campsites you will see this symbol:

If there is 80-100% wifi coverage, then you can access wireless internet on most of the campsite. In the editorial entry for these campsites you will see this symbol:

ACSI Club ID

On many campsites you can use the ACSI Club ID Card, this is a substitute identity card. When you can use the ACSI Club ID at a campsite, this is indicated in the facilities with the symbol. You will find more explanation of this Camping Carnet on page 30 of this guide.

3. Campsite number

The number in the blue CC logo refers to the number in the mini-atlas, included with this guide, which gives a good overview of where the campsite is located. See also: 'In the mini-atlas' on page 10.

4. Campsite name and star ratings

Here you can see the campsite name and possibly the number of stars. ACSI does not give stars or other classifications to campsites. Star ratings or other types of classification are awarded to the campsite by local or national organisations and are shown after the campsite name. Stars do not always indicate the quality but more often the comfort that a campsite offers. The more stars there are, the more amenities. The judgement of whether a campsite is good or not and whether you think it deserves two stars or four is something you must decide for yourself. Some good advice: if things are not what you expect, don't stay for ten days moaning about the unfriendly receptionist. Pack your bags and leave. Who knows what lovely places are just around the corner!

5. Address

The postal address of the campsite. You will find the postal address including the post code in the uppermost block of the editorial entry. Sometimes, in France and Italy for example, you will see that there is no postal address. You will discover that you will usually be able to find the campsite yourself once you have arrived in the town. To make it easier to find the campsite we have included a route description and the GPS coordinates in the editorial entry.

6. Telephone and fax

The telephone and fax numbers in this guide are preceded by a + sign. The + is the international access code (00 in the United Kingdom). The digits after the + denote the country where the campsite is located. For example: the phone number of a German campsite is shown as +49 followed by the area code with the 0 (in brackets) and the subscriber number. In most European countries, you should not dial the first zero of the area code after dialling the international access code. So for Germany you dial 0049 and then the area code, without the zero, followed by the subscriber's number. In general you do need to dial the zero in Italy.

7. Opening period 🔒

The periods advised by the campsite management during which the site will be open in 2018. TAKE NOTE: campsites do not offer the CampingCard ACSI discount for the entire period that they are open. For dates when the CampingCard ACSI discount is available you will need to refer to the acceptance periods in the lower block of the campsite's editorial entry. See also: 'Acceptance period' on page 17.

The opening and acceptance data have been compiled with the greatest care. It is possible that circumstances may cause these dates to change after publication of this guide. Go to www.CAMPINGCARD.com/modifications before you leave to see whether there have been changes at your chosen campsite.

8. E-mail address @

The campsite's e-mail address. The e-mail address is especially useful to make a reservation or enquiries in the low season, when the reception may be staffed less frequently.

9. Facilities

CampingCard ACSI is a discount card for the low season. Participating campsites will ensure that the most important facilities will also be available and functioning in the acceptance period of the discount card.
You will find a complete summary of all the facilities that are included in this guide in the fold-out cover at the front of the guide. If you leave the cover folded out you can see precisely which facilities are available at each campsite. By the numbers 1 to 6 you will find six categories with facilities:

1 Regulations
2 Location, ground and shade
3 Sports and play
4 Water recreation / Shops and restaurants
5 Washing up, laundry and cooking / Washing
  and toilet facilities
6 Miscellaneous

The letters after the numbers relate to the facilities in each category. Some facilities have a period shown in brackets, showing the day and month. These are the dates that you can expect these facilities to be available.
If a small key  is shown, this facility can be used at least during the entire opening period of the campsite (amenities such as restaurants may in a few cases stay open longer than the campsite itself).

Take note:
- These are the facilities that are present at the campsite. This does not mean that all these facilities are available on standard pitches and can be used by CampingCard ACSI guests. For example, when there is a mention of facility 6S, this means that the campsite offers pitches with radio/tv access. In most cases, these pitches will be comfort pitches, which are not meant for CampingCard ACSI guests.
- If a swimming pool or other facility is right next to the campsite, and campsite guests are allowed to use those facilities, the letters of those facilities are also shown in the campsite information.
- Some facilities on the fold-out cover have a *. Facilities with a * that are in **bold** script in the campsite information are not included in the overnight rate at that campsite. There are two

exceptions for CampingCard ACSI guests: in the CampingCard ACSI rate, one dog (assuming they are allowed on the campsite) and one warm shower per person per day are included, even if the facility is printed in bold and therefore belongs to the facilities at the campsite that require payment. Facilities without a * are never in bold, but this does not mean they are free of charge.

10. Surface area of the campsite

The surface area of the campsite is given in hectares. 1 ha = 10,000 m² (square metres) or approximately 2.5 acres).

11. Number of touring pitches

As a camper on the move, it is interesting to know how many overnight pitches a site offers. The size of the pitches is shown in brackets, in m². If it says > 100 m², then the pitches are larger than 100 m². < 100 m² means smaller than 100 m². Every campsite makes some of these touring pitches available for campers with CampingCard ACSI. A standard pitch is included in the CampingCard rate. See page 20 for more explanation.

12. Maximum loading available for electrical connections

With your CampingCard ACSI a connection with maximum 6A or power consumption to a maximum of 4 kWh per day, including the connection fee, is included in the overnight rate. If you use more, for example 5 kWh it is quite likely you have to pay a surcharge. You will find the minimum and maximum amperage available for the electrical connection for each campsite in the block with facilities. When the campsite information mentions 6-10A, this means that at this campsite there are pitches with an amperage of minimum 6 and maximum 10. This does not mean that 10A is included in the CampingCard ACSI rate.

State clearly on arrival at the campsite if you want a higher amperage than the included 6A, but be aware that you may have to pay a surcharge. Only when there is no lower amperage than 10A available at the campsite, you will not have to pay extra. Take note: on a connection that allows maximum 6A you cannot connect devices with a combined power consumption of more than 1380 Watt.

13. CEE

This indication means that you will need a three pin euro-adapter.

14. Rate and extra discount

A rate of 11, 13, 15, 17 or 19 euros is shown for each campsite. The rates offered by CampingCard ACSI are already low but could be even lower. Some campsites give an extra discount if you stay longer.
If, for example a campsite is showing '7=6' this means that you pay only 6 nights at the CampingCard ACSI rate for a 7 night stay. Be sure to indicate the number of nights you wish to stay when arriving or reserving. The campsite will make one booking for the entire period and will apply the discount. The discount may not apply if you decide to stay longer during your stay and thereby reach the required number of days.
Take note! If a campsite has several of these discounts you only have the right to one of these offers. For example: the special offers are 4=3, 7=6 and 14=12. If you stay for 13 nights you only have the right to one 7=6 discount and not to multiples of 4=3 or a combination of 4=3 and 7=6.

15. Acceptance period

Each campsite decides its own acceptance period and so defines its own low season. For dates when the CampingCard ACSI discount is available you will need to look at the acceptance periods in the lower blue block of the editorial entry for the campsite. The last date specified in a period is always the last possible day of arrival in order to stay overnight with a CampingCard ACSI discount. An acceptance period of 1/1 - 30/6 means that the first night you are entitled to a discount is the night from 1 January to 2 January, and the last night you are entitled to a discount is the night from 30 June to 1 July. So, on the night from 1 July to 2 July, you will pay the normal rate.

The opening and acceptance periods are compiled with the greatest care.
It is possible that circumstances may cause these dates to change after publication of this guide.
Check www.CAMPINGCARD.com/modifications to see whether we have been informed of any changes at the campsite of your choice.

16. Description

In this section you will get an idea of the layout of the campsite and its characteristics. Some examples: on the coast, by a lake, quiet family campsite, high specification of facilities, pleasant views, plenty of shade, privacy, pitches separated by shrubbery, stony ground, grass, terraced, etc.

17. Route description

The written directions in this route description will assist you in finding your way for the last few miles to the campsite entrance and will advise you which motorway exit to take and which signs to follow.

18. Sectional map

The sectional map shows where the campsite is located in its immediate surroundings. The precise location of the campsite is shown with the blue CampingCard ACSI logo.

19. GPS coordinates 🏕🔺

If you make use of a navigation system the GPS coordinates are almost indispensable. ACSI has therefore noted the GPS coordinates in this guide. Our inspectors have measured the coordinates right next to the campsite barrier, so nothing can go wrong. Take care: not all navigation systems are configured for cars with a caravan so always read the route description that is included with each campsite and don't forget to watch out for the signs. The shortest route is, after all, not always the easiest one. The GPS coordinates are shown in degrees, minutes and seconds. Check when you enter the data into your navigation system that it is also configured in degrees, minutes and seconds. The letter N is shown by the first number. By the second number there is a letter E or W (right or left of the Greenwich meridian).

There are five CampingCard ACSI rates:

At campsites in countries which use currencies other than the euro, you will normally pay in that country's currency. In this case, the CampingCard ACSI rate is converted to that currency using the daily exchange rate that is valid at that moment (average of highest and lowest rate of that day). Please take into account that exchange rates can be subject to large changes.

Inclusive

Participating campsites offer the following in the CampingCard ACSI rate on touring pitches:
- A camping pitch.*
- Overnight stay for 2 adults.
- Car & caravan & awning, or car & folding caravan, or car & tent, or motor home & awning.
- Electricity. A connection of maximum 6A or a consumption of maximum 4 kWh per day is included in the CampingCard ACSI rate. When a campsite only has pitches with a lower amperage, this lower amperage will apply. If you use excess, for example 5 kWh, it is possible that you might have to pay extra. See also 'Maximum loading available for electrical connections' on page 17.
- Hot showers. In campsites where showers are operated by tokens, CampingCard ACSI holders are entitled to one token per adult per day.**

- Maximum one dog staying on campsites which accept dogs. For a second (or additional) dog you might have to pay extra.
- VAT.

* Some campsites make a distinction between standard, luxury or comfort pitches. Luxury or comfort pitches are in general larger and equipped with their own water supply and drainage. CampingCard ACSI gives you the right to a standard pitch but it may occur that you are able to have a more expensive pitch at the CampingCard ACSI rate. The campsite has the right to decide this; you can NEVER insist on a luxury or comfort pitch.
Be aware also that some campsites have a different policy with regard to twin-axled caravans and mobile homes which are so large that they will not fit on a standard pitch.

** The campsite is required to allow the CampingCard ACSI holder one shower per day in accordance with the CampingCard ACSI conditions. Consequently each CampingCard ACSI holder has the right to one shower token per person per overnight stay. Where a campsite operates a different 'shower system' such as coins, a key or a SEP key, the above conditions still apply but the camper will need to make the necessary arrangements with the campsite.
Hot water in washing up sinks is not included in the price. Unused shower tokens cannot be exchanged for money.

Not included in the overnight rate

In general the CampingCard ACSI rate is sufficient to pay for the overnight charge. The campsite may however make extra charges for a number of items:

- Tourist taxes, environmental taxes, waste disposal charges or local authority requirements are not included in the CampingCard ACSI rate. These taxes can differ greatly by country and region. In Switzerland and Austria in particular, and also in the Netherlands, you should be prepared for high charges for some of these taxes.
- Reservation and administration charges are not included in the CampingCard ACSI rate. You can read more about reserving with CampingCard ACSI on page 8.
- A campsite may make a surcharge for a luxury or comfort pitch (unless the campsite only has comfort pitches).
- Campsites make pitches available for two adults. The campsite may decide if more guests may stay on these pitches, apart from the two adults who can stay for the CampingCard ACSI rate (for example the guests' children or more adults), for payment of the regular rate per guest. If this is not allowed, then the camping group will be directed to pitches that are not meant for CampingCard ACSI users and for which the regular low season rates must be paid. However, at campsites which display the following symbol 🏃👶, (a maximum of) three children up to and including the age of 5 are included in the CampingCard ACSI rate. Items such as shower coins and tourist tax (if applicable) for these children are not included.
- Extra services such as facilities for which the campsite makes a charge, such as a tennis court, can be charged to you at the applicable low season rate.
- Electricity, if more is consumed than is specified on page 20. See also 'Maximum loading available for electrical connections' on page 17.

New: online booking!

Nothing is more irritating than finding a campsite, and then arriving there to find there's no space left. In the low season, that luckily won't happen too often, but for those who prefer to err on the side of caution, it's possible to reserve a space online at a growing number of campsites.

You can do this, from home or on the road, via www.CAMPINGCARD.com or using the CampingCard ACSI app. These bookable campsites have an extra orange button. You book directly with the campsite, and you can pay online straight away, of course getting the bargain CampingCard ACSI rate.

Booking a campsite

Once you've found a bookable campsite that suits your tastes, just click on the orange button. Then select your preferred date of arrival and length of stay, click 'Book now'** in the calendar, and follow the steps below.

1. Fill in the names of the people you're travelling with.
2. Select any extras.

Sample booking form

3. Fill in any other details, and the details of your camping vehicle.
4. Choose your payment method.
5. Check your details, and click on 'Confirm booking'.

You will be redirected to the payment page, and pay the full booking amount immediately. Your booking is final, and is made under the terms and conditions of the campsite. If you cancel, this is also under the terms and conditions of the campsite.

The advantages of booking online

- You can be sure that there will be space for you.
- All costs will be clear in advance.
- The price is the same as you would pay at the campsite.

Important: don't forget to bring your CampingCard ACSI with you! Even if you book online, it's still necessary to show your discount card at the campsite reception. This is the only way you are entitled to camp at the reduced rate.

More and more campsites bookable via ACSI

The number of campsites that you can book via ACSI is increasing all the time. So keep an eye on the website, and check the app regularly. If you want to know more about booking a camping pitch via ACSI, check out www.CAMPINGCARD.com/bookonline.

Holiday exhibitions

A chance to meet us! The start of a new year is the perfect time to begin making your holiday plans. And to get yourself into the holiday mood.

We enjoy listening to your experiences of previous holidays, and welcome your ideas and suggestions.

Person to person

We would like to meet you in person at the 2018 Holiday Exhibitions and tell you more about the CampingCard ACSI formula. You can also get to know more about other ACSI products, such as ACSI Camping Tours (group trips with lots of individual freedom).

You're more than welcome!

In 2018:

Caravan Camping & Motorhome Show, Birmingham
20 - 25 February
www.ccmshow.co.uk

Motorhome & Caravan Show, Birmingham
October
www.mcshow.co.uk

Please visit www.CAMPINGCARD.com/fairs for more information about trade fairs.

CampingCard ACSI app

Now even more convenience with the CampingCard ACSI app

With the CampingCard ACSI app you have all campsite information at your fingertips! The app, which can also be used without an internet connection, includes all CampingCard ACSI campsites and has many handy functionalities and search filters. The campsite information in the CampingCard ACSI app is updated several times a year. The app is suitable for smartphones and tablets (Android and iOS) and for devices with Windows 10!

The CampingCard ACSI app has very handy filters to allow you to quickly find a suitable campsite. And, using the map, you can easily find campsites that are close to you!

J. Dielhof

• **Search by name**
You can search campsites by country, region, place, campsite number or campsite name. Enter a search term and view the campsite(s) on the map. The database is very extensive and contains more than 500,000 search terms!

• **Search in the area**
Is location awareness activated on your device? If so the app will identify your location and show the CampingCard ACSI campsites that are close to you. If you prefer to search for a specific place on the map you can set your location on the map manually. That way you'll always find a campsite close by. Perfect if you're looking for a place to stay overnight.

• **Search filters**
The app contains really useful search filters. You can filter by more than 150 amenities, the CampingCard ACSI rates, periods of stay and stopover campsites.

• **View the campsite**
You will find comprehensive information about the grounds and the amenities for each campsite. Check if it's suitable by looking at the photos, map resources and campsite reviews from other campers.

- **Favourites**

When you have found one or more campsites that meet your requirements, you can add them to your favourites so you can find them again quickly. Your favourites will then also be recognisable on the map.

- **Contacting the campsite**

When you have chosen a campsite you can call the site directly from the app to check availability. You can also send an e-mail from the app.

Campsite reviews

It is also possible to review a campsite in the app. Even when there is no internet connection. The app will save the review and send it automatically when your device connects to the internet at a later time!

Attention:
In order to be able to take advantage of the low, fixed rates you will always need to be able to show a physical, valid discount card at the reception. Showing only the app or campsite guide does not suffice.

New!

Are you going on the road with your motorhome? You can also buy motorhome pitch information in the CampingCard ACSI app now! Use your unique purchase code on the order form, and tick the box 'motorhome pitch information'.

Go to www.CAMPINGCARD.com/appinfo for more information and an explanation on how to purchase access to the app.

All CampingCard ACSI campsites in one app!

Campsite information at your fingertips, anytime, anywhere, with the CampingCard ACSI app

- 3,330 CampingCard ACSI campsites, inspected annually.
- Useful filters, and detailed maps
- Free updates, including campsite reviews
- New: information on 9,000 motorhome pitches!

From just € 3.59

Your unique purchase code

In order to gain access to the CampingCard ACSI app you will need a unique purchase code. With this code, we can verify that you have a valid CampingCard ACSI. You will find the code on the back of your discount card, as pictured below:

Comparison of ACSI apps

	ACSI Campsites Europe app	CampingCard ACSI app	ACSI Great Little Campsites app
Price	Packages with campsite information from € 0.99	Complete app with campsite information: € 3.59	Complete app with campsite information: € 2.99
Number of campsites	8,200	3,330	More than 2,000
Type of campsite	All campsites in the ACSI Campinggids Europa	All campsites that accept CampingCard ACSI	Small campsites with max. 50 touring pitches
New! Information about 9,000 motorhome pitches	For sale, together with campsite information	For sale, together with campsite information	For sale, together with campsite information
Suitable for	Smartphone, tablet, laptop and computer	Smartphone, tablet, laptop and computer	Smartphone, tablet, laptop and computer
Can be used on three devices at the same time	✓	✓	✓
Free updates	✓	✓	✓
Can be used offline	✓	✓	✓
Search by country, region, town or campsite name	✓	✓	✓
Search on map/GPS	✓	✓	✓
Search by CC rate and CC acceptance period		✓	
Total search filters	250	150	150
Special filters for motorhome pitches	✓	✓	✓
Book, call or mail campsite via app	✓	✓	✓
Read and submit campsite reviews	✓	✓	✓
Plan route	✓	✓	✓
More information	EUROCAMPINGS.eu/app	CAMPINGCARD.com/app	greatlittlecampsites.co.uk/app

The ACSI Club ID, the leading Camping Carnet for Europe, is indispensable for every camper. You will benefit from it both during your camping holiday and at home! Become a member at once and pay only € 4.95 a year.

Advantages of the ACSI Club ID

We have listed all the advantages of the ACSI Club ID below:

- **Alternative identity card**

You can hand in your Camping Carnet, the ACSI Club ID, at participating ACSI Club ID campsites instead of your passport or identity papers. Passport fraud is an ongoing issue in Europe and with the ACSI Club ID you remain in control of your valuable passport or ID card. You will not have to hand in your identity papers but can always keep them safely in your pocket.*

* Take note: It is possible that in some countries, including Spain, Italy and Croatia, you will still have to hand in your identity document at the campsite due to local regulations.

- **Liability insurance coverage**

If you are in possession of the ACSI Club ID, you and your travelling companions (max 11 people) are insured against liability during your camping holiday or when staying in a hotel or rented accommodation. This insurance applies when you cause damage for third parties, for example if you accidentally let your bicycle fall onto your neighbour's tent during your holiday

- **Benefit from various offers**

As an ACSI Club ID member, you'll always pay the lowest price in the ACSI Webshop.

Visit www.ACSIclubID.eu to stay informed about the latest developments concerning ACSI's Camping Carnet.

- **Accepted at almost 9,000 campsites in Europe**

Almost 9,000 campsites in the ACSI campsite guides accept the ACSI Club ID. The amenity that shows that a campsite accepts the ACSI Club ID is mentioned in the list of amenities as 1A. You can also recognise these campsites by the 'ID' logo in the orange bar above the campsite's entry.

If you are going camping in Scandinavia, there is a chance that you will need a special card that you must show at reception. You can purchase this card at the relevant campsite.

Take note: the ACSI Club ID does not entitle you to a discount at campsites.

Differences between CampingCard ACSI and ACSI Club ID

There are differences between CampingCard ACSI and the ACSI Club ID. We have put these differences in a table for your benefit.

ACSI Club ID

The Camping Carnet, a substitute means of identification	
A membership	
Liability insurance and discounts on ACSI products in the ACSI webshop	
Accepted as alternate means of identification at almost 9,000 campsites in 29 countries	
Valid for 1 year, until the expiration date	
€ 4.95 per year	
www.ACSIclubID.eu	

CampingCard ACSI

The discount card for camping in low season

A loose product or a subscription

Gives you the right to a fixed low overnight rate during low season

Accepted at 3,330 participating campsites in 21 countries

Valid for one calendar year, from 1 January until 31 December

From € 11.95 per year, including two-part guide

www.CAMPINGCARD.com

Application

You can apply for the ACSI Club ID via www.ACSIclubID.eu. Your card can be ordered in just a few steps. Be sure to have your identity papers handy when ordering.

The ACSI Club ID can be used by campers with one of the following nationalities: Dutch, Belgian, French, German, Austrian, Swiss, British (English, Scottish, Welsh and Northern Irish), Irish, Spanish, Italian, Norwegian, Swedish, Finnish and Danish.

Take note: campers with one of the above nationalities but not resident in the Netherlands, Germany, France, Belgium, Denmark, Switzerland, Austria, Ireland, the

United Kingdom, Norway, Sweden, Finland, Portugal, Spain or Italy cannot apply for the ACSI Club ID for insurance-related reasons.

Internet

Let your computer do the work!

On www.CAMPINGCARD.com, you will find a campsite that meets your needs quickly and easily. Very handy to use in conjunction with this guide.

If you do not have internet access while you are on the road, you can download the CampingCard ACSI app before you leave. You will find more information on page 26.

On the website there are various easy ways to search for a campsite, including:

- **By place name, region or country**
  Simply type in (part of) the name of the town, region or country in the search field. The website recognises more than 500,000 place names throughout Europe. This way, you will always find a campsite that is located close to you.

- **By map**
  You are searching for a campsite in a particular area. Each time you click on the map you reduce the search area. The result is a summary list of campsites from which you can make a choice. By clicking the tent symbol on the map the details of your chosen campsite will be displayed.

- **By campsite name or campsite number**
  Simply type in the name of the campsite. In these guides, and in the mini-atlas, you will also find the campsite number for each campsite. This will give you more information about a campsite quickly and easily.

- **By holiday period**
  When you search by holiday period you will see a summary of campsites that (partly) meet the search criteria. You will find more information about a campsite's acceptance period on page 17.

- **By facilities**
  You can also easily filter for particular facilities at the campsite. The 'advanced search' button on the website will allow you to search by more than 150 facilities! That way you can quickly find the right campsite for you.

- **By theme**
  Here you will find campsites with various themes, such as sites adapted for the disabled, wintersports campsites and naturist campsites.

Plan your route

When you have found the campsite where you want to go on holiday, you can use the

route planner on the campsite page under the 'Address & Route' tab to plan the journey completely from your home address to the campsite via Google Maps. You can also plan out the return journey. Convenient and quick!

Read and write reviews

Would you like to know what other campers think of a campsite? You can read other campers' reviews per campsite on www.CAMPINGCARD.com. These campers have reviewed a campsite for its staff, value for money and the surroundings, among other things. In this way you will get an independent and extensive impression of the campsite.

We would love to hear what you yourself thought about the campsite. By leaving a review you will enter a draw for great prizes! Also see page 35.

Always stay up to date with the CampingCard ACSI newsletter

If you sign up to our newsletter you will receive useful tips, special offers and information about CampingCard ACSI once a month! This way you will always be kept up to date on the latest news. You can sign up for this newsletter via www.CAMPINGCARD.com/newsletter.

Check the latest modifications

There may be some changes in the campsite information which is displayed in the course of a year. So check www.CAMPINGCARD.com/modifications before you leave.

Tips, comments or suggestions?

If you have any tips, comments or suggestions for CampingCard ACSI, please visit www.CAMPINGCARD.com/customerservice.

Your opinion matters

Give your opinion and have the chance to win wonderful prizes!

A beautiful swimming pool, well maintained toilet facilities or friendly staff at the campsite: you can submit a review for every campsite on our www.CAMPINGCARD.com website. Useful for you and for other campers. Your review can even win you prizes. So don't wait any longer and share your opinion!

How do you review a campsite?
Go to www.CAMPINGCARD.com and search for the campsite you visited. Click on the tab 'Reviews' and then on the button 'Add a review'. You can now fill in your campsite review.

If you have any questions about CampingCard ACSI, for example about the acceptance period or the rate of a campsite, you can contact ACSI via www.CAMPINGCARD.com/customerservice.

France

Dunkerque
Calais
Tourcoing
BRUSSEL
D
Nord-Pas-de-Calais Roubaix
41 Lille
B
Hauts-de-France
Amiens
St-Quentin
Haute-Normandie Charleville-
Le Havre **55** **Picardie** Mézières
Caen Rouen **44** **L**
Basse-Normandie LUXEMBURG
63 Normandie Reims Metz
PARIS **Champagne-** **Grand-Est**
Brest Île-de-France **Ardenne** Nancy
Bretagne Chartres **225** **229** **Lorraine** Strasbourg
Quimper **75** Le Mans Troyes **235** **Alsace**
Rennes **245**
Lorient Orléans Colmar
Pays de la Loire Mulhouse
St-Nazaire **114** Angers **Centre-Val de Loire** **Bourgogne** Besançon
Nantes Tours **251** **270** Dijon **Franche-Comté** BERN
Châteauroux Bourges **286**
Bourgogne- **CH**
La Rochelle Niort Poitiers Franche-Comté
Calvi Bastia **Poitou-Charentes** **Auvergne**
Corte **151** **Limousin** **302** Genève
Ajaccio **Corsica** Limoges **295** Lyon **Rhône-Alpes**
522 Clermont- **317** **I**
Sartène Bonifacio **Nouvelle Aquitaine** Brive- Ferrand **Auvergne-**
la-Gaillarde **Rhône-Alpes**
Bordeaux Grenoble
Aquitaine
176
Occitanie
Montauban Avignon **Provence-Alpes-**
Toulouse Nîmes **Côte d'Azur** Monaco
Pau **Midi-Pyrénées** Montpellier Nice **Provence-Alpes-** **Rivièra-**
E **379** **Languedoc-** Marseille **Côte d'Azur** **Côte d'Azur**
Roussillon **469** **519**
416
Perpignan

General
France is a member of the EU.

Time
The time in France is the same as Amsterdam,
Berlin and Rome and one hour ahead of
London.

Language
French. You can also get by in English in tourist
areas.

Border formalities
Many formalities and agreements about matters
such as necessary travel documents, car papers,

requirements relating to your means of transport and accommodation, medical expenses and taking pets with you do not only depend on the country you are travelling to but also on your departure point and nationality. The length of your stay can also play a role here. It is not possible within the confines of this guide to guarantee the correct and most up to date information with regard to these matters.

We advise you to consult the relevant authorities before your departure about:
- which travel documents you will need for yourself and your fellow passengers
- which documents you need for your car
- which regulations your caravan must meet
- which goods you may import and export
- how medical treatment will be arranged and paid for in your holiday destination in cases of accident or illness
- whether you can take pets. Contact your vets well in advance. They can give you information about the necessary vaccinations, proof thereof and obligations on return. It would also make sense to enquire whether any special regulations apply to your pet in public places at your holiday destination. In some countries for example dogs must always be muzzled or transported in a cage.

You will find plenty of general information on ▶ *www.europa.eu* ◀ but make certain you select information that is relevant to your specific situation.

For the most recent customs regulations you should get in contact with the authorities of your holiday destination in your country of residence.

Currency
The currency in France is the euro. Approximate exchange rates September 2017: £ 1 = € 1.09.

In general you can pay in France using your debit card.

Credit cards
You can pay almost everywhere by credit card, including motorway tolls. You usually have to validate a purchase with a signature and you may sometimes be asked for identification.

Opening times/Public holidays
Banks
French banks are open from Tuesday to Friday between 9:00 and 18:00. Banks are open on Saturday mornings.

Shops
Shops are open from Tuesday to Saturday until 19:00/20:00. Most shops in country areas are closed between 13:00 and 14:00. Many shops are closed on Monday morning or for the whole day.

Chemists
French chemists are open on weekdays until 19:00.

Public holidays
New Year's Day, Easter, 1 May (Labour Day), 8 May (1945 Armistice), Ascension Day, Pentecost, 14 July (Bastille Day), 15 August (The Assumption), 1 November (All Saints), 11 November (1918 Armistice), Christmas Day.

Communication

(Mobile) phones
The mobile network works well throughout France, except in some areas in the Alps and the Massif Central. There is a 4G network for mobile internet.

Wifi, internet
You can make use of a wifi network at more and more public locations, often for free.

Post
Post offices are open from Monday to Friday until 18:00 and on Saturday until 12:00.

Roads and traffic

Road network
You are advised not to drive after dark in rural areas. France does not have any roadside assistance organisations. There are orange emergency phones ('les bornes SOS') along the motorways, which you can use in emergency situations to request breakdown or recovery services ('dépanneur').

Traffic regulations
Remember, all traffic in France drives on the right and overtakes on the left! Headlight deflectors are advisable to prevent annoying oncoming drivers. France uses the metric system, so distances are measured in kilometres (km) and speeds in kilometres per hour (km/h).

Traffic from the right has priority except on main roads. Uphill traffic on narrow mountain roads has priority over descending traffic. You have priority on a roundabout if this is indicated by a triangular sign showing a roundabout. If there is no such sign drivers entering the roundabout will have priority.

Maximum speed

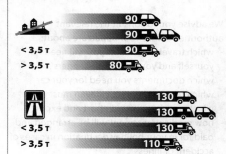

Maximum permitted alcohol level is 0.5‰. You must use dipped headlights in poor visibility. You must phone hands-free.
You are required to wear a high visibility jacket in the event of a breakdown. Children under 10 must always sit in the back. Take note: never cross continuous white road markings, not even with one wheel! Children under 12 years of age must wear a bicycle helmet, even if they are sitting on the back of the bike. The fine for not wearing a helmet is €135. Winter tyres are not compulsory but if you have an accident in adverse winter conditions and your vehicle does not have winter tyres, you could be held (jointly) liable.

You are required to carry a breathalyser in your vehicle, but you won't be fined if you don't. You can buy breathalysers at filling stations, supermarkets and chemists.

Caravans, motorhomes

If your caravan weighs more than 3.5 tonnes lower speed limits apply. Overnight stays in your caravan or motorhome in built up areas and beside the motorway are prohibited, except in specially designated areas and for a maximum of 24 hours.

Caravans with a twin axle are generally not permitted on municipal campsites.

Maximum allowed measurements of combined length

Height unlimited, width 2.55 metres and maximum length 18.75 metres (of which the trailer maximum 12 metres).

Environmental zones

Environmental zones to target air pollution are being introduced in more and more French cities. In cities with an environmental zone, you are only allowed to drive into the city if you have an environmental sticker on your car. The so-called Crit'Air Ecovignet is only available online via the official website

▶ *www.certificat-air.gouv.fr* ◀

There are 6 different environmental stickers, for different vehicles. If you enter an environmental zone without an environmental sticker in your windscreen, you risk a fine of dozens of euros.

Fuel

Euro 95 has been replaced almost totally by E10. Check before your holiday whether E10 is suitable for your vehicle. Superplus 98 is a suitable alternative for euro 95. Diesel and LPG are easily available at the pumps.

Filling stations

Most filling stations on motorways are open 24 hours. Some service stations on 'routes

nationales' are also open day and night, but many close at 21:00. Take note that an increasing number of service stations away from motorways are closed on Sunday.

Credit cards and most bank cards showing the Maestro logo are accepted at filling stations.

Tolls
Tolls apply to most French motorways. Blue signs indicate a road leading to a motorway. The indication 'péage' shows that it is a toll road. If you don't wish to pay a toll, follow the green signs which show alternative routes. You can pay the toll by credit card. Some of them can only be paid in cash. Take note that your toll ticket is only valid for 24 hours. More information about toll roads in France: ▸ www.autoroutes.fr ◂ (also in English).

Black Saturday
The busiest Saturdays in the summer season are known as 'black Saturdays'. Black Saturdays occur in the last week of July and the first week of August every year.

Emergency numbers
- 112: the national emergency number for fire, police and ambulance
- 17: police
- 18: fire
- 15: ambulance

Camping
With more than 11,000 campsites, France is Europe's biggest camping country. Be sure to reserve early if you want to go to the Ardèche or Dordogne in the interior, or to large seaside resorts. Pitches inland are often more spacious, better equipped and better value than on the coast.

It is worth noting that certain amenities such as the swimming pool, restaurant, snack bar, pizzeria and such like may only open in July and August. In all swimming pools, proper swimming trunks/costumes are obligatory and women are often required to wear a bathing cap. For hygienic reasons, boxer shorts, Bermuda shorts and other similar clothing is not allowed. On campsites in France you may come across signs 'Inondation par temps de grosse pluie', meaning that the area is prone to flooding during heavy rainfall.

Practical
- Prices for electrical hook-ups are high and can vary from € 1.50 to € 4.50 per day. (These are included in the CampingCard ACSI rate!)
- Make sure you have a world adaptor for electrical appliances.
- Drink bottled (mineral) water in preference to mains water.

Corsica
Most campsites on Corsica are on the coast and are usually well indicated. The roads, especially in the west, are narrow and sinuous. French is the official language but an accent similar to Italian is also spoken. There are few service stations inland!
Corsica can be reached by various routes.

Autingues, F-62610 / Nord-Pas-de-Calais (Pas-de-Calais) 👫 👥 ♿ 📶 iD (1264)

🏕 St. Louis***
📧 223 rue de Leulène
☎ +33 (0)3-21354683
📅 1/4 - 18/10
@ camping-saint-louis@sfr.fr

2ha 30T(80-110m²) 10A CEE

1 ACDGIJKLMOPQ
2 FRTVX
3 AGHJRU
4 (Q 1/5-17/9) (R 📅)
   (T+U+X+Z 1/5-9/9)
5 AFGIJKMNPUZ
6 EGJ(N 2km)TV

💬 A quietly located campsite in the Calais-Boulogne-St. Omer triangle. Spacious, marked-out pitches. A site with nice new toilet facilities and a lovely bar, eatery.

🚗 Take the A26 Calais-St. Omer. Exit Ardres/Nordausque. In Ardres RN43 direction Calais. Campsite signposted.

Fréthun, Coulogne, Guînes, D231, D218, D219 E1, A26, D943, D191, D217, D224

CC € 17 1/4-7/7 25/8-17/10 7=6, 15=13   📍 N 50°50'18'' E 1°58'36''

Boiry-Notre-Dame, F-62156 / Nord-Pas-de-Calais (Pas-de-Calais) ♿ 📶 iD (1265)

🏕 La Paille Haute**
📧 145 rue de Sailly
☎ +33 (0)3-21481540
📠 +33 (0)3-21220724
📅 1/4 - 15/10
@ lapaillehaute@wanadoo.fr

5ha 60T(80-100m²) 6A CEE

1 ACDGIJKLMPQ
2 FJKLRVWXY
3 BCDGRUW
4 (C+H 1/6-15/9) KN(Q 📅)
   (T+U+V+W+X+Z 8/6-31/8)
5 ABDFGIJKLMNPUW
6 EGIK(N 2km)TV

💬 Child-friendly, a swimming pool and various types of play equipment. Ideal campsite when travelling to northern or southern Europe. Rural location with spacious marked-out pitches. Ideal for exploring the area around Arras. Free wifi. There is a branch of the Louvre (Paris) in Lens (31 km). The Louvre in Lens is free.

🚗 From Lille A1 direction Paris, exit 15, then D939 direction Cambrai. Left after about 3 km to Boiry-Notre-Dame. Campsite signposted.

Sin-le-Noble, D919, D40, Arras, D39, D9, D939, D917, A1, A26, D956, D5

CC € 17 1/4-24/6 1/9-14/10 7=6, 15=13   📍 N 50°16'25'' E 2°56'56''

Éperlecques, F-62910 / Nord-Pas-de-Calais (Pas-de-Calais) ♿ 📶 iD (1266)

🏕 Château du Gandspette****
📧 D207, rue du Gandspette
☎ +33 (0)3-21934393
📠 +33 (0)3-21957498
📅 1/4 - 30/9
@ contact@
   chateau-gandspette.com

11ha 110T(80-120m²) 6-10A CEE

1 ACDGIJKLMOPRS
2 BLRTUVWX
3 ABFGMNRU
4 (C 15/5-15/9) (Q 1/5-15/9)
   (T+U+X+Z 27/4-21/9)
5 ABEFGIJKLMNOPUW
6 CDEGIK(N 1km)ORTV

💬 Castle site in beautiful park (11 ha). Two outdoor pools, tennis court, fitness equipment outside and good, attractive restaurant with reasonable prices. Modern, good toilet facilities. Visit Das Blockhaus from WWII, St. Omer (cultural town) and the Marais Audomarois (lakes).

🚗 From St. Omer take N943. Turn right at Blockhaus sign. Site signposted with arrows (± 6 km). From Calais D943 dir. St. Omer. Left in Nordausques dir. Éperlecques D221. Then D207. Follow signs.

D218 E1, D300, D11, D224, D218, D943, D928, A26, D217, Saint-Omer, Arques

CC € 19 1/4-6/7 1/9-29/9   📍 N 50°49'9'' E 2°10'43''

Equihen-Plage, F-62224 / Nord-Pas-de-Calais (Pas-de-Calais) 🛜 iD (1267)

🏕 Mun. La Falaise***
📧 rue Charles Cazin
☎ +33 (0)3-21312261
📠 +33 (0)3-21805401
🗓 28/3 - 7/11
@ camping.equihen.plage@
   orange.fr
8ha 95T(100-120m²) 10-16A CEE

1 ACD**G**IJKLMPQ
2 AEFIRSVX
3 BGNRUY
4 (**C** 1/6-30/9)
   (**F**+**H** 1/5-30/9) J
5 ABFJKLN**P**UW
6 CEGJ(N 1km)T

💬 A large municipal campsite with marked-out pitches which are positioned only 150 metres from the sea. There is plenty of shade. A good base for visiting Boulogne-sur-Mer and Le Touquet-Paris-Plage. With a large, partly covered new pool. Bakery 200 metres from the campsite.

🚗 N1 Boulogne-Abbeville, exit Le Portel/Hardelot or A16 Boulogne-Paris, exit Neuchâtel. From there campsite is signposted.

Boulogne-sur-Mer
CC · D341 · A16 · D901 · D940

CC € **17** 28/3-7/7 26/8-6/11 · 📐 N 50°40'15'' E 1°34'18''

Etaples-sur-Mer, F-62630 / Nord-Pas-de-Calais (Pas-de-Calais) ♿ 🛜 ✿ iD (1268)

🏕 La Pinède***
📧 940 chemin Départemental
☎ +33 (0)3-21943575
🗓 1/4 - 15/11
@ lapinede.etaples@gmail.com

NEW

5ha 68T(80-120m²) 6-10A CEE

1 ACD**G**IJKLM**P**Q
2 ABFRVWX
3 ABGHJKR
4 (Q 🔲) (U+V+Z 1/7-30/8)
5 **AB**DFGIJKLMNPUZ
6 CDEGJOT

💬 On the Canche estuary which flows into the Channel. Beautiful dunes and routes for walks and bike rides. Restaurant next to the site. Visit Le Touquet Paris Plage. Peaceful camping area with adequate shade. 2km from a sandy beach.

🚗 From Belgium on the A16 take exit 27 Etaples-Le Touquet D940. After 10 km turn right towards British Military Cemetery. The campsite is on the right. From Amiens-Rouen take exit 26. In Etaples head towards Boulogne-sur-Mer, following D940.

Sainte-Cécile
A16 · D901 · CC · **Étaples** · D939 **Attin** · D940 · D143

CC € **17** 1/4-6/7 27/8-14/11 7=6, 14=12 · 📐 N 50°31'57'' E 1°37'33''

Guines, F-62340 / Nord-Pas-de-Calais (Pas-de-Calais) ♿ 🛜 ✿ iD (1269)

🏕 La Bien Assise*****
📧 D231, avenue de la Libération
☎ +33 (0)3-21352077
📠 +33 (0)3-21367920
🗓 31/3 - 29/9
@ castels@bien-assise.com

15ha 149T(100-300m²) 10-16A CEE

1 ACD**G**IJKLMOPQ
2 FLRVX
3 ABGH**M**N**Q**RU
4 (E+H 1/4-15/9) J
   (Q+S+T+U+X 1/4-15/9)
   (Y 1/4-1/10) (Z 1/4-15/9)
5 **AB**DEFGIJKLMNOPUVWX
   YZ
6 ADEGIJ**K**(N 1km)ORTV

💬 Lovely, well-maintained castle campsite. Varied surroundings and only 8 km from the coast. The campsite is equipped with modern toilet facilities, a restaurant with an excellent menu, an indoor pool and spacious pitches.

🚗 From Calais A16, exit 43 to Guines D305. Follow signs in Guines. Site located on roundabout. From Boulonge exit 36 to Guines. From St. Omer take D943 to Ardres, then D231 past Guines. Follow signs to campsite.

Calais Marck
D940 · D127 · A16 · D943 · **Guînes** · CC · D238 · D231 · A26 · D243 · D224 · D127 E5 · D217

CC € **19** 31/3-29/6 3/9-28/9 7=6, 14=12, 21=18 · 📐 N 50°51'59'' E 1°51'30''

Licques, F-62850 / Nord-Pas-de-Calais (Pas-de-Calais) 🚻 ♿ 🛜 iD (1270)

🔺 Pommiers des Trois Pays****
✉ 273 rue du Breuil
☎ +33 (0)3-21350202
☎ 15/3 - 31/10
@ contact@pommiers-3pays.com

2,5ha 36T(100-150m²) 16A CEE

1 ACD**G**IJKLMOPQ
2 FRUVWX
3 ABGHJRU
4 (E+F+H 1/4-20/9)
   (Q 1/4-15/10) (R 1/4-25/10)
   (T+U+V+X+Z 1/4-15/10)
5 **AB**DEFGIJKLMNOPUXYZ
6 CDEGK(N 0,8km)TUV

💬 The campsite is located in a former apple orchard, with spacious marked-out pitches, situated in Parc Natural Régional des Caps et Marais d'Opale. Licques is just 25 km from the sea, there is a good restaurant with reasonable prices. Open nearly all the season. Arrival is possible until 22:00.

🚗 From Lille, to Saint-Omer via A26/E15. Exit 2 to Licques. Campsite signposted. From Calais head to Guines. Then D215 to Licques.

CC €**17** *15/3-6/7 27/8-30/10 7=6* 📐 N 50°46'47'' E 1°56'52''

Rang-du-Fliers, F-62180 / Nord-Pas-de-Calais (Pas-de-Calais) 🛜 iD (1271)

🔺 l'Orée du Bois****
✉ chemin Blanc
☎ +33 (0)3-21842851
FAX +33 (0)3-21842856
☎ 1/4 - 31/10
@ oree.du.bois@wanadoo.fr

18ha 50T(80-110m²) 6A CEE

1 ACD**G**IJKLMPQ
2 ABFGLRVX
3 B**F**GHJMNRUW
4 (C 1/6-15/9) (E 14/4-14/10)
   (H 1/6-15/9) **KLN**
   (Q+S+T+U+V+X+Y+Z ☎)
5 **AB**CFGJLNPUVW
6 BCDEGH**I**J**K**M(N 0,1km)TU
   V

💬 This French campsite with a leisure pool and marked-out pitches is situated in a natural wooded area and 4 km from the sea. Bar, restaurant (closed Wednesday), heated swimming pools and toilet facilities, jacuzzi and sauna. Some open-air fitness equipment. There is a supermarket next to the campsite.

🚗 A16 exit 25. Then D303 direction Rang-du-Fliers. After leaving Rang-du-Fliers, left just past Lidl entrance. Follow signs not SatNav for the last section.

CC €**17** *1/4-7/7 27/8-30/10 7=6* 📐 N 50°25'1'' E 1°36'42''

Sangatte, F-62231 / Nord-Pas-de-Calais (Pas-de-Calais) ♿ 🛜 iD (1272)

🔺 Camping des Noires Mottes***
✉ rue Pierre Dupuy
☎ +33 (0)3-21820475
☎ 1/4 - 31/10
@ campingdesnoiresmottes@
  orange.fr

3,5ha 94T(70-120m²) 6-10A CEE

1 ACDFIJKLMO**P**Q
2 AEFG**K**LRWXY
3 BGHK**OP**RUWY
4 (Q ☎) (U 10/7-22/8)
5 **AB**EFGIJKLMNOPUVZ
6 CEK(N 0,5km)RT

💬 Quiet campsite, beautiful clean grounds. Views over the hills. 100 metres from the sandy beach between le Cap Blanc-Nez and le Cap Gris-Nez. 5 km from the large Cité Europe shopping centre. Free wifi, 5 km from the Channel Tunnel and 8 km from the Dover-Calais ferry.

🚗 A16 from Calais towards Boulogne-sur-Mer. South of Calais exit 14 Coquelles, towards Sangatte.

CC €**17** *1/4-2/7 20/8-30/10* 📐 N 50°56'45'' E 1°45'30''

Wacquinghen, F-62250 / Nord-Pas-de-Calais (Pas-de-Calais) 🛜 iD (1273)

🏕 Camping l'Escale***
📧 15 Route Nationale
☎ +33 (0)3-21320069
📠 +33 (0)3-21337957
🗓 1/4 - 15/10
@ camp-escale@wanadoo.fr

11ha 40T(60-100m²) 10A CEE

1 ACDGIJKLMOPQ
2 FGRUWX
3 BGHIMNQRUW
4 (Q+R+U+V+Y+Z 🚿)
5 **AB**FGJLNPUVWZ
6 CEG**IK**(N 3km)OTV

💬 This 11 hectare parkland campsite invites you to take relaxing walks along the cliffs of Cap Gris-Nez and Cap Blanc-Nez. Just 5 km from the sandy beaches of the Opal Coast. Good connections to the Channel Tunnel and ferries to the UK. Good, affordable restaurant at the site.

🚗 A16 between Calais and Boulogne-sur-Mer exit 34 direction Wacquinghen. From Boulogne exit 33 dir. Wacquinghen.

D238
A16 D231
D940 D243
CC D127 E5
Boulogne-sur-Mer
Outreau D341 D127

CC € **17** 1/4-6/7 24/8-14/10 📍 N 50°47'2'' E 1°40'9''

Wimereux, F-62930 / Nord-Pas-de-Calais (Pas-de-Calais) ♿ 🛜 iD (1274)

🏕 Mun. L'Olympic***
📧 49 rue de la Libération
☎ +33 (0)3-21324563
🗓 19/3 - 21/10
@ camping.wimereux@orange.fr

3,8ha 91T(63-90m²) 6A CEE

1 ACD**G**HIJKLMPQ
2 EFGRVWX
3 ABF**GH**N**O**RUY
4 (Q 🚿)
5 **AB**DEFGIJKLMNOPUXYZ
6 EG**J**(N 0,8km)TV

💬 An unpretentious campsite marked out by hedges and close to the picturesque village of Wimereux. Located between Cap Gris-Nez, the Opal Coast and Boulogne-sur-Mer. 5 km from Nausicaá, the world-famous sea aquarium in Boulogne-sur-Mer. Easily accessible by bus.

🚗 A16, exit Wimereux Sud. Direction Wimereux. Campsite signposted and is located on the edge of the village.

D238
D940 D243
A16
CC
Boulogne-sur-Mer
D341

CC € **17** 19/3-9/7 27/8-20/10 📍 N 50°45'40'' E 1°36'28''

Albert, F-80300 / Picardie (Somme) ♿ 🛜 iD (1275)

🏕 Camping Le Vélodrome**
📧 avenue Henry Dunant
☎ +33 (0)3-64622253
🗓 1/4 - 10/10
@ campingalbert@laposte.net

1,6ha 75T(72-120m²) 6-10A CEE

1 ACDFIJKLMOPQ
2 CDGRTVWX
3 AHJR
4 (Q 🚿)
5 GIJKLMNOPUWXYZ
6 ACDEGJ(N 0,6km)T

💬 The campsite is located on the River Ancre and by several well-stocked fishing lakes. There is a free practice range for golf with 5 holes next to the site. The area around Albert formed the front line during the attacks of the Somme in 1916. The many graveyards and monuments are a silent witness to this. A visit to the welcoming historic centre of Albert is recommended. There is a special area for motorhomes.

🚗 Via D929 direction Albert. Then follow signs.

D919 D929
CC
D23 D938
Bray-sur-Somme
D1
Corbie D42 D329

CC € **17** 1/4-23/6 23/8-9/10 7=6 📍 N 50°0'41'' E 2°39'20''

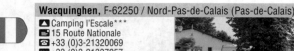

Berny-Rivière, F-02290 / Picardie (Aisne)

♿ 🛜 ✿ **iD** (1276)

🔺 La Croix du Vieux Pont*****
🏠 8 rue de la Fabrique
☎ +33 (0)3-23555002
📠 +33 (0)3-23550513
🗓 1/1 - 31/12
@ info@la-croix-du-vieux-pont.com

34ha 200T(100-450m²) 6A CEE

1 ACD**G**IJKLMOPRS
2 ACDLRVXY
3 ABCGHJK**M**N**O**P**Q**R**T**U**VW**Z
4 (C+E+H 1/4-31/10) IJK**M**N**O**
P(Q+S+T+U+V+W+X+Y+Z
1/4-31/10)
5 **AB**DEFGIJKLMNOPRUWXY
Z
6 BEG**IK**(N 0km)ORTV

💬 A very large, well equipped campsite on the River l'Aisne. All types of pitches. A family campsite suitable mainly for older children including a heated swimming pool and many other sports opportunities. Own bus connection to Paris and Disneyland.

🚗 In Vic-sur-Aisne take the D91 in the direction of Soissons. The campsite is located to the right after 1 km in Berny-Rivière.

D935
Attichy | Cuffies
CC | N31 | **Soissons**
D335
D973 | N2

CC € **19** 1/1-6/7 1/9-31/12 | 🧭 N 49°24'19'' E 3°7'44''

Bresles, F-60510 / Picardie (Oise)

♿ 🛜 **iD** (1277)

🔺 Camping de la Trye
🏠 34 rue de Trye
☎📠 +33 (0)3-44078095
🗓 1/1 - 31/12
@ camping.bresles@sfr.fr

3ha 60T(100-250m²) 6A CEE

1 ACDGIJKLM**P**Q
2 FGRVWXY
3 AGHJK**MOP**RW
4 (A 1/7-31/8) (C 1/5-30/9)
(Q+T 1/7-31/8)
5 **AB**GIJMNOPUXZ
6 ABCEGHJ(N 1km)O

💬 A congenial campsite near Beauvais in natural surroundings and with plenty of walking and cycling opportunities. You can visit Paris by car or train. Special pony, horse and donkey activities for young and old. The Parc Asterix and Saint Paul theme parks are close by.

🚗 N31 from Compiègne to Beauvais, exit Bresles. Then follow Stade or camping signs.

D149 | D1001 | Saint-Just-en-Chaussée
A16 | D938
Beauvais | D151 | D916
CC | N31
D927 | D12 | D929
D2 | D44 | **Mouy** | D137

CC € **15** 1/1-6/7 27/8-31/12 7=6, 14=12 | 🧭 N 49°24'19'' E 2°15'29''

Brighton-les-Pins, F-80410 / Picardie (Somme)

♿ 🛜 **iD** (1278)

🔺 Le Bois de Pins***
🏠 rue Guillaume le Conquérant
☎ +33 (0)3-22267104
📠 +33 (0)3-22266081
🗓 1/4 - 30/10
@ info@campingleboisdepins.com

4ha 61T(82-200m²) 10A CEE

1 ABCD**G**IJKLM**P**Q
2 BENRSVX
3 AGHNR
4 (Q+R 🖵)
5 **AB**DEFGJLNPU
6 ACEGH**K**(N 3km)

💬 A modest campsite where you will be able to relax. The (pebble) beach is about 500m from the campsite. Cayeux-sur-Mer is about 1 km away and there you can swim in the sea.

🚗 At Abbeville go from the A28 to the D40 then D940. After St. Valéry-sur-Somme to the D3. Right in La Mollière to the D102. Campsite signposted before Brighton.

CC
Cayeux-sur-Mer
D940 | D48 | D3

CC € **17** 1/4-7/7 25/8-29/10 | 🧭 N 50°11'51'' E 1°31'0''

Feuillères, F-80200 / Picardie (Somme)

♿ 🛜 **iD** (1279)

🏰 Château de l'Oseraie***
✉ 10, rue du Château
☎ +33 (0)3-22831759
🕐 15/3 - 31/10
@ jsg-bred@wanadoo.fr

3ha 30T(80-120m²) 6-10A CEE

1 ACD**G**IJKLM**P**Q
2 CFLRTVWXY
3 BGJ**M**NR
4 (C+H 1/5-30/9) (Q 1/5-15/10)
  (R 🔲) (T+Z 1/4-30/9)
5 **AB**DGJLNPUXZ
6 ABCDEGIK(N 8km)OTV

💬 Welcoming camping grounds in a small village. Many sports options. The area around the river Somme is perfect for nice days out. Fishing is possible nearby. Close to the town of Peronne. Receptionists speak French, English and Dutch.

🚗 Exit Autoroute A1 at 13.1 km, Feuillères 2 km further, road on right by the church goes to the campsite. Site is 2.5 km from A1.

CC € **17** 15/3-8/7 26/8-30/10

📐 N 49°56'54'' E 2°50'27''

Forest-Montiers, F-80120 / Picardie (Somme)

♿ 🛜 **iD** (1280)

🏰 Camping de la Mottelette**
✉ Ferme de la Mottelette
☎ +33 (0)3-22283233
🕐 1/4 - 31/10
@ fermedelamottelettemanier@wanadoo.fr

1ha 35T(100-150m²) 6-10A CEE

1 AD**G**IJKLMO**P**RS
2 DFLMRWX
3 AGRW
4 (Q 1/7-31/8) (R 🔲)
  (Z 1/7-31/8)
5 **A**CGJLNPUXZ
6 ACDEGJ(N 4km)OTV

💬 A small farmyard campsite close to the Bay of the Somme. You will be welcomed in friendly surroundings to spend an enjoyable holiday.

🚗 A16, exit 24 direction Rue. Follow signs at roundabout.

CC € **15** 1/4-7/7 25/8-30/10

📐 N 50°15'10'' E 1°42'45''

Fort-Mahon-Plage, F-80120 / Picardie (Somme)

🛜 **iD** (1281)

🏰 Le Royon****
✉ 1271 route de Quend
☎ +33 (0)3-22234030
📠 +33 (0)3-22236515
🕐 23/3 - 1/11
@ info@campingleroyon.com

4,5ha 38T(95-130m²) 6A

1 ACD**F**IJL**P**Q
2 GLRVX
3 A**F**GKMNQRU**W**
4 (C 1/7-31/8) (F 1/5-30/10)
  (G 1/7-31/8) (Q 🔲)
  (R+T+U+X+Z 1/7-31/8)
5 **AB**CDEFGIJKLNPUXZ
6 CDEGHI**K**(N 1km)ORTV

💬 A campsite with plenty of amenities and an indoor swimming pool. Pitches on grassland and separated by trees and hedges. 3 km from the resort of Fort-Mahon-Plage with its lovely sandy beach and good fish restaurants.

🚗 Motorway A16 take exit Quend. Then, in direction Fort-Mahon-Plage. Campsite is signposted.

CC € **17** 23/3-6/7 26/8-31/10

📐 N 50°19'57'' E 1°34'46''

La Mollière-d'Aval, F-80410 / Picardie (Somme) ♿ 🛜 **iD** (1282)

🏕 Les Galets de la Mollière***
🏠 rue Faidherbe
☎ +33 (0)3-22266185
FAX +33 (0)3-22266568
🔑 1/4 - 30/10
@ info@
campinglesgaletsdelamolliere.com
6ha 56T(80-120m²) 10A CEE

1 ABCD**G**IJKLM**P**Q
2 BLNRSVX
3 AGHJMRU**W**
4 (C+H 1/5-15/9) K(Q+R 🔑)
(T+Z 1/7-31/8)
5 **AB**CFGJLNPUZ
6 ACEH**K**(N 3km)T

💬 The campsite is located near a lovely shingle and sandy beach (no swimming), close to the dunes and pine forests. The campsite has a heated swimming pool. Kite-surfing possible in the bay when wind is good. Cayeux-sur-Mer is worth a visit, lovely beach.

🚗 Follow A16 motorway to the A28, then dir. Cayeux-sur-Mer. Turn right at the first village La Mollière. Signs on the right side of the road.

Saint-Valery-sur-Somme
CC
D940 D48 D3
Ault

(CC) € **17** 1/4-7/7 25/8-29/10 | N 50°12'10'' E 1°31'34''

Laon, F-02000 / Picardie (Aisne) 🛜 **iD** (1283)

🏕 La Chênaie
🏠 alleé de la Chênaie
☎ +33 (0)3-23233863
🔑 1/4 - 30/9
@ contact.camping.laon@
gmail.com
2ha 55T(100-120m²) 10A CEE

1 ACD**G**IJKLMO**P**
2 BDFGILRSTVWXY
3 AGR**W**
4 (E+H+Q+R+Z 🔑)
5 **AB**GIJKLMNOPUZ
6 CEGH**K**(N 3km)T

💬 Spacious, quiet campsite with many trees on the outskirts of the town of Laon. Ideal base for walking and cycling tours or a visit to the town.

🚗 Take the Laon exit from the D1044 and follow camping signs.

Versigny
D967 N2
D1044
Chambry
Laon A26 D977
D7
CC
D5
Vauxaillon D23

(CC) € **17** 1/4-30/6 1/9-29/9 7=6 | N 49°33'44'' E 3°35'44''

Le Crotoy, F-80550 / Picardie (Somme) 🛜 **iD** (1284)

🏕 Camping le Tarteron***
🏠 route de Rue, BP 70034
☎ +33 (0)3-22270675
FAX +33 (0)3-22270249
🔑 1/4 - 31/10
@ contact@letarteron.fr

7ha 50T(100-140m²) 6A

1 ACDGIJKLMPQ
2 AFMRVWX
3 AGHJMNRW
4 (F+H+Q+R 🔑) (Z 1/7-31/8)
5 **AB**CFGIJKLNPRUWX
6 AGJ**K**(N 1,5km)T

💬 The camping grounds have a peaceful location in the heart of the Bay of Somme. Partly marked out pitches, partly on large grassy fields. Lovely indoor swimming pool. Lovely cycle paths.

🚗 From A16, exit 23 route Le Crotoy. In Le Crotoy turn right at first roundabout. Signposted.

D12
D1001
CC
Cayeux-sur-Mer Le Crotoy A16 D32
D940 D48 D3
D40

(CC) € **17** 1/4-1/7 26/8-30/10 | N 50°13'50'' E 1°38'25''

Le Crotoy, F-80550 / Picardie (Somme)

🚭 📶 **iD** (1285)

🔺 Flower Camping Les
  Aubépines★★★★
🏠 rue de la Maye - St. Firmin
☎ +33 (0)3-22270134
� 30/3 - 4/11
@ contact@
  camping-lesaubepines.com
4ha 74T(90-180m²) 3-10A CEE

1 ACD**G**IJKLMOP**Q**
2 AFGLRVX
3 ADF**G**HJKMR
4 (A 9/7-31/8) (C 17/6-3/9)
  (F 1/4-1/10,20/10-4/11)
  (H 17/6-3/9)
  (Q+S+T+U+V+X ⌐)
5 **AB**CDEFGHIJKLMNPUWX
  YZ
6 ACEGI**K**(N 3km)ORTV

💬 Les Aubépines, a family campsite with a lovely indoor pool, is located in the heart of the Somme bay region, in natural surroundings and 1 km from the beach. A paradise for cyclists and walkers. You can bring your own horse. The campsite can arrange half board.

🚗 From A16 exit 23, follow road to Le Crotoy. At Le Crotoy, follow D4 Crotoy/St. Firmin de C. Left at St. Firmin sign. The campsite is signposted. Do not follow SatNav on last section.

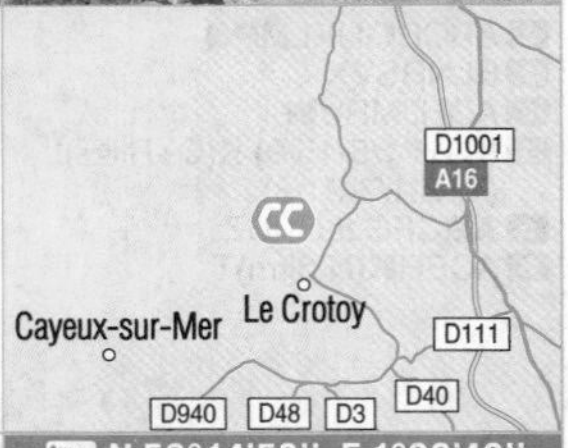

Cayeux-sur-Mer CC Le Crotoy
D1001 A16 D111
D940 D48 D3 D40

CC € **17** 30/3-4/5 14/5-6/7 27/8-31/10   🏕 N 50°14'59'' E 1°36'43''

Le Crotoy, F-80550 / Picardie (Somme)

🚭 📶 **iD** (1286)

🔺 Les Trois Sablières★★★★
🏠 1850 rue de la Maye
☎ +33 (0)3-22270133
📠 +33 (0)3-22271006
⌐ 30/3 - 8/11
@ contact@
  camping-les-trois-sablieres.com
2ha 30T(100-120m²) 6-10A CEE

1 ACD**G**IJKLMOP**Q**
2 AERUVX
3 AGHJRUV
4 (C+H 1/5-15/9) K**N**(Q+R ⌐)
  (T 1/7-30/8) (U+Z ⌐)
5 **AB**CEFGIJKLMNOPRUWXZ
6 ADEGK(N 4km)ORTV

💬 The campsite is located in one of the loveliest bays in the world. Sabine and Jean-Michel welcome you to their campsite for a wonderful holiday. The site is located ± 300m from a fine sandy beach (no swimming). Only campers are allowed in the toilet block (with key) and (free) showers.

🚗 From the A16 exit 24 direction Rue. Follow Le Crotoy road. At Le Crotoy follow D4 Crotoy/St. Firmin de C. Left at St. Firmin sign. Campsite signposted.

D1001 A16
CC Le Crotoy
Cayeux-sur-Mer D111
D940 D48 D3 D40

CC € **17** 30/3-7/7 26/8-7/11   🏕 N 50°14'54'' E 1°35'55''

Mers-les-Bains, F-80350 / Picardie (Somme)

📶 **iD** (1287)

🔺 Flower Camping Le Rompval★★★
🏠 Lieu dit Blengues
☎ +33 (0)2-35844321
⌐ 30/3 - 4/11
@ campinglerompval@gmail.com

3ha 79T(90-100m²) 6-13A CEE

1 ACD**G**HIJKLMOP**Q**
2 LRVWXY
3 AGKR
4 (E+H+Q+R+T+U+V+Z ⌐)
5 **AB**DFGHIJKLMNPQUWXYZ
6 ACEGK(N 2km)ORTV

💬 A quietly located Flowercamping site for those who appreciate the countryside. Located next to a protected wood less than 1 km from the Falaise. Mers-les-Bains and Tréport are worth a visit. Try ordering a delicious breakfast.

🚗 A28, exit 2 direction Le Tréport. Follow the D940 (Route d'Eu) direction St. Valery-sur-Somme. Left after 3 km. Signposted. Don't go via Mers-les-Bains with a caravan.

Le Tréport CC D940
Mers-les-
Bains Eu D1015 D48
D1314
D925 D22

CC € **17** 30/3-7/7 25/8-3/11 7=6, 14=11   🏕 N 50°4'39'' E 1°24'52''

Moyenneville, F-80870 / Picardie (Somme)

♿ 📶 ✿ iD **1288**

🏕 Le Val de Trie****
📧 rue des Sources
☎ +33 (0)3-22314888
🔑 1/4 - 1/10
@ raphael@camping-levaldetrie.fr

3ha 76T(100m²) 6-10A CEE

1 ACD**G**IJKLPQ
2 CFLRTUVXY
3 ABGHIJKN**P**RUW
4 (A 7/7-29/8) (E 15/4-1/10)
   (H 1/6-7/9) IK(Q+R 🔑)
   (T+U+X 28/4-31/8) (Z 🔑)
5 ABDEFGIJKLNPUWXYZ
6 CDEGJ(N 8km)OV

💬 Family campsite with a pleasant atmosphere in the green valley of the Trie, near the coast. Green, marked out pitches.

🚐 From Abbeville D925 direction Eu and Le Tréport. Don't follow Moyenneville! When leaving the village Miannay turn left D86 direction Toeufles. Campsite signs can be found on the left side of the road.

D940 | D40 | D1001
A16
D3
Friville-Escarbotin | **Abbeville**
CC
D86 | A28 | D901
D48 | D928
D22 | D29

CC € **17** *1/4-13/7 31/8-30/9 7=6, 14=11* | 📡 N 50°5'10'' E 1°42'56''

Nampont-St-Martin, F-80120 / Picardie (Somme)

📶 iD **1289**

🏕 La Ferme des Aulnes****
📧 Fresne
☎ +33 (0)3-22292269
📠 +33 (0)3-22293943
🔑 30/3 - 1/11
@ contact@fermedesaulnes.com

3,5ha 41T(100-120m²) 6-10A CEE

1 ACD**G**IJKLMOPQ
2 FLRTUVX
3 AC**F**GNRUV
4 (A 8/7-26/8) (E 🔑) **KN**
   (Q+R+T+U+V+Y+Z 🔑)
5 **AB**CDEFGJLNPUWXYZ
6 CDEGIK(N 10km)RTV

💬 The campsite is peacefully located in a rural area 5 km from the motorway, next to a traditional renovated farmhouse. Good cycling options and 2 km from a golf course. 2½ km from a fishing lake, free for campsite guests. The Marquenterre nature reserve is 15 km away. A campsite with a lovely ambiance.

🚐 A16, exit 25 direction Arras. After ± 2 km direction Abbeville as far as Nampont-Saint-Martin then right towards Villers/Fresne, campsite signposted.

Rang-du-Fliers
Berck | A16 | D939
D901
CC
D1001
D12
D940

CC € **17** *30/3-6/7 25/8-31/10* | 📡 N 50°20'11'' E 1°42'44''

Orvillers/Sorel, F-60490 / Picardie (Oise)

👨‍👩‍👧 ♿ 📶 ✿ iD **1290**

🏕 Camping de Sorel***
📧 24 rue St. Claude
☎ +33 (0)3-44850274
📠 +33 (0)3-44421165
🔑 1/1 - 31/12
@ contact@aestiva.fr

7ha 124T(110-170m²) 10A CEE

1 ACD**G**IJKLMOPQ
2 FLRVXY
3 A**F**GHJNRUV
4 (Q 🔑) (R 1/6-15/9)
   (T+U+V+X+Z 🔑)
5 **AB**GIJKLMNOPUVWXYZ
6 EG**K**(N 3km)OT

💬 You are welcome from 9.00 to 19.00 hours, every day of the week, in these quiet and green surroundings. 60 minutes from Paris and 90 minutes from Lille. Exit 11 from motorway A1 - E15 - E19, RN 17 Orvillers/Sorel.

🚐 When approaching from the north: after Roye take the N17. The campsite is located on the left side of the N17, after Orvillers.

D930 | D221 | D934
Montdidier
D929
A1 | D938
Tricot | CC
D142
Cambronne-lès-Ribécourt
D1017 | D935

CC € **17** *1/4-30/6 1/9-31/10 7=6, 14=12* | 📡 N 49°34'2'' E 2°42'29''

Pendé, F-80230 / Picardie (Somme) 📶 iD 1291

🏕 Camping De La Baie
📧 10 rue de la Baie
☎ +33 (0)3-22607272
📅 1/4 - 31/10
@ contact@campingdelabaie.eu

2ha 32T(80-110m²) 10A

1 ACDGIJLM**P**Q
2 FRSVWX
3 AGHJKQU
4 (Q+R+Z ▣)
5 **AB**DGIJKLMNPUV
6 EGKOT

💬 This basic campsite run by Vincent and Maud will appeal to those who appreciate simple campsites. The campsite is a useful stopover site, or for a longer stay, especially if you enjoy walking or cycling.

🚗 From the N drive onto D940 at roundabout at St. Valery-sur-Somme, Cap Hornu, Eu/Le Tréport, head towards Eu/Le Tréport. 1st road left towards Routhiauville. Campsite is signposted.

CC € **15** 1/4-5/7 25/8-30/10 7=6 ▨ N 50°10'35'' E 1°35'23''

Péronne, F-80200 / Picardie (Somme) 👫 ♿ 📶 iD 1292

🏕 Port de Plaisance***
📧 route de Paris
☎ +33 (0)3-22841931
📠 +33 (0)3-22733637
📅 1/3 - 31/10
@ contact@camping-plaisance.com

2ha 82T(80-150m²) 10A CEE

1 ACD**G**IJKLMPQ
2 CFGRVX
3 AGKRU**W**
4 (C+H 1/6-31/8) (Q+R ▣)
    (U 1/6-30/8) (Z ▣)
5 **AB**DGIJKLMNPUW
6 ACDEGH**IJK**(N 1km)V

💬 This campsite is located a few kilometres from the A1 near a yacht harbour close to Peronne. The grounds are level with a choice of shaded or non-shaded pitches. The area is known for its many historic World War I locations.

🚗 The campsite is located south of Péronne, on the N17.

CC € **17** 1/3-10/7 28/8-30/10 7=6 ▨ N 49°55'4'' E 2°55'57''

Poix-de-Picardie, F-80290 / Picardie (Somme) ♿ 📶 iD 1293

🏕 Le Bois des Pêcheurs***
📧 rue de Verdun
☎ +33 (0)3-22901171
📠 +33 (0)3-22903291
📅 1/4 - 30/9
@ camping@
    ville-poix-de-picardie.fr

2,4ha 88T(80m²) 6A

1 A**G**IJLMPRS
2 CFRTVWXY
3 ABR
5 **AB**FGIJMNPUWZ
6 ACDEGK(N 0,3km)V

💬 A very well maintained municipal campsite with marked out pitches. Quiet location, within walking distance of the village with opportunities for shopping. Free wifi. Stay three nights and pay for two.

🚗 D1029. From Amiens turn right at Poix-de-Picardie, town centre. From Rouen in Eplessier head for Poix-de-Picardie to the town centre. Follow camping signs. From Rouen A29/E44 exit 13.

CC € **17** 1/4-30/6 1/9-29/9 3=2 ▨ N 49°46'34'' E 1°58'28''

Port-le-Grand/Abbeville, F-80132 / Picardie (Somme)

🌐 📶 **iD** (1294)

🏕 Château des Tilleuls***
📧 rue de la Baie
☎ +33 (0)3-22240775
📠 +33 (0)3-22242380
🕐 1/3 - 1/11
@ contact@chateaudestilleuls.com

11ha 42T(120-150m²) 10A CEE

1 ACDGIJKLMPQ
2 FIJLRVX
3 AFGJKNPQRUV
4 (C+H 1/6-15/9) N(Q+S 🕐)
(T+U 1/6-1/9) (Z 🕐)
5 ABDFGIJKLMNOPUWXYZ
6 ACEGHIK(N 6km)OTV

💬 A campsite set in a park with trees more than a hundred years old. An oasis of peace in natural surroundings. Large pitches for a stopover or for longer stays. The new young owners are renovating the site beautifully.

🚗 Located on the D40. From Abbeville after about 6 km, direction St. Valéry/Le Crotoy, before Port-le-Grand. Short incline after barrier.

Saint-Valéry-sur-Somme D940 | D1001 | D12
A16 | D928 | D32
D48 | **Abbeville** | D183
D925 | D29 | D22 | A28 | D901 | D3

CC € 17 1/3-7/7 26/8-31/10

🧭 N 50°8'29'' E 1°45'48''

Quend, F-80120 / Picardie (Somme)

🌐 📶 **iD** (1295)

🏕 Des Deux Plages***
📧 15 rue des Maisonnettes
☎ +33 (0)3-22234896
📠 +33 (0)3-22234869
🕐 1/4 - 31/10
@ camping@camping2plages.com

2ha 30T(100-120m²) 4-6A CEE

1 AGIJKLPRS
2 FRTVX
3 AFGJRUW
4 (E 1/4-15/9) (G 1/7-31/8)
(Q+R+T+U+Z 🕐)
5 ABFGIJKLMNPUVZ
6 AEGK(N 5km)ORTV

💬 A small, peaceful family campsite with an indoor swimming pool. 5 km from Fort-Mahon-Plage with its fine sandy beaches and good fish restaurants. Suitable for short or longer stays, also with children. 5 km from Marquenterre park. Excellent area for cycling.

🚗 A16 exit Quend. In Quend D32 direction Fort-Mahon-Plage. Campsite shown on small signs.

Berck Rang-du-Fliers D142
D901
CC A16 D12
D1001
D940

CC € 17 1/4-14/7 1/9-30/10

🧭 N 50°19'25'' E 1°37'28''

Quend-Plage-les-Pins, F-80120 / Picardie (Somme)

🌐 📶 ✿ **iD** (1296)

🏕 Flower Camping Les
Vertes Feuilles****
📧 25 route de la Plage-Monchaux
☎ +33 (0)3-22235512
📠 +33 (0)3-22190752
🕐 31/3 - 4/11
@ contact@lesvertesfeuilles.com

3,5ha 45T(70-100m²) 6-10A

1 ACDGIJKLMPRS
2 FRVXY
3 AFGHJKRU
4 (E 🕐) (H 1/6-15/9)
(Q+R+T+U+V+X+Z 🕐)
5 ABCDEFGIJKLMNOPUWXYZ
6 AEGK(N 2km)OTV

💬 A small family campsite surrounded by greenery. There is a heated swimming pool for your use. Close to cycle paths, an ornithological park, an extensive beach and the Golf de Belle Dune golf course.

🚗 From Calais A16. Exit Quend direction Quend/Plages Les Pins. Campsite signposted.

Berck
Verton D901
CC
Rue D1001
A16
D940

CC € 17 31/3-8/7 26/8-3/11

🧭 N 50°19'9'' E 1°36'24''

Ressons-le-Long, F-02290 / Picardie (Aisne)

🛇 🛜 **iD** (1297)

🏔 La Halte de Mainville★★★
✉ 18 rue du Routy
☎ +33 (0)3-23742669
📠 +33 (0)3-23740360
🗓 13/1 - 8/12
@ lahaltedemainville@wanadoo.fr

5ha 74T(120m²) 6A CEE

1 AGIJKLMOPRS
2 RVX
3 AGNRUW
4 (C+H 17/6-15/9)
5 **AB**CEGIJKLMNPUXZ
6 CEGJ(N 4km)RT

💬 Level grounds with marked out, partly shaded pitches. Good facilities. A peaceful family campsite with a swimming pool and tennis court. Close to the completely restored Pierrefonds chateau. Free carp fishing. Disneyland about one hour away, Parc Astérix half an hour's drive.

🚗 On the N31 Compiègne-Soissons about 15 km from Soissons follow the D17 southwards to Ressons-le-Long. Follow camping signs.

Trosly-Breuil
N31 CC **Soissons**
D335 N2
D973

CC € **17** 13/1-30/6 1/9-30/11
🧭 N 49°23'34'' E 3°9'6''

Rue, F-80120 / Picardie (Somme)

🛇 🛜 **iD** (1298)

🏔 Camping de la Maye★★
✉ 32 rue du Moulin
☎ +33 (0)3-22250955
🗓 1/4 - 31/10
@ campingdelamaye@orange.fr

2,5ha 100T(70-150m²) 6-10A CEE

1 ACD**G**IJKLMO**P**Q
2 CDFLRVX
3 AGRW
4 (Q+R 🅿)
5 **AB**DEFGJKLMNPQUVZ
6 CDEG**K**(N 0,040km)OT

💬 This refurbished campsite is close to the historic village of Rue, close to the Bay of Somme and the Marquenterre nature reserve. A stopover campsite, but also suitable for longer stays.

🚗 D940 from Berck to Rue. Follow Rue Centre (D175) at roundabout. Campsite entrance opposite Carrefour Market.

D901
D12
D1001
A16
D940
Nouvion
Cayeux-sur-Mer D111 D32

CC € **15** 1/4-7/7 26/8-30/10
🧭 N 50°16'31'' E 1°39'39''

Sailly-le-Sec, F-80800 / Picardie (Somme)

🛇 🛜 ✿ **iD** (1299)

🏔 Les Puits Tournants★★★★
✉ 6 rue du Marais
☎ +33 (0)3-22766556
🗓 1/4 - 31/10
@ camping.puitstournants@
   wanadoo.fr

NEW

4,5ha 32T(100-300m²) 6A

1 ACDFIJKLMO**P**Q
2 DFLRUWX
3 B**F**HJ**Q**RW
4 F(H 🅿) **KN**(R 🅿)
   (U 1/6-30/9)
5 **A**DGJKNPWXYZ
6 BCDEG**K**(N 4km)OT

💬 Close to the lovely Somme River with excellent fishing, this campsite is in a small village. Close to the large cities of Peronne and Amiens, with lots of things to see.

🚗 From Amiens towards Peronne D1. Beyond Corbie in Sailly-le-Sec immediately past church turn right to campsite.

Albert
D919 D938
D929 D349
CC
D1 D42 D329
Villers-
Bretonneux A29 D337
D935 D23

CC € **17** 1/4-6/7 24/8-30/10 7=6
🧭 N 49°55'10'' E 2°34'48''

Seraucourt-le-Grand, F-02790 / Picardie (Aisne)

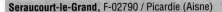

🅰 Camping du Vivier aux Carpes***
📧 10 rue Charles Voyeux
☎ +33 (0)3-23605010
📅 20/3 - 20/10
@ contact@camping-picardie.com

1,8ha 67**T**(100m²) 10A CEE

1 ACD**G**IJKLMPQ
2 DFGKRTUVX
3 ADGHJKRU**W**
4 (Q+R 🖾) (T+U+V 15/6-31/8)
5 **AB**DFGIJKLMNPQUWZ
6 CDEG**K**(N 0,1km)ORTV

💬 The campsite is located on the edge of a village. A perfect site for carp fishing, walking or cycling. You can fish in the natural pond from a number of pitches. A well maintained site with nicely marked out pitches. It has a friendly, amicable ambiance.

🚗 Leave A26 at exit 11 St. Quentin-Sud, direction Gauchy. Via D321 to Seraucourt-le-Grand. Signposted.

CC € **17** 20/3-2/6 1/9-19/10 7=6   📡 N 49°46'55'' E 3°12'51''

St. Quentin-en-Tourmont, F-80120 / Picardie (Somme)

🅰 Le Champ Neuf****
📧 8 rue du Champ Neuf
☎ +33 (0)3-22250794
📠 +33 (0)3-22250987
📅 1/4 - 31/10
@ campinglechampneuf@orange.fr

4,3ha 83**T**(100-140m²) 6-10A CEE

1 ACD**G**IJKLMO**P**RS
2 FLRSTVX
3 A**F**GHJKMNPRUV
4 (F+H 🖾) IKNP(Q+R 🖾) (T+U+Z 8/4-16/9)
5 **AB**DEFGJLNPUWXYZ
6 ACEG**K**(N 5km)ORTV

💬 This lovely campsite is located in the heart of the Marquenterre close to the Ornithological Park. Marked out pitches in natural surroundings. You can enjoy the indoor leisure pool and the adjacent sun terrace. Your horse is also welcome here. 2 km from a good restaurant.

🚗 The campsite is located in Le Bout des Crocs and can be reached via the D204 by following the 'Parc Ornithologique' signs. Follow the campsite signs, not the SatNav for the last section.

CC € **17** 1/4-6/7 25/8-30/10   📡 N 50°16'13'' E 1°36'4''

St. Valery-sur-Somme, F-80230 / Picardie (Somme)

🅰 Domaine de Drancourt*****
📧 BP 80022
☎ +33 (0)3-22269345
📠 +33 (0)3-22268587
📅 13/4 - 23/9
@ chateau.drancourt@wanadoo.fr

17ha 187**T**(< 120m²) 10A CEE

1 ACD**G**IJKLMO**P**Q
2 LRVX
3 BHJKMN**P**QRUVW
4 (C 15/6-11/9) (E+H 🖾) J (Q+S+T+U+V 🖾) (X 1/7-31/8) (Z 🖾)
5 **AB**DEFGJLNPUWZ
6 ADEGHJ(N 3km)RV

💬 This large campsite is located in an area with many places of interest. Large, partly marked out pitches on grass. Plenty of amenities are available on the campsite.

🚗 From Abbeville D40 and D940 direction St. Valery-sur-Somme. Campsite is signposted.

CC € **19** 13/4-30/6 25/8-22/9   📡 N 50°9'8'' E 1°38'9''

St. Valery-sur-Somme, F-80230 / Picardie (Somme)

♿ 📶 **iD** 1303

🏕 Le Walric****
🏠 345 route d'Eu
☎ +33 (0)3-22268197
📠 +33 (0)3-22607726
📅 1/4 - 30/10
@ info@campinglewalric.com

5,7ha 52T(95m²) 6A CEE

1 ABCD**F**IJKL**PQ**
2 LNRTVX
3 AGHJKMNRU
4 (E+H+Q+R+T+U+Z 🔌)
5 **AB**CDEFGJLNPU
6 ACEGH**IK**(N 3km)OT

💬 A campsite with spaciously appointed pitches marked out by natural bushes. The site has a lovely indoor swimming pool. Located close to the bay of Somme and near the medieval district of the village of St.Valery-sur-Somme with its large fish restaurants.

🚗 From Abbeville D40, D940 and D3 direction St. Valery-sur-Somme. Campsite beyond Cap Hornu on the right. Well signposted. Do not use SatNav for last section.

Cayeux-sur-Mer · CC · A16 · D1001 · D940 · D48 · D3 · D40 · Friville-Escarbotin · D925

CC € **17** 1/4-7/7 25/8-29/10 · 🏖 N 50°11'0'' E 1°37'4''

Suzy, F-02320 / Picardie (Aisne)

♿ 📶 **iD** 1304

🏕 Les Etangs du Moulin***
🏠 Le Champ Fercot
☎ +33 (0)3-23809286
📅 1/4 - 15/10
@ contact@etangsdumoulin.fr

7ha 30T(80-200m²) 6A

1 ACD**F**IJKLMOPQ
2 BDIRTUWXY
3 ABGHIJRUW
4 (F+H+Q+R+U+X+Z 🔌)
5 **AB**EFGJLNPQRUWZ
6 DEG**K**(N 6km)TV

💬 A spacious, quiet campsite in wild-west style close to Laon. There are marked-out and open pitches which vary in size. Good playing facilities for young and older children. Beautiful places for fishing (free of charge) on the campsite. Toilet facilities are clean and well-maintained.

🚗 Exit Chivi from N2. From N44 exit Cerny-lès-Bucy. In Suzy follow campsite signs.

Condren · D1044 · A26 · D7 · Chambry · D13 · Laon · CC · D5 · N2 · D1 · D23 · D15

CC € **17** 1/4-8/7 26/8-14/10 7=6 · 🏖 N 49°32'52'' E 3°28'14''

Villers-sur-Authie, F-80120 / Picardie (Somme)

♿ 📶 ✿ **iD** 1305

🏕 Sites & Paysages Le Val d'Authie*****
🏠 20 route de Vercourt
☎ +33 (0)3-22299247
📠 +33 (0)3-22299330
📅 1/4 - 30/9
@ camping@valdauthie.fr

7ha 60T(100-150m²) 6-10A

1 ACD**G**IJKLM**PQ**
2 FLRVX
3 A**F**GKMNRUV
4 (E 🔌) (H 15/5-30/9) **KLN** (Q+S+T+U+V+X+Z 🔌)
5 **AB**CDEFGIJKLNPUWXZ
6 CDEGH**IK**(N 6km)RTV

💬 This five-star campsite with excellent toilets and many facilities is 10 minutes from the coast, with Marquenterre nature reserve, and from the woods at Crécy. The site is an oasis of peace and has a good restaurant, indoor swimming pool and wellness room. Good cycling options.

🚗 D901 Boulogne-Abbeville, exit Nampont, direction Villers-sur-Authie.

Berck · D939 · Conchil-le-Temple · D901 · A16 · CC · D12 · D940 · D1001

CC € **17** 1/4-6/7 25/8-29/9 8=7, 14=12 · 🏖 N 50°18'49'' E 1°41'42''

Blangy-sur-Bresle, F-76340 / Haute-Normandie (Seine-Maritime) — 1306

Aux Cygnes d'Opale***
Zône de Loisirs
+33 (0)2-35945565
31/3 - 31/10
contact@auxcygnesdopale.fr

1ha 46**T**(80-120m²) 10A CEE

1 ACD**G**IJKLMP
2 CDFLRTWX
3 ABGHJKM**Q**R**W**
4 (E+H 15/4-15/10)
(Q+R+T+U+V+X+Z)
5 **AB**CDGHJKLMNPUZ
6 ACEGHK(N 1,5km)RT

A quiet family campsite located by a lake with fishing opportunities. Small, indoor pool with movable walls. Marked-out walking and cycling routes. Free wifi. Pleasant bar/restaurant with a large terrace.

From A28 exit 5. Then D49 to the right. Campsite is signposted (500m).

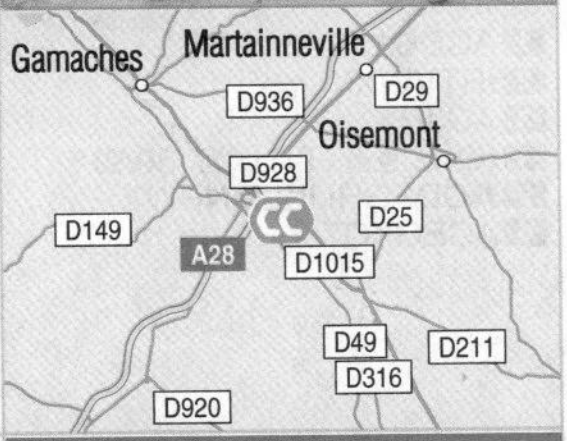

N 49°55'29'' E 1°39'27''

CC € 15 *31/3-30/6 1/9-30/10*

Bouafles, F-27700 / Haute-Normandie (Eure) — 1307

Château de Bouafles****
2 rue de Mousseaux
+33 (0)2-32540315
15/1 - 15/12
chateaudebouafles@gmail.com

13ha 25**T**(> 200m²) 15A CEE

1 ACD**G**IJKLMPQ
2 CGRUVWXY
3 B**F**GHJKMNQRU**W**
4 (Q+R+Z)
5 **AB**DEIJKLMNOPUWZ
6 EGJ(N 5km)TV

Ideal campsite for those who love very spacious pitches in natural surroundings. The famous Monet gardens are nearby.

From A15 to D14 and Les Andelys exit. Via D125 then D313 to Bouafles, then follow camping signs. Via A13 exit 17 via Gaillon and Courcelles to Bouafles.

N 49°12'47'' E 1°23'18''

CC € 17 *15/3-7/7 26/8-11/11*

Breteuil-sur-Iton, F-27160 / Haute-Normandie (Eure) — 1308

Les Berges de l'Iton***
53 rue du Fourneau
+33 (0)2-32627035
1/4 - 30/9
campinglesberges-de-liton@
orange.fr

1ha 25**T**(70-110m²) 6A CEE

1 ACFIJKLMPQ
2 CDGLRTUVWXY
3 ABGJUW
4 (D 15/5-15/9) (Q 15/6-15/9)
(T+U+V+Z)
5 **AB**DGIJKLMNOPUWZ
6 ACDEGK(N 0,3km)ORTV

Campsite close to a river and a pond, including special facilities for the disabled and an indoor swimming pool. 30 km from Evreux and 11 km from Verneuil-sur-Avre. You can go for nice walks in the woods close to the campsite, museums and other places to visit.

From Evreux on the D830 as far as Conches-en-Ouche. Then on the D840 as far as Breteuil, then follow the camping signs. From Verneuil-sur-Avre on the D840 as far as Breteuil then follow the cp signs.

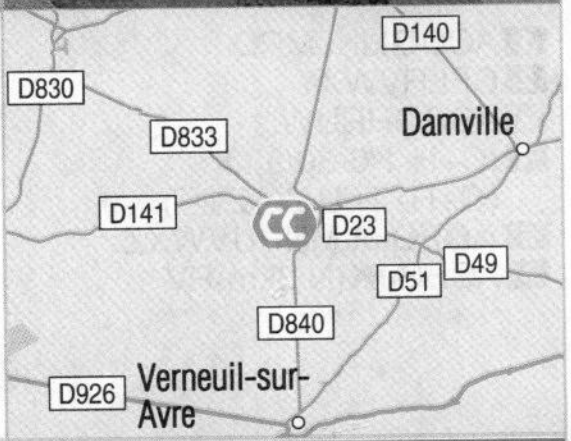

N 48°49'54'' E 0°54'45''

CC € 17 *1/4-30/6 1/9-29/9*

Forges-les-Eaux, F-76440 / Haute-Normandie (Seine-Maritime)

♿ 📶 iD **1309**

△ Camping la Minière**
🏠 3 boulevard Nicolas Thiessé
☎ +33 (0)2-35905391
🗓 30/3 - 15/10
@ campingforges@gmail.com

3ha 94T(100-120m²) 6A CEE

1 ACD**G**IJKLMOPRS
2 IRTVWXY
3 AGJR
4 (Q+S 🖊) (T+U 1/7-30/9)
5 **A**CDFGHIJKLMNPWZ
6 ACEGKOT

💬 Quiet campsite with spacious pitches in natural surroundings, just a five minute walk from the tourist centre of Forges-les-Eaux. Also on the 'Avenue Verte' cycle route.

🚗 A28 exit 10 towards Forges-les-Eaux (D1314). In Forges-les-Eaux take D921 and just outside of the centre follow campsite signs.

Serqueux — D135 — D9 — Formerie
Buchy — D919 — CC
Forges-les-Eaux
D41 — D915

CC € 15 30/3-30/6 1/9-14/10 3=2 ◰ N 49°36'22'' E 1°32'34''

Hautot-sur-Mer, F-76550 / Haute-Normandie (Seine-Maritime)

♿ 📶 iD **1310**

△ La Source***
🏠 63 rue des Tisserands
☎ +33 (0)2-35842704
FAX +33 (0)2-35822502
🗓 15/3 - 15/10
@ info@camping-la-source.fr

2,5ha 70T(80-130m²) 6-10A CEE

1 ACD**G**IJKLMOPRS
2 CLRTUVWX
3 ABGHJKNRU**W**
4 (C 15/6-15/9) (Q+R+T+Z 🖊)
5 **AB**DFGIJKLMNPUZ
6 CDEGK(N 1km)TV

💬 This very quiet campsite is located on a small river with fishing opportunities. Heated swimming pool. Ideally located 3 km from the beach and chalk cliffs. There is a wide cycle path from the campsite to the sea.

🚗 Follow route D925 between Dieppe and Valéry-en-Caux. The campsite is clearly signposted in Petit Appeville.

Dieppe
D75 — CC — D920
D925 — N27 — D154
Luneray — D915 — D107 — D1
D23 — D149

CC € 17 15/3-6/7 24/8-14/10 ◰ N 49°53'55'' E 1°3'25''

Honfleur/Fiquefleur, F-27210 / Haute-Normandie (Eure)

♿ 📶 iD **1311**

△ Sites & Paysages Domaine Catinière****
🏠 910 route de la Morelle
☎ +33 (0)2-32576351
FAX +33 (0)2-32421257
🗓 1/4 - 31/10
@ info@camping-catiniere.com

5,5ha 82T(80-100m²) 4-13A CEE

1 ACD**G**IJKLMPQ
2 CFLRVWXY
3 ABDGHRUW
4 (C+H 1/6-30/9) J (Q+R+T+U+X+Z 🖊)
5 **AB**FGIJLMNPUVWXZ
6 ACEGJ**K**(N 3km)RV

💬 A four-star campsite with modern toilet facilities in the middle of the countryside. An ideal base for visiting the picturesque town of Honfleur by bike along a quiet route.

🚗 From A13 exit 28 Beuzeville, then D22 direction Honfleur. Or from the Pont de Normandie 3.5 km on the left.

Le Havre
A131
Honfleur — A29 — D312
D579 — D22 — N178
D74 — CC — D180
Beuzeville
D17 — A13

CC € 17 1/4-8/7 26/8-30/10 7=6, 14=12 ◰ N 49°24'3'' E 0°18'24''

Jumieges, F-76480 / Haute-Normandie (Seine-Maritime)

♿ 📶 ✿ **iD** **1312**

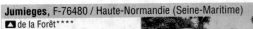

🏕 de la Forêt****
📧 582 rue Mainberte
☎ +33 (0)2-35379343
📠 +33 (0)2-35377648
⌚ 1/4 - 31/10
@ info@campinglaforet.com

3ha 78T(80-150m²) 10A CEE

1 ACDGHIJKLMPRS
2 BRVWXY
3 AFGHJKLMRU
4 (E 1/5-30/9) (H 1/7-31/8)
(Q+R ⌚) (T+U 1/6-31/8)
(Z ⌚)
5 **AB**DFGIJKLMNPUWXYZ
6 ACEG**KL**(N 0,6km)TV

💬 A campsite in wooded surroundings on one of the lovely meanders of the Seine. Only 600m from the famous Abbey of Jumièges. 25 km from the medieval city of Rouen. Completely new toilet facilities since 2015. Reception closed from 12:30 to 13:30.

🚗 On the A29 exit 9, direction Yvetot, then the D131e and D131 direction Pont-de-Brotonne. Before the bridge via D982 direction Rouen and via D143 to Jumièges. The campsite is signposted.

CC € **17** 1/4-8/7 27/8-30/10 · 🧭 N 49°26'5'' E 0°49'40''

Le Bec-Hellouin, F-27800 / Haute-Normandie (Eure)

♿ 📶 **iD** **1313**

🏕 Le Clos Saint Nicolas****
📧 15 rue St. Nicolas
☎ +33 (0)2-32448355
⌚ 15/3 - 15/10
@ campingstnicolas@orange.fr

2,8ha 67T(90-110m²) 10A CEE

1 ACD**G**IJKLMOPQ
2 BFLRVWX
3 AF**G**HJKMNRU
4 (E 1/4-30/9)
(Q+R+T+U+V+X+Z ⌚)
5 **AB**DEFGIJKLMNPUWZ
6 ACEGK(N 2km)ORTV

💬 This three star campsite in idyllic surroundings and surrounded by trees will welcome you for a stay in the countryside in peace and tranquillity. A place to relax. 18 hole golf within 10 km. Indoor pool at the campsite. You can enjoy your holiday here in your caravan, motorhome or tent.

🚗 From the A28 exit 13, direction Brionne. Take the D581 towards Malleville-sur-le-Bec. The campsite is signposted.

CC € **17** 15/3-8/7 26/8-14/10 · 🧭 N 49°14'5'' E 0°43'30''

Les Andelys, F-27700 / Haute-Normandie (Eure)

♿ 📶 **iD** **1314**

🏕 Flower Camping de l'Île
des Trois Rois***
📧 1 rue Gilles Nicolle
☎ +33 (0)2-32542379
📠 +33 (0)2-32511454
⌚ 15/3 - 15/11
@ campingtroisrois@aol.com

10ha 150T(100-250m²) 6-10A CEE

1 ACD**G**IJKLM**P**RS
2 CFGLRTUVWX
3 ABF**G**HJRUW
4 (C+H 15/5-30/9) (Q 1/7-31/8)
(T+U+V+X+Z 15/5-15/9)
5 **AB**DFGIJKLMNPUWZ
6 ABCEG**K**(N 0,5km)ORTV

💬 Peacefully located campsite on the banks of the Seine. Marked out pitches. Lovely heated swimming pool. Heated toilet facilities. The campsite is 500 metres from the centre. Wifi 100% (charges apply). 20 km from Giverny, with its famous Monet gardens.

🚗 In Les Andelys direction Évreux, the campsite is located before the bridge over the Seine; well signposted.

CC € **17** 15/3-7/7 26/8-14/11 7=6, 14=11 · 🧭 N 49°14'8'' E 1°24'1''

Les Loges, F-76790 / Haute-Normandie (Seine-Maritime)   ♿ 📶 **iD** `1315`

▲ L'Aiguille Creuse****
🏠 24 residence de L'Aiguille Creuse
☎ +33 (0)2-35295210
📠 +33 (0)2-35108664
🔓 1/4 - 16/9
@ camping@aiguillecreuse.com

3ha 135T(110-150m²) 10A CEE

1 ACD**G**IJLMPQ
2 GLRVWX
3 AB**F**GHMR
4 (E+H+Q 🔓) (T 1/7-31/8)
　(Z 🔓)
5 **AB**DEFGIJLNPQRUZ
6 ACDEGJ**K**(N 0,4km)RV

💬 A lovely campsite with marked out pitches; a bar, playground, football field, large tennis court, covered pool with sliding roof.

🚗 Les Loges is located along the D940 Fécamp-Le Havre. Campsite well signposted in the town.

Fécamp

CC €**17** 1/4-6/7　27/8-15/9   🏕 N 49°41'56'' E 0°16'33''

Lyons-la-Forêt, F-27480 / Haute-Normandie (Eure)   ♿ 📶 **iD** `1316`

▲ Camping Saint-Paul***
🏠 2 route St. Paul
☎ +33 (0)2-32494202
🔓 31/3 - 31/10
@ camping-saint-paul@orange.fr

3ha 57T(80-100m²) 6A

1 ACD**G**IJKLPRS
2 CGLRTVWX
3 ABGHJ**MNQRW**
4 (E 15/5-15/10) (Q+R 🔓)
　(T+U+Z 1/5-30/9)
5 **AB**DGIJKLMNPUWXZ
6 ACDEG**K**(N 0,6km)RTV

💬 A peacefully located campsite by a small stream (only fish). Municipal swimming pool next to the campsite is free for campers. Attractive small town with a lovely market place and restaurants within walking distance.

🚗 Campsite well signposted at the entrance to the village.

CC €**17** 31/3-30/6　3/9-30/10   🏕 N 49°24'12'' E 1°28'47''

Marcilly-sur-Eure, F-27810 / Haute-Normandie (Eure)   👫 ♿ 📶 **iD** `1317`

▲ Domaine de Marcilly****
🏠 rue de Saint André de l'Eure
☎ +33 (0)2-37484542
📠 +33 (0)2-37485111
🔓 1/1 - 31/12
@ domainedemarcilly@wanadoo.fr

15ha 100T(100-200m²) 10A CEE

1 ACGIJKLMPQ
2 BLRTVX
3 GKMNRU
4 (C 1/6-30/9) (Q+R 🔓)
5 **AB**GIMNPUVWXYZ
6 ACDEG**K**(N 1km)RTV

💬 A really lovely campsite in the middle of a wood with lovely marked out grounds, a wonderful (heated) swimming pool, 2 tennis courts, a large petanque alley. The reception is open from 09:00 to 12:00 and 14:00 to 18:00.

🚗 Coming from Dreux on the D928 turn left after about 15 km towards Marcilly. Then follow camping signs. From Annet on the D928 turn right after about 8 km. Follow route as shown above.

Dreux

CC €**19** 1/1-30/6　1/9-31/12   🏕 N 48°49'55'' E 1°19'47''

Martigny, F-76880 / Haute-Normandie (Seine-Maritime)   ♿ 🤶 **iD** (1318)

🏕 Municipal Des Deux Rivières***
🏠 D154
☎ +33 (0)2-35856082
🗓 30/3 - 7/10
@ martigny.76@orange.fr

6ha 75T(80-100m²) 10A CEE

1 ACD**G**IJKLMPQ
2 CDRTVWX
3 ABGRU**W**
4 (Q 15/6-31/8) (R 🔑)
5 **AB**FGIJKLMNPUZ
6 EGHJ(N 2km)RT

💬 A very peacefully located campsite on a 2 hectare lake with fishing opportunities. Located on the Avenue Verte, a 40 km cycling and walking path. 8 km from Dieppe, sea and beach.

🚗 From Dieppe about 8 km along the D154. Very well signposted beside the road.

Dieppe
D75 | Hautot-sur-Mer | CC | D920
N27 | D915
D927 | D149 | D154 | D1

CC € **17** 30/3-30/6 1/9-6/10   ☀️▲ N 49°52'14'' E 1°8'39''

Neufchâtel-en-Bray, F-76270 / Haute-Normandie (Seine-Maritime)   ♿ 🤶 **iD** (1319)

🏕 Sainte Claire***
🏠 19 rue Grande Flandre
☎ +33 (0)2-35930393
🗓 1/4 - 15/10
@ fancelot@wanadoo.fr

2,5ha 91T(60-180m²) 6-10A CEE

1 ACDGIJKLMOPQ
2 CFLRUVWX
3 HJ
4 (Q+R+T+U+X+Z 1/5-30/9)
5 **AB**FGIJKLMNPUZ
6 ABCDEG**K**(N 0,2km)

💬 The campsite is located in the grounds of a picturesque old farmstead in the shade of apple trees and a few steps from the 'Avenue Verte'. A dream for cyclists and walkers. Campers are welcome after 13:00.

🚗 Well signposted about 1 km from Neufchâtel-en-Bray. Coming from Amiens exit 7 and from Rouen exit 9 on A28/E402 motorway.

Les Grandes-Ventes
D1 | A28
D48 | CC | D929 | A29
Saint-Saëns
D928 | D1314 | D135
D915

CC € **15** 1/4-30/6 1/9-14/10   ☀️▲ N 49°44'16'' E 1°25'41''

Pourville-sur-Mer, F-76550 / Haute-Normandie (Seine-Maritime)   ♿ 🤶 **iD** (1320)

🏕 Le Marqueval***
🏠 1210 rue de la Mer
☎ +33 (0)2-35826646
📠 +33 (0)2-35845503
🗓 19/3 - 15/10
@ contact@
   campinglemarqueval.com

8,5ha 85T(80-120m²) 6A CEE

1 ACD**G**IJKLMO**P**RS
2 CGKLNQRVWX
3 ABGKNRUW
4 (C+H 1/6-30/9) **KN**(Q+R 🔑)
   (T+U+V+X 1/7-31/8)
   (Z 1/5-15/9)
5 **AB**DFGJLNPUWZ
6 CDEG**K**(N 5km)OR

💬 There are three fishing ponds and a small river on the campsite. 1500m from the beach with its lovely chalkstone cliffs. Heated swimming pool. Plenty of cycle and footpaths from the campsite to the coast.

🚗 Coming from Dieppe well signposted on the D75, follow the camping signs. Coming from Veules-les-Roses well signposted on the D75.

Dieppe
D68 | D75 | CC | Arques-la-Bataille
D925 | D154 | D1
D927 | D149
D915

CC € **17** 19/3-8/7 26/8-14/10   ☀️▲ N 49°54'32'' E 1°2'26''

St. Aubin-sur-Scie, F-76550 / Haute-Normandie (Seine-Maritime)

 ⚫ Dieppe Vitamín****
🏠 865 rue des Vertus
☎ +33 (0)2-35821111
📅 31/3 - 1/10
@ camping.vitamin@wanadoo.fr

🚷 🛜 iD 1321

5ha 69T(80-120m²) 10A CEE

1 ACD**G**IJKLMPQ
2 LRTVWX
3 ABGNRV
4 (C 15/6-15/9) (F+H 📅) JK**NP** (Q 📅) (T 1/7-31/8) (Z 📅)
5 **AB**EFGIJKLMNPUZ
6 DEGJ**K**(N 0,2km)RTV

💬 A really lovely and well run campsite 3 km from Dieppe centre. The indoor swimming pool is also enjoyable when the weather is not so good. There are various department stores close to the campsite.

🚗 Coming from the D925 direction Dieppe water tower. Coming from Rouen N27. Direction water tower.

Dieppe
D75 CC Saint-Nicolas-d'Aliermont
D925
D927 D154 D1
D915

CC € 17 31/3-7/7 25/8-30/9

🧭 N 49°54'1'' E 1°4'28''

St. Martin-en-Campagne, F-76370 / Haute-Normandie (Seine-Maritime)

 ⚫ Les Goélands****
🏠 11 rue des Grèbes
☎ +33 (0)2-35838290
📠 +33 (0)2-35832179
📅 1/4 - 31/10
@ contact@
camping-les-goelands.fr

🚷 🛜 iD 1322

4,5ha 70T(80-100m²) 16A

1 ACD**G**IJKLMOPQ
2 AEGJKNQRTUVWX
3 ABGHMNRUY
4 (A+Q 1/7-31/8) (R+T+U+Z 📅)
5 **AB**DEFGJKLMNOPQRUWX YZ
6 DEGHIK(N 2km)ORTV

💬 A very attractive terraced campsite within walking distance of a large sandy beach and chalk cliffs.

🚗 Follow D925 Dieppe-Le Treport. Turn off towards St. Martin-en-Campagne (D113). Campsite clearly signposted.

Le Tréport
D940
D925
CC
Dieppe
D920 D149
D56

CC € 17 1/4-30/6 20/8-30/10

🧭 N 49°57'59'' E 1°12'15''

St. Pierre-en-Port, F-76540 / Haute-Normandie (Seine-Maritime)

 ⚫ Les Falaises**
🏠 130 rue du Camping
☎ +33 (0)2-35295158
📅 1/4 - 5/10
@ lesfalaises@cegetel.net

🚷 iD 1323

4,2ha 72T(120-140m²) 10A CEE

1 AGIJKLMPQ
2 EGLNQRVWX
3 ABGHNRUY
4 (A 1/5-30/9) (U+V+Z 1/7-31/8)
5 **A**EGJLNPUVWZ
6 CEG(N 0,5km)T

💬 Extremely well located campsite high up on the cliffs and 300 metres from the sea. Access to beach via Le Rédillon is very easy. All necessary amenities available.

🚗 Take the D79 between Fécamp and St. Valéry. Signposted in St. Pierre-en-Port.

D68
CC D10
D79 D17 D925
Fécamp
Saint- D150 D50
D940 Léonard D131

CC € 15 1/4-6/7 26/8-4/10

🧭 N 49°48'35'' E 0°29'38''

St. Valéry-en-Caux, F-76460 / Haute-Normandie (Seine-Maritime)

👫 🛜 **iD** (1324)

🔺 Seasonova Etennemare***
✉️ 21 Hameau d'Etennemare
☎️ +33 (0)2-35971579
🔄 1/4 - 4/11
@ contact@
   camping-etennemare.com

4ha 70T(100m²) 10A

1 ACD**G**IJLMPRS
2 RTVWX
3 ABGKRU
4 (E 🔄) J(Q 🔄) (T 1/7-31/8)
5 **A**DEGIJKLMNPTUZ
6 EG**K**(N 2km)RV

💬 A beautiful, quiet campsite with marked out pitches and modern toilet facilities. The city centre is a 15 min walk.

🚗 Campsite well signposted coming from Cany-Barville (Fécamp) D925. If coming from Dieppe follow 'Centre Ville'. Campsite well signposted from there.

[map: Saint-Valery-en-Caux — D75, D68, D10, D20, D142, D925, D131, D50]

CC € 15 1/4-6/7 26/8-30/10   📐 N 49°51'31'' E 0°42'16''

Toutainville, F-27500 / Haute-Normandie (Eure)

♿ 🛜 ✿ **iD** (1325)

🔺 Camping Risle Seine Les Etangs***
✉️ 19 route des Etangs
☎️ +33 (0)2-32424665
🔄 +33 (0)2-32422417
🔄 1/4 - 31/10
@ camping.etangs@wanadoo.fr

1,5ha 50T(85-150m²) 10A CEE

1 ACD**G**HIJKLM**P**Q
2 CDFLRVWX
3 A**E**GHIJNRU**W**
4 (C 1/5-30/9)
   (Q+R+T+U+V+Z 🔄)
5 **AB**FGIJKLMNPUWXYZ
6 ACDEGK(N 2km)RTV

💬 A quiet campsite next to some beautiful small lakes. Pitches separated by beech hedges. Just 2 km from the picturesque town of Pont-Audemer with all its amenities. Close to Honfleur (20 km) and Rouen (46 km). A paradise for anglers. Golf course (9 holes) next to the campsite. Reception closed 12:00 to 13:30.

🚗 A13 motorway Rouen-Caen, exit 26 direction Pont-Audemer. Then follow the Toutainville signs. Campsite is signposted.

[map: D6178, D312, Sainte-Opportune-la-Mare, A131, D180, A13, Saint-Germain-Village, D675, D139, D89, D22, D810, D47]

CC € 17 1/4-6/7 25/8-30/10   📐 N 49°22'1'' E 0°29'15''

Veules-les-Roses, F-76980 / Haute-Normandie (Seine-Maritime)

👫 ♿ 🛜 ✿ **iD** (1326)

🔺 Seasonova Les Mouettes***
✉️ avenue Jean Moulin
☎️ +33 (0)2-35976198
🔄 +33 (0)2-35973344
🔄 1/4 - 15/10
@ contact@
   camping-lesmouettes-normandie.com

3,6ha 122T(80-150m²) 6A CEE

1 ACD**G**IJKLMPRS
2 EGRTVWX
3 ABGHKN**P**RUV
4 (E+H 15/4-1/10) **KN**
   (Q+R 🔄) (T+Z 1/7-31/8)
5 **AB**DFGIJKLMNOPUZ
6 CEG**K**(N 1km)V

💬 A lovely campsite with marked out pitches, located 300 metres from the beach. A beautiful village with France's shortest river, just 1100 metres long. This is an extremely peaceful campsite with excellent toilet facilities. Heated indoor swimming pool, children's pool and jacuzzi.

🚗 Campsite well signposted from the centre.

[map: Saint-Valery-en-Caux — D75, D237, D68, D20, D142, D925, D10, D50]

CC € 17 1/4-6/7 26/8-14/10   📐 N 49°52'33'' E 0°48'11''

Villequier-Rives-en-Seine, F-76490 / Haute-Normandie (Seine-Maritime) ♿ 📶 ✿ iD 1327

🔺 Barre-y-va****
🏠 D81, route de Villequier
☎ 📠 +33 (0)2-35962638
🗓 7/4 - 12/10
@ campingbarreyva@orange.fr

2ha 48T(90-130m²) 10A CEE

1 ACD**G**IJKLMPQ
2 CRTUVXY
3 ABGHJ**M**QRUV
4 (E 7/4-30/9) (H 1/5-30/9)
(Q+R+T+U+X+Z 🅿)
5 **AB**GIJKLMNOPUVWZ
6 CDFGI**K**(N 2km)V

💬 Campsite on the D81 with a quiet and beautiful location between Rouen and Le Havre, by the woods and on the Seine. Many boats on the river. There is a cycle path along the water, opposite the campsite. Indoor pool with slide, crazy golf, fitness, restaurant and wifi. A view of the Pont de Brotonne. The picturesque village of Villequier has a Victor Hugo museum.

🚐 Coming from Caudebec-en-Caux, take the D81 direction Villequier and follow the Seine.

CC € **17** 7/4-7/7 26/8-11/10 | 📡 N 49°31'29'' E 0°42'14''

Vittefleur, F-76450 / Haute-Normandie (Seine-Maritime) ♿ 📶 iD 1328

🔺 Les Prés de la Mer***
🏠 61 Grande Rue
☎ +33 (0)2-35975382
🗓 1/4 - 30/9
@ campinglespresdelamer@
orange.fr

2,7ha 76T(80-140m²) 16A CEE

1 ACG**G**IJKLMO**P**Q
2 CGLRTVWX
3 AGR**W**
4 (Q 1/7-31/8) (R 🅿)
5 **A**GIJKLMNO**P**UZ
6 EGK(N 1km)T

💬 Open, quiet campsite with spacious marked-out pitches, located in the valley between the falaises, by the river at walking distance from the picturesque village. Near Lac de Caniel, where there are many options for watersports, and 15 minutes' cycle from the sea.

🚐 In Cany-Barville take D10 towards Veulettes sur Mer. Site is 800 metres past Vittefleur village, across the river, on the left.

CC € **15** 1/4-30/6 15/7-27/7 1/9-29/9 | 📡 N 49°49'33'' E 0°38'2''

Yport, F-76111 / Haute-Normandie (Seine-Maritime) ♿ 📶 iD 1329

🔺 Flower Camping La Chênaie***
🏠 rue H. Simon / D104
☎ +33 (0)2-35273356
📠 +33 (0)2-22446562
🗓 30/3 - 30/9
@ camping.yport@
flowercampings.com

2,7ha 42T(80-90m²) 6A CEE

1 ACD**G**IJL**P**RS
2 BIJRVWX
3 AGHJRU
4 (E+H+Q+R+U+V 🅿)
5 **AB**EFGIJKLMNPQRUWZ
6 ACEGK(N 0,5km)V

💬 A natural campsite on the Alabaster coast 800 metres from the beach. The campsite is hidden in woodland and has an attractive ondoor swimming pool. Centrally located by the sea, the hinterland and towns such as Étretat and Fecamp.

🚐 On the D940 Fécamp-Le Havre, exit Yport (D211). Campsite on the left just before the village.

CC € **17** 30/3-29/6 1/9-29/9 7=6 | 📡 N 49°43'58'' E 0°19'14''

Bayeux, F-14400 / Basse-Normandie (Calvados) 👫 ♿ 📶 iD 〔1330〕

🔺 Camping des Bords de l'Aure★★★
🏠 boulevard d'Eindhoven
☎ +33 (0)2-31920843
📠 +33 (0)2-31227491
📅 30/3 - 4/11
@ campingmunicipal@
   mairie-bayeux.fr
2,5ha 136T(80-100m²) 6A CEE

1 ACDGHIJKLMPRS
2 CFGLRUVVWXY
3 AFGHJNRU
4 (F+H 🅿) N(Q 🅿)
5 ABGIJKMNPUVZ
6 CDEGHK(N 0,5km)RV

💬 Well-maintained campsite within walking distance of the very interesting historic centre of Bayeux. Public swimming pool offers free entrance for campsite guests. 10 km from D-Day beaches. Reception is closed between 12:00 and 14:00.

🚗 From A13 exit Bayeux then on the northern bypass towards Arromanches and Port-en-Bessin. Campsite is well signposted.

NEW

Map: D514, Ver-sur-Mer, D516, D65, Le Molay-Littry, D5, CC, Bayeux, D12, D572, D6

CC € 17 30/3-27/5 11/6-17/6 2/9-3/11   📍 N 49°17'3'' W 0°41'52''

Beauvoir, F-50170 / Basse-Normandie (Manche) ♿ 📶 iD 〔1331〕

🔺 Aux Pommiers★★★★
🏠 28 route du Mont-St-Michel
☎ +33 (0)2-33601136
📅 28/3 - 4/11
@ campingauxpommiers@
   gmail.com
1,8ha 72T(95-105m²) 10A CEE

1 ACDGIJKLMPRS
2 CFGLRTVX
3 ABGHJKNRUW
4 (F+H 🅿) J(Q+R+S 🅿)
    (T+U+V 1/7-31/8) (Z 🅿)
5 ABFGIJKLMNPRSUWXYZ
6 ACEGK(N 0km)TV

💬 A family campsite with a heated and covered swimming pool, only 4 km from Mont St. Michel which can easily be reached by bike. Also shuttle bus (charges apply) to Mont St. Michel. Arrival at the campsite from 12:00.

🚗 Via N175 from Avranches direction Pontorson, then via D976 direction Mont-St-Michel. Follow arrows.

Map: Avranches, Le Mont-Saint-Michel, Le Val-Saint-Père, D797, D275, D43, D975, N176, Pontorson, D998, D87, D30, A84, D155, D90, D40, D12

CC € 17 28/3-7/7 1/9-3/11 7=6   📍 N 48°35'47'' W 1°30'45''

Bernières-sur-Mer, F-14990 / Basse-Normandie (Calvados) 📶 iD 〔1332〕

🔺 Le Havre de Bernières★★★★
🏠 chemin de Quintefeuille
☎ +33 (0)2-31966709
📠 +33 (0)2-31973106
📅 1/1 - 31/12
@ campingnormandie@sfr.fr

5ha 102T(80-110m²) 20A CEE

1 ACDGIJKLMPQ
2 AEGRVWX
3 AFGKMNRUWY
4 (C+H 1/5-30/10) KN
    (Q 1/6-31/8) (R 1/7-31/8)
    (T+U+V+Y+Z 1/4-30/10)
5 ABDEFGIJKLMNPUWZ
6 ACEGIK(N 0,45km)TV

💬 A lively campsite with a heated swimming pool and a restaurant. There are both shaded and unshaded pitches. The campsite is just 200 metres from the sea, close to the World War Two Landing Beaches.

🚗 Coming from Caen on the Periphérique exit CHU/Côte de Nacre. Direction Courseules-sur-Mer then direction Bernières-sur-Mer. Campsite is on the left just outside the village.

Map: D514, D65, D12, Luc-sur-Mer, CC, D176, D404, Ouistreham, D22, D35

CC € 17 1/1-8/7 1/9-31/12   📍 N 49°19'56'' W 0°25'41''

Breville-sur-Mer, F-50290 / Basse-Normandie (Manche)   ♿ 🤟 📶 iD (1333)

▲ La Route Blanche★★★★
🏠 6 la Route Blanche
☎ +33 (0)2-33502331
🔑 6/4 - 23/9
@ larouteblanche@
   camping-breville.com

5,5ha 131T(90-120m²) 6-10A CEE

NEW

1 ABCDGIJKLMPRS
2 ALRSVX
3 ABEFGHIJNR
4 (C 1/5-14/9) (H 1/5-11/9) IJK
   (Q+S 🌙)
   (T+U+V+X+Z 1/7-31/8)
5 ABDEFGIJKLMNOPQRUWX
   YZ
6 CEGIK(N 3km)OTV

💬 Pretty campsite carpeted with flowers less than a kilometre from the sea. Beautiful heated pool. Good toilet facilities. Lots of days out in the area. The campsite has a golf course for those who enjoy playing golf. Hikers and cyclists will love it here.

🚗 From Caen on A84 towards Villedieu and Granville (exit 37). Before Granville take D971 towards Cherbourg-Brehal. After 2.5 km on the roundabout exit towards Bréville-sur-Mer, D135. Campsite is well signposted.

D20   D971   D13
Bréhal
Granville CC
D924
D911   D973   D7

CC € 15   6/4-7/7   25/8-22/9   N 48°52'10'' W 1°33'50''

Cahagnolles, F-14490 / Basse-Normandie (Calvados)   ♿ 📶 iD (1334)

▲ L'Escapade★★★★
☎ +33 (0)2-31216359
🔑 1/4 - 30/9
@ escapadecamping@orange.fr

7ha 43T(100-200m²) 10A CEE

1 ACDGHIJKLMOPRS
2 CDIJLRVWX
3 ADGHJKMNPRUW
4 (E 🌙) (H 15/6-15/9) J
   (Q+R+T+U 🌙) (V 1/7-31/8)
   (Z 🌙)
5 ABDEFGIJKLMNPUWZ
6 ACDEGJKRV

💬 Very spacious park-like site with big pitches in hilly, natural surroundings 25 km from the landing beaches and 15 km from Bayeux. Right next to a lake with plenty of free fishing. Toilet facilities renovated and heated in 2014. Reception closed from 12:30 to 14:00.

🚗 N13, exit Bayeux, direction St. Lo. At Subles D99 dir. St. Paul-du-Vernay. There D99 dir. Cahagnolles. Campsite signposted.

Le Molay-   D5   Bayeux
Littry
D10
D572   CC D13   D6
D28
D11   D71   D9
D54   A84

CC € 17   1/4-30/6   1/9-29/9   N 49°9'26'' W 0°45'37''

Carentan, F-50500 / Basse-Normandie (Manche)   ♿ 📶 (1335)

▲ Flower Camping Le Haut Dick★★★
🏠 30 chemin de Grand-Bas Pays
☎ +33 (0)2-33421689
📠 +33 (0)970065590
🔑 30/3 - 30/9
@ contact@
   camping-lehautdick.com

2,5ha 71T(100m²) 10A CEE

1 CDGIJKLMPRS
2 CFGRVWXY
3 BGHJKNRUW
4 (E+H 15/4-15/9)
   (Q+R+U+Y+Z 🌙)
5 ABFGIJKLMNPUWXZ
6 ACDEGK(N 0,5km)RTV

💬 A friendly, peaceful campsite with naturally separated pitches. Right next to the yacht harbour. About a 15-minute walk to the centre. The campsite has a heated swimming pool. The following sights are within a one hour drive: Mont St. Michel, Cherbourg, Cap de la Hague and the invasion beaches.

🚗 First direction Centre Ville. Then the campsite is clearly signposted.

Picauville   D14
D70
D913
Isigny-sur-Mer
D903   CC   N13   D5
Carentan
D971   N174

CC € 17   30/3-31/5   10/6-30/6   1/9-29/9   N 49°18'36'' W 1°14'21''

Colleville-sur-Mer, F-14710 / Basse-Normandie (Calvados)

  ♿ 🛜 iD (1336)

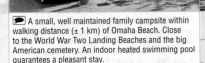

🏕 Le Robinson****
✉ 24 route d'Omaha Beach
☎ +33 (0)2-31224519
📅 31/3 - 30/9
@ dourthe.le.robinson@wanadoo.fr

2ha 32T(80-120m²) 6A CEE

1 ACD**G**HIJKLMPRS
2 AFGLRVWX
3 A**F**GHN**P**RU
4 (E+H 📅) J(Q+R 📅)
   (T+U+V+Z 1/7-31/8)
5 **AB**EFGIJLNPRUZ
6 ACEG**K**(N 5km)TV

💬 A small, well maintained family campsite within walking distance (± 1 km) of Omaha Beach. Close to the World War Two Landing Beaches and the big American cemetery. An indoor heated swimming pool guarantees a pleasant stay.

🚐 From A13 Caen-Cherbourg exit Vaucelles, direction Mosles, then D97 dir. Ste Honorine-des-Pertes. Then D514 direction Colleville-sur-Mer.

D517 CC — N13 — D6 D514 — Saint-Vigor-le-Grand — D5 Bayeux

CC € **17** 31/3-7/7 25/8-29/9   📍 N 49°21'1'' W 0°50'1''

Courtils, F-50220 / Basse-Normandie (Manche)

  🛜 iD (1337)

🏕 St. Michel***
✉ 35 route du Mont-Saint-Michel
☎ +33 (0)2-33709690
FAX +33 (0)2-33709909
📅 30/3 - 4/11
@ infos@campingsaintmichel.com

5,2ha 100T(90-100m²) 6-10A CEE

1 ACD**G**IJKLM**P**RS
2 FLRTVX
3 ABDGKRU
4 (C 1/5-30/9) (Q+S 📅)
   (U 1/6-31/8) (V 1/7-31/8)
   (Z 📅)
5 **AB**DFGIJKLMNOPUWZ
6 CDEGJ(N 0,5km)ORTV

💬 A beautifully floral family campsite with a heated pool. Close to Mont St. Michel, St. Malo and Dinard.

🚐 From Avranches via D43 direction Mont St. Michel. Campsite is located on the left just after Courtils.

D911 D973 D7 — Avranches — Le Val-Saint-Père D5 — D976 CC Ducey — D797 D975 — D40 A84 — D30

CC € **17** 30/3-7/7 25/8-3/11 7=6, 14=11   📍 N 48°37'41'' W 1°24'57''

Creully, F-14480 / Basse-Normandie (Calvados)

  ♿ 🛜 iD (1338)

🏕 Les Trois Rivières***
✉ rue de Tierceville
☎ +33 (0)2-31809017
📅 15/3 - 15/11
@ contact@
  camping-les-3-rivieres.com

1,5ha 65T 10A CEE

1 ACD**G**IJKLMO**P**RS
2 CGILRVWXY
3 AGHMRU
4 (Q+R 1/5-30/9)
   (T+U+Z 1/7-31/8)
5 **AB**FGIJKLMNOPUZ
6 EGJ(N 0,3km)ORTV

💬 Quiet campsite 500 metres from the little town of Creully with its castle which regularly hosts exhibitions. Ideal for visiting the WWII landing beaches. Bayeux 12 km, Caen 16 km, sea 7 km. Restaurant facilities open at weekends in May, June, September.

🚐 A13 in Caen on Périferique Nord take exit 6. Via D22 to Creully. From Bayeaux D12 to Creully. Site is signposted there.

D65 D514 — D12 CC Cresserons — Bayeux — D6 D22 D7 — D7

CC € **15** 15/3-7/7 25/8-14/11 7=6, 14=12   📍 N 49°17'23'' W 0°31'46''

Deauville/St. Arnoult, F-14800 / Basse-Normandie (Calvados)

♿ 📶 **iD** (1339)

🏠 La Vallée de Deauville*****
📧 rue des Genêts
☎ +33 (0)2-31885817
📠 +33 (0)2-31881157
📅 1/4 - 31/10
@ contact@camping-deauville.com

19ha 105T(80-120m²) 10A CEE

1 ACD**G**HIJKLMPQ
2 CDFGLRVWX
3 AB**F**GKNRUVW
4 (C 1/6-15/9) (E 1/5-30/9)
　(H 1/6-15/9) IJ**KN**
　(Q+R+T+U+V+X+Z 1/4-30/9)
5 **AB**DEFGIJKLMNPQRU
6 ACEG**IK**(N 0,8km)**P**V

💬 Large grounds with spacious pitches in natural surroundings. The campsite is near the famous seaside resorts of Deauville and Trouville. New heated leisure pool including indoor swimming pool with jacuzzi. Reception closed from 12:00 to 14:00.

🚗 From A13 exit Deauville. Direction Caen at roundabouts. Campsite is near the 3rd roundabout.

Honfleur
D513 D62 D74 A29
CC
D17
Dives-sur-Mer D118
D45
D27 D675 A13 D48

CC €**17** 1/4-8/7 26/8-30/10 ⛱ N 49°19'44'' E 0°5'11''

Etreham/Bayeux, F-14400 / Basse-Normandie (Calvados)

♿ 📶 **iD** (1340)

🏠 Reine Mathilde***
📧 Le Marais
☎ +33 (0)2-31217655
📅 30/3 - 30/9
@ campingreinemathilde@gmail.com

6ha 80T(100-150m²) 6A CEE

1 ACD**F**IJKLM**P**RS
2 FLRVWXY
3 A**F**GNRU
4 (C+H 15/6-15/9) (Q 1/5-15/9)
　(R 📅) (T+U+X 15/4-30/9)
　(Z 📅)
5 **AB**DEFGIJKLMNPUWZ
6 ACEGJ(N 4km)V

💬 This peaceful family campsite set in parkland is run by its friendly owners. It has very spacious marked out pitches and is located just 4 km from the renowned Omaha Landing Beach. This is an ideal base for visiting the many World War Two monuments and for trips inland, including Bayeux the regional capital

🚗 Leave N13 at exit 38. Take the N2013 direction Tour-en Bessin at the roundabout, then right onto D206. Campsite signposted from here.

D517
CC D6 D514
Saint-Vigor-le-Grand
Bayeux D12
D15 D5 N13

CC €**17** 30/3-7/7 25/8-29/9 7=6 ⛱ N 49°19'53'' W 0°48'9''

Falaise, F-14700 / Basse-Normandie (Calvados)

📶 **iD** (1341)

🏠 Camping du Château**
📧 1 rue du Val d'Ante
☎ +33 (0)2-31901655
📠 +33 (0)2-31905338
📅 1/5 - 30/9
@ camping@falaise.fr

1,5ha 60T(80-100m²) 10A CEE

1 ACD**F**IJKLMPQ
2 CGIJRVX
3 ABG**M**NRU**W**
4 (R 📅)
5 **AB**DGIJKLMNPUVWZ
6 CEGHJ(N 0,5km)TV

💬 Quiet, flowery campsite, pitches marked out by hedges, beautiful view of castle from 11th century and at 500 metres from medieval town centre.

🚗 From Caen N158 dir. Falaise, left on roundabout dir. 'centre ville', right on 2nd roundabout dir. 'Voie Panoramique', see campsite signs.

Potigny Soumont-Saint-Quentin
D6
D511 D63
CC
D658
A88
D509 D958

CC €**13** 1/5-2/7 22/8-29/9 ⛱ N 48°53'44'' W 0°12'18''

Formigny/Surrain, F-14710 / Basse-Normandie (Calvados)

♿ 🛜 **iD** (1342)

🏕 La Roseraie d'Omaha****
📧 Le Bourg
☎ +33 (0)2-31211771
📅 28/3 - 30/9
@ camping.laroseraie@gmail.com

3ha 49T(85-120m²) 10A CEE

1 ACD**G**IJKLM**P**RS
2 FLRVWXY
3 B**F**GHJKM**N**QRU
4 (F 1/4-30/9) (H 15/6-31/8) J
　 (Q+S 📅) (T 1/5-15/9) (U 📅)
　 (X 1/5-15/9) (Z 📅)
5 **AB**DFGIJKLMNPUWZ
6 EG**K**(N 4km)OTV

💬 A peaceful campsite with marked out pitches and a wide variety of planting 4 km from the sea and close to the American landing beaches from WWII. Beautiful grounds with excellent toilet facilities. 12 km from the medieval town of Bayeux. In April the reception is closed between 12:30 and 14:00.

🚐 N13 from Bayeux direction Cherbourg, exit 38. Follow Tour-en-Bessin/Mosles then Surrain. The campsite is in Surrain village. Signposted.

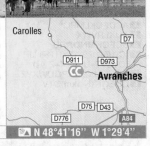

D517　D514
　CC
Saint-Vigor-le-Grand　D6
　Bayeux
D5
D15　D10　N13

CC € **15** 28/3-7/7　25/8-29/9
🗺 N 49°19'33'' W 0°51'53''

Genêts, F-50530 / Basse-Normandie (Manche)

♿ 🛜 **iD** (1343)

🏕 Les Coques d'Or****
📧 14 rue du Bec d'Andaine
☎ +33 (0)2-33708257
📅 1/4 - 30/9
@ contact@
　 campinglescoquesdor.com

7,5ha 70T(100-120m²) 6-10A CEE

1 ACD**G**IJKLM**P**RS
2 AFGRVWX
3 ABGKNRU
4 (C 1/7-31/8) (E+H 9/4-25/9) J
　 KLN
　 (Q+S+T+U+V+X+Y+Z 📅)
5 **AB**DEFGIJKLMNOPUWZ
6 CDEG**IK**(N 0,8km)ORTV

💬 Calm campsite located on the bay of Mont Saint-Michel. Nice restaurant, full board possible (all meals supplied).

🚐 At Avranches take exit Granville (D973). Then D911 direction Jullouville. The campsite is just past Genêts, left.

Carolles　　　　　　D7

D911　D973
　CC
　Avranches

D75　D43
D776　A84

CC € **17** 1/4-6/7　24/8-29/9
🗺 N 48°41'16'' W 1°29'4''

Grandcamp-Maisy, F-14450 / Basse-Normandie (Calvados)

♿ 🛜 **iD** (1344)

🏕 Camping Joncal***
📧 Quai du Petit Nice
☎ +33 (0)2-31226144
📠 +33 (0)2-31227399
📅 27/4 - 30/9
@ joncal@capfun.com

4ha 200T(80-100m²) 10A CEE

1 ACD**G**IJKLMOPQ
2 AEFGKQRTVWXY
3 BGHP**R**UWY
4 (Q 📅)
5 **AB**EFGIJKLMNPUWZ
6 BCEGHJ**K**(N 0,1km)RTV

💬 The campsite is located near the harbour of Grandcamp-Maisy. Just a few km from Pointe du Hoc. Perfect base for visiting the many WWII monuments such as Omaha Beach, the American Cemetery at Pointe du Hoc and the German military cemetery at La Cambe.

🚐 N13 exit Grandcamp-Maisy. Via D113 towards village centre. Campsite is next to the harbour, follow signs.

Grandcamp-Maisy　CC
D913
D514　D517
N13　D5

CC € **17** 27/4-30/6　3/9-29/9
🗺 N 49°23'17'' W 1°3'5''

Honfleur/Équemauville, F-14600 / Basse-Normandie (Calvados)   ♿ 🛜 **iD** (1345)

- 🏕 La Briquerie*****
- 🛣 D62
- ☎ +33 (0)2-31892832
- 🗓 31/3 - 30/9
- @ info@campinglabriquerie.com

11ha 200T(100m²) 6-10A

1 AGIJKLMPQ
2 FGLRVWXY
3 BFGHJMNQRU**V**
4 (C 25/6-10/9) (F 15/4-30/9) (H 15/5-15/9) IJ**KN** (Q+R+T+U+X+Y+Z 🔒)
5 **AB**DEFGIJKLMNPQRUXYZ
6 ACDEGHIKLM(N 0,1km)OPR TV

In easily accessible woodland with large, marked-out pitches. Easy access. 3 km from the sea and the picturesque town of Honfleur. 1 km from a large wood for walks. 100 metres from large supermarket. Luxury toilet facilities.

🚗 From A29 exit 1. Go towards Pont-l'Évêque. Right after 2 km on D579 dir. Honfleur. Third exit at Intermarché to D62. Campsite about 150m on the right.

Le Havre

Honfleur

A131 · A29 · D22 · D180 · D513 · D62 · D579 · D27 · D677 · D17 · A13

CC € **17** 1/4-8/7 26/8-29/9 7=6   🏖 N 49°23'53'' E 0°12'31''

Houlgate, F-14510 / Basse-Normandie (Calvados)   ♿ 🛜 **iD** (1346)

- 🏕 La Vallée*****
- 🛣 88 rue de la Vallée
- ☎ +33 (0)2-31244069
- 📠 +33 (0)2-31244242
- 🗓 29/3 - 5/11
- @ camping.lavallee@wanadoo.fr

14ha 87T(100-130m²) 6-10A CEE

1 ACD**F**IJKLMPQ
2 AIJKLRVWX
3 BC**F**GKM**NOP**RU
4 (C 1/5-15/9) (F+H 🔒) IJP (Q+S+T+U+V+X+Z 🔒)
5 **AB**FGIJKLMNP**Q**UWXYZ
6 CDEG**K**(N 1km)OTV

A spacious campsite with plenty of greenery, a 15 minute walk to the village and beaches. Beautiful views of the surrounding hills. The site offers all amenities and is well maintained. There is also entertainment in the early season. Reception closed between 12:30 and 14:00.

🚗 A13 exit Dozulé, then D400 direction Dives-sur-Mer/Houlgate and then follow the signs.

Ouistreham · Dives-sur-Mer

D163 · D118 · D27 · D45 · D513 · D400 · A13 · D16 · D37 · D675 · D49

CC € **17** 29/3-30/6 1/9-4/11   🏖 N 49°17'37'' W 0°4'6''

Isigny-sur-Mer, F-14230 / Basse-Normandie (Calvados)   🛜 **iD** (1347)

- 🏕 Le Fanal****
- 🛣 rue du Fanal
- ☎ +33 (0)2-31213320
- 📠 +33 (0)2-31221200
- 🗓 1/4 - 30/9
- @ info@camping-lefanal.com

8,4ha 93T(80-110m²) 16A CEE

1 ACD**F**IJKLMPRS
2 DFLRVWXY
3 BGHJMNRUVW
4 (C 15/6-31/8) (E 🔒) (H 15/6-31/8) IJ (Q+T+U+V+X+Y+Z 🔒)
5 **AB**DEFGIJKLMNPUWXZ
6 ACEG**IK**(N 1km)TV

An attractive, peaceful campsite located by a recreational lake. Fishing and surfing are permitted. Indoor swimming pool (sliding roof) and a large outdoor pool with slide and deckchairs. Good toilet facilities. An ideal location for visiting the Landing Beaches, Pointe du Hoc and the American and German war cemeteries.

🚗 Isigny-centre exit; then signposted. Follow route for heavy goods vehicles to avoid the town centre.

D14 · Grandcamp-Maisy · D913 · D514 · Isigny-sur-Mer · Carentan · N13 · D5 · D674 · D11

CC € **13** 1/4-29/6 28/8-29/9   🏖 N 49°19'8'' W 1°6'32''

Le Rozel, F-50340 / Basse-Normandie (Manche) ♿ 🛜 iD (1348)

🏕 Le Ranch*****
🏠 La Mielle
☎ +33 (0)2-33100710
📠 +33 (0)2-33100711
🗓 1/4 - 30/9
@ contact@camping-leranch.com

4ha 42T(100-130m²) 10A CEE

1 ACD**G**IJKLMPQ
2 AEJKRSVW
3 BGNRUVWY
4 (C 15/5-15/9) (E 🖐)
    (H 15/5-15/9) J**N**(Q+S 🖐)
    (T+U+V 1/5-15/9) (Z 🖐)
5 **AB**CDEFGIJKLMNOPUWXY
6 ACEG**K**(N 5km)ORTV

💬 Camping Le Ranch is located on the west coast of the Cotentin (La Manche) in the middle of a beautiful dune landscape and right on a wide sandy beach. The location and the amenities of this campsite ensure a unique ambiance in spring and autumn.

🚗 In Les Pieux follow the D904, direction Barneville-Carteret. Turn right just beyond Les Pieux. Signposted further on.

CC €**19** 1/4-30/6 1/9-29/9

📍 N 49°28'49'' W 1°50'32''

Le Vey, F-14570 / Basse-Normandie (Calvados) 🛜 iD (1349)

🏕 Des Rochers des Parcs***
🏠 La Cour, 8 rte du Viaduc
☎ +33 (0)2-31697036
🗓 1/4 - 30/9
@ camping.normandie@gmail.com

1,5ha 60T(80-140m²) 10A CEE

1 AC**G**IJKLMOPQ
2 CJRTUVX
3 ABGHJLR**W**X
4 (Q+R+T+Z 🖐)
5 **AB**DEFGIJKLMNOPUZ
6 BCDEJ(N 0,8km)T

💬 A green oasis of peace. Terraced campsite located on a river. At walking distance from a small, pretty village with shops and restaurants.

🚗 D562 Caen-Flers then D133A Le Vey, then follow signs. Turn right after Orne bridge.

CC €**17** 1/4-9/7 27/8-29/9 7=6

📍 N 48°54'49'' W 0°28'27''

Les Pieux, F-50340 / Basse-Normandie (Manche) 🚻♿🛜 iD (1350)

🏕 Le Grand Large*****
🏠 route du Grand Large
☎ +33 (0)2-33524075
📠 +33 (0)2-33525820
🗓 7/4 - 23/9
@ info@legrandlarge.com

4ha 123T(100m²) 10A CEE

1 ACD**F**IJKLMOPQ
2 AEKLRSVWX
3 BGHJ**M**NRUWY
4 (C+E+H 🖐) K(Q+R 🖐)
    (T+U 7/7-24/8) (Z 🖐)
5 **AB**CDEFGHIJKLMNOPUWX
    YZ
6 CEGH**I**K(N 3km)ORTV

💬 A family campsite in the dunes of Normandy on the west coast of the Cotentin area and near the British Channel Islands. The campsite is located right by the sea with a wide sandy beach. Pitches marked out by hedges. Lovely partially covered swimming pool with bubble bath.

🚗 From Valognes, take the D902. In Bricquebec direction Les Pieux. Clearly signposted from Les Pieux.

CC €**17** 7/4-6/7 26/8-22/9 7=6, 14=11

📍 N 49°29'40'' W 1°50'32''

69

Maupertus-sur-Mer, F-50330 / Basse-Normandie (Manche)

(1351)

🔺 L'Anse du Brick*****
📧 18 Anse du Brick
☎ +33 (0)2-33543357
📠 +33 (0)2-33544966
🔑 30/3 - 15/9
@ welcome@anse-du-brick.com

10ha 184T(90-150m²) 6-16A CEE

1 ACD**F**IJKLMOPQ
2 ABCEJKNOQRTVWXY
3 BF**GH**MNRUWY
4 (C 1/5-9/9) (F+H 🔑) JK
(Q+S+T+U+V+X+Y+Z 🔑)
5 **AB**CDEFGHIJKLMNOPQU
WXYZ
6 ACEGIJ**K**(N 8km)ORTV

💬 A lovely campsite with every comfort close to Cherbourg and by the sea. Large pitches on terraces, heated toilet facilities and two swimming pools. Direct access to footpaths and the beach. 30 minutes free wifi daily in the bar.

🚗 From Cherbourg via the D116 towards Bretteville-Barfleur. Follow the D116. Campsite signposted after about 4 km. Attention: difficult to reach via Maupertus, take D116 via Cherbourg.

Cherbourg-Octeville
D901 D355
D26
N13 D24

CC € 19 30/3-5/7 26/8-14/9   📍 N 49°40'4'' W 1°29'19''

Merville-Franceville-Plage, F-14810 / Basse-Normandie (Calvados)

(1352)

🔺 Les Peupliers****
📧 allée des Pins
☎ 📠 +33 (0)2-31240507
🔑 1/4 - 31/10
@ contact@camping-peupliers.com

4ha 100T(80-200m²) 10A CEE

1 ACD**F**HIJKLMPST
2 ACEFLRVWX
3 AF**GH**JNRU**W**Y
4 (C 1/6-30/9) (F+H 🔑) KP
(Q 🔑) (R 1/7-31/8)
(T+U 1/7-30/8) (Z 1/7-31/8)
5 **AB**DEFGIJLMNPQRUWXYZ
6 ACEGI**K**(N 2km)RV

💬 A peacefully located family campsite with large pitches. Grounds with plenty of flowers, close to Cabourg for all your shopping. Heated outdoor and indoor swimming pool and heated toilet facilities. 300 metres from the sandy beach. Walking and cycling routes right from the campsite. Reception closed from 12:00 to 14:00.

🚗 Drive from Cabourg via the D514 in the direction of Merville. The campsite is located on the left of this road and is signposted.

Hérouville-Saint-Clair
D163
D35 D514 D45
D513 D27
D400
A13
D49

CC € 19 1/4-30/4 22/5-30/6 1/9-30/10   📍 N 49°17'3'' W 0°10'8''

Merville-Franceville-Plage, F-14810 / Basse-Normandie (Calvados)

(1353)

🔺 Seasonova Le Point du Jour****
📧 75 route de Cabourg
☎ +33 (0)2-31242334
🔑 30/3 - 4/11
@ contact@
camping-lepointdujour.com

2,7ha 88T 10A CEE

1 ACD**G**HIJKLPQ
2 AEFGJKLRSVWX
3 AF**GH**IJKPRUVWY
4 (A 3/4-31/8)
(F+H 10/4-30/10) KN**P**
(Q+R+T+U+V+X+Y+Z 🔑)
5 **AB**DEFGJLMNPUWXY
6 ACEGI**K**(N 1,5km)**P**RTV

💬 Located right by the sea with an indoor swimming pool. Close to Caen and Cabourg with plenty of shops. A cycle path leads from the site to Cabourg. The centre of Merville is a 400m walk via the beach. Reception closed from 13:00 to 14:00.

🚗 A13 exit 29B Dozulé, direction Cabourg. Then via D514 towards Ouistreham. Campsite signposted. From the west: A13, exit 29 Dozulé, direction Cabourg. Then D514 direction Ouistreham.

Hérouville-Saint-Clair
Caen
D35 D45
D513 D27
D400
A13
D37 D49

CC € 17 30/3-6/7 26/8-31/10   📍 N 49°17'0'' W 0°11'29''

Moyaux, F-14590 / Basse-Normandie (Calvados) ⬙ 1354

△ Camping Le Colombier★★★★
✉ chemin du Val Sery
☎ +33 (0)2-31636308
↻ 18/5 - 23/9
@ info@
camping-normandie-lecolombier.com

4,5ha 180T(80-140m²) 10-14A CEE

1 CDGIJKLMOPQ
2 BLMRWXY
3 BIJKNQR
4 C(Q+R+T 🔒)
5 **AB**EFGIJKLMNOPUWXY
6 CEIJV

NEW

📺 This traditional-style campsite is located in the heart of a beautiful French estate around a castle. All amenities are available, and the surrounding area is rich in natural beauty.

🚗 A13 exit Pont-L'Evêque, via D579 to Lisieux and via D51 to Blangy-le-Château, then to Moyaux. Site is then signposted.

Épaignes
D534
D139 D27
D810
D579
D510
D28 D834
Lisieux
D613
Beuvillers
A28

CC € **15** 18/5-5/7 2/9-22/9   📐 N 49°12'35'' E 0°23'24''

Ouistreham, F-14150 / Basse-Normandie (Calvados) 👫 ♿ ⬙ iD 1355

△ Seasonova Riva Bella
✉ 1 rue de la Haie Breton
☎ +33 (0)2-31971266
↻ 30/3 - 4/11
@ camping-rivabella@
vacances-seasonova.com

5ha 286T(80-100m²) 10A CEE

1 ACD**G**HIJKLM**P**RS
2 CDLRUVWXY
3 AD**F**GHJK**M**PRW
4 (E+H 1/5-30/9) P(Q+R 🔒) (T+U+V+Z 1/5-15/9)
5 **AB**DEFGI**J**KLMNPQUXYZ
6 ABCDEGI**K**(N 0,8km)RT

NEW

📺 Large grounds with diverse landscaping, situated right on the Caen Ouistreham channel. New washing block, indoor pool, and close to both the sea and the WW2 landing beaches so you'll have a great holiday.

🚗 From A13, exit Ouistreham. Before Oistreham opposite supermarkets. On roundabout, first exit right. Campsite after 150 m.

Houlgate
Ouistreham
D35 CC D514
D7 D60 D27
D7 D513
Caen D226 D37 A13

CC € **17** 30/3-8/7 26/8-31/10 7=6, 14=11   📐 N 49°16'8'' W 0°15'19''

Pontaubault, F-50220 / Basse-Normandie (Manche) ⬙ iD 1356

△ Vallée de la Sélune★★
✉ 7 rue Maréchal Leclerc
☎ +33 (0)2-33603900
↻ 1/4 - 15/10
@ campselune@wanadoo.fr

1,6ha 70T(100-110m²) 10A CEE

1 ACDGIJKLMPQ
2 FGTVX
3 ABG**M**
4 (R+Z 🔒)
5 **AB**GIJKLMNPUZ
6 EGJ(N 0,2km)O

📺 Small, quiet campsite in a beautiful small village with shops and a restaurant. The campsite is only 15 km from Mont-Saint-Michel.

🚗 From N175 direction Mont-St-Michel D43. Exit Pontaubault; turn right over the bridge, then the second street to the left.

D973 D7
D911
D5
Avranches
D75 CC
Isigny-le-Buat
N175
D975 D40 A84
D998

CC € **17** 1/4-9/7 27/8-14/10 7=6   📐 N 48°37'49'' W 1°21'10''

Pontorson, F-50170 / Basse-Normandie (Manche)   ♿ 📶 iD 1357

🏕 Haliotis***
✉ boulevard Patton
☎ +33 (0)2-33681159
📠 +33 (0)2-33589536
🔓 30/3 - 4/11
@ camping@camping-haliotis.fr

8ha 150T(90-200m²) 16A CEE

1 ACD**G**IJKLM**P**Q
2 CFRTVX
3 ABDGHJKNRUW
4 (C+H 1/5-30/9) KN
  (Q+R+Z 🔓)
5 **AB**DFGIJKLMNP**S**UWZ
6 CEGIK(N 0,5km)RTV

💬 Beautiful, quiet and floral campsite within walking distance of the centre (market on Wednesday) and within cycling distance of Mont Saint-Michel.

🚍 N175 Avranches direction Pontorson, exit Pontorson. Follow the signs in the town.

CC € 17   30/3-7/7   25/8-3/11   7=6, 14=11   🏔 N 48°33'29'' W 1°30'52''

Ravenoville-Plage, F-50480 / Basse-Normandie (Manche)   ♿ 📶 ✿ iD 1358

🏕 Le Cormoran*****
✉ Ravenoville-Plage
☎ +33 (0)2-33413394
📠 +33 (0)2-33951608
🔓 31/3 - 30/9
@ lecormoran@wanadoo.fr

8ha 140T(100-150m²) 6-10A CEE

1 ACD**F**IJKLMOPRS
2 AEFLRUVWX
3 ABD**F**GHJKMN**OPQ**RUVWY
4 (C 1/7-31/8) (F+H 🔓) K**N**
  (Q+S 🔓) (T+U 1/7-31/8)
  (V+Z 🔓)
5 **AB**DEFGIJKLMNOP**ST**UWX
  YZ
6 ACDEGH**I**K(N 9km)ORTUV
  W

💬 A modern campsite with every comfort and luxury. Located right on Utah Beach by the sea. Spacious marked out pitches with plenty of greenery and flowers. Ideal base for sightseeing (WW II).

🚍 From St. Mère-Église follow the D15 towards Ravenoville. Then direction Plage. Campsite signposted.

CC € 19   31/3-6/7   25/8-29/9   7=6, 14=11   🏔 N 49°27'59'' W 1°14'8''

Servon, F-50170 / Basse-Normandie (Manche)   👫 📶 iD 1359

🏕 Campéole St. Grégoire***
✉ 47 rue Saint Grégoire
☎ +33 (0)2-33602603
📠 +33 (0)2-33606865
🔓 30/3 - 16/9
@ saint-gregoire@campeole.com

1ha 46T(80-100m²) 6A CEE

1 ACD**F**IJKLMOP**S**
2 FRTX
3 ABGR
4 (C 8/5-10/9) (Q 31/3-17/9)
  (R 🔓)
5 **AB**EFGIJKLMNPU
6 CEGH**K**RT

💬 A quiet natural campsite located between Avranches, Pontorson and Le Mont St. Michel.

🚍 From Avranches take N175 towards Pontorson. Take Servon exit (D107). 200m further on the right.

CC € 15   30/3-6/7   25/8-15/9   🏔 N 48°35'48'' W 1°24'45''

St. Aubin-sur-Mer, F-14750 / Basse-Normandie (Calvados) ♿ 🛜 iD (1360)

🔺 Sandaya La Côte de Nacre*****
📧 17 rue du Général Moulton
☎ +33 (0)2-31971445
📠 +33 (0)2-31972211
🔓 6/4 - 9/9
@ cotedenacre@sandaya.fr

10ha 142T(80-120m²) 10A

1 ACD**G**IJKLMPRS
2 GLRVWXY
3 B**F**GNRU
4 (C 15/6-31/8) (E+F+H 🔓) IJ
LNP(Q+S+T+U+V+Y+Z 🔓)
5 **AB**DEFGIJKLMNOPUWXYZ
6 ACEGHIJ**K**(N 0,5km)TV

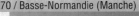 A beautiful parkland campsite with a leisure pool (open air and indoor and heated); sauna, Turkish bath, jacuzzi, restaurant, shopping facilities. Campsite is within walking distance of St. Aubin and 650 meters from the beach. All amenities are also open in the early and late seasons.

 On the Caen ring road exit Côte de Nacre, then via the D7 to Langrune-sur-Mer and St. Aubin-sur-Mer. Campsite is on the D7 and is signposted.

D65 D514
D12 D79
D404
D22 D35
Blainville-sur-Orne
CC

CC € **17** 6/4-6/7 1/9-8/9   ⛱ N 49°19'33'' W 0°23'26''

St. Jean-de-la-Rivière, F-50270 / Basse-Normandie (Manche) ♿ 🛜 iD (1361)

🔺 Camping du Golf****
📧 43 chemin des Mielles
☎ +33 (0)2-33047890
📠 +33 (0)9-70632192
🔓 1/4 - 30/9
@ contact@camping-du-golf.fr

3.2ha 90T(140-180m²) 6A CEE

1 ACD**F**IJKLMPRS
2 AEKRSVW
3 BE**G**HIJKNRUWY
4 (E+H 🔓) J(Q+R 🔓)
(T+U+V+Y+Z 1/5-15/9)
5 **AB**DEFGIJKLMNPQRUWX
6 ACEG**K**(N 3km)TV

 A family campsite with large pitches, located 500m from the Normandy Beaches, opposite the Channel Islands of Guernsey and Jersey. Covered and heated swimming pool. Bar, restaurant, pizzeria and shop on site. Plenty of activities available.

From Barneville-Carteret towards Barneville/St. Jean-de-la-Rivière. Signposted beyond there.

D904 D902 D900
D650 Saint-Jean-de-la-Rivière
CC D15
D903
La Haye-du-Puits

CC € **17** 1/4-6/7 25/8-29/9   ⛱ N 49°21'35'' W 1°44'55''

St. Pair-sur-Mer, F-50380 / Basse-Normandie (Manche) ♿ 🛜 ✿ iD (1362)

🔺 Lez-Eaux*****
📧 St. Aubin-des-Préaux
☎ +33 (0)2-33516609
📠 +33 (0)2-33519202
🔓 1/4 - 16/9
@ bonjour@lez-eaux.com

11ha 134T(100-150m²) 10-16A CEE

1 ACGIJKLMOPQ
2 DLRVX
3 ABG**K**M**N**RW
4 (C 15/5-10/9) (F+H 🔓) IJ
(Q+S+U+V+Z 🔓)
5 **AB**DEFGIJKLMNOPUWXYZ
6 CDEG**IK**(N 2km)RTV

 For an unforgettable holiday: a quiet flowery family campsite in a castle park, with a 1200 m² heated indoor swimming paradise close to Granville.

From Caen via the A84 and D924 towards Granville. Before Granville via the D971 and D973 towards Avranches. The campsite is well signposted on the right. Do not take direction St. Pair-sur-Mer or direction St. Aubin-des-Préaux.

D971
Granville
D924
Jullouville CC
D973
D7
D911

CC € **19** 1/4-8/7 3/9-15/9   ⛱ N 48°47'52'' W 1°31'30''

St. Vaast-la-Hougue, F-50550 / Basse-Normandie (Manche) ♿ 🛜 iD (1363)

🏕 La Gallouette★★★★
✉ 10 bis rue de la Gallouette
☎ +33 (0)2-33542057
🗓 1/4 - 30/9
@ contact@camping-lagallouette.fr

3,5ha 110T(85-105m²) 10A CEE

1 ACD**G**IJKLMPRS
2 AEQRVWX
3 BGHNRUWY
4 (C+H 15/5-15/9) (Q+R 🔲)
   (T+U+Z 1/6-31/8)
5 **AB**EFGJKLMNOPUWYZ
6 ACDEG**IK**(N 0,3km)TVW

💬 Quiet site with spacious pitches. Heated outdoor pool, jeu de boules, playground and wifi. 5 minutes' walk from the sea, harbour and shops. Outings to e.g. Vauban castle on the Tatihou island and Barfleur. Plenty of walking and cycling. Maritime atmosphere. Ideal stopover site: 30 minutes from Cherbourg (ferry).

🚗 N13 Caen-Cherbourg, at Valognes D902 dir. Quettehou and St. Vaast-la-Hougue. Right at traffic lights, turn right after 300m - Rue de la Galouette.

D901
D24 D355
D26
Saint-Vaast-la-Hougue CC
D902
D42
D14

CC €**17** 1/4-6/7 26/8-29/9   🧭 N 49°35'4'' W 1°16'8''

Ste Marie-du-Mont, F-50480 / Basse-Normandie (Manche) 🛜 iD (1364)

🏕 Flower Camping UTAH Beach★★★
✉ La Madeleine
☎ +33 (0)2-33715369
📠 +33 (0)2-33710711
🗓 1/4 - 22/9
@ utah.beach@wanadoo.fr

5ha 40T(80-100m²) 6A CEE

1 ACDGIJKLMOPQ
2 AELRSVWX
3 BF**H**JKMN**Q**RUWY
4 (F+H 🔲) **N**(Q+S 🔲)
   (U+V+X 1/6-31/8) (Z 🔲)
5 **AB**EFGIJKLMNPUWZ
6 ACEGK(N 6km)OTV

💬 A family campsite in Western style 100 metres from the sea. Close to Utah Beach landing beaches. The area is rich in history and architecture. Motorhome site also available, which is open all year.

🚗 From Carentan take the D913 direction Ste Marie-du-Mont (Utah Beach). Follow signs after Utah Beach monument.

D42
D14
D15
D67
CC
Grandcamp-Maisy
D913
D514

CC €**17** 1/4-26/5 11/6-30/6 1/9-21/9 7=6, 14=10   🧭 N 49°25'10'' W 1°10'55''

Ste Marie-du-Mont, F-50480 / Basse-Normandie (Manche) 👫 ♿ 🛜 iD (1365)

🏕 La Baie des Veys★★★
✉ Le Grand Vey
☎ +33 (0)2-33715690
🗓 30/3 - 30/9
@ la.bdv50@gmail.com

1,2ha 34T(100-120m²) 10A CEE

1 ACD**G**IJKLMOPRS
2 AFKRVWXY
3 BGHJRUW
4 (C+H 15/5-15/9)
   (Q+R+T+U+Z 🔲)
5 **A**FGIJKLMNPUZ
6 EGJ(N 5km)ORTV

NEW

💬 This medium-sized campsite lies on the the Grand Veys bay in a rural setting. Just a few kilometres from Utah Beach with a lovely pool and a bird sanctuary next door, where you might also find seals.

🚗 On N13 take exit D913 towards Utah Beach. After the village Ste Marie-du-Mont take exit on the right towards Grand Veys. Campsite is 4 km further.

Sainte-Mère-Église
D67 D14
D913 CC
D514
Carentan
D903
D5
D11

CC €**17** 30/3-31/5 8/6-6/7 24/8-29/9 7=6   🧭 N 49°21'56'' W 1°10'39''

Torigni-sur-Vire, F-50160 / Basse-Normandie (Manche)

🔥 📶 **iD** (1366)

🔺 Le Lac des Charmilles***
📧 route de Vire
☎ +33 (0)2-33758505
🗓 1/4 - 30/9
@ campingdulacdescharmilles@orange.fr

2,4ha 38T(100-150m²) 12A CEE

1 ACD**G**IJKLM**PQ**
2 DFJLRVWX
3 AGNRU**W**
4 (C 15/5-15/9) (Q+R 🖲) (T+U+V+Z 15/6-31/8)
5 **AB**DFGIJKLMNOPUWZ
6 CDEGK(N 0,5km)TV

💬 A well-located and well-maintained campsite by a lake and within walking distance of the small town of Torigni-sur-Vire. The campsite has a heated outdoor pool. Heated toilet facilities. One hour from Mont St. Michel and the Landing Beaches. Free wifi. Lovely footpath from the campsite around a fishing lake.

🚗 From A84 Caen-Rennes exit 40. Then D974 direction Torigni-sur-Vire. Campsite on the right before the town.

CC € **17** 1/4-8/7 26/8-29/9

📍 N 49°1'43'' W 0°58'20''

Villedieu-les-Poêles, F-50800 / Basse-Normandie (Manche)

🔥 📶 **iD** (1367)

🔺 Les Chevaliers de Malte***
📧 2 impasse Pré de la Rose
☎ +33 (0)2-33594904
📠 +33 (0)967734904
🗓 1/4 - 15/10
@ campingleschevaliersdemalte@gmail.com

1,5ha 78T(90-100m²) 8-16A CEE

1 ACD**G**IJKLM**PQ**
2 CFRTVX
3 ABGNRU**W**
4 (C 15/6-15/9) (Q+R+T+U+V+Z 🖲)
5 **AB**DEFGIJKLMNPUWZ
6 CDEGJ(N 0,3km)OV

💬 A small campsite in the countryside with marked out pitches. Located 300 metres from the centre. Copper works, bell-foundry and a typical weekly market.

🚗 From Caen A84 direction Mont St. Michel. In Villedieu take exit 38 towards the centre. Campsite well signposted.

CC € **17** 1/4-8/7 26/8-14/10 7=6, 14=11

📍 N 48°50'12'' W 1°13'2''

Ambon, F-56190 / Bretagne (Morbihan)

🔥 📶 **iD** (1368)

🔺 Camping de Cromenac'h**
📧 Lieu dit Cromenac'h
☎ +33 (0)2-97416747
🗓 1/4 - 31/10
@ villagedecromenach@orange.fr

1,5ha 94T(80-120m²) 6-10A CEE

1 ACD**G**IJKLMOPQ
2 ABEFKOQRUVWXY
3 AGHJRWY
4 (Q 🖲) (U 8/7-26/8)
5 **AB**GIJKLNOPUVXYZ
6 ACE**J**(N 4km)TV

💬 Quiet, simple campsite directly on a small beach. Modern toilet facilities, a few pitches with a view of the sea. Lovely, old chapel directly next to the pitches. Almost level region with walking and cycling paths. Reception closed from 12:00 to 14:00.

🚗 E60 Vannes-Nantes, exit Muzillac towards Sarzeau. On roundabout by shopping centre take direction Damgan. First roundabout take direction Cromenac'h.

CC € **11** 1/4-6/7 27/8-30/10 21=18

📍 N 47°31'33'' W 2°31'29''

Arradon, F-56610 / Bretagne (Morbihan)

⚿ 🛜 iD **1369**

🏕 Camping de l'Allée***
📧 L'Allée
☎ +33 (0)2-97440198
🗓 31/3 - 30/9
@ contact@camping-allee.com

124T(80-140m²) 10-15A CEE

1 ACD**G**IJKLMOPQ
2 EFIOQRVWXY
3 B**F**GHRUW
4 (C+F+H ⬚)
   (Q+R+T+U+Z 7/7-26/8)
5 **AB**DEFGIJKLMNOPQUVZ
6 ACE**K**(N 2km)OTV

💬 Peaceful campsite in the green belt between the town and the sea, rugged coastline with many coves and islands in the Gulf of Morbihan. Large level pitches between trees and hedges or open pitches with plenty of sun. Covered pool and heated toilet blocks. Low season reception hours: 10h-12h / 16h-19h.

🚗 N165/E60 Nantes-Lorient, exit Vannes Ouest/ Arradon. Via D101 and D127 to Arradon just past shopping centre. Follow cp signs on roundabout.

CC € **15** 31/3-1/7 3/9-29/9

📷 N 47°37'17'' W 2°50'25''

Arradon, F-56610 / Bretagne (Morbihan)

⚿ 🛜 ✿ iD **1370**

🏕 Sites & Paysages
   De Penboch****
📧 9 chemin de Penboch
☎ +33 (0)2-97447129
🗓 7/4 - 29/9
@ camping.penboch@wanadoo.fr

3,5ha 117T(85-110m²) 10A CEE

1 ACD**G**IJKLMOPQ
2 AEFKOQRVWXY
3 BC**F**GHJKN**Q**RUWY
4 (C 10/5-16/9) (F+H ⬚) IJK
   (Q+R ⬚) (T+U+Z 10/5-9/9)
5 **AB**CDEFGHIJKLMNOPQR**S**
   TUWXYZ
6 ACEGHI**K**(N 2km)RTV

💬 Excellently equipped campsite 300m from the north coast of the Golfe Du Morbihan and Grande Randonnée 34. Boat excursions on the Golfe Du Morbihan. Vannes is worth visiting, 8 km by bike. Excellent toilet facilities, a lovely indoor swimming pool and heated outdoor pool with slides. Low season reception hours: 9h-13h and 14h-19h30.

🚗 N165/E60 Vannes-Lorient, exit Vannes-Ouest/ Arradon. Via the D101 direction Arradon, then follow campsite signs or 'Pointe de Penboch'.

CC € **17** 7/4-6/7 27/8-22/9

📷 N 47°37'20'' W 2°48'4''

Arzano, F-29310 / Bretagne (Finistère)

👫 ⚿ 🛜 ✿ iD **1371**

🏕 Le Ty Nadan*****
📧 route d'Arzano
☎ +33 (0)2-98717547
📠 +33 (0)2-98717731
🗓 27/4 - 2/9
@ info@tynadan-vacances.fr

21ha 100T(90-200m²) 10A CEE

1 ACD**G**IJKLMOPQ
2 AC**K**LRVWXY
3 BCDGHJK**MNOP**RU**W**X
4 (A+C+F+H ⬚) IJKMP
   (Q+S+T+U+V+Y+Z ⬚)
5 **AB**DEFGJLMNPQ**ST**UWX
   YZ
6 CEGHI**K**(N 3km)O**P**RTV

NEW

💬 A family campsite in midst of the countryside. The swimming pools are always heated to minimum 28° C. There is an obstacle course in the trees. A few kilometres from the Devil's Rocks, well worth a visit.

🚗 North of Lorient via the N165/E60 towards Quimperlé, exit Quimperlé-Est. Take the D22 before Quimperlé-centre to Arzano. Head towards Locunolé just before Arzano-centre, or follow the signs.

CC € **13** 27/4-30/6 31/8-1/9

📷 N 47°54'17'' W 3°28'30''

Baden/Bourgerel, F-56870 / Bretagne (Morbihan) 👫 ♿ 📶 🆔 **1372**

🏕 Campéole Penn Mar***
✉ 21 route de Port Blanc
☎ +33 (0)2-97574990
📅 30/3 - 30/9
@ pennmar@campeole.com

6ha 72T(100-150m²) 10A CEE

1 ACD**G**IJKLMO**P**ST
2 AEGKOQRVWXY
3 A**F**GHJMNRUW
4 (E+H 📅) M(Q 1/7-31/8)
(R 📅) (T+U+Z 1/7-31/8)
5 **AB**CDFGHIJKLMNOPQRUZ
6 ACEGH**K**(N 4km)ORTV

💬 A family campsite with sufficient, modern toilet facilities close to the 'Golfe du Morbihan' with its hundreds of islands, the most famous of which, Île-aux-Moines, is especially worth a visit. Lovely new indoor pool with a fun open air water playground. Reception hours in low season: 9:00-12:00 and 15:00-18:00.

🚗 N165/E60 Vannes-Lorient, exit Vannes-Ouest/ Arradon. Via D101 dir. Baden/Île-aux-Moines. Then follow Île-aux-Moines via D316, campsite on the left.

Auray
Vannes
Sarzeau
D17 D19 D767 D28 CC

CC €**15** 30/3-6/7 25/8-29/9 · 🧭 **N 47°36'25'' W 2°52'32''**

Beg-Léguer/Lannion, F-22300 / Bretagne (Côtes-d'Armor) ♿ 📶 🆔 **1373**

🏕 Les Plages de Beg-Léguer***
✉ route de la Côte
☎ +33 (0)2-96472500
📅 28/4 - 30/9
@ info@campingdesplages.com

4,7ha 149T(80-120m²) 6A CEE

1 AC**G**IJKLMOPRS
2 AEF**G**LQRVXY
3 AB**F**GHJMNRUWY
4 (C 1/7-31/8) (D+G 📅) J
(Q+R 📅)
(T+U+V+X+Z 1/7-31/8)
5 **AB**EFGIJKLMNPUVWZ
6 AEGIK(N 4km)RV

💬 You will be warmly received at this beautiful campsite adorned by many flowers. Spacious pitches with glimpses of the sea. The sandy beach is 400 metres away and Lannion is just 5 km. Ideal base for the Côte de Granit Rose, Les Sept Îles and the Île Grande. A campsite worth going back to.

🚗 Lannion-Trébeurden (total 9 km). After about 6 km turn off at Champ Blanc (Bar-Tabac/Resto-Bar) towards Les Plages de Beg-Léguer. (Better not to drive through Servel).

Perros-Guirec
Lannion
D788 D64 D56 D11 D767 D786 D42 CC

CC €**15** 28/4-6/7 26/8-29/9 7=6, 14=12 · 🧭 **N 48°44'18'' W 3°32'41''**

Bénodet, F-29950 / Bretagne (Finistère) ♿ 📶 **1374**

🏕 Camping du Poulquer****
✉ 23 rue du Poulquer
☎ +33 (0)2-98570419
📠 +33 (0)2-98662030
📅 1/5 - 30/9
@ contact@
campingdupoulquer.com

3ha 148T(80-100m²) 6-10A

1 CD**G**IJKLOPQ
2 AERVWXY
3 B**F**GHJRUWY
4 (C 15/6-5/9) (E 1/5-15/9)
(H 15/6-5/9) IJKLNP
(Q+R+T+U+Z 1/7-31/8)
5 **AB**EFGIJKLMNOPUZ
6 ACEGIJ(N 1km)TV

💬 Family campsite close to the town and located near Bénodet and its beach. Modern and well maintained toilet facilities. Lovely heated outdoor pool with jacuzzi and slides, also an indoor pool with sliding roof, free hammam, sauna and wellness area with Balneo. Free wifi. Look out for the name of the campsite when you arrive!

🚗 From Quimper take the D34 to Bénodet. Continue Bénodet-plage. Turn left at the end of the boulevard. Follow the signs!

Fouesnant
Concarneau
D785 N165 D2 D34 D783 D53 CC

CC €**19** 1/5-10/7 28/8-29/9 · 🧭 **N 47°52'5'' W 4°5'54''**

Beuzec-Cap-Sizun, F-29790 / Bretagne (Finistère)

♿ 📶 **iD** (1375)

△ Camping Pors Peron**
☎ +33 (0)2-98704024
☖ 1/4 - 30/9
@ campingporsperon@hotmail.com

3ha 98T(60-120m²) 10A CEE

1 ACD**G**IJKLMPQ
2 AEJQRX
3 BGHJKRWY
4 (E+H 1/5-30/9) (Q+S ☖)
5 **AB**FGIJKLMNPUZ
6 AE**I**J(N 5km)OV

💬 This campsite has a peaceful rural location on the lovely headland of Cap Sizun in western Brittany. It has 98 marked out pitches. 250m from a sandy bay which can be reached via a footpath. Everything for a relaxing holiday. Heated indoor swimming pool. Free wifi. Shop. English owners.

🛣 From Châteaulin take the D7 direction Douarnenez and then follow Beuzec-Cap-Sizun. Turn right about 5 km before Beuzec-Cap-Sizun, direction Pors Peron, then follow camping signs.

CC Douarnenez

D765   D143
D784

CC € **15** 1/4-7/7   25/8-29/9   📍 N 48°5'3'' W 4°28'56''

Binic, F-22520 / Bretagne (Côtes-d'Armor)

♿ 📶 **iD** (1376)

△ Le Panoramic***
▭ rue Gasselin
☎ +33 (0)2-96736043
☖ 1/4 - 30/9
@ lepanoramic22@gmail.com

5,8ha 66T(80-130m²) 10A CEE

1 ACDFIJKLMOPQ
2 AFGIJLQRTVWXY
3 AB**F**GHN**OP**RUW
4 (C 1/7-31/8) (F+G ☖) IJ (Q+R ☖) (T+Z 2/7-27/8)
5 **AB**DEFGJLMNPRUZ
6 ADEGK(N 1km)ORTV

💬 A spacious and attractive campsite close to the harbour town of Binic. Heated, indoor swimming pool and terrace, cafe, bar and the welcome trees all give the place a pleasant feeling. Modern, heated toilet facilities. The pitches are separated by low hedges. Wifi.

🛣 Via the N12 after St. Brieuc, keep in direction Paimpol-par-la-Côte (D786). The campsite is signposted to the right, just before Binic. Turn right immediately.

D21
D9   D786
D6   **CC**
N12   **Saint-**
D7   D36   **Brieuc**

CC € **17** 1/4-30/6   1/9-29/9   📍 N 48°35'30'' W 2°49'29''

Brest, F-29200 / Bretagne (Finistère)

📶 **iD** (1377)

△ Le Goulet****
▭ chemin de Lanhouarnec
☎ +33 (0)2-98458684
☖ 1/4 - 30/9
@ campingduogoulet@wanadoo.fr

6ha 155T(< 100m²) 10A CEE

1 ACDFIJKLMPQ
2 EFGLRTUWXY
3 ABCGHQRUWY
4 (C+H 14/5-15/9) JKM (Q 1/7-30/8) (R ☖) (T+U+V+X+Z 1/7-30/8)
5 **AB**CDFGIJKLMNOPUVWXYZ
6 CDEGIJ(N 5km)ORTV

💬 Very well maintained campsite with a lovely heated swimming pool, also ideally located for visiting Brest and surroundings.

🛣 From Rennes or Morlaix turn right at 1st roundabout (Boulevard de L'Europe) to Plouzané-Le Conquet. Straight ahead ± 8 km. On D789 past Thalès company left at roundabout towards Technopole, Camping du Goulet.

D5   D68   D26
    Guipavas
D67
Brest
CC

CC € **17** 1/4-30/6   1/9-29/9   7=6   📍 N 48°21'55'' W 4°32'24''

Camaret-sur-Mer, F-29570 / Bretagne (Finistère) ♿ 📶 **iD**

▲ Le Grand Large****
🏠 Lambézen
☎ +33 (0)2-98279141
📠 +33 (0)2-98279372
🔑 30/3 - 30/9
@ contact@
  campinglegrandlarge.com
2,8ha 123T(80-130m²) 10A CEE

1 ACD**G**IJLPQ
2 AENRTVX
3 BGHM**Q**RUY
4 (C+H 15/6-15/9) J
  (Q+S+U+Z 15/6-15/9)
5 **AB**EFGIJKLMNOPUWXY
6 CEG**IJ**(N 3km)ORV

 A campsite that deserves its star rating; very clean and well-maintained new toilet facilities including showers and washbasins in the same room. 450m to the beach with spectacular panoramas of the sea and rocks.

🚐 From Cozon the D8 to Camaret. Just past Camaret the roundabout to the right, direction Roscanvel/D355 (1.8 km). At Lambézen follow signs to the right.

Locmaria-
Plouzané

CC

Crozon

CC € ⑮ 1/4-30/6 1/9-29/9 7=6, 14=11   🏕 N 48°16'51'' W 4°33'53''

Camaret-sur-Mer/Crozon, F-29160 / Bretagne (Finistère) ♿ 📶 **iD**

▲ Plage de Trez Rouz***
🏠 route de Camaret à Roscanvel
☎ +33 (0)2-98279396
🔑 15/3 - 15/10
@ contact@trezrouz.com

1,8ha 80T(85-100m²) 16A CEE

1 ACD**G**IJKLMPQ
2 AEKRVWX
3 BGHQRWY
4 (F 1/4-30/9) (Q+R 🔑)
  (T+U+V+Z 1/5-30/9)
5 **AB**DFGIJKLMNOPUVWZ
6 CEG**IJ**(N 3km)V

 A warm welcome by Isabelle and Yannick Trouplin on their beach campsite with views of Camaret. Sandy beaches, ochre coloured rocks, abundant greenery and small towns nearby. The views of Crozon are unique. Several boat trips possible. With a lovely heated indoor pool.

🚐 From Crozon take the D8 to Camaret. Just before Camaret turn right at the roundabout direction Pointe des Espagnols. Follow this road (D355) for 2.8 km.

Plouzané   **Brest**

CC

Crozon

CC € ⑮ 15/3-6/7 25/8-14/10 15=14   🏕 N 48°17'17'' W 4°33'55''

Carnac, F-56340 / Bretagne (Morbihan) 👫 ♿ 📶 **iD**

▲ Les Druides***
🏠 55 chemin de Beaumer
☎ +33 (0)2-97520818
📠 +33 (0)9-60538264
🔑 14/4 - 3/9
@ contact@
  camping-les-druides.com
2,5ha 90T(80-130m²) 6-10A CEE

1 ACD**G**HIJKLOPQ
2 EGRVWXY
3 BFGHJNRUY
4 (C+H 10/6-3/9) (Q 9/7-26/8)
5 **AB**CEFGHIJKLMNOPQRUV
  WXYZ
6 ACEG**J**(N 0,5km)TV

 A peaceful campsite. Well maintained toilet facilities. Pitches between hedges. Close to Carnac. Beach and supermarket 500m. Walking or cycling trips to the coast and the stone Megaliths. Reception open 09:00-12:00 and 14:00-18:00.

🚐 N165/E60 Nantes-Quimper exit Carnac/Quiberon, to Carnac Plage as far as roundabout at market place in Carnac centre. Then towards La Trinité as far as the roundabout with restaurant, then right, site entrance ± 1 km on the right.

D22 Auray
D781   D28
D768   Baden
Carnac CC

CC € ⑲ 14/4-7/7 25/8-2/9   🏕 N 47°34'48'' W 3°3'25''

Carnac-Plage, F-56340 / Bretagne (Morbihan)

👫 ♿ 📶 **iD**   (1381)

🔺 Le Dolmen***
🏠 58 chemin de Beaumer
☎ +33 (0)2-97521235
📠 +33 (0)2-97526391
🔓 2/4 - 23/9
@ camping.ledolmen@gmail.com

2,5ha 45T(80-120m²) 10A CEE

1 ACD**G**IJKLM**PQ**
2 RVWXY
3 A**F**GHNU
4 (E+H+Q 🔓)
   (T+U+Z 3/6-31/8)
5 **AB**EFGIJKLMNPQUXZ
6 BCEGK(N 0,9km)TV

💬 Lovely family campsite at 600 metres from the 'Men Du' beach and 3 km from the Carnac megaliths. The lovely covered and heated pool is always open. New toilet facilities with amenities for the disabled. Special 'city-Park' area and playroom for children.

🚗 N165, exit 34, take the D768 towards Carnac. In Carnac D781 direction La Trinité-sur-Mer. Left at roundabout after 1 km, campsite less than 1 km on the left.

Etel D22   Auray
D28
D781
D768
Quiberon

CC € **17** 2/4-9/7 27/8-22/9 7=6

📍 N 47°34'52'' W 3°3'27''

Carnac/Plouharnel, F-56340 / Bretagne (Morbihan)

👫 ♿ 📶 **iD**   (1382)

🔺 Les Bruyères***
🏠 Kerogile
☎ +33 (0)2-97523057
🔓 1/4 - 30/9
@ contact@
   camping-lesbruyeres.com

4,5ha 71T(80-120m²) 10A CEE

1 ACD**G**IJKLMOPQ
2 FGLQRVWXY
3 BDF**G**HJKN**OPR**TU
4 (E+H 7/4-30/9) (Q+R 🔓)
   (T+U+V+X 1/7-31/8) (Z 🔓)
5 **AB**CDEFGHIJKLMNOPUWZ
6 ACEG**K**(N 2km)TV

💬 A lovely, quiet campsite divided into shaded fields of six pitches, separated by green hedges. Well maintained toilet facilities. Perfect base for visiting historical remains and the Carnac beaches. Indoor, heated swimming pool open all season.

🚗 South of Auray, via D768 to Quiberon-Carnac. Beyond Carnac exit follow road to Quiberon as far as roundabout with blue and white building. Then left dir. Kerogile (C4). 300m to campsite.

Belz N165 D17
D22 Auray
D781
Crach
Carnac
D768

CC € **17** 1/4-6/7 24/8-29/9 7=6, 14=11

📍 N 47°36'28'' W 3°5'26''

Châteaulin, F-29150 / Bretagne (Finistère)

♿ 📶 **iD**   (1383)

🔺 de Rodaven***
🏠 Rocade de Parc Bihan
☎ +33 (0)2-98863293
🔓 1/4 - 30/9
@ contact@campingderodaven.fr

2ha 82T(80-120m²) 10A CEE

1 AC**G**HIJLPRS
2 CFRVWXY
3 AGJRW
4 (Q 1/5-30/9)
   (T+U+Z 15/4-10/9)
5 **AB**GIJKLMNPUWZ
6 CEJ(N 0,8km)O

💬 Located in the heart of Finistère (Brittany) on the banks of the 'Nantes à Brest' canal. The site is well maintained, quiet with plenty of greenery and within walking distance (800m) from the centre. A unique starting point for the many sights in this region. Cycling and walking beside the canal is well worth the effort.

🚗 From N125 and N164 intersection follow D887. Left at third roundabout, then first left. Then 1 km to the swimming pool. The campsite is opposite.

D791
Pleyben
Châteaulin
D47 D887 N164
D63
N165 D785
D107
D7 Briec D72

CC € **15** 1/4-7/7 25/8-29/9 7=6

📍 N 48°11'29'' W 4°5'19''

Châteaulin, F-29150 / Bretagne (Finistère) ♿ 🛜 iD (1384)

🔺 La Pointe***
📧 route de St. Coulitz
☎ +33 (0)2-98865153
📅 15/3 - 15/10
@ lapointecamping@aol.com

2ha 60**T**(80-120m²) 10A

1 ACD**G**IJKLMPQ
2 BCFRTVWXY
3 AKRU**W**
4 (Q+R 📵)
5 **AB**EFGIJKLMNOPQUWZ
6 CEGK(N 1,5km)

💬 A modest, quiet and well-maintained campsite where kindness, friendliness and hospitality are top of the list. Its central location in Finistére makes this a good campsite for trips out in the region. The centre is within walking distance (1,5 km) along the lovely 'Nantes-Brest' canal which can also be cycled.

🚗 In Châteaulin take direction Saint-Coulitz, then follow signs.

Pont-de-Buis-lès-Quimerch
Pleyben
D47 D887
D63
CC
D785
D107 N165
D7 Briec D72

CC € **15** 15/3-8/7 26/8-14/10 7=6 📡 N 48°11'15'' W 4°5'5''

Clohars-Carnoët, F-29360 / Bretagne (Finistère) ♿ 🛜 iD (1385)

🔺 Flower Camping Le Kergariou***
📧 Kervec
☎ +33 (0)2-98715465
📅 1/4 - 15/9
@ camping.lekergariou@wanadoo.fr

2,7ha 71**T**(80-150m²) 10A CEE

1 ACD**G**HIJKLPRS
2 FGQRVWXY
3 BCGHJNRU
4 (E+H 📵) **N**(Q 3/7-25/8)
　(T 7/4-7/5,1/7-31/8)
　(U+Z 2/7-31/8)
5 **AB**FGIJKLMNPQUXYZ
6 CDEG**K**(N 1,5km)TUV

💬 Peacefully located campsite with pitches between hedges and several mature trees. Well equipped toilet facilities. Cycling to the nearby small harbours is possible but watch out for some steep roads. The owner is a fervent angler and can inform you of the best places to fish. Indoor heated swimming pool open throughout the season.

🚗 E60/N165 Lorient-Quimper, exit Kervidanou. Via D16 to Clohars-Carnoët, straight through centre to roundabout. Direction Doëlan.

D22
D783 Quimperlé
D24 D62
D16 N165 D26
D224
CC D765
D152
Ploemeur

CC € **13** 1/4-13/7 1/9-14/9 📡 N 47°46'58'' W 3°35'20''

Clohars-Carnoët/Le Pouldu, F-29360 / Bretagne (Finistère) ♿ 🛜 ✿ iD (1386)

🔺 Les Embruns*****
📧 2 rue de Philosophe Alain
☎ +33 (0)2-98399107
📠 +33 (0)2-98399787
📅 6/4 - 23/9
@ contact@camping-les-embruns.com

6ha 65**T**(100-150m²) 16A CEE

1 ACD**G**IJKLMOPQ
2 AEFGQRVWXY
3 BDGHJK**M**N**OP**QRU**V**WY
4 (E 📵) (H 7/7-31/8) J**LN**
　(Q+S+T+U+V+Y+Z 📵)
5 **AB**DEFGIJKLMNOPQRUWXY
6 ACDEGHIJ**K**(N 0km)ORSTUVW

💬 Beautiful family campsite, 250m from beach. Located in village centre. Lovely indoor pool. Site with many flowers, awarded campsite with most beautiful planting in France. Restaurant. Excellent toilet facilities, sauna, hamam and beauty salon.

🚗 E60 Lorient towards Quimperlé. Exit Kervidanou or exit Kergostiou/Quimperlé centre. Via D16 to Clohars-Carnoët, straight through centre, D24 to Le Pouldu. Campsite in the town centre.

D783 D62
D24 D16 N165 D26
D224
D765
CC
Lorient
Ploemeur
D152

CC € **17** 6/4-9/7 27/8-22/9 14=12 📡 N 47°46'7'' W 3°32'42''

Combrit/Sainte-Marine, F-29120 / Bretagne (Finistère)   ♿ 🛜 iD (1387)

🔺 Le Helles***
🏠 55 rue du Petit Bourg
☎ +33 (0)2-98563146
🗓 1/4 - 30/9
@ contact@le-helles.com

2,7ha 80T(90-120m²) 10A

1 ACD**G**IJKLMPQ
2 AEGLRVWXY
3 BF**G**HJRWY
4 (C+E+H+Q+R 🗓)
  (T+U+V+Z 1/7-31/8)
5 **AB**EFGIJKLMNOPUZ
6 AEGK(N 0,5km)T

💬 An informal and quiet campsite with a heated outdoor swimming pool and new indoor swimming pool, opposite the renowned resort of Bénodet. 300 metres from a natural beach with fine sand and dunes and lots of opportunities to walk such as GR34. Wifi is free. 600 metres from Ste Marine harbour.

🚗 From Quimper to Bénodet. Then towards Pont-l'Abbé via D44. Over the bridge and 1st left to Ste Marine at roundabout. Then 2nd right and follow signs.

D785   D34   D783
Pont-l'Abbé   Fouesnant
D57   D2
D53

CC € ⑰ 1/4-7/7 26/8-29/9   📶 N 47°52'10'' W 4°7'42''

Concarneau, F-29185 / Bretagne (Finistère)   ♿ 🛜 iD (1388)

🔺 Flower Camping Le Cabellou Plage****
🏠 avenue du Cabellou
☎ +33 (0)2-98973741
🗓 28/4 - 15/9
@ info@le-cabellou-plage.com

5,4ha 159T(90-150m²) 10A CEE

1 ACD**G**HIJKLMOPRS
2 AEGKLQRVWXY
3 BF**G**HJKRUWY
4 (C+H 🗓) J
  (Q+S+T+U+V+Z 2/7-31/8)
5 **AB**EFGIJKLMNOPQUVWXYZ
6 CEGIJ(N 1,5km)TV

💬 Family campsite directly on the coast with well-equipped modern toilet facilities. Latge even pitches between hedges. Supermarket 1.5 km away, good area for walking and cycling along the varied coastline. Beautiful swimming pool with slides.

🚗 N165/E60 exit Coat Conq, direction Concarneau to roundabout with Hyper Leclerc, then direction Trégunc via D783 to Kerviniou roundabout 3 km. 2nd exit towards Cabellou, campsite 800m on the left.

D45   Rosporden
D70   D24
Concarneau
D783

CC € ⑰ 28/4-6/7 25/8-14/9 7=6   📶 N 47°51'23'' W 3°54'1''

Concarneau, F-29900 / Bretagne (Finistère)   👫 ♿ 🛜 iD (1389)

🔺 Les Prés Verts aux 4 Sardines***
🏠 chemin de Kernous
☎ +33 (0)2-98970974
🗓 1/5 - 30/9
@ info@presverts.com

3ha 131T(100-120m²) 10A CEE

1 ACD**G**HIJKLMOPRS
2 AEFKQRVWX
3 AB**F**HJQRWY
4 (C+H 18/5-31/8)
5 **AB**EGIJKLMNPUZ
6 ACEGK(N 2km)T

💬 A peaceful, well-equipped campsite with spacious, flat pitches and well maintained toilets. 300m from a sheltered beach with direct sea access. 3,9 km from the famous medieval walled town of Concarneau which can be reached by a footpath along the rocky coast. Shops ± 2 km away.

🚗 N165/E60, exit Concarneau, D70 until just before centre of Concarneau. Then direction Les Sables Blancs as far as the sea. Then direction Fouesnant. Signposted on fourth street on the left.

D36
D34   D765   D782
D45
Fouesnant   D70
   D24
Concarneau
D783

CC € ⑬ 1/5-7/7 25/8-29/9 7=6, 14=12, 21=18   📶 N 47°53'25'' W 3°56'19''

Concarneau, F-29900 / Bretagne (Finistère)

👫 ♿ 📶 **iD** (1390)

▲ Les Sables Blancs****
🏠 avenue du Dorlett
☎ +33 (0)2-98971644
📅 1/4 - 31/10
@ contact@
camping-lessablesblancs.com

2,9ha 99T(80-200m²) 10-16A CEE

1 ACD**G**IJKLMOPQ
2 AEFGJKQRVWXY
3 BF**G**HJKNRVWY
4 (C+H 14/4-16/9) KP
(Q+R+T+U+V+X+Y+Z 📅)
5 **AB**DEFGIJKLMNOPQRUWX
YZ
6 ACEGK(N 1,5km)TV

💬 Small quiet site with pool and restaurant in middle of countryside. 250m from a beach and a 15 min. walk from Concarneau, a lovely medieval walled town. Market twice a week in town centre. Modern, heated toilet facilities. Some pitches have sea views.

🚗 From N165 direction Concarneau, centre via D70, to the roundabout with supermarket, direction Concarneau. Third to the right to Les Sables Blancs, via 2 roundabouts to the sea, as far as the T-junction, then turn right.

CC € ⑮ 1/4-6/7 25/8-30/10 7=6, 14=12, 21=18

🧭 N 47°52'55'' W 3°55'43''

Crac'h, F-56950 / Bretagne (Morbihan)

♿ 📶 **iD** (1391)

▲ Flower Camping Le Fort
Espagnol****
🏠 rte du Fort Espagnol
☎ +33 (0)2-97551488
📅 7/4 - 22/9
@ fort-espagnol@wanadoo.fr

5,5ha 57T(75-140m²) 10A

1 ACD**G**IJKLMOPS
2 BFQRVWXY
3 BGHJKM**OP**RUW
4 (C 15/5-10/9) (E+H 📅) IJ
(Q 📅) (S 7/7-31/8)
(T+U+V+Z 📅)
5 **AB**DEFGIJKLNPQRUVWXY
Z
6 ACEGHJ**K**(N 0,6km)TUV

💬 Medium-sized campsite with homely atmosphere, large pitches at the back, in a pine forest. Modern toilet facilities. Located in a well-known and well-visited region. The campsite is quiet, with all sights within 20 km. Reception hours: 8:30-12:30 and 14:30-18:00.

🚗 N165/E60 Nantes-Vannes-Lorient, exit Crac'h. Via D28 until roundabout at centre. Left dir. Fort Espagnol, entrance on right after 600m.

CC € ⑮ 7/4-6/7 26/8-21/9

🧭 N 47°36'56'' W 2°59'24''

Crozon, F-29160 / Bretagne (Finistère)

iD (1392)

▲ L'Aber***
🏠 Tal-ar-Groas, 50 rte de l'Aber
☎ +33 (0)2-98270296
📅 1/4 - 1/11
@ contact@camping-aber.com

2ha 85T(100m²) 10A CEE

1 ACD**G**IJKLMPQ
2 ACJKLRTVWXY
3 AGHJRUW
4 (C+H+Q 15/6-15/9)
(R+T+U+V 1/4-1/10) (Z 📅)
5 AEJLMNPUV
6 EG(N 5km)V

💬 A panoramic terraced campsite about 1500m from the sea. The site has a heated swimming pool and a friendly bar. New and refurbished toilet facilities. Fantastic views of the sea, the beautiful coastline and the River l'Aber from anywhere on the site.

🚗 Follow the D887 from Chateaulin to Crozon. Follow camping signs in Tal-ar-Groas towards plage de L'Aber.

CC € ⑮ 1/4-7/7 25/8-31/10

🧭 N 48°14'32'' W 4°25'46''

Damgan, F-56750 / Bretagne (Morbihan)

👫 ♿ 📶 **iD** **1393**

🏕 Grand Air Cadu***
📧 rue de Cadu
☎ +33 (0)2-97411730
📅 1/4 - 31/10
@ info@campingcadu.com

7,8ha 93T(100-200m²) 16A CEE

1 ACD**G**IJKLM**P**ST
2 AEFGQRVWX
3 BGHJKLM**N**Q**R**UWY
4 (C+E+H 5/5-23/9) J
   (Q 1/7-31/8) (U+V 7/7-25/8)
5 **AB**FGIJKLMNOPUXYZ
6 ACDEG**K**(N 0,8km)OTUV

💬 Campsite 300m from the beach with pitches separated by bushes and hedges. Modern and well-maintained toilet facilities and a heated indoor swimming pool. Beaches within walking distance. Microclimate due to its proximity to the sea and the many tidal pools. Level area, so good for walking and cycling. Armbands compulsory everywhere on the campsite. Reception closed 12:00-15:30.

🚗 N165/E60 Vannes-Nantes. Exit Damgan or Muzillac, then to Damgan and follow camping signs.

Surzur · N165 · D153
· D20 · D5
Sarzeau · Muzillac
CC
D34
D83

CC € **17** 1/4-6/7 1/9-30/10   📍 N 47°31'19'' W 2°35'31''

Dinard/St.Lunaire, F-35800 / Bretagne (Ille-et-Vilaine)

♿ 📶 **iD** **1394**

🏕 La Touesse***
📧 171 rue de la ville Gehan
☎ +33 (0)2-99466113
📠 +33 (0)2-99160258
📅 1/4 - 6/10
@ camping.la.touesse@wanadoo.fr

3ha 80T(90-120m²) 5-10A CEE

1 ACD**G**IJLMPQ
2 AEGQRVWXY
3 ABF**G**HJKRUWY
4 (C 1/6-30/9) (F 📅)
   (H 1/6-30/9) IJKM**N**P
   (Q+R+T+U+V+X+Z 📅)
5 **AB**DFGHIJKLMNPUXYZ
6 ABCEG**IK**(N 1km)ORTV

💬 Intimate, sheltered site with leisure and covered pool. Nice restaurant with garden. 300m from sea, lovely sandy beach. Site is separated by hedges and trees into fields with 2 or 4 pitches. Close to historic town Dinard.

🚗 N137 via St. Malo over barrage. 1st rndbt with viaducts dir. Dinard. On dual carriageway after 500 metres 2nd exit left dir. St. Énogat. After 300 metres left at 1st traffic lights dir. St. Lunaire. Stay on D786. Follow signs.

Saint-Malo
D19 · **CC** Dinard
D786
D768 · D2 · D137

CC € **17** 1/4-6/7 25/8-5/10   📍 N 48°37'51'' W 2°5'3''

Dinéault/Châteaulin, F-29150 / Bretagne (Finistère)

♿ 📶 **iD** **1395**

🏕 Camping Panoramique Ty
   Provost
📧 rte de Dinéault
☎ +33 (0)2-98862923
📅 1/1 - 31/12
@ contact@typrovost.com

2ha 42T(> 150m²) 6A

1 ACD**G**IJKLMOPQ
2 JKLRVWXY
3 BCDGHIJU
4 (Q+R 1/6-15/9) (Z 8/7-31/8)
5 **AB**CDFGHIJKLMNOPWZ
6 ACDEGIJ(N 4km)RT

💬 Hospitable, familial campsite on an old, renovated farm with a lovely panoramic view of the 'Aulne valley'! Ideal base for lovers of walking, cycling, and those who wish to visit the Crozon headland.

🚗 N165 or N164 exit Châteaulin. After Châteaulin D887 direction Crozon. After 4 km D60 direction Dinéault, then follow signs.

D791 · Le Faou

CC Châteaulin
D887
D63
Plonévez- · D7 · D785
Porzay · D107

CC € **15** 1/1-7/7 25/8-31/12   📍 N 48°12'26'' W 4°7'27''

Dol-de-Bretagne, F-35120 / Bretagne (Ille-et-Vilaine)  ⬛ 1396

🔺 Le Vieux Chêne★★★★
🏠 D576, Baguer-Pican
☎ +33 (0)2-99480955
🔌 27/4 - 30/9
@ info@
camping-doldebretagne.com

12ha 200T(100-115m²) 10A CEE

1 ACD**F**IJKLMPS
2 DFILRVX
3 ABGHJMNQRUW
4 (C+H 20/5-15/9) IJ
(Q 1/6-31/8) (S 🔌)
(T+U+V+X+Z 4/7-31/8)
5 **AB**DEFGIJKLMNPRUWXYZ
6 CDEGJ(N 1km)TV

💬 A friendly family campsite in natural surroundings with a variety of old trees and with a wonderful leisure pool for the children. Located between St. Malo and Mont-St-Michel.

🚗 From Pontorson take the N176 in the direction of Dol-de-Bretagne. Exit Dol-de-Bretagne-Est. D576 direction Baguer-Pican. 1 km past the village turn right. From then clearly signposted.

CC € 15 27/4-5/7 2/9-29/9   📍 N 48°32'58'' W 1°41'2''

Douarnenez, F-29100 / Bretagne (Finistère) ♿ 🛜 ⬛ 1397

🔺 Trézulien★★★★
🏠 14 route de Trézulien
☎ +33 (0)2-98741230
📠 +33 (0)9-70063174
🔌 1/4 - 14/10
@ contact@camping-trezulien.com

3ha 179T(80-140m²) 10A

1 ACDGIJKLMOPQ
2 BIJKRVWXY
3 ABGRW
4 (C 15/6-15/9) J(Q 1/7-31/8)
(R 🔌)
5 **AB**FGHIJKLMNOPQRUVWX
YZ
6 ABDEGIJRT

💬 Lovers of nature and the sea will be enchanted by campsite Trézulien. The extraordinary location, the heated pool (27°C), jacuzzi and toddlers' pool, the homely atmosphere and the pitches on terraces offer peace and relaxation.

🚗 Follow D7 in Douarnenez towards Tréboul-Plages. After several roundabouts at Leclerc 'Centre Commercial' follow Tréboul and camping signs. At roundabout towards Trézulien.

CC € 15 1/4-7/7 25/8-13/10 7=6, 14=11   📍 N 48°5'34'' W 4°21'8''

Douarnenez/Tréboul, F-29100 / Bretagne (Finistère) 🛜 ⬛ 1398

🔺 Flower Camping de Kerleyou★★★
🏠 15 chemin de Kerleyou
☎ +33 (0)2-98741303
📠 +33 (0)2-98740961
🔌 14/4 - 22/9
@ campingdekerleyou@wanadoo.fr

3ha 41T(100-150m²) 10A CEE

1 AC**G**IJKLMPQ
2 LRTVX
3 BGRU
4 (E+H 🔌) (Q 1/7-31/8)
(R 1/6-15/9) (U 1/7-31/8)
(V+Z 1/7-1/9)
5 **AB**GIJKLMNOPUZ
6 EGJ(N 1km)V

💬 Well-situated in Douarnenez in natural surroundings, 1.3 km from the beach at Sables Blancs, with rest, comfort, and outstanding facilities. If it's just the two of you or you're with your whole family, this pleasant, floral campsite with a family atmosphere in the quiet countryside close to the beach and the shops will offer you a comfortable holiday.

🚗 In Douarnenez, drive direction Tréboul. Follow green sign to 'campings'. Then the campsite has it's own sign.

CC € 15 14/4-7/7 25/8-21/9   📍 N 48°5'56'' W 4°21'44''

Epiniac/Dol-de-Bretagne, F-35120 / Bretagne (Ille-et-Vilaine) 🛜 ✿ 🆔 1399

▲ Les Ormes Domaine &
Resort*****
🏠 Domaine des Ormes
☎ +33 (0)2-99735300
📠 +33 (0)2-99735355
🗓 14/4 - 16/9
@ info@lesormes.com

200ha 137T(80-150m²) 6-10A CEE

1 ACD**G**IJKLMOPRS
2 BDLMRVX
3 ABD**EF**GHJKL**MNOPQ**RU
VW
4 (C 26/5-2/9) (F+H 🔲) IJ
(Q+S+T+U+V+X+Y+Z 🔲)
5 **AB**DEFGJKLMNPUWZ
6 ACEGH**IJK**M(N 7km)OPTV

💬 A castle campsite in open countryside located in the heart of the Emerald Coast between St. Michel and St. Malo. The indoor heated aqua park (4000 m²) welcomes both young and old. Do not miss the wave pool. Many lodgings within the nature park (woods, forest).

🚗 From Dol-de-Bretagne take the D795 in the direction of Combourg. The campsite is located 7 km down the road at the left side.

🅲🅲 € ⑲ 14/4-5/7 1/9-15/9 7=6   🏕 N 48°29'15'' W 1°44'10''

Erdeven, F-56410 / Bretagne (Morbihan) ♿ 🛜 🆔 1400

▲ Des Mégalithes***
🏠 Kerfelicite, chemin des Saules
☎ +33 (0)2-97556876
🗓 1/5 - 23/9
@ campingdesmegalithes@
orange.fr

5ha 100T(90-160m²) 10A CEE

1 ACD**G**IJKLMOPQ
2 RVWXY
3 BFGHJNR
4 (C+H 5/5-16/9)
(Q+R 1/7-31/8)
5 **AB**FGIJKLMNOPUWZ
6 ACDEGK(N 1,5km)T

💬 A quiet, well equipped campsite with level pitches set between hedges and separated from the mobile homes. Megalith park within 500m. You can go for peaceful bike rides between the site and the sea, or make a trip to Quiberon via the cycle path.

🚗 N165/E60 Vannes-Lorient, exit Quiberon/Carnac, D768 direction Quiberon. At the crossroad in Plouharnel turn right to Erdeven via D781. After about 3.5 km turn left.

🅲🅲 € ⑰ 1/5-6/7 25/8-22/9   🏕 N 47°37'43'' W 3°8'46''

Erquy, F-22430 / Bretagne (Côtes-d'Armor) 👫 ♿ 🛜 🆔 1401

▲ Des Hautes Grées***
🏠 123 rue St. Michel les Hôpitaux
☎ +33 (0)2-96723478
📠 +33 (0)2-96723015
🗓 1/4 - 1/10
@ hautesgrees@wanadoo.fr

3,5ha 177T(80-98m²) 10A CEE

1 ACD**G**IJKLMOPQ
2 AEGLNQRTUVX
3 AB**EF**GHJN**OP**RUVWY
4 (A 1/7-31/8) (C+H 15/5-20/9)
LN(Q+R 🔲)
(T+U+V+X 1/7-31/8)
5 **AB**FGHIJKLMNPRUVWZ
6 ACEG**K**(N 2,5km)ORTV

💬 Quiet, well-maintained family campsite. Spaciously appointed, royal pitches, lots of flowers. Heated pool, at 400 metres from the beach. Close to fishing harbour, good base for anglers. Ideal for young families, but also for people seeking some peace and quiet in the low seasons.

🚗 Campsite located east of Erquy. At roundabout south-west of Erquy, where the D781 becomes the D34, direction 'Les Hôpitaux'. Then follow signs.

🅲🅲 € ⑰ 1/4-7/7 25/8-30/9   🏕 N 48°38'31'' W 2°25'27''

Erquy, F-22430 / Bretagne (Côtes-d'Armor)

🕴🚻 ♿ 🛜 iD (1402)

🔺 La Vallée***
📧 St. Pabu
☎ +33 (0)2-96720622
🅾 28/4 - 18/9
@ campinglavalleeerquy@
wanadoo.fr

1,5ha 30T(90-110m²) 10A CEE

1 ACD**G**IJKLMOPQ
2 AEJRTVWX
3 AB**F**GHJRWY
4 **KN**(Q+R 🅾)
5 **AB**EFGIJKLMNPUZ
6 ACEGJ(N 2km)ORTV

💬 A campsite located in the lovely, restful countryside of a valley. 700m from the sea and a sandy beach. Terraced campsite with modern toilet facilities. Pitches separated by small hedges. Unique relaxation room in oriental style including a sauna and jacuzzi.

🚗 Follow D786 between Val-André and Erquy. When the dual carriageway becomes a two-way road turn left immediately towards St. Pabu. Campsite signposted.

CC € 15 28/4-6/7   26/8-17/9

🗺 N 48°36'16'' W 2°29'19''

Erquy, F-22430 / Bretagne (Côtes-d'Armor)

🕴🚻 ♿ 🛜 iD (1403)

🔺 Les Roches***
📧 rue Pierre Vergos
☎ +33 (0)2-96723290
📠 +33 (0)2-96635784
🅾 1/4 - 30/9
@ jessica.lesroches@gmail.com

3ha 175T(80-120m²) 6-10A CEE

1 ACD**G**IJKLMOPQ
2 AGJKLQRTUVWXY
3 ABC**F**GHN**P**QRU
4 (Q+R 🅾) (U+V 1/7-30/8)
5 **AB**DEFGIJKLMNPUZ
6 ACEGIK(N 2,5km)ORTV

💬 In the middle of farm land, this peaceful campsite is 900m from the sea. The grounds are surrounded by tall hedges. Plenty of shelter against the wind. Lovely pitches with panoramic views of the sea. Modern toilet facilities provided. Free wifi.

🚗 Campsite located between Erquy and Pléneuf-Val-André, D786. Follow signs, well indicated.

CC € 13 1/4-7/7   25/8-29/9

🗺 N 48°36'37'' W 2°28'33''

Erquy, F-22430 / Bretagne (Côtes-d'Armor)

🕴🚻 ♿ 🛜 iD (1404)

🔺 Sites & Paysages Bellevue****
📧 route de la Libération
☎ +33 (0)2-96723304
🅾 31/3 - 16/9
@ info@campingbellevue.fr

3ha 128T(90-130m²) 10A CEE

1 ACD**G**IJKLMOPQ
2 KRTVXY
3 B**F**GHJLMNRU
4 (E 🅾) (H 31/3-15/9) (Q 🅾)
(R 1/5-1/9)
(T+U+V+Z 15/6-1/9)
5 **AB**EFGIJKLMNOPQRUWXY
Z
6 ACDEGIK(N 5km)ORTV

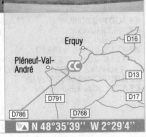

💬 Beautiful grounds with plenty of greenery and a lovely indoor swimming pool, children's pool, modern toilet facilities, playground and small cafe. Hedges provide the spacious camping pitches with plenty of privacy. Free wifi.

🚗 Between Erquy and Val André at the D786 near the village La Couture.

CC € 17 31/3-6/7   25/8-15/9

🗺 N 48°35'39'' W 2°29'4''

Fouesnant, F-29170 / Bretagne (Finistère)

♿ 📶 **iD** **1405**

- 🏕 Camping de la Piscine★★★★
- 📧 Kerleya-Beg Meil, BP 12
- ☎ +33 (0)2-98565606
- 🔑 28/4 - 9/9
- @ contact@
  campingdelapiscine.com

5ha 115T(85-110m²) 10A

1. ACD**G**IJKLMOPQ
2. ARVWXY
3. BDGHJKMNRU
4. (C 15/6-31/8) (F 28/4-8/9)
   (H 15/6-31/8) IJ**KLN**
   (Q+S 1/6-11/9)
   (T+U+Z 2/7-31/8)
5. **AB**CDFGIJKLMNPUWYZ
6. ACEGJ(N 3km)OTV

💬 A lovely quiet campsite with spacious marked out pitches. Wonderful water park with heated pool and bubble bath. Wellness area, sauna, hamam and jacuzzi. Access via a footpath (1000m) to a nice fine sandy beach. Ideal starting point for cycle trips and a visit to the region: Quimper, La Pointe du Raz, Locronan.

🚐 From Fouesnant take the D45 direction Mousterlin. Then follow camping signs.

[D785] [D34] [D783] [D765]
[D45] [N165]
[D70]
CC Concarneau
Tréguinc

CC € **17** 28/4-6/7 25/8-8/9 7=6, 14=11   🗺 N 47°52'1'' W 4°0'53''

Fouesnant/Beg-Meil, F-29170 / Bretagne (Finistère)

♿ 📶 **iD** **1406**

- 🏕 Le Kervastard★★★
- 📧 56 Hent Kervastard
- ☎ +33 (0)2-98949152
- 🔑 1/4 - 31/10
- @ camping.le.kervastard@
  wanadoo.fr

2,5ha 50T(90-100m²) 10A CEE

1. ACD**G**IJKLMOPQ
2. AEGQRVWX
3. BF**G**HJKRUWY
4. (C+H 15/6-15/9) (Q+R 🔑)
5. **AB**DFGIJKLMNOPUWYZ
6. ACDEG**K**(N 0,15km)TV

💬 Family campsite, located in the centre of the village of Beg-Meil. 150 metres from the shops and 300 metres from the beach. You can forget your car this holiday.

🚐 From Fouesnant to Beg-Meil. Left at the centre. See camping signs.

[D34]
[D45]
Fouesnant [D70]

CC Concarneau
[D783]

CC € **17** 1/4-7/7 27/8-30/10   🗺 N 47°51'37'' W 3°59'17''

Guidel, F-56520 / Bretagne (Morbihan)

♿ 📶 **iD** **1407**

- 🏕 Les Jardins de Kergal★★★★
- 📧 rte des Plages, Kangal Uhel
- ☎ +33 (0)2-97059818
- 🔑 29/3 - 31/10
- @ jardins.kergal@wanadoo.fr

5ha 57T(90-150m²) 16A CEE

1. ACD**F**HIJKLMPRS
2. AFLQRVWXY
3. BF**G**HJKMNQRU
4. (C 1/6-2/9) (E+H 🔑) J
   (Q 1/7-26/8) (R 🔑)
   (T+U+V+Z 7/7-25/8)
5. **AB**EFGIJKLMNPRUWZ
6. ACEG**K**(N 1,5km)TUV

💬 A lovely quiet campsite between Guidel and the sea. Lovely heated indoor pool, well maintained toilets, pitches among the trees and hedges. Supermarket 1 km, village 1.2 km with shops and a Sunday market. Lovely walking routes by the sea or the River Laïta.

🚐 From N165 Quimper-Lorient exit Guidel. Towards Guidel centre, round the church direction Guidel-plages via D306, left at roundabout after about 1,8 km, left at next crossroads, campsite entrance 500m on the right.

[D783] [D62]
[D24] [D26]
[D16] [N165]
[D224] [D765]
CC Lorient
Ploemeur
[D152]

CC € **15** 29/3-6/7 25/8-30/10   🗺 N 47°46'29'' W 3°30'23''

Huelgoat, F-29690 / Bretagne (Finistère) ♿ 🛜 iD (1408)

🔺 La Rivière d'Argent**
🏠 La Coudraie
☎ +33 (0)2-98997250
⌚ 1/4 - 30/9
@ contact@larivieredargent.com

5ha 84T(100m²) 6A CEE

1 ACD**G**IJKLPRS
2 BCGRTVWXY
3 BHMR**UW**
4 (A 1/7-31/8) (E 🔲)
   (Q+R 1/6-15/9)
   (T+U+Z 1/7-15/9)
5 **AB**GIJKLMNPUVZ
6 CEI**K**(N 3km)O

💬 Well maintained, very peaceful campsite set in woods by a lovely little river. You will wake up to the birds. A good starting point for walks. Opportunities for fishing. The north, south and west coasts can all be reached within an hour by car. Heated indoor pool.

🚗 From Guingamp take the N12 to Morlaix. Pass this town via the D785 and the D764 to Huelgoat. From the centre follow the signs 3 km in an eastern direction.

Plounéour-Ménez · D28 · D42 · D769 · CC · D54 · D14 · D764 · D36 · Carhaix-Plouguer

CC € **15** 1/4-7/7 25/8-29/9 7=6   🧭 N 48°21'47'' W 3°42'57''

Jugon-les-Lacs, F-22270 / Bretagne (Côtes-d'Armor) ♿ 🛜 iD (1409)

🔺 Au Bocage du Lac****
🏠 rue du Bocage
☎ +33 (0)2-96316016
📠 +33 (0)2-96317504
⌚ 7/4 - 15/9
@ contact@
   campinglacbretagne.com

7ha 183T(100-180m²) 10A CEE

1 AC**G**IJKLPRS
2 DFLMRVXY
3 ABGHK**MNPQ**RUV**W**
4 (**A** 1/7-31/8) (C 1/5-9/9)
   (F 10/4-9/9) (H 1/5-9/9) IJ
   (Q 1/7-31/8) (S 7/4-9/9)
   (T+U+V+X+Z 🔲)
5 **AB**EFGIJKLMNOPUVWZ
6 CDEGH**IJ**(N 0,8km)RTV

💬 A pleasant rural family campsite with safe direct access to a 70 hectare lake. A paradise for anglers. For those who like lazing around there is a heated indoor and outdoor swimming pool with a slide and a toddlers pool.

🚗 N176 exit Jugon-les-Lacs. The campsite is clearly signposted and is on the Jugon-les-Lacs to Mégrit road (D52).

Lamballe · D794 · N176 · D792 · CC · Plénée-Jugon · N12 · Broons · D793

CC € **17** 7/4-30/6 1/9-14/9   🧭 N 48°24'6'' W 2°19'0''

La Chapelle-aux-Filtzméens, F-35190 / Bretagne (Ille-et-Vilaine) ♿ 🛜 iD (1410)

🔺 Domaine du Logis*****
☎ +33 (0)2-99452545
📠 +33 (0)2-99453040
⌚ 30/3 - 1/10
@ domainedulogis@wanadoo.fr

8ha 180T(80-125m²) 16A CEE

1 ABCD**F**IJKLMOPQ
2 BCKLRTUVWXY
3 ABCGHJKLN**Q**RUV**W**
4 (C+H 1/5-30/9) **JKN**
   (Q+R 🔲)
   (T+U+X+Y 1/7-31/8)
   (Z 🔲)
5 **AB**DEFGIJKLMNOPQRUWX
   YZ
6 ABEGHKLTV

💬 This quiet campsite is located on the grounds of a 15th century castle. In the converted barn you will find a restaurant, bar and a shop with fresh croissants and bread every morning. During the day you can have fun in the heated pool, in the evening in the club house with games and billiards. There is also a BMX course for the young (at heart).

🚗 4 km east of the N137 Rennes-St.-Malo. On the D13 between St.-Domineuc and Combourg.

D73 · D83 · D794 · D2 · D137 · CC · D795 · Plouasne · D20 · Montreuil-sur-Ille

CC € **19** 30/3-7/7 25/8-30/9 7=6   🧭 N 48°22'55'' W 1°50'5''

La Forêt-Fouesnant, F-29940 / Bretagne (Finistère)

  🛆 De Kéranterec****
📧 1 route de Saint Laurent
☎ +33 (0)2-98569811
🔓 7/4 - 23/9
@ info@camping-keranterec.com

6,5ha 110T(90-150m²) 10-15A

1 ACD**G**IJKLMOPQ
2 AEFGIJKQRVWXY
3 BFGHJKMNRUWY
4 (C 19/5-23/9) (D+H 🔓) JK
  (Q 🔓) (R 19/5-22/9)
  (T+U+V 30/6-2/9)
  (Z 19/5-22/9)
5 **AB**CEFGHIJKLOPRUWXY
6 ACEGIJ(N 3km)TUV

💬 A rural campsite with an informal atmosphere. Right by the sea and direct access to the sandy beach. Excellent base for visiting Quimper-Concarneau and surroundings. Environmentally friendly, peaceful site with renewed toilet facilities (2016) and interesting, varied coast.

🚗 Between Lorient and Quimper via N165-E60, exit Fouesnant/Concarneau, through D44 direction Fouesnant till signs to Plage de Kerleven or Port la Forêt. Well signposted.

CC € **17** 7/4-7/7 25/8-22/9

🗺 N 47°53'55'' W 3°57'22''

La Forêt-Fouesnant, F-29940 / Bretagne (Finistère)

  🛆 Kerleven***
📧 4 route de Port-la-Forêt
☎ +33 (0)2-98569883
🔓 14/4 - 30/9
@ contact@
  campingdekerleven.com

4,5ha 79T(80-110m²) 10A CEE

1 ACD**G**IJKLOPQ
2 EFGIRVWX
3 AB**F**GHKNRUWY
4 (C 23/6-9/9) (E+H 🔓) J
  (Q+R+T+U+V+X+Z 🔓)
5 **AB**EFGJLNPQUZ
6 ACFG**K**(N 3km)T

NEW

💬 A family campsite with level pitches close to a swimming pool and street cafes. Indoor pool and outdoor pool with slide. Within walking distance of the beach.

🚗 N165 exit 51, direction La Foret-Fouesnant. Towards Plage Kerleven at first roundabout. Follow signs.

CC € **17** 14/4-6/7 1/9-29/9

🗺 N 47°53'55'' W 3°58'5''

La Trinité-sur-Mer, F-56470 / Bretagne (Morbihan)

  🛆 Kervilor****
📧 21 Kervilor
☎ +33 (0)297557675
🔓 30/3 - 30/9
@ camping.kervilor@wanadoo.fr

4,7ha 154T(80-120m²) 6-10A

1 ACD**F**IJKLMOPRS
2 CGQRVWXY
3 BFGHJK**M**NQRUV
4 (C 10/5-9/9) (E+H 🔓) JK
  (Q 🔓) (R 29/3-1/7,3/9-30/9)
  (S+T+U+V+Z 2/7-2/9)
5 **AB**EFGIJKLMNOPRUWXYZ
6 ACEGHJ**K**(N 1,5km)OTV

💬 Peaceful campsite in well-visited area. Free choice of pitches out of season. Heated indoor pool. Outdoor pool heated from 10 May. 3 km from the famous prehistoric megalith park at Carnac. The centre of La Trinité is 1.5 km away. Market twice weekly, large yacht harbour. The surroundings are wooded and good for cycling and walking.

🚗 South of Auray. D768 dir. Carnac, then D186 dir. La Trinité then via campsite signposts. Turn left before the centre.

CC € **17** 30/3-11/7 29/8-29/9 7=6, 14=12

🗺 N 47°36'8'' W 3°2'12''

Landéda, F-29870 / Bretagne (Finistère) ♿ 🛜 **iD** (1414)

▲ Des Abers****
🏕 Plage de St. Marguerite
☎ +33 (0)2-98049335
⌚ 28/4 - 30/9
@ camping-des-abers@wanadoo.fr

5,5ha 154T(90-120m²) 10A

1 ACD**G**IJKLMPQ
2 AEGJKRSTVWX
3 BGHJKNRUWY
4 (A 1/7-31/8) (Q ⌚)
(S 15/5-15/9) (U 1/7-31/8)
(V+Z ⌚)
5 **AB**FGIJKLMNO**P**UW
6 ACEGI**K**(N 2,5km)ORT

💬 Hubert and his team offer you a warm welcome in French, German or English to their lovely campsite positioned right on a sandy beach. Panoramic views of the ocean and countless small islands which are accessible at low tide. A wonderful site for an extended stay.

🚗 From Lannilis follow green 'campings' signs through Landéda. 1.7 km past Landéda follow camping signs.

Plouguerneau

CC

Ploudalmézeau
D68 D168 D26 D28 D13

(CC) € **17** 28/4-6/7 1/9-29/9 14=12   🔺 N 48°35'36'' W 4°36'9''

Landrellec/Pleumeur-Bodou, F-22560 / Bretagne (Côtes-d'Armor) ♿ 🛜 **iD** (1415)

▲ Camping Du Port****
🏕 3 chemin des Douaniers
☎ +33 (0)2-96238779
⌚ 31/3 - 14/10
@ renseignements@
  camping-du-port-22.com

3,8ha 44T(100-140m²) 5-15A CEE

1 ACD**G**IJKLMO**P**RS
2 AEJKORSVWX
3 B**F**HJKPRWY
4 (C+E+H 1/7-31/8) **KN**
(Q+R+T+U+V+X+Z 15/4-15/9)
5 **AB**DEFGIJKLMNPUWXZ
6 ACEGI**K**(N 0,3km)ORUV

💬 Beautiful campsite located south of Trégastel-Plage on the Landrellec headland. Spacious pitches on grass, partially divided by low bushes and trees. Some of the pitches have a magnificent view of the sea. Vehicle entrance ticket not available between 12.30 and 15.00. The 'Fruits de Mer' platter in the restaurant is recommended.

🚗 From Trégastel follow coastal route towards Trébeurden D788. Turn right at Landrellec. The road to the campsite is clearly signposted.

Perros-Guirec

CC

D788
D65 D6
Lannion D786

(CC) € **15** 31/3-8/7 26/8-13/10 15=14   🔺 N 48°48'35'' W 3°32'27''

Lanloup/Paimpol, F-22580 / Bretagne (Côtes-d'Armor) 👫 ♿ 🛜 **iD** (1416)

▲ Le Neptune****
🏕 Ker Guistin
☎ +33 (0)2-96223335
⌚ 2/4 - 5/10
@ contact@leneptune.com

1,5ha 57T(80-120m²) 10A CEE

1 ACD**F**IJKLMOPQ
2 AGLNQRTVWXY
3 BDF**G**HJNRU
4 (E+Q+S+T+U+X+Z ⌚)
5 **AB**DFGIJKLNPUVWXYZ
6 ACEGI**K**(N 5km)ORTV

💬 A hospitable natural campsite with a heated indoor swimming pool. Pleasantly small-scale. Pitches with plenty of privacy. 1 hour free wifi per day.

🚗 From Plouha direction Lanloup. Follow signs campsite.

Paimpol

D786
D7 **CC**
D6
D21
Étables-sur-Mer

(CC) € **17** 2/4-6/7 25/8-4/10   🔺 N 48°42'49'' W 2°58'1''

Lantic, F-22410 / Bretagne (Côtes-d'Armor) ♿ 🛜 iD (1417)

🏕 Les Etangs***
🛣 route de Châtelaudren
☎ +33 (0)2-96719547
📅 1/4 - 30/9
@ contact@campinglesetangs.com

2,1ha 65T(60-108m²) 6-10A CEE

1 ACD**G**IJKLOPQ
2 JRWXY
3 AB**F**GHJU**W**
4 (C+H 📅) (Q 1/7-28/8)
   (R 1/6-27/9)
   (T+U+V 1/7-28/8)
5 **AB**FGIJKLNPUV
6 ADEGJ(N 3km)ORTV

💬 An attractive, peaceful campsite in lovely countryside. Swimming pool. Pitches are sometimes separated by bushes or marked out by trees. Poplars and fruit trees give adequate shade. Free wifi.

🚗 D786, in Binic left direction Lantic. The campsite is located on the left after 3 km and is already signposted in Binic.

D7   D786
D21
D9   D6
CC
N12   Saint-Brieuc   Plérin

CC € **13** 1/4-7/7 25/8-29/9   📍 N 48°36'23'' W 2°51'42''

Le Roc-St-André, F-56460 / Bretagne (Morbihan) 👫 ♿ 🛜 iD (1418)

🏕 Domaine du Roc***
🛣 rue Beaurivage
☎ +33 (0)2-97749107
📅 31/3 - 4/11
@ domaine-du-roc@orange.fr

2,5ha 28T(90-150m²) 6-10A CEE

1 ACD**G**IJKLMOPQ
2 CFRVWXY
3 BGHJKL**OP**RUW
4 (E+H 7/4-30/9) (Z 📅)
5 **AB**FGIJKLMNOPQRUWXYZ
6 ACEGJ(N 0,3km)T

💬 A quiet campsite on the banks of the Oust. At the junction of two almost level cycle routes between several historic villages. Cycle tracks beside the river and an old railway track. Restored antique caravans, a tree house and a log cabin for rent. 300m from a small supermarket, baker and bar/restaurant.

🚗 N24 Rennes-Quimper, in Ploërmel towards Vannes via N166. Exit La Chapelle-Caro/Le Roc-St-André, via D4 over the bridge and beyond the church follow camping signs.

D766   D724
Ploërmel
D4   Augan
D10
CC   D8
Saint-Marcel   D776
D764
D774

CC € **15** 31/3-7/7 26/8-3/11 7=6, 14=12, 21=18   📍 N 47°51'49'' W 2°26'46''

Lesconil, F-29740 / Bretagne (Finistère) ♿ 🛜 ✿ iD (1419)

🏕 Camping des Dunes***
🛣 67 rue Paul Langevin
☎ +33 (0)2-98878178
📅 28/3 - 30/9
@ campingdesdunes@gmail.com

2,8ha 153T(80-100m²) 10-16A CEE

1 ACD**G**IJKLMOPQ
2 AEGRVWX
3 BGHJKNRUWY
4 (Q 1/6-15/9)
5 **AB**EFGIJKLMNOPUWXYZ
6 ACEG**IK**(N 0,8km)RT

💬 A well-maintained campsite located behind the dunes. Lovely plants mark out the large pitches. Selected as a natural floral campsite. The charm of outdoor life by the side of the sea. Well maintained toilet facilities, both old and new. Private access to the sea with a lovely sandy beach marked out by rocks.

🚗 In Pont-l'Abbé keep on to Lesconil(D102). Right after football stadium (camping sign). After 100m keep left at junction.

Pont-l'Abbé
D57
Guilvinec   D53
CC

CC € **17** 1/4-7/7 27/8-14/9 7=6   📍 N 47°47'50'' W 4°13'43''

Lesconil, F-29740 / Bretagne (Finistère)

♿ 🛜 **iD** (1420)

🏕 Flower Camping de la Grande Plage***
📧 71 rue Paul Langevin
☎ +33 (0)2-98878827
🗓 1/4 - 15/9
@ campinggrandeplage@hotmail.com

2,5ha 110T(80-120m²) 10A CEE

1 ACD**G**IJKLMOPQ
2 AEGRTVX
3 BGHJKRUWY
4 (C+H 1/5-14/9) IJ (Q+T+U+X+Z 15/6-14/9)
5 **AB**EFGIJKLMNPUVWZ
6 ACEGJ**K**(N 1km)TVX

💬 A campsite with direct access to a large beach with sand and granite rocks. Modern well maintained toilet facilities, water park with slides and bubble bath and a snack bar with takeaway meals. It also has its own restaurant.

🚗 From Pont-l'Abbé D102 to Lesconil. Turn right past the football stadium and skating park (camping signs). Keep left for 200m, campsite is another 1 km.

Pont-l'Abbé
D57
Penmarch
D2
D53
CC

CC € **15** *1/4-30/6 1/9-14/9 7=6*

🗺 N 47°47'52'' W 4°13'44''

Locmariaquer, F-56740 / Bretagne (Morbihan)

♿ 🛜 **iD** (1421)

🏕 Lann Brick***
📧 18 Lieu Dit Lann Brick
☎ +33 (0)2-97573279
🗓 17/3 - 31/10
@ camping.lannbrick@wanadoo.fr

1,5ha 39T(70-90m²) 6-10A CEE

1 ACD**G**IJKLMOPRS
2 AEGQRVWXY
3 BGHJKRUWY
4 (A 1/7-30/8) (C+H 10/5-16/9) (Q+R+T+U+Z 🅿)
5 **AB**CEFGHIJKLMNOPUVZ
6 AEGJ(N 3km)OTV

💬 A small, quiet campsite with well-maintained toilet facilities located on a headland between the ocean and the Golfe du Morbihan 300m from the beach. You can walk or cycle on a pathway which covers the entire length of the headland past many prehistoric sights. Reception is closed from 13h-14h.

🚗 N165/E60 Nantes/Quimper, exit Crach, via D28 direction Locmariaquer. towards La Trinité/Carnac. Via D781 direction Locmariaquer, after ± 2 km turn right.

Auray
D28
Baden
Carnac
D768
CC

CC € **15** *17/3-6/7 27/8-30/10 14=13, 21=19*

🗺 N 47°34'43'' W 2°58'28''

Locronan, F-29180 / Bretagne (Finistère)

♿ 🛜 **iD** (1422)

🏕 Camping Locronan***
📧 rue de la Troménie
☎ +33 (0)2-98918776
🗓 21/4 - 29/9
@ contact@camping-locronan.fr

2ha 103T(90-130m²) 10A CEE

1 ACD**G**IJKLMRS
2 ABJRVX
3 BHJM**O**R
4 (E+H 🅿) (Q 1/7-31/8)
5 **AB**FGJKNPRUZ
6 EGJ(N 0,4km)

💬 A rustic and informal campsite in the heart of La Montagne de Locronan, one of France's most beautiful villages. Ideal starting point for visiting Pointe Bretagne. Indoor heated swimming pool. A mecca for walking: GR38 and the Bois du Névet. Lovely views of the Baie de Douarnenez from the site. You can walk to the Montagne for sea views. Free wifi.

🚗 Take Locronan exit on N165 Quimper/Brest then follow camping signs after 15 km when entering Locronan.

D887
D63
D7
Douarnenez
CC
D143 Plogonnec
N165
D765 D39
D784

CC € **15** *21/4-6/7 24/8-28/9 7=6*

🗺 N 48°5'46'' W 4°11'53''

Loctudy, F-29750 / Bretagne (Finistère) ♿ 📶 iD 1423

🏕 Les Hortensias***
🏘 38 rue des Tulipes
☎ +33 (0)2-98874664
📅 1/4 - 30/9
@ hortensias@
   camping-loctudy.com

2ha 63T(80-110m²) 6-10A CEE

1 ACDGIJKLMOPQ
2 AEGQRVXY
3 BGHKNRWY
4 (C+E+H 🛏) K(Q 15/6-15/9)
  (R+T+U+V+Z 🛏)
5 ABEFGIJKLMNOPQUZ
6 AEGK(N 3km)OTV

💬 Quiet family campsite 300 metres from the sea in the south of the Finistère. This campsite welcomes families to an enormous area where nature is being preserved. Heated indoor swimming pool with sliding roof from 2017.

🚗 From Pont-L'Abbé dir. Loctudy. Right before the chapel, straight on through traffic lights. 1 km further site is on left.

Plonéour-Lanvern D2 D785 D34
D57
D53
CC

CC € 17 1/4-6/7 27/8-29/9 ◥ N 47°48'47'' W 4°10'54''

Loudéac, F-22600 / Bretagne (Côtes-d'Armor) ♿ 📶 iD 1424

🏕 Camping Aquarev***
🏘 Les Ponts es Bigots
☎ +33 (0)2-96262192
📅 30/3 - 15/10
@ contact@camping-aquarev.com

3,2ha 78T(80-150m²) 10A CEE

1 ACDGIJKLMPRS
2 DFKLRUVW
3 BGHIJKMNUW
4 (Q 1/4-15/10) (T 3/4-1/10)
5 ABCGIJKLMNOPUZ
6 ACDEGK(N 2km)TV

💬 A new family campsite since 2012. The site has spacious pitches. You can play tennis and football on the site. You can also go fishing. Or just enjoy yourself with the crazy water games.

🚗 Exit Loudéac centre direction Loudéac, left at roundabout towards Aquarev.

D35
N164 D768
Saint-Caradec D700
D7 CC Plémet
D32 D1
D41 D778 D14 A
Noyal-Pontivy D14
D11 D66

CC € 15 30/3-6/7 26/8-14/10 7=6 ◥ N 48°10'45'' W 2°43'41''

Matignon, F-22550 / Bretagne (Côtes-d'Armor) ♿ 📶 iD 1425

🏕 Le Vallon aux Merlettes***
🏘 43 rue Jobert
☎ +33 (0)2-96803799
📅 1/4 - 30/9
@ contact@
   campingdematignon.com

3,5ha 74T(100-130m²) 10A CEE

1 ACDGIJKLMPRS
2 CGLRVWXY
3 ABFGMNRUW
4 (A 1/7-31/8) (E+H+Q+R 🛏)
  (T 1/7-31/8) (Z 🛏)
5 ABEFGIJKLMNPUWZ
6 ACDEGJ(N 0,5km)RTV

💬 In green and very quiet surroundings, 400 metres from shops, 4 km from the beaches and many walking paths. Free: heated, indoor pool, wifi. Service: toilet facilities with all amenities, bread, sweet rolls, ice-cream, grocer, self-service freezer, laundry.

🚗 From Dinard: D168, exit D786 towards Matignon, follow camping signs. From Rennes N12 as far as Lamballe. Stay on the D768, then D13. Follow camping signs.

D16
Erquy Saint-Cast-le-Guildo
D34 D19
D794 D786 D2
D13 D17 D768
D792

CC € 13 1/4-1/7 25/8-29/9 ◥ N 48°35'28'' W 2°17'45''

Milizac, F-29290 / Bretagne (Finistère)

♿ 🛜 **iD** (1426)

🏕 Camping de la Récré****
📧 Le Lac des 3 Curés
☎ +33 (0)2-98079217
🗓 1/1 - 31/12
@ campingdelarecre@orange.fr

5,5ha 102T 10A CEE

1 ACD**G**IJKLMNOPQ
2 BDFJLRTUWXY
3 ABCGHJKNQ**W**
4 (F+H 1/5-15/9) JM
　(Q 1/5-15/9) (R 🔑)
　(T+U 1/5-15/9)
5 **AB**CFGHIJKLMNOPQRUV
　WZ
6 CDEGHIK(N 4km)ORTV

💬 A very attractive campsite in a peaceful location. Ideal for families as the campsite forms part of a lovely amusement park. Well located for visiting Brest and the surroundings.

🚗 From Brest Nord on the D26 exit 'Les Trois Curés'.

D28　D168　D26　D13　D788
CC
D68
D5
D67　　Guipavas
Plouzané　Brest

CC € **17** 1/1-30/6　1/9-31/12

📍 N 48°28'32'' W 4°31'37''

Névez, F-29920 / Bretagne (Finistère)

♿ 🛜 **iD** (1427)

🏕 Sandaya Les 2 Fontaines****
📧 Feunteun Vihan
☎ +33 (0)2-98068191
🗓 13/4 - 9/9
@ 2fontaines@sandaya.fr

6,5ha 56T(100-140m²) 10A CEE

1 ACD**G**HIJKLPRS
2 AQRVWXY
3 B**E**GH**J**M**NP**RU
4 (C 10/5-10/9) (E+H 🔑) IJ
　(Q+S+T+U+V+Z 🔑)
5 **AB**FGJLNPUWZ
6 ACEGHJ**K**(N 3,5km)TV

💬 Good family campsite. Lovely large pitches with plenty of foliage. Nice walking path along the rugged coast, small roads in the area undulate, but are excellent for cycling tours. 900 metres to the coast.

🚗 N165/E60 Lorient-Quimper, exit Kerampaou, via D24 and D77 direction Névez centre, church at roundabout. Direction Raguenès, left after 3 km. Campsite well signposted.

Concarneau　D24　D4
D783
Moëlan-sur-Mer
CC

CC € **17** 13/4-6/7　1/9-8/9

📍 N 47°47'58'' W 3°47'25''

Névez/Raguénez, F-29920 / Bretagne (Finistère)

👪 ♿ 🛜 **iD** (1428)

🏕 Camping du Vieux Verger**
📧 20, Keroren
☎ +33 (0)2-98068608
🗓 14/4 - 15/9
@ contact@
　campingduvieuxverger.com

2,5ha 99T(70-120m²) 4-10A CEE

1 ABCDGIJKLMOPRS
2 GRVWX
3 AB**F**GHK
4 (C+H 23/6-2/9) J(Q 23/6-2/9)
5 **AB**GIJKMNPUZ
6 EK(N 2,5km)

NEW

💬 This very well-maintained small-scale campsite lies under fruit trees. The main part of the campsite has a nice pool with slides. The part next to it is very quiet with lots of space.

🚗 N165 Laurent-Quimper, exit Kerampaou and then via D24 and D77 to Névez, then towards Ragvenar-Plage. Campsite is signposted.

D24
D783　D4
Moëlan-sur-Mer
CC

CC € **13** 14/4-30/6　1/9-14/9

📍 N 47°47'48'' W 3°47'54''

Noyal-Muzillac, F-56190 / Bretagne (Morbihan)

♿ 🛜 **iD** **1429**

🏕 Moulin de Cadillac★★★★
🛣 route de Berric
☎ +33 (0)2-97670347
🔑 7/4 - 16/9
@ infos@moulin-cadillac.com

7ha 129T(100-150m²) 16A CEE

1 ACD**G**IJKLMOPRS
2 CDFRVWXY
3 BDGHJMN**Q**RUVW
4 (C 19/5-2/9) (F+H 🔑) IJM
(Q 7/7-31/8) (R 🔑)
(U+Z 7/7-31/8)
5 **AB**CDEFGHIJKLMNOPQUV
WZ
6 ACDEGIJ**K**(N 5km)OTUV

💬 A quiet campsite in natural surroundings.
A stream flows through the site that turned the mill wheel, hence the name. Experienced cyclists can enjoy themselves in undulating landscape. In the morning all you can hear are the birds.

🚗 Between Nantes and Vannes via N165/E60 exit Muzillac, in the centre D5 towards Noyal-Muzillac. Follow the signs of the campsite. Turn left in the centre of Noyal-Muzillac before you reach the church, 4.5 km. Campsite entrance on the right.

CC €**15** 7/4-27/4 2/5-4/5 14/5-18/5 22/5-6/7 1/9-15/9

🧭 N 47°36'51'' W 2°30'5''

Pénestin, F-56760 / Bretagne (Morbihan)

🚻 ♿ 🛜 **iD** **1430**

🏕 Le Domaine d'Inly★★★★
🛣 BP 24, rte de Couarne
☎ +33 (0)2-99903509
🔑 7/4 - 23/9
@ inly-info@wanadoo.fr

16ha 40T(90-140m²) 10A CEE

1 ACD**F**IJKLMOPRS
2 ADGQRVWXY
3 BDGHJK**MN**O**P**RUW
4 (C 2/6-23/9) (E+F+H 🔑) IJM
(Q+S+T+U+V+X+Y+Z 🔑)
5 **AB**DEFGIJKLMNOPQRUWX
YZ
6 ACEGHJ**K**(N 1km)TV

💬 Campsite with fields divided into circles with an informal ambiance. All amenities open during the whole period. Wellness centre, open and covered swimming pools. 1 km from a village with market twice weekly. Large supermarket at 1 km. Beach and sea at 2 km. Good restaurant. Reception closed 13h-14h.

🚗 N165/E60 Nantes-Vannes, take exit Pénestin or exit Barrage d'Arzal towards Pénestin on the D34 or D139. Follow the signs to the campsite before the centre.

CC €**19** 7/4-1/7 3/9-22/9 15=14

🧭 N 47°28'17'' W 2°28'2''

Penmarc'h, F-29760 / Bretagne (Finistère)

♿ 🛜 **iD** **1431**

🏕 Flower Camping Les Genêts★★★★
🛣 20 rue Gouesnac'h Nevez
☎ +33 (0)2-98586693
🔑 7/4 - 29/9
@ campinglesgenets29@orange.fr

3,2ha 55T(100m²) 10A CEE

1 ACD**G**IJKLMOPQ
2 AGLRVWXY
3 BGHJKNRU
4 (C 15/6-5/9) (E+H 🔑) IJK
(Q 🔑) (R 1/7-31/8)
(T+U+V+Z 🔑)
5 **AB**DEFGIJKLMNOPUWZ
6 ACEGK(N 1km)T

💬 Brigitte and Pascal welcome you in a calm family atmosphere to Bigouden's loveliest beach with plenty of trees and surrounded by three large fishing harbours. Lovely new toilet facilities, partially heated. Swimming pool with sliding roof, slide, a playful toddlers' pool and heated toilets.

🚗 From Pont-L'Abbé take direction Plomeur and Penmarc'h. Turn left at roundabout 1 km before the centre; direction Plobannalec. Campsite on the left after about 500 metres.

CC €**15** 7/4-8/7 26/8-28/9

🧭 N 47°49'6'' W 4°18'34''

Penvénan, F-22710 / Bretagne (Côtes-d'Armor)

🏕 Les Hauts de Port Blanc***
📍 12 bis rue Keranscouc'h
☎ +33 (0)2-96928672
📠 +33 (0)2-96926197
🔑 31/3 - 30/9
@ contact@portblanc.com

1432

3ha 39T(80-200m²) 10A CEE

1 ACD**G**IJKLMOPRT
2 AKLNQRVWX
3 BCGHJKLNQRU
4 (C+F+H 🔑) **KN**(Q 🔑)
(U 1/7-31/8) (Z 🔑)
5 **AB**FGIJKLMNPUWXZ
6 ACEGI**K**(N 0,6km)UV

💬 Family campsite located on level grounds opposite the 7 islands. Distance to the beach is 2 km. Partially covered swimming pool and wellness. Marked out pitches. Opportunities for watersports and excursions around the beautiful wild coastline. 'Voies Vertes de Bretagne' cycle routes close to the campsite. A boat trip to the seabird colonies on Les Sept Îles islands is recommended.

🚗 From Tréguier in NW direction towards Plouguil and Penvénan. Follow signs in Penvénan.

Perros-Guirec

CC €**15** 31/3-5/7 27/8-29/9 7=6

🗺 N 48°49'5'' W 3°18'7''

Pléboulle, F-22550 / Bretagne (Côtes-d'Armor)

🏕 Le Frèche à l'Âne***
📍 Le Bourg,
6 rue du Champ St. Paul
☎ +33 (0)2-96410872
🔑 1/4 - 31/10
@ info@camping-frechealane.com

1433

2ha 66T(100-200m²) 6-10A CEE

1 ACD**G**IJKLMOPRS
2 GJKLRVWXY
3 ABC**F**GHJRU
4 (Q+R 🔑) (U 1/7-31/8)
5 **AB**FGHIJKLNPQUZ
6 ACEGHJ(N 3km)T

💬 Welcoming, hospitable campsite in the middle of the green Breton countryside. Lovely sandy beaches nearby plus tourist attractions such as Cap Fréhel, Fort de Latte, Dinan.

🚗 Coming from Matignon. D786 direction Fréhel, turn left onto D16. Follow signs.

Erquy
Ploubalay
Plancoët

CC €**11** 1/4-7/7 25/8-30/10

🗺 N 48°36'32'' W 2°20'13''

Pléneuf-Val-André, F-22370 / Bretagne (Côtes-d'Armor)

🏕 Campéole Les Monts Colleux***
📍 26 rue Jean Lebrun
☎ +33 (0)2-96729510
📠 +33 (0)2-96631049
🔑 30/3 - 23/9
@ monts-colleux@campeole.com

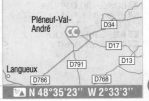

1434

3,7ha 114T(80-143m²) 10A CEE

1 AC**F**IJKLM**P**ST
2 AEGJKQRTVW
3 AB**F**GHJRUWY
4 (**F**+Q+R 🔑)
(T+U+Z 5/7-30/8)
5 **AB**EFGIJKLMNOPQRUZ
6 AEGH**J**(N 0,3km)RT

💬 A family campsite positioned on a hill. Lovely views of the Bay of Saint Brieuc. Shops and the beach are just 300m from the site.

🚗 In Rennes take the N12/E50, dir. Saint-Brieuc/Brest. Past Lamballe take the Pléneuf-Val-André exit and the D768 to Erquy-Cap Fréhel. In St. Alban take D58 to Pléneuf-Val-André. The campsite is in Val-André. Follow signs.

Pléneuf-Val-André
Langueux

CC €**15** 30/3-6/7 25/8-22/9

🗺 N 48°35'23'' W 2°33'3''

Ploëmel, F-56400 / Bretagne (Morbihan)

1435

▲ Le St. Laurent***
➤ Kergonvo, D186
☎ +33 (0)2-97568590
🔒 13/4 - 21/10
@ contact@
camping-saint-laurent.fr

3,5ha 41T(80-130m²) 10A CEE

1 ACDG**I**JKLMPST
2 BFLQRVWXY
3 A**F**GHJK**OP**RU
4 (E+H 13/4-30/9) (Q+R 🔒)
(T+U 1/5-15/10) (Z 🔒)
5 **AB**DEFGIJKLMNPUWZ
6 ACDEGJ(N 5km)TV

💬 A lovely campsite with modern heated toilet facilities, located in woods close to Carnac and 800m from a golf course. Relaxation is assured here, the only sound comes from the birds. Trips out by bike, car or on foot are perfectly possible.

🚗 N165/E60 Vannes/Lorient, exit Quiberon/Carnac. Via D22 direction Belz/Etel. Left after ± 9 km, campsite 100m on left.

Merlevenez · D33 · D19 · Brech · N165 · D17 · Auray · D28 · Baden · D781 · D768

CC € **15** 13/4-6/7 26/8-20/10 7=6, 14=12 · 🧭 N 47°39'48'' W 3°5'59''

Ploërmel/Taupont, F-56800 / Bretagne (Morbihan)

1436

▲ Camping du Lac**
➤ Les Belles Rives
☎ +33 (0)2-97740122
🔒 31/3 - 14/10
@ contact@
camping-du-lac-ploermel.com

2,5ha 92T(100-120m²) 6-10A

1 ACDG**I**JKLMOPRS
2 ADFKRVWXY
3 B**E**GHJL**MNPRWZ**
4 (Q+T+U 1/7-31/8) (Z 🔒)
5 **AB**GJKNP**ST**UXYZ
6 ACE**K**TV

💬 Family campsite directly on the Lac au Duc. Pitches with a view of the lake. 600 metres from a unique hydrangea garden via a cycle/walking path. 1300 metres from a shopping centre. 15 km cycle route around the lake.

🚗 N24 Rennes-Quimper, exit Ploërmel/Dinan/St. Malo, follow ring road to Lac au Duc. Campsite is located between the road and the lake and is signposted.

Lanouée · D793 · D8 · D766 · Josselin · D724 · Cruguel · **Ploërmel** · D772 · D4

CC € **15** 31/3-6/7 25/8-12/10 · 🧭 N 47°56'56'' W 2°25'16''

Ploërmel/Taupont, F-56800 / Bretagne (Morbihan)

1437

▲ La Vallée du Ninian***
➤ Le Rocher Ville Bonne
☎ +33 (0)2-97935301
🔒 31/3 - 30/9
@ infos@camping-ninian.fr

2,7ha 83T(100-160m²) 3-10A CEE

1 ACDG**I**JKLMOPRS
2 CFLRVWXY
3 BDF**G**HJKL**OP**RUW
4 (E 🔒) (H 1/7-31/8) (Q+R 🔒)
(T+U+X+Z 7/7-31/8)
5 **AB**FGJKLMNPQUWXYZ
6 ACEGK(N 7km)TV

💬 A lovely site with large 'grand confort' pitches among apple trees. An attractive area for walking and cycling trips. Region with many legends and places of interest. Modern, well maintained toilet facilities.

🚗 N24 Rennes-Quimper, exit Ploërmel/Dinan/St.Malo, follow ring road to Lac Au Duc, then direction Taupont. D8 towards the north. Follow the road just beyond the village with the camping sign on the left. Site located about 2.5 NW of Taupont.

D778 · Lanouée · D793 · D16 · D766 · Josselin · D724 · D4 · Ploërmel · N24 · D772 · N166 · D8

CC € **15** 31/3-6/7 25/8-29/9 · 🧭 N 47°58'9'' W 2°28'12''

Plonévez-Porzay, F-29550 / Bretagne (Finistère) 👫 🛜 iD (1438)

🔼 Campéole Trezmalaouen***
✉ 20 route de la Baie
☎ 🆑 +33 (0)2-98925424
🔓 27/4 - 16/9
@ trezmalaouen@campeole.com

4ha 33T(80-100m²) 10A

1 ACDFIJKLNPQ
2 AEIJKLQRVWX
3 BGHMRU**W**Y
4 (Q 🔑) (T+U+Z 1/7-31/8)
5 **AB**FIJKLMNOPWZ
6 CEGH**J**(N 5km)QRTV

💬 Sheltered from the wind with views of Douarnenez bay and the famous Sardines harbour. Direct access to the beach from the campsite.

🚗 From Quimper continue to Locronan. Follow signs beyond Plonévez-Porzay.

Plomodiern — D887
D63
D7
Douarnenez CC
D143 — D765 — D39

CC € **15** 27/4-6/7 25/8-15/9

📡 N 48°6'40'' W 4°16'37''

Plonévez-Porzay, F-29550 / Bretagne (Finistère) ♿ 🛜 iD (1439)

🔼 La Plage de Tréguer
✉ plage de Ste Anne-la-Palud
☎ +33 (0)2-98925352
🆑 +33 (0)2-98925489
🔓 28/4 - 22/9
@ camping-treguer-plage@wanadoo.fr

6ha 272T(90-130m²) 10A

1 ACD**F**IJKLMPRS
2 AELQRSVWX
3 BGHNRUWY
4 (C+H 15/6-15/9) K(Q+R 🔑) (T+U+V 1/7-31/8) (Y 🔑) (Z 1/7-31/8)
5 **AB**FGIJKLMNPUVYZ
6 CE**IJ**(N 4km)OV

💬 A family campsite by the sea, right behind the dunes. Gently sloping sandy beach. Suitable for children. Plenty of activities. Toilet facilities are very well maintained. Ideal starting point for visits to Douarnenez, Quimper and Pointe Duraz. The GR34 runs past the site by the dunes. Due to its location a wonderful climate!

🚗 From Châteaulin take the D7 in the direction of Douarnenez. Then take the D107 and D61 to Ste Anne-la-Palud. Then follow the camping signs.

D887
D47
CC
Douarnenez D63 — D7
Plogonnec
D765

CC € **15** 28/4-7/7 25/8-21/9

📡 N 48°8'40'' W 4°16'8''

Plouézec/Paimpol, F-22470 / Bretagne (Côtes-d'Armor) ♿ 🛜 iD (1440)

🔼 Le Cap de Bréhat****
✉ route de Port Lazo
☎ +33 (0)2-96206428
🆑 +33 (0)2-96206388
🔓 7/4 - 23/9
@ info@cap-de-brehat.com

5ha 95T(80-110m²) 16A CEE

1 ACD**F**HIJKLMPRS
2 EJKLNQRTUVX
3 BC**F**GHIJMNRUWY
4 (A 1/7-31/8) (E 🔑) (H 1/7-30/8) (Q+R+S+T+U+V 🔑) (X 1/7-31/8) (Z 🔑)
5 **AB**DEFGHIJKLMNPRUWXYZ
6 ACDEGJ**K**(N 2km)OTV

💬 Uniquely located terraced campsite with unforgettable views of the sea and the Isle de Bréhat. Oyster beds at low tide. Direct access to the sea and the GR34. The camping pitches are well secluded and offer plenty of privacy. Heated indoor swimming pool.

🚗 The campsite is located in Port-Lazo, 2.5 km from the D786. Follow the signs carefully; also the signs for one-way traffic with access only for residents and the campsite. (In other words, ignore the No Entry!)

Paimpol
Plouézec CC
D6 — D7 — D786

CC € **17** 7/4-7/7 25/8-22/9 7=6

📡 N 48°45'35'' W 2°57'44''

Plouézoc'h, F-29252 / Bretagne (Finistère) 🧗 ♿ 🛜 📱iD 1441

🔺 De la Baie de Térénez***
📧 Moulin de Caneret
☎ +33 (0)2-98672680
📅 7/4 - 29/9
@ campingbaiedeterenez@
  wanadoo.fr

2,3ha 65**T**(100-140m²) 10A

1 ACD**G**IJKLMPQ
2 AEGRVWXY
3 AHJ**Q**RUW
4 (C+G 15/5-15/9)
  (Q 15/6-15/9)
  (R+U+Z 1/7-31/8)
5 **A**BFGJKLMNPUWZ
6 ACDEG**J**(N 2,5km)V

💬 Baie de Térénez is located in a bay close to the old harbour town of Morlaix and is suitable for discovering the beautiful beaches and the typical Breton villages and harbours. Located between Perros-Guirrec en Carantec. The burial mounds at Barnénez, the largest in Europe are near the campsite. Spacious grassy stiches separated by low hedges and trees.

🚐 To Plouézoc'h-centre. Continue following signs to the campsite. The campsite is on the right after about 2.5 km.

Saint-Pol-de-Léon

D58 | ℂℂ D46 D78 D64
D769 | D786
D19 | **Morlaix** N12

ℂℂ € **13** *7/4-6/7   27/8-28/9 7=6* | 🔺 N 48°39'35'' W 3°50'53''

Plougastel-Daoulas, F-29470 / Bretagne (Finistère) ♿ 🛜 📱iD 1442

🔺 Saint Jean****
📧 1910 rte de la Chapelle Saint Jean
☎ +33 (0)2-98403290
📅 1/5 - 28/9
@ info@campingsaintjean.com

2ha 81**T**(70m²) 10A CEE

1 ACD**G**IJLPR
2 BEFJORVX
3 BGHKLNRUW
4 (C+F+H 🅿) JM
  (R+T+U+X+Z 2/7-27/8)
5 **A** **B**DFGJKLNPQUVWZ
6 ACEGI**J**(N 2,5km)V

💬 This green and flowery campsite should not be missed on your tour around Brittany. There is a heated indoor swimming pool and heated toilet buildings. Brest and the Océanopolis are just 10 km away.

🚐 Motorway Quimper-Brest. Exit Plougastel/Daoulas (Centre Commercial Leclerc). Then follow the camping signs (2 km).

D26 | N12
| D712
Brest | ℂℂ
Plougastel- | D770
Daoulas | N165

ℂℂ € **15** *1/5-7/7 25/8-27/9* | 🔺 N 48°24'6'' W 4°21'16''

Plouguerneau, F-29880 / Bretagne (Finistère) ♿ 🛜 ✿ 📱iD 1443

🔺 De la Grève Blanche**
📧 400 La Grève Blanche-St. Michel
☎ +33 (0)2-98047035
📅 23/3 - 8/10
@ lroudaut@free.fr

3ha 90**T**(80-120m²) 10A CEE

1 A**G**IJLO**P**Q
2 AEGJKLQRTVW
3 ABGHJNRUWY
4 (Q+R 🅿) (T+U 1/7-31/8)
  (Z 🅿)
5 CGIJKMNO**P**UZ
6 CEG**J**(N 3km)OR

💬 A modest campsite with very friendly staff and direct access to the beach. Spacious pitches on terrace-shaped grounds with an open view of the sea and of the highest lighthouse in Europe. Beautiful sandy beach, a welcoming bar and fresh bread daily. Nature and the environment are important at this campsite (eco-label). The GR 34 runs along this campsite.

🚐 Follow camping signs in centre of Plouguerneau.

ℂℂ
Plouguerneau | D10
| Lesneven
D28
D26

ℂℂ € **15** *23/3-6/7 3/9-7/10 14=12* | 🔺 N 48°37'49'' W 4°31'26''

Plouguerneau, F-29880 / Bretagne (Finistère)

♿ 📶 ✿ **iD** (1444)

▲ Du Vougot***
✉ 1037 rte de Prat Ledan, Le Vougot
☎ 📠 +33 (0)2-98256151
🗓 31/3 - 30/9
@ campingduvougot@hotmail.fr

2,5ha 38T(100-300m²) 10A CEE

1 ACDGIJKLMPRS
2 AERSVWXY
3 ABHJPRUW
4 (F+H 🖼) (Q 1/6-1/9) (R 🖼)
  (U 1/7-1/9) (X 15/5-15/9)
  (Z 1/5-30/9)
5 ABFGIJKLMNPUWZ
6 ACEGIK(N 5km)Q

💬 You will receive a warm welcome at this peaceful, small and well-run campsite which is sheltered from the wind. New: a lovely indoor and heated pool, toddler's pool and balneo. Plenty of greenery, flowers and spacious pitches 250 metres to the beautiful beach at Vougot. A good base for visiting Brest with its Oceanopolis and unique Abers or Meneham.

🚗 In Lesneven direction Plouguerneau. Follow signs. Campsite is situated on coastal road.

CC € ⑮ 31/3-6/6 25/8-29/9 7=6, 14=12   🧭 N 48°37'53'' W 4°26'59''

Plouhinec, F-56680 / Bretagne (Morbihan)

♿ 📶 **iD** (1445)

▲ Flower Camping Le Moténo****
✉ rue du Passage d'Etel
☎ +33 (0)2-97367663
📠 +33 (0)2-97858184
🗓 7/4 - 22/9
@ info@camping-le-moteno.com

5ha 55T(75-110m²) 10A CEE

1 ACDFHIJKLMPST
2 AEJRWXY
3 BGHKLNRUVW
4 (C 15/5-23/9) (E 🖼)
  (H 15/5-23/9) J(Q 🖼)
  (R 7/7-31/8)
  (T+U+V+Z 7/4-7/5, 7/7-31/8)
5 ABEFGIJKLMNOPQRUVWZ
6 FGJK(N 3km)T

💬 Spaciously appointed campsite with pitches under trees. Indoor and outdoor pool with various slides. Nice toilet facilities.

🚗 From N165, exit Port Louis direction Plouhinec. In Plouhinec centre, direction Carnac/Quiberon. Turn right about 1 km after the church and follow campsite signs towards Le Magouër.

CC € ⑮ 7/4-6/7 26/8-21/9   🧭 N 47°39'54'' W 3°13'16''

Plozévet, F-29710 / Bretagne (Finistère)

👫 ♿ 📶 **iD** (1446)

▲ Flower Camping La Corniche***
✉ chemin de la Corniche
☎ +33 (0)2-98913394
🗓 15/2 - 15/12
@ campinglacorniche@
  flowercampings.com

2ha 73T(80-120m²) 10A CEE

1 ACDGIJKLMOPRS
2 GKLRTVWXY
3 BGHJKNRU
4 (C+H 15/5-15/9)
  (Q+S 1/4-30/9) (T 🖼)
  (U+V+Z 1/4-30/9)
5 ABEFGIJLMNPUVWXYZ
6 CDEGK(N 0,5km)ORTV

💬 This natural campsite offers you every comfort and fun in a family atmosphere. 500m from the centre of Plozévet. 1.5 km from the beach. Perfectly maintained grounds and toilet facilities. Heated swimming pool from 15/5-15/9 and wifi. Snack bar open every day in high season.

🚗 In Plozévet, follow signs to 'Camping de la Corniche'. After the village, about 400 metres on the right.

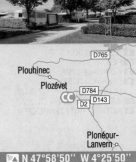

CC € ⑰ 15/2-9/7 27/8-31/10 7=6   🧭 N 47°58'50'' W 4°25'50''

Plurien/Sables d'Or-les-Pins, F-22240 / Bretagne (Côtes-d'Armor) ♿ 🛜 iD (1447)

🏕 Les Salines
✉ rue du lac/route de la ville Boulin
☎ +33 (0)2-96721740
🗓 1/4 - 31/10
@ campinglessalinesplurien@
gmail.com

4,2ha 150T 6A CEE

1 ACGIJKLMPRS
2 ACEGJLMQRTVWXY
3 ABFGHJKLPRUWY
4 (A+Q+R+Z 🔌)
5 ABCEFGHIJKLMNOPQUVY
Z
6 ACEGJ(N 2km)ORTV

💬 Spaciously appointed terraced campsite in natural surroundings. Close to lagoon area. Beautiful walking and cycling trips from the campsite.

🚗 From N12 Brest-Rennes exit Erquy, Pléneuf-Val-André. 2 km before Erquy exit Cap Fréhel, Sables d'Or-les-Pins. Follow campsite signs.

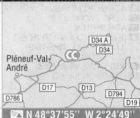

CC € 13 1/4-7/7 25/8-30/10 📍 N 48°37'55'' W 2°24'49''

Pont-Croix, F-29790 / Bretagne (Finistère) ♿ 🛜 iD (1448)

🏕 Entre Pierres et Mer
✉ Route de Lochrist
☎ +33 (0)7-85909108
🗓 1/1 - 31/12
@ campingentrepierresetmer@
orange.fr

59T 10-20A CEE

1 ACDGIJKLMOP
2 LRTUVWX
3 ABGHJKQRUW
4 (E+H+Q+R 🔌)
(T+U 15/7-30/9) (Z 🔌)
5 ABCFGHIJKLMNOPUXYZ
6 ACDEGJKORV

NEW

💬 The campsite lies in the hills of the small, characterful medieval Pont-Croix. Open all year round. Pitches from 90 to 150 m² in quiet, familiar surroundings. Free wifi, heated indoor pool (open all year round), bread service, large motorhome pitches, free water disposal outside the campsite. 500 m from the shops, and 10 minutes from the beaches at Beuzec-Cap-Sizun and Audierne.

🚗 N164 (E60) exit Quimper towards Douarnenez exit D43. Then D765 towards Pont-Croix.

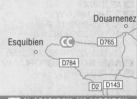

CC € 13 1/1-7/7 25/8-31/12 7=6, 14=11 📍 N 48°2'58'' W 4°28'56''

Pont-Scorff, F-56620 / Bretagne (Morbihan) ♿ 🛜 ✿ iD (1449)

🏕 Ty Nénez***
✉ route de Lorient
☎ +33 (0)2-97325116
🗓 1/1 - 31/12
@ camping-ty-nenez@wanadoo.fr

2,5ha 69T(100-200m²) 8-16A CEE

1 ACDGHIJKLMOP
2 FGLRVWX
3 ABFGHJRUW
4 (F+H+Q+R 🔌)
(T+U+Z 7/4-21/5,1/7-31/8)
5 ABDEFGIJKMNPQUXYZ
6 ACDEGHK(N 1km)OQTV

💬 Peacefully located campsite with lovely spacious pitches. Indoor swimming pool with water heated to 30° that is open for the entire season. 1 km to the shops and animal park nearby (500m).

🚗 N165 dir. Brest, exit Quéven dir. Pont-Scorff, 600 metres after zoo turn right. Then follow signs.

CC € 15 1/1-29/6 3/9-31/12 📍 N 47°49'13'' W 3°24'12''

Pordic, F-22590 / Bretagne (Côtes-d'Armor)   ♿ 🛜 iD (1450)

🏕 Les Madières***
🏢 Le Vau-Madec
☎ +33 (0)2-96790248
📅 9/4 - 21/10
@ campinglesmadieres@
  wanadoo.fr

2ha 75T(90-300m²) 10A CEE

1 ACDGIJKLMPQ
2 AFGKLNQRVWXY
3 ABGHJNRUW
4 (C 15/6-15/9) (Q 1/7-31/8)
  (R+T+U+V 📷) (Z 1/7-31/8)
5 **AB**CDFGIJKLMNPUVZ
6 ACDEGK(N 1,8km)RTV

💬 Beautifully appointed and well-maintained site with renovated toilet facilities (2014). Relaxing atmosphere in park-like surroundings. Lovely pool in Spanish style. Attractive small restaurant. Natural layout of the grounds, no permanent pitches. Very suitable for hikers. 10 minutes from sea. Free wifi.

🚗 N12, after Plérin exit Les Rampes to Pordic. D786 to Pordic. In Pordic follow centre, then 'campings' signs. Well signposted.

D21 D9 D786 D6 N12 D7 D36 **Saint-Brieuc** CC

CC € **15**   9/4-30/6   1/9-20/10   📍 N 48°34'58'' W 2°48'17''

Port-Manech/Névez, F-29920 / Bretagne (Finistère)   ♿ 🛜 iD (1451)

🏕 Le Saint Nicolas***
🏢 8 Kergouliou
☎ +33 (0)2-98068975
📅 1/5 - 16/9
@ info@campinglesaintnicolas.com

3,5ha 161T(80-130m²) 10A CEE

1 ACDGHIJKLMOPQ
2 AEGJQRVWXY
3 BGHJMNRUWY
4 (**A**+C 1/7-31/8) (E+H 📷) IJK
  P(Q 7/7-31/8)
5 **AB**CFGIJKLMNOPQRUVXY
  Z
6 ACEG**K**(N 0,3km)TV

💬 A lovely peaceful campsite within walking distance of the beach and harbour. A small shop (300m) sells fresh bread daily. 3 km from a beautifully restored Breton village. Numerous trips out possible. Indoor heated pool open all season. Outdoor pool open and heated from July.

🚗 From Lorient, take N165/E60 direction Quimper, exit Kerampaou via the D24 to Névez, then direction Port-Manech. Do not follow SatNav. On entering Port-Manech follow signs to the left.

Concarneau N165 D783 D104 CC Moëlan-sur-Mer D16

CC € **17**   1/5-7/7   25/8-15/9   📍 N 47°48'18'' W 3°44'44''

Poullan-sur-Mer/Douarnenez, F-29100 / Bretagne (Finistère)   👫 ♿ 🛜 iD (1452)

🏕 Camping de la Baie de
  Douarnenez****
🏢 30 rue Luc Robet
☎ +33 (0)2-98742639
📠 +33 (0)2-98745597
📅 27/4 - 9/9
@ info@camping-douarnenez.com

5,5ha 100T(100-150m²) 10A

1 ACD**G**HIJKLMPQ
2 RVX
3 BGMN**Q**RUW
4 (C+F+H 📷) J(Q+S 📷)
  (T+U+V+Y+Z 4/7-31/8)
5 **AB**FGIJKLMNPU
6 CEG**IK**(N 0,8km)ORV

💬 A friendly family campsite with plenty of greenery, spacious pitches and a lovely indoor swimming pool. The restaurant is recommended. Good base for exploring the beautiful surroundings, also by bike. The lovely little harbours and rugged cliffs contrast with sandy beaches and are a unique area for birdwatchers.

🚗 From Douarnenez D7 to Poullan-sur-Mer. Just before Poullan-sur-Mer, turn left direction campsite. Signposted further on.

CC **Douarnenez** D43 D143 D784 D765 Plozévet

CC € **15**   27/4-6/7   26/8-8/9   📍 N 48°4'54'' W 4°24'24''

Priziac, F-56320 / Bretagne (Morbihan)

♿ 🛜 iD (1453)

🏕 Le Lac ô Fées***
📧 Lac du Bel-air
☎ +33 (0)6-78332496
🗓 1/1 - 31/12
@ contact@campinglelacofees.fr

1,5ha 56T(100-200m²) 16A CEE

1 ACD**G**HIJKLMOP
2 ADKLMRVXY
3 BGHNRU**WZ**
4 (Q+R 🔌) (T+U+Z 1/4-30/9)
5 **AB**DGIJKLMNOPUZ
6 ACDEGJ(N 0,5km)RV

💬 Quiet campsite with spacious pitches under the trees with a view over the lake. Snack bar open from April to September. Ideal for people who like to enjoy life.

🚗 N165 exit 42 dir. Morlaix (D769). After Le Faouët take D132 to Priziac. Follow campsite/Lac du Bel-air signs.

CC € **13** 1/1-9/7 1/9-31/12

🛰 N 48°3'29'' W 3°24'58''

Quiberon, F-56170 / Bretagne (Morbihan)

👨‍👩‍👧 ♿ 🛜 ✿ iD (1454)

🏕 Do Mi Si La Mi***
📧 8 rue de la Vierge
☎ +33 (0)2-97502252
📠 +33 (0)2-97502669
🗓 31/3 - 30/9
@ camping@domisilami.com

5ha 184T(80-110m²) 10A CEE

1 ACD**G**IJKLMOPQ
2 AEGKNQRVWX
3 BC**F**GHJKLNRUWY
4 (Q+S+T+U+V+X+Z 🔌)
5 **AB**CEFGHIJKLMNOPQRUV XYZ
6 ACDEG**K**(N 0km)ORTV

💬 Campsite by a sandy beach, natural hedges ensure plenty of shade and privacy. Well maintained toilet facilities. Bar/restaurant and self service-shop (with fresh fruit and vegetables and a meat section). Lightly undulating cycle and footpaths close by. You will receive a surprise by using code ACSI-DoMi.

🚗 N165/E60 Nantes-Quimper exit Carnac/Quiberon, via D768 direction Quiberon. Turn left after St. Pierre/ Quiberon. Well signposted.

CC € **17** 31/3-29/6 1/9-29/9

🛰 N 47°29'59'' W 3°7'13''

Quiberon, F-56170 / Bretagne (Morbihan)

♿ 🛜 iD (1455)

🏕 Flower Camping Le Bois d'Amour***
📧 rue St. Clément
☎ +33 (0)2-97501352
🗓 30/3 - 30/9
@ camping.boisdamour@ flowercampings.com

5,5ha 65T(60-100m²) 6-16A CEE

1 ACD**F**IJKLM**P**RS
2 AEGQRSVWX
3 BF**G**HJK**MQ**R**T**UWY
4 (E+H+Q+R+T+U+V+Y+Z 🔌)
5 **AB**EFGIJKLMNOPUWZ
6 ACEGK(N 1,5km)T

💬 A good campsite with many facilities, 150m from a flat sandy beach. Noisy near the entrance, quieter at the rear. Located in an old dune area, so plenty of sand and long tent pegs are required. Indoor pool.

🚗 South of Auray, via the D768 to Quiberon. In Quiberon town direction Thalassotherapie or follow the camping signs.

CC € **17** 30/3-29/6 1/9-29/9 7=6

🛰 N 47°28'35'' W 3°6'15''

Quiberon, F-56170 / Bretagne (Morbihan) ✦✦ ♿ 📶 **iD** (1456)

🔺 Les Joncs du Roch★★★
✉ rue de l'Aérodrome
☎ +33 (0)2-97502437
📅 7/4 - 22/9
@ camping@lesjoncsduroch.com

2,3ha 105**T**(80-120m²) 10A CEE

1 ACD**G**HIJKLMOPRS
2 AEGQRVWX
3 B**F**GHJK**MNOP**RUWY
4 (E+H+Q 🅾)
5 **AB**EFGIJKLMNOPQUVXZ
6 ACEG**K**(N 1km)TV

💬 A hospitable campsite close to a lovely beach and town. 800m from a supermarket. Large level pitches and renewed toilet facilities (2016). You can watch light aircraft take off and land at the nearby airfield (open from 08:00 to 18:00). Indoor swimming pool, always heated to 30°C.

🚗 N165/E60 Nantes-Quimper, exit Carnac-Quiberon, via D768 to Quiberon. Left just before railway beyond St. Pierre/Quiberon. Follow Aerodrôme and Port-Haligven signs.

Locmariaquer
D768
CC

CC € **17** 7/4-6/7 24/8-21/9 | 🏕 N 47°28'45'' W 3°6'2''

Quimper, F-29000 / Bretagne (Finistère) ♿ 📶 ✿ **iD** (1457)

🔺 Domaine de L'Orangerie de Lanniron★★★★★
✉ allée/chemin de Lanniron/ Chât. de L
☎ +33 (0)2-98906202
📅 31/3 - 5/11
@ contact@lanniron.com

6,5ha 199**T**(80-150m²) 10A CEE

1 ACD**G**IJKLMOPQ
2 CFGKLRVWXY
3 B**E**F**G**HJK**MN**Q**RU**W
4 (A 9/7-31/8) (C+H 15/5-15/9) IJKMP
(Q+S+T+U+V+Y+Z 15/4-15/9)
5 **AB**DEFGIJKLMNOPUWXYZ
6 ACEGHJ**K**(N 2km)

💬 A unique site next to the Odet, the most beautiful river in France. Pitches, marked out by exotic trees and plants in a 17th century castle park (38 hectares). Restaurant and shop in authentic buildings. Lovely aqua park, 9 hole golf course, 3 fishing locations. Quimper is 2 km away via a woodland path. Superior, comfort or Castel premium pitches for a supplement.

🚗 In Quimper continue towards Pont-l'Abbé. Follow Lanniron camping signs.

D39
D765   N165
D784 **Quimper**   D15
CC
D785   D34   D783
D45
D2   **Fouesnant**

CC € **19** 31/3-30/6 1/9-4/11 | 🏕 N 47°58'46'' W 4°6'24''

Raguénès/Névez, F-29920 / Bretagne (Finistère) ♿ 📶 **iD** (1458)

🔺 Airotel Le Raguenès Plage★★★★
✉ 19 rue des Îles
☎ +33 (0)2-98068069
📅 20/4 - 1/10
@ leraguenesplage@orange.fr

7ha 218**T**(90-140m²) 6-15A CEE

1 ACD**G**IJKLMOPQ
2 AEKQRVWXY
3 BGHJKNRU**V**WY
4 (C 19/5-15/9) (E+H 🅾) IJ**N**
(Q+S+T+U+V+Y+Z 5/5-1/10)
5 **AB**EFGIJKLOPRUVWXYZ
6 ACEG**K**(N 2,5km)TV

💬 A lovely, luxurious campsite close to the sea. Choose a pitch with plenty or with little shade. There are a couple of nice walking and cycling routes close by. A lovely sandy beach 300m away via a footpath. Indoor pool heated all season, outdoor pool heated from the end of May. Sea views from 15 of the pitches.

🚗 N165 Lorient-Quimper, exit Kerampaou and via D24/D77 to Névez. Then direction Raguénès-Plage. Well indicated after 3 km.

Concarneau   N165
D783   D104
D24
CC

CC € **17** 20/4-9/7 27/8-30/9 7=6, 14=12 | 🏕 N 47°47'36'' W 3°48'3''

Rochefort-en-Terre, F-56220 / Bretagne (Morbihan)

♻ 📶 **iD** **1459**

▲ Sites & Paysages Au Gré
   Des Vents***
▤ 2 chemin de Bogeais
☏ +33 (0)2-97433752
⏲ 31/3 - 30/9
@ gredesvents@orange.fr

2,5ha 70T(85-150m²) 6-10A CEE

1 ACD**G**IJKLMOPRS
2 GIRVWXY
3 B**F**GHJKL**M**NRU**W**
4 (E+H 14/4-16/9) (Q+R 🔒)
   (T+U 28/4-9/9) (Z 🔒)
5 **AB**FGIJKLMNPUVW
6 ACEG**K**(N 1,5km)OTV

🗨 800m from one of the most beautiful villages in France, small characteristic village with folk arts. Campsite with greenery, large pitches separated by hedges. Modern toilet facilities, paths for walking, cycling and mountain biking. First two hours free wifi. Reception hours low season: 9h-12h30 and 16h-19h30.

🚙 N116 Ploërmel/Vannes exit D775, towards Redon, D777 towards Rochefort-en-Terre, then towards Limerzel, D774, take a right after 800m. See campsite signs.

D8
D774 D764
D5
D775   CC   D777
Questembert   D21
D7
D1   Caden   Allaire
D153

CC € **17** 31/3-6/7 26/8-29/9   🗺 N 47°41'43'' W 2°20'57''

Roz-sur-Couesnon, F-35610 / Bretagne (Ille-et-Vilaine)

📶 **iD** **1460**

▲ Les Couesnons***
▤ 8 l'Hopital
☏ +33 (0)2-99802686
⏲ 30/3 - 31/10
@ courrier@lescouesnons.com

0,9ha 41T(80-110m²) 6-10A CEE

1 ACD**G**IJKLMPRS
2 FGRTVX
3 ABGHJRU
4 (Q+R+X+Y+Z 🔒)
5 **AB**DEFGIJKLMNPRUWZ
6 CEGK(N 2km)T

🗨 Located at the entrance to the polders, 10 minutes from Mont Saint Michel, 20 minutes from Cancale, 30 minutes from Saint Malo. A friendly welcome at this family campsite, relaxing, comfortable, marked out pitches. Beautiful, typical Breton restaurant, closed in the off-season on Tuesday evening and all day Wednesday.

🚙 N175 Avranches direction Dol-de-Bretagne, exit Roz-sur-Couesnon, D797 direction St. Malo coastal road. Campsite signposted 7 km on the right.

D911
D75
Dol-de-   D797   CC
Bretagne   D976   N175
D576   Pontorson
D795   D155   D975
D90

CC € **15** 30/3-8/7 27/8-30/10 8=7   🗺 N 48°35'40'' W 1°35'55''

Sarzeau, F-56370 / Bretagne (Morbihan)

🚹 ♻ 📶 ✿ **iD** **1461**

▲ La Ferme de Lann Hoëdic***
▤ rue Jean de la Fontaine
☏ +33 (0)2-97480173
⏲ 31/3 - 31/10
@ contact@camping-lannhoedic.fr

3,6ha 106T(100-160m²) 10A CEE

1 ACD**G**IJKLMPQ
2 AOQRVWXY
3 BDF**G**HJKRUW
4 **N**(Q+R 🔒) (U 7/7-26/8)
   (Z 🔒)
5 **AB**CEFGHIJKLMNOPQUZ
6 ACEGHI**J**(N 2km)TUV

🗨 Near the sea, a natural campsite with rural charm and 3-star comfort. Beach 800 metres, supermarket 2 km, Sarzeau 2.5 km. Coastline with sandy beaches and cliffs. 15 mins free wifi per day. Reception hours 9h-12h / 15h-18h.

🚙 N165 Vannes-Nantes, exit Sarzeau via D20 or D780 (Do not enter Sarzeau). Follow the D20 direction Port Navalo to the roundabout with the Super U supermarket. On the roundabout turn left direction Roaliguen. Follow the sign to the site.

D780
D20
Saint-Gildas-de-   Sarzeau
Rhuys
CC

CC € **15** 31/3-9/7 27/8-30/10 14=13   🗺 N 47°30'26'' W 2°45'39''

Sarzeau, F-56370 / Bretagne (Morbihan)

♿ 📶 ⚙ 📱 iD **1462**

🏕 Manoir de Ker An Poul★★★★
✉ Lieu dit Penvins
☎ +33 (0)2-43530433
🔓 7/4 - 23/9
@ info@manoirdekeranpoul.com

6ha 107T(80-130m²) 10-16A CEE

1 ACD**F**IJKLMOPST
2 AEOQRVWXY
3 BHJKNRUWY
4 (**A** 1/7-31/8) (C 1/5-23/9)
(E+H 🔓) J(Q 1/7-31/8)
(T+U+V+X+Z 1/5-15/9)
5 **AB**EFGIJKLMNPQRUWXYZ
6 ACEGJ**K**(N 0,2km)RTV

NEW

📝 Large but quiet campsite close to the sea. Lots of mobile homes on the grounds, the touring pitches are grouped centrally between two toilet blocks and there is plenty of natural landscaping. Good campsite, particularly for families with children.

🚗 N165/E60 Vannes-Nantes. Via D780 direction Sarzeau and then the D199, direction Penvins until you see the campsite in the centre of Penvins.

D140
D20
Sarzeau
Saint-Gildas-de-Rhuys CC

CC €**17** 7/4-7/7 25/8-22/9 7=6

🌐 N 47°30'19'' W 2°40'59''

St. Benoît-des-Ondes, F-35114 / Bretagne (Ille-et-Vilaine)

📶 iD **1463**

🏕 de l'Ile Verte★★★★
✉ 42 rue de l'Ile Verte
☎ +33 (0)2-99586255
🔓 30/3 - 31/10
@ bienvenue@
campingdelileverte.com

1,8ha 40T(100-120m²) 6A CEE

1 ACD**G**IJKLMPRS
2 AEGLMRTVX
3 ABGKRUW
4 (F 1/4-30/9) (H 1/7-31/8)
(Q 🔓) (T+U+X+Z 1/7-31/8)
5 **AB**EFGIJKLMNOPQUWX
6 CEG**K**(N 0,5km)TV

📝 A peaceful and charming family campsite 400 metres from the sea (fishing possible) and shops. The campsite is close to Cancale, between St. Malo and Mont Saint Michel. Spacious, marked out wind-free pitches.

🚗 At Dol-de-Bretagne take exit Cancale (D155-D4). At La Fresnais take D207 and D7 to Vildé-la-Marine, then to St. Benoît. Turn left at service station in the village.

Saint-Malo
D155
D76 CC
D797
D4
Miniac-
Morvan D676 D795 N176

CC €**17** 30/3-6/7 1/9-30/10

🌐 N 48°36'58'' W 1°51'7''

St. Brieuc, F-22000 / Bretagne (Côtes-d'Armor)

👫 ♿ 📶 iD **1464**

🏕 Flower Camping les Vallées★★★
✉ boulevard Paul Doumer
☎ 📠 +33 (0)2-96940505
🔓 12/3 - 12/10
@ campingdesvallees@wanadoo.fr

3,2ha 35T(80-120m²) 10A CEE

1 ACD**F**IJKLPR
2 CFGRTUVX
3 BGHJKN**OP**RU
4 (**F+H** 🔓) **IJ**KMN
(Q+R+S+T+U+V+Z 1/7-31/8)
5 **AB**EFGIJKLMNOPQSUWXZ
6 ACDEGIJ**K**(N 1km)ORTV

📝 Campsite in natural surroundings, close to the centre of St. Brieuc. Lovely pitches beside a stream. Close to an indoor and outdoor leisure pool. Free wifi.

🚗 Via the N12 exit St. Brieux. Campsite well signposted throughout the town. Follow the Brézillet part of town.

D6
N12 Plérin
Saint-
Brieuc
D45 CC D786
D700
D790 D1 D765

CC €**15** 12/3-6/7 25/8-11/10

🌐 N 48°30'2'' W 2°45'31''

St. Cast-le-Guildo, F-22380 / Bretagne (Côtes-d'Armor)

♿ 📶 **iD** (1465)

🏰 Château de Galinée★★★★★
🏕 La Galinée
☎ +33 (0)2-96411056
📠 +33 (0)2-96410372
⌚ 5/5 - 8/9
@ info@chateaudegalinee.fr

14ha 272**T**(120-130m²) 10A CEE

1 ACD**G**IJKLM**P**RS
2 BLRTVXY
3 AB**FG**M**N**QRUW
4 (C 11/5-5/9) (F+H 19/4-5/9)
IJ**N**(Q+S 24/5-5/9)
(U+V+X+Z 24/5-31/8)
5 **AB**DEFGIJLMNPR**ST**UWXY
Z
6 AEGH**IK**(N 3km)RTV

💬 Beautiful family grounds in a castle park. Lovely water park with slides, bar and restaurant with views of the pool. Free fishing pond. Ancient trees in the castle park add ambiance. Marked out pitches with small hedges. Excellent heated toilet block. Swimming in the indoor heated pool when the weather is cool. Reception only open in the mornings 7/5-11/5.

🚗 From Dinard take the D168, then take the D786 and after leaving Notre Dame, signposted after 3 km on the left.

Les-Sables-d'Or-les-Pins

D786

CC

D168

D13 D17 D794 D19 D2

D768

CC € **17** 5/5-10/7 28/8-7/9

🗺 N 48°35'4'' W 2°15'26''

St. Cast-le-Guildo, F-22380 / Bretagne (Côtes-d'Armor)

👫 ♿ 📶 **iD** (1466)

🏰 Le Chatelet★★★★★
🏕 rue des Nouettes
☎ +33 (0)2-96419633
⌚ 16/4 - 14/9
@ lechateletcamping@gmail.com

9ha 105**T**(80-120m²) 8A CEE

1 ACD**G**IJKLM**P**RS
2 AEJK**Q**RTVWXY
3 AB**F**GHJN**OP**RUWY
4 (A 1/7-31/8) (E+H ⌚)
(Q+S 6/5-8/9)
(U+V 16/6-31/8) (Z 6/5-8/9)
5 **AB**CDEFGIJKLMNPQUWXY
Z
6 ACEGH**K**(N 0,8km)ORTV

💬 A lush campsite with beautiful sea views and a unique location. 150m from a fine sandy beach. Large pool with movable roof surrounded by terraces. Fishing lake, friendly clubhouse with bar. Many activities. Pitches are marked out by trees, hedges and bushes.

🚗 D786, first drive to Matignon. Then, D13 to St. Cast-le-Guildo. After the supermarket and garage, turn left direction 'le Port'. Site is clearly signposted. Avoid driving through the centre of St. Cast-le-Guildo.

Saint-Cast-Guildo **CC**

D786 D19

D13

D794 D2

D17 D768

CC € **19** 16/4-7/7 25/8-13/9

🗺 N 48°38'14'' W 2°16'10''

St. Coulomb/La Guimorais, F-35350 / Bretagne (Ille-et-Vilaine)

📶 ✿ **iD** (1467)

🏰 Des Chevrets★★★
☎ +33 (0)2-99890190
⌚ 30/3 - 12/10, 27/10 - 3/11
@ contact@campingdeschevrets.fr

13ha 254**T**(80-100m²) 6A CEE

1 ACD**G**IJKLM**P**RS
2 AEJRSVX
3 ABGHN**Q**RUWY
4 (Q+R+S+T+U ⌚)
(V 30/3-14/10) (X+Y+Z ⌚)
5 **AB**EFGIJKLNPUYZ
6 CEGI**K**(N 2km)OTV

💬 A peaceful, floral campsite with pitches marked out by plants. This site has a unique location: on high dunes with direct access to the beach and lovely views over the bay. There is a good restaurant for gourmets.

🚗 From Cancale via the D201 direction St. Malo. In La Guimorais turn right. The campsite is to the right of the D201 and is clearly signposted.

Saint-Malo D76

D155

CC

CC € **17** 30/3-8/7 26/8-11/10 27/10-2/11

🗺 N 48°41'24'' W 1°56'30''

St. Gildas-de-Rhuys, F-56730 / Bretagne (Morbihan)

🔥 🛜 **iD** 1468

- ⛺ Camping du Menhir★★★★
- ✉ 19 route du clos er bé
- ☎ +33 (0)2-97452288
- 📅 1/5 - 13/9
- @ campingmenhir@aol.com

3ha 121T(90-100m²) 6A

1 ACD**G**IJKLMPRS
2 AGQRVWXY
3 B**F**GHJKL**MQ**RUV
4 (C+H 10/5-16/9) J
   (Q+R+T+U+V 1/7-31/8)
   (X 1/7-10/9) (Z 1/7-31/8)
5 **AB**EFGIJKLMNPUWXYZ
6 ACEGJ(N 3km)TUV

💬 Very quiet, comfortable four-star campsite, especially in low season. Surroundings almost level, sea is nearby in three directions, beach 1 km. Free choice of pitches in low season. Cycling routes nearby. In low season it's not possible to pay by card. Reception closed 12h-14h.

🚗 N165/E60 Vannes-Nantes, exit direction Sarzeau, then via D20 or D780 direction Port Crouesty until the campsite signs direct you to the left.

Séné

Arzon

CC Sarzeau

CC € **15** 1/5-30/6 26/8-12/9

📐 N 47°31'44'' W 2°50'51''

St. Lunaire/Dinard, F-35800 / Bretagne (Ille-et-Vilaine)

🔥 🛜 **iD** 1469

- ⛺ Flower Camping Longchamp★★★★
- ✉ 773 boulevard de Saint Cast
- ☎ +33 (0)2-99463398
- 📅 1/4 - 30/9
- @ contact@
  camping-longchamp.com

4ha 156T(100-120m²) 10A CEE

1 ACD**G**HIJKLMOPQ
2 AEFGLRSWXY
3 ABF**G**HJKNRUWY
4 (C 1/6-6/9) (F+H 📅) IJM
   (Q+R+T+U+V+X+Z 📅)
5 **AB**CEFGJKLMNOPQRUW
6 ACEG**K**(N 0,6km)ORTV

💬 Rural family campsite 150m from the beach. Heated indoor and outdoor aquapark. Spacious pitches. Renovated toilet facilities. 800m from the centre of St. Lunaire. Ideally situated for St Malo, Dinard, Cap Fréhel, Mont St. Michel, Cancale.

🚗 N137 after passing Barrage de la Rance (reservoir) at Dinard take the D168. Turn right before the centre along the coast D786 direction St. Briac. Campsite located just outside the built-up area on the left. Well signposted.

Saint-Malo
CC Dinard

D19

D786 | D168

D768 | D2

D2 B

CC € **17** 1/4-6/7 1/9-29/9

📐 N 48°38'4'' W 2°7'14''

St. Malo, F-35400 / Bretagne (Ille-et-Vilaine)

🛜 **iD** 1470

- ⛺ Domaine de La Ville Huchet★★★★
- ✉ rte de la Passagère
- ☎ +33 (0)2-99811183
- 📅 7/4 - 23/9
- @ info@lavillehuchet.com

6,4ha 102T(100-120m²) 6-10A CEE

1 ACD**G**IJKLMOPRS
2 FGLRTX
3 ABG**K**LN**Q**RU
4 (C 1/6-24/9) (F+H 📅) IJ
   (Q+R+T+U+V 📅)
   (X 1/6-31/8) (Z 📅)
5 **AB**EFGIJKLMNPUWZ
6 ACEGJ**K**(N 2km)OV

💬 You can discover the Brittany region, the ancient city of Intra Muros, Saint-Malo from this friendly, peaceful family camping with its indoor pool (28°C). You will experience unforgettable, natural, culinary and historical richness.

🚗 N137 from Rennes to St. Malo, firstly direction 'centre ville'. At the roundabout exit La Ville Huchet Quelmer, straight ahead at the next roundabout turn 100 metres to the right under the bridge to the campsite.

Saint-Malo
Dinard
CC

D155

D786 | D76

D137 | D4

D766

D2

CC € **17** 7/4-6/7 1/9-22/9

📐 N 48°36'54'' W 1°59'14''

Nic, F-29550 / Bretagne (Finistère)

♿ 🛜 **iD** (1471)

Camping de Menéz Bichen✶✶✶
chemin des Dunes
☎ 📠 +33 (0)2-98265082
🕐 1/4 - 31/10
@ contact@menezbichen.fr

4ha 150**T**

1 ABD**G**IJKLMOQ
2 ACEFKLRVWX
3 ABGJKLNRV**W**Y
4 **KNP**(Q+R 🕐)
　(T+X 1/6-31/8) (Z 🕐)
5 **AB**FGHIJKLMNPQRTUVWZ
6 ABEGJ(N 7km)RTV

💬 Lightly sloping campsite with spacious pitches, located among the dunes close to the beach. Opportunities for surfing, swimming, kayaking, sailing, wellness and spa. A stylish restaurant where the owner himself is at the stove.

🚗 From end of N164 through Châteaulin to D887 (direction Crozon) to St. Nic exit, then follow Plage de Pentrez.

Crozon
D791
D887
CC
D47
D63　D107
Douarnenez
D7

CC € **15** 1/4-7/7　25/8-30/10

🧭 N 48°11'26'' W 4°18'1''

St. Pol-de-Léon, F-29250 / Bretagne (Finistère)

♿ 🛜 ⚙ **iD** (1472)

Ar Kleguer✶✶✶✶
avenue de la Mer
☎ +33 (0)2-98691881
🕐 31/3 - 23/9
@ info@camping-ar-kleguer.com

5,5ha 132**T**(90-120m²) 10A

1 ACD**G**IJLMOPRS
2 AEJKLRVWX
3 BCD**F**GHKMNQRUWY
4 (C 25/6-1/9) (F 🕐)
　(G 20/6-1/9) JL(Q+R 🕐)
　(S+T 1/7-31/8) (Y 🕐)
　(Z 1/7-31/8)
5 **AB**DFGHIJKLMNPQRUW
6 ACEGJ**K**(N 1km)OQRV

💬 Unique location, luxury 4-star campsite with lovely views of the bay of Morlaix and the many islands near St. Pol-de-Léon. Restaurant within walking distance. Spacious modern toilet facilities and a lovely indoor pool. The subtropical plants growing on the site will delight you. 5 km from the lovely town of Roscoff.

🚗 On the D58, take exit St. Pol-de-Léon and follow 'camping' and 'plage' signs. Don't use SatNav from Roscoff or Landivisian.

Saint-Pol-de-
Léon
CC Carantec
D10
D69　D58
D46
D19　D769

CC € **17** 31/3-6/7　27/8-22/9

🧭 N 48°41'26'' W 3°58'3''

St. Pol-de-Léon, F-29250 / Bretagne (Finistère)

♿ 🛜 **iD** (1473)

De Trologot✶✶✶
Grève du Man
☎ +33 (0)2-98690626
🕐 1/5 - 30/9
@ camping-trologot@wanadoo.fr

2,5ha 85**T**(80-100m²) 10A CEE

1 ACD**G**IJKLOPRS
2 AENQRVX
3 BGHRUWY
4 (C+H 10/6-10/9) (Q 1/6-15/9)
　(R+Z 1/7-31/8)
5 **AB**CFGIJKLMNPUVZ
6 EGJ(N 2km)V

💬 A well maintained peaceful campsite with excellent amenities for a pleasant stay on the coast. Close to St. Pol-de-Léon with its cathedral, Île de Batz with exotic gardens and Roscoff with its ferries. Extra service: special pitches outside the campsite for arrival and departure outside reception opening times.

🚗 On D58 take exit St. Pol-de-Léon. Turn SatNav off. Follow 'camping' and 'plage' signs. Then follow 'De Trologot'. Campsite is on the north east of the town.

Roscoff
Saint-Pol-
de-Léon **CC**
D58
D788　D46
D19　D58

CC € **15** 1/5-8/7　26/8-29/9 7=6, 14=12

🧭 N 48°41'36'' W 3°58'10''

St. Quay-Portrieux, F-22410 / Bretagne (Côtes-d'Armor) ♿ 📶 🆔 (1474)

🏕 Bellevue***
📧 68 boulevard du Littoral
☎ +33 (0)2-96704184
📠 +33 (0)2-96705546
🔓 19/4 - 18/9
@ campingbellevue22@orange.fr

4ha 151T(80-120m²) 6A CEE

1 ACD**G**IJKLMPRS
2 AEIJKOQRTVWX
3 B**F**GHNRWY
4 (C+H 1/6-17/9) (Q+R 🔓)
(U 1/7-31/8)
5 **AB**CEFGIJKLMNPUVWXYZ
6 CEGK(N 1km)ORTUV

NEW

💬 Uniquely located terraced site with lovely views of the sea. Swimming pool and toddlers' pool. Close to walks along the coast. St. Quay-Portieux is a lively resort. Sunny grounds with a few trees. Hedges give shelter against the wind. Free wifi.

🚗 From Étables-sur-Mer follow the D786 direction Paimpol, 50 metres after the second roundabout to the right. Exit Centre Ville. Continue straight to the beach and Casino. Turn left then continue straight and follow signs.

D7 D7 D21 CC Étables-sur-Mer D9 D6 D786 Pordic

CC € **17** 19/4-6/7 27/8-17/9 📍 N 48°39'47'' W 2°50'41''

Taden, F-22100 / Bretagne (Côtes-d'Armor) ♿ 📶 🆔 (1475)

🏕 La Hallerais****
📧 4 rue de la Robardais
☎ +33 (0)2-96391593
📠 +33 (0)2-96399464
🔓 10/3 - 11/11
@ contact@
camping-lahallerais.com

7ha 100T(84-133m²) 10A CEE

1 ACGIJLPQ
2 CFJRUVXY
3 BGHJKLMNOPQRUVW
4 (C+H 1/6-15/9)
(Q+R+T+U+X 15/3-1/11)
(Z 🔓)
5 **AB**DGIJKLMNOPRUXYZ
6 CDEGHIJ(N 0,5km)OTV

💬 Well-maintained campsite, consisting of different small terraced meadows. The campsite is located on the top of the banks of the Rance. Fishing possible. Pitches with hedges or bushes and trees.

🚗 N176 Dol-de-Bretagne - Dinan, exit D12 Taden. Campsite signposted from exit. Site is south of Taden.

Créhen Plerguer D2 D57 D29 D794 D137 CC Dinan D766

CC € **15** 10/3-18/5 1/6-15/6 1/9-10/11 📍 N 48°28'19'' W 2°1'24''

Telgruc-sur-Mer, F-29560 / Bretagne (Finistère) ♿ 📶 🆔 (1476)

🏕 Armorique****
📧 112 rue de la Plage
☎ +33 (0)2-98277733
🔓 1/4 - 30/9
@ contact@campingarmorique.com

3ha 100T(80-120m²) 10A CEE

1 ACD**G**IJKLPQ
2 AJKLQRVWXY
3 BGHJRU
4 (C 15/5-15/9) (H 15/6-30/9) J
(Q 15/6-30/9) (R 🔓)
(T+U 1/7-31/8) (Z 🔓)
5 **AB**FGIJKLMNOPUWZ
6 ACEGIJ(N 0,7km)OTV

💬 Very peaceful terraced campsite with heated swimming pool (± 27°C), children's pool and water slide (12 metres) with unique views over the bay of Douarnenez. Sandy beaches within 700 metres. The campsite is run by an enthusiastic couple with a passion for hygiene (toilets cleaned 3 times a day). Park-like entrance. In the centre of unspoiled scenery. The campsite is easily accessible.

🚗 D887 from Châteaulin to Crozon. Campsite is clearly marked in Telgruc.

N165 Crozon Telgruc-sur-Mer D791 CC D887 D47 D63

CC € **15** 1/4-7/7 25/8-29/9 7=6 📍 N 48°13'32'' W 4°22'17''

Telgruc-sur-Mer, F-29560 / Bretagne (Finistère)   ♿ 🛜 ✿ **iD** (1477)

🏕 Sites & Paysages Le Panoramic★★★★
✉ 130 route de la Plage le Penker
☎ +33 (0)2-98277841
📠 +33 (0)2-98273610
🗓 1/5 - 16/9
@ info@camping-panoramic.com
4ha 127**T**(100-160m²) 10A CEE

1 ACD**G**IJKLMPQ
2 JKRTVX
3 BGHJK**M**RU
4 (C+H 1/6-15/9) K
  (Q 1/7-30/8) (R+T 1/7-31/8)
  (U+V+X+Y 🗓) (Z 1/7-31/8)
5 **AB**FGJLNOPUVWXYZ
6 ACDEGIJ(N 1,5km)ORV

💬 A peaceful family campsite with plenty of privacy. Views of Douarnenez Bay in the middle of the regional nature park of Armorique. 500 metres from a lovely sandy beach. Plenty of opportunities for taking walks. The heated swimming pool is open from 1 June.

🚗 From Châteaulin, the D887, direction Crozon. In Telgruc continue straight ahead. The campsite is signposted.

N165 · Crozon · Telgruc-sur-Mer · **CC** D887 · D791 · D47 · D63

CC €**15** 1/5-7/7 25/8-15/9 7=6   📶 N 48°13'25'' W 4°22'21''

Tinténiac, F-35190 / Bretagne (Ille-et-Vilaine)   ♿ 🛜 **iD** (1478)

🏕 Domaine Les Peupliers★★★
✉ 21, La Besnelais
☎ +33 (0)2-99454975
🗓 1/4 - 1/10
@ contact@domainelespeupliers.fr

5ha 36**T**(100-130m²) 6A CEE

1 AC**G**IJLPQ
2 CFLRVWX
3 BGJMN**O**RUW
4 (C 15/6-15/9) (Q 15/4-15/9)
  (R+S 🗓) (U 15/5-15/9)
  (X+Y+Z 🗓)
5 **AB**GIJKLMNOPUW
6 CEG**K**(N 2km)OTUV

💬 A family campsite in a natural area of 5 hectares in the middle of a 16th century estate. Close to Rennes, St. Malo, Mont St. Michel. Ideal for families and senior citizens. Opportunities for walking (canal d'Ille et Rance), fishing and various trips out. Lake, swimming pool, tennis courts, various games and pitch & putt golf. Large pitches screened by hedges.

🚗 N137 Rennes-Dinard/St. Malo, exit Hédé/ Tinténiàc. Campsite is south of Tinténiàc.

Combourg · D794 · D2 · D795 · D137 · D68 · D20 · **CC** · D70 · D27 · D21 · D72 · Gévezé · Melesse

CC €**17** 1/4-6/7 26/8-30/9 7=6, 14=12   📶 N 48°18'34'' W 1°49'19''

Trédrez, F-22300 / Bretagne (Côtes-d'Armor)   👫 ♿ 🛜 **iD** (1479)

🏕 Flower Camping Les Capucines★★★★
✉ Ancienne Voie Romaine Kervourdon
☎ +33 (0)2-96357228
🗓 31/3 - 29/9
@ les.capucines@wanadoo.fr
4ha 89**T**(90-130m²) 10A CEE

1 ACD**G**IJKLMOPRS
2 AIJKLQRVWXY
3 BC**D**F**G**HJKLM**N**QRU
4 (D+H 🗓) J(Q 15/4-15/9)
  (R+U 🗓) (Z 15/4-15/9)
5 **AB**DEFGHIJKLMNOPUWXY
6 ACGIJ**K**(N 1km)RV

💬 A peaceful campsite with new owners. Locquémeau fishing village is worth a visit. Spacious pitches (comfort pitches without supplement) on parkland with beautiful views. On GR 34 walking route. Lovely heated indoor pool with a sliding roof.

🚗 From Lannion direction Morlaix D786. At Trédrez-Locquémeau intersection turn right then turn left three times. Follow signs.

Pleumeur-Bodou · Lannion · **CC** · D767 · D56 · D786 · D42 · D30 · D64 · D32 · D11

CC €**17** 31/3-7/7 25/8-28/9 7=6   📶 N 48°41'34'' W 3°33'26''

Trélévern, F-22660 / Bretagne (Côtes-d'Armor) ♿ 🛜 iD 1480

🏕 Camping RCN Port l'Épine***
✉ 10 Venelle de Pors Garo
☎ +31 034-3745090
🗓 20/4 - 24/9
@ reserveringen@rcn.nl

3ha 115T(80-150m²) 16A CEE

1 ACD**F**IJKL**P**ST
2 EKNQRSVWX
3 BGHRWY
4 (A 1/5-1/7)
(C+H+Q+T+U+X 🔑)
5 **AB**FGIJKLMNOPUWXYZ
6 CDEGHK(N 2km)

💬 Beautiful small campsite, situated on a promontory. The south of the site has beautiful views over the sea to the resort of Perros-Guirec. On the north side is a beach with views of seven islands. The level grass pitches are separated by hedges and trees. Wifi throughout the campsite free on one device.

🚗 From D6, towards Trélévern (+/- 5km), then follow signs to campsite and Port l'Epine. At carpark at seaside, left into dead end road. This ends at campsite.

Perros-Guirec CC
D788
D65 D11 D6 D8
D786
Lannion D33

CC € 15 20/4-7/7 25/8-23/9 📍 N 48°48'47'' W 3°23'9''

Trélévern, F-22660 / Bretagne (Côtes-d'Armor) 🧑‍🧑‍🧒 ♿ 🛜 iD 1481

🏕 Seasonova Les 7 Iles***
✉ Port L'Epine
☎ +33 (0)2-96917311
🗓 30/3 - 12/10
@ contact@camping-trelevern.com

2,8ha 127T(80-140m²) 10A CEE

1 ACD**G**IJKLMPQ
2 AEKLNORSTVW
3 AGHRUWY
4 (F+H+Q+R+T+U+Y+Z 🔑)
5 **AB**GJLMNPUVZ
6 ACEGHJ**K**(N 3km)V

💬 This long campsite is located directly on the coast and has a beautiful view over the 'Les 7 Îles' island group. The Côte le Granit Rose and Perros Guirec are nearby. The campsite has its own restaurant with fish specialities.

🚗 From Lannion dir. Trélévern via D38. In Trélévern follow signs Le Palud or Port L'Epine until the beach.

Perros-Guirec
D788
CC
D65 D11 D6 D8
Lannion D786
D33

CC € 15 1/4-6/7 26/8-11/10 7=6 📍 N 48°48'54'' W 3°22'59''

Vannes, F-56000 / Bretagne (Morbihan) ♿ 🛜 iD 1482

🏕 Flower Camping Le Conleau****
✉ 188 avenue Maréchal Juin
☎ +33 (0)2-97631388
🗓 30/3 - 30/9
@ camping.conleau@
flowercampings.com

5ha 104T(80-150m²) 6A CEE

1 ACD**G**IJKLMO**P**RS
2 AEFGIKPQRUVWXYZ
3 **B**FGHJKRUW
4 (E+H+Q+R+T+U+V+X 🔑)
(Z 1/5-15/9)
5 **ABC**DEFGHIJKLMNPUVWX
YZ
6 ACDEGIK(N 1km)TV

💬 Typical beach campsite near the sea with well-equipped toilet facilities. Choice of pitches with plenty of sun or shade. 2 km to historical city centre. 500m from a landscaped swimming lake with sea water and a small beach. Cycling and walking routes right by the entrance. Reception hours (low season): 9:00-12:00 and 14:30-18:30.

🚗 N165/E60 Nantes-Lorient exit Vannes Ouest/ Arradon. Then Vannes Centre and follow camping signs, each roundabout has a 'Le Conleau' sign.

D17 D779
D19
Ploeren N166
Vannes
CC Theix D7
D780
D20

CC € 17 30/3-6/7 25/8-29/9 7=6 📍 N 47°38'0'' W 2°46'48''

Allonnes, F-49650 / Pays de la Loire (Maine-et-Loire) ♿ 🛜 📱iD (1483)

🏕 Le Pô Doré****
✉ 51 route de Pô
☎ +33 (0)2-41387880
🗓 15/3 - 15/11
@ camping-lepodore@orange.fr

2,5ha 51T(100-120m²) 6-10A CEE

1 ACGIJKLMPQ
2 FGLRTVWXY
3 BDGHJNRUW
4 (B 15/5-15/9) (Q 1/7-31/8)
(R 🗓) (T+U+V 1/7-31/8)
(Z 🗓)
5 ABDFGIJKLMNOPUZ
6 ACEGIK(N 4km)TV

💬 A charming and quiet campsite with an unusually landscaped swimming lake and a sandy beach. Located in the countryside yet close to the Loire Valley with all its attractions.

🚐 From Saumur drive towards Allonnes, D10. Follow signs 1 km from the centre of Allonnes.

Longué-Jumelles · D53 · D347 · D767 · D952 · D751 · A85 · Bourgueil · D947 · Saumur · D7

CC € 15 15/3-14/7 1/9-14/11 7=6 | 🧭 N 47°17'57'' W 0°0'45''

Ambrières-les-Vallées, F-53300 / Pays de la Loire (Mayenne) 🛜 📱iD (1484)

🏕 Flower Camping Le Parc de Vaux***
✉ 35 rue des Colverts
☎ +33 (0)2-43049025
🗓 13/4 - 30/9
@ contact@parcdevaux.com

3,5ha 76T(80-110m²) 10A

1 ACDGJLMOPQ
2 CDGIJLRVWXY
3 ABGHJMNOPQRUWX
4 (A 1/7-31/8) (C+H 5/6-12/9) J
(Q+S 🗓)
(T+U+V+X+Z 1/7-31/8)
5 ABGIJKLMNOPQUWXYZ
6 ACEGJ(N 0,5km)ORV

💬 A small quiet campsite with pitches marked out by hedges on the banks of a river. The site forms part of a recreational park. Various sports facilities such as kayaking, pedal boats, tennis, swimming and mountain biking.

🚐 The campsite is located 2 km south of Ambrières-les-Vallées on the D23 from Domfront to Mayenne.

D962 · D117 · D33 Ambrières-les-Vallées · D5 · D34 · N12 · D23 · Mayenne · D113

CC € 15 13/4-6/7 25/8-29/9 7=6, 14=12, 21=18 | 🧭 N 48°23'31'' W 0°37'1''

Angers, F-49000 / Pays de la Loire (Maine-et-Loire) ♿ 🛜 📱iD (1485)

🏕 Camping d'Angers-Lac de Maine****
✉ avenue du Lac de Maine
☎ +33 (0)2-41730503
🗓 23/3 - 28/10
@ info@campingangers.com

4ha 146T(67-136m²) 10A CEE

1 ACDGIJKLMOPQ
2 ADFGLRTVWXY
3 BGHJNRWZ
4 (C 1/5-15/9) K(Q 25/3-10/10)
(V+Z 1/7-2/9)
5 ABDEFGIJKLMNOPQUWXYZ
6 CEGIJ(N 2km)TV

💬 In the heart of the Anjou in an unusual location: close to a famous historical town in the heart of 100 hectare area abundant in water. 1 hour from famous tourist towns, surrounded by renowned vineyards. Area of good living, gastronomy, heritage and a lovely climate. Recreation ground. Offers opportunities for sailing, swimming, swing golf, fishing. Bus stops 300m from the campsite.

🚐 Clearly signposted in Angers. Via Lac de Maine.

Montreuil-Juigné · D323 · A11 · Angers · D111 · D4 · D751 · A87 · D748

CC € 15 23/3-5/7 26/8-27/10 | 🧭 N 47°27'17'' W 0°35'47''

Assérac, F-44410 / Pays de la Loire (Loire-Atlantique) 👪 ♿ 📶 iD (1486)

🏕 Camping Du Domaine De Pont Mahé***
📧 rue Pont-Mahé 13
☎ +33 (0)2-40017498
📠 +33 (0)2-51102057
🔓 31/3 - 13/10
@ contact@pont-mahe.com

1,5ha 34T(90-120m²) 10A CEE

1 ACD**G**IJKLMOPRS
2 ABEGQRVWX
3 AGHJRUWY
4 (E+H+Q+R 🔓)
　(T+U+V 2/7-31/8) (Z 🔓)
5 **AB**FGIJLMNPUZ
6 ADEGKTV

💬 Small family campsite near the sea with pitches separated by hedges and well-maintained toilet facilities. The pitches behind the toilet block are quieter. Special coast with bay that you can walk across during low tide. Reception closed from 13:00 to 14:00.

🚗 N165 Nantes-Lorient exit La Roche Bernard, direction Guérande as far as Assérac. In the centre drive towards Pont-Mahe. Campsite is located on the right in the centre of this small village.

Damgan · La Porte-Garel

D34
D315
CC
D83
D33
D774

CC € **13** 31/3-6/7 1/9-12/10
🗺 N 47°26'50'' W 2°27'0''

Assérac, F-44410 / Pays de la Loire (Loire-Atlantique) 👪 ♿ 📶 iD (1487)

🏕 De la Baie***
📧 Keravelo Pen Bé
☎ +33 (0)2-40017116
🔓 31/3 - 30/9
@ contact@camping-delabaie.com

3ha 33T(80-100m²) 10A CEE

1 ACD**G**IJKLMOP
2 AEOQRVWX
3 BGHJN**P**RUWY
4 (C+H 1/5-16/9)
　(Q+R 1/5-2/9)
　(T+U+V+Z 7/7-2/9)
5 **AB**FGIJLMNPUVZ
6 ACDEG**K**(N 7km)OTV

💬 Quiet natural campsite close to the sea, homely atmosphere. Pitches with shade by the entrance next to the pool. Very sunny pitches around the toilet blocks. Lovely footpath along the bay which is dry in low tide. Indoor swimming pool and renovated toilet facilities in 2018.

🚗 E60/N165 Vannes-Nantes exit 15 and via D774 to Herbignac, roundabout by Super U take D33 to Assérac. Roundabout by church take Pen Bé D82, follow Pen Bé and campsite signs.

La Roche-Bernard
D34
D315
CC D83
D774
Guérande

CC € **15** 31/3-6/7 25/8-29/9 7=6, 14=12, 21=18
🗺 N 47°25'24'' W 2°26'46''

Assérac, F-44410 / Pays de la Loire (Loire-Atlantique) ♿ 📶 iD (1488)

🏕 Le Moulin de l'Eclis****
📧 5 bis rue de la Plage, Pont Mahé
☎ +33 (0)2-40017669
📠 +33 (0)2-40017775
🔓 1/4 - 4/11
@ info@camping-leclis.com

3,8ha 79T(90-140m²) 16A CEE

1 ACD**G**IJKLMPST
2 AEGKQRVWXY
3 AGHJKN**P**RUWY
4 (C 15/5-9/9)
　(D+H 15/4-31/10) IJ**KLP**
　(Q+S 🔓)
　(T+U+V+X+Z 2/7-25/8)
5 **AB**CDEFGHIJKLMNOPQRU
　WXYZ
6 ACEGHI**K**(N 5km)TV

💬 Pleasant site with covered and open pools. Beach. Some pitches have sea views. Shellfish can be dug from the sand. Good cycling and walking. Luxurious toilet facilities with Eco label. Kite surfing centre. Good restaurant. Reception closed 12:00-14:00. Wifi free out of season.

🚗 N165/E60 Nantes-Vannes, after La Roche-Bernard dir. Guérande/La Baule as far as Herbignac, then to Assérac. In centre at roundabout (with houses in middle) dir. Pont-Mahé and follow signs.

N165
D139
D34
D83
CC Herbignac
D33
Saint-Lyphard
La Turballe · D774 · D47

CC € **17** 1/4-3/5 22/5-6/7 3/9-3/11
🗺 N 47°26'41'' W 2°27'2''

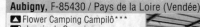

Aubigny, F-85430 / Pays de la Loire (Vendée)

♿ 🛜 iD **1489**

🏕 Flower Camping Campilô***
✉ chemin de Camping
☎ +33 (0)2-51316845
🗓 23/3 - 4/11
@ accueil@campilo.com

16ha 42T 16A CEE

1 A**G**IJKLMNOPST
2 DFLMRVXY
3 AGHJKN**Q**RW
4 (E 1/4-3/11)
(Q+R+T+U+V 1/7-31/8)
(Z 🗓)
5 **AB**CGIJKLMNOPUX
6 ACDEGK(N 3km)ORT

💬 A lovely new campsite in the countryside next to two lakes in the heart of the Vendée. Large fishing lake (carp/minnow/pike).

🚗 From La Roche-sur-Yon take A87 towards Les Sable d'Olonne; exit 32. Follow signs in Aubigny.

D978
D57
La Roche-sur-Yon
A87
CC
D12
D747 D746
D36
D4

CC € **17** 23/3-7/7 25/8-3/11

📍 N 46°37'22'' W 1°27'18''

Avrillé, F-85440 / Pays de la Loire (Vendée)

👫 🛜 iD **1490**

🏕 Flower Camping Beauchêne***
✉ avenue de Lattre de Tassigny
☎ +33 (0)2-51223049
🗓 1/4 - 30/9
@ contact@
campinglebeauchene.com

2,5ha 30T(80-120m²) 10A CEE

1 ACD**G**IJKL**P**RS
2 DRVWXY
3 BDGHJKNRUW
4 (E+H+Q+R 🗓)
(T+U+V+Z 1/7-31/8)
5 **A**FGIJKLMNPUVXZ
6 ACEG**K**(N 0,5km)RTV

💬 A peaceful, friendly campsite with a homely atmosphere and spacious pitches in natural surroundings. Fishing lake free of charge. A good starting point for cycling and walking tours.

🚗 Signposted from Avrillé.

D36
D21 D4 D12
D19
Talmont-Saint-
Hilaire
D949 CC
Longeville-sur-Mer
D46
D105 D747

CC € **13** 1/4-6/7 25/8-29/9 7=6, 14=12

📍 N 46°28'12'' W 1°29'13''

Barbâtre, F-85630 / Pays de la Loire (Vendée)

♿ 🛜 iD **1491**

🏕 Sandaya Domaine Le Midi****
✉ rue du Camping
☎ +33 (0)676082417
🗓 13/4 - 23/9
@ midi@originalcamping.com

13ha 207T(80-200m²) 16A CEE

1 ACD**G**IJKLMOPST
2 ABEIRSVWXY
3 ABGHJKMNQRWY
4 (C+F+H 🗓)
(Q+R+S+T 1/7-31/8)
5 **AB**EFGIJKLMNOPUZ
6 ACEGI**K**(N 0,5km)V

💬 This lovely campsite in the dunes has direct access to the beach and has an indoor and an outdoor pool, tennis court and a multi-sports pitch. In the vicinity you will find many beautiful sandy beaches and cycle routes. Various historic towns and villages in the area.

🚗 Dir. Noirmoutier. Left on 3rd roundabout after bridge. Follow signs to 'Du Midi' campsite.

Noirmoutier-en-
l'Île
D948
CC
D758
D38 D51 D59

CC € **17** 13/4-6/7 26/8-22/9

📍 N 46°56'43'' W 2°11'7''

Batz-sur-Mer, F-44740 / Pays de la Loire (Loire-Atlantique) ♿ 🛜 iD (1492)

🔺 Flower Camping Les Paludiers***
📧 rue Nicolas Appert
☎ +33 (0)2-40601728
🔛 30/3 - 30/9
@ paludiers@flowercampings.com

8ha 120T(80-120m²) 10A CEE

1 ACD**G**IJKLMO**P**RS
2 AEGQRSVWXY
3 BF**G**HJKN**Q**RUWY
4 (A 3/7-26/8) (C 1/7-2/9)
(E+G 🔛) I(Q 🔛)
(R 1/7-31/8)
(T+U+V+X+Z 🔛)
5 **AB**DEFGJLMNOPQRUVW
6 ACDEGK(N 1,5km)ORTUV

💬 Located on a neck of land about 500m wide on a headland, close to La Baule. Pitches separated by hedges and just 100m from a lovely sandy beach. Cycling to La Baule, St. Nazaire or Guérande. A trip through salt marshes on car-free roads is possible. Reception closed 12:00-15:00.

🚗 Nantes-Lorient N165, via N171 dir. St. Nazaire. Then follow Guérande, before Guérande turn onto the D774 at roundabout to Le Croisic and Batz-sur-Mer, then turn left just past Batz village.

D774 D47
D45 CC **La Baule-Escoublac**

CC €**17** 31/3-6/7 25/8-29/9 7=6

📡 N 47°16'42'' W 2°29'31''

Brain-sur-l'Authion, F-49800 / Pays de la Loire (Maine-et-Loire) ♿ 🛜 iD (1493)

🔺 Flower Camping Du Port Caroline***
📧 rue du Pont Caroline
☎ +33 (0)2-41804218
🔛 1/4 - 30/9
@ info@campingduportcaroline.fr

3,2ha 67T(110-200m²) 10A CEE

1 ACD**G**IJKLMPST
2 CFGRVWXY
3 ABDGHJKRU**W**
4 (F+H 🔛) (Q 15/6-31/8)
(R 🔛) (T+U+V+Z 15/6-31/8)
5 **AB**DEFGIJKLMNOPQUVWX
YZ
6 ACEGJ**K**(N 2km)TV

💬 Quiet campsite, 3 km from the Loire. There is a lovely heated indoor pool with removable sides. Located between Angers and Saumur. Many walking and cycling paths.

🚗 From Angers A87, exit 17, then follow signs.

Angers A11 D74
A85
Trélazé CC
Les Ponts-de-Cé
A87 D952
D751

CC €**15** 1/4-8/7 26/8-29/9 7=6, 14=11

📡 N 47°26'36'' W 0°24'31''

Brem-sur-Mer, F-85470 / Pays de la Loire (Vendée) ♿ 🛜 iD (1494)

🔺 L'Océan****
📧 rue des Gabelous
☎ 📠 +33 (0)2-51905916
🔛 7/4 - 4/11
@ locean@cybelevacances.com

7ha 97T(90-120m²) 16A

1 AC**G**IJKLMPST
2 ARSVX
3 BGHJKNRU**V**W
4 (C+F+H 🔛) IJ**P**
(Q+S+T+U+V+X+Z 🔛)
5 **AB**EFGIJKLMNOPUVWXZ
6 EGH**K**TV

💬 A large, welcoming family campsite, close to the sea. There is a water park of 1000 m² with slides, wellness and a toddler's pool on the campsite. Many activities in the surroundings such a local markets and a climbing park.

🚗 Via D38 from Bretignolles-sur-Mer follow road to Les Sables d'Olonne. In Brem-sur-Mer follow signs.

D6
D12
CC
D80 D32 D160
Olonne-sur-Mer

CC €**17** 14/5-7/7 1/9-3/11

📡 N 46°36'4'' W 1°50'39''

Brem-sur-Mer, F-85470 / Pays de la Loire (Vendée)

🛜 **iD** (1495)

▲ Yelloh! Village Le Chaponnet****
🏠 16 rue du Chaponnet
☎ +33 (0)2-51905556
📠 +33 (0)2-51909167
🕐 14/4 - 15/9
@ contact@le-chaponnet.com

6ha 90T(100-120m²) 10A CEE

1 ACD**F**IJKLMOPS
2 AGRSVWXY
3 ABGHJKMNRUVW
4 (C 1/5-15/9) (F 🕐)
  (H 1/5-15/9) JK**LNP**
  (Q 1/7-31/7)
  (T+U+V+X 1/6-31/8) (Z 🕐)
5 **AB**EFGIJKLMNOPUZ
6 ACEGI**K**(N 0,2km)TV

💬 An attractive well equipped campsite with an international flavour. Lovely swimming pool (also indoors), excellent restaurant and a favourable position by the ocean. This campsite is most pleasant throughout the season.

🚗 D38 from St. Gilles direction Brem, then the one-way street on the right.

Saint-Gilles-Croix-de-Vie

D6 D12 D32 D160 D80 D760 Olonne-sur-Mer D36

CC

CC € **17** 14/4-6/7 2/9-14/9   📍 N 46°36'15'' W 1°49'57''

Brétignolles-sur-Mer, F-85470 / Pays de la Loire (Vendée)

🛜 ✿ **iD** (1496)

▲ La Trévillière****
🏠 rue de Bellevue
☎ +33 (0)2-51330505
📠 +33 (0)2-51339404
🕐 30/3 - 29/9
@ info@chadotel.com

3,2ha 69T(100-130m²) 10A CEE

1 ACD**F**IJKLMOPRS
2 RTVXY
3 BGHJKN**Q**RU
4 (C+E+G 1/5-15/9) J
  (Q 15/5-15/9) (R 1/6-15/9)
  (T+U+V+X+Y 17/5-15/9)
  (Z 🕐)
5 **AB**EFGIJKLMNOPUWYZ
6 ACEG**K**(N 1km)ORTV

💬 A modestly sized campsite with shaded pitches on the edge of the village.

🚗 From St. Gilles-Croix-de-Vie take the D38 in the direction of Brétignolles. Overhead camping sign on bend after 8 km, indicating left.

Saint-Hilaire-de-Riez

D6 D12 CC D32 D160 D80

CC € **15** 30/3-12/7 30/8-28/9   📍 N 46°38'10'' W 1°51'30''

Brissac-Quincé, F-49320 / Pays de la Loire (Maine-et-Loire)

♿ 🛜 ✿ **iD** (1497)

▲ Sites & Paysages de l'Etang****
🏠 route de St. Mathurin
☎ +33 (0)2-41917061
🕐 21/4 - 16/9
@ info@campingetang.com

8ha 115T(120-150m²) 16A CEE

1 ACD**G**IJKLMOPRS
2 CDFLRTVWXY
3 ABD**F**GHJKRUW
4 (B+F+G+Q+R+S 🕐)
  (T+U+X+Z 17/6-31/8)
5 **AB**DEFGIJKLMNOPUWXYZ
6 AEGI**K**(N 1km)RTV

💬 Pleasantly sized campsite with spacious pitches, just right to find peace and quiet. The campsite offers a warm welcome to campers who are looking for a natural camping spot with the comfort necessary for an unforgettable stay in the Loire Valley. Plenty of amenities are available to you: wine tasting, free fishing lake, heated indoor pool, laundry room, sale of bread.

🚗 Take D761 at Brissac-Quincé direction St. Mathurin (D55). Follow signs. Parc de Loisirs.

Les Ponts-de-Cé Trélazé

D952 D751 A87 CC D55 D748 D70 D120 D24 D761 D69

CC € **17** 21/4-30/6 1/9-15/9 7=6, 14=11   📍 N 47°21'34'' W 0°26'4''

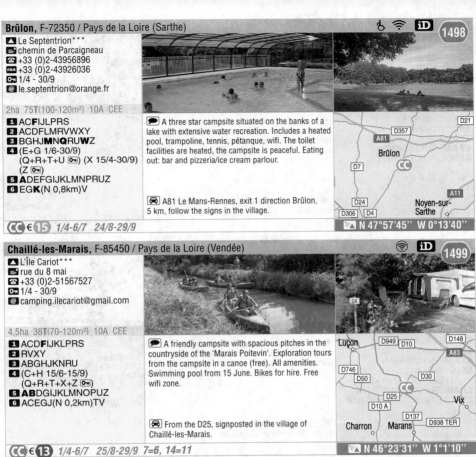

Brûlon, F-72350 / Pays de la Loire (Sarthe) ♿ 🛜 iD (1498)

🔺 Le Septentrion***
📧 chemin de Parcaigneau
☎ +33 (0)2-43956896
📠 +33 (0)2-43926036
🗓 1/4 - 30/9
@ le.septentrion@orange.fr

2ha 75T(100-120m²) 10A CEE

1 ACFIJLPRS
2 ACDFLMRVWXY
3 BGHJMNQRUWZ
4 (E+G 1/6-30/9)
  (Q+R+T+U 🗓) (X 15/4-30/9)
  (Z 🗓)
5 ADEFGIJKLMNPRUZ
6 EGK(N 0,8km)V

💬 A three star campsite situated on the banks of a lake with extensive water recreation. Includes a heated pool, trampoline, tennis, pétanque, wifi. The toilet facilities are heated, the campsite is peaceful. Eating out: bar and pizzeria/ice cream parlour.

🚗 A81 Le Mans-Rennes, exit 1 direction Brûlon, 5 km, follow the signs in the village.

CC € 15 1/4-6/7 24/8-29/9

📍 N 47°57'45'' W 0°13'40''

Chaillé-les-Marais, F-85450 / Pays de la Loire (Vendée) 🛜 iD (1499)

🔺 L'Île Cariot***
📧 rue du 8 mai
☎ +33 (0)2-51567527
🗓 1/4 - 30/9
@ camping.ilecariot@gmail.com

4,5ha 38T(70-120m²) 10A CEE

1 ACDFIJKLPRS
2 RVXY
3 ABGHJKNRU
4 (C+H 15/6-15/9)
  (Q+R+T+X+Z 🗓)
5 ABDGIJKLMNOPUZ
6 ACEGJ(N 0,2km)TV

💬 A friendly campsite with spacious pitches in the countryside of the 'Marais Poitevin'. Exploration tours from the campsite in a canoe (free). All amenities. Swimming pool from 15 June. Bikes for hire. Free wifi zone.

🚗 From the D25, signposted in the village of Chaillé-les-Marais.

CC € 13 1/4-6/7 25/8-29/9 7=6, 14=11

📍 N 46°23'31'' W 1°1'10''

Chalonnes-sur-Loire, F-49290 / Pays de la Loire (Maine-et-Loire) ♿ 🛜 iD (1500)

🔺 Les Portes de la Loire***
📧 route de Rochefort
☎ +33 (0)2-41780227
🗓 30/4 - 30/9
@ contact@
  campinglesportesdelaloire.fr

3ha 95T(60-80m²) 10A CEE

1 AGIJKLRS
2 CRWXY
3 JR
4 (Q 🗓)
5 AEFIJMNOPU
6 ACFJ(N 1km)

💬 Campsite located between the Loire and route D751 with lots of traffic. Near the Val de Loire bicycle routes. Good base for visiting the town of Angers and the Loire chateaux. Possible to visit vineyards and cellars with a tourist train. Beautiful area for walking. Canoe rental within 900 metres.

🚗 From Angers via D751 to Chalonnes-sur-Loire. Clearly signposted.

CC € 15 30/4-30/6 1/9-29/9

📍 N 47°21'3'' W 0°44'57''

Clisson, F-44190 / Pays de la Loire (Loire-Atlantique)

👫 ♿ 🛜 ✿ **iD** (1501)

🔺 Le Moulin***
🛏 route de Nantes
☎ +33 (0)2-40544448
📅 1/4 - 21/10
@ camping@clissonsevremaine.fr

1,8ha 51T(85-110m²) 10A CEE

1 ABCD**G**IJKLPST
2 CILRTUVWXY
3 ABGHR
5 **AB**DFIJKLMNOPW
6 BDEJK(N 0,2km)TV

💬 In the heart of the Muscadet vineyards, 20 minutes from Nantes, this campsite will welcome you near the historic centre of Clisson.

🚗 In Clisson, direction Clisson centre Zones d'activités.

Map: Vertou, Gesté, D37, D756, D74, D59, D149, CC, A83, D137, D762, D755, D7, D54, D763, Tiffauges

CC € (15) 1/4-10/6 27/6-6/7 27/8-20/10

📡 N 47°5'45'' W 1°17'2''

Coëx, F-85220 / Pays de la Loire (Vendée)

🛜 **iD** (1502)

🔺 Camping RCN La Ferme du Latois****
🛏 D40
☎ +31 034-3745090
📠 +33 (0)2-51600214
📅 6/4 - 24/9
@ reserveringen@rcn.nl

21ha 164T(110-250m²) 6-16A CEE

1 AC**F**IJKLMOPQ
2 DLRVWXY
3 ABF**GHJK**N**P**RUW
4 (A 1/6-31/8) (C+H 🔒) J (Q+S+T+U+V+X+Y+Z 🔒)
5 **AB**EFGIJKLMNOPRUWZ
6 ACDEGH**K**(N 1,5km)OTUV

💬 A lovely farm campsite with very varied vegetation and a pond. Large pitches and lovely fields with ample privacy.

🚗 Coëx, take the D40 in the direction of Brétignolles-sur-Mer. Signposted.

Map: D754, Saint-Gilles-Croix-de-Vie, Aizenay, D6, CC, D12, D978, D32, D57, D160

CC € (15) 6/4-7/7 25/8-23/9

📡 N 46°40'36'' W 1°46'8''

Concourson-sur-Layon, F-49700 / Pays de la Loire (Maine-et-Loire)

♿ 🛜 **iD** (1503)

🔺 La Vallée des Vignes****
🛏 La Croix Patron
☎ +33 (0)2-41598635
📅 1/4 - 30/9
@ info@campingvdv.com

3,5ha 71T(100-200m²) 10A CEE

1 ACD**G**IJKLMPST
2 CGLRTVWXY
3 ABGJNQRU**W**
4 (C+H 15/5-15/9) (Q+R+T+U+V+X+Z 🔒)
5 **AB**FGIJKLMNPUWXYZ
6 EGJ(N 5km)OV

💬 New young French owners have created a warm, welcoming atmosphere. Campsite located between Angers and Saumur, surrounded by vineyards and on the river Layon. Spacious pitches with plenty of greenery. Free heated pool and wifi.

🚗 Campsite located just outside Concourson on the D960 direction Cholet. Well signposted.

Map: D24, D70, D70E, D84, Doué-la-Fontaine, D748, CC, D960, D761, D69, Bouillé-Loretz, D87

CC € (15) 1/4-6/7 25/8-29/9 7=6, 14=12

📡 N 47°10'27'' W 0°20'51''

Damvix, F-85420 / Pays de la Loire (Vendée)

♵ 📶 **iD** （1504）

🏕 Camping des Conches***
✉ route du Grand Port
☎ +33 (0)2-51871706
🔓 1/4 - 15/10
@ campingdesconches@orange.fr

2,1ha 72T(80-120m²) 10A CEE

1 ACD**G**IJKLMPQ
2 CLRVXY
3 BGHIJKMR**W**
4 (C 15/5-15/9) (T+U+Z 🔓)
5 **A**FGHIJKLMNOPUVZ
6 ACEG**K**(N 0,3km)TV

💬 A friendly campsite, quietly located in 'Marais de Poitevin' in the peaceful village of Damvix. Ideal for cycling and trips out in the surrounding area.

🚗 From Fontenay-le-Comte direction Niort. Then direction Maillezais, then to Damvix. Campsite signposted in Damvix village.

D938 TER   D148   A83
D15   D25   D1
D116
D3
Saint-Sauveur-d'Aunis   D114

CC € ⑮ 1/4-29/6 1/9-14/10   📐 N 46°18'46'' W 0°43'57''

Durtal, F-49430 / Pays de la Loire (Maine-et-Loire)

♵ 📶 **iD** （1505）

🏕 Les Portes de l'Anjou***
✉ 9 rue du Camping
☎ +33 (0)2-41763180
🔓 30/3 - 12/10
@ contact-camping@
   lesportesdelanjou.com

3ha 88T(80-120m²) 10A CEE

1 AC**F**IJLPRS
2 CFGLRTVWXY
3 BGHJNRU**W**
4 (C+H+Q 1/7-31/8) (R 🔓)
   (T+U 1/6-8/9) (V 1/6-15/9)
   (Z 🔓)
5 **AB**FGIJKLMNPUWZ
6 CEG**K**(N 0,5km)RV

💬 Easy-going, well-kept small campsite on the banks of the Loir with large pitches, marked out by hedges in wooded surroundings. A paradise for anglers. Near a picturesque village with an imposing castle belonging to the dukes of Anjou. 5 minutes' walking distance from the shopping centre.

🚗 On the A11 take exit 11 Durtal, continue on the RD 859, right on the last roundabout to Durtal. Here, follow campsite signs.

D24   D23   D306
D859   D59
D308
D323 A11   D18   D938
Seiches-sur-le-Loir

CC € ⑬ 30/3-6/7 24/8-11/10 7=6   📐 N 47°40'16'' W 0°14'9''

Givrand/St.Gilles-Croix-de-Vie, F-85800 / Pays de la Loire (Vendée)

♵ 📶 **iD** （1506）

🏕 Le Domaine de Beaulieu****
✉ rue du Parc - Givrand
☎ +33 (0)2-51330505
📠 +33 (0)2-51339404
🔓 30/3 - 29/9
@ info@chadotel.com

8ha 127T(100-125m²) 6A CEE

1 AC**G**IJKLMOPRS
2 GRTVWX
3 B**F**GHJKM**N**QRU**W**
4 (C 10/5-20/9) (F 13/4-20/9)
   (H 10/5-20/9) J(Q 15/6-31/8)
   (S+T+U+V+X+Y 1/6-10/9)
   (Z 🔓)
5 **AB**FGIJKLMNOPUZ
6 AEG**JK**(N 3km)ORTV

💬 Good campsite on fine, green, maintained level grounds. The swimming pool and restaurant are the main features of this peaceful campsite.

🚗 From St. Gilles-Croix-de-Vie: D38 direction Les Sables-d'Olonne. Located to the left after 3 km.

D38   D69   D94
Saint-Hilaire-de-Riez   D754
D6
D12
D32

CC € ⑮ 30/3-12/7 30/8-28/9   📐 N 46°40'16'' W 1°54'13''

Guémené-Penfao, F-44290 / Pays de la Loire (Loire-Atlantique) 🛜 iD 1507

🏕 Flower Camping L'Hermitage***
✉ 46 avenue du Paradis
☎ +33 (0)2-40792348
⌛ 1/4 - 15/10
@ camping.hermitage@orange.fr

2,8ha 55T(36-70m²) 6A CEE

1 AGIJKLPST
2 BCGRTVXY
3 AGHJMNRUW
4 (A 1/7-31/8) (C 15/6-20/9)
(H 1/7-31/8) J(Q 🔒)
(R+T+U+V 1/7-31/8) (Z 🔒)
5 AGHIJKLMNPUZ
6 CEGJ(N 0,8km)OV

💬 A pleasant and informal campsite in natural surroundings with three rivers.

🚗 Redon-Châteaubriant, exit Guémené-Penfao. Campsite signposted.

[Map: D59, N137, D15, Derval, D775, Guémené-Penfao, D124, D3, D164, Nozay, Plessé, D2]

CC € 15 1/4-7/7 25/8-14/10 7=6 📷 N 47°37'33'' W 1°49'8''

Guérande, F-44350 / Pays de la Loire (Loire-Atlantique) 🚿 ♿ 🛜 iD 1508

🏕 Camping La Fontaine***
✉ rte de Saint Molf -D233-Kersavary
☎ +33 (0)2-40249619
⌛ 14/4 - 30/9
@ lafontaine.guerande@orange.fr

2,5ha 80T(100-150m²) 8-10A CEE

1 ACDGIJKLMOPQ
2 FGQRVWXY
3 AGHJR
4 (C+H 15/6-15/9)
(Q+T+Z 1/7-31/8)
5 ABEFGIJKLMNOPQRUWXYZ
6 AEK(N 2km)OT

💬 A campsite in the countryside. Pitches min. 100 m², in the sun or half-shaded. Comfortable, modern toilet facilities but not sheltered from the wind, heated swimming pools 100 m². Well located for visits to historic Guérande and nearby salt marshes. Reception closed from 12:30 to 14:30.

🚗 Nantes E60 and N171 direction St. Nazaire, N171 direction Guérande. Then past several roundabouts to Vannes, then D233 direction St. Molf, camping signs after 500m.

[Map: D83, D33, D774, D47, D45, La Baule-Escoublac]

CC € 13 14/4-6/7 25/8-29/9 📷 N 47°20'57'' W 2°26'3''

Guérande, F-44350 / Pays de la Loire (Loire-Atlantique) 👫 ♿ 🛜 iD 1509

🏕 Domaine de Léveno****
✉ Lieu dit Léveno
☎ +33 (0)2-40247930
📠 +33 (0)2-40620123
⌛ 7/4 - 23/9
@ domaine.leveno@wanadoo.fr

10ha 74T(100-250m²) 10A

1 ACDGIJKLMPR
2 BFQRVWXY
3 BCDFGHJKMNQRUV
4 (C 15/5-23/9) (E+H 🔒) IJLM
(Q+S+T+U+V+X+Y+Z 🔒)
5 ABDEFGIJKLMNOPQRSTUVWXYZ
6 ACEGHIJK(N 1,8km)OTV

💬 Large luxury site, pitches around toilet block, separated from mobile homes by trees and bushes. Well located for visiting medieval Guerande and salt marshes. Cycle and walking routes nearby. Shops and hypermarket 1800 metres. Reception closed 12:30 - 13:30. Excellent restaurant.

🚗 N165 Nantes-Lorient. Exit La Roche-Bernard. Dir. Guérande/La Baule via D774. At roundabout (near Guérande) with Super Leclerc supermarket follow signs. Site 1 km behind supermarket.

[Map: D83, D47, D50, D774, Guérande, D45, Saint-Nazaire]

CC € 19 7/4-1/7 3/9-22/9 15=14 📷 N 47°20'0'' W 2°23'26''

Guérande, F-44350 / Pays de la Loire (Loire-Atlantique) ♿ 🛜 iD 1510

🏕 Le Domaine de Bréhadour****
📧 route du Bréhadour
☎ +33 (0)2-40176515
🗓 7/4 - 23/9
@ info@domainedebrehadour.com

8ha 124T(100-150m²) 6-10A CEE

1 ACD**G**IJKLMOPST
2 BFIQRVWXY
3 BD**E**GHJKM**OP**R
4 (E+H 🔲) J(Q 🔲)
(R+T+U+V+X+Z 7/7-31/8)
5 **AB**EFGIJKLMNOPQUWXZ
6 ACDEGJ**K**(N 1,5km)OTUV

💬 Good, comfortable campsite with a number of sheltered pitches between trees and hedges, a number of other pitches with are more open and have more sun, close to the medieval town of Guérande. About 10 minutes from the beaches of La Turballe or the more crowded La Baule by car. Reception closed between 12h30 and 15h.

🚗 Nantes-Vannes via N165/E60 exit Guérande/ La Baule, at roundabout near Guérande follow signs Bréhadour.

CC € **17** 7/4-7/7 25/8-22/9 7=6 ⚐ N 47°20'32'' W 2°25'4''

Héric, F-44810 / Pays de la Loire (Loire-Atlantique) 👫 🛜 iD 1511

🏕 La Pindière***
📧 La Denais
☎ +33 (0)2-40576541
🗓 1/1 - 31/12
@ contact@
camping-la-pindiere.com

3ha 51T 6-10A CEE

1 ABC**G**IJKLMOPR
2 FLRUVX
3 ABGIJR
4 (E+H 1/5-30/9)
(Q+T+U 1/7-31/8)
(X+Y+Z 🔲)
5 **AB**DFGJLNPRUWXYZ
6 ACDEGJ(N 0,500km)ORV

💬 A friendly campsite with a relaxing atmosphere, heated indoor pool and a 3 hectare garden. The campsite offers space and marked out pitches. Ideally located between Rennes and Nantes and open all year. Close to the Nantes to Brest canal. Explore the Loire Atlantique and its lovely sandy beaches.

🚗 From the Nantes/Rennes dual carriageway in Héric continue towards Fay de Bretagne and turn left 500m after the Super U petrol station.

CC € **15** 1/1-7/7 25/8-31/12 7=6, 14=12 ⚐ N 47°24'48'' W 1°40'14''

Jard-sur-Mer, F-85520 / Pays de la Loire (Vendée) 🛜 iD 1512

🏕 L'Océano d'Or*****
📧 84 rue Georges Clémenceau
☎ +33 (0)2-51330505
📠 +33 (0)2-51339404
🗓 30/3 - 29/9
@ info@chadotel.com

8ha 200T(100m²) 10A

1 ACD**F**IJKLMOPRS
2 AGRTVWXY
3 BGKM**N**RUV
4 (C 1/5-15/9) (E+H 🔲) J
(Q+S+T+U+V+Z 1/5-15/9)
5 **AB**EFGIJKLMNOPUZ
6 CEG**K**(N 0,4km)RTUV

💬 A family campsite on the edge of the village with spacious pitches separated by hedges and a lovely swimming pool.

🚗 When leaving Jard-sur-Mer, located to the right of the road direction La Tranche on the D21.

CC € **17** 30/3-7/7 26/8-28/9 ⚐ N 46°25'15'' W 1°34'10''

Jard-sur-Mer, F-85520 / Pays de la Loire (Vendée)　　🛜 iD (1513)

🔺 La Ventouse****
📧 18bis rue Pierre Curie
☎ +33 (0)2-51335865
🔑 31/3 - 30/9
@ info@campinglaventouse.com

5,5ha 113T(80-100m²) 10A

1 ACD**F**IJKLPS
2 BEGIJRSXY
3 BGKNRU
4 (C+H 15/5-30/9) (Q 1/5-28/9)
　　(R 1/5-27/9) (T 1/7-30/8)
　　(U 1/7-31/8) (Z 1/7-30/8)
5 **AB**EFGIJKLMNPUVZ
6 ACEGJ**K**(N 0,5km)RTV

💬 The charm of bush-camping on a campsite. Lovely location in a forest withhin walking distance of the sea and the touristic Jard-sur-Mer. Good amenities and renovated toilet facilities. Free wifi zone.

🚗 In Jard-sur-Mer follow signs 'campings' and then signs 'Parfums d'Eté'.

Talmont-Saint-Hilaire

CC €⑮ 31/3-6/7 25/8-29/9　　　　📷 N 46°24'45'' W 1°34'53''

L'Épine, F-85740 / Pays de la Loire (Vendée)　　♿ iD (1514)

🔺 Sandaya Camping de la Bosse**
📧 rue du Port
☎ +33 (0)2-53469747
🔑 13/4 - 23/9
@ labosse@originalcamping.com

10,5ha 274T(60-150m²) 4A CEE

1 ACD**G**IJKLOP
2 ABEJKORSTWX
3 AGHJRWY
4 (Q 🔑)
5 **AB**GJLNPUVZ
6 AEG(N 2km)

💬 In a beautiful setting, this modest campsite for your holiday in the countryside is located between marshland, woods, the sea and the beach. Pitches in the sun or shade.

🚗 Follow L'Épine signs on Noirmoutier headland. Then follow road to stop sign at harbour (Port du Morin). Then left. Campsite is 1 km on the right.

Noirmoutier-en-l'Île

CC €⑬ 13/4-6/7 26/8-22/9　　　　📷 N 46°59'7'' W 2°17'0''

La Barre-de-Monts, F-85550 / Pays de la Loire (Vendée)　　👫 ♿ 🛜 iD (1515)

🔺 Campéole La Grande Côte***
📧 route de la Grande Côte
☎ +33 (0)2-51685189
📠 +33 (0)2-51492557
🔑 30/3 - 16/9
@ grande-cote@campeole.com

22ha 481T(80-120m²) 10A CEE

1 ACD**G**IJKLMO**P**ST
2 ABEIJSWXY
3 ABCHJKNRUWY
4 (C+H 1/6-15/9)
　　(Q+S+T+U+V+Z 1/7-31/8)
5 **AB**EFGIJLMNOPUVZ
6 ACGH**K**(N 1km)ORV

💬 A typical dune campsite in the middle of the countryside, with direct access to the beach. Relatively level pitches. The village of Fromentine is within walking distance.

🚗 From Nantes continue towards Noirmoutier as far as La Barre-de-Monts. Then take the Route de la Grande Côte. Follow campsite signs.

Saint-Jean-de-Monts

CC €⑮ 30/3-6/7 25/8-15/9　　　　📷 N 46°53'8'' W 2°8'51''

La Barre-de-Monts, F-85550 / Pays de la Loire (Vendée)

♿ 🛜 iD **1516**

🔺 Le Grand Corseau***
📧 Route de la Grande Cote
☎ +33 (0)2-51685287
📠 +33 (0)2-51497246
⌚ 31/3 - 1/10
@ accueil.grandcorseau@
vacances-ulvf.com

8ha 295T(80-120m²) 10A CEE

1 ACD**G**IJKLMOPST
2 ABERSVWXY
3 AGHJKNRUY
4 (C+H 1/5-30/9) (Q 🔒)
(R+T+U+V+Z 1/7-31/8)
5 **AB**CEFGJKLMNPUVZ
6 ACGHJ**K**(N 1,5km)ORV

NEW

💬 Beautiful campsite situated in the dunes and
the woods, just 400 metres from the beach, close
to the bridge to Noirmoutier and opposite the Île
d'Yeu. Ideally situated for walkers, cyclists, and beach
lovers.

🚗 From La Barre-de-Monts take D38 towards
Noirmoutier. 150m before the bridge, take
exit towards Grand Corseau. Follow signs.

D758
CC
D38 D51 D59
Saint-Jean-de-Monts

CC €⑬ 31/3-6/7 25/8-29/9

🗺 N 46°52'59'' W 2°8'50''

La Baule, F-44500 / Pays de la Loire (Loire-Atlantique)

♿ 🛜 iD **1517**

🔺 La Roseraie****
📧 20 avenue Jean Sohier
☎ +33 (0)2-40604666
⌚ 7/4 - 23/9
@ camping@laroseraie.com

5ha 110T(90-120m²) 6-25A

1 ACD**F**IJKLMOPRS
2 F**G**QRVWX
3 B**F**GHJK**MN**O**PQ**RUV
4 (C 1/7-31/8) (D+H 🔒) IJK
(Q+S+T+U+V+X+Z 🔒)
5 **AB**EFGIJKLMNOPQRUWXY
Z
6 ACDEG**K**M(N 0,3km)OTV

💬 A luxurious family campsite near La Baule.
The site has indoor and outdoor swimming pools.
2 km from one of France's most beautiful golf
courses. Cycling along the beach and on cycle paths
and roads with no traffic is recommended.

🚗 Between Guérande and St. Nazaire, via the N171
to La Baule Escoublac Golf de La Baule exit. On to
Escoublac. At roundabout drive to village as far as the
church, then Golf de La Baule, immediate right over
the bridge. See campsite signs.

D50
D774 D47
Guérande
CC
La Baule-Escoublac
Saint-Nazaire

CC €⑰ 7/4-6/7 27/8-22/9 7=6, 14=11

🗺 N 47°17'54'' W 2°21'27''

La Bernerie-en-Retz, F-44760 / Pays de la Loire (Loire-Atlantique)

♿ 🛜 iD **1518**

🔺 Les Écureuils****
📧 24 ave Gilbert Burlot
☎ +33 (0)2-40827695
⌚ 30/3 - 29/9
@ camping.les-ecureuils@
wanadoo.fr

5,5ha 155T(80-110m²) 10A

1 ACD**F**IJKLMOPRS
2 AEFGQRVWXY
3 B**F**GHJKLMNRWY
4 (C 1/5-10/9) (E+H 🔒) IJM
(Q+T+U+V+Z 1/7-31/8)
5 **AB**EFGIJKLMNOPUVWXYZ
6 ACEGIJ**K**(N 0,45km)ORTV

💬 350 metres from the sea and the centre of La
Bernerie-en-Retz. A beautiful sandy beach and cycle
routes. New toilet facilities. Pets maximum 10 kg
allowed on camping pitches. Attractive village with a
lovely beach. Reception closed from 12:30 to 14:00.

🚗 Ring road Nantes-West, exit Noirmoutier/Pornic
via D13 dir. Noirmoutier. Exit La Bernerie-en-Retz
dir. centre. After 400 metres (50 metres before the
railway line) right, then immediately left.

La Plaine-sur-Mer
Pornic
D751
CC
D5
D758 D13

CC €⑰ 30/3-7/7 26/8-28/9

🗺 N 47°5'3'' W 2°2'14''

La Chapelle-Hermier, F-85220 / Pays de la Loire (Vendée)

🏕 Yelloh! Village Le Pin
Parasol*****
📧 6 Châteaulong
☎ +33 (0)2-51346472
📠 +33 (0)2-51346462
📅 20/4 - 16/9
@ contact@campingpinparasol.fr
21ha 230T(150-250m²) 10A CEE

1 ACD**G**IJKLMOPQ
2 ADJKMRVWX
3 BF**G**HIJKL**MN**PRUV**W**
4 (A+C+F+H 📅) IJKLM
(Q+R+T+U+V+X+Z 📅)
5 **AB**DEFGJLOPQRUWXY
6 ABCDEGH**IK**(N 4km)ORTV

💬 A beautifully located campsite with excellent toilet facilities. Superb water recreation for children, and internet throughout the site. A lovely terrace with extraordinary views. A campsite for the camper who appreciates the French countryside!

🚗 From St. Gilles-Croix-de-Vie take the D6 in the direction of Coëx. Follow the road as far as the D21. Turn right. The campsite is signposted on the right after 2.5 km.

CC € **17** 20/4-6/7 1/9-15/9

🧭 N 46°39'56'' W 1°45'21''

1519

La Faute-sur-Mer, F-85460 / Pays de la Loire (Vendée)

🏕 Le Grand R***
📧 132, route de la Tranche-sur-Mer
☎ +33 (0)2-51564287
📅 1/4 - 30/9
@ grand-r@wanadoo.fr

2,5ha 91T 10A CEE

1 ACD**F**IJKLMOPQ
2 CEGRVWX
3 BF**G**HJR
4 (C+E 📅) (Q 15/6-15/9)
(Z 1/7-30/8)
5 **AB**FGIJKLNPUVY
6 ACEG**IK**(N 0,8km)TV

💬 Campsite with heated and covered pool between the sea and a river. 500 metres from a lovely sandy beach. Spacious, marked-out pitches. Cycling routes from the campsite. Shops at 800 metres.

🚗 From La Tranche-sur-Mer direction La Faute-sur-Mer take the first campsite on the left.

CC € **17** 2/4-6/7 24/8-29/9 7=6, 14=12, 21=18

🧭 N 46°20'25'' W 1°20'19''

1520

La Flèche, F-72200 / Pays de la Loire (Sarthe)

🏕 Camping Municipal de la
Route d'Or****
📧 allée du Camping
☎ +33 (0)2-43945590
📅 1/3 - 31/10
@ info@camping-laroutedor.com

4ha 190T(80-100m²) 10A CEE

1 ACD**G**IJKLMPQ
2 CRUVXY
3 BG**M**NR**W**
4 (C 15/6-15/9) (Q 1/7-31/8)
5 **AB**DFGIJKLMNOPUVYZ
6 CDEGJ(N 0,5km)QV

💬 Ideal location in the heart of town but still in the green, on the banks of the Loir. Spacious pitches, everything is available for your dream holiday! Cycle routes, canoe/kayak, recreation, archery...

🚗 The campsite is clearly signposted in the village and is located at the river.

CC € **13** 1/3-7/7 1/9-30/10 7=6

🧭 N 47°41'42'' W 0°4'46''

1521

La Guyonnière, F-85600 / Pays de la Loire (Vendée) ♿ 🛜 iD (1522)

🔺 Flower Camping du Lac de la Chausselière★★★
🏠 route des Herbiers
☎ +33 (0)2-51419840
⛔ 1/4 - 1/10
@ camping@chausseliere.fr

2,4ha 80**T**(100-200m²) 16A CEE

1 ACGIJKLMPRS
2 DLRVXY
3 AGHJKNRU**W**
4 (C+E ⛔)
  (Q+R+T+U+V+Z 1/7-31/8)
5 **A**FIJKLMNOPUWX
6 CEG**IK**(N 1km)ORTV

💬 Flowercamping site on a large lake with lovely large pitches in quiet surroundings. Now with an indoor swimming pool!

🚗 From Montaigu centre, towards Cholet to roundabout, right towards La Rochelle. 2nd roundabout left (D23) towards La Boissière; brown signs.

Boussay
D93 D763
D54 D753
Boufféré CC D755
D17 A83
Beaurepaire
D763 D6
D7 D137 A87

CC € **15** 1/4-7/7 26/8-30/9 | 🧭 N 46°57'25'' W 1°14'44''

La Plaine-sur-Mer, F-44770 / Pays de la Loire (Loire-Atlantique) 🚻 ♿ 🛜 iD (1523)

🔺 Flower Camping La Guichardière★★★
🏠 2 rue de Mouton
☎ +33 (0)2-40215509
⛔ 14/4 - 23/9
@ contact@camping-laguichardiere.net

5ha 46**T**(90-120m²) 10A CEE

1 ACD**G**IJKLMOPQ
2 AEFQRVWXY
3 BF**G**HJKMN**P**QRWY
4 (C+H 28/4-23/9) M(Q ⛔)
  (R+T+U+V+Z 28/4-23/9)
5 **AB**FGIJKLMNOPQUXYZ
6 ACEGJ(N 1,5km)OTV

💬 Family campsite on the coast, plenty of greenery for shade and flowers, walking and cycling along the sea which is 300 metres away, or on the marked routes in the lightly undulating interior. Beach at 400 metres. Reception closed from 12:00 to 14:00.

🚗 From D213 St. Nazaire-Pornic to exit La Plaine-sur-Mer. Then via D96 past Tharon Plage, and via D96 to Port de Gravette. Follow signs.

D213 D5
Tharon-Plage
CC D86
D213
Pornic

CC € **15** 14/4-12/7 30/8-22/9 7=6 | 🧭 N 47°9'8'' W 2°12'30''

La Plaine-sur-Mer, F-44770 / Pays de la Loire (Loire-Atlantique) 🚻 ♿ 🛜 ❁ iD (1524)

🔺 La Tabardière★★★★
🏠 2 rte d.l. Tabardière
☎ +33 (0)2-40215883
📠 +33 (0)2-40210268
⛔ 14/4 - 22/9
@ info@camping-la-tabardiere.com

6ha 148**T**(90-110m²) 6-10A CEE

1 ACD**G**IJKLMOPRS
2 FIJQRVWXY
3 BF**G**HJKMN**OP**QRUV
4 (C 5/5-15/9) (E+H ⛔) J
  (Q ⛔) (S 1/6-2/9)
  (T+U+V 2/7-31/8) (Z 1/6-2/9)
5 **AB**EFGIJKLMNOPQUVWXY
Z
6 ACDEGIK(N 3km)OTUV

💬 A pleasant and peaceful campsite with well maintained toilet facilities. There is a choice of pitches either on the level terraces or large open pitches higher up the campsite. The swimming pool is always heated to 28°C. Reception closed between 12:30 and 14:00.

🚗 D213 St. Nazaire-Pornic, take the exit La Plaine-sur-Mer/Pornic-Ouest. Subsequently, take the D13 towards La Plaine-sur-Mer until you see the signs to the campsite.

D5
D213
Tharon-Plage
D86
CC
Pornic D751
D13

CC € **17** 14/4-8/7 26/8-21/9 7=6, 14=11, 21=17 | 🧭 N 47°8'27'' W 2°9'12''

La Plaine-sur-Mer, F-44770 / Pays de la Loire (Loire-Atlantique) 〔1525〕

▲ Le Ranch★★★★
🏠 chemin des Hautes Raillères
☎ +33 (0)2-40215262
🕐 31/3 - 30/9
@ info@camping-le-ranch.com

3,5ha 83T(90-100m²) 10A

1 ACD**G**IJKLMOPRS
2 AFQRVWXY
3 BF**G**HJKLMN**P**RU
4 (A 5/7-31/8) (C 1/5-15/9)
   (F+H 1/4-30/9) JM
   (Q+R+T+U+V+Z 2/7-2/9)
5 **AB**EFGIJKLMNPRUWZ
6 ACEGJ**K**(N 3km)OTV

💬 Quiet, well-maintained campsite with pitches between hedges and shade-giving trees. 800 metres from the beach. New (2016) open-air and covered swimming pools. Wifi free on the entire site outside high season. Reception closed 12:00-14:00. Arrival possible until 23:00.

🚐 South of St. Nazaire via D213, La Route Bleu, exit La Plaine-sur-Mer and Tharon-Plage. Via D96 to La Plaine-sur-Mer and follow camping signs. (SatNav unreliable in immediate vicinity.)

Saint-Brevin-les-Pins — D86 — D213 — D5 — **Pornic** — D751 — D13

CC € **17** 31/3-6/7 27/8-29/9 14=13   N 47°9'17'' W 2°9'55''

La Tranche-sur-Mer, F-85360 / Pays de la Loire (Vendée) 〔1526〕

▲ Du Jard GC★★★★
🏠 123 bd Mar. de Lattre de Tassigny
☎ +33 (0)2-51274379
📠 +33 (0)2-51274292
🕐 8/5 - 15/9
@ info@campingdujard.fr

6ha 129T(100-120m²) 10A CEE

1 ACEIJKLMOPRS
2 ARVX
3 BGHJK**M**N**Q**RUW
4 (C 9/6-8/9) (F 🔑)
   (H 9/6-8/9) JK(Q 🔑)
   (S+T 8/7-26/8)
   (U+V 1/7-30/8)
   (X+Y 1/7-30/9) (Z 1/7-30/8)
5 **AB**EFGIJKLMNOPQUWZ
6 EGHIJ**K**(N 1km)RTV

💬 Very good family campsite in the village with spacious pitches separated by hedges. Indoor and giant outdoor swimming pool. Plenty of sports opportunities. Lovely beach within walking distance. Free wifi zone.

🚐 From La Roche-sur-Yon take the D747 to La Tranche. Follow the signs Grière-Plage, and then follow the camping signs.

D46 — D105 — D747 — CC La Faute-sur-Mer — La Tranche-sur-Mer

CC € **17** 8/5-9/7 27/8-14/9 7=6, 14=12, 21=17   N 46°20'52'' W 1°23'13''

La Tranche-sur-Mer, F-85360 / Pays de la Loire (Vendée) 〔1527〕

▲ La Grande Vallée★★
🏠 145 blvd de Lattre de Tassigny
☎ 📠 +33 (0)2-51301282
🕐 1/4 - 30/9
@ c.lagrandevallee@orange.fr

1ha 52T(80-140m²) 10A CEE

1 ACDFIJKLM**PQ**
2 GRWXY
3 BGJKR
4 (Q 🔑) (T+V+Z 1/5-15/9)
5 **AB**FGIJKLMNOPUZ
6 ACEGJ**K**(N 0,03km)RT

💬 A small, congenial campsite within walking distance of the sea and a beautiful sandy beach. Good cycling options (Vélodyssée). All basic facilities provided and a free wifi point at the bar.

🚐 From La Roche-sur-Yon D747 to La Tranche. Follow La Grière-Plage signs, signposted further.

D21 — D105 — D747 — CC D46 — D746 — La Tranche-sur-Mer

CC € **13** 1/4-10/7 28/8-29/9 7=6, 14=12, 21=18, 28=24   N 46°20'52'' W 1°22'59''

La Tranche-sur-Mer, F-85360 / Pays de la Loire (Vendée) 🛜 iD (1528)

▲ Le Cottage Fleuri****
✉ 4 impasse du cottage
☎ +33 (0)2-51303457
🗓 1/4 - 30/9
@ lecottagefleuri@wanadoo.fr

7,5ha 99T(80-130m²) 10A CEE

1 ACD**G**IJKLOP**S**
2 AEGRVXY
3 B**F**GKN**Q**RUVWY
4 (C 15/6-15/9) (F ⊙)
  (H 15/6-15/9) J**N**
  (Q+T+U+V+Z 1/7-31/8)
5 **AB**EFGIJKLMNOPUXZ
6 CEG**K**(N 0,05km)RTUV

💬 Large campsite with spacious, marked out pitches, 500 metres from a nice, sandy beach. Shops and baker within walking distance. Heated indoor pool. Ideal base for cycling and walking.

🚗 D105 Longeville towards La Tranche. Then at roundabout turn left then 1 km. In the centre of La Grière turn left.

Saint-Vincent-sur-Jard | D46 | D105 | D747 | D105 BIS | CC | La Faute-sur-Mer

CC € **17** 1/4-30/6 25/8-29/9   📍 N 46°20'59'' W 1°24'25''

La Turballe, F-44420 / Pays de la Loire (Loire-Atlantique) ♿ 🛜 iD (1529)

▲ La Falaise****
✉ 1 boulevard de Belmont
☎ +33 (0)2-40233253
🗓 30/3 - 28/10
@ info@camping-de-la-falaise.com

3ha 63T(100-130m²) 10A CEE

1 ACD**G**IJKLMOPQ
2 AEFGKQRSVWXY
3 AC**F**GHJKL**M**NWY
4 (E+H+Q+T+U+Z ⊙)
5 **AB**CDEFGHIJKLOPQRUWX
6 ABCDEGIK(N 0,4km)OTW

💬 Site directly at beach. Lovely, luxury toilet facilities. Indoor pool. Pitches divided by hedges. Located on edge of village, 400 metres from supermarket. 10 pitches with sea views. Please book in May and June. Reception closed between 12:30-13:30. CampingCard ACSI rate includes children up to 4 years.

🚗 N165/E60 Vannes-Nantes, exit Guérande/La Baule. Via D774 as far as Guérande, via D99 to La Turballe, follow camping signs or Super U on D99 when entering village.

D83 | D774 | CC **Guérande** | D45 | La Baule-Escoublac

CC € **19** 30/3-6/7 26/8-27/10   📍 N 47°21'13'' W 2°31'4''

Le Château-d'Olonne, F-85180 / Pays de la Loire (Vendée) 👫 🛜 iD (1530)

▲ Flower Camping Le Petit
  Paris****
✉ 41 rue du Petit Versailles
☎ +33 (0)2-51220444
📠 +33 (0)2-51331704
🗓 1/4 - 30/9
@ contact@campingpetitparis.com

3ha 55T(80-130m²) 10A CEE

1 ACDFIJKLOPQ
2 GRVWXY
3 AB**F**GJKNRU
4 (C 1/5-15/9) (E+H 9/4-30/9) J
  (Q+R ⊙) (T+U 1/7-30/8)
  (Z 1/7-31/8)
5 **AB**EFGIJKLMNPUX
6 AEG**JK**(N 3km)TV

💬 A pleasant child friendly family campsite between the ocean and the countryside. 5 minutes from the fine sandy beaches of Les Sables d'Olonne. Spacious separated pitches. Heated indoor swimming pool and swimming lake with lagoon beach. Good basic amenities.

🚗 From Les Sables-d'Olonne follow D949 towards Talmont-St. Hilaire. Straight on at traffic lights. Follow camping signs.

D80 | D32 | D160 | D36 | Les Sables-d'Olonne | D4 | CC | D949 | D21

CC € **15** 1/4-6/7 24/8-29/9 7=6, 14=12   📍 N 46°28'25'' W 1°43'16''

Le Château-d'Olonne, F-85180 / Pays de la Loire (Vendée) 👫 👫 📶 iD (1531)

🔺 Le Puits Rochais****
📧 25 rue de Bourdigal
☎ +33 (0)2-51210969
📠 +33 (0)2-51236220
🕐 14/4 - 29/9
@ info@puitsrochais.com

3,5ha 60T(100m²) 10A CEE

1 ACDFIJKLPS
2 AGRTVX
3 BFGHJKMNPRU
4 (C+H 1/5-29/9) J
(Q+S+T+U+V+W+Z 15/6-10/9)
5 ABDEFGIJKLMNOPUWX
6 ACEGJK(N 0,6km)RTV

💬 Good campsite on the outskirts of the village. Lovely swimming pool and clearly separated, shady pitches. New heated toilet facilities. Les Sables-d'Olonne is well worth a visit. The motor museum and amusement park Puy du Fou are also close by. La Rochelle is about one hour away by car.

🚗 Take the D949 from Talmont-St-Hilaire to Les Sables. Turn left at the first traffic lights in Le Château-d'Olonne.

Les Sables-d'Olonne
D80 D32 D160 D36 D21 D4 D949

(CC) € 15 14/4-13/7 31/8-28/9 7=6, 14=12, 21=18   🏕 N 46°28'53'' W 1°43'53''

Le Château-d'Olonne, F-85180 / Pays de la Loire (Vendée) 📶 iD (1532)

🔺 Les Fosses Rouges****
📧 8 rue des Fosses Rouges
☎ +33 (0)2-51951795
🕐 4/4 - 30/9
@ info@
  camping-lesfossesrouges.com

3,5ha 162T(75-120m²) 10A

1 ACDGIJKLMOPQ
2 GRVXY
3 ABGKMQR
4 (E+H+Q+R+S 🕐)
(U+Z 1/7-31/8)
5 ABFGIJKLMNPU
6 ACEGJK(N 1km)OTV

💬 Friendly family campsite close to the fine sandy beaches of Les Sables-d'Olonnes. Indoor swimming pool, bar and entertainment room. Ideal as base for walking and cycling trips. Free wifi zone at the bar.

🚗 From Talmont-St-Hilaire take the D949 direction Les Sables. Follow signs to the left at first traffic lights 7 km further on.

Les Sables-d'Olonne
D80 D32 D160 D36 D21 D4

(CC) € 15 4/4-6/7 24/8-29/9   🏕 N 46°28'46'' W 1°44'28''

Le Croisic, F-44490 / Pays de la Loire (Loire-Atlantique) 👫 👫 ♿ 📶 iD (1533)

🔺 de l'Océan Village et Spa*****
📧 route de la Maison Rouge
☎ +33 (0)2-40230769
📠 +33 (0)2-40157063
🕐 7/4 - 23/9
@ camping-ocean@wanadoo.fr

7,5ha 60T(90-120m²) 10A

1 ACDGIJKLMPQ
2 AEFGQRVWXY
3 BCEGHJKMNOPRUVWY
4 (C 15/5-23/9) (F+H 🕐) IJKL
MNP(Q+S+T+U+V+Y+Z 🕐)
5 ABDEFGIJKLMNOPQRUWX
YZ
6 ACEGJK(N 1km)OTV

💬 Campsite close to Le Croisic with outdoor leisure pool and super deluxe indoor pool with wellness centre. Highly recommended! The small town with attractive harbour is within walking distance. Salt marshes between headland and village of Guérande. Just 800m from a supermarket. Reception closed 12:30 - 14:00.

🚗 N165-E60 to Nantes, and N171 to Guérande. Before Guérande head towards Le Croisic (D774) at the roundabout. Just before centre of Le Croisic follow signs.

La Baule-Escoublac
D774

(CC) € 19 7/4-1/7 3/9-22/9 15=14   🏕 N 47°17'51'' W 2°32'7''

Le Givre, F-85540 / Pays de la Loire (Vendée) ♿ 📶 iD 1534

- ⛰ La Grisse***
- ☎ +33 (0)2-51308303
- ⌚ 1/1 - 31/12
- @ lagrisse@wanadoo.fr

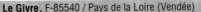

2,4ha 31T(120-350m²) 16A CEE

1 ACD**F**IJKLMOPQ
2 RTVXY
3 ABGKR
4 (Q+R 1/7-31/8)
5 **AB**FGJLMNOPUWXYZ
6 AEK(N 6km)

💬 A lovely friendly campsite open all year, ten minutes from the beaches at La Tranche sur Mer. A spectacular natural setting with large shaded pitches. Free wifi throughout the grounds. Plenty of footpaths from the campsite. A good base for trips out to the Vendée. You will find peace, space and comfort at Camping La Grisse.

🚗 From Moutiers to La Tranche via the D747. Left about 1 km past the D949 intersection. Campsite clearly signposted.

D4 · D12 · D19 · D949 · Jard-sur-Mer CC · D46 · D105 · D747 · La Tranche-sur-Mer

📡 N 46°26'41'' W 1°23'53''

CC € **13** 1/1-10/7 28/8-31/12

Le Grez, F-72140 / Pays de la Loire (Sarthe) ♿ 📶 iD 1535

- ⛰ Les Tournesols***
- 🏠 Le Landereau
- ☎ +33 (0)2-43201269
- ⌚ 1/5 - 30/9
- @ campinglestournesols@orange.fr

NEW

2,5ha 56T(80-120m²) 6-16A CEE

1 ABCD**G**IJKLMOPRS
2 LRVWXY
3 GJLQRU
4 (C 1/5-30/8) (Q+R ⌚) (T+U 1/7-15/8)
5 **AB**GIJKLMPZ
6 AEGJTUV

💬 A friendly welcome with a drink from the owners awaits you. Remond and Laëtitia make the campsite a friendly place to stay for the whole family. Rural location. Lovely large shaded pitches. Clean toilet facilities. Organised entertainment. TV room and wifi. Recreational lake 3 km away. Heated swimming pool (28 °C).

🚗 From Sillé-le-Guillaume keep on D304 direction Mayenne and take the 1st exit right past the picnic spot, the campsite is on the left. Signposted.

D16 · D35 · D310 · CC · D5 · D21 · Voutré · D4 · Domfront-en-Champagne · Tennie

📡 N 48°11'22'' W 0°8'28''

CC € **13** 1/5-6/7 25/8-29/9

Le Perrier, F-85300 / Pays de la Loire (Vendée) ♿ 📶 ⚙ iD 1536

- ⛰ Le Jardin du Marais****
- 🏠 208 route de Saint-Gilles/D59
- ☎ +33 (0)2-51680917
- ⌚ 10/4 - 3/10
- @ info@lejardindumarais.eu

NEW

60T(80-180m²) 16A CEE

1 ACD**F**IJKLMOPST
2 RVX
3 A**F**GHJKLNRUVW
4 (**A** 1/7-31/8) (C 15/6-15/9) (F ⌚) (H 15/6-15/9) J (Q 1/7-31/8) (S 1/4-30/9) (T+U+V+X+Y+Z ⌚)
5 **AB**EFGIJKLMNOPUWXZ
6 CEG**IJK**(N 2km)ORTV

💬 Beautiful campsite surrounded by greenery, just 7 km from the ocean. Family atmosphere. Close to St-Jean-de-Monts, but in a quiet area.

🚗 From Challans D205 to exit St. Hilaire-de-Riez. Then D59. Follow signs.

D71 · D32 · D38 · D59 · Challans · CC · D69 · D32 · D754 · Saint-Hilaire-de-Riez

📡 N 46°48'18'' W 1°58'48''

CC € **17** 10/4-7/7 31/8-2/10

Les Epesses, F-85590 / Pays de la Loire (Vendée)

👫 ♿ 📶 🌼 **iD** **1537**

🏕 La Bretèche***
📧 Base de Loisirs de Bretèche
☎ +33 (0)2-51204194
🔓 7/4 - 4/11
@ breteche.reception@gmail.com

3,5ha 94T(80-110m²) 10A CEE

1 ACD**F**IJKLMOPST
2 DFLRVWXY
3 ABHJRU**W**
4 (A 1/4-24/9) (C+H 1/5-5/9)
(Q 1/4-24/9)
(R+T+U+V+X+Z 🔓)
5 **AB**FGIJKLMNPUVWZ
6 ACEGHJ(N 1km)RTV

💬 A well run campsite situated by a lake and a stone's throw from the Puy du Fou theme park. The site has many sports and recreational amenities and is a good base for many excursions in the region. The pitches are spacious, as is the 300 m² heated swimming pool.

🚐 Campsite signposted in Les Epesses.

CC € **17** *7/4-7/7* *1/9-3/11*

🧭 N 46°53'23'' W 0°53'57''

Les Moutiers-en-Retz, F-44760 / Pays de la Loire (Loire-Atlantique)

♿ 📶 **iD** **1538**

🏕 Flower Camping Les Brillas***
📧 Le Bois des Tréans
☎ +33 (0)2-40827978
🔓 6/4 - 30/9
@ info@campinglesbrillas.com

4,5ha 53T(82-278m²) 10A

1 ACD**G**IJKLMOPRS
2 AFGKLQRVWXY
3 BD**F**GHJKLRUW
4 (E+H+Q 🔓)
(R+T+U+V+X+Z 1/7-31/8)
5 **AB**FGIJKLMNOPUWXYZ
6 ACDEGK(N 1km)TV

💬 A campsite with a choice of pitches between hedges or on an open field. Well maintained toilets. All amenities open from early May. Peaceful and close to a small town and the sea with its special coastline. Centre for farming oysters and mussels. Reception closed 12:00-14:00. Bar/restaurant open weekends out of season.

🚐 From ring Nantes-West, exit Noirmoutier/Pornic, continue towards Noirmoutier/Pornic as far as Les Moutiers-en-Retz village, then follow camping signs.

CC € **17** *6/4-6/7* *1/9-29/9*

🧭 N 47°4'30'' W 2°0'27''

Les Rosiers-sur-Loire, F-49350 / Pays de la Loire (Maine-et-Loire)

♿ 📶 **iD** **1539**

🏕 Yelloh! Village Les
Voiles d'Anjou****
📧 6 rue Sainte Baudruche
☎ +33 (0)2-41519433
🔓 1/4 - 1/10
@ contact@camping-valdeloire.com

4,5ha 111T(100-130m²) 10A

1 ACD**F**IJKLPQ
2 FRVWXY
3 ABGHJMN**Q**RU
4 (C+F+H 🔓) **KN**
(Q+R+T+V 🔓) (Z 1/6-30/9)
5 **AB**EFGIJKLMNOPUWXYZ
6 CEGK(N 0,8km)OTVW

💬 Located in the UNESCO heritage site of the Loire, with its beautiful chateaux, 500m from a lively village. Two swimming pools, one outdoor and one indoor with a lovely terrace. New toilet facilities. Also a playground, bike hire, attractively furnished restaurant with room for music and theatre and many opportunities for cycling and walking in the vicinity.

🚐 Via D952. Towards Beaufort at the traffic lights in the village. Follow signs. Campsite well signposted.

CC € **15** *1/4-30/6* *1/9-30/9* *7=6*

🧭 N 47°21'32'' W 0°13'32''

Longeville-sur-Mer, F-85560 / Pays de la Loire (Vendée) 🚻 📶 iD (1540)

🔺 Le Petit Rocher****
✉ 1250 avenue de Docteur Mathevet
☎ +33 (0)2-51204194
📠 +33 (0)2-51221109
🕗 7/4 - 23/9
@ contact@camp-atlantique.com

4,5ha 70T(85-120m²) 10A CEE

1 ACD**F**IJKLPS
2 ABEGJRSVWXY
3 ABCGHJKNRUY
4 (E+H 🕗) JKM
　(Q+S+T+U+V+Z 🕗)
5 **AB**EFGIJKLMNPUWZ
6 EGHJ**K**(N 2km)TV

💬 A lovely terraced campsite with spacious pitches under tall deciduous trees. Within walking distance of the sea and a sandy beach. Heated indoor swimming pool, wellness and snack bar.

🚙 Follow the D105 as far as Longeville-sur-Mer. At roundabout, take the D91a direction Le Rocher as far as the sea. Campsite signposted.

CC € **17** 7/4-7/7 1/9-22/9 　　🧭 N 46°24'13'' W 1°30'27''

Marçon, F-72340 / Pays de la Loire (Sarthe) ♿ 📶 iD (1541)

🔺 Le Lac des Varennes***
✉ route du Port Gauthier/Saint Lezin
☎ +33 (0)2-43441372
🕗 1/4 - 29/10
@ contact@lacdesvarennes.com

7ha 170T(100-300m²) 10A CEE

1 AC**G**IJKLMPRS
2 ACDLRVWXY
3 AGHK**M**RU**W**XZ
4 (Q+R 🕗)
　(T+U+V+Z 1/7-31/8)
5 **AB**DEFGJLMNPUWZ
6 EG**K**(N 6km)T

💬 This peaceful and spacious campsite borders both a large lake and the Loir. There is plenty of countryside around with footpaths and fishing on the site.

🚙 Drive via the D305 to Marçon. In the centre pass the Post Office/Town Hall (on the left). Follow the road. Signposted.

CC € **15** 1/4-7/7 25/8-28/10 7=6, 14=12, 21=17 　🧭 N 47°42'45'' E 0°29'58''

Mervent, F-85200 / Pays de la Loire (Vendée) ♿ 📶 iD (1542)

🔺 La Joletière***
✉ Departementale D99
☎ +33 (0)2-51002687
🕗 1/4 - 15/10
@ camping.la.joletiere@wanadoo.fr

1,4ha 40T 16A CEE

1 ACD**G**IJKLPST
2 RVWXY
3 ABGHJLRU
4 (F 🕗) (H 1/5-31/8)
　(Q+R 1/7-31/8) (T 🕗)
　(X 1/7-31/8) (Z 🕗)
5 **A**GIJKLMNOPUVYZ
6 AEG**K**OV

💬 Familial campsite in the heart of the woodland area 'Mervent-Vouvant'. 300 metres from a lake. Many options for walking and cycling.

🚙 From A83, exit 7.1 Fontenay-le-Comte Ouest, direction La Chataignerie D338. Then follow D99 for 3 km towards Mervent.

CC € **17** 1/4-29/6 1/9-14/10 7=6 　　🧭 N 46°31'17'' W 0°46'9''

Montjean-sur-Loire/Mauges, F-49570 / Pays de la Loire (Maine-et-Loire) 👫 ♿ 📶 iD (1543)

🔺 Flower Camping La Promenade★★★
✉ quai des Mariniers
☎ +33 (0)2-41390268
🔓 1/4 - 17/10
@ contact@campinglapromenade.com

3ha 150T(85-125m²) 10A

1 ACD**G**IJKLMOPQ
2 ACGRVWXY
3 ABGHJKRU**W**
4 (C+H 15/5-15/9) (Q+R+T+U+V+Z 🔓)
5 **AB**FGIJKLMNOPQRUWXYZ
6 ACEGK(N 1km)TV

💬 Near a small village in the middle of Anjou at the banks of the Loire. In the area between Angers and Nantes, famous for the unusual Corniche Angevine. Plenty of walking and cycling possibilities. Wine regions, Puy de Fou and lovely villages invite you for a visit. Spacious marked out pitches, lovely swimming pool, new toilet facilities, snack bar and hospitable owners.

🚗 From Angers to the D751. Follow this as far as Montjean-sur-Loire. Campsite well signposted.

D10 D6 D51 A11 D15
Varades D723
D150
D751
Chalonnes-sur-Loire
D752 D762
D961
D17

CC € 15 1/4-7/7 25/8-16/10 7=6, 14=12 📐 N 47°23'31'' W 0°52'13''

Montreuil-Bellay, F-49260 / Pays de la Loire (Maine-et-Loire) ♿ 📶 iD (1544)

🔺 Flower Camping Les Nobis d'Anjou★★★★
✉ rue Georges Girouy
☎ +33 (0)2-41523366
🔓 31/3 - 30/9
@ contact@campinglesnobis.com

3ha 69T(80-145m²) 10A

1 ACD**G**IJKLMOPQ
2 CRTVWXY
3 BGHJKRU**W**
4 (C 1/5-30/9) (Q+R+T+Y+Z 🔓)
5 **AB**EFGIJKLMNOPUWX
6 ACEGHK(N 0,5km)RTV

💬 Located in medieval Montreuil-Bellay at the foot of a castle and on the banks of the River Thouet. Many modern facilities: large pitches, heated swimming pool, restaurant, lively bar and entertainment. Plenty of walking and cycling tours, and also the heritage of the Loire region; everything therefore for a wonderful stay in this beautiful region.

🚗 Via N147 from either Saumur or Thouars. Follow camping signs once you get to the roundabout

D84 Doué-la-Fontaine
D761
D69 Montreuil-Bellay CC
D87
D31
D37 D938 D347
D39

CC € 15 31/3-3/7 27/8-29/9 7=6, 14=12 📐 N 47°7'54'' W 0°9'33''

Morannes, F-49640 / Pays de la Loire (Maine-et-Loire) ♿ 📶 iD (1545)

🔺 Camping Morédéna★★
✉ rue du Pont
☎ +33 (0)679109715
🔓 1/4 - 31/10
@ contact@camping-moredena.com

2,5ha 85T(70-250m²) 15-16A CEE

1 ABCD**F**IJKLMPQ
2 CLRVWXY
3 AGHKNRU**W**
4 (B 1/7-3/9) (Q 4/7-31/8)
5 **A**FGJLMNPUWZ
6 CEJK(N 0,3km)V

NEW

💬 Quiet campsite with some shady pitches, on the edge of a village and on the banks of the River Sarthe. A good base for discovering the historic places in the vicinity.

🚗 A11 direction Angers, exit 11 Durtal, then direction Châteauneuf. Follow the signs in Morannes.

Sablé-sur-Sarthe
D309
D27 D306
D24
CC
D859
D768
D770 A11
D89

CC € 11 1/4-7/7 25/8-30/10 📐 N 47°44'50'' W 0°25'14''

Nantes, F-44300 / Pays de la Loire (Loire-Atlantique) ♿ 🛜 ✿ iD 1546

🏕 Nantes Camping★★★★★
🏠 21 boulevard du Petit Port
☎ +33 (0)2-40744794
📠 +33 (0)2-40742306
🔓 1/1 - 31/12
@ nantes-camping@nge-nantes.fr

8,5ha 83T(100-200m²) 16A CEE

1 ACD**G**IJKLMPQ
2 BCFGLRTUVXY
3 ABF**G**HJKQRU**W**
4 (F 🔓) J**L**M
(Q+R+T+U+V 1/5-11/9)
(X+Y 1/7-31/8) (Z 🔓)
5 BDEFGJLNPUWXYZ
6 BEGHIK(N 0,2km)TV

💬 Nantes Camping is located in grounds covering 8.5 hectares and is a natural campsite, a few minutes from the centre of Nantes.

🚗 Take N39 Nantes from the ring road north, exit Porte de la Chapelle. Direction Nantes Centre. Campsite signposted and located on roundabout.

N137 · A11 · N165 · D751 · **Nantes** · CC · **Saint-Sébastien-sur-Loire** · D74 · D59

CC € **19** 1/1-13/7 3/9-31/12 📡⛰ N 47°14'36'' W 1°33'24''

Noirmoutier-en-l'Île, F-85330 / Pays de la Loire (Vendée) ♿ 🛜 iD 1547

🏕 Huttopia Noirmoutier★★★
🏠 23, allée des Sableaux
☎ +33 (0)2-51390624
🔓 13/4 - 23/9
@ noirmoutier@huttopia.com

12ha 386T(80-100m²) 10A CEE

1 ACD**F**IJKLM**P**ST
2 ABEKNRSWXY
3 ABGHJKRWY
4 (Q+R 🔓) (T+U 1/5-30/9)
5 **AB**FGIJKLMNPRUWZ
6 ABCEGIJ(N 2km)

💬 A campsite by the sea alongside the beach at Les Sableaux in a pine forest. Uniquely situated on the island of Noirmoutier. Direct beach access in several places. Quality amenities. CampingCard ACSI is only valid for standard pitches.

🚗 From Nantes direction Noirmoutier. Via the bridge to the island towards Noirmoutier-en-l'Île. Then follow Plage des Sableaux from centre.

CC · D38 · **Beauvoir-sur-Mer**

CC € **17** 13/4-22/6 27/8-22/9 📡⛰ N 46°59'49'' W 2°13'14''

Nort-sur-Erdre, F-44390 / Pays de la Loire (Loire-Atlantique) ♿ 🛜 iD 1548

🏕 Seasonova Port Mulon★★★
🏠 rue des Mares Noires
☎ +33 (0)2-40722357
🔓 1/4 - 31/10
@ contact@
camping-portmulon.com

2ha 100T(88-347m²) 10A CEE

1 ABCD**G**IJKLMPQ
2 BCLRVXY
3 AHIJKR**W**
4 C(Q 🔓) (T 1/6-15/9) (Z 🔓)
5 **AB**CEFGHIJKLMNPRUXYZ
6 ADEG**K**(N 1km)T

💬 A pleasant, refurbished campsite with many opportunities for the water enthusiast. Modern toilet facilities. Located by a river and close to a marina.

🚗 Direction Sucé-sur-Erdre. Follow 'camping' on the left.

Saffré · D33 · D121 · D178 · D164 · D16 · CC · D31 · **Casson** · D537 · D69 · **Sucé-sur-Erdre** · A11

CC € **15** 1/4-7/7 27/8-30/10 7=6 📡⛰ N 47°25'42'' W 1°29'51''

Notre-Dame-de-Riez, F-85270 / Pays de la Loire (Vendée)

🛰 ❀ **iD** **1549**

🔺 Domaine des Renardières***
🏠 13 chemin du chêne vert
☎ FAX +33 (0)2-51551417
🔑 1/4 - 30/9
@ campinglesrenardieres@
orange.fr

3,5ha 67**T**(90-130m²) 10A

1. **AF**IJKLMOPST
2. BRSVXY
3. AB**F**GHJKNRU**W**
4. (C+F+H 🔑) (Q 1/7-31/8)
   (R 5/4-2/9) (T+U+V 1/7-25/8)
   (Z 🔑)
5. **AB**EFGIJKLNOPTUVXZ
6. ACDEGH**K**(N 1km)OTV

💬 A beautiful campsite for the whole season. Covered saltwater pool (always 27°C), fine toilet facilities, spacious pitches. Excellent motorhome pitches in park-like surroundings. More than worth a visit. Bicycles for hire.

🚗 Challans direction Sable d'Olonne (8 km), first intersection after the level crossing (right). In Notre-Dame-de-Riez sharp turn to the right. Signposted.

Challans

D51 · D948 · D59 · D69 · D754 · D38 · **CC** · D94 · Saint-Hilaire-de-Riez · D32 · D6

CC € **17** *1/4-13/7 1/9-29/9* 🔻 N 46°45'18'' W 1°53'53''

Olonne-sur-Mer, F-85340 / Pays de la Loire (Vendée)

♿ 🛰 **iD** **1550**

🔺 Le Nid d'Été****
🏠 2 rue de la Vigne Verte
☎ +33 (0)2-51953438
FAX +33 (0)2-51953464
🔑 1/4 - 30/9
@ info@leniddete.com

3ha 100**T**(100-160m²) 10-16A CEE

1. ACD**G**IJKLMOPQ
2. AFRVX
3. AF**G**HJKNRUW
4. (C+D+H 3/4-25/9) JK**P**
   (Q+R 1/7-31/8)
   (T+U+V 1/6-31/8)
   (X 1/7-31/8) (Z 🔑)
5. **AB**FGIJKLOPUVWZ
6. AEG**K**(N 2km)QRTV

💬 This family campsite is a nice place to stay in the early and late seasons, just 3 km from a lovely sandy beach. The swimming pool is open from the beginning of April. There is excellent cycling in the lovely area.

🚗 From Angers follow the A87 as far as La Roche-sur-Yon. Then take the Les Sables d'Olonne route. Follow the signs in Olonne-sur-Mer.

D12 · D32 · D160 · D21 · D80 · **CC** · D760 · D36 · **Les Sables-d'Olonne**

CC € **17** *1/4-14/7 1/9-29/9* 🔻 N 46°32'0'' W 1°47'37''

Piriac-sur-Mer, F-44420 / Pays de la Loire (Loire-Atlantique)

♿ 🛰 **iD** **1551**

🔺 Parc du Guibel***
🏠 route de Kerdrien
☎ +33 (0)2-40235267
🔑 1/4 - 30/9
@ camping@parcduguibel.com

14ha 300**T**(100-200m²) 10A CEE

1. ACD**G**IJKLMOPQ
2. ABQRVWXY
3. BGHJN**OP**QRUW
4. (C+F+H 15/4-30/9) IJ(Q 🔑)
   (S+T+U+V+Y+Z 7/7-31/8)
5. **AB**EFGIJKLOPUVXYZ
6. CDEGHJ(N 3,5km)TV

💬 Lovely wooded site with marked out pitches among pine trees. You will be assigned a quiet pitch if you wish. Comfortable toilet facilities. Nice heated indoor and outdoor pools, you can swim from inside to outside. Peaceful almost level surroundings 1200 meters from a quiet beach and village at 3.5 km.

🚗 N165/E60 Nantes-Vannes. Guérande/La Baule exit. Via D774 direction Guérande and via D52 to St. Molf and Piriac-sur-Mer. Campsite located on the D52.

D192 · D83 · **CC** · La Turballe · D774 · D47 · **Guérande** · D45

CC € **15** *1/4-14/7 1/9-29/9* 🔻 N 47°23'10'' W 2°30'36''

Pornic, F-44210 / Pays de la Loire (Loire-Atlantique) ♿ 🛜 iD (1552)

🏕 La Boutinardière****
📧 23 rue de la Plage
de la Boutinard.
☎ +33 (0)2-40820568
📅 7/4 - 23/9
@ info@laboutinardiere.com

8ha 100T(80-120m²) 6-10A CEE

1 ACD**G**IJKLMOPRS
2 AEFGQRVWXY
3 BCF**G**HJK**MN**P**Q**RUVWY
4 (C 10/5-30/9) (F+H ☑) IJ**KL**
MN
(Q+S+T+U+V+X+Y+Z ☑)
5 **AB**DEFGHIJKLMNOPQRUV
WXYZ
6 ACDEGIJ**K**(N 2km)ORTV

💬 Family campsite with well maintained toilet facilities. The pitches are separated by hedges. 200m from the sea with a sheltered sandy beach between two cliffs. Open air swimming pool 400 m², indoor pool 300 m² with sauna, steam bath and beauty centre, good restaurant. Reception closed from 12:30 to 14:00.

🚐 Take the exit La Boutinardière/La Rogère at the D13 between Pornic and Bourgneuf-en-Retz, west of Nantes. Follow the signs to the campsite.

Saint-Michel-Chef-Chef — Pornic — D58 — D86 — D751 — D5 — D13 — D758

CC €**19** 6/5-8/5 13/5-18/5 21/5-6/7 2/9-22/9 15=14 ⛺ N 47°5'52'' W 2°3'7''

Pornic, F-44210 / Pays de la Loire (Loire-Atlantique) ♿ 🛜 ✿ iD (1553)

🏕 Le Patisseau****
📧 29 rue du Patisseau
☎ +33 (0)2-40821039
📅 7/4 - 23/9
@ contact@lepatisseau.com

4,5ha 67T(80-120m²) 10A CEE

1 ACD**F**IJKLMOPRS
2 BFGJQRVWXY
3 BF**G**HJKLNRUV
4 (C 1/6-23/9) (F+H ☑) IJKMN
P(Q+S+T+U+V+X+Y+Z ☑)
5 **AB**DEFGIJKLMNOPQRUWX
YZ
6 ACDEGI**K**(N 1km)RTVW

💬 Lovely site with luxurious heated toilet facilities and indoor swimming pool. 300 m² outdoor pool. Nice restaurant. The campsite is located in a green belt close to Pornic. Marked out footpaths, a sports complex and gently sloping cycle tracks nearby. Category 1 and 2 dogs are not permitted. Reception closed 12:30-14:00.

🚐 South of St. Nazaire via the D213 as far as the Pornic/Le Clion-sur-Mer exit. Follow the camping signs at the roundabout towards Le Clion-sur-Mer.

Saint-Michel-Chef-Chef — Pornic — D723 — D58 — D213 — D86 — D751 — D13 — D5

CC €**17** 7/4-6/7 1/9-22/9 7=6, 14=12, 21=18 ⛺ N 47°7'8'' W 2°4'23''

Pornichet, F-44380 / Pays de la Loire (Loire-Atlantique) 👨‍👩‍👧 ♿ 🛜 iD (1554)

🏕 Du Bugeau***
📧 33 avenue de Loriettes
☎ +33 (0)2-40610202
📅 7/4 - 30/9
@ campingdubugeau@wanadoo.fr

2ha 61T(70-95m²) 10A

1 ACDGIJKLMPRS
2 AEFGRVWXY
3 BF**G**HJRUWY
4 (E ☑) (G 1/7-2/9)
(Q+R+T+U+V+Z ☑)
5 **AB**EFGIJKLMNOPUWZ
6 ACEG**K**(N 0,5km)RTV

💬 Quiet campsite close to the beach. It is divided into small fields separated by hedges, with several trees between the pitches providing shade. The large promenade with its well-known half-moon beach is 1 km away. ± 1 km from supermarket, 700 metres from the beach.

🚐 Via the D92 from St. Nazaire direction La Baule and Pornichet. At roundabout with Carrefour supermarket, direction St. Sébastien. Turn left before the church, 400 metres further, entrance on the left.

Saint-Nazaire — D47 — D50 — N171 — D213

CC €**17** 7/4-6/7 26/8-29/9 ⛺ N 47°15'10'' W 2°19'10''

137

Préfailles, F-44770 / Pays de la Loire (Loire-Atlantique)

♿ 📶 **iD** **1555**

NEW

▲ Eléovic★★★★
✉ Route de la pointe Saint-Gildas
☎ +33 (0)2-40216160
🗓 30/3 - 30/9
@ contact@camping-eleovic.com

56**T**(80-130m²) 10A CEE

1 ACD**F**IJKLMOPST
2 AEFIJKNQRVWXY
3 BF**G**HJKLN**P**RUVWY
4 (E+H+Q+R 🚗)
   (T+U+V 31/3-16/9)
   (X 9/7-1/9) (Y+Z 31/3-16/9)
5 **AB**EFGIJKLMNPUWXZ
6 ABCEGIJ**K**(N 1km)OTV

💬 Campsite in Préfailles (Loire-Atlantique) with shady and sunny marked out pitches. View of and direct access to the sea. 900 m from shops and close to cycling and walking routes. Enjoy the indoor heated pool, warm all year round, and it's hydromassage beds. Spacious and extensive toilet facilities with clothes washers.

🚗 D213 St. Nazaire-Pornic exit La Plaine-sur-Mer/Préfailles. Via D96 head towards Préfailles until you see campsite signs.

Saint-Brevin-○ l'Océan D5
D213
D86
CC D213
Pornic

CC € **17** 30/3-3/5 13/5-17/5 22/5-5/7 3/9-29/9 🚩 N 47°7'58'' W 2°13'53''

Rochefort-sur-Loire, F-49190 / Pays de la Loire (Maine-et-Loire)

♿ 📶 ✿ **iD** **1556**

▲ Seasonova Les Plages de Loire★★★
✉ route de Savennières
☎ +33 (0)2-41685591
🗓 31/3 - 30/11
@ contact@ camping-lesplagesdeloire.com

6ha 116**T**(80-140m²) 10A CEE

1 ACD**G**IJKLMOPQ
2 ACDFGKLRVWXY
3 AGHJQRU**W**X
4 (A+C+F+H 1/7-31/8) **KLN**
   (Q+R+T+U+Z 🚗)
5 **AB**FGIJKLMNOPUWZ
6 ACEGJ**K**(N 0,5km)W

💬 A new campsite designed by a landscape architect and very attractively laid out. Close to all the amenities in the village and positioned by a small river.

🚗 Via the A11 to N160 dir. Les Ponts-de-Cé. Rochefort is indicated here on the D751. A87 exit 23 dir. Denée, D160, D123, D751.

A11
D723 Saint-Barthélemy-d'Anjou
D751
D762 **CC** A87
D961 D160 D55
D120

CC € **13** 31/3-7/7 29/8-29/11 7=6, 14=11 🚩 N 47°21'37'' W 0°39'24''

Saumur, F-49400 / Pays de la Loire (Maine-et-Loire)

♿ 📶 **iD** **1557**

▲ Flower Camping L'Ile d'Offard★★★★★
✉ boulevard de Verden
☎ +33 (0)2-41403000
📠 +33 (0)2-41673781
🗓 17/3 - 28/10
@ iledoffard@flowercampings.com

4,5ha 187**T**(100-120m²) 10A CEE

1 ACD**G**IJKLPQ
2 CFGKLRTVWX
3 BF**G**HJKMNR**W**
4 (C+H 1/5-30/9) **KLN**
   (Q+S+T+U+X+Y+Z 1/5-30/9)
5 **AB**DFGIJKLMNOPQUWXYZ
6 ACDEGIK(N 1km)V

💬 The campsite is located in a verdant 4.5 hectare park between both banks of the Loire. 15 minute walk from the centre of Saumur, where a number of events are organised throughout the year. An exceptional location. Vineyards, culture and tradition. CampingCard ACSI is valid for comfort pitches, not for privilege pitches.

🚗 The campsite is on an island in the Loire opposite Saumur castle. Easily accessible via the N152, D947 or N147.

D767
D751 Allonnes
Saumur A85 D10
CC Chouzé-sur-Loire
D960 D952
D761 D347

CC € **17** 17/3-29/6 1/9-27/10 7=6 🚩 N 47°15'36'' W 0°3'52''

Sillé-le-Guillaume, F-72140 / Pays de la Loire (Sarthe)

    ♿ 🛜 📱 **iD** (1558)

🏕 Flower Camping de La Forêt***
📧 Sillé-Plage
☎ +33 (0)2-43201104
📠 +33 (0)2-43208482
⏱ 1/4 - 31/10
@ campingsilleplage@wanadoo.fr

4ha 143**T**(100-150m²) 10A

1 ACG**I**JLPT
2 BDLMRVXY
3 ABGHJ**MNPQ**RU**W**Z
4 (**A** 1/7-30/8) (Q 🔌)
5 **AB**FGIJKLMNPUWZ
6 CDEGIJ(N 3km)OTV

💬 A level campsite on the edge of a deciduous forest and by a lake with opportunities for watersports. The campsite has shaded and sundrenched pitches. Country walking possible from the campsite in 3500 hectares of woods.

🚗 From Sillé-le-Guillaume direction Le Lac and La Forêt. Follow signs.

CC € **13** 1/4-30/6 1/9-30/10   🏔 N 48°12'33'' W 0°8'5''

Sillé-le-Guillaume, F-72140 / Pays de la Loire (Sarthe)

    ♿ 🛜 **iD** (1559)

🏕 Huttopia Lac de Sillé***
📧 Sillé-Plage
☎ +33 (0)2-43201612
📠 +33 (0)2-43245684
⏱ 27/4 - 23/9
@ lac-sille@huttopia.com

9ha 122**T**(100-150m²) 10A CEE

1 ACD**G**IJKLMPST
2 BDRWXY
3 ABGHJK**OP**RU**W**Z
4 (C 1/5-28/9) (Q+R 🔌)
   (T+U+V 1/7-31/8) (Z 🔌)
5 **AB**FGIJKLMNPTUW
6 CDEIJ(N 1,5km)

💬 A campsite on the shores of Lake Sillé in the middle of municipal woodland. Opportunities for walking and water recreation. Heated swimming pool and recreation facilities. CampingCard ACSI is only valid on standard pitches.

🚗 From Sillé-le-Guillaume direction Le Lac and La Forêt. Follow signs as far as La Crêperie du Lac. Turn right just before La Crêperie du Lac. Look out for campsite signs.

CC € **13** 27/4-5/7 26/8-22/9   🏔 N 48°12'13'' W 0°7'39''

St. Brévin-les-Pins, F-44250 / Pays de la Loire (Loire-Atlantique)

    ♿ 🛜 **iD** (1560)

🏕 La Courance***
📧 110, avenue Marechal Foch
☎ +33 (0)2-40272291
⏱ 1/1 - 31/12
@ info@campinglacourance.fr

4ha 61**T**(80-120m²) 10A

1 ACD**G**IJKLMOPST
2 ABEFGIKMRSVWXY
3 AGHJRUWY
4 (E+G 1/4-4/11)
   (Q+R+T+U+V+X+Z 7/7-31/8)
5 **AB**DGIJKLNPUZ
6 ACEGI**K**T

NEW

💬 Campsite right on the coast, located between two village centres. Pitches are in a pine forest with lots of trees, plenty of shade and shelter, but some problems with satellite TV reception. Supermarket less than 1 km away. Good value restaurant on the other side of the street. The campsite is open all year round.

🚗 D213 St. Nazaire/Pornic exit St. Brévin L'Ocean, follow signs L'Ocean and Casino to roundabout west of D213. Follow signs to campsite.

CC € **17** 1/1-6/7 1/9-31/12   🏔 N 47°14'17'' W 2°10'14''

St. Brévin-les-Pins, F-44250 / Pays de la Loire (Loire-Atlantique) ✲✲ ✿ 🛈 **(1561)**

🏕 Le Fief*****
✉ 57 chemin du Fief
☎ +33 (0)2-40272386
📅 31/3 - 23/9
@ camping@lefief.com

7ha 127**T**(80-130m²) 8-10A CEE

1 ACD**G**IJKLMOPRS
2 AEFGQRVWXY
3 BGHJKMNRU**V**WY
4 (C 1/5-23/9) (F+H 📅) IJ**KL**M
NP(Q+S+T+U+V+Y+Z 📅)
5 **AB**DEFGIJKLMNOPQRUW
XYZ
6 ACDEGHI**J**K(N 0,8km)**P**RT
V

💬 A family campsite 900m from the beach, between the two village centres of St. Brévin-les-Pins with a market 3 times a week. Own restaurant with very reasonable prices. Beautiful outdoor and indoor swimming pools. Only CampingCard ACSI for touring pitches, not for seasonal pitches. Larger motorhomes are permitted.

🚗 South of St. Nazaire via the D213, exit D5 then Casino. Follow St. Brevin-l'Océan and camping signs.

CC € **19** 31/3-3/5 14/5-17/5 22/5-6/7 2/9-22/9 · N 47°14'7'' W 2°10'3''

St. Christophe-du-Ligneron, F-85670 / Pays de la Loire (Vendée) ✿ 🛈 **(1562)**

🏕 Domaine de Bellevue***
✉ Bellevue de Ligneron
☎ +33 (0)2-51933066
📅 1/3 - 1/11
@ campingdebellevue85@orange.fr

13ha 50**T**(100-200m²) 16A CEE

1 ACD**G**IJKLMOPQ
2 DRVX
3 ABGHJNRUW
4 (E+H 📅)
(Q+R+T+U+V+X 1/7-31/8)
(Z 📅)
5 **AB**EFGIJKLMNOPUXYZ
6 CDEG**K**(N 2km)ORTV

💬 A beautiful, spaciously appointed campsite with excellent facilities. Gorgeous fishing water on the campsite and a lovely indoor pool and indoor leisure pool for children.

🚗 From La Roche-sur-Yon take D948 dir. Challans. In village St. Christophe-du-Ligneron follow signs.

CC € **13** 1/3-1/7 27/8-31/10 · N 46°48'54'' W 1°46'30''

St. Hilaire-de-Riez, F-85270 / Pays de la Loire (Vendée) ✿ 🛈 **(1563)**

🏕 Domaine des Salins****
✉ 43 chemin du Quart du Matelot
☎ +33 (0)2-51593628
📅 1/4 - 30/9
@ contact@domainedessalins.com

3ha 32**T**(80-100m²) 6A

1 ACD**G**IJKLMOPST
2 AGRVWX
3 BFGHJKRU
4 (C 5/5-20/9) (F+H 6/4-29/9) K
(Q+R+T 1/7-31/8)
5 **AB**CFGHIJKLPQUZ
6 ACEG**K**(N 0,4km)RV

💬 Pleasant and quiet campsite with heated swimming pools (an outdoor pool and a new indoor pool with luxurious toilet facilities). The pitches on the campsite are separated from the mobile homes. Good location at 800 metres from the sea, between St. Hilaire-de-Riez and St. Jean-de-Monts.

🚗 From St. Jean-de-Monts take the RD38 dir. St. Hilaire. In Orouet dir. les Mouettes, then dir. les Becs. Then follow camping signs.

CC € **17** 1/4-7/7 1/9-29/9 11=10 · N 46°45'46'' W 2°1'32''

St. Hilaire-de-Riez, F-85270 / Pays de la Loire (Vendée)

⚲ La Plage****
✉ 106 av. de la Pège
☎ +33 (0)2-51543393
📠 +33 (0)2-51559702
🔓 1/4 - 30/9
@ campinglaplage@
  campingscollinet.com

5,5ha 46T(100-120m²) 10A

1 ACGIJKLMPST
2 AERSVX
3 ABFGJMNRTUWY
4 (C 15/5-15/9) (F 7/4-30/9)
  (H 8/4-30/9) JK
  (Q+R+T+U+V 8/4-15/9)
  (X 15/6-31/8) (Z 🔓)
5 ABEFGIJKLMNOPUVZ
6 ACEGJ(N 1km)OQRTV

(1564)

💬 A large campsite with many facilities on a coastal road. Deciduous and conifer trees alternate with bushes, quiet avenues and busier sections at the entrance to the campsite. Cycle tracks in area and lovely swimming pool (also covered).

🚗 Take the D38 around St. Hilaire as far as the roundabout (Fina service station). Then take the D123 in the direction of La Pège. Signposted after 4.5 km.

D51   **Challans**
D38
     D59
      D69
CC Saint-Hilaire-de-Riez
       D32

CC € **17** 1/4-7/7 31/8-29/9   🧭 N 46°44'43'' W 2°0'36''

St. Hilaire-de-Riez, F-85270 / Pays de la Loire (Vendée)

⚲ La Plage de Riez***
✉ avenue des Mimosas
☎ +33 (0)2-51543659
🔓 1/4 - 30/9
@ riez85@free.fr

11ha 289T(80-140m²) 6A CEE

1 ACDFIJKLMOPT
2 ABERSVXY
3 AGHJKNRUWY
4 (C+H 8/5-15/9)
  (Q+R+T+U+V 15/5-15/9)
  (X 1/7-31/8) (Z 🔓)
5 ABEFGIJKLMNOPUXZ
6 ACDEGK(N 0,2km)OTV

(1565)

💬 You will be camping 'with your feet in the water' at this friendly and hospitable campsite in the middle of woods and with direct access to the beach. Extensive network of cycle paths, including one to Sion where you can go shopping.

🚗 From Nantes: Ri La Roche-sur-Yon via Route Départementale, then Challans, St. Hilaire-de-Riez/ St. Gilles-Croix-de-Vie and dir. Sion-sur-L'Ocean (not towards centre).

D38
   D59
    D69   D754
Saint-Hilaire-de-Riez CC
     D32
      D6
    D12

CC € **15** 1/4-30/6 1/9-29/9   🧭 N 46°43'22'' W 1°58'46''

St. Hilaire-la-Forêt, F-85440 / Pays de la Loire (Vendée)

⚲ Flower Camping La Grand'
  Métairie****
✉ 8 rue de la Vineuse en Plaine
☎ +33 (0)2-51333238
🔓 7/4 - 23/9
@ info@
  camping-grandmetairie.com

3,8ha 42T(80-100m²) 10A

1 ACDFIJKLMOPRS
2 RTVXY
3 BDGJKNRU
4 (C 1/6-8/9) (F+H 🔓) **N**
  (Q+R+T+U+V+X+Y+Z 🔓)
5 ABEFGIJKLMNOPUXYZ
6 CEGJK(N 0,1km)ORTV

(1566)

💬 A lovely family campsite with petting zoo and many amenities within walking distance of the village. Indoor heated swimming pool, bar and restaurant are open all season. Free wifi zone. Ideal location between Sables d'Olonne and La Tranche-sur-Mer.

🚗 La Roche-sur-Yon D747 as far as Moutiers; D19 via Avrillé to St. Hilaire-la-Forêt. Signposted from here.

D36
    D4   D12
D21   D19
Talmont-Saint-Hilaire
CC
     D949
      D46
D105
   D747

CC € **13** 7/4-13/7 1/9-22/9 7=6, 14=12, 21=18   🧭 N 46°26'55'' W 1°31'35''

St. Hilaire-St-Florent, F-49400 / Pays de la Loire (Maine-et-Loire) ♿ 🛜 ❁ 🆔 1567

🏕 Huttopia Saumur★★★★
📧 1, chemin Chantepie
☎ +33 (0)2-41679534
🗓 13/4 - 14/10
@ saumur@huttopia.com

12ha 100**T**(100-140m²) 10A CEE

1 AC**D**G**IJKLP**ST
2 FKRVWXY
3 B**F**GHJKL**P**RUV**W**
4 (B+E+G+Q+S ⌨)
　(T+U+V+W+X+Z 1/7-31/8)
5 **AB**DEFGIJKLMNOPQUWXY
　Z
6 ABCEGHIJ(N 5km)V

💬 Unusual location among vineyards with views of the Loire. 10 hectares of countryside, spacious marked-out pitches, two swimming pools (one heated) grocery shop, bar, take-away meals, pizzeria. Quality campsite hallmark. 6 km from Saumur. Rest and relaxation. CampingCard ACSI not valid alongside the river.

🚗 From Saumur direction Cholet. After the roundabout direction St. Hilaire, turn right at the end of the road. Follow 'Gennes touristiques' (D751). Follow the signs.

CC € **17** 13/4-5/7 2/9-13/10 　　🧭 N 47°17'38'' W 0°8'33''

St. Jean-de-Monts, F-85160 / Pays de la Loire (Vendée) ♿ 🛜 ❁ 🆔 1568

🏕 Aux Coeurs Vendéens★★★★
📧 251 rte Notre-Dame-de-Monts
☎ +33 (0)2-51588491
🗓 14/4 - 15/9
@ info@coeursvendeens.com

2ha 48**T**(60-120m²) 10A CEE

1 AC**D**F**IJKLMOP**ST
2 AGRVXY
3 ABF**G**HJKNRUV
4 (C 10/5-15/9) (F ⌨)
　(H 10/5-15/9) KLN
　(Q 1/6-15/9) (R 1/7-31/8)
　(T+U+Z 8/7-31/8)
5 **AB**EFGIJKLMNOPUVWXY
6 ACEGH**I**K(N 0,4km)RV

💬 A peaceful family campsite 700m from the sea, with spacious pitches. The campsite has two heated swimming pools, one of which is covered and has a free spa, sauna and hammam. Fitness equipment. Free wifi throughout the campsite. A paradise for cyclists with cycle routes from the campsite.

🚗 Follow the D38 from St. Jean-de-Monts to the north to Noirmoutier. The campsite is situated directly on the D38.

CC € **17** 14/4-6/7 1/9-14/9 7=6, 14=12, 21=18 　🧭 N 46°48'35'' W 2°6'35''

St. Jean-de-Monts, F-85164 / Pays de la Loire (Vendée) 👫 ♿ 🛜 🆔 1569

🏕 Campéole Les Sirènes★★★
📧 71 avenue des Demoiselles
☎ +33 (0)2-51580131
📠 +33 (0)2-51590367
🗓 30/3 - 30/9
@ sirenes@campeole.com

15ha 280**T**(> 90m²) 10A CEE

1 AC**G**IJKLMO**P**ST
2 ABRSWXY
3 ABF**G**HJKNR
4 (C+H 1/6-15/9)
　(Q+R+S+T 1/7-31/8)
5 **AB**EFGIJKLMNOPU
6 ACEGH**K**(N 0,4km)RT

💬 A beautiful dune campsite located in the woods with large open and shaded pitches. Large heated swimming pool. Beach and village nearby. Many cycling and walking opportunities.

🚗 Direction Nantes/La Roche-sur-Yon. Follow Challans and St. Jean- de- Monts. Then Le Bourg, La Plage and Palais des congrès. Enter Avenue des Demoiselle at roundabout. Campsite located 500 metres on the left.

CC € **15** 30/3-6/7 25/8-29/9 　　🧭 N 46°46'49'' W 2°3'18''

St. Jean-de-Monts, F-85161 / Pays de la Loire (Vendée) ♟ ♿ 📶 **iD** 1570

◣ Campéole Plage des Tonnelles - Dornier****
🏠 18 route de la Tonnelle
☎ +33 (0)2-51588116
📠 +33 (0)2-51584168
🗓 13/4 - 16/9
@ plage-tonnelles@campeole.com

25ha 200**T**(70-110m²) 10A CEE

1 ACD**G**IJKLMOPST
2 ABEGISWX
3 AB**F**GHJKNQRUVY
4 (C+H 1/6-13/9) **KN**
  (Q+S 5/5-5/9)
  (T+U 1/7-31/8)
5 **AB**EFGIJKLMNOPQRUVZ
6 ACEGH**J**(N 0,2km)RV

💬 A dune campsite with outdoor pool in sheltered surroundings. Access to the beach via a gate and through the dunes. Shop in immediate vicinity. Fitness room and sauna with jacuzzi. Walking and cycling.

🚗 Coming from Nantes, dir. Noirmoutier/Challans/ St. Jean-de-Monts, continue towards D38 Notre Dame-de-Monts/Noirmoutier. Turn left at the Tonnelles roundabout and follow camping signs.

CC € **15** 13/4-6/7 25/8-15/9 | 🧭 N 46°48'37'' W 2°7'12''

St. Jean-de-Monts, F-85160 / Pays de la Loire (Vendée) ♿ 📶 ❀ **iD** 1571

◣ Camping-Caravaning La Forêt****
🏠 190 chemin de la Rive
☎ +33 (0)2-51588463
🗓 14/4 - 22/9
@ camping-la-foret@orange.fr

1ha 45**T**(88-120m²) 10A CEE

1 ACD**G**IJKLMOPST
2 AEGRSVX
3 AB**F**GHJKLRUY
4 (**C+H** 1/5-21/9)
  (Q+R+T+U 1/6-31/8)
5 **AB**CFGHIJKLMNOPQUWXYZ
6 CEGH**K**(N 0,8km)RVW

💬 Camping la Forêt is a smaller, quiet family campsite and is geared to its clients. High standards. Heated swimming pool. On the edge of a wood. 400m from the beach which is accessible via a wood path. Various walking and cycling opportunities opposite the site. 1 km from the centre of Notre-Dame-de-Monts.

🚗 In St. Jean-de-Monts take the D38 towards Notre-Dame-de-Monts. Turn left at Notre-Dame-de-Monts sign, Chemin de la Rive. Campsite 300m on the left.

CC € **17** 14/4-6/7 25/8-21/9 8=7 | 🧭 N 46°49'6'' W 2°7'48''

St. Jean-de-Monts, F-85160 / Pays de la Loire (Vendée) ♿ 📶 **iD** 1572

◣ l'Océan****
🏠 67 rue de Notre Dame de Monts
☎ +33 (0)2-51580388
📠 +33 (0)2-51582463
🗓 13/4 - 16/9
@ info@campinglocean.com

4,2ha 94**T**(80-120m²) 10A

1 ACD**G**IJKLMOPRS
2 AGRSVWXY
3 AB**F**GHJNRU
4 (C+H 15/5-15/9)
  (Q+T+U 1/7-31/8)
5 **AB**EFGIJKLMNPUZ
6 AEG**J**(N 1,0km)RV

💬 Christophe and Valérie welcome you to their friendly campsite with a heated pool (26°C) and lovely, semi-shaded pitches. Located on the edge of the dunes with marked-out cycle tracks, 1 km from the beach and the town centre.

🚗 From St. Jean-de-Monts direction Notre-Dame-de-Monts on the D38. At the end of the town it is the 1st campsite on the left, beside the D38.

CC € **15** 13/4-6/7 25/8-15/9 7=6 | 🧭 N 46°48'1'' W 2°4'42''

St. Jean-de-Monts, F-85160 / Pays de la Loire (Vendée) ♿ 📶 iD (1573)

🏕 La Davière Plage***
📧 197 rte de N.D. / ch. de la Davière
☎ +33 (0)2-51582799
🗓 28/4 - 29/9
@ contact@daviereplage.com

3ha 133T(90-135m²) 10A CEE

1 ACD**G**IJKLMPST
2 AGRSVWXY
3 B**F**GHJKNR
4 (C+H 1/5-29/9) K
(Q+R+S+T+U+X 1/7-31/8)
5 **AB**FGIJKLMNPRUVZ
6 ACEGJ(N 3km)V

💬 This family campsite welcomes you on the edge of a beautiful wood and the St. Jean-de-Monts dunes and 900 metres from a lovely sandy beach. Spacious pitches, heated swimming pool, sun meadow and jacuzzi. Excellent cycling and walking in the immediate surroundings. Free wifi.

🚗 The campsite is located 1.5 km north of St. Jean-de-Monts. Follow D38 direction Notre-Dame-de-Monts. Campsite on the left on Chemin de la Davière.

CC € **15** 28/4-11/7 29/8-28/9   📍 N 46°48'20'' W 2°6'5''

St. Jean-de-Monts, F-85160 / Pays de la Loire (Vendée) ♿ 📶 ❄ iD (1574)

🏕 La Prairie****
📧 146 rue du Moulin Cassé
☎ +33 (0)2-51581604
🗓 6/4 - 30/9
@ contact@campingprairie.com

2ha 39T(85-100m²) 6A

1 ACD**G**IJKLMOPST
2 AGRVWX
3 AB**F**GHJKNRUV
4 (C 5/5-20/9) (F+H 6/4-29/9) J
K(Q 1/7-31/8) (R+T 🍽)
(X 1/7-31/8)
5 **AB**EFGIJKLMNPUVXZ
6 ACEG**K**(N 2km)OV

💬 A pleasant, peaceful campsite close to dunes and woods with direct access to the beautiful sandy beaches and with walking and cycle paths beside the campsite. Located 2.5 km from the town centre. Heated outdoor swimming pool and heated indoor pool with spa. Spacious marked out, half-shaded pitches.

🚗 From St. Jean-de-Monts take the D38 towards Notre-Dame-de-Monts. Campsite about 1500m north of St. Jean-de-Monts, follow camping signs.

CC € **17** 6/4-7/7 28/8-29/9 15=14   📍 N 46°48'15'' W 2°5'36''

St. Jean-de-Monts, F-85160 / Pays de la Loire (Vendée) ♿ 📶 iD (1575)

🏕 La Yole****
📧 chemin des Bosses
☎ +33 (0)2-51586717
📠 +33 (0)2-51590535
🗓 7/4 - 22/9
@ contact@la-yole.com

9ha 172T(90-150m²) 10A

1 ACD**F**IJKLMOPS
2 RSVXY
3 B**F**GHIJK**M**NRUVW
4 (C+F+H 🍽) JKP
(Q+S+T+U+V+X+Y 1/5-15/9)
(Z 🍽)
5 **AB**DEFGIJKLMNOPQRUWYZ
6 ACEGH**JK**(N 3km)OTV

💬 A well-organised campsite just near the coast with varied landscaping and playgrounds. Playfully designed swimming pool.

🚗 From St. Hilaire take the D38b north-west as far as Le Pissot. Then take the D38, signposted to the left after 4 km. Or from St. Jean-de-Monts direction St. Hilaire 6 km on the right.

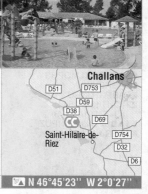

CC € **17** 7/4-13/7 31/8-21/9 7=6, 14=11   📍 N 46°45'23'' W 2°0'27''

St. Jean-de-Monts, F-85160 / Pays de la Loire (Vendée) ♿ 📶 **iD** (1576)

🏕 Le Bois Joly★★★★
📧 46 route de Notre Dame
☎ +33 (0)2-51591163
🔓 1/4 - 16/9
@ info@camping-leboisjoly.com

7,5ha 171T(80-110m²) 10A CEE

1 ACDFIJKLMOPS
2 AGRUVWXY
3 ABFGHJKNRU
4 (C+F+H 🅿) IJKM
(Q+T+U+X 1/7-31/8)
5 ABDEFGIJKLMNOPQUVXY
Z
6 ACEGHIJK(N 0,9km)OTV

💬 Pleasant campsite with spacious pitches. Heated toilet facilities. Outdoor and indoor swimming pool (expansion in 2017), new bar/restaurant. Free wifi point. At walking distance from St. Jean-de-Monts. Beautiful beach nearby. Plenty of options for cycling and walking.

🚗 Take the D38 from St. Jean-de-Monts direction Notre-Dame-de-Monts. The campsite is located on the edge of the village, right on the D38.

Saint-Jean-de-Monts CC
D51 D948 D753 D59 D38 D69

CC € **17** 1/4-30/6 1/9-15/9   📍 N 46°47'59'' W 2°4'28''

St. Jean-de-Monts, F-85169 / Pays de la Loire (Vendée) ♿ 📶 **iD** (1577)

🏕 Les Amiaux★★★★
📧 223 rte Notre Dame de Monts
☎ +33 (0)2-51582222
📠 +33 (0)2-51582609
🔓 2/5 - 30/9
@ accueil@amiaux.fr

16ha 300T(100-120m²) 10A CEE

1 ACDFIJKLMOPST
2 AGRVWXY
3 ABFGHJKMNRUV
4 (C 1/7-31/8) (F+H 5/5-9/9) JK
M(Q+S+T+U 5/5-31/8)
5 ABFGIJKLMNOPUXYZ
6 EGHK(N 3,5km)ORV

💬 Large four star campsite with spacious separated pitches. Many facilities are available, including a small supermarket (open until August), a fitness room and a large indoor swimming pool with water slides. 700 metres from a lovely beach. Next to a cycle path and a wood, perfect for lovely walks.

🚗 From St. Jean-de-Monts, the D38 in northerly direction to Noirmoutier. The campsite is directly on the D38.

D948 D38 D51 D59 CC
Saint-Hilaire-de-Riez

CC € **17** 5/5-30/6 31/8-29/9   📍 N 46°48'28'' W 2°6'17''

St. Julien-de-Concelles, F-44450 / Pays de la Loire (Loire-Atlantique) ♿ 📶 **iD** (1578)

🏕 du Chêne★★★
📧 1 route du Lac
☎ +33 (0)2-40541200
🔓 30/3 - 14/10
@ contact@campingduchene.fr

2,5ha 70T(70-150m²) 10A CEE

1 ABCDGIJKLMPQ
2 DFGLMRUVWXY
3 ABFGHJKLMRW
4 (E+H+Q 1/5-30/9)
(T+U+Z 🅿)
5 ABEFGJLMNPQUVWZ
6 CDEGK(N 0,25km)RTV

💬 The campsite has a friendly atmosphere and is located between the Loire and several vineyards, on the edge of a lake. This is a lovely natural area for complete relaxation.

🚗 Exit 44 Porte du Vignoble direction St. Julien-de-Concelles.

La Chapelle-sur-Erdre
D723 D751 A11 D23 D115 CC D37 D763
Nantes

CC € **17** 30/3-7/7 26/8-13/10   📍 N 47°14'57'' W 1°22'17''

St. Julien-des-Landes, F-85150 / Pays de la Loire (Vendée) ♿ 📶 **iD** (1579)

▲ Flower Camping La
   Bretonnière****
☎ +33 (0)2-51466244
FAX +33 (0)2-51466136
☷ 7/4 - 30/9
@ info@la-bretonniere.com

5,5ha 119T(140-200m²) 12A CEE

1 ACD**G**IJKLMOPQ
2 ADRWXY
3 AFGHJK**M**NRUW
4 (**A** 15/6-31/8) (C 10/5-20/9)
   (D+H 10/5-30/9) M(Q+R ☷)
   (T 15/6-30/9)
   (U+V 15/6-31/8) (Z ☷)
5 **AB**EFGIJKLMNPUVWZ
6 ACEGJ**K**(N 2km)OTV

💬 A beautiful campsite located in the countryside
around a former farmhouse with its own fish pond
and large pitches.

📷 From Angers take the A87 in the direction of
Cholet, Roche-sur-Yonne. Here continue to Sables
d'Olonne. At the exit La Mothe-Achard / St. Julien
drive in the direction of St. Gilles.

CC € **15** 7/4-6/7 25/8-29/9   🚩 N 46°38'39'' W 1°43'57''

St. Julien-des-Landes, F-85150 / Pays de la Loire (Vendée) ♿ 📶 ❉ **iD** (1580)

▲ La Garangeoire*****
☎ +33 (0)2-51466539
FAX +33 (0)2-51466985
☷ 4/5 - 24/9
@ info@garangeoire.com

20ha 174T(120-180m²) 12A CEE

1 ACD**G**IJKLMOPST
2 ADLRSVXY
3 BDFGHJKL**MNOP**QRUW
4 (A 5/5-20/9) (C+H ☷) J**KN**
   (Q+S+T+U+V+X+Y 5/5-20/9)
   (Z ☷)
5 **AB**DEFGIJKLMNOPRSUWX
   Y
6 ABCEGH**I**JL(N 3km)OPRTV

💬 A large castle campsite on a beautiful wooded
estate. Paths criss-cross woods and fields.
An international campsite also for teenagers. Horse
and pony riding also in early and late seasons. Sandy
beach on campsite.

📷 On the N160 Les Sables d'Olonne - La Roche-
sur-Yon, at La Mothe-Achard take the D12 in the
direction of St. Julien-des-Landes. Located to the
right after 3 km on the D21 in the direction of La
Chapelle.

CC € **19** 4/5-29/6 1/9-23/9   🚩 N 46°39'39'' W 1°42'56''

St. Julien-des-Landes, F-85150 / Pays de la Loire (Vendée) 📶 **iD** (1581)

▲ Yelloh! Village Château
   La Forêt****
☎ +33 (0)2-51466211
FAX +33 (0)2-51466087
☷ 4/5 - 5/9
@ camping@chateaulaforet.com

50ha 150T(100-140m²) 10A

1 ACD**G**IJKLMOPS
2 BDKLMRVXY
3 ABCDGHJK**MNOP**QRUW
4 (C 1/7-31/8) (**F**+H ☷) JK**P**
   (Q+R ☷) (T+U 13/5-5/9)
   (V+Y+Z ☷)
5 **AB**EFGHIJKLNPUWXY
6 ACDEGH**I**J**K**(N 0,3km)RTV

💬 Château La Forêt is a lovely international
campsite on a 50 hectare estate. The site opens on
28/4 and most amenities, such as the swimming pool,
can be used immediately. The campsite is up to full
strength from 13/5. Well worth a visit!

📷 D12 La Chaize-Giraud direction St. Julien-des-
Landes. Then pass the church and turn left unto the
D55. Signposted.

CC € **17** 4/5-6/7 26/8-4/9   🚩 N 46°38'36'' W 1°42'41''

St. Laurent-sur-Sèvre, F-85290 / Pays de la Loire (Vendée)

🚫 📶 **iD** (1582)

🏕 Le Rouge Gorge★★★
📧 route de la Verrie
☎ 📠 +33 (0)2-51678639
🔄 31/3 - 30/9
@ campinglerougegorge@
wanadoo.fr

2ha 53T(100-180m²) 8-13A CEE

1 ACD**G**IJKLMPST
2 FLRVWXY
3 ABGHJNRU
4 (F+H 8/4-25/9) K
(Q+R+T+U+V+Z 1/7-31/8)
5 **AB**DEFGIJKLMNPUVXYZ
6 AEJ(N 0,8km)OTV

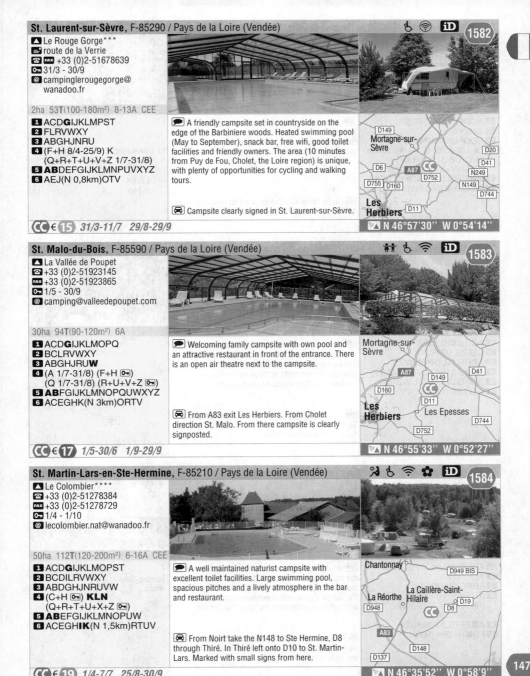

💬 A friendly campsite set in countryside on the edge of the Barbiniere woods. Heated swimming pool (May to September), snack bar, free wifi, good toilet facilities and friendly owners. The area (10 minutes from Puy de Fou, Cholet, the Loire region) is unique, with plenty of opportunities for cycling and walking tours.

🔜 Campsite clearly signed in St. Laurent-sur-Sèvre.

Mortagne-sur-Sèvre — D149 — D20 — D6 — A87 CC — D41 — D752 — N249 — D755 — D160 — N149 — Les Herbiers — D11 — D744

CC € **15** 31/3-11/7 29/8-29/9 📍 N 46°57'30'' W 0°54'14''

St. Malo-du-Bois, F-85590 / Pays de la Loire (Vendée)

👫 🚫 📶 **iD** (1583)

🏕 La Vallée de Poupet
☎ +33 (0)2-51923145
📠 +33 (0)2-51923865
🔄 1/5 - 30/9
@ camping@valleedepoupet.com

30ha 94T(90-120m²) 6A

1 ACD**G**IJKLMOPQ
2 BCLRVWXY
3 ABGHJRU**W**
4 (A 1/7-31/8) (F+H 🔄)
(Q 1/7-31/8) (R+U+V+Z 🔄)
5 **AB**FGIJKLMNOPQUWXYZ
6 ACEGHK(N 3km)ORTV

💬 Welcoming family campsite with own pool and an attractive restaurant in front of the entrance. There is an open air theatre next to the campsite.

🔜 From A83 exit Les Herbiers. From Cholet direction St. Malo. From there campsite is clearly signposted.

Mortagne-sur-Sèvre — A87 — D149 — D41 — D160 — CC — D11 — Les Epesses — Les Herbiers — D752 — D744

CC € **17** 1/5-30/6 1/9-29/9 📍 N 46°55'33'' W 0°52'27''

St. Martin-Lars-en-Ste-Hermine, F-85210 / Pays de la Loire (Vendée)

☂ 🚫 📶 ✿ **iD** (1584)

🏕 Le Colombier★★★★
☎ +33 (0)2-51278384
📠 +33 (0)2-51278729
🔄 1/4 - 1/10
@ lecolombier.nat@wanadoo.fr

50ha 112T(120-200m²) 6-16A CEE

1 ACD**G**IJKLMOPST
2 BCDILRVWXY
3 ABDGHJNRUVW
4 (C+H 🔄) **KLN**
(Q+R+T+U+X+Z 🔄)
5 **AB**EFGIJKLMNOPUW
6 ACEGH**IK**(N 1,5km)RTUV

💬 A well maintained naturist campsite with excellent toilet facilities. Large swimming pool, spacious pitches and a lively atmosphere in the bar and restaurant.

🔜 From Noirt take the N148 to Ste Hermine, D8 through Thiré. In Thiré left onto D10 to St. Martin-Lars. Marked with small signs from here.

Chantonnay — D949 BIS — La Caillère-Saint-Hilaire — La Réorthe — D19 — D948 — D8 — CC — A83 — D148 — D137

CC € **19** 1/4-7/7 25/8-30/9 📍 N 46°35'52'' W 0°58'9''

St. Michel-en-l'Herm, F-85580 / Pays de la Loire (Vendée)

♿ 📶 **iD** (1585)

La Dive****
12 route de la Mer
☎ +33 (0)2-51302694
☀ 1/4 - 30/9
@ camping-la-dive@wanadoo.fr

9ha 85T 10A CEE

1 ACD**F**IJKLMOPRS
2 GRVWXY
3 BDGHJKN**OPQ**RV
4 (**A** 1/7-31/8) (C+H ☀) IJ**K**M
N(Q 1/6-31/8) (R ☀)
(T+U+V+X+Z 1/7-31/8)
5 **AB**EFGIJKLMNOPQUWX
6 ACEGH**K**(N 0,5km)TUV

💬 A lovely campsite between land and sea. 5 minutes from the lovely sandy beaches and close to the 'Vénise Verte'. Bar, small shop and a beautiful jacuzzi and sauna. Wonderful atmosphere.

🚗 In St. Michel-en-l'Herm direction l'Aiguillon-sur-Mer. Right at end of village and follow camping signs.

CC € ⑰ 1/4-13/7 1/9-29/9

📐 N 46°20'57'' W 1°14'53''

St. Philbert-de-Grand-Lieu, F-44310 / Pays de la Loire (Loire-Atlantique)

♿ 📶 **iD** (1586)

Village Les Rives de Grand Lieu
1 avenue de Nantes
☎ +33 (0)2-40788879
☀ 1/4 - 31/10
@ accueil@lesrivesdegrandlieu.com

4,5ha 100T(100-200m²) 10A CEE

1 ACD**G**IJKLM**P**S
2 CDF**G**LMPRVXY
3 ABGHJKL**OP**RU**W**Z
4 (A 1/7-31/8) (Q+T+U+Z ☀)
5 **A**DFGIJKLMNPUWZ
6 AEGJ(N 0,5km)OTV

💬 Camping Les Rives de Grand Lieu is a lovely campsite full of character and on shaded grounds. The pitches are mainly separated by greenery. You can go swimming in the natural waters or sunbathe on the supervised sandy beach.

🚗 From Nantes direction Bordeaux then towards St. Philbert-de-Grand-Lieu. Campsite located between Super U and the town centre.

CC € ⑪ 1/4-9/7 28/8-30/10

📐 N 47°2'31'' W 1°38'29''

St. Vincent-sur-Jard, F-85520 / Pays de la Loire (Vendée)

📶 **iD** (1587)

La Bolée d'Air****
route du Bouil
☎ +33 (0)2-51330505
📠 +33 (0)2-51339404
☀ 30/3 - 29/9
@ info@chadotel.com

6ha 90T(80-100m²) 10A CEE

1 ACD**F**IJKLMOPRS
2 ALRVWX
3 ABFGK**MN**QRU
4 (C+F+H ☀) JK**N**
(Q+R+T+U 15/5-10/9)
(Z 1/5-15/9)
5 **AB**EFGIJKMNPUZ
6 FG**K**(N 2km)RTV

💬 A large campsite with marked out pitches next to the route Départementale (D21). The site is 1000m from the unguarded beach at Bouil and 1500m from the village. Lovely indoor-outdoor swimming pool with extensive entertainment for young and old.

🚗 Les Sables d'Olonne direction La Tranche-sur-Mer, 1500m beyond St. Vincent-sur-Jard (D21), on the right of the road.

CC € ⑮ 30/3-12/7 30/8-28/9

📐 N 46°25'5'' W 1°31'38''

Ste Reine-de-Bretag./Pontchât., F-44160 / Pays de la Loire (Loire-Atlantique) 👫👭 ♿ 🛜 iD (1588)

- 🏕 Camping Le Deffay****
- 🏠 D33
- ☎ +33 (0)2-40880057
- 🗓 26/4 - 30/9
- @ campingledeffay@gmail.com

13ha 171T(100-150m²) 10-16A CEE

1. **ACDF**IJKLMOPRS
2. DFJLRVWXY
3. B**F**GHJKMRUVW
4. (E+H+Q+R+T+U+V+Y+Z 🚐)
5. **AB**EFGIJKLMNPUWXYZ
6. ACDEGI**K**(N 5km)TVW

💬 Deffay, a lovely 18th century family estate. Pitches surrounded by flowering bushes and greenery, a number of them with a view of the ponds. Four-star comfort and tranquillity. Toilet facilities renovated in 2017.

🚗 N165/E60 Nantes-Vannes, exit Pontchâteau at the roundabout before the town direction Ste Reine-de-Bretagne or Calvaire via D33. Campsite clearly signposted.

CC €15 26/4-6/7 27/8-29/9

🧭 N 47°26'28'' W 2°9'36''

Talmont-St-Hilaire, F-85440 / Pays de la Loire (Vendée) 👫👭 ♿ 🛜 iD (1589)

- 🏕 Sun Océan***
- 🏠 538 av. des Sables
- ☎ 🖨 +33 (0)2-51906124
- 🗓 31/3 - 29/9
- @ camping-sunocean@wanadoo.fr

2,2ha 58T(100-140m²) 10A CEE

1. ACD**F**IJKLMOPRS
2. GRVWXY
3. BGHJNRU
4. (E+H 🚐) (T+Z 1/7-31/8)
5. **A**GIJKLMNPUXYZ
6. EGJ(N 0,1km)RTV

💬 A wonderfully peaceful campsite with a friendly ambiance and spacious marked out pitches. Very well-maintained toilet facilities. Heated indoor pool. A good starting point for walking and cycling tours. Bakery and shops within walking distance.

🚗 On the D949 when leaving Talmont-St-Hilaire towards Les Sables. On the right.

CC €15 31/3-13/7 31/8-28/9 7=6, 14=12, 21=18

🧭 N 46°28'14'' W 1°38'6''

Tharon-Plage, F-44730 / Pays de la Loire (Loire-Atlantique) ♿ 🛜 iD (1590)

- 🏕 Camping du Vieux Chateau***
- 🏠 54 avenue d'Anjou
- ☎ +33 (0)2-40278347
- 🗓 17/3 - 10/11
- @ campingduvieuxchateau@gmail.com

1,1ha 27T(80-120m²) 10A CEE

1. ACD**G**IJKLMO**PQ**
2. AEFGQRVWXY
3. B**F**GHJKLRUWY
4. (E+H 🚐) (Q 7/7-2/9) (R 🚐) (T+U+V+Z 7/7-2/9)
5. **AB**DEFGIJKLMNOPUZ
6. ABEGK(N 0,5km)TV

💬 Quiet family campsite 500 metres from the level sandy beach. Adequate and pleasantly clean toilet facilities. Centre for 'Peche a Pied'. Located in the characteristic beach village Tharon Plage. Almost level area, supermarket 2 km away.

🚗 D213, Route Bleue St. Nazaire-Pornic, exit La Plaine sur Mer, D96 to the big roundabout, then direction Tharon-Plage. Turn left and follow campsite signs. Take care with GPS.

CC €15 17/3-7/7 26/8-2/11 7=6, 14=12, 21=18

🧭 N 47°9'36'' W 2°9'47''

Tuffé, F-72160 / Pays de la Loire (Sarthe) 👪 ♿ 📶 ✿ 🆔 **1591**

🏕 du Lac****
✉ route de Prévelles
☎ +33 (0)2-43938834
📠 +33 (0)2-43934354
🗓 7/4 - 7/10
@ campingdulac.tuffe@orange.fr

4ha 115**T**(85-200m²) 6A CEE

1 ACD**G**HIJKLMPRS
2 ACDGLMRTVWXY
3 ABGHJKM**N**OPQRUW**Z**
4 (C+E+H+Q+R+Z ⌂)
5 **AB**DEFGJLMNPQUWZ
6 ACDEG**K**(N 0,7km)RTV

💬 This fine municipal campsite with an indoor swimming pool, fishpond and plenty of recreational opportunities is located in lovely natural surroundings. Well worth a visit!

🚗 Follow the D323 to Connerré, then via the D33 to Tuffé and follow the 'Base de Loisirs' camping signs. Camping du Lac is next door.

La Ferté-Bernard
D6 D7 D1
D19
D301 CC A11
D33
Connerré
D323 D85 D98

CC € **15** 7/4-7/7 25/8-6/10 7=6, 14=12, 21=18 📍 N 48°7'6'' E 0°30'36''

Vendrennes, F-85250 / Pays de la Loire (Vendée) 📶 🆔 **1592**

🏕 de la Motte****
✉ La Motte
☎ +33 (0)2-51635967
🗓 1/1 - 21/12
@ contact@camping-lamotte.com

3ha 43**T**(100-140m²) 16A CEE

1 ACD**G**IJKLMOPQ
2 FGRVXY
3 ADGHJNUW
4 (C+H 1/6-15/9) JK
   (Q+R 1/6-30/9)
   (T+U+V 1/6-15/9) (Z ⌂)
5 **AB**DGIJKLMNOPUZ
6 AEGJ(N 0,5km)ORTV

💬 This friendly campsite with large pitches in the interior of the Vendée is a guarantee for relaxation and space. Right next to the A83/A87 motorways.

🚗 From the A83 or A87 take the Les Essarts exit, then the D160 towards Cholet. Campsite signposted in the village of Vendrennes.

D6 D23 D755
Saint-Fulgent **Les Herbiers**
A83 A87 CC
D137
D98
D160 D7 D39 D48

CC € **15** 1/1-9/7 27/8-20/12 📍 N 46°49'38'' W 1°7'2''

Yvré-l'Evêque, F-72530 / Pays de la Loire (Sarthe) ♿ 📶 ✿ 🆔 **1593**

🏕 Camping Le Pont Romain****
✉ allée des Ormeaux
☎ +33 (0)2-43822539
🗓 16/3 - 11/11
@ contact@campinglepontromain.fr

2,5ha 67**T**(80-150m²) 16A CEE

1 ACD**G**IJKLNPQ
2 FGLRTUVWXY
3 BGHJQRU
4 (C+H 15/6-15/9)
   (Q 1/5-30/10) (R ⌂)
   (T 1/7-31/8)
5 **AB**DEFGIJKLMNPUWXYZ
6 ACDEGJ(N 0,5km)T

💬 This campsite is located in a natural oasis a few kilometres from the centre of the art and history town of Le Mans. A convenient location for visiting the tourist attractions. The campsite has a swimming pool, toddlers' pool, activity room and snack bar with terrace to guarantee you a pleasant stay.

🚗 From E50/A11, at exit 6 head south to the A28. On A28, exit 23 Le Mans-Centre.

D300
D304
A11
D301
Le Mans CC D323
Allonnes Changé D357
A28
D338

CC € **17** 16/3-30/6 1/9-10/11 📍 N 48°1'8'' E 0°16'46''

Aigrefeuille-d'Aunis, F-17290 / Poitou-Charentes (Charente-Maritime)   ♿ 🛜 iD 1594

▲ La Taillée***
✉ 3 rue du Bois Gaillard
☎ +33 (0)546355048
⌖ 1/4 - 30/10
@ lataillee@hotmail.fr

2ha 42T(80-120m²) 6-10A CEE

1 ABCD**F**IJLM**P**T
2 LRTVWXY
3 ABGH**P**QRU**W**
4 (C+H 15/6-15/9) (Q 1/7-31/8)
(R ⌖) (T 1/6-31/8)
(U 1/7-31/8) (Z ⌖)
5 **AB**FGIJKLMNPUZ
6 ACEG**K**(N 0,8km)TV

💬 Campsite is in a green, quiet and friendly location close to La Rochelle and Rochefort and 15 minutes from the beach at Châtelaillon. Free wifi, bar, mini golf (free), playground, gym, swimming pool open from 15 June to 15 September. Shops within 5 minutes' walk. Not far from Lac de Frace, where you can fish and hike.

🚗 Follow signs to centre of Aigrefeuille-d'Aunis, then follow signs to campsite.

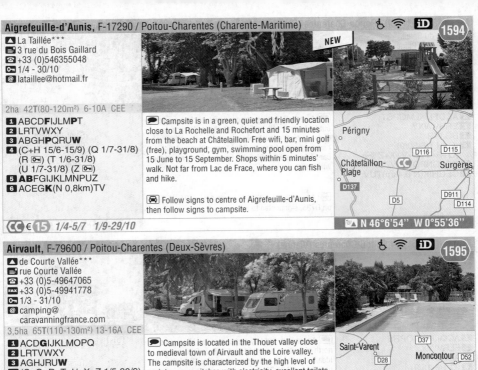

CC € **15** 1/4-5/7 1/9-29/10   🗺 N 46°6'54'' W 0°55'36''

Airvault, F-79600 / Poitou-Charentes (Deux-Sèvres)   ♿ 🛜 iD 1595

▲ de Courte Vallée***
✉ rue Courte Vallée
☎ +33 (0)5-49647065
📠 +33 (0)5-49941778
⌖ 1/3 - 31/10
@ camping@
caravanningfrance.com

3,5ha 65T(110-130m²) 13-16A CEE

1 ACD**G**IJKLMOPQ
2 LRTVWXY
3 AGHJRU**W**
4 (C+Q+R+T+U+X+Z 1/5-30/9)
5 **AB**GIJKLMNPUWZ
6 ABDEGK(N 1,5km)TV

💬 Campsite is located in the Thouet valley close to medieval town of Airvault and the Loire valley. The campsite is characterized by the high level of maintenance; pitches with electricity, excellent toilets, swimming pool. Wireless internet and nice terrace. The English family is hospitable and will do a lot to offer you a wonderful holiday.

🚗 From Thouars take the D938. Then take the D725-bis as far as Airvault. In the village follow the camp signs 'de Courte Vallée'.

CC € **19** 1/3-14/7 1/9-30/10   🗺 N 46°49'59'' W 0°8'53''

Argenton-les-Vall./Argentonnay, F-79150 / Poitou-Charentes (Deux-Sèvres)   ♿ 🛜 iD 1596

▲ Camping du Lac d'Hautibus**
✉ rue de la Sablière
☎ +33 (0)6-16101096
⌖ 1/4 - 30/9
@ campinghautibus@orange.fr

0,7ha 45T(100-120m²) 6A CEE

1 ACD**G**IJLMPST
2 DJKLRVWXY
3 ABCGHJMNRU**W**
4 (A 1/7-31/8) (C 7/7-31/8)
(H 1/7-31/8) J
5 **AB**FIJKLMNOPUV
6 AEGJ(N 0,5km)

💬 A family campsite, quiet and in natural surroundings, close to all the shops.

🚗 In Argenton-les-Vallées centre, D748 direction Thouars. Campsite indicated by 'complexe sportive'.

CC € **11** 1/4-30/6 1/9-29/9   🗺 N 46°59'16'' W 0°27'6''

Ars-en-Ré, F-17590 / Poitou-Charentes (Charente-Maritime) 🛜 iD 1597

🏕 Camp du Soleil***
🏠 route de la Plage
☎ +33 (0)5-46294062
📠 +33 (0)5-46294174
🔓 2/4 - 30/9
@ contact@campdusoleil.com

2ha 67T(70-120m²) 10A CEE

1 ACD**F**IJKLMOPST
2 ERSVWXY
3 BGJKR
4 (C+H 1/5-30/9)
(Q+R+T+U+V+X+Z 🔓)
5 DEFGNPQRUWZ
6 CEGHIK(N 0,4km)TUV

💬 A peaceful family campsite with pitches marked-out by hedges with and without shade. At walking distance from a lovely beach and the welcoming harbour town of Ars-en-Ré. All amenities and with a bar and restaurant. Bicycles for rent. Free wifi on the whole site.

🚗 After tolbridge D735 towards Ars-en-Ré. At Ars on D735, signposted to left.

Saint-Clément-des-Baleines Loix

CC € **17** 2/4-6/7 26/8-29/9 ⛰ N 46°12'14'' W 1°31'13''

Avanton, F-86170 / Poitou-Charentes (Vienne) 🧑‍🧒 ♿ 🛜 iD 1598

🏕 Du Futur***
🏠 9 rue des Bois
☎ +33 (0)5-49540967
🔓 1/4 - 4/11
@ contact@camping-du-futur.com

3ha 50T(100-120m²) 6-10A CEE

1 AC**G**IJKLMOPRS
2 FLRVWX
3 AB**F**GNQR
4 (C 1/6-15/9)
(Q+R+T+U+Z 🔓)
5 **AB**FGIJLMNPUWZ
6 ACDEG**JK**(N 0,5km)V

💬 A spacious and tidy campsite a few kilometres north of Poitiers and right next to Parc Futuroscope. Ideally located as a stopover campsite. Check-in possible until 23:00.

🚗 N10 exit Avanton, follow arrows, on D757 (the road to Poitiers). Or via motorway exit 29.

D18
D757
D30
D20
Migné-Auxances A10 N147
D7
Poitiers

CC € **17** 1/4-8/7 26/8-3/11 ⛰ N 46°39'22'' E 0°18'7''

Aytré/La Rochelle, F-17440 / Poitou-Charentes (Charente-Maritime) 🛜 iD 1599

🏕 Les Sables****
🏠 chemin du Pontreau
☎ 📠 +33 (0)5-46454030
🔓 1/4 - 14/10
@ camping_les_sables@yahoo.fr

5,5ha 298T(100-140m²) 6A CEE

1 ACD**F**IJLPQ
2 AERTVWX
3 ABGKMN**OP**RUVWY
4 (C 1/5-15/9) (F 1/5-30/9)
(H 1/5-15/9) IJ**LMNO**
(Q+R+T+U 1/7-31/8)
(V 15/6-31/8) (X+Z 1/7-31/8)
5 **AB**EFGIJKLMNPRUVZ
6 CFGIK(N 2km)RTV

💬 A wonderful family campsite with every amenity. Spacious pitches separated by hedges. Sandy beach within walking distance. Heated indoor swimming pool. Free wifi throughout the site. Close to La Rochelle.

🚗 N137 La Rochelle-Rochefort. Exit Aytré (D939). Turn right at the roundabout. At the following roundabout third exit left onto the D937. Turn left at the second traffic lights. Follow the signs 'La Plage'.

D735
D9 N11
La Rochelle
Aytré
CC
D109
D137
D5

152 CC € **19** 1/4-30/6 1/9-13/10 ⛰ N 46°6'59'' W 1°7'10''

Bignac, F-16170 / Poitou-Charentes (Charente)

♿ 🛜 iD **1600**

🏠 Marco de Bignac***
📧 2 chemin de la Résistance
☎ +33 (0)5-45217841
🔓 1/2 - 30/11
@ info@marcodebignac.com

8ha 84T(100m²) 6A

1 ABCDGIJKLMOPQ
2 DFGRVWXY
3 ADGHJKMNRW
4 (B 1/7-31/8) (Q+R 🔓)
　(U+Y+Z 1/4-15/10)
5 ABDFGHIJKLMNPQRUWZ
6 AEGJ(N 3km)T

💬 An idyllic and relaxing campsite located by a beautiful fishing lake. Shady and sunny pitches. Renovated and heated toilet facilities. Swimming pool, sports facilities and restaurant (ask about opening times) with a waterside terrace.

🚗 Leave the RN10 at the La Touche D'Anais sign. Follow the 'Vars', 'Bignac' and then 'Camping Marco de Bignac' signs.

D739　D6
D736　N10
CC　Vars
D14　D939　D737　Brie
Asnières-sur-Nouère　Champniers

CC € **17** 1/2-7/7 25/8-29/11 7=6　🧭 N 45°47'51'' E 0°3'47''

Bois Vert/Com. du Tallud, F-79200 / Poitou-Charentes (Deux-Sèvres)

♿ 🛜 iD **1601**

🏠 Le Bois Vert****
📧 14 rue de Boisseau
☎ +33 (0)5-49647843
📠 +33 (0)5-49959668
🔓 2/4 - 26/10
@ campingboisvert@orange.fr

3ha 88T(70-130m²) 16A CEE

1 ACDGIJKLMPST
2 CLRTUVWXY
3 ABGHJMRUW
4 (C+G 1/6-15/9)
　(Q+R+T+U+V+X+Z 15/5-15/9)
5 ABCDEFGHIJKLMNOPQRU
　WXYZ
6 ADEGIK(N 2km)ORTUV

💬 Medium sized campsite on a lake and a river with opportunities for fishing. Close to the medieval town of Parthenay. Well marked-out cycling and walking paths.

🚗 From Niort take the D743 as far as the southwest edge of Parthenay, then turn left onto the D949bis, over the bridge and immediately right.

D19　N149
　　Châtillon-sur-Thouet
Parthenay
　CC
D748
D743　D938　D738

CC € **17** 2/4-5/7 23/8-25/10 7=6　🧭 N 46°38'30'' W 0°16'3''

Boyardville, F-17190 / Poitou-Charentes (Charente-Maritime)

🛜 iD **1602**

🏠 Les Saumonards**
📧 route des Saumonards
☎ +33 (0)5-46472320
🔓 1/4 - 15/10
@ campingmunicipal.
　stgeorgesdoleron@wanadoo.fr

267T(60-120m²) 5A CEE

1 ACDGHIJKLMOPST
2 ABESWXY
3 AFGHJR
4 (Q 15/5-15/9)
　(T+U+V+Z 15/6-15/9)
5 ABFGIJKLMNOPUZ
6 J(N 1,2km)T

💬 A peaceful campsite in pine woods with access to the beach.

🚗 From the viaduct towards Dolus and then Boyardville. Over the bridge in Boyardville. Campsite shown as 'Municipal'.

Saint-Denis-d'Oléron　Châtelaillon-Plage
Saint-Georges-d'Oléron
　CC
Saint-Pierre-d'Oléron　Port-des-Barques

CC € **15** 1/4-30/6 1/9-14/10 7=6　🧭 N 45°58'42'' W 1°14'28''

Boyardville, F-17190 / Poitou-Charentes (Charente-Maritime)

👫 📶 **iD** 1603

- 🏔 Signol****
- 📧 121 avenue des Albatros
- ☎ +33 (0)2-51204194
- 🔓 7/4 - 23/9
- @ contact@camp-atlantique.com

8ha 44T(60-100m²) 16A CEE

- **1** BCD**F**HIJKLOPST
- **2** ABISVX
- **3** B**F**GJKNRUV**W**
- **4** (C 28/4-23/9) (F+H 🔓) J**K**LM
  N(Q+S+T+U+V+X+Z 🔓)
- **5** **AB**FGIJKMNOPUWZ
- **6** CEGHIJ**K**(N 6km)TV

💬 Renovated campsite on sandy ground. Large playground and indoor/outdoor pool with pool slide. Close to the centre of Boyardville, known for its harbour and festivities.

🚗 From bridge towards Dolus, on roundabout 1st road on right towards Boyardville.

Châtelaillon-Plage

Saint-Pierre-d'Oléron

CC € **17** 7/4-7/7 1/9-22/9 | 🧭 N 45°58'5'' W 1°14'40''

Brossac, F-16480 / Poitou-Charentes (Charente)

👫 📶 **iD** 1604

- 🏔 Camping de l'Etang Vallier
- 📧 Etang Vallier
- ☎ +33 (0)5-45980783
- 🔓 8/1 - 21/12
- @ campingetangvallier@orange.fr

48ha 60T(100-150m²) 16A

- **1** AC**F**IJKLOPST
- **2** ADKLMRWXY
- **3** AGHJK**QS**WZ
- **4** (A 5/7-31/8) **KLN**
  (Q+R+T+V+X+Z 🔓)
- **5** **A**DIJMNOPU
- **6** ADEGJ**K**(N 1km)O

💬 Well-maintained campsite with plenty of trees on a lake with swimming and fishing. Separate artificial sandy beach.

🚗 N10 from Angoulême, do not take Barbezieux nord exit but the 2nd exit to Barbezieux, then follow Chillac-Brossac. Coming from Bordeaux exit Montguyon then Brossac, drive round the lake, no entrance on the front. The front of the chalets is not the campsite.

Baignes-Sainte-Radegonde

CC € **15** 8/1-8/7 1/9-20/12 | 🧭 N 45°19'40'' W 0°3'54''

Chalandray, F-86190 / Poitou-Charentes (Vienne)

♿ 📶 **iD** 1605

- 🏔 Du Bois de St. Hilaire
- 📧 route de la Gare
- ☎ 📠 +33 (0)5-49602084
- 🔓 6/4 - 30/9
- @ info@camping-st-hilaire.eu

8ha 34T(100-198m²) 10A CEE

- **1** ACDGIJKLMOPQ
- **2** BRVWXY
- **3** A**F**GHKMNQRU
- **4** (B 1/6-31/8) (Q 🔓)
  (T+V 1/7-31/8) (Z 🔓)
- **5** **AB**GIJKLMNOPUW
- **6** AEK(N 0,7km)TV

💬 A peaceful campsite in a wood with plenty of tall trees, but 1 km from the local shops. The site has a lovely swimming pool, a tennis court with practice wall and a friendly English owner. You can stand on the prime meridian on the campsite. Plenty of cycling and walking in the immediate surroundings.

🚗 From Poitiers take the N149 direction Partenay (or vice versa). In Chalandray take the D24 direction Vauzailles. The campsite is located about 750 metres on the right.

La Peyratte

Ayron

Vouillé

CC € **15** 6/4-29/6 1/9-29/9 | 🧭 N 46°40'4'' W 0°0'11''

Châtelaillon-Plage, F-17340 / Poitou-Charentes (Charente-Maritime) 📶 ✿ iD (1606)

🏕 Camping Au Port-Punay***
📧 allée Bernard Moreau,
    Les Boucholeur
☎ +33 (0)5-17810000
📠 +33 (0)5-46568644
📅 4/5 - 23/9
@ contact@camping-port-punay.com
3ha 116T(100m²) 10A CEE

1 ACDFIJKLMP**Q**
2 AEGRSTVWXY
3 ABGJKRUWY
4 (C+H 📅) K(Q+R+S 📅)
    (T+U+V+X+Z 15/6-15/9)
5 **AB**EFGJLMNOPQRUVWXY
    Z
6 ACEGH**IK**(N 0,2km)OTUV

💬 A friendly campsite, partly under trees and 200m from a sandy beach. Heated swimming pool. Excellent toilet facilities and large pitches. Starting point for visiting the islands Ré and Aix, situated between the towns La Rochelle and Rochefort. Châtelaillon can be visited by bike. Wifi. The site has an Ecolabel.

🚗 N137 La Rochelle-Rochefort, exit D109 Châtelaillon-Plage. First left at the second roundabout. Follow 'Les Boucholeurs' then follow campsite signs.

Aytré
Châtelaillon-Plage
CC
D5
D137
D911

CC € ⑲ 4/5-6/7 25/8-22/9 | N 46°3'18'' W 1°5'0''

Châtelaillon-Plage, F-17340 / Poitou-Charentes (Charente-Maritime) ♿ 📶 iD (1607)

🏕 L'Océan***
📧 2 bis, Square des Terriers
☎ +33 (0)5-46568797
📅 19/5 - 30/9
@ reception@oceancamping.fr

1,9ha 97T(85-120m²) 10A CEE

1 ACD**F**IJKLMOPST
2 AGRVWXY
3 BGHJKLRU
4 (B 1/6-15/9) (Q 📅)
    (T+U 1/7-31/8)
5 **AB**EFGIJKLMNOPUVZ
6 CEG**K**(N 1km)TV

💬 Pure camping pleasure (only touring pitches) within walking distance (600m) of the sea. Congenial atmosphere and excellent toilet facilities. Lovely swimming lake. Walking and cycling paradise. A good base for visiting La Rochelle, Fort Boyard, les îles de Ré, Oléron en Aix and le Marais Poitevin.

🚗 N137 La Rochelle southwards, exit Angoulins. Then D202 Châtelaillon-Plage. Campsite is signposted on entering Châtelaillon.

La Rochelle
D939
CC
Châtelaillon-Plage
D137
D5

CC € ⑲ 19/5-1/7 26/8-29/9 7=6 | N 46°5'12'' W 1°5'39''

Châtelaillon-Plage, F-17340 / Poitou-Charentes (Charente-Maritime) 📶 iD (1608)

🏕 Le Village Corsaire des
    2 Plages****
📧 av. d'Angoulins
☎ +33 (0)5-46562753
📠 +33 (0)5-46435118
📅 31/3 - 30/9
@ reception@2plages.com
4,5ha 97T(80-150m²) 10A CEE

1 ACD**F**IJKLMOPST
2 AEGPRSTVXY
3 ABF**G**JKLMNRUWY
4 (C+H+Q+R+S+T+U+V+X+Z
    1/5-30/9)
5 **AB**EFGIJKLMNOPUVWZ
6 CGH**K**(N 1km)ORTV

💬 An attractive campsite with a lovely heated swimming pool. Walking distance from the sea. Spacious partly shaded pitches under high deciduous trees. Good base for cycle and walking tours.

🚗 N137 La Rochelle direction south, exit Angoulins. Then the D202 Châtelaillon-Plage. You will see the campsite when entering Châtelaillon.

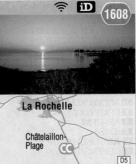

La Rochelle
Châtelaillon-Plage
CC
D5
D137

CC € ⑲ 28/4-6/7 25/8-29/9 7=6, 14=11 | N 46°5'3'' W 1°5'36''

Chef-Boutonne, F-79110 / Poitou-Charentes (Deux-Sèvres) ♿ 🛜 iD 1609

🏕 Le Moulin***
📧 Treneuillet, 1 route de Niort
☎ +33 (0)5-49297346
🔑 1/1 - 6/7, 22/7 - 31/12
@ info@campingchef.com

1,2ha 37T(40-150m²) 10-16A

1 ACD**G**IJKLM**P**RS
2 CGLRUVWXY
3 AGHJR
4 (C 1/5-30/9) (T 1/7-31/8)
(U 1/3-1/12) (Y 1/6-30/9)
(Z 1/7-31/8)
5 **A**GIJKLMNPUWZ
6 ACDEG**K**(N 2km)T

💬 A peaceful, family campsite by an old watermill. Level grounds, swimming pool and restaurant. Children's playground. Close to an active silver mine, Chateau de Javarzay, with fishing opportunities and guided tours.

🚗 In Chef-Boutonne follow the D740 towards Brioux. Campsite signposted.

CC € **17** 1/1-5/7 1/9-29/12 📡 N 46°6'28'' W 0°5'38''

Condac, F-16700 / Poitou-Charentes (Charente) 👫 🛜 iD 1610

🏕 Le Réjallant***
☎ +33 (0)9-83882906
🔑 1/1 - 31/12
@ camping@lerejallant.fr

2ha 70T(80-150m²) 10A CEE

1 ACDGIJKLMOPRS
2 CDRTUVWXY
3 ABGHJKR
4 (C+G 1/5-15/9) (Q 1/7-31/8)
(R 🔑) (T+U+Z 1/6-15/9)
5 **AB**DFGIJKLNPUXYZ
6 ACDEGK(N 1,5km)OT

💬 Located in the Charente, 150m from the river which bears its name, you can enjoy a holiday in the countryside throughout the year. 50 km from Futuroscope and Cognac.

🚗 Coudac village is 50 km south of Poitiers. Follow Coudac signs direction 'Aire de Réjallant'.

CC € **13** 1/1-30/6 1/9-31/12 7=6 📡 N 46°0'54'' E 0°12'46''

Confolens, F-16500 / Poitou-Charentes (Charente) 👫 🛜 iD 1611

🏕 des Ribières***
📧 route de St. Germain de Confolens
☎ +33 (0)5-45853527
🔑 1/4 - 1/10
@ camping-les-ribieres@orange.fr

2,3ha 119T(80-250m²) 16A CEE

1 ACD**G**IJKLMPQ
2 CRUVWXY
3 ABHJR**W**
4 (Q 🔑)
5 **AB**CIJKLMNPUV
6 CDEGK(N 0,6km)

💬 Quiet campsite on the Vienne (and on the D95), 5 minutes walking distance from Confolens centre. Excellent base for walking and cycling in the peaceful Charente region. The area has many culinary options.

🚗 In Confolens dir. St. Germain. Campsite on left of road after 500 metres.

CC € **13** 1/4-30/6 1/9-30/9 📡 N 46°1'9'' E 0°40'30''

Couhé, F-86700 / Poitou-Charentes (Vienne)

♿ 🛜 **iD** (1612)

▲ Sites & Paysages Les Peupliers****
🚏 RN10
☎ +33 (0)5-49592116
🅾 2/5 - 30/9
@ info@lespeupliers.fr

16ha 187**T**(80-140m²) 16A

1 ACGIJKLMOPQ
2 BCFLRVWXY
3 ABGHN**Q**RUW
4 (C+H 🅾) J(Q+S 🅾)
(V+Z 1/7-31/8)
5 **AB**CDEFGIJKNOP**ST**UWXY
Z
6 ACEG**K**(N 1km)OTV

💬 A lovely campsite with a relaxed atmosphere. Marked out pitches. On both sides of the river. A campsite with plenty of recreational facilities, heated toilets, located in a rural area. Reception is very customer-friendly.

🚗 At the N10, exit Couhé-Nord.

Château-Larcher
D150
D950
D14 | D2
Couhé
D15 | N10
D55 | D7 | D1

CC €**19** 2/5-9/7 27/8-29/9 7=6, 14=12   📍 N 46°18'44'' E 0°10'55''

Coulon, F-79510 / Poitou-Charentes (Deux-Sèvres)

♿ 🛜 ✿ **iD** (1613)

▲ Flower Camping La Venise Verte****
🚏 178 route des Bords de Sèvre
☎ +33 (0)5-49359036
🅾 1/4 - 15/10
@ accueil@camping-laveniseverte.fr

2,2ha 97**T**(80-187m²) 10A CEE

1 ACD**F**IJKLMPQ
2 BCFRTVWXY
3 ABGHJKLNRU**W**
4 (A 15/7-20/8)
(C+G 15/6-15/9) (Q+R 🅾)
(T+U+X 1/5-30/9) (Z 🅾)
5 **AB**EFGIJKLMNOPUWXYZ
6 ACEGHJ(N 2km)OSTV

💬 A campsite 2 km from Coulon, in the heart of the Marais Poitevin. Lovely cycling and walking trips are possible. 97 pitches, large swimming pool, restaurant and many recreational opportunities. The campsite has been awarded the European Eco label, thanks to the sustainable tourism that is practiced here. A lovely campsite for a relaxing stay.

🚗 From Niort dir. Coulon (D9), then from Coulon D123 direction Irleau. Site on this road.

D148 | A83
D15
D1 | D744
D25
Magné | **Niort**
D3 | Aiffres
Frontenay-Rohan-Rohan
N248 | D650

CC €**17** 1/4-9/7 27/8-14/10   📍 N 46°18'54'' W 0°36'33''

Dolus-d'Oléron, F-17550 / Poitou-Charentes (Charente-Maritime)

♿ 🛜 **iD** (1614)

▲ Flower Camping La Cailletière***
🚏 route de Boyardville
☎ +33 (0)5-46753633
🅾 7/4 - 23/9
@ camping.la.cailletiere@wanadoo.fr

3ha 40**T**(80-120m²) 10A

1 ACD**G**HIJKLMPST
2 ABQRUVXY
3 A**F**GHJKNR
4 (E 🅾) (G 1/6-30/9)
(Q 1/7-30/8)
(T+U+V+Z 1/7-31/8)
5 **AB**EFGIJKLMNOPUWZ
6 E**K**(N 0,8km)OV

💬 A peaceful, wooded campsite in the middle of an island, close to shops and cycle routes. Heated indoor swimming pool. Large marked out pitches.

🚗 From the viaduct direction St. Pierre. At the roundabout in Dolus (by the Intermarché) direction Boyardville. Signposted thereafter.

Saint-Pierre-d'Oléron
CC
D26

CC €**15** 7/4-6/7 1/9-22/9   📍 N 45°54'59'' W 1°15'10''

Dolus-d'Oléron, F-17550 / Poitou-Charentes (Charente-Maritime)

  ♋ 📶 **iD** **1615**

🔺 Ostrea****
📧 route des Huitres
☎ +33 (0)5-46476236
📠 +33 (0)5-46752001
🗓 1/4 - 30/9
@ camping.ostrea@wanadoo.fr

2ha 60**T**(75-120m²) 6A

1 ACG IJKLMPRS
2 AEKRSTVWX
3 BF GJKNRUWY
4 (E+F+H 🖱) K(Q+R 🖱)
(U+V 1/7-31/8) (Z 🖱)
5 **AB** EFGIJKMNOPUVWZ
6 CEG **K**(N 3,5km)O **P**UV

💬 A small, peaceful family campsite located right by the sea. Indoor heated swimming pool with jacuzzi. Pontoon for boats provided. Very well maintained toilet facilities.

🚌 Turn right over the bridge direction Le Château, through the village right on the coast road. Campsite 3 km further on.

Saint-Pierre-d'Oléron ○

Ⓒ Ⓒ

D26

Ⓒ Ⓒ € **17** 1/4-30/6   1/9-29/9   📷🔺 N 45°54'46'' W 1°13'26''

Exideuil-sur-Vienne, F-16150 / Poitou-Charentes (Charente)

  ♋ 📶 **iD** **1616**

🔺 Camping de la Rivière**
📧 La Rambaudie
☎ +33 (0)6-07987379
🗓 1/1 - 31/12
@ christophe.derveaux@gmail.com

2ha 34**T**(100-120m²) 16A CEE

1 AG IJKLMOPQ
2 CFGJKMRTUVWXY
3 AGHJNQRU **W**X
4 (B 1/4-1/11) (Q 1/7-31/8)
(R+T+U+Y+Z 1/5-30/9)
5 **A**GIJKLMNOPQUWXYZ
6 CDEGIK(N 1km)TUV

💬 Welcoming campsite by the river Vienne with large camping pitches. The campsite and the Charente have plenty to offer for all ages. You can enjoy delicious food in the restaurant, explore the Vienne by canoe, have a drink in the bar or play pool.

🚌 RN141 Limoges-Angoulême, continue to roundabout and cross narrow bridge over River Vienne in Exideuil-sur-Vienne.

D30

D951

D948

N141   Ⓒ Ⓒ   D29

Chassenon

Rochechouart

D10

Ⓒ Ⓒ € **11** 1/1-30/6   1/9-31/12   📷🔺 N 45°53'21'' E 0°40'36''

Eymouthiers/Montbron, F-16220 / Poitou-Charentes (Charente)

  ♋ 📶 ❊ **iD** **1617**

🔺 Castel Camping Les
   Gorges du Chambon****
📧 861, rue de la Tardoire
☎ +33 (0)5-45707170
🗓 1/5 - 15/9
@ info@
   camping-gorgesduchambon.com

28ha 109**T**(132-300m²) 10A CEE

1 ACD **G** IJKLM **P**RS
2 ACIKLRVWXY
3 BF **G**HJLM **P**QRU **W**X
4 (C+H+Q+R+T+U+V+X 🖱)
(Y 1/7-31/8) (Z 🖱)
5 **AB** DEFGHIJKLMNOPUWXZ
6 ACDEG **JK**(N 7km)ORTV

💬 This castle campsite is located in the middle of unspoilt countryside on the borders of the Dordogne and the Charente. Attractively landscaped with plenty of space. Heated swimming pool and restaurant.

🚌 N10 Poitiers-Angoulême, in Mansle turn left on the D6 direction La Rochefoucauld and Montbron. Signposted in Montbron. Turn left in La Tricherie, take the D163 (follow the signs).

La Rochefoucauld

D699

D6   Ⓒ Ⓒ

D91   Piégut-Pluviers

D4

D16   D75   D675

Ⓒ Ⓒ € **19** 1/5-30/6   1/9-14/9   📷🔺 N 45°38'39'' E 0°32'27''

Fouras, F-17450 / Poitou-Charentes (Charente-Maritime) ♿ 🛜 ❀ 🆔 (1618)

NEW

🔺 Municipal Le Cadoret***
📧 boulevard de Chaterny
☎ +33 (0)5-46821919
📠 +33 (0)5-46845159
🗓 1/1 - 31/12
@ campinglecadoret@
mairie17.com

7,6ha 300T(40-130m²) 6-10A

1 ACD**G**IJKLPST
2 AEFGRTVWXY
3 AB**F**GHJKLNRUWY
4 (C+H 1/5-15/9) J
(Q+R 1/5-31/10) (T 1/5-15/9)
(U 1/7-31/8) (X 1/5-15/9)
(Z 1/4-31/10)
5 **AB**CDEFGIJKLMNOPUXZ
6 EGHK(N 0,6km)ORTV

💬 Le Cadoret campsite welcomes you in quiet and cosy style. Situated on the coast, in a forested, park-like area, 500m from the city centre. The numerous pitches are located in partial shade, or in the sun closer to the sea, both are marked out and have a grassy surface for maximum comfort.

🚗 From La Rochelle to Rochefort. Exit Fouras (D937). Turn to the right after 2 km. Turn to the right at the first junction. Signposted.

Châtelaillon-Plage

D137 D5

CC

Rochefort

CC €**15** 1/1-29/6 3/9-31/12

📍 N 45°59'35'' W 1°5'14''

Ingrandes, F-86220 / Poitou-Charentes (Vienne) 👫 ♿ 🛜 🆔 (1619)

🔺 Le Petit Trianon de
Saint Ustre****
📧 1 rue du Moulin St. Ustre
☎ +33 (0)5-49026147
🗓 27/4 - 30/9
@ contact@petit-trianon.com

7ha 116T(120-150m²) 10A

1 AC**G**IJKLMOPRS
2 FIKLRVWXY
3 ABGHJKN**Q**RU
4 (C+H 🗓) K(Q+R 🗓)
(V 1/7-31/8) (Y 25/5-31/8)
(Z 🗓)
5 **AB**DEFGIJKLOPUWXYZ
6 CDEGIJ**K**(N 3km)OQRV

💬 This family campsite is located around a castle in a rural setting, and has spacious pitches and a heated swimming pool. Excellent base for visiting Roman churches, castles, Futuroscope and the Poitou and Touraine rivers.

🚗 N10 Tours-Poitiers, turn left before Ingrandes, follow the signs.

Descartes

D749 A10 D750

CC

D14 D910

Châtellerault D725

CC €**19** 27/4-6/7 27/8-29/9 7=6

📍 N 46°53'16'' E 0°35'13''

La Couarde-sur-Mer, F-17670 / Poitou-Charentes (Charente-Maritime) 👫 ♿ 🛜 🆔 (1620)

🔺 La Tour des Prises****
📧 route d'Ars
☎ +33 (0)5-46298482
📠 +33 (0)5-46298899
🗓 1/4 - 28/9
@ camping@lesprises.com

2,5ha 85T(85-120m²) 16A CEE

1 ACD**F**IJKLMOPST
2 GRSVWXY
3 BGJKLRU
4 (C+F+H+Q+R+S 🗓)
(T+U 1/6-20/9) (V 15/5-20/9)
(X 🗓) (Z 15/5-20/9)
5 **AB**CDEFGIJKLMNOPRSTU
VZ
6 ACDEGHIK(N 1,5km)RTV

💬 A peaceful family campsite in the middle of Ile de Ré and 600 metres from a fine sandy beach and the sea. Heated indoor swimming pool. A paradise for cyclists and walkers. Free wifi on the entire site.

🚗 Take D735 dir. La Flotte after the bridge, then to St. Martin-de-Ré and past Couarde-sur-Mer dir. Ars-en-Ré. Turn right on roundabout in Couarde. Signposted.

Saint-Martin-de-Ré
CC
D735

CC €**17** 1/4-7/7 29/8-27/9 14=12, 28=24

📍 N 46°12'16'' W 1°26'47''

La Flotte-en-Ré, F-17630 / Poitou-Charentes (Charente-Maritime) ♨ 📶 iD (1621)

▲ La Grainetière****
✉ route de St. Martin
☎ +33 (0)5-46096886
📠 +33 (0)5-46095313
⚬ 1/4 - 30/9
@ la-grainetiere@orange.fr

2,6ha 60T(80-120m²) 10A CEE

1 ACD**F**IJKLMO**P**ST
2 BSVXY
3 AB**F**GHJKLN**OP**RU
4 (C+F+H ⚬) K
   (Q+R+S+T+U+V+Z ⚬)
5 **AB**DEFGIJLMNOPQRUWXY
   Z
6 ACEGHIJK(N 1km)ORTV

💬 A friendly family campsite close to the idyllic town of La Flotte in the middle of wooded surroundings with spacious pitches. Heated in- and outdoor swimming pool with free jacuzzi, bar, shop, snack bar and bike hire. Heated top class toilet facilities. Free wifi on the entire site.

🚗 D735 towards La Flotte after the toll bridge. Just past La Flotte take direction St. Martin. Well signposted.

Nieul-sur-Mer
CC
Sainte-Marie-de-Ré

CC € 19 1/4-5/7 26/8-29/9 | 🏖 N 46°11'15'' W 1°20'37''

La Roche-Posay, F-86270 / Poitou-Charentes (Vienne) ♨ 📶 iD (1622)

▲ La Roche-Posay Vacances****
✉ route de Lesigny
☎ +33 (0)5-49862123
⚬ 7/4 - 22/9
@ info@
   larocheposay-vacances.com

8,5ha 200T(80-140m²) 10A CEE

1 AC**F**IJKLMPQ
2 CGLRVWXY
3 B**F**GHJKNRU**W**
4 (B+E+H ⚬) IJK
   (Q+R+T+U+V+X+Z ⚬)
5 **AB**DEFGIJKLMNOPSUVWZ
6 ADEGHIJ**K**(N 0,7km)RV

💬 Family campsite situated on the River Creuse, 1.5 km from the village. Large pitches marked out by trees. Indoor heated swimming pool open all season.

🚗 A10 exit 26 Châtellerault-Nord (km 273). Follow La Roche-Posay signs. Then D275 to La Roche-Posay. Follow camping-hippodrome signs at roundabout.

D60 D50
D725
Yzeures-sur-
CC Creuse
D14
D5 D750
Tournon-Saint-
Martin D6
D3

CC € 17 7/4-28/6 1/9-21/9 | 🏖 N 46°47'57'' E 0°48'34''

Le Bois-Plage-en-Ré, F-17580 / Poitou-Charentes (Charente-Maritime) 🗣🗣 📶 iD (1623)

▲ Campéole Les Amis de la
   Plage***
✉ 68 avenue du Pas des Boeufs
☎ +33 (0)5-46092401
⚬ 30/3 - 30/9
@ les-amis-de-la-plage@
   campeole.com

5ha 136T(80-110m²) 10A CEE

1 ABCD**G**IJKLO**P**ST
2 AEIJSVWXY
3 BGJKRUWY
4 (Q+R 1/7-31/8)
5 **AB**EFGHIJKLMNOPQUVZ
6 ACEGH**K**(N 1km)RT

💬 A family campsite with direct access to the beach. Swimming pool (entrance charge) and shops at the site entrance. Most suitable for visiting the beach, fishing from the beach, watersports and cycle trips between saline pools, oyster beds and bird sanctuaries.

🚗 Follow La Rochelle then cross the (toll) bridge to Ile de Ré island.

Saint-Martin-
de-Ré
CC
D735

CC € 17 30/3-6/7 25/8-29/9 | 🏖 N 46°10'39'' W 1°23'12''

Le Bois-Plage-en-Ré, F-17580 / Poitou-Charentes (Charente-Maritime)

♙♙ ♿ 🛜 **iD** (1624)

🏕 Les Varennes****
📧 Raise Maritaise
☎ +33 (0)5-46091543
📠 +33 (0)5-46094727
🔓 7/4 - 30/9
@ info@les-varennes.com

2,5ha 56T(80-100m²) 10A CEE

1 ACD**F**IJKLPST
2 AERSVWX
3 ABGKRY
4 (C 15/6-15/9) (F+H 🔓) K
(Q+R+S+Z 🔓)
5 **AB**DEFGJLNOPUVWZ
6 ACEGHK(N 0,8km)RTV

💬 A small, happy, family campsite under tall conifers with good amenities. Fairly sheltered pitches. There is a nice sandy beach within walking distance. Heated indoor pool with free jacuzzi. Free wifi on the whole campsite.

🚗 From the toll bridge, via the roundabout, onto the D201. In Le Bois-Plage follow the signs 'Les Varennes'.

Saint-Martin-de-Ré

D735

CC € **19** 7/4-6/7 3/9-29/9

🗺 N 46°10'43'' W 1°22'59''

Le Château-d'Oléron, F-17480 / Poitou-Charentes (Charente-Maritime)

♿ 🛜 **iD** (1625)

🏕 Airotel Oléron****
📧 19 avenue de la Libération
☎ +33 (0)5-46476182
🔓 1/4 - 30/9
@ info@
camping-airotel-oleron.com

7,4ha 123T(80-150m²) 10A CEE

1 ACG**HIJKLMPQ**
2 DRTVWXY
3 BF**G**HJK**MNOP**RUW
4 (C+H 🔓) (Q 1/7-31/8)
(R 15/6-15/9)
(T+U+V+X+Y+Z 1/6-15/9)
5 **AB**DFGIJKLMNOPUVZ
6 EGI**K**(N 1km)ORTUV

💬 Campsite close to the centre of Château-d'Oléron. Perfect for horse lovers. With a swimming pool and other sports opportunities.

🚗 Direction Le Château beyond bridge, then left towards centre. Follow signs by 'Crédit Agricole'.

Saint-Pierre-d'Oléron

D26

D728 E

CC € **17** 1/4-7/7 25/8-29/9 7=6, 14=11, 21=17

🗺 N 45°52'57'' W 1°12'24''

Le Château-d'Oléron, F-17480 / Poitou-Charentes (Charente-Maritime)

♿ 🛜 **iD** (1626)

🏕 La Brande*****
📧 route des Huîtres
☎ +33 (0)5-46476237
🔓 1/4 - 4/11
@ info@camping-labrande.com

5,5ha 109T(100-200m²) 10A

1 ACD**F**HIJKLMPST
2 AELRSTVWXY
3 BF**G**HJKL**M**N**Q**R**T**UWY
4 (A 1/7-30/8) (D+F+H 🔓) JKL
N(Q+R 🔓)
(T+U+V+X+Y+Z 1/7-31/8)
5 **AB**EFGIJKLMNOPR**ST**UVW
XY
6 CEGJ(N 3km)ORV

💬 A family campsite located in a rural area at 300 metres from the sea. Indoor heated swimming pool with slide. Free wifi hot spot.

🚗 From Le Château take the coastal road Route des Huîtres in a north-westerly direction. The campsite is located to the left after about 3 km.

Saint-Pierre-d'Oléron

D26

CC € **17** 1/4-6/7 27/8-3/11

🗺 N 45°54'15'' W 1°12'55''

Le Château-d'Oleron/La Gaconn., F-17480 / Poitou-Charentes (Charente-Maritime) 🚿 📶 iD 1627

🔺 Le Fief Melin***
🏠 rue des Alizés
☎ +33 (0)5-46476085
🔑 1/5 - 30/9
@ lefiefmelin@wanadoo.fr

3ha 81T(82-130m²) 10A CEE

1 ACDGHIJKLMOPQ
2 GRTVX
3 BFGHJKNRU
4 (E 🔒) (Q 1/7-30/8)
　　(T+U+V+Z 1/7-31/8)
5 AGIJKLMNPUVZ
6 EGK(N 1km)RUV

💬 A peacefully located campsite with a lovely indoor swimming pool. 1 km from the beach.

🚌 From the bridge towards Le Château, then direction Dolus to La Gaconnière, follow Rue des Illexés 400m on the right.

Saint-Pierre-d'Oléron °

CC

D26

D728 E

CC € 15 1/5-7/7 25/8-29/9 8=7　　　　🏕 N 45°53'37'' W 1°12'52''

Le Fouilloux, F-17270 / Poitou-Charentes (Charente-Maritime) 👫 🚿 📶 iD 1628

🔺 La Motte*
🏠 D270, Lieu-dit La Motte
☎ +33 (0)5-46042691
🔑 22/1 - 14/12
@ camping-la-motte17@orange.fr

3,5ha 45T(125-200m²) 16A CEE

1 ACGIJKLMOPST
2 DKLMRTUVWXY
3 AGHJOW
5 GIJKLMNOPUWZ
6 CDEGK(N 3,6km)O

💬 The campsite owner has deliberately opted for peace and quiet, ideal for walkers and cyclists. Anglers can indulge themselves in the small lake at the campsite. Swimming possible in the nearby lake.

🚌 N10 exit Montguyon. At Montguyon dir. St. Aigulin (D730). At Intermarché roundabout continue to St. Aigulin (D730). 2nd left after viaduct (D270). Campsite 1800m. 12 km from exit N10.

N10　D731
D910 BIS
D730
Montguyon CC
La Roche-Chalais
D674

CC € 15 22/1-14/7 1/9-13/12　　　　🏕 N 45°12'45'' W 0°8'16''

Le Grand-Village-Plage, F-17370 / Poitou-Charentes (Charente-Maritime) 📶 iD 1629

🔺 Camping-Club Les Pins****
🏠 6 allée des Pins
☎ +33 (0)5-46475013
🔑 15/3 - 15/11
@ contact@lespinsdoleron.com

6ha 70T(80-100m²) 10A CEE

1 ABCDGHIJKLMOPST
2 ABISVWXY
3 BFGHJKRUW
4 (B 🔒)
　　(Q+T+U+V+Z 1/5-30/9)
5 ABEFGIJKLMNOPQRUWXY
6 CEGK(N 0,2km)OTV

💬 A campsite located in pine woods. Friendly reception, every comfort provided. Swimming lake with sandy beach.

🚌 From viaduct straight on at 1st roundabout, 2nd roundabout direction Grand-Village, 3rd roundabout direction Centreville-Plage, 4th roundabout straight on. Campsite then signposted.

Saint-Pierre-d'Oléron °

CC

D728 E
La Tremblade °

CC € 17 15/3-7/7 25/8-14/11 7=6　　　　🏕 N 45°51'44'' W 1°14'26''

Le Grand-Village-Plage, F-17370 / Poitou-Charentes (Charente-Maritime) 🛜 iD (1630)

🔺 Le Maine****
📧 24 route du Maine
☎ +33 (0)5-46754276
📅 1/2 - 15/11
@ camping.lemaine@wanadoo.fr

1,7ha 23T(85-100m²) 10A CEE

1 ABCD**G**HIJKLMO**PQ**
2 ARTUVWXY
3 A**F**GHJKLRU
4 M(Q 1/7-31/8) (R 📦)
   (V 1/4-30/9)
5 **AB**DFGIJKLMNOPUXYZ
6 DEGHK(N 2,5km)ORVX

💬 A small family campsite 1.5 km from the sea. Every comfort. Free wifi.

🚐 From the viaduct towards St. Pierre-d'Oléron, 3rd exit at roundabout after 1st crossroads. Then direction Vert Bois. Left at traffic lights. 100m on the left.

Saint-Pierre-d'Oléron ○

CC

D26

D728 E

CC € **17** 1/2-30/6 1/9-14/11   🗺 N 45°52'53'' W 1°14'56''

Les Mathes, F-17570 / Poitou-Charentes (Charente-Maritime) ♿ 🛜 iD (1631)

🔺 La Palombière***
📧 1551 route de la Fouasse
☎ +33 (0)5-46226925
📠 +33 (0)5-46224458
📅 1/4 - 15/10
@ camping.lapalombiere@
   wanadoo.fr

9,5ha 218T(100-200m²) 6-10A CEE

1 A**G**IJKLMOPS
2 BGRUWXY
3 ABF**G**HJKLNR**W**
4 (C+H 1/6-30/9)
   (Q+R 15/6-15/9)
   (T+U+V+X+Z 1/7-31/8)
5 **AB**DFGIJKLMNOPQRUZ
6 ACDEGH**K**(N 1,5km)TV

💬 A campsite idyllically situated in the woods with luxurious toilet facilities and just 3 km from the sandy beaches of the Côte Sauvage. An ideal base for interesting trips out. Restaurant and optical fibre wifi available (for a fee).

🚐 Take exit 35 on the A10 at Saintes direction Royan N150. Then follow La Palmyre signs. Direction Les Mathes at the large roundabout. Campsite signposted at the next roundabout.

D728 E

D728

D14

D25 CC

Saint-Sulpice-de-Royan ○

CC € **17** 1/4-2/7 27/8-14/10   🗺 N 45°43'24'' W 1°10'27''

Les Mathes, F-17570 / Poitou-Charentes (Charente-Maritime) 👫 🧎 ♿ 🛜 iD (1632)

🔺 Le Petit Dauphin**
📧 1696 route de la Fouasse
☎ +33 (0)5-46063823
📅 1/4 - 30/9
@ lepetitdauphin2@wanadoo.fr

1,7ha 99T 10A CEE

1 ACD**G**IJKLMOPST
2 AGRSVWXY
3 **EFQ**R
4 (E+H+Q+T+V+X+Z 📦)
5 ADEFGIJKLMNOPQUW
6 AGJ**K**(N 5km)OTV

💬 Naturist campsite located close to the Atlantic coast. Heated pool from June to September. Surroundings with lots of plantlife and flowers.

🚐 On A10 from Saintes take exit 35, towards Royan N150. From Royan towards La Palmyre. In Palmyre towards Les Mathes. Signposted from there.

Marennes ○
La Tremblade ○   D728

D14

CC

Les Mathes ○

D25

CC € **17** 1/4-7/7 25/8-29/9   🗺 N 45°43'27'' W 1°10'28''

Les Mathes/La Palmyre, F-17570 / Poitou-Charentes (Charente-Maritime) ⊗ ♿ 📶 iD (1633)

🏠 La Pinède★★★★
✉ 2103 route de la Fouasse
☎ +33 (0)8-26965772
📠 +33 (0)5-46225021
🗓 30/3 - 23/9
@ contact@campinglapinede.com

11ha 145T(80-140m²) 10A CEE

1 ACDEIJKLPS
2 ABSVWXY
3 BDFGHKNQRU
4 (B 1/7-31/8) (F+H 🗓) IJM
(Q+R+T+U+V+X+Z 🗓)
5 **AB**EFGIJKLMNOP**ST**UWXY
Z
6 ACEGHJ**K**(N 4km)RTV

💬 Family campsite, located in a peaceful area just 5 minutes from the beach, equipped with modern comforts with five water slides, two swimming pools and a variety of activities.

🚗 On the A10 near Saintes take exit 35 towards Royan, N150. At Royan towards La Palmyre. In Palmyre direction Les Mathes and the campsite is signposted from there.

Marennes
La Tremblade   D728
D14
D25

(CC) € ⑰ 30/3-30/6 3/9-22/9   📷 N 45°43'41'' W 1°10'33''

Loix (Île de Ré), F-17111 / Poitou-Charentes (Charente-Maritime) ♿ 📶 iD (1634)

🏠 Flower Camping Les Ilates★★★★
✉ route du Grouin
☎ +33 (0)5-46290543
🗓 31/3 - 30/9
@ camping.les.ilates@
flowercampings.com

69T(90-115m²) 10A CEE

1 ACD**G**IJKL**P**Q
2 RVWX
3 BGKLMR
4 (C+H 1/5-30/9) K(Q 🗓)
(R 15/6-15/9)
(T+U+V+X+Z 🗓)
5 **AB**EFGIJKLMNOPUWXY
6 CEGIJ**K**(N 2km)RTV

💬 A large campsite with separate camping pitches. Lovely swimming pool and sports opportunities.

🚗 Follow the D102 almost to Loix. Then well signposted.

(CC)

Sainte-Marie-
de-Ré

(CC) € ⑰ 31/3-29/6 1/9-29/9 7=6   📷 N 46°13'35'' W 1°25'34''

Magné, F-79460 / Poitou-Charentes (Deux-Sèvres) ♿ 📶 iD (1635)

🏠 Le Martin-Pêcheur★★★★
✉ 155 avenue du Marais Poitevin
☎ +33 (0)5-49357181
🗓 1/5 - 18/9
@ info@
camping-le-martin-pecheur.com

2,5ha 57T(100-200m²) 10A CEE

1 ACD**G**IJKLMPQ
2 GLRVWXY
3 AB**F**GHJRU**W**
4 (C+H 15/6-30/8) (R 🗓)
5 **AB**DEFGIJKLMNOPQUW
6 AEGK(N 1km)T

💬 A well-maintained campsite with good facilities. Located 8 km from Niort and 6 km from Coulon. In the middle of the 'Marais de Poitevin'. The campsite is an ideal starting point for walking and cycling tours. Boat trips are also available. Lovely big free swimming pool.

🚗 From Niort D9 direction Coulon. Before Coulon direction Magné. Magné and Coulon are about 3 km from each other. Campsite next to the D9.

A83 D25 E
D744 Chauray
D25 D1 D743
(CC) **Niort**
D3 D611 Aiffres A10
N248 D650

(CC) € ⑰ 1/5-6/7 28/8-17/9   📷 N 46°18'49'' W 0°32'6''

Marennes, F-17320 / Poitou-Charentes (Charente-Maritime)

♔♔ 🛜 iD **1636**

🔺 Au Bon Air***
✉ 9 avenue Pierre Voyer
☎ +33 (0)5-46850240
⌚ 1/4 - 30/9
@ contact@aubonair.com

2,3ha 40T(80-120m²) 16A CEE

1 ACD**F**IJKLM**P**ST
2 AERTVXY
3 BGHJRUWY
4 (C+H 1/5-30/9) (Q ⌚)
(R 1/5-30/9) (T+U 1/7-31/8)
(V ⌚) (Z 1/7-31/8)
5 **AB**FGIJKLMNOPUVZ
6 AEG**K**(N 3km)ORT

💬 A small, quiet and shaded family campsite 150 metres from the beach. Located at the entrance to l'île d'Oléron and its rugged coast. Heated swimming pool and a paddling pool open from May to the end of the season.

🚗 From Saintes direction Ile d'Oléron to Marennes, then direction Marennes (Plages) where the campsite is signposted.

Dolus-d'Oléron

D26 · D123

D18

La Tremblade
D25 · D728

D14 · D131
D141

🔲€**17** 1/4-6/7 1/9-28/9

🔺 N 45°49'8" W 1°8'4"

Meschers, F-17132 / Poitou-Charentes (Charente-Maritime)

♿ 🛜 iD **1637**

🔺 Le Soleil Levant****
✉ 33 allée de la Longée
☎ +33 (0)5-46027662
📠 +33 (0)5-46025056
⌚ 14/4 - 30/9
@ info@camping-soleillevant.com

3ha 132T(76-100m²) 10A CEE

1 ACD**F**IJLPQ
2 AGQRTVWXY
3 BGJKN**OP**RUW
4 (B+G 20/6-15/9) J
(Q+R+S+T+U+V+X+Y+Z 1/7-31/8)
5 **AB**FGIJKLMNPUVXY
6 CDEGHI**K**(N 1km)OTV

💬 A peacefully located campsite with swimming pool and slide, close to a lively harbour and 1 km from the sea. Separate grounds with service point for motorhomes.

🚗 In Meschers drive in the direction of the harbour and turn left just before it. The campsite is located here. Clearly signposted.

N150

Royan
D17

Saint-Georges-de-Didonne
D730
D114 · D732

D1215 · D145

🔲€**17** 14/4-30/6 1/9-29/9

🔺 N 45°33'25" W 0°56'47"

Port-des-Barques, F-17730 / Poitou-Charentes (Charente-Maritime)

🛜 ✿ iD **1638**

🔺 Municipal de la Garenne***
✉ av. de l'Ile Madame
☎ +33 (0)5-46848066
📠 +33 (0)5-46849833
⌚ 1/3 - 31/10
@ camping@ville-portdesbarques.fr

7ha 242T(83-130m²) 10A CEE

1 ACD**G**IJKLMOPST
2 AEGRSVWXY
3 BGKM**N**RUWY
4 (B+G 15/6-15/9) (Q ⌚)
(T+U+V 15/5-15/9) (X ⌚)
(Z 15/5-15/9)
5 **AB**FGIJKLMNPUVZ
6 AEGHJ**K**(N 1km)T

💬 This campsite welcomes you in superb surroundings opposite 'l'Ile Madame' island. On offer: fishing, watersports, visiting special sights and other activities. Ideally situated by the sea between La Rochelle and Royan. Amenities include: playground, swimming pool. Motorhome service point.

🚗 N137 La Rochelle to the southern edge of Rochefort (becomes the D733). Right after Charente bridge onto D238 and D125. 12 km on the left, just past the small village.

D137 · D5

Breuil-Magné

Rochefort

Ors
D26 · D733

🔲€**15** 1/3-7/7 26/8-30/10

🔺 N 45°56'53" W 1°5'45"

Puilboreau/La Rochelle, F-17138 / Poitou-Charentes (Charente-Maritime) 📶 iD 1639

🏕 Le Beaulieu****
📧 3 rue du Treuil Gras
☎ +33 (0)5-46680438
📅 31/3 - 30/9
@ contact@
camping-la-rochelle.com

5ha 35T(85-120m²) 10A CEE

1 ACDFIJKLPST
2 RUVWXY
3 BGHJMNR
4 (C 15/5-15/9) (E+H 🌙) IJKM
N(Q 🌙) (R 1/7-31/8)
(T+U 🌙) (V 1/7-31/8)
(X+Z 🌙)
5 ABDEFGIJKLMNPUWZ
6 ADEGHJK(N 0,1km)TV

💬 A lovely town campsite with new, marked out pitches. Within cycling distance of La Rochelle, cycle track from the campsite and Île de Ré. Heated indoor swimming pool, heated toilets, sauna, jacuzzi. Free wifi zone. Good starting point for visiting La Rochelle and 'Marais Poitevin'.

🚘 From Niort, 2 km before La Rochelle, take 'Centre Commercial Beaulieu' exit. Follow camping signs at first roundabout.

D9 D20 D137
La Rochelle Aytré
D137 D939

CC €19 31/3-5/7 27/8-19/9 🌐 N 46°10'40'' W 1°6'55''

Rivedoux-Plage, F-17940 / Poitou-Charentes (Charente-Maritime) 🚻 📶 iD 1640

🏕 Campéole Le Platin***
📧 125 avenue Gustave Perreau
☎ +33 (0)5-46098410
📅 30/3 - 23/9
@ platin@campeole.com

3,7ha 139T(60-171m²) 10A CEE

1 ACDFIJKLMOPST
2 AEFGKRSTUWXY
3 ABJKLRUWY
4 (Z 1/7-31/8)
5 ABEFGIJKLMNOPQUZ
6 ACDEGHK(N 0,01km)RTV

💬 Campsite with sea views and modest facilities.

🚘 Over the bridge to the Île de Ré direction Rivedoux-Plage. Thereafter signposted.

D9
CC La Rochelle

CC €17 30/3-6/7 25/8-22/9 🌐 N 46°9'35'' W 1°15'59''

Royan, F-17200 / Poitou-Charentes (Charente-Maritime) 🚻 ♿ 📶 iD 1641

🏕 Campéole Clairefontaine****
📧 16 rue du Colonel Lachaud
☎ +33 (0)5-46390811
📠 +33 (0)5-46381379
📅 30/3 - 30/9
@ clairefontaine@campeole.com

5ha 124T(80-100m²) 10A CEE

1 ACDGIJKLMPQ
2 AEGRTWXY
3 BFMNRUWY
4 (C+H 15/5-15/9) (Q 🌙)
(T+U+V+Z 1/6-15/9)
5 ABEFGIJKLMNOPQRUVW
6 ACEGHIK(N 0,3km)TV

💬 A lovely camping ground in natural surroundings yet still close to shops, restaurants, the beach and providing everything you could need for an enjoyable holiday.

🚘 A10, near Saintes take exit 35 direction Royan (N150). In Royan drive in the direction of Pontaillac (west of Royan). From there the campsite is clearly signposted.

D1
D14 Saujon
Saint-Palais-
sur-Mer CC Royan D17
D25
D730
D1215 D25 D145

CC €17 30/3-6/7 25/8-29/9 🌐 N 45°37'52'' W 1°3'0''

Saujon, F-17600 / Poitou-Charentes (Charente-Maritime)

♿ 📶 **iD** (1642)

🏕 Camping du Lac de Saujon***
📧 Voie des Tourterelles
☎ +33 (0)5-46068299
📅 1/3 - 31/10
@ campingdesaujon@gmail.com

3,7ha 150T(120-250m²) 10A CEE

1 ACD**G**IJLPQ
2 DLRTVWXY
3 A**F**GHJK**MOP**RU**W**
4 (C+F 1/4-30/10) J
(Q 1/6-31/8)
(R+S+T+U+V+Y 1/7-31/8)
(Z 15/6-15/9)
5 **AB**FGIJKLMNOPUVWXY
6 ACDEG**J**(N 1km)TV

💬 A well-maintained campsite. Ideal base for visits to many old towns such as Talmont-sur-Gironde, Mornac-sur-Seudre, Royan, La Rochelle and L'Ile d'Oléron.

🚗 On the N50 Royan-Saintes, exit Saujon, centre. From there follow campsite signs.

D733 D131 D117
D14 D1 D142
CC
Royan D17 D114
Saint-Georges-de-
Didonne D730

©© € **17** 1/3-7/7 25/8-30/10

📍 N 45°40'59'' W 0°56'16''

St. Augustin-sur-Mer, F-17570 / Poitou-Charentes (Charente-Maritime)

♿ 📶 **iD** (1643)

🏕 Le Logis du Breuil****
📧 36 rue du Centre
☎ +33 (0)5-46232345
📠 +33 (0)5-46234333
📅 5/5 - 30/9
@ info@logis-du-breuil.com

9ha 390T(150-250m²) 10A CEE

1 ACD**G**IJKLMOPST
2 BGJRVWXY
3 B**F**GK**M**NRU
4 (F+H 10/5-30/9) IJKM(Q 📅)
(S+T+U+V+X+Y+Z 15/5-15/9)
5 **AB**EFGIJKLMNPQR**ST**UVW
XYZ
6 ACEG**J**(N 0,2km)RTV

💬 Located in the heart of the Arvert peninsula. You can enjoy the friendly, rural atmosphere of our grounds on a spacious pitch (± 200 sq.m.)in a woodland setting. With the ocean close by you can also enjoy the beach and sea. The surroundings are also well worth the effort. A holiday just made for relaxing.

🚗 On the A10 at Saintes take exit 35 towards Royan, N150. At Royan follow direction St. Palais as far as the St. Augustin exit. Indicated from there.

D14 D131
D141 D1
D25 CC Saujon
Saint-Palais-
sur-Mer N150
Royan

©© € **19** 5/5-14/6 1/9-29/9

📍 N 45°40'32'' W 1°5'42''

St. Christophe, F-16420 / Poitou-Charentes (Charente)

♿ 📶 **iD** (1644)

🏕 Camping & Gîtes
"en Campagne"***
📧 Essubras
☎ +33 (0)5-45316757
📅 1/4 - 30/9
@ info@encampagne.com

1,5ha 30T(150-240m²) 10A CEE

1 A**G**IJKLM**P**RS
2 KLRTVWXY
3 ABGHJKR
4 (C+H 15/5-15/9) (Q+T+X 📅)
5 **AB**CFGHIJKLMNOPUWXY
6 CDEGIK(N 9km)V

💬 Easy-going and welcoming campsite in Charente-Limousin. Close to the war-time village of Oradour-sur-Glane. Regular communal meals. Free wifi.

🚗 From the D82 in the centre of St. Christophe, take D330 to Nouic. Campsite is indicated.

D99 **Bellac**
D951
D675
D29 D82 CC
D30 D711
D948 Oradour-sur-
D21 **Glane**

©© € **15** 1/4-7/7 25/8-29/9

📍 N 46°0'52'' E 0°52'45''

St. Clément-des-Baleines, F-17590 / Poitou-Charentes (Charente-Maritime) ♿ 🛜 iD (1645)

🏔 La Plage★★★★
📧 408 rue du Chaume
☎ +33 (0)5-46294262
🔓 13/4 - 16/9
@ info@la-plage.com

30T 10A CEE

1 ACD**G**IJKLOPST
2 AEGRVX
3 BF**G**JKM**N**RUVWY
4 (C+H 🔲) LN
(Q+R+T+U+V+X+Y+Z 🔲)
5 **AB**DEFGIJKLMNOPQUVWZ
6 ACEGIK(N 4km)QTV

💬 Sunny campsite behind the dunes with an attractive beach. Lovely, heated pool and many amenities. Wellness facility with sauna and hamam. Free wifi throughout the campsite.

🚗 On Ile de Ré follow D735 past Ars-en-Ré. Follow signs 'Phare des B'. After St. Clément-des-Baleines campsite is clearly indicated.

La Grière Plage

CC

Ars-en-Ré

CC € 19 13/4-30/6 1/9-15/9 · N 46°14'28'' W 1°33'12''

St. Clément-des-Baleines, F-17590 / Poitou-Charentes (Charente-Maritime) 👫 ♿ 🛜 ✿ iD (1646)

🏔 Les Baleines★★★
📧 Le Gillieux
☎ +33 (0)5-46294076
🔓 28/4 - 22/9
@ contact@
camping-lesbaleines.com

4,6ha 157T(80-140m²) 10A CEE

1 ACD**F**IJKLMOPST
2 AEGJOQRSVWXY
3 ABFGHJKLRWY
4 (Q+R+S 🔲)
(T+U+Z 5/7-31/8)
5 **AB**EFGIJKLMNOPUWZ
6 ACEGHJL(N 1km)TVW

💬 Camping in a nature reserve with spacious pitches and direct access to the beach (50 metres). All amenities with top-notch toilet facilities. Views of the bay and Phare des Baleines. European Eco label. Electrical car for rent. Free wifi zone.

🚗 From the bridge direction 'Phare des Baleines' (± 30 km). Turn left before 'Le Phare' car park (signposted) in the Rue du Chaume and Rue de la Madeleine, then straight ahead to the campsite.

Les Portes-en-Ré

CC

Saint-Clément-
des-Baleines

Ars-en-Ré

CC € 19 28/4-6/7 1/9-21/9 · N 46°14'23'' W 1°33'35''

St. Cyr, F-86130 / Poitou-Charentes (Vienne) 👫 ♿ 🛜 ✿ iD (1647)

🏔 Camping
du Lac de Saint-Cyr★★★★
☎ +33 (0)5-49625722
🔓 1/4 - 30/9
@ contact@
campinglacdesaintcyr.com

5ha 157T(90-120m²) 10A CEE

1 ACG**G**IJKLMOPST
2 ADLORTVWXY
3 AB**E**GKLMN**P**RUV**W**XY
4 (C+H 1/6-29/9)
(Q+R+T+U+V+Z 🔲)
5 **AB**GIJKLPUWXYZ
6 EGHJ(N 7km)OV

💬 A campsite with spacious pitches and plenty of vegetation located in an oasis of greenery by a lake and just 10 minutes from Futuroscope. Heated swimming pool (28°C), bird sanctuary and opportunities for fishing, watersports, walking and golf (27 holes).

🚗 Left in Beaumont-La Trichérie (after 15 km) and follow signs. Coming from Poitiers, take N10 towards Châtelleraut. Right in Baumont-La Trichérie and follow signs.

Châtellerault

D757 · D14
D910 · D749
A10
CC
Migné-
Auxances · D20 · D3 · D1

CC € 15 1/4-30/6 1/9-29/9 7=6, 14=11 · N 46°43'9'' E 0°27'33''

St. Denis-d'Oléron, F-17650 / Poitou-Charentes (Charente-Maritime)

🛈 (1648)

△ Les Seulières**
🏠 1371 rue des Seulières
☎ +33 (0)5-46479051
📅 1/4 - 30/10
@ campinglesseulieres@ wanadoo.fr

2,5ha 58T(80-100m²) 10A CEE

1 ABCD**G**HIJKLPST
2 AERTUWXY
3 **F**GHJKRUWY
4 (Q 1/5-30/9) (R 📅) (V 1/7-31/8) (Z 📅)
5 **AB**EFGIJKLMNOPUZ
6 CE**J**(N 4km)OV

💬 An informal campsite with Dutch owners, 300 metres from the sea. There are watersports and cycling opportunities in the immediate vicinity. Wifi hotspot. Fully renovated toilet facilities.

🚗 Continue towards St. Pierre D734 from the viaduct, direction St. Denis, left just before village, direction Les Seulières. Campsite signposted after ± 3 km.

CC (cc) Saint-Pierre-d'Oléron ○

CC € **17** 1/4-6/7 25/8-29/10

🗺 N 46°0'17'' W 1°22'59''

St. Georges-d'Oléron, F-17190 / Poitou-Charentes (Charente-Maritime)

♿ 🛈 (1649)

△ La Campière****
🏠 route des Huttes - Chaucre
☎ +33 (0)5-46767225
📅 7/4 - 30/9
@ contact@la-campiere.com

1,6ha 48T(80-120m²) 10A CEE

1 ACD**G**HIJKLMOPT
2 ABERSVWXY
3 BF**G**HJKM**R**U
4 (C 15/5-1/10) (Q 1/5-1/10) (R 📅) (T+U+V+Z 1/5-30/9)
5 **AB**CEFGIJKLMNOPQUVWXYZ
6 CEG**K**(N 3km)RSV

💬 A small family campsite beautifully located at the edge of a wood. Swimming pool. Close to the dunes.

🚗 From the viaduct direction St. Pierre-d'Oléron, then direction St. Denis-d'Oléron, exit Cheray. 2nd road on left after football field. Right in Chaucre.

Saint-Denis-d'Oléron

CC (cc) Saint-Georges-d'Oléron

Saint-Pierre-d'Oléron ○

CC € **17** 7/4-29/6 1/9-29/9

🗺 N 45°59'28'' W 1°22'54''

St. Georges-d'Oléron, F-17190 / Poitou-Charentes (Charente-Maritime)

♿ 🛈 (1650)

△ Le Domaine d'Oléron****
🏠 La Jousselinière
☎ 📠 +33 (0)5-46765497
📅 30/3 - 29/9
@ info@chadotel.com

3,5ha 56T(80-120m²) 10A CEE

1 ABCD**F**HIJKLMOPS
2 RTVWXY
3 BF**G**JKNRU
4 (C+H 1/5-15/9) J (Q+T+U+V+X+Z 15/5-10/9)
5 **AB**CEFGIJKLMNPQUZ
6 CEG**K**(N 1,5km)TV

💬 Peacefully located campsite. Swimming pool with slides.

🚗 From the overpass direction St. Pierre. Right at Leclerc supermarket. Left at next roundabout direction Bois Fleurie. Turn right then immediately left after airfield.

Saint-Pierre-d'Oléron

CC € **17** 30/3-7/7 26/8-28/9

🗺 N 45°58'4'' W 1°19'7''

St. Georges-d'Oléron, F-17190 / Poitou-Charentes (Charente-Maritime) ♿ 🛜 iD (1651)

🏕 Le Suroit****
📧 1720 rue Ponthézières
☎ +33 (0)5-46470725
📠 +33 (0)5-46750424
🗓 1/4 - 30/9
@ info@camping-lesuroit.com

5ha 226T(80-130m²) 10A CEE

1 ACD**G**IJKLMPST
2 AEIJNRSTVWXY
3 B**F**GJKNRUWY
4 (C+E+H 🔒) IJKM
　(Q+R+T+U+V+X+Y+Z 🔒)
5 **AB**DFGIJKLMNOPR**S**UVXZ
6 EGH**K**L(N 4km)OTUVW

💬 Friendly four-star campsite with an attractive restaurant and an indoor pool with three water slides. Located close to the sea. Wifi.

🚗 From the bridge N734 as far as St. Gilles. Campsite on the left 3 km further on.

Saint-Pierre-d'Oléron

CC € **17** 1/4-6/7 26/8-29/9　　　🧭 N 45°56'53'' W 1°22'22''

St. Georges-d'Oléron, F-17190 / Poitou-Charentes (Charente-Maritime) ♿ 🛜 ✿ iD (1652)

🏕 Les Gros Joncs GC*****
📧 850 route de Ponthezière, BP 17
☎ +33 (0)5-46765229
📠 +33 (0)5-46766774
🗓 1/1 - 31/12
@ info@campinglesgrosjoncs.com

5,1ha 50T(94-240m²) 16A CEE

1 ACGHIJLMPST
2 AEINRSTVWXY
3 BFGJKNRU**V**WY
4 (A 1/7-31/8) (C 1/4-30/9)
　(F 🔒) (H 1/4-30/9) IJK**LP**
　(Q 1/4-30/9) (R 🔒)
　(S 15/6-15/9) (T 🔒)
　(U+V 15/6-15/9)(Y+Z 30/4-15/9)
5 **AB**EFGIJKLMNPUVWXYZ
6 BCDEG**IK**M(N 1,5km)RTV

💬 Family campsite close to the woods and the sea. Heated outdoor pool and wifi. The site has wellness with a beauty centre, massages and baths.

🚗 From the bridge direction St. Pierre. Turn left at Chéray, direction Sables Vigniers, left direction La Cotinière.

Saint-Pierre-d'Oléron

CC € **17** 1/1-6/7 26/8-31/12　　　🧭 N 45°57'2'' W 1°22'48''

St. Georges-de-Didonne, F-17110 / Poitou-Charentes (Charente-Maritime) ⊗ ♿ 🛜 iD (1653)

🏕 Ideal Camping***
📧 16 avenue de Suzac
☎ +33 (0)5-46052904
📠 +33 (0)5-46063236
🗓 2/5 - 9/9
@ info@ideal-camping.com

8ha 400T(90-100m²) 6-10A

1 ACDEHIJLPST
2 ABEGRSUVWXY
3 BCGHJRUWY
4 (C+H 10/6-5/9) IJK(Q 🔒)
　(S 1/6-1/9)
　(T+U+V+W+X+Y+Z 🔒)
5 **AB**GIJKLMNOPUVZ
6 CEG**K**(N 2km)OTV

💬 Very well maintained campsite near the sea (300m). Beautiful heated leisure pool. 2 km from St. Georges de Didonne. A peaceful campsite with plenty of sports and games for children.

🚗 Drive on the D25 from Royan to St. Georges-de-Didonne. The campsite is signposted before the centre of St. Georges-de-Didonne.

D25　Saujon
Saint-Georges-de-Didonne
Royan　D17
CC　D730
D145　D114
D1 E4
D1215

CC € **15** 2/5-1/7 25/8-8/9　　　🧭 N 45°35'6'' W 0°59'7''

St. Georges-de-Didonne, F-17110 / Poitou-Charentes (Charente-Maritime) ♿ 📶 iD 1654

△ Océan Vacances★★★★
🏠 63 allée des Bruyères
☎ +33 (0)5-46068000
📠 +33 (0)5-46064546
☼ 14/3 - 13/10
@ contact@oceanvacances.com

4,6ha 45T(80-142m²) 10A CEE

1 ACD**F**HIJKLN**P**ST
2 BEFGVWXY
3 AGHJK**P**QRUVY
4 (B+G 1/6-30/8) J**KLNOP**
(Q 1/4-30/9)
(S+T+U+V+W+Y 1/4-30/8)
(Z 15/6-15/9)
5 **AB**EFGIJKLMNOPUWXZ
6 AGK(N 1km)**P**QTV

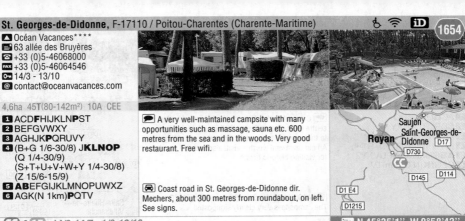

💬 A very well-maintained campsite with many opportunities such as massage, sauna etc. 600 metres from the sea and in the woods. Very good restaurant. Free wifi.

🚗 Coast road in St. Georges-de-Didonne dir. Mechers, about 300 metres from roundabout, on left. See signs.

Saujon
Saint-Georges-de-
Royan Didonne D17
D730
CC
D145 D114
D1 E4
D1215

CC € **15** 14/3-14/7 1/9-12/10 · N 45°35'1'' W 0°58'42''

St. Georges-lès-Baillargeaux, F-86130 / Poitou-Charentes (Vienne) 🚸 ♿ 📶 iD 1655

△ Le Futuriste★★★★
☎ +33 (0)5-49524752
📠 +33 (0)5-49372333
☼ 1/1 - 31/12
@ camping-le-futuriste@
wanadoo.fr

2ha 113T(100-120m²) 6-16A

1 ACG**I**JKLMOPQ
2 FGKLRTVWX
3 B**F**GNRUW
4 (C 1/7-30/8) (E+H 1/4-31/10)
J(Q ☼) (R 1/5-30/9)
(T+U+V+X+Z 1/7-30/8)
5 **AB**DGIJKLMNOPSUWXYZ
6 CE**K**(N 0,5km)R

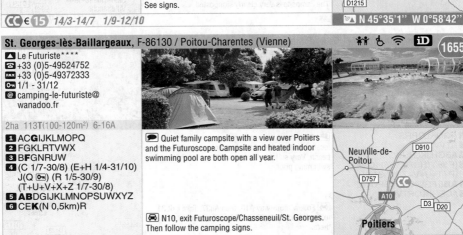

💬 Quiet family campsite with a view over Poitiers and the Futuroscope. Campsite and heated indoor swimming pool are both open all year.

🚗 N10, exit Futuroscope/Chasseneuil/St. Georges. Then follow the camping signs.

Neuville-de- D910
Poitou
D757 CC
A10
D3 D20
Poitiers

CC € **19** 1/1-8/7 26/8-31/12 7=6 · N 46°39'52'' E 0°23'41''

St. Hilaire-la-Palud, F-79210 / Poitou-Charentes (Deux-Sèvres) ♿ 📶 iD 1656

△ Camping Le Lidon★★★
🏠 Lieu-dit Lidon
☎ +33 (0)5-49353364
📠 +33 (0)5-49353263
☼ 30/3 - 30/9
@ info@le-lidon.com

4ha 115T(90-120m²) 10A

1 ACD**F**IJLMPQ
2 CLRTVWXY
3 ABHJKRU**W**
4 (C+G+Q+R+T+U+V+X+Z
1/7-31/8)
5 **AB**DFGIJKLMNOPUWZ
6 EG**J**(N 4km)

NEW

💬 A peaceful, attractive and natural campsite in the rural area of the Marais (= plenty of water). Swimming pool and children's pool. Attractive toilet buildings. Many opportunities for fishing, ideal for cycling. Boats and canoes available for rent.

🚗 From Niort N11 continue in direction Rochefort, turn right onto D3, just past St. Hilaire-la-Palud take Lidon exit on the right. Indicated from here.

Benet
D938 TER
D15 D25
D116 CC
D114 D116 E2 D3 D1
D115 Mauzé-sur-le-
Mignon N11

CC € **17** 30/3-30/6 1/9-29/9 · N 46°17'3'' W 0°44'36''

St. Jean-d'Angely, F-17400 / Poitou-Charentes (Charente-Maritime)

🏁 Val de Boutonne***
📧 56 quai Bernouët
☎ +33 (0)5-46322616
🔑 1/4 - 30/9
@ campingvaldeboutonne@
gmail.com

1657

1,9ha 99T(95-120m²) 10A CEE

1 ACG**I**JKLM**PQ**
2 CDFLRTVWXY
3 AGKNR**W**
4 (B+G 1/7-31/8) (Q+R 🔑)
5 **AB**GIJKLMNOPUVXYZ
6 CEG**I**K(N 0,7km)TV

💬 Campsite with plenty of shade located in the centre of St. Jean-d'Angly. Well-maintained, close to the river and a large lake in quiet surroundings. An old town well worth a visit, also suitable as a base for visiting historic towns.

🚗 A10 exit 34 direction St. Jean-d'Angely (Ouest). The campsite is very clearly signposted.

[Map: D120, D121, D939, D739, D950, D739 E, CC, A10, D130, D18, D150, D129, D124, Saint-Hilaire-de-Villefranche]

CC € 15 1/4-6/7 27/8-29/9 7=6

🧭 N 45°56'55'' W 0°32'11''

St. Nazaire-sur-Charente, F-17780 / Poitou-Charentes (Charente-Maritime)

🏁 Flower Camping L'Abri-Cotier***
📧 26 La Bernardière
☎ FAX +33 (0)5-46848165
🔑 30/3 - 30/9
@ abri-cotier@wanadoo.fr

1658

46T(90-145m²) 6A CEE

1 AG**I**JKLOPRS
2 RTVWXY
3 ABGHJKLRUW
4 (F 🔑) (H 1/7-31/8) (Q 🔑)
(R+T+U+V+Z 1/7-31/8)
5 **AB**EFGIJKLMNOPUWZ
6 ACEG**I**KORTV

💬 This campsite, with very spacious pitches, is located on the edge of a nature area, 3 km from the beach. Very suitable for bird spotting. Indoor heated swimming pool.

🚗 Follow motorway A10, then A837. Take exit 31 to Rochefort-centre/Royan/Marennes. Indicated from there.

[Map: D137, D5, Port-des-Barques, Tonnay-Charente, CC, Rochefort, D26, D733, D123, D117]

CC € 15 1/5-7/7 27/8-29/9

🧭 N 45°56'1'' W 1°3'37''

St. Palais-sur-Mer, F-17420 / Poitou-Charentes (Charente-Maritime)

🏁 Des Deux Plages****
📧 41 avenue des Acacias
☎ +33 (0)5-46231142
🔑 1/4 - 30/9
@ contact@campingdes2plages.fr

1659

3ha 70T(80-140m²) 10A CEE

1 ACD**F**IJKLMOPST
2 AGGQRUVWXY
3 B**F**GKRUW
4 (C+H 15/4-30/9) **KN**(Q 🔑)
(R+T+U+V+Y+Z 1/7-31/8)
5 **AB**EFGIJKLMNPUWZ
6 AEG**I**K(N 0,6km)ORTV

💬 A very peaceful campsite overlooking 2 beaches in the distance (600m). Lovely pitches on an flat site near the centre of St Palais-sur-Mer.

🚗 From the A10 near Saintes, take exit 35 to Royan. At large roundabout near Royan diretion St. Palais. Campsite well signposted in the centre.

[Map: D141, D131, D14, D733, D25, D1, Saujon, CC, Royan, D730, Saint-Georges-de-Didonne]

CC € 17 1/5-7/7 1/9-29/9

🧭 N 45°38'45'' W 1°4'48''

St. Palais-sur-Mer, F-17420 / Poitou-Charentes (Charente-Maritime)

👫 ♿ 🛜 **iD** 1660

🏕 Le Puits de l'Auture★★★★
✉ 151 av. de la Grande Côte
☎ +33 (0)5-46232031
📠 +33 (0)5-46232638
🔓 27/4 - 3/10
@ contact@
  camping-puitsdelauture.com

4ha 186T(100-200m²) 10A

1 ACD**G**IJKLMOPST
2 AEGKQRTVWXY
3 BFGHJRUVWY
4 (Q+R 20/5-15/9) (V 1/7-30/8)
5 **AB**CDEFGIJKLMNOPUWXYZ
6 ACEGI**JK**(N 0,25km)RTUV

💬 A traditional and homely four star campsite conveniently facing the ocean. Cycle path past the site, and 250m from 'la Grande Côte' beach, restaurants, bars and shops. A very quiet campsite with no entertainment. Spacious, level pitches with grass in both sun and shade. New toilet facilities.

🚗 From the A10 take exit 35 towards Royan. In Royan direction St. Palais-sur-Mer, then direction La Grande Côte on the boulevard.

D141 · D131 · D733 · Saint-Palais-sur-Mer · D14 · CC · N150 · **Royan** · D25

CC € **17** 27/4-2/7 20/8-2/10

🗺 N 45°38'59'' W 1°7'3''

St. Pierre-d'Oléron, F-17310 / Poitou-Charentes (Charente-Maritime)

🛜 **iD** 1661

🏕 Fleur d'Oléron★★
✉ 1 rue des Vignes
☎ +33 (0)5-46361140
🔓 7/4 - 29/9
@ contact@
  camping-fleur-oleron.com

2ha 73T(90-100m²) 16A CEE

1 ABCD**F**HIJKL**P**ST
2 AGORSVWXY
3 A**F**GJRU
4 (C 1/6-10/9) (Q+T 1/7-31/8)
5 **AB**EFGIJKLMNOPQUYZ
6 EGK(N 2km)

💬 Completely new and welcoming family campsite among the trees. New heated swimming pool. Modern toilet facilities. Quiet location.

🚗 The D734 takes you to a roundabout. Left in St. Pierre dir. La Natonnière. Campsite on the left.

Saint-Pierre-d'Oléron · CC · D26

CC € **13** 7/4-5/7 23/8-28/9 7=6

🗺 N 45°55'6'' W 1°17'53''

St. Pierre-d'Oléron, F-17310 / Poitou-Charentes (Charente-Maritime)

🛜 **iD** 1662

🏕 La Perroche Plage★★★
✉ 18 rue du Renclos (la Perroche)
☎ +33 (0)5-46753733
🔓 25/3 - 1/10
@ laperroche@oleron-camping.eu

1,8ha 70T(80-100m²) 6-10A CEE

1 ACG**H**IJKLMPST
2 AEORSVWXY
3 BFGJKLNRWY
4 **KN**(Q+R 1/7-31/8)
5 **AB**FGHIJKLMNOPUVZ
6 ACEGJ(N 2,5km)O

💬 A small, peaceful family campsite with direct access to the dunes and the sea. Opportunites for many watersports. 2 minutes from La Cotinière. Take advantage of the wellness (jacuzzi, sauna).

🚗 After the bridge direction Grand Village Plage, then turn right and follow the coast road. Located to the left after 8 km. 3 km before La Cotinière.

Saint-Pierre-d'Oléron · CC · D26

CC € **15** 25/3-7/7 25/8-30/9

🗺 N 45°54'6'' W 1°18'9''

St. Pierre-d'Oléron, F-17310 / Poitou-Charentes (Charente-Maritime)

♿ 🛜 iD **1663**

🏕 Le Sous Bois***
📧 avenue des Pins, La Cotinière
☎ +33 (0)5-46472246
🔓 1/4 - 31/10
@ resa.lesousbois@orange.fr

2,5ha 139T(80-130m²) 10A CEE

1 ABCD**G**HIJKLMPT
2 ABEGNORVWXY
3 AGJKNRUWY
4 **KN**
5 **A**BFGIJKLMNOPUWZ
6 EG**K**(N 1km)RUV

💬 A small, friendly campsite in the countryside. Located next to fishing village La Cotinière. The peaceful atmosphere is especially appealing!

🚐 From the bridge direction St. Pierre. In St. Pierre direction La Cotinière. In La Cotinière direction L'Ileau. Signposted thereafter.

Saint-Georges-d'Oléron
Saint-Pierre-d'Oléron
CC
D26

CC € **17** 1/4-30/6 1/9-30/10

🏕 N 45°55'23'' W 1°20'29''

St. Thomas-de-Cônac, F-17150 / Poitou-Charentes (Charente-Maritime)

♿ 🛜 iD **1664**

🏕 Camping de l'estuaire****
📧 3, route de l'estuaire
☎ +33 (0)5-46860820
📠 +33 (0)5-46860918
🔓 1/1 - 31/12
@ lestuaire@wanadoo.fr

9ha 65T(120-240m²) 10A

1 AFIJLMPRS
2 CDEKLQVXY
3 BG**J**M**R**V**W**
4 (B 15/6-15/9) **N**(Q+R 🔓)
(T+U 15/6-15/9) (V 🔓)
(X+Y 1/7-31/8) (Z 15/6-15/9)
5 **AB**DEFIJKLMNOPUXYZ
6 ACDEGIKORTV

💬 Family campsite with spacious and lovely swimming pool, all amenities. Sea at 500 metres (not for swimming), fishing possible on campsite lake. Walking and cycling in quiet surroundings among the kilometre-long tidal creeks.

🚐 From Bordeaux A10 exit 37 Mirambeau, then follow St. Bonnet-sur-Gironde D149. From Saintes A10 exit 37 and follow direction St. Georges-des-Agouts.

Saint-Genis-de-Saintonge
D145 D730
CC
A10
D146 D137
D18

CC € **15** 1/1-9/7 27/8-31/12

🏕 N 45°22'56'' W 0°43'19''

St. Trojan-les-Bains, F-17370 / Poitou-Charentes (Charente-Maritime)

♿ 🛜 iD **1665**

🏕 Camping St-Tro'Park****
📧 36 avenue des Bris
☎ +33 (0)5-46760047
🔓 15/4 - 30/9
@ info@st-tro-park.com

4ha 99T(80-120m²) 10A CEE

1 ACD**F**HIJKLMOPST
2 ABISVWXY
3 B**F**GHJKNRUVW
4 (A 1/7-30/8) (C+H 15/5-15/9)
KLN
(Q+S+T+U+V+Z 1/5-30/9)
5 **AB**EFGIJKLMNOPUVXYZ
6 CEG**K**(N 1,5km)OST

💬 A peaceful campsite in wooded surroundings. The site has a heated swimming pool, jacuzzi, hammam and sauna. Toilet facilities for the disabled. Wifi.

🚐 From the bridge, direction St. Pierre 'autres directions', follow St. Trojan as far as the harbour. Straight ahead at harbour roundabout. Turn right at roundabout with fountain. Keep left at junction. Then signposted.

D26
CC Marennes
D728 E
La Tremblade
D25
D14

CC € **17** 15/4-30/6 1/9-29/9

🏕 N 45°49'46'' W 1°13'1''

St. Trojan-les-Bains, F-17370 / Poitou-Charentes (Charente-Maritime)

🛜 📱iD (1666)

🔺 Huttopia Oléron Les Pins***
✉ 17 avenue des Bris
☎ +33 (0)5-46760239
🔓 4/5 - 23/9
@ oleron-pins@huttopia.com

5ha 203T(80-150m²) 10A CEE

1 ACD**F**IJKLMNO**P**ST
2 ABJKLSWXY
3 BGHJK**P**R
4 (C+Q+R 🔒)
　(T+U+V+Z 1/7-31/8)
5 **AB**FGIJKLMNOPQRUW
6 CDEGIJL(N 1,5km)

💬 In a majestic pine wood, close to the centre of Saint Trojan-les-Bains, this campsite offers you plenty of activities. You can make use of the many services at the campsite and the village: swimming pool, refurbished toilet facilities, leisure products.

🚗 From Bordeaux: follow A10. Exit 35 dir. Saintes and then dir. Ile d' Oléron. From Paris/Nantes: follow A10, take exit 33 La Rochelle/Rochefort and then follow Surgères/Rochefort/Ile d' Oléron.

CC Marennes
D728 E
La Tremblade
D25
D14

CC € **17** 4/5-5/7 2/9-22/9

🧭 N 45°49'53'' W 1°12'49''

St. Yrieix-sur-Charente, F-16710 / Poitou-Charentes (Charente)

♿ 🛜 ❀ 📱iD (1667)

🔺 du Plan d'eau****
✉ 1 rue du Camping
☎ +33 (0)5-45921464
🔓 1/4 - 31/10
@ camping@grandangouleme.fr

6ha 85T(100-120m²) 10A CEE

1 ACGIJKLMOPQ
2 FGRVWX
3 ABGHJLNR
4 (C 15/5-15/9) **I**
　(Q+R+T+U+X+Z 🔒)
5 **AB**DEFGIJKLMNOPUWXZ
6 CDEGIK(N 3km)ORV

NEW

💬 A campsite with spacious pitches. Very quiet and child-friendly. Clean toilet facilities. Good base for visiting the surroundings (Angoulême). Leisure pool close by, campsite guests receive a discount.

🚗 N10 (Poitiers-Bordeaux) north east of Angoulême. Exit St. Jean d'Angely/St. Yrieix. Direction Plan d'eau/Nautilis. Campsite signposted

D11
D939　　Brie
D737
CC
D14
D41　**Angoulême**
D699　La Couronne
D4

CC € **15** 1/4-30/6 1/9-30/10

🧭 N 45°41'31'' E 0°8'41''

Ste Marie-de-Ré, F-17740 / Poitou-Charentes (Charente-Maritime)

♿ 🛜 📱iD (1668)

🔺 Huttopia Île de Ré
✉ Route de La Flotte
☎ +33 (0)5-46302375
🔓 13/4 - 4/11
@ iledere@huttopia.com

4,8ha 197T(80-110m²) 10-16A CEE

1 ACD**F**IJKLPST
2 BSVY
3 AB**F**GJKRU
4 (C+G+Q+R 🔒)
　(T+V+Z 6/7-21/9)
5 **AB**FGIJKLMNOPQUW
6 ACEGIJ(N 2km)V

NEW

💬 Quiet, cosy campsite on the edge of the forest. The cycle route between Ste Marie and La Flotte runs alongside the campsite. Large, shady, marked-out pitches. The campsite has been fully renovated.

🚗 From bridge head towards Ste Marie-de-Ré and follow signs Huttopia Île de Ré. Campsite is next to the Les Clémorinants business park.

Nieul-sur-Mer
CC D735
La Rochelle

CC € **17** 13/4-28/6 2/9-3/11

🧭 N 46°9'56'' W 1°20'6''

Surgères, F-17700 / Poitou-Charentes (Charente-Maritime) ♿ 🛜 🆔 (1669)

🏕 Camping de la Gères***
✉ 10 rue de la Gères
☎ +33 (0)5-46077997
🗓 5/2 - 30/11
@ contact@campingdelageres.com

1ha 30T(80-120m²) 6-16A CEE

1 ACD**F**IJKLM**P**Q
2 CGRUVXY
3 ABGJR**W**
4 (C+H 1/5-30/9) (Q 1/7-31/8)
(T+U+Z 15/6-15/9)
5 **AB**DFGIJKLMNOPUZ
6 ACDEGK(N 0,2km)T

💬 Close to La Rochelle, Camping de la Gères is located on the shady banks of a river and 30 minutes from the beaches. A traditional family campsite, quiet and hospitable, 5 minutes by foot from Surgères centre and 300 metres from a supermarket. Many places to visit in La Rochelle, Rochefort, Le Marais Poitevin, etc. Free wifi throughout the campsite.

🚐 Campsite well signposted in Surgères (avoid centre of Surgères).

Ⓒ€**15** 25/2-6/7 26/8-29/11 　🧭 N 46°6'5'' W 0°45'12''

Vaux-sur-Mer, F-17640 / Poitou-Charentes (Charente-Maritime) ♿ 🛜 🆔 (1670)

🏕 Flower Camping Le Nauzan-Plage****
✉ 39 ave de Nauzan Plage
☎ +33 (0)5-46382913
🗓 1/4 - 30/9
@ contact@
campinglenauzanplage.com

4,5ha 137T(90-160m²) 10A CEE

1 ACD**G**IJKLOPQ
2 AEGRTVWXY
3 AB**FM**NRUW
4 (C+F+H+Q+S+T+U+V+X+Z 🗓)
5 **AB**DEFGIJKLMNOPUWYZ
6 ACEG**K**(N 0,7km)RTV

💬 Located 450 metres from the beach, this 4 star campsite offers you all the ingredients of an enjoyable stay. All amenities are available on site or in the immediate surroundings. Horse riding, golf, sailing, swimming, fishing, walking and cycling are just some of the possibilities. There are also plenty of interesting sights in the vicinity.

🚐 From the A10 near Saintes take exit 35 towards Royan, N150. At Royan direction Vaux-sur-Mer. Campsite well signposted in Vaux.

Ⓒ€**17** 1/4-14/7 1/9-29/9 7=6 　🧭 N 45°38'34'' W 1°4'20''

Agen/St. Hilaire-de-Lusignan, F-47450 / Aquitaine (Lot-et-Garonne) ♿ 🛜 🆔 (1671)

🏕 Le Moulin de Mellet***
✉ D107
☎ +33 (0)5-53875089
🗓 1/4 - 15/10
@ moulin.mellet@orange.fr

5ha 47T(130-200m²) 10A CEE

1 ACD**G**IJKLMPQ
2 BCDLRVWXY
3 BDGHKMNRUW
4 (B 15/5-15/9) (G 15/6-15/9)
(Q+R+T+U+V+X+Z 🗓)
5 **A**FGJKLMNOPQUZ
6 ACDEGJ(N 3km)ORTV

💬 Small scale, peaceful rural family campsite, also suited to families with children. A good out-of-season base for discovering the area. Fishing possible. Very large swimming pools. Modern, attractive and clean toilet facilities. Spacious pitches and hardened motorhome pitches.

🚐 N113. 7 km west of Agen at Colayrac-St-Cirq, take route D107 direction Prayssas. Campsite signposted from here.

Ⓒ€**17** 1/4-6/7 27/8-14/10 7=6 　🧭 N 44°14'38'' E 0°32'33''

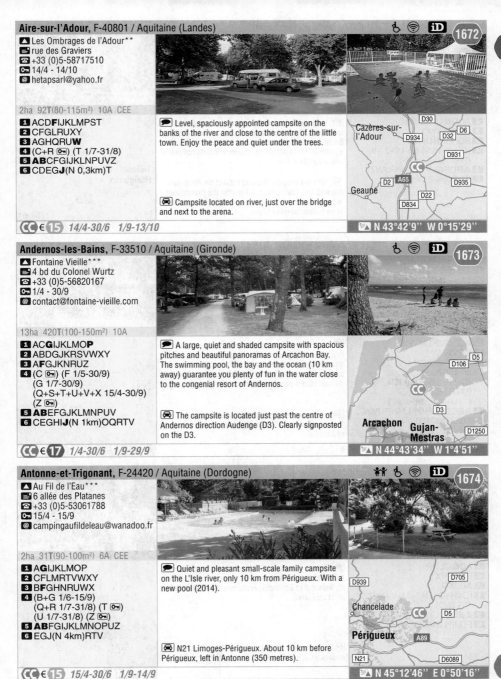

Aire-sur-l'Adour, F-40801 / Aquitaine (Landes)

♿ 📶 **iD** 1672

🔺 Les Ombrages de l'Adour**
✉ rue des Graviers
☎ +33 (0)5-58717510
📅 14/4 - 14/10
@ hetapsarl@yahoo.fr

2ha 92T(80-115m²) 10A CEE

1 ACD**F**IJKLMPST
2 CFGLRUXY
3 AGHQRU**W**
4 (C+R 📅) (T 1/7-31/8)
5 **AB**CFGIJKLNPUVZ
6 CDEG**J**(N 0,3km)T

💬 Level, spaciously appointed campsite on the banks of the river and close to the centre of the little town. Enjoy the peace and quiet under the trees.

🚗 Campsite located on river, just over the bridge and next to the arena.

D30
Cazères-sur-l'Adour
D934 D32 D6
D931
D2 A65 D935
Geaune D22
D834

CC € **15** 14/4-30/6 1/9-13/10 · 🧭 N 43°42'9'' W 0°15'29''

Andernos-les-Bains, F-33510 / Aquitaine (Gironde)

♿ 📶 **iD** 1673

🔺 Fontaine Vieille***
✉ 4 bd du Colonel Wurtz
☎ +33 (0)5-56820167
📅 1/4 - 30/9
@ contact@fontaine-vieille.com

13ha 420T(100-150m²) 10A

1 AC**G**IJKLMOP
2 ABDG**J**KRSVWXY
3 A**F**GJKNRUZ
4 (C 📅) (F 1/5-30/9)
   (G 1/7-30/9)
   (Q+S+T+U+V+X 15/4-30/9)
   (Z 📅)
5 **AB**EFGJKLMNPUV
6 CEGH**IJ**(N 1km)OQRTV

💬 A large, quiet and shaded campsite with spacious pitches and beautiful panoramas of Arcachon Bay. The swimming pool, the bay and the ocean (10 km away) guarantee you plenty of fun in the water close to the congenial resort of Andernos.

🚗 The campsite is located just past the centre of Andernos direction Audenge (D3). Clearly signposted on the D3.

D106 D5
D3
Arcachon Gujan-Mestras D1250

CC € **17** 1/4-30/6 1/9-29/9 · 🧭 N 44°43'34'' W 1°4'51''

Antonne-et-Trigonant, F-24420 / Aquitaine (Dordogne)

👫 ♿ 📶 **iD** 1674

🔺 Au Fil de l'Eau***
✉ 6 allée des Platanes
☎ +33 (0)5-53061788
📅 15/4 - 15/9
@ campingaufildeleau@wanadoo.fr

2ha 31T(90-100m²) 6A CEE

1 A**G**IJKLMOP
2 CFLMRTVWXY
3 B**F**GHNRUWX
4 (B+G 1/6-15/9)
   (Q+R 1/7-31/8) (T 📅)
   (U 1/7-31/8) (Z 📅)
5 **AB**FGIJKLMNOPUZ
6 EG**J**(N 4km)RTV

💬 Quiet and pleasant small-scale family campsite on the L'Isle river, only 10 km from Périgueux. With a new pool (2014).

🚗 N21 Limoges-Périgueux. About 10 km before Périgueux, left in Antonne (350 metres).

D939 D705
Chancelade D5
Périgueux A89
N21 D6089

CC € **15** 15/4-30/6 1/9-14/9 · 🧭 N 45°12'46'' E 0°50'16''

Antonne-et-Trigonant, F-24420 / Aquitaine (Dordogne) ♿ 🛜 iD 1675

🏕 Le Bois du Coderc***
🛣 route des Gaunies
☎ +33 (0)5-53059983
📅 1/1 - 31/12
@ coderc-camping@wanadoo.fr

3ha 38T(100-160m²) 10A CEE

1 ACDGIJKLMPRS
2 CLRTVWXY
3 BGHJKNORWX
4 (C 1/5-15/9) (Q 1/6-31/8)
(R+T+U+X+Z 📅)
5 ABDFGIJKLMNPRUWZ
6 CEGJ(N 2,5km)RTV

💬 Very well-maintained campsite, partly situated in the woods. Spacious pitches and clean toilet facilities. Suitable for those looking for some peace and quiet as well as for families with children. Sports options in and around the site.

🚗 A20 to Limoges. Then N21 direction Périgueux. After 85 km, past Sarliac. 2 km after the roundabout in Laurière hamlet left after Les Routiers restaurant. Then follow camping signs.

Trélissac
Périgueux

CC € 15 1/1-30/6 1/9-31/12   🧭 N 45°13'11'' E 0°51'47''

Aramits, F-64570 / Aquitaine (Pyrénées-Atlantiques) ♿ 🛜 ✿ iD 1676

🏕 Barétous-Pyrénées****
☎ +33 (0)5-59341221
📅 31/3 - 15/10
@ contact@camping-pyrenees.com

2,5ha 34T(90-130m²) 10A CEE

1 ACDGIJKLMPRS
2 CRVWXY
3 AGHJKLRUW
4 (A 1/7-30/8)
(C+H 15/5-20/9) KN
(Q+R 📅)
(T+U+X+Z 1/6-20/9)
5 ABCDFGHIJKLMNPUVWZ
6 ACEGKL(N 0,6km)V

💬 Very well-maintained campsite with pitches marked-out by greenery. Heated outdoor pool. In a small village in a beautiful natural area. Good base for all ages for walking and/or (electric) cycling. Easy and difficult routes possible. Wifi on the entire site.

🚗 In Oloron-Ste-Marie take the D919 towards Arette (about 13 km). Campsite indicated in the centre of Aramits.

Oloron-Sainte-Marie

CC € 15 31/3-11/7 29/8-14/10 7=6, 14=11   🧭 N 43°7'17'' W 0°43'56''

Arès, F-33740 / Aquitaine (Gironde) ♿ 🛜 iD 1677

🏕 Flower Camping La Canadienne****
🛣 82 rue du Général de Gaulle
☎ +33 (0)5-56602491
📠 +33 (0)5-57704085
📅 15/3 - 31/10
@ info@lacanadienne.com

2ha 35T(80-120m²) 15A

1 ACGIJLOP
2 BFRSVXY
3 AGJKR
4 (C+H+Q+R+T+U+V+X+Z 1/6-15/9)
5 ABDEFGIJKLMNPUWXZ
6 EGJ(N 2km)ORTV

💬 Shaded campsite with large swimming pool from 1/6 till 15/9 and bike hire, 7 km from the ocean. Ideal for trips out to Bordeaux, Arcachon, the Pilat dunes and Cap Ferret.

🚗 La Canadienne is located 1 km from Arès centre in direction Lège-Cap-Feret on the right hand side.

Andernos-les-Bains

CC € 17 15/3-6/7 1/9-30/10   🧭 N 44°46'43'' W 1°8'35''

Atur, F-24750 / Aquitaine (Dordogne)

🏕 Le Grand Dague****
✉ route du Grand Dague
☎ +33 (0)5-53042101
📠 +33 (0)5-53042201
📅 27/4 - 30/9
@ info@legranddague.fr

22ha 86T(100-120m²) 16A CEE

1 AF**I**JKLQ
2 FHIKLRVWX
3 BCFGHJKNRU
4 (C+G 📅) IJ
(Q+R+S+T+U+V+X+Y+Z 📅)
5 **AB**DEFGIJKLMNOPQUZ
6 EGH**IJ**(N 1km)RTV

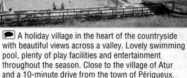

📺 A holiday village in the heart of the countryside with beautiful views across a valley. Lovely swimming pool, plenty of play facilities and entertainment throughout the season. Close to the village of Atur and a 10-minute drive from the town of Périgueux. Free wifi in low season.

🚗 Coming from Brive follow Atur signs at 2nd roundabout. Then follow signs. On the A89 exit 16 St. Laurent-sur-Manoire and the follow Atur and camping signs.

Chancelade
D6089 **Périgueux** D5
A89 CC
N21 D8 D710

1678

CC € **13** 27/4-29/6 3/9-29/9 | 📍 N 45°8'52'' E 0°46'40''

Audenge, F-33980 / Aquitaine (Gironde)

🏕 Le Braou***
✉ 26 route de Bordeaux
☎ +33 (0)5-56269003
📠 +33 (0)5-57760366
📅 1/4 - 30/9
@ info@camping-audenge.com

90T(66-180m²) 6A

1 ACD**G**IJKLM**P**ST
2 FGRSVWXY
3 A**F**GHJM**N**RU
4 (C 📅) (G 25/6-15/9)
(Q+T+U+V+X+Z 1/7-31/8)
5 **AB**FGIJKLMNOPUVXZ
6 CDEGK(N 1km)OQT

📺 A peaceful campsite with very large pitches and a lovely swimming pool. Ideal for cycling and walking tours or trips out to Arcachon, Bordeaux, the ocean or the Dune of Pilat.

🚗 D3 Biganos-Andernos. In Audenge right at second roundabout. Campsite 700m on the right.

D5
Arcachon CC
Gujan- D1250
Mestras D216
D652 A660 A63
D3

1679

CC € **17** 1/4-13/7 31/8-29/9 | 📍 N 44°41'3'' W 1°0'15''

Bayas/St. Émilion, F-33230 / Aquitaine (Gironde)

🏕 Le Chêne du Lac***
✉ 3 Lieu-dit Châteauneuf
☎ +33 (0)5-57691378
📅 1/3 - 30/11
@ lechenedulac@orange.fr

4,6ha 54T(96-180m²) 10A

1 A**G**IJKLM**P**ST
2 ABCDFLMRSTVWXY
3 AGHJKNRU**V**XZ
4 (Q 1/5-15/5)
(R+T+U+V+Z 1/5-15/10)
5 A**G**IJKLMNPUXYZ
6 CEGJK(N 3km)V

📺 A wooded campsite within walking distance of the town of Guitres. After visiting the Benedictine abbey you can board a steam train, rent a canoe / kayak or go fishing in one of the many streams. Close to a lake with a sandy beach and swimming area. Choose a well-shaded or less-shaded pitch. Opportunities for football, basketball and table tennis. Covered terrace.

🚗 N10 Bordeaux-Angoulême exit Laruscade/Guitres. Bayas is on the D247 coming from Guitres.

N10 D730
D910 BIS
CC D17 D674
D18 **Coutras** D21
D10
Saint-Denis-de- A89
Pile

1680

CC € **15** 1/3-14/7 1/9-29/11 | 📍 N 45°4'45'' W 0°12'24''

Beauville, F-47470 / Aquitaine (Lot-et-Garonne) ♿ 🛜 iD 1681

▲ Les 2 Lacs***
☎ +33 (0)5-53954541
🔓 1/4 - 31/10
@ camping-les-2-lacs@wanadoo.fr

22ha 50T(100m²) 6A CEE

1 ACD**G**IJKLMPRS
2 ABDLMPRVWXY
3 ABGHJKLMRUWZ
4 (B+G 1/5-30/9) (Q+T 🔓)
(U+V+Y 1/5-30/9) (Z 🔓)
5 **AB**DFGIJKLMNOPRUWX
6 AEG**K**(N 1km)RTV

💬 Lovely, spacious campsite with its own woods and walks. Walking and cycling (hilly, but electric bikes can be rented) in beautiful surroundings. Fishing lake (3 hectares) with carp, pike, perch (no licence required). Swimming lake (0.8 hectares) with top quality water. Delicious food, beautiful countryside, peace and space. Dutch owners who speak English.

🚗 From Cahors D656 direction Agen. Roundabout with exit Beauville. Follow signs in the village.

Saint-Antoine-de-Ficalba
D103 D18 D2 D656 CC D953

CC € **15** 1/4-30/6 1/9-30/10 ⛺ N 44°16'20'' E 0°53'17''

Belvès, F-24170 / Aquitaine (Dordogne) ♿ 🛜 ✿ iD 1682

▲ Camping RCN Le Moulin de la Pique*****
🏠 La Pique
☎ +33 (0)34-3745090
📠 +33 (0)5-53282909
🔓 20/4 - 2/10
@ reserveringen@rcn.nl
10ha 170T(80-140m²) 10A CEE

1 ACD**F**IJKLMOPQ
2 CDLRVXY
3 AB**F**GH**MNOPQ**RUVWXZ
4 (A 1/5-15/9) (C+H 🔓) IJ
(Q+R+T+U+V+Y+Z 🔓)
5 **AB**DEFGIJKLMNPRUWXYZ
6 ACDEGHKL(N 2km)OTV

💬 A very well maintained, child friendly five star campsite located on an estate with 18th century buildings. Aquaparc la Pique with swimming pools and 3 water slides. Plenty of trips out in the Dordogne Périgord Noir, with its many castles and historic towns. Canoe trips on the Dordogne every week for guests. Hardened motorhome pitches.

🚗 The campsite is located on the D710 Fumel-Belvès. About 2 km south of Belvès. Clearly signposted.

Le Buisson-de-Cadouin
D703 D53 D710 D60 D2 D660

CC € **17** 20/4-30/6 25/8-1/10 ⛺ N 44°45'43'' E 1°0'51''

Bergerac, F-24100 / Aquitaine (Dordogne) ♿ 🛜 iD 1683

▲ La Pelouse***
🏠 8b rue J.J. Rousseau
☎ +33 (0)5-53570667
🔓 1/4 - 31/10
@ campinglapelouse24@orange.fr

2,5ha 62T 10A CEE

1 ACD**G**IJL**P**S
2 CMRXY
3 AGHJQUX
4 (Q 🔓)
5 **AB**DGIJKLMNOPUZ
6 ACDEGJ(N 1km)RTV

💬 The campsite is located on the southern banks of the Dordogne just west of the centre. You can walk to the historic town centre in 10 minutes. The campsite is often used as a stopover campsite and favoured by wine lovers (Bergerac-Monbazillac). Plenty of activities in the Dordogne. Tranquility and nature. No big attractions.

🚗 Campsite located on the south bank of the Dordogne. Around Bergerac follow signs to Bergerac centre, then the campsite is signposted.

Bergerac Creysse
Prigonrieux
D709 D936 D21 E1 D21 CC D933 N21 D14

CC € **17** 1/4-1/7 1/9-30/10 7=6 ⛺ N 44°50'57'' E 0°28'35''

Bias, F-40170 / Aquitaine (Landes)

🏕 Camping Municipal Le Tatiou***
📧 route de Lespecier
☎ +33 (0)5-58090476
🗓 31/3 - 30/9
@ camping-le-tatiou@bias40.fr

1684

10ha 222**T**(100m²) 10A CEE

1 ACDGIJKLMOPST
2 BRSVWX
3 B**F**GHJKMN**Q**RU
4 (C+H+Q+S+T+U+V+X+Y+Z
15/6-15/9)
5 **AB**EFGIJKLMNOPUZ
6 EHIJ(N 7km)OQV

💬 This municipal campsite is located in a beautiful wooded area with fantastic walking routes, and just a few kilometres from the ocean. Good amenities, shop and swimming pool. Bicycles can be hired here.

🚗 A10 to Labouheyre then D626 towards Mimizan, from there to Bias where the campsite is signposted.

Mimizan-Plage Mimizan

CC €**13** 31/3-6/7 25/8-29/9

N 44°8'40'' W 1°14'24''

Bidart, F-64210 / Aquitaine (Pyrénées-Atlantiques)

🏕 Camping + Residence Oyam****
📧 chemin Oyamburua
☎ +33 (0)5-59549161
📠 +33 (0)5-59547687
🗓 14/4 - 21/9
@ accueil@camping-oyam.com

1685

4,5ha 54**T**(80-100m²) 6A

1 ACG**I**JKLMPRS
2 FGJRVXY
3 A**F**GNRU
4 (C+H 1/5-19/9) IJ(Q 🅿)
(T+U+X+Z 1/7-31/8)
5 **AB**EFGIJKLMNOPUWZ
6 CDEG**IK**(N 0,8km)TV

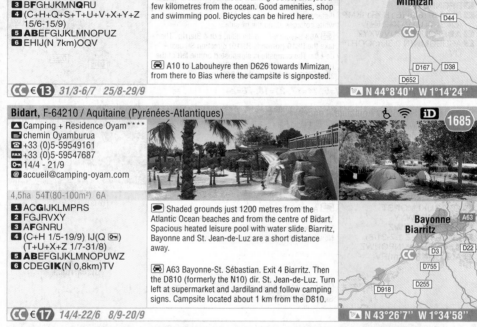

💬 Shaded grounds just 1200 metres from the Atlantic Ocean beaches and from the centre of Bidart. Spacious heated leisure pool with water slide. Biarritz, Bayonne and St. Jean-de-Luz are a short distance away.

🚗 A63 Bayonne-St. Sébastian. Exit 4 Biarritz. Then the D810 (formerly the N10) dir. St. Jean-de-Luz. Turn left at supermarket and Jardiland and follow camping signs. Campsite located about 1 km from the D810.

Bayonne
Biarritz

CC €**17** 14/4-22/6 8/9-20/9

N 43°26'7'' W 1°34'58''

Bidart, F-64210 / Aquitaine (Pyrénées-Atlantiques)

🏕 Sunêlia Berrua****
📧 rue Berrua
☎ +33 (0)5-59549666
📠 +33 (0)5-59547830
🗓 29/4 - 30/9
@ contact@berrua.com

1686

5ha 85**T** 6A

1 ACG**I**JKLMPQ
2 FGJRVWXY
3 B**F**G**M**NRU
4 (C+E+G 🅿) IJK**L**P
(Q+S+T+U+V+Y+Z 🅿)
5 **AB**EFGJLPUWZ
6 CEGH**IK**(N 1km)OTV

💬 A terraced campsite with plenty of shade and good amenities. About 1 km from a sandy beach and the picturesque village. Extensive swimming pool complex with indoor pool and heated outdoor pool.

🚗 A63 Bayonne-St. Sebastián, exit 4 Biarritz. Then D810 direction St. Jean-de-Luz. Campsite signposted on the left of the road in Bidart centre and at the 'Intermarché'. Site about 800m from the D810.

Bayonne
Anglet

CC €**17** 29/4-30/6 1/9-29/9

N 43°26'18'' W 1°34'55''

Bidart, F-64210 / Aquitaine (Pyrénées-Atlantiques)

♿ 📶 **iD** **1687**

🏕 Ur-Onea***
✉ 489 rue de la Chapelle
☎ +33 (0)5-59265361
📅 7/4 - 16/9
@ contact@uronea.com

5ha 125T(80-140m²) 10A

1 ACG HIJKLMPRS
2 EFGJRVXY
3 BFGNRU
4 (C 15/5-18/9) (E+H 🅿) IKMP
(Q+S+T+U+V+X+Z 🅿)
5 AB EFGIJKLNPUVWXYZ
6 ACDEGIJK(N 0,5km)OQRT
UV

💬 Ur-Onea is a well maintained campsite with paved paths with shade for tents and caravans. It has a heated indoor and outdoor pool. Within walking distance of the ocean and the town centre with the white cottages along the hillside.

🚗 A63 Bayonne-St. Sebastián, exit 4 Biarritz. Then take the D810 (formerly RN10) direction St. Jean-de-Luz. The campsite is signposted on the left of the road just beyond the centre of Bidart and is located about 400 metres from the D810.

Bayonne
Biarritz

CC

D3 D22
D755
D255
D918

CC €17 7/4-7/7 27/8-15/9 7=6, 14=12, 21=18, 28=24

⛰ N 43°26'1'' W 1°35'25''

Biscarrosse, F-40600 / Aquitaine (Landes)

🚻 📶 **iD** **1688**

🏕 Campéole Navarrosse****
✉ 712 chemin de Navarrosse
☎ +33 (0)5-58098432
📠 +33 (0)5-58098622
📅 23/3 - 30/9
@ navarrosse@campeole.com

8ha 162T(80-110m²) 10A CEE

1 ACD GIJKLMOP ST
2 ABCDMRSWXY
3 BFGHJKMRU WZ
4 (A+Q+T+V+Z 1/7-31/8)
5 AB EFGIJKLMNPQUWZ
6 ACEGH K(N 3km)RV

💬 An ideal campsite for watersports enthusiasts thanks to its exceptional location on the Biscarrosse lake. The shallow water makes it safe for children. New toilets and spacious pitches on wooded grounds.

🚗 From Biscarrosse direction Biscarrosse-Plage, Sanguinet and Navarrosse.

D218 D216
D652
D146 CC
D46
Biscarrosse

CC €15 23/3-6/7 25/8-29/9

⛰ N 44°25'54'' W 1°10'10''

Biscarrosse, F-40600 / Aquitaine (Landes)

♿ 📶 **iD** **1689**

🏕 Flower Camping Bimbo****
✉ 176 chemin de Bimbo
☎ +33 (0)5-58098233
📅 30/3 - 30/9
@ info@campingbimbo.fr

6ha 45T(80-150m²) 10A

1 ACD FHIJKLOP ST
2 GRSVXY
3 ABF GHJKMNRUV
4 (C+H 🅿) KNP(Q 1/4-30/9)
(R+T+U+V+X+Z 15/6-15/9)
5 AB DEFGIJKLMNOPUX
6 ACEGIJK(N 2km)QRV

💬 Family campsite with well-maintained infrastructure. Within walking distance of a lake. Heated swimming pool, sauna, jacuzzi, spa, massage and fitness room. Watersports options and cycling routes nearby. Keywords: lakes, ocean, leisure pool and countryside.

🚗 On the Sanguinet-Biscarrosse road (D652), on roundabout take 'Route des Lacs'. Campsite is signposted. Enter Chemin de Bimbo.

D218 D216
D83
D146 CC
D46
Biscarrosse
D652
D43

CC €15 30/3-30/6 1/9-29/9

⛰ N 44°25'37'' W 1°9'36''

Biscarrosse, F-40600 / Aquitaine (Landes)

🏕 Mayotte Vacances★★★★★
✉ 368 chemin des Roseaux
☎ +33 (0)5-35371411
📠 +33 (0)5-58820052
🗓 30/3 - 23/9
@ camping@mayottevacances.com

1690

15ha 140T(90-140m²) 16A CEE

1 ACD**F**IJKLMO**P**S
2 ABDLMRSVWXY
3 ABF GHJKLNQRUV**W**Z
4 (C+F+H ⊙) IJKLNP
  (Q+S+T+U+V+X+Y+Z ⊙)
5 **AB**DEFGIJKLMNPRUWXY
6 ACEGH**K**(N 5km)O**P**RV

💬 Five-star campsite with sandy beach on lake. A 600 m² outdoor swimming pool, water slide, jacuzzi, hammam, sauna, hydromassage and heated indoor pool. Multi-sports area with plenty of options, fitness room and outdoor exercise equipment.

🚗 The campsite is on Lake Biscarrosse between Sanguinet and Biscarrosse. Clearly signposted.

CC € **17** 30/3-6/7 24/8-22/9
📷 N 44°26'7'' W 1°9'17''

D218 D216
D652
D146
D46
Biscarrosse
Parentis-en-Born

Biscarrosse-Plage, F-40600 / Aquitaine (Landes)

🏕 Campéole Le Vivier★★★
✉ 681 rue du Tit
☎ +33 (0)5-58782576
📠 +33 (0)5-58783523
🗓 27/4 - 16/9
@ vivier@campeole.com

1691

25ha 348T(100-250m²) 10-16A CEE

1 ACD**G**IJKLO**P**
2 ABRSVXY
3 BF GHJKLM NRU
4 (C+G 15/5-15/9)
  (Q 1/7-31/8) (R ⊙)
  (T+U+V 1/7-31/8)
  (Z 1/7-15/9)
5 **AB**DEFGIJKLMNOPQUZ
6 ACEGH**K**(N 0,8km)RV

💬 A large campsite offering every comfort located in a wood and 800 metres from the sea. Excellent starting point for trips out, cycling and walking.

🚗 From Biscarrosse direction Biscarrosse-Plage. Follow camping signs.

CC € **17** 27/4-6/7 25/8-15/9
📷 N 44°27'31'' W 1°14'25''

D218
CC
D146 D652
Biscarrosse
D46

Biscarrosse-Plage, F-40600 / Aquitaine (Landes)

🏕 Campéole Plage Sud★★★
✉ 230 rue des Bécasses
☎ +33 (0)5-58782124
🗓 30/3 - 14/10
@ plagesud@campeole.com

1692

35ha 491T(70-110m²) 6-16A CEE

1 ACD**G**IJKLMO**P**ST
2 BRSVWXY
3 ABF GHJKLNRU
4 (C+H ⊙) K(Q ⊙)
  (T+U+V 1/7-31/8)
  (Y+Z 15/6-15/9)
5 **AB**EFGIJKLMNOPQRUZ
6 ACDFGH**K**(N 0,05km)RV

💬 A large campsite in a shaded wood. 800 metres from the sea and from the lively resort of Biscarrosse-Plage. Lovely heated swimming pool and water slide. Campsite completely renovated. Plenty of walking and cycling opportunities in the area.

🚗 From Biscarrosse direction Biscarrosse-Plage. Follow 'Plage-Sud' camping signs.

CC € **15** 30/3-6/7 25/8-13/10
📷 N 44°26'29'' W 1°14'44''

D218
CC
D146 D652
Biscarrosse

Bouzic, F-24250 / Aquitaine (Dordogne)

♿ 🛜 **iD** `1693`

▲ Le Douzou***
🖃 D52
☎ +33 (0)5-53284160
📅 1/4 - 30/9
@ contact@campingledouzou.fr

2,5ha 39T(100-200m²) 10A CEE

1 ACD**G**IJKLMOPQ
2 BCJLMRVWXY
3 BFGHJKLN**P**RU**W**X
4 (C+H+Q+R 🔑)
(T+U+V 1/7-31/8) (Z 🔑)
5 **A**DEFGIJKLMNPQRUZ
6 ABCDEGJL(N 5km)ORTV

💬 A hospitable, intimate and small-scale terraced campsite with every amenity. Enjoy the relaxing ambiance away from all the pressure. Lovely swimming pool and a fast flowing stream. Enjoy nature, relaxation and space. La douce France!

🚗 D673 Gourdon-Fumel. Then D46 direction Domme, after 3 km take D52 towards Daglan. Campsite 2 km before Bouzic. From Daglan D60 direction Domme. Right after about 2 km to Bouzic on the D52. Campsite 2 km on the right beyond Bouzic.

La Roque-Gageac · D704 · D46 · D60 · CC · Gourdon · D673 · D6

CC € **13** 1/4-13/7 31/8-29/9 7=6, 14=11

📍 N 44°43'51'' E 1°14'18''

Brantôme, F-24310 / Aquitaine (Dordogne)

👫 ♿ 🛜 **iD** `1694`

▲ Brantôme Peyrelevade***
🖃 46 avenue André Maurois
☎ +33 (0)5-53057524
📅 28/4 - 30/9
@ info@camping-dordogne.net

4ha 127T(100-200m²) 10A CEE

1 ACD**G**IJKLMPRS
2 ACLMRVWXY
3 BGHJ**M**N**O**PRW**X**
4 (C+H+Q+R+T+U+Z 🔑)
5 **AB**DEFGHIJKLMNOPQUW XYZ
6 ABCDEGK(N 1km)TV

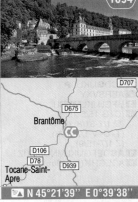

💬 A peaceful parkland campsite on the banks of the Dronne river. Large pitches within walking distance of Brantôme. Plenty of walking and cycling opportunities, swimming pool and good toilet facilities. Free wifi available throughout the campsite, faster internet for a fee.

🚗 Continue from Perigueux/Brantôme towards Thiviers. From Angoulême towards centre then direction Thiviers. About 1 km from centre. Follow camping signs.

D707 · D675 · Brantôme · CC · D106 · D78 · D939 · Tocane-Saint-Apre

CC € **15** 28/4-4/7 25/8-29/9 7=6, 14=12, 21=18

📍 N 45°21'39'' E 0°39'38''

Carcans, F-33121 / Aquitaine (Gironde)

🛜 **iD** `1695`

▲ Huttopia Carcans**
🖃 Domaine de Bombannes
☎ +33 (0)5-56039502
📅 4/5 - 16/9
@ lac-carcans@huttopia.com

13ha 170T(100-250m²) 16A CEE

1 ACD**F**IJKLMNO**P**ST
2 ABDGSUVXY
3 BFGHJK**M**NRU**W**Z
4 (C+H+Q 🔑)
(T+U+V+X+Z 1/7-31/8)
5 **AB**EFGIJKLMNOPUWZ
6 CDEG**I**J(N 0,1km)RTV

💬 Authentic camping in the free countryside. Open air swimming pool and toddlers' pool. The campsite is 13 hectares of the state forest of Bombannes, on the banks of Carnas Lake, the largest fresh water lake in France. A paradise for water sports and sun lovers. Plenty of opportunities for walking and cycling.

🚗 From D3 in Carcans D207 continue towards Maubuisson. Right on the roundabout beyond village towards 'Domaine de Bombannes'. Campsite 3 km on the right.

CC · D207 · D3 · Lacanau Océan · D650

CC € **17** 4/5-5/7 2/9-15/9

📍 N 45°5'47'' W 1°8'52''

Carcans, F-33121 / Aquitaine (Gironde)

🛜 iD **1696**

🔺 Flower Camping Le Médoc Bleu***
📧 35 route de Lacanau
☎ +33 (0)5-56033712
🗓 28/4 - 30/9
@ campinglemedocbleu@orange.fr

4ha 52**T**(120-180m²) 16A CEE

NEW

1 ACD**F**IJKLMPST
2 ABRSVWXY
3 BGJKNRU
4 (C+H 15/6-15/9)
(Q+T+U+V+X+Z 1/7-31/8)
5 **AB**CJKMOPUWZ
6 EGJ(N 1,5km)OT

💬 Quiet, shady family campsite with swimming pool close the centre of Carcans and just 5 km from the lake. Situated between the sea, a surfer's paradise (with Lacanau among others) and a Haut-Médoc vineyqrd. Cycling routes close to the campsite.

🚐 Campsite is on the D3 15 km south of the centre of Carcans.

D3

CC D207

Lacanau
Océan

Brach

D650

D104

CC €**15** 28/4-8/7 1/9-29/9

🗺 N 45°3'59'' W 1°2'53''

Cassy-Lanton, F-33138 / Aquitaine (Gironde)

♿ 🛜 iD **1697**

🔺 Le Coq Hardi***
📧 3 av. de la République
☎ +33 (0)5-56820180
📠 +33 (0)5-56828293
🗓 1/4 - 30/9
@ violesgalyon@aol.com

8ha 330**T**(100-120m²) 10A

1 ACG**G**IJKLMOP
2 ADGKLRSVWXY
3 BF**GH**JK**M**NQRU
4 (B 15/6-30/9) (G 15/6-15/9) J
(Q+R+U+V+Z 1/7-31/8)
5 **AB**FGIJKLNPUXZ
6 CEI**K**(N 2km)TV

💬 Quiet, welcoming family campsite with a very large playground, directly on Arcachon Lake and 10 km from the ocean. Well-maintained, with a swimming pool with slides, spacious pitches. Trips by bicycle or by car to Bordeaux, Cap Jerret or Pilat are possible.

🚐 Campsite on right of the D3 just south of Andernos in Cassy. Well signposted.

D106

D5

CC

D3

Gujan-
Mestras

D1250

D218

A660

CC €**17** 1/4-30/6 1/9-29/9

🗺 N 44°42'50'' W 1°3'39''

Castelnaud-la-Chapelle, F-24250 / Aquitaine (Dordogne)

🧍 ♿ 🛜 ❀ iD **1698**

🔺 Camping Maisonneuve***
☎ +33 (0)5-53295129
📠 +33 (0)5-53302706
🗓 1/4 - 31/10
@ contact@
campingmaisonneuve.com

6ha 140**T**(90-120m²) 6-10A CEE

1 ACD**G**IJKLMOPQ
2 CMRVWXY
3 AB**F**GHJKLN**Q**RU**W**X
4 (C+H+Q 🅾)
(R+T+U+V+Y 1/7-30/8)
(Z 🅾)
5 **AB**DEFGIJKLMNOPQUWZ
6 ACEGJ(N 1km)ORTV

💬 Typical Dordogne campsite with pitches on the River Céou. The grassland and peace and quiet day and night are all you need for good camping. Heated toilet facilities. Ideal for canoeing. Dordogne scenery all around. Castelnaud is a tourist village.

🚐 From the D703 via the D57 in the direction of Daglan. The campsite is signposted after passing Castelnaud. From Daglan take the D57 towards St. Cybranet and Castelnaud. Campsite signposted on the right before Castelnaud.

Saint-Cyprien

Sarlat-la-
Canéda

D703

CC

D710

D704

D46

D60

CC €**17** 1/4-5/7 31/8-29/10

🗺 N 44°48'18'' E 1°9'30''

Cénac-et-Saint-Julien, F-24250 / Aquitaine (Dordogne)

👪 ⛷ 🛜 **iD** **1699**

🏕 Le Pech de Caumont***
☎ +33 (0)5-53282163
📅 7/4 - 30/9
@ info@pech-de-caumont.com

10ha 100T(80-120m²) 10-16A

1 ACDGIJKLMPQ
2 BJKLRTVXY
3 BFGHJKRUW
4 (B+G 1/5-30/9) (Q 📅)
(R+T+U+V+X+Z 1/7-30/8)
5 ABEFGIJKLMNPUVWXZ
6 ACEGJ(N 1,5km)RTV

💬 A large spacious, beautifully laid out terraced campsite with lovely views. The site is located about 1 km outside Domme. Relaxation, space and views are the keywords. Lovely swimming pool.

🚗 From the A20, exit 55 Souillac direction Carsac D703. Then Vitrac D703. Then towards Cénac on the D46. Campsite located about 1.5 km south of the Dordogne. Signposted.

Saint-Cyprien | D57
Beynac-et-Cazenac | D703
CC
D704
D46 | Gourdon
D60 | D673

CC €**13** 7/4-6/7 26/8-29/9

📐 N 44°47'12'' E 1°12'33''

Champs-Romain, F-24470 / Aquitaine (Dordogne)

👪 ⛷ 🛜 ✿ **iD** **1700**

🏕 Château Le Verdoyer****
🏠 Le Verdoyer
☎ +33 (0)5-53569464
📅 21/4 - 30/9
@ chateau@verdoyer.fr

NEW

25ha 109T(100-150m²) 10A CEE

1 ACDGIJKLMOPRS
2 ADIJLMRVWXY
3 ABFGHJKMNRUWZ
4 (C+E+H 📅) J
(Q+S+T+U+X+Y+Z 📅)
5 ABCDEFGIJKLMNPQSUWX
YZ
6 CEGHIJK(N 3km)OQRTV

💬 Castle campsite in the Parc Naturel Regional Perigord Limousin. Well-maintained campsite that offers plenty of relaxation opportunities, both at the campsite as well as in the immediate vicinity. Indoor and outdoor pools. Ideal for a sportive holiday.

🚗 D21 Limoges-Chalus, right onto D6bis and D85 towards Nontron. After 20 km left at sign Chateau Le Verdoyer. Well signposted.

D91
D15 | D6 BIS
Nontron | D85 CC
Saint-Pardoux-la-Rivière
D707
D675 | N21

CC €**17** 21/4-6/7 25/8-29/9 7=6, 14=11

📐 N 45°33'2'' E 0°47'43''

Coux-et-Bigaroque, F-24220 / Aquitaine (Dordogne)

⛷ 🛜 **iD** **1701**

🏕 Le Clou***
🏠 Meynard route D703 📅
☎ +33 (0)5-53316332
📅 20/4 - 30/9
@ info@camping-le-clou.com

4ha 87T(80-150m²) 10A CEE

1 ACDGIJLPRS
2 IKLQRSTVXY
3 ABFGHJNRUW
4 (B+H 📅) J
(Q+R+T+U+V+X+Z 📅)
5 ABEFGIJKLMNPQRSUWZ
6 AEGJL(N 3,5km)TV

💬 A Dutch owned campsite. A wonderful location in the Dordogne with its mild climate and beautiful landscapes, caves, castles, monasteries and medieval villages. You will receive a personal and warm welcome. 'Mediterranean' swimming complex. From early in the season camping guests can enjoy the various facilities. Many walking opportunities in the vicinity. Walking routes available.

🚗 Campsite located between Le Bugue and Coux-et-Bigaroque on the D703 and is signposted.

D706
D31 E1 | D35 | D47
Le Buisson-de-Cadouin | CC
D25 | D703
D710

CC €**15** 20/4-7/7 25/8-29/9 21=14

📐 N 44°51'42'' E 0°58'53''

Créon, F-33670 / Aquitaine (Gironde)

♿ 📶 iD **1702**

🏠 Bel-Air***
🚏 D671 Lorient-Sadirac
☎ +33 (0)5-56230190
📠 +33 (0)5-56230838
🕐 15/1 - 15/12
@ info@camping-bel-air.com

3,5ha 62**T**(80-90m²) 5-10A

1 ACD**G**IJKLMPQ
2 FGLRVWXY
3 BGHJN**OP**QRU
4 (B+G 15/5-30/9)
   (Q+T+U+V+Z 1/4-30/9)
5 **AB**DGIJKLNPUZ
6 ADEGJ(N 1,8km)TV

💬 Perfectly maintained and quiet family campsite close to Bordeaux with a bus connection to the centre from the campsite. Swimming pool, heated toilet facilities, bar and small restaurant. Free wifi point.

🚐 The campsite is located on the D671 between Bordeaux and Créon, 2 km before Créon.

Cenon
D936
D671 D20
Cadaujac D14
D10
Langoiran D13
D1113

CC € **17** 15/1-6/7   27/8-14/12   ⛰ N 44°47'2'' W 0°22'16''

Daglan, F-24250 / Aquitaine (Dordogne)

♿ 📶 iD **1703**

🏠 La Peyrugue***
🚏 D57
☎ +33 (0)5-53284026
🕐 1/4 - 1/10
@ camping@peyrugue.com

5ha 78**T**(95-160m²) 6-10A CEE

1 ACD**G**IJKLPQ
2 BJKLRTVXY
3 B**F**GHJN**O**R**UW**
4 (B+G+Q+R+T+U+V+X+Z
   1/5-1/10)
5 **AB**CFGJLNOPQUWX
6 AEGK(N 1km)ORTV

💬 Emmy and Phlip Cappetti have turned this site into one of the nicest family sites. The pitches are spacious and well maintained. Walking, cycling and canoeing close by. In the middle of the scenic area of the Dordogne.

🚐 A20 Limoges-Toulouse, exit 55 Souillac, D820 direction Gourdon, then D673 direction Gourdon, turn right D801 direction Gourdon. Through Gourdon and again the D673 direction Fumel. D6, D46, D60 and D57 through Daglan direction St. Cybranet.

Calviac-en-
Périgord
Beynac-et-
Cazenac
D46 D704
CC
D60 D673 D6

CC € **15** 1/4-13/7   31/8-30/9   ⛰ N 44°45'9'' E 1°11'15''

Daglan, F-24250 / Aquitaine (Dordogne)

👪 ♿ 📶 iD **1704**

🏠 Le Moulin de Paulhiac****
🚏 D57
☎ +33 (0)5-53282088
📠 +33 (0)5-53293345
🕐 29/4 - 16/9
@ francis.armagnac@wanadoo.fr

5ha 160**T**(100-120m²) 6-10A CEE

1 ACDGIJKLMOPQ
2 CLNRVXY
3 AB**F**GHJKLNRU**W**X
4 (C+F+H 🕐) IJMP
   (Q+S+T+U+V+Y+Z 🕐)
5 **AB**EFGIJKLMNOPQRUWXY
   Z
6 ACEGH**J**L(N 1,5km)ORTV

💬 This spectacular four-star campsite with refreshing and varying swimming opportunities is noted for its spacious marked out pitches. The 'Céou' which borders one side of the site offers a safe descent by boat. Restaurant with competitive prices. Beautiful new toilet facilities.

🚐 From Souillac, direction Sarlat, Vézac, Castelnaud (D57). Campsite signposted beyond St. Cybranet. Or from Daglan take the D57 direction St. Cybranet. Campsite situated ± 4 km on the right.

D703 Beynac-et- D57 Calviac-en-
Cazenac Périgord
CC D704
D46
D673
D60 D6

CC € **17** 29/4-5/7   25/8-15/9   ⛰ N 44°46'4'' E 1°10'35''

Dévillac/Villeréal, F-47210 / Aquitaine (Lot-et-Garonne)

♿ 📶 **iD** (1705)

🏔 Sites & Paysages
Fontaine du Roc***
🏕 Aux Moulaties
☎ +33 (0)5-53360816
📅 1/4 - 15/10
@ reception@fontaineduroc.com

2ha 60T(120-175m²) 10A

1 ACD**G**IJKLMOPST
2 KLRTVWXY
3 BGHJN**OP**RUVW
4 (B+G 15/5-30/9) JK**N**
(Q+R 🔲)
(T+U+X 15/5-15/10) (Z 🔲)
5 **AB**EFGIJKLMNPUWZ
6 ACDEGJ(N 6km)ORTV

💬 Three-star campsite on the border of the Dordogne/Lot-et-Garonne provinces, well-known for its Southern French climate, rolling hills and friendly villages, streams and caves. You will find peace and quiet and have spectacular panoramic views of Chateau Biron. Swimming pool, children's pool, bar, restaurant, shop, new toilet facilities. Excellent amenities.

🚗 Campsite is located 500 metres from the D255 (Villeréal-Lacapelle-Biron) and the D272 crossroads. Signposted.

CC € **15** 1/4-6/7 25/8-14/10 | 🧭 N 44°36'51'' E 0°49'8''

Domme, F-24250 / Aquitaine (Dordogne)

👫 ♿ 📶 **iD** (1706)

🏔 Le Bosquet***
🏕 La Rivière
☎ +33 (0)5-53283739
📠 +33 (0)5-53294195
📅 7/4 - 22/9
@ info@lebosquet.com

1,5ha 36T(100-140m²) 10A CEE

1 ACD**F**IJKLMPQ
2 CLRTVXY
3 AFGHJKLRU**W**X
4 (A 1/7-30/8) (C+Q+R 🔲)
(T+U+V+Z 20/5-15/9)
5 **AB**EFGIJKLMNOPUWZ
6 ACEG**K**(N 3km)TV

💬 Beautifully located campsite 300 metres from the Dordogne. Quiet location, lovely countryside and extensive views over the hills, close to Domme. Heated swimming pool, free wifi. Walking routes from the campsite. Beautiful indoor toilet facilities. New building for reception and snacks.

🚗 From Souillac and Sarlat, direction Vallée de-la-Dordogne as far as Vitrac Port. Over bridge. Campsite 300m and is signposted.

CC € **13** 7/4-6/7 25/8-21/9 8=7 | 🧭 N 44°49'20'' E 1°13'36''

Domme, F-24250 / Aquitaine (Dordogne)

👫👫 ♿ 📶 **iD** (1707)

🏔 Le Perpetuum***
🏕 D50 Griffoul
☎ +33 (0)5-53283518
📅 19/5 - 12/10
@ luc.parsy@wanadoo.fr

4,5ha 120T(80-120m²) 10-16A

1 A**G**IJKLMOPQ
2 CNRTXY
3 ABF**G**HJKLNRU**W**X
4 (C+G 20/5-30/9) (Q+R 🔲)
(T+U+V+X 1/6-30/9) (Z 🔲)
5 **AB**DEFGIJKLMNOP**S**UZ
6 ACDEGJ(N 2,5km)V

💬 Lovely site on banks of Dordogne. Canoeing and kayaking from the site. The lovely town Domme and the beautiful countryside of the Lot and Dordogne are close by. Walking and cycling trips from the site. Nice swimming pools, one is heated. Free wifi. New restaurant.

🚗 Coming from Sarlat, Souillac, Gourdon or Bergerac, follow dir. Vitrac Port on the D703. Cross Vitrac bridge and follow signs (turn right towards the D50 at crossroads). Don't go to Domme.

CC € **15** 19/5-5/7 23/8-11/10 | 🧭 N 44°48'56'' E 1°13'14''

Douville, F-24140 / Aquitaine (Dordogne) ♿ 🏕 📶 **iD** (1708)

🏕 Lestaubière***
🚏 Pont-St-Mamet
☎ +33 (0)5-53829815
🕐 15/4 - 30/9
@ lestaubiere@gmail.com

20ha 104T(160-250m²) 6-10A

1 ACD**G**IJKLMPQ
2 ABDFIKLMRTVXY
3 BGHJ**M**N**O**RUWZ
4 (B+G 1/5-15/9) (Q 🕐)
(R 4/7-21/8) (T+U+V 🕐)
(X 1/5-15/9) (Z 🕐)
5 **AB**FGJKLMNPQUWX
6 ACEGJ(N 1km)OTV

💬 A magnificently located campsite with Dutch owners, close to the historic towns of Bergerac and Périgueux. The campsite has modern toilet facilities and very spacious pitches (more than 160 m²). Breathtaking views of the campsite and the surrounding area from the terrace under the plane trees (with free wifi). Enjoy the peace, space and countryside!

🚗 19 km north of Bergerac. Take exit Pont-St-Mamet from the N21. Campsite 2 km further on.

CC € **17** 15/4-6/7 25/8-29/9 7=6, 14=12, 21=18 〽 N 44°59'33'' E 0°35'50''

Douville, F-24140 / Aquitaine (Dordogne) 🚻👪 ♿ 🏕 **iD** (1709)

🏕 Orphéo Negro
🚏 RN21, Les Trois Frères Lieu-dit
☎ +33 (0)5-53829658
🕐 1/4 - 31/10
@ camping@orpheonegro.com

11ha 50T(80-150m²) 6A CEE

1 ACD**G**IJKLMPQ
2 BDLMRTVWXY
3 BGHJKMN**OP**QTUW
4 (B+G 15/5-30/9) **J**KL**N**
(Q+R+T+V+Y+Z 🕐)
5 **AB**FGIJKLMNOPUWYZ
6 EG**K**L(N 4km)ORTV

💬 A very spacious campsite in naturally wooded surroundings. Recreational lake on the site. Suitable for an active holiday.

🚗 From Périgueux follow the RN21 towards Bergerac. On the right after 25 km. Signposted.

CC € **15** 1/4-14/7 1/9-30/10 7=6, 14=12, 21=18 〽 N 45°1'39'' E 0°37'3''

Espelette, F-64250 / Aquitaine (Pyrénées-Atlantiques) ♿ 🏕 **iD** (1710)

🏕 Biper Gorri****
🚏 chemin de Lapitxague
☎ +33 (0)5-59939688
📠 +33 (0)5-59939689
🕐 3/4 - 3/11
@ info@camping-biper-gorri.com

2,5ha 56T(100-120m²) 6-10A CEE

1 AC**G**IJKLMPQ
2 CRVWXY
3 BFGNPRU**VW**
4 (C+E+H 🕐) KL**N**P
(Q+R 15/6-15/9)
(T+U+V+Y+Z 🕐)
5 **AB**DEFGJLNPUWXY
6 CDEGH**I**K(N 1,5km)TV

💬 The campsite is located 1.5 km from Espelette in a rocky area. The campsite has a typical Basque character. Biper Gorri means 'red pepper' for which Espelette is renowned. Swimming pool heated in early season.

🚗 A63 exit 5 Bayonne-Sud. Then D932 direction Ustaritz and via Cambo-les-Bains towards Espelette. Campsite well signposted from there.

CC € **17** 3/4-6/7 1/9-2/11 〽 N 43°21'12'' W 1°26'59''

Fumel, F-47500 / Aquitaine (Lot-et-Garonne) 🛜 iD (1711)

🏕 Les Catalpas***
🚪 La Tour
☎ +33 (0)5-53711199
📅 1/4 - 1/11
@ contact@les-catalpas.com

2ha 47T(70-100m²) 10A CEE

1 ACD**G**IJLMPQ
2 CKLRTUVWXY
3 BF**G**HJKNRU**W**X
4 (B 1/6-31/8) (Q 🔑)
(T+U 15/5-15/9) (V 1/7-30/8)
(X+Z 15/5-15/9)
5 **AB**DFGIJKLMNOPQUYZ
6 CDFG**K**(N 1,5km)RTV

💬 Campsite with lovely location directly on the Lot. One part located on the water, the other part on slightly higher ground close to 79 beautiful old catalpa trees. A good base for walking and cycling by the Lot, fishing, exploring the surroundings or just unwinding. Ideally located on the Lot valley cycle route (160 km of level cycling).

🚗 In Fumel follow dir. Puy- l'Évêque, campsite is located 3 km after the village of Fumel and is clearly signposted from Fumel.

Frayssinet-le-Gélat — D710
Fumel — D124 — D811 — Duravel — CC
D911 — D102
D656

€ 15 1/4-10/7 28/8-30/10 | 📶 N 44°29'18'' E 0°59'48''

Groléjac, F-24250 / Aquitaine (Dordogne) 👫 ♿ 🛜 iD (1712)

🏕 Camping du Lac de Groléjac***
🚪 Le Roc Percé
☎ +33 (0)5-53594870
📅 28/4 - 22/9
@ contact@
camping-dulac-dordogne.com

3ha 96T(90-120m²) 10A CEE

1 ACD**G**IJKLMOPQ
2 ADLRTVXY
3 BGHJKMNRU**W**Z
4 (**A** 1/7-30/8) (C+G 🔑)
(Q 15/6-15/9) (R 🔑)
(T+U+V+X+Z 15/6-15/9)
5 **AB**EFGIJKLMNPRUWZ
6 CEGJ(N 1,5km)OTV

💬 This campsite is located on Groléjac lake and exudes peace and quiet. A restaurant and a beautiful pool will complete your holiday. A really homely campsite, with a welcoming atmosphere and lots of space.

🚗 From Groléjac centre in the direction of Gourdon. Campsite is signposted after 2 km.

Sarlat-la-Canéda
D57
D703 — Groléjac — CC
D46 — D704
D673

€ 13 28/4-30/6 1/9-21/9 7=6 | 📶 N 44°48'7'' E 1°17'41''

Groléjac, F-24250 / Aquitaine (Dordogne) 👫 ♿ 🛜 iD (1713)

🏕 Les Granges****
☎ +33 (0)5-53281115
📠 +33 (0)5-53285713
📅 14/4 - 15/9
@ contact@lesgranges-fr.com

6ha 90T(90-100m²) 6A CEE

1 ACD**F**IJKLPR
2 BLRTVXY
3 BF**G**HJN**Q**RU**W**
4 (C+G 🔑) IJ
(Q+T+U+V+Y+Z 🔑)
5 **AB**EFGIJKLMNOPUWXYZ
6 AEGH**K**(N 0,5km)RTV

💬 A modern 4-star campsite 600m from the Dordogne and 1.5 km from a large fishing lake. Lovely terraced campsite with 3 swimming pools and 2 large slides. Attractive restaurant area with bar. All this in the authentic ambiance of the Périgord. Plenty of opportunities for kayaking.

🚗 The campsite is clearly signposted from the D704 in Groléjac.

Sarlat-la-Canéda
D704 A
D57
D703 — CC
D704
D46 — Gourdon
D60

€ 15 14/4-8/7 27/8-14/9 | 📶 N 44°48'57'' E 1°17'28''

Hendaye, F-64700 / Aquitaine (Pyrénées-Atlantiques)

♣ 📶 **iD** 1714

▲ Ametza****
✉ 156 boulevard de l'Empereur
☎ +33 (0)5-59200705
🕐 1/5 - 30/9
@ contact@camping-ametza.com

5ha 140**T**(80-100m²) 6-10A CEE

1 AC**G**IJKLMPRS
2 AFGJKRSVXY
3 AGJKMNRU
4 (**A** 1/7-31/8)
(C+G+Q+S+T 🔒)
(U 1/5-15/9) (V+X+Z 🔒)
5 **AB**EFGJLOPUWZ
6 ACDEGHIK(N 2,5km)OQTVX

💬 Close to Hendaye Plage. It has a swimming pool, bar and restaurant (open from 1 May). Spacious marked-out pitches amongst the flowers. 3 specially equipped motorhome pitches with amenities!

🚗 Exit A63 in St. Jean-de-Luz (Sud). Then follow the D912 Socoa - Hendaye-Plage over the Corniche Basque. Campsite signposted 4 km on the left.

Hendaye **CC**
Errenteria

D918
N-121-A

CC € **19** 1/5-30/6   1/9-29/9

🗺 N 43°22'22'' W 1°45'21''

Hourtin-Port, F-33990 / Aquitaine (Gironde)

♣ 📶 **iD** 1715

▲ Les Ourmes****
✉ 90 avenue du Lac
☎ +33 (0)5-56091276
🕐 21/4 - 22/9
@ info@lesourmes.com

7ha 300**T**(80-100m²) 10A

1 AC**F**IJKLMPST
2 ADGRSVWXY
3 BGJ**M**N**OP**RU**W**Z
4 (B+H 🔒) M(Q 🔒)
(S 1/7-31/8)
(T+U+V+X+Z 🔒)
5 **AB**EFGHIJKMNOPUVWZ
6 CDEGJ**K**(N 1km)ORTV

💬 Just 400 metres from a lake with a beach and watersports opportunities and 10 km from the ocean beaches, with cycle paths from the campsite, the prestigious Médoc wine chateaux, lively markets and tranquillity: these are just some of the top features of this clean and well equipped campsite.

🚗 Drive from the centre of Hourtin direction Hourtin-Port. Located about 1 km outside Hourtin on a corner. Clearly signposted.

Naujac-sur-Mer
D101

Hourtin
CC

D3

CC € **17** 21/4-1/7   26/8-21/9

🗺 N 45°10'55'' W 1°4'32''

Itxassou, F-64250 / Aquitaine (Pyrénées-Atlantiques)

♣ 📶 **iD** 1716

▲ Hiriberria***
✉ D918
☎ +33 (0)5-59299809
📠 +33 (0)5-59292088
🕐 1/1 - 31/12
@ hiriberria@wanadoo.fr

4,5ha 175**T**(100-120m²) 6-10A

1 AC**G**IJKLMPQ
2 JKRUVXY
3 BGHNRU
4 (A+E 1/4-31/10)
5 **AB**CDEFGIJKLMNPUVWXY Z
6 CDEGHK(N 1km)TV

💬 A quiet family campsite at the foot of the Basque mountains in floral surroundings. Spacious, level, marked out pitches. Close to the sea and the Spanish border. Shuttle available for guests. Heated swimming pool and toilet facilities.

🚗 A63 exit 5 Bayonne-Sud. Then D932 via Ustaritz and Cambo-les-Bains direction St. Jean-Pied-de-Port. Campsite located 3 km south of Cambo on the left of the D918. Drive past site entrance to roundabout then back to the entrance.

D755   D21
Saint-Pée-sur-
Nivelle   Cambo-les- D10   D22
            Bains
D3   D14
D4   D20   **CC**

N-121-B   D918

CC € **17** 1/1-7/7   26/8-31/12

🗺 N 43°20'19'' W 1°24'3''

La Roque-Gageac, F-24250 / Aquitaine (Dordogne)

🏕 Beau Rivage***
🏠 Lieu-dit 'Gaillardou'
☎ +33 (0)5-53283205
📠 +33 (0)5-53296356
🔑 21/4 - 8/9
@ camping.beau.rivage@wanadoo.fr

9ha 152T(80-200m²) 6A

⚥ 🛜 iD **1717**

1 ACFIJKLMPRS
2 CLMNRVXY
3 BFGHJMRUWX
4 (C+F 🔑) (H 15/5-10/9)
(Q+R 🔑) (S 1/6-10/9) (T 🔑)
(U+V+Y 1/6-10/9) (Z 🔑)
5 ABEFGIJKLMNOPRUVWXZ
6 DEGJ(N 2km)ORTV

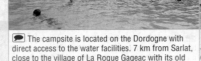

💬 The campsite is located on the Dordogne with direct access to the water facilities. 7 km from Sarlat, close to the village of La Roque Gageac with its old houses, cliffs and meanderings.

🚗 A20 exit 55 Souillac, direction Calviac-Carsac-Sarlat-Vitrac, then follow signs (advisable for caravans).

Sarlat-la-Canéda — D57 — D704 A — D703 CC — D704 — D46 — D60 — Gourdon

CC € **13** 21/4-30/6 18/8-7/9

🗺 N 44°48'58'' E 1°12'53''

Lacanau-Lac, F-33680 / Aquitaine (Gironde)

🏕 Le Tedey***
🏠 route de Longarisse
☎ +33 (0)5-56030015
📠 +33 (0)5-56030190
🔑 21/4 - 22/9
@ camping@le-tedey.com

14ha 700T(80-100m²) 10A CEE

⚥ 🛜 iD **1718**

1 ACDGIJKLOPST
2 ABDSVXY
3 BFGJKNQRUWZ
4 (Q+S 🔑) (U 25/6-5/9)
(V 25/6-15/9) (Z 🔑)
5 ABEFGIJKLMNPUVXZ
6 CEGHIK(N 6km)ORTV

💬 This site offers relaxation and nature in the middle of a 14-hectare pine forest. It has its own access to the shores of Lake Lacanau and is ideal for families with children and for watersports activities. The campsite offers every amenity. The ocean beaches are easily reached by bicycle (7.5 km).

🚗 From Lacanau towards Lacanau-Océan, D6 direction Le Moutchic. Follow road to the end of Le Moutchic, also to the end of the lake, then turn left. Follow campsite signs.

Carcans — CC Lacanau — D6 — D650 D5 E3 — D3 D5 E4

CC € **17** 21/4-30/6 1/9-21/9

🗺 N 44°58'56'' W 1°8'32''

Le Bugue, F-24260 / Aquitaine (Dordogne)

🏕 Les Trois Caupain***
🏠 725 allée Paul-Jean-Souriau
☎ +33 (0)6-85484425
🔑 1/4 - 30/10
@ info@camping-bugue.com

4ha 116T(110-170m²) 16A CEE

⚥ 🛜 iD **1719**

1 ACDGIJKLMPRS
2 BCRVWXY
3 ABFGHJKNRUWX
4 (A 3/7-27/8) (C+F+G 🔑)
(Q 1/7-30/8)
(T+U+V+X+Y 15/4-30/9)
(Z 🔑)
5 ABDEFGIJKLMNOPRUVXY
6 ACEGJ(N 0,9km)TV

💬 Les Trois Caupain campsite offers shaded pitches with every comfort. There are three swimming pools, one of which is covered. A perfect base for visiting the valley of Vézère. 900 metres from the lively village of Le Bugue with shops and places to eat. Good restaurant on the campsite. The campsite is located on the River Vézère.

🚗 On the right of the D703 from Le Bugue to Les Eyzies and indicated by signs.

D710 D32 E — D706 — D47 — CC — D31 E1 D703 — D49 — Le Buisson-de-Cadouin — D25

CC € **15** 1/4-11/7 29/8-29/10

🗺 N 44°54'33'' E 0°55'55''

Le Bugue, F-24260 / Aquitaine (Dordogne)   👫 ♿ 📶 iD 1720

🏔 Rocher de la Granelle***
📧 La Borie
☎ +33 (0)5-53072432
📅 12/4 - 17/9
@ info@lagranelle.com

7,5ha 102**T**(80-150m²) 10A CEE

1 ACDGIJKLMPRS
2 BCKLMRUVXY
3 BGK**M**NRU**W**
4 (B 1/5-15/9) (G 1/7-31/8) J
(Q 1/5-30/9) (R 📅)
(T+U+V 1/5-15/9) (Z 📅)
5 **AB**EFGIJKLNPUZ
6 ACDEG**K**(N 0,8km)ORTV

💬 Peaceful family campsite with its own typical French ambiance. You can swim in the River Vézère or in the swimming pool with slide. The Périgord-Noir region is renowned for its sumptuous gastronomy, caves and castles. Extensive sports facilities, attractive pitches.

🚗 Campsite located on the south side of Le Bugue on the D31E direction Le Buisson and is well signposted.

CC € **13**   12/4-7/7   25/8-16/9   7=6, 18=15   🗺 N 44°54'42'' E 0°55'0''

Le Buisson-de-Cadouin, F-24480 / Aquitaine (Dordogne)   ♿ 📶 iD 1721

🏔 Du Pont de Vicq En Périgord***
📧 avenue de La Dordogne
☎ +33 (0)5-53220173
📠 +33 (0)5-53220670
📅 1/4 - 30/10
@ le.pont.de.vicq@wanadoo.fr

5,5ha 130**T**(100-110m²) 10A CEE

1 ACDGIJKLMOPRS
2 CSWXY
3 B**F**GHJKLR**W**
4 (C+H 1/6-30/9) (Q 📅)
(T+U+V+X 1/7-31/8)
(Z 15/6-15/9)
5 **AB**DEFGIJKLMNOPUZ
6 CDEGJ(N 1km)RV

💬 The campsite borders about 500m of the Dordogne bank and has a heated swimming pool. Lovely, marked out pitches and good toilet facilities. Close to the lovely town of Le Buisson.

🚗 Fom Le Buisson-de-Cadouin direction Le Bugue. Campsite on the right just before the Dordogne bridge.

CC € **15**   1/4-7/7   27/8-29/10   7=6, 15=13   🗺 N 44°51'13'' E 0°54'38''

Les Eyzies-de-Tayac, F-24620 / Aquitaine (Dordogne)   ♿ 📶 iD 1722

🏔 La Rivière****
☎ +33 (0)5-53069714
📅 7/4 - 7/10
@ la-riviere@wanadoo.fr

7ha 109**T** 6-10A

1 ACDGIJKLPRS
2 CKLRTVWXY
3 AGHJKMRU**W**
4 (C+G+Q+R+S+T+U+V+X+Y
+Z 📅)
5 **AB**CDEFGIJKLMNPUWXY
6 EGIJ(N 0,5km)ORUV

💬 A 16th-century mansion in Périgord style has been transformed into a lovely campsite-hotel-restaurant. Close to the many sights in the region.

🚗 In Les Eyzies continue towards Périgueux, left immediately after the (River Vézère) bridge, 200m to campsite.

CC € **15**   7/4-7/7   25/8-6/10   14=12, 21=17   🗺 N 44°56'12'' E 1°0'22''

Les Eyzies-de-Tayac, F-24620 / Aquitaine (Dordogne)   ♿ 📶 iD 1723

🏔 Le Pech Charmant***
☎ +33 (0)5-53359708
🗓 10/5 - 15/9
@ info@lepech.com

17ha 83T(100-180m²) 10A CEE

1 ACDGIJKLPS
2 BIJRTVWXY
3 AGHJKNOPRU
4 (B+H ⚡) KN
  (Q+R+T+U+V ⚡) (X+Y 25/4-12/9) (Z ⚡)
5 ABFGJLMNOPRUWZ
6 ACDEGHJ(N 2km)OV

💬 'Le Pech Charmant' lives up to its name. The original 'camping à la ferme' has developed into a modern campsite but has kept its unique farmhouse atmosphere. The chance to enjoy typical 'communal' French meal, donkey trips and the outdoor life make a stay on this site well worthwhile.

🚐 Set SatNav to the village Les Eyzies. Then follow signs to campsite as road is one way for motorhomes and caravans.

CC €15 10/5-7/7 25/8-14/9 14=13, 21=19   📐 N 44°55'26'' E 1°1'46''

Lestelle-Bétharram, F-64800 / Aquitaine (Pyrénées-Atlantiques)   ♿ 📶 iD 1724

🏔 Le Saillet***
🚩 rue Soum de Castet
☎ +33 (0)5-59719865
🗓 1/5 - 30/9
@ le-saillet@orange.fr

4ha 70T(100m²) 10A CEE

1 ACDGIJKLMOPQ
2 CGKLRVX
3 BGHJKMNRUWX
4 (B 1/6-30/9) (T+U+Z ⚡)
5 ABCGHIJKLMNPUVS
6 ACEGJ(N 0,05km)TU

💬 Come relax in peaceful surroundings where you can hear the rushing water. Spacious shaded and sunny pitches with view of the river and Pre-Pyrenees. Easy access to river. 5 minutes' walk to the village with shops and restaurants. Beautiful walking and cycling options from the campsite, via the Voie Verte Pau-Lourdes. Bus to Lourdes and Pau (bus stop on village square). Free wifi.

🚐 Campsite located between Pau and Lourdes (D937). Signposted in village.

CC €13 1/5-9/7 27/8-29/9 7=6, 14=10   📐 N 43°7'46'' W 0°12'24''

Limeuil, F-24510 / Aquitaine (Dordogne)   ♿ 📶 iD 1725

🏔 La Ferme de Perdigat****
☎ +33 (0)5-53633154
🗓 24/3 - 4/11
@ accueil@perdigat.com

7ha 60T(90-220m²) 10A

1 ACGIJKLOPRS
2 CDLMRTUVWXY
3 BGHJKNRUVWX
4 (C+H 1/5-15/9) (Q ⚡)
  (R 1/5-30/9) (T+U 1/5-15/9)
  (V 1/7-30/8) (X 1/5-15/9)
  (Z 1/5-30/9)
5 ABEFGIJKLMNOPQRUWXZ
6 ACDEGK(N 3,5km)RT

💬 This relaxing campsite alongside the Vézère is situated in the grounds of an old farmhouse, and has many types of trees, bushes and flowers. The camping pitches are separated by bushes. Beautifully maintained grounds. Excellent toilet facilities. A good base for visiting Limeuil, the caves and the Dordogne. Hardened motorhome pitches. New owner

🚐 From Port de Limeuil to Le Bugue. Signposted.

CC €15 24/3-6/7 26/8-3/11   📐 N 44°53'37'' E 0°54'52''

Limeuil/Alles-sur-Dordogne, F-24480 / Aquitaine (Dordogne)   ♿ 📶 iD (1726)

🏕 Le Port de Limeuil****
🚏 D31
☎ +33 (0)5-53632976
📅 27/4 - 24/9
@ leportdelimeuil@orange.fr

7ha 90T(100-200m²) 6-10A CEE

1 ACD**G**IJKLMPRS
2 CLNRSVXY
3 BGHJKMN**O**RU**W**X
4 (C+H 📅) K
   (Q+S+T+U+V+X+Z 📅)
5 **AB**DEFGIJKLMNOPRUWXZ
6 ACDEGJ**K**(N 0,5km)ORTV

💬 Port de Limeuil campsite is located where the Dordogne and Vézère rivers converge, and on the other side from Limeuil, one of France's most beautiful villages. The site has its own 400m beach for swimming and fishing and canoes can be rented. The site has a shop, bar and snack bar. Wifi and tennis are free. Lovely swimming pool and heated jacuzzi. Hardened motorhome pitches.

🚗 From Le Bugue follow the D31 direction Limeuil. Campsite is sign posted in plenty of time.

D47
D706
D703 CC D35
Le Buisson-de-
D29 Cadouin
D660 D25
D710

CC € 15 27/4-5/7 26/8-23/9   🧭 N 44°52'47'' E 0°53'9''

Lisle, F-24350 / Aquitaine (Dordogne)   ♿ 📶 iD (1727)

🏕 Camping Le Pont**
🚏 8, rue de Pont
☎ +33 (0)6-30533827
📅 1/4 - 31/10
@ campingdelisle.24@gmail.com

NEW

2,5ha 49T(80-110m²) 16A CEE

1 AGIJKLMOPQ
2 ACLMRVWXY
3 BGHJK**MOP**RW**X**
4 (Q 1/7-31/8) (T+U+Z 📅)
5 **AB**FGHIJKMNOPUZ
6 CDEGK(N 1,5km)T

💬 A rural and peaceful campsite on the banks of the River Dronne. Spacious, shaded and marked out pitches. Well-kept toilet facilities.

🚗 D939 Angoulême-Périgueux. South of Brantôme D78 direction Boudeilles then Lisle, turn right just before village. On the right just before the bridge.

D106
D78 D939
CC
D710
Coulounieix-Chamiers

CC € 11 1/4-30/6 1/9-30/10   🧭 N 45°16'52'' E 0°32'25''

Louvie-Juzon, F-64260 / Aquitaine (Pyrénées-Atlantiques)   ⛷ ♿ 📶 ✿ iD (1728)

🏕 Le Rey***
🚏 route de Lourdes
☎ +33 (0)5-59057852
📅 1/1 - 27/10, 22/12 - 31/12
@ celine@campinglerey.com

2,5ha 38T(80-120m²) 10A CEE

1 ACD**F**IJKLM**P**Q
2 IJLRVXY
3 AGHJKLN**OP**RU**W**
4 (**A** 1/7-31/8) (C+H 1/7-15/9)
   (Q+R+T+U+V+Z 📅)
5 **AB**DGIJKLMNOPUWZ
6 ABDEGJ(N 0,9km)

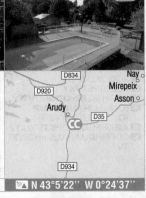

💬 A well maintained small campsite (3 hectares) just outside Louvie-Juzon with a natural character. This is because a lot of the natural vegetation is not used for camping pitches. Good walking and cycling area. Free wifi. Central location for the sights of the Pyrenees on your way to Spain (via the Col de Pourtalet). Please telephone if arriving after 18:00 in the winter.

🚗 In Louvie-Juzon direction Lourdes (D35). Start following signs about 400 metres after village.

D834
D920 Nay
Mirepeix
Arudy Asson
CC D35
D934

CC € 15 1/1-29/6 1/9-26/10 22/12-31/12 7=6   🧭 N 43°5'22'' W 0°24'37''

Mareuil-en-Périgord, F-24340 / Aquitaine (Dordogne) 🔥 📶 iD (1729)

🔺 Parc Touristique L'Etang Bleu
📧 D93
☎ +33 (0)5-53609270
📅 1/4 - 20/10
@ letangbleu@orange.fr

10ha 50T(100-160m²) 10A

1 ACGIJKLMOPQ
2 LRVXY
3 AGHJNRUVWX
4 (B 15/5-30/9)
(Q+R+T+U+V+Y+Z 🔒)
5 ABFGJLMNPUWX
6 AEGK(N 5km)OV

💬 This well run campsite is an excellent base from which you can explore the Dordogne countryside and visit its lovely villages such as Brantôme. Plenty of leisure opportunities in the near vicinity. Large, marked out pitches.

🚐 Along the D939, from Angoulême. In Vieux-Mareuil (half way between Angoulême and Périgueux). Turn left (1500 metres). Clearly signposted.

CC € 15 1/4-5/7 26/8-19/10 📍 N 45°26'46'' E 0°30'32''

D16 — Nontron
D5
CC
D12 — D708 — D675
Verteillac — D939 — Brantôme

Messanges, F-40660 / Aquitaine (Landes) 🔥 📶 iD (1730)

🔺 Albret-Plage***
📧 100 chemin du Junca
☎ +33 (0)5-58480367
📠 +33 (0)5-58482191
📅 1/4 - 30/9
@ albretplage@wanadoo.fr

6ha 117T(80-100m²) 6A CEE

1 ACGIJLMOPST
2 ABEGRSTUVWXY
3 BFGHJNRUWY
4 (Q+S+T+U+V+Y+Z 15/6-15/9)
5 ABEFGIJKLMNOPUVZ
6 ACDEGHIJK(N 1km)OQTV

💬 Camping grounds 1 km from the centre of Vieux Boucau. The campsite is predominantly level but there is also a slightly sloping section that is set in a pine forest. There is direct access to the Atlantic Ocean (300 metres). The swimming section of the beach has lifeguards.

🚐 D652 Léon-Vieux-Boucau, 1 km north of Vieux-Boucau. The campsite is situated next to Le Vieux Port, but has its own access road on the D652.

CC € 15 1/4-30/6 1/9-29/9 📍 N 43°47'47'' W 1°24'4''

Léon — D142
CC
Soustons — D116
D79
D652 — D17

Messanges, F-40660 / Aquitaine (Landes) 🔥 📶 ✿ iD (1731)

🔺 Camp. Village Resort & Spa Le Vieux Port*****
📧 850 route de la Plage Sud
☎ +33 (0)5-58482200
📠 +33 (0)5-58480169
📅 24/3 - 4/11
@ levieuxport@resasol.com

30ha 400T(100-120m²) 6A CEE

1 ACGIJKLMPS
2 ABEGIRSTVXY
3 BFGHJKLMNOPQRUVWY
4 (C+F+H 🔒) IJKLMNP
(Q+S+T+U+V+Y+Z 🔒)
5 ABDEFGIJKLOPSTUWXYZ
6 CDFGHIKM(N 0,5km)OPQR TV

💬 A large, spaciously planned campsite, but still peaceful as many of the facilities are near the reception. Located in a large pine forest that is divided into coloured zones, each with its own toilet facilities. Large leisure pool with heated swimming pool and slides.

🚐 D652 Léon - Vieux-Boucau, 1 km north of Vieux-Boucau. Well signposted.

CC € 19 24/3-27/3 2/4-23/6 1/9-3/11 📍 N 43°47'52'' W 1°24'4''

D142
CC
Soustons — D116
D79
Le Penon — D652 — D17

Messages, F-40660 / Aquitaine (Landes)   ♿ 🛜 iD 1732

🏕 La Côte★★★★
✉ 361 chemin de la Côte
☎ +33 (0)5-58489494
⏲ 1/4 - 30/9
@ info@campinglacote.com

3,5ha 113T(100-130m²) 6A

1 ACG IJKLMPST
2 RVXY
3 BFGHJKNRU
4 (B+H 15/5-20/9) K
   (Q+R 15/6-15/9)
   (U+V 1/7-31/8)
5 AB EFGIJKLOPUWXYZ
6 ACEG IK (N 2km)OQRTV

💬 A campsite on level ground with spacious shaded pitches. Ideal for families thanks to the playground, lovely swimming pool with toddlers' pool and bubble bath. The swimming complex is open from 15 May. Just 1 km to the Atlantic beaches. Refurbished toilet facilities in 2015.

🚗 In Bordeaux follow Bayonne A63 and D810 as far as exit 11 Magescq. In Magescq centre direction Azur and Messanges. Then direction Vieux-Boucau, D652. 2 km past centre of Messanges on the right.

CC € 13 1/4-3/7 27/8-29/9   📡 N 43°48'1'' W 1°23'30''

Messages, F-40660 / Aquitaine (Landes)   ♿ 🛜 iD 1733

🏕 Les Acacias★★★
✉ 101 chemin du Houdin
☎ +33 (0)5-58480178
⏲ 25/3 - 15/10
@ lesacacias@lesacacias.com

3,4ha 74T(90-120m²) 6-10A CEE

1 ACDG IJKLMPST
2 RSUVWXY
3 BFGHJKNRU
4 (Q 🚿) (S 1/6-30/9)
   (U+V 4/7-31/8)
5 AB EFGIJKLMNPUWXYZ
6 ACDEGHK(N 1,5km)OQRT

💬 Friendly family campsite about 2 km from the Atlantic coast. Although you are here in Les Landes you will not be camping among pine trees. However there is sufficient shade. Very well maintained toilet facilities.

🚗 A63 and N10 Bordeaux-Bayonne to exit 11 Magescq. Then dir. Azur and Messanges. Then dir. Vieux-Boucau. Left at roundabout 2 km before Messanges centre (Quartier Caliot road). Campsite 1 km further on the left.

CC € 13 25/3-6/7 25/8-14/10   📡 N 43°47'54'' W 1°22'33''

Mimizan-Plage-Sud, F-40200 / Aquitaine (Landes)   👪 ♿ 🛜 iD 1734

🏕 Airotel Club Marina-Landes★★★★
✉ rue Marina
☎ +33 (0)5-58091266
📠 +33 (0)5-58091640
⏲ 5/5 - 16/9
@ contact@clubmarina.com

9ha 353T(80-110m²) 10A CEE

1 ACDG IJKLMOPST
2 BERSVWXY
3 BFGHJKLM NQRUVW Y
4 (B+E+H 🚿) IJKMP
   (Q+S+T+U+V+X+Y+Z 🚿)
5 AB DEFGIJKLMNOPUZ
6 ACEGHJ K (N 1km)OQRV

💬 A lovely campsite with all the amenities to ensure a wonderful stay. You will enjoy the heated indoor pool and if the weather is good in the large outdoor pool. The sea and dunes are 500 metres away and back on the site you will find a good restaurant, jeu de boules, minigolf and direct access to Les Landes cycle route network.

🚗 In Mimizan drive in the direction of Mimizan-Plage (6 km). The campsite is located on this road.

CC € 17 5/5-7/7 25/8-15/9   📡 N 44°12'17'' W 1°17'27''

Moliets-Plage, F-40660 / Aquitaine (Landes)

🛁 🛜 **iD** (1735)

🏕 Le Saint Martin★★★★
✉ 2655 avenue de l'Océan
☎ +33 (0)5-58485230
📠 +33 (0)5-58485073
🔑 1/4 - 28/10
@ contact@camping-saint-martin.fr

18ha 450T(80-150m²) 15A CEE

1 ACGIJKLMOPST
2 AEIJKRSVWXY
3 BFGHJKLNRU**W**Y
4 (B 1/6-15/9) (**F**+**H** 🔑) **KN**
    (Q 🔑) (S+T 1/4-15/10)
    (V 20/6-15/9) (Y+Z 🔑)
5 **AB**DEFGIJKLPUXYZ
6 ACDEGH**IK**M(N 2km)OQRT
    V

💬 The campsite has direct access to the Atlantic. You can use the outdoor pool, the heated indoor pool, sauna and bubble bath for free in low season. Wifi is also free in this period.

🚗 From Bordeaux direction Bayonne over the A63 and N10. Take exit 'Castets' then direction Léon. Turn left just before the centre of Léon towards Messanges. In Moliets take the road to Moliets-Plage. Last campsite before the ocean.

D42
D652
D142
CC
Magescq
Soustons

CC € **17** 1/4-29/6 3/9-27/10

🏕 N 43°51'9'' W 1°23'13''

Monflanquin, F-47150 / Aquitaine (Lot-et-Garonne)

🤸 🛁 🛜 **iD** (1736)

🏕 Domaine Laborde★★★★
✉ Commune Paulhiac
☎ +33 (0)5-53631488
📠 +33 (0)5-53616023
🔑 1/4 - 15/10
@ domainelaborde@wanadoo.fr

20ha 150T(120-160m²) 6-15A

1 ACD**G**IJKLMNOPST
2 CDLRTVWXY
3 ABDGHJMN**OP**RUVWZ
4 (A 🔑) (B 15/5-30/9)
    (F+H 🔑) J**K**LN
    (Q+S+T+U+V 🔑)
    (Y 1/5-30/9) (Z 🔑)
5 **AB**DEFGIJKLMNOPUVWZ
6 ACDEGJ(N 7km)ORTV

💬 Four-star naturist campsite directly on the border of the Dordogne and Lot et Garonne, famous for its Southern French climate, small villages, castles, creeks and caves. Indoor leisure pool, sauna with hammam, outdoor pool with 2 slides, restaurant, shop, bar and internet. Great campsite.

🚗 D255 from Villeréal to Lacapelle-Biron. The road to the campsite is on the left, 10 km from Villeréal. Indicated by Domaine Laborde signs.

D676
D53
D14
Monpazier
D207
D2
D104
CC
Blanquefort-sur-Briolance
Monflanquin
D124
D710

CC € **19** 1/4-7/7 25/8-14/10

🏕 N 44°36'50'' E 0°50'8''

Monplaisant, F-24170 / Aquitaine (Dordogne)

🛁 🛜 **iD** (1737)

🏕 La Lénotte★★★
✉ D710
☎ +33 (0)5-53302580
🔑 1/4 - 30/9
@ contact@la-lenotte.com

8ha 33T(90-120m²) 10A CEE

1 ACD**F**IJKLMPQ
2 CLMRTVX
3 BFGHJQRUW
4 (C+G 1/6-30/9) (Q 1/7-30/8)
    (R 🔑) (T+U+V 1/7-31/8)
    (X 1/7-30/8) (Z 🔑)
5 **A**FGIJKLMNOPRUX
6 ACDEGHJ(N 4km)ORTV

💬 A spacious, peaceful campsite where you will be welcomed by the young, enthusiastic owners. A lovely brook meanders through the campsite, suitable for fishing. The Dordogne, Sarlat and the fortified towns are close by, as well as castles and caves. Level grounds and easy access, making it suitable as a stopover campsite (Bis-Toulouse). Hardened motorhome pitches.

🚗 Bergerac-Sarlat 7 km east of Le Buisson-de-Cadouin. Follow the D710 at Siorac for 5 km (Bis-Toulouse).

Le Buisson-de-Cadouin
D35
D25
D703
CC
D53
D710
D60

CC € **13** 1/4-7/7 25/8-29/9 7=6

🏕 N 44°47'46'' E 1°0'29''

Montalivet, F-33930 / Aquitaine (Gironde)

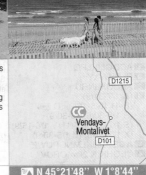

🛖 📶 iD (1738)

🔺 Centre Helio-Marin (CHM) Montalivet***
🏠 46 av. de l'Europe
☎ +33 (0)5-33092092
📠 +33 (0)5-56093215
📅 31/3 - 29/10
@ reservations@socnat.fr
200ha 561T(100m²) 16A CEE

1 ACD**G**IJKLMPST
2 AEGSVWXY
3 BGHJKL**M**NQRU**V**Y
4 (E+H 📶) IJ**KLNP**
  (Q+S+T+U+V+W+X+Y+Z 📶)
5 **AB**DEGIJKLMNOPUVXYZ
6 CDEGH**I**K**M**(N 1km)ORTV

💬 This naturist campsite extends over 200 hectares of pine forest with direct access to a two kilometre Atlantic sandy beach. Leisure pool and spa complex. Many sporting opportunities with cycling and walking routes right from the site. Further afield the vineyards of the Médoc and the Pointe du Verdon lure.

🚗 A10 to Saintes, N105 to Royan, boat to Verdon, D1215 to Lesparre, D102, right to Vendays-Montalivet. Left at fire station Ave de l'Europe to 46. Site is on right.

CC € 17 31/3-6/7 25/8-28/10   📍 N 45°21'48'' W 1°8'44''

Montalivet-les-Bains, F-33930 / Aquitaine (Gironde)

🚻 📶 iD (1739)

🔺 Campéole Médoc Plage****
🏠 av. de l'Europe
☎ +33 (0)5-56093345
📠 +33 (0)5-56093312
📅 27/4 - 16/9
@ medoc-plage@campeole.com

30ha 393T(100-120m²) 10-16A CEE

1 ACD**G**IJKLMOP
2 GRSVWXY
3 BGJK**M**NRU
4 (C+H 📶) IJ
  (Q+R+T+U+V+Z 1/7-31/8)
5 **AB**EFGIJKLMNOPUVZ
6 CEGH**J**(N 0,5km)RTUV

💬 A large well equipped campsite with a number of sporting opportunities 700m from the beach.

🚗 From D101 in Vendays direction Montalivet (D102). Just before Montalivet-les-Bains (D102) left at filling station. Campsite on left after 800m, well indicated.

CC € 17 27/4-6/7 25/8-15/9   📍 N 45°22'12'' W 1°8'41''

Montignac, F-24290 / Aquitaine (Dordogne)

♿ 📶 iD (1740)

🔺 Le Moulin du Bleufond-Lascaux***
🏠 avenue Aristide Briand
☎ +33 (0)5-53518395
📠 +33 (0)9-82631828
📅 1/4 - 15/10
@ info@bleufond.com

1,3ha 81T(70-120m²) 10A CEE

1 ACD**G**IJKLMOPST
2 CLRTVWXY
3 BGHIJKL**M**NQRUW
4 (A 1/7-31/8) (C+H 📶) **KN**
  (Q+R+T+U+V+X+Z 📶)
5 **AB**CDFGJLNPUXYZ
6 ACEGIJL(N 0,5km)RTVW

💬 You will receive a warm welcome on this comfortable rural campsite, located 2 minutes from Lascaux. Very attractive with heated toilets. The swimming pool is also heated. The campsite is within walking distance of the village where you can do all your shopping. Plenty of sights in the immediate vicinity. An ideal location for visiting the Lascaux caves.

🚗 On the A89 exit Thenon, direction Montignac/Lascaux. In Montignac direction Valojoux Sergeac. Follow the signs.

CC € 17 1/4-6/7 27/8-14/10   📍 N 45°3'36'' E 1°9'31''

Montignac/Lascaux, F-24290 / Aquitaine (Dordogne)   ♿ 📶 iD (1741)

🏕 La Fage****
📧 la Chapelle-Aubareil
☎ +33 (0)5-53507650
🔓 7/4 - 7/10
@ contact@camping-lafage.com

2,5ha 61T(80-150m²) 10A

1 ACD**G**IJKLPQ
2 BLRVWXY
3 ABCGHJNRU
4 (**A** 1/7-31/8)
  (E+H 15/5-15/9) (Q 🔓)
  (R 1/5-30/6, 1/9-30/9)
  (S 1/7-31/8)(T+U+V 1/6-15/9)
  (X 1/7-31/8) (Z 1/5-30/9)
5 **AB**EFGIJKLMNOPUWZ
6 CEGHK(N 2km)ORUV

💬 The campsite is located between Montignac and Sarlat, close to the caves at Lascaux and les Eyzies and the many beautiful castles in the Dordogne. Definitely worth a visit.

🚗 On the D704 after 8 km between Montignac and Sarlat, south of the Lascaux caves. Then follow camping signs.

Montignac
Saint-Léon-sur-Vézère
D62
D706   D704   D60
D47

CC € **13** 7/4-7/7 25/8-6/10   📷 N 45°1'4'' E 1°11'17''

Montignac/Thonac, F-24290 / Aquitaine (Dordogne)   ♿ 📶 iD (1742)

🏕 La Castillonderie***
☎ +33 (0)5-53507679
🔓 1/4 - 15/9
@ contact@
  dordogne-castillonderie.fr

5ha 48T(80-300m²) 3-10A CEE

1 ACD**G**IJKLMPST
2 BDLMRTVWXY
3 ABDGHJ**OP**RUW
4 (C+G 15/5-15/9) (Q+R 🔓)
  (T+U+V+X 1/5-15/9) (Z 🔓)
5 **AB**DFGIJKLMNPQRUWXZ
6 ACDEG**K**L(N 2,5km)ORTV

💬 Comfortable campsite surrounded by woods, in a lovely part of the Dordogne. Family atmosphere. Spacious pitches. Renovated toilet facilities with spacious showers. Swimming and children's pools and a lovely fishing lake. Opportunities for walking and cycling. An excellent base for many places of interest.

🚗 Turn right on the D706 Montignac-Les Eyzies and Thonac; at the roundabout towards Fanlac. Turn right after 1 km. Follow the signs.

D6089   D67   D65
Rouffignac-Saint-Cernin-de-Reilhac
D704   D62
Montignac
CC
Thonac
D47   D706
Les Eyzies-de-Tayac   D60

CC € **17** 1/4-8/7 26/8-14/9 7=6, 14=13, 21=19   📷 N 45°2'27'' E 1°7'10''

Neuvic-sur-L'Isle, F-24190 / Aquitaine (Dordogne)   ♿ 📶 iD (1743)

🏕 Le Plein Air Neuvicois***
📧 avenue de Planèze
☎ +33 (0)5-53815077
🔓 1/4 - 1/10
@ pleinairneuvic@gmail.com

NEW

2ha 54T(100-120m²) 10A CEE

1 ACD**G**IJKLMOPQ
2 CFLMRTVWXY
3 BGHJK**M**RU**W**X
4 (C+H 1/7-31/8) J
  (Q+R+T+U 1/7-31/8)
5 **AB**DEFGIJKLMNPUZ
6 CEGK(N 0,8km)TV

💬 Very well maintained family campsite on the L'Isle. Owner is expanding the facilities. Located in a recreational area.

🚗 From Périgueux N89 towards Bordeaux. After 25 km exit Neuvic towards centre. Campsite is in the Planèze neighbourhood. See campsite signs. Or on A89 take exit Neuvic. Campsite is close to the bridge opposite the recreational centre.

D710
D709   Saint-Astier
CC
A89   Neuvic
Mussidan

CC € **15** 1/4-30/6 1/9-30/9   📷 N 45°6'28'' E 0°28'12''

Oloron-Ste-Marie, F-64400 / Aquitaine (Pyrénées-Atlantiques) 👫♿🛁📶 iD 1744

🔺 Pyrénées Nature***
📧 chemin de Lagravette
☎ +33 (0)5-59391126
🔚 1/1 - 31/12
@ camping.pyrenees.nature@gmail.com

NEW

3,5ha 110T(80-130m²) 10A CEE

1 ACD**G**IJKLMPST
2 CGKLRVWY
3 BGHNRW
4 (Q+R 🛁) (T+U+Z 1/6-30/9)
5 **A**DFGIJKLMNPUWX
6 ACEGJ(N 0,3km)OT

💬 Situated just outside Oloron, this campsite still offers you all the relaxation you need. Pitches, many of which are shady, are marked out with green hedges. Bus connection from the campsite to the centre (1 km). Supermarket (300 m). Free wifi point. Good base for walks and excursions. Pourtalet, the Petit Train d'Artouste and more.

🚗 In Oloron on the ringroad, follow signs 'poids lourds' towards Zaragoza or Col du Sampart. Follow signs to campsite. Avoid the centre.

D25 · D936 · D9 · **Oloron-Sainte-Marie** · D919 · N134 · D920 · D918

CC €17 1/1-29/6 1/9-31/12 7=6, 14=12 📍 N 43°10'43'' W 0°37'26''

Ondres, F-40440 / Aquitaine (Landes) 👫♿🛁📶✿ iD 1745

🔺 Du Lac*****
📧 518 rue de Janin
☎ +33 (0)5-59452845
🔚 2/3 - 31/10
@ contact@camping-du-lac.fr

3ha 60T(100-120m²) 10A CEE

1 ABCF**IJ**LP
2 CDFGIJRSVWX
3 BGJK**M**RUW
4 (C+H 1/6-30/9) IK**LN**P(Q 🛁) (T+U+Y+Z 1/7-31/8)
5 **AB**DEFGIJKLMNOPQRUWXYZ
6 ACEGHIK(N 0,5km)RTV

💬 The touring pitches are between the swimming pool and a lovely little lake. The seasonal pitches are on another part of the campsite. Flemish-French owners.

🚗 In Bordeaux direction Bayonne A63 as far as exit 7. Then take D810. Stay on D810 till about 1 km before Ondres centre. Take the road to the left to Ondres-Plage. Left at the 1st roundabout and follow the signs.

D810 · CC · D817 · A63 · **Biarritz** · **Bayonne**

CC €17 2/3-6/7 27/8-30/10 📍 N 43°33'56'' W 1°27'12''

Ondres, F-40440 / Aquitaine (Landes) ♿📶 iD 1746

🔺 Lou Pignada****
📧 741 avenue de la Plage
☎ +33 (0)5-59453065
🔚 28/4 - 30/9
@ info@camping-loupignada.com

4,5ha 93T(80-120m²) 10A CEE

1 ACD**G**HIJKLMOPST
2 BFRSVXY
3 BGHJKNRU
4 (C+H 15/6-15/9) K (Q+T+U+V+Y+Z 15/6-15/9)
5 **AB**EFIJKLMNPUZ
6 EG**I**K(N 0,3km)TV

💬 Family campsite at 2 km from the beach of Ondres-Plage. Heated swimming pool. Spacious and shaded pitches. Hossegor, Bayonne and Biarritz are nearby.

🚗 A63 Bordeaux-Bayonne to exit 7. Then follow D810 till 1 km before Ondres centre. Then left to Ondres-Plage. Campsite 3 km on the left.

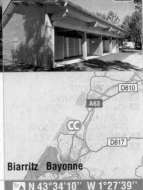

D810 · A63 · CC · D817 · **Biarritz** **Bayonne**

CC €15 28/4-7/7 25/8-29/9 📍 N 43°34'10'' W 1°27'39''

Parentis-en-Born, F-40160 / Aquitaine (Landes)

1747

L'Arbre d'Or****
1037 route du Lac
+33 (0)5-58784156
FAX +33 (0)5-58784962
31/3 - 30/10
@ contact@arbre-dor.com

5ha 109**T**(90-120m²) 10A CEE

1 ACDGIJKLMOPST
2 RSVWXY
3 B**F**GHJKLNRU**W**
4 (C 15/5-1/10) (E)
(G 15/5-1/10) KP(Q+R)
(T+U+V+X+Y+Z 7/4-30/9)
5 **AB**EFGIJKLMNOPUWZ
6 ACEGJ**K**(N 1km)ORTV

An excellent campsite for exploring parts of Landes in the early or late season by foot, on a bike or in the car. 500 metres from the lake of Biscarrosse. Heated indoor swimming pool with jacuzzi and spacious pitches. Friendly and hospitable management.

Leave the Bordeaux motorway A63/N10 in Liposthey and drive towards Parentis (D43). The campsite is signposted in Parentis.

D146
Biscarrosse
Parentis-en-Born
D43
D652
D46
D87

CC € 13 *31/3-6/7 25/8-29/10 14=13*

N 44°20'46'' W 1°5'35''

Pineuilh/Ste Foy-la-Grande, F-33220 / Aquitaine (Gironde)

1748

Camping de la Bastide***
allée de Camping
FAX +33 (0)5-57461384
1/4 - 31/10
@ contact@camping-bastide.com

1,2ha 28**T**(60-100m²) 10A

1 ACD**G**IJKLMPRS
2 CORTVY
3 AGHJKLRU**W**X
4 (B 20/5-30/9)
5 **AB**GIJKLMNPUWXY
6 ACDEG**K**(N 0,5km)RTV

Campsite is located right next to the village of St. Foy-la-Grande on the Dordogne. The popular market has a reputation throughout the region. A hospitable, cozy campsite run by a very friendly English family. Internet bookings also possible. Small-scale and tranquil. Beautiful surroundings.

From Bordeaux D936 to Bergerac, dir. Ste. Foy. Continue via the D936 to the roundabout by Super U. Third exit towards hospital. Signposted after 500m.

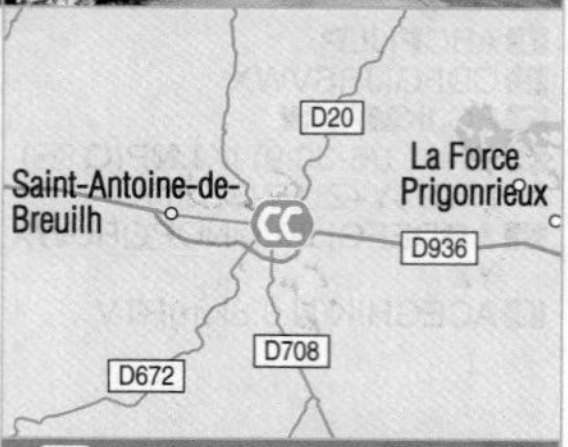
D20
La Force
Saint-Antoine-de-Breuilh
Prigonrieux
D936
D708
D672

CC € 17 *1/4-9/7 1/9-30/10*

N 44°50'39'' E 0°13'29''

Plazac, F-24580 / Aquitaine (Dordogne)

1749

Domaine Du Lac***
Lieu dit Le Lac
+33 (0)5-53507586
FAX +33 (0)5-53505836
8/5 - 30/9
@ contact@domainedulac-dordogne.com

8ha 75**T**(100-180m²) 10A

1 ACDGIJKLPQ
2 ADLMRTVWXY
3 BGHMN**O**QRUWZ
4 (C+H 1/6-30/9) (Q)
(S 8/5-15/9)
(T+U+V+X+Z 15/5-30/9)
5 **AB**CEFGJLNPUVXYZ
6 ACDEGJ(N 1km)TV

For 40 years this top-quality family campsite has been located in the middle of Dordogne with its beautiful countryside, picturesque villages, countless castles and prehistoric caves. Positioned by a lake and with a lovely heated swimming pool which guarantees hours of fun in the water under the French sun.

A20, then A89, exit 17, direction Montignac, Thonac, Plazac. Campsite signposted.

D6089
D67
D704
Rouffignac-Saint-Cernin-de-Reilhac
Montignac
D45
D47
D32 E
D706
D710

CC € 15 *8/5-7/7 25/8-29/9*

N 45°1'52'' E 1°2'53''

Pomport/Sigoulès, F-24240 / Aquitaine (Dordogne)

♿ 📶 iD (1750)

🔺 Pomport Beach★★★★
✉ route de la Gardonnette
☎ +33 (0)5-24106113
🕐 6/5 - 8/9
@ info@pomport-beach.com

1,3ha 70T(100-150m²) 10A CEE

1 ACD**G**IJKLMPRS
2 ADLMRTUVWXY
3 B**F**GHJKM**NOP**QRUWZ
4 (A 1/7-30/8) (C+E+H 🕐) IJ
(Q 🕐) (T+U+V 1/7-30/8)
(Z 🕐)
5 **AB**EFGIJKLMNPUWX
6 CDEGK(N 1km)RTV

NEW

💬 This modern, 4 star campsite is close to Bergerac. The campsite has a small lake to swim and fish in, a heated pool, a heated indoor pool and a lovely restaurant. Beautiful surroundings.

🚗 From Bergerac take the D933 towards the south. In Pomport the campsite is signposted.

Prigonrieux • **Bergerac**
D936 — D19 — D933 — N21

CC € **17** 6/5-7/7 25/8-7/9

🗺 N 44°46'17'' E 0°24'41''

Pujols, F-47300 / Aquitaine (Lot-et-Garonne)

♿ 📶 iD (1751)

🔺 Lot & Bastides à Pujols★★★
✉ allée de Malbentre
☎ +33 (0)5-53368679
🕐 31/3 - 3/11
@ contact@
camping-lot-et-bastides.fr

12ha 83T(115-140m²) 16A CEE

1 ACD**G**IJKLMOPQ
2 GRVWX
3 B**F**GHJKLRUW
4 (C+G 15/5-15/9) K
(Q 1/5-30/9) (R 🕐)
(T+U+V+X+Z 15/5-15/9)
5 **AB**DEFGIJKLMNOPQRUW
XY
6 ACDEGK(N 1km)OTV

💬 The campsite is located at the foot of the medieval village of Pujols; Pujols is listed as one of the most beautiful villages of France and a stone's throw from Villeneuve-sur-Lot. Comfortable camping pitches in a brand new, well designed park.

🚗 On the N21 from the north dir. Villeneuve-sur-Lot (D661) at first roundabout. Follow Bordeaux then Pujols signs. Then follow Piscine de Malbentre and/or campsite.

D133 — D676 — N21 — D667 — **Villeneuve-sur-Lot** — D911 — **CC** — D661 — D103 — D13

CC € **15** 31/3-6/7 25/8-2/11

🗺 N 44°23'41'' E 0°41'13''

Pyla-sur-Mer, F-33115 / Aquitaine (Gironde)

📶 iD (1752)

🔺 Pyla Camping★★★
✉ rte de Biscarosse
☎ +33 (0)5-56227456
📠 +33 (0)5-56221031
🕐 1/4 - 1/10
@ reception@pylacamping.fr

8,5ha 260T(35-100m²) 10A CEE

1 ABC**G**IJKLMO**P**S
2 ABEGIJKSUVWXY
3 B**F**GJKLNRUWY
4 (C 🕐) (G 15/5-30/9)
(Q+R+S+T+U+V+X+Y+Z
1/5-24/9)
5 **AB**FGIJLMNPU
6 CEG**J**(N 7km)QRTV

💬 Quiet family campsite by the Pilat dune, the largest dune in Europe with options for swimming and parasailing.

🚗 A660, N250 Bordeaux-Arcachon, exit Dune de Pyla. Follow 'Campings'. 3rd campsite on the right.

D106 — **La Teste-de-Buch** — **CC** — D218 — D652

CC € **17** 1/4-30/6 1/9-30/9

🗺 N 44°34'40'' W 1°12'47''

Rauzan, F-33420 / Aquitaine (Gironde)

👪 ♿ 📶 iD (1753)

🏔 du Vieux Château***
📧 6 Blabot-Bas
☎ +33 (0)5-57841538
📅 30/3 - 18/10
@ contact@vieuxchateau.fr

2,5ha 45T(110-130m²) 6A

1 ACD**G**IJKLMPST
2 BRVWXY
3 ABGJKNRU
4 (C+G 15/5-15/9) K
 (Q 8/7-26/8) (R 🔑)
 (T+U+X 15/6-31/8) (Z 🔑)
5 **A**BFGIJKLMNPUWZ
6 ACDEGJ(N 0,5km)TV

💬 Experience the magic and peace of a castle park with centuries old trees and a feudal castle built on the orders of the English monarchy. Visit a Celestine cave under the village with a subterranean river. You can walk to the shops in the town in minutes.

🚗 In Rauzan towards 'gendarmerie' take the D123 opposite and follow signs to 'du Vieux Château'. 300m to campsite. Select Rue Peyruc on SatNav and follow signs to campsite.

D19 · D21 · D122 · D936 · D670 · D17 · D671 · D672 · D11 · Sauveterre-de-Guyenne

CC € 15 30/3-6/7 24/8-17/10

📍 N 44°47'6'' W 0°7'32''

Saint-Martial-de-Valette, F-24300 / Aquitaine (Dordogne)

♿ 📶 iD (1754)

🏔 L'Agrion Bleu***
📧 120 route du Stade
☎ +33 (0)5-53560204
📅 8/1 - 14/12
@ camping@lagrionbleu.fr

NEW

2ha 54T(80-120m²) 10A CEE

1 ACD**G**IJKLMPQ
2 CGLRVWXY
3 BGHJ**M**NRU**W**
4 **KLN**(Q+R+T+U+X 🔑)
5 **A**DFGIJKLMNOPUVZ
6 BCEGJ(N 1km)OTV

💬 Small, modest family campsite next to the municipal sports complex and swimming pool (campers receive discounted entry to both). Very clean toilet block. Perfect as a stopover campsite.

🚗 South of the town, along the N675 direction Brantôme, turn left next to the swimming pool and the sports centre.

D4 · D91 · D75 · Nontron D85 · CC Saint-Pardoux-la-Rivière · D708 · D675 · D707 · D939

CC € 15 8/1-30/6 1/9-13/12

📍 N 45°31'15'' E 0°39'29''

Salies-de-Béarn, F-64270 / Aquitaine (Pyrénées-Atlantiques)

♿ 📶 iD (1755)

🏔 Domaine d'Esperbasque**
📧 route de Sauveterre
☎ 📠 +33 (0)5-59382104
📅 1/4 - 31/10
@ info@esperbasque.com

3ha 100T(80-100m²) 6-10A CEE

1 A**G**IJKLPRS
2 FIJKLRXY
3 A**F**GHJN**OP**RU
4 (B+G 25/4-15/10) (Q 🔑)
 (U 1/7-31/8) (Z 🔑)
5 **A**BGJKLMNPU
6 DEJ(N 3km)V

💬 Esperbasque Estate (16 hectares) is set on a hillside with splendid views of the pastures where horses graze. Lovely countryside and plenty of space. Home-baked bread, occasional communal meals, gardening, horses and other animals, pétanque, archery, visits to wine growers and the salt town of Salies-de-Béarn.

🚗 Campsite on the east side of the D933 between Salies-de-Béarn and Sauveterre. From the north do not turn left, turn around at next exit. See signs.

D103 · D29 · A64 · D817 · D46 · D28 · Salies-de-Béarn · Orthez · CC · D936 · D11 · D933 · D23 · D947

CC € 17 1/4-30/6 1/9-30/10

📍 N 43°27'11'' W 0°55'15''

Sanguinet, F-40460 / Aquitaine (Landes)

‡‡ ♿ 🛜 **iD** (1756)

▲ Campéole Le Lac de Sanguinet★★★
📧 526 rue de Pinton
☎ +33 (0)5-58827080
📠 +33 (0)5-58821424
🕐 30/3 - 30/9
@ lac-sanguinet@campeole.com
10,6ha 147T(80-150m²) 10A CEE

1 ACD**G**IJKLM**O**P
2 ADMRSVWXY
3 BGHJRU**WZ**
4 (C 10/6-16/9) (H 1/6-16/9) P
(Q 10/6-16/9) (R 1/7-31/9)
(T+U+V+X+Z 10/6-16/9)
5 **AB**EFGJLNPQUZ
6 ACEGH**K**(N 1km)RUV

💬 Family campsite near the welcoming village of Sanguinet in the heart of the Landes forests. Quiet location on the shore of one of the most beautiful and largest lakes of Europe. Direct access to a sandy beach.

🚙 A10, exit Arcachon. Follow d'Arcachon road. Exit Mios/Biscarrosse, then direction Sanguinet. Campsite in Sanguinet by the lake. Signposted.

D218 — D216 — Sanguinet — CC — D146 D652 D46 — **Biscarrosse**

CC € **15** 30/3-6/7 25/8-29/9 ⛺ N 44°28'53" W 1°5'36"

Sanguinet, F-40460 / Aquitaine (Landes)

♿ 🛜 **iD** (1757)

▲ Les Grands Pins★★★★★
📧 1039 avenue de Losa
☎ +33 (0)5-58786174
📠 +33 (0)5-58786915
🕐 31/3 - 16/9
@ info@campinglesgrandspins.com

8ha 65T(80-130m²) 10A CEE

1 ACD**G**IJKLM**P**
2 ADMRSVWXY
3 AB**F**GHJ**KM**NRU**WZ**
4 (C+E+H 🕐) JM
(Q+S+T+V+X+Y+Z 🕐)
5 **AB**CDEFGIJKLMNOPRUZ
6 ACEGH**K**(N 1km)V

💬 Campsite on sandy beach of Lake Sanguinet for a successful holiday in Landes. Outdoor pool and heated indoor pool. Various types of water recreation. Network of cycle paths.

🚙 The campsite is located in Sanguinet. Clearly signposted and positioned by a lake.

D218 — D216 — Sanguinet — CC — D146 D652 D46 — **Biscarrosse**

CC € **17** 31/3-30/6 1/9-15/9 ⛺ N 44°29'2" W 1°5'24"

Sarlat, F-24200 / Aquitaine (Dordogne)

🚫🐕 ♿ 🛜 **iD** (1758)

▲ Le Moulin du Roch★★★★★
📧 route des Eyzies
☎ +33 (0)5-53592027
🕐 18/5 - 22/9
@ moulin.du.roch@wanadoo.fr

8ha 195T(100-120m²) 10A CEE

1 ACDEIJKL**PRS**
2 JRTVY
3 BGHN**OP**RUW
4 (A 1/6-31/8) (C+G 🕐)
(Q 1/7-31/8) (S+U+V 🕐)
(X 1/7-31/8) (Y+Z 🕐)
5 ABDEFGIJKLMNOPUXYZ
6 EG**K**(N 10km)OTV

💬 This shaded campsite offers amenities for a holiday packed with variety. Entertainment programme, heated swimming pool, a trip on the Dordogne river and delicious meals in the restaurant. Perfect for a successful holiday in the Dordogne.

🚙 On the D47 Sarlat-Les Eyzies.

D706 — D60 — D704 — D47 — Sarlat-la-Canéda — CC — D35 — Saint-Cyprien — D703 — D57 — D710

CC € **17** 18/5-6/7 26/8-21/9 ⛺ N 44°54'30" E 1°6'54"

Sarlat-la-Canéda, F-24200 / Aquitaine (Dordogne) ⬤ 🛜 iD 1759

🏕 Huttopia Sarlat****
📧 route de la Croix d'Allon
☎ +33 (0)5-53590584
📠 +33 (0)5-53285751
📅 30/3 - 4/11
@ sarlat@huttopia.com

6ha 109T(100-115m²) 10A CEE

1 ACDGIJKLPRS
2 JRVXY
3 ABGMNRU
4 (B 2/4-28/9) (F+G ⊙) N (Q+R+T+U+V+Z ⊙)
5 ABDFGIJKLMNOPUWXZ
6 CEGHJ(N 0,8km)OTUV

💬 The closest campsite to Sarlat, just 10 minutes walk from the historic centre of the capital of the Périgord Noir. Beautiful wooded grounds laid out in terraces. Swimming pools (one of which is indoors), tennis courts, social activities. CampingCard ACSI valid only on standard pitches.

🚗 From Paris and Toulouse: A20, exit Souillac. From Bordeaux: A89, exit Périgueux.

D60 D62
D47 Sarlat-la-Canéda CC
D57
D703
D704 A
D704

CC € 17 30/3-5/7 2/9-3/11

📡 N 44°53'36'' E 1°13'41''

Sarlat-la-Canéda, F-24200 / Aquitaine (Dordogne) ♿ 🛜 iD 1760

🏕 Les Acacias***
📧 avenue-de-la-Canéda
☎ +33 (0)5-53310850
📅 12/4 - 30/9
@ camping-acacias@wanadoo.fr

4ha 102T(80-150m²) 10A

1 ACDFIJKLPRS
2 BGIJKLRTVXY
3 BFGHJKNRU
4 (C+F+G ⊙) KP (Q+R 12/4-25/9) (T+U+V 1/6-10/9) (Z ⊙)
5 ABDEFGIJKLMNOPUZ
6 ACEGJ(N 1,3km)UV

💬 A compact French campsite in the centre of La Canéda. Located in the heart of the loveliest tourist sights. Within cycling distance of Sarlat for those who prefer to leave the car behind. Even inexperienced walkers can easily walk the 2.5 km to the centre. There is a bus stop near the campsite. Modern toilet facilities. Free wifi-point. Heated indoor swimming pool with jacuzzi.

🚗 In Sarlat direction Cahors, exit La Canéda. Campsite signposted.

D62
D47 Sarlat-la-Canéda Calviac-en-Périgord
D703
D46
D704

CC € 15 12/4-5/7 23/8-29/9 21=20

📡 N 44°51'27'' E 1°14'15''

Sarlat-la-Canéda, F-24200 / Aquitaine (Dordogne) ♿ 🛜 ✿ iD 1761

🏕 Les Terrasses du Périgord***
📧 Pech d'Orance
☎ +33 (0)5-53590225
📠 +33 (0)5-53591648
📅 14/4 - 22/9
@ terrasses-du-perigord@wanadoo.fr

6ha 75T(120m²) 16A CEE

1 ACDFIJKLPQ
2 JKLRTVXY
3 BFGHJKNQRTUV
4 (B+H ⊙) K(Q 1/7-31/8) (R ⊙) (T+U 1/7-20/9) (W+X 1/7-10/9) (Z ⊙)
5 AFGIJKLMNOPUWXY
6 CEGKL(N 2,7km)ORUV

💬 The campsite has beautiful panoramic views but is still easy to reach, just 2 km from the medieval village of Sarlat. Central location for exploring the many sights.

🚗 When entering Sarlat from the north, direction Ste Nathalène. After 2 km follow signs at the junction to the left.

D60 D62
D704
D47 CC
Sarlat-la-Canéda D704 A
D46
D703

206

CC € 15 14/4-30/6 1/9-21/9

📡 N 44°54'23'' E 1°14'13''

Sarlat/Carsac, F-24200 / Aquitaine (Dordogne) ♿ 🛜 **iD** (1762)

🔺 Le Plein Air des Bories***
📧 Les Bories
☎ +33 (0)5-53281567
📅 5/5 - 8/9
@ contact@
   camping-desbories.com

3ha 80T(100-120m²) 6-16A

1 ACD**G**IJLPRS
2 ACLRSWXY
3 BGHJMNRUWX
4 (B+E+G 💶)
   (Q+R+T+U+V+X 1/7-31/8)
   (Z 💶)
5 **A**EFGJKLNPUVZ
6 CEG**J**(N 0,6km)V

💬 A really quietly located campsite. Suitable for families. Hidden away in wooded countryside and located right by the River Dordogne it is an ideal spot to enjoy peace and watersports. The swimming pool can be covered over.

🚗 On the A20 exit Souillac, direction Sarlat via D703. Left past Calviac towards 'Vallée de la Dordogne'. Go under the railway bridge in Carsac and take the second left. Follow the signs.

CC € 15 5/5-8/7 26/8-7/9

🗺 N 44°49'59'' E 1°16'5''

Sarlat/Marcillac, F-24200 / Aquitaine (Dordogne) ♿ 🛜 **iD** (1763)

🔺 Les Tailladis***
📧 Marcillac/St. Quentin
☎ +33 (0)5-53591095
📠 +33 (0)5-53294756
📅 15/4 - 31/10
@ tailladis@wanadoo.fr

4,5ha 78T(80-110m²) 6A

1 ACD**F**IJLPRS
2 CIJKLRXY
3 ABGHJNRUW
4 (C+G+Q+S+T+U+V+X+Y+Z
   💶)
5 **AB**DFGIJKLMNOPUWZ
6 EGI**K**(N 8km)OQRV

💬 Located in the Beune valley between Montignac and Sarlat, by a brook with a natural pool and heated swimming pool. Heated toilet facilities, excellent cuisine and a special welcome. Ideal starting point in all seasons for discovering the locality and the many places of interest.

🚗 In Brive direction Montignac. Then D704 direction Sarlat. After St. Genies name board (± 8 km) right on D48 towards Tamniès. To next junction then left to Marcillac (± 6 km). Follow signs.

CC € 15 15/4-13/7 31/8-30/10

🗺 N 44°58'29'' E 1°11'16''

Sarlat/Ste Nathalène, F-24200 / Aquitaine (Dordogne) ♿ 🛜 **iD** (1764)

🔺 La Palombière*****
☎ +33 (0)5-53594234
📠 +33 (0)5-53284540
📅 7/4 - 23/9
@ contact@lapalombiere.fr

6,5ha 68T(100-110m²) 10A CEE

1 ACD**F**IJKLPRS
2 JKLRTVWXY
3 BGHJKMNQRUV
4 (C+H 💶) IJ**KNP**
   (Q+S+T+U+V+Y+Z 💶)
5 **AB**CDEFGIJLNPQUWXY
6 EGH**I**K(N 6km)ORUV

💬 An entrance that gives camping guests a wonderful feeling at this beautiful and enchanting site located on a hillside. The reception and excellent restaurant built in Perigord style offer a warm welcome. The stunning views and beautifully maintained grounds, with sports areas, will please everyone. New since 2016: indoor leisure pool.

🚗 A20 exit Souillac, D704 direction Sarlat. Turn right in Rouffiac, D47 Carlux-Sarlat. 8 km from Sarlat in Ste Nathalène.

CC € 17 7/4-8/7 27/8-22/9

🗺 N 44°54'23'' E 1°17'31''

Sauveterre-la-Lémance, F-47500 / Aquitaine (Lot-et-Garonne)

♿ 🛜 **iD** `1765`

🔼 Camping Moulin du Périé****
☎ +33 (0)5-53406726
🗓 12/5 - 22/9
@ moulinduperie@wanadoo.fr

5ha 125T(80-120m²) 6-10A CEE

1 ACD**G**IJKLMOPQ
2 ACDLRVXY
3 B**F**GHJKNRU**W**Z
4 (B+Q+R+T+U+V+Y+Z 🖵)
5 **AB**EFGIJKLMNOPRUWXYZ
6 ACDEGJ(N 3km)TV

💬 The Baudot family welcomes you in a park around an old mill in the south of the Périgord Noir. Lovely pitches in the sun or in shade, a natural spring lake with a beach, plenty of peace and quiet: an ideal campsite for relaxing. From here you can easily visit the many attractions of the Dordogne and the Lot.

🚗 Campsite signposted in Sauveterre-la-Lémance. Follow road over railway to the left. Campsite is located about 3 km past the village towards Loubejac.

D2 D660 D710
D60
D57
CC
D673
Fumel Puy-l'Évêque Prayssac

CC € **15** 12/5-5/7 23/8-21/9 7=6

🔼 **N 44°35'26'' E 1°2'52''**

Socoa/Urrugne, F-64122 / Aquitaine (Pyrénées-Atlantiques)

♿ **iD** `1766`

🔼 Juantcho**
📧 875 route de la Corniche
☎ +33 (0)5-59471197
🗓 27/4 - 15/10
@ juantcho64@gmail.com

6ha 215T(80-100m²) 5A

1 AC**G**IJKLMPRS
2 EFIJKQRUVWXY
3 A**F**GR
4 (Q+U 1/7-31/8)
5 **AB**FGIJKLNPUV
6 CDE(N 0,5km)R

💬 Juantcho is located at the 'Corniche Basque'. This route runs along the coast and is one of France's most beautiful. You have wonderful views of the ocean and St. Jean-de-Luz bay from the Corniche.

🚗 A63 exit 2 St. Jean-de-Luz Sud towards Socoa. 1st exit at 1st roundabout, 1st exit at second roundabout, straight on towards Hendaye - 3rd roundabout, 1st exit towards Socoa on the D912 and the campsite is about 1 km on the right.

Biarritz

A63
Hendaye CC
Irún D918 D255
D3
N-121-A D306 D4

CC € **17** 27/4-8/7 1/9-14/10 7=6, 14=12, 21=18

🔼 **N 43°23'38'' W 1°41'30''**

Soulac-sur-Mer, F-33780 / Aquitaine (Gironde)

👫 🛜 ✿ **iD** `1767`

🔼 Flower Camping des Pins****
📧 213 Passe de Formose
☎ +33 (0)5-56098252
📠 +33 (0)5-56736558
🗓 28/5 - 30/9
@ contact@campingdespins.fr

3,4ha 66T(90-100m²) 6A CEE

1 ACD**F**IJLM**P**S
2 ABIJSTVWXY
3 BGKNRW
4 (C+H+Q+R 🖵)
   (T+U+V+X 1/7-31/8)
5 **AB**FIJKLMNOPXZ
6 ADEGIK(N 3km)TV

💬 A campsite located in a quiet natural setting, away from the bustle of everyday life. The 3.4-hectare grounds are 2 minutes from the Atlantic with a wide beach. It has a new swimming pool and modern enery efficient toilet facilities. Environmentally friendly campsite.

🚗 On the A10 exit 25 towards Saintes Royan. Take ferry across the Gironde to Le Verdon. In Soulac take the Route-des-Lacs southbound. After leaving built-up area 1st right, 2nd left.

D25
Soulac-sur-Mer
CC
D101 D1215

CC € **17** 28/5-1/7 27/8-29/9

🔼 **N 45°28'58'' W 1°7'38''**

Soulac-sur-Mer, F-33780 / Aquitaine (Gironde)

♿ 📶 iD (1768)

🔺 Les Lacs★★★★★
📧 126 route des Lacs
☎ +33 (0)5-56097663
📠 +33 (0)5-56099802
🕐 7/4 - 31/10
@ info@camping-les-lacs.com

5,8ha 98T(102-170m²) 10A CEE

1 ACD**G**IJKLMOPST
2 ARSVWXY
3 ABDGKLNQRUW
4 (A 1/7-31/8) (B 15/6-15/9)
(F ⏱) (H 15/6-15/9) IJ
(Q+S+T+U+V ⏱)
(X+Y 1/6-15/9) (Z ⏱)
5 **AB**DEFGIJKLMNOPUWXYZ
6 ACDEGHI**K**(N 4km)OTV

💬 This campsite offers everything you could wish for on holiday near the ocean. In addition you can enjoy two lovely swimming pools, one of them indoors and heated. Ideally located for trips out.

🚗 From Bordeaux: Rocade exit 7. Then N215 Le Verdon or D2 Pauillac along the D101. From the boat: first to Soulac then direction L'Amélie. Follow Route des Lacs. On the left outside the built up area.

Soulac-sur-Mer

D25
D101
D1215

CC € **17** 7/4-14/7 1/9-30/10

📐 N 45°29'0'' W 1°7'8''

Soulac-sur-Mer, F-33780 / Aquitaine (Gironde)

♿ 📶 iD (1769)

🔺 Sandaya Soulac Plage★★★★
📧 Lieu-dit l'Amélie
☎ +33 (0)5-56098727
📠 +33 (0)5-56736426
🕐 20/4 - 16/9
@ soulacplage@sandaya.fr

10ha 210T(75-240m²) 10A CEE

1 ACD**G**IJKLPST
2 ABEIKSVWXY
3 BGKLNRUWY
4 (B 15/6-9/9) (E ⏱)
(G 15/6-9/9) IJ
(Q+S+T+U+V+X+Z ⏱)
5 **AB**EFGIJKLMNPUW
6 AEGH**K**(N 0,2km)ORTV

💬 This campsite located right by the sea offers you a leisure pool. The surrounding countryside is fine for cycling, walking and horse riding.

🚗 In L'Amélie-Plage directly in the direction of the beach.

Soulac-sur-Mer

D101
D1215

CC € **17** 20/4-6/7 1/9-15/9

📐 N 45°28'55'' W 1°9'4''

St. André-d'Allas/Sarlat, F-24200 / Aquitaine (Dordogne)

📶 iD (1770)

🔺 Les Charmes★★★
📧 Malartigue Haut
☎ +33 (0)5-53310289
🕐 30/3 - 30/9
@ lescharmescamping@gmail.com

5ha 80T(100-110m²) 10A

1 ACD**F**IJLPRS
2 BIRVWY
3 ABGHJKMNRU
4 (A 1/7-31/8) (B 1/6-15/9)
(E ⏱) J(Q+R ⏱)
(T+U+X 1/7-1/8) (Z ⏱)
5 **AB**FGJLMNOPU
6 CEGHK(N 4km)OV

💬 This campsite with a very peaceful location is in the heart of the Dordogne, so you can easily visit 40 sights in an area of 30 km. The shaded pitches, surrounded by shoulder-high hedges, offer welcome privacy.

🚗 South of Sarlat take the D25 towards Meyrals/Bergerac.

D32 E | D706
D47
D704
D35
D703
D57
D710

Sarlat-la-Canéda

CC € **13** 30/3-7/7 25/8-29/9

📐 N 44°53'39'' E 1°6'51''

St. Antoine-d'Auberoche, F-24330 / Aquitaine (Dordogne) 👫 ♿ 📶 iD (1771)

▲ de La Pélonie***
🏠 La Pélonie
☎ +33 (0)5-53075578
📠 +33 (0)5-53037427
🔓 16/4 - 10/10
@ info@campinglapelonie.com

3ha 71T(100-120m²) 10A CEE

1 ACDGIJKLMPRS
2 FJLRUVXY
3 BCGHJN**OP**RU
4 (C 1/5-30/9) (E 🔓)
(G 1/5-30/9) IJ(Q+R 🔓)
(T+U+V 15/6-31/8)
(Y 1/7-31/8) (Z 15/6-30/9)
5 **AB**DEFGIJKLMNPRUWYZ
6 ACDEGIK(N 5km)OTV

💬 Nice family campsite, well maintained. Located in the countryside, in the heart of Dordogne, 15 km from Périgueux. Suitable for discovering touristic sights in Dordogne. Two heated pools (1 covered) and various water slides. Wifi free in low season.

🚗 On the D6089 (don't take the A road) Brive-Périgueux, 5 km past Fossemagne on the right side, turn in and continue for 200 metres, or coming from Périgueux 5 km past St. Pierre on the left.

Trélissac
Boulazac D5
A89
CC D6089
D710 D67
Rouffignac-Saint-Cernin-de-Reilhac
D45

CC € **13** 16/4-9/7 27/8-9/10   📷 N 45°7'54'' E 0°55'43''

St. Antoine-de-Breuilh, F-24230 / Aquitaine (Dordogne) 👫 ♿ 📶 iD (1772)

▲ La Rivière Fleurie***
🏠 180 rue T. Cart, Saint Aulaye
☎ +33 (0)5-53248280
🔓 21/4 - 23/9
@ info@la-riviere-fleurie.com

2,4ha 66T(100-200m²) 10A CEE

1 ACD**G**IJKLMO**P**ST
2 CRTVWXY
3 ABHJK**M**NQRU**W**
4 (C+H 20/5-23/9) (Q+R+T 🔓)
(U+V+X+Y 20/5-23/9) (Z 🔓)
5 **AB**FGIJKLMNOPQUXZ
6 AEGJ(N 2km)RTV

💬 Quiet, beautiful, quality campsite with fine spacious pitches in a familial atmosphere. Campsite is close to the Dordogne. Child-friendly. Good swimming pool and restaurant. Lovely surroundings.

🚗 Campsite is signposted when coming from St. Foy on the D936 direction Bordeaux, and when leaving St. Antoine-de Breuilh.

Saint-Genès-de-Castillon D708 D20
D21
Le Fleix
D936 Sainte-Foy-la-Grande
CC Pineuilh
D672 D708 E3

CC € **17** 21/4-8/7 26/8-22/9 7=6, 14=12, 21=18   📷 N 44°49'44'' E 0°7'21''

St. Astier, F-24110 / Aquitaine (Dordogne) ♿ 📶 iD (1773)

▲ Le Pontet***
🏠 Lieu dit Le Pontet (D41)
☎ +33 (0)5-53541422
🔓 2/4 - 15/9
@ mail.lepontet@gmail.com

3ha 142T(100-120m²) 6A CEE

1 ACD**G**IJKLMPQ
2 CFLMRVWXY
3 AGHJNQRU**WX**
4 (B+G 🔓) (Q 1/6-28/8)
(T+U+X 24/6-31/8)
(Z 15/6-31/8)
5 **AB**FGJLMNPUVWZ
6 EG**K**(N 0,5km)TV

💬 An unpretentious, well maintained campsite beside River L'Isle in a parkland setting and within walking distance of St. Astier. A lovely base to explore the countryside. Suitable for anglers and outdoor sports enthusiasts.

🚗 N89 Périgueux-Bordeaux or A89 direction Bordeaux, exit 14 direction St. Astier. In Quatre Routes turn right in the direction of St. Astier, take the D41 (3 km).

D710 D939
Coulounieix-Chamiers
D709 CC A89
Saint-Astier
N21
D6089

CC € **13** 2/4-7/7 25/8-14/9   📷 N 45°8'49'' E 0°32'0''

St. Avit-de-Vialard, F-24260 / Aquitaine (Dordogne)   ♿ 🛜 ✿ iD (1774)

🏕 Saint Avit Loisirs*****
☎ +33 (0)5-53026400
📠 +33 (0)5-53026439
🗓 29/3 - 24/9
@ contact@saint-avit-loisirs.com

52ha 199T(100m²) 6-10A CEE

1 ACD**G**IJKLMOPQ
2 BDJKLMPRTVXY
3 AB**EF**GHJKM**NOQ**RUVW
4 (C+F+H 🔒) IJKMOP
(Q+S+T+U+V+Y+Z 🔒)
5 **AB**DEFGIJKLMNOPRUWXY
6 ACDEGHI**K**(N 4km)OPRTV

💬 A luxurious five-star, 52-hectare campsite surrounded by meadows in a very tranquil area. Every comfort on offer, from swimming pool to jacuzzi, from thermal bath to hydro massage. Beautiful restaurants and shops.

🚗 From Le Bugue D710 direction Périgueux. Campsite is signposted.

Ⓒ €**17** 29/3-7/7 25/8-23/9   🧭 N 44°57'7'' E 0°51'1''

St. Crépin-Carlucet/Sarlat, F-24590 / Aquitaine (Dordogne)   ♿ 🛜 iD (1775)

🏕 Les Peneyrals*****
▤ Le Poujol
☎ +33 (0)5-53288571
🗓 5/5 - 12/9
@ camping.peneyrals@wanadoo.fr

13ha 117T(100-120m²) 10A

1 ACD**F**IJL**P**RS
2 JRTVX
3 BGHJKM**NQ**RUW
4 (A 5/6-31/8) (C+D+H 🔒) J
(Q+S+T+U+V+X+Y+Z 🔒)
5 **AB**DEFGIJKLMNOPUWZ
6 CEGHI**K**(N 4km)ORTUV

💬 The campsite is 12 km from the spectacular medieval town of Sarlat and blends well into the surroundings. The heated pools, 1 indoors, paddling pool and toilet facilities ensure every comfort, even in early and late season. Excellent restaurant and café with Belgian beers. A hospitable welcome and peaceful surroundings. Free wifi in May, June and September.

🚗 A20 exit Brive or Souillac, direction Salignac/Sarlat. Campsite signposted. Located 12 km north of Sarlat.

Ⓒ €**17** 5/5-7/7 25/8-11/9 14=12, 21=18   🧭 N 44°57'28'' E 1°16'20''

St. Félix-de-Bourdeilles, F-24340 / Aquitaine (Dordogne)   ♿ 🛜 iD (1776)

🏕 Les Etangs du Plessac***
☎ +33 (0)5-53463912
🗓 1/4 - 15/10
@ contact@campingdeplessac.fr

8ha 26T(100-200m²) 16A CEE

1 ACD**G**IJKLMOPQ
2 ADGLMRVWXY
3 BGHRW
4 (C 1/5-15/9)
(Q+R+U+V+Y+Z 🔒)
5 **AB**DGIJKLMNOPUYZ
6 CDEGJ(N 9km)OT

NEW

💬 Beautiful campsite located on a small lake. Quiet, spacious pitches. Very clean toilet block. Heated pool and a spacious playground for children. Restaurant with terrace and view of the lake. New owner since 2017.

🚗 From Brantôme towards Mareuil (D939). Turn right at Saint-Félix-de-Mareuil and the Bourdeilles. Then follow signs to campsite.

Ⓒ €**11** 1/4-9/7 27/8-14/10 7=6   🧭 N 45°24'50'' E 0°34'23''

St. Girons-Plage, F-40560 / Aquitaine (Landes)

⛺ Campéole Les Tourterelles***
🛣 route de la Plage
☎ +33 (0)5-58479312
📠 +33 (0)5-58479203
📅 30/3 - 30/9
@ tourterelles@campeole.com

20ha 460T(80-150m²) 10-16A CEE

1 ACGIJKLMP
2 ABEGIJKRSVWXY
3 BGJKNRY
4 (C+H 🔑) IKM(Q 15/5-30/9)
(T+U+V 1/7-31/8)
(Z 15/6-15/9)
5 ABEFGIJKLMNPUZ
6 ACDEGHIK(N 0,2km)QRTV

💬 Campsite in Les Landes in a pine forest with two direct entrances to the beach. Spacious heated swimming facilities with a large paddling pool. Large camping pitches with space for an extra tent (must be paid for). Ideal for surfers.

🚗 In Bordeaux dir. Bayonne on the A63 and the N10 as far as exit 12 Castets. In Castets centre continue towards Linxe and St. Girons. Then towards St. Girons-Plage till almost at the beach. Campsite on the right.

Saint-Julien-en-Born

D652

Linxe
D42

Léon
D142

CC € 17 30/3-6/7 25/8-29/9   🏕 N 43°57'16'' W 1°21'24''

St. Girons-Plage, F-40560 / Aquitaine (Landes)

⛺ Eurosol****
🛣 4756 route de la Plage
☎ +33 (0)5-58479014
📠 +33 (0)5-58477674
📅 8/5 - 23/9
@ contact@camping-eurosol.com

18ha 322T(70-120m²) 10A CEE

1 ACFHIJKLPST
2 BIRSVXY
3 BGHJKLMNQRU
4 (B+E 🔑) (G 1/6-11/9) I
(Q+S 🔑)
(T+U+V+Y 1/6-17/9) (Z 🔑)
5 ABEFGIJLPUWXYZ
6 ACDEGHK(N 8km)OQRTV

💬 Located in an area with hills, run by French-Dutch management. At the reception there is a small square with a bar-restaurant and shop and swimming pools, one of which is indoors. You will camp under coniferous trees 600 metres from the ocean.

🚗 In Bordeaux take direction Bayonne A63 and N10 as far as exit 12 (Castets); in Castets centre keep in direction Linxe and St. Girons. Then direction St. Girons-Plage. Campsite located 5 km on the left of the road (D42).

Lit-et-Mixe

D652

Linxe
D42

Léon
D142

CC € 19 8/5-1/7 25/8-22/9 14=12, 21=17   🏕 N 43°57'6'' W 1°21'7''

St. Jean-de-Luz, F-64500 / Aquitaine (Pyrénées-Atlantiques)

⛺ Atlantica****
🛣 15 ch. de
Miquelenia-Quartier Acotz
☎ +33 (0)5-59477244
📅 28/3 - 1/10
@ atlantica@cielavillage.com

3,5ha 51T(80-120m²) 6A

1 ACGIJKLPRS
2 EFGIJRVWXY
3 BFGJKLNQRUV
4 (C+H 🔑) IKN
(Q+R+T+U+V+X+Z 🔑)
5 ABFGIJKLPUWXYZ
6 ACEGIK(N 1km)QRTV

💬 You could not tell by looking at the entrance how lovely this campsite is. Hidden behind a hedge and a small wall is a lovely, heated swimming pool. An extended reception building houses a games room and a restaurant.

🚗 A63 Bayonne-St. Sebastián, exit 3 St. Jean-de-Luz (Nord). D810 (formerly N10) direction Bayonne. Continue 1 km and take exit 'Acotz-plages'.

Anglet

A63 D3
D755

Hendaye
D918 D255

N-121-A

CC € 17 28/3-6/7 26/8-30/9   🏕 N 43°24'56'' W 1°36'58''

St. Jean-de-Luz, F-64500 / Aquitaine (Pyrénées-Atlantiques) ♿ 📶 iD 1780

△ Bord de Mer***
✉ 71, chemin d'Erromardie
☎ +33 (0)5-59262461
🔁 31/3 - 4/11
@ bord-de-mer64@orange.fr

1ha 62T(90-120m²) 10A

1 AGIJKLMPQ
2 AEFGKQRTVWX
3 AWY
4 (Q+R+T+U+V+X+Z 🔒)
5 ABFGIJLMNPUZ
6 ACEGK(N 1km)

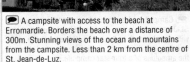

💬 A campsite with access to the beach at Erromardie. Borders the beach over a distance of 300m. Stunning views of the ocean and mountains from the campsite. Less than 2 km from the centre of St. Jean-de-Luz.

🚗 A63 Bayonne-St. Sébastian, exit St. Jean-de-Luz (Nord). Then dir. St. Jean-de-Luz on the D810 (formerly RN10). Just over 1 km turn right to Plage Erromardie. Follow road ± 2 km to the campsite on the left.

Biarritz
Saint-Jean-de-Luz · A63 · D3 · D755
D912 · D255
Irún · D810 · D918
N-121-A

CC € **17** 31/3-6/7 25/8-3/11 · N 43°24'24'' W 1°38'31''

St. Jean-de-Luz, F-64500 / Aquitaine (Pyrénées-Atlantiques) ♿ 📶 iD 1781

△ Flower Camping La Ferme Erromardie****
✉ 40 chemin Erromardie
☎ +33 (0)5-59263426
🔁 17/3 - 6/10
@ contact@camping-erromardie.com

2ha 110T(70-120m²) 16A

1 ACDGHIJKLMPRS
2 AEFGNOQRVWXY
3 BFGJKLRUWY
4 (E 17/3-5/10) (H 🔒) P (Q+R+U+V+Y+Z 🔒)
5 ABEFGIJKLOPUVWZ
6 ACEGHK(N 2,5km)STV

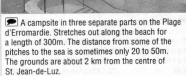

💬 A campsite in three separate parts on the Plage d'Erromardie. Stretches out along the beach for a length of 300m. The distance from some of the pitches to the sea is sometimes only 20 to 50m. The grounds are about 2 km from the centre of St. Jean-de-Luz.

🚗 A63 Bordeaux-Bayonne-San Sébastian, exit 3 St. Jean-de-Luz Nord. Then dir. St. Jean-de-Luz centre and after ± 1 km turn right to Plage Erromardie. Campsite then signposted.

Biarritz
Saint-Jean-de-Luz CC · A63 · D3 · D755
D912 · D255
Irún · D810 · D918
N-121-A

CC € **15** 17/3-6/7 25/8-5/10 7=6, 14=12, 21=18 · N 43°24'20'' W 1°38'30''

St. Jean-de-Luz, F-64500 / Aquitaine (Pyrénées-Atlantiques) ♿ 📶 iD 1782

△ Inter-Plages****
✉ 305 route des Plages-Acotz
☎ +33 (0)5-59265694
🔁 1/4 - 30/9

1,5ha 63T(20-100m²) 6-10A

1 AFIJKLPST
2 AEFJKNQRTUVX
3 BFGKRUWY
4 (C+G 🔒) (Q+S 15/6-15/9) (T+U+V+X 1/7-31/8)
5 ADEFGIJKLNOPUVXYZ
6 CEGJ(N 1,5km)OTV

💬 As its name suggests, the site is located between two beaches. You will have a beautiful panoramic view of the Atlantic ocean. It is 3 km to St. Jean-de-Luz from the campsite. The pool is heated.

🚗 Bayonne - St. Jean-de-Luz motorway. Exit 3 St. Jean-de-Luz Nord towards Bayonne on the RD 810 to the Plages 'Acotz'. After entering the quartier Acotz turn left and follow this road to the campsite.

Biarritz
CC · D755
Hendaye · Saint-Jean-de-Luz · D255
Irún · D918
N-121-A · D3

CC € **15** 1/4-20/6 18/9-29/9 · N 43°24'54'' W 1°37'36''

St. Jean-de-Luz, F-64500 / Aquitaine (Pyrénées-Atlantiques)   ♿ 🛜 iD   (1783)

🔺 International Erromardie****
📧 235 allée de la Source / Erromardie
☎ +33 (0)5-59260774
📠 +33 (0)5-59511211
⌛ 30/3 - 5/11
@ info@chadotel.com

4ha 70T(80-120m²) 10A CEE

1. **AC**F**I**JKLMPRS
2. AEFGKQRSVWXY
3. **BF**GHJKRUWY
4. (C 15/5-15/9) M (Q+S+T+U+V+Y+Z ⊙)
5. **AB**EFGJLNPUWY
6. ACEG**K**(N 3km)RTV

💬 Campsite at less than 2 km from the centre of St. Jean-de-Luz. Large pitches on level grounds with direct access to the ocean. A stream in the undergrowth divides the site into two parts. It has all the amenities of a four-star campsite.

🚗 A63 Bayonne-St. Sébastian, exit St. Jean-de-Luz (Nord). Then dir. St. Jean-de-Luz on D810 (formerly RN10). Right after ± 1 km to Plage Erromardie. Follow road and turn right just past 1st campsite on the right. Site signposted.

Bayonne
Anglet
Saint-Jean-de-Luz
Bayonne · D3 · A63 · D755 · D912 · D255 · D810 · D918 · N-121-A

CC € **17** 30/3-30/6   2/9-13/10   📍 N 43°24'26'' W 1°38'19''

St. Jean-de-Luz, F-64500 / Aquitaine (Pyrénées-Atlantiques)   ♿ 🛜 iD   (1784)

🔺 Itsas Mendi****
📧 115 chemin de Duhartia-Acotz
☎ +33 (0)5-59265650
📠 +33 (0)5-59265444
⌛ 22/3 - 4/11
@ itsas@wanadoo.fr

9ha 230T(80-100m²) 10A CEE

1. ACD**G**IJKLOPQ
2. AEFGIJKRVXY
3. **BF**GHJKLMNRUWY
4. (C+E+H ⊙) IJKM**N**P (Q+S+T+U+V+Y+Z ⊙)
5. **AB**DEFGIJKLMNOPUWZ
6. ACEGH**I**K(N 1km)OQRTV

💬 Come with family and friends and enjoy this campsite with its spacious shaded and half-shaded pitches separated by bushes and trees and 500m from the Basque coast. There is a leisure pool in the middle of the campsite with a toddlers' pool, waterfalls, steam baths, slides, lawns and an indoor heated swimming pool with a jacuzzi.

🚗 N10 Bayonne-St. Jean-de-Luz. 3 km north of St. Jean-de-Luz exit 'Acôtz-plages' (A63, exit 3 north).

Bayonne
Biarritz
CC · D755 · D912 · D255 · A63 · D918 · N-121-A · D3

CC € **17** 22/3-30/6   1/9-3/11   7=6, 14=12, 21=18   📍 N 43°24'50'' W 1°37'0''

St. Jean-de-Luz, F-64500 / Aquitaine (Pyrénées-Atlantiques)   🛜 iD   (1785)

🔺 Municipal Chibau Berria**
📧 525 chemin de Chibau Berria
☎ +33 (0)5-59261194
⌛ 12/5 - 30/9
@ camping.municipal@ saintjeandeluz.fr

5ha 213T(70-110m²) 10-A CEE

1. AC**G**IJKLPQ
2. EFKNQRVX
3. AJKRU
4. (Q 1/7-31/8)
5. **AB**GIJKLMNOPUVZ
6. EHJ(N 0,8km)TV

💬 Campsite on a hill with a lovely view of the Erromardie beach and the Atlantic Ocean. The beach is accessible from the campsite. Great cycling and walking routes next to the campsite. Many pitches are marked-out with hedges.

🚗 Bayonne-St. Jean-de-Luz motorway. Exit 3 St. Jean-de-Luz Nord dir. Bayonne on RD 810 as far as Plages "Acotz". Left immediately on entering quartier Acotz. Left at first roundabout. Campsite signposted. Follow road to site.

Biarritz
Irun · CC · D755 · D912 · D255 · A63 · D918 · N-121-A

CC € **15** 12/5-29/6   1/9-29/9   📍 N 43°24'30'' W 1°38'11''

St. Jean-de-Luz, F-64500 / Aquitaine (Pyrénées-Atlantiques) ♿ 📶 iD (1786)

🏕 Tamaris Plage****
✉ 720 route des Plage - Acotz
☎ +33 (0)5-59265590
📠 +33 (0)5-59477015
🔓 6/4 - 4/11
@ tamaris1@wanadoo.fr

31T(80-120m²) 7A

1 ACD**G**IJKLM**PQ**
2 AEFGKNOQRVXY
3 AJRUV
4 (E 🔓) KLN(Q 🔓)
(T+U 1/5-15/10) (V 🔓)
(Z 1/5-15/10)
5 **AB**DEFGIJKLMNPUZ
6 ACEG**K**(N 1,5km)QTV

💬 A small, friendly campsite on the edge of the Atlantic Ocean with wonderful views of the ocean from the entrance. Toilet facilities in Spanish style.

🚗 From Bordeaux direction Bayonne on the A63. Take exit 3 in St. Jean-de-Luz Nord. Then the D810 direction Bayonne. Take 'Acotz-plages' exit on left after about 2 km. Then another 1500m following camping signs.

Bayonne
Biarritz
Saint-Jean-de-Luz
D912 A63 D755 D255 D918 D3

CC € **17** 6/4-6/7 1/9-3/11   📍 N 43°25'3'' W 1°37'26''

St. Jean-Pied-de-Port, F-64220 / Aquitaine (Pyrénées-Atlantiques) ♿ 📶 iD (1787)

🏕 Narbaïtz - Vacances Pyrénées Basques****
✉ route de Bayonne (Ascarat)
☎ +33 (0)5-59371013
🔓 5/5 - 16/9
@ camping-narbaitz@wanadoo.fr

2,8ha 101T(80-140m²) 10A

1 AGIJKLMPQ
2 CKRVXY
3 AGHR**UW**
4 (**A** 1/7-31/8) (C+H+Q 🔓)
(R+T+U+X+Z 1/7-31/8)
5 **AB**DEFGJKLOPUWZ
6 ACEGK(N 2km)OTV

💬 The campsite is on the route to St. Jean-Pied-de-Port, a well-known stop for pilgrims on their way to Santiago de Compostela. Hydrangea bushes are everywhere. The swimming pool is heated to 28°C the entire season. Cash-only payment when using CampingCard ACSI.

🚗 A63 exit 5 Bayonne-Sud. Then take the D932 via Ustaritz and Cambo-les-Bains to St. Jean-Pied-du-Port. The campsite is located on the right of a bend on the D918 2.5 km before the town of Ascarat.

Saint-Étienne-de-Baïgorry
D918 D948 D933 N-135

CC € **19** 5/5-7/7 25/8-15/9   📍 N 43°10'39'' W 1°15'34''

St. Jory-de-Chalais, F-24800 / Aquitaine (Dordogne) 👫 ♿ 📶 iD (1788)

🏕 Camping Maisonneuve**
✉ 1 chemin de Maisonneuve/D98
☎ +33 (0)5-53551063
🔓 30/3 - 20/10
@ camping.maisonneuve@wanadoo.fr

10,5ha 40T(100-150m²) 10A CEE

1 A**G**IJKLMPQ
2 CDFLRVWXY
3 AGHJKMN**OP**RUW
4 (B 1/5-30/9) (T+U+Y+Z 🔓)
5 **AB**FGIJKLMNOPUVWYZ
6 CDEGK(N 0,4km)V

💬 A peaceful, family-run campsite in the Périgord countrysyide, only 4 km from the N21 between Limoges and Périgueux. Ideal stopover en route to Spain or Portugal. Excellent facilities with 4-star shower block, swimming pool, free wifi, fishing lake, on-site bar and restaurant with home-cooked meals 7 nights a week.

🚗 N21 south from Limoges. Right at Mavaleix onto D98 to St. Jory-de-Chalais. Campsite well signposted and on your left just as you enter St. Jory de Chalais.

D6 BIS D67 D85 N21 D707 D78
Saint-Paul-la-Roche
Villars Thiviers

CC € **17** 30/3-6/7 1/9-19/10   📍 N 45°29'58'' E 0°54'21''

St. Julien-de-Lampon, F-24370 / Aquitaine (Dordogne) ♿ 🛜 iD (1789)

🏠 Le Mondou***
📧 Le Colombier
☎ +33 (0)5-53297037
🕐 1/4 - 15/10
@ lemondou@
  camping-dordogne.info

1,7ha 46T(80-130m²) 6A

1 AGIJKL**P**RS
2 ILRVXY
3 AGHJNRU
4 (B+G 1/5-15/9)
  (Q+T+U 15/4-15/10)
  (V 1/5-15/10) (X 1/5-15/9)
  (Z 🔒)
5 **AB**EFGIJKLMNPUWZ
6 AEG**K**(N 0,6km)TV

💬 John, Lia and Nick Doejaaren have run this pleasant and peaceful campsite in the Dordogne for over 15 years. They provide an informal and friendly atmosphere and are very helpful. The beautiful swimming pool (up to 2 metres deep) is striking. Totally renovated toilet facilities. Good cycling and walking opportunities.

🚐 A20 exit 55 Souillac. Then D804 direction Sarlat. Over the bridge at Rouffillac direction St. Julien-de-Lampon. Campsite signposted in the village.

Sarlat-la-Canéda
D62 D165 D15
D704 A CC
D703 D820 A20
D704 D673

CC € **13** 1/4-6/7 25/8-14/10 7=6 🏖 N 44°51'48'' E 1°22'24''

St. Justin, F-40240 / Aquitaine (Landes) ♿ 🛜 iD (1790)

🏠 Le Pin***
📧 1529 route de Roquefort
☎ +33 (0)5-58448891
🕐 15/4 - 15/10
@ camping.lepin@wanadoo.fr

3ha 45T(100-120m²) 10A

1 ACD**F**IJKLMPST
2 BFLRSVWXY
3 BGHNRUW
4 (B 15/6-30/9) (Q+U+Y+Z 🔒)
5 **AB**EFGIJKLMNOPUZ
6 CEG**K**(N 2km)TV

💬 This dream-come-true campsite is located between oak and fir trees and will allow you to relax completely. Here, children can play safely and freely. There is a welcoming little restaurant with an atmospheric terrace next to the swimming pool. Free wifi (10 minutes a day).

🚐 The campsite is situated between Roquefort and St. Justin at the D626.

D932
Roquefort
A65 D933 N
Pouydesseaux CC
D626 D35
D934
Cazaubon
D32

CC € **15** 15/4-14/7 1/9-14/10 7=6, 14=12, 21=18 🏖 N 44°0'7'' W 0°14'5''

St. Léon-sur-Vézère, F-24290 / Aquitaine (Dordogne) ♿ 🛜 ✿ iD (1791)

🏠 Le Paradis*****
📧 La Rebeyrolle
☎ +33 (0)5-53507264
📠 +33 (0)5-53507590
🕐 1/4 - 20/10
@ le-paradis@perigord.com

8ha 144T(80-200m²) 10A CEE

1 ACD**G**IJKLMOPQ
2 CLRTVXY
3 BGHKL**M**NRU**W**X
4 (A 🔒) (C 15/5-15/9) (E 🔒)
  (H 15/5-15/9) KLN
  (Q+S+T+U+Y+Z 🔒)
5 **AB**CDEFGJLNPQUWXYZ
6 ACEGHIKLORTVW

💬 A very luxurious campsite on the banks of the Vézère. Spacious pitches surrounded by lovely vegetation. Many historic sights in the immediate vicinity. Plenty of sports opportunities and entertainment. Very clean and comfortable toilet facilities.

🚐 The campsite is located on the D706 Montignac-Les Eyzies (do not turn off towards the village St. Léon). Follow the signs.

Montignac
Plazac D704
D47
D32 CC
D32 E D706
Le Bugue

CC € **19** 1/4-7/7 1/9-19/10 🏖 N 45°0'6'' E 1°4'17''

St. Michel-Escalus, F-40550 / Aquitaine (Landes)

☺ 📶 **iD** (1792)

▲ Camping Huttopia Landes Sud
▫ 450 route Léon
☎ +33 (0)5-58902630
☉ 4/5 - 23/9
@ lac-leon@huttopia.com

133T(60-150m²) 10A

1 ACD**F**IJKL**P**ST
2 BCFRSVXY
3 BGKRU
4 (C+G+Q+R 🔒)
　(T+U+V+X+Z 1/7-31/8)
5 **A**BFGIJKLMNPUW
6 CEGIJ(N 6km)V

🗪 Camp in Les Landes close to Le Lac Léon, a few kilometres from the ocean on completely renovated grounds in the middle of a beautiful forest. Enjoy the heated pools, grab a bite to eat at the Pizza Grill, play some beach volleyball, little ones will love the new playground... A new Huttopia destination, suitable for discovering the Les Landes heritage during a 100% natural stay!

🚌 From Bordeaux: A63, exit 12 (8 km).

Vieux-Boucau-
les-Bains

CC € **15** 4/5-5/7 26/8-22/9   **N 43°52'46'' W 1°14'5''**

St. Palais, F-33820 / Aquitaine (Gironde)

☺ 📶 ❈ **iD** (1793)

▲ Chez Gendron**
▫ 2 chez Jandron
☎ +33 (0)5-57329647
☉ 1/3 - 15/10
@ info@chezgendron.com

3,5ha 50T(100-160m²) 10A CEE

1 ACD**G**IJKLPST
2 BFIJLRTUWXY
3 AGHJKNO**P**RU
4 (B 1/5-15/9) (G 1/5-30/9)
　(Q+T+U+X+Y 1/5-15/9)
　(Z 1/3-15/9)
5 **AB**DFGIJKLMNOPRUWXZ
6 EGK(N 3km)TV

🗪 Situated in an undulating landscape with woods, wine and sunflower fields. Sander, Aletta and kids manage the campsite with heart for environment and guests. Modern toilet blocks with solar water heater, bio-uv pool filter, organic restaurant products and extended opening hours at reception.

🚌 From north: A10 exit 37, then D137 through Mirambeau, D151 towards St. Ciers; follow signs. From south: A10 exit 38, then to St. Ciers and dir. St. Palais, follow signs.

Braud-et-Saint-
Louis

Etauliers

CC € **15** 1/3-7/7 1/9-14/10   **N 45°18'50'' W 0°36'12''**

St. Paul-en-Born, F-40200 / Aquitaine (Landes)

☺ 📶 ❈ **iD** (1794)

▲ Flower Camping La Clairière***
▫ 1151 route de Talucat
☎ +33 (0)5-58048307
☉ 28/4 - 30/9
@ contact@camping-laclairiere.fr

3,4ha 80T(100-130m²) 10A CEE

1 ACD**G**IJKLMOPST
2 CRSVWXY
3 B**F**GHJKQ**R**U**W**
4 (C 1/6-30/9) (H+Q+R 🔒)
　(S 8/7-31/8)
　(T+U+V+X+Z 🔒)
5 **AB**EFGIJMNPQUWZ
6 ACEGHJ**K**(N 1km)RTV

🗪 Welcoming, quiet family campsite on a little babbling river. Many options for families that like a 'real' holiday in beautiful surroundings under high oaks. Beautiful heated pool. Direct connection to cycling network through the wooded Landes area.

🚌 Take A10 as far as Labouheyre, then D626 direction Mimizan as far as St. Paul-en-Born. In the centre of St. Paul-en-Born take first right (before church on left). Campsite is signposted.

Mimizan-
Plage

Mimizan

CC € **13** 28/4-1/7 25/8-29/9   **N 44°14'3'' W 1°9'5''**

St. Paul-lès-Dax, F-40990 / Aquitaine (Landes) ♿ 📶 iD (1795)

△ Les Pins du Soleil★★★★
🚏 route des Minières
☎ +33 (0)5-58913791
🗓 1/4 - 31/10
@ pinsdusoleil@gmail.com

6ha 37T(100-120m²) 10A

1 ACG HIJKLMPST
2 RSVWXY
3 AGRUV
4 (C 1/5-30/9) (G 1/6-15/9) K
(Q+R ⊙)
(T+U+V+X+Z 1/6-15/9)
5 AB DEFGIJKLOPUWXY
6 CEGK(N 2,5km)OSTV

💬 Campsite in the heart of Landes not far from the Atlantic Ocean and on the edge of the French Basque Country. The well-known spa Dax is a few kilometres away. Heated toilet facilities in low season. Reasonably spacious pitches. Grounds are slightly undulating. Restaurant/bar open from June to September.

🚗 St. Paul is west of Dax in dir. of Bayonne. Take exit on roundabout just outside built-up area. Campsite is signposted.

CC € 15 1/4-30/6 1/9-30/10

⛺ N 43°43'14'' W 1°5'37''

St. Pée-sur-Nivelle, F-64310 / Aquitaine (Pyrénées-Atlantiques) ♿ 📶 iD (1796)

△ d'Ibarron★★★
🚏 D918
☎ +33 (0)5-59541043
🗓 16/4 - 1/10
@ camping.dibarron@wanadoo.fr

3ha 119T(80-130m²) 6-10A

1 ACG IJKLPRS
2 CFGRVWXY
3 BGHJKNRU
4 (C 1/5-20/9) (G 15/6-15/9)
(Q 15/5-15/9) (R ⊙)
(U+V 1/7-31/8)
5 AB DEFGIJKLMNOPUVWZ
6 CDEGJK(N 0,2km)TV

💬 Large, level, shaded pitches at the foot of the Pyrenees. 8 km from the Spanish border and 10 km from the Atlantic coast in St. Jean-de-Luz. Beautiful heated swimming pool. Marked out footpaths. Bus stop outside campsite. Large supermarket close by.

🚗 A63 exit 3 St. Jean-de-Luz Nord. Then D810 direction St. Jean-de-Luz. Left just before the centre towards Ascain and St. Pée-sur-Nivelle. Campsite located 2 km before St. Pée by a roundabout and opposite Intermarché.

CC € 15 16/4-5/7 1/9-30/9

⛺ N 43°21'28'' W 1°34'29''

St. Pée-sur-Nivelle, F-64310 / Aquitaine (Pyrénées-Atlantiques) ♿ 📶 iD (1797)

△ Goyetchea★★★★
🚏 route d'Ahetze
☎ +33 (0)5-59541959
🗓 18/5 - 23/9
@ info@camping-goyetchea.com

3,5ha 100T(80-120m²) 6-10A

1 ACG IJKLMPRS
2 FRTVWXY
3 BCGRU
4 (C+G ⊙)
(Q+T+U+V+X+Z 1/7-31/8)
5 AB EFGIJKLPUVW
6 CEGJK(N 0,8km)V

💬 Family campsite not far from St. Pée-sur-Nivelle, 10 km from the Atlantic coast and 5 km from St. Pée lake. Spacious sunny and shady pitches. Heated pool (excl. toddler's pool). Outdoor and indoor playground.

🚗 On A63 take exit 3 'St. Jean-de-Luz Nord' and drive in dir. of town. Left just before centre, dir. Ascain and St. Pée-sur-Nivelle. Continue to St. Pée. Another 1 km from roundabout and supermarket and then left to campsite. Signposts there.

CC € 13 18/5-30/6 1/9-22/9

⛺ N 43°21'45'' W 1°33'56''

St. Saud-Lacoussière, F-24470 / Aquitaine (Dordogne) 📶 iD (1798)

🏕 La Bûcherie**
📧 La Bûcherie
☎ +33 (0)5-24121130
📅 1/1 - 31/12
@ info@labucherie.nl

7,5ha 48T(80-250m²) 10A CEE

1 AGIJKLMPRS
2 BIRTVWXY
3 ADHJNU
4 (Q+T+U+X+Z ⊡)
5 AEFGIJKLMNPRUZ
6 ADEGJ(N 3,5km)T

💬 Small, natural campsite in the Périgord Limousin regional park. Spacious, naturally appointed pitches. Good toilet facilities. Recreational lake within walking distance. Suitable for people who love peace, space and nature. Walking options.

🚗 From Limoges follow Périgueux signs (N21). In Châlus D6bis dir. Dournazac to Les Trois Cerisiers. Towards Nontron. Then follow signs for 4 km to campsite. Take note, from St Saud keep right after the lake (± 1 km) on paved road.

Châlus · D91 · D15 · D675 · D6 BIS · Nontron D85 · N21 · Saint-Front-la-Rivière D707 · CC

CC € 13 1/1-7/7 25/8-31/12 7=6, 14=12   N 45°34'1'' E 0°50'16''

St. Symphorien, F-33113 / Aquitaine (Gironde) 🚻 ⛺ 📶 iD (1799)

🏕 Vert Bord'Eau**
📧 2 Au Moulin de Lescroumpes
☎ +33 (0)5-56257954
📅 1/3 - 17/11
@ vertbordeau@live.fr

4ha 48T(100-200m²) 10A

1 ACDGIJKLMPST
2 BCDLRSVWXY
3 BGHJKRW
4 (C 1/6-15/9) (Q 1/7-31/8)
   (T+U+X 1/5-30/9) (Z ⊡)
5 ABGIJKLMNOPUWZ
6 AEJ(N 0,2km)T

💬 Welcoming family campsite in the heart of Parc Régional des Landes. Heated pool and free wifi point. Many cycling and walking routes and wine tasting events ('route du vin', by bike).

🚗 From St. Symphorien D220 direction Sore. Campsite on the other side of the Intermarché supermarket.

Hostens · D110 · D8 · D3 · D11 · Villandraut · D220 · Préchac · D651 · D114 · D43 · CC

CC € 15 1/3-6/7 25/8-16/11   N 44°25'5'' W 0°29'39''

Ste Eulalie-en-Born, F-40200 / Aquitaine (Landes) ⛺ 📶 iD (1800)

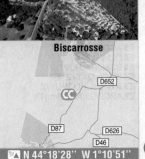

🏕 Municipal Le Camping du Lac***
📧 1590 route du Lac
☎ +33 (0)5-58097010
📅 31/3 - 27/10
@ contact@lecampingdulac.com

6ha 127T(80-150m²) 10A CEE

1 ACDGHIJKLMOPST
2 ABDLMRSVWXY
3 ABFGHJKRWZ
4 (B+G 15/6-15/9)
   (Q+R+T+U+X+Z 1/6-31/8)
5 ABEFGIJKLMNOPUVX
6 ACEGHK(N 4km)TV

💬 A peaceful campsite located by the lake. Own harbour close by, perfectly suitable for all watersports. Adjacent to the Les Landes cycle route network.

🚗 In Parentis-en-Born on the D652 continue in direction Mimizan. Campsite clearly signposted between Gastes and Ste Eulalie-en-Born.

Biscarrosse · D652 · CC · D87 · D626 · D46

CC € 13 31/3-30/6 1/9-26/10   N 44°18'28'' W 1°10'51''

Tamniés (Dordogne), F-24620 / Aquitaine (Dordogne) 🛜 iD 1801

▲ Le Pont de Mazerat★★★★
☎ +33 (0)5-53291495
🔓 15/4 - 15/9
@ le.pont.de.mazerat@wanadoo.fr

2ha 47T(80-110m²) 10A

1 ACDGIJKLMPRS
2 CJLRVY
3 BGHJNQRUW
4 (C+H+Q+R 🔒)
(T+U 1/6-15/9) (V 1/7-15/9)
(X 1/7-30/9) (Z 1/6-15/9)
5 ABFGIJKLPUVWZ
6 CDEGHK(N 8km)ORUV

💬 Campsite with a very peaceful location between the picturesque Montignac and the medieval Sarlat. 2 km from the swimming lake in Tamnies, a quiet Dordogne village with a welcoming restaurant. Spacious marked-out pitches.

🚗 On D704 from Montignac to Sarlat, take exit to D48 dir. Les Eyzies. Campsite is near Tamnies' lake.

D62 · D706 · D704 · D60 · D47 · **Sarlat-la-Canéda** · D35

CC €15 15/4-14/7 1/9-14/9   🧭 N 44°57'54'' E 1°9'54''

Tardets/Abense-de-Haut, F-64470 / Aquitaine (Pyrénées-Atlantiques) 🚹 🛜 ✿ iD 1802

▲ du Pont d'Abense★★
🏠 Abense-de-Haut
☎ +33 (0)6-78735359
🔓 1/1 - 31/12
@ camping.abense@wanadoo.fr

1,5ha 50T(90-100m²) 10A

1 AGIJKLMP
2 CGKNRWXY
3 HJWX
4 (A 1/7-30/8) (Q 🔒)
5 CGHIJKLMNOPUVWZ
6 ABCDEK(N 0,5km)O

💬 A friendly campsite in the heart of the French Basqueland with many different types of birds and flowers on the site and where you can fish for trout to your heart's content. Plenty of excursion possibilities within 15 km of the site. Lovely area with plenty of walking opportunities. Basic toilet facilities. Free wifi.

🚗 Follow the D918 as far as Tardets. Just south of the town centre Pont d'Abense is indicated. The campsite is over the bridge on the right.

Etchepay · **Barcus** · D919 · D918 · D26 · Larrau · D132

CC €17 1/4-2/7 20/8-11/11 7=6   🧭 N 43°6'42'' W 0°51'49''

Thiviers, F-24800 / Aquitaine (Dordogne) 🚻 🚹 🛜 iD 1803

▲ Le Repaire★★★
🏠 Le Repaire
☎ +33 (0)5-53526975
🔓 1/4 - 1/11
@ contact@camping-le-repaire.fr

8ha 80T(100-150m²) 6A

1 ACDGIJKLMPST
2 DLMRVWXY
3 BGHJKMRUW
4 (E+G+Q+T+Z 🔒)
5 ABGHIJKLOPUWZ
6 ABCEGJ(N 0,8km)TV

💬 A beautiful, park-like campsite within walking distance of a village. Lovely swimming pool and close to a lake with opportunities for swimming (1 km).

🚗 N21 Limoges-Périgueux, at the second traffic lights (large intersection) in Thiviers turn left onto the D707 in the direction of Lanouaille. Follow the signs.

Saint-Jory-de-Chalais · D707 · D78 · N21 · Négrondes · D76 · D705

220

CC €15 1/4-14/7 1/9-31/10 7=6, 14=11   🧭 N 45°24'47'' E 0°55'56''

Urrugne, F-64122 / Aquitaine (Pyrénées-Atlantiques) ♿ 🛜 iD (1804)

🏕 Col d'Ibardin***
📧 220 route d'Olhette
☎ +33 (0)5-59543121
📠 +33 (0)5-59546228
📅 1/4 - 30/9
@ info@col-ibardin.com

8ha 105T(80-100m²) 6-10A

1 ACGIJKLMPQ
2 FIJKRSTVXY
3 BFGNRU
4 (A 1/7-31/8) (C+G 1/5-30/9)
M(Q 🍴) (S 15/6-15/9)
(T+U+V+Y+Z 1/5-15/9)
5 ABEFGIJKLMNPUXYZ
6 ACDEHIJ(N 4km)OQTV

💬 Under centuries old oak trees on the Spanish border at the foot of the Col d'Ibardin. Bargain shopping there on te col. Restaurant and swimming pool with a splash pool for children.

🚗 A63 Bayonne-St. Sébastian. Exit 2 St. Jean-de-Luz. D810 dir. Urrugne/Hendaye. At roundabout just before Urrugne dir. D4 (Col D'Ibardin). Don't go up the hill, but turn left by the customs house. Campsite 200 metres on the right.

CC € **17** 1/4-30/6 1/9-29/9 🏕 N 43°20'2'' W 1°41'5''

Urrugne, F-64122 / Aquitaine (Pyrénées-Atlantiques) ♿ 🛜 iD (1805)

🏕 Flower camping de la Corniche****
📧 chemin Antziola
☎ +33 (0)5-59200687
📅 31/3 - 30/9
@ contact@camping-corniche.com

6ha 60T(80-120m²) 10A

NEW

1 ACDGIJKLPQ
2 ABFGIJNQRVWXY
3 BFGHJNRUW
4 (C+H 1/5-30/9)
(Q+R+T+U+V+Y+Z 1/7-31/8)
5 ABEFGIJKLMNOPQUV
6 CDEGHJ(N 5km)OTV

💬 A campsite on the Basque Corniche. Many marked out and shaded pitches. You have lovely views of the Bay of Biscay in the Atlantic Ocean from the Corniche. Spain 6 km, San Sebastian 25 km.

🚗 A63 Bordeaux to Spain exit 2, St. Jean-de-Luz Sud. Direction Socoa-Hendaye Plage on the D192. At 3rd roundabout direction Hendaye Plage along the Corniche Basque. Campsite about 3 km on the left in a small valley.

CC € **19** 31/3-30/6 1/9-29/9 7=6, 14=12, 18=16, 21=18 🏕 N 43°22'37'' W 1°43'59''

Urrugne, F-64122 / Aquitaine (Pyrénées-Atlantiques) ♿ 🛜 ✿ iD (1806)

🏕 Larrouleta***
📧 210 route de Socoa
☎ +33 (0)5-59473784
📅 1/1 - 31/12
@ info@larrouleta.com

10ha 327T(80-120m²) 5-10A

1 ACDGIJKLMPQ
2 ACDFGKLRTUVWXY
3 BFGHMNRUWZ
4 (E 🍴) (G 15/6-30/9) M(Q 🍴)
(S 15/6-15/9)
(T+U+Y+Z 1/4-15/9)
5 ABDEFGIJKLMNPUWXYZ
6 CDEGIK(N 0,5km)OQRTV

💬 The owner is a real, proud Basque. He can be proud of his campsite. The part in the front is less beautiful than the part in the back. Here are the pleasant pitches by a small lake, with a quiet part for swimming, sunbathing and fishing. There is also an indoor swimming pool!

🚗 From Bordeaux A63 direction Bayonne-St. Sébastian exit 2 (St. Jean-de-Luz Sud). Then drive towards the coast and the Corniche Basque. Take second on the left after the bridge then follow signs.

CC € **17** 1/1-30/6 1/9-31/12 🏕 N 43°22'13'' W 1°41'10''

Urrugne, F-64122 / Aquitaine (Pyrénées-Atlantiques)

 ♿ 📶 **iD** **1807**

🔺 Suhiberry****
▪️ 1575 route de Socoa
☎ +33 (0)5-59470623
🔓 1/5 - 30/9
@ suhiberry@wanadoo.fr

4ha 119T(80-120m²) 6-10A

1 ACGIJKLPQ
2 CFJRVY
3 BFGHMNRUW
4 (C+G 1/6-30/9) **KN**
(Q+R+T+U+V+X+Z
15/6-15/9)
5 ABEFGIJKLMNPUWXYZ
6 ACEGIK(N 1km)OTV

💬 Suhiberry is located between the hills of the Basque coast. Located on a side road between Urrugne and Socoa. It is peaceful here but you can be at a large department store or the lively St. Jean-de-Luz fishing harbour within minutes. There is a heated pool.

🚗 From Bordeaux take A63 dir. Bayonne-St. Sebastián, exit 2 St. Jean-de-Luz Sud. Then towards Socoa-Hendaye. Second left after the bridge. Then follow signs.

Biarritz

Hendaye

A63

CC

D255

D918

Irun N-121-A

D3

D4

D406

CC € **17** *1/5-7/7 25/8-29/9* 7=6, 14=12   🏕 N 43°22'46'' W 1°41'28''

Valeuil, F-24310 / Aquitaine (Dordogne)

📶 ✿ **iD** **1808**

🔺 Du Bas-Meygnaud**
▪️ D939
☎ +33 (0)5-53055844
🔓 1/4 - 30/9
@ camping-du-bas-meygnaud@
wanadoo.fr

1,7ha 50T(100-120m²) 6A CEE

1 AGIJKLPQ
2 BILRWXY
3 BGHJNRU
4 (B+G 15/5-30/9) (Q 1/7-31/8)
(R 1/6-30/9) (T 1/7-30/9)
(U+V 🔓) (X+Z 1/7-30/9)
5 AFGJLMNPUZ
6 AEGJ(N 4km)T

💬 A small, peaceful campsite with plenty of shade in the Dronne valley. Child-friendly and very suitable for nature lovers. Dutch owners. Located 4 km from the tourist town of Brantôme. Lovely cycling and walking routes start from the campsite.

🚗 In Brantôme D939 direction Périgueux. Right after about 4 km. Take second Lasserre exit then follow signs. Take note: do not go via Valeuil. From Périgueux 4 km before Brantôme on the left.

D675

Brantôme

D106 CC

D78

D1 D939

Château-l'Évêque

D710

CC € **13** *1/4-30/6 1/9-29/9*   🏕 N 45°19'48'' E 0°38'16''

Vézac, F-24220 / Aquitaine (Dordogne)

📶 **iD** **1809**

🔺 La Plage***
▪️ La Malartrie
☎ +33 (0)5-53295083
🔓 15/3 - 20/10
@ campinglaplage24@orange.fr

3,5ha 83T(80-120m²) 10A

1 ACGIJKLMPQ
2 CKLNRWXY
3 ABGHIJKLRU**W**X
4 (B+G 1/5-20/10)
(Q+R 1/7-31/8) (T 1/6-31/8)
(U 1/7-31/8) (V 1/6-31/8)
(Z 🔓)
5 ABEFGJLMNPUZ
6 EGK(N 2km)OV

💬 Located on the Dordogne within walking distance of La Roque-Gageac (1 km) and cycling distance to Domme (4 km). Easily accessible site in the centre of Perigord Noir by the Marqueyssac gardens.

🚗 From Sarlat direction Vézac, direction Roque-Gageac, campsite is signposted.

D47 **Sarlat-la-Canéda**

D35

D49

D57 D704 A

D703

CC

D704

D46

D60

CC € **15** *15/3-6/7 24/8-19/10*   🏕 N 44°49'26'' E 1°10'16''

Vézac, F-24220 / Aquitaine (Dordogne) 👫 ♿ 📶 iD (1810)

🔺 Les Deux Vallées***
🚉 La Gare
☎ +33 (0)5-53295355
🔓 14/3 - 7/10
@ contact@
campingles2vallees.com

3,3ha 94T(90-160m²) 10A CEE

1 ACD**G**IJKLMPQ
2 KRSVWXY
3 ABF**G**HJKNRUW
4 (C+G 1/4-1/10)
(Q+R 15/4-1/10)
(U+X+Y+Z 1/5-1/10)
5 **AB**DFGIJKLMNPUZ
6 ACEGKL(N 0,5km)OV

💬 A beautiful, relaxed campsite in stunning countryside west of Sarlat, with views of Beynac Castle. 'La Roque Gageac', Domme, Castelnau and the river Dordogne are all close by, making it an ideal place for exploring. The region is well known for its excellent cuisine and good wine. Free wifi. Heated toilet facilities.

🚗 On the D57 from Sarlat, turn right just after Vézac sign. Campsite is marked.

CC € **15** 14/3-6/7 24/8-6/10 16=14 📍 N 44°50'8'' E 1°9'30''

Vielle-St-Girons, F-40560 / Aquitaine (Landes) 🏄 ♿ 📶 ✿ iD (1811)

🔺 Arnaoutchot (FKK)***
🚉 5006 route de Pichelèbe
☎ +33 (0)5-58491111
📠 +33 (0)5-58485712
🔓 1/4 - 23/9
@ contact@arna.com

25ha 250T(100-120m²) 3-6A

1 AC**F**IJLPST
2 ABEIRSVXY
3 BF**G**HJKL**M**NQRUV**W**Y
4 (B+F+H 🚗) IJ**KLNP**(Q 🚗)
(S+T+U+V+Y+Z 28/4-23/9)
5 **AB**DEFGIJKLMNOPUVWZ
6 CDEGHI**J**K(N 8km)OQRTV

💬 Undulating grounds for naturists. Right on a lovely sandy beach. It has swimming pools (one of which can be covered) and many activities are organised.

🚗 A63 and N10 Bordeaux-Bayonne. Exit 12 Castets. Towards Léon (14 km) in Castets centre. From Léon centre direction St. Girons as far as Vielle. Left at water tower to Arnaoutchot.

CC € **17** 1/4-6/7 25/8-22/9 14=11, 21=18 📍 N 43°54'24'' W 1°21'42''

Vielle-St-Girons, F-40560 / Aquitaine (Landes) ♿ 📶 ✿ iD (1812)

🔺 Sandaya Le Col Vert****
🚉 1548 route de l'Etang
☎ +33 (0)5-58429406
📠 +33 (0)5-58429188
🔓 23/3 - 9/9
@ contact@colvert.com

30ha 270T(100-130m²) 6-10A

1 AC**F**IJKLMPST
2 ABDKLRSVXY
3 BD**F**GHJKL**M**N**OP**Q**R**UVW Z
4 (B 1/4-20/9) (E+H 🚗) IJ**KLN** P(Q+S+T+U+V+Y+Z 🚗)
5 **AB**DEFGIJKLMNP**ST**UWXY Z
6 ACDEGHI**K**(N 3km)OPQRT UV

💬 A campsite next to the Léon lake in Les Landes. Lovely view of the lake. Most amenities are also available in low season, such as entertainment. CampingCard ACSI holders are entitled to a comfort pitch in low season.

🚗 A63 and N10 Bordeaux-Bayonne. Exit 12 Castets. Head for Léon in the centre of Castets (14 km). From Léon centre direction St. Girons as far as Vielle. Campsite indicated along this road.

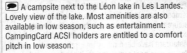

CC € **17** 23/3-6/7 2/9-8/9 📍 N 43°54'10'' W 1°18'38''

Villefranche-du-Périgord, F-24550 / Aquitaine (Dordogne)   ♿ 🛜 iD (1813)

🏕 La Bastide★★★★
🛣 route de Cahors
☎ +33 (0)5-53289457
🔓 7/4 - 11/11
@ contact@
camping-la-bastide.com

2,5ha 41T(80-130m²) 6-10A CEE

1 ACDFIJKLMOPRS
2 JKLRTUVWXY
3 ABGHJRUW
4 (A 1/7-30/8) (C+G 15/5-15/9)
(Q+R 1/7-30/8)
(T+U+V+X+Z 🔓)
5 ADEFGIJKLMNPQUWXYZ
6 ACDEGIK(N 0,3km)TV

💬 Lovely terraced campsite with panoramic views of the stunning surroundings. The historic medieval centre of Villefranche du Périgord is just 250 metres away with a good selection of shops. Suitable for those who like relaxation. Plenty of excursion opportunities. Free wifi. Also good as a stopover site.

🚐 On the D660. 500 metres from Villefranche-du-Perigord and 45 km from Cahors. Campsite signposted.

D53   Saint-Pompont
D60
Villefranche-du-Périgord CC
D660
D673
D710

CC € ⑬ 7/4-12/7   30/8-10/11   7=6   📍 N 44°37'40'' E 1°4'57''

Villefranche-du-Queyran, F-47160 / Aquitaine (Lot-et-Garonne)   ♿ 🛜 iD (1814)

🏕 Moulin de Campech★★★
🛣 D11
☎ +33 (0)5-53887243
📠 +33 (0)5-53880652
🔓 14/4 - 1/10
@ camping@
moulindecampech.co.uk

5ha 46T(80-150m²) 6A CEE

1 ACDGIJKLOPQ
2 BCFLRUVWXY
3 AFGHJKRW
4 (C 7/5-19/9) (Q 2/5-20/9)
(R 🔓)
(T+U+X+Y+Z 2/5-20/9)
5 ABGIJKLNPUVWX
6 DEGJ(N 10km)RTU

💬 An English family runs this campsite in wooded surroundings near an old water mill. Toilet facilities are good. Lovely grounds, alternating well and less shaded level pitches. Swimming pool higher up with panoramic views. Opportunities for trout fishing in the lake.

🚐 Exit 6 on autoroute A62. Then towards Montmarsan. After about 3 km direction Casteljaloux (D11). Campsite 5 km on the right.

Casteljaloux D120 D813
D655 Aiguillon
CC A62
D933 N D642
D8 D930
Lavardac

CC € ⑰ 14/4-29/6   1/9-30/9   📍 N 44°16'18'' E 0°11'27''

Vitrac, F-24200 / Aquitaine (Dordogne)   ♿ 🛜 iD (1815)

🏕 Domaine de Soleil Plage★★★★★
🛣 Plage De Caudon
☎ +33 (0)5-53283333
📠 +33 (0)5-53283024
🔓 7/4 - 30/9
@ info@soleilplage.fr

6ha 106T(80-120m²) 16A

1 ABCDGIJLPQ
2 ACKLNORSTVXY
3 BGHJKMNQRUVWX
4 (C+E 🔓) (H 13/4-29/9) IJK
(Q 🔓)
(R+S+T+U+V 4/5-16/9)
(X 4/5-18/9) (Y 4/5-17/9)(Z 🔓)
5 ABDEFGIJKLMNOPQRUWX
Y
6 CDEGHK(N 5km)ORTUV

💬 Beautifully located on the Dordogne river, this campsite is split up into two parts. With its excellent leisure pool and spacious pitches this campsite exudes space. Centrally located reception, bar and restaurant have been nicely integrated into the valley. Has its own boat rental and multisports grounds.

🚐 The campsite is located on the D703 and is signposted at Vitrac and Montfort.

D47
Sarlat-la-Canéda
D704 A
D57
D703 CC
D704
D46

CC € ⑲ 7/4-5/7   30/8-29/9   📍 N 44°49'28'' E 1°15'11''

Vitrac, F-24200 / Aquitaine (Dordogne) ♿ 🛜 iD 1816

🔼 La Bouysse de Caudon***
🏠 Caudon/Vitrac
☎ +33 (0)5-53283305
🗓 8/4 - 16/9
@ info@labouysse.com

5ha 142T(100m²) 10A CEE

1 ACDGIJLPQ
2 CKNORVWXY
3 BGHJKMNRUWX
4 (A 1/7-31/8) (B+G 15/5-15/9) (Q+R+T+U 15/6-31/8) (Z 🔒)
5 ABFGIJKLMNPUZ
6 ACEGHIK(N 4km)ORTUV

💬 Located on the banks of the Dordogne with its own canoes for hire. This homely campsite offers the necessary relaxation and opportunities to enjoy the sporting facilities in the vicinity and to explore the many sights. Free wifi.

🚐 Located on the Dordogne. Signposted on the D703 at Vitrac and Montfort.

CC € 15 8/4-2/7 25/8-15/9 14=12, 21=18   📷 N 44°49'26'' E 1°15'3''

Vitrac/Sarlat, F-24200 / Aquitaine (Dordogne) ♿ 🛜 iD 1817

🔼 Flower Camping La Sagne***
🏠 Lieu dit Lassagne
☎ +33 (0)5-53281836
🗓 7/4 - 22/9
@ info@camping-la-sagne.com

3,5ha 100T(100-120m²) 16A CEE

1 ACDFIJKLMPST
2 CRVWXY
3 AGHJWX
4 (E+H 🔒) K(Q 1/7-31/8) (R 🔒) (T+V 1/7-31/8) (Z 🔒)
5 ABEFGIJKLMNOPUWXY
6 EK(N 1km)UV

💬 Campsite in the Dordogne and on the Dordogne, close to the picturesque commune of Vitrac. Excellent base for discovering the many sights.

🚐 Situated on the Dordogne. Indicated on D703 near Vitrac and Montfort.

CC € 15 7/4-7/7 25/8-21/9   📷 N 44°49'31'' E 1°14'32''

Boulancourt, F-77760 / Ile-de-France (Seine-et-Marne) 🛜 ✿ iD 1818

🔼 Ile de Boulancourt***
🏠 6 allée des Maronniers
☎ +33 (0)1-64241338
🗓 9/1 - 22/12
@ campingiledeboulancourt@orange.fr

5,3ha 32T(120m²) 6A

1 ACGIJKLMOPQ
2 BCLRSWXY
3 AFHJRW
5 ABDFGIJKLMNOPUVZ
6 CDEGIK(N 0,4km)T

💬 Quiet, environmentally friendly campsite with spacious pitches and high trees (Clef Verte, Camping Qualité). Many options in surroundings: rock climbing (close to Fontainebleau), fishing, walking, cycling. Paris easily accessible by train. Ideal for nature lovers!

🚐 A6, exit 14 Ury, direction Malesherbes, then D410 direction Puiseaux, and then Boulancourt. Then follow signs.

CC € 15 1/4-14/7 1/9-30/10   📷 N 48°15'19'' E 2°26'3''

Dourdan, F-91410 / Ile-de-France (Essonne) 🛜 iD 1819

🔺 Les Petits Prés***
📧 11 ave Mendes France
☎ +33 (0)1-64596483
⌚ 1/4 - 30/9, 20/10 - 4/11
@ camping@mairie-dourdan.fr

7,5ha 70T(80-110m²) 6A CEE

1 ACDFHIJKLMPQ
2 FGIRVWX
3 AGRU
4 (Q 1/7-15/8)
5 DFGIJKLMNPUVZ
6 EGJ(N 0,5km)TV

💬 A hospitable oasis of peace on your way to and from the south. Department store and leisure pool close by. A 10-minute walk to the centre of Dourdan. Camping with CampingCard ACSI is also possible during the weekends of 17/18 and 24/25 March and in the weekends of October.

🚐 A10 exit Dourdan; D116 Dourdan. Direction Étampes. Signposted, located on the eastern ring road in Dourdan.

D936 — Bonnelles — Bruyères-le-Châtel
A11 / D168 — A10 — CC
D291 — D838 — D836 — N20
Étampes

CC € **15** 1/4-30/6 1/9-29/9 20/10-3/11 📡 N 48°31'35'' E 2°1'41''

Jablines, F-77450 / Ile-de-France (Seine-et-Marne) ♿ 🛜 iD 1820

🔺 International de Jablines***
📧 Base de Loisirs
☎ +33 (0)1-60260937
📠 +33 (0)1-60264333
⌚ 24/3 - 3/11
@ welcome@camping-jablines.com

3,5ha 139T(90-100m²) 10A CEE

1 ACDGHIJKLMPQ
2 ADFGLMRUVWXY
3 BFGHJKMNOPQRWZ
4 (Q+R+S ⌚)
5 ABDEFGIJKLMNPUYZ
6 CEGHIK(N 3km)RT

💬 A lovely, hospitable campsite in natural surroundings of 450 hectares. Marked out pitches, free wifi, ticket sales and shuttle bus to Disneyland. The largest beach in the Paris region (an enormous lake) for swimming and many types of watersport is next to the campsite. Close to Paris, 9 km from Disneyland and 30 km from Parc Asterix.

🚐 A104 exit 8 or N3 exit D404 'Base de Plein Air et de Loisirs-Jablines'. Follow signs. The campsite is along the D45.

N330
D404 — D129
A104 — D139 — **Meaux**
CC
Noisy-le-Grand
N36

CC € **19** 24/3-6/7 25/8-2/11 📡 N 48°54'49'' E 2°44'4''

Maisons-Laffitte, F-78600 / Ile-de-France (Paris) ♿ 🛜 iD 1821

🔺 Sandaya Paris Maisons Laffitte****
📧 1 rue Johnson
☎ +33 (0)1-39122191
📠 +33 (0)1-39127050
⌚ 6/4 - 4/11
@ maisonslaffitte@sandaya.fr

6,5ha 210T(80-110m²) 10-16A CEE

1 ABCDGIJKLMPST
2 CFRVWXY
3 BGNRW
4 (Q+S+V+X+Y+Z ⌚)
5 ABDGIJKLMNPUZ
6 ABCFGHK(N 1,5km)ORT

💬 Ideal for a visit to Paris or Disneyland. The campsite is located on an island with views of the Seine. Just a 12 minute walk to the RER station, and 20 minutes later you will be in Paris.

🚐 Coming from the north A1 and then A86 as far as Bezons, exit 2 and then D308 direction Houilles to Maisons-Laffitte. Follow camping signs instead of using SatNav.

D22
CC **Argenteuil**
A13
D7 — A86 — **Paris**

CC € **17** 6/4-6/7 1/9-3/11 📡 N 48°56'23'' E 2°8'45''

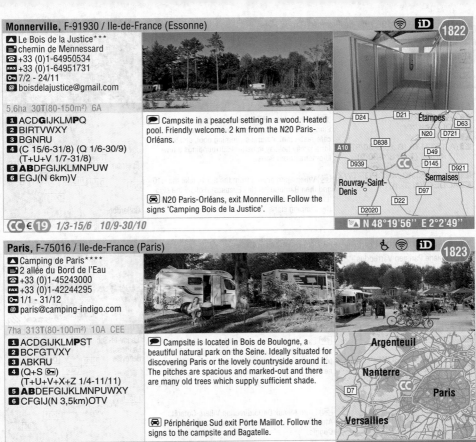

Monnerville, F-91930 / Ile-de-France (Essonne)

🔺 Le Bois de la Justice***
📧 chemin de Mennessard
☎ +33 (0)1-64950534
📠 +33 (0)1-64951731
🔒 7/2 - 24/11
@ boisdelajustice@gmail.com

1822

5,6ha 30T(80-150m²) 6A

1 ACD**G**IJKLM**P**Q
2 BIRTVWXY
3 BGNRU
4 (C 15/6-31/8) (Q 1/6-30/9)
  (T+U+V 1/7-31/8)
5 **AB**DFGIJKLMNPUW
6 EGJ(N 6km)V

💬 Campsite in a peaceful setting in a wood. Heated pool. Friendly welcome. 2 km from the N20 Paris-Orléans.

🚗 N20 Paris-Orléans, exit Monnerville. Follow the signs 'Camping Bois de la Justice'.

CC € **19** 1/3-15/6 10/9-30/10

N 48°19'56'' E 2°2'49''

Paris, F-75016 / Ile-de-France (Paris)

🔺 Camping de Paris****
📧 2 allée du Bord de l'Eau
☎ +33 (0)1-45243000
📠 +33 (0)1-42244295
🔒 1/1 - 31/12
@ paris@camping-indigo.com

1823

7ha 313T(80-100m²) 10A CEE

1 ACD**G**IJKLM**P**ST
2 BCFGTVXY
3 ABKRU
4 (Q+S 🔒)
  (T+U+V+X+Z 1/4-11/11)
5 **AB**DEFGIJKLMNPUWXY
6 CFGIJ(N 3,5km)OTV

💬 Campsite is located in Bois de Boulogne, a beautiful natural park on the Seine. Ideally situated for discovering Paris or the lovely countryside around it. The pitches are spacious and marked-out and there are many old trees which supply sufficient shade.

🚗 Périphérique Sud exit Porte Maillot. Follow the signs to the campsite and Bagatelle.

CC € **19** 7/1-6/4 21/5-14/6 2/9-22/12

N 48°52'6'' E 2°14'5''

Pommeuse, F-77515 / Ile-de-France (Seine-et-Marne)

🔺 Iris Parc Le Chêne Gris****
📧 24 place de la Gare
  de Faremoutiers
☎ +33 (0)1-64042180
🔒 30/3 - 28/10
@ info@lechenegris.com

1824

7ha 47T(75-120m²) 6A CEE

1 ACD**G**IJKLPQ
2 FGIJRTUVWXY
3 BC**F**RU
4 (C 🔒) (E 1/4-1/11)
  (H+Q+S+T+U+V+X+Y+Z 🔒)
5 **AB**DEFGIJKLNPUWX
6 BCFGH**IJ**(N 2km)TV

💬 The campsite is terraced with marked out pitches surrounded by old trees. Modern toilet facilities, restaurant, shop and swimming pool. Something for young families.

🚗 A4 exit 13 Serris. D231 direction Provins; left to Faremoutiers 3 km beyond roundabout with obelisk. Opposite Pommeuse/Faremoutiers station.

CC € **19** 30/3-6/7 2/9-27/10

N 48°48'30'' E 2°59'36''

Rambouillet, F-78120 / Ile-de-France (Paris)

▲ Huttopia Rambouillet***
✉ route du Château d'Eau
☎ +33 (0)1-30410734
📠 +33 (0)1-30410017
⌚ 30/3 - 4/11
@ rambouillet@huttopia.com

4,7ha 149T(100-200m²)

1 ABCD**F**IJKLNPST
2 BDLRTUVXY
3 ABGHJKR**W**
4 (A 1/7-31/8) (B 15/6-30/9)
(Q+S ⌚) (T+U 3/4-30/9)
(V+W 1/7-31/8) (Z ⌚)
5 **AB**DEFGIJKLMNOPQRTWX
6 ACDEG**I**(N 3km)TV

💬 In the middle of woods on the banks of the Etang d'Or, this is a campsite with excellent facilities: café-restaurant, natural swimming pool, etc. Ideal for a family holiday in natural surroundings a few kilometres from Paris.

🚗 When approaching from the north, take the N10 and then Rambouillet (les Eveuses). Follow the sign 'Laboratoires Garnier'. Pass under the N10 and follow the camping signs.

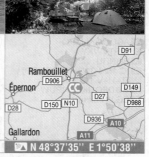

CC € ⑰ 30/3-29/6 2/9-3/11 — 📍 N 48°37'35'' E 1°50'38''

Varreddes, F-77910 / Ile-de-France (Seine-et-Marne)

▲ Le Village Parisien Varreddes****
✉ rue des Otages
☎ +33 (0)2-51204194
📠 +33 (0)1-60228984
⌚ 7/4 - 4/11
@ contact@camp-atlantique.com

7ha 52T(50-70m²) 10-16A CEE

1 ACDFIJKL**P**RS
2 CFGLRVWXY
3 ABGHJKMNQRU**W**
4 (B 29/4-24/9) (F+H ⌚)
(Q 7/4-24/9) (R 1/5-15/9)
(T 7/4-24/9) (U 1/5-24/9)
(V 7/4-24/9) (X 15/4-24/9)
(Z 7/4-24/9)
5 **AB**DEFGIJKLMNPUWZ
6 AEGH**K**(N 0,5km)TV

💬 Large level terrain with plenty of sports and recreational opportunities. Ideal starting point for trips to Paris, Disneyland and Parc Asterix. Bus stop next to campsite entrance.

🚗 From Meaux D405 direction Villers-Coterêts. After about 7 km route D97, then D121 direction Congis.

CC € ⑰ 7/4-7/7 1/9-3/11 — 📍 N 49°0'10'' E 2°56'29''

Veneux-les-Sablons, F-77250 / Ile-de-France (Seine-et-Marne)

▲ Les Courtilles du Lido***
✉ chemin du Passeur
☎ +33 (0)1-60704605
📠 +33 (0)1-64706265
⌚ 20/3 - 24/9
@ lescourtilles-dulido@wanadoo.fr

5ha 161T(100-300m²) 10A CEE

1 ACD**G**IJKLMPQ
2 CRTVXY
3 B**F**G**MQ**RW
4 (C 1/5-20/9)
(Q+R+V+Z 20/3-20/9)
5 **AB**FGJKNPUWZ
6 CEGK(N 1km)TV

💬 This is the place to relax. Heated swimming pool, tennis, minigolf. Paris and Fontainebleau within easy reach by train or car. Free internet on the entire campsite. Climbing opportunities in the vicinity.

🚗 From Fontainebleau N6 towards Sens. Exit Veneux-les-Sablons. Left at traffic lights after bridge and follow camping signs.

CC € ⑲ 20/3-1/7 31/8-23/9 — 📍 N 48°22'59'' E 2°48'6''

Versailles, F-78000 / Ile-de-France (Paris)

♿ 🛜 **iD** (1828)

🏕 Huttopia Versailles***
📧 31 rue Berthelot
☎ +33 (0)1-39512361
📅 30/3 - 4/11
@ versailles@huttopia.com

4ha 126**T**(70-130m²) 10A CEE

1 ACD**F**HIJKLM**P**ST
2 BFGIRSVXY
3 B**F**GHJKRU
4 (C+H 30/4-20/9) (Q 🔲)
    (T+U+V+X+Z 15/4-15/10)
5 **AB**DEFGIJKLMNOPRUWZ
6 BCEGIJ(N 0,2km)TV

💬 Huttopia Versailles is a natural campsite close to Paris, just a five minute drive from the Palace of Versailles. The campsite offers very good amenities: an attractive café-restaurant, heated swimming pool, comfortable toilet facilities. The nearby RER-C station offers easy access to central Paris.

🚗 From Paris: A13 direction Rouen, exit Versailles Centre, then 'Camping'. From A86: N12, then exit Porchefontaine, follow 'Camping'.

CC € (19) 30/3-23/6 2/9-3/11

🏔 N 48°47'39'' E 2°9'40''

Andelot-Blancheville, F-52700 / Champagne-Ardennes (Haute-Marne)

♿ 🛜 **iD** (1829)

🏕 Le Moulin***
📧 5 rue du Moulin
☎ +33 (0)3-25306948
📅 7/2 - 28/10
@ info@lemoulin-andelot.com

2,6ha 57**T**(80m²) 10A

1 ACDGIJKLMPQ
2 CRTVWXY
3 AGHJ**QRW**
4 (D 1/5-15/9)
    (Q+T+U+V+Y+Z 🔲)
5 **AB**CGIJKLMNPUZ
6 ACEGJ(N 1km)TV

💬 A peaceful, small campsite by a river with large pitches and a service point for motorhomes. It has a heated swimming pool that can be covered, an 18 hole minigolf course, free wifi and delicious food in the restaurant/pizzeria. Walking, cycling and fishing in the area. The site is Dutch managed.

🚌 Andelot is located on the D674 Neufchâteau-Chaumont. Campsite clearly signposted in the centre of Andelot. Campsite just 500m from the main Route Nationale.

CC € (15) 7/2-30/6 1/9-27/10

🏔 N 48°15'8'' E 5°17'56''

Arrigny, F-51290 / Champagne-Ardennes (Marne)

🛜 **iD** (1830)

🏕 De la Forêt
📧 Presqu'île de Larzicourt
☎ +33 (0)3-26726317
📅 1/4 - 30/9
@ laforet51@wanadoo.fr

4ha 99**T**(80-130m²) 6-16A CEE

1 ACD**G**IJLMPQ
2 ABDJLRTVWXY
3 BGHJRU**W**Z
4 (C+H 1/5-15/9) (Q 1/5-30/9)
    (T+V+X+Z 5/7-25/8)
5 **AB**FGJKLMNOPUWXYZ
6 ACEKOUV

💬 A wooded campsite 100m from Lac-du-Der-Chantecoq. Ideal for families with children. Plenty of nature and water sports opportunities and cycling. A paradise for ornithologists. Heated swimming pool.

🚗 From Vitry-le-François follow 'Lac du Der'. Signposted on the D13. On north side of lake and ± 2 km south of Arrigny. From Châlons-en-Champagne follow N4 direction St. Dizier. Turn south halfway towards Orconte, Larzicourt, Arrigny. Then follow signs.

CC € (15) 1/4-6/7 24/8-29/9

🏔 N 48°36'14'' E 4°42'55''

Bannes, F-52360 / Champagne-Ardennes (Haute-Marne) 📶 iD 1831

🏕 Hautoreille
📧 6 rue Boutonnier
☎ +33 (0)3-25848340
🕐 8/1 - 25/11
@ campinghautoreille@orange.fr

3,5ha 100T(100-150m²) 10A CEE

1 ACDGIJKLMPQ
2 RTVWXY
3 BGKR
4 (Q 1/3-25/11) (R+U 🖾)
   (X 2/5-21/10) (Z 1/5-30/9)
5 ADFGIJKLMNPUWZ
6 ACDEGK(N 6km)T

💬 Shaded site in the countryside, quiet location 7 km from Langres and close to lakes (3 km). Heated toilet facilities. Restaurant open from April (only weekends) to mid-October. Charming terrace, take-away meals. Ideal for stopovers or for a longer stay.

🚗 From south (A31: exit 7), via N19 10 km dir. Langres. Turn left at traffic lights before Langres, dir. Neufchâteau. Via D74 to Bannes. From the north (A31: exit 8), via D74. Dir. Langres. 15 km. Signposted.

Map: Rolampont, D1, D74, D35, D14, D3, D120, Langres, A31, D974, D619, D428, Chalindrey

CC €**17** 16/3-8/7 27/8-31/10 📷 N 47°53'42'' E 5°23'41''

Bourbonne-les-Bains, F-52400 / Champagne-Ardennes (Haute-Marne) 📶 iD 1832

🏕 Montmorency***
📧 rue du Stade / BP 7
☎ +33 (0)3-25900864
FAX +33 (0)9-71701367
🕐 24/3 - 4/11
@ camping.montmorency@sfr.fr

4ha 74T(85-150m²) 6-10A CEE

1 ACDGIJKLMPQ
2 IKRTUVWXY
3 AGHJRU
4 (Q+R+T+X+Z 🖾)
5 ABGIJKLNPUWZ
6 CDEGJ(N 0,8km)ORTV

💬 Homely atmosphere, warm and friendly, for a quiet and relaxing stay in green surroundings. Wonderful walks and cycling tours through the Haut Marnaise forest. This spa resort is called la Petite Provence de l'Est and is situated in Bourbonne les Bains. Montmorency *** campsite offers classic surroundings at the foot of the Vosges mountains.

🚗 From the centre of Bourbonne-les-Bains follow the (information)signs Montmorency. Then follow the camping signs.

Map: A31, D429, D460 A, D14, D417, Villars-Saint-Marcellin, D460, D5, Melay, D3

CC €**17** 24/3-30/6 1/9-3/11 7=6, 14=12 📷 N 47°57'26'' E 5°44'25''

Buzancy, F-08240 / Champagne-Ardennes (Ardennes) ♿ 📶 iD 1833

🏕 Flower Camping La Samaritaine***
📧 3 rue des Étangs
☎ +33 (0)3-24300888
🕐 13/4 - 14/9
@ contact@ camping-lasamaritaine.fr

2,5ha 106T(80-100m²) 10A CEE

1 ACDGIJKLMOPQ
2 ACDLMRTUVWXY
3 ABGHJRUWZ
4 (Q+R 🖾) (T 1/7-31/8)
5 ABFGIJKLMNOPQRUWXYZ
6 CDEGK(N 1,5km)TV

💬 A friendly and well maintained family campsite in the south of the French Ardennes. Enjoy peace and nature with every comfort. Free wifi.

🚗 D947 to Buzancy. Campsite is signposted. The end of the access road is not in a very good state.

Map: Le Chesné, Buzancy, D947, D6, D15, D946, D12, Grandpré, D998

CC €**15** 13/4-6/7 25/8-13/9 📷 N 49°25'35'' E 4°56'24''

Châlons-en-Champagne, F-51000 / Champagne-Ardennes (Marne)

♿ 🛜 iD (1834)

🏕 Camping de Châlons-en-Champagne****
✉ rue Plaisance
☎ +33 (0)3-26683800
⌚ 5/3 - 4/11
@ camping.chalons@orange.fr

7,5ha 138T(100-120m²) 10A

1 ACD**G**IJKLM**P**Q
2 DFGLRUVWXY
3 BGJKMNQRUW
4 (Q 🅿)
　(R+T+U+X+Z 15/4-15/10)
5 **AB**DEFGIJKLOPUWXYZ
6 ACDEGJ**K**(N 0,2km)UV

💬 Level, peaceful city campsite with pitches marked out by hedges. Ideal for city visits (cycling distance), and visits to the Champagne region. Older but clean toilet facilities. Also suitable as stopover campsite. Disabled parking and pitches must be reserved.

🚗 A26, exit 18. When entering the town keep to the right. The campsite is signposted. From the A4, exit 27 to the N44. In Châlons on the ring road exit St. Memmie. Follow the camping signs 'camping Municipal'.

CC € 15 5/3-7/7 25/8-3/11

📷 N 48°56'9'' E 4°22'59''

Dienville, F-10500 / Champagne-Ardennes (Aube)

♿ 🛜 iD (1835)

🏕 Du Tertre***
✉ rue Fontaine du Mont (rotonde)
☎ 📠 +33 (0)3-25922650
⌚ 22/3 - 8/10
@ campingdutertre@wanadoo.fr

3,5ha 102T(100-120m²) 10A

1 ACD**G**IJKLMOPQ
2 ADRUVX
3 BGHJNRU**WZ**
4 (C+H 20/5-15/9) (Q+R 🅿)
　(T+U+Y 1/7-31/8) (Z 🅿)
5 **A**GIJKLMNOPUWXYZ
6 ACEGJ(N 0,2km)OTUV

💬 A lovely level site with sections separated by hedges and bushes and with its own swimming pool, restaurant and snack bar. This and the proximity of the sport harbour and village make it an ideal family campsite.

🚗 From Troyes take the D960 as far as Piney. Then take the D11 from Piney to Dienville. From Brienne-le-Chateau take the D443 direction Vendeuvre-sur-Barse as far as Dienville. Located opposite 'Port Dienville'.

CC € 15 22/3-6/7 27/8-7/10

📷 N 48°20'56'' E 4°31'39''

Flagey, F-52250 / Champagne-Ardennes (Haute-Marne)

♿ 🛜 iD (1836)

🏕 Ferme de la Croisée
✉ 3 route de Auberive
☎ +33 (0)3-25880126
⌚ 1/1 - 31/12
@ yannick.durenne52@orange.fr

5ha 106T(90-130m²) 10A CEE

1 ACD**G**IJKLMPRS
2 FRUVWX
3 ADG
4 (Q 🅿) (T+X+Z 15/5-15/9)
5 GIJKLMNOPUZ
6 ACDEGK(N 8km)T

💬 Located close to the motorway exit but still quiet and in the countryside.

🚗 A31 exit 6 direction Langres via D428. Campsite on your left after 1 km.

CC € 15 1/4-30/6 1/9-31/10

📷 N 47°47'43'' E 5°13'58''

Géraudot-Plage, F-10220 / Champagne-Ardennes (Aube)

♛ ♿ 📶 **iD** (1837)

🔺 Les Rives du Lac/L'Epine
aux Moines**
🏠 rue de Fort St. Georges, RD43
☎ +33 (0)3-25412436
🔓 2/1 - 23/12
@ camping.lepineauxmoines@
orange.fr

3,5ha 156T(80-150m²) 10A

1 ACD**G**IJKLMOPQ
2 ADLMRTUVWXY
3 BF**G**HJK**MQR**W**Z**
4 (Q 1/3-31/10) (R 🔓)
   (T+U+V+X+Z 1/5-30/9)
5 **AB**DGIJKLNPUVZ
6 ACDEG**K**L(N 7km)OU

💬 Convivial family campsite with pitches more
or less separated by the trees. Good toilet facilities.
Separate section for teenagers. Close to a lovely
(patrolled) beach, also suitable for small children.
Cycling possible close by.

🚗 From Troyes D960 direction Piney. In or before
Piney exit towards Geraudot. From the RN19 Troyes
- Bar-sur-Aube direction north, take the D619 in
Lusigny or the D79/D43 in Vendeuvre to Geraudot.
Located on the north side of Lac d'Orient.

Piney — D960 — D11 — D43 — CC — D79 — Lusigny-sur-Barse — D443 — D619 — N19

CC € **15** 2/1-5/7 23/8-22/12

📍 N 48°18'10'' E 4°20'15''

Les Mazures, F-08500 / Champagne-Ardennes (Ardennes)

♿ 📶 **iD** (1838)

🔺 Du Lac des Vieilles Forges***
☎ +33 (0)3-24401731
📠 +33 (0)3-24408035
🔓 7/4 - 16/9
@ campinglesvieillesforges@
homair.com

12ha 200T(80-100m²) 10A CEE

1 AC**F**IJKLMOPQ
2 ABDIJTUVXY
3 BGHMNR**U**W**Z**
4 (Q+T 🔓)
5 **AB**GJLNPU
6 CFGHJ**K**(N 7km)RV

💬 A terraced campsite located in a wood and by
a reservoir where you can go swimming, surfing,
sailing and fishing. Spacious marked out pitches on
paved surfaces.

🚗 Lac des Vieilles Forges is signposted on the D40
from Renwez to Les Mazures/Revin.

N964 — Revin — D877 — D988 — D1 — N51 — CC — Bogny-sur-Meuse — D8043 — D985 — N43 — Nouzonville — D978 — D2 — D989

CC € **13** 7/4-7/7 2/9-15/9

📍 N 49°52'21'' E 4°36'18''

Matton-et-Clemency, F-08110 / Champagne-Ardennes (Ardennes)

♿ 📶 ✿ **iD** (1839)

🔺 Résidence du Banel***
🏠 11 rte du Banel
☎ +33 (0)3-24271589
📠 +33 (0)3-24265561
🔓 20/3 - 31/10
@ residence-du-banel-sarl@
wanadoo.fr

13ha 32T(< 200m²) 16A CEE

1 ACDGIJKLMOPQ
2 BCRTVWXY
3 BHIJLR
4 **KLN**(Q 🔓)
   (T+U+X+Y+Z 15/6-15/9)
5 **AB**GIJKLMNOPSTUXYZ
6 CEG**K**(N 5km)T

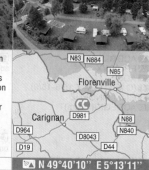

💬 Small, green and dog-friendly campsite. Hidden
away at the edge of the woods. Separate field for
tourists with large pitches and private toilet facilities
in a wooden cabin. Tasteful restaurant (in low season
only open at weekends, 15/6 to 15/9 open every
day except Tuesday). Sights nearby. Countryside for
walking and cycling. If reception is closed please
choose your own pitch.

🚗 From Florenville direction Carignan, after Les
Deux-Villes follow campsite signs.

N83 N884 — N85 — Florenville — CC — N88 — Carignan — D981 — N840 — D964 — D8043 — D19 — D44

CC € **17** 20/3-30/3 3/4-26/4 2/5-8/5 14/5-18/5 22/5-6/7 25/8-30/10

📍 N 49°40'10'' E 5°13'11''

Mesnil-St-Père, F-10140 / Champagne-Ardennes (Aube)

♿ 📶 **iD** 1840

⛺ Camping Le Lac D'Orient
✉ 17 route du Lac
☎ +33 (0)3-25406185
FAX +33 (0)3-25709687
🕐 7/4 - 22/9
@ info@camping-lacdorient.com

4ha 160T(80-160m²) 10A CEE

1 ACD**G**IJKLMOPQ
2 ADL**R**TUVWX**Y**
3 BHJNRU**WZ**
4 (C 12/5-16/9) (F 🔒)
(H 12/5-16/9) J(Q 🔒)
(R 1/5-15/9)
(U+V+X+Z 28/4-16/9)
5 **AB**DEFGIJKLMNOPUWXYZ
6 ACDEGIJ**K**(N 8km)TUV

💬 Large, beautiful campsite on even grounds with parts marked out with hedges and bushes. Restaurant and indoor and outdoor pools. Close to a beautiful beach and little marina. Options and facilities for water freaks, outdoor enthusiasts, anglers and nature lovers.

🚗 From the D619 Troyes - Bar-sur-Aube, D43 direction North (between La Villeneuve-au-Chêne and Lusigny-sur-Barce) to Mesnil-St-Père. Located on the south side of the Lac d'Orient, on the D43.

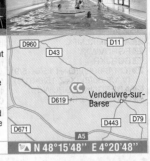

CC € **17** 7/4-5/7 23/8-21/9 7=6

🧭 N 48°15'48'' E 4°20'48''

Montigny-le-Roi, F-52140 / Champagne-Ardennes (Haute-Marne)

♿ 📶 **iD** 1841

⛺ Du Chateau***
✉ rue Hubert Collot
☎ FAX +33 (0)3-25873893
🕐 15/4 - 30/9
@ camping@
communevaldemeuse.fr

6ha 75T(90-110m²) 6-10A CEE

1 ACDGIJKLMPQ
2 FIJK**R**TVWX**Y**
3 BGHMR
4 (Q 15/6-15/9) (R 🔒)
(T 15/5-30/9)
5 GIJKLMNPUW
6 CDEGK(N 0,1km)T

💬 This lovely well maintained campsite is an ideal stopover location on your way south and invites you to stay longer. Close to the motorway but still very quiet. Pitches are spacious and marked out, some with extensive panoramas. The village is close by within walking distance.

🚗 From the A31 exit 8, Montigny-le-Roi, direction centre. From there on, campsite is clearly signposted.

CC € **17** 15/4-30/6 20/8-29/9

🧭 N 48°0'3'' E 5°29'47''

Peigney, F-52200 / Champagne-Ardennes (Haute-Marne)

♿ 📶 ❄ **iD** 1842

⛺ Le Lac de la Liez*****
✉ rue des Voiliers
☎ +33 (0)3-25902779
FAX +33 (0)3-25906679
🕐 31/3 - 30/9
@ contact@camping-liez.fr

6ha 157T(90-140m²) 10A CEE

1 ACD**G**IJKLMPQ
2 ADIJKLM**R**UVWX**Y**
3 BGHJ**KMN**P**R**U**WZ**
4 (B 15/6-15/9) (F+G 🔒) JK**N**
(Q+S 🔒)
(U+V+Y+Z 15/4-25/9)
5 **AB**DEFGIJKLMNOP**S**UWXY
Z
6 CDEGI**JK**(N 4km)TV

💬 These terraced grounds overlooking a lake are ideally located between Champagne and Burgundy. Direct access from the campsite to the sandy beach for swimming, sailing and pedalos. Indoor water complex with swimming pool, sauna, spa and waterslide. Bar, restaurant and tennis court. New toilet block with large comfort cabin.

🚗 From Langres N19 direction Vesoul. Or D74 direction Montigny. Follow camping signs.

CC € **19** 31/3-8/7 27/8-29/9

🧭 N 47°52'19'' E 5°22'50''

Pont-Ste-Marie/Troyes, F-10150 / Champagne-Ardennes (Aube)

♿ 📶 **iD** (1843)

🔺 Municipal de Troyes***
📧 7 rue Roger Salengro (N77)
☎ 📠 +33 (0)3-25810264
📅 1/4 - 17/10
@ info@troyescamping.net

4ha 150T(80-150m²) 10A CEE

1 ACD**G**IJKLMPQ
2 FGRUVWXY
3 BCGJKR
4 (C 1/6-30/9) (Q+R 15/6-15/9)
(V 1/5-30/8) (X+Z 15/6-31/8)
5 **AB**EFGIJKLNOPUWZ
6 CDEGJ(N 0,1km)UV

💬 Atmospheric municipal campsite with many trees and squirrels. About 2 km of walking/cycling to the medieval centre or you can take bus 1. Suitable as stopover campsite or for a longer stay. Heated pool from 15 May. Cycling routes in the area, mostly level. 1001 half-timbered houses, museums, churches etc. Check-out before 15.00 h.

🚗 A26, exit Troyes/Pont-Ste-Marie. Then follow signs Municipal. Other approach roads direction Pont-Ste-Marie. Follow the signs in the town.

D442 | D78 | D677
D619 | | D960
| | A26
D660 | **Troyes** | D619
Saint-André-les-Vergers
N77 | A5

CC € ⑲ 1/4-24/6 1/9-16/10

🗺 N 48°18'40'' E 4°5'50''

Saints-Geosmes/Langres, F-52200 / Champagne-Ardennes (Haute-Marne)

♿ 📶 **iD** (1844)

🔺 La Croix d'Arles***
📧 route de Dijon
☎ +33 (0)3-25882402
📅 15/3 - 31/10
@ croix.arles@yahoo.fr

7ha 100T(85-100m²) 10A CEE

1 ACDGIJKLMPQ
2 BFRTVWXY
3 BGHJR
4 (B+G 15/5-15/9) **N**(Q+R 📅)
(U+X 31/3-15/10) (Z 📅)
5 **AB**DFGIJKLMNOPU
6 ACEGJ(N 3km)OT

💬 A busy stopover site with a friendly restaurant and swimming pool. The old fortified town of Langres is close by. You can cycle to Langres via the 'Voie Verte' (7 km). There are quiet pitches at the back of the campsite among the trees which are recommended for longer stays.

🚗 A31 exit 6 Langres-Sud. Dir. Langres via D428, then to Dijon via D974. After 2 km the campsite is clearly signposted on your right.

D3 | D74
| **Langres**
Saints-Geosmes | D619
D428 | | **Chalindrey**
A31 | D6
D974
D67
N74

CC € ⑮ 15/3-30/6 31/8-30/10

🗺 N 47°48'47'' E 5°19'16''

St. Hilaire-sous-Romilly, F-10100 / Champagne-Ardennes (Aube)

♿ 📶 ✿ **iD** (1845)

🔺 La Noue des Rois****
☎ +33 (0)3-25244160
📠 +33 (0)3-25243418
📅 1/1 - 31/12
@ contact@lanouedesrois.com

30ha 70T(120-200m²) 16A

1 AC**F**IJKLM**P**Q
2 DLMRUVX
3 ABGHJMNQRU**W**
4 (C+E 15/5-15/9) (H 1/5-30/9)
J(Q 1/5-30/9) (R 📅)
(T 1/6-8/9) (Z 16/1-15/12)
5 **AB**DGIJKLMNPRUVXY
6 CDEGJ(N 1km)TV

💬 Relaxation by a lake in very natural surroundings (30 hectares). Indoor and outdoor swimming pool heated by solar panels and with slide; minigolf, everything included in the price.

🚗 Follow D619 Troyes - Romilly-sur-Seine. Follow St. Hilaire-sous-Romilly. Site is clearly signposted. Or Paris dir. Provins. Then dir. Nogent-sur-Seine. Then dir. St. Hilaire-sous-Romilly and follow signs.

D60 | D373
D76 | D5
D951 | D48 | D50 | D52
CC **Romilly-sur-Seine**
D442 | D440 | D619
D374 | D54 | D33

CC € ⑰ 1/1-1/7 31/8-31/12

🗺 N 48°31'32'' E 3°39'53''

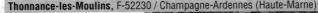

Thonnance-les-Moulins, F-52230 / Champagne-Ardennes (Haute-Marne) ♿ 🛜 ✿ iD (1846)

🏕 La Forge de Ste Marie*****
🛣 D427
☎ +33 (0)3-25944200
📠 +33 (0)3-25944143
🗓 21/4 - 7/9
@ info@laforgedesaintemarie.com

11ha 144T(100-200m²) 6-10A CEE

1 ACD**G**IJKLMPQ
2 BCJLRUVWXY
3 BDGHJKN**P**RU**W**
4 (A+F+H 🗓) K
   (Q+R+T+U+V+Y+Z 🗓)
5 **AB**DEFGIJKLMNPRUWXYZ
6 ACEG**K**(N 5km)OTV

💬 This luxurious five star campsite is located in wooded surroundings in the heart of the Champagne region. Lovely and peaceful. Enjoy the new jacuzzi and the heated indoor pool with outside its terrace. All facilities open during the opening period. Spacious pitches, trout fishing, 100% wifi coverage.

🚗 From Joinville via the D60 to Thonnance-les-Joinville (2 km), then via the D427 through Poissons and Noncourt in the direction of Thonnance-les-Moulins (10 km).

CC € **17** 21/4-7/7 26/8-6/9 7=6, 14=12   N 48°24'23'' E 5°16'16''

Map references: D960, D335, D32, Joinville, D60, D16, N67, D427, CC, D25, D67 A, Doulaincourt-Saucourt

---

Villegusien-le-Lac, F-52190 / Champagne-Ardennes (Haute-Marne) ♿ 🛜 iD (1847)

🏕 Camping du Lac***
🛣 rue le Bocage
☎ +33 (0)3-25884524
🗓 15/3 - 15/10
@ campingdulacdevillegusien@
   gmail.com

NEW

2ha 80T(100m²) 16A CEE

1 ACDFIJLMPQ
2 DILRTVWXY
3 BGHJMRU**W**
4 (B 15/6-30/9) (Q 🗓)
   (R 15/6-30/9)
   (T+U+V+X+Z 🗓)
5 **AB**FGIJKLMNPUVWXYZ
6 CEGK(N 3km)TV

💬 Mainly used as a stopover site but one which invites you to stay longer, with market out pitches and excellent toilet facilities. Swim in the small pool or in the lake next to the campsite with a lovely beach 1 km away.

🚗 From the A31 exit 5 when approaching from the south and exit 6 or 7 when approaching from the north, the campsite can be reached via the RN74 Dijon-Langres. Clearly signposted.

CC € **15** 15/3-30/6 1/9-14/10   N 47°44'24'' E 5°18'23''

Map references: Chalindrey, D428, D6, A31, CC, D974, D67, D7, Prauthoy, Vaux-sous-Aubigny

---

Baerenthal, F-57230 / Lorraine (Moselle) ♿ 🛜 iD (1848)

🏕 Ramstein Plage***
☎ +33 (0)3-87065073
🗓 1/4 - 30/9
@ camping.ramstein@wanadoo.fr

12ha 100T(100m²) 6-16A CEE

1 ACD**G**IJKLMPQ
2 ADLRTVX
3 BGHJMNU**W**Z
4 (A+C 1/7-31/8)
   (T+U+V+X+Y 🗓)
5 **AB**DFGIJKLNPUX
6 ACEGHK(N 0,4km)TV

💬 The campsite has an idyllic location next to a small lake which is suitable for swimming. The surrounding area is heavily wooded and has been designated by UNESCO as a site of ecological world importance.

🚗 From Sarreguemines take the D662 direction Haguenau. At Phillipsbourg turn right onto D36 to Baerenthal. Follow signs.

CC € **17** 1/4-30/6 1/9-29/9   N 48°58'53'' E 7°30'53''

Map references: Bitche, D35, D3, D37, D662, D36, Niederbronn-les-Bains, Reichshofen, D12, CC, D919, D1062, D28

Bulgnéville, F-88140 / Lorraine (Vosges) ♨ 🤚 📶 iD (1849)

🔺 Porte des Vosges***
🏭 ZA la Grande Tranchée
☎ +33 (0)3-29091200
🗓 30/3 - 1/11
@ contact@
 camping-portedesvosges.com

3,5ha 100**T**(85m²) 10A CEE

1 ACDGIJLMPQ
2 FITWXY
3 AGHNR
4 (C 15/5-15/9) (Q+T+U+Z 🔑)
5 DFGIJKLMNPUWX
6 CEGJ(N 0,8km)TV

💬 Well-maintained stopover campsite, located near the motorway exit. Restaurants and shops at walking distance. Heated pool. Snackbar also open in both low seasons. The well-known spa resorts Contrexéville and Vittel are only a few minutes drive away.

🚗 A31 exit 9, through Bulgnéville via D164 dir. Contrexéville. Follow campsite signs.

La Neuveville-sous-Châtenois
D14 D13
D5 A31 CC
D17
Contrexéville
D1 D429 D164
D2

(CC) € **17** 30/3-6/7 1/9-31/10   📐 N 48°11'57'' E 5°50'41''

Burtoncourt, F-57220 / Lorraine (Moselle) ♨ 🤚 📶 iD (1850)

🔺 La Croix du Bois Sacker**
🏭 D53a
☎ +33 (0)3-87357408
🗓 1/4 - 8/10
@ camping.croixsacker@
 wanadoo.fr

11ha 49**T**(80-120m²) 6A

1 ACG IJKLMP RS
2 ABDLMRVWX
3 AGHJNRUWZ
4 (Q 1/6-31/8) (R+Z 🔑)
5 A GJMNPUVXYZ
6 ABEGJ(N 8km)ORTV

💬 Not too big a site surrounded by woods on a natural lake where you can fish and swim. Opportunities for sports and games and for walking and cycling in the area. Sunny terrace. The lovely Metz is only 25 minutes away by car. Arrival no later than 8 pm.

🚗 A4 (north of Metz) direction Strasbourg, exit 37. D38 Malroy-Chieulles-Vany. Then take the D3 towards Bouzonville. After ± 13 km direction Burtoncourt. Follow camping signs.

D8 D918 Bouzonville
D19 D23
CC Boulay- D954
D3 Moselle
D25
A4

(CC) € **17** 1/4-30/6 18/8-30/9   📐 N 49°13'25'' E 6°23'59''

Bussang, F-88540 / Lorraine (Vosges) ⛷ 🤚 📶 iD (1851)

🔺 Le Domaine de Champé*****
🏭 14 rue des Champs-Navets
☎ +33 (0)3-29616151
📠 +33 (0)3-29615690
🗓 1/1 - 31/12
@ info@domaine-de-champe.com

5,5ha 110**T**(90-110m²) 10A CEE

1 ACD**F**IJKLMOPQ
2 CGLRVWXY
3 ABCDGHIJKLMNRUV**W**
4 (A 1/7-31/8) (C 1/5-30/9)
 (**F** 🔑) (H 1/5-30/9) IJ**KLMN**
 OP(Q+T 1/6-30/9) (U 🔑)
 (V 1/6-30/9) (Y+Z 🔑)
5 **AB**CDFGHIJKLNPQRUWXY
 Z
6 ACDEGH**K**(N 0,5km)OTVW

💬 A well-maintained, sportive campsite, partly divided by hedges. Very relaxed ambiance.
The 3.5 km long Old Moselle river flows through the campsite. Paragliding takes place on the hill above the campsite and you can take your maiden flight here.

🚗 The campsite is signposted in Bussang from the RN66. At the church follow the camping signs.

Cornimont
D43 D430
D13 BI
D13 BIS
Le Thillot N66
CC
Fresse-sur-
D486 Moselle
D465 D466

(CC) € **17** 1/4-5/7 23/8-20/11 7=6, 14=12   📐 N 47°53'20'' E 6°51'27''

Celles-sur-Plaine, F-88110 / Lorraine (Vosges)

♿ 🛜 🆔 **1852**

🏕 Camping des Lacs***
✉ 6 Place de la Gare
☎ +33 (0)3-29412800
📅 1/4 - 30/9
@ camping@paysdeslacs.com

3ha 123T(75-140m²) 10A

1 ACD**G**IJKLMPRS
2 ACDLRTVX
3 ABGHJMN**Q**RU**W**XZ
4 (B+H 1/6-15/9)
(Q+R 1/7-31/8)
(T+U+X+Z 1/6-31/8)
5 **AB**DEFGIJKLNPQUY
6 EG**K**(N 0,1km)TV

💬 A lovely campsite with many activities for young and old. New heated toilet facilities, heated outdoor swimming pool. Wifi on the site. All watersports activities are a ten minute walk from the campsite.

🚗 From Nancy, first the N4, then the N59. In Raon-l'Étape follow 'Lacs de Pierre Percée'. In Celles-sur-Plaine, the campsite is signposted.

Raon-l'Étape
Moyenmoutier

D20
D935 D992 D392
D392 A
D424

CC €**17** 1/4-6/7 1/9-29/9 7=6, 14=12

🧭 N 48°27'18'' E 6°56'52''

Charmes, F-88130 / Lorraine (Vosges)

♿ 🛜 🆔 **1853**

🏕 Les Îles***
✉ 20 rue de l'Écluse
☎ +33 (0)3-29388771
📅 1/4 - 30/9
@ violettefleurs@gmail.com

3,5ha 67T(100-200m²) 10A CEE

1 AGIJKLPQ
2 CFRSX
3 AGHKN**Q**RU**W**X
4 (Q+R+T+U 🖾)
5 **A**GIJKLMNOPUZ
6 CEGH**K**(N 1km)OT

💬 Simple, quiet campsite situated between a tributary of the Moselle and the l'Est canal. Medium-sized trees on the corners of the pitches.

🚗 From Nancy take N57 direction Epinal.
At Charmes take exit Charmes/Mirecourt (D55) and follow the camping signs in the village.

D112 D22
N57
D913 D904 D570
D9
CC
D55
Châtel-sur-Moselle
Mirecourt D10
D12

CC €**13** 1/4-6/7 25/8-29/9 7=6, 14=12

🧭 N 48°22'37'' E 6°17'23''

Corcieux, F-88430 / Lorraine (Vosges)

🛜 🆔 **1854**

🏕 Camping au Mica**
✉ 8 route du plafond
☎ +33 (0)3-29507007
📅 28/4 - 15/9
@ info@campingaumica.com

NEW

1,5ha 62T(80-150m²) 6-10A CEE

1 AC**G**IJLP**Q**
2 ACRVX
3 ABHIJU
4 (**A** 6/7-26/8)
(C+**H** 20/5-15/9)
(Q+R+T+Z 🖾)
5 **AB**FGJKLMNOPQRUW
6 AEGJ(N 1km)ORT

💬 A peaceful family campsite with a lovely swimming pool and a small beach by a shallow babbling brook.

🚗 From St. Dié take the N415 direction Gérardmer/Colmar. In Anould turn right direction Gérardmer. 3 km further on turn right direction Corcieux. Located just before the village, on the left of the road.

D420 Taintrux D23
D60 D415
D423 D8
Le Tholy
D417 Gérardmer

CC €**15** 28/4-30/6 31/8-14/9

🧭 N 48°9'57'' E 6°53'38''

Corcieux, F-88430 / Lorraine (Vosges)

 ♿ 🛜 ✿ **iD** (1855)

🔼 Sites & Paysages Au Clos de la Chaume***
🏠 21 rue d'Alsace
☎ +33 (0)3-29507676
⌚ 21/4 - 20/9
@ info@ camping-closdelachaume.com

5ha 100T(80-150m²) 6-10A

1 ACD**G**IJKLMPQ
2 CLRTVXY
3 BGHJNRU**W**
4 (**A** 1/7-31/8) (E 1/5-20/9) (Q+R+U 1/7-31/8)
5 **AB**EFGJLNPRUWXYZ
6 ACDEGJ**K**(N 0,6km)OT

💬 Pascaline and Michael, an Anglo-French couple, welcome you to their quiet campsite with large pitches, swimming pool and new toilet facilities. Ideal for visiting the Vosges and Alsace. New: the pool is heated and covered.

🚗 From St. Dié take the N415 in the directon of Gérardmer/Colmar. In Anould turn right direction Gérardmer. 3 km further on turn right direction Corcieux. Located just before the village on the right side of the road.

D420 — Taintrux — D23 — Fraize — D60 — CC — D415 — D423 — D8 — D61 — Gérardmer — D417 — D23 H

CC € 15 21/4-6/7 25/8-19/9 7=6, 14=12

📷 N 48°10'5'' E 6°53'24''

Épinal, F-88000 / Lorraine (Vosges)

 👫 🛜 **iD** (1856)

🔼 Parc du Château**
🏠 37 chemin du Petit Chaperon Rouge
☎ +33 (0)3-29344365
⌚ 15/2 - 15/11
@ camping.parcduchateau@ gmail.com

1,7ha 43T(60-200m²) 16A CEE

1 ACDGIJKLMOPRS
2 FGRUVWXY
3 AGHJ
4 (B+G+Q+T+U+X+Y+Z 1/6-1/9)
5 **AB**DFGIJKLMNOPUWZ
6 ACDEGIK(N 0,5km)TV

💬 Pleasant, quiet, small campsite. No entertainment. Located on the grounds of a castle park with swimming pool and free wifi. Restaurant with varied and tasty dishes. You can stay on the campsite outside the opening period by reserving in advance.

🚗 From Nancy or Besançon, direction Épinal, take exit 'Razimont' or 'Parc des Expositions'. Drive towards centre. Signposted from here on. The campsite is located 500 metres from the exit, 1st road on right.

Thaon-les-Vosges — D10 — D46 — D420 — D6 — Épinal — CC — D159 BIS — D460 — D11 — D157 — D44 A — N57 — D44 — D434

CC € 17 15/2-7/7 25/8-14/11 7=6, 14=12

📷 N 48°10'47'' E 6°28'5''

Gérardmer, F-88400 / Lorraine (Vosges)

 ♿ 🛜 **iD** (1857)

🔼 Les Sapins**
🏠 18 chemin de Sapois
☎ +33 (0)3-29631501
⌚ 1/4 - 15/10
@ les.sapins@ camping-gerardmer.com

1,3ha 67T(80-120m²) 6-10A

1 A**G**IJKLMOPQ
2 DLMRVY
3 BHJNRU**WZ**
4 (Q+R ☞) (T 1/7-31/8) (Z ☞)
5 EFGIJKLMNPUVY
6 EGIJ(N 1,5km)TV

💬 Pleasant, peaceful campsite within walking distance of the tourist town of Gérardmer. Spacious pitches with views of the wooded hills. Gérardmer Lake is 200 metres away from the campsite.

🚗 The campsite is located at the start of the southern section of the Gérardmer ring road (chemin du Tour du Lac D69).

D23 — D423 — D8 — D11 — Gérardmer — D61 — D417 — CC — D486 — D34 D — Vagney — D43 — D34 — Cornimont — D430

CC € 17 1/4-6/7 31/8-14/10 7=6, 14=12

📷 N 48°3'48'' E 6°51'21''

Granges-sur-Vologne, F-88640 / Lorraine (Vosges)

🏕 Flower Camping La Sténiole***
📧 1 le Haut Rain
☎ +33 (0)3-29514375
📅 2/4 - 16/10
@ steniole@wanadoo.fr

♿ 🛜 **iD** (1858)

7ha 119T(80-200m²) 10A CEE

1 ACD**G**IJKLPQ
2 CDIJLRTX
3 ABGHJNRUW
4 (E 29/4-15/9) (Q 1/6-31/8)
  (R+T+U+V+Z 1/7-31/8)
5 **AB**DFGIJKLMNPQRUVWZ
6 CEGK(N 3km)OV

💬 A friendly family campsite by a small lake. Large pitches. Campfires permitted on your pitch. New, heated pool with retractable roof.

🚗 From Gérardmer take the D423 in the direction of Granges-sur-Vologne. Turn left just before Granges. Follow the signs.

CC € **13** 2/4-8/7 26/8-15/10 7=6, 14=12

📍 N 48°7'16'' E 6°49'43''

Map: Bruyères, D415, D44, D60, D423, D8, D11, **CC**, Gérardmer, D417, D486, Saint-Amé

Herpelmont, F-88600 / Lorraine (Vosges)

🏕 Domaine des Messires****
📧 rue des Messires
☎ +33 (0)3-29585629
📅 13/4 - 30/9
@ mail@domainedesmessires.com

♿ 🛜 **iD** (1859)

12ha 115T(80-100m²) 10A CEE

1 ACD**G**IJKLMPRS
2 ADMRSTVXY
3 AGHJRUWZ
4 (Q+R 📷) (T 1/7-31/8)
5 **AB**EFGHIJKLPQRUWXZ
6 AEGJ(N 1,5km)V

💬 Lovely four-star campsite on a small lake in unspoilt nature. Fishing is free. New toilet facilities. Walking and mountainbiking possible from the campsite.

🚗 N57, exit N420 direction St. Dié. After 27 km D423 direction Bruyères/Gérardmer. Turn right after 4 km towards Herpelmont/Lac des Messires.

CC € **17** 13/4-6/7 27/8-29/9 14=12

📍 N 48°10'43'' E 6°44'34''

Map: D48, D420, Taintrux, D44, **CC**, D60, D159 BIS, Pouxeux, D11, Éloyes, D423, D8

Jaulny, F-54470 / Lorraine (Meurthe-et-Moselle)

🏕 Camping de la Pelouse***
📧 chemin de Fey
☎ +33 (0)3-83819167
📅 31/3 - 30/9
@ campingdelapelouse@orange.fr

iD (1860)

3ha 94T(110-115m²) 6A CEE

1 ACD**G**IJLMPQ
2 CIRTUVWXY
3 AGU**W**
4 (C 1/6-15/9) (Q+R 📷)
  (X 1/5-30/9) (Z 📷)
5 **AB**GIJKMNPU
6 ACFGH(N 4km)

💬 A site with shaded pitches in the old part. Walking, cycling and visits to WW1 Museum. Trains may be heard in the distance. Restaurant is open Sunday and holiday afternoons, closed Monday, open Tuesday to Saturday evenings.

🚗 From the A31, exit 31 dir. Ars-sur-Moselle via the D6, Then D91 dir. Arnaville, then D952 dir. Onville. Then D28 to Jaulny, follow camping signs.

CC € **15** 31/3-14/7 1/9-29/9

📍 N 48°57'57'' E 5°53'7''

Map: D13, D901, D6, D657, **CC**, D904, D952, D3, Pont-à-Mousson, D958

La Bresse, F-88250 / Lorraine (Vosges)

🎿 ⛷ ♿ 📶 **iD** (1861)

🏔 Domaine du Haut des Bluches***
✉ 5 rte des Planches
☎ +33 (0)3-29256480
🕐 1/1 - 11/11, 14/12 - 31/12
@ hautdesbluches@labresse.fr

4,2ha 109T(100m²) 4-13A CEE

1 ACD**G**IJKLMPQ
2 CJKRVX
3 ABHJN**O**PRU**W**
4 (Q+R+U+X+Z 🕐)
5 **AB**DEFGIJKLMNPRU
6 CDEGIJ(N 4km)TV

💬 Campsite in hilly surroundings. A mountain stream runs through the site. During the winter there is a shuttle bus service to the ski area 5 km higher up. Excellent sanitary facilities. Rooms for rent on half or full board basis.

🚗 In La Bresse take the D34 direction La Schlucht. Campsite is 4 km further on, on your right.

Gérardmer — D61 / D417
La Bresse — D34 D / D10
Cornimont — D27
D43 — D486 — D13 BI — D430 — D13 BIS — D431

ℂℂ € **13** 1/4-6/7 27/8-10/11 7=6, 14=12

🗻 N 47°59'56'' E 6°55'5''

Le Tholy, F-88530 / Lorraine (Vosges)

♿ 📶 **iD** (1862)

🏔 JP Vacances - camping de Noirrupt****
✉ 15 chemin de l'Étang
☎ +33 (0)3-29618127
🕐 1/5 - 30/9
@ info@jpvacances.com

3ha 77T(90-200m²) 2-10A CEE

1 ACD**G**IJKLPQ
2 JKRVXY
3 BGHJM**O**RTU**W**
4 (C 1/6-15/9) **N**
   (Q+R+U+V+Z 5/7-24/8)
5 **AB**FGJKLNPUVWZ
6 ACEG**K**(N 1km)ORTV

💬 An attractive campsite, peacefully located and surrounded by lovely big trees. Five minutes from Gérardmer. Panoramic views. Heated swimming pool.

🚗 From Gérardmer take D417 direction Remiremont. Turn right onto D11 at Le Tholy. Turn left 0.5 km after leaving Le Tholy. Follow arrows.

D44 — D60
D159 BIS
D11 — D423
N57 — D417 — Gérardmer
Saint-Étienne-lès-Remiremont — D486
D23 — D43

ℂℂ € **17** 1/5-6/7 24/8-29/9 7=6, 14=12, 21=18

🗻 N 48°5'20'' E 6°43'44''

Liverdun, F-54460 / Lorraine (Meurthe-et-Moselle)

🚶‍♀️🚶 ♿ 📶 **iD** (1863)

🏔 Les Boucles de la Moselle**
✉ 7 avenue Eugène-Lerebourg
☎ +33 (0)3-83244378
🕐 1/5 - 1/10
@ contact@lesbouclesdelamoselle.com

2,1ha 187T(70-90m²) 6-10A CEE

1 ACD**G**IJKLMOPQ
2 CFGLMRTWXY
3 BFHJK**M**NRW
4 (C 1/6-30/9) (Q+R 🕐)
   (T 30/6-10/9) (U 1/5-30/9)
   (X 15/6-15/9) (Z 🕐)
5 AGIJKLMNPUZ
6 CGJ(N 2,5km)T

💬 A campsite with swimming pool in the natural area between Metz and Nancy. At the foot of medieval Liverdun and the Moselle. Enjoy the untouched countryside by bike, foot or boat.

🚗 Leave the A31 at exit 22 direction Frouard. Then at 2nd traffic lights past Lidl, left to Liverdun. Left at traffic lights and follow camping signs.

D657 — D44 — D44 A
D907
D611
ℂℂ — A31
Vandoeuvre-lès-Nancy — Nancy
Toul — D909 — A33

ℂℂ € **15** 1/5-7/7 25/8-30/9 7=6

🗻 N 48°44'51'' E 6°3'28''

Lutzelbourg, F-57820 / Lorraine (Moselle)

♿ 📶 **iD** **1864**

🏔 Piscine du Plan Incliné***
🛣 D98
☎ +33 (0)3-87253013
🔑 1/4 - 15/10
@ campingplanincline@orange.fr

2ha 45**T**(100m²) 6-16A CEE

1 ACD**G**IJKLMPRS
2 FGKLRX
3 AGHJNRU**W**
4 (B+G 2/7-28/8)
　(Q+R+U+X+Y+Z 🔑)
5 **AB**DEGIJKMNPUX
6 CDG**J**(N 2km)OR

💬 This campsite is located on the Marne-Rhine Canal in a beautiful, wooded area. Wifi for 1 Euro per day!

🚗 From Phalsbourg D38 to Lutzelbourg. Then the D98 direction Dabo. The campsite is located near the boat lift, 2 km outside Lutzelbourg, on the right.

D1　D661　D178　D133
D122
A4
D43　D46　D38　**Saverne**
Sarrebourg CC D132
D45　D98 C
D1004
D218
D44　D224

CC € **17** 1/4-6/7　25/8-14/10

🧭 N 48°43'10''　E 7°13'35''

Nancy/Villers-lès-Nancy, F-54600 / Lorraine (Meurthe-et-Moselle)

👫 ♿ 📶 **iD** **1865**

🏔 Campéole Le Brabois***
🛣 2301 avenue Paul Muller
☎ +33 (0)3-83271828
📠 +33 (0)3-83400643
🔑 30/3 - 14/10
@ brabois@campeole.com

4ha 182**T**(70-100m²) 6-15A CEE

1 ACD**G**IJKLMOPQ
2 FGRTUVWXY
3 BGNRU
4 (Q+R 🔑)
　(T+U+X+Z 15/4-15/9)
5 **AB**DFGIJKLMNOPUWZ
6 ACEGH**IJ**(N 2km)TV

💬 Easily accessible from the A33 (exit 2B). Parkland setting with spacious, shaded pitches. Excellent bus connections to historic Nancy. Covered picnic area with cooking facilities, modern toilet facilities. Attractive snack bar (self-grown products) and terrace. Internet and wifi. Reductions for various sights from the reception.

🚗 A33, exit 2B (Brabois). Keep on the left to turn left at the roundabout. Follow camp signs.

Villers-lès-Nancy **Nancy**
D909
CC
A33
D570　D112
D974
N57

CC € **15** 30/3-6/7　25/8-13/10

🧭 N 48°39'26''　E 6°8'25''

Plombières-les-Bains, F-88370 / Lorraine (Vosges)

📶 **iD** **1866**

🏔 de l'Hermitage***
🛣 54 rue du Boulot
☎ +33 (0)3-29300187
🔑 15/4 - 15/10
@ camping.lo@wanadoo.fr

1,4ha 47**T**(77-135m²) 10A CEE

1 ACD**G**IJKLM**P**Q
2 CJRTVWXY
3 ABGHIJKRU
4 (C 15/6-15/9)
　(Q+R+T+U+V+X 🔑)
5 **AB**DFGIJKLMNPUWZ
6 ACEGJ(N 1,5km)OTV

💬 Located in the 'Ballons des Vosges' nature park. 1.5 km from a thermal centre with a Roman bathhouse, fitness centre and casino. The campsite has over 40 marked out shaded pitches and a swimming pool. Quiet family campsite.

🚗 From Épinal take the N57 to Plombières-les-Bains. In built up area follow signs direction Xertigny/Ruaux. Campsite located just in Plombières-les-Bains, on the right of the D20.

D4　D3
D434
D63　N57
D164
CC　D23
D64　D57 BIS
Saint-Loup-sur-Semouse D83　D6

CC € **13** 15/4-30/6　18/8-14/10　7=6, 14=12, 21=18

🧭 N 47°58'2''　E 6°26'48''

Plombières-les-Bains/Ruaux, F-88370 / Lorraine (Vosges)

👫 🎿 ♿ 📶 **iD** (1867)

🏕 Camping Fraiteux***
📧 81 rue du Camping - Ruaux
☎ +33 (0)3-29660071
🗓 1/1 - 31/12
@ campingfraiteux@orange.fr

0,8ha 28T(80-120m²) 16A

1 **AG**IJKLMOPQ
2 JRTVWX
3 AHJRU
4 (Q+R+T+U+X+Z 🖭)
5 **AB**DGIJKLMNPUVWZ
6 ADEGK(N 4km)OT

💬 Well maintained; large pitches separated by hedges. Totally peaceful location with lovely views.

🚗 From Épinal take the N57 to Plombières-les-Bains. In the outskirts follow sign dir. Route des Chalots. Campsite located in Ruaux (± 4 km). Coming from Luxeuil follow Route Thermale.

D4 D3
D434
D63
D164 CC D23
D64 N57
Saint-Loup-sur-
Semouse D83
D6

CC € **17** 1/1-30/6 18/8-31/12 7=6, 14=11, 21=18   📍 N 47°57'55'' E 6°24'59''

Sanchey, F-88390 / Lorraine (Vosges)

👫 ♿ 📶 **iD** (1868)

🏕 Club Lac de Bouzey****
📧 19 rue du Lac
☎ +33 (0)3-29824941
📠 +33 (0)3-29642803
🗓 1/2 - 31/12
@ lacdebouzey@orange.fr

3,5ha 155T(58-100m²) 10-16A

1 ACD**G**IJKLMOPQ
2 ADFGJLRTVWXY
3 ABF**G**HJKLMNR**TUW**Z
4 (A 1/7-31/8) (C+H 15/6-15/9) (Q+S 🖭)
    (T+U+V+X+Y+Z 1/5-30/9)
5 **AB**DEFGIJKLNPUVXYZ
6 CDEGHJ(N 0,5km)OPRTV

💬 A lovely family campsite located by a lake, suitable for a longer stay. Extensive recreational opportunities: tennis, carting, golf, rock climbing, kayaking, horse riding, Jorkeyball. Lovely unusually shaped swimming pool. The campsite has the 'Camping Qualité' hallmark.

🚗 From Nancy take the N57/E23 in the direction of Épinal. Exit Chavelot direction Uxegney. In Uxegney take the D41 in the direction of Lac de Bouzey. Then follow the signs.

D46
D166 Thaon-les-
Vosges
D6 D157 D420
Épinal D11
D4 D460 N57
D44 A
D3 D44 D434

CC € **19** 1/2-6/7 25/8-30/12 7=6   📍 N 48°10'1'' E 6°21'35''

St. Maurice-sur-Moselle, F-88560 / Lorraine (Vosges)

📶 **iD** (1869)

🏕 Les Deux Ballons***
📧 17 rue du Stade
☎ +33 (0)3-29251714
🗓 22/4 - 23/9
@ stan0268@orange.fr

4ha 153T(80-120m²) 10A CEE

1 **AG**IJKLMO**P**Q
2 CGJRTVXY
3 BGHJMRUW
4 (C 1/6-31/8) (H 1/6-15/9) J (Q+V+Z 1/7-31/8)
5 **AB**CDFGIJKLNPUWZ
6 ACDEG**K**(N 1km)ORV

💬 This campsite, dissected by the young River Mosel is located at the foot of the Ballon d'Alsace and the Ballon de Servance. Large heated swimming pool with water slide. Enthusiastic warden.

🚗 N66 Épinal-Mulhouse. In St. Maurice follow the camping signs.

Rupt-sur- D43
Moselle D13 BIS
D6 Le Thillot N66
CC
D465
D466
D486

CC € **15** 22/4-7/7 25/8-22/9   📍 N 47°51'19'' E 6°48'40''

Sturzelbronn, F-57230 / Lorraine (Moselle)

♿ 🛜 📱 **1870**

🏕 Camping Muhlenbach★★★★
🏠 10 route du Muhlenbach
☎ +33 (0)3-87062015
📅 1/4 - 30/9
@ info@camping-muhlenbach.com

12,5ha 40T(100m²) 6A CEE

1 ACDFIJLPQ
2 ADJKRTVX
3 ABGHJNRU**W**Z
4 **LN**(Q+S 1/7-31/8)
   (T+V+Z 8/7-20/8)
5 **AB**FGIJKLMN**P**UWZ
6 CEGIJT

💬 A peaceful campsite located by a small lake where you can go fishing and swimming; in the middle of a stunning nature reserve. Free wifi-spot.

🚗 From Sarrequemines take the N62 direction Haguenau. Via Bitche take the D35 to Sturzelbronn. Here take the Rue du Muhlenbach. The campsite is located at the end of this road.

ⓒ € **19** 1/4-14/7 1/9-29/9

🧭 N 49°3'56'' E 7°35'37''

Villey-le-Sec, F-54840 / Lorraine (Meurthe-et-Moselle)

♿ 🛜 📱 **1871**

🏕 Villey-le-Sec★★★
🏠 34 rue de la Gare
☎ +33 (0)3-83636428
📅 31/3 - 30/9
@ info@campingvilleylesec.com

3ha 90T(90-120m²) 6-10A CEE

1 ACD**G**IJKLMPQ
2 CFRTVWX
3 BG**QRW**
4 (Q 15/4-15/9) (S 📅)
   (T+U+Y+Z 7/4-30/9)
5 **AB**DEFGIJKLMNPUYZ
6 AF**GJ**(N 5km)R

💬 A pleasant campsite for overnight and longer stays in natural surroundings right on the Mosel. 8 km from the old town of Toul. Some noise from jet fighters. Lovely walking and cycling. Good catering. Ideal for fishing in the Mosel.

🚗 From Nancy: A31, exit 15. Take the 2nd road D909 direction Villey-le-Sec after 1 km on the roundabout near the Leclerc supermarket. Follow signs to 'Camping/Base de Loisirs' in the village 4 km further on.

ⓒ € **17** 31/3-30/6 18/8-29/9

🧭 N 48°39'10'' E 5°59'33''

Vilsberg, F-57370 / Lorraine (Moselle)

👫 ♿ 🛜 📱 **1872**

🏕 Les Bouleaux★★★
🏠 5 rue des Trois Journaux
☎ +33 (0)3-87241872
📅 1/4 - 15/10
@ info@campinglesbouleaux.fr

7ha 85T(100-200m²) 6-10A

1 ACD**G**IJKLMPRS
2 FRTX
3 AGHNQRU
4 (C 1/6-15/9) (Q+T+X+Z 📅)
5 **AB**FGIJKLMNPUZ
6 EGJ(N 2km)OTV

💬 A peaceful family campsite, also suitable for longer stays. Lovely spacious pitches with plenty of grass. You will be welcomed by a Dutch-German couple. Free wifi.

🚗 The campsite is 2 km outside Phalsbourg on the N61 to Sarreguemines. Don't turn at the 'Vilsberg' sign but at the next sign: 'Camping'.

ⓒ € **17** 1/4-7/7 25/8-14/10 7=6, 14=12, 21=18

🧭 N 48°47'0'' E 7°14'58''

Vittel, F-88800 / Lorraine (Vosges) ♿ 🤚 📶 **iD** (1873)

⛰ Camping de Vittel***
🏠 270 rue Claude Bassot
☎ +33 (0)3-29080271
🔑 30/3 - 21/10
@ vittel.camping@orange.fr

2ha 125T(85-125m²) 10A CEE

1 ACD**G**IJKLM**P**Q
2 GRTUVWXY
3 B**F**GRU
4 (Q+R 🔒)
5 **AB**DEFGIJKLMNOPQRUZ
6 CDEGJ(N 0,8km)V

💬 A campsite for those passing through or anyone wanting to visit the chique resort of Vittel. Numbered pitches and surrounded by lovely hedges.

🚗 From A31 exit 9, via D165 direction Vittel (new road) or D164 (old road). Campsite signposted in Vittel.

CC € **15** 30/3-7/7 25/8-20/10   📐 N 48°12'28'' E 5°57'19''

Xonrupt-Longemer, F-88400 / Lorraine (Vosges) 👫 🎿 ♿ 📶 **iD** (1874)

⛰ Flower Camping Verte Vallée***
🏠 4092 route du Lac
☎ +33 (0)3-29632177
🔑 1/1 - 31/10, 15/12 - 31/12
@ contact@
   campingvertevallee.com

3,5ha 82T(80-140m²) 4-10A

1 ACD**G**IJKLM**P**Q
2 CTVWX
3 ABHJKLMNRU**W**
4 (**A** 8/7-25/8)
   (C+D+H 1/5-30/9)
   (Q+R 1/6-15/9) (U 1/7-31/8)
   (Z 1/6-30/9)
5 **AB**DFGJLMNOPUWZ
6 AEGIJK(N 8km)TV

💬 A beautiful campsite with a new, heated indoor pool with a sliding roof. The campsite is located 300 metres from the lake.

🚗 From Gérardmer take the D417 towards Colmar. Just past Xonrupt, at Hotel du Lac de Longemer turn right onto D67. Campsite at the end of the lake.

CC € **17** 1/3-30/6 1/9-30/10 7=6, 14=12   📐 N 48°3'45'' E 6°57'53''

Xonrupt-Longemer, F-88400 / Lorraine (Vosges) ♿ 📶 **iD** (1875)

⛰ Les Jonquilles***
🏠 2552 route du Lac
☎ +33 (0)3-29633401
🔑 21/4 - 30/9
@ info@camping-jonquilles.com

4,5ha 228T(80-120m²) 6-10A

1 ACD**G**IJKLM**P**Q
2 DIKLORTVX
3 BGHJNRTU**WZ**
4 (Q+S 🔒)
   (T+U+V+X 1/6-31/8)
5 **AB**FGIJKLMNOPUV
6 ACDEGJ(N 2,5km)OTV

💬 Beautiful, pleasant family campsite on the shores of the lake of Longemer. Suitable for longer visits. Large pitches, which nearly all have a view over the lake. Many different walking (hiking) routes start from the campsite.

🚗 Take the D417 from Gérardmer to Xonrupt-Longemer. Take the D67a in this village to the campsite, which is situated 2.5 km from the church in Xonrupt-Longemer left of the road.

CC € **13** 21/4-6/7 25/8-29/9 7=6, 14=12, 21=18   📐 N 48°4'4'' E 6°56'53''

Altkirch, F-68130 / Alsace (Haut-Rhin) 📶 iD (1876)

🏕 Les Acacias
📍 Rue de Hirtzbach
☎ +33 (0)3-89406940
📅 30/3 - 31/10
@ deborahdietsch@hotmail.fr

2ha 49T(80-160m²) 16-A CEE

1 ACD**G**IJKLMP
2 KRWXY
3 AGHJR
4 (U+Y+Z 🔌)
5 **AB**CFGHIJKLMNPUW
6 ACFGJ(N 2km)T

💬 Small quiet campsite with spacious pitches on grass under the trees. Good stopover campsite with a nice restaurant. Modern toilet block. Swimming pool and tennis courts nearby.

🚗 In Altkirch drive in the direction of Centre-Ville. Then follow the signs 'camping'. Clearly signposted.

D466 | D18 V — Dietwiller
D68
D419
D103
CC
D432 | D9 B
D13
D463 | Seppois-le-Bas

🅲🅲 € 15 30/3-6/7 25/8-30/10　　🧭 N 47°36'48'' E 7°14'0''

Bassemberg, F-67220 / Alsace (Bas-Rhin) 👫 ♿ 📶 iD (1877)

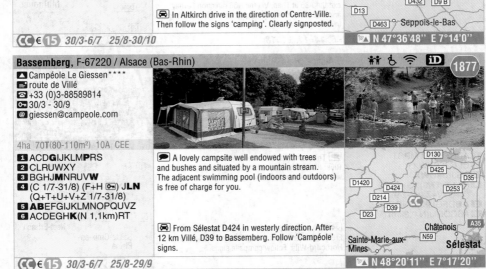

🏕 Campéole Le Giessen****
📍 route de Villé
☎ +33 (0)3-88589814
📅 30/3 - 30/9
@ giessen@campeole.com

4ha 70T(80-110m²) 10A CEE

1 ACD**G**IJKLM**P**RS
2 CLRUWXY
3 BGHJ**M**NRUV**W**
4 (C 1/7-31/8) (F+H 🔌) J**LN** (Q+T+U+V+Z 1/7-31/8)
5 **AB**EFGIJKLMNOPQUVZ
6 ACDEGH**K**(N 1,1km)RT

💬 A lovely campsite well endowed with trees and bushes and situated by a mountain stream. The adjacent swimming pool (indoors and outdoors) is free of charge for you.

🚗 From Sélestat D424 in westerly direction. After 12 km Villé, D39 to Bassemberg. Follow 'Campéole' signs.

D130
D425
D1420 | D424 | D35
D214 | D253
D23 | D39
CC
Châtenois
Sainte-Marie-aux-Mines | N59 | A35
Sélestat

🅲🅲 € 15 30/3-6/7 25/8-29/9　　🧭 N 48°20'11'' E 7°17'20''

Burnhaupt-le-Haut, F-68520 / Alsace (Haut-Rhin) 👫 📶 iD (1878)

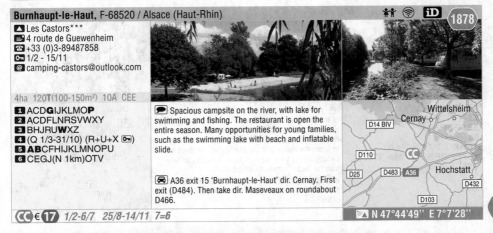

🏕 Les Castors***
📍 4 route de Guewenheim
☎ +33 (0)3-89487858
📅 1/2 - 15/11
@ camping-castors@outlook.com

4ha 120T(100-150m²) 10A CEE

1 ACD**G**IJKLMO**P**
2 ACDFLNRSVWXY
3 BHJRU**W**XZ
4 (Q 1/3-31/10) (R+U+X 🔌)
5 **AB**CFHIJKLMNOPU
6 CEGJ(N 1km)OTV

💬 Spacious campsite on the river, with lake for swimming and fishing. The restaurant is open the entire season. Many opportunities for young families, such as the swimming lake with beach and inflatable slide.

🚗 A36 exit 15 'Burnhaupt-le-Haut' dir. Cernay. First exit (D484). Then take dir. Masevaux on roundabout D466.

Wittelsheim
D14 BIV | Cernay
D110 | CC
D25 | D483 A36 | Hochstatt
D432
D103

🅲🅲 € 17 1/2-6/7 25/8-14/11 7=6　　🧭 N 47°44'49'' E 7°7'28''

Cernay, F-68700 / Alsace (Haut-Rhin)

♿ 📶 iD **1879**

🏕 Les Cigognes***
✉ 16, rue René Guibert
☎ +33 (0)3-89755697
🗓 1/4 - 30/9
@ campinglescigognes@orange.fr

4ha 146T(80-100m²) 6A CEE

1 ACD**G**IJKLM**P**Q
2 RVWXY
3 BGHJ**M**NU
4 (C+**F**+H 🔌)
5 **AB**DFGIJKLMNPU
6 CEG**K**(N 0,5km)T

💬 A large, spacious and peaceful campsite on level grounds located in a natural setting, surrounded by storks and the River Thur and close to the town centre of Cernay. Storks fly from their nests and ask to be fed. New heated outdoor swimming pool. 500m from a large shopping centre. Level grounds.

🚗 A5 direction Basel, then A36 direction Mulhouse, exit the A36 at Than. Via the N66 direction Cernay and D483 and follow the signs. Left before the bridge in Cernay.

CC € **15** 1/4-6/7 25/8-29/9 7=6, 14=11, 21=18

🧭 N 47°48'16'' E 7°10'12''

Colmar/Horbourg-Wihr, F-68180 / Alsace (Haut-Rhin)

♿ 📶 iD **1880**

🏕 Camping de l'Ill - Colmar***
✉ 1 allée du Camping
☎ +33 (0)3-89411594
🗓 30/3 - 31/12
@ colmar@camping-indigo.com

4ha 150T(80-100m²) 10A CEE

1 ACD**F**HIJKLM**P**ST
2 CFGJLRVWXY
3 AGJK**MU**WX
4 (C 1/5-17/9) (G+Q 🔌) (T+U+V+Z 2/7-2/9)
5 **AB**DFGIJKLMNOPUXZ
6 ABCDGIJ(N 0,3km)TV

💬 This campsite is located on the banks of the River Ill. Ideally located for visiting Colmar. Snack bar with pavement cafe. Heated pool.

🚗 Leave the A35 via exit 25, then D415 direction Freiburg. After 3 km on roundabout via D418 to Horbourg-Wihr. Follow campsite signs.

CC € **17** 30/3-1/6 2/9-23/11

🧭 N 48°4'51'' E 7°23'12''

Eguisheim, F-68420 / Alsace (Haut-Rhin)

♿ 📶 iD **1881**

🏕 Les Trois Châteaux***
✉ 10 rue du Bassin
☎ +33 (0)3-89231939
🗓 23/3 - 5/11, 30/11 - 24/12
@ reception@camping-eguisheim.fr

1,8ha 133T(80-100m²) 8-10A CEE

1 ACD**G**HIJLM**P**Q
2 FGRTVWXY
3 A**F**GHJRU
4 (R 🔌)
5 **AB**GIJKLMNOPUW
6 ABCDEGJ(N 0,3km)OTV

💬 A restful campsite in the wine region on the edge of the stunning town of Eguisheim, which is a great place to look around. You can walk into this floral medieval pearl of Alsace from the campsite and get to know the delicious local specialities. Walking and cycling routes from the campsite. Marked pitches, also for motorhomes, shade possible.

🚗 E35 exit 28. Then take the D1B dir. Herrlisheim. After ± 7 km direction Eguisheim then follow camping signs.

CC € **17** 23/3-29/6 29/8-4/11

🧭 N 48°2'34'' E 7°17'58''

Masevaux, F-68290 / Alsace (Haut-Rhin)

👪 ♿ 📶 **iD** (1882)

🏕 Les Rives de la Doller***
📧 14 rue du Stade
☎ +33 (0)3-89398394
📅 30/3 - 20/10
@ info@masevaux-camping.com

3,5ha 115T(80-110m²) 6A CEE

1 ACD**G**IJKLMPST
2 CGRUVWXY
3 AGHJKNRU**W**
4 (F 📅) (Q 15/6-31/8) (R 📅)
(T 1/7-31/8) (U 15/6-31/8)
(Z 📅)
5 **AB**CDEFGHIJKLMNOPUWZ
6 AEGJ(N 0,2km)TV

💬 Lovely, welcoming campsite in the countryside, with spacious pitches. Near the centre of Masevaux, an ideal base for exploring the Doller area on foot or by bike.

🚗 From the A36 take exit 15 to Masevaux. Exit N466 Pont d'Aspach and via the N83 to Masevaux. In the town follow 'Centre-Ville' signs, then 'Zone de Sport Loisirs' signs.

N66   D13 BVI
D465   D431
D466   **Cernay**
CC   Thann
Burnhaupt-le-Haut
D13   D2   A36
D12

CC € **15** 30/3-7/7 25/8-19/10 7=6, 14=12   📐 N 47°46'42'' E 6°59'27''

Molsheim, F-67120 / Alsace (Bas-Rhin)

♿ 📶 **iD** (1883)

🏕 Municipal Molsheim**
📧 6 rue des Sports
☎ +33 (0)3-88498245
📅 31/3 - 28/10
@ camping-molsheim@orange.fr

1,6ha 95T(80-100m²) 10A CEE

1 ACD**G**IJKLPQ
2 CFLRTVWXY
3 BGHJ**OPRW**
4 (C+G 27/5-3/9) (Q+R 📅)
5 **AB**DGIJKLOPUWZ
6 ABCEGHJ(N 0,1km)T

💬 This site is located on the edge of an attractive craftsmen's village, typical of the Alsace. The municipal swimming complex with a lovely new playground is next to the site and is free for campers. Lovely linden trees. Within walking distance of the Super-U supermarket. Free wifi.

🚗 On the A4 exit Saverne. N4 to Wasselone. Via the D422 to Molsheim. Turn left just past the centre, before the bridge. Follow the signs.

D224
D30   N4
D75   D45
Lingolsheim
D218
CC
D35   A35
Obernai
D214   D426

CC € **15** 31/3-7/7 25/8-27/10 5=4   📐 N 48°32'29'' E 7°29'58''

Neuf-Brisach, F-68600 / Alsace (Haut-Rhin)

👪 ♿ 📶 **iD** (1884)

🏕 Vauban**
📧 Entrée Porte de Bâle
☎ +33 (0)3-89725425
📅 30/3 - 31/10
@ contact@camping-vauban.fr

4ha 140T(< 100m²) 10A CEE

1 ACD**F**IJKLMPQ
2 GRWXY
3 AGJK
4 **N**(Q+R 📅)
5 **AB**DGLMNPUZ
6 CEGK(N 0,3km)T

💬 A 4-hectare site next to the famous fortress of Neuf Brisach dating from 1699 (UNESCO World Heritage Site) in a striking rural setting. You will be on one of the spacious sunny or shaded places to relax and enjoy woodpeckers, pheasants and the many other birds around you.

🚗 Leave the A35 at Colmar (sortie 25), N415 direction Freiburg. Left at second roundabout after 15 km to Neuf-Brisach and follow signs.

Colmar   D52
L104
D415   D468   L114
Sainte-Croix-en-Plaine
CC
A35   D1 BIS   Neuf-Brisach   B31
A5
D2

CC € **17** 30/3-30/6 1/9-30/10 11=10   📐 N 48°0'57'' E 7°32'8''

Obernai, F-67210 / Alsace (Bas-Rhin)

♿ 🛜 ✿ **iD** (1885)

🏔 Mun. Le Vallon de l'Ehn***
✉ 1 rue de Berlin
☎ +33 (0)3-88953848
📅 1/1 - 7/1, 16/3 - 31/12
@ camping@obernai.fr

3ha 142T(90-95m²) 16A CEE

1 ACD**G**HIJKLMPQ
2 GRVWXY
3 BGHIKRU**W**
4 (**A** 1/7-31/8) (Q 1/5-31/10)
   (R 📅)
5 **AB**DFGIJKLMNOPUWYZ
6 CDEGHK(N 1km)QRT

💬 A lovely campsite close to a tourist village. Level pitches with some shade. Good modern amenities.

🚗 From Molsheim or Strasbourg take Obernai exit. Not to Centre Ville, but follow Le Mont-Ste-Odile at roundabouts. Right at end of ring road then immediate left. Campsite 100m on the left.

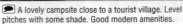

Molsheim   Dachstein
Urmatt
A352
D35
A35
D214
D854   D206   D1083
D5

CC € **17** 1/1-6/1 16/3-30/6 1/9-31/12 11=10

📐 N 48°27'53'' E 7°28'3''

Osenbach, F-68570 / Alsace (Haut-Rhin)

🛜 **iD** (1886)

🏔 Osenbach
✉ rue du Stade
☎ +33 (0)3-89470522
📅 1/4 - 31/10
@ contact@camping-osenbach.fr

3,5ha 128T(100-120m²) 10A CEE

1 ACD**G**IJLPQ
2 BIKRTWXY
3 AGHJLNR
4 (Q+T+Z 📅)
5 CHI**J**KLMNOPU
6 CEGHJV

💬 New campsite, aimed at returning to nature and outdoor activities. Many possibilities for walking in the area, cycling and climbing with stunning views.

🚗 On D83 take exit to D15 Orschwir. Then follow D18BIS to Orschwir. Right after 5 km to Rue d'Osenbach on route D18BIS. Finally, turn left after 2.5 km. Site is signposted.

Wintzenheim   **Colmar**
D10
D83
D27   A35
D430
Guebwiller

CC € **15** 1/4-6/7 26/8-30/10

📐 N 47°58'50'' E 7°13'8''

Ranspach, F-68470 / Alsace (Haut-Rhin)

♿ 🛜 **iD** (1887)

🏔 Flower Camping Les Bouleaux****
✉ 8 rue des Bouleaux
☎ +33 (0)3-89826470
📠 +33 (0)3-89391417
📅 1/1 - 31/10, 1/12 - 31/12
@ contact@alsace-camping.com

2,8ha 56T(80-100m²) 6-10A CEE

1 ACD**G**IJKLMOPQ
2 CGIKLRVXY
3 BGHJNRU**W**
4 (F+H 📅) K**LP**(Q 1/7-31/8)
   (R 1/4-30/9) (U+V+X+Z 📅)
5 **AB**CDEFGHIJKLMNOPUWZ
6 ABDEGJ(N 1km)OTV

💬 This peaceful campsite with marked out pitches, partly under trees, is located in floral surroundings on the route des vins d'Alsace. Views of the wooded hillsides. It has a heated indoor swimming pool, spa-hammam, massage and a daily menu with local produce for a reasonable price.

🚗 From Nancy take the N57 to Remiremont, then follow the N66 for about 10 km. Ranspach is beyond Col de Bussang. Follow signs in Ranspach.

D27
Cornimont   D430
D43   D13 BIS
Fellering
N66   D431
D466   D14 BIV   **Cernay**

CC € **17** 1/1-6/7 26/8-30/10 1/12-31/12

📐 N 47°52'48'' E 7°0'37''

Riquewihr, F-68340 / Alsace (Haut-Rhin) ♿ 🛜 iD 1888

▲ Camping de Riquewihr★★★★
✉ 1 route du Vin
☎ +33 (0)3-89479008
📅 1/4 - 4/11, 24/11 - 24/12
@ info@campingriquewihr.com

4ha 148T(80-150m²) 16A CEE

1 ACD**G**HIJKLM**P**Q
2 FRTVWXY
3 B**F**GHJKL**M**NRU
4 (Q 🚿)
5 **AB**DEFGIJKLMNPQUWXYZ
6 BCDFGK(N 1km)

💬 Located on the Route des Vins and close to the picturesque medieval town of Riquewihr. Similar villages such as Ribeauville and Kaysersberg are close by. Level, spacious marked out pitches, some with shade. Brilliant heated toilet facilities.

🚐 Leave the N83 at exit 21 if coming from Strasbourg (or exit 22 if coming from Mulhouse/Colmar) and take direction Ostheim/Riquewihr. Campsite signposted.

CC €17 1/4-9/5 14/5-13/7 10/9-3/11 | 📍 N 48°9'45'' E 7°19'1''

Saverne, F-67700 / Alsace (Bas-Rhin) 🧑‍🤝‍🧑 ♿ 🛜 iD 1889

▲ Seasonova Les Portes d'Alsace★★★
✉ 40, rue du Père Liebermann
☎ +33 (0)3-88913565
📅 31/3 - 4/11
@ contact@camping-lesportesdalsace.com

3ha 145T(80-120m²) 10A CEE

1 ACD**G**IJLPQ
2 FRTXY
3 AGHKL**M**RU
4 (E+H 1/5-30/9) (Q+U+V 🚿)
5 **AB**DGIJKLMNPUWX
6 EGH**K**(N 1km)TV

💬 A peaceful campsite with lovely big trees within walking distance of the small town of Saverne. It has a small heated swimming pool with a sliding roof.

🚐 From the A4 exit 45 direction Saverne. Campsite signposted from the centre.

CC €17 31/3-6/7 26/8-3/11 7=6, 14=11 | 📍 N 48°43'52'' E 7°21'19''

Ste Croix-en-Plaine, F-68127 / Alsace (Haut-Rhin) 🚫 ♿ 🛜 iD 1890

▲ ClairVacances★★★★
✉ route de Herrlisheim
☎ +33 (0)3-89492728
📅 20/4 - 8/10
@ reception@clairvacances.com

4ha 135T(90-100m²) 16A CEE

1 ACDEHIJKLPST
2 FRTVWY
3 BGJRU
4 (C 1/5-15/9) (H 15/6-1/9) (Q+R 🚿) (T 1/7-31/8) (U 🚿)
5 **AB**DEFGJLMNPUW
6 ABDEGK(N 2km)OT

💬 ClairVacances is located near Colmar and tourist attractions, in a green heart with a large variety of bushes and flowers. The site is known for its excellent amenities which are superbly maintained. Heated swimming pool from 1 May. ClairVacances will enchant you.

🚐 Exit 27 on the A35 direction Herrlisheim. Then follow camping signs.

CC €17 20/4-29/6 29/8-7/10 | 📍 N 48°0'58'' E 7°21'1''

Ste Marie-aux-Mines, F-68160 / Alsace (Haut-Rhin) 👫 ♿ 📶 iD (1891)

🏕 Les Reflets du Val d'Argent★★★
✉ 20 route d'Untergrombach
☎ +33 (0)3-89586431
🔓 1/1 - 31/12
@ reflets@calixo.net

3ha 110T(90-110m²) 16A

1 ACDGIJKLMPQ
2 CGJRTVWXY
3 ABF GHJMRU W
4 (A 1/7-31/8) (C 1/5-30/9) N
(Q 15/6-15/9) (R 15/4-1/11)
(U+V+X+Z 🔓)
5 A GIJKLMNOPUVZ
6 ACDEGJ(N 1km)ORTV

💬 Situated among hills and woods in the centre of Alsace and set in a beautiful valley on the edge of an old town close to a silver mine. This family campsite offers many amenities for an enjoyable stay, such as a restaurant, bar and swimming pool.

🚗 N59 Sélestat-St. Dié. Follow the signs to the campsite in Ste Marie-aux-Mines.

CC € **13** 1/1-20/6 1/9-31/12 7=6, 14=11   🧭 N 48°14'7'' E 7°10'14''

Strasbourg, F-67200 / Alsace (Bas-Rhin) ♿ 📶 iD (1892)

🏕 Camping de Strasbourg★★★★
✉ 9 rue de l'Auberge de Jeunesse
☎ +33 (0)3-88301996
🔓 1/1 - 31/12
@ strasbourg@
  camping-indigo.com

2,2ha 98T(80-100m²) 10A CEE

1 ACDF IJKLMP ST
2 FGRTWXY
3 BGKRU
4 (B 30/4-18/9) (Q 🔓)
(T+U+X 1/4-30/9) (Z 🔓)
5 AB DEFGIJKLMNPUWZ
6 ABCEGK(N 0,5km)V

💬 Campsite is located in surroundings with lots of plantlife and large trees, a few km away from the touristy centre of town.

🚗 From A35, exit 4. Follow signs 'Montagne Verte - camping'.

CC € **19** 2/1-31/5 5/9-23/11   🧭 N 48°34'28'' E 7°43'5''

Turckheim, F-68230 / Alsace (Haut-Rhin) ♿ 📶 iD (1893)

🏕 Le Médiéval
✉ 5 quai de la Fecht
☎ +33 (0)3-89270200
🔓 28/3 - 22/10, 30/11 - 24/12
@ reception@camping-turckheim.fr

2ha 117T(80-100m²) 16A CEE

1 ACDG HIJKLMPQ
2 CRTVWXY
3 AF HJMRU
4 (Q 7/7-31/8)
5 AB EFGIJKLMNOPUYZ
6 ACDFGK(N 0,4km)TV

💬 Located 300m from intimate medieval Turckheim between vineyards and close to the Route des Vins. You can be in Colmar by bus or train within 10 minutes. Enjoy the Alsatian wines and agreeable restaurants. A former municipal campsite which has now been renovated.

🚗 Leave the A35 at Colmar, exit 24 to Logelbach. Direction Turckheim at roundabout and turn left immediately after the level crossing to the campsite.

CC € **15** 28/3-4/7 22/8-21/10   🧭 N 48°5'7'' E 7°16'21''

Wattwiller/Cernay, F-68700 / Alsace (Haut-Rhin) 🛜 iD 1894

🏕 Camping Huttopia Wattwiller***
✉ route des Crêtes
☎ +33 (0)3-89754494
FAX +33 (0)3-89757198
🗓 27/4 - 23/9
@ info@campingwattwiller.com

15ha 118**T**(80-100m²) 6A CEE

1 ACD**G**IJKLOPRS
2 BJLSTVWXY
3 B**F**GHMN**OP**QRU
4 (A+B 1/7-31/8) (F 🔌)
　(G 1/7-31/8) (Q+R 🔌)
　(T+U+V 1/7-31/8) (X 🔌)
　(Z 1/7-31/8)
5 **AB**DFGIJKLMNPU
6 CDEGHIJ(N 7km)**P**T

💬 A terraced campsite located in woods between Mulhouse and Colmar. It has indoor and outdoor swimming pools.

🚗 From the N83 take the exit Cernay-Nord/Wattwiller, through Uffholtz to Wattwiller. Then follow signs to the campsite.

N66　D431　　D2
　　　　CC　D83
D14 BIV　D35
　　　　　　　Illzach
D466　　　**Mulhouse**

CC € 15 27/4-5/7　26/8-22/9　🧭 N 47°50'1'' E 7°9'56''

Wihr-au-Val, F-68230 / Alsace (Haut-Rhin) ♿ 🛜 iD 1895

🏕 La Route Verte**
✉ 13 rue de la Gare
☎ +33 (0)3-89711010
🗓 25/4 - 30/9
@ info@camping-routeverte.com

0,9ha 55**T**(80-105m²) 4-10A CEE

1 ACD**G**IJKLPQ
2 GIRSVWXY
3 AGHJKRU
4 (A 1/7-31/8) (Q+R+V+Z 🔌)
5 **A**FGIJKLMNPUW
6 CEGK(N 0,1km)OT

💬 Small-scale, hospitable campsite on the edge of a village. Well-maintained and full of flowers. Located in the Munster valley countryside in the Vosges. Close to the Route des Vins, Route des Crêtes and the Route du Fromage. Ideally situated for beautiful mountain hikes, but also for castles, lakes, cycling and picturesque little towns.

🚗 Leave D8 west of Colmar and follow D417. After ± 10 km right turn to Wihr-au-Val. After ± 400 metres La Route Verte is on your left.

D415
D61　D48　　**Colmar**
　　D11 VI
D417　　　　D30
　　CC
D10　　Sainte-Croix-en-
　　　　Plaine
　　　D83

CC € 13 25/4-30/6　25/8-29/9　🧭 N 48°3'6'' E 7°12'18''

Argenton-sur-Creuse, F-36200 / Centre-Val de Loire (Indre) ♿ 🛜 iD 1896

🏕 Les Chambons***
✉ 37 rue des Chambons
☎ +33 (0)966840601
🗓 1/2 - 30/11
@ campingleschambons@gmail.com

1,3ha 54**T**(100m²) 10A CEE

1 ACDGIJKLMOPQ
2 CFGLMRTVWXY
3 HJKRU**W**X
4 (Q 1/7-31/8)
5 **AB**FGIJKLMNOPUZ
6 CEGK(N 1km)T

💬 A friendly campsite with tall trees situated by the River Creuse in the town of Argenton, sometimes called 'the Venice of the Berry', with several medieval and Roman remains (Museum Argentomagus). Close to the centre (a 15 minute walk). The long 'Voie Verte' is close by.

🚗 From the north take the A20 Orléans-Limoges, exit 17, follow camping signs. Enter Saint-Marcel into SatNav.

　　　　　　　　D14
　　　D11
　　　N151
D927　Argenton-sur-　Saint-Marcel
　　　Creuse
　　　　CC
D29　　　A20
D46　　D1　D913　D48
　　　　　　　D40

CC € 15 1/2-30/6　1/9-29/11　🧭 N 46°35'47'' E 1°30'23''

Aubigny-sur-Nère, F-18700 / Centre-Val de Loire (Cher)

♿ 🛜 **iD** (1897)

🏕 Des Étangs***
📧 Avenue du Parc des Sports
☎ +33 (0)2-48580237
🗓 1/4 - 30/9
@ camping.aubigny@orange.fr

2ha 85T(80-200m²) 10A

1 ACDGIJKLMOP**Q**
2 DLRSTVWXY
3 ABGHJMRU**W**
4 (C+H 1/6-15/9) (Q 1/7-31/8)
 (R 🌙) (T 15/6-15/9)
 (U+V+Y+Z 1/7-31/8)
5 **AB**GIJKLMNPUWXZ
6 AEGIKL(N 2km)TV

💬 A well maintained campsite with excellent toilet facilities close to a fishing pond. Marked out spacious pitches mostly with shade. An indoor 25 metre swimming pool with toddlers' pool is next to the campsite.

🚗 In Aubigny-sur-Nère, east of the town, 200 metres past sports centre. Clearly signposted.

Argent-sur-Sauldre
D923
Aubigny-sur-Nère CC
D8
D21
D79
D30
D940
D926
D11

CC € **15** 1/4-2/7 27/8-29/9

📐 N 47°29'5'' E 2°27'21''

Azay-le-Rideau, F-37190 / Centre-Val de Loire (Indre-et-Loire)

♿ 🛜 **iD** (1898)

🏕 Municipal Le Sabot***
📧 Parc de Sabot
☎ +33 (0)2-47454272
🗓 20/4 - 4/11
@ camping.lesabot@wanadoo.fr

NEW

9ha 150T(80-100m²) 10A CEE

1 ACDGIJKLMOPQ
2 CFGLRVX
3 BGHJ**M**NRU**W**
4 (C+H+Q 1/7-31/8)
5 **AB**EFGIJKLMNPUVYZ
6 CEGHJ(N 0,3km)TV

💬 Municipal campsite located on the Indre, a stone's throw from the famous castle.

🚗 Via D751 exit Azay-le-Rideau. Close to the castle. Campsite is signposted.

Savonnières
A85
D952
Monts
D7
D17 CC
Artannes-sur-Indre
D751
D757 D57
A10

CC € **15** 20/4-30/6 1/9-3/11

📐 N 47°15'32'' E 0°28'11''

Ballan-Miré, F-37510 / Centre-Val de Loire (Indre-et-Loire)

👫 ♿ 🛜 **iD** (1899)

🏕 La Mignardière****
📧 22 avenue des Aubépines
☎ +33 (0)2-47733100
🗓 1/4 - 12/9
@ info@mignardiere.com

3,5ha 118T(80-150m²) 6-10A CEE

1 ACD**G**IJKLMOPQ
2 FGRVXY
3 B**F**GHJKN**Q**RU**W**
4 (C+F+G 🌙) **KNP**
 (Q+S+T+U+V+X+Y 🌙)
5 **AB**EFGIJKLMNOPUWZ
6 ACEG**K**(N 2km)RTV

💬 A lovely family campsite with good toilet facilities. Heated swimming pool (also covered), tennis. Playground opposite. There is a lake close by for surfing. A good base for cycle trips or visiting the chateaux of the Loire.

🚗 Via A10 past Tours, take exit 24 Joué-les-Tours, centre direction Ballan-Miré. Right at first traffic lights and follow camping signs.

D952
Tours
Saint-Avertin
D976
D7 CC
A85
D751
A10
D17
D84

CC € **17** 1/4-5/7 26/8-11/9 7=6

📐 N 47°21'19'' E 0°38'2''

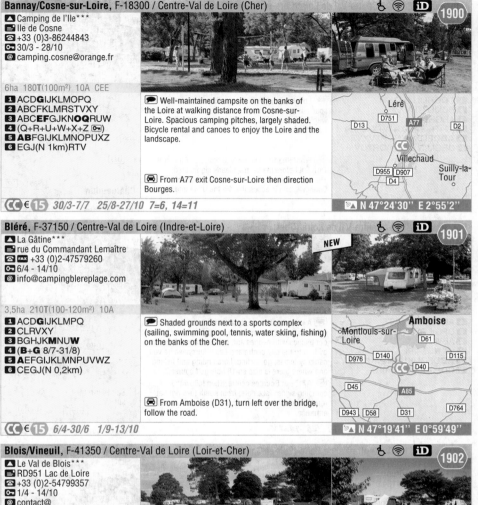

Bannay/Cosne-sur-Loire, F-18300 / Centre-Val de Loire (Cher) ♿ 🛜 iD 1900

🏕 Camping de l'Ile***
📧 Ile de Cosne
☎ +33 (0)3-86244843
🗓 30/3 - 28/10
@ camping.cosne@orange.fr

6ha 180T(100m²) 10A CEE

1 ACD**G**IJKLMOPQ
2 ABCFKLMRSTVXY
3 ABC**EF**GJKN**OQ**RUW
4 (Q+R+U+W+X+Z 🅿)
5 **AB**FGIJKLMNOPUXZ
6 EGJ(N 1km)RTV

💬 Well-maintained campsite on the banks of the Loire at walking distance from Cosne-sur-Loire. Spacious camping pitches, largely shaded. Bicycle rental and canoes to enjoy the Loire and the landscape.

🚗 From A77 exit Cosne-sur-Loire then direction Bourges.

CC € 15 30/3-7/7 25/8-27/10 7=6, 14=11 — N 47°24'30'' E 2°55'2''

Bléré, F-37150 / Centre-Val de Loire (Indre-et-Loire) ♿ 🛜 iD 1901

🏕 La Gâtine***
📧 rue du Commandant Lemaître
☎ FAX +33 (0)2-47579260
🗓 6/4 - 14/10
@ info@campingblereplage.com

NEW

3,5ha 210T(100-120m²) 10A

1 ACD**G**IJKLMPQ
2 CLRVXY
3 BGHJK**M**NU**W**
4 (**B+G** 8/7-31/8)
5 **A**EFGIJKLMNPUVWZ
6 CEGJ(N 0,2km)

💬 Shaded grounds next to a sports complex (sailing, swimming pool, tennis, water skiing, fishing) on the banks of the Cher.

🚗 From Amboise (D31), turn left over the bridge, follow the road.

CC € 15 6/4-30/6 1/9-13/10 — N 47°19'41'' E 0°59'49''

Blois/Vineuil, F-41350 / Centre-Val de Loire (Loir-et-Cher) ♿ 🛜 iD 1902

🏕 Le Val de Blois***
📧 RD951 Lac de Loire
☎ +33 (0)2-54799357
🗓 1/4 - 14/10
@ contact@
    camping-loisir-blois.com

10ha 120T(> 100m²) 16A

1 ACD**G**IJKLMPQ
2 CFKRSVWX
3 BGJK**W**
4 (**B+G** 1/6-31/8) (Q+R 🅿) (T 1/7-31/8)
5 **AB**GIJKLMNOPUX
6 EJ(N 3km)OT

💬 For your holiday or weekend in Lorie et Cher: discover the peace of Val de Loire campsite on the banks of the Loire (Vineuil). Perfect starting point for cultural or tourist trips out by car or bike (route Loire a Vélo next to the campsite).

🚗 Via A10 exit Blois, then towards Vierzon, turn right over the bridge direction Orléans (D951). 3 km east of Blois.

CC € 17 1/4-6/7 1/9-13/10 — N 47°36'23'' E 1°22'35''

Bonneval, F-28800 / Centre-Val de Loire(Eure-et-Loir) 1903

Camping du Bois de Chièvre***
29 route de Vouvray
+33 (0)237475401
1/4 - 31/10
campingduboisdechievre@gmail.com

4,5ha 62T(25-65m²) 16A CEE

1 CDGHIJLMPQ
2 BCIJLRTUVXY
3 ABGHIJNU
4 (Q+R+S+T+U+W+X+Z)
5 **AB**DEIJKLMNOPTVXYZ
6 DEGIJ(N 0,5km)ORTUV

Lovely campsite in a peaceful setting with spacious pitches. Playground and climbing course with 4 different distances. Restaurant. Chip & Pin possible from Euro15.

From Chartres via the N10 direction Bonneval. Turn left before the centre, clearly signposted. The campsite is located about 1.5 km east of Bonneval, and is accessible via the D144 and C1.

CC € 15 1/4-30/6 1/9-30/10 N 48°10'16'' E 1°23'11''

Bourges, F-18000 / Centre-Val de Loire (Cher) 1904

Robinson***
26 bd de l'Industrie
+33 (0)2-48201685
+33 (0)2-48503239
30/3 - 28/10
camping.bourges@orange.fr

2,2ha 107T(80-182m²) 10-16A CEE

1 ABC**G**IJKLMPST
2 CFGILRSTUVWXY
3 AB**W**
4 (C 18/6-4/9)
5 **AB**DFGIJKLMNOPUVWXYZ
6 CDEGJ(N 0,8km)RT

A well maintained city and stopover campsite. Campers have free use of the swimming pool. Marked out pitches with hedges and partial shade. 15 minutes by foot to the city centre and Lac d'Auron where you can play tennis, go surfing, horse riding and fishing and where there is also an 18 hole golf course.

A71, exit Bourges centre. Then follow the camping signs. Take note: from south turn right at fourth roundabout, then cross over to the campsite entrance.

CC € 17 30/3-7/7 25/8-27/10 7=6, 14=11 N 47°4'21'' E 2°23'41''

Bracieux, F-41250 / Centre-Val de Loire (Loir-et-Cher) 1905

Huttopia Les Châteaux***
11 rue Roger Brun
+33 (0)2-54464184
30/3 - 4/11
leschateaux@huttopia.com

8ha 202T(100-120m²) 10A CEE

1 ACD**F**IJLMO**P**ST
2 CGLRSTVWXY
3 BF**G**HJK**M**RU**W**
4 (C+E+H+Q+R)
  (T+V 3/7-30/8) (Z)
5 **AB**DFGIJKLMNPRUW
6 ACEGJ(N 0,3km)OTV

Located just 8 km from the chateau of Chambord, this completely renovated campsite offers quality amenities with numerous opportunities for hiking and cycling. The closest camp site to Chambord. CampingCard ACSI is valid only on standard pitches.

From Paris A10, exit 16 Mer. From Tours A10, exit 17 Blois, then D923. In Bracieux cross the bridge and turn right.

CC € 17 30/3-5/7 2/9-3/11 N 47°33'5'' E 1°32'21''

Bréhémont, F-37130 / Centre-Val de Loire (Indre-et-Loire)

♿ 🛜 iD **1906**

🏕 Loire et Châteaux***
🏠 Lieu-dit Le Stade
☎ +33 (0)6-61910142
🗓 1/2 - 30/11
@ camping@loireetchateaux.com

1,5ha 51**T**(100-150m²) 16A CEE

1 ACD**G**IJKLM**P**Q
2 FRVW
3 AGJKLU**W**
4 (C+H 1/4-30/9) (Q 1/4-31/10) (R+T+U+V+Z 1/4-30/9)
5 **AB**CDEFGHIJKLMNOPQRUWXYZ
6 ACDEGIJ(N 8km)RTV

💬 A campsite in rural surroundings with a friendly atmosphere. Enjoy the comfort including the brand new toilet facilities. The campsite is set among castles and in countryside listed as a Unesco World Heritage Site. Heated swimming pool (with facilities for the disabled), snack bar and playground. Close to the 'Loire à vélo' cycle route.

🚐 Via D16 direction Bréhémont. Left in village after church. Follow signs. Right at crossroads.

ⓒⓒ € **17** 1/2-6/7 24/8-29/11 | 📷 N 47°17'27'' E 0°21'13''

Briare-le-Canal, F-45250 / Centre-Val de Loire (Loiret)

♿ 🛜 iD **1907**

🏕 Le Martinet***
🏠 Val du Martinet
☎ 📠 +33 (0)2-38312450
🗓 30/3 - 30/9
@ contact@campinglemartinet.fr

4,2ha 160**T**(80-100m²) 10A CEE

1 AC**G**IJKLMPQ
2 CFLRSVWXY
3 BGQ**W**
4 (Q 1/6-1/9)
5 **A**DGIJKLMNOPUVXZ
6 CDEGJ(N 1km)T

💬 A relaxing campsite beside the Loire, close to the touristy Briare-le-Canal which is famous for its water works and the canal bridge over the Loire. Ideal for cyclists (Loire à vélo cycle route). The campsite has pitches partly marked out by hedges and with some shade.

🚐 Via A77 Paris-Nevers. From Montargis drive south on the N7. Near Briare exit towards Briare. In the town keep on towards Nevers, cross the bridge at the marina and turn right. Clearly signposted.

ⓒⓒ € **17** 30/3-30/6 1/9-29/9 | 📷 N 47°38'30'' E 2°43'33''

Candé-sur-Beuvron, F-41120 / Centre-Val de Loire (Loir-et-Cher)

♿ 🛜 ✿ iD **1908**

🏕 La Grande Tortue*****
🏠 route de Pontlevoy
☎ +33 (0)2-54441520
🗓 7/4 - 15/9
@ camping@grandetortue.com

6ha 90**T**(100-200m²) 10A CEE

1 ACD**G**IJKLMO**P**Q
2 BRSVXY
3 BF**G**HJKLN**P**RU**W**
4 (C+E+F+H 🖼) IJKM**N** (Q+S+T+U+V+X+Z 🖼)
5 **AB**DFGIJKLMNP**S**UVWXYZ
6 ACEGH**K**(N 6km)ORTV

💬 Child-friendly five-star site in an old oak wood. Surrounded by chateaux in the Loire Valley. An inspiring destination for nature and culture lovers. Heated indoor pool, open air leisure pool with slides and toddlers' pool. 'La Loire à vélo' cycle routes 500m from the site.

🚐 From Blois direction Vierzon. Via southern Loire-route (D751) direction Montrichard, Pont-le-Voye. Follow the Loire as far as Candé. Straight ahead at bend in the centre of Candé. Signposted.

ⓒⓒ € **19** 7/4-6/7 25/8-14/9 | 📷 N 47°29'23'' E 1°15'31''

Chartres, F-28000 / Centre-Val de Loire(Eure-et-Loir) ♛♛ ♿ 🛜 iD `1909`

▲ Les Bords de l'Eure***
🏠 9 rue de Launay
☎ 📠 +33 (0)2-37287943
🔓 1/3 - 31/10
@ camping-roussel-chartres@
wanadoo.fr

3,8ha 97T(100-150m²) 6A CEE

1 ACGIJKLO**PQ**
2 CFLRWX
3 BGKNR**W**
4 (R 1/7-31/8) (S+T 1/4-30/9)
(U 1/7-31/8)
(V+W+X 1/4-30/9)
5 **AB**FGIJKLMNPUV
6 CDEGIK(N 0,03km)ORTV

💬 A lovely overnight campsite in the centre of the town with plenty of trees and greenery all around. A lovely footpath leads from the campsite through the park to the cathedral. The river flows past the campsite. Refurbished playground for the children.

🚗 The campsite is located the southeast of the city. Drive via the N10 and take the ring road N123 until the intersection with the N154. Then follow the signs 'Centre Douane' and afterwards follow the camping signs.

Mainvilliers
Chartres
Lucé
D906 D32 D24 D939 D921 D910 A11 D935 N154 D29

🆑 € **17** 1/3-30/6 1/9-30/10   📐 N 48°26'3'' E 1°29'57''

Châteauneuf-sur-Loire, F-45110 / Centre-Val de Loire (Loiret) 🛜 iD `1910`

▲ La Maltournée**
🏠 route de Châteauneuf
☎ +33 (0)2-38584246
🔓 1/4 - 31/10
@ contact@
camping-chateauneufsurloire.com

5ha 190T(80m²) 10A CEE

1 ACG**I**JLQ
2 ACFIRSWX
3 BGJKRU**W**X
4 (Q+R+Z 🔓)
5 **AB**FGIJKLMNPUWX
6 CDEGJ(N 1km)TV

💬 Very well-maintained campsite with new toilet facilities. Large beach along the Loire. Spacious pitches, partly shaded. Baby and wheelchair-friendly. Good base for lovers of nature.

🚗 In Châteauneuf-sur-Loire direction Sigloy. Left immediately over the bridge (300m).

D9 D2060 D11 D2060 D2060 Mardié D960 Châteauneuf-sur-Loire Saint-Martin-d'Abbat D952 D14 D60 D83 Sully-sur-Loire

🆑 € **15** 1/4-30/6 1/9-30/10   📐 N 47°51'24'' E 2°13'48''

Châteauroux, F-36000 / Centre-Val de Loire (Indre) ♿ 🛜 iD `1911`

▲ Le Rochat Belle-Isle***
🏠 17 rue du Rochat
☎ +33 (0)2-54089629
🔓 1/1 - 31/12
@ campinglerochat@gmail.com

2,5ha 152T(80-130m²) 10A CEE

1 ABCD**G**IJKLMO**PQ**
2 ACDFGLMRTVWXY
3 AB**F**GHJKR**TW**Z
4 (F+G 🔓) J(R 1/2-30/11)
(X+Z 🔓)
5 **AB**DEFIJKLMNOPUZ
6 CDFGK(N 2km)OTV

💬 Nice stopover campsite (also for longer stays) located in parkland surroundings near the town centre. Close to recreational lake with playground. Restaurant on the lake. Free pool 100 metres from site. Cycle routes from campsite. Free bus service to centre.

🚗 A20 exit 13, dir. Châteauroux centre. Left at 1st traffic lights. Continue on road. Straight on at roundabout. Straight on through traffic lights. Left after green building. Campsite located on left.

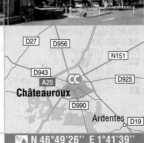

D27 D956 N151 D943 A20 D925 **Châteauroux** D990 Ardentes D19

🆑 € **15** 1/1-30/6 1/9-31/12   📐 N 46°49'26'' E 1°41'39''

Chemillé-sur-Indrois, F-37460 / Centre-Val de Loire (Indre-et-Loire) 👫 ♿ 📶 🌀 iD 1912

🏕 Les Coteaux du Lac****
☎ +33 (0)2-47927783
🕐 24/3 - 7/10
@ lescoteauxdulac@wanadoo.fr

2,5ha 60T(100-170m²) 16A CEE

1 ACD**G**IJKLMOPQ
2 ADK**L**RVWX
3 BGHJKN**Q**RUV**W**Z
4 (C+H 15/4-15/9) J
(Q 15/6-15/9) (R+T+U 🕐)
(V 1/7-31/8) (X+Z 🕐)
5 **AB**FGIJKLMNOPRUWXYZ
6 ACDEGK(N 3km)RTV

💬 Situated on the shore of a lake. Ideal place for family holidays and for discovering the Châteaux of the Loire. Heated swimming pool, children's toilets, shop, television room. Also: paddle boats, canoes, supervised beach, fishing (carp), bar/restaurant.

🚗 From St. Aignan via the D675 to Nouans, then D760 direction Montrésor and via the D10 to Chemillé. After passing the village cross the bridge and turn right. Follow the signs.

CC € **17** 24/3-8/7 26/8-6/10 7=6　　🏕 N 47°9'28'' E 1°9'35''

Cheverny, F-41700 / Centre-Val de Loire (Loir-et-Cher) 👫 ♿ 📶 🌀 iD 1913

🏕 Sites & Paysages Les Saules****
🏠 les Saules
☎ +33 (0)2-54799001
🕐 1/4 - 15/9
@ contact@camping-cheverny.com

8ha 164T(100-140m²) 10A CEE

1 ACD**G**IJL**PQ**
2 BLRVXY
3 B**EF**HJKLN**Q**RUW
4 (C 1/4-14/9) (E 15/4-14/9)
(G 1/4-14/9) (Q 🕐)
(S+T+U+V 15/5-14/9)
(X 1/7-31/8) (Z 15/5-14/9)
5 **AB**EFGIJKLMNPUWXZ
6 ACEGHIJ(N 3km)OTVW

💬 The woods around Les Saules offer relaxation. The campsite fits in perfectly with spacious shaded pitches and well maintained toilets. The friendly ambiance provides the rest. Good walking and cycling opportunities such as the 'Loire à vélo' cycle route which can be reached from the site. Golf course 2 km away.

🚗 A10, exit 17 Blois direction Vierzon. From centre Cheverny take direction Château. Campsite on the right 1.4 km after castle.

CC € **17** 1/4-8/7 26/8-14/9 7=6, 14=12　　🏕 N 47°28'40'' E 1°27'3''

Cloyes-sur-le-Loir, F-28220 / Centre-Val de Loire(Eure-et-Loir) 👫 ♿ 📶 🌀 iD 1914

🏕 Parc de Loisirs Le Val Fleuri****
🏠 route de Montigny
☎ +33 (0)2-37985053
📠 +33 (0)2-37983384
🕐 15/3 - 15/11
@ info@val-fleuri.fr

5ha 196T(100-150m²) 6A CEE

1 AC**G**IJKLPR
2 CDGLRTVWXY
3 ABGJNPQRU**W**
4 (C 1/5-30/9) (E 🕐)
(H 1/5-30/9) IJ**K**
(Q+S+T+U+V+X+Z 🕐)
5 **AB**EFGIJKLMNOPUWYZ
6 CEGH**IK**(N 0,5km)OQRTV

💬 A lovely, large campsite for young and old in a beautiful area close to the chateaux of the Loire and not far from Paris and Versailles. Lovely outdoor heated swimming pool with slide, toddlers' pool, indoor pool and jacuzzi (free). Also minigolf, sailing, pony riding and bouncy castle.

🚗 Drive from Châteaudun via the N10 and D35. Turn right before the built up area of Cloyes-sur-le-Loir. Camping signs indicate the route clearly.

CC € **17** 15/3-30/6 1/9-14/11　　🏕 N 48°0'8'' E 1°13'59''

Éguzon, F-36270 / Centre-Val de Loire (Indre)

  ⛺ 🛜 **iD** **1915**

- 🏕 Éguzon La Garenne****
- 📧 1 rue Yves Choplin
- ☎ +33 (0)2-54474485
- 🕐 10/3 - 15/10
- @ info@campinglagarenne.eu

2ha 78T(100-150m²) 6-10A CEE

1 ACDGIJKLMOPQ
2 FIJLRTUVWXY
3 BGHJNRU
4 (**A** 1/5-15/9) (C 1/6-13/9)
  (H 17/6-2/9) (T+V 24/5-15/9)
  (Z 9/5-15/9)
5 **AB**CDFGHIJKLNPUWXYZ
6 ACDEG**K**(N 0,3km)V

💬 A Dutch run campsite with heated pool. 3 km from Lac d'Eguzon with all watersports opportunities, 300m from the centre with shopping and small restaurants. Lovely walking and cycling routes (partly hilly, partly level). Privacy, rest and space. Heated toilet facilities in low season.

🚗 On A20 exit 20 direction Éguzon. In centre D45 direction Pont des Piles. The campsite is 300m further on. It is located in Éguzon. Follow the Camping 'La Garenne' signs in Éguzon.

(CC) €15 10/3-6/7 24/8-14/10 7=6, 14=11   📐 N 46°26'46'' E 1°34'56''

Faverolles-sur-Cher, F-41400 / Centre-Val de Loire (Loir-et-Cher)

  ⛺ 🛜 **iD** **1916**

- 🏕 Couleurs du Monde****
- 📧 1 Rond Point de Montparnasse
- ☎ +33 (0)2-54320608
- 📠 +33 (0)2-54326135
- 🕐 26/3 - 28/9
- @ touraine-vacances@wanadoo.fr

4ha 100T(120m²) 6-10A CEE

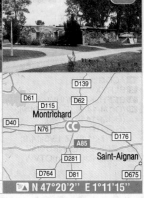

1 ACD**G**IJKLMOPQ
2 GLRVXY
3 BDGHJKLNRUV**W**
4 (C+E+H 🔒) **KLN** 🔒
  (Q+S+T+U+V+X+Z 🔒)
5 **AB**EFGIJKLMNOPUWZ
6 ACEG**K**M(N 0,05km)ORTV

💬 Surrounded by beautiful castles and vineyards in the Loire Valley. A stone's throw from the historic town of Montrichard. Parkland grounds (4 hectares). Family atmosphere: 'la douce France'. Hospitable, good facilities, peace and space. Heated swimming pool on site, restaurant, bar, bike hire. Supermarket within walking distance.

🚗 From Blois D764 direction Montrichard/Loches. From Montrichard direction Faverolles. Campsite on left after second roundabout.

(CC) €15 26/3-13/7 31/8-27/9 7=6, 14=12   📐 N 47°20'2'' E 1°11'15''

Francueil/Chenonceaux, F-37150 / Centre-Val de Loire (Indre-et-Loire)

  ⛺ 🛜 **iD** **1917**

- 🏕 Le Moulin Fort***
- ☎ +33 (0)2-47238622
- 🕐 5/5 - 30/9
- @ lemoulinfort@wanadoo.fr

3ha 130T(80-100m²) 6A CEE

1 ACD**G**IJKLMOPRS
2 CLRVX
3 BGHJ**Q**RU**W**
4 (B+G 26/5-23/9) (Q+S 🔒)
  (T+U+X+Z 26/5-23/9)
5 **AB**FGIJKLMNOPUWZ
6 CEG**J**(N 7km)OTV

💬 Well maintained campsite very close to Chenonceaux Castle. Site located on the banks of the River Cher. Good amenities and good leisure opportunities in and around the grounds.

🚗 From Bléré via the D976, after 6 km turn left towards Chenonceaux. Before you reach the bridge turn right. Clearly signposted.

(CC) €17 5/5-6/7 27/8-29/9   📐 N 47°19'35'' E 1°5'1''

Illiers-Combray, F-28120 / Centre-Val de Loire(Eure-et-Loir)   ♿ 🛜 iD 1918

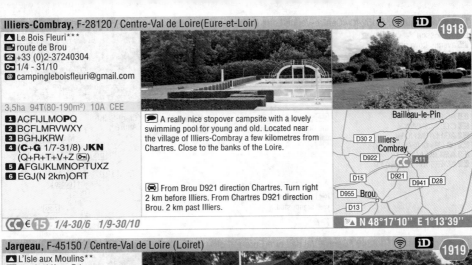

▲ Le Bois Fleuri***
🏠 route de Brou
☎ +33 (0)2-37240304
🗓 1/4 - 31/10
@ campinglebois fleuri@gmail.com

3,5ha 94T(80-190m²) 10A CEE

1 ACFIJLMO**PQ**
2 BCFLMRVWXY
3 BGHJKRW
4 (C+G 1/7-31/8) J**KN**
  (Q+R+T+V+Z 🔒)
5 AFGIJKLMNOPTUXZ
6 EGJ(N 2km)ORT

💬 A really nice stopover campsite with a lovely swimming pool for young and old. Located near the village of Illiers-Combray a few kilometres from Chartres. Close to the banks of the Loire.

🚗 From Brou D921 direction Chartres. Turn right 2 km before Illiers. From Chartres D921 direction Brou. 2 km past Illiers.

Bailleau-le-Pin
D30 2 Illiers-Combray
D922 CC A11
D15 | D921 | D941 | D28
D955 Brou
D13

CC € 15 1/4-30/6 1/9-30/10   📍 N 48°17'10'' E 1°13'39''

Jargeau, F-45150 / Centre-Val de Loire (Loiret)   🛜 iD 1919

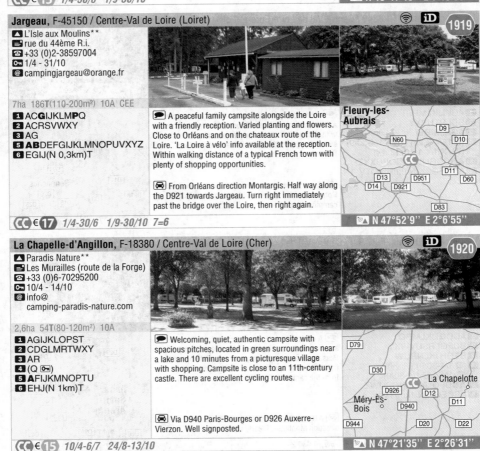

▲ L'Isle aux Moulins**
🏠 rue du 44ème R.i.
☎ +33 (0)2-38597004
🗓 1/4 - 31/10
@ campingjargeau@orange.fr

7ha 186T(110-200m²) 10A CEE

1 ACG**I**JKLMO**PQ**
2 ACRSVWXY
3 AG
5 **AB**DEFGIJKLMNOPUVXYZ
6 EGIJ(N 0,3km)T

💬 A peaceful family campsite alongside the Loire with a friendly reception. Varied planting and flowers. Close to Orléans and on the chateaux route of the Loire. 'La Loire à vélo' info available at the reception. Within walking distance of a typical French town with plenty of shopping opportunities.

🚗 From Orléans direction Montargis. Half way along the D921 towards Jargeau. Turn right immediately past the bridge over the Loire, then right again.

Fleury-les-Aubrais
D9
N60 | D10
CC
D11
D13 | D951 | D60
D14 | D921
D83

CC € 17 1/4-30/6 1/9-30/10 7=6   📍 N 47°52'9'' E 2°6'55''

La Chapelle-d'Angillon, F-18380 / Centre-Val de Loire (Cher)   🛜 iD 1920

▲ Paradis Nature**
🏠 Les Murailles (route de la Forge)
☎ +33 (0)6-70295200
🗓 10/4 - 14/10
@ info@
  camping-paradis-nature.com

2,6ha 54T(80-120m²) 10A

1 AGIJKLOP**ST**
2 CDGLMRTWXY
3 AR
4 (Q 🔒)
5 **A**FIJKMNOPTU
6 EHJ(N 1km)T

💬 Welcoming, quiet, authentic campsite with spacious pitches, located in green surroundings near a lake and 10 minutes from a picturesque village with shopping. Campsite is close to an 11th-century castle. There are excellent cycling routes.

🚗 Via D940 Paris-Bourges or D926 Auxerre-Vierzon. Well signposted.

D79
D30
La Chapelotte
D926 | D12
Méry-Ès-Bois | D940 | D11
D944 | D20 | D22

CC € 15 10/4-6/7 24/8-13/10   📍 N 47°21'35'' E 2°26'31''

La Ferté-St-Aubin, F-45240 / Centre-Val de Loire (Loiret) 🛜 iD 1921

🏕 du Cosson**
✉ avenue Lowendal
☎ +33 (0)2-38765590
🔑 30/3 - 30/9
@ campingducosson45@outlook.fr

50T 6A CEE

1 ACD**G**IJLMPRS
2 CGLRSVWXY
3 AGHJ**K**M**R**U**W**
4 (B+F+G 🔑) J(Y 🔑)
5 **AB**IJKLMNPU
6 ADEGJ(N 0,5km)TV

💬 Situated in parkland grounds on the banks of the Cosson. A stone's throw away from a castle, the centre and a leisure pool.

🚗 In centre follow dir. castle via D2020. Campsite is well signposted.

Cléry-Saint-André
Marcilly-en-Villette — D13
D18 — D921
A71 CC
D15 — D61
D2020
D922
N20

CC € 15 15/4-30/6 1/9-29/9 7=6 — ⛺ N 47°43'31'' E 1°56'1''

La Ferté-Vidame, F-28340 / Centre-Val de Loire(Eure-et-Loir) 👫👶 ♿ 🛜 iD 1922

🏕 Les Abrias du Perche
✉ route de la Lande
☎ +33 (0)2-37376400
🔑 1/2 - 31/12
@ lesabriasduperche@orange.fr

2ha 48T(70-100m²) 10A CEE

1 AC**F**IJKLMPST
2 BDLRTUVXY
3 AGHJ**M**R**W**
4 (E 15/4-30/9) (Q+T 1/4-30/9)
   (W+X 1/4-1/10) (Z 🔑)
5 **AB**CDGIJKLMNOPUXYZ
6 ACDEGHK(N 0,8km)OTV

💬 A beautifully located campsite in the middle of a wood with many lakes. Good marked out pitches with plenty of shade. Large playground and heated swimming pool. Modern toilet facilities and wifi throughout the campsite.

🚗 From Verneuil-sur-Avre direction Nogent-le-Rotrou as far as La Ferté-Vidame and then follow camping signs.

D939
N12 — La Ferté-Vidame — D4
CC
D11 — D941
D918 — Senonches
D8 — D15 — D20 — D25

CC € 13 1/2-7/7 1/9-30/12 — ⛺ N 48°36'28'' E 0°53'23''

La Ville-aux-Dames, F-37700 / Centre-Val de Loire (Indre-et-Loire) ♿ 🛜 iD 1923

🏕 Tours Les Acacias***
✉ rue Berthe Morisot
☎ +33 (0)2-47440816
🔑 1/1 - 31/12
@ contact@camplvad.com

3,5ha 88T(100-120m²) 10A CEE

1 ACD**G**IJKLM**P**Q
2 BCFGLRSUVWXY
3 B**F**GHJKLNRU**W**
4 (Q 1/4-30/9) (R 🔑)
   (T+V+X+Z 1/4-30/9)
5 **AB**DFGIJKLMNOPUWZ
6 ABCEGK(N 1km)TV

💬 A quiet and partly shaded campsite where peace and hospitality are the order of the day all year round. Passers-by and longer stayers can benefit optimally from the many opportunities. Route 'Loire à Velo' from the campsite. Free wifi.

🚗 A10 exit 21. Accessible from Tours. 6 km direction Montlouis. Clearly signposted.

A28 — D910
D938 — D29 — D46
A10
D76 — D751
Tours CC
Saint-Avertin — D40
D976
D86 — A85 — D943 — D45

CC € 17 1/1-8/7 26/8-31/12 7=6, 14=12 — ⛺ N 47°24'7'' E 0°46'48''

Loches, F-37600 / Centre-Val de Loire (Indre-et-Loire) ♿ 🛜 iD 1924

🏕 La Citadelle****
🍴 Aristide Briand
☎ +33 (0)2-47590591
🗓 30/3 - 5/10
@ camping@lacitadelle.com

4ha 115T(50-180m²) 10-20A CEE

1 ACD**G**IJKLMOPQ
2 CGLRVXY
3 **BEF**GHJ**M**RU**W**
4 (C 9/4-5/10) (F 🚿)
　(**G** 9/4-5/10) (Q+R 🚿)
　(T+U+V+X+Z 1/7-31/8)
5 **AB**EFGIJKLMNPUVWXY
6 ACEG**K**(N 0,5km)ORTUV

💬 Hospitable campsite on the edge of the historic town of Loches with its interesting castle. Both the town and the surroundings offer various leisure opportunities. On the site itself a heated swimming pool, bar/snack/restaurant and good toilet facilities. Low season opening times: 08:00-12:15 and 14:00-19:30. Discount offered at restaurant and wellness centre in town. Wifi Euro2/day, Euro1/night after 7 nights and free from 7 nights.

🚗 Follow camping signs in the centre.

Tauxigny D58 — Genillé D764 D10 — Loches D760 CC D9 — D31 — D59 D41 D943

CC € **17** 30/3-6/7 25/8-4/10 　　🧭 N 47°7'22'' E 1°0'8''

Luynes, F-37230 / Centre-Val de Loire (Indre-et-Loire) ♿ 🛜 iD 1925

🏕 Flower Camping Les Granges***
🍴 avenue de l'Europe
☎ +33 (0)2-47557905
FAX +33 (0)2-47409243
🗓 26/3 - 30/9
@ reception@campinglesgranges.fr

1,8ha 30T(> 100m²) 10A CEE

1 ACD**G**IJKLM**P**RS
2 FGRVX
3 BGHJN**P**RUV**W**
4 (C+H+Q+R 🚿)
　(T+U+Z 15/4-15/9)
5 **AB**GIJKMNOPUXZ
6 ACEGHIK(N 0,5km)TV

💬 A peacefully located campsite near the town of Luynes. Good amenities and shop. Improved toilet facilities. Good cycling and walking opportunities in the area. Free wifi, heated pool. Loire castles (Ussé, Langeais, Villandry) nearby. Futuroscope (1 hours' drive).

🚗 Easily accessible via the D952, west of Tours direction Saumur. Campsite signposted

D959 D29 — D34 — **Tours Saint-Avertin** CC D952 — D15 — D57 D7 — A85 D86

CC € **15** 26/3-6/7 27/8-29/9 　　🧭 N 47°22'52'' E 0°33'31''

Luzeret, F-36800 / Centre-Val de Loire (Indre) 🌀 ♿ 🛜 iD 1926

🏕 La Petite Brenne
🍴 La Grande Métairie
☎ +33 (0)2-54250578
🗓 21/4 - 1/10
@ info@lapetitebrenne.com

42ha 150T(200-300m²) 10A CEE

1 ACEHIJKLMNOPQ
2 ACDFKLMRUWXYZ
3 ABCDGHJNOPRUVW
4 (**A**+B+E+G 🚿) **N**
　(Q+R+T+U 🚿) (V 1/7-31/8)
　(Y+Z 🚿)
5 **AB**CEFGHIJKLMNOPQRU
　WZ
6 CDEH**K**L(N 6km)OTV

NEW

💬 A very spaciously appointed naturist campsite surrounding a small lake. The campsite provides everything for a carefree and relaxing holiday in the middle of the countryside.

🚗 A20 exit 18 direction Prissac/Luzeret. Follow 'La Petite Brenne' signs in centre.

D927 — Argenton-sur-Creuse — D29 — A20 D48 — CC — D10 D46 D1 D913 — Saint-Benoît-du-Sault

CC € **19** 21/4-8/6 1/9-30/9 　　🧭 N 46°32'33'' E 1°24'11''

Montbazon, F-37250 / Centre-Val de Loire (Indre-et-Loire) ♿ 🛜 **iD** 1927

🏕 La Vallée de l'Indre***
🛣 D910
☎ +33 (0)2-47260643
🗓 1/4 - 31/12
@ contact@
   camping-montbazon.com

3ha 110T(100-120m²) 10A CEE

1 ACD**G**IJKLMPQ
2 CFGLRVX
3 HJ**M**N**QRW**
4 (B 15/5-15/9) (Q+R 1/7-31/8)
   (T+U+X+Y+Z 1/4-30/9)
5 **AB**FGIJKLMNOPUV
6 ACEK(N 0,1km)T

💬 Quietly located in the heart of the Touraine, on the banks of the Indre. A good stopover site, close to the N910. Also suitable for longer stays. Restaurant and playground with bouncy castles on campsite. Shops within walking distance. In the midst of the Azay le Rideau-Amboise-Villandry-Ussé castles and Honoré de Balzac museum (Saché).

🚗 Via A10 exit 23 Chambray to D910 in southerly dictrection. Turn right at Office de Tourisme. Well signposted.

CC €**15** 1/4-7/7 25/8-30/12 4=3, 8=6

🧭 N 47°17'25'' E 0°42'59''

Montlouis-sur-Loire, F-37270 / Centre-Val de Loire (Indre-et-Loire) ♿ 🛜 **iD** 1928

🏕 Camping Les Peupliers***
🛣 D751
☎ +33 (0)2-47508190
🗓 30/3 - 21/10
@ camping.lespeupliers@
   wanadoo.fr

4ha 72T(100-120m²) 10A CEE

1 ACD**G**IJKLMPQ
2 CRUVXY
3 BGHJK**M**RU**W**
4 (C 4/7-31/8) (Q+R+T+Z 🔑)
5 **A**BFGIJKLMNOPUXYZ
6 DEGJ(N 0,5km)TV

💬 This campsite has sunny and shaded pitches. Good amenities.

🚗 From Tours via the D751 direction Amboise, well signposted.

CC €**15** 30/3-7/7 25/8-20/10

🧭 N 47°23'40'' E 0°48'42''

Muides-sur-Loire, F-41500 / Centre-Val de Loire (Loir-et-Cher) ♿ 🛜 **iD** 1929

🏕 Sandaya Château
   des Marais*****
🛣 27 rue de Chambord
☎ +33 (0)2-54870542
🗓 13/4 - 9/9
@ chateaudesmarais@sandaya.fr

8ha 116T(100-120m²) 10A CEE

1 ACD**G**IJKLMOPQ
2 BFLRVX
3 BHJK**M**N**PQ**RUW
4 (C+F+G 🔑) IJ**KLN**
   (Q+S+T+U+V+X+Y+Z 🔑)
5 **A**BFGIJKLMNOPUWXY
6 CDEGH**I**K(N 0,2km)ORTV

NEW

💬 Rurally located family campsite with many opportunities for young and old. Water park! Ideally located for visiting the chateaux in the Loire Valley. The chateau of Chambord is 500 metres from the campsite.

🚗 From A10 (Mer exit) direction Muides/Chambord. Campsite signposted. Also via D951 Blois-Orléans.

CC €**17** 13/4-6/7 1/9-8/9

🧭 N 47°39'59'' E 1°31'45''

Néret, F-36400 / Centre-Val de Loire (Indre) 📶 🆔 1930

🏕 Le Bonhomme**
🍽 Mulles
☎ +33 (0)2-54314611
🗓 1/4 - 1/10
@ info@camping-lebonhomme.com

1,5ha 37T(100-120m²) 6A CEE

1 AG**I**J**L**PQ
2 ILRTVWXY
3 GIJR
4 (Q+V+X 🖙)
5 A**C**GIJKLMNOPUWZ
6 CEG**K**(N 6km)T

💬 A small, friendly campsite among fruit and nut trees in a very peaceful, undulating landscape. The surroundings are a paradise for walking and cycling. The campsite is Dutch run. Communal meals and bread at your tent.

🚗 Exit 12 Chateauroux from Vierzon on the A20. Then D943 direction Montluçon. Left at Néret exit. In Néret follow the 'Aire Naturelle' signs, 2 km beyond Néret sign to 'Le Bonhomme' on the left of the road.

CC € 15 1/4-7/7 25/8-30/9   N 46°35'19'' E 2°7'59''

Nouan-le-Fuzelier, F-41600 / Centre-Val de Loire (Loir-et-Cher) ♿ 📶 🆔 1931

🏕 La Grande Sologne***
🍽 rue Cauchoix
☎ 📠 +33 (0)2-54887022
🗓 1/4 - 16/10
@ info@campingrandesologne.com

10ha 150T(80-120m²) 10A

1 ACD**G**IJKLPRS
2 BCDFGLRVWXY
3 BGHJK**M**N**OP**QRTUW
4 (C 1/6-15/9) (H 15/6-31/8) J
   (Q 1/7-31/8) (R 🖙)
   (T+U+X 1/7-23/8)
5 **AB**EFGIJKLMNPUWZ
6 ACDEGK(N 0,5km)OTV

💬 A friendly family campsite located around a fish pond; spacious shaded pitches, extensive sports facilities including tennis and swimming pool next to the site. Children's playground, free wifi. Close to the chateaux of the Loire (including Chambord). Various cycling and walking routes.

🚗 From the north A71, exit 3 dir. RD2020. From Orléans follow the RD2020 dir. Vierzon until past the town of Nouan-le-Fuzelier. From the south A71 exit 4 dir. Orléans.

CC € 15 1/4-2/7 20/8-15/10 7=6, 14=11   N 47°31'58'' E 2°2'12''

Poilly-lez-Gien/Gien, F-45500 / Centre-Val de Loire (Loiret) 🚻 ♿ 📶 ✿ 🆔 1932

🏕 Les Bois du Bardelet*****
🍽 Le Petit Bardelet
☎ +33 (0)2-38674739
📠 +33 (0)2-38382716
🗓 14/4 - 16/9
@ contact@bardelet.com

15ha 120T(100-300m²) 16A CEE

1 ACD**G**IJKLMOPQ
2 ADLRSTUVXY
3 BGHJK**M**NQRUV**W**
4 (C 1/5-3/9) (F 🖙)
   (H 1/5-3/9) JKM**NP**
   (Q+S+U+V+X+Y+Z 8/4-10/9)
5 **AB**DEFGJLNPS**U**WXYZ
6 CDEGI**JK**(N 6km)TV

💬 Luxury holiday resort with indoor and outdoor pools, and indoor playing pool 'Robin' for children up to 12. All the amenities you can think of, including for groups. Spacious marked-out pitches, partly with shade. Fishing lake of 1 hectare. Cycling options (Loire á vélo). Full wifi coverage. Water slide by pool.

🚗 D940 in Gien direction Bourges. Left in 'La Ruellée' hamlet. SatNav: Le Petit Bardelet 45500 Poilly-lez-Gien. Campsite is clearly signposted.

CC € 17 14/4-30/6 1/9-15/9   N 47°38'29'' E 2°36'54''

Poilly-lez-Gien/Gien, F-45500 / Centre-Val de Loire (Loiret)   ♿ 🛜 iD   1933

▲ Sites & Paysages Camping de Gien***
🏠 rue des Iris
☎ +33 (0)2-38671250
FAX +33 (0)2-38671218
⌚ 3/3 - 4/11
@ camping-gien@wanadoo.fr
6ha 200T(100-120m²) 10A CEE

1 ACGIJKLMPQ
2 ACFKLORTVXY
3 AHIJKLNQRUW
4 (A 1/7-31/8)
(C+E+G 1/6-30/9) (Q 1/6-31/8) (S+T 1/5-30/9)
(U 15/5-30/9) (W ⌂)
(Y+Z 1/5-30/9)
5 ABDFGIJKLMNOPUWXYZ
6 ACDEGIK(N 0,5km)OQTV

💬 A campsite with shaded but unreserved pitches alongside the banks of the Loire. Views of the town of Gien, famous for its pottery. The swimming pool can be covered. You can make canoe trips from the campsite. This part of the Loire is perfect for walking and cycling trips.

🚗 Campsite is located on the Loire, close to the old bridge, opposite the castle. Take first exit Gien-Centre from roundabout, then follow signs 'Bord de Loire'.

CC € 17 3/3-8/7 26/8-3/11 7=6   📷 N 47°40'56'' E 2°37'23''

Romorantin-Lanthenay, F-41200 / Centre-Val de Loire (Loir-et-Cher)   ♿ 🛜 iD   1934

▲ Le Tournefeuille***
🏠 32 rue des Lices
☎ +33 (0)2-54761660
⌚ 15/4 - 30/9
@ entreprisefrery@orange.fr

1,9ha 90T(80-130m²) 10A CEE

1 ACDGIJKLMPQ
2 CFRVWX
3 BGJKMRU
4 (C+E+H+Q+T+Z ⌂)
5 ABFGIJKLMNOPSUXY
6 CDEJ(N 0,3km)TV

💬 On the banks of the Sauldre on the edge of the historic town Romorantin. The possibilities are many: fishing, walking, visiting museums (Matra).

🚗 In centre via D922/D922a or D764. Follow signs 'Complexe Sportif'.

CC € 15 15/4-6/7 24/8-29/9 7=6   📷 N 47°21'18'' E 1°45'20''

Salbris, F-41300 / Centre-Val de Loire (Loir-et-Cher)   ♿ 🛜 iD   1935

▲ Camping de Sologne***
🏠 8 alleé de la Sauldre
☎ +33 (0)2-54970638
⌚ 1/4 - 30/9
@ campingdesologne@wanadoo.fr

2ha 85T(60-100m²) 10A CEE

1 ACGHIJKLMOP
2 CDFRVWX
3 AGHJMRW
4 (C 1/6-15/9) (Q 15/6-15/8)
(R ⌂) (T+X+Z 1/5-31/8)
5 ABFGIJKLMNPUXYZ
6 FGIK(N 0km)TV

💬 A beautiful, relaxing campsite by a lake. Located 2 km from the motorway. Restaurants and shops within walking distance of the pleasant and quiet Salbris. Close to a swimming pool.

🚗 From Orléans via the N20 towards Vierzon, turn left at Salbris onto the D55 to Pierrefitte. Campsite after 300m right.

CC € 15 1/4-17/6 1/9-29/9   📷 N 47°25'49'' E 2°3'16''

Savonnières, F-37550 / Centre-Val de Loire (Indre-et-Loire)

♿ 📶 **iD** `1936`

🏔 La Confluence***
✉ route du Bray
☎ +33 (0)2-47500025
📅 30/4 - 30/9
@ contact@campinglaconfluence.fr

80T(95-100m²) 10A CEE

1 ACD**G**IJKLMPQ
2 CFGMRVWXY
3 BGHJMNR**W**
4 (Q 1/7-31/8)
5 **AB**EFGIJKLMNOPQRUXYZ
6 DEGJ(N 0,6km)T

💬 La Confluence is located on the banks of the Cher with a view of the village. Spacious pitches. The stalactite caves and mushroom farms in the vicinity are worth a visit. Don't forget to visit Ussé castle (Sleeping Beauty castle) and Villandry with its beautiful gardens.

🚗 Accessible via A58, exit Villandry. Follow dir. Villandry/Savonnières. Left after centre. Via D37 exit Savonnières. Right before centre. Well signposted.

CC € **17** 30/4-30/6 1/9-29/9

📐 N 47°20'59'' E 0°33'0''

Sonzay, F-37360 / Centre-Val de Loire (Indre-et-Loire)

👫 ♿ 📶 **iD** `1937`

🏔 L'Arada Parc****
✉ rue de la Baratiere
☎ +33 (0)2-47247269
📅 30/3 - 30/9
@ info@laradaparc.com

1,7ha 59T(85-115m²) 10A CEE

1 ACD**G**IJKLMPQ
2 FGLRSVWX
3 ABC**F**GHJK**M**PRU
4 (C 15/5-15/9) (F+H 🔑) **LN**
(Q+R+T+U+V+X+Z 🔑)
5 **AB**EFGIJKLMNOPUWXYZ
6 ACDEG**K**(N 6km)OTV

💬 A beautiful campsite in the countryside between the valleys of the Loire and the Loir, close to the chateaux. Indoor and outdoor swimming pools, indoor playground, wellness accommodation and spa. On presentation of CampingCard ACSI during acceptance period, free wifi for one device.

🚗 From Château-Renault D766 to Neuillé-Pont-Pierre then follow camping signs. From the A28 take exit 27 to Neuillé-Pont-Pierre, then follow camping signs.

CC € **17** 30/3-7/7 25/8-29/9 7=6

📐 N 47°31'37'' E 0°27'11''

St. Amand-Montrond, F-18200 / Centre-Val de Loire (Cher)

♿ 📶 **iD** `1938`

🏔 La Roche***
✉ chemin de la Roche
☎ 📠 +33 (0)2-48960936
📅 1/4 - 30/9
@ camping-la-roche@wanadoo.fr

4ha 120T(100-120m²) 6A CEE

1 AGIJKLM**P**Q
2 CFGRVWXY
3 ABG**M**NRU**W**
4 (Q 🔑)
5 **AB**DGIJKLMNOPUV
6 EGK(N 1km)TV

💬 A well maintained campsite by a canal and near the Cher. Pitches with sufficient shade separated by bushes. The centre is within walking distance and there is a bus stop next to the site. A free bus goes to the centre (where there is a swimming pool).

🚗 A71 exit 8, through the centre direction Montluçon. Just before the bridge, when leaving the city, turn right and keep on the side of the river.

CC € **15** 1/4-30/6 1/9-29/9 7=6

📐 N 46°43'4'' E 2°29'26''

St. Avertin, F-37550 / Centre-Val de Loire (Indre-et-Loire)

♿ 🤍 **iD** 1939

🏕 Tours Val de Loire****
📧 61 rue de Rochepinard
☎ +33 (0)2-47278747
🔄 2/2 - 16/12
@ contact@
camping toursvaldeloire.fr

2,6ha 90T(80-100m²) 10A CEE

1 ACD**G**IJKLMPQ
2 CDFGLRUVX
3 GJMRU**W**
4 (Q+R 1/7-31/8)
5 A**B**FGIJKLMNPUW
6 CEGJ(N 0,2km)TV

💬 Near the centre of the art and history city of Tours, this site is located in shaded, well-maintained surroundings on the banks of the Cher. A convenient location for visiting the tourist attractions. Swimming pool and playground. The site is located on the cycle route 'La Loire à Vélo'.

🚗 A10 exit Tours-Sud/St. Avertin. Follow direction Bléré via N76 direction Vierzon. Also A85 exit Bléré (Est) and exit St.Avertin (Ouest). Campsite signposted.

CC € **17** 2/2-30/6 1/9-15/12

📐 N 47°22'15'' E 0°43'25''

St. Gaultier, F-36800 / Centre-Val de Loire (Indre)

🤍 **iD** 1940

🏕 Oasis du Berry****
📧 rue de la Pierre Plate
☎ +33 (0)2-54471704
🔄 1/1 - 31/12
@ oasisduberry@gmail.com

2,5ha 41T(64-100m²) 20A CEE

1 ACDGIJKLO**P**Q
2 BCGIJRVY
3 ABGHIJK**OP**QRU
4 (C 1/6-30/8) (G 15/5-30/9)
(Q 1/7-31/8) (T 1/7-15/12)
(U 1/7-31/8) (V 1/2-11/11)
(X+Y+Z 1/7-15/12)
5 A**B**DFGIJMNOPUWZ
6 BEGK(N 1km)T

NEW

💬 Oasis du Berry is situated in an oasis of green 2½ hectares large, close to the town of Saint Gaultier. The campsite offers a large pool, plenty of entertainment options, and a good restaurant. Ideal for the sporty holiday maker.

🚗 From the north A20 exit 15 from the south exit 17 towards St. Gaultier. Then follow signs to campsite.

CC € **13** 1/2-8/7 26/8-31/8 5/9-15/12

📐 N 46°38'1'' E 1°24'34''

St. Satur, F-18300 / Centre-Val de Loire (Cher)

♿ 🤍 **iD** 1941

🏕 Flower Camping Les
Portes de Sancerre***
📧 Quai de Loire
☎ +33 (0)2-48721088
🔄 30/3 - 30/9
@ camping.sancerre@
flowercampings.com

2,5ha 85T(80-120m²) 6A CEE

1 AC**G**IJKLMPQ
2 ACLRSVXY
3 AFGHJK**MQ**RW
4 (**B**+G 1/7-31/8)
(Q 1/5-15/9) (R 5/4-30/9)
5 A**B**FIJKLMNPUWXZ
6 AEGIK(N 1km)TV

💬 Well-maintained campsite on the Loire. Spacious marked out pitches with sufficient shade. Opportunities for tennis, golf and canoeing on site. Outdoor pool next to the site. Very close to Sancerre, famous for its wine.

🚗 From Cosne take the D955 in the direction of Bourges. In St. Satur drive in the direction of St. Thibault (D2). The campsite is located on the left of the road by the river, just before the bridge over the Loire.

CC € **13** 30/3-29/6 1/9-29/9 7=6

📐 N 47°20'32'' E 2°51'58''

Ste Catherine-de-Fierbois, F-37800 / Centre-Val de Loire (Indre-et-Loire) ♿ 📶 **iD** (1942)

🏕 Parc de Fierbois*****
☎ +33 (0)2-47654335
📅 27/4 - 2/9
@ contact@fierbois.com

30ha 189T(130-150m²) 10A CEE

1 ACDFIJKLMOPRS
2 ADFLMRVXY
3 BGHJKMNP**PQ**RUVW
4 (C+F+G 📅) IJ(Q+S+T+U 📅)
(V 1/7-31/8) (X+Z 📅)
5 **AB**EFGJLNPUWXYZ
6 ACEGI**J**(N 1km)RTV

💬 This Castel campsite is located in 30-hectare grounds around a lake that is surrounded by an old wood. The facilities include an indoor heated swimming pool, aquatic park with slides, skate park, bar and restaurant. Many castles and vineyards in the area.

🚗 Can be reached via the A10 exit St. Maure (25) and Sorigny (24.1), then Tours. Via the N10, located 16 km south of Montbazon.

Sorigny Saint-Branchs
D57
CC
D760 A10
D58 D910 D50
D59

CC € **19** *27/4-30/6 25/8-1/9* 🛰 N 47°8'49'' E 0°39'10''

Suèvres, F-41500 / Centre-Val de Loire (Loir-et-Cher) ♿ 📶 **iD** (1943)

🏕 Camping La Grenouillère*****
🏠 Chât. de la Grenouillère, RN152
☎ +33 (0)2-54878037
📠 +33 (0)2-54878421
📅 14/4 - 9/9
@ grenouillere@capfun.com

11ha 69T(90-150m²) 10A

1 ACDFIJKLPRS
2 BFLRVXY
3 B**F**GJKM**N**RU**V**W
4 (C+F+H 📅) IJKM**N**
(Q+S+T+U+V+X+Y+Z 📅)
5 **AB**DEFGIJKLMNOPSTUW
XZ
6 ACEGJ**K**(N 2,5km)TV

💬 This chateau campsite is located between Orléans and Blois and can be reached via the RN152 (via A10 exit Mer). Rural location. Good facilities such as well maintained toilets, heated indoor swimming pool. Bar restaurant, pizzeria, spacious shop. A good base for exploring further in the Loire Valley.

🚗 From Blois via RN152 direction Orléans. 3 km beyond Suèvres on the left.

D110 Beaugency
D925
D924 Mer D951
A10 CC
N2152 D112 D103
D84 D33
Blois

CC € **15** *14/4-30/6 3/9-8/9* 🛰 N 47°41'8'' E 1°29'14''

Sully/St. Père-sur-Loire, F-45600 / Centre-Val de Loire (Loiret) 📶 **iD** (1944)

🏕 Le Jardin de Sully***
🏠 1 rue d'Orleans
☎ +33 (0)2-38671084
📠 +33 (0)9-71706705
📅 1/1 - 31/12
@ info-camping-lejardindesully@orange.fr

5ha 80T(90-120m²) 10A CEE

1 ACG**I**JKLMOQ
2 ACGLMRSUVXY
3 AB**F**GHJKMQRU**W**
4 (C 1/7-1/9) (H 1/7-10/9)
(Q+R 1/7-1/10)
(T+U+V+Z 1/7-1/9)
5 **AB**DFGIJKLMNPSUWXYZ
6 CEGHI**K**(N 1,5km)TV

💬 A very peaceful campsite with spacious pitches and attention to planting. An area rich in nature, right by the Loire. An excellent starting point for light walking and cycling in level surroundings. Various castles, towns and villages with plenty of sights close by. Sully has an attractive centre.

🚗 Approaching from Lorris or Bellegarde towards Sully, turn right at the roundabout before the Loire bridge. Campsite indicated.

Châteauneuf-sur-Loire D952 D961
D11 D60
Sully-sur-Loire CC D119
D83 D951
D59 D948

CC € **17** *1/1-7/7 25/8-31/12 7=6* 🛰 N 47°46'16'' E 2°21'44''

Thoré-la-Rochette, F-41100 / Centre-Val de Loire (Loir-et-Cher)

♻ 📶 ⚙ **iD** `1945`

🏕 La Bonne Aventure***
✉ route de la Cunaille
☎ +33 (0)2-54720059
⊙ 1/5 - 30/9
@ campingthore@orange.fr

8,4ha 58T(150-200m²) 6A CEE

1 AGIJKLM**P**RS
2 CRVWXY
3 AGHJKMR**W**
5 AGIJKLMNOPUWXZ
6 EGJ(N 3km)T

💬 Located on the river Loir in the beautiful green countryside. For lovers of nature. Many activities, cycling, canoeing, mountain climbing, visiting castles and much more. In and around the Loir valley.

🚗 From Thoré-la-Rochette via D82. Then follow Route de la Conaille. Signposted.

CC € **13** 1/5-7/7 25/8-29/9 7=6

N 47°48'7'' E 0°57'30''

Trogues, F-37220 / Centre-Val de Loire (Indre-et-Loire)

♻ 📶 **iD** `1946`

🏕 Château de la Rolandière****
☎ +33 (0)2-47585371
⊙ 1/5 - 16/9
@ contact@larolandiere.com

4ha 50T(90-110m²) 10A CEE

1 ACD**G**IJKLM**P**Q
2 FLRVXY
3 BHJN**Q**RU**V**
4 (B+G+Q+R ⊙)
(T+U 15/7-15/8) (Z ⊙)
5 **AB**FGIJKLMNOPUWZ
6 AEG**K**(N 6km)RTV

💬 The elegant château is the centre of this rural campsite. Next to the castle are shaded camping pitches, a park, swimming pool, minigolf, restaurant and clubhouse. Hospitality and relaxation are high on the list here. Good starting point for walking and cycle trips.

🚗 A10 exit 25. Or via RD910. Follow D760 for 6 km direction Chinon/l'Ile Bouchard. After Noyant-de-Touraine straight ahead at roundabout towards Chinon/l'Ile Bouchard. Site located about 3 km on the left.

CC € **19** 1/5-7/7 25/8-15/9

N 47°6'42'' E 0°30'58''

Valloire-sur-Cisse, F-41150 / Centre-Val de Loire (Loir-et-Cher)

♻ 📶 **iD** `1947`

🏕 Camping-Ferme de Prunay****
✉ Ferme de Prunay
☎ +33 (0)2-54700201
⊙ 31/3 - 3/11
@ contact@prunay.com

6ha 69T(300-400m²) 12A CEE

1 ACD**G**IJKLMOP**Q**
2 LRVWXY
3 BDGHJKNPRUW
4 (A 1/7-31/8) (C+H 1/5-30/9)
(Q+R+T+U+V+X+Z ⊙)
5 **AB**EFGHIJKLMNOPQRUWX
YZ
6 ACDEGJ(N 2km)RTV

💬 'Le Prunay' is located in quiet surroundings in the heart of the Loire, close to both castles and countryside. Camping pitches from 300 to 400 m2. Heated pool. Bar/restaurant on site. Campsite is the set off point for several walking and cycling routes.

🚗 A10, exit Blois dir. Angers/Château-Renault. D131 Molineuf - Chambon-sur-Cisse, in Molineuf continue towards Seillac (D135 and D760). Campsite signposted.

CC € **15** 31/3-30/6 18/8-2/11 10=9, 22=21

N 47°33'17'' E 1°10'50''

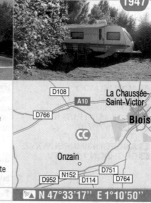

Velles, F-36330 / Centre-Val de Loire (Indre) ♿ 🛜 iD (1948)

🏕 Les Grands Pins★★★
🚐 D920 Les Maisons-Neuves
☎ +33 (0)2-54366193
📅 1/4 - 30/9
@ contact@les-grands-pins.fr

5ha 46T(120-140m²) 10A CEE

1 ACD**G**IJKLO**P**
2 BFLRVWXY
3 BG**M**Q**R**
4 (B+Q 1/7-31/8)
  (U+X 10/5-25/9) (Y 🔒)
  (Z 10/5-25/9)
5 ADGHIJKLMNOPUXYZ
6 CEGJ(N 7km)TV

💬 A spacious campsite with partially shaded pitches. Suitable as a stopover campsite and as a starting point for trips out. Ideal for an overnight stop on your way south (A20). The restaurant has been completely refurbished. New interior and new chef.

🚗 7 km south of Châteauroux. Located 5 min. from the A20 between exit 14 and 15. On the D920 direction 'Les Maisons Neuves'.

CC € **17** 1/4-30/6 25/8-29/9

N 46°44'30'' E 1°37'16''

Vendôme, F-41100 / Centre-Val de Loire (Loir-et-Cher) ♿ 🛜 iD (1949)

🏕 Au Coeur de Vendôme★★★
🚐 rue Geoffroy Martel
☎ +33 (0)2-54770027
📅 14/4 - 30/10
@ aucoeurdevendome@
  camp-in-ouest.com

2,5ha 140T(80-100m²) 10A CEE

1 ACD**G**IJKLM**P**Q
2 CGLRVWXY
3 BGHJK**M**R**W**
4 (B+F+H 1/4-30/9) J(Q 🔒)
5 A**B**DGIJKLMNPUYZ
6 ACEG**K**(N 0,4km)TV

💬 400 metres from the centre of historic and cultural town. Located next to N10 on the banks of the River Loir. Suitable for those passing through or staying. Touraine and Loire castles all around the site.

🚗 Via N10 from north. In Vendôme, turn right at third traffic light Quartier des Grands Prés, then first left and left again. Follow signs to swimming pool and sports centre.

CC € **15** 14/4-8/7 26/8-29/10 7=6, 14=13

N 47°47'28'' E 1°4'19''

Vouvray, F-37210 / Centre-Val de Loire (Indre-et-Loire) ♿ 🛜 iD (1950)

🏕 Le Bec de Cisse★★
☎ +33 (0)2-47760722
📅 28/3 - 3/10
@ camping.vouvray@gmail.com

1,5ha 35T(80-100m²) 16A CEE

1 ACD**G**IJKLM**P**Q
2 CFGRVX
3 AGKR**W**
4 (Q 🔒)
5 A**B**FGHIJKLMNPUWZ
6 EG**K**(N 1km)T

NEW

💬 Quiet, green, and cosy campsite situated on the banks of the Cisse in the heart of the Loire Valley. 200m from the centre of Vouvray. Good toilet facilities. New enthusiastic owner.

🚗 A10 exit 20 Tours. In Tours follow N152 towards Vouvray/Blois. At traffic lights in the village turn right. The campsite is 200m from the centre by the river.

CC € **13** 28/3-13/7 31/8-2/10

N 47°24'32'' E 0°47'47''

Andryes, F-89480 / Bourgogne (Yonne)

🏕 Sites & Paysages Au Bois Joli***
📧 2 route de Villeprenoy
☎ +33 (0)3-86817048
🗓 1/4 - 30/9
@ info@campingauboisjoli.com

4,5ha 89T(100-250m²) 10A CEE

1 ACD**FI**JKLPQ
2 BIKRTXY
3 ABGHJKMNR
4 (C+H 5/6-15/9) (Q+R+S 🖭)
(T 1/7-1/9) (V 🖭)
5 **AB**DEFGIJKLMNOPQRUWX
YZ
6 ACDEG**IJ**(N 5km)ORT

💬 On the edge of the Morvan natural park, near a cycle track along the Canal du Nivernais. Wonderfully peaceful, pleasant natural campsite, with orchids in spring. Heated swimming pool and view over the hills. Located close to Vézelay and Guédelon. Many options for cultural and sportive days out.

🚗 From Auxerre or Clamecy follow N151.
In Coulanges-sur-Yonne take D39 dir. Andryes. From there follow signs to campsite.

1951

D950
D73 Coulanges-sur-Yonne
D104
Billy-sur-Oisy Clamecy
D19 N151 D34

CC € **17** 1/4-30/6 27/8-29/9   N 47°31'0'' E 3°28'48''

Arnay-le-Duc, F-21230 / Bourgogne (Côte-d'Or)

🏕 Camping de l'Étang de
Fouché - Arnay****
📧 8, rue du 8 Mai 1945
☎ +33 (0)3-80900223
🗓 30/3 - 7/10
@ info@campingfouche.com

8ha 158T(80-140m²) 10A CEE

1 ACD**G**IJKLM**P**ST
2 ADLMRVWXY
3 ABGHJ**M**N**P**RU**W**Z
4 (C 30/4-30/9) (H 🖭) P
(Q+R+T 🖭) (U 1/7-31/8)
(V+Z 🖭)
5 **AB**DEFGIJKLMNPQUWZ
6 ABCEGIJ(N 1km)OV

💬 A campsite situated by a lake with large marked out pitches offering sufficient shade. Plenty of watersports opportunities at the lake.

🚗 Follow camping signs in Arnay-le-Duc.
The campsite is located 1.2 km east of the N6.

1952

A6
D970
Arnay-le-Duc CC
D981 D17
D4 D906 Lacanche D33
N81 Viévy D36

CC € **15** 30/3-5/7 2/9-6/10   N 47°8'5'' E 4°29'49''

Athée, F-21130 / Bourgogne (Côte-d'Or)

🏕 De l'Arquebuse***
📧 D24
☎ +33 (0)3-80310689
📠 +33 (0)3-80311362
🗓 15/1 - 23/12
@ camping.arquebuse@wanadoo.fr

4,5ha 100T(100m²) 10A CEE

1 ACD**G**IJKLMPQ
2 CFLRTVWXY
3 BGR**W**
4 (**C**+**G** 15/5-31/8) (Q 🖭)
(R 15/5-15/10)
(U+V+Y+Z 🖭)
5 **AB**DGIJKLMNPUVXZ
6 AEGI**K**(N 1km)OTV

💬 A peaceful campsite right next to the River Saône. Bar/restaurant with big screen TV. Large open air swimming pool next to the site and all sorts of watersports in the river. Restaurant closed Sunday and Monday in low season. You can walk along the Saône to Auxonne with its various shops and restaurants.

🚗 From Dijon take the N5 in the direction of Auxonne. Before Auxonne exit D24, dir. Athée. The campsite is located on the right after about 500 metres.

1953

Lamarche-sur-Saône D459
Genlis D112
A39 CC
Auxonne
D475
D976 D20 D905
A36 D6

CC € **17** 1/5-25/6 9/9-30/9   N 47°11'56'' E 5°22'57''

Autun, F-71400 / Bourgogne (Saône-et-Loire) 🛜 **iD** 1954

🏕 Camping de la Porte d'Arroux***
📧 Les Chaumottes
☎ +33 (0)3-85521082
🗓 5/3 - 4/11
@ camping.autun@orange.fr

2,5ha 77T(50-100m²) 16A CEE

1 ACD**G**IJKLMPQ
2 CLMRVWXY
3 A**F**GHJRU**W**
4 (Q 1/4-30/9) (R 🅾) (T+U+Z 1/7-31/8)
5 **AB**FGIJKLMNPUWZ
6 ACEG**K**(N 2km)V

💬 A peaceful campsite, conveniently located for visiting the historic town of Autun. Shaded pitches some of which are marked out by tall hedges.

🚗 A6 afslag 24.1 Beaune-Centre. D973 to Autun. Leave Autun via the D980 towards Saulieu/ St. Forgeot. Signposted.

CC € **15** 5/3-7/7 25/8-3/11 7=6, 14=11   📍 N 46°57'53'' E 4°17'34''

Bourbon-Lancy, F-71140 / Bourgogne (Saône-et-Loire) 🛜 **iD** 1955

🏕 Camping du Breuil***
📧 11 rue des Eurimants
☎ +33 (0)3-85892098
🗓 5/3 - 4/11
@ camping.chaletsdubreuil@ orange.fr

2ha 40T(80-105m²) 10A CEE

1 ACD**G**IJKLMPQ
2 DLRTVWXY
3 A**F**GHJRU**W**
4 (B+G 1/6-15/9) (Q+R 🅾)
5 **AB**DFGIJKLMNPUZ
6 ACDEGJ**K**(N 0,4km)V

💬 Campsite close to the centre of Bourbon/Lancy. Pitches marked out by hedges.

🚗 The campsite is on the edge of Bourbon/Lancy. Follow signs Camping du Breuil.

CC € **17** 5/3-7/7 25/8-3/11   📍 N 46°37'9'' E 3°45'13''

Chagny, F-71150 / Bourgogne (Saône-et-Loire) 👫 ♿ 🛜 **iD** 1956

🏕 Pâquier Fané***
📧 20 rue du Pâquier Fané
☎ +33 (0)3-85872142
🗓 1/4 - 31/10
@ camping-chagny@orange.fr

1,8ha 91T(80-100m²) 16A CEE

1 ACD**G**IJKLMPQ
2 CLRVWXY
3 AGHJMNRU**W**
4 (C+**H** 1/5-31/8) (Q 🅾) (T+U+V+X+Z 1/5-31/8)
5 **AB**EFGIJKLMNOPU
6 ACDEGK(N 0,3km)R

💬 Lovely camping pitches (on grass) with some shade from a few tall trees. Close to the centre of Chagny. Lovely cycle routes. Free wifi. Municipal swimming pool next to the campsite.

🚗 A6 exit 24.1 Beaune-Centre, D974 direction Chalon-sur-Saône. After 13 km head for Chagny. In Chagny follow 'complexe sportif'/'camping' signs.

CC € **15** 1/4-3/7 21/8-30/10 7=6, 14=12   📍 N 46°54'43'' E 4°44'44''

Chalon-sur-Saône/St. Marcel, F-71380 / Bourgogne (Saône-et-Loire)

👫 ♿ 🛜 **iD** (1957)

🔺 Du Pont de Bourgogne***
📧 12 rue Julien Leneveu
☎ +33 (0)3-85482686
🔑 1/4 - 30/9
@ campingchalon71@wanadoo.fr

3ha 91T(50-100m²) 10A CEE

1 ACD**G**HIJKLMOPQ
2 CFLRTUVWXY
3 A**F**JRW
4 (Q+R 🔑) (T+U+V 1/5-30/9) (Z 🔑)
5 **AB**EFGIJKLMNOPQUWZ
6 ACFGHJ(N 1,5km)OV

💬 A campsite located along the Saône with shaded pitches. Near exit 26 Chalon Sud on the A6. Within walking distance (15 min) from the centre of Chalon-sur-Saône. Starting point for cycling: Voie Verte. Modern toilet facilities.

🚗 In Chalon-sur-Saône follow campsite and Roseraie St. Nicolas signs.

Chalon-sur-Saône
D19 D5 D673 D981 D678 A6 D977 D906 D978 D18 D6

CC € **17** 1/4-6/7 26/8-29/9 7=6, 14=12

📐 N 46°47'3'' E 4°52'21''

Charny, F-89120 / Bourgogne (Yonne)

♿ 🛜 **iD** (1958)

🔺 Les Platanes***
📧 41 route de la Mothe
☎ 📠 +33 (0)3-86918360
🔑 1/4 - 31/10
@ info@campinglesplatanes.fr

2ha 87T(100-120m²) 16A CEE

1 ACD**G**IJLMPQ
2 CGRVXY
3 AGHJK**M**RUW
4 (C 🔑) (Q 1/7-31/8) (R+Z 🔑)
5 **AB**DGIJKLMNOPUVWXYZ
6 DEGK(N 0,7km)TV

💬 Located between Auxerre, Sens and Montargis. Within walking distance of Charny. A campsite with plenty of plant life and flowers, with level pitches, partly partitioned camping pitches. Guests can use a heated pool. Wifi everywhere. A multi-lingual reception offers comfort and quality.

🚗 A6 exit 18. Follow the recommended route to the campsite.

D37 Triguères D34 D943 A6 Château-Renard D16 CC Charny D3 D56 D950 D41

CC € **11** 1/4-7/7 25/8-30/10 7=6, 14=12

📐 N 47°53'29'' E 3°5'39''

Châtillon-sur-Seine, F-21400 / Bourgogne (Côte-d'Or)

♿ 🛜 **iD** (1959)

🔺 Municipal Louis Rigoly**
📧 Esplan. St. Vorles
☎ +33 (0)3-80910305
🔑 1/4 - 30/9
@ camping-chatillon-sur-seine@orange.fr

0,8ha 43T(80-120m²) 4-6A CEE

1 ACDGIJKLMPQ
2 RUVWXY
3 AGHJUW
4 (F+H 🔑) **KN**(Q 🔑)
5 **AB**FGIJKLMNPUXYZ
6 CEGJ(N 0,5km)UV

💬 In the Côte d'Or on the edge of the Champagne region in natural surroundings near a large wood. Intimate and shaded, near the town centre and next to a swimming pool (free for long-stay campers). Free wifi, TV room. Suitable for sportive and cultural holidays.

🚗 From Paris A5 to Troyes, exit 21 Magnant. Then D971 to Bar-sur-Seine, then Châtillon-sur-Seine. Follow signs. From A6 Paris-Lyon exit 23 Bierre-lès-Semur. Then D988 to Montbard, then Châtillon-sur-Seine.

Châtillon-sur-Seine D13 D965 D965 D928 CC D21 D980 D971 D971

CC € **15** 1/4-6/7 27/8-29/9

📐 N 47°51'34'' E 4°34'47''

Decize, F-58300 / Bourgogne (Nièvre) ♿ 🛜 iD (1960)

🏕 Camping Des Halles***
📧 rue Marcel Merle
☎ +33 (0)3-86251405
🔑 30/3 - 28/10
@ camping.decize@orange.fr

3,5ha 79T(80-100m²) 16A

1 ACD**G**IJKLM**P**Q
2 CLRTVWXY
3 AGK**M**N**Q**R**W**
4 (C+F 1/7-31/8) J
  (Q+R 1/5-1/10)
  (T+Z 1/6-31/8)
5 **AB**FGIJKLMNPU
6 CDEGJ**K**(N 0,8km)OV

💬 The campsite is located right beside the Loire, water sports are possible. Within walking distance of the centre of Decize. The pitches are shaded by tall trees.

🚗 In Decize head towards Moulins. Keep to the right after the Loire bridge; follow signs.

CC €15 30/3-7/7 25/8-27/10 7=6, 14=11   📍 N 46°50'7'' E 3°27'21''

Digoin, F-71160 / Bourgogne (Saône-et-Loire) 🛜 iD (1961)

🏕 La Chevrette***
📧 41 rue de la Chevrette
☎ +33 (0)3-85531149
📠 +33 (0)3-85885970
🔑 1/4 - 30/9
@ info@lachevrette.com

1,6ha 85T(60-100m²) 10A CEE

1 ACD**G**IJKLMPQ
2 CGRTVY
3 BGHJQRU**W**
4 (C 1/5-7/9) (Q+R 🔑)
  (T+U+X+Z 1/7-31/8)
5 **AB**DFGJLNPUWX
6 ACEGK(N 0,5km)RV

💬 The campsite is located on the banks of the Loire with opportunities for cycle trips over the Voie Verte and canoe trips. The campsite has free wifi internet.

🚗 The campsite is signposted in Digoin by the side of the D979 from Moulin to Paray-le-Monial.

CC €17 1/4-6/7 27/8-29/9   📍 N 46°28'47'' E 3°58'3''

Dompierre-les-Ormes, F-71520 / Bourgogne (Saône-et-Loire) ♿ 🛜 iD (1962)

🏕 Le Village des Meuniers****
📧 344 rue du Stade
☎ +33 (0)3-85503660
🔑 1/4 - 13/10
@ contact@
villagedesmeuniers.com

4ha 76T(80-300m²) 10-16A CEE

1 ACD**G**IJKLM**P**Q
2 IJKLMRVWXY
3 ABDGHJKMNP**Q**RUW
4 (C+H 1/5-15/9) J(Q+R 🔑)
  (T+U+V+Y 1/5-30/9) (Z 🔑)
5 **AB**DEFGIJKLMNOPQUWXY
  Z
6 ACEJ**K**(N 0,3km)OV

💬 Friendly campsite with spacious pitches in the sun or shade. Heated pool. Walking and cycling trips through the area possible. Restaurant with extensive menu.

🚗 A6 Mâcon-Sud direction Charolles N79. Dompierre-les-Ormes is signposted via D41. Follow camping signs in Dompierre.

CC €17 1/4-6/7 27/8-12/10 14=12   📍 N 46°21'50'' E 4°28'29''

Étang-sur-Arroux, F-71190 / Bourgogne (Saône-et-Loire)   🚴 📶 **iD** (1963)

🔺 Des 2 Rives**
📧 26-28 rue de Toulon
☎ +33 (0)3-85823973
📅 1/1 - 31/12
@ camping@des2rives.com

2,5ha 100T(85-150m²) 6A CEE

1 ACD**G**IJKLPQ
2 CGLMRSVWXY
3 AGHJNRU**W**X
4 (Q+T 1/7-31/8)
5 **A**DFGIJKLNPUZ
6 ADEGHK(N 0,3km)O

💬 The camping terrain is peacefully located in parkland between two rivers: the Mesvrin and the Arroux. The pitches are separated by tall trees. The toilet block is heated in early and late season. Dutch owners. Free wifi.

🚗 From Autun to Étang-sur-Arroux on D681 direction Moulins-Luzy. Via D994 to Étang. In 'centre ville' direction Toulon-sur-Arroux. Campsite just outside Étang-sur-Arroux at the D994.

[Map: D18, D3, Autun, N81, Étang-sur-Arroux CC, D61, D981, Marmagne, D994]

CC € **15** 1/1-6/7 25/8-31/12   📷 N 46°51'42'' E 4°11'31''

Gigny-sur-Saône, F-71240 / Bourgogne (Saône-et-Loire)   🚴 📶 **iD** (1964)

🔺 Château de l'Epervière*****
☎ +33 (0)3-85941690
📅 1/4 - 30/9
@ info@domaine-eperviere.com

10ha 114T(100-130m²) 10A CEE

1 ACD**G**IJKLMOPQ
2 LRTUVWX
3 AGHJKRUW
4 (C 30/4-20/9) (F 📅)
   (H 30/4-20/9) (Q 📅)
   (S 30/4-30/9)
   (U+V 30/4-17/9) (Y 📅)
   (Z 30/4-30/9)
5 **AB**EFGIJKLMNOPUW
6 CDEGHJ(N 7km)OV

💬 A lovely castle campsite in southern Bourgogne. Spacious pitches, a restaurant in the castle and heated indoor and outdoor pool. Wine tasting from the end of May to mid-September. A good base for exploring southern Burgundy, and good for cycling (15 km from Voie Bleue).

🚗 From Sennecy-le-Grand leave the D906 direction Gigny-sur-Saône (D18). Follow camping signs.

[Map: Epervans, D678, D6, D978, D18, A6, CC, D906, D971, Tournus, Cuisery]

CC € **19** 1/4-30/6 2/9-29/9   📷 N 46°39'16'' E 4°56'39''

La Celle-en-Morvan, F-71400 / Bourgogne (Saône-et-Loire)   🚴 📶 **iD** (1965)

🔺 Les Deux Rivières***
📧 Le Pré Bouché
☎ +33 (0)3-45740138
📅 9/5 - 15/9
@ info@les2rivieres.com

1,8ha 48T(80-220m²) 10A CEE

1 A**G**IJLMPQ
2 CLRVWXY
3 ABFGHIJRU**W**X
4 (C+**H**+Q+R+T+U 📅)
5 **AB**FGIJKLMNPQRUWZ
6 ABCEG**K**(N 9km)O

💬 The campsite is located by two rivers on the edge of the Morvan nature reserve. Starting point for hikers and cyclists. Many antiquities in the area; Autun, Vezelay, Bibracte, the Burgundy wine route and routes through the Morvan lakes. Heated swimming pool. Dutch owners.

🚗 In La Celle-en-Morvan D978, follow camping signs from Autun-Château-Chinon. Campsite is 300m from the D978.

[Map: D15, D2, D4, D980, D978, CC, Tavernay, Saint-Forgeot, D3, D18, N81, Autun]

CC € **17** 9/5-4/7 27/8-14/9   📷 N 47°0'44'' E 4°11'30''

La Clayette, F-71800 / Bourgogne (Saône-et-Loire)

👫 ♿ 📶 **iD** **1966**

🏕 Les Bruyères***
📧 9 route de Gibles, D79
☎ +33 (0)3-85280915
📅 1/4 - 1/11
@ contact@campingbruyeres.com

2ha 70T(90-150m²) 10A CEE

1 ACD**G**IJKLMO**P**Q
2 DILRSTUVWXY
3 BGHJKLM**N**Q**RW**
4 (C+G 1/6-31/8) J(Q 📅)
(T+U+V+X 1/7-31/8) (Z 📅)
5 **AB**DFGIJKLMNPUWZ
6 CDEGJK(N 0,6km)V

💬 A spacious family campsite with a swimming pool. Overlooking a lake and castle. Close to the centre with restaurants, bars and all amenities. A good base for exploring Charolais by bike or on foot. For experienced cyclists there are many opportunities: various villages with artists with their own studios, Beaujolais wine route.

🚗 Leave the town in the direction of Mâcon/Lyon. At the edge of the town take the D79, where the campsite is located on the left.

D34 · D25 · D79 · D989 · CC · D20 · D987 · D985 · D43 · Saint-Edmond · Chauffailles · D10

Ⓒ € **17** 1/4-6/7 25/8-31/10 📐 N 46°17'30'' E 4°19'10''

La Tagnière, F-71190 / Bourgogne (Saône-et-Loire)

♿ 📶 **iD** **1967**

🏕 Le Paroy
☎ +33 (0)3-85545927
📅 15/4 - 30/9
@ info@campingleparoy.com

1,2ha 24T(100-250m²) 6-10A CEE

1 ACD**G**IJKL**P**Q
2 DJKRTVWXY
3 DGHJNRUW
4 (Q 15/5-15/9) X
5 **A**FGIJKLMNPUXYZ
6 AEGK(N 2km)V

💬 A very quiet campsite in the Morvan, a paradise for nature lovers and birdwatchers. Lovely walking routes from the campsite. Table d'hôte, free wifi. Dutch owner. Modern toilet facilities.

🚗 From Autun via N81 richting Moulin/Luzy. After 10 km left through Étang-sur-Arroux direction Toulon. 3 km after Etang left to La Tagnière (D224). Follow camping signs in Tagnière.

D61 · D981 · N80 · D994 · CC · D980 · D985 · D102 · **Montceau-les-Mines**

Ⓒ € **13** 15/4-30/6 1/9-29/9 📐 N 46°46'38'' E 4°12'20''

Laives, F-71240 / Bourgogne (Saône-et-Loire)

👫 ♿ 📶 **iD** **1968**

🏕 La Héronnière***
📧 2 Les Lacs
☎ +33 (0)3-85449885
📅 3/3 - 4/11
@ camping.laives@wanadoo.fr

2ha 80T(100m²) 10A CEE

1 ACD**G**IJKLMOP**R**S
2 ACDLRVXY
3 ABGJKNRU**WZ**
4 (C+H 1/5-13/10) (Q+R 📅)
(T+U 1/5-31/8) (Y 1/5-30/9)
(Z 1/5-31/8)
5 **AB**DFGIJKLMNPUVWZ
6 ACDEGK(N 6km)ORV

💬 Peaceful campsite 200 metres from large recreational lake, plenty of fishing opportunities, swimming pool on campsite. Suitable for cycle trips.

🚗 From North: A6 exit 26 Chalon-sur-Saône. D906 dir. Mâcon. At Varennes-le-Grand: D6 to Ferté. D18 dir. Lacs-des-Laives. From South: A6 exit 27 Tournus. In Sennecy-le-Grand: D18 dir. Lacs-des-Laives.

Saint-Rémy · N78 · Lux · D978 · D977 · Saint-Germain-du-Plain · D6 · CC · D18 · A6 · D981 · N6

Ⓒ € **17** 3/3-30/6 1/9-3/11 7=6, 14=12 📐 N 46°40'19'' E 4°49'58''

Lormes, F-58140 / Bourgogne (Nièvre)

👫 ♿ 📶 **iD** 1969

🔺 Camping de l'Etang du
  Goulot***
🏠 rue des Campeurs
☎ +33 (0)3-86228237
📅 1/5 - 30/9
@ campingetangdugoulot@
  gmail.com

2,7ha 64T(75-300m²) 16A CEE

1 **A**G**IJKLMPQ
2 ADKLRTVWXY
3 AGHJK**M**QRU**W**Z
4 (Q 1/7-31/8) (T+U+X+Z ☺)
5 **A**GIJKLMNOPQRUWXZ
6 ACEGHJ(N 0,4km)O

💬 In the heart of the Morvan (an area of large lakes). A shady and peaceful campsite with a friendly family atmosphere located on the Etang du Goulot. Offers 64 spacious pitches. Supermarket and shops within walking distance (400 metres).

🚗 Take the D944 between Avalon and Chateau-Chinon. The campsite is located on the southern edge of Lormes. Well signposted.

CC € **13** 1/5-30/6 1/9-29/9 5=4, 10=8

🧭 N 47°16'57'' E 3°49'21''

Louhans, F-71500 / Bourgogne (Saône-et-Loire)

👫 ♿ 📶 **iD** 1970

🔺 Municipal Les Trois Rivières***
🏠 10 chemin de la Chapellerie
☎ +33 (0)3-85751902
📠 +33 (0)3-85767511
📅 1/4 - 30/9
@ camping@
  louhans-chateaurenaud.fr

1,2ha 53T(100-140m²) 10A CEE

1 **A**G**IJKLMOPQ
2 CLRUVWXY
3 AGRU**W**
5 **A**GIJKLMNPUVY
6 DEGK(N 1km)T

💬 A well-maintained campsite on the edge of town. Large traditional weekly market on Monday (extra big on first Monday of the month). Louhans is also known for its arcades and its 15th-century facades. Within walking distance of the baker (500m).

🚗 D996 as far as Louhans then follow signs to the campsite or swimming pool.

CC € **11** 1/4-8/7 26/8-29/9 7=6, 14=11

🧭 N 46°37'51'' E 5°13'1''

Louvarel/Champagnat, F-71480 / Bourgogne (Saône-et-Loire)

♿ 📶 **iD** 1971

🔺 Yelloh! Village Le
  Domaine de Louvarel****
☎ +33 (0)3-85766271
📅 30/3 - 30/9
@ info@louvarel.com

8ha 110T(80-110m²) 10A CEE

1 ACD**G**IJKLMOPQ
2 ADFJLRVWX
3 BGHJR**W**Z
4 (E+H+Q+T+U+V+Y+Z ☺)
5 **AB**EFGIJKLMNPUWXYZ
6 ACDEGJ**K**(N 4km)TV

💬 A campsite with excellent toilet facilities and young landscaping on Lake Louvarel. There is a heated indoor swimming pool, and a swimming lake with a sandy beach and a swimming zone that is patrolled in high season. There is also a fishing pond.

🚗 A39 exit 9, then follow signs. Campsite is signposted. Or exit Champagnat on the N83 and follow Louvarel or camping signs. Campsite located on the 'Base de Loisirs Louvarel'.

CC € **17** 30/3-14/7 1/9-29/9

🧭 N 46°29'50'' E 5°19'30''

Luzy, F-58170 / Bourgogne (Nièvre) 🏃 ♿ 📶 iD `1972`

🏕 Domaine de la Gagère****
☎ +33 (0)3-86304811
🔓 1/4 - 30/9
@ info@la-gagere.com

5ha 120T(100-120m²) 4-16A CEE

1 ACD**G**IJKLMNPST
2 KLMRSTVWXY
3 AGHINR
4 (A 1/5-14/9) (C+H 🔓) **N**
(Q 🔓) (R 1/5-30/9)
(S 15/5-15/9) (T+U 1/5-15/9)
(X+Z 🔓)
5 **AB**DEFGIJKLMNOPUWZ
6 CDEGIK(N 9km)RV

💬 A lovely naturist campsite high up in the middle of the countryside with extensive views of the Morvan. Guided walking tours to Mont Dône.

🚐 From Autun take D981 to Luzy. La Gagère is signposted about 6 km before Luzy on the left. Campsite 3 km uphill on narrow road.

Étang-sur-Arroux / N81 / D27 / D985 / D981 / D994 / Luzy / CC / D973

CC € **19** 1/4-6/7 27/8-29/9 🗺 N 46°49'0'' E 4°3'23''

Luzy/Tazilly, F-58170 / Bourgogne (Nièvre) ♿ 📶 iD `1973`

🏕 Château de Chigy****
🚩 route Moulins
☎ +33 (0)3-86301080
🔓 1/5 - 29/9
@ reception@
chateaudechigy.com.fr

10ha 100T(100-150m²) 6A CEE

1 ACD**G**IJKLPQ
2 DIJLRSTVWXY
3 AGHJNQRU**W**
4 (B 15/6-30/9) (D+Q 🔓)
(R 15/6-30/9)
(T+U+X+Z 7/7-31/8)
5 ABDFGIJKLOP**S**UWZ
6 AEJ(N 4,5km)V

💬 Large grounds with very spacious pitches, heated swimming pool, shaded by tall trees. Apartments and chalets for rent, 25 hectare fishing lake, indoor swimming pool in 70 hectares of grounds. Fresh bread available.

🚐 In Luzy D973 direction Moulins. Campsite signposted.

Millay / D981 / D27 / Luzy / D3 / CC / Issy-l'Évêque / D985 / D973 / Uxeau

CC € **17** 1/5-6/7 25/8-28/9 🗺 N 46°45'28'' E 3°56'39''

Marcenay, F-21330 / Bourgogne (Côte-d'Or) ♿ 📶 iD `1974`

🏕 Camping Les Grèbes du
Lac de Marcenay***
🚩 5 rue du Lac
☎ +33 (0)3-80816172
🔓 1/5 - 30/9
@ info@campingmarcenaylac.com

3,6ha 90T(80-120m²) 10A

1 ACD**G**IJKLMPQ
2 ADLMRVVWXY
3 BGHJKNRU**W**Z
4 (B+G 1/6-30/9) (Q 🔓)
(T 1/7-25/8)
5 **AB**EGIJKLPUWZ
6 EGJ(N 4,8km)UV

💬 A meeting place for musicians. Many trees on the site. Avoid toll roads and enjoy a country drive! Discover Burgundy: trips out, walking, cycling, sailing, fishing (free boats). Indoor and outdoor play facilities. 3 swimming pools, free wifi. Call manager Dirk in EN, FR, DE or NL.

🚐 Half way between Troyes and Dijon (D971) and near village of Laignes. Close to the D965. Also signposted 'Lac de Marcenay'.

D452 / D453 / D952 / CC / Châtillon-sur-Seine / D965 / Ampilly-le-Sec / D971 / D953 / D5 / D21 / D980

CC € **13** 1/5-7/7 25/8-29/9 🗺 N 47°52'12'' E 4°24'17''

Matour, F-71520 / Bourgogne (Saône-et-Loire)

♿ 🛜 **iD** (1975)

⛺ Flower Camping Le Paluet***
🏠 2 rue de la Piscine
☎ +33 (0)3-85597092
🗓 7/4 - 30/10
@ lepaluet@matour.fr

3ha 61**T**(80-120m²) 10A CEE

1 ACD**G**IJKLMOPQ
2 DLRTVWXY
3 ABGHJNRU**W**
4 (C+H 27/5-31/8) JKN
   (T+U+Z 20/5-15/9)
5 **AB**FGIJKLOPUWZ
6 ACEHJ**K**(N 0,3km)V

💬 A family campsite with sunny and shaded places next to a free municipal swimming pool. Located in the beautiful area known as 'Little Switzerland'. Hiking trails in the area. Within walking distance of the centre and all shops. 30 minutes free wifi close to the campsite reception. Free sauna.

🚐 Follow the camping signs in the town.

Verosvres [N79]
[D79]
La Clayette [CC] Tramayes
[D987]
[D43]
[D10]

CC € **15** 7/4-9/7 27/8-29/10 7=6, 14=10

📍 N 46°18'16'' E 4°28'43''

Merry-sur-Yonne, F-89660 / Bourgogne (Yonne)

👫 ♿ 🛜 **iD** (1976)

⛺ Camping Merry-sur-Yonne****
🏠 5 Impasse des Sables
☎ +33 (0)3-86345955
🗓 1/1 - 31/12
@ campingmerrysuryonne@
   yahoo.com

2ha 50**T**(70-180m²) 16A CEE

1 ACDGIJKLMOPQ
2 CGRSUWXY
3 AGHJKM**W**
4 (Q+S+T+U+V+Y+Z 🔑)
5 **AB**GIJKLMNOPUWZ
6 ACEGIKORV

💬 No ordinary campsite, but a campsite where you, the guest, come first. The restaurant has an international and regional menu. Tennis and wifi are free. Level grounds. Excellent cycling along the Yonne and the Canal du Nivernais. Climbing activities on Le Rocher de Saussois.

🚐 Follow the D100 from north or south. Follow the D950 from east or west and switch off GPS. In Mailly-la-Ville follow D100 towards Merry-sur-Yonne. Over 2 bridges, left at church. GPS off.

Courson-les-
Carrières
[D950] [D100]
[N151] [D606]
[CC]
[D951]
Asquins

CC € **13** 1/1-8/7 31/8-31/12 7=6, 14=11

📍 N 47°33'46'' E 3°38'46''

Montbard, F-21500 / Bourgogne (Côte-d'Or)

♿ 🛜 **iD** (1977)

⛺ Municipal de Montbard
   'Les Treilles'***
🏠 rue Michel Servet
☎ +33 (0)3-80926950
🗓 1/4 - 31/10
@ camping.lestreilles@montbard.fr

2,5ha 78**T**(100-150m²) 16A CEE

1 ACD**G**IJKLM**P**Q
2 KRUVWXY
3 ABGHJNRU**W**
4 (A 1/7-31/8)
   (C+F+H 15/4-31/8,15/9-30/10)
   JKLNP(Q 1/6-30/9)
   (T 1/7-31/8) (Z 1/6-30/9)
5 **AB**DFGIJKLMNPUWXYZ
6 ACDEGHK(N 1km)V

💬 A campsite with large shaded pitches in a region that is rich in historical heritage and gastronomy. Located near a swimming pool complex (free entry for campers, closed till 18/4 and from 1/9 to 15/9) and the Canal de Bourgogne. Bakery service, bar, wifi, tennis, volleyball, billiards.

🚐 Follow D980 around Montbard town. Turn off to the north at sharp bend between the Canal de Bourgogne and the D5 to Laignes. Signposted 'Camping/Piscine'.

[D956] [D5]
[D957] [CC] [D19]
Montbard [D905]
[D980]
Venarey-les-
Laumes

CC € **15** 1/4-6/7 24/8-30/10

📍 N 47°37'52'' E 4°19'56''

Montsauche-les-Settons, F-58230 / Bourgogne (Nièvre) ｲｲ 🛜 iD 1978

▲ La Plage des Settons***
🏠 Rive Gauche Aval
☎ +33 (0)3-86845199
🔓 27/4 - 30/9
@ camping-plages-des-settons@
   wanadoo.fr

2,3ha 46T(80-120m²) 3-15A

1 ACDGIJKLMOPQ
2 BDJKLMPRTVWXY
3 AHJR**W**Z
4 (Q 1/7-31/8)
5 **A**BGIJKLMNOPUZ
6 AEGJ(N 0,6km)RV

💬 Campsite is located near the Barrage of Lac des Settons. Options for walking and cycling around the lake, boating and fishing on the lake.

🚌 In Montsauche towards Lac des Settons. Then follow Rive Gauche Aval and camping signs to Barrage.

Saulieu
D236
D977 BIS
D12 CC D37 D193 D302
Remoillon D17 Le Guidon

CC € **13** 27/4-30/6 1/8-8/8 27/8-29/9 ⚐ N 47°11'36'' E 4°3'36''

Montsauche-les-Settons, F-58230 / Bourgogne (Nièvre) ｲｲ ♿ 🛜 iD 1979

▲ Les Mésanges***
🏠 Rive Gauche
☎ FAX +33 (0)3-86845577
🔓 14/5 - 15/9
@ campinglesmesanges@orange.fr

5ha 100T(100-200m²) 16A

1 ACD**G**IJKLMOPQ
2 ADKLMRTVWXY
3 BGHJNRWZ
4 (Q+R 🔓) (U+V 1/7-1/9)
5 **AB**EFGIJKLPUVXYZ
6 EGJ(N 3km)T

💬 A peaceful campsite with large, fenced, well maintained pitches, opposite Lac des Settons in the heart of the Morvan. Plenty of walking and cycling routes in the rural surroundings. You will find relaxation here. Clean toilet facilities, large fishing lake.

🚌 Take the D977 bis from Saulieu to Montsauche-les-Settons. In Montsauche follow the dir. of Lac des Settons, then Rive Gauche. Then follow camping signs.

D6 Saulieu
D236
Ouroux-en- D977 BIS
Morvan D193
CC
D980
D37 D17
D944 D2

CC € **15** 14/5-7/7 25/8-14/9 7=6 ⚐ N 47°10'54'' E 4°3'10''

Nevers, F-58000 / Bourgogne (Nièvre) 🛜 iD 1980

▲ Camping de Nevers***
🏠 rue de la Jonction
☎ +33 (0)3-86364075
🔓 5/3 - 4/11
@ campingdenevers@orange.fr

1,6ha 73T(85-110m²) 16A CEE

1 ACD**G**IJKL**P**Q
2 CFMRSTUVWXY
3 AGJ**W**
4 (Q 🔓) (T 1/5-15/9) (Z 🔓)
5 **AB**DFGIJKLMNPUXYZ
6 ACEGJ(N 1km)V

💬 A campsite with spacious shaded pitches on the banks of the Loire opposite the town centre. The town is within walking distance and is suitable for cyclists, anglers and canoeists. A limited number of pitches with electricity are available.

🚌 A77 exit 37 direction Nevers. Campsite is in Nevers on the right before the bridge. Signposted. In Nevers follow Moulins signs.

D45 D977 D26
**Varennes-
Vauzelles** A77
D920 **Nevers** D958
CC D978
D976 D18
D907
D13 D981

CC € **17** 5/3-7/7 25/8-3/11 7=6, 14=11 ⚐ N 46°58'56'' E 3°9'39''

Ouroux-en-Morvan, F-58230 / Bourgogne (Nièvre)

👫 🛜 iD 1981

🏕 Les Genêts du Morvan***
📧 route de L'Ormes
☎ +33 (0)3-86672288
📅 14/4 - 1/10
@ camping.ouroux@orange.fr

1,7ha 42T(80-120m²) 10-16A CEE

1 ACDGIJKLPQ
2 KRVWXY
3 AGHJR
4 (B 15/5-15/9) (Q 🔒)
(T+U+Z 1/7-31/8)
5 ABEFGJLNPUWZ
6 EGIKM(N 0,6km)R

💬 A rurally located campsite in 'Le Morvan' nature reserve with lovely panoramic views. Good spacious pitches with dividing hedges.

🚗 Take the D37 from the D978 Château-Chinon then follow D17. From Lormes follow the D17 as far as Ouroux. Campsite signposted in Ouroux.

D170 D6 D236
Cervon D977 BIS
Montsauche-les-Settons
CC
D944 D193
D37 D17
D2

CC € 15 14/4-6/7 26/8-30/9 7=6, 14=12

🧭 N 47°11'19'' E 3°56'21''

Paray-le-Monial, F-71600 / Bourgogne (Saône-et-Loire)

♿ 🛜 iD 1982

🏕 de Mambré****
📧 19 rue du Gué Léger
☎ +33 (0)3-85888920
📅 2/5 - 29/9
@ camping.plm@gmail.com

6ha 141T(80-100m²) 10A CEE

1 ACDGIJLPQ
2 FRTVWXY
3 ABGJKNR
4 (B+G 15/5-29/9) (Q 🔒)
(R+Z 1/7-31/8)
5 ABDFGIJKLMPUWZ
6 AEGK(N 1km)V

💬 A shaded campsite in a parkland setting at the edge of the historical town of Paray-le-Monial. Shaded and sunny pitches. Car and cycle trips possible in the surrounding area. Good cycling opportunities along the canal (Voie verte). Dutch owner.

🚗 Leave the N70 and N79 at Paray-le Monial-Sud. The campsite is signposted along Canal-du-Centre on the D979 on the edge of Paray-le-Monial.

D994 N70
Digoin Paray-le-Monial
N79 CC
D352 BIS
D982 D34 D10
D985

CC € 17 2/5-6/7 24/8-28/9

🧭 N 46°27'26'' E 4°6'18''

Pontailler-sur-Saône, F-21270 / Bourgogne (Côte-d'Or)

🛜 iD 1983

🏕 La Chanoie***
📧 46 rue de la Chanoie
☎ +33 (0)3-80672198
📅 15/3 - 15/10
@ camping.municipal1@orange.fr

NEW

6ha 160T(80-120m²) 10A

1 ACDGIJKLMPQ
2 ACLMRVWXY
3 ABGHJNWX
4 (Q 🔒) (U+X+Z 1/5-15/9)
5 ABEFIJKLMNOPRUVYZ
6 EGJ(N 1km)OT

💬 Campsite located on the Saône, with a large lawn and a small sandy beach. There's a lovely view of the river from the restaurant's terrace. The surrounding area is great for water sports, walking, and cycling.

🚗 Coming from Dijon on D959, drive through Pontailler-sur-Saone and turn left before bridge. Follow campsite signs.

D70 D475
Belleneuve
D959 D976
D961
Pontailler-sur-Saône Pesmes
A39 D112
D20

CC € 15 15/3-6/7 24/8-14/10

🧭 N 47°18'31'' E 5°25'32''

Pouilly-en-Auxois, F-21320 / Bourgogne (Côte-d'Or)

♿ 📶 **iD** `1984`

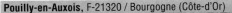

⛺ Camping Vert Auxois***
🏠 15 rue du Vert Auxois
☎ +33 (0)3-80907189
🕐 1/4 - 7/10
@ contact@camping-vert-auxois.fr

1,5ha 66**T**(80-100m²) 16A CEE

1 ACD**G**IJKLM**P**Q
2 CFGKLMRUVWXY
3 FHIJU**W**
4 (C 1/5-30/9) (Q 15/6-15/9)
(T 25/5-15/9) (U+X 🅿)
(Z 30/4-15/9)
5 **AB**DGIJKLMNOPUXYZ
6 AEGJ(N 0,5km)OT

💬 A small, peaceful campsite in the countryside next to a canal and a stone's throw from the town. The pitches are separated by high hedges.

🚗 Campsite located in Pouilly-en-Auxois and signposted.

CC € **17** 1/5-8/7 27/8-1/10

📍 N 47°15'55'' E 4°32'56''

Prémeaux/Prissey, F-21700 / Bourgogne (Côte-d'Or)

♿ **iD** `1985`

⛺ Du Moulin de Prissey
🏠 14 rue du Moulin de Prissey
☎ +33 (0)3-80623115
📠 +33 (0)3-80613729
🕐 1/4 - 30/9
@ cpg.moulin.prissey@free.fr

1,1ha 64**T**(83-120m²) 6-10A CEE

1 ACG**H**IJKLMOP**S**T
2 FILRVWXY
3 AGHIJR**W**
4 (Q+T+U 15/5-15/9)
5 A**G**IJKLMNOPUVXYZ
6 CEG(N 4km)T

💬 A very peacefully located level campsite among the vineyards. The pitches are reasonably shaded. Snacks and a small restaurant. Ideal starting point for visiting the wine region.

🚗 On A31 motorway between Dijon and Beaune take the Nuits-St-Georges exit. Take the D974 from here to Prémeaux/Prissey. Then follow camping signs.

CC € **15** 2/4-8/7 26/8-29/9

📍 N 47°6'13'' E 4°56'29''

Santenay, F-21590 / Bourgogne (Côte-d'Or)

♿ 📶 **iD** `1986`

⛺ Camping des Sources***
🏠 avenue des Sources
☎ +33 (0)3-80206655
🕐 30/3 - 28/10
@ camping-de-santenay@orange.fr

3,1ha 150**T**(90-120m²) 6A CEE

1 ACG**IJ**KLM**P**RS
2 LRTVWX
3 BGHJ**M**RU
4 (**C+H** 28/5-2/9)
(Q+R 1/5-30/9)
5 **AB**GIJKLMNPU
6 ACE**K**(N 1,5km)V

💬 A family campsite in the middle of the Côte de Beaune vineyards. Next to the municipal swimming pool. Large pitches in the shade of several trees.

🚗 A6 exit 24.1 Beaune-Centre. In Beaune D974 direction Chalon-sur-Saône to Santenay. Follow camping signs in Santenay.

CC € **15** 30/3-7/7 25/8-27/10 7=6, 14=11

📍 N 46°54'26'' E 4°41'8''

Saulieu, F-21210 / Bourgogne (Côte-d'Or)

♿ 📶 iD **1987**

🔺 Camping de Saulieu***
📧 Le Perron
☎ +33 (0)3-80641619
🕐 30/3 - 28/10
@ camping.saulieu@wanadoo.fr

6ha 63T(100-110m²) 10A CEE

1 ACD**G**IJKLMO**PQ**
2 LRTVWXY
3 BGHJKMN**OP**QRU**W**
4 (**A** 1/7-31/8) (B+G 1/6-15/9) (Q+R 🔌) (T+V 1/7-31/8) (Z 🔌)
5 **AB**DFGIJKLMNPUWXYZ
6 ACEGJ**K**(N 0,8km)QRTV

💬 A campsite located in the countryside with large, sunny camping pitches and a swimming pool. Countless recreational possibilities in the immediate vicinity.

🚐 Campsite located near the north exit of the town on the N6.

A6

D906

D6
D977 BIS

Thoisy-la-Berchère

D15

D980

La Croix

CC € **15** 30/3-7/7 25/8-27/10 7=6, 14=11

📷 N 47°17'22'' E 4°13'26''

Seurre/Pouilly-sur-Saône, F-21250 / Bourgogne (Côte-d'Or)

♿ 📶 iD **1988**

🔺 de la Plage**
📧 3 le Portail (RD973)
☎ +33 (0)3-80204922
📠 +33 (0)3-80210069
🕐 28/4 - 1/10
@ camping.seurre@orange.fr

6ha 110T(98-100m²) 6-10A CEE

1 A**G**IJKLMOPQ
2 CFLRWXY
3 BGJKR**W**
4 (C+**G** 1/7-31/8) **J** (Q 1/7-31/8) (T+U+X+Y 🔌) (Z 29/4-26/9)
5 **AB**GJLNPUVXYZ
6 EGHJ(N 1,0km)T

NEW

💬 Situated on cycle route Eurovélo 6, centrally located between the towns of Dijon, Beaune, Dole and Chalon, you'll find the Seurre municipal campsite. The site is on the banks of the Saone, and offers a large number of (water sports) activities: canoe rental, pedal boating, water skiing, and fishing. Restaurant. Close to the charming city centre and shops.

🚐 Campsite located alongside the D973 towards Beaune west of Seurre.

Maison-Dieu

A36 D996 D968

D976

Chevigny-en-Valière CC

D973 D673

D5

D73

CC € **13** 28/4-15/6 30/6-6/7 25/8-30/9

📷 N 47°0'1'' E 5°8'14''

St. Boil, F-71390 / Bourgogne (Saône-et-Loire)

📶 iD **1989**

🔺 Moulin de Collonge****
☎ +33 (0)3-85440032
📠 +33 (0)3-85440040
🕐 1/4 - 30/9
@ millofcollonge@wanadoo.fr

1ha 50T(80-100m²) 6A CEE

1 ACDGIJKLMPQ
2 ADLMRVWX
3 AGHJKNRUWZ
4 (E+H+Q+R+U+V+X+Z 🔌)
5 **AB**DEFGIJKLNPUWZ
6 AEGJ(N 5km)OV

💬 A small, flower-filled campsite with an indoor heated swimming pool, a lake for swimming, a small fish pond and pizzeria. Ideal departure point for cyclists (voie verte) to discover the Route des Vins from Beaune to Cluny.

🚐 On the D981 at the southern end of St. Boil take the small V5 road and follow the camping signs.

D977

Sevrey N6

D28

Varennes-le-Grand

D981 A6

D983

D18

CC

D67

D980 D14

CC € **17** 1/4-9/7 27/8-29/9 7=6, 14=12, 21=18

📷 N 46°38'47'' E 4°41'41''

St. Honoré-les-Bains, F-58360 / Bourgogne (Nièvre)   ♿ 📶 **iD** 1990

🏕 Camping et gîtes des Bains***
✉ 15 ave Jean Mermoz
☎ +33 (0)3-86307344
🗓 21/3 - 25/10
@ campinglesbains@gmail.com

4,5ha 130T(80-100m²) 10A CEE

1 ACD**G**IJKLMPQ
2 CLRTVWXY
3 BGHJ**M**N**Q**RUV**W**
4 (B+G 8/6-20/9) J**OP**
  (Q+R+T+U+X+Z 🔒)
5 **AB**DEFGIJKLMNPUVWZ
6 AEG**K**(N 0,8km)ORV

💬 The campsite is located in St. Honoré village. The site has pitches marked out by trees and bushes. The area offers plenty of chance to take in the nature: rest and space.

🚗 In St. Honoré-Les-Bains direction Vandenesse, follow signs to Des Bains. The campsite is 200 metres to the left after the park.

CC € 15 *21/3-6/7 26/8-24/10*   📍 N 46°54'23'' E 3°49'42''

St. Léger-de-Fougeret, F-58120 / Bourgogne (Nièvre)   👨‍👩‍👧 ♿ 📶 ✿ **iD** 1991

🏕 Sites & Paysages La Fougeraie****
✉ Hameau du Champs
☎ +33 (0)3-86851185
🗓 1/4 - 30/9
@ info@campingfougeraie.fr

10ha 63T(90-600m²) 10A CEE

1 ACD**G**IJKLMPRS
2 BCDIJKLMORTVWXY
3 ABHJR**W**Z
4 (C+H 1/6-30/9) K
  (Q+R+S+U+V+X+Z 🔒)
5 **AB**CEFGHJKLNPUWZ
6 CEGIJORV

💬 A friendly family campsite at an altitude of 440 metres in the Morvan regional nature reserve, located by a small lake with a beach for swimming and fishing. Space, rest, nature, calm, walking tours, table tennis, jeu de boules. Bar, restaurant and terrace with splendid views.

🚗 From Château-Chinon D27 direction Onlay. After about 4 km turn right onto the D157 towards St. Léger-de-Fougeret. Follow the camping signs for 2 km in St. Léger.

CC € 15 *1/4-30/6 1/9-29/9*   📍 N 47°0'23'' E 3°54'18''

St. Léger-sous-Beuvray, F-71990 / Bourgogne (Saône-et-Loire)   ♿ 📶 **iD** 1992

🏕 De La Boutière
✉ La Boutière
☎ +33 (0)6-80408128
🗓 15/4 - 15/10
@ camping@la-boutiere.com

2ha 36T(100-150m²) 10A CEE

1 A**G**IJKLM**P**Q
2 RSVWX
3 GHJNR**W**
5 **A**DGIJKLMNOPUXYZ
6 ADEG**K**(N 0,6km)O

💬 You will experience the nostalgia of camping on this small, rural campsite. Within walking distance of a village, in the Morvan regional park. A paradise for walkers. More than 30 marked out routes. Plenty of opportunities close by for anglers. Free wifi.

🚗 From Autun to St. Léger-sous-Beuvray on the D681 direction Moulins-Luzy. After 4 km turn right towards St. Léger (D3) and continue until the campsite is signposted.

CC € 13 *15/4-6/7 25/8-14/10 14=12*   📍 N 46°55'54'' E 4°6'4''

St. Péreuse-en-Morvan, F-58110 / Bourgogne (Nièvre)

👫 ♿ 📶 **iD** 1993

🏕 Le Manoir de Bezolle****
✉ Lieu-Dit-Bezolle
☎ +33 (0)3-86760189
🗓 31/3 - 29/9
@ campingmanoirdebezolle@
gmail.com

8ha 100T(150-250m²) 10A

1 ACGIJKLMOPQ
2 BDGIJKLRSTVWXY
3 BDGHJPQRW
4 (B+G 1/5-30/9) (Q 1/7-31/8)
(R 🔌) (T+U+X 1/7-31/8)
(Z 🔌)
5 **AB**FGIJKLMNOPUWXZ
6 AEGHK(N 10km)TV

💬 This campsite with its country house, pitches for tents, caravans or motorhomes is located at the foot of the Morvan between hills, valleys and fields. Everything is possible here, where nature rules. The sound of crickets and birds predominates from May to October in these grounds of almost 8 hectares.

🚗 On route D978 from Autun to Nevers. 11 km after Château Chinon take a right off the D978 to the D11 towards Manoir de Bezolle and Saint-Péreuse.

D944
D945 Château-
Chinon(ville)
D978 CC
D985 D27
D10 Moulins-
Engilbert
D18
D37

CC € **17** 31/3-6/7 25/8-28/9

🏕 N 47°3'27'' E 3°48'57''

Tonnerre, F-89700 / Bourgogne (Yonne)

♿ 📶 **iD** 1994

🏕 La Cascade*
✉ 8 avenue Aristide Briand
☎ +33 (0)3-86551544
🗓 31/3 - 14/10
@ contact@revea-vacances.fr

2ha 54T(100m²) 6A CEE

1 ACD**G**HIJKL**P**Q
2 BCLRTWXY
3 ABGHJNRU
4 (C 1/5-15/9) (Q+R+T 🔌)
5 **A**DGIJKLMNPUWZ
6 CDEGJ(N 1km)TV

💬 Spacious campsite with large, non-marked-out pitches along a river, close to the centre of Tonnerre. There's a railway line (TGV) next to the campsite. 15% discount in the low season with a stay of 7 nights or more.

🚗 Located between the towns of Troyes and Avalon. Campsite signposted in Tonnerre. Don't follow GPS as there is a low and very narrow tunnel.

D444
Flogny-la-
Chapelle
D952
CC D114
Chablis D965
D944 D905

CC € **15** 31/3-7/7 25/8-13/10

🏕 N 47°51'36'' E 3°59'3''

Tournus, F-71700 / Bourgogne (Saône-et-Loire)

♿ 📶 **iD** 1995

🏕 Camping de Tournus***
✉ 14 rue des Canes
☎ +33 (0)3-85511658
🗓 29/3 - 1/10
@ camping-tournus@orange.fr

1,5ha 94T(80-100m²) 10A CEE

1 ACDFIJKLMOPST
2 CFRUVWX
3 AJKR**W**
4 (**C+H** 1/7-31/8) **J**
(Q+T+U+Z 🔌)
5 **AB**FGIJKLMNOPUVWXZ
6 ACDEGK(N 1km)V

💬 A campsite with spacious pitches, close to the centre of the historic town of Tournus, famous for its many restaurants, 1000-year-old abbey and the starting point of the Voie Bleue cycle path along the Saône. Most suitable as a stopover campsite.

🚗 A6 exit 27 Tournus. Follow D906 towards Tournus. Turn off opposite the station. Campsite signposted.

Laives
A6
CC Cuisery D971
Tournus
D14 D906 D975
D56 D933

CC € **17** 29/3-1/7 20/8-30/9 7=6, 14=12

🏕 N 46°34'25'' E 4°54'34''

Uchizy, F-71700 / Bourgogne (Saône-et-Loire)

👫 ♿ 🛜 **iD** `1996`

🏕 Camping d'Uchizy**
📧 Port d'Uchizy
☎ +33 (0)3-85405390
📅 1/4 - 30/9
@ camping.uchizylen6@wanadoo.fr

6ha 95T(100m²) 6A CEE

1 **AG**IJKLMP**Q**
2 CLR**V**WXY
3 AGJRU**W**X
4 (B+G 1/6-15/9)
  (Q+S+T+U 15/4-15/9)
  (V 1/7-31/8) (X 15/4-15/9)
  (Z 📅)
5 **A**EFGIJKLMNPUV
6 EJ(N 5km)V

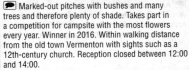

💬 A quiet campsite located on the banks of the Saône with shaded pitches, swimming pool and restaurant. The Voie Bleue cycle route goes beside the Saône.

🚗 Campsite on left of the D906, near Uchizy (on the banks of the Saône) when arriving from the north. Follow camping signs.

Tournus   Cuisery   D971
D975
D14   D56   A6   Romenay
CC
D82
D15   D906   D2
D933   D26

CC € **17** 1/4-30/6 1/9-29/9   📍 N 46°29'16'' E 4°54'45''

Vandenesse-en-Auxois, F-21320 / Bourgogne (Côte-d'Or)

👫 ♿ 🛜 **iD** `1997`

🏕 Lac de Panthier****
📧 1 chemin du Lac
☎ +33 (0)3-80492194
📠 +33 (0)3-80492580
📅 30/3 - 30/9
@ info@lac-de-panthier.com

7ha 127T(110-150m²) 6A CEE

1 ACD**G**IJKLMP**RS**
2 ADFKLPRTVWXY
3 ABF**G**HIJK**P**RUV**W**Z
4 (B 15/6-15/9) (F 📅)
  (G 15/6-15/9) JMN
  (Q+R+U+V+X+Y+Z 📅)
5 **AB**DEFGIJKLMNOPQUWXY
  Z
6 ABCDEGH**IJK**(N 4km)ORTV

💬 A campsite located between a lake and the edge of a wood. Pitches marked out by hedges with sufficient shade, some of which have a view of the lake. There is also an indoor swimming pool. The restaurant and pavement cafe have a panoramic view.

🚗 Leave motorway at A6 and A38 intersection near Pouilly-en-Auxois. Then follow Dijon, Créancey and camping signs.

D9   D7
D905   A38
Pouilly-en-   Créancey
Auxois   A6   CC
D33
D981   D970
D18   D25

CC € **17** 30/3-6/7 26/8-29/9 7=6, 14=11   📍 N 47°14'13'' E 4°37'41''

Vermenton, F-89270 / Bourgogne (Yonne)

👫 ♿ 🛜 **iD** `1998`

🏕 Les Coullemières***
📧 route de Coullemières
☎ +33 (0)3-86815302
📅 1/4 - 30/9
@ contact@
  camping-vermenton.com

1ha 47T(80-120m²) 6A CEE

1 ACD**G**IJKLPQ
2 ACGLRTUVWXY
3 BGMNRU**W**X
4 (Q+R 📅)
5 **AB**DGIJKLMNOPUVW
6 CDEGK(N 1km)TV

💬 Marked-out pitches with bushes and many trees and therefore plenty of shade. Takes part in a competition for campsite with the most flowers every year. Winner in 2016. Within walking distance from the old town Vermenton with sights such as a 12th-century church. Reception closed between 12:00 and 14:00.

🚗 On the N6 Auxerre-Avalon the campsite is clearly signposted before Vermenton. Pay attention to the name. Site is located behind a small train station.

Irancy   D956
Cravant   A6
Migé   CC   D11
D606   D944
D100   D32

CC € **13** 1/4-6/7 25/8-29/9   📍 N 47°39'31'' E 3°43'51''

Vincelles, F-89290 / Bourgogne (Yonne)

♿ 🛜 **iD** 1999

🏕 Les Ceriselles★★★★
🛏 route de Vincelottes
☎ +33 (0)3-86425047
⊙ 1/4 - 1/10
@ camping@cc-payscoulangeois.fr

2,5ha 76T(90-150m²) 10A CEE

1 ACD**G**IJKLPQ
2 CGRTVWX
3 BGHJKL**MNQ**RU**W**
4 (**E**+Q+R+T+U+X+Z ⊙)
5 **AB**DFGIJKLMNOPUXYZ
6 ACDEGIK(N 0,2km)TV

💬 A lovely quiet 4-star campsite full of flowers in the heart of the Burgundy vineyards and among cherry trees. Hallmarks:'Camping Qualité' and 'Tourisme et Handicap'. The site is located alongside the Yonne, Canal du Nivernais with its cycle routes, not far from lake (4 ha) offering plenty of opportunities for anglers. You can visit the lovely countryside of Sud de l'Yonne.

🚐 South of Auxerre, 10 km from the D606. Campsite signposted from Vincelles.

🇨🇨 € **15** 1/4-7/7   25/8-30/9

📍 N 47°42'25'' E 3°38'8''

Bonlieu, F-39130 / Franche-Comté (Jura)

♿ 🛜 **iD** 2000

🏕 Camping L'Abbaye★★★
🛏 2 route du Lac
☎ +33 (0)3-84255704
⊙ 1/5 - 30/9
@ camping.abbaye@wanadoo.fr

4ha 80T(100-120m²) 10A CEE

1 ACD**G**IJKLMOPQ
2 CJRUVWXY
3 BGHJN**OP**R**W**
4 (Q+R+T+U+V+X+Y+Z ⊙)
5 **AB**FGJKLNPUZ
6 ACDEGK(N 5km)V

💬 A terraced campsite with spacious pitches marked out by bushes and hedges. Lovely views of the cliffs. Ideal starting point for walks and cycle trips. The campsite is only a few minutes from the Herrisson waterfalls and has an excellent restaurant with the 'Tourisme' and 'Maître-restaurateur' hallmarks.

🚐 From Clairvaux-les-Lacs continue on to Geneva on the N78 through Bonlieu. Turn right at end of built up area about 1 km further to 'Lac de Bonlieu' and the campsite.

🇨🇨 € **15** 1/5-6/7   27/8-29/9

📍 N 46°35'48'' E 5°52'17''

Chalezeule/Besançon, F-25220 / Franche-Comté (Doubs)

🛜 **iD** 2001

🏕 Camping de Besançon - La Plage★★★
🛏 12 route de Belfort
☎ +33 (0)3-81880426
⊙ 15/3 -31/10
@ contact@ campingdebesancon.com

2,5ha 99T(75-120m²) 16A CEE

1 ACD**G**IJKLMPQ
2 CFGRUWXY
3 A**F**GHJN**QR**W
4 (Q+T 20/6-30/8)
5 **AB**CDEFGHIJKLMNOPUVW Z
6 ACDFGIK(N 0,2km)TV

💬 A campsite with a good location for visiting the World Heritage Site of Besançon. There are many opportunities for sports in and around the campsite. Fast connection to centre of Besançon with new tram.

🚐 RD683, Belfort-Besançon. Campsite signposted from there.

🇨🇨 € **17** 15/3-1/7   25/8-30/10 7=6

📍 N 47°15'57'' E 6°4'18''

Champagnole, F-39300 / Franche-Comté (Jura)

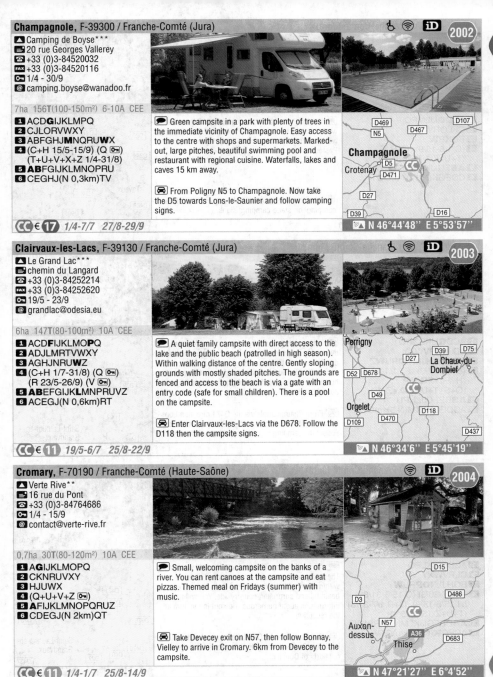

♿ 📶 **iD** `2002`

🏕 Camping de Boyse***
✉ 20 rue Georges Vallerey
☎ +33 (0)3-84520032
📠 +33 (0)3-84520116
🔑 1/4 - 30/9
@ camping.boyse@wanadoo.fr

7ha 156**T**(100-150m²) 6-10A CEE

1 ACD**G**IJKLMPQ
2 CJLORVWXY
3 ABFGHJ**M**NQRU**W**X
4 (C+H 15/5-15/9) (Q 🔑)
   (T+U+V+X+Z 1/4-31/8)
5 **AB**FGIJKLMNOPRU
6 CEGHJ(N 0,3km)TV

💬 Green campsite in a park with plenty of trees in the immediate vicinity of Champagnole. Easy access to the centre with shops and supermarkets. Marked-out, large pitches, beautiful swimming pool and restaurant with regional cuisine. Waterfalls, lakes and caves 15 km away.

🚗 From Poligny N5 to Champagnole. Now take the D5 towards Lons-le-Saunier and follow camping signs.

D469 N5 D467 D107
Champagnole
Crotenay ○ D5 CC
D471
D27
D39 D16

CC € **17** 1/4-7/7 27/8-29/9   ⛺ N 46°44'48'' E 5°53'57''

Clairvaux-les-Lacs, F-39130 / Franche-Comté (Jura)

♿ 📶 **iD** `2003`

🏕 Le Grand Lac***
✉ chemin du Langard
☎ +33 (0)3-84252214
📠 +33 (0)3-84252620
🔑 19/5 - 23/9
@ grandlac@odesia.eu

6ha 147**T**(80-100m²) 10A CEE

1 ACD**F**IJKLMO**P**Q
2 ADJLMRTVWXY
3 AGHJNRU**W**Z
4 (C+H 1/7-31/8) (Q 🔑)
   (R 23/5-26/9) (V 🔑)
5 **AB**EFGIJKL**L**MNPRUVZ
6 ACEGJ(N 0,6km)RT

💬 A quiet family campsite with direct access to the lake and the public beach (patrolled in high season). Within walking distance of the centre. Gently sloping grounds with mostly shaded pitches. The grounds are fenced and access to the beach is via a gate with an entry code (safe for small children). There is a pool on the campsite.

🚗 Enter Clairvaux-les-Lacs via the D678. Follow the D118 then the campsite signs.

Perrigny
D39 D75
D27
La Chaux-du-
D52 D678 Dombief
D49
Orgelet CC
D109 D470 D118
D437

CC € **11** 19/5-6/7 25/8-22/9   ⛺ N 46°34'6'' E 5°45'19''

Cromary, F-70190 / Franche-Comté (Haute-Saône)

📶 **iD** `2004`

🏕 Verte Rive**
✉ 16 rue du Pont
☎ +33 (0)3-84764686
🔑 1/4 - 15/9
@ contact@verte-rive.fr

0,7ha 30**T**(80-120m²) 10A CEE

1 A**G**IJKLMOPQ
2 CKNRUVXY
3 HJUWX
4 (Q+U+V+Z 🔑)
5 **A**FIJKLMNOPQRUZ
6 CDEGJ(N 2km)QT

💬 Small, welcoming campsite on the banks of a river. You can rent canoes at the campsite and eat pizzas. Themed meal on Fridays (summer) with music.

🚗 Take Devecey exit on N57, then follow Bonnay, Vielley to arrive in Cromary. 6km from Devecey to the campsite.

D15
D3 D486
CC
Auxon- N57
dessus A36 D683
Thise

CC € **11** 1/4-1/7 25/8-14/9   ⛺ N 47°21'27'' E 6°4'52''

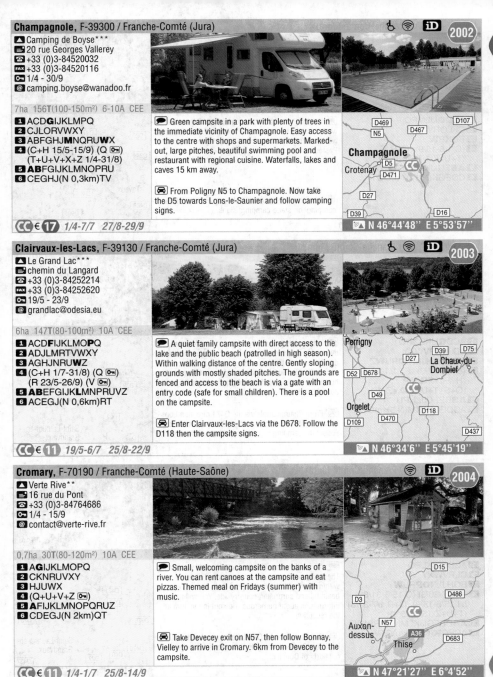

Dole, F-39100 / Franche-Comté (Jura) ♿ 📶 iD 2005

🏕 Du Pasquier***
📧 18 ch. Victor et Georges Thévenot
☎ +33 (0)3-84720261
📠 +33 (0)3-84792344
🕐 15/3 - 15/10
@ lola@camping-le-pasquier.com

2ha 120T(80-110m²) 10A

1 ACD**G**IJLMPQ
2 CFLORVWXY
3 BGKR**W**
4 (C 1/6-15/9) (Q+R 📅)
　(T+U+Z 1/7-31/8)
5 **AB**FGIJKLMNOPUW
6 CDEGK(N 1,0km)OQT

💬 A friendly and attractive campsite 15 minutes' walk from the town centre. The town of Dole is a well-preserved historic town, the birthplace of Louis Pasteur.

🚗 From the A36 take the Dole exit. In Dole follow 'camping' or 'stade-camping' signs.

CC € 15 15/3-6/7 25/8-14/10 ▧ N 47°5'22'' E 5°30'11''

Doucier, F-39130 / Franche-Comté (Jura) ♿ 📶 iD 2006

🏕 Domaine de Chalain****
☎ +33 (0)3-84257878
📠 +33 (0)3-84257006
🕐 27/4 - 17/9
@ chalain@chalain.com

30ha 417T(90-120m²) 10A CEE

1 ACD**G**IJKLO**P**Q
2 ADJLORVWXY
3 ABDE**GH**J**M**N**QR**U**W**Z
4 (B 1/6-17/9) (F 21/4-13/9)
　(H 📅) IJK**LNP**
　(Q+S+T+U+V+X+Z 📅)
5 **AB**DEFGJLNPU
6 ACDEGH**IK**M(N 3km)OQRT
　V

💬 A campsite located by a lake and surrounded by a richly wooded and hilly landscape. An excellent departure point for discovering the area: rivers, panoramas, waterfalls. Water park with 400 m² indoor heated swimming pools and from the beginning of June 500 m² outdoor pools.

🚗 From Champagnole via the D471 direction Lons-le-Saunier. Via the D27 direction Clairvaux-les-Lacs. Follow the camping signs in the village of Doucier.

CC € 17 27/4-6/7 1/9-16/9 ▧ N 46°39'51'' E 5°48'50''

Doucier, F-39130 / Franche-Comté (Jura) ♿ 📶 iD 2007

🏕 Les Merilles***
📧 rue des 3 Lacs
☎ +33 (0)3-84257306
🕐 15/4 - 30/9
@ camping.lesmerilles@wanadoo.fr

2ha 96T(80-140m²) 6-10A CEE

1 ACD**G**IJKLPQ
2 CLRVWXY
3 BGHJLN**OP**RU**W**
4 (A 1/7-30/8) (C 15/6-31/8)
　(H 15/5-15/9) (Q+R 1/7-31/8)
　(T+U+Z 15/6-15/9)
5 **AB**DEFGIJKLMNOPR**S**UVZ
6 ACEG**K**(N 0,5km)OTV

💬 A friendly campsite close to lakes and waterfalls. The village with various restaurants and shops is within walking distance. You can walk and cycle in beautiful and surprising countryside. You will find information about numerous trips out in the Jura at the reception.

🚗 In Doucier via the D27 follow signs to Clairvaux-les-Lacs. Campsite located 150 metres from the outskirts of Doucier.

CC € 15 15/4-30/6 31/8-29/9 ▧ N 46°39'6'' E 5°46'29''

Ecrille, F-39270 / Franche-Comté (Jura)

 ♿ 📶 **iD** `2008`

🏕 La Faz***
📧 4 Pont de Vaux
☎ +33 (0)3-84254027
🔓 1/5 - 30/9
@ campinglafaz@gmail.com

6ha 99T(100-150m²) 6A CEE

1 **A**FIJKLMOPRS
2 CLRVXY
3 BGHJNRU**W**
4 (C 1/6-30/9)
　(Q+R+T+U+V+Z 🔓)
5 **A**GIJKNPUZ
6 CEJ**K**(N 1,5km)RTV

💬 A campsite located in extensive grounds by a river and a stone's throw from Lake Vouglans. The area is perfect for rest, relaxation and nature walks. Pitches marked out by hedges. There is a snack bar and a swimming pool. No toilet facilities in April and October.

🚌 From Lons-le-Saunier D52 direction Orgelet via the D678 and then D52e and D52 as far as Orgelet. Take the D470 and turn immediately right to Ecrille. Follow camping signs.

Beaufort / D678 / D52 / D49 / D118 / D27 / D117 / CC Meussia Maisod / D109 / D470

CC €**15** 1/5-6/7 27/8-29/9

🗺 N 46°30'35'' E 5°37'14''

La Tour-du-Meix, F-39270 / Franche-Comté (Jura)

📶 **iD** `2009`

🏕 Domaine du Surchauffant***
📧 Le Pont de la Pyle
☎ +33 (0)3-84254108
📠 +33 (0)3-84355688
🔓 27/4 - 17/9
@ info@camping-surchauffant.fr

3ha 156T(80-110m²) 10A CEE

1 ACD**G**IJKLMOPQ
2 ADJLRVWXY
3 ABGHIJRU**WZ**
4 (C+G+Q+R+T+U+V+X+Y+Z 🔓)
5 **AB**EFGIJKLMNPUXZ
6 CEGH**K**(N 5km)QRTV

💬 An extensive campsite sloping down to the lake. Marked out pitches, some with shade. Various watersports possibilities in the swimming pool and in the lake.

🚌 From Lons-le-Saunier take the N78 then the D52. In Orgelet take D470 towards St. Claude. Follow camping signs.

D117 / D52 / D49 / D678 / Orgelet / CC / D27 / D109 / D470 / D118 / Moirans-en-Montagne

CC €**13** 27/4-6/7 1/9-16/9

🗺 N 46°31'24'' E 5°40'27''

Leval, F-90110 / Franche-Comté (Territoire-de-Belfort)

📶 **iD** `2010`

🏕 Flower Camping du Lac de la Seigneurie***
📧 3 rue de la Seigneurie
☎ +33 (0)3-84230013
🔓 1/4 - 31/10
@ contact@camping-lac-seigneurie.com

3,8ha 77T(90-360m²) 6-10A

1 ACD**G**HIJKLMPQ
2 BDFMRTUVXY
3 BF**G**HJNRU**W**
4 (C+H 1/7-31/8)
5 **AB**IJKLMNOPUVWZ
6 CDEG**J**(N 5km)TV

💬 A peaceful campsite on the shores of 'Lac de la Seigneurie'. 20 minutes from Belfort and Mulhouse, 25 minutes from Ballon d'Alsace. Natural grounds with outdoor activities 20 minutes away. The restaurant next to the site is open every day except Monday. Arrival after 14:00, otherwise a 2 Euros supplement.

🚌 E36 exit 14.1 'Fontaine', third exit on roundabout D60A. Next roundabout 1st exit D12, turn right onto the D83. Campsite signposted from there, located on the D11.

Cernay / D14 BIV / D466 / D12 / D25 / A36 / CC / D483 / D11 / Valdoie D83 / D103 / Belfort D419

CC €**15** 1/4-14/7 1/9-30/10 7=6

🗺 N 47°44'9'' E 7°0'58''

Levier, F-25270 / Franche-Comté (Doubs)

⌃ Camping de la Forêt***
▤ route de Septfontaine
☎ +33 (0)3-81895346
☉ 27/4 - 16/9
@ camping@
camping-dela-foret.com

📶 ✿ **iD** 2011

2ha 67T(100-120m²) 6-10A CEE

1 ACDGIJKLMOPRS
2 LRVWXY
3 BGHJLNRU
4 (A 9/7-31/8) (C 1/6-31/8)
(Q+R+U+Z 1/7-31/8)
5 ABEFGIJKLMNPUWZ
6 EGJK(N 0,5km)ORT

💬 Family-friendly, very well-maintained campsite located on a plateau with direct access to a wooded walking area. 800 metres from a supermarket. Cycling opportunities from the campsite. Mushroom picking in September in the woods around the campsite. Lovely heated pool.

🚗 Levier is located on the D72 between Salins-les-Bains and Pontarlier. The campsite is located just 1 km northeast from the towncentre. Along the D41 direction Septfontaine.

[Map: Reugney, D67, D492, D41, D9, D72, Dommartin, D472, Courvières, D471]

CC € 15 27/4-12/7 30/8-15/9 7=6, 14=12 📐 N 46°57'35'' E 6°7'58''

Lons-le-Saunier, F-39000 / Franche-Comté (Jura)

⌃ La Marjorie****
▤ 640 boulevard de l'Europe
☎ +33 (0)3-84242694
🖷 +33 (0)3-84240840
☉ 1/4 - 15/10
@ info@camping-marjorie.com

♿ 📶 **iD** 2012

7,5ha 192T(100-120m²) 6-10A CEE

1 ACDGIJKLMOPQ
2 CFGLRUVWXY
3 ABFGHJLNRU
4 (A 1/7-21/8) **B**(Q+R ☉)
(T 1/5-30/9) (U+Z ☉)
5 ABDEFGIJKLMNPUWXYZ
6 CDEGIJK(N 0,5km)ORTV

💬 A neat campsite with pitches marked out by hedges. Near the town of Lons with its health resort. Free swimming in the municipal indoor heated swimming pool (200m) if staying a minimum of 5 days.

🚗 A39, exit 7 from the north, 23 km on the dual carriageway (N83). Exit 8 from the south, 9 km op N78. Follow campsite signs.

[Map: D122, D120, D5, A39, D471, D39, Lons-le-Saunier, D678, D1083, D117, D470, D27]

CC € 15 1/4-7/7 1/9-14/10 📐 N 46°41'3'' E 5°34'7''

Malbuisson, F-25160 / Franche-Comté (Doubs)

⌃ Locahome Les Fuvettes***
▤ 24 route de la Plage des Perrières
☎ +33 (0)3-81693150
☉ 1/4 - 30/9
@ les-fuvettes@wanadoo.fr

♿ 📶 **iD** 2013

6ha 200T(80-140m²) 6A CEE

1 ACDGIJKLMOPRS
2 ADORVWXY
3 ABDGHJNQRUWZ
4 (C 1/6-31/8) (F+H ☉) IJ
(Q+S+T+U+V+X+Z 1/6-31/8)
5 ABEFGJKLMNPUWZ
6 ACEGK(N 1km)OT

💬 Campsite on the St. Point Lac with opportunities for watersports recreation opportunities and fishing. Ideal base for long and short walks and for trips out in the ever-changing countryside of the 'Haut-Jura'. Indoor heated leisure pool and outdoor pool.

🚗 After Pontarlier (on the N57) turn right and follow route D437 to Malbuisson direction Lac St. Point-Rive Droite. In the village turn right and follow signs to the campsite.

[Map: Frasne, D67 B, D471, D6, D9, D107, Jougne, D45, N57, A9, D437, Vallorbe]

CC € 17 1/4-30/6 1/9-29/9 📐 N 46°47'31'' E 6°17'36''

Marnay, F-70150 / Franche-Comté (Haute-Saône)

ﾙﾙﾙ ♿ 🛜 **iD** 2014

🔺 Vert Lagon★★★★
📧 route de Besançon
☎ 🖷 +33 (0)3-84317316
⌚ 1/5 - 30/9
@ contact@camping-vertlagon.com

3ha 77T(100-120m²) 10A CEE

1 ACD**G**IJKLMPQ
2 CRVWXY
3 AGHJRU**W**
4 (B+G 15/5-15/9) (Q 1/7-31/8)
(T+U+Z ⌾)
5 **AB**DFGJMNPUW
6 CDFGK(N 0,1km)TV

💬 Located at walking distance from the old village of Marnay. This campsite is an ideal place for sportive campers. Kayaking, mountain biking and other activities.

🚐 From A36 exit 3. Dir. Graz via D67. Then D29 to Marnay. Entrance is left of road, just before centre.

D1
D67
D12   Auxon-
          Dessous
D459   A36
          Dannemarie-
          sur-Crête

CC € **15** 1/5-30/6 1/9-29/9   📐 N 47°17'20'' E 5°46'38''

Mesnois/Clairvaux-les-Lacs, F-39130 / Franche-Comté (Jura)

♿ 🛜 **iD** 2015

🔺 Sites & Paysages
Beauregard★★★★
📧 2 Grande rue Mesnois
☎ 🖷 +33 (0)3-84483251
⌚ 29/3 - 30/9
@ reception@
juracampingbeauregard.com

6ha 195T(100-120m²) 6A

1 ACDGIJKLMOPRS
2 RVXY
3 BGHJMNQRU**W**
4 (B 15/6-1/9) (F+H ⌾) IJKLNP
(Q 1/6-31/8) (R ⌾)
(U 1/5-30/9) (V 25/6-31/8)
(X+Y 1/5-30/9) (Z 25/6-31/8)
5 **AB**DEFGJLNPUVYZ
6 ACDEG**K**(N 1km)T

💬 A well-maintained, friendly family campsite with fitness apparatus, playground and bouncy castle in rustic surroundings. An ideal location for exploring this surprising region. Excellent restaurant! New indoor pool with water slide.

🚐 From Lons-le-Saunier via the D52 direction Clairvaux-les-Lacs. Caravans go via the D678 (D52 prohibited for caravans). Follow the camping signs.

Lons-le-Saunier
D39
D117
CC
D52   D49   D678
D27
D109   D470   D118

CC € **17** 29/3-6/7 26/8-29/9   📐 N 46°35'59'' E 5°41'18''

Montbarrey, F-39380 / Franche-Comté (Jura)

♿ 🛜 **iD** 2016

🔺 Flower Camping Les 3 Ours★★★
📧 28 rue du Pont
☎ +33 (0)3-84815045
⌚ 31/3 - 23/9
@ h.rabbe@orange.fr

3,5ha 68T(100-140m²) 10A

1 ACD**G**IJKLMPQ
2 CLORSVWXY
3 BGHJNR**W**X
4 (B+G 1/6-15/9)
(Q+R+U+Y+Z ⌾)
5 **A**EFGIJKLMNPUWZ
6 CEGJ(N 3km)TV

💬 A delightfully quiet campsite by the River Loue. Perfect fishing. Enjoy the flora and fauna. Excellent cycling and many marked out walks in the area. The campsite has an excellent restaurant with local dishes. Privilege pitches by the river are not included in the CampingCard ACSI rate.

🚐 South of Dole via N5 or D405, go through Parcey. Then keep on towards Pontarlier-Lausanne via D472. Follow campsite signs.

Dole
Arc-et-
Senans
D405
CC
D475   D472   Mouchard
A39
D905   D469   N83

CC € **15** 31/3-3/7 26/8-22/9   📐 N 47°0'44'' E 5°37'50''

Ornans, F-25290 / Franche-Comté (Doubs) ♿ 🛜 iD 2017

🔺 Le Chanet***
📧 9 chemin du Chanet
☎ +33 (0)3-81622344
🔓 30/3 - 1/10
@ contact@lechanet.com

2,5ha 68T(80-120m²) 10A CEE

1 ACD**G**IJLPQ
2 IJKLRUVWXY
3 BGHJKM**R**UV**W**
4 (B+G 🔓) **N**(Q+S 🔓)
(T+U+Z 1/7-31/8)
5 **AB**DEFGIJKLMNPUWZ
6 ACDEGK(N 2km)ORTV

💬 Good campsite for short or long stays, located between Besançon and Pontarlier. Perfect for anglers, walkers and cyclists. Eco-friendly swimming. The area is noted for its gastronomy in the historic picturesque town of Ornans.

🚗 Leave the D67 in Ornans and follow D241 direction Chassagne-St-Denis. Turn right over the bridge and follow the signs.

CC € 15 30/3-1/7 26/8-30/9 7=6, 14=11   📍 N 47°6'1'' E 6°7'40''

Ornans, F-25290 / Franche-Comté (Doubs) 👫 ♿ 🛜 iD 2018

🔺 Sites & Paysages La Roche d'Ully****
📧 5 allée de la Tour de Peilz
☎ +33 (0)3-81571779
🔓 2/4 - 7/10
@ contact@larochedully.com

3ha 75T(120-250m²) 16A CEE

1 ACD**G**IJKLMPQ
2 CKLRSVWX
3 ABGHJN**OP**RUW**X**
4 (**A** 1/7-31/8) (C 15/6-1/9)
(F+H 🔓) J**KLN**
(Q+R+T+U+Y+Z 🔓)
5 **AB**CDEFGIJKLMNPUWXYZ
6 CDEGJL(N 2km)TV

💬 Luxury family campsite which puts nature first. Covered swimming pool. A centre for climbing trees, canoeing, kayaking and spelunking just outside the campsite. Free use of a dishwasher.

🚗 Follow D67 through Ornans centre. Towards Pontarlier. After Ornans (after overpass) immediately left. Left over the same bridge after 100 metres (traffic lights).

CC € 17 2/4-7/7 25/8-6/10 7=6   📍 N 47°6'2'' E 6°9'37''

Ounans, F-39380 / Franche-Comté (Jura) ♿ 🛜 iD 2019

🔺 Huttopia La Plage Blanche***
📧 2 rue de la Plage
☎ +33 (0)3-84376963
🔓 27/4 - 23/9
@ plageblanche@huttopia.com

17ha 180T(120-200m²) 6-10A CEE

1 ACD**G**IJKLMPQ
2 CLMNRVWXY
3 ABGHJNRU**W**X
4 (B 🔓)
(F+G 27/4-30/6,1/9-23/9)
(Q+R 🔓)
(T+U+V+Z 5/7-31/8)
5 **AB**DEFGIJKLMNOPUWZ
6 ACEGIJ(N 1km)RTV

💬 An extensive grassy campsite along the river, partly shaded. Countless opportunities for walking and cycling in the wooded surroundings. The Jura with its waterfalls, lakes, villages and towns is not far away. Free wifi. CampingCard ACSI is not valid for pitches on the river.

🚗 N5 Dole-Poligny. After about 18 km from Dole at Mont-sous-Vaudrey take the D472 in the direction of Pontarlier. Then follow the camping signs.

CC € 17 27/4-5/7 26/8-22/9   📍 N 47°0'9'' E 5°39'49''

Ounans, F-39380 / Franche-Comté (Jura)

♿ 🛜 iD 2020

🏕 Le Val d'Amour***
✉ 1 rue du Val d'Amour
☎ +33 (0)3-84376189
📠 +33 (0)3-84377869
🗓 1/4 - 30/9
@ camping@levaldamour.com

3,5ha 97**T**(140m²) 6-10A CEE

1 ACD**G**IJKLMPRS
2 LRVXY
3 BGHJNRU
4 (B 15/6-15/9) J
   (T+U+Z 1/7-31/8)
5 **AB**GIJKLMNOPUVWZ
6 CEGJ(N 0,2km)TV

💬 Family campsite, lovely pitches in the sun and shade, partly with fruit trees. Nice toilet facilities and swimming pool with slides. Quiet location in wooded area, plenty of opportunity for cycling and walking. Dijon, Dole and characteristic towns such as Arbois and Ornans and also the Jura with waterfalls, lakes and mountains at a short distance.

🚗 Follow N5 Dole-Poligny. Follow D472 dir. Pontarlier about 18 km from Dole near Mont-sous-Vaudrey. Follow signs in Ounans.

Dole
Villette-lès-Dole
CC — D472
A39 — D905 — N83
D475 — D469 — Arbois

CC € **11** 1/4-14/7 1/9-29/9 7=6, 14=11

📐 N 46°59'36'' E 5°40'15''

Parcey, F-39100 / Franche-Comté (Jura)

♿ 🛜 iD 2021

🏕 Les Bords de Loue***
✉ chemin du Camping
☎ +33 (0)3-84710382
🗓 1/4 - 29/9
@ contact@jura-camping.fr

17ha 240**T**(100-200m²) 10A

1 ACD**G**IJKLMPQ
2 CFLORTVWXY
3 B**E**GHKMN**P**QRU**W**X
4 (C+H 5/5-9/9) J
   (Q+R 1/5-29/9)
   (T+U+V 1/7-31/8)
   (Z 1/5-29/9)
5 **AB**EFGIJKLMNPUWZ
6 ACDEGJ**K**(N 7km)OTV

💬 An attractively-located campsite on the river Loue, ideal for trout fishing. Archery and golf close to the site. Shops and good restaurants are within walking distance in the village. The area invites you to go walking or cycling.

🚗 Follow the N5 south of Dole in the direction of Genève up to Parcey. Campsite is well marked in both directions.

Foucherans **Dole**
A36
Tavaux — D405
CC
D673 — D475 — D472
D469 — A39
D468 — D905

CC € **15** 1/4-30/6 26/8-28/9 7=6, 14=10

📐 N 47°0'59'' E 5°28'53''

Patornay, F-39130 / Franche-Comté (Jura)

♿ 🛜 iD 2022

🏕 Le Moulin****
✉ chemin du Camping
☎ +33 (0)3-84483121
📠 +33 (0)3-84447121
🗓 27/4 - 16/9
@ contact@camping-moulin.com

5ha 217**T**(80-100m²) 6A CEE

1 ACD**F**IJKLPRS
2 CLORVXY
3 ABGJNRU**W**X
4 (C+E+H 🔆) JKLN(Q 🔆)
   (R+T+U+V+Z 15/6-5/9)
5 **AB**EFGIJKLNPUWZ
6 ACEG**IJK**(N 0,8km)ORTV

💬 A campsite with plenty of greenery and shade. Outdoor swimming pool with slide and indoor pool with sauna by means of a sliding roof. Located by a river with a beach and plenty of water sports opportunities.

🚗 From Lons-le-Saunier via the D52 direction Clairvaux-les-Lacs. Caravans via the D678. D52 is prohibited for caravans. Follow camping signs in Patornay.

Lons-le-Saunier — D39

D52 — D49 — D678
D27
D109 — D470 — D118

CC € **17** 27/4-6/7 26/8-15/9 7=6

📐 N 46°35'14'' E 5°42'3''

Pont-les-Moulins, F-25110 / Franche-Comté (Doubs)

📶 **iD** (2023)

🏕 de L'Île*
📧 1 rue Pontarlier
☎ +33 (0)3-81841523
🗓 27/4 - 9/9
@ info@campingdelile.fr

1,5ha 35T(120-200m²) 6A

1. AGIJKLPQ
2. CFRWX
3. AHJKNRU**W**X
4. (T+Z 🔓)
5. **AB**GIJKMOPUV
6. FG**J**(N 0,5km)

💬 A modest campsite by a small river with spacious (unmarked) pitches in beautiful natural surroundings.

🚐 Take the N83. In Beaume-les-Dames exit Pont-les-Moulins. The campsite is located in the beginning of Pont-les-Moulins, on the left side of the road.

D486 — Baume-les-Dames — A36 D683 — D73
D464 — D50
Nancray — D492

CC € **11** 27/4-14/7 1/9-8/9 📐 N 47°19'30'' E 6°21'41''

Port-Lesney, F-39600 / Franche-Comté (Jura)

👫 ♿ 📶 **iD** (2024)

🏕 Les Radeliers***
📧 1 rue Edgar Faure
☎ +33 (0)3-84738144
🗓 1/5 - 30/9
@ lesradeliers@woka.fr

3,5ha 100T(< 80m²) 8A CEE

1. ACD**G**IJKLMO**P**Q
2. CNORTVWXY
3. BGHJ**M**RU**W**X
4. (T+Z 1/6-31/8)
5. **AB**CEFGIJKLMNPRU
6. ACDEGK(N 0,1km)

💬 Neat campsite along the Loue with pebble beach and located just beside the church in the village. Shops for groceries and restaurants beside the campsite.

🚐 Campsite located on D48 in Port-Lesney between the church and the river Loue.

D472 — **CC**
D467 — D492
N83 — Salins-les-Bains — Arc-sous-Montenot
D469

CC € **15** 1/5-30/6 1/9-29/9 📐 N 47°0'12'' E 5°49'25''

Rioz, F-70190 / Franche-Comté (Haute-Saône)

♿ 📶 **iD** (2025)

🏕 Camping du Lac***
📧 14 rue de la Faïencerie
☎ +33 (0)3-84919159
🗓 1/4 - 30/9
@ camping@rioz.fr

3ha 52T(80-130m²) 16A

1. ACD**G**IJKLM**P**Q
2. DGJKRUVWXY
3. BG**M**NRU**W**
4. (B+G 1/6-15/9) J(Q+R 🔓)
5. DFGIJKLMNPUWXY
6. EGK(N 0,4km)V

💬 Spaciously appointed municipal campsite with accessible toilet facilities. Swimming pool with water slide next to the campsite. The campsite is located next to a lake with various sports options.

🚐 Leave the N57 at Rioz, in Rioz take D5 and D232 then D15 towards Montbozon. Follow the signs.

Frasne-le-Château
Rioz D15
D5 — **CC**
D3 — D486
D1 — N57 — Pouligney-Lusans

CC € **15** 1/4-29/6 1/9-29/9 📐 N 47°25'31'' E 6°4'29''

Villard-Saint-Sauveur, F-39200 / Franche-Comté (Jura)

2026

Flower Camping Le Martinet***
12 le Martinet
+33 (0)3-84450040
1/4 - 30/9
contact@camping-saint-claude.fr

3ha 110**T**(50-100m²) 10A CEE

1 ACD**G**IJKLMPQ
2 CIJLRTUVWXY
3 A**F**GHJ**M**RU**W**
4 (C+H 1/6-1/9) (Q+R)
(T+U+V+X+Z 15/5-10/9)
5 **AB**DEFGIJKLMNPUWXYZ
6 CDEGK(N 3km)RV

A very large and completely renovated campsite on the River Tacon. It has a large swimming pool complex. St. Claude is a picturesque village in the south of the high Jura with views of the beautiful rock formations.

On entering St. Claude from the west, cross the bridge over the Bienne via de D436. Immediately right at the cathedral. Follow campsite signs. Narrow entrance to campsite. Beware of oncoming traffic.

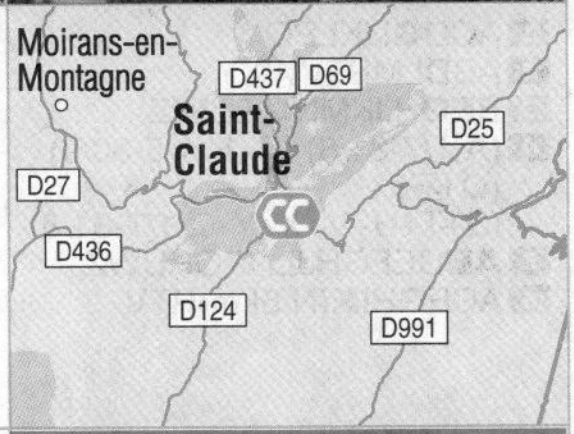
Moirans-en-Montagne
D437
D69
Saint-Claude
D25
D27
D436
D124
D991

CC € 15 *1/4-7/7 1/9-29/9*

N 46°22'18'' E 5°52'21''

Argentat, F-19400 / Limousin (Corrèze)

2027

Au Soleil d'Oc****
Monceaux-sur-Dordogne
+33 (0)5-55288484
+33 (0)5-55281212
25/4 - 30/10
info@campingsoleildoc.com

3,5ha 99**T**(120-140m²) 6-10A CEE

1 ACDFIJKLMPQ
2 CGJLNRTVWXY
3 BGHJN**OPQ**RUV**W**X
4 (B 1/7-30/9) (F)
(G 1/7-30/9) KN(Q 1/5-15/9)
(R 1/7-31/8)
(T+U+V+X+Z 15/6-30/9)
5 **AB**DEFGJLMNOPRUVZ
6 ACEGJ**K**(N 4,5km)RTV

A campsite on the Dordogne with pitches by the water. Plenty to see in the area in terms of nature and culture. Also well suited in low season for lovers of peace and tranquillity. 4 km from picturesque Argentat. The indoor swimming pool is in use from the opening date of the campsite.

A20 exit 45. D1120 Uzerche-Tulle-Argentat. In Argentat D12 direction Beaulieu, in Laygues (after 3.5 km) left, over the bridge, direct left.

Saint-Chamant
D18
Argentat
D980
D940
D12
D41
D1120

CC € 15 *25/4-7/7 25/8-29/10 7=6, 14=11, 21=16*

N 45°4'31'' E 1°55'2''

Argentat, F-19400 / Limousin (Corrèze)

2028

Le Vaurette****
Monceaux-sur-Dordogne
+33 (0)5-55280967
1/5 - 21/9
info@vaurette.com

4ha 120**T**(90-140m²) 6A CEE

1 ACD**F**IJKLMOPRS
2 CJKLNRTVWXY
3 BGHK**M**NRUV**W**X
4 (A 5/7-25/8) (C+G+Q+R)
(S+T+U+V 1/7-31/8) (Z)
5 **AB**CEFGJLNPUWZ
6 ACEGJ(N 9km)OTV

Campsite with tranquillity and friendliness directly on the Dordogne river. Spacious pitches. Lots to see in the surroundings, suitable for walking. Fly fishing and angling at the site. You can enjoy the beautiful, heated pool during the entire opening period. There is always fresh bread. Tennis free in low season.

A20 exit 45 direction Tulle. Then take the D1120 to Argentat. At the roundabout take the D12 towards Beaulieu. Then follow the signs and the river.

D921
D18
Argentat
D980
D38
D41
D1120
D12
Beaulieu-sur-Dordogne
D940

CC € 17 *1/5-4/7 25/8-20/9*

N 45°2'44'' E 1°53'2''

Aubazine, F-19190 / Limousin (Corrèze)

▲ Campéole Le Coiroux★★★★
🏠 Parc Touristique du Coiroux
☎ +33 (0)5-55272196
📠 +33 (0)5-55271916
🗓 27/4 - 30/9
@ rsage@andretriganogroupe.com

2029

7ha 62T(100-200m²) 10A CEE

1 ACDG IJKLPQ
2 ABDLMRTVWXY
3 BEGHJKMNQRUWZ
4 (A 1/7-31/8) (C+H 1/5-30/9)
(Q 🗓)
(S+T+U+V+X+Y+Z 1/7-31/8)
5 ABCEFGHJLNPQRUWZ
6 ACEGHIK(N 5km)RTV

💬 Very peacefully located campsite with spacious pitches. Walking and cycling routes in the wooded surroundings. Swimming and fishing possible in the lake. Heated swimming pool. Golf course with 27 holes. Day trips to historic sights or picturesque villages.

🚗 A89 exit Tulle dir Beaulieu-Figeac. 2 km after St. Fortunade turn right towards Centre Touristique Coiroux. Or take A20 exit 49 towards Tulle. Right at Gare d'Aubazine village. Follow Centre touristique de Coiroux.

CC € **15** 27/4-6/7 25/8-29/9   N 45°11'10'' E 1°42'26''

Beaulieu-sur-Dordogne, F-19120 / Limousin (Corrèze)

▲ Huttopia Beaulieu sur
Dordogne★★★
🏠 bd Rodolphe de Turenne
☎ +33 (0)5-55910265
📠 +33 (0)5-55910519
🗓 20/4 - 30/9
@ beaulieu@huttopia.com

2030

5ha 145T(80-120m²) 10A CEE

1 ACDG IJKLMPRS
2 CNRTVWXY
3 ABGHKRUWX
4 (A 1/7-31/8) (C+H+Q+R 🗓)
(T+U+V+Z 1/7-31/8)
5 ABDFGIJKLMNPUVWZ
6 ACEGIK(N 0,2km)TV

💬 The campsite is situated on an island making it ideal for water sports enthusiasts. Only a bridge separates it from the friendly medieval town of Beaulieu with its many pavement cafes and restaurants. During May there is a 'strawberry festival' and as well as visiting the many places of interest locally you can also relax on the site. CampingCard ACSI is not valid for pitches on the river.

🚗 Direction to the campsite is marked in the centre of Beaulieu.

CC € **17** 20/4-5/7 2/9-29/9   N 44°58'46'' E 1°50'25''

Beynat, F-19190 / Limousin (Corrèze)

▲ Camping du Lac de Miel★★★★
🏠 Centre Touristique de Miel
☎ +33 (0)5-55855066
🗓 30/4 - 5/9
@ info@camping-miel.com

2031

7ha 61T(150-300m²) 6-10A CEE

1 ACDFIJKLMPQ
2 ADGIKLMRTVWXY
3 BFGHJMNQRUWZ
4 (E+H 🗓) JM(Q+R 1/7-31/8)
(T+U+V+X+Z 🗓)
5 ABEFGJLNPUVZ
6 CEGHK(N 4km)V

💬 Comfortable, child-friendly campsite on a lake with a sandy beach. Spacious pitches with views of the lake. Swimming possible in the swimming pool with sliding roof or in the lake (Pavillon Bleu) with a water slide.

🚗 Take the N120 as far as Tulle, then N940 direction Beaulieu/Figeac to Beynat. The campsite is signposted. Or take the A20 as far as Brive, D921 direction Argentat.

CC € **15** 30/4-9/7 27/8-4/9 7=6, 14=11   N 45°7'54'' E 1°45'47''

Bonnac-la-Côte, F-87270 / Limousin (Haute-Vienne) ♿ 🛜 iD 2032

🏯 Du Château de Leychoisier*****
📮 route de Leychoisier
☎ 📠 +33 (0)5-55399343
🔑 16/4 - 20/9
@ contact@leychoisier.com

4ha 80T(80-200m²) 10A CEE

1 AG**IJKLMP**RS
2 DFLRTVWXY
3 AGHMRUWZ
4 (B 15/5-20/9) (Q+R 🔲)
(U+X 22/4-20/9) (Z 🔲)
5 **AB**FGJLNPRUWXYZ
6 AEG**J**(N 2,5km)RV

💬 This castle campsite is located close to the Bonnac-la-Côte turning. A private park with a lake, next to a listed 9th-century castle ensures a unique setting. Here you will have every comfort for a successful holiday: spacious pitches, peaceful surroundings, comfortable toilets, swimming pool, restaurant. Golf course in the immediate vicinity.
🚗 A20 Châteauroux-Limoges, ca. 10 km before Limoges turn right (exit 27) direction Bonnac-la-Côte. Clearly signposted.

N147 D220 D5 D7 A20 D914 D920 D20 D56 A Le Palais-sur- D29 Vienne N141 **Panazol** D941

CC € **19** 16/4-8/7 1/9-19/9 📐 N 45°56'0'' E 1°17'23''

Boussac, F-23600 / Limousin (Creuse) 🏃 🎣 ♿ 🛜 ✿ iD 2033

🏯 Creuse Nature Naturiste****
📮 route de Bétête, D15
☎ +33 (0)5-55651801
🔑 1/4 - 15/10
@ creuse.nature@wanadoo.fr

19ha 120T(80-160m²) 10A

1 ACD**G**HIJKLMNOPS
2 BDLRTUVXY
3 A**F**GHJNRUW
4 (A 1/5-30/9) (B 1/6-15/9)
(F 🔲) (G 1/6-15/9) K**N**
(Q 🔲) (R 1/7-30/8)
(T+U+V+X+Z 🔲)
5 **AB**GIJKLMNOPUWXYZ
6 ACDEGHI**K**(N 2km)ORTUV

💬 A lovely naturist campsite in a woodland setting. Heated indoor pool and sauna. Good facilities and spacious pitches. A lovely area for walking and cycling. French, English, German and Dutch spoken. There is a restaurant and fresh bread every morning.

🚗 Boussac is located in the La Châtre-Montluçon-Guéret triangle. In Boussac via the D15 direction Bétête. Campsite is beside this road, well signposted.

Préveranges D917 D2 Betête D15 **Boussac** D916 D11 **Soumans** D990 D997

CC € **19** 1/4-6/7 24/8-14/10 📐 N 46°20'57'' E 2°11'11''

Boussac/Bourg, F-23600 / Limousin (Creuse) ♿ 🛜 ✿ iD 2034

🏯 Le Château de
Poinsouze/les Castels****
📮 route de la Châtre
☎ +33 (0)5-55650221
🔑 12/5 - 13/9
@ campingpoinsouze@gmail.com

23ha 123T(110-250m²) 6-25A CEE

1 ACD**G**HIJKLMP**Q**
2 DILRTVX
3 ABGHJNRUW
4 (B+G 🔲) J
(Q+R+T+U+X+Z 🔲)
5 **AB**FGIJKLMNPUWXYZ
6 CDEG**JK**(N 2,5km)RV

💬 A beautiful castle campsite with very spacious and grassy level pitches. The toilet facilities are excellent. There is a lovely small lake, with possibilities for canoeing and suitable for the novice surfer. There is also a swimming pool with water slide. There are many trips out possible nearby in 'La Creuse'.
🚗 From La Châtre, drive via the D917 in the direction of Boussac. Signposted on the right side of the road 2 km before Boussac.

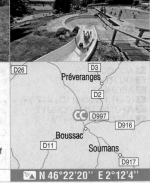

D26 D3 **Préveranges** D2 CC D997 D916 **Boussac** D11 **Soumans** D917

CC € **17** 12/5-3/7 30/8-12/9 📐 N 46°22'20'' E 2°12'4''

Bugeat, F-19170 / Limousin (Corrèze)

  ♿ 🛜 iD **2035**

🏕 Sites& Paysages Portes des Mille Sources***
📧 16, rue des 3 Ponts
☎ +33 (0)5-55943212
📅 31/3 - 30/9
@ auxportesdesmillesources@orange.fr

8,5ha 40T(100-300m²) 10A CEE

1 ABDFIJKLMPR
2 BCGKLRTUVWXY
3 ACGHJMQRUVW
4 (Q+R 1/7-31/8)
  (T+U+V+Z 1/5-30/9)
5 ABDGJLNPUWZ
6 CDEK(N 0,7km)TV

💬 A very spacious, natural and quiet campsite with large pitches. Large sports hall. Plenty of cycling and walking options. Free wifi on the entire campsite. Pleasant snack bar. Lively shopping village within 600m.

🚗 From Paris A20 dir. Toulouse. Exit Eymoutiers and follow Bugeat. In Bugeat D97 and follow signs.

D69 · D940 · D78 · D164 · D16 · D157 · D32 · D979 · Barsanges · Bonnefond · CC

CC € ⑬ 31/3-7/7 25/8-29/9 7=5, 14=11

📡 N 45°36'20'' E 1°55'22''

Châteauneuf-la-Forêt, F-87130 / Limousin (Haute-Vienne)

  🛜 iD **2036**

🏕 Le Cheyenne***
📧 avenue Michel Sinibaldi
☎ +33 (0)5-55693929
📅 1/4 - 30/9
@ contact@camping-le-cheyenne.com

1,4ha 49T(90-120m²) 6A CEE

1 ACDGIJKLMPRS
2 ADKLMRTVWXY
3 AGHJMRUWZ
4 (C 1/5-30/9)
  (Q+T+U+V+X+Y+Z 📅)
5 ABEGJKLNPUVZ
6 CEGJ(N 0,5km)RTV

💬 Quiet campsite on a lake with a sandy beach. Walking, cycling, swimming. Have a drink afterwards or head to the restaurant.

🚗 A20, exit 35 dir. Eymoutiers. D979 Châteauneuf-la-Forêt follow signs 'Le Lac'.

Bujaleuf · D979 · Eymoutiers · D940 · Linards · CC · D12 · D30 · D7 BIS · D16 · D3

CC € ⑮ 1/4-8/7 26/8-29/9

📡 N 45°42'59'' E 1°36'5''

Cognac-la-Forêt, F-87310 / Limousin (Haute-Vienne)

  ♿ 🛜 iD **2037**

🏕 Camping des Alouettes***
📧 1 les Alouettes
☎ +33 (0)5-55032693
📅 1/4 - 30/9
@ info@camping-des-alouettes.com

4ha 68T(150m²) 10A CEE

1 ACDGIJKLPS
2 FKLRTVWXY
3 ABGHIJRU
4 (C+H 1/5-30/9) (Q+X+Z 📅)
5 AFGIJKLMNOPQRUYZ
6 ACEGIK(N 1km)TV

💬 Very spacious pitches on the edge of a wood at 25 km from Limoges. Dutch owners. An ideal area for relaxation, walking and exploring this beautiful region. Heated pool. Unlimited wifi for 1 Euro per day. Table d'hôtes on Monday and Friday.

🚗 A20, exit 28 direction Périgueux (N520). Continue towards Périgueux (D2000) as far the roundabout with Cognac-la-Fôret turning (D10). Follow signs beyond Cognac-la-Fôret to the campsite. Parking near the entrance of the camping.

Saint-Junien · N141 · D9 · Verneuil-sur-Vienne · D10 · CC · D2000 · D901 · D21 · N21 · D20 · D699

CC € ⑮ 1/4-6/7 24/8-29/9

📡 N 45°49'30'' E 0°59'48''

Dun-le-Palestel, F-23800 / Limousin (Creuse)   ♿ 🤝 **iD** (2038)

🏕 Camping Dun-le-Palestel**
📧 Promenade Maurice Rollinat 2
☎ +33 (0)6-52718939
🗓 1/3 - 1/11
@ info@campingdunlepalestel.fr

2ha 42T(130m²) 10-16A CEE

1 ACD**G**IJKLMPS
2 FKLRVWXY
3 AHJKR
4 (B 1/5-15/9) (Q+T+V ☕)
5 **AB**CGHIJKLMNPUWZ
6 ACEGJ(N 0km)T

💬 Small, pleasant campsite with a panoramic view and spacious pitches, run by a welcoming young Dutch couple. Lively village with all the amenities nearby. Lovely cycling and walking routes through the undulating surroundings begin directly from the campsite. Regular lively communal meals and fresh pizzas, even in the low season. Daily bread service and free wifi.

🚗 From Dun-le-Palestel towards Crozant. At roundabout straight on, turn right after 1 km.

Saint-Sébastien
D913
D49   D951
La Celle-Dunoise
CC
D5

CC € **15** 1/3-6/7 25/8-31/10   📐 N 46°19'2'' E 1°39'55''

Fourneaux, F-23200 / Limousin (Creuse)   👫 🤝 **iD** (2039)

🏕 La Perle***
📧 Commune de
   St. Médard-la-Rochette
☎ +33 (0)5-55830125
🗓 1/4 - 30/9
@ info@camping-laperle.nl

3ha 33T(50-120m²) 10A

1 A**G**IJKLMPST
2 IJKLRUVWXY
3 ABD**F**GHJNPR**W**
4 (B+G 1/6-30/8)
   (Q+X+Y+Z ☕)
5 **A**FGIJKLMNPQUWXZ
6 DEG**K**(N 0,5km)

💬 A homely campsite with friendly Dutch owners. Countryside, hospitality, breathtaking views, lovely sights and the River Creuse within walking distance. Plenty of walking, cycling, golf and fishing opportunities. Restaurant/bar/terrace, swimming pool, spacious camping pitches and well maintained toilet facilities. Wifi and bakery service.

🚗 A20 exit 23 direction Guéret, then D942 direction Aubusson. Campsite well signposted.

Ahun
D55   D4
D13
D942
Saint-Sulpice-les-Champs   CC
D990 D993
D942 A
Aubusson
D941   D988
D7   D982

CC € **15** 1/4-30/6 1/9-29/9 7=6, 14=12   📐 N 46°1'18'' E 2°8'22''

Guéret, F-23000 / Limousin (Creuse)   👫 ♿ 🤝 **iD** (2040)

🏕 de Courtille***
📧 rue Georges Aulong
☎ FAX +33 (0)5-55819224
🗓 1/4 - 30/9
@ contact@camping-courtille.com

2,7ha 60T(80-100m²) 10A CEE

1 ACD**G**IJLPST
2 ADFKLMRVWXY
3 AHJR**W**Z
4 (Q+R ☕)
5 **AB**GIJKLMNPUVWZ
6 ACEGK(N 3km)TV

💬 Well-maintained campsite in a parkland setting, spaciously positioned next to a small lake with water sports activities (20 hectares). Marked out pitches.

🚗 From the A20 exit 23 direction Guéret (N145). Then exit 49 and follow signs. SatNav is correct. The route is very tricky. It's better to follow directions on the signs.

D913
Saint-Vaury
D4   **Guéret**   N145
CC
D914   Sainte-Feyre
D940 D942
D50

CC € **13** 1/4-7/7 25/8-29/9   📐 N 46°9'45'' E 1°51'31''

Limoges, F-87280 / Limousin (Haute-Vienne)
♿ 🛜 **iD** **(2041)**

🔺 Camping d'Uzurat***
📧 40 avenue d'Uzurat
☎ 📠 +33 (0)5-55384943
🔓 15/3 - 31/10
@ contact@campinglimoges.fr

2,5ha 155T(70-80m²) 10A CEE

1 ACD**G**HIJKLMOPR
2 BCDFKLMNRTUVWXY
3 ABCGHJMQRUW
4 (B 1/7-31/8) (Q+V 🔓)
5 ABDEFJLMNPUVZ
6 CE**K**(N 0,3km)TV

💬 Less than 2 km from motorway exit. Site is clearly signposted. Ideal stopover site with clean new toilet facilities. Also ideally suited for visiting Limoges and its natural surroundings. Walking, cycling, sports and recreation options close by. Friendly welcome. Wifi 1 Euro for 24 hours.

🚗 From north along the A20, take exit 30. From south exit 31 and follow Zone Industriël (ZIN) Lac Uzurat.

CC € **15** 15/3-8/7 27/8-30/10 — 📐 N 45°52'14'' E 1°16'32''

Lissac-sur-Couze, F-19600 / Limousin (Corrèze)
♿ 🛜 **iD** **(2042)**

🔺 Flower Camping Le Lac du Causse***
📧 Lieu-dit la Prairie
☎ +33 (0)5-55853797
🔓 1/4 - 30/9
@ camping.causse@brive-tourisme.com

4ha 82T(80-100m²) 16A CEE

1 ABCD**F**IJKLMP
2 ADFJKLMRTUVWXY
3 AB**F**GHIKLNRU**WZ**
4 (B 10/6-30/9) (Q 🔓)
(R 1/7-31/8) (T 🔓)
(U+X 1/7-31/8) (Z 🔓)
5 **AB**DEFGJLNPUWY
6 CDEGH**IK**(N 7km)TV

💬 Campsite located on a slightly undulating hill on the Lac du Causse. Enjoy the sandy beach by the lake, the many water sports options and the beautiful countryside. With spacious, sometimes hardened pitches and many shaded pitches.

🚗 A20 Limoges-Toulouse, exit 51 Bordeaux/Périgueux. Then direction Lissac-sur-Couze and follow 'Lac du Causse' signs.

CC € **15** 1/4-6/7 25/8-29/9 7=6, 14=11 — 📐 N 45°5'59'' E 1°27'4''

Marcillac-la-Croisille, F-19320 / Limousin (Corrèze)
♿ 🛜 **iD** **(2043)**

🔺 Camping du Lac***
📧 28 route du Viaduc
☎ +33 (0)5-55278138
🔓 30/3 - 21/10
@ campingdulac19@wanadoo.fr

3,5ha 80T(80-120m²) 6A

1 ACD**G**IJKLMO**P**Q
2 ADIJKLMRVWXY
3 ABGH**M**RU**WZ**
4 (B 15/6-15/9) (Q+R+T 🔓)
(X 1/4-15/10) (Z 🔓)
5 **AB**EFGIJKLMNPUWZ
6 CEGJ(N 2km)TV

💬 A beautifully located campsite with plenty of parking space; lovely touring pitches with reasonable privacy; plenty of shade. Ideal for water sports enthusiasts. The campsite is located 2 km from the centre of the village.

🚗 D978 Tulle-Mauriac. Follow signs in the village. Or D18 Egleton-Argentat, follow 'Complexe Touristique du Lac la Valette' in the village.

CC € **15** 30/3-7/7 25/8-20/10 7=6, 14=11 — 📐 N 45°16'9'' E 2°0'33''

St. Germain-les-Belles, F-87380 / Limousin (Haute-Vienne)

iD **2044**

▲ de Montréal***
rue du Petit Moulin
☎ +33 (0)5-55718620
1/1 - 31/12
@ contact@campingdemontreal.com

2ha 47**T**(80-130m²) 10A CEE

1 ACD**F**IJKLMPRS
2 ADFJLRTVWXY
3 ABGH**M**NRU**W**Z
4 (B 15/5-15/10)
(Q 15/4-31/10)
(T+U+V 1/4-31/10)
(X 15/4-31/10) (Z 1/4-31/10)
5 **AB**DEFGJLNPUWZ
6 AEG**K**(N 1km)RTV

A quietly located campsite by a lake with a sandy beach. Clean comfortable toilet facilities. Plenty of opportunities for sports. Within walking distance of an attractive village.

A20, exit 42. Direction St. Germain-les-Belles. Then follow signs (Plan d'eau de Montréal). Now quicker to take new ring road. Campsite very well signposted.

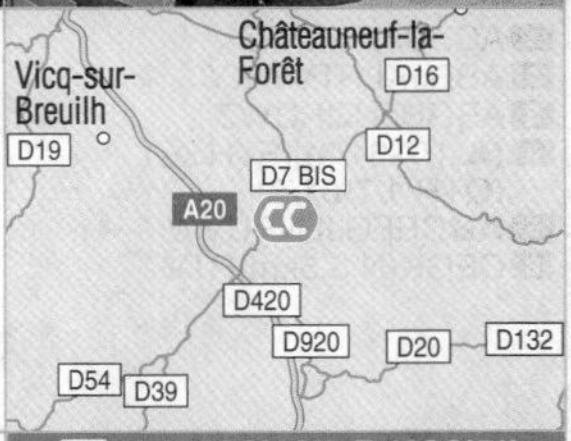
Châteauneuf-la-Forêt
Vicq-sur-Breuilh
D16
D19
D12
D7 BIS
A20
CC
D420
D920
D20
D132
D54
D39

CC € 15 1/1-1/7 19/8-31/12 7=6

N 45°36'42'' E 1°30'5''

St. Léonard-de-Noblat, F-87400 / Limousin (Haute-Vienne)

iD **2045**

▲ Camping de Beaufort***
Lieu-dit Beaufort
☎ +33 (0)6-17128618
14/4 - 3/11
@ info@campingdebeaufort.fr

NEW

2,5ha 76**T**(90-120m²) 15A

1 ACD**G**HIJKLMPQ
2 CLRTVWXY
3 BGHJRU**W**
4 (Q+R 29/5-20/9) (X)
5 **AB**FGJLNPRUZ
6 CEGIJ(N 4km)TV

A campsite in a quiet location on the banks of the Vienne and on the pilgrimage route to Santiago de Compostela. Spacious pitches and comfortable toilet block. An ideal base for getting to know the region. Possibility of guided kayaking.

A20 exit 34 from the north, exit 35 from the south. D941 dir. Clermont-Ferrand. In St. Léonard-de-Noblat follow camping signs.

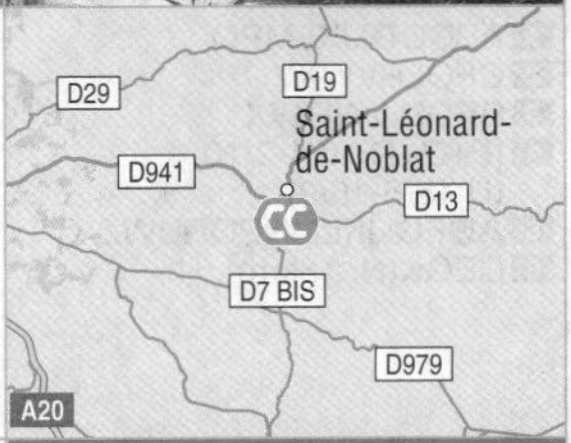
D29
D19
Saint-Léonard-de-Noblat
D941
D13
CC
D7 BIS
D979
A20

CC € 11 28/4-29/6 27/8-22/9

N 45°49'23'' E 1°29'31''

St. Pardoux, F-87250 / Limousin (Haute-Vienne)

iD **2046**

▲ Camping Fréaudour****
Site de Freaudour
☎ +33 (0)5-55765722
5/3 - 4/11
@ camping.freaudour@orange.fr

4,5ha 103**T**(80-150m²) 10-16A CEE

1 ACD**G**IJKLM**P**Q
2 ABDFGIKLMRVWXY
3 AGHJKN**OP**RU**W**Z
4 (B 5/6-11/9) (Q 1/5-30/9)
(R 1/4-30/9)
(T+U+Z 1/7-31/8)
5 **AB**EFGIJKLMNPUWZ
6 ACEJ(N 7km)RTV

By the lake (Lac de Saint-Pardoux) in wooded surroundings with First Aid post and a supervised swimming area. Lovely outdoor swimming pool on the grounds.

Take the A20 in the direction of Limoges. Exit 25 Lac de St. Pardoux, then 'Site de Fréaudour'.

D1
D711
D28
CC
A20
Nantiat
D44
D7
N147
D220
D5
Neuvillas
Ambazac
D914

CC € 15 5/3-7/7 25/8-3/11 7=6, 14=11

N 46°2'59'' E 1°16'44''

Treignac-sur-Vézère, F-19260 / Limousin (Corrèze) ♿ 🛜 iD (2047)

🏕 Flower Camping La Plage***
🏖 Lac des Bariousses
☎ +33 (0)5-55980854
📅 30/3 - 30/9
@ camping.laplage@
   flowercampings.com

3,7ha 83T(80-150m²) 6A

1 ACD**G**IJLM**P**RS
2 ABDJKLRTVWXY
3 ABGHJNQRUWZ
4 (**A** 1/7-31/8) (E+H 🔒)
   (Q+R 1/7-31/8)
5 **AB**CEFGJLNPUVW
6 CEGK(N 3,5km)RTV

💬 A comfortable campsite by a lake with a sandy beach. Quiet location and close to a lively village. Spacious pitches marked out by bushes.

🚗 A20 exit 43 towards Treignac. Treignac direction Gueret via D970.

Chambéret
Treignac
Affieux
D30 · D979 · D164 · D20 · D32 · D157 · D3 · D16 · D940

CC € **13** 30/3-6/7 25/8-29/9 7=6 · 📐 N 45°33'35'' E 1°48'48''

Abrest/Vichy, F-03200 / Auvergne (Allier) ♿ 🛜 iD (2048)

🏕 La Croix St-Martin en
   bordure d'Allier***
🏖 allée du cp, avenue des Graviers
☎ +33 (0)4-70326774
📅 2/4 - 2/10
@ camping-vichy@orange.fr

3ha 72T(100-200m²) 10A CEE

1 ABCD**G**IJKLMPQ
2 CFGLRVWXY
3 B**F**GHJLNR**W**X
4 (F+Q+R 10/4-2/10)
   (U 15/5-15/9)
5 **AB**FGIJKLMNPQRUWZ
6 CEGK(N 1,5km)

💬 A peaceful campsite on the banks of the Allier, within walking distance of the spa resort of Vichy. An ideal location for trips out into the Auvergne. Heated indoor swimming pool and free wifi. Reception open 08:30 to 12:00 and 13:30 to 20:00.

🚗 In Vichy keep in direction Thiers. The campsite is signposted and is located along this road.

Bellerive-sur-Allier · Vichy · Cusset
D6 · D907 · D906 B · D2209 · D25 · D995 · D984 · D1093 · D906

CC € **13** 2/4-9/7 27/8-1/10 · 📐 N 46°6'28'' E 3°26'12''

Ambert, F-63600 / Auvergne (Puy-de-Dôme) ♿ 🛜 iD (2049)

🏕 Les Trois Chênes***
🏖 route du Puy
☎ 📠 +33 (0)4-73823468
📅 27/4 - 30/9
@ tourisme@ville-ambert.fr

5ha 94T(100-150m²) 10A CEE

1 ACD**G**IJLPQ
2 CLRVX
3 AGHRU**W**
4 (C 1/7-31/8) (F 🔒)
   (H 1/7-31/8) IJ(Q 1/7-31/8)
   (T+U 15/5-7/9) (V 1/5-30/9)
   (X 15/6-15/9) (Z 1/5-30/9)
5 **AB**FGIJKLMNPUVZ
6 CDEGHJ(N 2km)V

💬 Spacious campsite located in the south of the Auvergne. Very spacious shady pitches, marked out by hedges.

🚗 Take the D906 south of Ambert. The campsite is located on the left 3 km down the road.

Cunlhat · La Forie · Ambert
D66 · D996 · D39 · D906 · D38

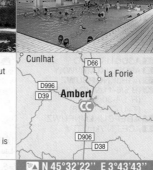

CC € **15** 27/4-1/7 19/8-29/9 · 📐 N 45°32'22'' E 3°43'43''

Aydat, F-63970 / Auvergne (Puy-de-Dôme)   ♿ 🛜 iD   **2050**

🏕 Le Camping du Lac d'Aydat***
✉ 16 boulevard du Lac -
    Forêt du Lot
☎ +33 (0)4-73793809
⌚ 1/4 - 15/10
@ info@camping-lac-aydat.com

8ha 80T(80-130m²) 16A CEE

1 ACD**G**HIJKLMPRS
2 ABDJLRTVWXY
3 ABHJN**PQR**U**WZ**
4 (Q+T+U+V+X+Y+Z 🔑)
5 **AB**DEFGIJKLMNPUVWZ
6 EGJ**K**(N 1km)TV

💬 Ideally situated campsite, 20 km south east of Clermont Ferrand, in the heart of regional natural park Des Volcans d'Auvergne. On Aydat Lake, in a pine tree forest with shade. Beautiful area with lots of sights.

🚗 A75, exit 5. Follow signs on D213 Aydat.

CC € **15** 1/4-6/7 1/9-14/10   📐 N 45°40'7'' E 2°59'21''

Bellerive-sur-Allier, F-03700 / Auvergne (Allier)   ♿ 🛜 iD   **2051**

🏕 Les Acacias au Bord du Lac****
✉ rue Claude Decloître
☎ +33 (0)4-70323622
📠 +33 (0)4-70598852
⌚ 31/3 - 1/10
@ camping-acacias03@orange.fr

3ha 75T(100m²) 10A CEE

1 ACD**G**IJKLMOPRS
2 CFLRVWXY
3 B**F**GNRU**W**
4 (C 15/6-15/9) (H 15/6-15/9) J
    (Q 15/5-15/9) (R 🔑)
    (T+U 1/6-15/9) (Z 🔑)
5 **AB**FGIJKLMNOPQRUVWZ
6 CEG**K**(N 0,5km)QRSV

💬 A well-kept campsite not far from River Allier and 1.5 km from Vichy. The campsite is characterised by its colourful appearance and by the peace of its spacious pitches. The campsite has a large terrace since 2017. There is also a heated swimming pool and an open air fitness circuit.

🚗 In Bellerive follow the signs 'campings'. Follow the river.

CC € **17** 31/3-30/6 31/8-30/9   📐 N 46°6'59'' E 3°25'33''

Bellerive-sur-Allier/Vichy, F-03700 / Auvergne (Allier)   ♿ 🛜 iD   **2052**

🏕 Beau Rivage sur les
    berges de l'Allier****
✉ rue Claude Decloître 15-17
☎ +33 (0)4-70322685
⌚ 1/4 - 6/10
@ camping-beaurivage@
    wanadoo.fr

2ha 37T(100m²) 10A CEE

1 ACD**G**IJKLMPRS
2 CFLRUVWXY
3 B**F**GKNRUV**W**
4 (E+H 15/5-15/9) J
    (Q 1/5-15/9) (R 🔑)
    (T 1/6-1/9) (Z 🔑)
5 **AB**DFGIJKLMNOPQUVWZ
6 CEG**K**(N 1km)QUV

💬 A well-kept comfortable campsite with spacious camping pitches and many facilities close to Vichy. The site is directly on the River Allier and offers (water)sports, but enjoying the peace and quiet on the riverside terrace is also one of the possibilities.

🚗 In Bellerive continue towards Hauterive and follow the green 'Berges de l'Allier' signs. At Allier enter 'rue Claude Decloître'. Campsite is on the left at the end of the road.

CC € **17** 1/4-9/7 27/8-5/10   📐 N 46°6'56'' E 3°25'49''

Blot-L'Église, F-63440 / Auvergne (Puy-de-Dôme) 🛜 iD (2053)

🔺 La Coccinelle**
🏠 Le Bourg
☎ +33 (0)4-73649315
📅 3/4 - 28/9
@ info@campingcoccinelle.com

1,6ha 41T(80-110m²) 6A CEE

1 ABCD**G**IJKLPS
2 KRTVWXY
3 ABGHJ**M**NR
4 (B 15/6-15/9) (X+Z 🔌)
5 **AB**CDFGJKMNPUW
6 ACDEGK(N 0,5km)

💬 A peacefully located family campsite on the edge of the village of Blot. In beautiful natural surroundings with many places of interest. This is the place for people who like walking, (electrically rechargeable) cycling, fishing, countryside and relaxation. With wifi. Dutch owners.

🚗 From A71 toll road exit 12.1 continue to St. Pardoux. Then follow camping signs. From Montluçon D2144, follow camping signs in Pouzol.

Ébreuil
D109 D2144 D207
CC
D227 A71
Manzat Combronde
D19 A89

CC € 13 3/4-4/7 22/8-27/9 30=25 🧭 N 46°1'56'' E 2°57'23''

Brioude, F-43100 / Auvergne (Haute-Loire) ♿ 🛜 ❀ iD (2054)

🔺 Camping de la Bageasse***
🏠 La Chaud
☎ +33 (0)4-71500770
📅 5/3 - 4/11
@ labageasse@orange.fr

2ha 49T(80-160m²) 10A CEE

1 ACD**G**IJKL**P**
2 CJMRTVWXY
3 AGHJRU**W**X
4 (B+G 1/7-31/8)
   (Q+R 1/6-15/9)
   (T+X+Z 1/6-30/9)
5 **AB**GIJKLMNPUVZ
6 EGJ(N 3km)RTV

💬 Campsite along the Allier river with swimming pool and paddling pool. Marked-out, shady pitches.

🚗 A75 exit 20 to Brioude. Then follow campsite signs. About 3 km from town centre.

Champagnac-le-Vieux
A75 Lamothe
Brioude
D588 CC
D12
D585 N102
D10

CC € 15 5/3-7/7 25/8-3/11 7=6, 14=11 🧭 N 45°16'53'' E 3°24'16''

Buxières-sous-Montaigut, F-63700 / Auvergne (Puy-de-Dôme) 🛜 iD (2055)

🔺 Les Suchères**
🏠 Les Suchères
☎ +33 (0)4-73859266
📅 1/4 - 30/9
@ sucheres@gmail.com

7,5ha 35T(100-140m²) 6A

1 ACD**G**IJKLPRS
2 IRVX
3 AD**F**GJKNRU
4 (A 1/5-31/8) (B 1/6-15/9)
   (Q+R+T+U+X+Z 🔌)
5 **A**BCEFGHIJKLMNPQRUW
6 EGJ(N 1,5km)V

💬 A charming family campsite on the edge of the Auvergne on the border between the Allier and Puy de Dôme departments. The campsite has 40 spacious pitches, a swimming pool, restaurant with garden, excellent toilet facilities. Dutch owners.

🚗 From Montmarault direction St. Eloy-les-Mines and keep on D13 as far as the camping signs.

Commentry
D998 D13
D4 D502 CC
Saint-Éloy-les-Mines
D987 D2144
D988

CC € 15 1/4-7/7 26/8-29/9 7=6 🧭 N 46°11'36'' E 2°49'10''

Ceyrat, F-63122 / Auvergne (Puy-de-Dôme)   👍 ⛄ 📶 iD 2056

🏨 Hôtel de Plein Air Le Chanset***
✉ rue du Chanset
☎ 📠 +33 (0)4-73613073
🕰 1/3 - 31/12
@ camping.lechanset@gmail.com

6ha 114T(100-150m²) 10A CEE

1 **ACDG**IJLPQ
2 GKRSTVY
3 BGNQRU
4 (A 1/7-31/8) (C 15/5-30/9)
(Q+R+T+U+X 🅿)
5 **AB**GIJKLMNOPUVWZ
6 CEGHK(N 0,8km)TV

💬 Quiet, family-run campsite on the slopes of the 'Parc des Volcans d'Auvergne', surrounded by plenty of trees. A lovely view of the valley.

🚗 In Clermont-Ferrand take exit Le Mont Dore/La Bourboule and keep following these signs. Take the N89 as far as Ceyrat. The campsite is signposted.

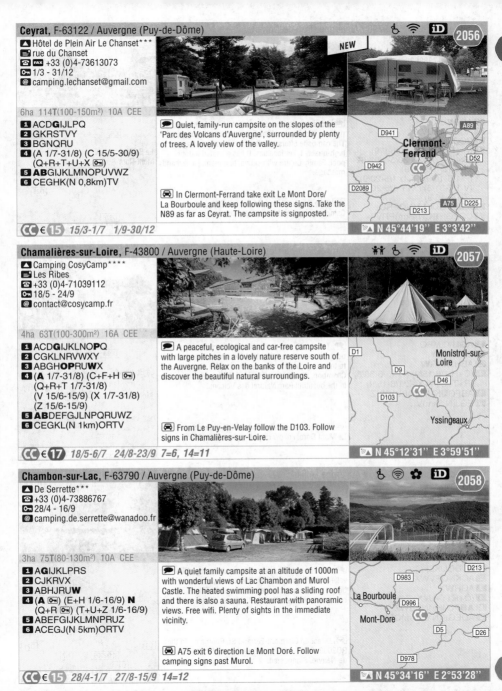

Clermont-Ferrand

CC €15 *15/3-1/7 1/9-30/12*   📍 N 45°44'19'' E 3°3'42''

Chamalières-sur-Loire, F-43800 / Auvergne (Haute-Loire)   👫 👍 📶 iD 2057

🏨 Camping CosyCamp****
✉ Les Ribes
☎ +33 (0)4-71039112
🕰 18/5 - 24/9
@ contact@cosycamp.fr

4ha 63T(100-300m²) 16A CEE

1 **ACDG**IJKLNO**P**Q
2 CGKLNRVWXY
3 ABGH**OP**RUWX
4 (**A** 1/7-31/8) (C+F+H 🅿)
(Q+R+T 1/7-31/8)
(V 15/6-15/9) (X 1/7-31/8)
(Z 15/6-15/9)
5 **AB**DEFGJLNPQRUWZ
6 CEGKL(N 1km)ORTV

💬 A peaceful, ecological and car-free campsite with large pitches in a lovely nature reserve south of the Auvergne. Relax on the banks of the Loire and discover the beautiful natural surroundings.

🚗 From Le Puy-en-Velay follow the D103. Follow signs in Chamalières-sur-Loire.

Monistrol-sur-Loire

Yssingeaux

CC €17 *18/5-6/7 24/8-23/9 7=6, 14=11*   📍 N 45°12'31'' E 3°59'51''

Chambon-sur-Lac, F-63790 / Auvergne (Puy-de-Dôme)   👍 ⛄ ✿ iD 2058

🏨 De Serrette***
☎ +33 (0)4-73886767
🕰 28/4 - 16/9
@ camping.de.serrette@wanadoo.fr

3ha 75T(80-130m²) 10A CEE

1 **AG**IJKLPRS
2 CJKRVX
3 ABHJRU**W**
4 (**A** 🅿) (E+H 1/6-16/9) **N**
(Q+R 🅿) (T+U+Z 1/6-16/9)
5 ABEFGIJKLMNPRUZ
6 ACEGJ(N 5km)ORTV

💬 A quiet family campsite at an altitude of 1000m with wonderful views of Lac Chambon and Murol Castle. The heated swimming pool has a sliding roof and there is also a sauna. Restaurant with panoramic views. Free wifi. Plenty of sights in the immediate vicinity.

🚗 A75 exit 6 direction Le Mont Doré. Follow camping signs past Murol.

La Bourboule

Mont-Dore

CC €15 *28/4-1/7 27/8-15/9 14=12*   📍 N 45°34'16'' E 2°53'28''

Chambon-sur-Lac, F-63790 / Auvergne (Puy-de-Dôme) 🔊 📶 ❀ iD 2059

△ Le Pré Bas*****
🏕 Lac Chambon
☎ +33 (0)4-73886304
📠 +33 (0)4-73886593
⊙ 21/4 - 15/9
@ prebas@campingauvergne.com

3,5ha 63T(90-130m²) 6A CEE

1 ACD**F**IJKLPRS
2 ACDLMRUVXY
3 BCGJNRU**VW**Z
4 (A 1/7-30/8) (C 20/5-9/9)
(E 4/5-17/9) (H 20/5-9/9) J**K**
L**M**N(Q 1/5-20/9)
(R 1/6-10/9) (T+U 1/5-20/9)
(V 1/7-31/8) (X+Y 1/5-20/9)
(Z 1/5-15/9)
5 **AB**EFGIJKLMNOPRU
6 CDEGH**IK**(N 2km)PRV

💬 Located in the volcanic heart of the Auvergne, right on the shores of the beautiful Lac Chambon. The campsite offers excellent facilities including high-quality toilet facilities. It has a heated indoor pool. Family Centre with sauna, hammam, jacuzzi and massage.

🚗 Take the D996 from Murol to Le Mont-Dore. Campsite is marked with green signs.

CC € **17** 21/4-30/6 1/9-14/9   📍 N 45°34'31'' E 2°54'51''

Chambon-sur-Lac, F-63790 / Auvergne (Puy-de-Dôme) 🔊 📶 ❀ iD 2060

△ Les Bombes***
🏕 chemin de Pétary
☎ +33 (0)4-73886403
⊙ 27/4 - 17/9
@ lesbombes@orange.fr

5ha 126T(100-124m²) 10A

1 A**G**IJKLMPQ
2 CKLRVXY
3 ABHJKNR**W**
4 (C+H 1/6-15/9) (Q 15/6-30/8)
(R+T+U+V+X+Z 1/6-15/9)
5 ABFGIJKLMNOPUVXYZ
6 EGJ(N 3km)V

💬 This lovely and well run campsite with swimming pool, restaurant and beautiful mountain views is close to the village of Chambon-sur-Lac and 1 km from Lac Chambon. Plenty of walking and cycling trips possible in the beautiful Parc Naturel des Volcans.

🚗 From exit 6 on the A75 to the 996 direction Le Mont Doré. Follow camping signs after Muro.

CC € **15** 27/4-5/7 29/8-16/9   📍 N 45°34'11'' E 2°54'8''

Châtel-de-Neuvre, F-03500 / Auvergne (Allier) 🔊 📶 iD 2061

△ Deneuvre***
🏕 route de Moulins
☎ +33 (0)4-70420451
📠 +33 (0)9-72256263
⊙ 1/4 - 16/10
@ campingdeneuvre@wanadoo.fr

1,2ha 58T(90-115m²) 6A

1 ACDGIJKLPQ
2 ACKNORVWXY
3 AGR**W**X
4 (Q+R+T+U+X+Z ⊙)
5 **AB**FGJKMNPUWZ
6 ADEGK(N 0,8km)ORV

💬 A quiet, beautiful campsite located in the Allier valley. Pitches by the river. The river has a small beach where you can spend some time. This is also a campsite for those who like fishing or bird-watching.

🚗 Direction Clermont-Ferrand/St. Pourçain. On the RD2009 (RN9) turn left before the small town Châtel-de-Neuvre. Signposted.

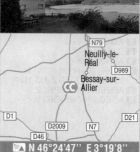

CC € **15** 1/4-30/6 1/9-15/10   📍 N 46°24'47'' E 3°19'8''

Châtel-Guyon, F-63140 / Auvergne (Puy-de-Dôme)

♿ 🛜 **iD** 2062

▲ Le Ranch des Volcans***
✉ route de la Piscine
☎ +33 (0)4-73860247
📠 +33 (0)4-73860564
🕐 17/3 - 28/10
@ contact@ranchdesvolcans.com

5ha 239T(80-200m²) 6A

1 ACD**G**IJKLMO**P**Q
2 FGRSVXY
3 ABGHJN**OP**QRU
4 (B+G 15/5-30/9)
(Q+R+T+U 🔩) (X 1/7-31/8)
(Y 🔩) (Z 15/5-30/9)
5 **AB**DFGIJKLMNPUV
6 ACDEGJ(N 0,5km)OV

💬 The three-star Le Ranch des Volcans campsite is located in Châtel-Guyon, a resort in the regional park of the volcanoes of the Auvergne. Near the towns of Volvic en Clermont-Ferrand. Lakes and volcanoes are close by. The campsite has a swimming complex with three pools, a playground, mini-golf and other sports activities. The restaurant serves regional specialities and is open on Friday, Saturday and Sunday.

🚗 A71, exit Riom. Then direction Châtel-Guyon. Signposted.

CC € **15** 17/3-6/7 25/8-27/10 7=6   🏕 N 45°54'54'' E 3°4'38''

Dallet, F-63111 / Auvergne (Puy-de-Dôme)

🛶 ♿ 🛜 **iD** 2063

▲ Les Ombrages***
✉ rue de pont du Chateau
☎ 📠 +33 (0)4-73831097
🕐 12/5 - 15/9
@ lesombrages@hotmail.com

3ha 90T(120-250m²) 6A CEE

1 ACDEIJKLPST
2 CFLNORSTVY
3 AHJNRUW**X**
4 (B+G+Q+T+U+X+Z 🔩)
5 **A**GIJKLMNPQUZ
6 AEJ(N 0,5km)V

💬 A friendly campsite on the banks of the Allier in the middle of the Auvergne plains. Numerous deciduous trees give the pitches plenty of shade. Dutch owners. Dogs not allowed. A 5-minute walk to the village. Cycle and walking route maps available. Baby and children's toilet facilities.

🚗 From Pont-du-Château via the D1 direction Cournon. Signposted.

CC € **13** 12/5-6/7 25/8-14/9   🏕 N 45°46'31'' E 3°14'31''

La Bourboule, F-63150 / Auvergne (Puy-de-Dôme)

⛷ ♿ 🛜 ✿ **iD** 2064

▲ Flower Camping
Les Vernières***
✉ 170 ave Mar. de Lattre de Tassigny
☎ +33 (0)4-73811020
🕐 3/2 - 4/3, 1/4 - 13/10
@ contact@
camping-la-bourboule.fr

5,5ha 165T(100-150m²) 10A CEE

1 AC**G**IJKLMPQ
2 CFGLRVWXY
3 **B**FGHIJNRUW
4 (**A** 1/7-31/8) (E 15/5-15/9) J
M(Q+T+U+V+Z 1/7-31/8)
5 **AB**DEFGJLNPZ
6 ACEG**JK**(N 0,5km)TV

💬 The campsite is located on the banks of the Dordogne between La Bourboule and the Mont Dore. In a natural area with centuries old trees and large pitches. Indoor heated swimming pool from 15-5 to 15-9.

🚗 A86 Gare de Laqueille. Between La Bourboule and Le Mont Dore.

CC € **15** 1/4-30/6 25/8-12/10   🏕 N 45°35'24'' E 2°45'9''

La Bourboule/Murat-le-Quaire, F-63150 / Auvergne (Puy-de-Dôme)

♿ 🎿 ⚡ 📶 iD 2065

🏔 Le Panoramique****
🏕 Le Pessy
☎ +33 (0)4-73811879
🗓 10/2 - 12/3, 7/4 - 30/9
@ info@campingpanoramique.fr

2,7ha 50T(70-100m²) 6A

1 ACGIJKLMPST
2 FJKLRTVX
3 ABDFGHJNRU
4 (C+H 15/6-31/8) (Q+R 🔒)
  (T+U+V+Z 15/6-27/8)
5 ABDEFGIJKLNPUVWXYZ
6 CEGJK(N 2km)OV

💬 The campsite lives up to its name: all pitches have spectacular views of the nearby Auvergne mountains. You can enjoy sunny days and fresh nights, especially in early and late season (1000 metres altitude). Perfect if you like walking, sports cycling or simply fresh mountain air. Excellent sanitation. La Bourboule (2 km) and Mont-Dore (6 km) are popular mountain areas.

🚗 A89, exit 25. Then the 219 to Murat-le-Quaire. Then follow camping signs.

D2089 A89 Saint-Sauves-d'Auvergne D987 D983 Mont-Dore D996 D203 D922 D47 CC

CC € 15 10/2-11/3 7/4-9/7 27/8-29/9 14=13

📍 N 45°35'49'' E 2°45'4''

Lanobre, F-15270 / Auvergne (Cantal)

⚡ 📶 iD 2066

🏔 Le Lac de la Siauve***
🏕 La Siauve
☎ +33 (0)4-71403185
🗓 8/4 - 17/9
@ campinglelacdelasiauve@orange.fr

NEW

17ha 171T(80-120m²) 6-16A CEE

1 ACGIJLMPQ
2 ADIJKLNORSVXY
3 ABGHKNRUWZ
4 (C+H 🔒) M(Q+R 🔒)
  (T+U+V+Z 1/7-31/8)
5 ABEFGIJKLMNOPUVWYZ
6 BCDEGJK(N 2,5km)TV

💬 Large, fun, terraced campsite in very green surroundings with a beautiful view of the Lac des Bort-les-Orgues. Indoor heated pool. Direct access to the lake and also to the pontoon/ramp for boats. Luxurious toilet block.

🚗 From Clermont-Ferrand exit Bordeaux, then the N89 in Laqueraille. Then take the D922 direction Bort-les-Orgues. The campsite is signposted beyond Lanobre.

Bagnols D47 D979 Bort-les-Orgues D922 D679 Ydes D3 CC

CC € 17 8/4-6/7 1/9-15/9

📍 N 45°25'50'' E 2°30'14''

Le Monastier-sur-Gazeille, F-43150 / Auvergne (Haute-Loire)

⚡ 📶 iD 2067

🏔 Estela**
🏕 route du Moulin de Savin
☎ +33 (0)4-71038224
🗓 15/4 - 29/9
@ estelacamping@gmail.com

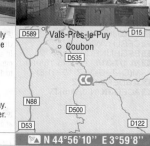

50T(70-110m²) 16A

1 AGIJKLOPQ
2 CDRVWXY
3 AFHJMRUWXZ
4 (A 1/7-31/8) (C 15/6-15/9)
  (Q 1/5-29/9) (T+Z 🔒)
5 AJLMNPUXYZ
6 AEGJ(N 0,8km)T

💬 This quiet and peaceful campsite is set in a hilly landscape, close to Le-Puy-en-Velay and next to the Gazeille, a Loire tributary. Heated swimming pool. Renovated barn for having a drink, a bite to eat or asking for information. The village is the starting point for the Stevenson path (GR70) to Alès in the Cevennes.

🚗 N88 direction St. Etienne from Le-Puy-en-Velay. Right after a few kilometres onto D535 to Monastier. Well indicated at entrance to village.

D589 Vals-Près-le-Puy D15 Coubon D535 N88 D500 D53 D122 CC

CC € 15 15/4-7/7 25/8-28/9

📍 N 44°56'10'' E 3°59'8''

Le Puy-en-Velay, F-43000 / Auvergne (Haute-Loire)

🛗 📶 **iD** 2068

△ de Bouthezard***
✉ chemin de Bouthezard Aiguilhe
☎ 📠 +33 (0)4-71095509
⌚ 30/3 - 28/10
@ camping.puyenvelay@orange.fr

1,5ha 72T(50-100m²) 6A CEE

1 A**G**IJKLM**P**Q
2 CGRSTX
3 H**M**R**W**
4 (Q 15/4-30/9) (R 1/4-30/9)
5 **AB**FGIJKLMNPUZ
6 CDFGJ(N 1km)TV

💬 Welcoming, small, town campsite with plenty of shade on the foot of one of Le Puy's most famous volcanic cones. Suitable base for visiting the town.

🚗 Signposted in Le Puy-en-Velay. Campsite located on the foot of the high rock church on the N88.

Map: N102, D103, Saint-Germain-Laprade, D906, D590, D15, **Le Puy-en-Velay**, Coubon, D589, D535, N88

CC € **15** 30/3-7/7 25/8-27/10 7=6, 14=11 📷 N 45°3'2'' E 3°52'51''

Lempdes-sur-Allagnon, F-43410 / Auvergne (Haute-Loire)

🛗 📶 **iD** 2069

△ Le Pont d'Allagnon***
✉ rue René Filiol
☎ +33 (0)4-71765369
⌚ 1/3 - 3/11
@ centre.auvergne.camping@orange.fr

1,7ha 60T(80-140m²) 10A CEE

1 ACFIJKLMPQ
2 CFLMRTVXY
3 BDGHJMNQRU**W**
4 (C+H 15/6-15/9) (T+Z 1/6-30/9)
5 **AB**FGIJKLMNOPUVWZ
6 ACDEGHIJ(N 0,5km)RTV

💬 A well-maintained, quiet campsite on the edge of a village, with heated swimming pool and toddlers' pool. Modern sports complex including tennis courts. About 500 metres from the A75, suitable for stopovers or longer stays. Base for walks in the surrounding area.

🚗 From Clermont-Ferrand follow the A75/E11. Exit 19 Lempdes direction Lempdes. Follow signs. From St. Flour follow the A75 as far as exit 20 direction 'Centre Ville'. Then follow camping signs.

Map: D214, Brassac-les-Mines, D17, D16, D5, A75, D909, N102, Brioude

CC € **15** 1/3-7/7 25/8-20/10 7=6 📷 N 45°23'13'' E 3°15'57''

Les Pradeaux/Issoire, F-63500 / Auvergne (Puy-de-Dôme)

🛗 📶 **iD** 2070

△ Château de Grange Fort***
✉ La Grange Fort
☎ +33 (0)4-73710243
📠 +33 (0)4-73710769
⌚ 5/4 - 31/10
@ chateau@lagrangefort.eu

7ha 120T(80-120m²) 6A CEE

1 ACD**G**IJKL**P**Q
2 BCFIKLORTVWXY
3 B**G**HJ**MNOP**RU**W**X
4 (A 1/5-31/10) (B 15/6-15/9) (F 15/4-1/7,31/8-15/10) (G 15/6-15/9) **N** (Q+R 1/5-15/9) (T+U+V+X+Z 1/5-30/9)
5 **AB**EFGIJKLMOPUZ
6 CDEG**IJ**(N 1km)OV

💬 This castle campsite located in the heart of the Auvergne offers peace, ambiance and numerous leisure activities. You can enjoy the heated indoor swimming pool and a delicious meal in the castle in early and late seasons. Dutch owners.

🚗 On A75 exit 13 direction Parentignat. 1st turn to right at roundabout after 1.5 km, direction St. Rémy-de-Chargnat via D999. Then right again at 2nd roundabout after 1.5 km, direction Les Pradeaux (D34). Campsite 1 km on the right.

Map: D229, D996, A75, D26, **Issoire**, D999, D214, Brassac-les-Mines

CC € **17** 5/4-7/7 25/8-30/10 14=12 📷 N 45°30'31'' E 3°17'5''

Mauriac, F-15200 / Auvergne (Cantal)

♿ 📶 **iD** (2071)

🏔 Le Val Saint-Jean****
🏖 Plan d'eau
☎ +33 (0)4-71673113
📅 1/5 - 16/9
@ valsaintjean@mauriac.fr

3,5ha 91**T**(110-120m²) 16A

1 ACD**G**IJLMOPQ
2 ADJLMRVWXY
3 AB**E**GHJNRU**W**Z
4 (A+C+H 1/7-31/8) J
  (Q+R+T+U+X+Z 🔲)
5 **AB**DFGIJLMNOPUZ
6 CEGHK(N 1,5km)RTV

💬 In natural surroundings between Dordogne and the Cantal mountains, you will be welcomed to spend a pleasant holiday on this campsite with many entertainment options: leisure pool, swimming lake, water sports, golf course, adventure park, amusement park, laser games, scavenger hunts, paths for walking...

🚗 When approaching from Aurillac follow Mauriac (D922). Signposted before the centre. From Clermont-Ferrand: exit Bordeaux N89/D922 to Bort-les-Orgues/Mauriac.

Lapleau · D982 · D682 · D978 · D105 · D678 · Mauriac · D12 · D122 · Ally · D922 · D22 · Pleaux · D680 · Salers

CC € **17** 1/5-7/7 25/8-15/9 7=6, 14=11, 21=17   **N 45°13'7'' E 2°18'56''**

Murol, F-63790 / Auvergne (Puy-de-Dôme)

♿ 📶 **iD** (2072)

🏔 Le Repos du Baladin***
🏕 Groire
☎ +33 (0)4-73886193
📅 29/4 - 16/9
@ reposbaladin@free.fr

2,4ha 67**T**(80-120m²) 10A CEE

1 A**G**IJL**PQ**
2 CJKLRVWXY
3 BGHJNRU**W**
4 (C 1/6-16/9)
  (Q+R+T+U+V+Z 15/6-31/8)
5 **AB**DEFGIJLMNPQRUVXYZ
6 AEGIJ**K**(N 1km)RV

💬 A peaceful campsite with sheltered pitches in a very natural setting. Small family campsite about 2 km from the really attractive town of Murol. This is absolutely the place for anyone who enjoys a restful holiday. Fine marked-out pitches with plenty of shade, excellent sanitary facilities and a lovely swimming pool. The surroundings are perfectly wonderful for walks and excursions.

🚗 In Murol direction Syndicat d'Initiative. Then follow the signs 'Le Repos du Baladin'.

D213 Tallende · Aydat · D983 · D996 · Champeix · D5 · D26 · D978

CC € **15** 29/4-1/7 26/8-15/9 8=7, 14=12   **N 45°34'25'' E 2°57'27''**

Nêbouzat, F-63210 / Auvergne (Puy-de-Dôme)

♿ 📶 **iD** (2073)

🏔 Les Dômes***
🏕 Les 4 routes de Nêbouzat
☎ +33 (0)4-73871406
📅 28/4 - 30/9
@ contact@les-domes.com

1ha 40**T**(80-100m²) 10A CEE

1 ACD**G**IJKLMPQ
2 GLRTUVX
3 A**F**GJRU
4 (A 10/7-25/8)
  (E+Q+R+T+U+V+X 1/5-15/9)
  (Y 🔲)
5 **AB**DEFGHIJKLMNOPUVWYZ
6 ACDEGIJ(N 1,3km)ORTV

💬 A fine family campsite with facilities for motorhomes. Level rectangular grounds with plenty of flowers and well maintained camping pitches. Indoor heated swimming pool in early and late seasons. The largest number of volcanoes in the Auvergne is in this region. Close to Vulcania and Le Puy de Dôme.

🚗 From the A75 exit 5 direction Aydat. Take the Col de la Ventouse D2089 in the direction of Ussel and pass Nêbouzat. Signposted.

A89 · D941 · D204 · D986 · Chamalières · D942 · Royat · D2089 · D983 · D5 · D213

CC € **15** 28/4-6/7 27/8-29/9   **N 45°43'33'' E 2°53'25''**

Neuvéglise, F-15260 / Auvergne (Cantal)

🏕 Flower Camping
Le Belvédère****
🏠 Lanau
☎ +33 (0)4-71235050
📅 30/3 - 22/9
@ belvedere.cantal@orange.fr

3,5ha 80T(80-100m²) 6-15A

1 ACDGIJLMPRS
2 JKRTVX
3 ABGHNRU**VW**
4 (**A** 1/7-31/8) (E 1/5-25/9)
(G 1/7-15/9) **N**(Q 📷)
(R 1/7-8/10)
(T+U+V+X+Z 📷)
5 **AB**CFGIJKLMNOPUWYZ
6 ACEGJ(N 6km)ORTV

💬 This terraced campsite is located on a south-facing slope with beautiful views of the valley, some pitches have a view of Lanau Lake. Snacks available, indoor and heated pool. Sportive as well as cultural outings are possible. The health spa Chaudes-Aigues is 5 km away with a hot water spring of 82 °C.

🚐 On D921 take exit St. Flour/Chaudes-Aigues. Pass Neuvéglise on right. Dir. Lanau, 1st right when you have reached the dam (signposted).

2074

CC € 15 30/3-6/7 29/8-21/9

🧭 N 44°53'42'' E 3°0'5''

Nonette, F-63340 / Auvergne (Puy-de-Dôme)

🏕 Les Loges***
☎ +33 (0)4-73716582
📅 31/3 - 13/10
@ les.loges.nonette@wanadoo.fr

3ha 143T(80-130m²) 6A CEE

1 ACD**F**IJKLMOPR
2 CFNORSTVXY
3 ABGRU**W**X
4 (C 20/6-9/9) (H 1/6-9/9) J**N**
(Q 1/7-31/8) (R 1/6-9/9)
(T+U+V+X+Z 1/7-31/8)
5 **AB**FGIJKLMNPUZ
6 AEG**JK**(N 5km)OTV

💬 Peaceful campsite on the Allier. Shaded pitches. Walking and cycling tours possible. An ideal overnight site just a few kilometres from the A75, with static caravans for rent. With swimmingpool in June and September.

🚐 A75, from Clermont-Ferrand exit 17 Nonette, then turn left. Follow campsite signs (± 5 km).

2075

CC € 15 31/3-6/7 25/8-12/10

🧭 N 45°28'10'' E 3°16'20''

Olliergues, F-63880 / Auvergne (Puy-de-Dôme)

🏕 Les Chelles***
☎ +33 (0)4-73955434
📅 1/4 - 31/10
@ info@camping-les-chelles.com

3,5ha 41T(80-180m²) 10A CEE

1 ACD**G**IJKLMPQ
2 BIJKRTVXY
3 AGHJMRUW
4 (C+G 1/6-31/8)
(Q+R+T+U+X+Z 📷)
5 **AB**FIJKLMNOPQUVZ
6 CDEGIJ(N 5km)V

💬 Peaceful family campsite with plenty of ambiance and lovely pitches on various terraces. The campsite has a swimming pool. Located in the Livradois-Forez nature reserve. English, French, Dutch and German spoken at the reception.

🚐 Take the D906 from Thiers to Ambert. Campsite clearly marked by arrows in Olliergues village.

2076

CC € 15 1/4-6/7 26/8-30/10 8=7, 14=12

🧭 N 45°41'25'' E 3°37'59''

Orcet, F-63670 / Auvergne (Puy-de-Dôme)

🏕 Le Clos Auroy****
✉ 15, rue de la Narse
☎ 📠 +33 (0)4-73842697
📅 1/1 - 31/12
@ orcet@wanadoo.fr

2,5ha 82T(100-120m²) 5-10A CEE

1 ACD**G**IJKLPQ
2 CFGJLRTVX
3 ABGHN**O**R**UW**
4 (C 15/5-15/9) (**G** 1/7-31/8) IJ
K(Q 🔲) (T+U+Z 1/7-31/8)
5 **AB**FGIJKLMNOPUVWZ
6 ACEG**K**(N 0,2km)OV

💬 Open all year. Reception open from 14:00-19:00. When not available you can check at the automatic check-in machine. Wifi. Heated swimming pool, bubble bath, children's pool and slides. 5A connection in early and late seasons. 10A also possible. Close to all amenities.

🚗 At 2.5 km from autoroute A75 Clermont-Ferrand/Issoire. Take exit 5 direction Orcet/Cournon. Then follow camping signs.

🆔 (2077)

Clermont-Ferrand
D52 · D212 · D213 · D229 · A75 · D225 · D978

€ **17** 1/4-6/7 24/8-30/10   N 45°42'1'' E 3°10'9''

Pers, F-15290 / Auvergne (Cantal)

🏕 Du Viaduc***
✉ Au Bord du Lac
☎ +33 (0)4-71647008
📅 21/4 - 13/10
@ campingduviaduc@wanadoo.fr

1,3ha 49T(80-110m²) 10A CEE

1 ACD**G**IJLMPQ
2 DJKMRTVWXY
3 B**F**GRU**WZ**
4 (B 15/6-15/9) (Q 21/6-31/8)
(R 🔲) (T+U+V+Z 1/6-30/9)
5 **AB**CDFGIJKLMNOPUWZ
6 ACGJ(N 7km)

💬 The large lake on which all types of water sports are permitted is directly accessible from this small, well maintained terraced campsite. Every pitch has wide views of this lake. Anglers are of course very welcome. You can swim in the swimming pool and in the lake a reasonable distance away. Delicious pizzas are also made to order.

🚗 From Aurillac take the N122 towards Figeac. After Sansac keep right D61 direction Pers. The campsite is signposted from here.

🆔 (2078)

Laroquebrou
D2 · D653 · D120 · D7 · Ytrac · N122 · Le Rouget

€ **15** 21/4-30/6 26/8-12/10   N 44°54'21'' E 2°15'14''

Royat, F-63130 / Auvergne (Puy-de-Dôme)

🏕 Huttopia Royat****
✉ route de Gravenoire
☎ +33 (0)4-73359705
📠 +33 (0)4-73356769
📅 23/3 - 4/11
@ royat@huttopia.com

8ha 125T(80-120m²) 10A

1 ACD**F**IJKLMOPS
2 FGJKRSVX
3 BGHJMNRU
4 (C+H 30/4-15/9) K
(Q 29/4-2/11) (R 29/4-3/11)
(T+V+X 1/7-31/8) (Z 🔲)
5 **AB**DFGJKLNPUWZ
6 CEGIJ(N 1,5km)V

💬 In the spa town of Royat, at the foot of the Puy de Dôme. This terraced campsite is located in beautiful natural surroundings. Various top-quality amenities: heated swimming pool, tennis courts, central facilities, playground.

🚗 On the A71 continue to A75. Take exit Le Mont Dore/La Bourboule just after Clermont-Ferrand. Follow N89 until you are in Ceyrat. Take the exit and follow signs to Royat.

🆔 (2079)

Clermont-Ferrand
D402 · A71 · A89 · D2 · D52 · D942 · D2089 · D983 · D213 · A75 · D225

€ **17** 23/3-28/6 2/9-3/11   N 45°45'31'' E 3°3'16''

Ruynes-en-Margeride, F-15320 / Auvergne (Cantal)   👤 🆔 (2080)

🔺 Le Petit Bois***
☎ +33 (0)4-71234226
📠 +33 (0)9-72508069
🔓 14/4 - 29/9
@ contact@revea-vacances.com

7ha 90T(100-150m²) 10A CEE

1 ACD**G**IJKLMPQ
2 BFIKLMRTVWXY
3 AGHJMRU
4 (C+H+Q 1/7-31/8)
   (R 1/6-15/9)
5 **A**EGIJKLMNOPUWZ
6 CEG(N 0,3km)QTV

💬 Lightly undulating meadow on the edge of a wood with a wide view over the hills of Auvergne with some pitches that are marked-out and some that are not. Swimming pool. There are also many pitches in the pine forest. 15% discount for a stay from 7 nights (not in July and August).

🚐 Leave the A75 at exit 30 after St. Flour. Via the D4 towards Ruynes-en-Margeride, then follow camping signs.

CC € **17** 14/4-7/7   25/8-28/9   📷 N 44°59'56'' E 3°13'8''

Sainte Sigolène, F-43600 / Auvergne (Haute-Loire)   👫 ♿ 📶 ✿ 🆔 (2081)

🔺 Camping Sites & Paysages de Vaubarlet****
☎ +33 (0)4-71666495
🔓 1/5 - 30/9
@ camping@vaubarlet.com

3,5ha 100T(80-120m²) 16A CEE

1 ACD**G**IJKLMPQ
2 CLRTVWXY
3 AGHJNRU**W**
4 (A 1/7-31/8) (C+H 15/5-15/9)
   (Q+R 🔓) (T+U 15/5-15/9)
   (V+Z 🔓)
5 **AB**FGIJKLMNP**S**UVW
6 EGJ(N 6km)OTVW

💬 A family campsite with character and a heated swimming pool, bar and restaurant in the south of the Auvergne. Fourteen hectares of unspoilt countryside in a valley, surrounded by rolling hills. On the banks of the river Dunière.

🚐 Leave the N88 at Monistrol-sur-Loire/Ste Sigolène exit. Follow Ste Sigolène (D44). Before Sigolène take D43 to Grazac. Follow campsite signs.

CC € **17** 1/5-8/7   26/8-29/9   7=6, 14=11   📷 N 45°12'59'' E 4°12'45''

Singles, F-63690 / Auvergne (Puy-de-Dôme)   ♿ 📶 ✿ 🆔 (2082)

🔺 Hôtel de Plein Air Le Moulin de Serre***
🚩 D73, Vallée de La Burande
☎ +33 (0)4-73211606
🔓 7/4 - 16/9
@ moulindeserre@orange.fr

7ha 59T(90-150m²) 10A

1 ACD**G**IJKLM**P**Q
2 CRVWXY
3 BGH**M**NRU**W**
4 (A 9/7-31/8) (C 26/5-15/9) **K**
   (Q+R+T+U 🔓) (X 5/7-30/8)
   (Z 🔓)
5 **AB**DFGIJKLMNOPUWXZ
6 CEGJ**K**(N 9km)OTV

💬 Friendly well-run campsite with heated pool in beautiful surroundings. Fishing and sailing in the Bort lake, trout fishing in the Dordogne and the Burande, where you can pan for gold under supervision. Close to many sights.

🚐 A89 exit 25. D922 in direction of Bort-les-Orgues. Turn right 1 km south of Tauves D29. Follow camping signs.

CC € **15** 7/4-28/6   24/8-15/9   📷 N 45°32'35'' E 2°32'34''

St. Didier-en-Velay, F-43140 / Auvergne (Haute-Loire) ♿ 📶 iD (2083)

▲ Camping Municipal
La Fressange***
☎ FAX +33 (0)4-71662528
☉ 21/4 - 30/9
@ camping.lafressange@gmail.com

2ha 65T 15A CEE

1 ACD**G**IJKLMPQ
2 GIJRTXY
3 AGHJNR**W**
4 (C+Q 1/7-31/8) (R 🔑)
(Z 4/7-31/8)
5 **A**IJKLMNOPUVW
6 DEGJ(N 0,8km)T

💬 An attractive terraced campsite by a lovely municipal swimming pool. The campsite is located in a beautiful, peaceful area.

🚌 Leave St. Étienne N88 at exit St. Didier-en-Velay. At La Séauve-sur-Semène turn left towards St. Didier-en-Velay. Follow the signs in the village.

CC € **17** 21/4-30/6 1/9-29/9   📍 N 45°18'4'' E 4°16'59''

St. Flour, F-15100 / Auvergne (Cantal) 📶 iD (2084)

▲ International Roche Murat***
▣ N9
☎ +33 (0)4-71604363
FAX +33 (0)4-71600210
☉ 8/4 - 4/11
@ courrier@camping-saint-flour.com

3ha 120T(50-100m²) 16A CEE

1 AC**G**IJKLMPQ
2 FJRTVWX
3 BGU
4 (Q+R 🔑)
5 **AB**DFGIJKLMNPUXYZ
6 CEGJ(N 1,5km)TV

💬 Terraced campsite close to entrance and exit of the A75. Excellent stopover campsite. A good base to visit the historic town of St. Flour. 15% discount for a stay from 7 nights (not in July and August).

🚌 The campsite is located on the A75 just north of St. Flour. Take exit 28. Follow the signs at the roundabout.

CC € **15** 8/4-7/7 25/8-3/11   📍 N 45°3'2'' E 3°6'28''

St. Maurice-de-Lignon, F-43200 / Auvergne (Haute-Loire) ♿ 📶 iD (2085)

▲ Camping du Sabot
▣ 813 route du Stade
☎ +33 (0)4-71653268
☉ 16/4 - 15/10
@ contact@campingdusabot.fr

3,5ha 29T(80-120m²) 6-10A

1 AGIJKLMOPQ
2 BJKRTUWXYZ
3 AGR
4 (Q 🔑)
5 **A**GIJKLMNPUV
6 DEGJ(N 1,5km)T

💬 Lovers of the outdoors, nature and relaxation will enjoy staying in these extraordinary surroundings. Located between the Loire Gorges and Lignon at 30 minutes from Puy-en-Velay. There are fishing and walking options in this country of old volcanoes. Village within walking distance, jeu de boules, table football, table tennis and a weekly market.

🚌 RN88 St. Etienne - Le Puy-en-Velay, exit St. Maurice-de-Lignon. Left at entrance to village and follow signs.

CC € **15** 16/4-8/7 26/8-14/10   📍 N 45°13'23'' E 4°9'6''

St. Nectaire, F-63710 / Auvergne (Puy-de-Dôme) ♿ 📶 iD (2086)

🏕 Flower Camping
La Vallée Verte***
🚩 route des Granges
☎ 📠 +33 (0)4-73885268
🗓 14/4 - 16/9
@ contact@valleeverte.com

2,5ha 74T(80-100m²) 8A

1 ACDGIJKLMPQ
2 CRVWXY
3 BGHNRU**W**
4 (E+H+Q+R 🗓)
(T+U+Z 1/7-31/8)
5 **AB**DFGJLMNOPUWZ
6 CEGJ(N 0,5km)RV

💬 A quiet, green campsite of 2.5 hectares. Pitches are marked out by plants. Covered heated swimming pool, snack bar, fresh bread and produce, ice cream, etc. In the heart of the Massif du Sancy and the Parc des Volcans d'Auvergne, at a height of 700 metres in St. Nectaire. Lakes and waterfalls nearby.

🚗 From Murol via D996 to Issoire. Or from A75 exit 6 dir. Champaix. Campsite is signposted and is 2nd site on the left after 200m on rue des Granges.

CC € **13** 14/4-7/7 25/8-15/9 8=6, 14=11   🏔 N 45°34'31'' E 2°59'58''

St. Nectaire, F-63710 / Auvergne (Puy-de-Dôme) ♿ 📶 iD (2087)

🏕 La Clé des Champs***
🚩 route des Granges
☎ 📠 +33 (0)4-73885233
🗓 7/4 - 22/9
@ campingcledeschamps63@
orange.fr

2ha 63T(75-150m²) 6A

1 ACF IJKLMOPQ
2 CRVXY
3 BGHJRU**W**
4 (E+G 🗓) J(Q+R 1/7-31/8)
(T 🗓) (U+X 1/7-31/8) (Z 🗓)
5 **AB**DFGIJKLMNOPUV
6 CDEGJ(N 0,3km)OV

💬 This campsite in the spa resort of St. Nectaire offers plenty of opportunities for relaxation. Walking, cycling, historical visits. Located in wooded surroundings with a babbling brook running through the site. Indoor heated swimming pool.

🚗 From Murol to Issoire via the D996. The campsite is located directly after St. Nectaire-Bas village. Or from A75 exit 6 dir. Champaix. In Champaix dir. St. Nectaire. Campsite indicated just before St. Nectaire.

CC € **13** 7/4-6/7 25/8-21/9 7=6, 14=11   🏔 N 45°34'31'' E 3°0'7''

St. Nectaire, F-63710 / Auvergne (Puy-de-Dôme) ♿ 📶 iD (2088)

🏕 Le Viginet***
🚩 2 chemin du Manoir
☎ +33 (0)4-73885380
🗓 7/4 - 30/9
@ info@camping-viginet.com

3,5ha 63T(90-140m²) 10A CEE

1 ACD**G**IJKLMPST
2 KLRUVWXY
3 ABGHNRU
4 (C+H 15/6-15/9) (Q 1/6-10/9)
(R 1/6-31/8)
(T+U+V 1/7-30/8)
(Z 15/5-22/9)
5 **AB**EFGIJKLMNOPQ**R**UVWX
YZ
6 ACDEGJK(N 2km)RV

💬 Set in the beautiful Auvergne countryside, a true paradise for walkers and nature lovers, you can choose from the spacious marked-out pitches in this beautifully-maintained parkland campsite. Snack bar, pizzeria, small shop, library, free wifi and freshly baked bread. In just 5 minutes you can walk to St. Nectaire with its various restaurants and sights.

🚗 A75 exit 6 to St. Nectaire. First road right in the village.

CC € **15** 7/4-8/7 26/8-29/9 7=6, 14=11, 21=16   🏔 N 45°34'46'' E 3°0'10''

St. Paulien, F-43350 / Auvergne (Haute-Loire) 🏃‍♂️ ♿ 📶 **iD** (2089)

🔺 Flower Camping
   La Rochelambert★★★★
📧 route de Lanthenas
☎ 📠 +33 (0)4-71005402
🔓 1/4 - 30/9
@ infos@
   camping-rochelambert.com
4ha 80**T**(80-120m²) 16A CEE

1 ACD**G**IJKLMPQ
2 CIJLMRTVWX
3 BGHJMNRU**W**
4 (C+H 20/5-15/9) **N**
   (Q 1/5-30/9) (R 🔓)
   (T+U+V+X 26/6-26/8) (Z 🔓)
5 **AB**DEFGIJKLMNPUWXYZ
6 ACEGHJ(N 3km)TV

💬 Well-maintained, quite campsite with an informal ambiance in the undiscovered east of the Auvergne, 15 km from Le Puy. Starting point for walks. The site is located by a river in natural surroundings with a heated pool and toddlers' pool. Own tennis court.

🚗 The campsite is signposted from the N102 Le Puy - Clermont-Ferrand in the direction of St. Paulien. Follow camp signs (3 km) from St. Paulien centre (D906).

N102 D13
        CC
              D103
D590
         Le Puy-en-
D906   Velay

CC €**17** 1/4-7/7 27/8-29/9   🏕 N 45°7'13'' E 3°47'38''

St. Rémy-sur-Durolle, F-63550 / Auvergne (Puy-de-Dôme) ♿ 📶 **iD** (2090)

🔺 Camping Les Chanterelles★★★
📧 Chapon
☎ +33 (0)4-73943171
🔓 7/4 - 6/10
@ campingleschanterelles@yahoo.fr

4ha 140**T**(100-120m²) 10A CEE

1 ACD**G**IJKLMPRS
2 DFIJKLRSVXY
3 AGHNRU**W**Z
4 (**A** 1/7-31/8) (Q+R+Z 🔓)
5 **A**GIJKLMNOPUVW
6 CDEJ(N 2km)RV

💬 A campsite located within walking distance of a recreational lake at St. Rémy-sur-Durolle. This terraced campsite has large trees which provide sufficient shade. Heated toilet facilities, 10A electricity.

🚗 A89, exit 30 Thiers-Est. In St. Rémy, the Parc de Loisirs with campsites are clearly signposted.

Puy-   D995 D7
Guillaume

   D906
                CC
D224   A89
         Thiers D2089   D1
D212   D1089

CC €**15** 7/5-12/7 30/8-5/10 7=6   🏕 N 45°54'11'' E 3°35'56''

Tauves, F-63690 / Auvergne (Puy-de-Dôme) ♿ 📶 ✿ **iD** (2091)

🔺 Les Aurandeix★★★
☎ +33 (0)3-86379583
🔓 30/3 - 30/9
@ camping.lesaurandeix@
   gmail.com

2,5ha 75**T**(45-110m²) 10A CEE

1 AC**G**IJKLM**P**
2 FLRVXY
3 BGHMNRU
4 (C 15/6-5/9) (H 1/7-30/9)
   (Q 1/6-30/9) (R 15/6-30/8)
5 **AB**DFGIJKLMNPRUVWZ
6 CDEGJ(N 0,2km)OT

💬 A well-maintained campsite on the foot of the Massif du Sancy and by the Parc des Volcans. Own field for football, basketball and volleyball. Heated swimming pool. Close to the village of Tauves.

🚗 From the A71 to the A89. Exit 25 on the D922 to Tauves. Follow camping signs.

D1089
A89   Laqueuille
Messeix D987
              D219
         D922
              CC

         D47   D203
                   Picherande

CC €**15** 30/3-7/7 25/8-29/9 7=6, 14=11   🏕 N 45°33'40'' E 2°37'29''

Vic-sur-Cère, F-15800 / Auvergne (Cantal) 📶 iD 2092

▲ La Pommeraie****
☎ +33 (0)4-71475418
📠 +33 (0)4-71496330
📅 28/4 - 9/9
@ pommeraie@wanadoo.fr

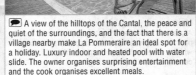

4ha 40T(60-110m²) 10A

1 ACF**IJ**LPRS
2 JKLRTUVWXY
3 BCGHJMNRU
4 (A 1/7-31/8) (C 1/5-30/8)
(F+H 🅾) **I**JP
(Q+S+T+U+V+X+Y+Z 🅾)
5 **AB**DEFGHIJKLMNPQUWXY
6 AEG**K**(N 2km)OTV

💬 A view of the hilltops of the Cantal, the peace and quiet of the surroundings, and the fact that there is a village nearby make La Pommeraire an ideal spot for a holiday. Luxury indoor and heated pool with water slide. The owner organises surprising entertainment and the cook organises excellent meals.

🚗 In Vic-sur-Cère leave the N122. In village follow signs dir. municipal sports field/ swimming pool. Stay on road for about 3 km. Follow 'la Pommeraie'.

D17 Thiézac

N122
Arpajon-sur-Cère D59
D990
D600

CC € **15** 28/4-6/7 27/8-8/9

N 44°58'17'' E 2°37'59''

Vorey-sur-Arzon, F-43800 / Auvergne (Haute-Loire) ♿ 📶 iD 2093

▲ Les Moulettes****
✉ chemin de Félines
☎ +33 (0)4-71037048
📅 1/5 - 15/9
@ contact@
camping-les-moulettes.fr

2ha 55T(90-150m²) 10A

1 A**FI**JKLMPQ
2 CGLRTVX
3 BGHJNRU**W**
4 (A 1/7-31/8) (C+H 1/6-31/8) I
J(T+U+V+X+Z 1/7-31/8)
5 **AB**EFGIJKLMNPUWXYZ
6 ACDEGJK(N 0,2km)TV

💬 A hospitable campsite in the beautiful valley of the Haute Loire, 22 km from Le Puy-en-Velay and close to the centre of the village of Vorey. The pitches are sheltered and are mostly semi-shaded. The site is near a small river with a lovely pool with two slides on the opposite side. Free for camping guests. Free wifi.

🚗 From Puy-en-Velay follow the D103. Campsite signposted in Vorey village.

D1
D9 D46
D906 Retournac
D103
D13
Saint-Paulien CC
Rosières
N102 N88

CC € **17** 1/5-30/6 1/9-14/9

N 45°11'11'' E 3°54'23''

Aigueblanche, F-73260 / Rhône-Alpes (Savoie) ♿ 📶 iD 2094

▲ Eliana***
✉ 176 rue des Pommiers
☎ +33 (0)4-79242387
📅 20/3 - 31/10
@ campingeliana@hotmail.com

1ha 40T(120-220m²) 4-15A CEE

1 ACD**G**IJKLMOPQ
2 GKRUVXY
3 BHJRUV**W**
4 (C+H+Q 15/6-15/9)
5 **AB**CDGHIJKLMNOPUV
6 CEGJ(N 0,8km)TV

💬 Small, peacefully located campsite with very large marked-out pitches located in a one hectare garden. A free shuttle bus will take you to the spa resort Léchère-les-Bains. 800 metres from Aigueblanche centre.

🚗 N90 Albertville-Moutiers, exit 38. Follow campsite signs. Campsite located in dead-end street opposite swimming pool car park (Base de Loisir du Morel).

Cevins Aime
D1090
CC
Moûtiers
D117

CC € **11** 20/3-7/7 26/8-30/10

N 45°30'25'' E 6°29'29''

Aigueblanche, F-73260 / Rhône-Alpes (Savoie)

♿ 📶 **iD** **2095**

🏔 Marie-France***
✉ 453 avenue de Savoie
☎ +33 (0)6-09473230
📠 +33 (0)4-79229481
🗓 10/3 - 21/10
@ sarlmariefrance@gmail.com

1ha 27T(100-150m²) 6-16A CEE

1 ACD**G**IJKLMPST
2 GJKRVWXY
3 AHIJU
4 (Q 1/7-31/8)
5 **AB**CDGIJKLMNPUZ
6 AEGJ(N 0,6km)V

💬 Campsite with quiet location at 300 metres from Aigueblanche centre. The pitches, which are marked-out with hedges, are located on spacious terraces, with hardened walking paths for comfort. Beautiful countryside in the Savoie.

🚗 N90 Albertville-Moutiers, exit 38. Follow camping signs. Campsite 300m beyond roundabout near the edge of the village.

Aime
D1090
CC
Moûtiers
D117 Bozel

CC € **11** 10/3-6/7 24/8-20/10

📡 N 45°30'38'' E 6°29'18''

Albertville, F-73200 / Rhône-Alpes (Savoie)

⛷ ♿ 📶 **iD** **2096**

🏔 Les Adoubes
✉ 24 avenue du Camping
☎ +33 (0)4-79320662
🗓 1/1 - 21/10, 6/11 - 31/12
@ hello@camping-albertville.fr

3ha 70T(100-120m²) 6-32A CEE

1 ACDGIJKLMOPRS
2 CFGKRTWXY
3 AGNV
4 (Q 🔒) (Z 1/5-1/9)
5 **AB**DGJKLMNPUVWZ
6 FG**K**(N 0,2km)ORTV

💬 Campsite located in a green area, yet still also close to Albertville centre. Suitable for longer stays or as a stopover campsite, especially for winter sports. In spring and autumn there is great cycling over a secured cycle path of about 40 km up to Annecy. Albertville and the medieval area of Conflans are worth a visit.

🚗 Take exit Albertville centre and follow campsite signs or Médiévale de Conflans.

Saint-Ferréol
Ugine D1212
D1212 D925
Albertville
CC
D1090
D1090
A430

CC € **15** 1/1-7/7 25/8-20/10 6/11-31/12 7=6, 14=11

📡 N 45°40'41'' E 6°23'43''

Allemont, F-38114 / Rhône-Alpes (Isère)

♿ 📶 **iD** **2097**

🏔 Le Grand Calme
☎ +33 (0)6-84302175
🗓 1/5 - 30/9
@ info@campinglegrandcalme.com

3ha 114T(100-110m²) 10A

1 ACD**G**IJKLMOPQ
2 CGKRVWXY
3 AGHJ
4 (V 1/7-31/8)
5 **A**EFGIJKLMNO**PQ**UWZ
6 BCEJ(N 0km)O

💬 Le Grand Calme is situated in the centre of Allemont, the last village before the Glandon and Croix de Fer cols. You have a view of the surrounding mountains from the spacious pitches.

🚗 D1091 towards Briançon. In Rochetaillée D526 towards Allemont/Col du Glandon. Site is in the middle of the village on the right of the road. Well signposted.

Le Versoud
D111
CC
Alpe d'Huez
D1091
D211
D526

CC € **13** 1/5-1/6 10/6-30/6 18/8-29/9

📡 N 45°7'41'' E 6°2'18''

Allevard-les-Bains, F-38580 / Rhône-Alpes (Isère)

♿ 🛜 iD **2098**

△ Clair Matin***
🏠 20 rue de Pommiers
☎ +33 (0)4-76975519
FAX +33 (0)4-76458715
☷ 14/4 - 14/10
@ contact@
   camping-clair-matin.com
5,5ha 195T(100-110m²) 2-10A

1 ACD**G**IJKLMO**P**Q
2 BGJKRVXY
3 BGHJNRU
4 (**A** 1/7-31/8)
   (B+G 15/6-15/9) (Q 1/7-31/8)
   (T+U+X+Z 🔲)
5 **AB**FGIJKLMNPRUVZ
6 ABCDEG**K**(N 0,5km)ORV

💬 Clair Matin is located 500 metres from the Allevard-les-Bains spa. Thanks to its sheltered location in the Belledonne-Massif it enjoys pleasant temperatures, even in spring and autumn. Recommended for both sportive and not-so-sportive campers. Camping Qualité.

🚗 A41, exit 23 Le Touvet. Then via D29 towards Goncelin. Then D525 direction Allevard. Campsite is on the left before the roundabout.

D912 — La Rochette
D1090
Allevard
Le Touvet — CC
D525
A41
D523

CC €15 *14/4-7/7 25/8-13/10* 🏔 N 45°23'19'' E 6°3'53''

Allevard-les-Bains, F-38580 / Rhône-Alpes (Isère)

♿ 🛜 iD **2099**

△ Idéal Camping***
🏠 67 avenue de Savoie
☎ +33 (0)4-76975023
☷ 28/4 - 14/10
@ camping.ideal@wanadoo.fr

1,8ha 62T(80-120m²) 4-10A CEE

1 ACD**G**IJKLM**P**Q
2 CGKRVXY
3 AGHJNRU
4 (C+H 15/5-25/9) (Q 1/7-31/8)
   (T+U+V 🔲)
5 **AB**EFGIJKLMNOPZ
6 CFGI**K**OV

💬 Idéal Camping has undulating grounds with plenty of shade. The centre and the spas are 700 metres away. Enthusiastic owners.

🚗 A41 exit 23 Le Touvet. Via D29 to Concelin. Then D525 to Allevard. Campsite opposite the swimming pool, 1st right at the roundabout.

Les Marches — D925
A41 D523 B
Saint-Pierre- CC
d'Allevard
D525
D1090
Lumbin

CC €15 *28/4-8/7 26/8-13/10* 🏔 N 45°24'3'' E 6°4'51''

Anneyron, F-26140 / Rhône-Alpes (Drôme)

🚻 ♿ 🛜 ✿ iD **2100**

△ Flower Camping La
   Châtaigneraie****
🏠 50 route de Font-Flacher
☎ +33 (0)4-75314333
FAX +33 (0)4-75038467
☷ 7/4 - 23/9
@ contact@chataigneraie.com
2ha 29T(90-120m²) 10A

1 ACD**G**IJKLPS
2 IJKLRTVWXY
3 BF**G**HJLMN**O**R**UW**
4 (C+H 15/5-15/9) **KN**
   (Q+S+T+U+V+Y+Z 🔲)
5 **AB**EFGIJKLMNOPQUWYZ
6 ACEGI**J**K(N 3km)ORTV

💬 Peaceful, beautifully located campsite on the Anneyron hills. Views of the Rhône valley and the Ardèche mountains. You can also treat yourself to gastronomic delights. Enquire about restaurant opening times in the low season.

🚗 From A7 exit 12 Chanas. N7 direction Valence, before Le Creux-de-la-Tine take D1 towards Anneyron. Follow signs to the campsite on the hill in Anneyron.

Salaise-sur- — D519 — Beaurepaire
Sanne
D86 — D1 — D538
D82 — CC — D51
A7
N7

CC €15 *7/4-6/7 27/8-22/9 7=6, 14=12, 21=18* 🏔 N 45°15'18'' E 4°54'13''

319

Anse, F-69480 / Rhône-Alpes (Rhône)

♿ 📶 ✿ **iD** (2101)

🔺 Les Portes du Beaujolais****
📧 495 avenue Jean Vacher
☎ +33 (0)4-74671287
🔓 1/3 - 31/10
@ contact@
   camping-beaujolais.com

10ha 198T(100m²) 16A CEE

1 ACD**G**IJKLM**P**Q
2 CFLRTVWXY
3 BGJKLM**N**Q**R**U**W**
4 (B+G 1/5-30/9) J**KLN**
   (Q+R 🔓)
   (T+U+V+X+Z 20/6-31/8)
5 **A**DEFGIJKLMNPUXYZ
6 CFG**K**(N 0,5km)TV

💬 A very-well-maintained campsite on the edge of the village of Anse. A tourist train takes you from the campsite to the village. You will enjoy the countryside.

🚗 From the north A6 exit 31.2 Anse then N6 direction Anse/Villefranche. Turn right after Saône bridge and follow signs. Exit 33.1 from the south.

Villefranche-sur-Saône

CC € **17** 1/3-5/7 25/8-30/10 7=6, 14=11   🌄 N 45°56'26'' E 4°43'36''

Ars-sur-Formans, F-01480 / Rhône-Alpes (Ain)

⊗ ♿ 📶 **iD** (2102)

🔺 Du Bois de la Dame**
📧 590 chemin du Bois de la Dame
☎ +33 (0)4-74007723
🔓 1/4 - 30/9
@ camping.boisdeladame@
   orange.fr

103T(80m²) 10-16A CEE

1 AEIJKLPQ
2 BJRTXY
3 ABGHJKLMRW
5 ABGIJKLMNOPUVZ
6 CDEGJ(N 0,5km)T

💬 Peaceful campsite with spacious pitches, flowers and lots of plant life all around. Ideal base offering value for money. Close to a (fishing) lake and a historic village centre. Close to Beaujolais, Lyon and the beautiful Dombes with its iconic Parc des Oiseaux. The imposing 'basilique Saint-Sixte' is just 800m from the campsite.

🚗 A6 exit Villefranche-sur-Saône. D904 direction Bourg/Ars-sur-Formans. Campsite signposted.

Villefranche-sur-Saône CC

CC € **13** 1/4-30/6 1/9-29/9   🌄 N 45°59'27'' E 4°49'1''

Artemare, F-01510 / Rhône-Alpes (Ain)

♿ 📶 ✿ **iD** (2103)

🔺 Sites & Paysages Le Vaugrais***
📧 2 chemin le Vaugrais
☎ 📠 +33 (0)4-79873734
🔓 10/3 - 1/11
@ contact@camping-le-vaugrais.fr

1,6ha 50T(80-120m²) 10A CEE

1 AC**G**IJKLM**P**R
2 CRUVWX
3 AHJKRU**W**
4 (C 1/6-30/9) (Q 1/5-30/9)
   (T+U 1/6-31/8)
5 **A**FGIJKLMNPUVWXYZ
6 AGJ**K**(N 0,2km)

💬 A small family campsite on the edge of the Savoie 10 km from Lake Bourget. 50 level, shaded pitches. The heated swimming pool and snack bar with takeaway meals are open from 1 June. Free wifi near the reception. Lovely walking and cycle routes from the campsite.

🚗 From Belley N504 dir. Ambérieu and Bugey, right after Pugieu onto D904 as far as Artemare. From Ambérieu and Bugey N504 dir. Belley, left before Pugieu, follow D904 as far as Artemare. Follow camping signs.

Cormaranche-en-Bugey

Culoz

CC € **13** 10/3-6/7 1/9-31/10 7=6, 14=12   🌄 N 45°52'28'' E 5°41'2''

Auberives-sur-Varèze, F-38550 / Rhône-Alpes (Isère)

♿ 🛜 **iD** ②2104

🔺 Camping des Nations***
🏠 RN7, 8 Bis Louze
☎ +33 (0)4-74849513
🔓 1/3 - 31/10
@ contact@
campingdesnations.com

1,5ha 63T(100m²) 8-10A

1 ACDGIJKLMOPST
2 FGRUVWXY
3 AGRU
4 (B 1/6-15/9) (Q 🔓)
(U+X+Z 15/4-15/9)
5 ABDFGIJKLMNOPUZ
6 EGJ(N 2km)TV

💬 A small, pleasant stopover campsite on the RN7 between Vienne and Chanas. Shaded, marked out pitches. Suitable for day trips to the Ardèche and the Vercors. Friendly, helpful reception. Free wifi.

🚗 A7 exit Vienne, follow the N7 as far as Auberives-s-V. Campsite on the right side south of the village. You are advised to take exit 11 from north and exit 12 from south of the A7.

CC € **17** 1/3-30/6 1/9-30/10

N 45°24'46'' E 4°48'48''

Baix, F-07210 / Rhône-Alpes (Ardèche)

🛜 **iD** ②2105

🔺 Domaine du Merle Roux -
Capfun****
🏠 Le Roux Est
☎ +33 (0)4-75858414
FAX +33 (0)4-75858307
🔓 7/4 - 23/9
@ merle-roux@capfun.com

15,8ha 89T(80-250m²) 10A CEE

1 ACDGIJKLMPST
2 FJKRTVWXY
3 BGHJNQRU
4 (C+H 🔓) IJ
(Q+R+T+U+V+Y+Z 🔓)
5 ACDEFGIJKLMNOPRUWZ
6 AEGHJK(N 5km)ORTV

💬 This terraced campsite has a lovely swimming complex with water slides. There is a special pool for small children. Wonderful views over the Rhône valley in good weather. Plenty of activities. The restaurant is open regularly in early and late seasons. New waterslide.

🚗 Campsite located 6 km NW of Baix. A7 exit 16 Loriol. Via Le Pouzin N86 dir. Le Teil. At the level crossing left D22a. Left after a few kilometres. Continue to campsite.

CC € **13** 7/4-30/6 3/9-22/9

N 44°42'18'' E 4°44'17''

Balbigny, F-42510 / Rhône-Alpes (Loire)

👫 ♿ 🛜 **iD** ②2106

🔺 La Route Bleue***
🏠 Pralery, D56
☎ +33 (0)4-77272497
🔓 15/3 - 31/10
@ camping.balbigny@wanadoo.fr

2ha 100T(100m²) 10A

1 ACDGIJKLMPQ
2 CFLRTVWXY
3 GJUW
4 (B+G 10/6-10/9)
(Q+T+U+V+Z 15/5-15/9)
5 ABGIJKLMNOPUVWZ
6 CEGK(N 2km)OTV

💬 A peaceful campsite with a friendly atmosphere. Direct access to the Loire shores. Easy access. Tourist region. Ideal for a holiday in the open air. You can go fishing and walking here. The site has a bar, snack bar, take away meals. Swimming pool and toddlers' pool.

🚗 On the north side of Balbigny. From the N82 take the D56. Campsite signposted.

CC € **15** 15/3-2/7 20/8-30/10

N 45°49'45'' E 4°9'39''

Barbières, F-26300 / Rhône-Alpes (Drôme)

♿ 🛜 **iD** (2107)

🏕 Le Gallo-Romain★★★★
📧 1090 route du Col de Tourniol
☎ 📠 +33 (0)4-75474407
🗓 23/4 - 15/9
@ info@legalloromain.net

3ha 75**T**(80-100m²) 6A CEE

1 ACD**G**IJKLMPST
2 CFJKLRTVXY
3 AB**F**GHJN**OP**RU
4 (A 18/6-25/8)
(B+G+Q+R+T+U+V+Y+Z ⊙)
5 **AB**DEFGIJLMNOPRUWXZ
6 AEG**I**J(N 7km)RTV

Romans-sur-Isère

💬 A beautiful campsite, proclaimed to be one of the loveliest in France, located close to the Vercours which can be explored on foot, by bike or in the car. Orchid season from the beginning of May to mid-June, with more than 20 varieties near the campsite.

🚗 A7 exit 14, dir. A49 Grenoble exit 5 towards Alixan. In Alixan D101 to Barbières, via Besayes and follow the camping signs. You will find the campsite beyond the village of Barbières on the right.

CC € **17** 23/4-6/7 24/8-14/9 7=6, 14=12   📶 **N 44°56'40'' E 5°9'4''**

Belmont-Tramonet, F-73330 / Rhône-Alpes (Savoie)

♿ 🛜 **iD** (2108)

🏕 Des Trois Lacs★★★★
☎ +33 (0)4-76370403
🗓 14/4 - 15/9
@ info@les3lacs.com

5ha 63**T**(100-250m²) 10A

1 ACD**G**IJKLM**P**RS
2 CFRVXY
3 BGH**M**NRU**W**X
4 (C+G ⊙) I(Q+S ⊙)
(T+U+V+Y+Z 10/6-30/8)
5 **AB**EFGIJKLMNOPUWZ
6 AEGJ**K**(N 3km)OV

Les Avenières
Dolomieu

💬 A campsite in a lovely park with 2 small rivers (trout fishing and canoeing). Very spacious pitches, camp shop. Plenty of walking opportunities. Lovely swimming pool with water slide and toddlers' pool. Restaurant only open at weekends in low season.

🚗 A43 Lyon-Chambéry. Exit 11: St. Génix/Belmont-Tramonet. Left at the end of the exit road towards Belmont-Tramonet and Pont de Beauvoisin. Located beyond the small bridge on the right of the D916a.

CC € **17** 14/4-7/7 27/8-14/9   📶 **N 45°33'33'' E 5°40'33''**

Bourg-St-Andéol, F-07700 / Rhône-Alpes (Ardèche)

♿ 🛜 **iD** (2109)

🏕 Le Lion★★★
📧 chemin Ile Chenevier
☎ +33 (0)4-75545320
🗓 1/4 - 30/9
@ contact@campingdulion.com

5ha 121**T**(100-250m²) 6A CEE

1 ACD**G**IJKLMPST
2 BCFGLMORTVXY
3 AGHJLNQRU**W**X
4 (B+G 1/6-30/9) (Q ⊙)
(T+U+V+X 14/5-30/9) (Z ⊙)
5 **AB**EFGIJKLMNPUVZ
6 AEGJ(N 0,6km)RV

Pierrelatte
Saint-Paul-Trois-Châteaux
Bollène

💬 The camping pitches at Le Lion are under tall trees, giving it a typical French ambiance. They are spacious, between 100 and 250 m². There are opportunities for watersports on the Rhône. Supermarket at 600 metres. Close to Via Rhôna cycle route.

🚗 Site located north of Bourg-St-Andéol 800 metres from centre. From the north: N86 dir. village, left after supermarket. Follow signs. From the south: N86 to village, dir. Viviers. Right before supermarket. Follow signs.

CC € **17** 1/4-6/7 25/8-29/9 7=6, 14=12, 21=18   📶 **N 44°22'53'' E 4°38'55''**

Bourg-St-Maurice, F-73700 / Rhône-Alpes (Savoie) ♿ 🚿 🛜 iD (2110)

🏔 Huttopia Bourg-St-Maurice***
📧 route des Arcs
☎ +33 (0)4-79070345
🕐 25/5 - 21/10
@ bourgsaintmaurice@
huttopia.com

5ha 153T(50-200m²) 10A CEE

1 ACGIJKLMOPST
2 CKRUVWX
3 BGHMNRUW
4 (A 2/7-27/8) (C+G 27/5-17/9)
(Q 🕐) (U+V 1/7-31/8)
5 ABDEFGIJKLMNPQWZ
6 CDFGIJ(N 0,3km)TV

💬 Within walking distance of the centre and a supermarket. Level grounds shaded by several trees. Fully refurbished toilet facilities, also geared up to winter sports. New swimming pool and playground.

🚗 From Albertville via Moutiers to Bourg-St-Maurice. Turn right at the station direction Les Arcs. Then continue for about 300 metres.

D925 / SS26

Bourg-Saint-Maurice CC
Aime D1090 D902

CC € **17** 25/5-6/7 2/9-20/10   📶🏔 N 45°37'21'' E 6°47'6''

Bramans-en-Vanoise, F-73500 / Rhône-Alpes (Savoie) ♿ 🚿 🛜 iD (2111)

🏔 Val d'Ambin Bramans-Vanoise***
📧 602 route de l'Église
☎ +33 (0)4-79050305
📠 +33 (0)4-79052316
🕐 1/1 - 31/12
@ campingbramans@gmail.com

4ha 155T(100-115m²) 6A CEE

1 ACDFIJKLMOPQ
2 FGJKRTVWXY
3 BGHJLMNRUW
4 (A 1/7-31/8) (Q 1/7-30/8)
5 ABDFGIJKLMNPUVZ
6 ACEGK(N 8km)V

💬 The campsite is set on undulating ground 500 metres from Bramans. The pitches are marked out with stakes. The views of the surrounding mountains are an invitation to go walking.

🚗 D1006 St. Jean-de-Maurienne - Col du Mt. Cenis. You will find the site just across town centre behind the church of Bramans and at a distance of only 200 metres from N6.

D902
Bramans-en-Vanoise
Aussois
Modane CC
D1006
Fourneaux

CC € **15** 6/1-9/2 10/3-30/3 14/4-29/6 28/8-21/12   📶🏔 N 45°13'44'' E 6°46'51''

Buis-les-Baronnies, F-26170 / Rhône-Alpes (Drôme) 👫 🚿 🛜 iD (2112)

🏔 Domaine La Gautière***
📧 La Penne-sur-Ouvèze
☎ +33 (0)4-75280268
🕐 30/3 - 31/10
@ accueil@camping-lagautiere.com

3,5ha 20T(100-120m²) 6A

1 ACGHIJKLMPST
2 IJKTVWX
3 BDGHJNUW
4 (B+G 15/5-30/9)
(Q+R 1/5-15/9) (S 🕐)
(T+U+V+X+Z 1/5-15/9)
5 AEFGIJKLMNOPUZ
6 CDEGK(N 4km)OTV

💬 Charming rural campsite set among olive groves and the vineyards of warm Provence. Located in a large valley with rustic wooded mountains. Restaurant, terrace and swimming pool protected from the mistral. Close to the historic holiday resort of Buis-les-Baronnies.

🚗 Vaison-la-Romaine direction Buis-les Baronnies, left before village and follow the signs.

D108
D538 D546
Vaison-la-Romaine
D5
Entrechaux CC
D938 D72
D41
D40
D974

CC € **17** 30/3-8/7 26/8-30/10   📶🏔 N 44°15'8'' E 5°14'35''

Buis-les-Baronnies, F-26170 / Rhône-Alpes (Drôme)

👫 ♿ 📶 **iD** (2113)

🔼 La Fontaine d'Annibal***
📧 Quai de l'Ouvèze
☎ +33 (0)4-75280312
📅 1/4 - 7/10
@ contact@
   vacances-baronnies.com

2ha 42T(70-120m²) 10A CEE

1 ACD**G**IJKLP
2 CKRTVWX
3 BGHJRU
4 (B 1/6-1/9)
   (Q+R+T+U+V+X+Z 1/7-31/8)
5 **A**BFIJKLMNOPUZ
6 AEGK(N 0,8km)PTV

💬 The campsite is 800m from Buis-les-Baronnies with shops, restaurants and a large weekly market. Protected countryside and a starting point for walking and cycle routes. Here you will smell the flowers and the aromatic herbs of Provence.

🚗 From Vaison-la-Romaine/Nyons direction Buis-les-Baronnies and towards Séderon in centre. Left 300m further on at Quai du Pont Neuf towards site.

Nyons
D64
D108
CC
D546
Saint-Romain-en-Viennois
D72
D41

CC € **17** 1/4-6/7 24/8-6/10 7=6

🗺 N 44°17'3'' E 5°16'55''

Buis-les-Baronnies, F-26170 / Rhône-Alpes (Drôme)

👫 📶 **iD** (2114)

🔼 Sites & Paysages L'Orée
   de Provence***
📧 D108, route du col d'Ey
☎ +33 (0)4-75281078
📅 20/4 - 14/10
@ info@loree-de-provence.com

130ha 81T 6A CEE

1 ACDGIJKLOP
2 BJKTVWXY
3 ABGHNQR
4 (**A** 1/7-31/8) (B 15/5-15/9)
   (F 21/4-14/10) (G 15/5-15/9)
   JKLN(Q 📅) (R 15/6-15/9)
   (T+U+V 1/7-31/8)
   (X 15/6-15/9) (Z 1/6-30/9)
5 **AB**GIJKLMNOPUWXZ
6 ABEJOV

💬 Discover the true countryside at this campsite, with extraordinary natural life all around. There is also a water complex with a large outdoor pool and a small (heated) indoor pool with a sauna and jacuzzi.

🚗 Montélimar-Nyons-Buis-les-Baronnies-Col d'Ey.

Nyons
D64
D108
CC
D546
Buis-les-Baronnies
Mollans-sur-Ouvèze
D13

CC € **15** 20/4-30/6 1/9-13/10 7=6

🗺 N 44°18'10'' E 5°16'24''

Challes-les-Eaux, F-73190 / Rhône-Alpes (Savoie)

♿ 📶 **iD** (2115)

🔼 Municipal Le Savoy***
📧 av. du Parc
☎ +33 (0)4-79729731
📅 1/4 - 30/9
@ contact@
   camping-challesleseaux.com

2,8ha 66T(80-150m²) 6-10A CEE

1 ACD**G**IJLM**P**ST
2 DFGNRUVWX
3 AGHJ**M**RU**W**
4 (Q+T+U+Z 1/7-31/8)
5 **AB**DFGIJKLMNOPUWXYZ
6 CDEG**K**(N 0,2km)OTV

💬 A quiet, well-maintained campsite with spacious, partly marked-out pitches and paved roads. Heated toilet facilities by the entrance. Walking, cycling, swimming and fishing close by. Many tourist sights in the vicinity. Close to Chambéry. Snack bar is only open at weekends in low season.

🚗 A43 Lyon-Chambéry. In Chambéry direction Grenoble as far as Challes-les-Eaux exit. Then D1006 Albertville-Grenoble. Campsite located just before the centre on the left of the road.

La Motte-Servolex
A41
D913
D911
Chambéry
CC
D1006
D912
A43
D1090
D925

CC € **15** 1/4-7/7 2/9-29/9

🗺 N 45°33'5'' E 5°59'3''

Chantemerle-les-Blés, F-26600 / Rhône-Alpes (Drôme)

♿ 🛜 **iD** (2116)

▲ Chante Merle***
✉ 390 route de Tain
☎ +33 (0)4-75074973
🕐 1/2 - 15/12
@ campingchantemerle@
wanadoo.fr

2ha 37T(100m²) 10-16A CEE

1 AGIJKLPST
2 FRTVXY
3 BGRUW
4 (C 15/4-15/10)
(Q+T+X+Z 🕐)
5 ABDFGIJKLMNOPUZ
6 FJ(N 2km)

NEW

💬 Shady campsite between the hills of the Droôme, with a family-friendly and relaxed atmosphere. 49 pitches, a (snack) bar, a takeaway restaurant, and an ice cream stand are all available. Enjoy a tranquil stay at Chante Merle. At the lakeside there's an enclosure with various types of animals.

🚗 In Tain-l'Hermitage follow signs to Chantemerle-les-Blés. Campsite is on the D109 and is signposted.

D51 · D538 · D112 · D53 · D532 · A7 · D534 · **Romans-sur-Isère** · D86 · N7

CC € **15** 1/2-30/6 1/9-14/12 · 📍 N 45°6'26'' E 4°53'27''

Châteauneuf-de-Galaure, F-26330 / Rhône-Alpes (Drôme)

👫 ♿ 🛜 **iD** (2117)

▲ Iris Parc Le Château de
Galaure****
✉ 31 rue de Stade
☎ +33 (0)4-75686522
🕐 27/4 - 30/9
@ info@chateaudegalaure.com

12ha 165T(100-120m²) 10-16A

1 ACDGHIJKLMOPQ
2 CRVWXY
3 BCGHJKLMNORW
4 A(C+H 🕐) JN
(Q+R+T+U+V+X+Z 🕐)
5 ABGIJKMNPUZ
6 CEGHIJ(N 0,2km)TV

💬 A peaceful, friendly family campsite. This is an ideal campsite to relax in a pleasant way, where children can develop and where you can enjoy real camping.

🚗 Exit Chanas, then take the N7 direction Valence, until just past St. Vallier. Then take the D51 to St. Uze and Hauterives. The campsite is located about 10 km behind St. Uze on the D51, before Châteauneuf-de-Galaure.

Chanas · Anneyron · D1 · Hauterives · D51 · D86 · A7 · CC · D538 · N7 · D112

CC € **13** 27/4-29/6 3/9-29/9 · 📍 N 45°13'26'' E 4°57'3''

Châteauneuf-sur-Isère, F-26300 / Rhône-Alpes (Drôme)

👫 ♿ 🛜 **iD** (2118)

▲ Le Soleil Fruité****
✉ 480 chemin des Communaux
☎ +33 (0)4-75841970
🕐 21/4 - 15/9
@ contact@lesoleilfruite.com

3,5ha 138T(140m²) 10A CEE

1 ACDFIJKLMPST
2 FKRTVWX
3 BFGHJKRU
4 (B 28/4-15/9) (E 🕐)
(H 28/4-15/9) J
(Q+R+T+U+V+X+Z 🕐)
5 ABEFJKLMNOPQUZ
6 CEGIJ(N 8km)TV

💬 A family campsite located in an orchard and with magnificent views of the Drôme valley. Modern toilet facilities. Sports lovers will find everything to their satisfaction. Cycle trips and canoeing/kayaking make everything complete. The campsite has an indoor heated swimming pool.

🚗 Exit Valence North A7. Direction Lyon N7. Direction Pont d'Isère. Follow camping signs.

D532 · D238 · **Romans-sur-Isère** · A7 · CC · N532 · D538 · D86 · N7 · D14 · D533 · **Valence** · D68

CC € **19** 21/4-8/7 26/8-14/9 · 📍 N 45°0'7'' E 4°53'42''

Châtillon-en-Diois, F-26410 / Rhône-Alpes (Drôme) ♀♂ ♿ 📶 iD (2119)

🏔 Le Lac Bleu★★★
🏕 Quartier la Touche
☎ +33 (0)4-75218530
📅 14/4 - 22/9
@ info@lacbleu-diois.com

6,5ha 75T(100-130m²) 6A CEE

1 ACD**G**IJKLMOPST
2 ACDKLMRTVWXY
3 ABGHJKRU**W**XZ
4 (E+H+Q+R+T+U+V+X+Z 🔓)
5 **A**EFIJKLMNOPUWZ
6 AEGIJ(N 3km)OTV

💬 Located on the shores of a lake where swimming is possible from early in the season. Wonderful views of the lake and the surrounding mountains from the terrace. The valley is wide and flat. An excellent location for making lovely trips out. Restaurant and shop are open for the whole season. Lovely indoor pool with jacuzzi.

🚐 From Loriol direction Die; then D539 direction Châtillon-en-Diois. Right 1 km beyond St. Roman. The campsite is well signposted.

CC € **17** 14/4-30/6 1/9-21/9 🏔 N 44°40'59'' E 5°26'56''

Châtillon-en-Diois, F-26410 / Rhône-Alpes (Drôme) ♿ 📶 iD (2120)

🏔 Municipal Les Chaussières★★
🏕 Les Chaussières
☎ +33 (0)6-43002500
📅 30/3 - 14/10
@ camping.chatillonendiois@ wanadoo.fr

2ha 159T(60-110m²) 10A CEE

1 ACD**G**IJKLMOPST
2 CGKRTVWXY
3 ABGHJ**M**NR**W**
4 (C+H 15/6-10/9) J
(Q 1/7-31/8)
(T+X+Z 1/5-15/9)
5 **A**FGIJKMNPUVZ
6 ACEGH**IJ**(N 0,5km)

💬 Camp in the Drôme, at the foot of the Vercors in the medieval wine village of Châtillon-en-Diois. Plenty of shade, along the river, surrounded by mountains. Many options for walking, cycling and mountain-biking. 3 swimming pools and 1 slide. Snack bar, tennis, games for children.

🚐 From Valence D93 to Die. After Die D539 dir. Châtillon-en-Diois. Drive into village. After 1 km turn right after bridge. Site is then after 500 metres.

CC € **15** 30/3-14/7 1/9-13/10 🏔 N 44°41'38'' E 5°29'1''

Chauzon, F-07120 / Rhône-Alpes (Ardèche) ♿ 📶 iD (2121)

🏔 La Digue★★★★
🏕 860 chemin des Diques
☎ +33 (0)4-75396357
📅 23/3 - 23/9
@ info@camping-la-digue.fr

2,5ha 69T(80-130m²) 6-10A CEE

1 ACD**G**IJKLMOPST
2 ABCNORTVXY
3 AGHJMNRU**W**X
4 (C+H+Q+S+T+U 🔓)
(V 1/7-25/8) (Y 24/3-15/9)
(Z 🔓)
5 **AB**DEFGIJKLMNOPQRUWZ
6 AEGJ**K**(N 3km)OTV

💬 Attractive site, good toilet facilities, enthusiastic French owner speaks English and will do all she can.

🚐 A7 exit Montélimar-Nord. N7 to Le Teil. N102 to Aubenas. Past Villeneuve-de-Berg left at roundabout, D103. Left D579 to Vallon. In Pradons right to Chauzon at supermarket. Left before village, keep right at end of road (route des Gras). Right at end of road, then keep left (route d'Uzer). Left before village, follow signs.

CC € **13** 7/4-6/7 24/8-22/9 🏔 N 44°29'15'' E 4°22'14''

Choranche, F-38680 / Rhône-Alpes (Isère) 📶 iD 2122

🔺 Le Gouffre de la Croix***
📧 1050 route du Pont de Vezor
☎ +33 (0)4-76360713
🗓 28/4 - 16/9
@ camping.gouffre.croix@
    wanadoo.fr

2,5ha 52**T**(80-100m²) 10A

1 ACD**G**IJKL**P**Q
2 CGJKMORUVXY
3 AHJNR**W**X
4 (Q 1/6-31/8)
    (R+T+U+X+Z 🔧)
5 **AB**FGIJKLMNPUZ
6 ACFG**J**OV

💬 Campsite with picturesque location on the banks of a little river with overhanging rocks. Once voted France's most beautifully situated campsite. Friendly owners.

🚗 A49 exit St. Marcellin, via St. Romans (D518) as far as Pont-en-Royans. In Pont-en-Royans turn left in the direction of Choranche (D531). When leaving Choranche site is signposted on right after small bridge.

Saint-Marcellin
A49
D1532
Villard-de-Lans
D531 CC D103
D54
D612
D76

CC € 15 28/4-6/7 27/8-15/9 ◼ N 45°3'52'' E 5°23'45''

Cordelle, F-42123 / Rhône-Alpes (Loire) 👨‍👩 ♿ 📶 iD 2123

🔺 Flower Camping de Mars****
📧 Les Rivières
☎ +33 (0)4-77649442
🗓 1/4 - 15/10
@ campingdemars@gmail.com

1,8ha 46**T**(5-41m²) 10-16A CEE

1 ACD**G**IJKL**P**Q
2 JKRVX
3 A**F**GHJKNR**W**
4 (A 1/7-31/8) (C+G 1/5-30/9)
    (Q+S+T+U+V+X+Z 🔧)
5 **AB**DFGIJKLMNPUVWXYZ
6 EGJ(N 5km)OT

💬 Quiet, beautifully located terraced campsite. You will have a view of the nearby reservoir of Villerest. Great for surfing and sailing. The campsite has a restaurant.

🚗 From Roanne (N7) at Le Coteau follow D43 and D56 towards Comelle-Verney, Cordelle and then towards Château de la Roche. Site is to the right 5 km from Cordelle.

D207
D9
D53
Saint-Symphorien-de-Lay
D1082
D8 CC
D1
D1082
A89
Balbigny

CC € 15 1/4-7/7 25/8-14/10 7=6, 14=11 ◼ N 45°55'8'' E 4°3'53''

Cormoranche-sur-Saône, F-01290 / Rhône-Alpes (Ain) 👨‍👩 ♿ 📶 iD 2124

🔺 du Lac****
📧 Base de Loisirs,
    365 chemin du Lac
☎ +33 (0)3-85239710
🗓 1/5 - 30/9
@ contact@lac-cormoranche.com

4ha 90**T**(80-100m²) 10A CEE

1 ACD**G**IJKLM**P**Q
2 ADFLMRSVWX
3 B**F**GHJKNRU**W**Z
4 (A 1/7-31/8)
    (Q+R+T+U+V+X+Z 🔧)
5 **AB**EFGIJKLPUWXY
6 ACFGHIJ**K**(N 5km)RTV

💬 A family campsite by a large swimming and fishing lake with pitches of 100 m² in the sun or in the shade. The campsite has a bar/restaurant and free wifi at reception. 5 minutes from a supermarket. A very touristy region, including wine cellars in Mâcon, Beaujolais and Bourgogne.

🚗 In Mâcon-centre D906 dir. Lyon. In Crêches left (D51) over the Saône. In Cormoranche follow Base de Loisirs signs. A40 dir. Bourg. Exit 3 Mâcon-Sud via Pont-de-Veyle to Cormoranche.

N79 **Mâcon** D28
A40
CC
La Chapelle-de-Guinchay D933 D2
A6
N6
D7

CC € 15 1/5-14/7 1/9-29/9 7=6, 14=12 ◼ N 46°15'5'' E 4°49'33''

Crest, F-26400 / Rhône-Alpes (Drôme) ⚲ 🛜 iD 2125

🏕 Les Clorinthes***
✉ Quai Soubeyran
☎ +33 (0)4-75250528
FAX +33 (0)4-75767509
📅 29/4 - 16/9
@ clorinthes@wanadoo.fr

4ha 154T(90-120m²) 6A CEE

1 AC**G**IJKLM**P**ST
2 CLORTVW**X**Y
3 AB**F**GHJK**MOP**RUW**X**
4 (B+G 1/5-10/9) (Q 📅)
   (T+U+V+Z 1/7-31/8)
5 **AB**FGIJKLMNPUZ
6 ACEGK(N 0,8km)TV

💬 Nice park with shade-giving trees. Modern toilet facilities. Swimming in swimming pool or in the Drôme, the river that flows past the campsite. Good start for cycling, walking or car trips. Medieval Crest within walking distance. Free wifi for CampingCard ACSI-holders.

🚗 Leave the A7 at Loriol. D104 dir Crest. Left at 2nd traffic lights towards centre. Over railway line. Turn right at large roundabout with monument. Continue for 600 metres beside the river to campsite.

(CC) € **17** 29/4-5/7 23/8-15/9   🧭 N 44°43'27'' E 5°1'40''

Cublize/Amplepuis, F-69550 / Rhône-Alpes (Rhône) 👫 ⚲ 🛜 iD 2126

🏕 Campéole Le Lac des Sapins****
✉ rue du Stade
☎ +33 (0)4-74895283
📅 30/3 - 23/9
@ lacdessapins@campeole.com

8ha 79T(50-100m²) 16A CEE

1 ACD**G**IJKLM**P**RS
2 ACDLMRTUVWXY
3 BGHJMN**OPQ**RW**Z**
4 (B+Q 1/7-31/8) (R 📅)
   (T+Z 1/7-31/8)
5 **AB**EFGIJKLMNOPUVXYZ
6 ACEGH**J**(N 0,5km)

💬 Family campsite located close to the lake with plenty of water sports. It has a bar and restaurant at the lake.

🚗 Follow the camping signs in the village. Drive past the village campsite. The entrance to the campsite 'Du Lac des Sapins' is located after about 600 metres.

(CC) € **17** 30/3-6/7 25/8-22/9   🧭 N 46°0'47'' E 4°22'54''

Cuisiat/Val-Revermont, F-01370 / Rhône-Alpes (Ain) 👫 ⚲ 🛜 iD 2127

NEW

🏕 Mun. La Grange du Pin***
✉ 330 chemin de la Grange du Pin
☎ +33 (0)4-74513414
📅 1/4 - 30/9
@ camping@val-revermont.fr

75T(80-100m²) 10A CEE

1 ACD**G**IJKLMO**PQ**
2 ABDKLMPRTUVWXY
3 AGHJKMNR**W**Z
4 (Q+R 1/7-31/8)
   (T+U+Y+Z 📅)
5 **A**FGIJKLMNOPUVXZ
6 EGJ(N 10km)TV

💬 This peaceful and spacious campsite is located on the edge of a wood and by a lovely lake with a nice beach. There is an extensive Forest Adventure Trail.

🚗 From A39, exit 10 direction Saint-Amour. Then D1083 direction Bourg-en-Bresse. Follow signs in St-Etienne du Bois.

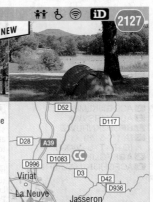

(CC) € **15** 1/4-7/7 1/9-29/9   🧭 N 46°18'22'' E 5°21'19''

Culoz, F-01350 / Rhône-Alpes (Ain) ♿ 🛜 iD (2128)

▲ Le Colombier***
🏠 Ile de Verbaou
☎ +33 (0)4-79871900
📅 14/4 - 23/9
@ info@camping-alpes.net

1,5ha 55T(70-100m²) 10A

1 ACGIJKLMPQ
2 ADLMRTVWXY
3 BGHJMNQRUZ
4 (Q+T+U+Z 15/5-15/9)
5 ABDFGIJKLMNPUVWXYZ
6 EGJ(N 0,3km)OV

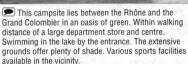

💬 This campsite lies between the Rhône and the Grand Colombier in an oasis of green. Within walking distance of a large department store and centre. Swimming in the lake by the entrance. The extensive grounds offer plenty of shade. Various sports facilities available in the vicinity.

🚗 A40 dir. Genève. Exit 11: Éloise. RN508 as far as Frangy. In Frangy dir. Seyssel. Via D992 dir. Culoz. Campsite is located on the right of the road by the roundabout in Culoz.

CC € **15** 14/4-30/6 26/8-22/9 7=6, 14=11 🏔 N 45°51'6'' E 5°47'38''

Darbres, F-07170 / Rhône-Alpes (Ardèche) 🛜 (2129)

▲ Camping Les Charmilles***
🏠 Le Clapas, D258
☎ +33 (0)4-75885627
📅 28/4 - 30/9
@ info@campinglescharmilles.fr

5ha 58T(80-135m²) 5-10A CEE

1 BCDGIJKLPST
2 JKRTVWXY
3 BDGHJMNRU
4 (A+C+G+Q+R+T+U+V+Y+Z 🔑)
5 ABCEFGIJKLMNOPQRUWZ
6 AEGHK(N 8km)ORV

💬 Charming campsite with welcoming owners in the heart of the Ardèche. Think of a spellbinding view and the perfect mix of nature and relaxation, including walks, jeu de boules, sports, or dancing during the musical evenings. Enjoy delicious dishes made from fresh local produce in the restaurant.

🚗 A7 exit 17 to Le Teil. There N102 to Aubenas. In Lavilledieu right, D224 to Lussas and Darbres. Then to Mirabel. Site left. Don't use SatNav.

CC € **17** 28/4-7/7 25/8-29/9 14=12, 21=18 🏔 N 44°38'0'' E 4°30'30''

Die, F-26150 / Rhône-Alpes (Drôme) ♿ 🛜 iD (2130)

▲ Chamarges**
🏠 route de Valence
☎ FAX +33 (0)4-75221413
📅 24/3 - 6/10
@ campingchamarges@orange.fr

3,5ha 150T(80-110m²) 3-6A CEE

1 ACDFIJKLMPST
2 CKLNORWXY
3 AGHJNRWX
4 (B 2/4-30/9) (Q+T+U+V+X+Y+Z 🔑)
5 GIJKLMNOPUVWZ
6 EJK(N 1,5km)TV

💬 Level, sunny and shaded grounds. Beautiful views. Canoeing and kayaking on the Drôme right from the campsite. Swimming pool. Good restaurant with nice terrace. Lovely trips into the beautiful countryside and picturesque villages. Free wifi.

🚗 From Valence take the D93. Campsite just before Die. Take campsite exit at roundabout. Camping sign on the right.

CC € **13** 24/3-1/7 19/8-5/10 🏔 N 44°45'44'' E 5°20'47''

Die, F-26150 / Rhône-Alpes (Drôme) ⚓ 🛜 iD (2131)

🏕 Le Glandasse***
✉ 550 route de Gap
☎ +33 (0)4-75220250
🗓 10/4 - 30/9
@ camping-glandasse@wanadoo.fr

3,5ha 120T(80-120m²) 10A CEE

1 ACD**G**IJKLOPST
2 BCKLNORSTVWXY
3 ABGHJN**Q**RU**W**X
4 (C+H 25/4-30/9) K
(Q+R+T+U+V 1/5-25/9)
(X 15/4-30/9) (Z 🖙)
5 **AB**EFGIJKMNOPUZ
6 EGK(N 1km)ORTV

💬 Located right by the river in a wide valley. Lovely pitches with shady trees. Discover the natural area of the Vercors on foot, by bike or in your car. Good restaurant, lovely swimming pool, minigolf, fitness. 1 km from Die.

🚗 Exit Valence, then dir. Crest/Die. After centre of Die, 1 km south of town continue towards Gap. Campsite clearly signposted. You reach campsite via tunnel (max. height 2.80m). Not accessible for high motorhomes or extra-wide caravans.

Saint-Étienne | D518
Die
D93 | CC | Menée
D120
D539

CC € **13** 10/4-6/7 24/8-29/9 📷 N 44°44'41'' E 5°23'7''

Die, F-26150 / Rhône-Alpes (Drôme) ⚓ 🛜 ✿ iD (2132)

🏕 Le Riou-Merle***
✉ route de Romeyer
☎ 📠 +33 (0)4-75222131
🗓 1/4 - 10/10
@ lerioumerle@gmail.com

2,5ha 97T(70-300m²) 6A CEE

1 AFIJKLMPST
2 KRTVWXY
3 BGHJR
4 (B 15/5-30/9) (Q 1/6-30/9)
(U+X+Y+Z 🖙)
5 **A**FGIJKLMNPUVZ
6 CEG**K**(N 0,4km)

💬 Quiet campsite close to the medieval town of Die. Modern toilet facilities. Swimming pool. Mountain views. Tall trees give necessary shade and the small trees do not obstruct the sun. A base for making excursions through the countryside. Lovely new restaurant with excellent cuisine. Wifi on entire campsite.

🚗 From Crest take direction Gap before Die centre. Drive round the centre. Towards the centre again at the large roundabout. Just before the centre on the right.

Saint-Étienne | D518
Die
D93 | CC | Menée
D120
D539

CC € **15** 1/4-6/7 25/8-9/10 📷 N 44°45'16'' E 5°22'40''

Dieulefit, F-26220 / Rhône-Alpes (Drôme) ⚓ 🛜 iD (2133)

🏕 Domaine Provençal***
✉ Les Grands Prés
☎ +33 (0)4-75499436
🗓 23/3 - 4/11
@ contact@domaineprovencal.com

1,9ha 41T(80-100m²) 10A CEE

1 ACD**F**IJKLMPST
2 CGRTVWXY
3 AGHJL**M**RU
4 (C 30/4-20/9) **KN**
5 **AB**DEFGIJKLMNOPUVZ
6 EGJ**K**(N 0,3km)RTV

💬 A lovely campsite with plenty of shade near the picturesque village of Dieulefit, where you will find many artists. All shops are within walking distance. The fresh air invites you to go walking and cycling in the unique countryside.

🚗 A7 exit Montélimar-Nord, direction Dieulefit (D540). At the entrance to the town on the south side of the road, right. Follow signs.

D6 | Cléon-d'Andran
D540
D9 | CC
D538
Taulignan
D4

CC € **15** 23/3-7/7 25/8-3/11 📷 N 44°31'18'' E 5°3'41''

Divonne-les-Bains, F-01220 / Rhône-Alpes (Ain)　♿ 🛜 iD　2134

🏔 Huttopia Divonne-les-Bains***
✉ Quart. Villard, 2465 Vie de l'Etraz
☎ +33 (0)4-50200195
📠 +33 (0)4-50200035
📅 27/4 - 30/9
@ divonne@huttopia.com

8ha 175T(80-150m²) 10A CEE

1 ACD**G**IJKL**P**ST
2 CF**I**JKRVWXY
3 B**F**GHJ**M**NRU**W**
4 (A 5/7-30/8) (C+G 30/4-11/9) (Q+R 🔑) (T+U+V+X+Z 4/7-28/8)
5 **AB**DFGIJKLMNOPUW
6 CEGIK(N 3km)TV

💬 A lovely wooded campsite laid out in terraces. Pitches delightfully set among trees. A large swimming pool, plenty of amenities for children, fun activities. Switzerland, Geneva and Lake Geneva are close by.

🚗 From Gex D984 direction Divonne. Take the road to St. Gixet before Divonne and follow the camping signs.

D1005　Gland
D25
CC　Nyon
A1
Gex　D984 C
D991
Versoix　N5

CC € **17** 27/4-5/7　26/8-29/9　　🧭 N 46°22'29'' E 6°7'16''

Doussard, F-74210 / Rhône-Alpes (Haute-Savoie)　👨‍👧 ♿ 🛜 iD　2135

🏔 Campéole La Nublière***
✉ 30 allée de la Nublière
☎ +33 (0)4-50443344
📠 +33 (0)4-50443178
📅 27/4 - 30/9
@ nubliere@campeole.com

11ha 350T(100-110m²) 6A CEE

1 AC**G**IJKLMPRS
2 ACD**G**KLORTUVXY
3 B**F**GJK**M**N**Q**RU**W**Z
4 (Q+S 🔑) (T+U+V 15/6-15/9) (Y 🔑) (Z 15/6-15/9)
5 **AB**CDEFGIJKLMNPQUZ
6 ACEGH**J**(N 1,5km)ORTV

💬 Quite a big campsite with a beach and a meadow by a lake. Interesting for water sports enthusiasts. Shade present everywhere. A nice view from the beach on the surrounding mountains and the lake.

🚗 D1508 Annecy-Albertville. The campsite is located near this road. Well signposted on the southwest shore of the lake, follow the camping signs in the community of Doussard.

Seynod　D909　Thônes
D909 A
D1508　D12
D912
CC
D911　Faverges

CC € **17** 27/4-6/7　25/8-29/9　　🧭 N 45°47'24'' E 6°13'4''

Doussard, F-74210 / Rhône-Alpes (Haute-Savoie)　♿ 🛜 iD　2136

🏔 La Ferme de la Serraz*****
✉ rue de la Poste
☎ +33 (0)4-50443068
📅 1/5 - 15/9
@ info@campinglaserraz.com

3,5ha 79T(100-200m²) 10-16A CEE

1 A**G**IJKLPRS
2 G**R**VWXY
3 B**F**HJKRU**W**
4 (C+**H** 🔑) (Q+T+U+V+X+Z 1/7-31/8)
5 **AB**EFGIJKLMNPUWXYZ
6 ACEGHI**K**(N 0,3km)TV

💬 There is a lovely swimming pool and a paddling pool here. There is a bar and a restaurant. Good impression as you drive onto the site. Sunny grassland or shade provided by trees.

🚗 Route D1508 Annecy-Albertville. The campsite is signposted on the south side of the lake at the roundabout which leads to Doussard centre.

D909 A
D1508　D12
Doussard
CC　Faverges
D911
D912　Albertville

CC € **15** 1/5-14/7　1/9-14/9　　🧭 N 45°46'31'' E 6°13'34''

Duingt, F-74410 / Rhône-Alpes (Haute-Savoie) ♿ 🛜 iD 2137

🔺 Mun. Les Champs Fleuris**
🏠 631 voie Romaine
☎ +33 (0)4-50685731
📠 +33 (0)4-50770317
🔑 14/4 - 22/9
@ camping@duingt.fr

1,5ha 111**T**(80-120m²) 3-10A

1 AGIJKLMPQ
2 GJKRVWXY
3 BFGHJR
4 (Q+T+Z 🔑)
5 ABFGIJKLMNPUVZ
6 ACEGIJ(N 1km)T

💬 Grounds with wide terraces from which some pitches have views of Lake Annecy. The Annecy-Faverges-Marlens cycle route goes right past the campsite. For shopping, Duingt centre is 1 km away. It is 10 km to Annecy and about 25 km to Albertville.

🚗 D1508 Annecy-Albertville. The campsite is on the right of the D1508 between St. Jorioz and Duingt, exit Entrevernes. Clearly signposted.

Cran-Gevrier **Annecy**
D16 · D909
A41 · D909 A
D1201
D912 · D1508
D3 · D12
D911

CC € **17** 14/4-30/6 27/8-21/9 N 45°49'36'' E 6°11'19''

Eclassan, F-07370 / Rhône-Alpes (Ardèche) ♿ 🛜 iD 2138

🔺 l'Oasis****
🏠 810 chemin du Petit Chaléat
☎ +33 (0)4-75345623
🔑 28/4 - 2/9
@ info@oasisardeche.com

5ha 40**T**(90-250m²) 3-6A CEE

1 ACD**F**IJLPST
2 CJKLMRVWXY
3 BGHJNQRU**W**
4 (C+H 8/5-1/9) (Q+T+U 🔑) (V 8/5-2/9) (X 1/7-31/8) (Z 🔑)
5 A DEFGIJKLMNPQRUWZ
6 AEGJ(N 4km)ORTV

💬 Terraced campsite in beautiful country, a small paradise on earth with attention and care for nature, a real oasis. The swimming pool is heated from 8 May. Walking and cycling maps are available. You can get a delicious dish of the day and home made pizzas. Call them, and they will pitch your caravan for you.

🚗 A7, exit 12 Chanas. Then N7 dir. Valence as far as St. Vallier. D86 over the Rhône to Sarras. Then D6 dir. Eclassan and then following the camping signs.

Davézieux
Annonay · Anneyron
D121 · N7
CC · A7
D578 A · D86
D578
D532

CC € **15** 28/4-2/7 20/8-1/9 14=12 N 45°10'45'' E 4°44'22''

Entre-deux-Guiers, F-38380 / Rhône-Alpes (Isère) ♿ 🛜 iD 2139

🔺 L'Arc en Ciel
🏠 37 chemin des Berges
☎ +33 (0)4-76660697
🔑 1/4 - 15/10
@ info@camping-arc-en-ciel.com

1,3ha 60**T**(100-110m²) 4-6A CEE

1 ACD**G**IJKLMOPRS
2 CGORSVXY
3 BGHJ**MRW**
4 (C 15/5-15/9) (G 15/5-25/9) (V 🔑)
5 A**B**GJKLNOPUVZ
6 ACDEGJ(N 0,1km)OV

💬 Peaceful grounds situated in a village. Pitches are shaded by tall trees. The low altitude makes it ideal for exploring the Chartreuse highlands and surrounding district in spring and autumn. The mountain stream with its pebble beach next to the site is an added attraction.

🚗 D1006 from Chambéry towards Les Echelle. Then take the D520 direction St. Laurent-du-Pont. On the roundabout follow campsite signs.

D82 · D1006 · D912
D512
Saint-Laurent-du-Pont
Voiron
Coublevie · D520 B

CC € **15** 1/4-6/7 27/8-14/10 N 45°26'5'' E 5°45'22''

Excenevex-Plage, F-74140 / Rhône-Alpes (Haute-Savoie) 👥 ♿ 📶 iD **2140**

🏕 Campéole La Pinède***
✉ 10 avenue de la Pinède
☎ +33 (0)4-50728505
📠 +33 (0)4-50729300
🔑 27/4 - 30/9
@ pinede@campeole.com

12ha 246T 16A CEE

1 ACD**F**IJKLM**PQ**
2 ABDGLMRSVXY
3 BGHK**MN**O**Q**RUWZ
4 (A 1/7-31/8) (C 1/6-15/9)
(E 🔑) (H 1/6-15/9) K**N**P
(Q+S 1/5-30/9)
5 **AB**FGIJKLMNPUV
6 CEGH**JK**(N 1km)TV

💬 A large family campsite set in a wood right next to Lake Geneva with its sandy beaches. Quite secluded but with all amenities next to the entrance. Pitches spread out among the permanent camp facilities.

🚗 N5 Genève direction Thonon-les-Bains. Before Bonnatrait turn left to Yvoire/Excenevex. The campsite is 500 metres to the right after the roundabout.

CC € **17** 27/4-6/7 25/8-29/9   📍 N 46°20'45'' E 6°21'29''

Fleurie, F-69820 / Rhône-Alpes (Rhône) 👥 📶 iD **2141**

🏕 La Grappe Fleurie****
✉ rue de la Grappe Fleurie
☎ +33 (0)4-74698007
🔑 7/4 - 13/10
@ info@beaujolais-camping.com

3,5ha 59T(100-150m²) 16A CEE

1 ACD**G**IJKLMO**PS**
2 JKRVWX
3 BGHJ**M**RU
4 (A 1/7-31/8) (B 15/5-15/9)
(E+Q+R 🔑)
(T+U+Z 1/5-30/9)
5 **AB**DFGHJLMNOPUWXYZ
6 ACEGK(N 0,8km)RV

💬 A quiet campsite with pitches on terraces, surrounded by the Beaujolais vineyards. Marked out pitches separated by hedges, spaciously appointed.

🚗 A6 exit Mâcon-Sud. D906 (N6) direction Villefranche. Right after La Maison Blanche on D32 to Fleurie. Follow campsigns.

CC € **17** 7/4-7/7 25/8-12/10 7=6, 14=11, 21=16   📍 N 46°11'16'' E 4°41'56''

Gex, F-01170 / Rhône-Alpes (Ain) 📶 iD **2142**

🏕 Les Genêts de Gex***
✉ 400 avenue des Alpes
☎ +33 (0)4-50428457
🔑 1/3 - 31/10
@ auxamisdugolin@gmail.com

3,2ha 122T(80-130m²) 16A

1 ACD**G**IJLPT
2 GKLRUVWXY
3 AD**F**GHJN**O**RUW
4 (**A** 15/6-15/9)
(**E**+Q+R+T+U+Z 🔑)
5 **AB**DFGIJKLMNOPUVWXYZ
6 CDEGHJOTV

💬 Campsite near the town of Gex on even grounds with large and very large pitches marked-out by hedges. Separate corners between bushes for guests camping in tents. Lots of space on separate grounds for sports and/or communal entertainment.

🚗 In Gex take the D984 to Divonne-les-Bains. Clearly signposted, on the right of the road.

CC € **15** 1/3-6/7 24/8-30/10 7=6, 14=12   📍 N 46°20'4'' E 6°4'4''

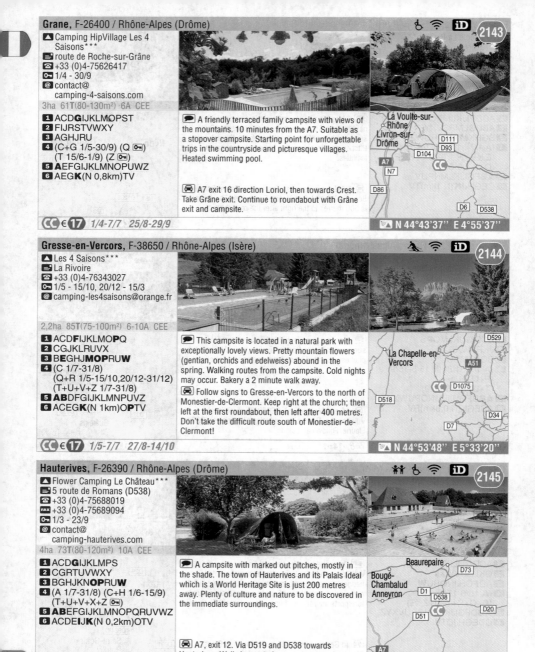

Grane, F-26400 / Rhône-Alpes (Drôme)

🖰 ⬚ 📶 iD (2143)

🔺 Camping HipVillage Les 4 Saisons***
✉ route de Roche-sur-Grâne
☎ +33 (0)4-75626417
📅 1/4 - 30/9
@ contact@camping-4-saisons.com

3ha 61T(80-130m²) 6A CEE

1 ACD**G**IJKLM**O**PST
2 FIJRSTVWXY
3 AGHJRU
4 (C+G 1/5-30/9) (Q 📅)
(T 15/6-1/9) (Z 📅)
5 **A**EFGIJKLMNOPUWZ
6 AEG**K**(N 0,8km)TV

💬 A friendly terraced family campsite with views of the mountains. 10 minutes from the A7. Suitable as a stopover campsite. Starting point for unforgettable trips in the countryside and picturesque villages. Heated swimming pool.

🚗 A7 exit 16 direction Loriol, then towards Crest. Take Grâne exit. Continue to roundabout with Grâne exit and campsite.

La Voulte-sur-Rhône · Livron-sur-Drôme — D111 / D93 / D104 / A7 / N7 / CC / D86 / D6 / D538

CC € **17** 1/4-7/7 25/8-29/9 | 📐 N 44°43'37'' E 4°55'37''

Gresse-en-Vercors, F-38650 / Rhône-Alpes (Isère)

🎿 📶 iD (2144)

🔺 Les 4 Saisons***
✉ La Rivoire
☎ +33 (0)4-76343027
📅 1/5 - 15/10, 20/12 - 15/3
@ camping-les4saisons@orange.fr

2,2ha 85T(75-100m²) 6-10A CEE

1 ACD**F**IJKLMO**P**Q
2 CGJKLRUVX
3 B**E**GHJ**MOP**RUW
4 (C 1/7-31/8)
(Q+R 1/5-15/10,20/12-31/12)
(T+U+V+Z 1/7-31/8)
5 **AB**DFGIJKLMNPUVZ
6 ACEG**K**(N 1km)O**P**TV

💬 This campsite is located in a natural park with exceptionally lovely views. Pretty mountain flowers (gentian, orchids and edelweiss) abound in the spring. Walking routes from the campsite. Cold nights may occur. Bakery a 2 minute walk away.

🚗 Follow signs to Gresse-en-Vercors to the north of Monestier-de-Clermont. Keep right at the church; then left at the first roundabout, then left after 400 metres. Don't take the difficult route south of Monestier-de-Clermont!

La Chapelle-en-Vercors — D529 / A51 / CC / D1075 / D518 / D34 / D7

CC € **17** 1/5-7/7 27/8-14/10 | 📐 N 44°53'48'' E 5°33'20''

Hauterives, F-26390 / Rhône-Alpes (Drôme)

👫 ♿ 📶 iD (2145)

🔺 Flower Camping Le Château***
✉ 5 route de Romans (D538)
☎ +33 (0)4-75688019
📠 +33 (0)4-75689094
📅 1/3 - 23/9
@ contact@camping-hauterives.com

4ha 73T(80-120m²) 10A CEE

1 ACD**G**IJKLMPS
2 CGRTUVWXY
3 BGHJKN**OP**RUW
4 (A 1/7-31/8) (C+H 1/6-15/9)
(T+U+V+X+Z 📅)
5 **AB**EFGIJKLMNOPQRUVWZ
6 ACDEI**JK**(N 0,2km)OTV

💬 A campsite with marked out pitches, mostly in the shade. The town of Hauterives and its Palais Ideal which is a World Heritage Site is just 200 metres away. Plenty of culture and nature to be discovered in the immediate surroundings.

🚗 A7, exit 12. Via D519 and D538 towards Hauterives. Well signposted.

Beaurepaire — Bougé-Chambalud · Anneyron — D73 / D1 / D538 / CC / D51 / D20 / A7

CC € **15** 1/3-7/7 26/8-22/9 7=6 | 📐 N 45°15'10'' E 5°1'37''

Hauteville-Lompnès, F-01110 / Rhône-Alpes (Ain)

▲ Les 12 Cols★★★
✉ chemin de Cormaranche
☎ +33 (0)4-37865587
⌚ 1/4 - 30/9
@ contact@camping-les12cols.fr

2146

100T(85-135m²) 10A CEE

1 ACD**F**IJKLP
2 JLRVWXY
3 ADF**G**HJK**M**NR**S**U**W**
4 (B 1/6-30/9) (Q 1/7-30/8)
(Z ⌁)
5 **A**BDGIJKLMNOPUWXZ
6 CDEG**I**K(N 1km)

💬 A peaceful campsite at an altitude of 800m with terraced pitches on flowery and well landscaped grounds with clean, modern facilities. Perfect for nature lovers. Various sports activities are possible on the Plateau d'Hauteville, an ideal location for cycling or exploring the waterfalls.

🚗 A40, exit St. Martin-du-Fresne. Then follow signs to Hauteville-Lompnes. A42, exit Ambérieu-en-Bugey direction Belley RN504 Tenay. Direction Hauteville-Lompnes.

CC € **15** 1/4-30/6 1/9-29/9

📐 N 45°58'15'' E 5°35'44''

Joyeuse, F-07260 / Rhône-Alpes (Ardèche)

▲ La Nouzarède★★★
✉ chemin d'Orival
☎ +33 (0)4-75399201
⌚ 21/4 - 15/9
@ campingnouzarede@wanadoo.fr

2147

2ha 53T(80-120m²) 10A

1 ACD**G**IJKLMOPST
2 ABCLNRTVXY
3 AG**M**NR**W**X
4 (C+H ⌁) K
(Q+R+T+U+V+Z ⌁)
5 **A**DEFGIJKLMNPQUXYZ
6 AEGJ(N 0,8km)TV

💬 All the charm of the Ardèche at La Nouzarède, 5 min. from the centre of the village and 100m from the river. Walking, swimming and excursions. All you need on holiday at this site. Swimming pool and jacuzzi heated in late season.

🚗 A7 exit Montélimar-Nord dir. Le Teil/Aubenas. In Le Teil N102 to Aubenas. Then D104 direction Alès. From roundabout at Joyeuse to the village. After 1 km, after garage, turn right. Left at stop sign. 2nd left after bridge.

CC € **17** 21/4-14/7 1/9-14/9 7=6, 14=11

📐 N 44°29'2'' E 4°14'8''

La Motte-Chalancon, F-26470 / Rhône-Alpes (Drôme)

▲ La Ferme de Clareau★★★
✉ route de Die (RD 61)
☎ +33 (0)4-75272603
⌚ 15/4 - 15/10
@ campingfermeclareau@
   wanadoo.fr

2148

9ha 42T(100-500m²) 10A CEE

1 AGIJKLM**P**ST
2 BCIKRWXY
3 AGHJRU**W**
4 (**A** 1/7-31/8) (B 1/6-1/9)
(Q+U+V+Z ⌁)
5 **A**IJKMNOPUV
6 AEJ(N 1,5km)

💬 Christine and Olivier welcome you to this undulating campsite with 42 pitches on 9 hectares of grounds. Plenty of space, lovely views, also from the swimming pool. You can swim and fish in the river, go cycling and walking. There are Provençal markets in the area at Nyons, Die and Vaison la Romaine.

🚗 A7, exit Montélimar south. D94 dir Nyons and Gap. At Rémuzat take the D61 towards La Motte-Chalancon. Follow signs on the D61, through centre and follow camping signs.

CC € **15** 15/4-6/7 24/8-14/10

📐 N 44°28'43'' E 5°23'43''

La Plagne Tarent./Montchavin, F-73210 / Rhône-Alpes (Savoie)

🎿 🛜 iD **2149**

🔺 de Montchavin**
📧 2 allée du Mont Blanc
☎ +33 (0)4-79078323
🕐 1/1 - 30/9, 1/11 - 31/12
@ campingmontchavin@orange.fr

1,3ha 45T(80-100m²) 4-10A

1 ACGIJKLMP**Q**
2 JKRTUVWX
3 GHRU
4 (Q 1/7-30/8,20/12-20/4)
5 **AB**DEGIJKLMNPUVWZ
6 CEG**JK**(N 0,3km)V

💬 High-altitude terraced campsite with extensive view over the valley from every pitch. Very welcoming village at 5 minutes from the campsite on foot. Ideal for skiing in winter.

🚗 From Moutiers take the N90. After Bellentre drive in the direction of Montchavin-les-Coches. Signposted from here on. The campsite is located on the left of the village centre.

Bourg-Saint-Maurice

D1090   D902

CC

CC € **15** 15/4-8/7 26/8-29/9

🏔 N 45°33'38'' E 6°44'22''

La Roche-sur-Grane, F-26400 / Rhône-Alpes (Drôme)

👫 🛜 iD **2150**

🔺 La Magerie
📧 Les Fayes
☎ +33 (0)4-75627177
🕐 1/3 - 30/11
@ la.magerie@wanadoo.fr

NEW

2,5ha 38T(120-350m²) 10A CEE

1 AGIJKLMPST
2 JKRTVWXY
3 ADGHJU
4 (B 1/5-15/11) **K**(Q 🕐)
5 **AB**GIJKLMNPUZ
6 DEIJ(N 7km)OV

💬 Those who have calm, quiet, extra spacious pitches, a beautiful view of the fields and the mountains of the Vercors Massif and stunning toilet facilities on their wish list will be glad of a visit here. You can enjoy the lovely Provençal weather until the end of October.

🚗 A7 exit 16 Loriol. Follow De Diou until Grane then D119 towards La Roche-sur-Grane. Directly after 30 km sign to La Roche-sur-Grane turn right towards campsite (don't enter village).

Livron-sur-Drôme   D93
Loriol-sur-Drôme   D104
A7
N7   CC
          D6   D538
          D9

CC € **17** 1/3-10/6 1/9-29/11

🏔 N 44°40'46'' E 4°56'38''

Lalley, F-38930 / Rhône-Alpes (Isère)

♿ 🛜 iD **2151**

🔺 Sites & Paysages Belle Roche***
☎ +33 (0)6-32613882
🕐 1/4 - 14/10
@ camping.belleroche@gmail.com

2,5ha 57T(100-250m²) 10A CEE

1 ACD**G**IJKLMOPST
2 CGKLRTVWX
3 BGHIJLMN**P**RUVW
4 (A 1/6-31/8) (C 10/5-30/9) (Q+T+U+V+Y+Z 🕐)
5 **A**DFGIJKLMNOPUWXZ
6 ACDEGH**IK**(N 0,5km)TV

💬 A sunny campsite at an altitude of 900 metres in mountainous surroundings. Heated swimming pool. Plenty of walking and cycling tours possible. Electric bikes for rent on the campsite. The surrounding mountains form a beautiful panorama. Restaurant and terrace with mountain views and with 'Montignard' specialities.

🚗 N57 Grenoble-Sisteron. Indicated before the Col de la Croix-Haute by signs at Lalley.

Chichilianne   D526   Mens
                Prébois   D66
          D7
        D120   CC
          D1075
Mensac   D539

CC € **17** 1/4-5/7 23/8-13/10 7=6, 14=12

🏔 N 44°45'17'' E 5°40'44''

Lamastre, F-07270 / Rhône-Alpes (Ardèche) 2152

🔥 🛜 iD

🔺 Camping de Retourtour***
✉ 1 rue de Retourtour
☎ +33 (0)4-75064071
🗓 1/4 - 21/9
@ campingderetourtour@wanadoo.fr

2,9ha 80T(90-120m²) 8A CEE

1 ACG IJKLMPST
2 ACDLMNRTUVWXY
3 BGHJKLNQRUVWXZ
4 (Q+R+T+U+V+X+Z 🔒)
5 AFGIJKLMNOPUVZ
6 CEGK(N 1,5km)ORTV

💬 A quiet family campsite in the heart of the Ardèche just 1.5 km from Lamastre. Ideal for a holiday with family or friends. Less than 100m from Le Doux river.

🚗 From Tournon take the D534 to Lamastre, then towards Saint Agrève. Camping sign after 1.5 km, then turn right and go downhill.

CC € 15 1/4-7/7 25/8-20/9

🏔 N 44°59'30'' E 4°33'55''

Lanslevillard, F-73480 / Rhône-Alpes (Savoie) 2153

⛷ 🔥 🛜 iD

🔺 Camping Caravaneige de Val Cenis***
☎ +33 (0)4-79059052
FAX +33 (0)4-79052685
🗓 26/5 - 30/9, 19/12 - 30/4
@ campoland@orange.fr

2,5ha 86T(100-140m²) 10A CEE

1 ACDFHIJKLMOPQ
2 CGKRTVW
3 AGHJMNRU
4 (A 1/7-31/8) N (Q+T+U+V+X+Z 🔒)
5 ABDEFGIJKLMNOPQUZ
6 ACEGK(N 0,5km)OV

💬 A spacious level campsite with 360° panorama views of the mountain range and village. All pitches are marked out. 200 metres from the ski lifts.

🚗 A43 exit Modané. Then D1006 direction Mont-Cenis. Campsite located on the left of the village.

CC € 17 8/1-9/2 12/3-19/4 26/5-13/7 31/8-29/9

🏔 N 45°17'28'' E 6°54'32''

Largentière, F-07110 / Rhône-Alpes (Ardèche) 2154

🛜 ✿ iD

🔺 Sunêlia Domaine Les Ranchisses*****
✉ route de Rocher
☎ +33 (0)4-75883197
FAX +33 (0)4-75883273
🗓 14/4 - 23/9
@ reception@lesranchisses.fr

10ha 102T(95-120m²) 10A CEE

1 ACDG IJKLMOPST
2 CORSTVXY
3 BGHIJMNQRUVWX
4 (C+F+H 🔒) IJKLNP (Q+S+T+U+V+Y+Z 🔒)
5 ABCDEFGJLNPRUWXYZ
6 ACEGJKL(N 2,5km)TV

💬 This campsite has various amenities such as a large aquapark and extensive wellness and sports activities. Delicious dining in the auberge, but there is also a campsite restaurant. A supplement applies for a comfort pitch.

🚗 A7 exit Montélimar-Nord dir. Le Teil/Aubenas. In Le Teil N102 to Aubenas. Then N104 dir. Alès. After Uzer take D5 to Largentière. At the end of the village left onto D5 dir. Rocher. Campsite is on left after a few km.

CC € 19 14/4-29/6 1/9-22/9

🏔 N 44°33'38'' E 4°17'5''

Lathuile, F-74210 / Rhône-Alpes (Haute-Savoie) ♿ 📶 iD (2155)

🏔 l'Idéal****
📧 715 route de Chaparon
☎ +33 (0)4-50443297
📅 1/5 - 16/9
@ contact@campingideal.com

3ha 180T(80-110m²) 10A

1 ACGIJKLPRS
2 IJKRVWXY
3 BFGHJKLMNQRUV
4 (B 6/5-16/9) (E 📅)
(H 6/5-16/9) IJKMP(Q+R 📅)
(T 15/5-4/9)
(U+V+Y+Z 15/5-9/9)
5 ABEFGIJKLPUWZ
6 ACDEGHJ(N 2km)OTV

💬 A beautifully located campsite with lovely swimming pools, of which the indoor pool is heated. The restaurant and bar are only open at weekends in low season. Open-air fitness equipment for all ages.

🚗 Route Annecy-Albertville D1508. The campsites are signposted on green signs at the lights in Brédannaz (Lathuile).

Seynod Sévrier Menthon-Saint-Bernard
A41
D1508 D12
CC
D911
D912

CC € **19** 1/5-1/7 26/8-15/9 📐 N 45°47'43'' E 6°12'21''

Lathuile, F-74210 / Rhône-Alpes (Haute-Savoie) ♿ 📶 iD (2156)

🏔 Les Fontaines****
📧 1295 route de Chaparon
☎ +33 (0)4-50443122
📠 +33 (0)4-50448780
📅 7/5 - 9/9
@ info@campinglesfontaines.com

2ha 105T(80-100m²) 6A

1 ACGHIJKLMPRS
2 JKRVXY
3 BFGHJKLNRU
4 (C 1/6-9/9) (E 📅)
(H 1/6-9/9) JK(Q 📅)
(S 15/6-15/9)
(T+U+V+Y+Z 25/5-5/9)
5 ABDEFGIJKLPUWZ
6 EGIK(N 3km)OTV

💬 Campsite with all facilities, beautiful swimming pools for young and old. Good restaurant and bar. Near the lake and an autonomous cycle path.

🚗 Route Annecy-Albertville D1508. Signposted at the traffic lights in Brédannaz (Lathuile).

Annecy Sévrier
A41 D909 A
D1201 D1508
D912 CC D12
D911 Doussard
Faverges

CC € **17** 7/5-30/6 31/8-8/9 📐 N 45°48'2'' E 6°12'17''

Laurac-en-Vivarais, F-07110 / Rhône-Alpes (Ardèche) ♿ 📶 iD (2157)

🏔 Les Châtaigniers Camping***
📧 515 route de Rabette
☎ +33 (0)4-75368626
📅 1/4 - 30/9
@ chataigniers07@orange.fr

1,2ha 57T(90-100m²) 10A CEE

1 ACDFIJKLPST
2 JKRTVWXY
3 AGHJRU
4 (A 13/7-24/8) (B+G 1/5-30/9)
(Q+Z 📅)
5 AFGHJKMNPUXYZ
6 AEGJ(N 0,5km)RT

💬 Wonderfully peaceful here by the chestnut trees. A small campsite with good toilet facilities close to the owner's vineyards. The village of Laurac-en-Vivarais is close by and there is a supermarket 4 km away. No noisy evening entertainment, therefore quiet.

🚗 A7 exit Montélimar-Nord direction Le Teil/Aubenas. At Le Teil N102 to Aubenas. Follow the D104 direction Alès from there. The campsite is beyond Prends-Toi-Gardes to the right.

Lavilledieu
D24 D5 D579 D103
CC
D104 D4
Les Vans Saint-Alban-Auriolles

CC € **15** 1/4-29/6 1/9-29/9 📐 N 44°30'14'' E 4°17'40''

Le Bourg-d'Oisans, F-38520 / Rhône-Alpes (Isère)

🔥 🤿 iD **2158**

▲ Camping RCN Belledonne★★★★
🏠 Rochetailleé
☎ +31 034-3745090
📠 +33 (0)4-76791295
� 11/5 - 2/10
@ reserveringen@rcn.fr

4ha 175**T**(80-140m²) 10A

1 ACD**F**IJKLMPQ
2 GRSVXY
3 BGHJM**N**RU
4 (A 1/7-30/8) (C+H 15/5-31/8)
LN(Q+R �) (T 1/7-31/8)
(U+V+X+Z ☿)
5 **AB**CEFGIJKLMNOPRUVWZ
6 ABEGH**I**J**K**(N 8km)OV

💬 A spacious campsite with extensive facilities. Lovely views from the marked out pitches. The site is located in a mountainous landscape. Thanks to its location at the beginning of a valley (l'Eau d'Olle), the park-like grounds are level and easy accessible. A large number of trees provide plenty of shaded areas.

🚗 D1091 Grenoble-Briançon. In Rochetaillée turn right towards Allemont (D526). Campsite is on the right after 500 metres and is signposted.

Saint-Martin-d'Uriage
Allemond
D111
Alpe d'Huez
D1091
D211
D526

CC € **15** 11/5-5/6 8/6-6/7 25/8-1/10

📐 N 45°6'53'' E 6°0'32''

Le Bourg-d'Oisans, F-38520 / Rhône-Alpes (Isère)

⛷ 🔥 🤿 iD **2159**

▲ La Cascade★★★★
🏠 route de l'Alpe d'Huez
☎ +33 (0)4-76800242
📠 +33 (0)4-76802263
☿ 1/1 - 30/9, 15/12 - 31/12
@ lacascade@wanadoo.fr

2,5ha 128**T**(90-100m²) 16A

1 ACDGIJKLMPQ
2 CGKRSTVWXY
3 BGHJNRU**W**
4 (**A** 1/7-31/8)
(C+H 15/5-15/9)
(Q+T+V 1/7-31/8) (Z ☿)
5 **AB**DFGIJKLMNOPUVWZ
6 ABEGIK(N 1,2km)OTV

💬 A campsite on the first bend of the climb up l'Alpe d'Huez, well known from the Tour de France. The pitches are separated by hedges. Le Bourg d'Oisans just a stroll away. The l'Alpe d'Huez ski bus stops in front of the site.

🚗 Route D1091 Grenoble-Briançon. Turn left as you leave Le Bourg-d'Oisans via ring road direction l'Alpe d'Huez, the campsite 500 metres on the right.

Allemond
D111
D1091
CC
Le Bourg-d'Oisans
D526

CC € **17** 1/1-30/5 10/6-28/6 22/8-29/9

📐 N 45°3'51'' E 6°2'21''

Le Bourg-d'Oisans, F-38520 / Rhône-Alpes (Isère)

🔥 🤿 ❀ iD **2160**

▲ Sites & Pays. à la Rencontre du Soleil★★★★★
🏠 route de l'Alpe d'Huez
☎ +33 (0)4-76791222
📠 +33 (0)4-76802637
☿ 1/5 - 30/9
@ contact@rencontresoleil.fr

1,5ha 48**T**(80-120m²) 10A CEE

1 ACDFIJKLMPQ
2 CGKRSTVXY
3 BGHIJMNR
4 (C+D 1/5-20/9) (Q 20/5-31/8)
(T+U+V+X 15/5-15/9)
(Y 20/5-3/9) (Z 15/5-15/9)
5 **AB**DEFGIJKLMNPUVWY
6 AEGI**K**(N 0,8km)OV

💬 Well maintained grounds 1.3 km from le Bourg d'Oisans. The many flower borders and views of the surrounding mountain ranges make this a suitable base for your holiday.

🚗 D1091 Grenoble-Briançon. After leaving the Le Bourg-d'Oisans ring road, take direction L'Alpe-d'Huez on roundabout. Well signposted.

Allemond
D111
D1091
CC
Le Bourg-d'Oisans
D526

CC € **19** 1/5-1/6 9/6-30/6 18/8-29/9

📐 N 45°3'54'' E 6°2'24''

Le Crestet, F-07270 / Rhône-Alpes (Ardèche)

♿ iD 2161

🏠 Les Roches****
☎ +33 (0)4-75062020
FAX +33 (0)4-75062623
🗓 1/4 - 15/9
@ camproches@nordnet.fr

4ha 50T(100m²) 6-10A CEE

1 ACD**G**IJKLMPS
2 ABJKLMNRTVXY
3 BCGHJNRU**W**
4 (B+H+Q+R 🗝) (T 1/7-30/8)
(U+V 1/6-30/8)
(X+Y 1/7-30/8) (Z 1/6-30/8)
5 **AB**EFGJLNPUVXZ
6 DEG(N 5km)RTV

💬 A quiet family campsite in the heart of the rural Ardèche with wonderful views of the Doux valley. Panoramic restaurant.

🚗 From Tournon D534 direction Lamastre. Do not drive to village of Le Crestet but stay on the road till you see the Les Roches camping or restaurant sign on the right, then follow signs.

Lemps
Étables
D532
D236
D534
Désaignes
CC
D533
D2
D578
D14

CC € 15 1/4-6/7 26/8-14/9

🏖 N 45°0'38'' E 4°37'25''

Le Grand-Bornand, F-74450 / Rhône-Alpes (Haute-Savoie)

⛷ ♿ 📶 iD 2162

🏠 l'Escale***
🏢 33 chemin du Plein Air
☎ +33 (0)4-50022069
FAX +33 (0)4-50023604
🗓 18/5 - 23/9, 21/12 - 8/4
@ contact@campinglescale.com

3,2ha 142T(80-100m²) 2-10A CEE

1 AC**G**IJKLMOPQ
2 CGJKRTVWX
3 B**F**GHJKLM**Q**RU**W**
4 (C 1/7-27/8) (F+H 🗝) K
(Q 9/7-27/8,23/12-31/12)
(U+Y+Z 🗝)
5 **AB**DEFGIJKLOPRUWXYZ
6 ACDEGHIJ(N 0,2km)O**P**TV

💬 Campsite 150m from the centre of Le Grand-Bornand. Combined 240 m² indoor and outdoor swimming pool. Restaurant is located in an old farmhouse in traditional Savoy style. New toilet facilities and free wifi.

🚗 A41 exit Annecy-Nord, then direction Thônes. In Thônes head for St. Jean-de-Sixt. Go towards Le Grand-Bornand at the roundabout. Turn right before the centre towards 'Vallée du Bouchet'. Campsite 1 km on the right.

D4
CC
La Clusaz
Thônes
Manigod
D909
D12

CC € 19 28/3-7/4 18/5-6/7 31/8-22/9

🏖 N 45°56'26'' E 6°25'40''

Le Grand-Serre, F-26530 / Rhône-Alpes (Drôme)

♿ 📶 iD 2163

🏠 Le Grand Cerf****
🏢 3 Impasse du Grand Cerf
☎ +33 (0)4-75688614
🗓 7/4 - 30/9
@ contact@campingdrome.fr

2ha 60T(80-160m²) 10A

1 ACD**G**IJKLMPST
2 AGIJKLRVWXY
3 BDGHJKMNR
4 (C 28/4-30/9) (G 29/4-1/10)
(Q+T+U+V+X+Y 1/7-31/8)
(Z 🗝)
5 **A**FGIJKLMNPUWZ
6 ACEGJ(N 1km)OV

💬 A peaceful campsite with marked out pitches, partly shaded. As a guest of the campsite you can enjoy free swimming (heated pool from 28/04), play tennis or borrow a mountain bike (6 available). Children under 6 free until 22/6 and from 26/8.

🚗 N7 Valence-Vienne. In Sablon take D519 direction Beaurepaire. Right here towards Hauterive. Then D51 to Le Grand-Serre. Well signposted.

Beaurepaire
Saint-Siméon-de-Bressieux
D1
D51
CC
D20
D71
D538

CC € 11 7/4-12/7 30/8-29/9

🏖 N 45°16'17'' E 5°6'6''

Le Poët-Célard, F-26460 / Rhône-Alpes (Drôme) 👫 📶 iD 2164

🏔 Le Couspeau****
📧 Quartier Bellevue
☎ +33 (0)4-75533014
🔓 27/4 - 7/9
@ info@couspeau.fr

8ha 70**T**(100-180m²) 10A CEE

1 ACD**G**IJKLMPST
2 IJKRTVWXY
3 BGHJLNRU
4 (C+E+H 🔓) JM
　(Q+R+T+U+V+X+Y+Z 🔓)
5 **AB**EFGIJKLMNOPQUWXYZ
6 ACEGH**K**(N 4km)OTV

💬 A beautiful, terraced campsite with breathtaking views of the valley and the Vercors hills beyond. You can enjoy the wonderful Provençale sun and ambiance in the aqua park.

🚗 A7 exit 15 in Valence-Sud. D111 Valence-Crest. In Crest direction Dieulefit, Bourdeaux. In Bourdeaux dir. Dieulefit. Signposted south of Bourdeaux.

D6
Charols CC
La Bégude-de-Mazenc
D540 Dieulefit
D538

🆑 € **15** 27/4-30/6 2/9-6/9 　📐 N 44°35'47'' E 5°6'40''

Lépin-le-Lac, F-73610 / Rhône-Alpes (Savoie) ♿ 📶 iD 2165

🏔 Le Curtelet***
📧 Lac d'Aiguebelette
☎ +33 (0)4-79441122
🔓 14/4 - 30/9
@ campinglecurtelet@gmail.com

1,3ha 83**T**(90-110m²) 4-10A

1 ACG**G**IJKLPQ
2 DFLMRVWXY
3 BNR**WZ**
4 (Q 1/6-15/9) (T+Z 🔓)
5 **AB**FGJLNPUWZ
6 EGK**K**(N 1km)T

💬 A peaceful family campsite with direct access to Lake Aiguebelette, the warmest lake in France, with views of the mountains. Reliable toilet facilities.

🚗 A43 Lyon-Chambéry, exit Lac d'Aiguebelette. After péage turn right at roundabout, after 300 metres left at roundabout direction St. Alban-de-Montbel. Via south bank towards Lépin-le-Lac. Campsite on the left of the road on D921d.

D1516
D916 D921 La Motte-Servolex
D916 A CC Chambéry
A43
D912
D82
D1006

🆑 € **15** 14/4-6/7 27/8-29/9 7=6 　📐 N 45°32'23'' E 5°46'45''

Lépin-le-Lac, F-73610 / Rhône-Alpes (Savoie) ♿ 📶 iD 2166

🏔 Les Peupliers**
📧 D921d / Lac d'Aiguebelette
☎ +33 (0)4-79360048
🔓 1/4 - 31/10
@ info@camping-lespeupliers.net

3ha 114**T**(70-100m²) 6A CEE

1 ACD**G**IJKLMPRS
2 ADFLMRVWXY
3 AGNRU**WZ**
4 (Q+T+Z 🔓)
5 **AB**FGIJKLMNPUVS
6 ACE**K**(N 3km)O

💬 Extended grounds that slope gently down to Lake Aiguebelette. Swimming and fishing permitted via a direct access. The pitches are large, shaded and marked out by hedges. In the vicinity: paragliding, rock climbing, canoeing, kayaking, mountain biking and cycling. Wifi (not free).

🚗 A43 Lyon-Chambéry. Exit 'Lac Aiguebelette'. After the toll station left at the roundabout towards Aiguebelette and Lépin-le-Lac. Campsite after about 9 or 10 km on the right.

D1516
D916 D921 La Motte-Servolex
CC Chambéry
A43
D912
D82
D1006

🆑 € **15** 1/4-30/6 27/8-30/10 7=6 　📐 N 45°32'19'' E 5°47'57''

Les Abrets, F-38490 / Rhône-Alpes (Isère)

♿ 🛜 **iD** (2167)

🏕 Le Coin Tranquille★★★★
✉ 6 chemin des Vignes (Le Véroud)
☎ +33 (0)4-76321348
📠 +33 (0)4-76374067
📅 31/3 - 1/11
@ contact@coin-tranquille.com

10ha 176T(100-120m²) 6-10A

1 ACD**G**IJKLMPRS
2 FKRVWXY
3 BHJKNRU
4 (C 1/5-1/10) (G 15/5-30/9)
(Q+S 🔑) (T 9/7-19/8) (U 🔑)
(V 1/5-15/9) (X+Y+Z 🔑)
5 **AB**DFGIJKLMNOPUWZ
6 CEGJ(N 2,5km)OTV

💬 Welcoming family campsite with flowers and green fields all around. There is a heated swimming pool, a good restaurant and modern and well-maintained toilet facilities.

🚗 A43 Lyon-Chambéry. Exit 10 Les Abrets. Left on roundabout to centre. Then dir. Pont-de-Beauvoisin (N6). After 1.5 km campsite is indicated on left. Cross miniature train tracks and stay on road 1 km.

D16 | D1516
Saint-Jean-de-Soudain | D916
A43 | D916 A
D73 | D203
D1075 | D1006

CC € **17** 31/3-7/7 25/8-31/10 7=6

⛰ N 45°32'29'' E 5°36'29''

Les Contamines-Montjoie, F-74170 / Rhône-Alpes (Haute-Savoie)

⛷ ♿ 🛜 **iD** (2168)

🏕 Le Pontet★★★
✉ 2485 rte de Notre Dame
de la Gorge
☎ +33 (0)4-50470404
📅 1/1 - 23/9, 22/12 - 31/12
@ campinglepontet74@orange.fr

2,8ha 150T(90-120m²) 2-10A

1 ACGIJKLMOPQ
2 ACDGKLMRTVWXY
3 AGH**MNOPQ**RUW**Z**
4 (Q+R 🔑) (T+V+X 1/6-23/9)
5 **AB**DFGIJKLMNPUVWZ
6 CEG**J**(N 2,5km)OTV

💬 A campsite for winter and summer. You can already take mountain walks in April. Ideal base for touring Mont Blanc.

🚗 A40 exit St. Gervais, direction St. Gervais-centre. Another 9 km past the centre to Les Contamines. Site is located 3 km beyond the centre on the left of the D902, the Route de Notre Dame de la Gorge.

Saint-Gervais-les-Bains
Megève
D1212
CC

CC € **17** 1/4-9/7 27/8-22/9

⛰ N 45°48'9'' E 6°43'19''

Les Marches/Montmélian, F-73800 / Rhône-Alpes (Savoie)

♿ 🛜 **iD** (2169)

🏕 La Ferme du Lac★★★
✉ Lac St. André
☎ +33 (0)4-79281348
📅 15/4 - 15/9
@ campinglafermedulac@
wanadoo.fr

2,6ha 70T(90-200m²) 10A CEE

1 ACD**G**IJKLMPQ
2 FGNRTUVWXY
3 ACF**G**HJRU**W**
4 (C 1/6-15/9) (Q 1/7-30/8)
(T 1/5-15/9)
5 **A**FGIJKLMNOPQRUVZ
6 CDEGJ(N 0,3km)OV

NEW

💬 Lively campsite in green surroundings at the foot of Mont Granier. There is a heated pool and a decent toilet block.

🚗 On the D1090 Chambéry-Grenoble in Les Marches, exit in the bend to Lac St. André. Then continue 500m further on.

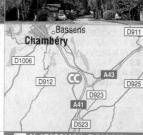

Bassens | D911
Chambéry
D1006
D912 | CC | A43 | D925
D923
A41
D523

CC € **15** 15/4-30/6 1/9-14/9

⛰ N 45°29'46'' E 5°59'35''

Les Ollières-sur-Eyrieux, F-07360 / Rhône-Alpes (Ardèche) ♿ 📶 **iD** (2170)

🏕 Camping Mas de Champel★★★★
📧 135 La Dolce Via
☎ +33 (0)4-75662323
📅 21/4 - 14/9
@ masdechampel@wanadoo.fr

4ha 56**T**(100-130m²) 10A CEE

1 ACD**F**IJKLMPS
2 ACGJKRSTVWXY
3 AGHJKNRU**W**X
4 (C+G 1/5-15/9) **KN**
　(Q 1/5-15/9) (R 📅)
　(T+U+V+Y 1/5-10/9) (Z 📅)
5 **AB**DEFGIJKLMNOPUVWXZ
6 AEGJ(N 0,4km)V

💬 Located along the River l'Eyrieux. Includes terraces with magnificent views over the mountains. Facilities are housed in a beautiful old farmhouse. Wellness room with jacuzzi and sauna. Restaurant with panorama terrace.

🚗 From the A7, exit Valence-Sud. Then D86 to La Voulte. Past La Voulte take the D120 to Les Ollières-sur-Eyrieux. From the south, A7 exit Loriol. Then N304 to Privas. Then the D2 and D120 to Les Ollières-sur-Eyrieux.

CC € **17** 21/4-6/7 25/8-13/9 7=6, 14=11　📐 N 44°48'26'' E 4°36'54''

Les Vans, F-07140 / Rhône-Alpes (Ardèche) ♿ 📶 **iD** (2171)

🏕 Lou Rouchetou★★★
📧 Chassagnes
☎ +33 (0)4-75373313
📅 1/4 - 30/9
@ info@rouchetou.com

5ha 98**T**(80-100m²) 10A CEE

1 A**G**IJKLMPST
2 ACNORTVXY
3 AGHLNRU**W**X
4 (B+G 1/5-15/9)
　(Q+R+U+V+Y+Z 1/4-23/9)
5 **A**DEFGIJKLMNOPQUZ
6 ACDEG**K**(N 1,5km)ORTV

💬 A campsite in attractive surroundings 3 km from Les Vans. Plenty of space in the grounds and by the river. Swim and sail in the Chassezac. Lovely swimming pool and good restaurant open all season.

🚗 A7, exit 17 Montélimar-Nord. Then dir. Le Teil/Aubenas. In Le Teil Nioz dir. Aubenas. Then N104 dir. Alès. ± 3 km past Joyeuse turn right dir. Les Vans/Chambonas, D104A. Then D295 dir. Chassagnes. Follow road and in big bend turn right then left. Use SatNav coordinates.

CC € **17** 1/4-6/7 25/8-29/9　📐 N 44°24'38'' E 4°10'16''

Luc-en-Diois, F-26310 / Rhône-Alpes (Drôme) ♿ 📶 **iD** (2172)

🏕 Les Foulons★★★
📧 rue de la Piscine
☎ +33 (0)4-75213614
📅 31/3 - 31/10
@ contact@
　camping-luc-en-diois.com

1,8ha 100**T**(80-130m²) 10A CEE

1 ACDGIJKLMO**P**ST
2 CGKLRVVWXY
3 ABGHJKL**M**NRU**W**X
4 (**C**+H 15/6-15/9)
　(Q 10/4-31/10)
　(T+U+V+X+Z 24/6-20/8)
5 **AB**GIJKLMNPUXZ
6 ADEG**J**(N 0,6km)OTV

💬 A campsite with sun and shade on the Drôme. Good toilet facilities. Tennis court. Wonderful trips out from the campsite in the beautiful mountains and old villages. Recharging point for electric bikes. (E-) bikes for rent.

🚗 On the D93 from Die to Gap, in Luc-en-Diois on the west side of the road. Drive to the centre then follow signs.

CC € **13** 31/3-7/7 26/8-30/10　📐 N 44°36'56'' E 5°26'46''

Lugrin, F-74500 / Rhône-Alpes (Haute-Savoie)   ♿ 🛜 iD (2173)

🏕 La Vieille-Eglise***
✉ 53 route des Prés Parrau
☎ +33 (0)4-50760195
📠 +33 (0)4-50761312
📅 10/4 - 20/10
@ campingvieilleeglise@wanadoo.fr

2ha 73T(100-120m²) 4-10A CEE

1 ACD**G**IJKLPQ
2 JKLRVWX
3 AG**Q**RU
4 (C+H 1/5-30/9)
　　(Q+R 15/6-15/9)
　　(V+Z 1/6-30/9)
5 **AB**DFGIJKMNPRUWXYZ
6 AEGH**K**(N 0,8km)RTV

💬 A friendly, peaceful, shaded campsite with a heated swimming pool. Water supply, drainage and electricity on all pitches. Close to a supermarket, shops, Lake Geneva and Evian-les-Bains. Ideal for visiting the Swiss side of the lake.

🚗 From Evian-les-Bains on D1005 by the lake to the east. The campsite is clearly signposted near Lugrin.

CC € **17** 10/4-8/7 26/8-19/10 7=6, 14=12, 21=18　　　📷 N 46°24'2'' E 6°38'48''

Thonon-les-Bains
9 | A9
D1005
N5
D32
D26
D902 | D22

Lus-la-Croix-Haute, F-26620 / Rhône-Alpes (Drôme)   🛜 iD (2174)

🏕 Champ la Chèvre***
✉ Le Village
☎ +33 (0)4-92585014
📅 7/4 - 7/10
@ champlachevre@orange.fr

3,7ha 85T(80-150m²) 6A CEE

1 ABCD**G**IJKLM**P**RS
2 IJKLRXY
3 ABGHJRU**W**
4 (A 1/7-31/8) (C+E+H 📷) K
　　(Q+T+U+V 📷) (X 24/4-15/9)
　　(Y 📷) (Z 24/4-15/9)
5 **A**DEFGIJLMNOPQRUWZ
6 CDEI**K**(N 0,2km)OTV

💬 Beautiful peaceful campsite, with spacious feel. All around are mountains, shopping 200m from the campsite. Lovely restaurant. Perfect resting place for campers on their way south or returning home. 500 metres from the N1075 but you don't hear it. Also very suitable for longer stays.

🚗 From Grenoble N75 direction Sisteron. Past Col de la Croix-Haute, enter the town of Lus-la-Croix-Haute, then follow the signs. Not the first campsite. Drive on to village.

CC € **15** 7/4-7/7 25/8-6/10　　　📷 N 44°39'52'' E 5°42'26''

D120
Menée
D539
CC
D937
La Haute-Beaume
D1075
D320

Lussas, F-07170 / Rhône-Alpes (Ardèche)   🛜 iD (2175)

🏕 Ludo Camping***
✉ 70 chemin de Bourgeon
☎ +33 (0)4-84800189
📅 1/5 - 30/9
@ contact@ludocamping.com

6ha 143T(100-160m²) 10A CEE

1 ACD**G**IJKLMPST
2 CJNORTVWXY
3 ABGHJRU**W**
4 (A 16/5-24/9) (C 📷)
　　(H 1/6-24/9) (Q+R 📷)
　　(T+U+V+X+Z 13/5-17/9)
5 **AB**DEFGIJKLMNPUWX
6 CEGJ(N 2km)V

💬 This campsite is located by a stream. The level part of the site is pleasantly shaded. The terraced section has larger pitches. Toilet facilities in the lower grounds are new. New owner.

🚗 Via the A7, exit Montelimar-Nord dir. Le Teil. Then via Villeneuve-de-Berg (dir. Aubenas) to Lavilledieu. Via D224 to Lussas/Darbres. Turn right before the village.

Vals-les-Bains
Aubenas
D578
CC
D103
N102
D104 | D579
D107

CC € **17** 1/5-6/7 25/8-29/9 7=6, 14=11　　　📷 N 44°36'18'' E 4°28'17''

Lyon/Dardilly, F-69570 / Rhône-Alpes (Rhône) 👤♿🛜 iD 2176

🏕 Camping de Lyon****
allée du Camping International
☎ +33 (0)4-78356455
⏱ 19/2 - 31/12
@ lyon@camping-indigo.com

6ha 165T(80m²) 10A CEE

1 ACD**G**IJKLMPST
2 FGIJRTVXY
3 ABGNRU
4 (C+H 30/4-20/9) (Q 🔒)
  (T+U+V+X 1/6-31/8) (Z 🔒)
5 **AB**DFGIJKLMNOPUZ
6 CFGJ(N 0,5km)V

💬 A municipal campsite located in a landscaped park on the outskirts of Lyon. Ideal for a stopover on the way to your holiday destination or to visit the city of Lyon, included on the UNESCO World Heritage List. Tourist information centre, swimming pool, TV room on the site.

🚗 From Paris: A6 Lyon - Villefranche-sur-Saône. Exit 33. Follow the 'Complexe Touristique' and/or 'Camping Porte de Lyon' signs.

CC € **17** 19/2-28/6 3/9-1/12 🧭 N 45°49'12'' E 4°45'39''

Marlens, F-74210 / Rhône-Alpes (Haute-Savoie) 👤♿🛜 iD 2177

🏕 Champ Tillet***
D1508
☎ +33 (0)4-50443374
📠 +33 (0)4-50662344
⏱ 1/4 - 30/10
@ duchamptillet@wanadoo.fr

3ha 104T(80-110m²) 6-10A CEE

1 ACG**HIJKLMPRS**
2 GRSTVWXY
3 BF**G**JKR
4 (C+H 15/5-15/9) J(Q+U 🔒)
  (V 1/7-30/8) (Y+Z 🔒)
5 **AB**DEFGIJKLMNPUWZ
6 ACFGIJ(N 4km)TV

💬 Level, open grounds. Many campers choose this campsite to avoid the busy campsites around the lake. Shopping centre 4 km away. The campsite has a good restaurant.

🚗 D1508 Annecy-Albertville. The campsite is located along the D1508, 4 km past Faverges on the right side. Clearly signposted.

CC € **17** 1/4-6/7 25/8-29/10 🧭 N 45°45'43'' E 6°20'12''

Marsanne, F-26740 / Rhône-Alpes (Drôme) 👫♿🛜 iD 2178

🏕 Les Bastets****
335 chemin du Camping
☎ +33 (0)4-75903503
📠 +33 (0)4-75903505
⏱ 1/4 - 30/9
@ contact@campinglesbastets.com

3,5ha 67T(80-120m²) 10A CEE

1 ACDGIJKLMO**P**
2 FJKRSTVWXY
3 ABF**G**HJN**QR**U
4 (C+Q+R 🔒) (T 1/5-7/9)
  (U 🔒) (V+X+Y 1/5-7/9)
  (Z 🔒)
5 **AB**DEFGIJKLMNOPUWXZ
6 ACEGJ**K**(N 2km)V

💬 A terraced campsite with stunning views of the Plaine de la Valdaine. A unique swimming pool where you can look over the side into the valley. The new owners will do all they can to ensure you enjoy a wonderful holiday. Plenty of cycling opportunities in the Drôme Provençale!

🚗 A7, exit 17 Montélimar-Nord. Direction Tourette then towards La Coucourde. Left in centre towards Sauzet. Then direction Condillac/Marsanne.

CC € **17** 1/4-7/7 26/8-29/9 🧭 N 44°39'29'' E 4°53'28''

Massignieu-de-Rives, F-01300 / Rhône-Alpes (Ain)　♿ 🛜 **iD** (2179)

🏕 Lac du Lit du Roi****
📧 La Tuillière
☎ +33 (0)4-79421203
🗓 31/3 - 23/9
@ info@camping-savoie.com

2,5ha 84T(80-120m²) 10A

1 ACD**G**IJLM**P**R
2 DJLMRTVWXY
3 AGHJKMRU**W**Z
4 (B 15/5-15/9) (G 15/5-19/9)
M(Q+R 1/5-31/8)
(U+V+X+Z 1/6-31/8)
5 **AB**FGIJKLMNPUVWXYZ
6 EGJ(N 7km)OV

💬 Extensive grounds with three toilet blocks. Almost all pitches have views of the lake that is connected to the Rhône. There is also a small swimming pool. 300m from a small harbour with a slipway.

🚌 A40 direction Genève. Exit 11 Eloise. RN508 direction Frangy. D992 direction Culoz. Continue on D992 for a further 12 km past Culoz. Over the bridge to Massignieu-de-Rives. Well signposted.

D904　D1504　D921　D991　D914　Belley **CC**　D992　D48　A41　D10　D1516　**Aix-les-Bains**

CC € **17** 31/3-6/7 24/8-22/9 7=6, 14=11　🏕 N 45°46'7'' E 5°46'11''

Matafelon-Granges, F-01580 / Rhône-Alpes (Ain)　🛜 **iD** (2180)

🏕 Les Gorges de l'Oignin***
📧 724 rue du Lac
☎ +33 (0)4-74768097
🗓 15/4 - 29/9
@ camping.lesgorgesdeloignin@
orange.fr

2,6ha 128T 10A CEE

1 ACD**G**IJKLO**P**Q
2 DJKLMRTUVWXY
3 ABD**F**GHNRU**W**Z
4 (C+G 1/6-20/9)
(Q+R+T+U+V+X+Z 🔑)
5 **AB**DFGIJKLMNOPUXZ
6 AEGJ(N 3km)OTV

💬 A lovely modern and spacious terraced campsite with heated swimming pools by a small reservoir. The campsite has wonderful views. The Gorges de l'Ain are close by. For a day out, Geneva or Lyon, the Jura or the bird park at Villars-les-Dombes.

🚌 From Bourg-en-Bresse in the direction of Nantua, turn left at roundabout and take D18 as far as Matafelon, follow the signs. Matafelon is not signposted coming from Oyonax.

D109 E1　D436　D117　D31　D109　Oyonnax　D936 **CC**　D13　D18　A404　D42　Montréal-la-Cluse　A40

CC € **17** 15/4-6/7 25/8-28/9 7=6, 14=12　🏕 N 46°15'19'' E 5°33'26''

Mayres-Savel, F-38350 / Rhône-Alpes (Isère)　🛜 **iD** (2181)

🏕 Camping de Savel**
📧 D116
☎ 📠 +33 (0)4-76811479
🗓 1/4 - 31/10
@ contact@camping-savel.com

7ha 100T(100-120m²) 12A CEE

1 ACD**G**IJKLMPST
2 DJKLMNORTVWXY
3 ABGHJNRU**VW**Z
4 (B 1/5-30/9) **LN**(Q 🔑)
(R 1/4-15/10) (T+U 1/5-15/9)
(V 1/7-31/8) (X 🔑)
(Z 1/5-15/9)
5 **AB**EFGIJKLMNPUXZ
6 ACDEGHI**K**OTV

💬 The campsite is located right by a lake. Swimming pool. Ample trees which give necessary shade. Large restaurant with spacious terrace with views of the mountains and lake. 3 km from the campsite is one of Europe's most beautiful footpaths, La Passerelle du Drac with a footbridge over the lake. Beautiful countryside.

🚌 Grenoble N85 dir. Vizille-La Mure. In La Mure, at the roundabout drive Mayres-Savel and 'Camping de Savel', then another 15 km to the campsite.

A51　D529　Monestier-de-Clermont　La Mure　D26　D26 A　**CC**　D34　Mens　D7　D526　D1075　D66　

CC € **13** 1/4-30/6 1/9-30/10　🏕 N 44°52'56'' E 5°41'16''

Menglon, F-26410 / Rhône-Alpes (Drôme)

♿ 🛜 **iD** (2182)

🏕 L'Hirondelle★★★★
📧 Bois de St. Ferréol
☎ +33 (0)4-75218208
📠 +33 (0)4-75218285
🗓 14/4 - 30/9
@ contact@campinghirondelle.com

14ha 102T(80-300m²) 6-10A CEE

1 ACDGIJKLMOPST
2 BCKLNRSTXY
3 BGHJKLN**OP**QRU**W**X
4 (**A** 9/7-2/9) (C+H 1/5-2/10) IJ
P(Q+R+T+U+V+X+Y+Z 🗝)
5 **AB**EFGIJKLMNOPQRUWZ
6 AEHI**K**(N 3km)ORTV

💬 The campsite forms part of the countryside (10 hectares of forest, river and open views of the fields). There is a lake nearby. Plenty to do for young and old. Lovely leisure pool. Plenty of pitches at the edge of the woods with views over fields and the mountains.

🚗 From Die D93 towards the south, road beside the Drôme, then left onto D539 direction Châtillon-en-Diois. D140 after St. Roman. Cross bridge. Campsite on the right.

CC € **17** 14/4-7/7 25/8-29/9   📐 N 44°40'53'' E 5°26'49''

Mens, F-38710 / Rhône-Alpes (Isère)

🛜 **iD** (2183)

🏕 Le Pré Rolland★★★
📧 rue de la Piscine
☎ +33 (0)4-76346580
🗓 21/4 - 30/9
@ contact@prerolland.fr

2,5ha 90T(100-200m²) 10A CEE

1 ACD**G**IJKLMPST
2 GKLRTVWXY
3 AGHJK**M**N**OP**RUW
4 (**A** 1/7-31/8) (C 1/6-31/8)
(H 29/6-31/8) J(Q 1/7-31/8)
(T 1/5-1/10) (U+Z 1/5-31/8)
5 **AB**FGIJKLMNPUVWZ
6 ACEG**K**(N 0,2km)TV

💬 A very peaceful campsite within walking distance of a village in rural, mountainous surroundings. Spacious pitches separated by low trees and bushes.

🚗 N75 Grenoble-Sisteron. At Clelles take D526 towards Mens. In Mens follow signs.

CC € **15** 21/4-30/6 1/9-29/9   📐 N 44°48'54'' E 5°44'56''

Meyras, F-07380 / Rhône-Alpes (Ardèche)

🛜 **iD** (2184)

🏕 Le Ventadour★★★
📧 213 route du Puy en Velay
☎ +33 (0)4-75941815
🗓 14/4 - 7/10
@ info@leventadour.com

3,5ha 115T(70-150m²) 10A

1 ACD**G**IJKLM**P**ST
2 ACMORTVWXY
3 AGHJNRU**W**X
4 (Q 🗝)
(R+T+U+V+X+Z 30/6-26/8)
5 **AB**CDFGJLMNPRUVZ
6 ACFGJ**K**(N 2km)OV

💬 A park-like location with a hospitable family. Ideal for sports or trips to cultural and natural surroundings. Between mountains and volcanoes on the River Ardèche. Private beach. Spacious shaded level pitches. Renovated heated toilets. Wifi everywhere.

🚗 A7 exit Montélimar-Nord dir. Le Teil-Aubenas. N102 to Aubenas. In Aubenas N102. After Pont de Labeaume campsite on your left. From Le Puy first follow N88, before Pradelles N102 dir. Aubenas. Campsite on the right.

CC € **17** 14/4-6/7 25/8-6/10 14=13, 21=19   📐 N 44°40'6'' E 4°17'0''

Mirabel-et-Blacons, F-26400 / Rhône-Alpes (Drôme)   ⚲ 🤚 📶 iD (2185)

🔺 Gervanne Camping****
🏢 Bellevue
☎ +33 (0)4-75400020
🗓 1/4 - 30/9
@ info@gervanne-camping.com

3,8ha 138T(90-157m²) 6A CEE

1 ACD**G**IJKLMOPST
2 CGORTVWXY
3 ABGHJKLNRU**W**X
4 (**A** 15/5-30/9) (Q+S ⊙)
   (C+H 1/5-30/9) (Q+S ⊙)
   (T+U+V+X+Y 1/5-30/9)
   (Z ⊙)
5 **AB**DEFGIJKLMNOPRUVWX
   YZ
6 CEGH**IJK**(N 0,1km)ORTV

💬 There are pitches: around the swimming pool and beside the Drôme. Abundant with beautiful trees. Nice walks along the Drôme. You can also go kayaking and swimming. A good starting point for exploring the Vercors and the Drôme Provençale. Picturesque villages (including Crest) a short distance away. Good restaurant.

🚗 A7 exit Valence dir. Crest D111. Before Crest dir. Die D164. 6 km past Crest left and continue to Mirabel-et-Blacons. Campsite signposted.

Montoison
Allex
Crest
CC Saillans
D93
D6
D538

CC € **17** 1/4-6/7 25/8-29/9   🏔 N 44°42'39'' E 5°5'23''

Mirabel-et-Blacons, F-26400 / Rhône-Alpes (Drôme)   🚶🚶 🍽 📶 iD (2186)

🔺 Val Drôme Soleil
🏢 830 chemin Sans Souci
☎ +33 (0)4-75400157
🗓 1/4 - 27/10
@ camping@valdromesoleil.com

NEW

11ha 120T(40-150m²) 6-10A CEE

1 A**F**IJKLMPST
2 BJKLTUVWXY
3 ABGHJRUV
4 (A+B+F+G ⊙) **N**
   (Q+R+T+U+V+X+Y+Z ⊙)
5 **AB**DFGIJKLMNOPRUWZ
6 EGH**IK**(N 3km)V

💬 A naturist campsite hidden in the mountains with fields of lavender and the vineyards of the Drôme. The pitches on these sloping grounds have sun or shade and often wonderful views. The daily grind is far away from this campsite which has a swimming pool, restaurant, bar, boules, sauna and walks. The sun shines in early and late season.

🚗 A1 exit Valence D111 towards Crest. After Crest D93 towards Die. After Mirabel-et-Blacons turn left onto D617 to Charsac-Montclair.

Crest
D93
CC Saillans
Puy-Saint-Martin
D538

CC € **19** 1/4-2/6 1/9-26/10   🏔 N 44°42'25'' E 5°8'0''

Mirmande, F-26270 / Rhône-Alpes (Drôme)   ⚲ 📶 iD (2187)

🔺 La Poche***
🏢 Quartier la Poche
☎ +33 (0)4-75630288
🗓 1/4 - 30/9
@ camping@la-poche.com

3,5ha 72T(80-140m²) 2-6A CEE

1 ACDGIJKLMPST
2 BCFJLRTVWXY
3 AGHJN**O**RU
4 (A 1/7-1/9) (C+G 1/5-1/10)
   (Q+R 1/5-15/9) (T 15/6-31/8)
   (Y 1/7-31/8) (Z 15/6-31/8)
5 **AB**EFGIJKMNOPUVWZ
6 EGIJ(N 6km)OV

💬 A little way from the motorway (7 km from the Route du Soleil), La Poche offers an oasis of peace in the countryside with, among other things, a beautiful swimming pool. Mirmande is at walking distance (3 km) and has been voted one of the most beautiful villages in Europe.

🚗 From north: A7 exit 16 Loriol, left dir. Loriol/Montélimar. After ± 2 km left dir. Mirmande. From south: A7 exit 17 Montélimar-Nord dir. Valence. After 2 km right dir. Mirmande and follow signs.

Livron-sur-Drôme
D111
D104
D93
Crest
D22
A7
CC
D538
D2
D86
N7
D6
D9

CC € **13** 1/4-7/7 25/8-29/9   🏔 N 44°41'13'' E 4°51'16''

Montbrison/Moingt, F-42600 / Rhône-Alpes (Loire) 👪 📶 iD (2188)

🏕 Municipal du Surizet***
📧 31 rue du Surizet
☎ +33 (0)4-77580830
📅 15/4 - 15/10
@ campingmunicipal@
ville-montbrison.fr

2,5ha 88T(100m²) 10-16A

1 ACGIJKLMOPQ
2 CGRVWXY
3 BGNRW
4 (B 15/5-15/10) (Q 10/6-15/9)
5 ABDGHIJKLMNPUVWZ
6 CEGK(N 3km)T

💬 This municipal campsite on the banks of a river offers attractive pitches in natural, peaceful surroundings. Practical, as it's close to the town centre and its shops. A warm welcome, it is the only campsite in the area.

🚗 In Montbrison direction St. Anthème, St. Étienne via D496. Follow signs on left. In the south side of Montbrison.

CC € **11** 15/4-30/6 1/9-14/10

N 45°35'29'' E 4°4'41''

Montferrat, F-38620 / Rhône-Alpes (Isère) ♿ 📶 iD (2189)

🏕 Détente et Clapotis****
📧 1578 rue des Chevaliers de l'An Mil
☎ +33 (0)4-76553394
📅 15/4 - 15/9
@ campingmontferrat@gmail.com

6ha 140T(70-110m²) 6-10A

1 AGIJKLMRS
2 ADGKLMNRVWX
3 BGHJNRWZ
4 (C+E+H 🔒) N
(Q+T+U+V+Z 🔒)
5 ACEFGIJKLMNPQSUZ
6 CDEGHJ(N 3km)V

💬 This campsite was completely reconstructed in 2016. The lake and private beach have been retained. The grounds with park-like details contains a partially covered swimming pool and a substantial restaurant.

🚗 From Voiron take the D1075 as far as Montferrat. Left in the village towards Lac de Paladru/camping D50/D50c. Well signposted.

CC € **17** 15/4-6/7 27/8-14/9

N 45°28'4'' E 5°33'31''

Montrevel-en-Bresse, F-01340 / Rhône-Alpes (Ain) ♿ 📶 iD (2190)

🏕 La Plaine Tonique****
📧 599 route d'Etrez
☎ +33 (0)4-74308052
📠 +33 (0)4-74308800
📅 25/4 - 2/9
@ contact@laplainetonique.com

15ha 380T(100m²) 10A CEE

1 ACDGIJKLMOPQ
2 ACDFGLRVXY
3 BGHJMNPQRUWZ
4 (B 1/7-2/9) (E 🔒)
(G 1/7-2/9) IJMN
(Q+R+T+U 9/7-20/8)
(X+Z 🔒)
5 ABEFGIJKLMNOPUWZ
6 CDEGHIK(N 0,8km)RTV

💬 A very large, lovely family campsite with a big leisure pool. Located by a large lake with plenty of watersports opportunities. Suitable for older children. Located in fairly level countryside, therefore suitable for cycle trips. Swimming shorts not allowed in the pool.

🚗 In Montrevel-en-Bresse take the D28 in the direction of Etrez/Marboz. Campsite on the left of the road.

CC € **19** 25/4-1/7 27/8-1/9

N 46°20'21'' E 5°8'12''

Murs-et-Gélignieux, F-01300 / Rhône-Alpes (Ain)

♿ 📶 **iD** (2191)

🏕 L'Île de la Comtesse★★★★
✉ route des Abrets
☎ +33 (0)4-79872333
📅 27/4 - 16/9
@ camping.comtesse@wanadoo.fr

3ha 60T(100-120m²) 6A CEE

1 ACD**G**IJLM**P**RS
2 CDFRSVWX
3 AGJKNRU**W**
4 (A 5/7-27/8) (C+H 🔲) JM (Q+S+T+U 🔲) (V 1/7-31/8) (X+Z 🔲)
5 **AB**FGJKLNPUWXYZ
6 CEGIK(N 1km)OV

💬 A friendly four star campsite located between a lake and mountain, close to Chambéry and Lyon. It has a swimming pool, children's pool and slide. The campsite is located on the unique 'Via Rhôna' cycle route. Many kilometres of cycling beside the Rhône. The snack bar, pizzeria and restaurant are only open at weekends in low season.

🚗 A43 Lyon-Chambéry, exit 10 Chimilin/Aoste, then on the B592 direction Belley. Campsite located on the right after the 2nd bridge.

CC €**17** 27/4-6/7 25/8-15/9

📍 N 45°38'23'' E 5°38'56''

Neydens, F-74160 / Rhône-Alpes (Haute-Savoie)

♿ 📶 ❀ **iD** (2192)

🏕 Sites & Paysages La Colombière★★★★
✉ 166 chemin Neuf
☎ +33 (0)4-50351314
📠 +33 (0)4-50351340
📅 28/3 - 31/10
@ la.colombiere@wanadoo.fr

2,3ha 69T(80-120m²) 10-16A

1 ACD**G**IJKLMPQ
2 FGKRUVWX
3 ABCGHIJKLNRU
4 (A 1/5-30/9) (C 1/6-15/9) (F 1/4-31/10) (G 1/6-15/9) K **LN**(Q 🔲) (R 15/6-15/9) (U 🔲) (V 1/7-31/8) (Y+Z 🔲)
5 **AB**DEFGIJKLMNOP**S**UWXYZ
6 ACDEGHK(N 0,3km)OQRTVW

💬 Pitches marked out by overgrowth. Peaceful location but close to Geneva. The warden organises guided visits to Geneva, also in low season (min. 6 participants). Indoor pool and excellent restaurant (open all year). Heated outdoor pool with children's section with slide and jacuzzi, also sauna and hammam.

🚗 From Lausanne follow signs to France. From Macon the A40. Exit St. Julien. Follow the green signs to Annecy, D1201 to the village Neydens/campsite.

CC €**19** 28/3-6/7 24/8-30/10

📍 N 46°7'11'' E 6°6'19''

Nyons, F-26110 / Rhône-Alpes (Drôme)

♿ 📶 **iD** (2193)

🏕 Les Clos★★★★
✉ route de Gap
☎ +33 (0)4-75262990
📠 +33 (0)4-75264944
📅 1/4 - 30/9
@ info@campinglesclos.com

2,2ha 82T(80-120m²) 10A

1 ABC**G**IJLPST
2 CJNOSTUVWXY
3 ABGHJNRUWX
4 (C 15/5-15/9) (G 1/7-24/8) (Q+R 🔲) (T+U 1/7-24/8)
5 **A**DFGIJKLMNOPUWXYZ
6 EGH**K**(N 1km)ORT

💬 At this campsite you will find peace, near to a river and surrounded by olive trees. At walking distance from Nyons, the centre of olives, apricots and wines. Bathing and fishing in the river and swimming in the pool. Swimming pool open and heated from 15 May to 15 September.

🚗 A7 exit Montelimar-Sud, towards Valréas/Nyons.

CC €**17** 1/4-30/6 19/8-29/9

📍 N 44°21'56'' E 5°9'14''

Nyons/Venterol/Novézan, F-26110 / Rhône-Alpes (Drôme)

🔥 📶 **iD** (2194)

🔺 Les Terrasses Provençales****
✉️ 450 route de Rousset
☎️ +33 (0)4-75279236
📅 31/3 - 30/9
@ lesterrassesprovencales@
gmail.com

2,5ha 69**T**(80-100m²) 10A CEE

1 ACG**I**JKLPST
2 JKRTUVWXY
3 BGHJKLRU
4 (C+Q 15/4-30/9) (R 🔑)
(T 15/4-30/9) (U+V+X 🔑)
(Z 15/4-30/9)
5 **A**BDFGIJKLMNPUWZ
6 CEGIJ(N 3km)OTV

💬 A terraced campsite with beautiful views of the mountains, vineyards, apricot and olive trees. The toilet facilities and swimming pool, with terrace and bar, are heated. Close to Mont Ventoux, Nyons, Vaison la Romaine and Orange.

🚗 Campsite located between Valréas and Nyons D538. From Valréas 3 km before Venterol.

CC € **15** 31/3-7/7 25/8-29/9

📐 N 44°24'30'' E 5°4'48''

Pelussin, F-42410 / Rhône-Alpes (Loire)

👫 📶 **iD** (2195)

🔺 Sites & Paysages
Bel'Epoque du Pilat***
✉️ 2 rte de la Vialle
☎️ +33 (0)4-74876660
📅 1/4 - 30/9
@ contact@camping-belepoque.fr

3,5ha 55**T**(50-150m²) 6A CEE

1 ACD**G**IJKLMPQ
2 BCIJKRTVXY
3 ABCGHJMRU**W**
4 (C 1/5-30/9) (Q 15/5-15/9)
(T+U 1/7-31/8) (Z 🔑)
5 **A**EFGJLNOPUW
6 EG**K**(N 1,5km)ORT

💬 A peaceful campsite 45 km south of Lyon. There are many marked footpaths and mountain bike trails in the Côte du Rhône wine area and the Pilat nature reserve. Heated pool from 1 May. Tennis courts.

🚗 A7, exit 10, Ampuis. On N86 direction Serrières, in Chavanay D7 to Pelussin. At roundabout follow D79 and signs. Do not follow GPS, use these directions.

CC € **15** 1/4-5/7 27/8-29/9 7=6, 14=12, 21=18

📐 N 45°24'50'' E 4°41'29''

Petichet/St. Théoffrey, F-38119 / Rhône-Alpes (Isère)

🔥 📶 **iD** (2196)

🔺 Ser Sirant***
✉️ Lac de Laffrey
☎️ +33 (0)4-76839197
📅 29/4 - 30/9
@ info@campingsersirant.com

2ha 87**T**(90-110m²) 10A

1 ACG**I**JKLMPQ
2 ADJKLMNRVWXY
3 ABGHJN**OP**RUW**Z**
4 (A 8/7-28/8)
(Q+R+T+U+V+X+Y+Z
1/5-30/9)
5 **AB**DEFGIJKLMNPQUWZ
6 ACEGIJ**K**(N 8km)TV

💬 A campsite right by a large lake where you can go rowing, surfing and sailing. It has the French quality hallmark 'Camping Qualité'. An active family campsite: activities during the day and relaxation in the evening. A wonderful area for (mountain) hiking, cycling and mountain biking.

🚗 N85 dir. Napoléon, 30 km south of Grenoble towards Gap. Turn left at traffic lights in village of Petichet. Follow signs.

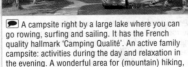

CC € **17** 29/4-6/7 25/8-29/9

📐 N 45°0'0'' E 5°46'39''

Piégros-la-Clastre, F-26400 / Rhône-Alpes (Drôme) 🛜 iD 2197

🏕 Camping les Chambers
📧 Les Chambers
☎ +33 (0)6-66303894
🔑 28/4 - 23/9
@ contact@leschambers.com

1,5ha 35T(80-150m²) 10A CEE

1 AGIJKLMO**P**ST
2 BCKNRTWXY
3 HJR**W**X
4 (Q 1/7-31/8) (T+V+Z 🔑)
5 A**I**JKLMNPU
6 AEG**K**(N 3km)V

💬 Welcoming, small-scale campsite with a lot of respect for nature. The little private beach on the Drôme river is perfect for swimming or just relaxing in the water. The owners welcome the guests with a number of original ideas. Only 8 km from the historical town of Crest with a hypermarché. Easily accessible by bike.

🚗 On D93 between Crest and Die at the Piégros-la-Clastre roundabout, follow signs to the campsite.

Montoison
Crest
D104   Saillans   D93
D538
D6

CC € **15** 28/4-6/7 1/9-22/9

🔼 N 44°41'52'' E 5°7'5''

Pont-de-Vaux, F-01190 / Rhône-Alpes (Ain) 👫 ♿ 🛜 iD 2198

🏕 Aux Rives du Soleil***
📧 D933A
☎ +33 (0)3-85303365
🔑 13/4 - 15/10
@ info@rivesdusoleil.com

7ha 160T(100m²) 6A

1 ACD**G**IJKLMOPQ
2 CFLMRTVWXY
3 ADF**G**HJKLNRU**W**X
4 (B+G 1/6-15/9) (Q+R 🔑)
   (T 1/6-30/9) (V 1/7-31/8)
   (Y+Z 🔑)
5 **AB**EFGIJKMNPUWZ
6 ACEGJ(N 3km)OV

💬 Spacious natural campsite on the banks of the Saône, suitable for cycling, walking and fishing. Separate overnight terrain.

🚗 From the north: A6, exit 27 Tournus. From the south: A6, exit Mâcon. Mâcon-Nord. Then the D906 direction Pont-de-Vaux. At roundabout Fleurville over the Saône. Campsite located on the Saône.

D14   N6
D56
D975
D933
D82   A6
D15   CC   D2
Saint-Martin-
Belle-Roche
Hurigny   D26

CC € **17** 13/4-2/7 1/9-14/10

🔼 N 46°26'49'' E 4°53'56''

Pont-de-Vaux, F-01190 / Rhône-Alpes (Ain) 👫 ♿ 🛜 iD 2199

🏕 Champ d'Été****
📧 Base de Loisirs
☎ +33 (0)3-85239610
🔑 24/3 - 13/10
@ info@camping-champ-dete.com

3,5ha 108T(80-100m²) 10A CEE

1 ACD**G**IJKLM**P**Q
2 DGLMRUVXY
3 AGHJKLNPRU**VW**
4 (C 1/7-31/8) (F+H 🔑) IJ**KLN**
   (Q 🔑) (R 1/6-31/8)
   (T 1/7-31/8) (Z 1/6-15/9)
5 **AB**EFGIJKLPUWXYZ
6 ACDEGIJ**K**(N 1km)V

💬 This quiet campsite is located in park-like surroundings, at walking distance from the vibrant village of Pont-de-Vaux, on a large fishing lake, beside the municipal pool (free entrance). The campsite is not far from the A6.

🚗 At Fleurville (D906) over the Saône to Pont-de-Vaux (D933). In Pont-de-Vaux follow Base-de-Loisirs and camping signs. Use GPS coordinates.

D56   D12
D906   D933   D975
D82   Saint-Trivier-de-
Courtes   D2
D15   A6
D26
Sancé

CC € **15** 24/3-6/7 24/8-12/10

🔼 N 46°25'46'' E 4°56'0''

Pont-de-Vaux, F-01190 / Rhône-Alpes (Ain)

♦ ⏚ 🛜 iD **2200**

🏕 Les Ripettes***
✉ 283 route des Ripettes
☎ +33 (0)3-85306658
🔓 1/4 - 30/9
@ info@camping-les-ripettes.com

2,5ha 55T(150-400m²) 10A CEE

1 ACD**G**IJKLOPQ
2 RUVXY
3 AGHJR
4 (B 15/5-15/9) (Q 🔧)
　(T 1/6-15/9)
5 **AB**GIJKLMNPUVWX
6 ADEGJ(N 2,5km)

💬 A lovely, quiet and friendly campsite with very spacious pitches just 4 km from the town of Pont-de-Vaux. The campsite is expertly run and is always kept perfectly clean. Cycle routes close by.

🚗 At Fleureville D906 cross the Saône to Pont-de-Vaux (D933). In Pont-de-Vaux dir. St. Trivier-de-Courtes. (D2). Campsite on the left 4 km past St. Bénigne next to the water tower.

CC € 15 1/4-6/7 26/8-29/9

📐 N 46°26'40'' E 4°58'50''

Pradons/Ruoms, F-07120 / Rhône-Alpes (Ardèche)

👫 ⏚ 🛜 iD **2201**

🏕 Camping de Laborie***
✉ 780 route de Ruoms
☎ +33 (0)4-75891837
🔓 7/4 - 23/9
@ contact@campingdelaborie.com

3ha 68T(100-150m²) 6-10A CEE

1 ACDGIJKLMOPST
2 BCNOPRTVXY
3 AGHJNRU**W**X
4 (C+H 🔧) K(Q 🔧)
　(R 1/5-31/8) (T 1/5-15/9)
　(V 4/7-25/8) (Z 🔧)
5 **AB**EFGJKMNOPQUWZ
6 AEGJ**K**(N 2,0km)OV

💬 Campsite located on the Ardèche with a beach. De Laborie is situated on the road to Ruoms and Vallon-Pont-d'Arc, two tourist villages with country markets. Nature and environment are held in high esteem. Very well-maintained. Playful children's water park. 30 minutes free wifi every 6 hours.

🚗 A7, exit Montélimar-Nord. Then dir. Le Teil. Then N102 dir. Aubenas. After Villeneuve-de-Berg left D103. At Vogüé left on roundabout D579. Follow road to site right of road.

CC € 15 7/4-24/6 26/8-22/9

📐 N 44°28'47'' E 4°22'41''

Pradons/Ruoms, F-07120 / Rhône-Alpes (Ardèche)

⏚ 🛜 iD **2202**

🏕 Du Pont****
✉ 225A, route du Cirque de Gens
☎ +33 (0)4-75939398
🔓 23/3 - 14/9
@ campingdupont07@wanadoo.fr

2ha 48T(80-110m²) 10A CEE

1 ACD**F**IJKLMOPST
2 ABCGRTVXY
3 AGHJRU**W**X
4 (A 9/7-26/8) (C+H+Q+T 🔧)
　(U+V 1/7-31/8) (Y+Z 🔧)
5 **AB**EFGJKLMNOPUWZ
6 ACDEGH**K**(N 0,3km)RTUV

💬 Du Pont is close to Pradons and just 300m from a supermarket. You have wonderful views of the Cirque de Gens rocks which are on the other side of the river. A neat, small-scale campsite with personal attention.

🚗 A7 exit Montelimar Nord, N7 to Le Teil, then N102 dir. Aubenas. Left at roundabout after Villeneuve-de-Berg, D103. Then left D579 dir. Vallon. Right in Pradons at supermarket. Campsite on left.

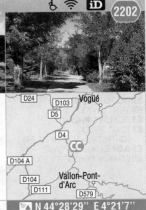

CC € 15 23/3-30/6 25/8-13/9

📐 N 44°28'29'' E 4°21'7''

Pradons/Ruoms, F-07120 / Rhône-Alpes (Ardèche)

🛴 📶 ✿ **iD** (2203)

🏕 Les Coudoulets★★★★
📧 125 chemin de l'Ardèche
☎ +33 (0)4-75939495
📠 +33 (0)4-75396589
🕐 7/4 - 16/9
@ camping@coudoulets.com

2,5ha 118T(80-160m²) 16A CEE

1 ACD**F**IJKLMPST
2 ACGJNORTVWXY
3 AGHJKLNRU**W**X
4 (A 1/7-31/8) (C+E+H 🔲) K (Q+T+U+V 🔲) (X 15/5-15/9) (Z 🔲)
5 **AB**DEFGIJKLMNOPQ**S**UVWXYZ
6 ACDEGH**K**L(N 0,1km)RTUVW

💬 A real family campsite with a lively atmosphere. The river with its large rocks flows past the site. Aquapark with, among other things, an indoor pool with jacuzzi and aqua-bikes. Pitches with private toilet facilities for extra fee.

🚗 A7, exit Montélimar-Nord direction Le Teil. In Le Teil N102 in the direction of Aubenas. Past Montfleury, turn left onto the D103. At Vogüé turn left onto the D579. The campsite is located on the right, before the village of Pradons.

CC € **17** 7/4-30/6 25/8-15/9 14=13, 21=19 📷 N 44°28'36'' E 4°21'30''

Privas, F-07000 / Rhône-Alpes (Ardèche)

🛴 📶 **iD** (2204)

🏕 Ardèche Camping★★★★
📧 chemin du Camping
☎ +33 (0)4-75640580
📠 +33 (0)4-75645968
🕐 14/4 - 28/9
@ ardechecamping07@gmail.com

5,5ha 111T(100-150m²) 10A CEE

1 ACD**G**IJKLMOPST
2 CJLORVXY
3 BGHKLNRU**W**
4 (A 1/5-31/8) (C 1/5-28/9) (E 🔲) (H 1/5-28/9) J (Q+T+U+V+Y+Z 🔲)
5 **A**EFGHJLMNPQUWZ
6 ACEGJ**K**(N 0,1km)UV

💬 Shaded campsite on the edge of Privas. Plenty of foliage in the grounds. Fishing in the river, swimming in the heated outdoor pool or the covered pool. Lovely market and many shops in Privas. The restaurant is open in the afternoon and evening.

🚗 A7, exit 16 Loriol. Dir. Le Pouzin. Then dir. Aubenas N304 (former D104). In Privas D2 dir. Montélimar. On 1st roundabout take dir. Villeneuve de Berg. Campsite left, next to Espace Ouvèze.

CC € **17** 14/4-6/7 24/8-27/9 7=6 📷 N 44°43'34'' E 4°35'53''

Recoubeau-Jansac, F-26310 / Rhône-Alpes (Drôme)

🛴 📶 **iD** (2205)

🏕 Domaine du Couriou★★★★
📧 D93
☎ +33 (0)4-85880138
🕐 1/5 - 30/9
@ contact@lecouriou.fr

7ha 90T(80-150m²) 10A CEE

1 ACD**G**IJKLMPST
2 JKRTVWXY
3 BGHJN**O**PRUW
4 (C+G 🔲) IJ (Q+R+T+U+V+X+Y+Z 🔲)
5 **AB**FGIJKLMNPUWZ
6 EGI**J**(N 1km)ORTV

💬 Camping Le Couriou is a lovely terraced campsite with panoramic views. The campsite is located in a wide valley that invites you to explore the mountains. The swimming pool is one of the largest in the area. Good restaurant with terrace offering stunning views of the mountains.

🚗 Exit Valence-Sud direction Gap/Crest/Die. After Die direction Gap. Campsite on the right before Recoubeau.

CC € **15** 1/5-6/7 28/8-29/9 7=6, 14=11 📷 N 44°39'31'' E 5°24'26''

Rosières, F-07260 / Rhône-Alpes (Ardèche)

👫 📶 **iD** (2206)

🔺 Domaine Arleblanc Camping****
📧 Domaine Arleblanc
☎ +33 (0)4-75395311
📠 +33 (0)4-75399398
⏱ 30/3 - 28/10
@ info@arleblanc.com

7ha 127T(100-150m²) 6-10A CEE

1 ACDGIJKLMOPST
2 ACNRTVWXY
3 AGHJKLM**N**Q**R**U**W**X
4 (A 1/7-31/8)
  (C+G 15/4-15/10)
  (Q+S+T ⏱)
  (U+V+Y+Z 30/3-15/9)
5 **AB**DEFGIJKLMNPQUXYZ
6 ACEGHIK(N 2,5km)ORTV

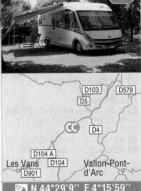

💬 Domaine Arleblanc has an excellent restaurant in a historic building. Excellent toilet facilities. It is heated in low season. The campsite has a typical French ambiance. It has extended grounds along the River Beaume with its lovely cliffs. There is free wifi on the grounds.

🚗 A7, exit 17, 2nd right on roundabout, follow route N7 to Le Teil. Take the N102 to Aubenas, then the D104 towards Alès. Left before Rosières at the supermarket. Site on right of road.

CC € **17** 30/3-1/7 25/8-27/10 14=12, 21=18 📍 N 44°27'51'' E 4°16'22''

Rosières, F-07260 / Rhône-Alpes (Ardèche)

📶 **iD** (2207)

🔺 La Plaine****
📧 Les Plaines
☎ +33 (0)4-75395135
⏱ 1/4 - 20/9
@ campinglaplaine@orange.fr

5ha 58T(80-150m²) 10A CEE

1 ACD**G**IJKLPST
2 BRTVXY
3 AGHMNQRUW
4 (C+H ⏱) KP(Q 7/7-25/8)
  (V 1/7-31/8) (Z ⏱)
5 **A**DEFGIJKLMNPUZ
6 AEGJ(N 0,8km)UV

💬 Very well-maintained campsite, 900 metres from La Beaume river. Friendly, homely atmosphere. There is a lake for anglers. Within walking distance of Lidl and Intermarché supermarkets. Large swimming pool with jacuzzi. Free wifi zone. Outdoor fitness.

🚗 A7, exit 17. N7 to le Teil. There N102 to Aubenas, there D104 dir. Alès. At Rosières roundabout turn directly right at the Pépiniéres. Continue to campsite.

CC € **15** 1/4-8/7 27/8-19/9 7=6, 14=12, 21=17 📍 N 44°29'9'' E 4°15'59''

Roybon, F-38940 / Rhône-Alpes (Isère)

♿ 📶 **iD** (2208)

🔺 Camping de Roybon***
📧 D20
☎ +33 (0)4-76362367
⏱ 15/4 - 30/9
@ campingroybon38@gmail.com

2,5ha 85T(80-110m²) 10A CEE

1 ACD**G**IJKLMPRS
2 CDGLNRVWXY
3 AGHJN**O**RUWZ
4 (C 1/5-15/9) (Q ⏱)
  (T+U+X 1/5-15/9) (Z ⏱)
5 **A**FGJKMPUVZ
6 ACEGJ(N 1km)OTV

💬 A peaceful campsite with a homely atmosphere on the shore of the lake and 800m from Roybon. The area has a Tuscan feel to it. Enjoy the heated swimming pool and the restaurant with delicious regional dishes.

🚗 A7/E15 exit 12, D519 direction Voiron. Turn right D71 Bressieux/Roybon. Campsite located 1 km out of the village and is indicated.

CC € **13** 15/4-14/7 1/9-29/9 6=5, 12=10 📍 N 45°14'49'' E 5°14'53''

Ruoms, F-07120 / Rhône-Alpes (Ardèche)

♿ 📶 **iD** (2209)

🏕 La Grand' Terre***
✉ 64 chemin de la Grand' Terre, D111
☎ +33 (0)4-75396494
📠 +33 (0)4-75397862
🕒 7/4 - 9/9
@ grandterre@wanadoo.fr

8ha 124T(> 100m²) 10A CEE

1 ACDGHIJKLMPST
2 ABCKLNRTVWXY
3 BGHJMNRUWX
4 (A+C+H+Q+S+T+U+V+Y+Z 🅱)
5 ABEFGIJKLMNPQUWZ
6 ACEGHJK(N 3km)OTUV

💬 Comfortable campsite on the Ardèche. Heated pool (420 m²) with lovely view. Good restaurant with reasonable prices. Characteristic surroundings with many sights. Motorhomes can stay in the campsite or on a commercial motorhome area, also in the campsite.

🚗 A7 exit Montélimar-Nord. Then N102 dir. Aubenas. Descend into Villeneuve-de-Berg left on the roundabout D103. Then left D579 dir. Vallon. After Ruoms dir. Alès, D111. Campsite on the left.

Ribes · D4 · Vallon-Pont-d'Arc · D104 A · CC · D104 · D579 · D290

CC € **17** 7/4-30/6 1/9-8/9 · 🧭 N 44°25'29'' E 4°19'55''

Ruoms, F-07120 / Rhône-Alpes (Ardèche)

♿ 📶 **iD** (2210)

🏕 Sites & Paysages Le Petit Bois***
✉ 87 rue du Petit Bois
☎ +33 (0)4-75396072
🕒 1/4 - 30/9
@ vacances@campinglepetitbois.fr

3,7ha 48T(100-120m²) 10A CEE

1 ACDGIJKLMOPST
2 JRTVXY
3 AGHJNRUW
4 (A+C+E 🅱) (H 1/7-30/9) JKL N(Q 🅱) (T 1/7-31/8) (U+V+X+Z 🅱)
5 ABEFGIJKLMNOPQRUVWZ
6 ADEGJK(N 0,8km)ORTV

💬 This well equipped campsite is located on the edge of Ruoms. The heated swimming pool can also be covered over, when it gets a bit colder. Usually not the case, the Ardèche has a good climate. There is a sauna and Turkish bath.

🚗 A7 exit Montélimar-Nord, dir. Le Teil. D102 towards Aubenas. At Villeneuve-de-Berg turn left on the roundabout, D103. At Vogüé take D579 towards Vallon. In Ruoms turn right at 1st roundabout. Right at Gamm Vert. Follow road, site on right.

Villeneuve-de-Berg · Vogüé · D5 · D4 · CC · D104 A · D104 · D111 · D579 · D290

CC € **15** 1/4-30/6 29/8-29/9 14=13, 21=19 · 🧭 N 44°27'41'' E 4°20'15''

Ruoms, F-07120 / Rhône-Alpes (Ardèche)

♿ 📶 ✿ **iD** (2211)

🏕 Sunêlia Aluna Vacances*****
✉ route de Lagorce
☎ +33 (0)4-75939315
📠 +33 (0)4-75939090
🕒 30/3 - 5/11
@ contact@alunavacances.fr

15ha 60T(120m²) 10A CEE

1 ACDFIJKLMPT
2 BJSTVXY
3 AGHMNOPRU
4 (A 1/7-31/8) (C+F+H 🅱) IJK LMP(Q+S+T+U+V+Y+Z 🅱)
5 ABDEFGIJKLMNOPQUWZ
6 ACEGHJKL(N 1km)OTV

💬 Campsite set in woodland with many naturally laid out pitches on a somewhat rugged terrain. Many sports opportunities. An Oriental style covered and heated 1000 m² leisure pool.

🚗 From Ruoms take the D559 direction Lagorce. After 1.5 miles you'll find the campsite on the right side.

Largentière · D4 · CC · D104 · D111 · Saint-Remèze · D290 · D579

CC € **19** 30/3-29/6 1/9-3/11 · 🧭 N 44°26'49'' E 4°21'55''

Saillans, F-26340 / Rhône-Alpes (Drôme) ♿ 📶 iD (2212)

▲ Les Chapelains***
✉ 1105 avenue Georges Coupois
☎ +33 (0)4-75215547
⟳ 6/4 - 30/9
@ bonjour@chapelains.com

1ha 40T(80-115m²) 10A

1 ACD**G**IJKLPS
2 BCKNRTVXY
3 AGHJKNRUW**X**X
4 (Q+T+U+V+X+Z ⌕)
5 AEFGIJKLMNOPQRUWZ
6 EGJ(N 1km)R

💬 Jean-Michel and Alice greatly value 'slow tourism'. This simply means enjoying a relaxing holiday close to nature, where you can swim in natural water and where you have time to exchange experiences and enjoy life. And all of this in combination with excellent toilet facilities make this the number one formula for real camping.

🚐 D104/D164 as far as roundabout before Saillans. Then turn onto D493, the campsite is just before the village on the right.

Crest Mirabel-et-Blacons D93
CC
D538

CC € **15** 6/4-6/7 24/8-29/9 · N 44°41'44'' E 5°10'53''

Samoëns, F-74340 / Rhône-Alpes (Haute-Savoie) ⛷ ♿ 📶 iD (2213)

▲ Camping Caravaneige Le Giffre***
✉ 1064 route du Lac aux Dames
☎ +33 (0)4-50344192
📠 +33 (0)4-50349884
⟳ 1/1 - 31/12
@ camping.samoens@wanadoo.fr

6,9ha 212T(80-110m²) 6-10A CEE

1 ACD**G**IJKLM**P**Q
2 CDGKLRTVWXY
3 BCGJMN**O**RW
4 (C 1/6-15/9) J(V ⌕)
   (X 15/6-15/9)
5 **AB**DFGIJKLMNOPUVWXYZ
6 ACDFGH**I**K(N 0,7km)T

💬 A beautiful campsite on level ground beside a river. Marked out pitches. Separate area for small tents. Several trees. Municipal swimming pool and tennis courts right beside the site (free for campsite guests). Small lake near the site with all types of sports facilities. Ice rink in winter also free. Village of Samoëns with its alpine garden within walking distance. Very suitable for wintersports.

🚐 Towards Samoëns via D907. Then follow camping signs.

D902
Taninges
CC
Cluses
Magland
A40

CC € **17** 6/1-2/2 28/4-29/6 25/8-14/12 · N 46°4'38'' E 6°43'7''

Sampzon, F-07120 / Rhône-Alpes (Ardèche) 👨‍👩‍👧 ♿ 📶 iD (2214)

▲ Flower Camping Le Rivièra****
✉ 3319 route du Rocher, D161
☎ +33 (0)4-75396757
⟳ 20/4 - 16/9
@ leriviera@wanadoo.fr

6,5ha 116T(85-100m²) 10A

1 ACD**G**IJKLMPS
2 ACGORSTVWXY
3 AGHJNRUW**X**X
4 (A 1/7-31/8) (C+H+Q+R ⌕)
   (T 1/5-15/9)
   (U+V+Y+Z 1/5-16/9)
5 **AB**DEFGIJKLMNOPQUWZ
6 AFGHK(N 3km)RTUV

💬 Site on the Ardèche river with private sandy beach. Pitches under acacia trees. Excellent toilet facilities with much comfort. Close to the Pont d'Arc and La Caverne du Pont d'Arc (Grotte Chauvet).

🚐 A7, exit Montélimar-Nord dir. Le Teil. In Le Teil N102 dir. Aubenas. Go down into Villeneuve-de-Berg and left at the roundabout, D103. At Vogüé left D579 towards Vallon. About 3 km past Ruoms right over the bridge.

D4
Saint-Alban-Auriolles CC Saint-Remèze
D104
D290
D579
D979

CC € **17** 20/4-30/6 25/8-15/9 21=18 · N 44°25'45'' E 4°21'19''

Sampzon, F-07120 / Rhône-Alpes (Ardèche) ⬩ 🚻 📶 iD **2215**

🏔 Le Chassezac***
🛣 RD111
☎ +33 (0)4-75396071
🔓 6/4 - 9/9
@ campinglechassezac@
　wanadoo.fr

4,3ha 118T(80-100m²) 10A CEE

1 ACDFIJKLMOPST
2 CNRTVXY
3 AGHJRU**W**X
4 (A 1/7-31/8) C(Q+R 🔓)
　(T+U+V+X 1/7-31/8) (Z 🔓)
5 **AB**DEFGIJKLMNOPQUWZ
6 ACDEG**K**(N 5km)RTV

💬 Situated in the peace and quiet on the banks of
the Chassezac. Thanks to a spring, there's always
water in the river. Great to swim, fish, or canoe in.
The famous Pont d'Arc is about a 15 km drive away.

🚗 A7 exit Montélimar-Nord, dir. Le Teil/Aubenas.
In Le Teil N102 dir. Aubenas. Descend into Villeneuve-
de-Berg, left at roundabout D103. Then left D579
dir. Vallon. After Ruoms dir. Alès D111. Campsite
on right.

CC € **13** *6/4-7/7 25/8-8/9 14=13* 　　　 🏕 N 44°25'27'' E 4°18'49''

Sampzon/Ruoms, F-07120 / Rhône-Alpes (Ardèche) ⬩ 🚻 📶 iD **2216**

🏔 Camping RCN La Bastide
　en Ardèche****
🛣 D111, 1 route d'Alès
☎ +31 034-3745090
🔓 23/3 - 17/9
@ reserveringen@rcn.nl

7,8ha 212T(100-140m²) 6-10A CEE

1 ACD**F**IJKLPST
2 ACNRTVWXY
3 AGHJKLN**OP**RUV**W**X
4 (A 28/4-15/9) (C+H 🔓) IJ
　(Q+S+T+U+V+Y+Z 🔓)
5 **AB**CDEFGIJKLMNOPQRU
　WXYZ
6 ACFGHKL(N 4km)RTV

💬 A family campsite with views of Mount Sampzon.
Many activities make it great for young and old.
The site has excellent toilet facilities. The weather in
low season is usually very agreeable.

🚗 A7, exit Montélimar-Nord, dir. Le Teil. Then N102
dir. Aubenas. Downhill at Villeneuve-de-Berg and left
onto D103 at roundabout. Then left on D579 direction
Vallon. Dir. Alès after Ruoms, D111. Campsite on the
left 1 km past the bridge.

CC € **17** *23/3-31/3 3/4-7/7 25/8-16/9* 　 🏕 N 44°25'23'' E 4°19'18''

Sandrans, F-01400 / Rhône-Alpes (Ain) 👫 🚻 📶 iD **2217**

🏔 Paradis des Dombes***
🛣 693 route de Saint Trivier
☎ +33 (0)4-28459407
🔓 1/4 - 31/10
@ campingsandrans@
　numericable.fr

75T(80-120m²) 10A CEE

1 ACD**G**IJKLMOPQ
2 DLMRTUVWXYZ
3 BGHJKRU**W**
4 (B 15/5-30/9) (Q+T+X+Z 🔓)
5 **AB**FGIJKLNPUVWZ
6 CDEGJ(N 6km)V

💬 Peacefully located in the heart of Dombes with
thousands of lakes, this level campsite with spacious
pitches is next to a 5 ha lake. It has a bar-restaurant
with terrace. Good cycling at L'Ain à Vélo. Parc des
Oiseaux, medieval city of Pérouges, golf course in
Villars-les-Dombes. Free wifi.

🚗 Sandrans is about 6 km south of Chatillon-sur-
Chalaronne in the centre of Sandrons, at the church,
head towards St. Trivier-sur-Mer, D27. After 700m the
campsite is on the left.

CC € **15** *1/4-5/7 23/8-30/10 7=6, 14=12* 　 🏕 N 46°3'40'' E 4°58'21''

Sciez-sur-Léman, F-74140 / Rhône-Alpes (Haute-Savoie)

♿ 🛜 ✿ iD (2218)

📐 Le Chatelet***
📧 658 chemin des Hutins Vieux
☎ +33 (0)4-50725260
🔓 1/4 - 31/10
@ info@camping-chatelet.com

3,4ha 42T(95-100m²) 10A CEE

1 ACD**G**IJKLMPQ
2 GLRTVX
3 ABGKNRWZ
4 (Q 1/7-31/8) (Z 🔓)
5 **AB**DFGIJKLMNOPUVWZ
6 CEG**K**(N 0,5km)ORT

💬 Campsite with quiet location. Spacious pitches. The nearby beach has all kinds of options for recreation on the water. Touring pitches separate from annual pitches. Site is only 300 metres from the lake and the water sports.

🚗 Follow the N5 from Genève to Thonon-les-Bains. After Bonnatrait the campsite is signposted at road on the left.

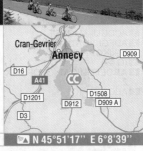

Nyon   Thonon-les-Bains

🆑 € **15** 1/4-29/6 1/9-30/10

🌐 N 46°20'28'' E 6°23'49''

Sévrier, F-74320 / Rhône-Alpes (Haute-Savoie)

♿ 🛜 iD (2219)

📐 Au Coeur du Lac***
📧 3233 route d'Albertville
☎ +33 (0)4-50524645
📠 +33 (0)4-50190145
🔓 29/3 - 30/9
@ info@aucoeurdulac.com

1,7ha 73T(70-100m²) 5-16A CEE

1 ACGIJKLMPRS
2 DFGIJKLRVWXY
3 AGHJK**M**QR**T**UWZ
4 (A 1/7-25/8) (Q+R 🔓) (U+V 10/6-9/9)
5 **AB**DFGIJKLMNOPUVXYZ
6 CDGJ(N 1km)TV

💬 Located right by the lake 4 km from Annecy in the small village of Sevrier, 40 km from Geneva. Camping pitches on terraces. Some have views of the lake and the mountains. The campsite has direct access to a 24 km paved, traffic-free cycle path. This is also the best way to arrive in Annecy without traffic tailbacks (approx. 15 minutes by bike).

🚗 Route Annecy-Albertville. From Annecy; when leaving Sévrier left of the D1508, 500 metres past McDonalds.

Cran-Gevrier   Annecy

🆑 € **17** 29/3-7/7 25/8-29/9

🌐 N 45°51'17'' E 6°8'39''

Sévrier, F-74320 / Rhône-Alpes (Haute-Savoie)

♿ 🛜 iD (2220)

📐 l'Aloua**
📧 492 route de Piron
☎ +33 (0)4-50526006
🔓 14/4 - 29/9
@ camping-de-l-aloua@orange.fr

2,3ha 173T(90-130m²) 6-10A

1 ACF**HIJ**KLPRS
2 FGRTVWXY
3 AF**G**JKLRU
4 (Q 🔓) (T+U+V+Z 1/7-31/8)
5 **AB**FGIJKNPUWZ
6 CFGJ(N 0,2km)TV

💬 A quiet family campsite with plenty of shade. There is a small nature reserve and a car-free cycle path next to the site. The pitches are level and on grass. 200 m from an entrance to the lake and to a supermarket.

🚗 D1508 Annecy-Albertville. The campsite is located between Sévrier and St. Jorioz, behind the Carrefour supermarket. Turn off at the roundabout.

Annecy-le-Vieux   Annecy

🆑 € **17** 14/4-7/7 26/8-28/9

🌐 N 45°50'38'' E 6°9'13''

Sévrier, F-74320 / Rhône-Alpes (Haute-Savoie) ⟨⚙⟩ 🚻 📶 **iD** `2221`

🏔 Le Panoramic***
✉ 1011 route de Cessenaz
☎ +33 (0)4-50524309
🔓 13/4 - 30/9
@ info@camping-le-panoramic.com

2ha 135T(80-110m²) 6-10A CEE

1 ACFHIJKLPQ
2 FIJKRVWXY
3 ABGHRU
4 (C+H 1/6-15/9) (Q 1/6-9/9)
(S 1/6-2/9)
(T+U+V+Y+Z 1/6-8/9)
5 ABEFGIJKLMNPUVZ
6 ACEGJ(N 1,5km)TV

💬 Campsite overlooking the lake of Annecy. Some pitches have panoramic views over the lake and surrounding villages; hence the name. Swimming pool is open from 1 June. The restaurant is open from June to the beginning of September. Renovated toilet facilities.

🚗 In Annecy continue to Albertville on the D1508. Just past Sévrier take first exit right at the first roundabout to the Col de Leschaux. Small bridge after about 3 km. Campsite is 300m further on the left.

Cran-Gevrier
Annecy | D909
D16
A41 | CC
D1201 | D909 A
D3 | D912
D911 | D1508

CC € **17** 13/4-6/7 25/8-29/9

🧭 N 45°50'35'' E 6°8'30''

Sévrier, F-74320 / Rhône-Alpes (Haute-Savoie) ⟨⚙⟩ 🚻 📶 **iD** `2222`

🏔 Les Rives du Lac***
✉ 331 chemin des Communaux
☎ +33 (0)4-50524014
🔓 31/3 - 30/9
@ lesrivesdulac-annecy@ffcc.fr

1,5ha 100T(80-100m²) 10A CEE

1 ACDGIJKLMOPST
2 ADFGKLMRTUVWX
3 BGJK**OP**RUWZ
4 (Q 🚻)
5 ABDEFGIJKLMNOPQRUWX
Z
6 ABCDEGHKT

💬 Campsite with private beach and direct access to Annecy lake. Very modern and well-maintained toilet facilities. There is a boat ramp and 20 berths for boat owners. You can rent bicycles at the campsite to explore the surroundings. Good cycle paths from the campsite. All kinds of options for watersports.

🚗 D1508 Annecy-Albertville. After about 5 km, just past 'LIDL', site is signposted on left.

Annecy
D16
Seynod | D909
A41 | CC
D1201 | D1508
D912

CC € **19** 31/3-29/6 3/9-29/9

🧭 N 45°50'55'' E 6°9'4''

St. Alban-Auriolles/Ruoms, F-07120 / Rhône-Alpes (Ardèche) ⟨⚙⟩ 🚻 ✿ **iD** `2223`

🏔 Sunêlia Le Ranc Davaine*****
✉ 500 chemin du Ranc Davaine
☎ +33 (0)4-75396055
📠 +33 (0)4-75393850
🔓 6/4 - 16/9
@ contact@rancdavaine.fr

13ha 93T(80-150m²) 10A CEE

1 ACDFIJKLMPT
2 CNRTVXY
3 BGH**MNOP**RUWX
4 (**A** 1/7-31/8) (B+E+H 🚻) IJ**K**
LMNP
(Q+S+T+U+V+Y+Z 🚻)
5 ABDEFGIJKLMNOPQRUWZ
6 ACEGHJ**K**L(N 1,5km)ORTV

💬 A large campsite. The small river is not very deep. Plenty of amusement, but still set peacefully under oak trees. There is a lovely leisure pool with an indoor pool for those who like swimming. Wellness facilities.

🚗 From Ruoms on the D579 turn onto the D111 towards Alès. Right after 5 km onto the D246 (at Grospierres). Left at end of road towards Chandolas. Campsite on your left.

Saint-Alban-
D104 | Auriolles
Les Vans | D4
D901 | CC
Saint-Paul-le- | D290
Jeune | D579
D979

CC € **19** 6/4-29/6 1/9-15/9

🧭 N 44°24'49'' E 4°16'18''

St. Alban-de-Montbel, F-73610 / Rhône-Alpes (Savoie)

♿ 🛜 iD 2224

▲ Le Sougey****
📧 Lac Rive Ouest
☎ +33 (0)4-79360144
🗓 20/4 - 30/9
@ info@
camping-aiguebelette-sougey.com

4ha 148T(85-150m²) 6-10A CEE

1 ACD**G**IJLM**P**ST
2 ADFLMRSV**W**XY
3 BGJNRU**WZ**
4 (Q+S 🖐)
(T+U+V+Z 1/7-31/8)
5 **A** **B**FGIJKLOPUWXYZ
6 EGIJ(N 3km)TV

💬 Relatively large pitches, separated by hedges. Several sanitary buildings are spread over the hilly site. A few trees provide shade. Within 100 metres is a beautiful meadow at the lake of Aiguebelette (550 hectare).

🚗 A43 Lyon-Chambéry, exit Lac d'Aiguebelette. After péage turn right at the roundabout then after 300 metres left at next roundabout direction St. Alban-de-Montbel. Campsite indicated after 2 km on the left.

D1516 D35
D916 D921 La Motte-Servolex
D916 A **Chambéry**
A43
D912
D82
D1006

CC € 15 20/4-28/6 2/9-29/9

📷 N 45°33'21'' E 5°47'27''

St. Avit, F-26330 / Rhône-Alpes (Drôme)

👫 ♿ 🛜 iD 2225

▲ Domaine La Garenne****
📧 156 chemin de Chablezin
☎ +33 (0)4-75686226
🗓 15/4 - 30/9
@ garenne.drome@wanadoo.fr

14ha 50T(150-300m²) 6A

1 ACD**G**IJKLMP
2 JKLRSVWXY
3 BGHNRU
4 (C+H 15/5-14/9) (Q 9/7-27/8)
(T 1/7-31/8) (U 9/7-26/8)
(Z 🖐)
5 **A**EFGIJKLMNOPUVZ
6 CEJ(N 3km)T

💬 A terraced campsite beside a hill with pine trees. The pitches are spread out in natural surroundings with fir and oak trees. The hedges and the height differences in the grounds offer you large pitches with privacy between the hills of the Drôme.

🚗 Chanas exit, N7 towards Valence until just past St. Vallier. D51 direction St. Uze and Hauterives. Right in Châteauneuf-de-Galaure towards St. Donat (D53). Campsite 4 km on the left.

D1 D51
Andancette
Beausemblant
A7 CC D538
N7 D112
D86

CC € 15 15/4-4/7 25/8-29/9

📷 N 45°12'7'' E 4°57'24''

St. Clair-du-Rhône, F-38370 / Rhône-Alpes (Isère)

👫 ♿ 🛜 iD 2226

▲ Le Daxia****
📧 route de Péage D4
☎ +33 (0)4-74563920
🗓 1/4 - 30/9
@ info@campingledaxia.com

7,5ha 116T(100-150m²) 6A

1 ACD**G**IJKLMOPQ
2 CRTVWXY
3 BCGHJNQRU**W**
4 (B+G 1/6-15/9) JM
(Q 1/5-30/9)
(T+U+V+X+Z 1/7-31/8)
5 **A****B**EFGIJKLMNPUVZ
6 CEJ(N 3km)

💬 A very friendly and attractive campsite in northern Isère. This campsite, which according to the French is one of the better ones in the area, can indulge tourists for long or short periods. Located in a rural and peaceful setting in Provençale ambiance and close to Lyon and Vienne. Spacious pitches in a lovely park.

🚗 A7 exit Vienne. Follow the N7 as far as D4 right direction St. Claire-du-Rhône. Follow camping signs in the village.

D59 E **Vienne**
D386
D62
D63 D7 D4
CC
Le Péage-de-Roussillon
D503 D86 N7

CC € 17 1/4-8/7 26/8-29/9

📷 N 45°25'26'' E 4°46'56''

St. Donat-sur-l'Herbasse, F-26260 / Rhône-Alpes (Drôme)

♿ 🤟 📶 **iD** (2227)

🏕 Les Ulèzes★★★★
✉ rte de Romans,
   400 av. Raymond Pavon
☎ +33 (0)4-75478320
🕐 1/4 - 31/10
@ contact@
   domaine-des-ulezes.com

3,5ha 76T(100m²) 6-10A CEE

1 ACD**G**IJKLMPST
2 CRS**V**WXY
3 BGHJNQRU**W**
4 (B 15/5-30/9) (Q+R 🔑)
   (T 15/4-15/9) (U 🔑)
   (V+X 15/4-15/9) (Z 🔑)
5 **AB**EFGIJKLMNPRUWXYZ
6 CEG**I**JK(N 0,6km)TV

💬 A lovely level and well maintained campsite with spacious pitches, bordered at the back by the 'Les Ulèzes' hills. There is a footpath from the site to the village. Friendly owners who try to please the campers. Toilet facilities close to every pitch. Located close to the Tain-l'Hermitage wine district.

🚗 A7 exit Tain-l'Hermitage, dir. Romans. At Curron D67 dir. St. Donat. Follow signs. Campsite is on right of D53.

D51 D112 A7 **CC** D538 D53
Romans-sur-Isère
N7 A49

CC € **17** 1/4-30/6 1/9-30/10   📍 N 45°7'9'' E 4°59'34''

St. Étienne-du-Bois, F-01370 / Rhône-Alpes (Ain)

📶 **iD** (2228)

🏕 Camping du Sevron
✉ 115 chemin du Moulin
   des Groboz
☎ +33 (0)6-47975073
🕐 1/1 - 31/12
@ campingdusevron@gmail.com

31T(60-100m²) 16A CEE

1 ACDGIJKLMO**P**RS
2 CFGLRTUVWXY
3 AGK
5 DGIJKLMNOPUVXY
6 CDGJT

💬 Friendly, small family campsite in the countryside, in a typical 'Pays de Bresse' area. The campsite has sunny and shaded pitches marked out with hedges. An interesting detail: Camping du Sevron is enthusiastically run by France's youngest campsite owner; Emile Polo is 19 years old! Free wifi at reception.

🚗 Campsite located along N83 between Bourg-en-Bresse and Lons-le-Saunier, to the south of St. Étienne-du-Bois.

D1083 D117
D28 A39
D996 **CC** D3
A40
D936
Bourg-en-Bresse

CC € **15** 1/1-7/7 25/8-31/12 7=6, 14=11   📍 N 46°17'1'' E 5°17'28''

St. Galmier, F-42330 / Rhône-Alpes (Loire)

👫 🤟 📶 **iD** (2229)

🏕 Campéole Le Val de Coise★★★★
✉ route de la Thiéry
☎ +33 (0)4-77541482
📠 +33 (0)4-77540245
🕐 30/3 - 30/9
@ val-de-coise@campeole.com

3,5ha 27T(80-100m²) 16A CEE

1 ACD**G**HIJKLO**P**Q
2 CIJLRVWX
3 BGNRU**W**
4 (C+H 15/6-15/9) (Q+R 🔑)
5 **AB**EFGIJKLMNPUZ
6 CEG**K**(N 2,5km)V

💬 A small but friendly terraced campsite with views of the river, just outside the centre of the flower-filled town of St. Galmier. Nature lovers will certainly find this campsite to their liking.

🚗 Past Lyon via the A7 and the A47 direction St. Étienne. Then follow the A72 as far as St. Galmier exit. Follow the signs in St. Galmier.

D389 D34
D1089
D2
D1082 **CC**
A72
Saint-Just-Saint-Rambert
D3

CC € **15** 30/3-6/7 25/8-29/9   📍 N 45°35'34'' E 4°20'8''

St. Genix-sur-Guiers, F-73240 / Rhône-Alpes (Savoie)

♿ 🛜 iD 2230

▲ Les Bords du Guiers**
✉ 640 route de la Glière
☎ +33 (0)4-76317140
📅 14/4 - 23/9
@ lesbordsduguiers@orange.fr

1,5ha 55T(120-160m²) 6-10A CEE

1 ACD**G**IJLMP**Q**
2 CFLRTVWXY
3 AGHJK**MQ**R**W**X
4 (B 15/5-10/9) (Q+T+U+X 🔲)
5 **AB**CGIJLMNPUVWZ
6 AFHJ(N 0,1km)OV

💬 Family campsite with quiet location. Pool. The campsite is located 200 metres from the centre, in the middle of a network of walking and cycling routes. Supermarket at 150 metres from the campsite. Dutch owners.

🚗 From A43 exit 11 towards St. Genix-sur-Guiers. From D1075 Evrien, D1516 to Aoste, then St. Genix-sur-Guiers. In St. Genix take first exit right on the roundabout then follow camping signs.

Morestel · D19 · D10 · D33 · D1516 · D992 · D16 · D35 · CC · D916 · D921 · D1075 · Le Pont-de-Les Abrets · Beauvoisin · A43 · D73

CC € **13** 14/4-30/6 18/8-22/9

N 45°35'45'' E 5°38'5''

St. Gervais-les-Bains, F-74170 / Rhône-Alpes (Haute-Savoie)

♿ 🛜 ✿ iD 2231

▲ Nature & Lodge Les Dômes de Miage****
✉ 197 route des Contamines
☎ +33 (0)4-50934596
📠 +33 (0)4-50781075
📅 14/5 - 16/9
@ info@camping-mont-blanc.com

2,5ha 150T(90-200m²) 3-12A CEE

1 ACG IJKLMOPQ
2 FGKLMRVWXY
3 BGHNRU
4 (Q+S 1/6-31/8)
5 **AB**DEFGIJKLMNPUWZ
6 ACDFGHIJ(N 2km)ORTV

💬 Level grassy base with excellent toilet facilities. Lovely views of the snowy mountain tops. A stream divides the ground in two. St. Gervais is a pretty tourist village. There is a restaurant right next to the campsite.

🚗 A40 exit St. Gervais (no. 21). To St. Gervais centre then Les Contamines. Campsite on the left after 2 km.

Chamonix-Mont-Blanc · A40 · D909 · D1205 · CC · D1212

CC € **19** 14/5-7/7 25/8-15/9

N 45°52'25'' E 6°43'13''

St. Jean-de-Chevelu, F-73170 / Rhône-Alpes (Savoie)

♿ 🛜 iD 2232

▲ Camping des Lacs***
☎ +33 (0)6-59498394
📅 28/4 - 16/9
@ campingdeslacs73@gmail.com

4ha 95T(100-150m²) 16A CEE

1 ACD**G**IJKLMP**Q**
2 ACDFGKLMRVWXY
3 AGHJRU**W**XZ
4 (A 5/7-30/8) (Q 🔲)
(T+U+Z 1/7-31/8)
5 **AB**EFGIJKLMNOPRUWZ
6 CDEGJ(N 6km)OV

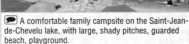

💬 A comfortable family campsite on the Saint-Jean-de-Chevelu lake, with large, shady pitches, guarded beach, playground.

🚗 A41 as far as Chambéry exit 13, N504 direction Aix-les-Bains tunnel direction Yenne, then D210 direction St. Jean-de-Chevelu; campsite signposted from there.

Belley · D991 · D1201 · D992 · D914 · A41 · CC · Aix-les-Bains · D1516 · D1504 · D913 · D35 · D916 · D921

CC € **15** 28/4-6/7 25/8-15/9

N 45°41'38'' E 5°49'29''

St. Jean-de-Maurienne, F-73300 / Rhône-Alpes (Savoie) ♨ 📶 iD (2233)

🔺 Des Grands Cols***
🏠 422 ave du Mont-Cenis
☎ +33 (0)9-52174655
🔓 10/5 - 22/9
@ info@
   campingdesgrandscols.com

2ha 92T(80-100m²) 16A CEE

1 ACD**G**HIJKLMOPQ
2 FGKRTUVWXY
3 BGHJLNRUV
4 (Q+R 1/6-31/8) (T 1/7-31/8)
   (Z 1/6-31/8)
5 **AB**EFGIJKMNOPUVXYZ
6 ACDEG**J**(N 1km)OV

💬 Located in the heart of the Maurienne valley at the foot of the prestigious 'cols' such as the Glandon, Croix de Fer and Madeleine. The warden will be pleased to help you plan your bike rides, walks or cultural trips out. Cycle shop and free cycle storage available. Easy to reach via the D1006. 500m from town centre.

🚗 D1006 Chambéry - St. Jean-de-Maurienne. In St. Jean direction centre, then follow 'Toutes directions' and 'camping' signs.

CC € **17** 10/5-30/6 25/8-21/9   🗺 N 45°16'15'' E 6°21'2''

St. Jean-de-Muzols/Tournon-s-R, F-07300 / Rhône-Alpes (Ardèche) 🚼 ♨ 📶 iD (2234)

🔺 Le Castelet****
🏠 113 route du Grand Pont
☎ +33 (0)4-75080948
🔓 28/4 - 8/9
@ courrier@
   camping-lecastelet.com

3ha 63T(88-110m²) 10A CEE

1 A**G**IJKLPST
2 CFGJLMORTVXY
3 BGHJLN**PRUW**X
4 (C+G 10/5-19/9) (Q+Z 🔓)
5 **A**EFGJLNPUW
6 ACEGJ(N 3km)OTV

💬 A well maintained campsite on the river, just 3 km from a village. Lovely heated swimming pool. Lively bar with terrace and views of the pool. Free wifi point. Spacious toilet facilities. Also facilities for motorhomes. Walking and cycling routes from the campsite. Fresh bread in the morning.

🚗 A7, exit 13 Tournon. Over the Rhône D86, follow direction Tournon, then St. Jean-de-Muzols. When entering St. Jean-de-Muzols left onto D238. CP indicated on the left after 4 km.

CC € **15** 28/4-5/7 23/8-7/9 7=6, 14=11, 21=18, 28=24   🗺 N 45°4'4'' E 4°47'6''

St. Jean-le-Centenier, F-07580 / Rhône-Alpes (Ardèche) ♨ 📶 iD (2235)

🔺 Les Arches****
🏠 Le Cluzel, route de Mirabel, D458
☎ +33 (0)4-75367519
🔓 27/4 - 23/9
@ info@camping-les-arches.com

10ha 152T(70-200m²) 10A CEE

1 ACD**F**IJKLMPST
2 CJMRTVWXY
3 AGHJLRUV**W**X
4 (**A** 18/7-24/8) (C+H 🔓)
   (Q 1/5-10/9) (T 1/7-31/8)
   (U 1/6-15/9) (V 6/7-26/8)
   (Y 1/6-15/9) (Z 🔓)
5 **A**DEFGIJKLMNOPRUWZ
6 ACDEGHIJ**K**(N 1km)RTV

💬 Parkland campsite with plenty of trees and bushes. Pick your own cherries, enjoy the view, the quiet, the birds and the river. Walking and cycling area. Sightseeing close by, shops, doctors. EN, NL, DE and SP spoken. Heated swimming pool. Restaurant open often.

🚗 A7 exit Montélimar-Nord. Then towards Le Teil. Then the N102 direction Aubenas. Drive past St. Jean-le-Centenier exit. Towards Mirabel (D458) before the service station. Continue on road. Don't use SatNav.

CC € **17** 27/4-6/7 24/8-22/9 10=9, 19=17, 28=24   🗺 N 44°35'15'' E 4°31'33''

St. Jorioz, F-74410 / Rhône-Alpes (Haute-Savoie) ♿ 📶 iD (2236)

🔺 Europa★★★★
📧 1444 route d'Albertville
☎ +33 (0)4-50685101
🔓 28/4 - 14/9
@ info@camping-europa.com

3,2ha 141T(80-100m²) 6A CEE

1 AC**F**IJKLPS
2 FGKRVXY
3 B**F**GHJKNRU
4 (C 🔓) (**H** 18/5-2/9) IJKMP
　(Q 1/7-31/8)
　(V+Y+Z 18/5-2/9)
5 **AB**EFGIJKLMNPUWXYZ
6 AG**K**(N 1,5km)TV

💬 An excellent site 400 metres from the lake, 9 km from Annecy, with excellent toilets. The lovely leisure pool has 3 open-air pools with additional facilities (deckchairs with water massage), slides and child-friendly water games. Excellent restaurant. Direct access to a cycle path beside the lake. Comfort pitches for extra fee.

🚗 D1508 Annecy-Albertville. The campsite is located along this road, just past St. Jorioz it is the second site on the right hand side.

Cran-Gevrier **Annecy**
D16　D909
A41　D909 A
D1201　CC　D12
　D912　D1508
D3
　D911

CC €**17** 30/4-6/7 27/8-13/9　🧭 N 45°49'48'' E 6°10'54''

St. Jorioz, F-74410 / Rhône-Alpes (Haute-Savoie) ♿ 📶 iD (2237)

🔺 International du Lac
　d'Annecy★★★★
📧 1184 route d'Albertville (D1508)
☎ +33 (0)4-50686793
🔓 14/4 - 15/9
@ contact@
　camping-lac-annecy.com

2,5ha 110T(85-110m²) 6-10A CEE

1 AC**G**IJKLPS
2 FGK**RV**WXY
3 A**F**GJKNRU
4 (C+H 5/5-15/9) IJ
　(Q 1/7-31/8)
　(T+U+V+X+Z 1/6-31/8)
5 **AB**EFGIJKMNPUWXYZ
6 AG**K**(N 1,5km)RTV

💬 Campsite with excellent toilet facilities is an attractively lit building. Shaded pitches 400 metres from Lake Annecy and 1 km from the beach. Heated, child-friendly and tropical leisure pool with slide. Direct access to a guarded cycle path.

🚗 D1508 Annecy-Albertville. Campsite located on this road, just past the centre of St. Jorioz.

Cran-Gevrier **Annecy**
D16　D909
A41　D909 A
D1201　CC　D12
D3　D912　D1508
　D911

CC €**19** 14/4-5/7 27/8-14/9　🧭 N 45°49'51'' E 6°10'42''

St. Jorioz, F-74410 / Rhône-Alpes (Haute-Savoie) ♿ 📶 iD (2238)

🔺 Le Crêtoux★★★
📧 1059 route d'Entredozon
☎ +33 (0)4-50686194
🔓 1/4 - 15/11
@ info@campinglecretoux.com

6ha 75T(100-120m²) 3-10A

1 AC**G**IJLPRS
2 IJKRVWXY
3 B**F**RUW
4 (Q 1/7-31/8)
5 **AB**DEFGIJKLMNPUVZ
6 ACDEGIJ(N 2km)V

💬 A basic campsite in natural surroundings on a hill just outside the centre of St. Jorioz. You have views over Annecy Lake from certain pitches. The site is recommended for anyone who appreciates peace and nature. The steep access road is short, but that need not be a problem.

🚗 D1508 Annecy-Albertville. At traffic lights in St. Jorioz D10a direction St. Eustache. Signposted (about 2 km). Short, steep access road.

Meythet **Annecy**　D16
Seynod　　　D909
　D1201
A41　CC　D909 A
D3　D912
　　D1508
　D911

CC €**17** 1/4-7/7 25/8-14/11　🧭 N 45°49'4'' E 6°8'49''

St. Jorioz, F-74410 / Rhône-Alpes (Haute-Savoie)

2239

Le Solitaire du Lac***
615 route de Sales
+33 (0)4-50685930
7/4 - 23/9
contact@campinglesolitaire.com

4,5ha 185**T**(80-120m²) 5-6A

1 ACGIJKLMPRS
2 ADFLRTVWXY
3 BFGJKRUWZ
4 (Q+R 1/5-23/9) (U 1/7-31/8)
5 **AB**EFGIJKLMNPUWZ
6 ACEG**IJK**(N 1km)OV

Well-cared-for campsite divided in parallel avenues. The pitches are under the trees. The pitches are separated from the lake by a playing field. On the shore is a narrow passage to the water.

D1508 Annecy-Albertville. Just before you reach St. Jorioz centre drive to the lake. Follow the camping signs.

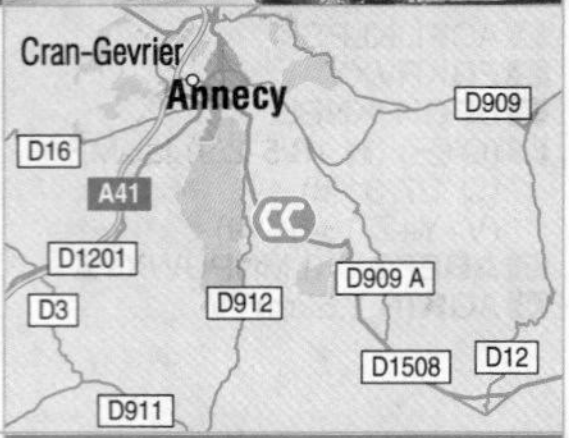

Cran-Gevrier
Annecy
D909
D16
A41
D1201
D909 A
D3
D912
D1508
D12
D911

CC € 17 *7/4-7/7 25/8-22/9*

N 45°50'27'' E 6°9'53''

St. Julien-en-St-Alban, F-07000 / Rhône-Alpes (Ardèche)

2240

L'Albanou***
280 chemin de Pampelonne
+33 (0)4-75660097
+33 (0)9-60112471
13/4 - 31/10
campingalbanou@orange.fr

2ha 84**T**(100-110m²) 10A CEE

1 ACD**G**IJKLMO**P**ST
2 CFGLORTVWXY
3 AGHJNRU**WX**
4 (C+G) K
(Q+R+T+U+V+Z)
5 **AB**GHIJKLMNOPUZ
6 ACDEGJ(N 1km)

Ideal springboard to your holiday destination, but also suitable for longer stays. Swimming pool with jacuzzi. Heated toilet facilities. Free wifi point. Well maintained landscaping on this level terrain. Nearly all pitches are marked out by hedges. Easily reached from the A7 autoroute.

A7 exit 16 Loriol, then towards Le Pouzin. Then dir. Aubenas via D104. Site is signposted on left before village (at small industrial site). Then left again and 2nd site on right.

D120
D86
N7
Livron-sur-Drôme
A7
Privas
D104
D22
D2

CC € 17 *13/4-3/7 21/8-30/10 8=7, 14=12, 21=18, 28=24*

N 44°45'26'' E 4°42'46''

St. Laurent-du-Pape, F-07800 / Rhône-Alpes (Ardèche)

2241

Camping La Garenne***
383 Montée de la Garenne
+33 (0)4-75622462
1/4 - 30/9
info@
campinglagarenne-ardeche.fr

6ha 117**T**(80-125m²) 6-10A CEE

1 A**G**IJKLP
2 GJRSTVWXY
3 BGHJRU
4 (A 26/5-15/9) (B 5/5-20/9)
(G 22/4-20/9) M(Q+R)
(T+U+V+Y+Z 5/5-17/9)
5 **AB**EFGIJKLMNOPRUWZ
6 AEGK(N 0,4km)OV

On the edge of a wood, close to the village centre. Friendly atmosphere. Plenty of walking and cycling opportunities. A wide range of daily menus. Jeu de boules. Friendly Dutch wardens. Dutch, French, English and German spoken.

A7, exit 16 (Loriol). D104 to Privas. After Rhônebrug right D86 to La Voulte s/Rhône. Roundabout in La Voulte, dir. St. Laurent-du-Pape. After La Voulte left D120 to St. Laurent. Cross bridge and left. Right after 200m (before La Poste).

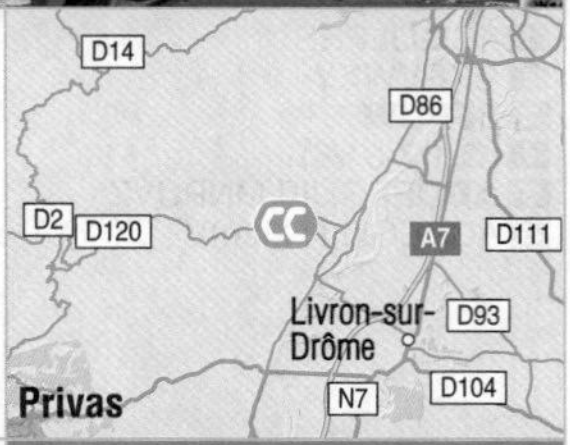

D14
D86
D2
D120
A7
D111
Livron-sur-Drôme
D93
Privas
N7
D104

CC € 19 *1/4-7/7 25/8-29/9*

N 44°49'34'' E 4°45'44''

St. Martin-d'Ardèche, F-07700 / Rhône-Alpes (Ardèche)

👫 📶 **iD** (2242)

⛺ Camping Le Pontet***
✉ quartier Le Pontet
☎ +33 (0)4-75046307
🕐 6/4 - 24/9
@ contact@campinglepontet.com

NEW

2,5ha 82**T**(80-120m²) 16A CEE

1 ACDGIJKLPQ
2 BGTVXY
3 AGHJNRU
4 (B+G 1/5-24/9)
(Q+R+T+U 🕐)
(V+Y 1/7-31/8) (Z 🕐)
5 AEFGIJKLMNPUVZ
6 CDEG**K**(N 1km)V

💬 Nice, smaller campsite with young, enthusiastic owners. The swimming pool and the play and sports facilities are on separate grounds. The famous Route des Gorges de L'Ardèche begins in St. Martin d'Ardèche (1 km). Free wifi in the low season.

🚗 A7, exit Bollène, direction Pont St. Esprit. Then N86 as far as St. Just. Then follow St. Martin d'Ardèche. Then Sauze débarcadière. Campsite on the left.

CC € **15** 6/4-6/7 24/8-22/9 7=6

📡 N 44°18'14'' E 4°35'4''

St. Martin-d'Ardèche, F-07700 / Rhône-Alpes (Ardèche)

♿ 📶 **iD** (2243)

⛺ Des Gorges****
✉ Sauze
☎ 📠 +33 (0)4-75046109
🕐 27/4 - 16/9
@ info@camping-des-gorges.com

3,5ha 114**T**(80-120m²) 10A CEE

1 ACDGIJKLMPST
2 ACJORTVWXY
3 AGHNRU**W**X
4 (C+H 🕐) K
(Q+S+T+U+V+Y+Z 🕐)
5 **AB**DEFGIJKLMNOPQUVWZ
6 ACEG**K**(N 1km)RTV

💬 Des Gorges has a lovely pool with a wall of bubbles. Lovely views from the terraces. Pitches under tall trees and the Ardèche flows past the grounds. St. Martin d'Ardèche is a lovely tourist village. Toilet facilities partially renovated. Family shower. Free wifi in low season throughout the grounds.

🚗 Route A7, exit Bollène dir. Pont-St-Esprit. Then N86 to St. Just. Then follow St. Martin-d'Ardèche and Sauze débarcadère. Campsite on left.

CC € **17** 27/4-30/6 1/9-15/9

📡 N 44°18'40'' E 4°33'22''

St. Martin-d'Ardèche, F-07700 / Rhône-Alpes (Ardèche)

📶 **iD** (2244)

⛺ Huttopia Le Moulin***
✉ Le Moulin
☎ +33 (0)4-75046620
🕐 20/4 - 30/9
@ lemoulin@huttopia.com

7ha 111**T**(100-200m²) 10A CEE

1 ACD**F**IJKLMPST
2 CKLNORTVWXY
3 BGHNRU**W**X
4 (C+G+Q+R 🕐)
(T+U+V+X+Z 1/6-31/8)
5 **AB**FGIJKLMNOPQRUWZ
6 ACEGIJ(N 0,2km)V

💬 The campsite is located near the Gorges de l'Ardèche in natural surroundings. An ideal location for taking trips out. Located at the end of the famous descent of the Ardèche by canoe. Lovely pitches on the banks of the river. 300 metres from the village.

🚗 A7 exit Bollène. From there towards Pont Saint Esprit. Then follow 'Gorges de l'Ardeche' signs as far as Saint Martin-d'Ardèche.

CC € **17** 20/4-28/6 2/9-29/9

📡 N 44°18'2'' E 4°34'17''

St. Maurice-de-Gourdans, F-01800 / Rhône-Alpes (Ain) 📶 iD (2245)

▲ Les Plages de l'Ain***
🏠 11 chemin du Stade
☎ +33 (0)4-74358293
🔄 1/4 - 30/9
@ contact@camping-plage-ain.fr

3ha 50T(150-200m²) 10-16A

1 ACD**F**IJKLMO**P**Q
2 CFNRTVWXY
3 AGHRUW**X**
4 (B+G 1/6-30/9) (Q 1/7-31/8)
　 (T+U+V+X+Z 1/6-30/9)
5 **AB**GIJKLNOPUVYZ
6 CDEGJ**K**(N 2km)OTV

💬 A campsite positioned by the River Ain with a pebble beach. The pitches are spacious and the many lovely old trees offer plenty of shade. A perfect place for kayaking, cycling, walking or just enjoying yourself. Swim safely in the two pools.

🚗 A42 exit 7 Pérouges/Meximieux, D65B direction St. Maurice-de- Gourdans and follow signs to Stade and the campsite.

CC € 15 1/4-6/7 27/8-29/9　　　　N 45°48'31'' E 5°11'4''

St. Paul-de-Varax, F-01240 / Rhône-Alpes (Ain) ♿ 📶 iD (2246)

▲ Domaine de la Dombes****
🏠 Etang du Moulin,
　 chemin de Verfey
☎ +33 (0)4-74303232
🔄 3/3 - 4/11
@ contact@
　 domainedeladombes.com

30ha 30T(100-200m²) 10A CEE

1 AC**G**IJKLMO**P**RS
2 ABCDLRTUVWXY
3 ABD**F**GHJKN**Q**RU**W**
4 (B 15/6-30/9) **KN**(Q+U 🔄)
　 (Z 1/5-30/9)
5 **A**DFGIJMNOPRUWZ
6 ACDEGJ(N 3km)OTV

💬 This campsite is in an extensive nature reserve with many lakes, the Dombes. It has a very large swimming pool with a sandy beach and a forest adventure trail, one of the largest in Europe.

🚗 From Lyon or Bourg-en-Bresse take the N83. In St. Paul-de-Varax take the D70a direction St. Nizier-le-Desert. Follow signs.

CC € 15 3/3-6/7 27/8-3/11 7=6, 14=12　　N 46°5'11'' E 5°9'7''

St. Paul-de-Vézelin, F-42590 / Rhône-Alpes (Loire) ♿ 📶 iD (2247)

▲ D'Arpheuilles***
☎ +33 (0)4-77634343
🔄 1/5 - 23/9
@ arpheuilles.camp@gmail.com

3,5ha 66T(120m²) 6-10A

1 ACDGIJLPRS
2 ACDHJKLRVWXY
3 BCGNQRUW**Z**
4 (C+G 1/5-4/9) (Q+R 🔄)
　 (T+U+X+Z 1/7-31/8)
5 **AB**FGJKLMNPUVZ
6 EGJ(N 10km)OT

💬 A lovely well-run campsite on the shores of a reservoir. This campsite offers some type of water recreation for every camper. The nature lover will enjoy exploring the hilly surroundings.

🚗 From St. Paul-de-Vézelin follow the D8 direction Dancé. Campsite located a few km outside village. Campsite signposted.

CC € 15 1/5-6/7 24/8-22/9　　　　N 45°54'42'' E 4°3'57''

St. Pierre-d'Albigny, F-73250 / Rhône-Alpes (Savoie)

♿ ✈ **iD** (2248)

🏕 Lac de Carouge***
🏠 Base de Loisirs
☎ +33 (0)6-25913831
⏱ 28/4 - 15/9
@ contact@lacdecarouge.com

1,9ha 64T(100-150m²) 10A CEE

1 ACG**I**JKLM**P**Q
2 ADFKMNRVWXY
3 BGHKN**P**R**U**W**Z**
4 (Q 15/6-31/8)
  (R+T+U+V+Z ⊙)
5 **AB**EFGIJKLMNOPQUWZ
6 ACGJ(N 1km)OTV

💬 Campsite is at a lake. The camping pitches are minimum 100 m² in size and nearly all of them marked out by hedges. Swimming in the lake is permitted in the patrolled area. The Arbin vineyards and Miolans castle are in the neighbourhood. Good toilet facilities.

🚗 From Chambéry A43, exit 23 St. Pierre-d'Albigny which is well signposted 3.5 km from the campsite. From Albertville A43, exit 24 drive to St. Pierre-d'Albigny then follow the camping signs.

Montmélian
La Rochette
D1090 A430 D912 D911 A43 CC D1006 D925 A41

♿ € **17** 28/4-6/7 25/8-14/9 7=6, 14=12, 21=18   📷 N 45°33'24'' E 6°9'59''

St. Pierre-de-Chartreuse, F-38380 / Rhône-Alpes (Isère)

♿ ✈ **iD** (2249)

🏕 Sites & Paysages De Martinière***
🏠 route du Col de Porte
☎ +33 (0)4-76886036
⏱ 5/5 - 16/9
@ camping-de-martiniere@orange.fr

2,5ha 85T(80-110m²) 6-10A

1 ACD**G**IJKLMO**P**ST
2 GKRTVWXY
3 AGHJNRU
4 (C+H 15/5-15/9) (Q 1/7-31/8)
  (R 1/6-15/9)
  (T+X+Z 1/7-31/8)
5 **A**GIJKLMNPUVWZ
6 ACEGJ(N 3km)OT

💬 Peacefully located campsite within the walls of a Cartusienne farm with a magnificent view on the Chartreuse range. Well maintained area with a lovely swimming pool. Separated pitches, partially with the help of hedges.

🚗 Driving with a caravan we advise the route via St. Laurent-du-Pont, direction St. Pierre-de-Chartreuse. 1 km before St. Pierre in the town of Diat turn right direction Col de Porte. From there, it's only 2 km to the campsite.

Voreppe
Saint-Égrève
Crolles
D520 D520 B D520 A D1090 D512 A41 CC

♿ € **17** 5/5-6/7 25/8-15/9 7=6   📷 N 45°19'32'' E 5°47'51''

St. Privat, F-07200 / Rhône-Alpes (Ardèche)

♿ ✈ **iD** (2250)

🏕 Flower Camping Le Plan d'Eau***
🏠 route de Lussas
☎ +33 (0)4-75354498
⏱ 28/4 - 22/9
@ info@campingleplandeau.fr

3ha 75T(80-150m²) 8A CEE

1 ACD**G**IJKLMO**P**S
2 ACLORTVXY
3 AGHIJNRU**W**X
4 (C+H+Q+R+T+U+V+Y+Z ⊙)
5 **A**DEFGIJKLMNOPUZ
6 ACEGHJ**K**(N 2km)OTV

💬 A campsite with direct access to the River Ardèche. Sandy beach with deckchairs. Lovely views of the surrounding rock formations. Not far from Aubenas. Pitches often surrounded by hedges. You pay extra for XL pitches.

🚗 A7 exit Montélimar-Nord, dir. Le Teil/Aubenas. Right onto D304 towards St. Privat/Privas before Aubenas. After bridge dir. Lussas on roundabout. Campsite on the right. Do not use SatNav!

Vals-les-Bains
Aubenas
D578 D579 N102 D103 D5 D104 CC

♿ € **15** 28/4-6/7 25/8-21/9 27=24   📷 N 44°37'8'' E 4°25'56''

St. Remèze, F-07700 / Rhône-Alpes (Ardèche) ♿ 📶 ✿ iD **2251**

🏕 Domaine de Briange***
🛣 route de Gras
☎ +33 (0)4-75041443
⌛ 28/4 - 16/9
@ contact@campingdebriange.com

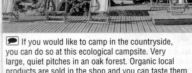

4ha 49T(150-300m²) 6A CEE

1 ACD**G**IJKLMPS
2 BKRTVXY
3 AGHLRU
4 (A 1/7-31/8) (C+H 15/5-16/9) (Q+R+T+U+V+X+Z ⌚)
5 **A**EFGJLNPUWZ
6 AEGJ(N 2km)RUV

💬 If you would like to camp in the countryside, you can do so at this ecological campsite. Very large, quiet pitches in an oak forest. Organic local products are sold in the shop and you can taste them in the restaurant. Large swimming pool. Close to La Caverne du Pont d'Arc.

🚗 A7, exit 18. Follow Pierrelatte, then Bourg-Saint-Andéol. Then dir. Vallon Pont d'Arc via D4. Right before St. Remèze D362 dir. Gras and Lamas. Campsite 2 km on the right.

[Map: Vallon-Pont-d'Arc, Lapalud, D107, D4, D86, D579, D290]

CC € 15 28/4-10/7 28/8-15/9   📍 N 44°24'27'' E 4°30'56''

St. Romans (Isère), F-38160 / Rhône-Alpes (Isère) ♿ 📶 iD **2252**

🏕 Flower Camping Le Lac du Marandan***
🛣 657 route des Marandans
☎ +33 (0)4-76644177
⌛ 7/4 - 30/9
@ contact@ camping-lac-marandan.com

3ha 100T(80-130m²) 6-10A CEE

1 AC**G**IJKLMO**PQ**
2 ABDFKLRTVXY
3 BGHJKMNRUWZ
4 (Q+R+T+U+V+X+Z 1/7-31/8)
5 **AB**EFGIJKLMNOPUVWZ
6 ACEGHJ**K**(N 2km)OT

💬 A family campsite by a shallow lake with a sandy beach. Also suitable for exploring Vercors (altitude 200m) among other places. Restaurant with views of the lake.

🚗 Take the D1532 between Grenoble and Valence. Clearly signposted in St. Romans. Through Base de Loisirs to Lac du Marandan campsite. Or take motorway A49, exit 9 St. Marcellin.

[Map: Saint-Marcellin, Saint-Jean-en-Royans, D71 K, D1532, A49, D1092, D325, D518, D531, D54, D103, D612]

CC € 15 7/4-7/7 1/9-29/9   📍 N 45°6'11'' E 5°17'32''

St. Sauveur-de-Cruzières, F-07460 / Rhône-Alpes (Ardèche) ♿ 📶 iD **2253**

🏕 Camping de la Claysse****
🛣 La Digue
☎ +33 (0)4-75354065
📠 +33 (0)4-75366865
⌛ 15/4 - 15/9
@ camping.claysse@wanadoo.fr

1ha 47T(70-90m²) 10A CEE

1 ACDGIJKLPST
2 CJMRTVXY
3 AGHJNRUV**W**X
4 (A 1/7-31/8) (B ⌚) (Q 1/7-31/8) (T+U+V+X+Z ⌚)
5 **A**DEFGIJKLMNOPQUWZ
6 AEG**K**(N 0,2km)TV

💬 Located by the small River Claysse. Views of the mountains and the village. There is a working olive mill on the campsite, great for souvenirs! The Gorges de L'Ardèche and Vallon Pont d'Arc are 20 km away and Barjac with its lively market is 8 km.

🚗 A7, exit 19 Bolléne. N86 to Pont St. Esprit. Then D6086 towards Bourg St. Andéol. Then left after 2.5 km on D901. In Barjac continue to St. Sauveur. Don't turn off in the village, turn left a bit further by the car park.

[Map: Bessèges, Saint-Ambroix, D111, D104, D579, D979, D901, D37, D51, D904]

CC € 15 15/4-7/7 25/8-14/9   📍 N 44°18'2'' E 4°14'57''

St. Sauveur-de-Montagut, F-07190 / Rhône-Alpes (Ardèche)

♿ 📶 iD (2254)

▲ l'Ardéchois*****
🏠 Le Chambon Gliuras, D102
☎ +33 (0)4-75666187
⊙ 19/5 - 22/9
@ ardechois.camping@wanadoo.fr

6,5ha 78T(90-160m²) 10A CEE

1 ACD**G**IJKLMOPST
2 ACJKLMORTVWXY
3 AGHJNRU**W**X
4 (**A**+C+H+Q+R ⊙)
(T 7/7-26/8) (U+Y+Z ⊙)
5 **AB**DEFGIJKLMNOPQRUWZ
6 ACEGI**K**(N 8km)OUV

💬 A beautiful 5-star campsite located in the middle of the Ardèche. The ideal site if you are seeking rest, space, luxury and friendliness. A site where you are not just a number but where a family atmosphere and a personal approach are important.

🚗 A7 exit 15 Valence-Sud. Dir. Le Puy-en-Velay. N7 Montélimar. Right on D111a to Carmes-sur-Rhone. D86 to Privas. In Beauchastel D21. D120 dir. Le Cheylard to St. Sauveur. Then D102 to. Mezilhac. Campsite on right after 8 km.

CC € 19 19/5-6/7 1/9-21/9

🏔 N 44°49'44'' E 4°31'23''

St. Theoffrey/Petichet, F-38119 / Rhône-Alpes (Isère)

📶 iD (2255)

▲ Au Pré du Lac***
☎ +33 (0)4-76839134
⊙ 3/3 - 27/10
@ aupredulac@aupredulac.eu

3,5ha 80T(60-120m²) 10A CEE

1 ACD**G**IJKLMPQ
2 DGJKLMRWXY
3 ABGHJNRU**W**Z
4 (Q+X+Y+Z ⊙)
5 **A**DEFGJKLMNPU
6 ACEGJ(N 10km)RV

💬 The campsite is located directly next to a beautiful lake with wonderful views of the mountains all around. Plenty of sports opportunities and well positioned for trips out in the area. Both sunny and shaded pitches available. Restaurant with terrace overlooking the lake and the mountains. Private beach.

🚗 Grenoble direction Gap. A480, exit 8 direction Vizille. In Vizille direction Gap via the N85. Through Laffrey. Then follow camping signs.

CC € 17 3/3-30/6 18/8-26/10

🏔 N 45°0'5'' E 5°46'21''

St. Thomé, F-07220 / Rhône-Alpes (Ardèche)

📶 iD (2256)

▲ Le Médiéval***
🏠 120 Impasse du Médiéval
☎ +33 (0)4-75526876
⊙ 27/4 - 30/9
@ contact@
campinglemedievalardeche.fr

4ha 84T(90-120m²) 10-16A CEE

1 ACD**G**IJKLMPST
2 CFGORTVXY
3 AGHJRU**W**
4 (A 15/7-15/8) (C+H+Q+R ⊙)
(T+U 1/5-30/9) (V 1/6-31/8)
(X 1/5-30/9) (Z ⊙)
5 **AB**DFGIJKLMNOPQUWZ
6 AEG**K**(N 0,5km)OV

💬 Genuine French ambiance. Views from the terrace over the pool or authentic reception building. Some pitches under old tall trees. New toilet facilities. Wifi on nearly the entire grounds.

🚗 A7 exit Montélimar-Sud/Viviers. After 1 km on N7 dir. Montélimar take D126/D73 to Viviers, then N86 dir. Le Teil. After 6 km take D107 dir. St. Thomé. Site on the left. From North: continue to 1st roundabout St. Thomé, then turn back to D107, site on left.

CC € 13 27/4-6/7 1/9-29/9 7=6, 14=11

🏔 N 44°30'25'' E 4°37'9''

Tain-l'Hermitage, F-26600 / Rhône-Alpes (Drôme) ♿ 🛜 **iD** (2257)

▲ Mun. les Lucs***
🏠 56 avenue Pres. Roosevelt
☎ +33 (0)4-75083282
🔓 1/3 - 31/10
@ camping.tainlhermitage@
orange.fr

NEW

1,3ha 54T(100m²) 10A CEE

1 ACD**G**IJLP
2 CFKRSTVWXY
3 GLR**W**
4 (F+H 🔓) J(Q 🔓)
5 ACDGIJKLMNPUVWZ
6 FGJ(N 0,5km)TW

💬 A peaceful, spacious campsite on the banks of the Rhône. The site is located in the centre of Tain-l'Hermitage, famous for its wine and 'art de vivre'. Double axled trailers are not permitted on the campsite.

🚐 A7 Lyon-Marseille, exit Tain-l'Hermitage. Take the N95 in the direction of Tain-l'Hermitage. After the level crossing take the first road to the left onto the N7. Follow the camping signs. (Caravans max. 5.5 metres long).

Map: N7, D112, D532, Tournon-sur-Rhône, D53, D534, D238, CC, A7, Châteauneuf-sur-Isère, D86

CC € **15** 1/3-6/7 25/8-30/10   📍 N 45°4'0'' E 4°51'6''

Thonon-les-Bains, F-74200 / Rhône-Alpes (Haute-Savoie) 👪 ♿ 🛜 **iD** (2258)

▲ Saint Disdille***
🏠 117 avenue de Saint-Disdille
☎ +33 (0)4-50711411
📠 +33 (0)4-50719367
🔓 1/4 - 30/9
@ camping@disdille.com

12ha 250T(90-120m²) 10A CEE

1 ACD**G**IJKLMPQ
2 BDGLNRTVWXY
3 BGHKMNR**W**Z
4 (Q+S+T+U+V+X+Y+Z 🔓)
5 **AB**EFGIJKLMNPUWYZ
6 ACDEGH**I**J**K**(N 3km)QRTV

💬 Large family campsite with spacious pitches in wooded surroundings. The banks of Lake Geneva are in a park 150 metres from the entrance. Public transport, restaurant, supermarket, newspaper kiosk. Nature reserve next to the campsite. Excellent cycling in the mountainous area around the lake. Bike rental.

🚐 N5 Genève-Evian, exit Vongy-Lac, then direction St. Disdille. Campsite signposted.

Map: A1, CC, N5, D21, Thonon-les-Bains, D903, D902, D32, D22, D12, D26

CC € **17** 1/4-8/7 26/8-29/9   📍 N 46°23'58'' E 6°30'14''

Tournon-sur-Rhône, F-07300 / Rhône-Alpes (Ardèche) ♿ 🛜 **iD** (2259)

▲ Camping de Tournon HPA***
🏠 1 prom. Roche Defrance
☎ +33 (0)4-75080528
🔓 4/1 - 22/12
@ camping@camping-tournon.com

1,1ha 56T(60-100m²) 6A CEE

1 AC**G**IJKLMPST
2 CFGKRUVWXY
3 AHJRU**W**
5 **AB**DEFGIJKMNPUVWZ
6 CDEGK(N 0,1km)OT

💬 A pleasant campsite near the town centre on the banks of the Rhône, overlooking the vineyards of L'Hermitage. This shaded campsite with heated toilet facilities is open all year round. Reception open till 19:00.

🚐 A7 exit 13 Tain l'Hermitage. Over the bridge to Tournon and turn right by the water. Follow camping signs.

Map: D112, D578, D532, N7, Tournon-sur-Rhône, CC, A7, D534, Mauves, D86

372

CC € **17** 4/1-30/6 1/9-21/12   📍 N 45°4'18'' E 4°49'40''

Tournon-sur-Rhône, F-07300 / Rhône-Alpes (Ardèche)

♿ 🛜 **iD** (2260)

▲ Les Acacias***
🏠 190, route de Lamastre
☎ +33 (0)4-75088390
🗓 1/4 - 30/9
@ info@acacias-camping.com

2,4ha 44**T**(80-200m²) 6-20A CEE

1 AC**G**IJKLMOPST
2 CFGNRWXY
3 BGHIJNQRU**W**X
4 (B+G 15/5-15/9)
   (Q+T+U+V+X+Z 1/7-31/8)
5 **A**GIJKLMNOPUW
6 EGH**J**(N 3km)ORV

💬 A quiet, attractive family campsite in the heart of the Ardèche and close to Tournon. Spacious shaded pitches, swimming pool. Opportunities for walking from the campsite.

🚗 A7, exit 13 Tournon. Over the Rhône turn right. Follow D532. 1.5 km from Tournon, campsite is on right.

🆑 € **13** 1/4-6/7 25/8-29/9

📍 **N 45°3'57'' E 4°47'41''**

Treffort, F-38650 / Rhône-Alpes (Isère)

♿ 🛜 **iD** (2261)

▲ Camping de la Plage**
🏠 Sous Jullières
☎ 📠 +33 (0)4-76340631
🗓 7/4 - 12/10
@ contact@camping2laplage.com

2ha 75**T**(80-150m²) 10A CEE

1 ACD**G**IJLPST
2 DFJKMNOTVWXY
3 BGHJLNR**W**Z
4 (G 1/7-31/8) J(Q+R+T 🅿)
   (U+V 1/7-31/8) (X+Z 🅿)
5 **AB**GIJKLMNPUWXYZ
6 AEG**K**TV

💬 A campsite located by the lake. Plenty of facilities for the sportive camper. Good restaurant. Convenient for a boat trip on the lake and a walk across the Himalaya suspension bridge.

🚗 From N: Via Grenoble A51, exit 13 to Lac de Monteynard. Then Sinard/Treffort. Campsite signposted at lake. Keep left. From S: N1075 through Monestier (not A51), then Sinard/Treffort.

🆑 € **13** 7/4-29/6 3/9-11/10

📍 **N 44°54'34'' E 5°40'13''**

Trept, F-38460 / Rhône-Alpes (Isère)

♿ 🛜 **iD** (2262)

▲ Les 3 Lacs du Soleil****
🏠 La Plaine de Serrières
☎ +33 (0)4-74929206
🗓 28/4 - 9/9
@ les3lacsdusoleil@hotmail.fr

26ha 160**T**(100-120m²) 6A

1 ACD**G**IJLM**P**RS
2 ADGLMORVWXY
3 BGHJKLMNQRU**VW**Z
4 (B 1/5-10/9) (G 🅿) JK
   (Q+R 🅿) (T 15/6-31/8)
   (V+X+Z 🅿)
5 **AB**FGIJKLMNOPUWZ
6 EGHI**K**(N 2,5km)OV

💬 A family campsite with a swimming pool and toddlers' pool located in grounds with three lakes, one of which has a water slide. Lovely area for walking and cycling. Spacious level pitches and a restaurant in the grounds.

🚗 Bourg-en-Bresse direction Lyon. Exit Ambérieu. N75 direction Lagnieu. Then direction Lancin. Follow D522 and D517 towards Trept and Crémieu. Campsite located 3 km before Trept. Well signposted.

🆑 € **15** 28/4-6/7 27/8-8/9 7=6, 14=11

📍 **N 45°41'21'' E 5°21'6''**

Trévoux, F-01600 / Rhône-Alpes (Ain)

♿ 🛜 ✿ **iD** (2263)

△ Sites & Paysages Kanopee Village***
✉ rue Robert Baltié
☎ +33 (0)4-74084483
⊶ 1/4 - 30/9
@ contact@kanopee-village.com

2,5ha 160T(100-140m²) 10A CEE

1 ACDGIJKLMOPQ
2 CRVXY
3 AGHIJKLRU
4 (A 1/7-1/9) (C 1/6-31/8) (H 1/7-31/8) IJ(Q+R ⊶)
5 CIJKLMNPUZ
6 ABCEG**K**(N 1km)RT

💬 This campsite on the edge of the River Saône is just 30 km from Lyon. Camping pitches for tents, caravans and motorhomes in natural surroundings.

🚗 From the north A46 exit 2 (Trévoux). Follow signs to town. Campsite signposted. From the south A6 take exit 32.

Villefranche-sur-Saône

D933 D936 D44 D904 D28 D4 D338 A6 A46 D30 D16 A89 D42 D483

CC € **17** 1/4-5/7 25/8-29/9 7=6, 14=11 ⛺ N 45°56'21'' E 4°46'6''

Tulette, F-26790 / Rhône-Alpes (Drôme)

👫 ♿ 🛜 **iD** (2264)

△ Les Rives de l'Aygues***
✉ 142 chemin des Rives de l'Aygues
☎ +33 (0)4-75983750
⊶ 22/4 - 7/10
@ camping.aygues@wanadoo.fr

3,5ha 100T(80-300m²) 6-10A CEE

1 ACF IJKLM**P**S
2 BCRSTUVWXY
3 ABGHJNRUX
4 (C+G+Q+R+T+U+V ⊶) (X 6/7-8/9,1/6-30/9) (Z ⊶)
5 **A**DFGIJKLMNOPUXZ
6 EG**K**(N 2,5km)OTV

💬 A campsite located in the middle of the countryside on the edge of extensive vineyards and in a wood by a river. Plenty of privacy provided by the hedges which screen the pitches, a very basic shop (with bread each morning) and a well-heated pool from May to October. Free wifi on entire site in low season.

🚗 Motorway exit Bollène direction Vaison-la-Romaine, in Tulette turn right and follow signs.

Saint-Paul-Trois-Châteaux

D59 D20 D94 CC D976 D977 D8 D43

CC € **17** 22/4-8/7 26/8-6/10 ⛺ N 44°15'52'' E 4°55'59''

Ucel/Aubenas, F-07200 / Rhône-Alpes (Ardèche)

♿ 🛜 **iD** (2265)

△ Domaine de Gil****
✉ 91 route de Vals
☎ +33 (0)4-75946363
⊶ 27/4 - 23/9
@ resa@domaine-de-gil.com

4,5ha 28T(80-130m²) 10A CEE

1 ACD**F**IJKLM**P**ST
2 ACLNORTVXY
3 AGHJ**M**N**Q**RU**W**X
4 (C+H ⊶) K(Q+R+T+U+V ⊶) (Y 16/6-26/8) (Z ⊶)
5 **AB**EFGIJKLMNOPUVWZ
6 ACEG**IJK**(N 2km)OTUV

💬 A campsite with ambiance and beautiful landscaping. Several natural springs in the area including Vals-les-Bains. Heated swimming pool (27°C). Not far from Aubenas, plenty of shops. Outdoor fitness by the river.

🚗 A7 exit Montélimar-Nord direction Le Teil/Aubenas. Just before Aubenas turn right D304 to St. Privat/Privas. Exit St. Privat, follow St. Privat/Ucel. In Pont d'Ucel, direction Vals-les-Bains/Ucel at roundabout. Campsite on left after 2 km. Don't use SatNav!

D536 D578 N102 Vals-les-Bains CC Aubenas D104 D24 D5 D103 D579

CC € **17** 27/4-30/6 26/8-22/9 14=13, 21=19 ⛺ N 44°38'33'' E 4°22'47''

Valbonnais, F-38740 / Rhône-Alpes (Isère) 👫 📶 iD (2266)

🏕 Au Valbonheur***
☎ +33 (0)4-76302128
⌚ 27/4 - 30/9
@ perron38@orange.fr

20ha 180T(200-300m²) 10A CEE

1 ACDFIJKLMPQ
2 ACDGKLMRWXY
3 ABGHJLMN**OP**R**UW**XZ
4 (A 10/7-20/8)
    (Q+R+T+U+V+Y+Z ⌨)
5 **AB**CEFGHJLNPQRUVZ
6 ACEGHJ**K**(N 0,8km)ORTV

💬 Beautiful, large family campsite with sunny part and part with lots of shade. Located on a swimming lake surrounded by green hills. Ideal for sportive cyclists and hikers.

🚗 From Grenoble with a caravan follow diversion routes for heavy vehicles. Signposted on N85 in La Mur as Le Plan d'eau.

La Motte-d'Aveillans
Le Villaret
D526
D26
D26 A
D66 N85

CC € 15 27/4-30/6 1/9-29/9   📷 N 44°53'33'' E 5°54'15''

Vallon-Pont-d'Arc, F-07150 / Rhône-Alpes (Ardèche) ♿ 📶 iD (2267)

🏕 Beau Rivage****
✉ quartier les Mazes
☎ +33 (0)4-75880354
⌚ 28/4 - 8/9
@ campingbeaurivage@wanadoo.fr

2,2ha 86T(100-110m²) 10A CEE

1 ACD**G**IJKLMPST
2 ACRTVXY
3 BGNRU**W**X
4 (A 28/6-31/8) (C+H+Q+R ⌨)
    (T+U+V+Y 30/5-31/8) (Z ⌨)
5 **A**DEFGIJKLMNOPUVWZ
6 ADEGJ(N 2km)RTV

💬 4 star campsite Beau Rivage is located among the vineyards by the river. It has a wide beach and there is enough water in the Ardèche for swimming and sailing. The lovely heated swimming pool has a wall of bubbles. Plenty of shaded pitches. Heated toilet facilities. The owners are very friendly and hospitable.

🚗 From Ruoms take D579 dir. Vallon-Pont-d'Arc. Turn right at Les Mazes, left at end of road, campsite on right. Don't use SatNav but this route description.

Ruoms   Lagorce
D104   D111   CC   Saint-Remèze
D290   D4
D579
D979

CC € 17 28/4-6/7 24/8-7/9 14=13, 21=19   📷 N 44°24'23'' E 4°21'51''

Vallon-Pont-d'Arc, F-07150 / Rhône-Alpes (Ardèche) ♿ 📶 iD (2268)

🏕 Domaine de l'Esquiras****
✉ 1280 chemin du Fez
☎ +33 (0)4-75880416
⌚ 1/4 - 30/9
@ esquiras@orange.fr

3ha 48T(80-120m²) 10A CEE

1 ACD**G**IJKLMPST
2 KRTVWXY
3 AGHJKRU
4 (**A** 1/7-31/8) (B+E+H ⌨) IJ
    (Q+R ⌨)
    (T+U+V+Y 13/4-16/9) (Z ⌨)
5 **A**EFGIJKLMNPQUWZ
6 ACDEGKL(N 1,5km)RTVW

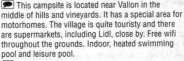

💬 This campsite is located near Vallon in the middle of hills and vineyards. It has a special area for motorhomes. The village is quite touristy and there are supermarkets, including Lidl, close by. Free wifi throughout the grounds. Indoor, heated swimming pool and leisure pool.

🚗 From Ruoms D579 continue towards Vallon-Pont-d'Arc. Left at the Prassarat roundabout just before the village (3/4 round) and follow camping signs.

Saint-Alban-Auriolles
D104   CC   Saint-Remèze
D4
D579
D979   D290

CC € 19 1/4-8/7 26/8-29/9   📷 N 44°24'55'' E 4°22'41''

Vallon-Pont-d'Arc, F-07150 / Rhône-Alpes (Ardèche) ♿ 🛜 iD (2269)

🏕 International Camping****
✉ 65 Impasse de la Plaine
☎ +33 (0)4-75880099
⌚ 28/4 - 7/10
@ inter.camp@wanadoo.fr

3ha 117T(90-130m²) 10A

1 ACD**G**IJKLMOPST
2 CGNORTVXY
3 AGHJNRUV**W**X
4 (C+H 🖢) K
(Q+R+T+U+V+Y+Z 🖢)
5 **A**EFGIJKLMNPUZ
6 ACFGJ**K**(N 1km)TUV

💬 Four-star campsite with green zone for sports and games. Heated swimming pool. Good toilet facilities. Restaurant. Pitches with panoramic views by the river. Close to the centre of Vallon and 5 km from the Caverne du Pont d'Arc.

🚗 A7 exit 17. N86 dir. Le Teil, then N102 dir. Aubenas. After Villeneuve-de-Berg left at the roundabout D103 dir. Vallon-Pont-d'Arc. Then D579 to Vallon-Pont-d'Arc. Follow road dir. Salavas. Campsite on right after the bridge.

Ruoms · Lagorce
D104 · D111 · Saint-Remèze · D4
D579
D979 · D290
D901

CC € 17 28/4-7/7 26/8-6/10 📍 N 44°23'52'' E 4°22'59''

Vallon-Pont-d'Arc, F-07150 / Rhône-Alpes (Ardèche) ♿ 🛜 iD (2270)

🏕 Mondial Camping****
✉ route des Gorges de l'Ardèche
☎ +33 (0)4-75880044
📠 +33 (0)4-75371373
⌚ 23/3 - 23/9
@ reserv-info@
mondial-camping.com

5,2ha 207T(90-110m²) 10A CEE

1 ACD**G**IJKLMOPST
2 ACGNORTVXY
3 AGHMN**OPQ**RUWX
4 (C+H 🖢) J
(Q+S+T+U+V+Y+Z 🖢)
5 **AB**DEFGIJKLMNOPQRUWX
YZ
6 ACEGJ**K**(N 1km)ORTUV

💬 This lovely campsite is close to Vallon-Pont-d'Arc. The varying greenery provides plenty of shade. There are also luxury pitches with water supply and drainage. You can sunbathe beside the pool. Canoeing on the River Ardèche from the campsite. Refurbished restaurant. New toilet facilities. Friendly owners.

🚗 From Vallon-Pont-d'Arc follow the D290 (Route des Gorges). After 1 km, the campsite is the third on the right.

Pradons
D111
Maisonneuve · D4
D579 · D290
Bessas
D979

CC € 19 23/3-6/7 26/8-22/9 📍 N 44°23'50'' E 4°24'4''

Vallon-Pont-d'Arc/Lagorce, F-07150 / Rhône-Alpes (Ardèche) ♿ 🛜 iD (2271)

🏕 Domaine de Chadeyron****
✉ Quartier de Chadeyron, D1
☎ +33 (0)4-75880481
⌚ 30/3 - 13/10
@ infos@campingchadeyron.com

3ha 30T(100-150m²) 10-16A CEE

1 ACD**G**IJKLM**P**ST
2 JKRTVWXY
3 AGHJRU
4 (C+H 1/5-30/9) JM
(Q+R+T+U+V+Z 🖢)
5 **AB**CDEFGHIJKLMNOPQRU
WXYZ
6 ACDEGK(N 2,5km)V

💬 Terraced site on 43 hectare grounds with lovely views. Peaceful homely ambiance. Free wifi. Good base for lovely walks and cycle rides. Supplement for grand comfort pitches. Luxurious new toilet facilities. Heated pool. EN, NL, FR and DE spoken.

🚗 A7 exit Montélimar-Nord. N7 dir. Le Teil, then N102 to Aubenas. After Villeneuve-de-Berg left at roundabout onto D103. At Vogüé left towards Vallon on roundabout. Then left and follow D1. Site on right. Ok to use SatNav.

D103 · D5 · Vogüé · Villeneuve-de-Berg
D104
D4
D111
D579 · D290

CC € 17 30/3-6/7 24/8-12/10 21=19 📍 N 44°28'13'' E 4°25'1''

Vallon-Pont-d'Arc/Salavas, F-07150 / Rhône-Alpes (Ardèche) 🛜 iD 2272

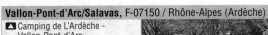

🏕 Camping de L'Ardèche - Vallon-Pont-d'Arc
🏠 100 chemin de la Plage
☎ +33 (0)4-75880473
🔓 24/3 - 30/9
@ campingvallonpontdarc@ gmail.com

3,5ha 150T(75-120m²) 6-10A CEE

1 ACDGIJKLMOPST
2 ACGORTVXY
3 AGHJRW**X**
4 (Q+T+U+V+X+Z 🔒)
5 **A**DEFGIJKLMNPUZ
6 ACEGHJ**K**RTV

💬 Easy-going and quiet campsite. Direct access from the site to the beach and the river. Close to the centre of Vallon-Pont-d'Arc. The owner is making improvements. German spoken.

🚗 A7, exit 17 N86 dir Le Teil, then N102 dir Aubenas. After Villeneuve-de-Berg left on roundabout dir Vallon-Pont-d'Arc, D103. Then 579 to Vallon-Pont-d'Arc. Follow road to Salavas. Over Ardèche bridge. 3rd exit left on 1st roundabout past Le Chauvieux follow road. Campsite on right.

Saint-Sauveur-de-Cruzières
D104 D111 D579 D4 D290

CC € **13** 24/3-7/7 25/8-29/9 📷 N 44°23'50'' E 4°23'1''

Vercheny, F-26340 / Rhône-Alpes (Drôme) 🛁 🛜 iD 2273

🏕 Les Acacias***
🏠 Les Tours
☎ +33 (0)4-75217251
📠 +33 (0)4-75217398
🔓 1/4 - 15/9
@ infos@campinglesacacias.com

3,6ha 90T(80-120m²) 6A CEE

1 ACD**G**IJKLPST
2 BCKNTVXY
3 BGHJRU**W**X
4 (Q 🔒)
  (R+T+U+X+Z 1/5-15/9)
5 **A**GIJKLMNOPUVWZ
6 AEGK(N 1,5km)OTV

💬 Well shaded campsite on the Drôme, ideal as a starting point for exploring the beautiful surroundings by bike (in a large flat area with small towns) or by car (lovely mountains close by). Basic but good and inexpensive restaurant. You can hire canoes and kayaks for sailing on the Drôme. Free wifi.

🚗 A7 exit Valence, direction Crest (D111). After Crest direction Die (D93). Campsite located between Crest and Die on the D93, 2 km before Vercheny on the south of the road.

Die
D518
Mirabel-et-Blacons
D93 CC
D538

CC € **15** 1/4-5/7 24/8-14/9 📷 N 44°41'44'' E 5°14'29''

Vernioz, F-38150 / Rhône-Alpes (Isère) 🛁 🛜 iD 2274

🏕 Le Bontemps****
🏠 5, Impasse du Bontemps
☎ +33 (0)4-74578352
📠 +33 (0)4-74578370
🔓 15/4 - 1/10
@ info@camping-lebontemps.com

8ha 120T(100-150m²) 10-16A CEE

1 ACD**G**IJKLMOPQ
2 CLMRUVWXY
3 BGHJ**M**N**Q**RUVW
4 (E 🔒) (H 15/5-1/10) J
  (Q 1/5-30/9) (T+U+Y+Z 🔒)
5 **AB**EFGIJKLMNOPUVWXYZ
6 CEG**JK**(N 2km)ORTUV

💬 High-class campsite in beautiful park with a rich variety of trees. Many activities: fitness and fishing for free. Located in the Rhône, a few kilometres from Vienne.

🚗 A7 exit 9 Condrieu, N7 dir. Valence. In Reventin-Vaugris D31 and follow signs, well signposted.

Vienne
D518
D502
D4
A7 CC
N7
Salaise-sur-Sanne

CC € **17** 15/4-8/7 26/8-29/9 7=6, 14=11 📷 N 45°25'42'' E 4°55'42''

Villars-les-Dombes, F-01330 / Rhône-Alpes (Ain) ♿ 🛜 iD (2275)

▲ Le Nid du Parc****
📧 164 avenue des Nations
☎ +33 (0)4-74980021
🔓 6/4 - 4/11
@ camping@parcdesoiseaux.com

4,5ha 148T(80-100m²) 6A CEE

1 ACD**G**IJKLM**P**ST
2 CLMRTUVWXY
3 ABF**G**HJKLM**N**RU**W**
4 (**A** 25/4-20/9) (B 1/7-31/8)
   (Q 🔓) (T 1/5-5/9)
   (U+X 1/6-31/8)
5 **AB**EFGIJKLMNOPUWXYZ
6 CDEGJ(N 0,1km)TV

💬 A pleasant, friendly campsite located in a beautiful natural area with many lakes and ponds. Plenty of opportunities for (nature) excursions, including the Jura, Gorges de l'Ain and les Dombes. Close to a large bird park. An ideal area for cycle trips. The campsite has new toilet facilities.

🚗 From Bourg-en-Bresse follow the RD1083, then follow signs in the village.

D936 · D2 · Ambérieux-en-Dombes · D7 · D22 · CC · D904 · D1083 · D22 A · D4 · D43

🔲 N 45°59'49'' E 5°1'51''

(CC) € **17** 6/4-14/7 1/9-3/11

Villeneuve-de-Berg, F-07170 / Rhône-Alpes (Ardèche) 🛜 iD (2276)

▲ Domaine le Pommier*****
📧 Quartier Forcemâle, RN102
☎ +33 (0)4-75948281
📠 +33 (0)4-75948390
🔓 13/4 - 12/9
@ lepommier@cielavillage.com

40ha 171T(80-120m²) 6-10A CEE

1 ACDFIJKLM**P**ST
2 CGJKNORTVWXY
3 BGHJL**M**N**Q**RU
4 (**A**+C+H 🔓) IJK
   (Q+S+T+U+V+W+Y+Z 🔓)
5 **AB**DEFGIJKLMNOPQRUWZ
6 ACDEGH**K**L(N 1,5km)OTUV

💬 For those who like to have lots of fun, this place will suit them perfectly. There is always something fun to do. There is a level part and there are terraces with wonderful views of Mirabel. Various restaurants. Lovely swimming pools. New management.

🚗 A7 exit Montélimar-Nord direction Le Teil/Aubenas. In Le Teil take the N102 to Villeneuve-de-Berg. Just before the village and the roundabout you'll find the campsite on the right hand side.

Aubenas · D104 · CC · Villeneuve-de-Berg · N102 · D107 · D579

🔲 N 44°34'21'' E 4°30'40''

(CC) € **19** 13/4-22/6 1/9-11/9

Villerest, F-42300 / Rhône-Alpes (Loire) 🛜 iD (2277)

▲ L'Orée du Lac***
📧 68 route du Barrage
☎ +33 (0)4-77696088
🔓 14/4 - 28/10
@ camping@loreedulac.net

2,5ha 50T(80-100m²) 10A CEE

1 ACD**G**IJKLMQ
2 CDJLRVWXY
3 AGHJR**W**Z
4 (B+G 1/6-30/9)
   (Q+R 1/6-30/8)
   (T+Z 1/5-20/9)
5 **AB**FGJKLNPUVZ
6 CEG**K**(N 6km)RTV

💬 Small terraced campsite just behind the Villerest dam. The lake with its many water sports opportunities is located 400 metres from the campsite. Pitches with a lot of shade. There is a library for the guests.

🚗 From Roanne follow the N7 to Lyon, exit Le Coteau D43 and then take the D84. Follow signs Barrage-Villerest. Campsite is on right after the dam.

Renaison · Riorges · **Roanne** · D504 · D8 · N7 · D9 · CC · D53 · D1082

🔲 N 45°59'18'' E 4°2'41''

(CC) € **15** 14/4-30/6 1/9-27/10

Vizille, F-38220 / Rhône-Alpes (Isère)

♿ 🛜 **iD** (2278)

🏔 Le Bois de Cornage***
✉ 110 chemin du Camping
☎ +33 (0)4-76681239
🗓 1/4 - 1/11
@ campingvizille@orange.fr

3,6ha 115T 6-16A CEE

1 ACD**G**IJKLMOPST
2 BGKRVY
3 B**F**GHJNR
4 (B+G 1/6-15/10)
 (Q+T+U+V+X+Z 1/6-31/8)
5 **AB**FGIJKLMPUVWY
6 ACEJ**K**(N 1km)TV

💬 A campsite with spacious marked pitches under large trees. The centre and historic castle are 1 km from the campsite. An ideal location to explore the Alpine Cols from here in spring or autumn (280m).

🚗 D1085 Grenoble-Sisteron. Follow signs from roundabout in Vizille (1,4 km). Campsite clearly signposted.

Grenoble
D106 **Échirolles**
D5 D111
CC D1091
A51 D1085
D529
D1075

CC € **17** 1/4-6/7 1/9-31/10

📐 N 45°5'11'' E 5°46'12''

Vonnas, F-01540 / Rhône-Alpes (Ain)

🛜 **iD** (2279)

🏔 Le Renom***
✉ 240 avenue des Sports
☎ +33 (0)4-74500275
🗓 31/3 - 30/9
@ campingvonnas@wanadoo.fr

2,6ha 82T(80-100m²) 16A CEE

1 ACD**G**IJKLMOPQ
2 CRVWX
3 AGJK**M**NRU**W**
4 (C+H 1/7-31/8) J
 (Q+T+X+Z 🖘)
5 **AB**FGIJKLMNPUZ
6 CDEGK(N 0,3km)V

💬 The campsite is located 300m from the centre of Vonnas with many amenities in the Bresse region, which is known for its good food. The site is located beside two rivers, has spacious pitches marked out by hedges which are about 2m high and is filled with flowers. Free wifi.

🚗 Campsite is signposted in the town of Vonnas.

Mâcon D28
D26
A406 A40
D933 D26 C D1079
Saint-Didier-sur- CC
Chalaronne D2 D80
D936
D7

CC € **15** 31/3-29/6 17/8-29/9

📐 N 46°13'15'' E 4°59'15''

Agos-Vidalos, F-65400 / Midi-Pyrénées (Hautes-Pyrénées)

⛷ ♿ 🛜 **iD** (2280)

🏔 La Châtaigneraie***
✉ 46 avenue du Lavedan
☎ +33 (0)5-62970740
🗓 1/1 - 15/10, 1/12 - 31/12
@ camping.chataigneraie@
 wanadoo.fr

1,8ha 60T(80-100m²) 2-10A

1 ACD**G**IJKLMOPQ
2 GJKLRVXY
3 BGHJRU
4 (C+H 1/5-30/9) J(Q 1/7-31/8)
5 **AB**CDEFGHIJKLMNPQRUW
6 ACEGK(N 2km)TV

💬 A peaceful family campsite with lovely new toilet facilities in a fine wooden building. Shaded pitches on the edge of a chestnut wood with lovely views of the mountains. Heated swimming pool. A good base for all types of excursions and for enjoying some relaxation. Free wifi everywhere.

🚗 In Lourdes take D821/N21 to Argelès-Gazost. Then exit Agos-Vidalos. In Agos village centre. Signposted.

D937 D940 N21
Lourdes
D821
Argelès- CC
Gazost
D921

CC € **13** 1/4-10/7 28/8-14/10 7=6, 14=13, 21=19, 30=27

📐 N 43°1'55'' W 0°4'31''

Aguessac, F-12520 / Midi-Pyrénées (Aveyron)

👫 ♿ 🛜 **iD** (2281)

🏕 Camping la Belle Etoile***
✉ chemin des Prades
☎ +33 (0)5-65729107
📅 1/5 - 30/9
@ contact@camping-labelleetoile.fr

2,5ha 69**T**(150-300m²) 6A CEE

1 ACDGIJKLMOPQ
2 CFGKLNRVWXY
3 BGHIJQRU**W**X
4 (T+U+V+X+Y 📅)
  (Z 1/7-31/8)
5 **A**EFGIJKLMNOPUZ
6 ACDEGHJM(N 0,3km)RTV

💬 This charming campsite with lovely views is on the river Tarn. The site is within walking distance of the village. Large pitches and new toilet facilities. The owners are very helpful, friendly and speak English.

🚐 From the north: A75, exit 44.1 Aguessac. Left at chemists. From the south: A75, exit 47 Millau. Direction Aguessac. Right after railway line.

Map: D809, D907 BIS, D911, D9, D907, Saint-Beauzély, La Cresse, A75, D30, **CC**, D991, **Millau**, D992

CC € **13** 1/5-7/7 25/8-29/9 7=6 | 🧭 N 44°9'13'' E 3°5'53''

Alliat/Niaux, F-09400 / Midi-Pyrénées (Ariège)

♿ 🛜 **iD** (2282)

🏕 Des Grottes****
☎ +33 (0)5-61058821
📅 1/3 - 15/10
@ info@campingdesgrottes.com

7ha 120**T**(90-110m²) 16A CEE

1 ACG IJKLMOPQ
2 CKLRVX
3 BGHJN**O**RUVW
4 (C+G 1/6-15/9) IJKN
  (Q 1/5-30/9) (S 1/7-31/8)
  (T+U+V+X 1/6-31/8) (Z 📅)
5 **AB**CDEFGHIJKLMNOPUWZ
6 ACEG**K**(N 3km)OV

💬 A lovely campsite with plenty of atmosphere. Attractive separated pitches in avenues. Now with a heated toilet block. Good starting point for cultural trips and mountain hiking. Good views of the Niaux cave.

🚐 From Foix N20 direction Andorra. Turn right just past Tarascon towards Niaux/Vicdessos. Campsite 2 km on the right.

Map: Saint-Paul-de-Jarrat, D618, Tarascon-sur-Ariège, **CC**, N20

CC € **15** 1/3-3/7 21/8-14/10 7=6, 14=11, 21=14 | 🧭 N 42°48'47'' E 1°35'21''

Arcizans-Avant, F-65400 / Midi-Pyrénées (Hautes-Pyrénées)

♿ 🛜 **iD** (2283)

🏕 Les Châtaigniers***
✉ 11 rue Deth Bas
☎ +33 (0)5-62979477
📅 1/5 - 30/9
@ contact@
  camping-les-chataigniers.com

5ha 45**T**(140-180m²) 2-6A CEE

1 A**G**IJKLMPQ
2 JKLRTVWXY
3 BFGHJRU**W**
4 (A 1/7-30/8) (E+Q 📅)
5 **AB**CFGHIJKLMNPRUVZ
6 ABEGJ(N 2km)RV

💬 Small, quiet, in the green countryside, beautiful view of the valley and the Pyrenees. Peaceful and easy-going. There is no ongoing traffic nearby. Helpful, jovial owner (also speaks English). Heated pool, very clean toilet facilities. Free wifi. Fresh bread, many options for excursions and good little restaurants nearby.

🚐 From Lourdes the D821: 1st roundabout: Argelès D821a, 2nd roundabout: final exit, 3rd roundabout: Arcizans-Avant. Then follow signs.

Map: D821, Argelès-Gazost, Arras-en-Lavedan, **CC**, D921

CC € **15** 1/5-29/6 1/9-29/9 | 🧭 N 42°59'8'' W 0°6'19''

Argelès-Gazost, F-65400 / Midi-Pyrénées (Hautes-Pyrénées) ♿ 🛜 iD 2284

🏔 Les Trois Vallées★★★★
✉ avenue des Pyrénées
☎ +33 (0)5-62903547
📠 +33 (0)5-62903548
🔓 30/3 - 14/10
@ 3-vallees@wanadoo.fr

15ha 200**T**(100-170m²) 6-10A

1 ACD**G**IJKLMPQ
2 CGKLRTVXY
3 BCGHJKL**M**NRU**W**
4 (**A** 1/7-31/8) (C 1/6-30/9)
  (E 🔓) (H 1/6-30/9) IJKMP
  (Q+T+U+V+W 15/6-11/9)
  (Z 🔓)
5 **AB**CDEFGHIJKLMNPQRUX
  YZ
6 ABCFGHI**K**L(N 0,5km)TUV

💬 A modern campsite with large indoor and outdoor leisure pools with water slides and whirlpools. Restaurant and snack bar with garden. New indoor club room for all ages. Beautiful modern toilet facilities. Wifi is free in low season. 300m from centre. Excursions: Gavarnie, Tourmalet, zoo, Lourdes, bird of prey show etc. Campsite is easily accessible. Starting point for many Tour de France 'cols'.

🚗 D821 from Lourdes. 1st roundabout turn right. Next roundabout 1st exit.

CC €**19** 30/3-6/7 1/9-13/10   🏖 N 43°0'44'' W 0°5'50''

Argelès-Gazost/Ayzac-Ost, F-65400 / Midi-Pyrénées (Hautes-Pyrénées) ♿ 🛜 iD 2285

🏔 La Bergerie★★★
✉ 8 chemin de la Bergerie
☎ +33 (0)5-62975999
📠 +33 (0)5-62975189
🔓 1/5 - 30/9
@ sarl.campingdelabergerie@
  aliceadsl.fr

3,5ha 51**T**(100-130m²) 2-6A

1 ACD**G**IJKLMOPQ
2 GKRVWY
3 BGHJRU
4 (C+H 1/6-15/9) JKMP
  (Q 1/7-30/8) (V 🔓)
  (Z 15/6-31/8)
5 **A**CEFGHIJKLMNOPUZ
6 ACEG**K**(N 0,2km)OUV

💬 Level, centrally located campsite with nice large shaded pitches, close to a supermarket and within walking distance of the centre of Argelès-Gazost. New, modern and clean toilet facilities. Heated swimming pool. Wifi. The campsite is located right on the level cycle path to Lourdes.

🚗 From Lourdes right at first roundabout. 2nd exit at next roundabout. First exit to Ayzac-Ost at next roundabout.

CC €**15** 1/5-5/7 23/8-29/9 14=13, 21=19, 30=27   🏖 N 43°1'9'' W 0°5'44''

Argelès-Gazost/Lau-Balagnas, F-65400 / Midi-Pyrénées (Hautes-Pyrénées) 🚻 ♿ 🛜 iD 2286

🏔 Le Lavedan★★★★
✉ 44 route des Vallées
☎ +33 (0)5-62971884
📠 +33 (0)5-62972068
🔓 31/3 - 28/10
@ contact@lavedan.com

2ha 54**T**(80-100m²) 6-10A

1 ACD**G**IJKLMPQ
2 GKRVXY
3 BGHJRU
4 (**A** 1/7-30/8)
  (E+H 15/4-15/9) JK
  (Q 1/6-15/9) (R 🔓)
  (T+U+V+Z 15/5-15/9)
5 **AB**CDEFGHIJKLMNOPUWX
  YZ
6 ACEGIJ**K**(N 2km)ORTUV

💬 Sabine, Michel and Thomas welcome you to the Pyrenees. After a warm greeting you will stay in lovely, natural surroundings. There are unique locations to be discovered, such as Gavarnie, de Pic du Midi, Lourdes, Cauterets and the Pont d'Espagne. Heated swimming pool, wifi. Natural, level pitches. Very clean toilets.

🚗 From Lourdes follow D921. On 1st roundabout take 1st exit (D921b). Next roundabout last exit. Then through south of Argelès-Gazost. Site is signposted.

CC €**17** 31/3-6/7 25/8-27/10 7=6, 14=12   🏖 N 42°59'17'' W 0°5'22''

Ascou, F-09110 / Midi-Pyrénées (Ariège)

2287

Ascou la Forge***
Ascou la Forge
+33 (0)5-61646003
1/4 - 1/10
info@ascou-la-forge.fr

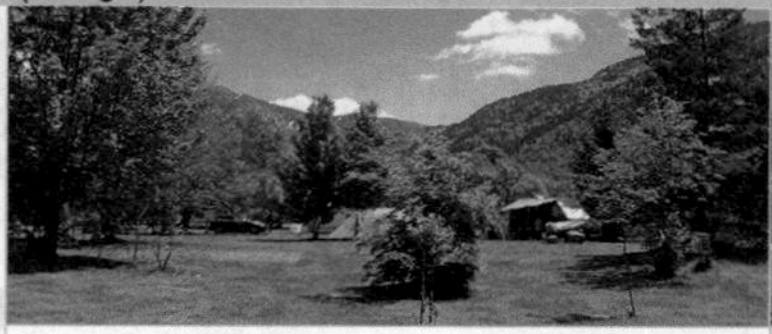

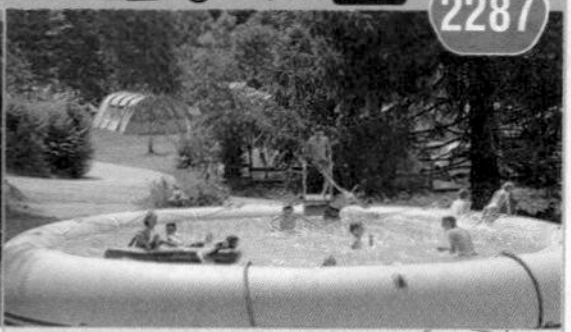

1,5ha 55T(100-120m²) 6-10A CEE

1 A**G**IJKLMO**P**Q
2 CDKRX
3 AGHNRU**W**
4 (**A**) (B 1/6-18/9) (Q+R) (S 1/7-31/8) (T 1/7-30/8) (Y+Z)
5 **AB**EFGIJKLMNPQRUZ
6 E**K**(N 7km)OV

Small campsite, located in a beautiful natural area with plenty of options for walking. Numerous outdoor sports are organised, from rafting to rock climbing. The campsite is run by a Dutch couple. Close to the border of Andorra and Spain.

From the roundabout at Ax-les-Thermes follow the signs Ascou/Pailhères. The campsite is located 3 km past the town of Ascou.

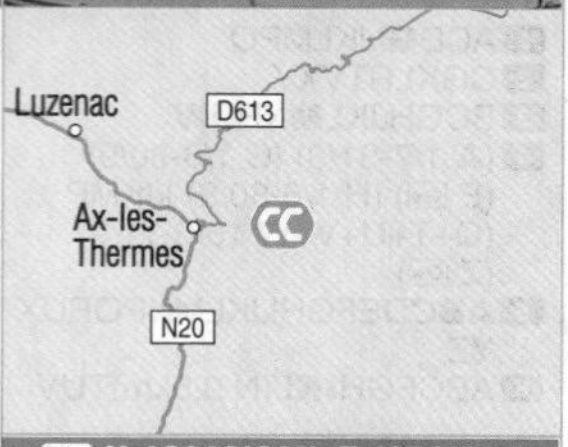
Luzenac
D613
Ax-les-Thermes
CC
N20

CC € 15 *1/4-7/7 25/8-30/9 7=6*

N 42°43'28'' E 1°53'35''

Ax-les-Thermes, F-09110 / Midi-Pyrénées (Ariège)

2288

Le Malazéou****
RN20
+33 (0)5-61646914
13/4 - 10/11, 7/12 - 2/4
contact@campingmalazeou.com

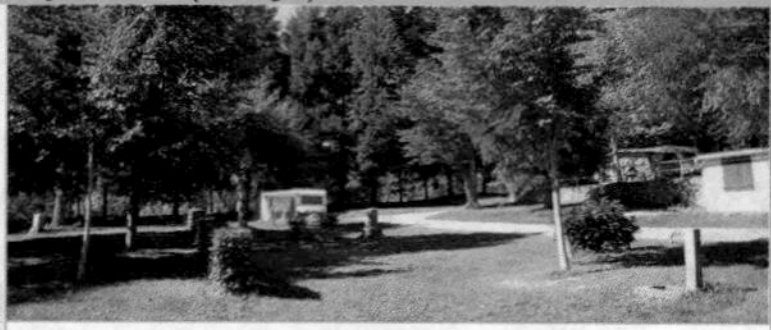

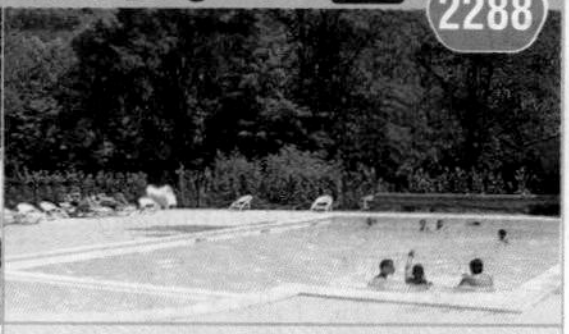

6ha 103T(90-100m²) 10A

1 ACDGIJKLMO**P**Q
2 CRTVWXY
3 BGRUV**W**
4 (C 1/6-30/9) N (T+U+X+Z 1/7-31/8)
5 **AB**DEFGJLMNPUVW
6 AFGHI**K**(N 0,8km)TV

Campsite situated by a fast-flowing river within walking distance of the town centre. Lovely swimming pool and lovely new cafeteria.

Coming from Foix, leave the motorway and continue to Ax-les-Thermes. Campsite is located on the N20 1 km before entering Ax.

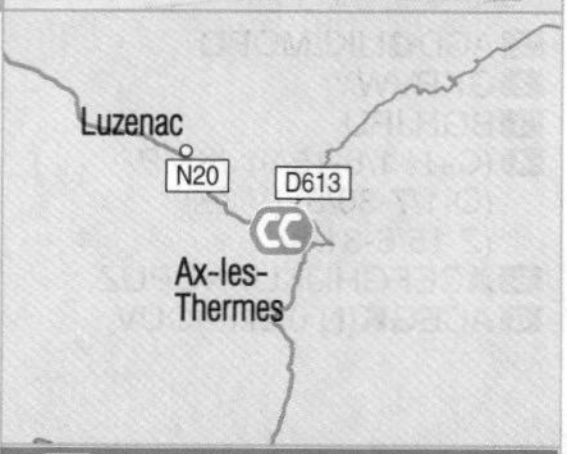
Luzenac
N20
D613
CC
Ax-les-Thermes

CC € 17 *7/1-8/2 11/3-1/4 13/4-6/7 25/8-3/11 7/12-20/12 7=6, 14=11, 21=17*

N 42°43'43'' E 1°49'32''

Bagnères-de-Bigorre, F-65200 / Midi-Pyrénées (Hautes-Pyrénées)

2289

Le Monlôo****
6 route de la Plaine
FAX +33 (0)5-62951965
15/1 - 15/12
campingmonloo@yahoo.com

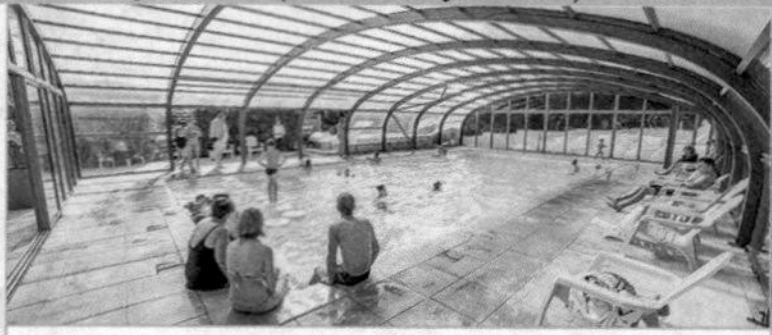

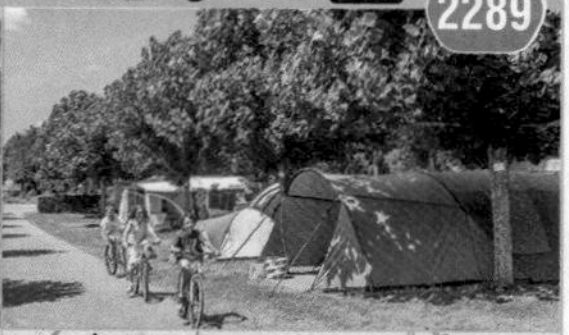

3,5ha 122T(100-120m²) 10A

1 ACD**G**IJKLMPQ
2 ACDGIKLRTVXY
3 AB**F**GJ**M**NRUZ
4 (F 1/5-30/10) (H 15/5-30/9) J (Q 15/6-15/9) (R+T 1/7-15/9) (U 5/7-23/8)
5 **AB**DFGIJKLMNOPQU
6 CDE**K**(N 2km)V

Spacious, quiet, shady campsite. Heated indoor pool 15/5 - 15/10 and an artificial swimming lake 15/6 - 15/9 with a sandy beach and deckchairs. Free wifi for CampingCard ACSI guests. Good base for visiting the Pyrenees.

From Tarbes take the D935 as far as Bagnères-de-Bigorre. Left at the first roundabout, left again at the next roundabout. Then follow camping signs.

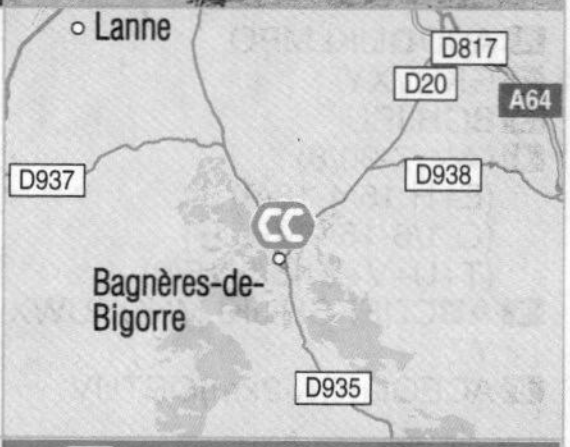
Lanne
D817
D20
A64
D937
D938
CC
Bagnères-de-Bigorre
D935

CC € 17 *15/1-29/6 27/8-14/12 21=19*

N 43°4'51'' E 0°8'57''

Bagnères-de-Luchon, F-31110 / Midi-Pyrénées (Haute-Garonne)

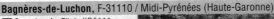

🏕 Camping Au Fil de l'Oô***
🏠 37 avenue de Vénasque
☎ +33 (0)5-61793074
🕐 10/3 - 2/11
@ campingaufildeloo@gmail.com

2,5ha 104T(80-120m²) 2-10A

1 ACDGHIJKLMPQ
2 CKLRVWXY
3 A**F**GHJKRU**W**
4 (Q 1/5-15/10) (T+U 1/6-15/9)
(V 15/6-30/9) (X 1/6-15/9)
5 **AB**DGIJKLMNOPUV
6 CEGK(N 0,5km)TV

💬 Very structured and well maintained campsite with views of majestic mountains and the town in Belle Epoque style. There is a path beside the river via a gate at the back of the campsite which takes you into the town past sports fields and a swimming pool.

🚗 In Bagnères-de-Luchon follow road to Superbagnères, second campsite on left.

2290

(CC) € **13** 10/3-5/7 21/9-1/11

📡 N 42°46'40'' E 0°36'1''

Boô-Silhen, F-65400 / Midi-Pyrénées (Hautes-Pyrénées)

🏕 Deth-Potz**
🏠 40 route de Silhen
☎ +33 (0)5-62903723
🕐 1/1 - 10/10, 10/12 - 31/12
@ contact@deth-potz.fr

4ha 74T(85-110m²) 10A

1 ACD**G**IJLPQ
2 IJKRTVWXY
3 AGHJNQRU
4 (B+G 15/6-15/9) (Q 1/7-31/8)
(R 🕐)
5 A**C**DEFGHIJKMNOPQUV
6 ABCEJ(N 2km)OTV

💬 This campsite is located in an oasis of greenery and relaxation at the foot of a 16th-century chapel, two kilometres from Argelès-Gazost in the heart of the Pyrenees. Modern toilet facilities, motorhome service point, playing field. Ideally located for countless sports activities and discovery trips in the countryside.

🚗 From Lourdes towards Luz-St-Sauveur, Gavarnie. Last exit on 2nd roundabout, over bridge, immediate left. Campsite 1500m on the left.

2291

(CC) € **13** 1/1-30/6 1/9-9/10 10/12-31/12

📡 N 43°0'40'' W 0°4'39''

Boyne/Rivière-sur-Tarn, F-12640 / Midi-Pyrénées (Aveyron)

🏕 Camping Moulin de la Galinière**
🏠 chemin des Condamines
☎ +33 (0)5-65626560
🕐 28/4 - 15/9
@ info@moulindelagaliniere.fr

2ha 57T(90-150m²) 6A CEE

1 ABG**IJ**KLPRS
2 CFKLMNRSTVWXY
3 AGHJRU**W**X
4 (Q+T 🕐) (U 15/5-13/9)
(V 🕐) (X 15/5-13/9)
(Z 15/5-15/9)
5 **A**CEFGHIJKLMNOPQRUV
6 ABEGJ(N 5km)TU

💬 Close to the Gorges du Tarn in the heart of the 'Parc des Grands Causses'. A homely campsite where you can go kayaking and canoeing. Friendly restaurant. Special flora (wild orchids) and fauna (more than 50 species of birds). English, German and Dutch also spoken.

🚗 A75 Clermont-Ferrand, exit 44.1 Aguessac. Follow signs to 'Gorges du Tarn'. Go to Boyne, campsite just outside Boyne village on the right by the Tarn.

2292

(CC) € **15** 28/4-30/6 25/8-14/9

📡 N 44°12'4'' E 3°9'34''

Boyne/Rivière-sur-Tarn, F-12640 / Midi-Pyrénées (Aveyron)

▲ Le Pont***
✆ +33 (0)5-65599633
🕒 1/4 - 31/10
@ camping-le-pont@wanadoo.fr

♿ 📶 **iD** (2293)

2ha 30T(90-100m²) 6A CEE

1 ACDGIJKLOPQ
2 BCFKLMRVVWXY
3 AGHIJRU**W**X
4 (C+Q+R+S+Z 🔒)
5 **A**CEGHIJKLMNOPUWZ
6 ABCEGK(N 2km)OTV

🗨 Small, hospitable campsite in the middle of the town of Boyne. Driving from Riviere sur Tarn this is the first campsite directly after the cheese factory in Peyrelade. The campsite is situated in a bend in the river and has its own beach and woods. Many great outings possible from this campsite into the Tarn countryside.

🚗 A75 Gorges du Tarn. After Rivière-sur-Tarn (2km). After cheese factory Peyrelade it is the 1st campsite on right before Boyne.

©© € **11** 1/4-7/7 25/8-30/10

🌴 N 44°12'10'' E 3°9'26''

Canet-de-Salars, F-12290 / Midi-Pyrénées (Aveyron)

▲ Camping Soleil Levant***
✉ Pont des Vernhes / D993
✆ +33 (0)5-65460365
🕒 1/5 - 30/9
@ contact@
camping-soleil-levant.com

♿ 📶 **iD** (2294)

7ha 146T(100-110m²) 6A CEE

1 ACG**I**JKLMPRS
2 ADIJKRVVWXY
3 BGHJNRU**W**Z
4 (Q 🔒) (T+U+V 1/7-31/8) (Z 🔒)
5 **AB**EFGJLNPRUVZ
6 AEGJ(N 4km)OUV

🗨 Located on a peninsula. Slightly undulating wooded grounds. Large pitches directly on the shores of Lake Pareloup. The shores are like beaches. The large area lends itself to strolling or walking the dog. Free wifi spot.

🚗 A75 exit 44.1 in the direction of Pont-de-Salars. Follow D911 (27 km) till just before Pont-de-Salars, turn left onto the D993 towards Salles-Curan. Campsite about 8 km on the left just before the bridge.

©© € **13** 1/5-10/7 28/8-29/9 14=11, 21=18

🌴 N 44°12'55'' E 2°46'41''

Capvern, F-65130 / Midi-Pyrénées (Hautes-Pyrénées)

▲ Les Craouès***
✉ 682 rue du 8 Mai 1945
✆ +33 (0)5-62390254
🕒 1/4 - 30/10
@ camping-les-craoues@orange.fr

♿ 📶 **iD** (2295)

NEW

1,5ha 66T(85-150m²) 8A CEE

1 ACD**G**IJKLMPQ
2 FGRUVVWXY
3 A**F**GR
4 (B+G 21/6-21/9) (Q 🔒)
5 **AB**EFIJKLMNOPUV
6 CDFG**K**(N 0,6km)V

🗨 Quiet, shady campsite located on the roundabout, ideal for those stopping over before the heading through the Bielsa Tunnel. Good base for visiting the pretty region Les Baronnies. Cycling enthusiasts can take a ride up the Col d'Aspin from here.

🚗 Campsite is on the 1st roundabout on D817 1 km after the exit from A64.

©© € **15** 1/4-14/7 1/9-29/10

🌴 N 43°6'20'' E 0°19'24''

Carennac, F-46110 / Midi-Pyrénées (Lot) ♟♿ 🛜 iD (2296)

🔺 L'Eau Vive★★★★
🏠 Prés Nabots
☎ +33 (0)5-65109739
📠 +33 (0)5-55281212
🔓 20/5 - 30/9
@ info@dordogne-soleil.com

3ha 100T(80-120m²) 6A CEE

1 AGIJKLMPRS
2 CRVWXY
3 BFGHJNQRU**W**X
4 (B+G 1/6-30/9) (Q 1/6-31/8)
(R+T+U+V 1/7-31/8)
(Z 15/6-15/9)
5 **AB**FGIJKLMNOPUZ
6 CEGJ(N 1km)RTV

💬 A campsite just outside Carennac, one of France's most beautiful villages, in the middle of the countryside on the Dordogne. Plenty of opportunities for tourist trips out: culture (villages, markets, caves) and nature (walking, cycling, canoeing). Lovely in summer but also in the early and late seasons. Pitches with sun or shade. Family atmosphere.

🚐 From Martel to Carennac via Vayrac (D703), then via Bétaille and via the D20 to Carennac. Campsite signposted.

CC € ⑮ 20/5-7/7 31/8-29/9 7=6, 14=11   📷 N 44°54'36'' E 1°44'27''

Castelnau-Magnoac, F-65230 / Midi-Pyrénées (Hautes-Pyrénées) ⅍♿ 🛜 ✿ iD (2297)

🔺 l'Eglantière
🏠 Ariès-Espenan
☎ +33 (0)5-62398800
📠 +33 (0)5-62398144
🔓 7/4 - 14/10
@ infos@leglantiere.com

50ha 80T(90-200m²) 16A CEE

1 AC**G**IJKLMPQ
2 CLMNRVWXY
3 AGHJKNRU**W**X
4 (A 1/6-15/9) (C+H 🔲) N
(Q 🔲) (R+S 15/6-15/9)
(T 🔲) (U 15/5-15/9)
(V 1/6-15/9) (X 15/5-30/9)
(Y 1/6-15/9) (Z 1/6-15/10)
5 **AB**EFGIJKLMNOPQUWZ
6 DEG**I**J(N 5km)OV

💬 Naturist campsite located between Gascony and the Pyrenees in a 50 hectare organic agricultural area. The River Gers passes through the campsite. A good spot for lovers of nature, walking and fishing. Heated swimming pool and sauna, wine bar, snack bar, restaurant, free wifi. Welcoming atmosphere, French/Dutch staff. Ideal stopover site on way to Spain.

🚐 Follow the D929 from Lannemezan to Castelnau-Magnoac. Campsite signposted about 2 km before Castelnau-Magnoac.

CC € ⑰ 7/4-6/7 25/8-13/10 14=13, 21=17   📷 N 43°15'49'' E 0°31'15''

Castres, F-81100 / Midi-Pyrénées (Tarn) ♿ 🛜 iD (2298)

🔺 Camping de Gourjade★★★
🏠 Av. de Roquecourbe/
Parc de Gourjade
☎ 📠 +33 (0)5-63593351
🔓 1/4 - 30/9
@ contact@campingdegourjade.net

4ha 100T(80-200m²) 16A CEE

1 AC**G**IJKLMPQ
2 BCGJLRVWXY
3 AFGHJN**P**QRU
4 (A 1/7-31/8) (B 15/6-15/9) M
(Q+R 🔲) (T+X+Y 1/4-15/9)
(Z 🔲)
5 **AB**EFGIJKLMNOPUVZ
6 CEGJK(N 2km)

💬 Beautiful campsite located between the banks of a river and a large park on the edge of Castres with a large sports and water complex. There is a golf course next to the campsite. Public transport is free.

🚐 In Castres follow dir. Brassac and then follow campsite signs and signs Parc de Loisirs de Gourjade.

CC € ⑬ 1/4-30/6 1/9-29/9   📷 N 43°37'14'' E 2°15'14''

Cauterets, F-65110 / Midi-Pyrénées (Hautes-Pyrénées)

♿ 🛜 iD (2299)

🏠 Cabaliros***
✉ 93 avenue du Mamelon Vert
☎ +33 (0)5-62925536
🗓 18/5 - 30/9
@ info@camping-cabaliros.com

2ha 93T(85-130m²) 6A

1 ACD**G**IJKLMOPQ
2 CGIJKLRVWX
3 AHJRU**W**
4 (Q+R 🖩)
5 **AB**CEFGHIJKLMNOPUVX
6 ACEJ**K**(N 0,3km)TV

💬 An attractive campsite by a mountain stream close to Cauterets and the National Park with its lakes and waterfalls (including the Pont d' Espagne). Spacious pitches with lovely views of the mountains. Free shuttle buses for most of the year. Good explanation of the various sights and fantastic walks at the reception. Wifi on entire campsite and bread service.

🚗 D920. After Carrefour supermarkt 1st road right over bridge.

Lau-Balagnas

CC

Cauterets | D921 | D918

CC € **15** 18/5-6/7 26/8-29/9

📷 N 42°54'11'' W 0°6'26''

Caylus, F-82160 / Midi-Pyrénées (Tarn-et-Garonne)

♿ 🛜 iD (2300)

🏠 De la Bonnette***
✉ 672 route de la Bonnette
☎ +33 (0)5-63657020
🗓 24/3 - 1/10
@ info@campingbonnette.com

1,5ha 50T(100m²) 10A CEE

1 A**G**IJKLMPQ
2 CGKLRVXY
3 AGHJNR**W**
4 (B 15/4-30/9) (Q 1/5-30/9) (T+U+X 🖩) (Y 1/4-1/10) (Z 🖩)
5 **AB**CFGIJKLMNOPUWXZ
6 CEG**K**(N 0,5km)T

💬 An extremely friendly campsite run by a friendly Dutch couple, with good facilities, a swimming pool, bar, restaurant and snacks, wifi, large camping pitches, and all this in a charming and rural setting with old villages. Also good for cyclists.

🚗 Until Caussade A20. Exit 59 dir. Rodez (D926). Drive through village of Caylus as far as garage on left. Turn right here and follow the camping signs.

D42

D17 | Caylus | D926

CC

Septfonds

D19

Saint-Antonin-Noble-Val | D115 | D958

CC € **17** 24/3-6/7 25/8-30/9 14=13

📷 N 44°14'2'' E 1°46'31''

Cayriech, F-82240 / Midi-Pyrénées (Tarn-et-Garonne)

♿ 🛜 iD (2301)

🏠 Le Clos de la Lère***
✉ Lieu dit Clergue
☎ +33 (0)5-63312041
🗓 1/3 - 15/11
@ le-clos-de-la-lere@wanadoo.fr

1,5ha 40T(80-130m²) 10A

1 ACF**IJ**LPQ
2 CLRVX
3 BGHJMNRU**W**
4 (C 1/5-31/10) (Q+S+T+U+X+Z 🖩)
5 **AB**DEFGIJKLMNPUWZ
6 ACDEG**K**(N 5km)ORTV

💬 A family campsite in a picturesque village in a quiet, natural and rural setting. Heated swimming pool and wifi. Interesting for groups and cyclists. Small restaurant with local products, breakfast service.

🚗 D820 from Cahors to Caussade. After 30 km turn off to Lapenche (D103), then to Cayriech and follow signs.

D820 | D42

Montpezat-de-Quercy | D17

A20 CC

| D926

Caussade | D5 | D19

D964 | D115

CC € **15** 1/3-7/7 25/8-14/11 7=6, 14=12, 21=19

📷 N 44°13'3'' E 1°36'47''

Conques/Sénergues, F-12320 / Midi-Pyrénées (Aveyron) ♿ 📶 ✿ iD (2302)

🔺 Etang du Camp***
☎ +33 (0)5-65460195
📅 1/4 - 30/9
@ info@etangducamp.fr

5ha 40T(100-200m²) 6A

1 AGIJKLMPQ
2 DKLRUVWXY
3 AGHJNRUW
4 (Q 1/5-30/9) (R 🔑)
5 ACDEFGIJKLMNOPQUVWX
6 EGJ(N 3km)T

💬 A peaceful campsite in the heart of nature near a fishing lake. English/German owned. Warm welcome. Spacious, marked-out partly shaded pitches. Ideal for exploring charming Aveyron. The celebrated medieval abbey at Conques is nearby. Bread, themed meals, campfires, ice cream, soft drinks and coffee. Bike collection service.

🚍 From Rodez dir. Conques (D901). In St. Cyprien follow D46 to Peyrelebade. Left D242 dir. Sénergues. From there campsite is signposted.

CC € 15 1/4-11/7 29/8-29/9

📐 N 44°33'34'' E 2°27'43''

Cordes-sur-Ciel, F-81170 / Midi-Pyrénées (Tarn) 📶 iD (2303)

🔺 Camping Camp Redon***
🛣 D107
☎ +33 647461362
📅 28/4 - 30/9
@ annelientomassen@gmail.com

2ha 43T(100-120m²) 10-16A CEE

1 ACDGIJKLPQ
2 KLRTVWXY
3 AGHJKLNRU
4 (B+G+Q+R+U+V+X+Z 🔑)
5 ABCFGIJKLMNOPUWZ
6 ADEGHJ(N 5km)OT

💬 Between the bastide Cordes-sur-Ciel (France's favourite village) and the lovely town of Albi (UNESCO Heritage Site) you will find Camp Redon campsite in lovely hilly surroundings. In addition to the good amenities (including free wifi) at this small and friendly campsite, you will find camping pitches with lovely views and sunsets.

🚍 Signposted on the D107 Cordes-Albi, 5 km direction Albi.

CC € 17 28/4-6/7 26/8-29/9

📐 N 44°2'30'' E 2°1'1''

Cordes-sur-Ciel, F-81170 / Midi-Pyrénées (Tarn) ♿ 📶 iD (2304)

🔺 Le Moulin de Julien***
🛣 D922
☎ +33 (0)5-63561110
📅 1/5 - 29/9
@ contact@
   campingmoulindejulien.com

8ha 82T(100-120m²) 5-10A CEE

1 ACGIJLMPRS
2 CJLRTVWXY
3 BGNQRW
4 (B 🔑) J(Q 1/7-31/8) (Z 🔑)
5 AEFGIJKLMNPUW
6 EGK(N 0,8km)OTV

💬 An extensive campsite set in parkland and located at the foot of Cordes-sur-Ciel. Excellent toilet facilities, lovely swimming pool and large pitches. An ideal base for trips out in the surrounding area and for gastronomic delights.

🚍 Leave Cordes via D600 in direction of Albi. Take the D922 after 500 metres towards Gaillac. The entranceway is after 300 metres on the left.

CC € 17 1/5-6/7 25/8-28/9

📐 N 44°3'14'' E 1°58'19''

Crayssac, F-46150 / Midi-Pyrénées (Lot) ♔♔ 🛜 iD (2305)

🔼 Campéole Les Reflets du Quercy★★★★
🏠 Mas de Bastide
☎ +33 (0)5-65300027
🔓 27/4 - 16/9
@ reflets-du-quercy@campeole.com

8ha 37T(80-100m²) 10A CEE

1 ACF**I**JKL**P**RS
2 BIJKTUVWXY
3 BGHMN**O**RU
4 (C+H 1/6-15/9) M(Q 🕐)
   (R+T+U+V+X+Z 1/7-31/8)
5 **AB**CEFGIJKLMNOPUW
6 ACEGHI**K**(N 5km)RTV

💬 Spaciously laid out terraced campsite situated high up overlooking the Lot on the rocky plateau of Quercy. Plenty of sun, swimming pool with solarium and sports facilities. You can taste the Cahor wines and regional products(foie gras, truffles, gastronomy) at the local producers.

🚗 On the D811 (Cahors-Puy-l'Évèque) signposted at Crayssac, from the D911 about another 3 km.

CC € 15 *27/4-6/7 25/8-15/9*   📐 N 44°30'37'' E 1°19'22''

Creysse, F-46600 / Midi-Pyrénées (Lot) ♿ 🛜 iD (2306)

🔼 Du Port★★★
☎ +33 (0)5-65322082
📠 +33 (0)5-65410532
🔓 21/4 - 30/9
@ contact@campingduport.com

5ha 86T(100-300m²) 10A CEE

1 ACD**G**IJKLPRS
2 CLNRVWXY
3 ABGHJKRU**W**X
4 (B 1/5-30/9) (Q 1/5-10/9)
   (R 🕐) (S+T+U 1/7-31/8)
   (Z 🕐)
5 **A**EFGIJKLMNOPUZ
6 EGJ(N 5km)OV

💬 Direct access to the Dordogne. Close to the historic village of Creysse. The restaurant/brasserie is open during the CampingCard ACSI validity period. You can book canoeing, climbing and potholing trips at the campsite. Beautiful pool. Free wifi.

🚗 A20 exit Rocamadour/Martel. Via the N140 as far as Martel. In Martel via the D23 towards Creysse. Then follow the camping signs.

CC € 15 *21/4-30/6 26/8-29/9*   *10=8*   📐 N 44°53'7'' E 1°35'58''

Damiatte, F-81220 / Midi-Pyrénées (Tarn) ♿ 🛜 iD (2307)

🔼 Le Plan d'Eau Saint Charles★★★
🏠 La Cahuziere
☎ +33 (0)5-63706607
🔓 1/4 - 31/10
@ sournisseurs@
   campingplandeau.com

6ha 33T(100-150m²) 6A CEE

1 ABCD**G**IJKL**P**ST
2 ADLRVWXY
3 A**F**GHJNRUW
4 (A 7/7-31/8) (**B** 🕐) JM
   (Q+R+T+V+X+Z 1/7-31/8)
5 **A**FGJKLMNOPUVZ
6 EGJL(N 2km)TV

💬 A family campsite with marked-out pitches. The campsite has a natural lake for swimming with a water slide. Bar-restaurant with wifi. Various routes for walking and mountain biking nearby.

🚗 Take the Graulhet (D84) exit St. Paul-de-Joux. Campsite is situated in Damiatte and is signposted.

CC € 15 *1/4-30/6 1/9-30/10*   📐 N 43°39'47'' E 1°58'17''

Deyme, F-31450 / Midi-Pyrénées (Haute-Garonne) 👫 ♿ 📶 iD (2308)

▲ Les Violettes
🚇 17 R5 813
☎ +33 (0)5-61817207
⏱ 1/1 - 31/12
@ campinglesviolettes@wanadoo.fr

2,7ha 58T(80-150m²) 6-10A

1 CDF**I**JKLMOPQ
2 FGRTUVX**Y**
3 ABGHJR
4 (Q+R+T 🔒)
5 **AB**DGIJKLMNOPUVWXYZ
6 ACDGIJ**K**(N 5km)OV

💬 Les Violettes campsite in Deyme, south east of Roulouse, is open all year round. Feel at home in these natural surroundings close to the Canal du Midi. Cycling routes nearby, renovated heated toilet block. Adventure and natural surroundings close to Toulouse and Lauraguais: relaxation, discovery, culture, gastronomy, shopping. All of these elements combine for a wonderful stay.

🚗 Follow A61 Toulouse, exit 19 direction Ramonville on RD813. Follow signs.

Toulouse · Quint-Fonsegrives · Castanet-Tolosan · D813 · D16 · D2 · A61 · D4 · D19 · D38 · A66

CC € **15** 1/1-7/7 26/8-31/12 7=6   🏔 N 43°29'12'' E 1°31'57''

Entraygues-sur-Truyère, F-12140 / Midi-Pyrénées (Aveyron) 👫 ♿ 📶 ✿ iD (2309)

▲ Camping le Val de Saures***
☎ +33 (0)5-65445692
⏱ 28/4 - 23/9
@ info@camping-valdesaures.com

4ha 115T(70-120m²) 10A

1 ACG**I**JKLMPQ
2 CKLORVWXY
3 BGHJMNRUW**X**
4 (C+H 1/7-31/8)
5 **AB**CFGIJKLMNOPUWZ
6 CFK(N 0,3km)RTV

💬 A campsite with 115 shaded pitches. A footbridge takes you to the characteristic village of Entraygues-sur-Truyère. Enjoy the charm of the village with its lovely shops and the delicious Aveyron food. Opportunities close by for kayaking, canoeing and rafting.

🚗 From Aurillac take the D920 as far as Entraygues, where the campsite is signposted, or exit 42 on the A75 past Laissac and Espaillon to Entraygues.

D19 · Saint-Amans-des-Cots · D34 · CC · D904 · D920 · Estaing

CC € **13** 28/4-7/7 25/8-22/9   🏔 N 44°38'34'' E 2°33'54''

Estaing, F-65400 / Midi-Pyrénées (Hautes-Pyrénées) ♿ 📶 iD (2310)

▲ Pyrénées Natura****
🚇 route du Lac
☎ +33 (0)5-62974544
⏱ 19/5 - 30/9
@ info@
camping-pyrenees-natura.com

2ha 47T(90-150m²) 4-10A CEE

1 ACDG**I**JKLOPQ
2 CIKMRUX
3 AGHJRU**W**
4 N(Q+R+T+U+Z 🔒)
5 **AB**CEFGHJLNPUWZ
6 ACDEGHJ**K**ORTV

💬 A four-star campsite set in parkland near the village of Estaing. Set in a beautiful valley in the Pyrenees next to the National Park. A campsite to 'crash out' with food and drink at cheap prices. Walking and cycle trips at all levels.

🚗 From Argeles-Gazost follow the D918 (direction Col d'Aubisque) as far as the D13 direction Bun. Then follow Lac d'Estaing signs. Do not take the earlier exit to Estaing on the D918 with a caravan!

Argelès-Gazost · D821 · Arras-en-Lavedan · CC · D921

CC € **17** 19/5-14/7 1/9-29/9   🏔 N 42°56'29'' W 0°10'41''

Estang, F-32240 / Midi-Pyrénées (Gers)

♿ 🛜 **iD** **2311**

🏕 Les Lacs de Courtès***
🚩 Base de Loisirs
☎ +33 (0)5-62096198
📠 +33 (0)5-62096313
⌚ 1/1 - 31/12
@ contact@lacsdecourtes.com

7ha 55T(100-130m²) 6-10A CEE

1 ACD**G**IJKLMOPQ
2 CDJLRTUVWXY
3 BGH**M**NQRUW
4 (C 1/5-29/9)
　(G+Q+T+U+X+Z 1/7-31/8)
5 **AB**DEFGIJKLMNOPQUWYZ
6 CDEGI**K**(N 2,4km)OTV

💬 Lively terraced campsite with a lovely swimming pool, large fishing lake and many activities for young people.

🚗 Campsite on the D152 Estang towards Panjas, left beyond the church just outside the village.

Cazaubon — D626 — D37
Estang — N524
D1 — D30
Panjas
D32
D6 — D931 — Manciet

ⒸⒸ € **17** 1/1-6/7　25/8-31/12

📍 N 43°51'53'' W 0°6'11''

Flagnac, F-12300 / Midi-Pyrénées (Aveyron)

♿ 🛜 **iD** **2312**

🏕 Camping Le Port de
　Lacombe - Escapade****
☎ +33 (0)5-65435918
📠 +33 (0)4-90360989
⌚ 1/4 - 30/9
@ reservation@
　escapade-vacances.fr

2,5ha 97T(80-120m²) 10A CEE

1 CD**F**IJLPT
2 CLMRTVY
3 BHJN**P**RUW
4 (C+H 15/6-15/9) J
　(Q+T+U+V+X+Z 15/6-15/9)
5 **AB**EFGIJKLMNPWXY
6 ACEGKTV

NEW

💬 High hedges separate the camping pitches at this level campsite. The River Lot flows slowly past and there is a heated swimming pool.

🚗 Follow the camping signs from the D963 between Aurillac and Decazeville close to Flagnac.

D663
N122 — D601 — D42
D963
Capdenac-Gare — D901
Decazeville
D994 — D221
D5 — D840 — D22

ⒸⒸ € **15** 1/4-14/7　1/9-29/9

📍 N 44°36'34'' E 2°14'9''

Foix, F-09000 / Midi-Pyrénées (Ariège)

👫 ♿ 🛜 **iD** **2313**

🏕 Du Lac***
🚩 D919 Labarre
☎ +33 (0)5-61600909
⌚ 15/3 - 31/10
@ camping-du-lac@wanadoo.fr

5ha 135T(90-110m²) 10A CEE

1 ACD**G**IJKLMPQ
2 CDLRVX
3 AGMNRU**W**
4 (B+G 1/6-30/9) (Q 1/6-5/9)
　(T+V 15/6-15/9) (Z 1/6-15/9)
5 **AB**DFGIJKLMNPUVZ
6 CFGJ(N 0,2km)RTV

💬 Comfortable campsite with nice pool and renovated toilet facilities (2015). Located on the northern edge of the town. Very easily accessible. Cycling and walking options from the campsite.

🚗 The campsite is located on the north side of Foix, dir. Touolouse, on the N20.

Les Pujols
D919 — Dalou
D117
Foix
N20
D618

ⒸⒸ € **15** 15/3-7/7　25/8-30/10 7=6, 14=11

📍 N 42°59'22'' E 1°36'56''

Garganvillar, F-82100 / Midi-Pyrénées (Tarn-et-Garonne)

♿ 🛜 iD (2314)

🔺 Camping Des Etangs★★★
✉ 2315 route d'Angeville
☎ +33 (0)5-63290228
⏱ 31/3 - 30/9
@ camping-des-etangs@orange.fr

5ha 44T(80-150m²) 10A CEE

1 ACD**G**IJKLPQ
2 RVWX
3 AGNRUW
4 (B 19/5-30/9) (G 1/7-31/8) J (Q+R+T+U+Z 🔲)
5 A GIJKLOPUZ
6 AEGJ(N 6km)TV

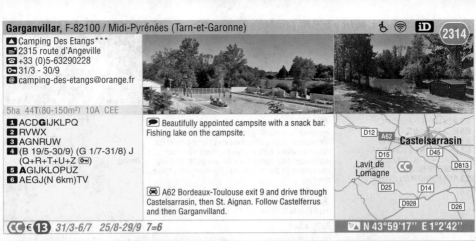

💬 Beautifully appointed campsite with a snack bar. Fishing lake on the campsite.

🚗 A62 Bordeaux-Toulouse exit 9 and drive through Castelsarrasin, then St. Aignan. Follow Castelferrus and then Garganvilland.

CC € 13 *31/3-6/7 25/8-29/9 7=6*

📐 N 43°59'17'' E 1°2'42''

Gavarnie, F-65120 / Midi-Pyrénées (Hautes-Pyrénées)

🎿 ♿ 🛜 iD (2315)

🔺 Le Pain de Sucre★★
✉ quartier Couret
☎ FAX +33 (0)5-62924755
⏱ 29/5 - 30/9, 15/12 - 15/4
@ camping-gavarnie@wanadoo.fr

1,5ha 36T(88-130m²) 2-10A

1 ACD**G**IJKLMOPQ
2 CGKRVX
3 AGHRU**W**
4 (**A**+Q 🔲) (T+U+V 1/6-30/9) (Z 🔲)
5 AB CDGHIJKLMNOPUWZ
6 CEK(N 3km)V

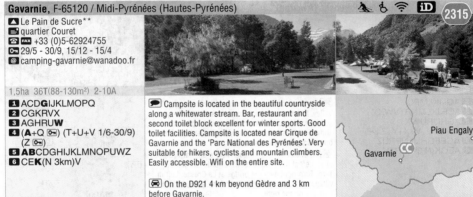

💬 Campsite is located in the beautiful countryside along a whitewater stream. Bar, restaurant and second toilet block excellent for winter sports. Good toilet facilities. Campsite is located near Cirque de Gavarnie and the 'Parc National des Pyrénées'. Very suitable for hikers, cyclists and mountain climbers. Easily accessible. Wifi on the entire site.

🚗 On the D921 4 km beyond Gèdre and 3 km before Gavarnie.

CC € 13 *1/1-14/4 29/5-29/6 1/9-29/9 14=12*

📐 N 42°45'34'' E 0°0'2''

Gourdon, F-46300 / Midi-Pyrénées (Lot)

♿ 🛜 iD (2316)

🔺 Domaine Le Quercy★★★★
✉ Ecoute s'il pleut
☎ +33 (0)5-65410619
⏱ 14/4 - 22/9
@ domainequercy@orange.fr

5ha 90T(80-120m²) 10A CEE

1 ACDFIJKLMOPRS
2 BDJLRTUVXY
3 BGHJK**M**N**R**W**Z**
4 (C+G 🔲) J(Q 1/7-31/8) (R 1/7-30/8) (T+U+V+Z 🔲)
5 AB EFGIJKLMNOPUWXYZ
6 ACEGHJ(N 2km)TV

💬 A peaceful terraced campsite in early and late seasons and close to an artificial lake. Lovely swimming pool with slides. Completely renewed toilet facilities. The town of Gourdon is close by and the site is ideally located for exploring the lovely surroundings.

🚗 A20, exit 55 or 56 direction Gourdon. In Gourdon centre take the D704 Sarlat. Follow 'Domaine Le Quercy'.

CC € 13 *14/4-28/6 25/8-21/9*

📐 N 44°44'57'' E 1°22'31''

La Bastide-de-Sérou, F-09240 / Midi-Pyrénées (Ariège)

👫 ♿ 📶 **iD** (2317)

🏕 Flower Camping L'Arize****
🚩 Bourtol
☎ +33 (0)5-61618151
📅 6/4 - 28/10
@ mail@camping-arize.com

3ha 69T(100-200m²) 6A CEE

1 ACD**G**HIJKLMOPQ
2 BCLRUVWXY
3 B**F**GHJKN**OP**RU**W**
4 (B 1/6-30/9) (Q+R 🔑) (T+U 1/7-31/8) (Z 🔑)
5 **AB**DEFGIJKLOPUWXYZ
6 ACDEGI**JK**(N 2km)RTV

💬 The campsite is positioned at the foot of the Pyrenees by a babbling brook in the Pyrenées Ariegeoises. nature area. Excellent starting point for mountain walks, historical and cultural trips out. Restaurant 400 metres from the campsite. Walking and cycling on the 'Voie Verte'. Excellent golf course close by.

🚗 La Bastide-de-Sérou is located by the main road from Foix to St. Girons (D117). Campsite signposted.

D119 D919
D15 D31
Crampagna
Rimont ╋ D117
Foix
D618

CC € **15** 6/4-8/7 27/8-27/10 8=7, 14=11

📐 N 43°0'7'' E 1°26'44''

La Cresse, F-12640 / Midi-Pyrénées (Aveyron)

♿ 📶 **iD** (2318)

🏕 Le Papillon***
🚩 Les Canals
☎ +33 (0)5-65590842
📅 21/4 - 29/9
@ info@campinglepapillon.com

1,5ha 41T(80-123m²) 10A CEE

1 A**G**IJKLMPQ
2 ACFJKLMNRTVWXY
3 AGHIJRU**W**X
4 (Q+T+U+V+X+Y+Z 🔑)
5 **A**CEFGHIJLNPRUZ
6 AEGK(N 3km)RTV

💬 Terraced campsite with magnificent views of Tarn Valley. Friendly owners, Hans and Annette offer you sunny, spacious pitches, modern clean toilet facilities and a lively restaurant. Weekly pizza evenings. Fresh bread daily in the season.

🚗 A75, exit 44.1 Aguessac/Rivière-sur-Tarn (SatNav off!). Left at mini-roundabout towards Gorges-du-Tarn. Turn right over the bridge at La Cresse. Left in village at church D187 dir. Peyreleau. After 1500m first site on the right.

D32 D907 BIS
D9
D911 Rivière-sur-Tarn ╋ D907 D996
A75 D809
D30
D991
Millau

CC € **13** 21/4-1/7 20/8-28/9

📐 N 44°11'12'' E 3°8'11''

La Romieu, F-32480 / Midi-Pyrénées (Gers)

♿ 📶 **iD** (2319)

🏕 Le Camp de Florence****
🚩 Au Camp
☎ +33 (0)5-62281558
📅 27/4 - 24/9
@ info@lecampdeflorence.com

15ha 95T(100-250m²) 10A CEE

1 ABCD**G**IJKLMOPQ
2 BLRUVWXY
3 BDGHJKL**M**NRUV
4 (A 1/6-15/9) (C+H 1/5-23/9) K (Q+T+U 1/5-30/9) (Y 1/5-23/9) (Z 1/5-30/9)
5 **AB**DEFGIJKLMNOPRUWXYZ
6 CDEGHI**JK**M(N 0,5km)TV

💬 A gently undulating campsite near a 19th-century farmhouse. 500 metres from the fortified village of La Romieu with its magnificent collegiate church, cloister and tower. Armagnac, Floc, Madiran and local wines are in close proximity and there are plenty of opportunities for walking.

🚗 From Agen D931 to Condom. D36 at Ligarde then D166 direction Collegiale de la Romieu. Left in village and follow signs.

Astaffort
N21
Condom ╋ Lectoure
D931 D7
D930
D654

CC € **17** 27/4-7/6 1/9-23/9

📐 N 43°59'0'' E 0°30'7''

Lamontélarié, F-81260 / Midi-Pyrénées (Tarn)

👫 ♿ 📶 **iD** (2320)

- 🏕 Le Rouquié du Lac
- 📫 Rouquié
- ☎ +33 (0)5-63709806
- 🕐 1/5 - 31/10
- @ contact@campingrouquie.fr

NEW

3ha 82T(85-148m²) 6A CEE

1 ACDGIJKLM**P**Q
2 ADJKLMRVWXY
3 ABHJRUWZ
4 (C 15/6-15/9)
(Q+R 14/7-31/8)
(T+U+Z 1/7-31/8)
5 **AB**FGIJKLMNOPUWZ
6 EGI**J**(N 10km)ORTV

💬 Family-run campsite in the heart of the regional park Haut Languedoc. Campsite overlooks the Lac de La Ravièoe. Plenty of (water) sports and recreational activities.

🚗 Clermont-Ferrand-Millau from Millau towards St. Afrique on the D992. Then follow D32 to Lacaune. Then follow D607/D52 to Lamontélarié.

Le Moulin de Terral
D53
D622
Anglès
D907

CC € **15** *1/5-8/7 26/8-30/10*

🗺 **N 43°35'49'' E 2°36'28''**

Larnagol, F-46160 / Midi-Pyrénées (Lot)

♿ 📶 **iD** (2321)

- 🏕 Camping Ruisseau du Treil**
- ☎ +33 (0)5-65312339
- 🕐 5/5 - 8/9
- @ contact@lotcamping.com

3,2ha 46T(100-350m²) 6A CEE

1 A**G**IJKLPRS
2 CGLMRVXY
3 BGHJKLNRU**W**X
4 (B+G 20/6-30/8) (Q 1/6-31/8)
(R 🕐) (T 1/6-31/8) (U 🕐)
(V 1/6-31/8) (Z 🕐)
5 **A**CEFGIJKLMNOPUWZ
6 E**K**(N 5km)V

💬 A very welcoming English owner runs this rural campsite which exudes tranquillity. Beautifully situated on a river, the very large pitches invite you to have a restful stay.

🚗 Camping du Ruisseau du Treil is located on the D662 between Cahors and Cajarc, on the double bend 300 metres outside Larnagol village in the direction of Cajarc.

D19
D662
D24
Limogne-en-Quercy
D911 Martiel

CC € **17** *5/5-30/6 27/8-7/9*

🗺 **N 44°28'24'' E 1°47'1''**

Le Mas-d'Azil, F-09290 / Midi-Pyrénées (Ariège)

♿ 📶 **iD** (2322)

- 🏕 Le Petit Pyrénéen***
- 📫 route de Sabarat, Castagnès
- ☎ +33 (0)5-61697137
- 🕐 30/3 - 8/10
- @ contact@
  campinglepetitpyreneen.com

1,6ha 42T(100-200m²) 10-16A CEE

1 ACD**G**IJKLMPQ
2 CLMRVWXY
3 AGHM**R**X
4 (B 1/6-30/9)
(Q+R+T+U+Z 🕐)
5 **AB**FGIJKLMNPUVWZ
6 ACEK(N 1km)OT

💬 A small, friendly family campsite with lovely sheltered pitches 1500m from the centre with all its shopping opportunities. Ideal for visiting the caves or one of the surrounding lakes. Service station for motorhomes.

🚗 A64 exit 27 Carbonne/Montesquieu/Volvestre. Take the D628 as far as Sabarat. Then follow Le Mas-d'Azil signs.

Carla-Bayle
D626 A
La Bastide-de-Besplas
Sabarat
D15
D919
D119
D117

CC € **15** *30/3-6/7 27/8-7/10*

🗺 **N 43°4'44'' E 1°22'41''**

Lelin-Lapujolle, F-32400 / Midi-Pyrénées (Gers) ♿ 🛜 iD (2323)

🔺 La Solanilla***
✉ Lieu-dit Lahount
☎ +33 (0)5-62696409
🕐 1/1 - 31/12
@ info@campinglasolanilla.com

3ha 86T 10A CEE

1️⃣ ACDGIJKLMOPST
2️⃣ JRVWXY
3️⃣ ADGHRUW
4️⃣ (B 1/5-30/9) (G 1/6-30/9)
   (Q+R+T+V+X+Z 🕐)
5️⃣ ABDEFGJKLNOPUVWZ
6️⃣ ACDEGJ(N 7km)OTV

💬 Welcoming campsite in a rural area with many amenities such as: croissants, a little shop, snack bar and bar. Wine tasting sessions in the vicinity and all through the year. Free wifi.

🚘 From A65, exit 6 dir. Tarbes. In Saint-Germé dir. Lelin-Lapujolle. Then follow signs.

Cazères-sur-l'Adour — D32 — D6
Aire-sur-l'Adour — D2 — D931 — D25
A65 — CC — D3
D834 — D22 — D946 — D935

CC € 15 1/1-29/6 25/8-31/12 7=6, 14=12, 21=18 🧭 N 43°41'49'' W 0°8'17''

Léran, F-09600 / Midi-Pyrénées (Ariège) ♿ 🛜 iD (2324)

🔺 La Régate***
✉ avenue Montjean - route du Lac
☎ +33 (0)5-61030917
🕐 31/3 - 15/10
@ contact@campinglaregate.com

2ha 38T(90-110m²) 10A CEE

1️⃣ ACGIJKLPR
2️⃣ BDJRTVY
3️⃣ BGHJKNRUWZ
4️⃣ (A 1/4-30/9) (B 15/6-31/8)
   (Q 30/6-2/9) (R 🕐)
   (W+X+Z 30/6-2/9)
5️⃣ AEFGJLNPUWZ
6️⃣ EGJ(N 6km)OTV

💬 The reservoir is one of La Régate's attractions. The campsite has homely, attractive pitches with plenty of peace. Lovely views of the lake from the restaurant. Many activities are organised. Only electric boats/jet skis are permitted (no motor boats).

🚘 From the D625 Lavelanet-Mirepoix, take the Léran exit at Aiges-Vives. Follow camping signs or lake in Léran. Do not follow SatNav.

D119 — D626
D7
D625
Laroque-d'Olmes — CC — D12
Lavelanet — D620 — D16
D117

CC € 15 31/3-6/7 25/8-14/10 7=6, 10=8 🧭 N 42°59'2'' E 1°56'8''

Loudenvielle, F-65510 / Midi-Pyrénées (Hautes-Pyrénées) ⛷ ♿ 🛜 iD (2325)

🔺 La Vacance Pène Blanche**
☎ +33 (0)5-62996885
🕐 1/4 - 3/11
@ info@peneblanche.com

3,5ha 76T(80-120m²) 10A CEE

1️⃣ ACDGIJKLMPQ
2️⃣ CJKLRUWX
3️⃣ BHJLR
4️⃣ (Q 1/7-31/8)
5️⃣ ABDGIJKLMNPUWZ
6️⃣ AEGJ(N 0,2km)

💬 A lovely well-maintained terraced campsite in an open and sunny valley by a large lake where you can try or watch paragliding or delta flying. The starting point for 30 walking and mountain tours. Well maintained toilet facilities and a friendly atmosphere.

🚘 Follow the D929 as far as Arreau then continue left on the D618. At the junction with the D25 continue to Loudenvielle. Campsite 50m before the town on the right.

Bourg-d'Oueil
D19
Saint-Lary-Soulan
D929 — CC — D618

CC € 15 1/4-29/6 3/9-2/11 7=6 🧭 N 42°47'48'' E 0°24'23''

Lourdes, F-65100 / Midi-Pyrénées (Hautes-Pyrénées)   ♿ 🛜 iD (2326)

▲ Camping de Sarsan***
4 avenue Jean Moulin
☎ FAX +33 (0)5-62944309
⌚ 1/4 - 15/10
@ camping.sarsan@wanadoo.fr

1,8ha 67T(100-150m²) 2-10A

1 AGIJKLMOPQ
2 CKLRTVXY
3 AFGHJRU
4 (D 1/5-30/9) (Q 1/4-30/9)
(R 1/7-31/8)
5 ABCGHIJKLMNOPUZ
6 ABCEGK(N 0,8km)RT

📝 Level campsite (with lovely views) in a rural location and close to the town of Lourdes. Spacious sunny or shaded pitches under old trees. The centre of the town can be easily reached from the campsite (800m). Bus stop in front of the site. Supermarket. Free wifi on the entire campsite and free motorhome service.

🚗 From Tarbes as you enter Lourdes take first on the left, zône industrielle du Monge, keep following this road. Campsite signposted.

CC € **13** 1/4-7/7 25/8-14/10   🏔 N 43°6'9'' W 0°1'39''

Lourdes, F-65100 / Midi-Pyrénées (Hautes-Pyrénées)   👫 ♿ 🛜 iD (2327)

▲ D'Arrouach***
9 rue des Trois Archanges
☎ +33 (0)5-62421143
⌚ 15/3 - 31/10
@ contact@camping-arrouach.com

13ha 36T(90-130m²) 5-10A CEE

1 ACDGIJKLMOPQ
2 BGJKRVWY
3 BFGHJKLRUV
4 (A 🅿) N
(Q+R+T+U+X+Z 🅿)
5 ABCFGHIJKLMNOPUW
6 ACDEGK(N 1km)ORTUV

📝 It is a 15-minute walk from the campsite to the lake and the entrance to Lourdes golf course. The shrine is 2 km away (bus stop at campsite entrance). Modern toilet facilities, also for the disabled. Free wifi, shop, tapas bar, restaurant with local specialities, fitness room and sauna.

🚗 From Pau RD940 after entering Lourdes (sign) 2nd road right La Rue des Trois Archanges. Follow signs.

CC € **13** 15/3-13/7 3/9-30/10 7=6, 14=12   🏔 N 43°6'13'' W 0°4'4''

Lourdes, F-65100 / Midi-Pyrénées (Hautes-Pyrénées)   👫 ♿ 🛜 iD (2328)

▲ Le Moulin du Monge***
28 avenue Jean Moulin
☎ +33 (0)5-62942815
⌚ 1/4 - 9/10
@ camping.moulin.monge@
wanadoo.fr

1,3ha 55T(100-140m²) 2-6A CEE

1 ACDGIJKLMOPQ
2 FGKRVXY
3 BFGHJNRU
4 (A 1/6-30/9)
(E+G 21/5-16/9) N(Q 🅿)
(R 1/5-10/10) (S 15/6-15/9)
5 ABCDEFGHIJKLMNOPUWZ
6 ACDGK(N 0,4km)RTV

📝 A three-star campsite located on the edge of Lourdes. Good amenities. Spacious pitches and reasonable shade. Camp shop, sauna and heated swimming pool. Basic, clean toilets. 5 minutes from the centre. Supermarket close by. Bus stop by the entrance to the campsite. Free wifi on entire campsite.

🚗 From Tarbes turn left just before Lourdes (Zône industriele de Monge). Campsite 100 metres on the left.

CC € **11** 1/4-7/7 25/8-8/10   🏔 N 43°6'56'' W 0°1'53''

Lourdes, F-65100 / Midi-Pyrénées (Hautes-Pyrénées) 🔥 📶 iD (2329)

🏔 Le Vieux Berger**
📧 2 route de Julos
☎ +33 (0)5-62946057
🔓 1/4 - 31/10
@ levieuxberger@gmail.com

1,8ha 54T(80-100m²) 6-10A

1 AGIJKLMPQ
2 GKRVWXY
3 BFG
4 (T 1/6-30/9)
5 ABGIJKLMNPUVZ
6 BCDEK(N 0,7km)T

NEW

💬 Campsite is close to the centre of Lourdes on slightly sloping grounds, with flat pitches. From the campsite you have a lovely view of the Pyrenees. Free wifi.

🚗 From north, on 1st roundabout take 2nd exit to Argelès/Gavarnie. After 300m, get into left-hand lane. From south, turn back at roundabout due to sharp bend at entrance road.

CC € 13 1/4-29/6 1/9-30/10 | 📡 N 43°6'16'' W 0°1'59''

Lourdes, F-65100 / Midi-Pyrénées (Hautes-Pyrénées) 👫 🔥 📶 iD (2330)

🏔 Sites et Paysages la Forêt***
📧 route de la Forêt
☎ +33 (0)5-62940438
🔓 24/3 - 3/11
@ hello@
   camping-hautes-pyrenees.com

4,5ha 71T(85-120m²) 3-10A

1 ACDGIJKLMOPQ
2 BCGKLRTVWXY
3 BDFGHJKLNRUW
4 (C+H 1/6-30/9)
   (Q+R+T+U+Y+Z 🔓)
5 ABCEFGHIJKLMNOPUWZ
6 ABCEGK(N 2km)TV

💬 Stylish campsite 800 metres from the Shrine, easily accessible on foot via a marked footpath or by bike or bus. Many amenities, heated pool, informal restaurant and wifi everywhere. Peaceful and natural surroundings. Service point for motorhomes.

🚗 In Lourdes direction Pau. Direction St. Pé/Bétharram after 1.5 km. Cross railway left after 1 km. Right over the bridge before sanctuary then signposted direction Ségus.

CC € 15 24/3-8/7 26/8-2/11 7=6, 14=12, 21=18 | 📡 N 43°5'44'' W 0°4'29''

Luchon/Moustajon, F-31110 / Midi-Pyrénées (Haute-Garonne) 🔥 📶 iD (2331)

🏔 Pradelongue****
📧 D125
☎ +33 (0)5-61798644
📠 +33 (0)5-61791864
🔓 1/4 - 1/10
@ camping.pradelongue@
   wanadoo.fr

4,1ha 119T(90-140m²) 2-16A

1 ACDGIJKLMPQ
2 CKLRSTVWXY
3 BCFGHJNRU
4 (A 1/7-1/9) (C+G 1/6-30/9)
   (Q 1/7-1/9)
5 ABCDEFGHIJKLMNOPQRU
   WXYZ
6 ACDEGKM(N 0,1km)TV

💬 This campsite has the peace and space of a park in a wide, sunny valley. Reading, TV and billiard room. All types of sports fields, plenty of play and fitness apparatus and a lovely swimming pool. Modern toilet facilities. Supermarket next door.

🚗 Follow the D125 and take the exit Antignac and Moustajon approximately 2 km before Luchon. Campsite is next to the supermarket.

CC € 15 1/4-30/6 1/9-30/9 | 📡 N 42°48'31'' E 0°35'50''

Luz-St-Sauveur, F-65120 / Midi-Pyrénées (Hautes-Pyrénées) 👫 ♿ 📶 iD 2332

▲ International****
✉ B.P. 4
☎ +33 (0)5-62928202
☼ 19/5 - 30/9
@ camping.international.luz@
wanadoo.fr

4,5ha 110T(75-120m²) 2-10A CEE

1 ACDGIJKLMPQ
2 IKRVX
3 BGHJNQRW
4 (E+H ☼) JK
(Q+R+S 1/6-15/9)
(U+Z 1/7-30/8)
5 ABCDFGHJKLNPUW
6 ACEGK(N 1km)T

💬 4-star family campsite, 1 km from the lovely mountain village of Luz-St.-Saveur. The site is easily accessible. Shaded, spacious pitches. Shop and heated, indoor swimming pool with 2 jacuzzis. Centrally located for trips out to Gavarnie, Tourmalet, Cirque de Troumouse and the National Parc des Pyrénées. Free wifi (1 connection per pitch). Secure covered storage for bicycles.

🚐 D921 direction Luz-St-Saveur. Campsite 1 km before Luz-St-Saveur.

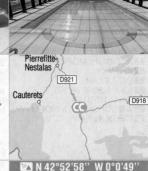

CC € 15 19/5-8/7 26/8-29/9 7=6, 14=12   🏔 N 42°52'58'' W 0°0'49''

Luz-St-Sauveur, F-65120 / Midi-Pyrénées (Hautes-Pyrénées) 👫 ♿ 📶 iD 2333

▲ Sites & Paysages
Pyrénévasion****
✉ route de Luz-Ardiden/Sazos
☎ +33 (0)5-62929154
☼ 1/4 - 15/10
@ info@campingpyrenevasion.com

2,5ha 68T(80-130m²) 3-10A

1 ACDGIJKLMOPQ
2 IJKRTVX
3 BGHJMNRUVW
4 (C 1/6-15/9) (F ☼)
(H 1/6-15/9) KNP
(Q 1/6-15/9) (R ☼)
(T+U+V 1/7-30/8) (Z ☼)
5 ABCDEFGHIJKLMNPUWXYZ
6 ABCEGK(N 3km)OV

💬 Terraced campsite with modern toilet facilities. Located in the mountains around Luz-St.-Saveur valley. Heated outdoor pool with sundeck and free jacuzzi. Lovely new indoor pool and hydro massage. Bar and terrace. Excursions possible to Tourmalet, Gavarnie and Troumouse. An excellent area for walking. Free wifi (1 per pitch).

🚐 Take the road to Luz-Ardiden in Luz-St-Sauveur and follow this road for 3 km up to the village of Sazos. Campsite is signposted here.

CC € 15 1/4-10/7 28/8-14/10 7=6, 14=12, 21=18, 30=25   🏔 N 42°52'56'' W 0°1'20''

Luz-St-Sauveur/Esquièze-Sère, F-65120 / Midi-Pyrénées (Hautes-Pyrénées) ♿ 📶 iD 2334

▲ Airotel Pyrénées*****
✉ 46 avenue du Barège
☎ +33 (0)5-62928918
☼ 1/5 - 24/9
@ airotel.pyrenees@wanadoo.fr

2,8ha 66T(80-100m²) 3-10A

1 ACDGIJKLOPQ
2 IJKLRVX
3 BGHJNRUV
4 (C 15/6-10/9) (F ☼)
(G 15/10-10/9) JKLN
(Q 15/5-15/9) (R ☼)
(U 1/7-30/8)
5 ABCDEFGHIJKLNPUVW
6 ACEGK(N 0,8km)ORV

💬 A challenging campsite. Plenty of fitness equipment, a sauna, indoor and outdoor swimming pools on site. Rafting and cycling. Sports ground for multi-sports. Wifi on entire campsite.

🚐 D921 to Luz-St-Sauveur. Located ca. 1 km before Luz-St-Sauveur left of the D921. Clearly signposted.

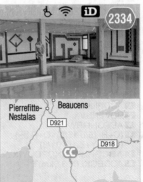

CC € 15 1/5-1/7 27/8-23/9   🏔 N 42°52'49'' W 0°0'40''

Luz-St-Sauveur/Sassis, F-65120 / Midi-Pyrénées (Hautes-Pyrénées)

🏔 🚴 🤿 📶 **iD** (2335)

🏔 Le Hounta***
🏕 Le Village
☎ +33 (0)5-62929590
📅 10/2 - 14/10
@ info@campinglehounta.com

2ha 84T(75-100m²) 2-10A CEE

1 ACD**G**IJKLMOPQ
2 KRTVXY
3 BGHJRU**W**
4 (Q 1/6-30/9) (R 📅)
(U+V 1/7-31/8)
5 **AB**CDFGHIJKLMNOPUVWZ
6 CEG**K**(N 1,5km)OTV

NEW

💬 Campsite just above Luz-St-Saveur, accessible via a footbridge. Quiet, spacious level pitches with wifi. Very clean toilets and well-equipped motorhome service point. Centrally located for visits to Gavarnie, Tourmalet, Lourdes, Pont d'Espagne, Pyrenees etc. Ideal if you like cycling in the hills.

🚗 D921 from Argelès, right before Luz-St. Sauveur. D12, campsite on left after Sassis.

Soulom

D921 Esquièze-Sère D918
CC

CC € **13** 1/5-14/7 1/9-13/10 7=6   🏔 N 42°52'19'' W 0°0'53''

Marciac, F-32230 / Midi-Pyrénées (Gers)

🤿 📶 **iD** (2336)

🏔 Flower Camping Du Lac***
☎ +33 (0)5-62082119
📅 24/3 - 6/10
@ info@camping-marciac.com

4,5ha 72T(100-120m²) 10A CEE

1 ACD**G**IJKLMPQ
2 IJLRUVWXY
3 BF**G**HJMNRU
4 (C 1/5-30/9) (Q+R+T+Z 📅)
5 **A**CDFGHJKLMNOPUVWXZ
6 CDEG**K**(N 0,7km)O

💬 Located by a lake suitable for water recreation, 800m from a 'bastide' fortified town with a jazz museum. With the exception of the annual jazz festival, peace and quiet are the order of the day.

🚗 Follow the D943 in Marciac direction Bassoues, after about 300m over the bridge turn left. From the lake; follow signs. From Plaisance; turn left on D3.

Plaisance du Gers   Bassoues
D14   D3   D946
D5   **CC**
D943   D34
N21

CC € **15** 24/3-7/7 25/8-5/10 7=6   🏔 N 43°31'56'' E 0°10'0''

Martiel, F-12200 / Midi-Pyrénées (Aveyron)

📶 **iD** (2337)

🏔 Flower Camping Lac aux Oiseaux***
🏕 Moulin de Bannac
☎ +33 (0)5-65656759
📅 1/4 - 14/10
@ info@campinglacauxoiseaux.fr

7ha 63T(80-120m²) 10-16A CEE

1 ACD**F**IJKLMPQ
2 BDKLRUVX
3 ABF**G**HQRW
4 (C+H 15/6-15/9) (Q+R 📅)
(T+U+Y+Z 1/7-31/8)
5 **AB**CGHIJKLMNOPQUWXY
6 ACDEGKL(N 3,5km)T

💬 Simple natural campsite around a historic building that is being renovated. Located on a recreational lake with an adventure trail in the treetops.

🚗 D911 from Villefranche, 10 km westward to Martiel then follow signs.

D662   D24
D19   D911   **CC**
Villefranche-de-Rouergue
D926   D922

CC € **15** 1/4-6/7 26/8-13/10   🏔 N 44°23'3'' E 1°53'12''

Martres-Tolosane, F-31220 / Midi-Pyrénées (Haute-Garonne) ♿ 🛜 ✿ 🆔 2338

▲ Sites & Paysages Le Moulin★★★★
🏠 avenue de Saint Vidian
☎ +33 (0)5-61988640
🕑 26/3 - 29/9
@ info@campinglemoulin.com

10ha 61T(80-200m²) 6-10A

1 ACD**G**IJKLMPQ
2 CFLMRVXY
3 ABCDGHJKMNRUV**W**
4 (C+H 1/6-15/9) JK
(Q 2/5-28/9)
(R+T+U 1/6-15/9)
(V+X 7/7-25/8) (Z 1/6-15/9)
5 **AB**DEFGIJKLMNOPUWXYZ
6 ACEG**K**(N 2km)ORTV

💬 The campsite is located on the banks of the Garonne at the edge of the Pyrenees. Ideal for a relaxing stay in open countryside for discovering the immediate vicinity. You can swim, fish, play tennis and relax here. Lovely shaded pitches, comfortable toilet facilities.

🚗 Martres-Tolosane is located on the A64 Toulouse-Tarbes, exit 22 or 21 if coming from the south. The campsite is signposted.

Le Fousseret
D10
D8 D635 A64 D6
D13 CC
D817
D117
Salies-du-Salat

ⓒⓒ € **17** 26/3-5/7 26/8-28/9 7=6 🏕 N 43°11'29'' E 1°1'0''

Mazères, F-09270 / Midi-Pyrénées (Ariège) ♿ 🛜 🆔 2339

▲ La Bastide★★★
🏠 chemin de la Plage
☎ +33 (0)9-67737241
🕑 14/5 - 29/9
@ la-bastide@orange.fr

6ha 66T(100-130m²) 10A CEE

1 ACD**G**HIJKLMOPRS
2 BCFJLMRWXY
3 BGMRW
4 (B 15/6-15/9)
(Q+T+U+Z 1/6-31/8)
5 **AB**JKLNPUVWZ
6 FGJ(N 0,5km)T

💬 A peaceful, shaded campsite on the banks of a river. Perfect for fishing.

🚗 A66 motorway, exit Mazères/Saverdun. Follow 'Belpech' in Mazères.

Cintegabelle D91 A61
D35 D16
A66 D625
CC
D624 Belpech
D820 D25

ⓒⓒ € **15** 14/5-7/7 26/8-28/9 🏕 N 43°14'58'' E 1°40'59''

Mercus-Garrabet, F-09400 / Midi-Pyrénées (Ariège) ♿ 🛜 🆔 2340

▲ Du Lac Mercus★★★
🏠 1 Promenade du Camping
☎ 📠 +33 (0)5-61059061
🕑 31/3 - 13/10
@ info@campingdulacmercus.com

1,4ha 39T(80-150m²) 6-10A CEE

1 ACDGIJLPQ
2 DFHJKLMRTVWXY
3 AGHRUW
4 (**A** 1/7-30/8)
(C+G 15/5-15/9) **KLN**
(Q+R+Z 🕑)
5 **A**EFGJKLMNOPRUVWZ
6 EGJ**K**(N 2km)T

💬 An oasis of peace and hospitality. Everything very well maintained. Friendly owners. Not too far from the motorway between Foix and Tarascon.

🚗 N20 from Foix dir. Andorra. Exit 14 Mercus. In Mercus follow signs Camping du Lac.

Foix
D117
N20
D618
Tarascon-sur-Ariège CC

ⓒⓒ € **15** 31/3-6/7 24/8-12/10 7=6, 14=11 🏕 N 42°52'18'' E 1°37'20''

Millau, F-12100 / Midi-Pyrénées (Aveyron)   ♿ 🛜 iD (2341)

🏕 Camping des Deux Rivières***
🏠 61 avenue de l'Aigoual
☎ +33 (0)5-65600027
🗓 1/4 - 22/10
@ camp2rivieres@yahoo.fr

1ha 64T(80-120m²) 10A CEE

1 AGIJKLMPQ
2 CFGKLMRVXY
3 BGHJKRU**W**X
4 (Q+R+T+U+V+Z ♿)
5 **AB**DGIJKLMNPQRUWZ
6 ACEGK(N 0,5km)TV

💬 This campsite is the closest to Millau centre. Quiet, child-friendly and clean on the banks of the Tarn with private beach, shaded, lovely views of 'La Pouncho' (paragliders). Catering: breakfast, snacks and bar. New toilets since 2016. Free wifi.

🚗 Southwards A75 exit 45 Millau. Northwards A75 exit 47 (toll-free) La Cavalerie-Millau or toll on Viaduc de Millau, exit 45. In Millau follow 'Campings' signs as far as Cureplat bridge, over the bridge, 1st site on the left.

CC € **13** 1/4-29/6 25/8-30/9   🏔 N 44°6'10'' E 3°5'14''

Millau, F-12100 / Midi-Pyrénées (Aveyron)   ♿ 🛜 iD (2342)

🏕 Du Viaduc****
🏠 121 avenue de Millau-Plage
☎ +33 (0)5-65601575
🗓 14/4 - 30/9
@ info@camping-du-viaduc.com

5ha 185T(80-130m²) 6A CEE

1 ACD**F**IJKLMOPQ
2 ABCFGKLORSVWXY
3 BGHIJKLNRUV**W**X
4 (C+H 1/5-2/10) IJP
  (Q+S+T+U+V ♿)
  (X+Y 1/5-2/10) (Z ♿)
5 **AB**CDEFGHIJKLMNOPQRU
  WXYZ
6 CEG**K**(N 0,8km)OTV

💬 500 metres from the centre of Millau. Spacious pitches in lovely natural surroundings. Private beach with sun loungers on the River Tarn. Heated, modern toilet facilities. Unlimited wifi for 1.50 Euros per day per device. Heated leisure pool with slide from 1 May.

🚗 From Clermont-Ferrand A75, exit 45 (turn off SatNav). From Montpellier A75, exit 47. Then follow camping signs as far as 'Pont de Cureplat', towards Paulhe D187 at the roundabout, 1st campsite on the left.

CC € **15** 14/4-7/7 27/8-29/9   🏔 N 44°6'18'' E 3°5'18''

Millau, F-12100 / Midi-Pyrénées (Aveyron)   ♿ 🛜 iD (2343)

🏕 Huttopia Millau***
🏠 455 avenue de l'Aigoual
☎ +33 (0)5-65611883
🗓 27/4 - 30/9
@ millau@huttopia.com

3,5ha 119T(100-190m²) 6-10A CEE

1 ACD**F**IJKLM**P**ST
2 CFGKLMNRVWXY
3 BGHIJKRU**W**X
4 (C+G+Q+R ♿)
  (T+U+V 1/7-31/8) (Z ♿)
5 **AB**DEFGHIJKLMNPUVWXZ
6 ACDEGIJ(N 0,5km)OTV

💬 A peaceful, natural family campsite close to the centre of Millau. Plenty of sport and leisure activities possible close by. A friendly family site. Spacious pitches, both shaded and sunny. Heated toilet facilities. CampingCard ACSI is not valid for pitches on the river.

🚗 From Clermont-Ferrand take the A75, exit 45 (turn off SatNav). From Montpellier A75, exit 47. Follow camping signs to 'Pont de Cureplat', take D991 at roundabout then 1st site on the right.

CC € **15** 27/4-28/6 2/9-29/9   🏔 N 44°6'9'' E 3°5'27''

Millau, F-12100 / Midi-Pyrénées (Aveyron)

♿ 📶 iD (2344)

▲ Larribal***
✉ avenue de Millau-Plage
☎ +33 (0)5-65590804
⌚ 1/4 - 31/10
@ camping.larribal@wanadoo.fr

1,7ha 72T(80-110m²) 6A CEE

1 ACDGIJKLMOPQ
2 BCFGKLMNRSVXY
3 AGHJ**OP**RU**W**X
4 (B+G+Q+R ⊙) (U 1/7-31/8) (Z ⊙)
5 A EFGIJKLMNPQUWZ
6 ACEGK(N 1,5km)ORTV

💬 A campsite right on the banks of the Tarn. Shaded and quiet, nice swimming pool with bar. Free wifi throughout the site. You can be in Millau by bike in 5 minutes for sports opportunities, restaurants and various markets.

🚗 From Clermont-Ferrand (A75) take exit 45 (turn SatNav off!), or from Montpellier (A75), exit 47. Then follow 'Campings' sign to the 'Pont de Cureplat' bridge. Over the bridge and towards Paulhe D187 at roundabout, 3rd site on the left.

CC € **11** 1/4-30/6   25/8-30/10   📍 N 44°6'37'' E 3°5'13''

Millau, F-12100 / Midi-Pyrénées (Aveyron)

♿ 📶 iD (2345)

▲ Les Erables***
✉ avenue de Millau-Plage
☎ +33 (0)5-65591513
⌚ 1/4 - 30/9
@ camping-les-erables@orange.fr

1,5ha 72T(100m²) 10A CEE

1 ACDGIJKLMOPQ
2 BCFGKLMNRVWXY
3 ABGHIJKLNRU**W**X
4 (Q ⊙) (S 1/7-31/8) (T+U+Z ⊙)
5 A CDGHJLNPUWXY
6 ACEGK(N 2km)ORTV

💬 Quiet grounds close to a river and near the town centre, the Millau bridge and leisure activities. Spacious marked out pitches; shaded or sunny. Everything you need for an agreeable holiday in a friendly atmosphere. Free wifi. Friendly new owners.

🚗 Over the bridge in Cureplat, 3rd exit at roundabout direction Paulhe. In Millau follow camping signs, second campsite on the left. Or take the A75, exit 45 Millau centre. Look out for camping signs (turn SatNav off).

CC € **13** 1/4-5/7   23/8-29/9 7=6   📍 N 44°6'20'' E 3°5'16''

Millau, F-12100 / Midi-Pyrénées (Aveyron)

♿ 📶 iD (2346)

▲ Les Rivages****
✉ 860 avenue de l'Aigoual
☎ +33 (0)5-65610107
⌚ 7/4 - 30/9
@ info@campinglesrivages.com

7,5ha 277T(100-160m²) 10A CEE

1 ACD**G**IJKLMOPQ
2 CFKLMNRVWXY
3 BCGHIJK**M**N**OPQR**S**UVW**X
4 (**A** 1/7-30/8) (C+H 1/5-30/9) I K(Q 13/4-30/9) (S 15/6-15/9) (T+U+V+Y+Z ⊙)
5 **AB**CDEFGHIJKLMNPQRUXYZ
6 ACDEG**JK**(N 0,8km)OTV

💬 Enormous pitches, indoor tennis/ squash hall, magnificent restaurant, heated pools, private beach on the river Dourbie. Only campsite in Millau with a view of the famous viaduct. The site is really peaceful, you cannot hear any noise from traffic.

🚗 A75 from north, exit 45 Millau. Exit 47 from south (SatNav off!). Follow 'campings' signs up to Cureplat bridge. 1st exit D991 on roundabout after bridge. Campsite 800m further at next small roundabout.

CC € **15** 7/4-5/7   23/8-29/9 7=6, 14=12   📍 N 44°6'3'' E 3°5'45''

Millau, F-12100 / Midi-Pyrénées (Aveyron) ⚓ 🏕️ 📶 **iD** (2347)

🏕️ St. Lambert***
✉️ 2050 avenue de l'Aigoual
☎️ +33 (0)5-65600048
🗓️ 27/4 - 30/9
@ contact@campingsaintlambert.fr

3,5ha 107**T**(80-160m²) 6A

1 ACDGIJKLMPRS
2 ABCFKLMNORSVWXY
3 BGHJKNQRU**W**X
4 (B 1/5-30/9) (Q+S ⊡)
(T+U+V+X 1/7-25/8) (Z ⊡)
5 **AB**CEFGHIJKLMNPQRUZ
6 ACDEGJ**K**(N 2,5km)ORTV

💬 A campsite quietly located at the entrance to the Gorges du Tarn, between the Grands Causses and the Cévennes, 2,5 km from the centre of Millau. It has a lovely big private pebble beach on the River Dourbie. Friendly atmosphere.

🚗 A75 exit 44.1 Millau and follow camping signs. Take D991 direction La Roque-Sainte-Marguerite. Turn right after the bridge in Cureplat and follow camping signs again.

CC € **13** 27/4-6/7 27/8-29/9 7=6, 14=12   🧭 N 44°5'59'' E 3°6'42''

Moissac, F-82200 / Midi-Pyrénées (Tarn-et-Garonne) 📶 **iD** (2348)

🏕️ Le Moulin du Bidounet***
✉️ Saint Benoit
☎️ +33 (0)5-63325252
🗓️ 1/4 - 30/9
@ camping-bidounet@moissac.fr

2,5ha 97**T**(70-90m²) 6A CEE

1 AC**G**IJKLMPRS
2 CFKLRTVXY
3 AGHNRU**W**
4 (A 1/7-31/8) (B+G 15/6-15/9)
(Q+R 1/7-31/8)
5 ABFGIJKLMNPUVZ
6 ACDEGJ(N 0,5km)TV

💬 An attractive stopover campsite with swimming pool. Enjoy the peace of a shaded island in the River Tarn on the pilgrims' route to Compostella. Close to the historic village of Moissac.

🚗 Castelsarrasin to Moissac RD813. Follow camping signs just before Moissac.

CC € **15** 1/4-6/7 25/8-29/9   🧭 N 44°5'47'' E 1°5'21''

Molières (Tarn-et-Gar.), F-82220 / Midi-Pyrénées (Tarn-et-Garonne) 👫 📶 **iD** (2349)

🏕️ Domaine de Merlanes****
✉️ Merlanes
☎️ +33 (0)6-11524247
🗓️ 21/4 - 29/9
@ simone.merlanes@gmail.com

6ha 51**T**(200-300m²) 6-10A CEE

1 ACD**G**IJKLMPQ
2 ADIKLRVWXY
3 BDGN**O**PRUW
4 (C+G+Q+T+U+Z ⊡)
5 **AB**EFGIJKLMNPRUWZ
6 AEGHJ(N 3,5km)TV

💬 Site (35 hectares) with large pitches in a valley, ideal for those seeking peace and quiet. Excellent amenities: heated pool, terrace, bread, farm and stables. A good base for Moissac, Montauban, St. Antonin-Noble-Val.

🚗 D820 Cahors-Montauban. Exit Montpezat-de-Q (D20). Just before Molières turn left towards St. Christophe. Follow camping signs. From Toulouse exit 60 (Montauban-Nord). RN20 as far as Réalville then dir. Molières, then follow camping signs.

CC € **17** 21/4-6/7 25/8-28/9 10=9, 15=13   🧭 N 44°11'6'' E 1°23'17''

Montcabrier, F-46700 / Midi-Pyrénées (Lot)

2350

🏕 Moulin de Laborde***
📧 Laborde
☎ +33 (0)5-65246206
📅 10/5 - 13/9
@ moulindelaborde@wanadoo.fr

12ha 90T(100-150m²) 6-10A

1 AEIJKLPQ
2 CLRTVXY
3 B**F**GHJMNRUW
4 (B 20/5-10/9) (G 1/7-31/8)
(Q+R+T+U+V+X+Z 10/5-10/9)
5 **AB**FGIJKLNOPUWZ
6 AEGJ(N 8km)ORTV

💬 The Van Bommel family welcome you to their child-friendly campsite with spacious pitches. The attractive interior of a 17th-century water mill has a terrace, bar and restaurant. The site has a brook and a small lake. Unique walking area, bastides and the Cahors vineyards. Free wifi.

🚗 A20 direction Cahors, exit 56. Then via the D1 towards Gourdon. Then the D673 direction Fumel. Signposted 11 km before Fumel.

CC € **17** 10/5-6/7 25/8-12/9 — N 44°32'52" E 1°5'1"

Montgailhard, F-09330 / Midi-Pyrénées (Ariège)

2351

🏕 La Roucateille***
📧 15 rue du Pradal
☎ +33 (0)5-61640592
📅 15/3 - 15/10
@ info@roucateille.com

2ha 71T(90-130m²) 10A CEE

1 ACD**G**IJKLMPQ
2 BCFGLMRSVY
3 AGHJLRU**W**
4 (Q 🅿) (U 1/7-30/8)
5 **A**FGIJKLMNPUVWZ
6 EGIJ(N 2km)V

💬 Peaceful, high-quality campsite with friendly welcome. Everything is in great order with modern, clean toilet facilities. Electric bicycles for rent. Only 4 km from Foix, which has a beautiful medieval castle.

🚗 From Toulouse road 61, exit 11, Montgailhard. 1st right on roundabout (Montgailhard centre). Arrow to camps. onleft after 2 km. From Andorra, exit 12 dir. Lowanalet. 3rd right on roundabout dir. Montgailhard. Camps. sign on right after 2 km.

CC € **11** 15/3-9/7 27/8-14/10 — N 42°55'51" E 1°38'19"

Montgeard/Nailloux, F-31560 / Midi-Pyrénées (Haute-Garonne)

2352

🏕 Camping du Lac de la Thésauque***
📧 Lac de la Thésauque
☎ +33 (0)5-61813467
📠 +33 (0)5-61810012
📅 1/1 - 31/12
@ camping@thesauque.com

5ha 57T(75-90m²) 6A CEE

1 ACDGIJLPST
2 DFJLRVXY
3 BGHQRW**Z**
4 (B 1/6-30/9) (Q 1/7-31/8)
(R+T+X+Y+Z 🅿)
5 **A**DGIJKLMNPUZ
6 EG**K**(N 4km)OTV

💬 Terraced campsite with many trees. Located beside the Thésauque lake. Ideal for walking or for outings to Toulouse or Carcassonne.

🚗 The campsite is located on the D622 Auterive-Villefranche. The lake at Thésauque is signposted from Nailloux and the A61.

CC € **13** 1/1-8/7 26/8-31/12 7=6, 14=11 — N 43°21'18" E 1°38'55"

Montréjean, F-31210 / Midi-Pyrénées (Haute-Garonne) ♿ 🛜 iD (2353)

▲ Midi Pyrénées****
✉ chemin de Loubet
☎ +33 (0)6-52754830
⊙ 1/3 - 30/11
@ camping.midi-pyrenees@
wanadoo.fr

10ha 110T(100-120m²) 6A CEE

1 ACDFIJLPQ
2 FIJKLRUXY
3 AFGMNRU
4 (B 1/6-30/9) P(Q ⊙)
(T+U 1/5-30/9) (Z ⊙)
5 ABDFGIJKLMNOPUV
6 CDEGJK(N 0,6km)OV

💬 People come and people stay. Very relaxing friendly atmosphere. Overflowing swimming pool 1/6 to 30/9 in stunning surroundings. Fields with views of the valley and mountains and quiet fields in the countryside. Own new food truck 1/5 to 30/9 for relaxing cooking-free evenings. 500m from a supermarket.

🚗 A64 exit 17 and D817, at roundabout with Lidl on your left, drive onto an uphill road. Camping signs at the end.

CC € 15 1/3-7/7 25/8-29/11   📡 N 43°5'31'' E 0°33'14''

Montricoux, F-82800 / Midi-Pyrénées (Tarn-et-Garonne) 🛜 iD (2354)

▲ Le Clos Lalande***
✉ 359 route de Bioule
☎ FAX +33 (0)5-63241889
⊙ 31/3 - 4/11
@ contact@
camping-lecloslalande.com

3ha 58T(100-150m²) 6A CEE

1 AGIJKLMPQ
2 CGLRVWXY
3 BDGHJMNOPRUW
4 (B+G 1/5-15/9)
(Q+T+U+V+Z 15/5-15/9)
5 ABEFGIJKLMNOPQRUVWZ
6 ACEGJ(N 0,5km)RTV

💬 A peaceful campsite with swimming pool, toddlers' pool, tennis, children's farm and many amenities. Large pitches, new toilets and motorhome facilities. At the entrance to the Gorges de l'Aveyron and 500m from the village and shopping. Close to some of the most beautiful villages in France: Cordes, St.-Cirq-Lapopie, Bruniquel, Puycelci, Penne, Najac...

🚗 A20 to Montauban, exit 61. Then D115 direction St. Antonin. Signposted in Montricoux.

CC € 15 31/3-7/7 26/8-3/11 7=6, 14=12   📡 N 44°4'39'' E 1°36'40''

Nant, F-12230 / Midi-Pyrénées (Aveyron) ♿ 🛜 iD (2355)

▲ Sites & Paysages Les 2 Vallées**
✉ route de l'Estrade Basse
☎ +33 (0)5-65622689
⊙ 13/4 - 15/10
@ contact@lesdeuxvallees.com

2ha 63T(80-140m²) 6A CEE

1 ACDGIJKLMPST
2 BCFGKLRVWXY
3 BGHJKMNOPRUW
4 (A 1/7-31/8) (C 31/5-24/9)
(Q+R 1/7-31/8)
(T+U+X+Z 23/6-9/9)
5 ABCDFGIJKLMNPUVWXYZ
6 ACEGIK(N 0,8km)OTV

💬 A quiet, shaded and lovely campsite with many facilities. Free wifi. Heated swimming pool. Located in beautiful countryside with lovely views of the surroundings. Close to an authentic medieval village (800m).

🚗 A75, exit 47 La Cavalerie. D999 direction Nant. Then follow camping signs 800m from 1st sign.

CC € 11 13/4-13/7 1/9-14/10   📡 N 44°1'2'' E 3°18'5''

Nant-d'Aveyron, F-12230 / Midi-Pyrénées (Aveyron) ♿ 🛜 iD (2356)

🏕 Camping RCN Val de Cantobre****
☎ +31 034-3745090
📅 20/4 - 24/9
@ reserveringen@rcn.nl

6,5ha 139T(60-150m²) 6A CEE

1 ACD**G**IJKLMOPRS
2 BCFIJKLNRTUVWXY
3 BGHJMN**Q**RU**W**X
4 (A 29/5-26/6) (C+H ⏰) IJK (Q+S+T+U+V+Y+Z ⏰)
5 **AB**CEFGHIJKLMNOPQRUW XZ
6 ABCEGH**K**(N 4km)ORTV

💬 A terraced, luxury campsite with stunning views of the beautiful Vale of Dourbie. Lovely touring pitches. Good catering facilities. The service and customer focus is a strong asset here!

🚗 After Clermont-Ferrand take the A75 over the Millau Bridge (toll) exit 47 direction Nant/La Cavalerie. Through La Cavalerie towards Nant. Campsite signposted in Nant. Turn left immediately to D991.

Lanuéjols ○ D986
D991
Saint-Sauveur-Camprieu
CC
A75
D809
D7
D999

CC € ⑰ 20/4-2/7 25/8-23/9 | 🧭 N 44°2'44'' E 3°18'8''

Naucelle, F-12800 / Midi-Pyrénées (Aveyron) ♿ 🛜 iD (2357)

🏕 Flower Camping du Lac de Bonnefon***
🚩 route de Bonnefon
☎ +33 (0)5-65693320
📅 1/4 - 30/9
@ info@ camping-du-lac-de-bonnefon.com

4,5ha 67T(80-165m²) 10A CEE

1 ACD**F**IJKL**P**RS
2 DIJRVWXY
3 BGHJ**Q**RUW
4 (A 7/7-27/8) (C 1/6-30/9) (H 1/7-30/9) KM(Q ⏰) (T 1/5-30/9) (U+V 1/7-15/9) (Z ⏰)
5 **AB**EGIJKLMPQUVWXYZ
6 CDEGJ**K**(N 1km)RV

💬 Open from 1 April to 30 September. Close to a lake abundant with fish (free fishing) in peaceful, richly planted surroundings. Campsite with swimming pool and jacuzzi. 1200 metres from the town of Naucelle.

🚗 N88 Rodez-Albi, exit Naucelle/Sauveterre-de-Rouergue. Then follow Naucelle. Then follow campsite signs.

Baraqueville Calmont
Naucelle
CC
D905
N88
D78
D53 D263

CC € ⑰ 1/4-6/7 25/8-29/9 7=6 | 🧭 N 44°11'17'' E 2°20'54''

Peyrouse/Lourdes, F-65270 / Midi-Pyrénées (Hautes-Pyrénées) ♿ 🛜 iD (2358)

🏕 À l'Ombre des Tilleuls***
🚩 31 route de Pau
☎ +33 (0)5-62418154
📅 31/3 - 30/9
@ contact@ombredestileuls.com

4,8ha 99T(100-200m²) 6-10A CEE

1 ACD**G**IJKLMOPQ
2 KRVWXY
3 A**F**GHJMNRU
4 (B 1/6-30/9) (Q 1/7-31/8) (R ⏰) (T+U+V+X 1/7-31/8) (Z ⏰)
5 **AB**CFGHIJKLMNOPUVWXZ
6 ACEG**K**(N 2km)V

💬 A fair-sized campsite with very spacious pitches. There is plenty of shade under old linden (lime) trees. Excursions possible, among other places, to Lourdes (6 km to the site of the pilgrimage), Tourmalet, Gavarnie and Pont d'Espagne.

🚗 The campsite is signposted on the D937 in the direction of Pau (via Bétharram), at approximately 6 km from Lourdes.

Coarraze D936 Ossun
D35 D940 N21
D937 CC Lourdes
D821

CC € ⑬ 31/3-30/6 1/9-29/9 14=12 | 🧭 N 43°6'3'' W 0°7'43''

Pont-de-Salars, F-12290 / Midi-Pyrénées (Aveyron)

🛆 Flower Camping Les Terrasses du Lac★★★★
📧 route du Vibal/La Souquette
☎ +33 (0)5-65468818
📅 1/4 - 30/9
@ campinglesterrasses@orange.fr

6ha 180**T**(80-100m²) 10A CEE

1 ACD**G**IJKLPRS
2 DIJKORTVWXY
3 AGR**WZ**
4 (A 1/7-31/8) (C+G 1/6-15/9) J K(Q+R+T+U+V+X 1/7-31/8) (Z 1/6-30/9)
5 **AB**FGIJKLMNOPUWXYZ
6 AEGJ(N 4km)ORV

💬 An attractive terraced campsite by a reservoir. The differences in height give optimal privacy to the pitches which are quite a distance from each other. Most of the pitches have fine views of the lake.

🚗 A75 exit 44.1 Pont-de-Salars. D911 direction Rodez. Turn right after Pont-de-Salars village onto the D523. Campsite well signposted.

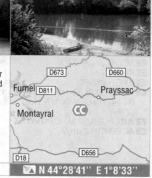

CC € **15** 1/4-7/7 27/8-29/9 7=6

📷🛆 N 44°18'17'' E 2°44'7''

Pouylebon, F-32320 / Midi-Pyrénées (Gers)

🛆 Camping Pouylebon
📧 Lieu dit "Haouré" D216
☎ +33 (0)5-62667210
📅 1/4 - 15/10
@ campingpouylebon2@wanadoo.fr

1ha 30**T**(120m²) 8A CEE

1 ABCDGIJLPRS
2 KLRXY
3 A**F**GHJRU
4 (B 15/5-15/9) (Q+T+X+Z 📷)
5 **AB**CGHIJKLMPRUWZ
6 AEJ(N 6km)

💬 Campsite with its own swimming pool, very peacefully located around a Gascony farmhouse on grass with trees and lovely views of the Gers country-side. Sunflowers and corn are grown all around. There are 25 spacious pitches with good toilet facilities on 1 hectare of grounds at the end of a no through road.

🚗 Follow the D159 to the west from the D34 at Monclar. Then continue to Pouylebon D216 in northerly direction, take track to campsite 500 metres on the left.

CC € **15** 15/4-7/7 25/8-14/10

📷🛆 N 43°33'13'' E 0°18'11''

Puy-l'Évêque, F-46700 / Midi-Pyrénées (Lot)

🛆 Camping Les Vignes★★★
📧 Lieu dit le Meouré
☎ +33 (0)5-65308172
📅 26/3 - 31/10
@ campinglesvignes46@gmail.com

5ha 90**T**(86-120m²) 10A CEE

1 ACG**G**IJKLM**P**ST
2 ACLMRVXY
3 BGHJKMNRU**W**X
4 (C 15/5-30/9) (Q+R 📷) (T+U+V+X 1/7-31/8) (Z 📷)
5 **AB**DFGHIJKLMNOPUWZ
6 EGK(N 3km)TV

NEW

💬 Idyllically located on a beach next to Lot, in the middle of the Cahors vineyards. Plenty of options for swimming and canoeing, renovated heated pool, and simple but good restaurant.

🚗 Coming from the direction of Cahors on D811 (D911) campsite is signposted just before Puy-l'Évêque (left turn).

CC € **15** 26/3-29/6 1/9-30/10

📷🛆 N 44°28'41'' E 1°8'33''

Rivière-sur-Tarn, F-12640 / Midi-Pyrénées (Aveyron) ⚓ 🤿 iD (2362)

🏕 Flower Camping Le Peyrelade★★★★
✉ rte des Gorges du Tarn
☎ +33 (0)5-65626254
📅 9/5 - 15/9
@ contact@campingpeyrelade.com

4ha 137T(90-130m²) 10A CEE

1 ACD**G**IJKLMPQ
2 ABCFJKLNRVXY
3 BGHIJKL**MQ**RU**W**X
4 (C+H 📷) IKMOP(Q 📷)
(S 1/7-31/8)
(T+U+V+Y+Z 📷)
5 **AB**CEFGHIJKLMNOPQRUW
Z
6 ABCEGJ**K**(N 1km)OTUV

💬 A beautiful site in every way: nature, toilet facilities, pitches, beach, entertainment! And the longest pebble beach on the Tarn. New leisure pool including a Balnéo room and children's play area. Relaxation on holiday with all facilities imaginable: restaurant, supermarket, etc.

🚗 A75 exit 44.1.Turn left in Aguessac to get on the D907. The first campsite after the village Rivière-sur-Tarn. The campsite is situated exactly at the entrance of the Gorges du Tarn.

CC € 17 9/5-6/7 25/8-14/9 7=6, 14=12, 21=18   📍 N 44°11'27'' E 3°9'25''

Rivières, F-81600 / Midi-Pyrénées (Tarn) 👫 ⚓ 🤿 iD (2363)

🏕 Les Pommiers d'Aiguelèze★★★★
✉ Espace Loisirs d'Aiguelèze
☎ +33 (0)5-63330249
📅 1/4 - 30/9
@ info@camping-lespommiers.com

2,7ha 53T(80-120m²) 13A CEE

1 ACD**G**IJKLMPST
2 CFL**R**TUVWXY
3 AB**F**GJKMN**Q**R**W**X
4 (C+H 15/4-30/9)
(Q+R+X+Z 📷)
5 **A**BFGIJKLMNPUWZ
6 ACEGK(N 5km)TV

💬 A peaceful and informal campsite located next to the watersports centre in the Tarn. There are plenty of vineyards in the area and you will encounter the culture and history of the UNESCO Heritage Sites like Albi, the 'Route des Bastides' and beautiful panoramas.

🚗 A68, exit 10 Lagrave. Then follow Espace Loisirs d'Aiguelèze.

CC € 17 1/4-6/7 27/8-29/9   📍 N 43°54'32'' E 1°59'0''

Rocamadour, F-46500 / Midi-Pyrénées (Lot) ⚓ 🤿 iD (2364)

🏕 Padimadour★★★★
✉ La Châtaigneraie-Varagnes
☎ +33 (0)5-65337211
📅 30/3 - 30/9
@ camping@padimadour.fr

3ha 49T(120-180m²) 10A CEE

1 ACD**G**IJKLMP
2 ILRVWXY
3 ACGHRUV
4 (E+H 📷) KMP(Q 📷)
(R+T+U+V 1/6-30/9)
(X 1/7-31/8) (Z 1/6-30/9)
5 **AB**DEFGIJKLMNOPQUWXY
Z
6 ACDEGK(N 1,5km)RTV

💬 A peacefully located family campsite in the middle of the countryside. Park-like grounds with very spacious pitches. Ideally situated for visiting the Lot and the Dordogne or for walking. Extremely pleasant heated toilet facilities. The swimming pool is heated. Free Wifi. Very friendly welcome.

🚗 From A20, exit 54 (from north) dir. Gramat D840, exit 56 (from south) dir. Brive D840; follow Padimadour camping signs in Rocamadour.

CC € 17 30/3-6/7 25/8-29/9 7=6   📍 N 44°49'5'' E 1°41'11''

Salles-Curan, F-12410 / Midi-Pyrénées (Aveyron)

⚡ 🛜 **iD** (2365)

🏕 Les Genêts****
🏠 Lac de Pareloup
☎ +33 (0)5-65463534
📅 5/5 - 16/9
@ contact@camping-les-genets.fr

3ha 163T(80-100m²) 10A CEE

1 ACD**G**IJKLPST
2 ADMRSVWXY
3 BGKNQR**W**Z
4 (A 1/7-1/9) (C+H 🔑) K(Q 🔑)
(S 1/6-16/9) (T 1/7-8/9)
(U+V+X 23/6-9/9)
(Z 2/7-16/9)
5 **AB**EFGIJLMNOPRUWXYZ
6 CEGJ(N 6km)OV

💬 Pleasant family campsite on a peninsula with many spacious pitches on the water. Many amenities for children.

🚗 To the east of Pont-de-Salars D993 direction Salles-Curan. Take the D577 from Salles-Curan. Campsite signposted.

Canet-de-Salars
Arvieu
Salles-Curan
Montjaux
D911
D95
D199
D993
D25
D44

€ **17** 5/5-7/7 26/8-15/9 7=6, 14=11

N 44°11'21'' E 2°46'0''

Salles-Curan, F-12410 / Midi-Pyrénées (Aveyron)

🛜 **iD** (2366)

🏕 Sites & Paysages Beau Rivage****
🏠 route de Vernhes
☎ +33 (0)5-65463332
📅 1/5 - 30/9
@ camping@beau-rivage.fr

2ha 54T(80-120m²) 6A CEE

1 AC**G**IJLPRS
2 ADIJKRVWXY
3 AGRU**W**Z
4 (A 1/7-30/8) (C 10/6-15/9)
(Q 🔑) (R 15/6-15/9)
(T+U+V+X+Z 1/7-30/8)
5 **AB**FGIJKLMNOPUVWZ
6 CEG**K**(N 3km)OV

💬 Peaceful terraced campsite on Lake Pareloup. 3 km from the small town of Salles-Curan and its shops. Heated pool (from 10 June). Water sports, fishing, walking. Lovely surroundings.

🚗 A75, exit 44.1. Towards Salles-Curan/Lac de Pareloup.

Flavin
Pont-de-Salars
D911
D29
Salles-Curan
D25
D993
D30
Durenque
D44

€ **15** 1/5-9/7 28/8-29/9

N 44°12'9'' E 2°46'38''

Salles-et-Pratviel, F-31110 / Midi-Pyrénées (Haute-Garonne)

⛷ ♿ 🛜 **iD** (2367)

🏕 Le Pyrénéen***
🏠 7 Molles
☎ +33 (0)5-61795919
📅 15/1 - 15/10, 1/12 - 31/12
@ campinglepyreneen@orange.fr

1,6ha 36T(70-100m²) 4-10A CEE

1 ACD**F**HIJKL**P**R
2 CKLRVWX
3 A**F**GHIJNRU**W**
4 (C 15/6-15/9)
(Q+R+T 1/7-31/8)
5 ABDFGIJKLMNPUVW
6 CEG**K**(N 4km)OT

💬 Pleasant, level, well-maintained campsite in the sunny valley of Luchon, 4 km from a golf course. Many marked out mountain walks. Heated pool from 15/6 to 15/9. Hospitable welcome, free wifi. If arriving on a Sunday in low season please call in advance.

🚗 From Montréjeau N125 then D125 then A64 exit 17 and A645. Towards Spain this becomes the N125, then to Bagnères-de-Luchon on D125. Stay on this road until town name sign and camping sign on right. Then take D27.

D125
N125
N-230
Bagnères-de-Luchon
D618
N-141

€ **13** 15/1-8/7 26/8-14/10 1/12-30/12 7=6, 14=12

N 42°49'19'' E 0°36'21''

Seissan, F-32260 / Midi-Pyrénées (Gers)

♿ 📶 **iD** **2368**

🏕 Camping Domaine Lacs de Gascogne
🛣 route du Lac
☎ +33 (0)5-62662794
📅 31/3 - 30/9
@ info@domainelacsdegascogne.eu

14ha 50T(90-120m²) 16A CEE

1 ACD**F**IJKLMPQ
2 ABDJKLMRWXY
3 AB**F**GHJKMRUVWZ
4 (A 1/7-31/8) (B+G 1/5-30/9)
N(Q+T+U+X+Y+Z 🔒)
5 **AB**GIJKLMNOPUWZ
6 ACEGJ(N 2km)TV

💬 Enjoy the tranquillity among the century-old oak trees that are reflected by the lakes of these grounds. Excellent restaurant, open Thursday to Monday inclusive, lovely poolside terrace (1/5-30/9). Peacefully located fishing lake. Enthusiastic dynamic Dutch managers.

🚗 Follow the D929 as far as Seissan centre, then follow camping signs.

N21 — Castelnau-Barbarens
CC
D929
D2 Masseube — D40
D27 — D12

CC € **17** 31/3-6/7 25/8-29/9 7=6, 14=11, 21=17   📍 N 43°29'38'' E 0°34'47''

Séniergues, F-46240 / Midi-Pyrénées (Lot)

♿ 📶 **iD** **2369**

🏕 Flower Camping Domaine de la Faurie****
🛣 la Faurie
☎ +33 (0)5-65211436
📠 +33 (0)5-65311117
📅 7/4 - 29/9
@ contact@camping-lafaurie.com

27ha 54T(120-250m²) 6-10A CEE

1 ABCD**F**HIJKLMOPS
2 FIJKLRTUVWXY
3 A**F**GHJRU
4 (A 1/7-31/8)
(C+H+Q+R+T+U+V+X+Y+Z 🔒)
5 **AB**DFGIJKLMNOPUWZ
6 ACDEGJ(N 3km)TV

💬 Campsite located in the lovely Lot countryside on 27 hectares of grounds in the 'Parc Naturel Régional des Causses du Quercy'. Big, spacious pitches, tranquil location and a good base for days out. Recommended for nature lovers and gastronomy lovers!

🚗 A20, exit 56 Gourdon, at roundabout turn right exit St. Germain du Belair and continue for 5 km. Follow camping signs. Or from Souillac dir. Cahors via D820. Exit Montfaucon. Campsite signposted.

Gourdon
D704 — D801 — A20 — D807
D820 CC
D2
Labastide-Murat — D802

CC € **17** 7/4-7/7 25/8-28/9   📍 N 44°41'32'' E 1°32'5''

Septfonds, F-82240 / Midi-Pyrénées (Tarn-et-Garonne)

📶 **iD** **2370**

🏕 De Bois-Redon***
🛣 10 chemin de Bonnet
☎ +33 (0)5-63649249
📅 1/2 - 31/12
@ info@campingdeboisredon.com

2,5ha 34T(100-150m²) 10A CEE

1 A**F**IJKL**P**ST
2 B**F**RTXY
3 BGHJNRU
4 (A 1/7-31/8) (C 1/6-15/9)
(Q 1/4-1/11) (T+U 15/6-31/8)
(Z 1/6-30/9)
5 **A**DFGIJMNPUWZ
6 AEGJ(N 1km)TV

💬 A very peaceful and child-friendly campsite with large pitches in a parkland setting in Septfonds. Excellent amenities in an area with plenty of opportunities. Open from 1 February to 31 December. Free wifi.

🚗 A20 exit 59, then D926 to Rodez. Switch off SatNav in Caussade. In Septfonds after the roundabout take third on the left and follow signs. (121).

Caylus
D17
A20 — D926
Caussade — D19
D820 — D964 — Saint-Antonin-Noble-Val
D115

CC € **17** 1/2-6/7 25/8-30/12 7=6, 14=12, 21=17   📍 N 44°10'58'' E 1°36'13''

Sévérac-le-Château, F-12150 / Midi-Pyrénées (Aveyron) ⚹ 📶 iD (2371)

🏕 Les Calquières****
✉ 17 av. Jean Moulin
☎ +33 (0)5-65476482
🗓 1/4 - 30/9
@ contact@
camping-calquieres.com

2,4ha 85T(100-120m²) 10-16A CEE

1 ACD**G**IJKLMOPQ
2 FJKLRUVWXY
3 BFGHIJLMN**PRUW**
4 (**A** 1/7-31/8) (C 15/4-30/9)
(E 🗓) (F+H 15/4-30/9)
(Q+R+T+U+V+X+Y+Z 🗓)
5 **AB**DEFGHIJKLMNOPQRUW
Z
6 ACDEG**K**L(N 0,5km)RTUV

💬 Ideal for exploring the Gorges du Tarn and La Jonte. Many excursions in the area. In early and late season you can enjoy sunny days and fresh nights. Perfect stopover campsite on your way south and the last campsite before the breathtaking viaduct at Millau. Heated indoor swimming pool and restaurant.

🚐 From north A75 exit 42 or from south 43 Sévérac-le-Château. Follow signs. Campsite located next to municipal swimming pool.

Recoules-Prévinquières D2 A75
Sévérac-le-Château CC
D267
D995
D29 D809 D32
D911
D9

CC € **17** 1/4-8/7 26/8-29/9 7=6 ⛰ N 44°19'11'' E 3°3'51''

Sorèze, F-81540 / Midi-Pyrénées (Tarn) ⚹ 📶 iD (2372)

🏕 St. Martin***
✉ rue du 19 mars 1962
☎ +33 (0)5-63502019
🗓 30/3 - 21/10
@ campingsaintmartin@gmail.com

1,2ha 33T(100-120m²) 10A CEE

1 ACD**G**IJKLPQ
2 GLRVWXY
3 AGHJMNR
4 (B 1/6-30/9) (T+U+Z 🗓)
5 **AB**FGJLNPUWZ
6 ACDEGJ(N 0,5km)TV

💬 A village campsite in the heart of the Sorèze with shaded pitches and a swimming pool. Sorèze's heritage: half-timbered houses, the Saint Martin clock tower, Abbaye-école, protected historic monuments. Sorèze's culture: theatre, music festivals, braderies, festivities. Sorèze's natural setting: Rigole de la Plaine and Saint Ferréol lake, protected world heritage monuments.

🚐 In Revel follow the D85 towards Sorèze. Campsite signposted in village.

Viviers-lès-Montagnes
D46 D84
D1 Revel D85
CC
D622
D624 D629

CC € **15** 30/3-6/7 24/8-20/10 7=6 ⛰ N 43°27'16'' E 2°4'10''

Souillac, F-46200 / Midi-Pyrénées (Lot) 👫 ⚹ 📶 iD (2373)

🏕 Castels Domaine de la
Paille Basse*****
☎ +33 (0)5-65378548
FAX +33 (0)5-65370958
🗓 7/4 - 15/9
@ info@lapaillebasse.com

12ha 120T(100-110m²) 16A

1 ABCD**G**IJKLMPQ
2 FJKRTUVXY
3 BFGHJM**N**RU
4 (**A** 1/7-31/8) (C+H 🗓) J
(Q+R+S 🗓) (T 1/5-14/9)
(U 13/5-16/9) (X 20/5-10/9)
(Y+Z 13/5-16/9)
5 **AB**FGJLNPUW
6 EGH**J**(N 9km)OQTUV

💬 A medieval village (3 farmhouses) restored and reconstructed into an 80 hectare campsite, all of this without losing its authenticity. Positioned on a hill with lovely views and romantic sunsets. This, with all the facilities you would expect, means this Castels campsite deserves its five stars.

🚐 Don't use SatNav. Take exit 55 on A20. At 2nd roundabout dir. Salignac. Follow signs 'La Paille Basse'. Site is 8 km from Souillac.

D60
D820
D62 D840
CC A20
D803
Souillac
D703 Meyronne
Pinsac

CC € **17** 7/4-7/7 25/8-14/9 7=6, 14=12, 21=18 ⛰ N 44°56'44'' E 1°26'29''

Souillac, F-46200 / Midi-Pyrénées (Lot) 〒 iD (2374)

🔺 Flower Camping Les Ondines***
🚏 rue des Ondines
☎ +33 (0)5-65378644
🔓 1/5 - 30/9
@ camping.les.ondines@
flowercampings.com

4ha 135T(90-110m²) 6A CEE

1 ACD**G**IJLPRS
2 CFRVWXY
3 ABFGHJKOPR**W**X
4 (A 1/7-31/8) (C+H+Q+R 🔓)
(T 25/5-31/8) (Z 🔓)
5 **AB**CEFGHIJKLMNOPUWZ
6 AEGK(N 0,5km)RW

💬 A campsite located on the banks of the Dordogne, a five minute walk from the centre of Souillac. You can swim in the heated pool on the campsite or from the natural river beach 200m away. The campsite is located between Sarlat and Rocamadour.

🚗 A20, exit 55 Souillac and follow camping signs.

CC € 15 1/5-6/7 25/8-29/9 7=6   🧭 N 44°53'20'' E 1°28'29''

Souillac, F-46200 / Midi-Pyrénées (Lot) ♿ 〒 ✿ iD (2375)

🔺 Vakantiepark 'La Draille'****
☎ +33 (0)5-65326501
🔓 28/4 - 15/9
@ la.draille@wanadoo.fr

35ha 146T(100-120m²) 10A CEE

1 ACD**F**IJLPRS
2 ACFJLRTVY
3 B**F**GHJK**MNOPQ**RUW
4 (A 1/7-31/8) (C+G 🔓) J
(Q+S+T+U+V+X+Z 🔓)
5 **AB**FGIJKLMNOPUZ
6 EGHJ**K**L(N 6km)OPRTUV

💬 A beautiful four-star campsite: perfectly maintained pitches, toilet facilities and amenities. Set among the hills on the River Borrèze. Ideal as stopover campsite and/or starting point for many places of interest. Beautiful woodland walks in the 35 hectare park. Limited services on Sundays.

🚗 A20 exit Soulliac. When entering Soulliac turn right to the D15 and then the D62.

CC € 15 28/4-6/7 25/8-14/9   🧭 N 44°56'9'' E 1°26'14''

St. Antonin-Noble-Val, F-82140 / Midi-Pyrénées (Tarn-et-Garonne) 〒 iD (2376)

🔺 Flower Camping Les
Gorges de l'Aveyron***
🚏 Lieu dit Marsac Bas
☎ +33 (0)5-63306976
🔓 6/4 - 30/9
@ info@
camping-gorges-aveyron.com

3,8ha 80T(100-120m²) 6-10A

1 ABCD**G**IJKLPRS
2 CMRVWXY
3 AGHJNR**W**X
4 (C 🔓) (H 1/7-31/8)
(Q+S+T+U+V 1/6-15/9)
(Z 1/6-25/9)
5 **AB**FGIJKLMNPUZ
6 ACEGJ**K**(N 1,5km)V

💬 A peaceful campsite right by the river in the Gorges de l'Aveyron with lovely level grounds and views of the 'Gorges'. It has a beautiful new swimming pool. Beautifully refurbished toilet facilities. Especially friendly wardens. The village of St Antonin is worth a visit.

🚗 From Caussade on the N20 take the D5 to St. Antonin. Cross the bridge and enter tunnel to the left. Campsite about 1 km on the left.

CC € 15 6/4-29/6 1/9-29/9   🧭 N 44°9'5'' E 1°46'18''

411

St. Antonin-Noble-Val, F-82140 / Midi-Pyrénées (Tarn-et-Garonne)

🌐 **iD** (2377)

🏕 Les 3 Cantons★★★★
☎ +33 (0)5-63319857
📅 1/5 - 30/9
@ info@3cantons.fr

15ha 80T(80-150m²) 6-10A

1 ACD**F**IJLP
2 BFTXY
3 BGHJMN**OP**RU
4 (B+G 1/6-15/9) (Q 📅)
   (T+U+X 8/7-26/8) (Z 📅)
5 **A**CDFGIJLMNPRUWZ
6 ADEGKM(N 6km)TV

💬 A friendly campsite in the middle of woods and in a lovely walking area with orchid displays in the spring. Pleasant bar/terrace, refurbished swimming pool and sports on offer. Close to authentic villages, markets and gastronomic opportunities. Dutch owners.

🚗 From Caussade D926 direction Caylus, Villefranche-de-Rouergue. Past Septfonds do not take St. Antonin exit, but stay on main road for about 5 km. Turning on the right. Signposted.

CC € **17** 1/5-7/7 25/8-29/9 10=9

📍 N 44°11'37'' E 1°41'47''

St. Cirq-Lapopie, F-46330 / Midi-Pyrénées (Lot)

♿ 🌐 ✿ **iD** (2378)

🏕 Camping Restaurant De la Plage★★★★
🏠 Porte Roques
☎ +33 (0)5-65302951
📅 7/4 - 30/9
@ camping-laplage@wanadoo.fr

3ha 93T(100-120m²) 10-16A

1 ACD**G**IJKLMPQ
2 ACGKLMORTUVWXY
3 BGHJKLNRU**W**X
4 (A 1/7-30/8) (Q+R 📅)
   (T 1/7-31/8) (U 📅)
   (V 1/5-15/9) (Y 15/4-30/9)
   (Z 📅)
5 **AB**CDEFGIJKLMNOPQRUW
   XYZ
6 ACDEGIJ(N 0,5km)ORTV

💬 Superbly located at the foot of St. Cirq-Lapopie and the banks of the Lot, in the middle of Les Causses du Quercy regional park. Good amenities and plenty of sports (with discounts). Good restaurant with local products and an attractive terrace. St. Cirq is a popular village with the French.

🚗 Follow the D653 from Cahors direction Figeac. At Vers take the D662 direction St. Cirq. At Tour-de-Faure cross the bridge over the Lot. Campsite 500 metres right on the D40.

CC € **17** 7/4-30/6 1/9-29/9

📍 N 44°28'8'' E 1°40'51''

St. Cirq-Lapopie, F-46330 / Midi-Pyrénées (Lot)

🌐 **iD** (2379)

🏕 La Truffière★★★
🏠 D42
☎ +33 (0)5-65302022
📅 1/4 - 30/9
@ contact@camping-truffiere.com

4ha 83T(100-120m²) 6A CEE

1 AC**F**IJKLPST
2 BIJKLRTVWXY
3 BGHJNRU
4 (A 1/7-31/8) (C+G 1/5-20/9)
   (Q 1/5-15/9) (R 📅)
   (T+U 1/6-31/8) (V 1/6-15/9)
   (X+Z 1/6-31/8)
5 **AB**DEFGIJLMNOPUWXZ
6 CDEGJ(N 2,5km)OTV

💬 Spaciously laid out yet intimate terraced campsite in a parkland setting with lovely views. Ideal for those who love nature and relaxation. 3 km from the lovely village of St. Cirq (with free shuttle service).

🚗 Campsite is signposted in St. Cirq-Lapopie. Approximately 3 km from the village.

CC € **15** 1/4-6/7 26/8-29/9

📍 N 44°26'53'' E 1°40'29''

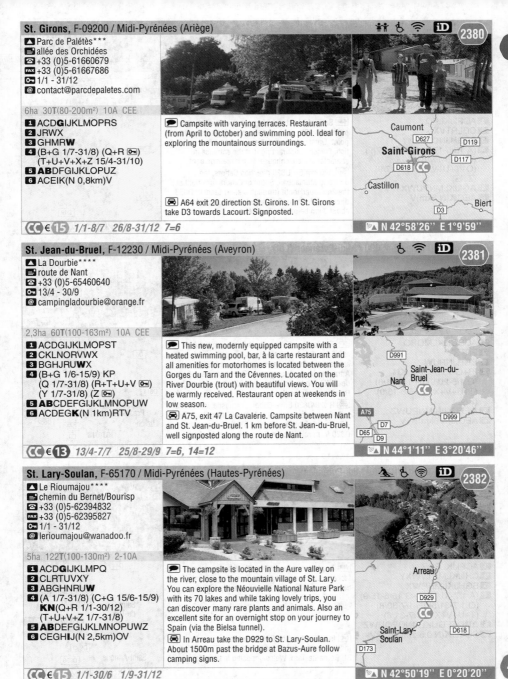

St. Girons, F-09200 / Midi-Pyrénées (Ariège) 2380

Parc de Palétès***
allée des Orchidées
☎ +33 (0)5-61660679
FAX +33 (0)5-61667686
⌚ 1/1 - 31/12
@ contact@parcdepaletes.com

6ha 30T(80-200m²) 10A CEE

1 ACDGIJKLMOPRS
2 JRWX
3 GHMRW
4 (B+G 1/7-31/8) (Q+R ☁) (T+U+V+X+Z 15/4-31/10)
5 ABDFGIJKLOPUZ
6 ACEIK(N 0,8km)V

💬 Campsite with varying terraces. Restaurant (from April to October) and swimming pool. Ideal for exploring the mountainous surroundings.

🚗 A64 exit 20 direction St. Girons. In St. Girons take D3 towards Lacourt. Signposted.

Caumont — D627 — D119
Saint-Girons — D117
D618 CC
Castillon — D3 — Biert

CC € 15 1/1-8/7 26/8-31/12 7=6 📐 N 42°58'26'' E 1°9'59''

St. Jean-du-Bruel, F-12230 / Midi-Pyrénées (Aveyron) 2381

La Dourbie****
route de Nant
☎ +33 (0)5-65460640
⌚ 13/4 - 30/9
@ campingladourbie@orange.fr

2,3ha 60T(100-163m²) 10A CEE

1 ACDGIJKLMOPST
2 CKLNORVWX
3 BGHJRUWX
4 (B+G 1/6-15/9) KP (Q 1/7-31/8) (R+T+U+V ☁) (Y 1/7-31/8) (Z ☁)
5 ABCDEFGIJKLMNOPUW
6 ACDEGK(N 1km)RTV

💬 This new, modernly equipped campsite with a heated swimming pool, bar, à la carte restaurant and all amenities for motorhomes is located between the Gorges du Tarn and the Cévennes. Located on the River Dourbie (trout) with beautiful views. You will be warmly received. Restaurant open at weekends in low season.

🚗 A75, exit 47 La Cavalerie. Campsite between Nant and St. Jean-du-Bruel. 1 km before St. Jean-du-Bruel, well signposted along the route de Nant.

D991
Saint-Jean-du-Bruel
Nant CC
A75 — D999
D65 — D7
D9

CC € 13 13/4-7/7 25/8-29/9 7=6, 14=12 📐 N 44°1'11'' E 3°20'46''

St. Lary-Soulan, F-65170 / Midi-Pyrénées (Hautes-Pyrénées) 2382

Le Rioumajou****
chemin du Bernet/Bourisp
☎ +33 (0)5-62394832
FAX +33 (0)5-62395827
⌚ 1/1 - 31/12
@ lerioumajou@wanadoo.fr

5ha 122T(100-130m²) 2-10A

1 ACDGIJKLMPQ
2 CLRTUVXY
3 ABGHNRUW
4 (A 1/7-31/8) (C+G 15/6-15/9) KN(Q+R 1/1-30/12) (T+U+V+Z 1/7-31/8)
5 ABDEFGIJKLMNOPUWZ
6 CEGHIJ(N 2,5km)OV

💬 The campsite is located in the Aure valley on the river, close to the mountain village of St. Lary. You can explore the Néouvielle National Nature Park with its 70 lakes and while taking lovely trips, you can discover many rare plants and animals. Also an excellent site for an overnight stop on your journey to Spain (via the Bielsa tunnel).

🚗 In Arreau take the D929 to St. Lary-Soulan. About 1500m past the bridge at Bazus-Aure follow camping signs.

Arreau
D929
CC
Saint-Lary-Soulan — D618
D173

CC € 15 1/1-30/6 1/9-31/12 📐 N 42°50'19'' E 0°20'20''

St. Pantaléon, F-46800 / Midi-Pyrénées (Lot)

◭ des Arcades***
🏚 Moulin de St. Martial
☎ +33 (0)9-61677498
🗓 12/5 - 15/9
@ info@des-arcades.com

2383

12ha 81T(70-140m²) 6A

1 ACFIJKLPQ
2 CDLRTVX
3 BFGHJNOPRUW
4 (A 15/5-17/9) (B 31/5-17/9)
(G 15/5-17/9) J
(Q+T+U+V+Y 15/5-17/9)
(Z ☍)
5 AGIJKLMNPUWX
6 AEGK(N 8km)V

💬 Set in 12 hectares of grounds with spacious pitches. A 13th-century water mill forms its centre point. Outstanding amenities, you can swim or fish. French restaurant right at the entrance in characteristic coachhouse. Dutch management.

🚗 A20 exit 57. D820 direction Cahors, then direction Montauban. South of Cahors turn right at the 2nd roundabout (through a short tunnel). D653 direction Montcuq. Campsite located on the left, about 3 km before St. Pantaléon.

CC € **17** 12/5-29/6 18/8-14/9

N 44°22'15'' E 1°18'28''

St. Pierre-Lafeuille, F-46090 / Midi-Pyrénées (Lot)

◭ Quercy Vacances****
🏚 Le Mas de Lacombe
☎ +33 (0)5-65368715
🗓 1/4 - 30/9
@ quercyvacances@wanadoo.fr

2384

5ha 80T(100-130m²) 16A CEE

1 ACDGIJKLMOPQ
2 FRTXY
3 BGHJNRUW
4 (B+G 15/6-15/9) KN
(Q 1/5-20/9) (R 1/7-31/8)
(T+U+V+X+Y 15/6-15/9)
(Z ☍)
5 AEFGIJKLMNPUWZ
6 AEGIJ(N 9km)RTV

💬 The lovely intimate site is 5km from the A20 exit 57 and suitable as a stopover site. Lovely sauna and jacuzzi close to an enormous swimming pool. Attractive bar and restaurant. The surroundings are beautiful and the tourist town of Cahors is close by. Relaxation assured!

🚗 RN20/D820 Brive-Cahors, campsite well indicated 800m before St. Pierre-Lafeuille, turn right. Site ± 700m on right. Or: A20 exit 57 dir. Cahors. Onto D820 from roundabout. Then follow route above.

CC € **15** 1/4-4/7 27/8-29/9

N 44°31'53'' E 1°27'33''

St. Rome-de-Tarn, F-12490 / Midi-Pyrénées (Aveyron)

◭ de la Cascade****
☎ +33 (0)5-65625659
📠 +33 (0)5-65625862
🗓 1/1 - 31/12
@ contact@
camping-cascade-aveyron.com

2385

4ha 99T(80-120m²) 6A CEE

1 ACFIJKLPRS
2 CHIJKLMRTVWXY
3 BGHJKLMNRWX
4 (A 1/7-31/8) (B+G 15/6-15/9)
(Q 1/7-31/8) (R 1/7-30/8)
(T+U+V+X+Z 1/7-31/8)
5 ABDEFGIJKLMNOPQUWX
6 CDEGK(N 0,5km)OPQRV

💬 An attractive campsite with terraces and excellent facilities situated right on the Tarn. You can ask for help when positioning your caravan.

🚗 In Millau take the D992 direction Albi.
In St. Georges-de-Luzençan take the D73 direction St. Rome-de-Tarn. Well signposted in the village.

CC € **15** 1/4-8/7 26/8-15/10

N 44°3'11'' E 2°53'59''

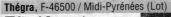

Thégra, F-46500 / Midi-Pyrénées (Lot)

 ♿ 🛜 ✿ iD (2386)

🏕 Sites & Paysages Le
   Ventoulou★★★★
🏠 Ventoulou
☎ +33 (0)5-65336701
🔓 1/4 - 4/11
@ contact@leventoulou.com

2ha 27T(100-120m²) 10A CEE

1 ACD**F**IJKLMPRS
2 JRTVWXY
3 B**F**GHJNRU
4 (A 1/7-31/8) (C+E ⌨)
   (G 1/7-31/8) (Q 1/6-31/8)
   (R ⌨) (T+U+V+X 1/7-31/8)
   (Z ⌨)
5 **AB**DEFGIJKLMNOPQUWYZ
6 ACEG**IK**(N 8km)RTV

💬 A lovely campsite, calm and peaceful, situated in protected countryside. Three minutes from Padirac and ten minutes from the medieval district of Rocamadour in the heart of the Vallée region of the Dordogne Lotoise. Ideal for discovering various nearby towns less than 15 kilometres away as the crow flies. Campsite guests can enjoy discounts at many sights in the surroundings.

🚗 Campsite signposted on D673 near Padirac. Site located on the D60.

CC € ⑰ 1/4-6/7 25/8-3/11 7=6, 14=11, 21=16, 28=21

🧭 N 44°49'32'' E 1°46'42''

Toulouse, F-31200 / Midi-Pyrénées (Haute-Garonne)

👫 ♿ 🛜 iD (2387)

🏕 Camping Toulouse Le Rupé★★★
🏠 21 chemin du Pont de Rupé
☎ +33 (0)5-61700735
FAX +33 (0)5-61709717
🔓 1/1 - 31/12
@ campinglerupe31@wanadoo.fr

4ha 84T(80-120m²) 10A CEE

1 ACD**G**IJKLMOPQ
2 DFGRUVWXY
3 ABG**M**RV**W**
4 **KN**(Q+R ⌨)
   (T+U+V+X+Z 1/7-31/8)
5 **AB**DEFGIJKLMNOPUXYZ
6 ACDEG**K**(N 3km)OTV

💬 A beautifully laid out town campsite. Ideal as a stopover campsite or as a starting point to visit Toulouse.

🚗 Toulouse ringroad (A620), exit Sesquieres (33). Campsite signposted. Located north of the town.

CC € ⑰ 1/1-7/7 26/8-31/12 7=6

🧭 N 43°39'21'' E 1°24'56''

Touzac, F-46700 / Midi-Pyrénées (Lot)

 ♿ 🛜 iD (2388)

🏕 Le Ch'timi★★★
🏠 La Roque
☎ +33 (0)5-65365236
🔓 1/4 - 30/9
@ info@campinglechtimi.com

3,5ha 77T(90-150m²) 6A CEE

1 ACD**G**IJKLPQ
2 CKLRTVXY
3 B**F**GHJMNRU**WX**
4 (B 15/5-30/9) (G 1/7-1/9)
   (Q 15/5-15/9) (R ⌨)
   (T+U+V+X 1/5-30/9) (Z ⌨)
5 **A**CFGIJKLMNPUWZ
6 ACEGHIJ(N 5km)OTV

💬 This campsite, laid out in the style of an old country estate offers spacious pitches and first rate amenities. Located in a charming valley of the Lot. It is a good base for cyclists and carp anglers.

🚗 A20 exit 57, D820 to Cahors. Sharp right just before Cahors roundabout follow D811 till Duravel, left on the D58 to Port de Vire. Right at the roundabout to Touzac. Campsite signposted from here.

CC € ⑮ 1/4-2/7 20/8-29/9

🧭 N 44°29'53'' E 1°3'59''

Touzac, F-46700 / Midi-Pyrénées (Lot) 🚿 📶 iD (2389)

🏕 Le Clos Bouyssac***
☎ +33 (0)5-65365221
🔓 1/4 - 30/9
@ camping.leclosbouyssac@
wanadoo.fr

1,5ha 85T(80-190m²) 10A CEE

1 ACFIJLMPQ
2 BCJLORVY
3 AEGHJNRUWX
4 (A 15/7-18/8) (B 1/6-15/9)
(G 1/7-18/8)
(Q+R+T+U 1/7-31/8)
(Z 1/6-1/9)
5 ABFGIJKLMNPUZ
6 CEJ(N 4km)V

💬 A wonderful, calm campsite with large riverside pitches, ideal for fishing or just relaxing. Specialised in bringing campers together with weekly activities such as wine tasting and barbecues. Surrounded by stunning countryside and vineyards. Worth a visit.

🚗 A20, exit 57 direction Cahors. Sharp right at the roundabout just before Cahors towards Fumel. Left at Duravel via the D58 to Port de Vire. Turn right at the roundabout to Touzac. Campsite signposted

CC € 15 1/4-29/6 17/8-29/9

📐 N 44°28'49'' E 1°3'7''

Villefranche-de-Rouergue, F-12200 / Midi-Pyrénées (Aveyron) 🚿 📶 iD (2390)

🏕 Le Rouergue***
🏠 35 avenue de Fondies
☎ +33 (0)5-65451624
🔓 14/4 - 30/9
@ campingrouergue@wanadoo.fr

2ha 93T(100-175m²) 16A CEE

1 ACDGHIJKLMPQ
2 CRUVWXY
3 AFGHRU
4 (A 🔲) (B 1/7-15/9) K
(Q+R 🔲) (T+Z 1/7-31/8)
5 ACFGIJKLMNOPUVWXYZ
6 ACEGHJ(N 2km)RTUV

💬 Camping du Rouergue is situated close to the Villefranche-de-Rouergue royal fortified town with its lovely market square. The site offers you rest and comfort in shady natural surroundings. This campsite has spacious pitches with water and electricity (grand comfort), the toilet facilities meet modern expectations completely.

🚗 The campsite is located 2 km from the centre of Villefranche-de-Rouergue. Follow 'Stade' signs towards Monteils-Najac.

CC € 13 14/4-7/7 25/8-29/9

📐 N 44°20'33'' E 2°1'35''

Agde, F-34300 / Languedoc-Roussillon (Hérault) 🚿 📶 iD (2391)

🏕 Camping Le Neptune****
🏠 route du Grau
☎ +33 (0)4-67942394
🔓 1/4 - 30/9
@ info@campingleneptune.com

2,7ha 100T(70-120m²) 10A CEE

1 ACDFIJKLMPST
2 ACFRVWXY
3 BFGJKNRUVW
4 (C+G 🔲) K(Q 🔲)
(R 10/5-15/9)
(T+U+V 27/6-21/8)
(Z 15/5-30/9)
5 ABEFGIJKLMNOPSUVWZ
6 ABEGHIK(N 0,8km)ORTUV

💬 Peaceful friendly family campsite with heated pool. 2 km from sea. Marked-out pitches, some with private toilets, motorhome services. Wifi, free fitness. Bike hire. Fresh bread daily. Free boat mooring.

🚗 A9 exit Agde dir Agde. Then exit Le Grau-d'Agde. 1st exit over bridge Grau d'Agde. 4th exit at 1st and 2nd roundabouts, 3rd and 4th roundabouts straight on, 2nd exit at 5th roundabout (Grau d'Agde). 800m beside river. Using GPS: 46, blvrd du Saint Christ, 34300 Agde.

CC € 15 1/4-6/7 24/8-29/9 7=6, 14=11

📐 N 43°17'53'' E 3°27'23''

Agde, F-34300 / Languedoc-Roussillon (Hérault)   👣 🤟 📶 iD (2392)

🔺 L'Escale***
✉ route de la Tamarissière
☎ +33 (0)4-67212109
📠 +33 (0)4-67211024
🔑 25/3 - 30/9
@ camping.lescale.agde@
  gmail.com
2,5ha 50T(80-90m²) 10A

1 ACD**G**IJKLMPST
2 ACFRVXY
3 B**F**GKLN**O**RUW
4 (B+G 15/5-30/9)
  (Q+R+T+U+V+X+Y+Z 🔒)
5 **AB**FGJLNPUVZ
6 AEGHIK(N 2,5km)OT

💬 Attractive, shaded family campsite located on the Hérault. River or sea fishing. Wonderful cycling to Cap d'Agde or inland. Bridge competitions for enthusiasts on the campsite. Free wifi.

🚗 A9 exit Agde. At the roundabout N312, direction Agde exit Tamarissière. Campsite about 3 km on the right.

CC €**17** 25/3-6/7 25/8-29/9   📷 N 43°17'49'' E 3°26'57''

Agde, F-34300 / Languedoc-Roussillon (Hérault)   🚹🚺 👣 🤟 📶 iD (2393)

🔺 La Pepinière***
✉ 3 route du Grau d'Agde
☎ +33 (0)4-67941094
🔑 15/3 - 15/10
@ reception@
  campinglapepiniere.com
1,9ha 36T(80-100m²) 10A CEE

1 ACDGIJKLM**P**ST
2 CGTVWXY
3 B**F**GJKLNRUW
4 (C+H 1/4-30/9) **N**
  (T+Z 1/7-31/8)
5 **AB**GIJKLMNPUZ
6 ABEGK(N 0,9km)RT

💬 This quiet family campsite is located near an old fishing harbour on the Mediterranean on the banks of the Hérault. Lovely cycle path to the beach (1200m) and shops. Very good fishing. Free heated swimming pool, bubble bath and sauna. Free wifi in low season throughout the campsite.

🚗 From the A9: exit Agde towards Agde. Then Le Grau d'Agde. Campsite is located on the left after about 3 km. Boulevard St. Christ (for GPS).

CC €**13** 15/3-6/7 25/8-14/10   📷 N 43°17'47'' E 3°27'9''

Agde, F-34300 / Languedoc-Roussillon (Hérault)   👣 🤟 📶 iD (2394)

🔺 Les Champs Blancs****
✉ 76 route de Rochelongue
☎ +33 (0)4-67942342
📠 +33 (0)4-67948781
🔑 1/4 - 15/10
@ contact@
  campingleschampsblancs.com
6,5ha 160T(80-130m²) 10A CEE

1 ACDGIJKLMOPST
2 AFGRTVWXY
3 B**F**GJKMNRU**W**
4 (C+H 🔒) IJKM(Q+S 🔒)
  (T+U+V 10/4-14/10)
  (Y 2/5-30/9) (Z 10/4-14/10)
5 **AB**GJLNOPSTUWXYZ
6 ABCEGHIK(N 1km)TUV

💬 Quiet family campsite, 2 km from the sea. Large, heated aquapark and large pitches, marked out by oleander hedges, a few even have private toilet facilities. Wifi on the grounds and many activities for everybody.

🚗 A9 exit 34 dir. Beziers/Agde. On D1612 dir. Grau d'Agde-Rochelonge. At roundabout (with statue) left dir. Grau d'Agde. Next rndbt 2nd exit right. Next rndbt 1st exit right. After bridge 1st right.

CC €**17** 1/4-6/7 24/8-14/10 7=6, 14=11   📷 N 43°17'47'' E 3°28'37''

Agde, F-34300 / Languedoc-Roussillon (Hérault) ♿ 🛜 iD (2395)

▲ Les Mimosas****
🏢 98 route de Guiraudette
☎ +33 (0)4-67016736
📠 +33 (0)4-67316406
🗓 17/3 - 13/10
@ lesmimosas-agde@outlook.fr

1,6ha 16T(80-110m²) 16A

1 ACD**G**IJLPST
2 GSVWXY
3 B**F**GJKRUW
4 (C+H 15/4-15/9)
 (Q+T+U+V+Z 🗝)
5 **A**EFGIJKLMNOPUXZ
6 AEGH**I**K(N 0,6km)T

💬 Small family campsite with agreeable ambiance and well maintained toilet facilities. Many options for cycling and for cultural trips to Cap d'Agde. Heated pool and free wifi (1 code pp) on entire site. Baker, restaurant and supermarket next to the campsite.

🚗 A9 exit Cap d'Agde then take N112. Then take exit Agde, Grau d'Agde, Rochlongue. 2nd exit at roundabout (Lidl). Straight on at 2nd roundabout, campsite on the left.

CC € **13** 17/3-6/7 27/8-12/10 7=6, 12=10, 14=11, 21=17 📲 N 43°17'17'' E 3°28'14''

Agde, F-34300 / Languedoc-Roussillon (Hérault) 👫 ♿ 🛜 iD (2396)

▲ Les Romarins****
🏢 6 route du Grau
☎ +33 (0)4-67941859
📠 +33 (0)4-67265880
🗓 31/3 - 6/10
@ contact@romarins.com

2,5ha 120T(80-115m²) 10-13A CEE

1 ACD**G**IJKLMOPST
2 ACF**G**RVWXY
3 B**F**GJKNRUW
4 (C+Q+R+T+U+V+X+Z 🗝)
5 **AB**EFGJKLMNPUZ
6 ABEG**IJ**K(N 0,6km)RTV

💬 A friendly campsite on the River Hérault 900m from the sea. A friendly couple who will do anything they can to help you. A good base for trips out, also by bike. Multifunctional sports field and some fitness apparatus. Heated swimming pool and free wifi on the terrace. Fishing on the campsite.

🚗 A9 exit Agde. Direction Agde. At Agde exit Le Grau d'Agde. Turn left after about 3 km.

CC € **15** 31/3-6/7 26/8-5/10 7=6, 14=12, 21=18, 28=24 📲 N 43°17'40'' E 3°27'0''

Agde, F-34300 / Languedoc-Roussillon (Hérault) 👫 ♿ 🛜 iD (2397)

▲ Les Sablettes***
🏢 55 chemin de Baluffe
☎ +33 (0)4-67943665
🗓 1/4 - 30/9
@ lessablettes@hotmail.fr

2,5ha 70T(60-100m²) 10A CEE

1 ACD**F**IJKLMPST
2 A**F**GSVWXY
3 B**F**GJKRUW
4 (C+H 🗝) J
 (Q+T+U+V+X+Z 🗝)
5 **AB**FGJLNPQUZ
6 ACEGHJ**K**(N 1,5km)TV

💬 A peaceful family campsite 800 metres from Agde beach. The site has a large swimming pool with slide. Free wifi at the bar in the restaurant. Trips out from the campsite to Agde or Sète. An afternoon sailing on the Canal du Midi is most enjoyable.

🚗 A9 exit Cap d'Agde (D112). Then take Grau d'Agde exit and 2nd exit at the roundabout with statue. 1st exit at next roundabout and follow camping signs.

CC € **13** 1/4-7/7 27/8-29/9 7=6, 14=12, 21=18, 28=24 📲 N 43°17'17'' E 3°27'46''

Anduze, F-30140 / Languedoc-Roussillon (Gard)   ♿ 📶 iD (2398)

🏕 Cévennes-Provence***
📫 Corbès-Thoiras
☎ +33 (0)4-66617310
📠 +33 (0)4-66616074
📅 20/3 - 1/10
@ info@campingcp.com

30ha 226T(80-200m²) 10A CEE

1 ACD**G**IJKLPST
2 ABCGJKLMNORSVWXY
3 B**G**HJ**MNPQR**U**W**X
4 (**A** 🕑) (Q 1/4-15/9)
　(S 1/4-30/9)
　(T+U+V+X+Y+Z 15/4-9/9)
5 **AB**CDEFGHIJKLMNOPQRU
　VZ
6 ACEGHIJ(N 2km)O**P**RTUV

💬 Lovely, peaceful, natural campsite between two branches of the river Gardon. Direct access to a private beach. Swimming in the clear river water. Its micro-climate supports more than 120 types of trees and many different plants. New toilet block since 2017. Run by the same family for 60 years.

🚗 Leave the A7 at Bollène. At Alès drive in dir. of Montpellier. In Anduze take the D907 dir. St. Jean-du-Gard. 3 km after Anduze turn tright at bus stop (D284 Rte de Corbes).

CC € **17** 20/3-30/6 1/9-30/9 🧭 N 44°4'41'' E 3°57'53''

Anduze, F-30140 / Languedoc-Roussillon (Gard)   ♿ 📶 iD (2399)

🏕 Le Castel Rose****
📫 610 chemin Recoulin
☎ +33 (0)4-66618015
📅 7/4 - 16/9
@ castelrose@wanadoo.fr

7ha 182T(100-260m²) 10A CEE

1 A**G**IJKLMPST
2 ABCGKLMNORSVWXY
3 B**F**GHIJN**P**RUV**W**X
4 (C+H 🕑) IJ**KL**MN
　(Q+S+T+U+V+X+Y+Z 🕑)
5 **AB**CDEFGHIJKLMNOPQRU
　VWXY
6 ABCEGIJ**K**(N 0,5km)ORTV

💬 Family campsite on the banks of the Gardon with private beaches and views of the bamboo plantation. Large shaded pitches, level grounds with heated 1800 m² water park. Wellness, petanque, table tennis, trampoline and playgrounds. Bar, snack bar, supermarket and restaurant. Free wifi. Pitches by the river and larger than 130 m²: 1 Euros per day extra.

🚗 From Anduze the D907 dir. St. Jean-du-Gard. Turn right after the bend and continue to the end of the road.

CC € **17** 7/4-1/7 27/8-15/9 🧭 N 44°3'52'' E 3°58'37''

Anduze, F-30140 / Languedoc-Roussillon (Gard)   ♿ 📶 iD (2400)

🏕 Le Pradal****
📫 rte de Générargues
☎ +33 (0)4-66617981
📅 1/4 - 30/9
@ camping-le-pradal@orange.fr

3,5ha 106T(90-400m²) 10A CEE

1 ACD**G**IJKLMOPST
2 ABCGKLNORSVWXY
3 BGHIJ**MP**RU**W**X
4 (B 15/5-30/9) (G 1/7-30/9)
　(Q+S+T+U+V 🕑)
　(X 1/6-31/8) (Z 🕑)
5 **AB**DEFGIJKLMNOPQUXYZ
6 ACEG**JK**(N 1km)OTUV

💬 A ten-minute walk from Anduze and the bamboo garden, close to many interesting places. A pleasant campsite with a private beach on the River Gardon, large swimming pool. Peaceful, agreeable atmosphere. Large, level shaded pitches. Bar, restaurant with terrace, fresh bread, newspapers. Free tennis, jeu de boules, trampolines, table tennis, playground. Free wifi.

🚗 A7 Bollène. Then take Bagnols-Alès-Anduze road, turn right before the bridge, follow signs (500 metres).

CC € **17** 1/4-14/7 1/9-29/9 🧭 N 44°3'44'' E 3°58'58''

Anduze, F-30140 / Languedoc-Roussillon (Gard)

♿ 📶 iD (2401)

🏕 Les Fauvettes***
📧 rte de St. Jean-du-Gard
☎ +33 (0)4-66617223
🗓 21/4 - 30/9
@ camping-les-fauvettes@
wanadoo.fr

4ha 102T(90-140m²) 10A CEE

1 ACD**G**IJKLMOPS
2 BGJKLRVXY
3 BF**G**HIKN**P**RU**W**
4 (C+G 15/5-15/9) JK
 (Q 1/6-15/9)
 (T+U+V+X+Z 1/7-31/8)
5 **A**FGIJKLMNOPQRUVWZ
6 CEGJ(N 0,4km)TV

💬 A 10-minute walk from the centre. 500 metres to the river by a private footpath and the amenities are close by. Friendly campsite, marked out pitches with shade, heated swimming pool, toddlers' pool, water slides, jeu de boules, table tennis. Free wifi.

🚗 Campsite on the D907 Anduze - St. Jean-du-Gard. Signposted.

D9 D260   **Alès** D6
Saint-Christol-lès-Alès
N2106
CC
D24
D35   D907
D982   D6110

CC € **15** 21/4-3/7 21/8-29/9   🏔 N 44°3'37'' E 3°58'26''

Argelès-sur-Mer, F-66701 / Languedoc-Roussillon (Pyrénées-Orientales)

👫 ♿ 📶 iD (2402)

🏕 Albizia***
📧 avenue du Général de Gaulle
☎ +33 (0)4-68811562
📠 +33 (0)4-68958774
🗓 7/4 - 30/9
@ contact@camping-albizia.com

1ha 70T(70-90m²) 10A CEE

1 ACGHIJKLOPST
2 EGRTVX
3 **A**FNRUY
5 **AB**FGJLMNOPUVZ
6 ACGJ(N 0,2km)RT

💬 Camping Albizia, located between the sea and the mountains, is an ideal starting point for trips to the Pyrenees or Spain. Walk to the centre of Argelès-Plage, the lovely beach, the lively promenade, the little bars, the shops or the restaurants from the campsite.

🚗 A9, exit Perpignan-Sud, D914 direction Argelès-sur-Mer to exit 10, direction Argelès. At the second roundabout direction Argelès, Les Plages. In the village, follow signs to 'Centre Plage'.

D914
CC
Argelès-sur-Mer
Banyuls-sur-Mer

CC € **15** 7/4-7/7 25/8-29/9 7=6   🏔 N 42°33'5'' E 3°2'40''

Argelès-sur-Mer, F-66700 / Languedoc-Roussillon (Pyrénées-Orientales)

👫 ♿ 📶 iD (2403)

🏕 Camping Catalan**
📧 Avenue du Général de Gaulle
☎ +33 (0)4-68811226
📠 +33 (0)4-68810939
🗓 1/5 - 29/9
@ contact@campingcatalan.com

71T(70-80m²) 8-13A CEE

1 ACGIJKLPT
2 GTVXY
3 ABF**R**
5 **AB**EFGJLNPUVW
6 ACEGHIJ**K**RT

NEW

💬 You can leave your car at the Catalan campsite if you want to have a quick dip in the sea (150 m), walk down the boulevard, visit one of the inviting markets or the lively centre of Argelès-Plage. It's also ideal for day trips to Spain or the Pyrenees.

🚗 A9 exit Perpignan-Sud D914 towards Argelès-sur-Mer to exit 10 towards Argelès. At 2nd roundabout towards Argelès, Les Plages. In village follow signs to Centre Plage.

Saint-Cyprien
D914
CC
Argelès-sur-Mer
D914

CC € **15** 1/5-6/7 25/8-28/9   🏔 N 42°33'2'' E 3°2'45''

Argelès-sur-Mer, F-66700 / Languedoc-Roussillon (Pyrénées-Orientales) ⚹ 🛜 iD (2404)

🏕 de Pujol***
✉ avenue de la Retirada 1939
☎ +33 (0)4-68810025
🗓 15/5 - 31/10
@ postmaster@
campingdepujol.com

6,3ha 220T(80-120m²) 6A

1 ACDFIJKLMOPST
2 GLRTVWXY
3 ABFGJKNQRU
4 (B+G 1/5-12/10) K
(Q+R+T+U+V+X+Z 📷)
5 ABEFGJKLMNOPSTUVZ
6 ACEGJ(N 1,5km)OTV

💬 De Pujol is located between the sea and the 'Pyrénées Orientales' and has shaded and sunny pitches. There are lovely swimming pools and it is 1.2 km away from the beautiful beach and the welcoming village of Argelès. Take a trip to Spain or the Pyrenees.

🚐 A9 exit Perpignan-Sud, RN114 direction Argelès-sur-Mer as far as exit 10. Drive in the dir. of Argelès at the 1st roundabout, at the 2nd roundabout direction Pujols. At the 3rd roundabout direction Plage Nord.

Saint-Cyprien
D914
CC
Argelès-sur-Mer
D914

CC € 13 15/5-29/6 1/9-30/10 ⛰ N 42°33'25'' E 3°1'46''

Argelès-sur-Mer, F-66700 / Languedoc-Roussillon (Pyrénées-Orientales) ⚹ 🛜 iD (2405)

🏕 Flower Camping Le Romarin***
✉ route de Sorède, chemin des Vignes
☎ +33 (0)4-68810263
🗓 1/4 - 30/9
@ campingleromarin@gmail.com

2,5ha 35T(80-140m²) 6-10A CEE

1 ACDGHIJKLPST
2 BFRSVWXY
3 ABGHKNRU
4 (C+G+Q+R+T+U+V+X+Z 📷)
5 ABGIJKLMNPUWZ
6 ACEGHK(N 2km)OT

💬 This welcoming family campsite is surrounded by farmlands with olive trees, is shaded with beautiful landscaping and has a nice heated pool. The sea is close by (4 km) and there are many options for outings to the Pyrenees or Spain.

🚐 A9, exit Perpignan-Sud, D914 direction Argelès-sur-Mer as far as exit 11. At the roundabout diretion 'Les Olivettes'. After 1300 metres right at roundabout. Right at next roundabout. Campsite after 200m

Saint-Cyprien
D914
D900
Argelès-sur-Mer
CC
A9
D914
AP-7

CC € 15 1/4-29/6 1/9-29/9 ⛰ N 42°32'24'' E 2°59'43''

Argelès-sur-Mer, F-66701 / Languedoc-Roussillon (Pyrénées-Orientales) ⚹ 🛜 iD (2406)

🏕 La Chapelle****
✉ Place de L'Europe - avenue du Tech
☎ +33 (0)4-68812814
📠 +33 (0)4-68731730
🗓 21/4 - 29/9
@ contactlc@
camping-la-chapelle.com

9,7ha 299T(80-120m²) 6-10A CEE

1 ACDGIJKLMOPS
2 ACEGVY
3 BFGMNQRVY
4 (C+E+H 📷) J
(Q+R+U+V+Z 📷)
5 ABEFGIJKLMNOPQUVZ
6 ACDEGHJK(N 0,2km)RTV

💬 Campsite La Chapelle is ideally located in the centre of Argelès-Plage and 200m from the beautiful beach. Enjoy the peace, the shaded pitches, and the heated, partly covered pools and slides. The boulevard with its small shops, bars and restaurants is close by.

🚐 A9 exit 42 Perpignan-Sud, then D914 direction Argelès-sur-Mer. Take exit 10 direction Centre Plage, Office Tourisme via Chemin de Neguebous. Campsite located opposite the 'Office du Tourisme'.

D914
Argelès-sur-Mer
CC
Banyuls-sur-Mer

CC € 19 21/4-27/6 3/9-28/9 ⛰ N 42°33'10'' E 3°2'35''

Argelès-sur-Mer, F-66702 / Languedoc-Roussillon (Pyrénées-Orientales) 👫 ♿ 🛜 ✿ iD (2407)

La Marende★★★★
avenue du Littoral
☎ +33 (0)4-68811209
FAX +33 (0)4-68818852
⌖ 27/4 - 22/9
@ info@marende.com

2,5ha 133T(90-120m²) 6-10A CEE

1 ACGIJKLMPST
2 AEGRVXY
3 BFGHKNRUWY
4 (C+H ⌖) KP
(Q+S+T+U+V+X+Z ⌖)
5 ABCDEFGHIJKLMNOPQRU
VWXYZ
6 ACGIJ(N 0,5km)ORTV

💬 The friendly La Marende campsite with its lovely heated swimming pool, restaurant and new luxurious heated toilet facilities is just 100m from the beach. Close to Spain and the Pyrenees. An ideal starting point for many day trip possibilities.

🚗 A9, exit Perpignan-Sud, D914 direction Argelès-sur-Mer, as far as exit 10 direction Taxo-d'Avall. Left at the 2nd roundabout direction Plage Nord and continue on this road until the campsite is signposted.

CC € 17 27/4-29/6 1/9-21/9   ⛺ N 42°34'20'' E 3°2'28''

Argelès-sur-Mer, F-66701 / Languedoc-Roussillon (Pyrénées-Orientales) 👫 ♿ 🛜 iD (2408)

Le Dauphin★★★★★
route de Taxo à la Mer
☎ +33 (0)4-68811754
FAX +33 (0)4-68958260
⌖ 14/4 - 23/9
@ info@campingledauphin.com

7,5ha 144T(100-120m²) 10A

1 ACGIJKLOPST
2 GLRTVX
3 BFGKMNRU
4 (C+H ⌖) IJKP
(Q+S+T+U+V+X+Z ⌖)
5 ABDFGIJKLMNOPSUWXYZ
6 AEGIJK(N 3km)TV

💬 Campsite with spacious, marked-out pitches. 7000 m² aqua park with heated swimming pools and a toddler's pool. Bar/restaurant, supermarket and entertainment from April to September. For a small extra fee you can enjoy a pitch with private toilet facilities: shower, toilet and washing basin. In Argelès-sur-Mer!

🚗 A9 exit Perpignan-Sud, D914 dir. Argelès-sur-Mer as far as exit 10 Taxo-d'Avall. Left at 2nd roundabout dir. Taxo-d'Avall, Plage Nord. Follow signs.

CC € 19 14/4-29/6 1/9-22/9   ⛺ N 42°34'21'' E 3°1'18''

Argelès-sur-Mer, F-66702 / Languedoc-Roussillon (Pyrénées-Orientales) 👫 ♿ 🛜 iD (2409)

Le Soleil★★★★★
route du Littoral
☎ +33 (0)4-68811448
⌖ 5/5 - 22/9
@ contact@camping-le-soleil.fr

12ha 428T(90-120m²) 6-10A CEE

1 ACDGIJKLPST
2 ACEGRSVXY
3 BFGKNRUWY
4 (C+H ⌖) IJKP
(Q+S+T+U+V+X+Y+Z ⌖)
5 ABDFGIJKLMNOPUWXYZ
6 ACEGHIKM(N 1km)ORTUV

💬 All luxury amenities and activities are at your disposal for the entire season. Heated toilet facilities, heated pools and several direct access points to the sea. An ideal base for outings to the Pyrenees or Spain.

🚗 A9 exit Perpignan-Sud, D914 direction Argelès-sur-Mer as far as exit 10 direction Taxo-d'Avall. Turn left at the 2nd roundabout in the direction of Plage Nord, continue on this road and follow the camping signs.

CC € 19 5/5-6/7 25/8-21/9   ⛺ N 42°34'33'' E 3°2'33''

Argelès-sur-Mer, F-66701 / Languedoc-Roussillon (Pyrénées-Orientales) ♿ 🛜 iD (2410)

⛺ Les Criques de Porteils*****
🛏 RD114 - Corniche de Collioure
☎ +33 (0)4-68811273
📠 +33 (0)4-68958576
🗓 24/3 - 27/10
@ contactcdp@lescriques.com

5ha 179T(80-100m²) 10A CEE

1 ACD**G**IJKL**P**S
2 EIJKNOQRSTVXY
3 ABGHMNRY
4 (A+C+H 🅾) JKP
(Q+S+U+V+X+Z 🅾)
5 **AB**DEFGIJKLMNPUVW
6 ACDEGIJ**K**(N 2km)RTV

💬 Beautiful terraced campsite close to Collioure in an exceptional area with endless views of the sea and on the mountains of Roussillon. Private access to the sublime little creeks on the Mediterranean sea and all kinds of options for trips out.

🚗 A9 direction Perpignan. Exit 42 Perpignan-Sud direction Argelès-sur-Mer. D914 towards Collioure, take exit 13. 'Collioure par la Corniche' till l'Hotel du Golfe, turn right in direction of campsite.

Argelès-sur-Mer — CC Collioure — D914

CC € ⑲ 24/3-27/4 13/5-27/5 3/6-27/6 2/9-6/9 16/9-26/10 | 📡 N 42°32'2'' E 3°4'4''

Argelès-sur-Mer, F-66702 / Languedoc-Roussillon (Pyrénées-Orientales) ♿ 🛜 iD (2411)

⛺ Les Marsouins****
🛏 avenue de la Retirada
☎ +33 (0)4-68811481
🗓 13/4 - 1/10
@ lesmarsouins@cielavillage.com

12ha 337T(90-120m²) 5A CEE

1 ACGIJKLMOPS
2 GLRVXY
3 BFGKN**OP**RU
4 (C+H 🅾) J
(Q+S+T+U+V+X+Y+Z 🅾)
5 **AB**DEFGIJKLOPUWXYZ
6 ACDEGHK(N 1,5km)ORTV

💬 Welcoming campsite with a beautiful heated pool, spacious pitches and paved motorhome pitches. All amenities are available throughout the season. Located 800 metres from the sea and close to the Pyrenees and Spain.

🚗 A9, exit Perpignan-Sud, D914 direction Argelès-sur-Mer as far as exit 10. First roundabout direction Argelès, second roundabout direction Pujols. At the third roundabout direction Plage Nord.

D81 A — **Saint-Cyprien** — D914 — CC — D914

CC € ⑰ 13/4-29/6 1/9-30/9 | 📡 N 42°33'49'' E 3°2'5''

Argelès-sur-Mer, F-66702 / Languedoc-Roussillon (Pyrénées-Orientales) ♿ 🛜 iD (2412)

⛺ Les Pins****
🛏 avenue du Tech
☎ +33 (0)4-68811046
📠 +33 (0)4-68813506
🗓 7/4 - 7/10
@ camping@les-pins.com

4ha 173T(85-95m²) 6A CEE

1 ACG**G**IJKLOPST
2 AEGQRVY
3 ABFGNRUVWY
4 (C+H 🅾) J/Q 1/7-31/8)
(T+U+V+X 15/5-15/9)
(Z 1/5-15/9)
5 **AB**DEFGIJKLMNOPUWZ
6 AEGHJ**K**(N 0km)RTV

💬 A restful and shaded campsite close to the centre of Argelès-Plage. Enjoy the walks along the magnificent beaches or a dive in the heated swimming pool. The Pyrenees and Spain are close by and invite you for a stunning day trip.

🚗 A9, exit Perpignan-Sud, D914 direction Argelès-sur-Mer as far as exit 10 direction Argelès. At the second roundabout direction Argelès, les Plages. In the village follow the signs 'Centre Plage' and 'Plage des Pins'.

D914 — Argelès-sur-Mer — CC — Banyuls-sur-Mer

CC € ⑰ 7/4-3/7 24/8-6/10 | 📡 N 42°33'21'' E 3°2'32''

Arles-sur-Tech, F-66150 / Languedoc-Roussillon (Pyrénées-Orientales)

🛜 iD **2413**

🔺 Du Riuferrer**
☎ +33 (0)4-68391106
🗓 1/3 - 1/11
@ campingriuferrer@libertysurf.fr

4ha 150T(75-120m²) 10A CEE

1 ACFIJLMP
2 CRTVY
3 G**O**PUX
4 (A+T+U 1/7-31/8)
(V 1/6-31/8) (Z 1/7-31/8)
5 **A**FGIJKLMOPUV
6 EG**J**(N 0,6km)OT

💬 Campsite is now more easily accessible for motorhomes and caravans because of its new entrance. The site is located next to the authentic little town Arles-sur-Tech, and is surrounded by unspoiled countryside. This area has the lowest humidity in Europe, often lower than 20%, due to its micro-climate.

🚐 Campsite is 1 km from Arles-sur-Tech. Indicated with arrows along D115. New entrance to campsite.

CC € **15** 1/3-6/7 25/8-31/10

📡 N 42°27'26'' E 2°37'33''

Attuech/Anduze, F-30140 / Languedoc-Roussillon (Gard)

👫 ♿ 🛜 iD **2414**

🔺 Le Fief d'Anduze***
🖼 195 chemin du Plan d'Eau
☎ +33 (0)4-66618171
🗓 1/4 - 30/9
@ campingdufief@free.fr

6ha 90T(80-100m²) 6-10A CEE

1 ACDGIJKLMPS
2 ABCDKNORTVWXY
3 A**F**GHJNOPRU**W**X
4 (C+G 🔲) **KLN**
(Q+R+T+U+V+Y+Z 🔲)
5 **A**EFGIJKLMPUVWZ
6 AEGIK(N 5km)TV

💬 You will enjoy your stay here close to a lake and a river at the start of the Cévennes and a 5-minute drive from Anduze. Plenty of opportunities for visiting beautiful towns, cultural and sports activities. Free wifi on entire campsite. Two swimming pools.

🚐 Exit Bollène dir. Alès, then to Montpellier. In St. Christol-les-Alès dir. Anduze. Past Intermarché left to Lézan. After Gardon bridge to Anduze at roundabout. 2nd site on right.

CC € **15** 1/4-6/7 26/8-29/9 7=6, 14=12

📡 N 44°1'37'' E 4°1'40''

Bagnols-sur-Cèze, F-30200 / Languedoc-Roussillon (Gard)

♿ 🛜 iD **2415**

🔺 La Coquille***
🖼 route de Carmignan
☎ +33 (0)4-66890305
📠 +33 (0)4-66895986
🗓 23/4 - 14/9
@ campinglacoquille@wanadoo.fr

1,5ha 30T(90-110m²) 6-10A CEE

1 ACD**F**IJKLPST
2 CTVY
3 AGJQRWX
4 (A 🔲) (B+G 15/6-15/9)
(Q+T 🔲) (U+V 10/6-10/9)
(Z 🔲)
5 **AB**FGJLNOPUX
6 AEGK(N 2km)TV

💬 Small, idyllic child-friendly campsite on the banks of the Cèze with pitches in the sun or in the shade. The Ardèche, Provence and Camargue are all close by. Bread available on the site. Genuine campers will feel immediately at home here after a friendly welcome from José and Fifi Gimeno.

🚐 A7, exit 19 Bollène direction Pont-St-Esprit and Bagnols-sur-Cèze. The campsite is 1 km from the village at the D360.

CC € **17** 23/4-7/7 25/8-13/9

📡 N 44°10'34'' E 4°38'9''

Bagnols-sur-Cèze, F-30200 / Languedoc-Roussillon (Gard)

♨ 🤚 📶 ⚙ iD (2416)

🏕 Les Genêts d'Or****
📧 1840 chemin de Carmignan
☎ 📠 +33 (0)4-66895867
🗓 20/4 - 20/9
@ info@camping-genets-dor.com

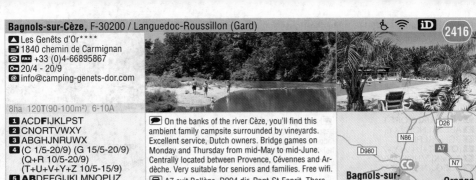

8ha 120T(90-100m²) 6-10A

1 ACD**F**IJKLPST
2 CNORTVWXY
3 ABGHJNRUWX
4 (C 1/5-20/9) (G 15/5-20/9)
(Q+R 10/5-20/9)
(T+U+V+Y+Z 10/5-15/9)
5 **AB**DEFGIJKLMNOPUZ
6 ACEGHK(N 2km)OTV

💬 On the banks of the river Cèze, you'll find this ambient family campsite surrounded by vineyards. Excellent service, Dutch owners. Bridge games on Monday and Thursday from mid-May to mid-June. Centrally located between Provence, Cévennes and Ardèche. Very suitable for seniors and families. Free wifi.

🚗 A7 exit Bollène. D994 dir. Pont-St-Esprit. There N86 dir. Bagnols-sur-Cèze. About 500 m. past the city limits sign, just before service station turn left. Follow signs.

CC € **19** 20/4-8/7 26/8-19/9

📍 N 44°10'25'' E 4°38'13''

Barjac, F-30430 / Languedoc-Roussillon (Gard)

🏃 ♿ 📶 ✿ iD (2417)

🏕 Domaine de la Sablière****
📧 St. Privat-de-Champclos
☎ +33 (0)4-66245116
📠 +33 (0)4-66245869
🗓 31/3 - 30/9
@ contact@villagesabliere.com

62ha 204T(100-120m²) 10A CEE

1 ACD**G**IJKLMNOPST
2 ABCIJKNORSTVWXY
3 ABGHJMNQRUV**W**X
4 (A 15/6-1/9) (C+E+G 🔑) **L**N
(Q+S 🔑) (T 15/6-31/8)
(U+V+X+Y+Z 🔑)
5 **AB**EFGIJKLMNOPUWXYZ
6 CEGHJ(N 6km)OQRTV

💬 This naturist site on the wooded slopes of the Cèze gorge includes: 2 swimming pools, 1 of which is covered, 2 saunas, a beauty centre, sports and other activities and a mini club. Shop, bar and restaurant (partly open, partly sheltered) contribute to your comfort in this dream paradise.

🚗 From Pont-Saint-Esprit take the D901, then the D266 on the left. Follow signs.

CC € **17** 31/3-30/6 1/9-29/9

📍 N 44°16'1'' E 4°21'7''

Barjac, F-48000 / Languedoc-Roussillon (Lozère)

♨ 📶 iD (2418)

🏕 Le Clos des Peupliers**
📧 2 chemin des Peupliers
☎ +33 (0)4-66470116
🗓 1/4 - 30/9
@ leclosdespeupliers@wanadoo.fr

3,2ha 61T(90-240m²) 10A CEE

1 ACD**G**IJLP
2 CGKRTVWXY
3 AGHJRU**W**X
4 (C+H 1/6-30/8) (Q 🔑)
(T+U+V 1/5-30/9) (Z 🔑)
5 **AB**DFGIJKLMNOPUVWXY
6 CEGJ(N 0,5km)T

💬 A homely, sunny and shady campsite in the heart of the beautiful Lozère, on the banks of the Lot. The heated pool and the trout in the Lot await you. The village is not far and the surrounding hills offer a beautiful panoramic view. It is a good base for exploring the Tarn and a number of typical French, active villages.

🚗 From A75 take exit 39.1. Follow RN88 dir. Mende until Barjac. Campsite is indicated.

CC € **15** 1/4-7/7 25/8-29/9

📍 N 44°30'3'' E 3°24'26''

Bédouès/Florac, F-48400 / Languedoc-Roussillon (Lozère)

♿ 🛜 **iD** (2419)

🏕 Camping Chantemerle**
📧 La Pontèze
☎ +33 (0)4-66451966
🗓 1/5 - 30/9
@ chante-merle@wanadoo.fr

2,5ha 66T(150-200m²) 10A CEE

1 ACD**G**IJKLMOPST
2 ABCJKLNORVXY
3 BGHIJKLRU**W**X
4 (Q+R+T+U+V+Y+Z 🔌)
5 **A**GIJKLMNOPQUVZ
6 ACEGJ(N 5km)TV

💬 A campsite in a fantastic setting, right on the beautiful banks of the Tarn where beavers have built a lodge. Chantemerle invites you to spend a well-earned holiday; laze around and at the same time enjoy the countryside and culture. Excellent restaurant, home-made pizzas and regional products.

🚗 A75 exit 39.1 via N106 direction Mende to Florac. Before Florac left at roundabout to Bedoues D998. Left at Roman bridge past village. Follow camping signs.

Ispagnac
Blajoux
Florac
D998
N106
D907
D983

CC € 15 1/5-30/6 1/9-29/9 📷 N 44°20'43'' E 3°36'38''

Boisseron/Sommières, F-34160 / Languedoc-Roussillon (Hérault)

👫 ♿ 🛜 ❄ **iD** (2420)

🏕 Flower Camping Domaine de Gajan****
📧 rue de Pie Bouquet
☎ +33 (0)4-66809430
🗓 7/4 - 23/9
@ info@campingdomainedegajan.com

3ha 45T(80-120m²) 10-16A CEE

1 ACD**G**IJKL**P**S
2 BCFSTVWXY
3 AGHJNRU**W**
4 (C+G 🔌) J(Q+R 🔌) (T+U+V+X+Z 1/7-31/8)
5 **AB**EFGJLMNPQUZ
6 ACEGJ**K**(N 2,5km)TV

💬 Peacefully located by the cycle path to Sommières. Large heated swimming pool and restaurant next to each other. Renovated toilet facilities in 2016. Camping pitches in the sun or under oak trees. Positioned between the mountains and the sea. Perfect for cycling and walking.

🚗 A9, exit Lunel. Then about 7 km towards Boisseron. Follow signs in Boisseron and turn right before the bridge. 250m to the campsite.

D45 D35 D999
D6110
D40
Beaulieu D34
D610 A9 N113
Castries
Lunel

CC € 15 7/4-6/7 1/9-22/9 7=6 📷 N 43°46'1'' E 4°4'28''

Boisset-Gaujac/Anduze, F-30140 / Languedoc-Roussillon (Gard)

👫 ♿ 🛜 **iD** (2421)

🏕 Domaine de Gaujac***
📧 2406 chemin de la Madeleine
☎ +33 (0)4-66616757
📠 +33 (0)4-66605390
🗓 1/5 - 2/9
@ contact@domaine-de-gaujac.com

10ha 145T(80-110m²) 4-10A CEE

1 ACDGIJKLMO**P**ST
2 BCJNORSVY
3 BFGHJ**MQ**RU**W**X
4 (C+H 🔌) IJKP (Q+R+S+T+U+V+Z 🔌)
5 **AB**CDEFGIJKLMNOPUVXZ
6 CDEGH**I**J(N 5km)ORTV

💬 A large and green campsite, located just outside Anduze, 100 metres from River Gardon. Plenty of shade.

🚗 A7 exit Alès/Bollène. Before Alès direction Montpellier/St. Christol/Anduze. 5 km before Anduze turn left in Bagard towards Boisset and Gaujac.

Alès
Saint-Christol-lès-Alès N2106
D24
D35
D982 D907
D999 D6110

CC € 17 1/5-3/7 21/8-1/9 📷 N 44°2'9'' E 4°1'26''

Brousses-et-Villaret, F-11390 / Languedoc-Roussillon (Aude) 👣 📶 iD (2422)

🏔 Le Martinet Rouge***
🏠 2 chemin du Lac des Rochers
☎ +33 (0)4-68265198
📅 31/3 - 3/11
@ info@camping-martinet.com

51T(90-125m²) 10A CEE

1 ACD**F**IJKLPST
2 CLRXY
3 ABGHJNRU
4 (B+G 1/6-15/10) K
   (Q 15/5-15/9) (R 15/5-4/11)
   (T+U+X 1/7-31/8) (Z 📅)
5 **A**DFGIJLMNPQUZ
6 EGJ(N 5km)OTV

💬 Welcoming, child-friendly campsite with an attractive swimming pool on the edge of the Forêt Noire in a landscape of boulders.

🚗 Route D118 Carcassonne-Cestres, exit D103 to Brousses-et-Villaret. Campsite signposted in Brousses-et-Villaret.

CC € 15 31/3-30/6 1/9-2/11 🧭 N 43°20'21'' E 2°15'7''

Camurac, F-11340 / Languedoc-Roussillon (Aude) 🎿 👣 📶 iD (2423)

🏔 Les Sapins**
☎ +33 (0)4-68203811
📅 1/1 - 1/11, 15/12 - 31/12
@ info@lessapins-camurac.com

3,5ha 72T(80-100m²) 10A CEE

1 A**G**IJKLNO**P**ST
2 KLRVWXY
3 AGHIJN**OPQ**RUW
4 (**A** 1/7-30/8)
   (B+G 15/6-15/9) (Q 📅)
   (R+T 1/5-30/9)
   (U+V 1/5-1/11)
   (X+Z 15/4-1/11)
5 **AB**DFGIJMNPQRUZ
6 EJ(N 6km)OV

💬 Welcoming campsite in beautiful countryside with lovely views. The Cathar Ruin of Montaillou is visible. Various walks through flower meadows and villages. Nearby skiing area (altitude 1625m).

🚗 From Quillan follow Ax-Les-Thermes and Belcaire. Via Ax-Les-Thermes from dir. Quillan in Camurac follow 'Piste de ski' signs. Right after 1 km. Route for large vehicles via Foix-Lavelanet (D117). Then D117 dir. Belesta and D16/D29 and D613 until the 'Piste de ski' signs.

Fougax-et-Barrineuf

CC € 13 1/4-7/7 27/8-31/10 🧭 N 42°47'30'' E 1°55'30''

Canet-en-Roussillon, F-66140 / Languedoc-Roussillon (Pyrénées-Orientales) 👣 📶 iD (2424)

🏔 Ma Prairie****
🏠 avenue des Coteaux
☎ +33 (0)4-68732617
📠 +33 (0)4-68732882
📅 5/5 - 22/9
@ contact@maprairie.com

4,5ha 153T(65-100m²) 10A CEE

1 ACDFHIJKLOPST
2 GRVXY
3 B**F**GKNRUV
4 (C+H 15/5-15/9) J
   (Q 1/6-15/9)
   (T+U+V 1/7-31/8)
   (X 15/5-15/9) (Z 1/5-15/9)
5 **AB**FGIJKLMNOPUWXYZ
6 AEGHJ**K**(N 0,2km)ORTV

💬 A friendly family campsite 3 km from the beach with many amenities, some of which are located on the other side of a small road, such as the lovely heated swimming pool, restaurant, playground and fitness room. Ma Prairie is perfect for day trips out to the Pyrenees and Spain.

🚗 A9, exit 41 Perpignan-Centre direction Le Barcarès/Canet via the D83 and D81. Then D617 direction St. Nazaire. Right at roundabout after the St. Nazaire exit on the D11.

Canet-en-Roussillon

Perpignan

CC € 17 5/5-6/7 25/8-21/9 7=6, 25=20 🧭 N 42°42'4'' E 2°59'54''

Canet-en-Roussillon, F-66140 / Languedoc-Roussillon (Pyrénées-Orientales) ♿ 📶 iD (2425)

🏕 Mar Estang****
📧 Voie des Flamants Roses
☎ +33 (0)4-68803553
📠 +33 (0)4-68733294
🔓 14/4 - 16/9
@ contactme@marestang.com

13ha 150T(60-100m²) 6-10A CEE

1 ACDGIJKLMOPS
2 ADEFGRSUVX
3 ABFGKMNRUVY
4 (C+F+H 🔓) IJK
(Q+S+T+U+V+X+Y+Z 🔓)
5 ABEFGIJKLMNOPU
6 ACDEGHJK(N 2km)RTV

💬 Large campsite located between the Canet-en-Roussillon nature reserve and a beautiful beach, accessible via a tunnel (100m) directly from the campsite. Ample amenities including lovely heated swimming pools. Close to the centre of Canet and close to the Pyrenees and Spain.

🚗 A9, exit 41 dir. Le Barcarès and Canet-en-Roussillon. Continue towards St. Cyprien or Plage Sud from Canet. Campsite located south of Canet on the right.

Perpignan · Canet-en-Roussillon
CC
D914   D81 A

CC € **17** 14/4-6/7 25/8-15/9   📷 N 42°40'31'' E 3°1'52''

Canet-Plage, F-66140 / Languedoc-Roussillon (Pyrénées-Orientales) 👫 ♿ 📶 iD (2426)

🏕 Le Bosquet***
📧 av. des Anneaux du Roussillon
☎ +33 (0)4-68802380
🔓 31/3 - 5/10
@ campinglebosquet@
club-internet.fr

1,5ha 71T(70-100m²) 10A

1 ACGIJKLOPST
2 CEGRSTVWXY
3 ABFGKNRUWY
4 (B+G 🔓) K
(Q+R+T+U+V+Z 🔓)
5 ABDEFGJLMNPUVW
6 ACEGJK(N 1,5km)RTV

💬 A small, modest, intimate campsite with sunny and shaded pitches, with a snack bar and a lovely swimming pool. 400m to the beach via an entrance directly from the campsite. A 5 minute walk to the pleasure boat harbour and a little train to the centre of Canet-Plage.

🚗 A9 exit 41 Perpignan-Centre dir. Barcarès/Canet via D83 and D81. In Canet dir. Ste Marie at first roundabout then immediately right direction 'Zone Artisanale las Bigues' and follow camping signs.

A9
Perpignan · Canet-en-Roussillon   CC
D914   D81 A

CC € **15** 31/3-6/7 1/9-4/10 7=6   📷 N 42°42'33'' E 3°1'59''

Cap-d'Agde, F-34300 / Languedoc-Roussillon (Hérault) 👫 ♿ 📶 iD (2427)

🏕 La Mer***
📧 Impasse des Camarines
☎ +33 (0)4-67947221
📠 +33 (0)4-67947207
🔓 7/4 - 30/9
@ camping-la-mer@wanadoo.fr

3ha 93T(60-90m²) 6A

1 AFIJKLPST
2 AEFGRSVWXY
3 BFGJKRUWY
4 (Q+T 1/5-30/9) (V+Z 🔓)
5 ABEFGJLNPUVZ
6 AEGIJK(N 0,8km)TV

💬 Very peaceful family campsite where the camper is well taken care of. A paved footpath leads from the campsite right to the sea. The spacious beach is 100 metres away. Free wifi on the terrace.

🚗 A9 exit N34 Pézenas, Agde, Bessan, Vias. Towards Rochelongue at roundabout dir. Cap-d'Agde after bridge over the Herault. Left at first crossroads dir. "mail de Rochelongue" (follow Camping La Mer sign). Campsite signposted.

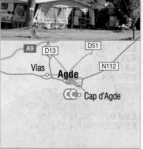

A9   D13   D51
Vias   N112
Agde
CC Cap d'Agde

CC € **15** 7/4-7/7 1/9-29/9   📷 N 43°16'43'' E 3°28'43''

Cap-d'Agde, F-34300 / Languedoc-Roussillon (Hérault)

✝✝ ⅋ 📶 iD **2428**

🏕 Le Rochelongue****
📧 route de Rochelongue
☎ +33 (0)4-67212551
🗓 15/4 - 14/10
@ le.rochelongue@wanadoo.fr

2,5ha 46T(80-90m²) 10A CEE

1 ACD**G**IJKLM**P**ST
2 AEFGRSVWX
3 B**F**GJNRUWY
4 (C+H 1/5-30/9)
(Q+R+T+U+V+X+Z 5/5-16/9)
5 **AB**EFGIJKLMNOPUVWXYZ
6 AEGIK(N 0,4km)ORTV

💬 Located in Cap d'Agde, close to the shopping centre and 500m from the sea. Perfectly suitable for children with its 'safe beach' (a wide stretch of shallow water). Lovely swimming pool with children's pool. 800m from a large water park (Aqualand), a lovely golf course with 24 holes and a disco. Entertainment for all ages!

🚘 On the A9 take the Cap d'Agde exit lane. 800m from Cap d'Agde follow camping signs showing Le Rochelongue.

A9   D13   D51
N112
Vias
Agde
CC

CC € **15** 15/4-7/7 1/9-13/10 14=12, 21=17   📷 N 43°16'45'' E 3°28'53''

Cardet, F-30350 / Languedoc-Roussillon (Gard)

⅋ 📶 iD **2429**

🏕 Beau Rivage**
📧 22 chemin du Bosquet
☎ +33 (0)4-66830248
🗓 15/3 - 15/10
@ receptie@
campingbeaurivage.com

5ha 124T(85-125m²) 6A

1 ACD**G**IJKLPQ
2 ABCLMNRSTWXY
3 B**F**GHJK**M**N**OP**RUWX
4 (C+G 1/5-15/10)
(Q+R 1/5-15/9)
(T+U+V+X 1/5-1/10) (Z 🔌)
5 **A**CDEFGIJKLMNPQRUWZ
6 ACEGHJ**K**(N 0,5km)OTV

💬 A lovely campsite right by the river. Spacious pitches, heated swimming pool, pleasant pizzeria and modern heated toilet facilities. The river is suitable for prospecting (searching for gold). The area is perfect for walks, cycling tours or visiting medieval villages and small markets. Good wifi throughout the campsite.

🚘 From Alès follow signs to Nîmes, 2nd exit direction Ledignan/Ners, then direction Anduze. After intersection with D6110, 4rd exit in Cardet.

Alès
Saint-Christol-
lès-Alès   N2106   D981
CC   N106
D982
D35   D6110
D999   D907

CC € **15** 15/3-6/7 25/8-6/10   📷 N 44°1'40'' E 4°4'27''

Castries, F-34160 / Languedoc-Roussillon (Hérault)

📶 iD **2430**

🏕 de Fondespierre***
📧 277 chemin du Pioch Viala
☎ +33 (0)4-67912003
🗓 8/1 - 21/12
@ campingfondespierre@outlook.fr

2,1ha 50T(60-120m²) 10-16A

1 ACD**F**IJLPT
2 FIJKTVWXY
3 BG**M**NRU
4 (B 1/5-15/10) (Q+R+T+Z 🔌)
5 **AB**DFGJLNPUVZ
6 ACEGJ**K**(N 2km)ORT

💬 The campsite has an exceptional location just 6 km from the motorway. Breathe the tranquillity and enjoy the many attractions: Montpellier's historic centre, wine regions, the Camargue, many cycling and hiking routes around the aqueduct and the castle near the campsite.

🚘 A9, A709 direction Montpellier, exit 28 towards Vendargues to Alès, then D610 and follow 'Domaine de Fondespierre' signs.

D17   D610
D34
D68   CC   A9
N113
Montpellier   Mauguio   D61

CC € **17** 8/1-7/7 25/8-20/12   📷 N 43°41'38'' E 3°59'46''

Chastanier, F-48300 / Languedoc-Roussillon (Lozère)

🦽 📶 ✿ **iD** 2431

🏕 Du Pont de Braye***
🏠 Lieu dit de Braye
☎ +33 (0)4-66695304
📠 +33 (0)5-31600523
🔓 1/5 - 20/9
@ accueil@
camping-lozere-naussac.fr

1,5ha 26T(80-100m²) 5-6A

1 ACD**G**IJKLMP
2 CJKLRVWXY
3 ABF**G**HKRU**W**X
4 (A 7/7-24/8)
(Q+R+T+U+V+Z 🔓)
5 **AB**CDFGIJKLMNPUVWZ
6 ACEG**K**(N 10km)TV

💬 It's great to camp on the banks of the Chapeauroux, a little river in the Margueride which can be tumultuous at times. Very quiet roads lead to this secluded, but easily accessible spot. You will be welcomed by a very enthusiastic and helpful owner.

🚌 N88 southwards from Langogne towards Naussac, left at the crossroads. Along the D34 past Chastanier. Campsite signposted.

Grandrieu — D5 — D88
Auroux
D985 — Langogne — D108
D988 — N88
D906

ⒸⒸ € ⑬ 1/5-7/7 25/8-19/9

📷 N 44°43'32'' E 3°44'52''

Clapiers, F-34830 / Languedoc-Roussillon (Hérault)

🦽 📶 ✿ **iD** 2432

🏕 Sandaya Le Plein Air des Chênes****
🏠 avenue Georges Frêche
☎ +33 (0)4-67020253
📠 +33 (0)4-67594219
🔓 13/4 - 9/9
@ pleinairdeschenes@sandaya.fr

8ha 69T(50-80m²) 10-16A

1 ACD**G**IJKLMOP
2 FGJTVXY
3 BCG**M**NO**Q**RU
4 (C 🔓) (G 1/6-10/9) IJKM
(Q 1/7-31/8)
(T+U+X+Y+Z 🔓)
5 **AB**FGJLMNP**S**UVZ
6 AEG**I**K(N 0,4km)QTV

💬 Quiet family campsite. On level grounds under the shade of trees. A good starting point for visiting Montpellier. CampingCard ACSI campers are received on comfort pitches.

🚌 A9, exit Vendargues. Continue towards Jacou/Clapiers via D21. Campsite on the D112 in Clapiers, signposted.

D986 — D17
D68 — D610
N113
A9
Montpellier **Mauguio**

ⒸⒸ € ⑰ 13/4-6/7 1/9-8/9

📷 N 43°39'6'' E 3°53'46''

Collioure, F-66190 / Languedoc-Roussillon (Pyrénées-Orientales)

🦽 📶 **iD** 2433

🏕 Camping Les Amandiers**
🏠 route des Campings
☎ +33 (0)4-68811469
🔓 31/3 - 9/10
@ info@
camping-les-amandiers.com

1,8ha 50T(60-90m²) 10A CEE

1 ACD**G**HIJKL**P**ST
2 BEHJNQRVWXY
3 AGHRWY
4 (Q+R+T+U+V+X+Y+Z 🔓)
5 **AB**GIJKLMNOPUVZ
6 ACDEGJ(N 1,5km)OTV

💬 Les Amandiers** campsite is a natural, quiet and shady departure point for trips to Spain or the Pyrenees. The beautiful village of Collioure is at walking distance and the 'La Crique de l'Ouille' beach is 200 metres from the campsite.

🚌 A9 to Perpignan, exit 42 Perpignan Sud to Argelès-sur-Mer. D914 to Collioure as far as exit 13 Collioure par la Corniche. Follow camping signs to Collioure then turn left.

D81
Argelès-sur-Mer
ⒸⒸ
Banyuls-sur-Mer
D914

ⒸⒸ € ⑰ 31/3-7/7 1/9-8/10

📷 N 42°31'53'' E 3°4'18''

Colombiers, F-34440 / Languedoc-Roussillon (Hérault)

🛖 👫 ♿ 📶 **iD** (2434)

🏔 Les Peupliers***
✉ 7 promenade de l'Ancien Stade
☎ 📠 +33 (0)4-67370526
🗓 1/1 - 31/12
@ contact@
camping-colombiers.com

1ha 50T(75-100m²) 10A CEE

1️⃣ ACD**G**IJKLMOPST
2️⃣ FRTVWXY
3️⃣ BGHJR
4️⃣ (B+G 1/6-30/9) (Q 15/4-30/9)
(T+U+V+X 15/6-9/9)
(Z 1/6-30/9)
5️⃣ **AB**DEFGJLMNPQRUWZ
6️⃣ ACEGJ**K**(N 0,6km)TV

💬 Small attractive campsite within walking distance of the village of Colombiers and the Canal du Midi. Open all year. Perfect for trips in the area and the Mediterranean beaches around Béziers. Heated toilets in winter. Free wifi 30 minutes every 6 hours.

🚐 Do not use SatNav! A9, exit 36 Béziers-West. Then towards D64 Castres/Mazamet at the roundabout, third road on right towards D11 Capastang/Montady. In Montady take Colombiers-Les Peupliers at the roundabout.

D14 D909
D612 N9
D16 **Béziers**
D5 D11 CC
D609 Sérignan
D13
Coursan A9

CC € **15** 1/1-8/7 26/8-31/12 ⛺ N 43°19'6'' E 3°8'35''

Crespian, F-30260 / Languedoc-Roussillon (Gard)

👫 ♿ 📶 **iD** (2435)

🏔 Mas de Reilhe****
✉ N110
☎ +33 (0)4-66778212
🗓 20/4 - 29/9
@ info@camping-mas-de-reilhe.fr

3ha 67T(70-100m²) 10A CEE

1️⃣ ACD**G**IJKLPST
2️⃣ BRSTVWXY
3️⃣ BGHKNRUV**W**
4️⃣ (C+H 🔌) K
(Q+R+U+V+Y+Z 🔌)
5️⃣ **AB**EFGJKLNPUWXYZ
6️⃣ ACEGH**K**(N 10km)RTV

💬 In the heart of the Gard, hidden between vineyards and forests with shrubberies, you will be very welcome at this homely campsite. Relax on the edge of the heated swimming pool with jacuzzi or on the terrace. Walking, cycling, visiting beautiful old sights.

🚐 A9 exit Nîmes-Ouest, then towards Le Vigan via D999. At crossroads with N110 Montpellier-Alès take direction Crespian. Site is signposted.

Sauve D907
D35 D6110 La Calmette
D45 D999 CC D22
D35 A
Villevieille D40

CC € **17** 20/4-29/6 17/8-28/9 7=6, 14=11 ⛺ N 43°52'43'' E 4°5'47''

Elne/St. Cyprien, F-66200 / Languedoc-Roussillon (Pyrénées-Orientales)

♿ 📶 **iD** (2436)

🏔 Le Florida****
✉ route Latour Bas Elne
☎ +33 (0)4-68378088
🗓 1/1 - 31/12
@ info@campinglefiorida.com

7ha 70T(100-180m²) 5-10A CEE

1️⃣ ACD**F**IJKLM**P**ST
2️⃣ GRTVXY
3️⃣ B**F**GMN**P**RU
4️⃣ (B+G 1/4-30/10) J(Q 🔌)
(T+U+V+Z 1/5-30/9)
5️⃣ **AB**DFGIJKLMNOPUWZ
6️⃣ ACDEGK(N 0,2km)RTUV

💬 Le Florida campsite has 3 km of beach, offers spacious, shady pitches and has a new 2000 m2 leisure pool with a jacuzzi, water games, waterfall, pool slides... You can enjoy the facilities, entertainment and good service all year round.

🚐 A9, exit Perpignan-Sud direction Argelès-sur-Mer. Take exit 7 from th N114 to Latour-Bas-Elne via D11 direction Elne-centre. Then via D40 direction St. Cyprien.

Perpignan **Canet-en-Roussillon**
D914 D81 A
CC
A9
D900

CC € **17** 1/1-29/6 1/9-30/12 7=6, 14=12, 21=18 ⛺ N 42°36'24'' E 2°59'24''

Err, F-66800 / Languedoc-Roussillon (Pyrénées-Orientales) 🎿 ♿ 📶 ✿ iD (2437)

🏕 Las Closas***
📧 1 place St. Genis
☎ +33 (0)4-68047142
📅 1/1 - 29/9, 1/11 - 31/12
@ reception@
camping-las-closas.com

2ha 114T(< 100m²) 6A

1 ACDFIJKLOPQ
2 KRVY
3 BGRW
4 (A 15/7-31/8) (**B** 15/6-15/9)
J(V 1/6-1/9)
5 ACGIJKLMNPUV
6 EGK(N 0km)RT

💬 Las Closas campsite is located in the village of Err with views of Pic Carlit and Puigmal. 100m from the heated municipal swimming pool (15/6 - 15/9). Enjoy the natural surroundings and the extensive walking trails in this mountainous area. A visit to the El Segre Gorge at Llo is a must.

🚗 The campsite is signposted at the exit Err on the N116 from Mont-Louis to Bourg-Madame.

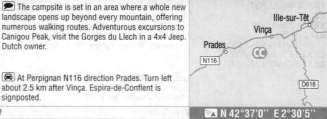

CC € ⑰ 29/4-30/6 26/8-28/9   📡 N 42°26'26'' E 2°1'55''

Espira-de-Conflent, F-66320 / Languedoc-Roussillon (Pyrénées-Orientales) ♿ 📶 iD (2438)

🏕 Le Canigou***
☎ +33 (0)4-68058540
📅 31/3 - 31/10
@ canigou@yahoo.com

4ha 115T(100m²) 10A

1 ACDGIJKLMOPS
2 CIORTVXY
3 AGHIJNRUWX
4 (A 1/7-31/8) (Q+R+T+U 📅)
(V 1/7-1/10) (X 1/6-30/9)
(Z 1/7-1/10)
5 **AB**CGIJKMNOPU
6 CEGJL(N 10km)OV

💬 The campsite is set in an area where a whole new landscape opens up beyond every mountain, offering numerous walking routes. Adventurous excursions to Canigou Peak, visit the Gorges du Llech in a 4x4 Jeep. Dutch owner.

🚗 At Perpignan N116 direction Prades. Turn left about 2.5 km after Vinça. Espira-de-Conflent is signposted.

CC € ⑮ 31/3-6/7 25/8-30/10   📡 N 42°37'0'' E 2°30'5''

Estavar/Cerdagne, F-66800 / Languedoc-Roussillon (Pyrénées-Orientales) 🎿 ♿ 📶 iD (2439)

🏕 L'Enclave***
📧 2 rue des Vynials
☎ +33 (0)4-68047227
📠 +33 (0)4-68040715
📅 1/1 - 30/9, 1/11 - 31/12
@ contact@camping-lenclave.com

4ha 175T(80-130m²) 3-10A

1 ACD**G**IJKLPST
2 CJKRVXY
3 BGHJMNQRU
4 (A 1/7-31/8) (C+H 15/6-15/9)
KN
(Q+R+T+U+V+X+Z 15/6-15/9)
5 **AB**DFGIJKLMNOPUVWZ
6 CEG**K**(N 0,1km)OTV

💬 This peacefully located campsite is not far from Font Romeu (15 minutes) and the Spanish enclave of Llívia (5 minutes). Marked out and unchallenging walking routes, fishing opportunities and plenty of nature make this campsite an ideal place to stay. Swimming pool.

🚗 From Puigcerda/Saillagouse N154 direction Llivia. Then follow the Estavar and camping signs. Campsite located on the D33.

CC € ⑮ 10/4-5/7 23/8-29/9   📡 N 42°28'8'' E 1°59'55''

Fabrègues, F-34690 / Languedoc-Roussillon (Hérault)

🏕 Le Botanic***
🏠 Launac-le-Vieux
☎ +33 (0)4-67855318
🗓 1/4 - 10/10
@ contact@
  camping-le-botanic.com

2ha 62T(90-180m²) 10A CEE

1 ACDFIJKLMO**P**ST
2 DFRTVWXY
3 ADGZ
4 (C+H+Q 🖢) (T+V 1/7-30/8)
  (Z 🖢)
5 **A**EFGIJKLMNOPUZ
6 ACEG**K**(N 2km)ORT

💬 Very well-maintained ecological campsite with exceptional advantages such as its location near Montpellier, the sea and the interior. The campsite has a unique natural lagoon with fine sandy beach.

🚗 A9, exit 32 or 33. Between Fabrègues and Gigean on the D613 towards Cournonterral. Campsite 800m on the left.

🆔 2440

CC € 15 1/4-5/7 25/8-9/10

N 43°32'28'' E 3°44'51''

Fitou, F-11510 / Languedoc-Roussillon (Aude)

🏕 Le Fun***
🏠 Domaine des Bergeries
☎ +33 (0)4-68457197
🗓 30/3 - 3/11
@ contact@lefun-camping.com

10ha 100T(80-180m²) 6A CEE

1 ACD**F**IJKLMP
2 DFIKLRTUVWXY
3 BGMNUW
4 (C+H 1/5-30/9) (Q+R 🖢)
  (T+U 1/7-31/8) (Z 🖢)
5 AEGJLNPUV
6 CDEGJ**K**(N 2km)TV

💬 This campsite, located on the Leucate lagoon offers watersports opportunities such as surfing and kite surfing. The site also has lovely views.

🚗 A9 exit 40 direction Perpignan via D6009. Campsite signposted.

🆔 2441

CC € 17 30/3-5/7 2/9-2/11

N 42°54'51'' E 2°59'56''

Fleury-d'Aude, F-11560 / Languedoc-Roussillon (Aude)

🏕 La Grande Cosse****
🏠 Saint-Pierre-sur-la-Mer
☎ +33 (0)4-68336187
📠 +33 (0)4-68333223
🗓 7/4 - 30/9
@ grande-cosse@capfun.com

15ha 200T(100-130m²) 10A CEE

1 ACD**G**IJKLMPT
2 AELRSTVWX
3 ABGHJKMRUY
4 (C+H 🖢) IJM(Q+S+T+U 🖢)
  (V 1/7-31/8) (X+Y 1/6-7/10)
  (Z 🖢)
5 **AB**FGIJLMNOPUWZ
6 ACEGHIJ**K**(N 5km)ORV

💬 This site is located between Béziers and the Pyrenees in a large sheltered natural area by the sea within walking distance of the beach. A campsite with a fine, friendly atmosphere. Well-appointed toilets spread over these large, well-maintained grounds. Renovated, heated pool with adjacent water slide.

🚗 A9 exit Béziers-Ouest direction Béziers. Then to Lespignan/Fleury. Straight ahead at roundabout towards Les Cabanes. Camping sign after ± 3 km.

🆔 2442

CC € 17 7/4-30/6 3/9-29/9

N 43°12'21'' E 3°12'39''

Florac, F-48400 / Languedoc-Roussillon (Lozère)

2443

Flower Camping Pont du Tarn***
route de Pont de Montvert, D998
+33 (0)4-66451826
7/4 - 14/10
contact@camping-florac.com

5,5ha 147**T**(80-150m²) 10A CEE

1 ABCD**G**IJKLMOPS
2 ACGKLMNORTVWXY
3 BGHIJKLNRU**WX**
4 (C+H 8/5-15/9) IM(Q) (T+U+X+Y 15/5-31/8) (Z 1/5-15/9)
5 **AB**CDEFGHIJKLMNOPQRU WXYZ
6 ABCEGK(N 0,5km)RTV

With direct access to the natural beaches of the Tarn, the wooded location, the wonderful countryside and just 5 minutes from the centre of Florac and its shops; this campsite is a quiet spot to enjoy the water, sun and nature. Ideal for staying with the family. Excellent services and amenities.

A75, exit 39 direction Florac. Then take the N106 and D998.

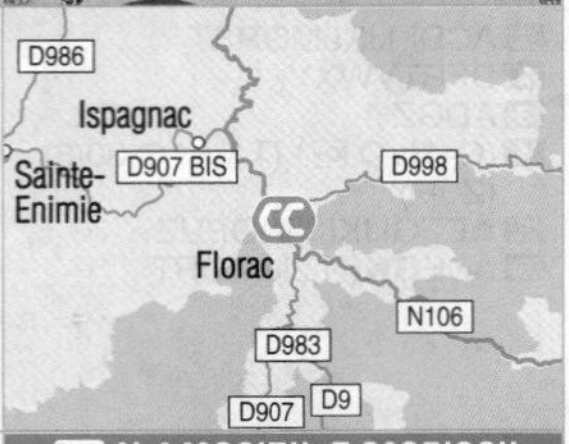

CC €17 *7/4-7/7 27/8-13/10 7=6*

N 44°20'7'' E 3°35'26''

Fontès, F-34320 / Languedoc-Roussillon (Hérault)

2444

L'Evasion***
route de Cabrières
+33 (0)4-67253200
12/3 - 25/10
cordierseverine@hotmail.fr

2,7ha 35**T**(80-120m²) 10A CEE

1 ACD**G**IJL**P**ST
2 FJKRSTVWX
3 BDHU
4 (C 1/5-15/9) (Q+R) (T+U+V+X+Z 5/4-10/9)
5 ABEFGIJLMNPUVXZ
6 AEGK(N 0,4km)OTV

Fontès offers an unusual mediterranean micro climate. Magical landscapes and beautiful cultural towns close by.

A75, from north exit 58, from south exit 59 towards Adissan. After Adissan direction Fontès. In Fontès D124 towards Cabrières. Site is located on this road.

CC €17 *13/3-6/7 24/8-24/10*

N 43°32'51'' E 3°22'48''

Frontignan-Plage, F-34110 / Languedoc-Roussillon (Hérault)

2445

La Lagune**
10 avenue des Vacances
+33 (0)4-99040430
24/3 - 7/10
contact@camping-la-lagune.com

1ha 38**T**(70-90m²) 6A CEE

1 ACD**G**IJKLPST
2 ADEGRVWXY
3 BHJWY
4 (Q+T+U+V+Z)
5 **A**FGIJKLMNOPQUXZ
6 ACDEG**K**(N 5km)T

Small, modest campsite with completely renewed toilet facilities (2016). The campsite is 150 metres from the sea in a small village which has excellent cycle paths into the area. Baker is 100 metres from the campsite. Bar, restaurant and pizzas on sale opposite the campsite.

Take exit 33 Sète on A9. Campsite on D612 direction Sète or Montpellier. Follow 'Les Campings' signs.

CC €13 *24/4-6/7 27/8-6/10*

N 43°25'48'' E 3°45'35''

Frontignan-Plage, F-34110 / Languedoc-Roussillon (Hérault)

♿ 📶 iD (2446)

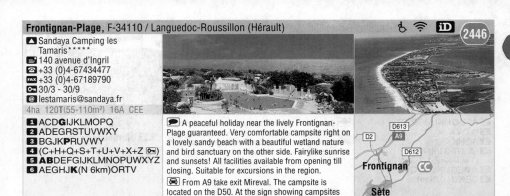

🏕 Sandaya Camping les Tamaris*****
📧 140 avenue d'Ingril
☎ +33 (0)4-67434477
📠 +33 (0)4-67189790
📅 30/3 - 30/9
@ lestamaris@sandaya.fr

4ha 120**T**(55-110m²) 16A CEE

1 ACD**G**IJKLMOPQ
2 ADEGRSTUVWXY
3 BGJK**P**RUVWY
4 (C+H+Q+S+T+U+V+X+Z ⌨)
5 **AB**DEFGIJKLMNOPUWXYZ
6 AEGHJ**K**(N 6km)ORTV

💬 A peaceful holiday near the lively Frontignan-Plage guaranteed. Very comfortable campsite right on a lovely sandy beach with a beautiful wetland nature and bird sanctuary on the other side. Fairylike sunrise and sunsets! All facilities available from opening till closing. Suitable for excursions in the region.

🚗 From A9 take exit Mireval. The campsite is located on the D50. At the sign showing campsites follow the sign to the left. Well signposted from then on.

D613
D2 — A9
D612

Frontignan ℂℂ

Sète

ℂℂ € **19** 30/3-6/7 1/9-29/9
N 43°27'0'' E 3°48'21''

Fuilla, F-66820 / Languedoc-Roussillon (Pyrénées-Orientales)

♿ 📶 iD (2447)

🏕 Le Rotja***
📧 avenue de la Rotja
☎ 📠 +33 (0)4-68965275
📅 24/3 - 13/10
@ camping@camping-lerotja.com

1,6ha 75**T**(80-100m²) 6A

1 ACD**G**IJKLMPST
2 BFKRTUVXY
3 BGHJR**W**
4 (A 15/6-15/9)
(B+G 1/5-10/10) (Q+R+T ⌨)
(X+Z 1/5-10/10)
5 **A**CEFGIJKLMNPRUWY
6 EGHK(N 3km)OTV

💬 Peacefully located attractive campsite in the Apple Valley of La Rotja river. Plenty of walking options with many places of historical interest. Mild climate in early and late seasons. The owner speaks English, French, Dutch and German. The site is positioned exactly on the Green Meridian, marked by a post on the site. Free wifi on entire site.

🚗 Take the N116 to Villefranche direction Mont-Louis. After about 500 metres, past Villefranche, take the exit to Fuilla.

Prades

Vernet-les-
ℂℂ Bains

N116

ℂℂ € **17** 24/3-6/7 25/8-12/10
N 42°33'45'' E 2°21'34''

Gallargues-le-Montueux, F-30660 / Languedoc-Roussillon (Gard)

♿ 📶 iD (2448)

🏕 Les Amandiers****
📧 20 rue des Stades
☎ +33 (0)4-66352802
📅 1/4 - 23/9
@ camping-lesamandiers@orange.fr

3ha 40**T**(70-120m²) 16A CEE

1 AC**G**IJKLMO**P**ST
2 FGRSTVWXY
3 BGHJKMN**O**P**RUVW**
4 (C+H 1/5-30/9) **K**L**N**O
(Q+T+U+V+X+Z 1/6-31/8)
5 **A**BEFJKLMNPUZ
6 AEG**K**(N 4km)OTV

💬 The campsite is located 2 km from the A9 motorway (exit 26) within walking distance of an old village on a hill. Several types of (heated) pools, spa, fitness room, sun terrace and large camping pitches. Valerie offers you a warm welcome.

🚗 A9, exit 26 to Gallargues. Well signposted from there.

D40
Bernis
D34 — A9 — D135
D610
ℂℂ
Mauguio — N113 — Lunel
D61 D979 D6572

ℂℂ € **17** 1/4-24/6 1/9-22/9 7=6
N 43°43'0'' E 4°10'1''

Gruissan, F-11430 / Languedoc-Roussillon (Aude)

👫 👤 🛜 **iD** (2449)

🔺 Campéole Barberousse**
📧 route de l'Ayrolle
☎ +33 (0)4-68490722
📅 27/4 - 30/9
@ barberousse@campeole.com

NEW

5ha 161T(90m²) 16A CEE

1 ACD**G**IJKLMOPST
2 GTWX
3 AGHK
4 (**A** 1/7-31/8) M
   (T+U+X+Z 1/7-31/8)
5 **AB**EGIJKLMNOPU
6 CE**K**(N 0,3km)

💬 Campsite is 300m from the picturesque fishing area of Gruissan, and 3 km from the beach. Ideally situated for a visit to the Narbonne Regional National Park and the hills of La Clape.

CC € **17** 27/4-6/7 25/8-29/9

🔺 N 43°6'7'' E 3°5'7''

Junas, F-30250 / Languedoc-Roussillon (Gard)

👫 👤 🛜 **iD** (2450)

🔺 L'Olivier***
📧 route de Congénies
☎ +33 (0)4-66803952
📅 7/4 - 13/10
@ camping.lolivier@wanadoo.fr

1ha 22T(50-70m²) 6-10A CEE

1 ACD**G**IJKL**P**S
2 BGSTVWXY
3 AGHJMQR**W**
4 (B 1/5-30/9) (G+Q 1/7-31/8)
   (R 📅) (T+V+Z 1/7-31/8)
5 **A**EFGIJKLMNPUVZ
6 AEG**K**(N 2km)ORTV

💬 Intimate campsite with differences in altitude, plenty of shade from hundred-year-old olive trees. The site is close to a medieval village. Excellent cycling and walking. Close to the 'voie verte' route from Nîmes to Sommières.

🚗 A9, exit 26 dir. Sommières. Then D22 to Junas. Follow signs.

CC € **15** 7/4-8/7 26/8-12/10

🔺 N 43°46'12'' E 4°7'33''

Junas, F-30250 / Languedoc-Roussillon (Gard)

👫 👤 🛜 🌸 **iD** (2451)

🔺 Les Chênes**
📧 95 chemin des Teullières Basses
☎ +33 (0)4-66809907
📅 7/4 - 14/10
@ chenes@wanadoo.fr

1,7ha 69T(80-100m²) 10A CEE

1 ACD**G**IJKL**P**ST
2 BFILRTVWXY
3 AGHJNR**W**
4 (B+G 15/5-15/10)
   (Q+R+T+U 📅)
5 **A**EFGJKNPUVWZ
6 AEGJ**K**(N 5km)OT

💬 Gilles and Nathalie will welcome you on holiday in the south of France in calm and informal surroundings, with a lovely swimming pool under the Languedoc sun in the shade of oak trees. Located 5 km from Sommières and 2 km from the 'voie verte' (lovely cycle route), and 30 minutes from the beaches, Nîmes and Montpellier, at the foot of the Cévennes.

🚗 On the A9 take the Gallargues exit, continue through village towards Sommières (6 km). Campsite signposted from there.

CC € **15** 7/4-8/7 26/8-13/10 15=13

🔺 N 43°45'41'' E 4°7'16''

La Franqui/Leucate, F-11370 / Languedoc-Roussillon (Aude)   ♿ iD (2452)

🏕 La Franqui**
📧 chemin des Coussoules
☎ +33 (0)4-68457493
📠 +33 (0)4-68453688
🔒 13/4 - 16/9
@ franqui@originalcamping.com

3,5ha 256T(60-80m²) 6A CEE

1 ACD**G**IJKLMOPST
2 AEFSTVWX
3 AWY
4 (Q+R 1/6-31/8) (U 1/7-31/8)
5 **A**FGIJKLMNOPUZ
6 AEG(N 2km)T

💬 La Fraqui is an unpretentious but attractive campsite with direct access to the wide flat beach and the sea. Beach surfing is a fun activity on the flat beach. The pitches are not all that big, but reasonably well shaded and marked out by beautiful planting.

🚗 A9 direction Perpignan, exit 40 Leucate. Stay on D627 to La Franqui exit. Follow camping signs at La Franqui.

Port-la-Nouvelle
D709
CC
A9
D6009
D627
D900

CC € **13** 13/4-6/7 27/8-15/9   📐 N 42°56'37'' E 3°1'50''

La Grande-Motte, F-34280 / Languedoc-Roussillon (Hérault)   ♿ 📶 iD (2453)

🏕 La Petite Motte***
📧 195 allée des Peupliers
☎ +33 (0)4-67565475
🔒 31/3 - 30/9
@ camping-lapetitemotte@ffcc.fr

196T(80-100m²) 6A CEE

1 ACD**G**HIJKLMOPT
2 ARSVWX
3 **A**FGHJKR
4 (Q+R+T+U+V+X+Z 🔒)
5 **A**DEFGIJKLMNOPUWZ
6 ACEGHJ**K**(N 0,5km)

💬 Shaded campsite located 700 metres from the beach and the La Grande-Motte harbour. There are various water sports possibilities for active campers. The Parc Naturel Régional de Camargue and Montpellier are half an hour's drive from the site.

🚗 From Lunel to La Grande Motte. In La Grande Motte keep right. Campsites are signposted from there.

D979
A9
D61
Montpellier
Aigues-Mortes
Lattes
D62
CC

CC € **19** 31/3-6/7 27/8-29/9   📐 N 43°33'52'' E 4°4'31''

La Palme, F-11480 / Languedoc-Roussillon (Aude)   👫 ♿ 📶 iD (2454)

🏕 Flower Camping Domaine de La Palme***
📧 79 chemin du Stade
☎ +33 (0)4-68485040
🔒 31/3 - 22/10
@ info@camping-la-palme.com

NEW

1ha 31T(65-120m²) 6A CEE

1 ACD**G**HIJKLM**P**ST
2 FGRVWX
3 AHKM
4 (C+H+Q 🔒)
5 **A**EIJKLMNP
6 EGJ(N 0,5km)TV

💬 Small, quiet family-run campsite with a heated pool. Situated in the wine village of La Palme, with spacious touring pitches. Near to Lencate, plenty of natural scenery and water sports at the nearby salt lakes, Mediterranean Sea 5 km away.

🚗 From Montpellier/Narbonne A9 towards Perpignan, exit 39 Sigean/Port-la-Nouvelle. Follow D6009 towards Perpignan. At Les Cabanes on roundabout turn left towards Port-la-Nouvelle and then La Palme. In the village 1st left.

D611 A
Portel-des-Corbières
A9
D709
CC
D6009

CC € **13** 31/3-30/6 1/9-21/10   📐 N 42°58'19'' E 2°59'51''

La Palme, F-11480 / Languedoc-Roussillon (Aude)

🏕️ 👤 📶 ✿ **iD** (2455)

▲ Le Clapotis**
✉️ 2000 chemin de Prade
☎ +33 (0)5-56737373
📠 +33 (0)556093215
📅 31/3 - 29/9
@ reservations@socnat.fr

6,5ha 107T(70-110m²) 6A CEE

1 CD**G**IJKLMOPT
2 DFKNTVWXY
3 ABDGJKNRUWZ
4 (C+H 1/6-30/9)
(Q+R+T+U+V+X+Z 15/6-15/9)
5 **AB**EFGIJKLMNOPUV
6 ABDEG**K**(N 4km)ORTV

NEW

💬 A basic naturist campsite with ambiance in natural surroundings and with a heated swimming pool, ideally located by the lake at La Palme for real surfing enthusiasts.

🚗 From Montpellier/Narbonne A9 direction Perpignan as far as exit 39 Sigean. Then towards Perpignan, via D6009. Left at La Palme roundabout then right after 400m, follow camping signs.

D3 — Port-la-Nouvelle
D709
CC
A9
D6009
D627

CC € **17** *31/3-6/7 25/8-28/9* ⛰️ N 42°57'28'' E 2°59'45''

La Roque-sur-Cèze, F-30200 / Languedoc-Roussillon (Gard)

👫 📶 **iD** (2456)

▲ La Vallée Verte****
✉️ route de Donnat
☎ +33 (0)4-66790889
📅 31/3 - 29/9
@ info@la-vallee-verte.com

36ha 80T(75-100m²) 6-10A CEE

1 ACD**G**IJKLPST
2 ABCIJKMNORSTVXY
3 ABGMNRUWX
4 (A 🔓) (B 25/4-19/9) (G 🔓) J (Q+R+U+V+Y+Z 🔓)
5 **A**FGJLNPUVW
6 AEGHJ(N 2km)V

💬 Terraced campsite in natural surroundings. Spacious pitches with privacy and beautiful views. New sanitation. Attractive restaurant. Swimming and fishing in the Cèze. Terrace with views of the swimming pool, tennis court and petanque.

🚗 A7 exit Bollène/Pont-St-Esprit. D994 dir. Pont-St-Esprit. Then N86 dir. Bagnols-sur-Cèze. D6 to Alès. After 3.5 km D143 dir. La Roque-sur-Cèze. 1.5 km past Donnat turn right. At fork right to La Roque. After 1.5 km site on the right.

N86
D980
CC — Bagnols-sur-Cèze
D6 — N580
D6086
D979 — D9

CC € **17** *31/3-7/7 25/8-28/9* ⛰️ N 44°10'53'' E 4°32'7''

La Roque-sur-Cèze, F-30200 / Languedoc-Roussillon (Gard)

👫 👤 📶 **iD** (2457)

▲ Les Cascades****
☎ +33 (0)4-66827297
📠 +33 (0)4-66826851
📅 20/4 - 23/9
@ infos@campinglescascades.com

6ha 76T(90-120m²) 10A CEE

1 ACD**G**IJKL**P**ST
2 BCDIJLNQRTVXY
3 AGHNRWXZ
4 (C+G+Q+S 🔓) (T 1/6-31/8) (U+V+Y+Z 🔓)
5 **AB**EFGIJKLMNOPUWYZ
6 DEGH**IK**(N 5km)RTV

💬 A particularly friendly family campsite on predominantly level and shaded grounds on the banks of the River Cèze. Lovely beaches and wonderful swimming waters. The lovely waterfalls are an added attraction. Heated swimming pool from 1/5 - 15/9.

🚗 Accessible for caravans and large cars only via the D6 Bagnols-Alès, exit Donnat (D143). Then 3 km further.

D901
D980
CC
N86
D6 — Bagnols-sur-Cèze
N580
D6086
D979 — D9

CC € **17** *20/4-6/7 25/8-22/9 7=6, 14=11* ⛰️ N 44°11'19'' E 4°31'31''

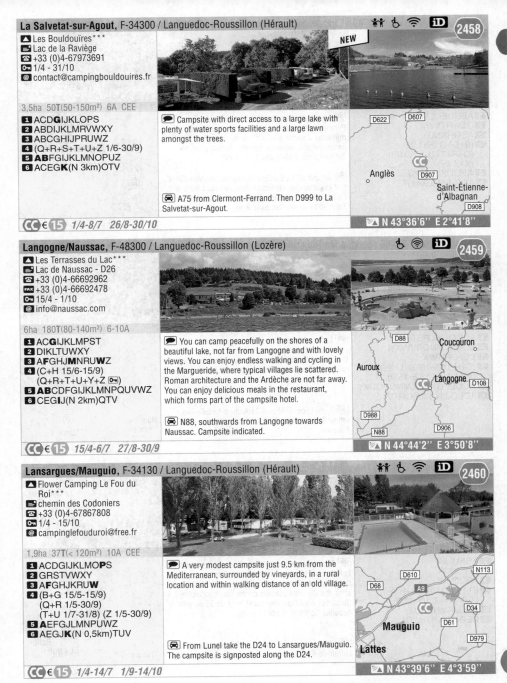

La Salvetat-sur-Agout, F-34300 / Languedoc-Roussillon (Hérault)   👪 ♿ 📶 iD (2458)

🏕 Les Bouldouïres***
📧 Lac de la Raviège
☎ +33 (0)4-67973691
🔑 1/4 - 31/10
@ contact@campingbouldouires.fr

3,5ha 50T(50-150m²) 6A CEE

1 ACD**G**IJKLOPS
2 ABDIJKLMRVWXY
3 ABCGHIJPRUWZ
4 (Q+R+S+T+U+Z 1/6-30/9)
5 **AB**FGIJKLMNOPUZ
6 ACEG**K**(N 3km)OTV

NEW

💬 Campsite with direct access to a large lake with plenty of water sports facilities and a large lawn amongst the trees.

🚗 A75 from Clermont-Ferrand. Then D999 to La Salvetat-sur-Agout.

CC € 15 1/4-8/7 26/8-30/10   📡 N 43°36'6'' E 2°41'8''

Langogne/Naussac, F-48300 / Languedoc-Roussillon (Lozère)   ♿ 📶 iD (2459)

🏕 Les Terrasses du Lac***
📧 Lac de Naussac - D26
☎ +33 (0)4-66692962
📠 +33 (0)4-66692478
🔑 15/4 - 1/10
@ info@naussac.com

6ha 180T(80-140m²) 6-10A

1 ACG**I**JKLMPST
2 DIKLTUWXY
3 AF**G**HJMNRU**W**Z
4 (C+H 15/6-15/9)
   (Q+R+T+U+Y+Z 🔑)
5 **AB**CDFGIJKLMNPQUVWZ
6 CEG**I**J(N 2km)QTV

💬 You can camp peacefully on the shores of a beautiful lake, not far from Langogne and with lovely views. You can enjoy endless walking and cycling in the Margueride, where typical villages lie scattered. Roman architecture and the Ardèche are not far away. You can enjoy delicious meals in the restaurant, which forms part of the campsite hotel.

🚗 N88, southwards from Langogne towards Naussac. Campsite indicated.

CC € 15 15/4-6/7 27/8-30/9   📡 N 44°44'2'' E 3°50'8''

Lansargues/Mauguio, F-34130 / Languedoc-Roussillon (Hérault)   👪 ♿ 📶 iD (2460)

🏕 Flower Camping Le Fou du Roi***
📧 chemin des Codoniers
☎ +33 (0)4-67867808
🔑 1/4 - 15/10
@ campinglefouduroi@free.fr

1,9ha 37T(< 120m²) 10A CEE

1 ACDGIJKLMO**P**S
2 GRSTVWXY
3 AF**G**HJKRU**W**
4 (B+G 15/5-15/9)
   (Q+R 1/5-30/9)
   (T+U 1/7-31/8) (Z 1/5-30/9)
5 **A**EFGJLMNPUWZ
6 AEG**J**K(N 0,5km)TUV

💬 A very modest campsite just 9.5 km from the Mediterranean, surrounded by vineyards, in a rural location and within walking distance of an old village.

🚗 From Lunel take the D24 to Lansargues/Mauguio. The campsite is signposted along the D24.

CC € 15 1/4-14/7 1/9-14/10   📡 N 43°39'6'' E 4°3'59''

Laroque-des-Albères, F-66740 / Languedoc-Roussillon (Pyrénées-Orientales) ⊗ ♿ 🛜 iD **2461**

🔺 Les Albères****
📧 route Moulin de Cassagnes
☎ +33 (0)4-68892364
📅 31/3 - 30/9
@ lesalberes@cybelevacances.com

7ha 128T(32-92m²) 16A CEE

1 ABCDEIJLMPST
2 GIJKRTVWX
3 ABGHKNU
4 (B+D+G 📅) IJM
    (Q+R+T+U 1/7-31/8)
    (X+Z 📅)
5 A FGIJKLMNPU
6 AEGJ(N 0,9km)T

💬 Homely campsite at the foot of the Eastern Pyrenees, located in a forest of cork oaks and mimosas. Leisure pool with many recreation amenities and wellness: a heated indoor pool, an outdoor pool, a slide and a whirlpool.

🚗 A9 exit 43 Le Boulou. To Argelès-sur-Mer (D618). Exit Laroque-des-Albères. Follow this road for 3 km. Left at village to Sorède. Right at next roundabout. Then 500 metres. Campsite is signposted.

Saint-Cyprien
A9 D914
Argelès-sur-Mer
ℭℭ
D900
AP-7

CC € **17** 31/3-7/7 1/9-29/9   🏕 N 42°31'26'' E 2°56'39''

Lasalle/Anduze, F-30460 / Languedoc-Roussillon (Gard) ♿ 🛜 iD **2462**

🔺 La Salendrinque***
📧 route de St. Hippolyte-du-Fort
☎ +33 (0)4-66852457
📅 1/5 - 15/9
@ info@campinglasalendrinque.fr

2,5ha 77T(80-140m²) 10A CEE

1 ACD**G**IJKL**P**ST
2 BCIJKLMNORVWXY
3 BGHJRU**WX**
4 (C+H 15/5-15/9) (Q 📅)
    (T+U+V+Z 15/6-15/9)
5 A CDEFGHIJKLMNOPQUXY
6 ACEGJ(N 1km)ORTV

💬 Lovely, friendly campsite on a river with cascades. Pitches on a level section and on the hill. Good toilet facilities. Very friendly and welcoming reception. Free wifi on terrace. Heated pool.

🚗 From Lyon-Bollène-Alès-Anduze-Lasalle-Rte. follow St. Hippolyte-du-Fort to the campsite left of the road.

D260
D907
ℭℭ
Moulès-et-Baucels
D982 D35
Sauve

CC € **17** 1/5-30/6 1/9-14/9   🏕 N 44°2'19'' E 3°51'42''

Latour-de-France, F-66720 / Languedoc-Roussillon (Pyrénées-Orientales) ♿ 🛜 iD **2463**

🔺 La Tour de France***
📧 ave du Général de Gaulle
☎ +33 (0)6-15142346
📅 1/4 - 14/10
@ contact@
    camping-latourdefrance.fr

1,5ha 70T(50-120m²) 6A CEE

1 AB**F**IJLMP
2 CRTVXY
3 ABGJMRU
4 (B 15/6-15/9) (Q+R 📅)
    (T+V+W+Z 1/7-31/8)
5 A FGJKMNPRUZ
6 DEGHJ(N 1km)TU

💬 The campsite is located in the Catalan hinterland between the Mediterranean and the Pyrenees. Centrally located for trips out to the many Cathar sites and the wide beaches on the coast, including 'Le Barcarès'. Also the rocky coast towards Spain with beautiful Collioure is not far away.

🚗 Millas direction Estnagel. In Estnagel direction Latour-de-France. Campsite signposted on the D17.

D12
D611
D117
ℭℭ
D612 D614
Baho
Ille-sur-Têt Le Soler

CC € **15** 1/4-6/7 25/8-13/10   🏕 N 42°45'57'' E 2°39'56''

Laurens, F-34480 / Languedoc-Roussillon (Hérault)

♿ 🛜 ✿ **iD** (2464)

🏕 Sites & Paysages L'Oliveraie****
🏠 chemin de Bédarieux
☎ +33 (0)4-67902436
📠 +33 (0)4-67901120
🗓 19/3 - 27/10
@ oliveraie@free.fr

7ha 78T(85-150m²) 10A CEE

1 ACDFIJKLPST
2 JTVXY
3 BGHJMNP**Q**RU
4 (B+G+Q 1/6-30/9)
(S+T+U+V+X+Z 1/7-31/8)
5 **A**DEFGIJLNOPUVWXZ
6 ACEGI**K**(N 1,5km)ORT

💬 The campsite is located at the entrance to the Parc Natural Regional du Haut Languedoc. Being only 30 km from the Mediterranean yet protected by the hills, this is an ideal place to stay in early and late seasons.

🚗 Campsite is located on a side-road of the D909. About 1.5 km north of Laurens. Along the D909 signs say 'Centre de Loisirs de l'Oliveraie'.

CC € **17** 19/3-6/7 25/8-26/10

🗺 N 43°32'10'' E 3°11'10''

Le Barcarès, F-66420 / Languedoc-Roussillon (Pyrénées-Orientales)

♿ 🛜 ✿ **iD** (2465)

🏕 L'Oasis - California****
🏠 route de St. Laurent
☎ +33 (0)4-68861243
📠 +33 (0)4-68864683
🗓 28/4 - 16/9
@ camping.loasis@wanadoo.fr

9,7ha 278T(80-100m²) 10A CEE

1 ACD**F**HIJKLMOPST
2 FGLRSTVWXY
3 ABGJK**M**NRU
4 (C+H 🗓) JKP(Q+R 🗓)
(T+U+V+X 1/6-1/9) (Z 🗓)
5 **AB**EFGIJKLMNPUVWZ
6 ACGHI**JK**(N 0,8km)RTV

💬 Close to the charming Port-Barcarès and a beautiful Mediterranean beach, with a heated pool and excellent amenities, L'Oasis-California offers its guests a pleasant stay. From here, great excursions to the Pyrenees and to Spain are possible.

🚗 A9 exit Perpignan-Centre. D83 direction Le Barcarès as far as exit 9. Take the D81 direction Canet as far as the first exit St. Laurent, direction Le Barcarès-Village.

CC € **13** 28/4-8/7 1/9-15/9

🗺 N 42°46'35'' E 3°1'29''

Le Barcarès, F-66420 / Languedoc-Roussillon (Pyrénées-Orientales)

♿ 🛜 **iD** (2466)

🏕 Le Floride & l'Embouchure*****
🏠 route de St. Laurent
☎ +33 (0)4-68861175
📠 +33 (0)4-68860750
🗓 30/3 - 5/11
@ contact@floride.fr

12ha 186T(80-130m²) 10A

1 ACD**F**IJKL**P**S
2 ACEFGTVXY
3 ABGKNRUVWXY
4 (C+F+H 🗓) IJK**LM**(Q+R 🗓)
(T 7/4-7/5,1/7-31/8)
(U+V+X+Y 1/4-20/9) (Z 🗓)
5 **AB**EFGIJKLMNP**ST**UVWXY
Z
6 ACGHK(N 0,6km)O**P**RTV

💬 The friendly site of Le Floride & l'Embouchure is located between Lake Leucate and the Mediterranean. It has heated swimming pools, its own entrance to the beach and for an extra charge pitches with individual sanitary facilities.

🚗 A9 exit Perpignan-Centre. D83 direction Le Barcarès. Continue to exit 9 via D81 direction Canet. First exit St. Laurent direction Le Barcarès-Village.

CC € **17** 30/3-29/6 1/9-4/11 7=6, 14=12

🗺 N 42°46'44'' E 3°1'47''

Le Rozier, F-48150 / Languedoc-Roussillon (Lozère) ♿ 📶 iD (2467)

🏕 Municipal de Brouillet★★★
✉ chemin de Brouillet
☎ +33 (0)5-65626398
📠 +33 (0)5-65626083
🗓 1/4 - 30/9
@ contact@campinglerozier.com

3ha 150T(100-120m²) 6A CEE

1 ACD**G**IJKLMOPST
2 BCGKLMNORSTVWXY
3 BGHIJK**M**NRU**WX**
4 (**A** 1/7-31/8) (C+H 1/6-13/9)
5 **A**CFGHIJKLMNOPUVYZ
6 ACEGKM(N 0km)RTV

💬 A very attractive campsite in the picturesque village of Le Rozier. Here you will find good shops and a restaurant. An ideal base for trips out in the area. Reservation is only possible between 1 January and 30 September.

🚗 In Augessac A75, take exit 44.1. (Turn off SatNav!) Follow the signs 'Gorges du Tarn' as far as Le Rozier. The campsite is located in the heart of Le Rozier.

D809 D32 D907 BIS D986
A75 D9 D907
Rivière-sur-Tarn CC
Compeyre
Millau D991

CC € 15 1/4-30/6 1/9-29/9   📡 N 44°11'29'' E 3°12'16''

Le Rozier/Peyreleau, F-12720 / Languedoc-Roussillon (Lozère) ♿ 📶 iD (2468)

🏕 Les Prades★★★★
✉ D187
☎ 📠 +33 (0)5-65626209
🗓 1/5 - 15/9
@ lesprades@orange.fr

5ha 178T(100-120m²) 6A CEE

1 ACDGIJKLMOPRS
2 CFKLNORSVWXY
3 BGHIJMNRU**WX**
4 (**A** 1/7-31/8) (C+H 🗓) IJKMN
P(Q 🗓) (S 1/7-31/8)
(T+U+V+Y+Z 🗓)
5 **AB**CDEFGHIJKLMNOPQRU
VWXYZ
6 ACDEGIJ(N 4km)O**P**TV

💬 A lovely campsite on the River Tarn. Clean toilet facilities, sauna, jacuzzi, bubble bath, the largest heated leisure pool in the area. Free tennis and 1 hour free use of canoe per family for use near campsite. The à la carte restaurant is open all season.

🚗 A75, exit 44.1 (navigation off!). N9 as far as Aguessac. Left onto the D907 Gorges du Tarn. Dir. La Cresse. In La Cresse turn left D187. Campsite on the left after 4 km.

D809 D32 D907 BIS
A75 D9 D907
Rivière-sur-Tarn CC
Compeyre
Millau D991

CC € 15 1/5-7/7 25/8-14/9   📡 N 44°11'59'' E 3°10'24''

Le Vigan, F-30120 / Languedoc-Roussillon (Gard) ♿ 📶 iD (2469)

🏕 Le Val de l'Arre★★★★
✉ route Du Pont de la Croix
☎ +33 (0)4-67810277
🗓 1/4 - 30/9
@ valdelarre@wanadoo.fr

8ha 133T(80-120m²) 10-16A

1 ACD**F**IJLPST
2 CLRTVXY
3 BGHJLN**OP**RU**WX**
4 (C 1/5-30/9) (G 15/6-10/9)
(Q 🗓) (S 1/6-31/8)
(T+U+X+Z 1/6-15/9)
5 **AB**FGIJKLNPUVWZ
6 ACEG**K**(N 2km)ORTV

💬 This campsite, where a family atmosphere predominates, is located in the south of the Cévennes amid the calm and the shade of the woods. Comfort in the middle of nature.

🚗 Via A75 take exit 48 Le Vignan D999. Right 2.5 km past Le Vignan on roundabout. Or via A6/A7/A9 exit Nîmes West. Ring round Nîmes dir. Alès. Then D999 and left at roundabout 2.5 km before Le Vignan.

D986
Le Vigan CC Sumène
D999
Ganges
D25
D48

CC € 15 1/4-5/7 23/8-29/9   📡 N 43°59'29'' E 3°38'14''

Les Vignes, F-48210 / Languedoc-Roussillon (Lozère) ♿ 📶 iD (2470)

⛺ Beldoire★★★
🚏 D907 Bis
☎ +33 (0)4-66488279
📅 27/4 - 9/9
@ camping-beldoire@orange.fr

5,5ha 118T(80-120m²) 6A CEE

1 ACDGIJKLMPRS
2 BCJKLMNOQRSVWXY
3 BDGHIJKLNRU**W**X
4 (A 1/7-16/8) (C+Q 🔑)
(S 1/6-7/9)
(T+U+V+X+Y+Z 15/6-28/8)
5 **AB**FGIJKLMNPUVZ
6 EGJ(N 0,8km)OTV

💬 Quiet campsite with nice pool. Located in a beautiful part of the Gorges du Tarn. Beautiful pitches on the water. Campsite is on the Plan d'Eau: swimming, canoeing, kayaking and fishing to the wetlands of Les Vignes at +/-800 m.

🚐 A75 exit 42 Sévérac-le-Château. Direction Gorges du Tarn, after that Le Massegros/Les Vignes.

CC € 15 27/4-5/7 26/8-8/9

📍 N 44°17'13'' E 3°14'2''

Les Vignes, F-48210 / Languedoc-Roussillon (Lozère) ♿ 📶 iD (2471)

⛺ La Blaquière★★★
🚏 RD 907 bis
☎ +33 (0)4-66485493
📅 20/4 - 14/9
@ contact@campingblaquiere.fr

1,5ha 64T(80-120m²) 6-10A CEE

1 ACDGIJKLPST
2 BCJKLNORSVWXY
3 BGHJNRU**W**X
4 (Q+S 🔑)
(T+U+V+X 1/7-31/8) (Z 🔑)
5 **AB**CEFGHJLNPQUWZ
6 ADEGJ**K**(N 6km)OTV

💬 A small, peaceful campsite with a lovely beach on the Tarn. Beautiful surroundings with plenty to see. Helpful warden.

🚐 Take A75 from Sévérac-le-Château to Les Vignes, exit 44 Le Massegros to Les Vignes. After Les Vignes 6 km direction Ste Enimie and follow signs.

CC € 15 20/4-7/7 31/8-13/9

📍 N 44°18'17'' E 3°16'5''

Lézan, F-30350 / Languedoc-Roussillon (Gard) 👪 ♿ 📶 iD (2472)

⛺ Le Mas des Chênes★★
🚏 D982, 760 route des Cévennes
☎ +33 (0)4-66544830
📅 1/5 - 15/9
@ info@
campingmasdeschenes.com

11ha 173T(100-120m²) 10A CEE

1 ACD**G**IJKLMNO**P**ST
2 CLNRVWXY
3 A**F**GHJRU**W**
4 (B+G 1/6-11/9)
(Q+R+X+Z 1/7-31/8)
5 **AB**EFGIJKLMNPQUZ
6 CEGJ(N 0,6km)V

💬 The campsite has large open pitches that are level and covered with grass. Cars are in a separate car park. Renovated toilet facilities from 2017.

🚐 From Alès follow signs to Nimes. 2nd exit towards Ledignan/Ners. Then towards Anduze. Campsite is before Cardet on the right of the D982.

CC € 15 1/5-14/7 1/9-14/9

📍 N 44°4'40'' E 4°3'8''

Lézignan-Corbières, F-11200 / Languedoc-Roussillon (Aude)   ♿ 🛜 iD (2473)

🏕 Camping la Pinède***
🏠 rue des Rousillous
☎ FAX +33 (0)4-68270508
🗓 1/4 - 30/10
@ lapinede.aude@gmail.com

3,5ha 69T(90-100m²) 6A CEE

1 ACG**I**JLP
2 FIJRTVXY
3 BGH**M**RU
4 (A 1/7-31/8) (C+G 1/6-30/9)
(Q 🔑) (R 16/6-31/8)
(T+U+X 25/6-31/8)
(Z 1/6-30/9)
5 **A**EFGIJKLNPUZ
6 EGJ**K**(N 0,7km)OTV

NEW

💬 Located in the town of Lézignan in the middle of the Aude, with a beautiful old town centre. Lovely pool next to the campsite.

🚘 Situated on the N113 1 km east of Lézignan on the right hand side of the road to Carcassonne.

(map: D5, D611, D610, D11, D6113, D111, Lézignan-Corbières, A61, D212, D613)

CC € **13** 1/4-3/6   1/9-29/10   N 43°12'12'' E 2°45'6''

Llauro, F-66300 / Languedoc-Roussillon (Pyrénées-Orientales)   🛜 iD (2474)

🏕 Al Comu
🏠 route Fourques
☎ +33 (0)4-68394208
🗓 31/3 - 15/10
@ alcomu@wanadoo.fr

2,5ha 35T(90-110m²) 16A

1 AGIJKLMOPST
2 ITUVXY
3 AGHJNR
4 (Q+R 🔑)
5 **A**CGIJKLMNOPUZ
6 EGJ(N 0,8km)T

💬 A perfect site for those who love tranquillity and nature. Walks directly from the campsite. A few pitches with lovely views of the Mediterranean and Perpignan. French/Dutch wardens.

🚘 D615 Thuir direction Llauro. Campsite located about 800 metres before Llauro on the right.

(map: Canohès, D618, A9, Le Boulou, D615, Céret, D900)

CC € **15** 31/3-6/7   2/9-14/10   N 42°32'55'' E 2°45'13''

Lodève, F-34700 / Languedoc-Roussillon (Hérault)   👫 ⊗ 🍴 🛜 iD (2475)

🏕 Domaine de Lambeyran***
🏠 Hameau de Lambeyran
☎ +33 (0)4-67441399
FAX +33 (0)4-67440991
🗓 15/5 - 30/9
@ lambeyran@wanadoo.fr

345ha 130T(100-160m²) 5-10A CEE

1 ACDEIJKLMOPST
2 CFIJKRVWXY
3 ABGHNRU
4 (C+G 15/5-15/9)
(Q 1/6-15/9) (R 15/6-30/8)
(S+T+U 1/6-30/8)
(Z 10/6-10/9)
5 **A**FGIJKLMNOPUVZ
6 EGIJ(N 5km)OV

NEW

💬 Flanked by wooded hills, this extremely peaceful campsite is ideally suited to enjoy naturism to the full.

🚘 A75 to Lodève then follow direction Lunas. Turn off to L'Ambayran. Follow the D35e4 uphill to the campsite.

(map: Ceilhes-et-Rocozels, D9, D142, D25, D8, D902, Lodève, A75, D35)

CC € **17** 15/5-6/7   27/8-29/9   N 43°44'11'' E 3°15'52''

Lodève, F-34700 / Languedoc-Roussillon (Hérault)

♿ 🛜 iD (2476)

▲ Les Vals***
✉ 2000 route de Puech
☎ +33 (0)4-30401780
📅 1/4 - 30/9
@ campinglesvals@yahoo.fr

3,5ha 65**T**(80-180m²) 6-16A CEE

1 ACDGIJLN**P**T
2 CFJRSTVXY
3 ABGHIKMNQRU**W**X
4 (B 15/5-15/9) (Q 🔚)
(R+T 6/7-24/8) (U+V 🔚)
(X+Z 6/7-24/8)
5 **AB**EGJLNPUZ
6 AEG**K**(N 2km)OV

💬 The site is 5 minutes from Lake Salagou in the middle of the vineyards on the banks of a river. The camp pool, activities such as tennis, mini golf and table tennis and the region's vast cultural heritage ensure a successful holiday.

🚗 From north: A75 exit 52 dir. Lodève. Follow av. Fumel, not the centre. Left over Vinas bridge dir. Puech. 2 km on the D148. From south: A75 exit 53 dir. Lodève centre. First roundabout left dir. Puech. 2 km on the D148.

CC € **17** 1/4-7/7 25/8-29/9

📍 N 43°42'43'' E 3°19'19''

Loupian, F-34140 / Languedoc-Roussillon (Hérault)

♿ 🛜 iD (2477)

▲ Municipal de Loupian***
✉ route de Mèze
☎ +33 (0)4-67435767
📠 +33 (0)4-67437316
📅 6/4 - 14/10
@ camping@loupian.fr

1,7ha 90**T**(60-100m²) 6A CEE

1 ACD**G**IJKLOPST
2 FGRTVWXY
3 AGJMR
4 (Q+T+U+X+Z 1/5-30/9)
5 **A**FGIJKLMNPUZ
6 AEG**K**(N 2km)T

💬 Lovely clean municipal campsite with spacious pitches in a beautiful rural setting. A well cared for campsite. Quietly located, ideal for visiting Sète and Agde

🚗 A9 exit Mèze. Continue towards Mèze to the roundabout, then right (dir. Loupian). Campsite on the left on the D158 E4.

CC € **13** 6/4-26/6 24/8-13/10

📍 N 43°26'42'' E 3°36'55''

Lunel, F-34400 / Languedoc-Roussillon (Hérault)

♿ 🛜 iD (2478)

▲ Bon Port****
✉ 383 chemin du Mas St. Ange
☎ +33 (0)4-67711565
📠 +33 (0)4-67836027
📅 7/4 - 23/9
@ contact@campingbonport.com

5ha 150**T**(80-100m²) 6A

1 ACD**G**HIJKLMOPS
2 FGRTVXY
3 BF**G**HJKN**OP**RUW
4 (C+H 1/5-25/9) IJK(Q+S 🔚)
(T+U+V+X+Z 1/7-31/8)
5 **AB**EFGIJKLMNPRUZ
6 ACEGH**K**(N 2km)O

💬 This familial, shaded but also sunny campsite in the 'petite Camargue' is located 10 km from the beaches. Lovely leisure pool. Ideal location for plenty of outings into the area. Wifi free before 1 July and after 31 August.

🚗 Located on the D61 from Lunel to La Grande Motte. Signposted 2 km outside Lunel on the left side of the road.

CC € **17** 7/4-7/7 25/8-22/9

📍 N 43°39'20'' E 4°8'31''

Marseillan-Plage, F-34340 / Languedoc-Roussillon (Hérault) ⚓ ♿ 🛜 iD (2479)

🏕 Beauregard Plage***
✉ 250 chemin de l'Airette
☎ +33 (0)4-67771545
🗓 30/3 - 15/10
@ reception@
  camping-beauregard-plage.com

3,3ha 200T(80-155m²) 6A CEE

1 ACD**G**IJKLMPST
2 AEGRSVWXY
3 AB**F**GJRUWY
4 (Q 1/5-15/9)
  (T+U+X+Z 1/5-30/9)
5 A**C**FGIJKLNOPUZ
6 ABCEG**K**(N 0km)TV

💬 An authentic and lovely campsite with direct beach access, where respect for nature is tangible. There are only tents, caravans and motorhomes. Genuine campers will feel at home. Restaurant and bar overlooking the sea and beach. The shops and cafes on Marseillan-Plage are around the corner.

🚗 A9 exit Agde. Continue towards Sète and take D612 direction Marseillan-Plage. Right at 2nd roundabout, follow signs to campsite.

CC € **17** 30/3-30/6 1/9-14/10   🏖 N 43°18'54'' E 3°32'56''

Marseillan-Plage, F-34340 / Languedoc-Roussillon (Hérault) ⚓ ♿ 🛜 iD (2480)

🏕 Dunes et Soleil****
✉ 380 chemin de l'Airette
☎ +33 (0)4-67771868
📠 +33 (0)4-67012080
🗓 7/4 - 7/10
@ campingdunesetsoleil@
  homair.com

3ha 38T(70-130m²) 10A CEE

1 ACD**F**IJKLMOPS
2 AEFGRSVWXY
3 B**F**GJRUWY
4 I(Q 7/4-30/9)
  (T+U+V+X+Z 🔒)
5 **AB**EFGJLMNOPUWXZ
6 ACEGHJ**K**(N 0,1km)TUV

💬 The second site on your left in the centre of the lively Marseillan-Plage. Camping pitches with direct private access to the sandy beach. Enjoy a blissful holiday here on the Mediterranean which is a great place to be in both early and late seasons.

🚗 D112 from Agde direction Sète. Right at first roundabout direction Plage du Rieu. Left at next roundabout. Straight ahead at next roundabout. Campsite on the right.

CC € **17** 7/4-7/7 2/9-6/10   🏖 N 43°18'50'' E 3°32'52''

Marseillan-Plage, F-34340 / Languedoc-Roussillon (Hérault) ⚓ ♿ 🛜 iD (2481)

🏕 Flower Camping Robinson***
✉ Quai de Plaisance
☎ +33 (0)4-67219007
🗓 21/4 - 22/9
@ reception@
  camping-robinson.com

2,5ha 128T(60-120m²) 10A CEE

1 ACD**G**IJKLMOPST
2 AEGRSVWXY
3 B**F**GJKNRUWY
4 (B+G 1/5-22/9)
  (Q+R+T+U+V+Z 🔒)
5 **A**EFGJLNPUWXZ
6 ABEGHIK(N 1km)OTV

💬 Located between the Mediterranean and the Bassin de Thau lake, renowned for its shellfish. The campsite is located on the canal that flows out into the harbour of Marseillan-Plage and has direct access to the beach. Anyone who likes being beside the sea and enjoys a quiet campsite has found the right place. Plenty of fishing opportunities and many other forms of sports and games.

🚗 A9 exit Agde or Sète, then direction Marseillan-Plage. Follow camping signs.

CC € **17** 21/4-30/6 1/9-21/9   🏖 N 43°19'9'' E 3°33'24''

Marseillan-Plage, F-34340 / Languedoc-Roussillon (Hérault)   👫 ♿ 📶 iD (2482)

🔺 La Créole***
📧 74 av. des Campings
☎ +33 (0)4-67219269
🕐 24/3 - 14/10
@ campinglacreole@orange.fr

1,5ha 91T(80-95m²) 6-10A CEE

1 ACD**G**IJKLMPS
2 AEFGRSTVWXY
3 B**F**GJKLRUVWY
4 (T+X+Z 1/5-30/9)
5 **A**EFGJKLMNOPUWZ
6 ACDEG**K**(N 0km)RT

💬 The campsite is located in the centre of lively Marseillan-Plage. It offers shaded pitches, good toilet facilities and has a private entrance to the lovely sandy beach. Multilingual receptionist. Suitable for a beach holiday and for promenading around the lively resorts.

🚗 D112 from Agde to Sète. Turn right at the second roundabout, direction Marseillan-Plage. Then follow the signs.

CC € **17** 24/3-24/6 2/9-30/9   🧭 N 43°18'46'' E 3°32'47''

Marseillan-Plage, F-34340 / Languedoc-Roussillon (Hérault)   👫 ♿ 📶 iD (2483)

🔺 Le Galet***
📧 233 avenue des Campings
☎ +33 (0)4-67219561
📠 +33 (0)4-67218723
🕐 1/4 - 30/9
@ reception@camping-galet.com

2,9ha 136T(50-80m²) 10A

1 ACD**G**IJLPST
2 AEGHSVWXY
3 BFJNRUWY
4 (C 16/4-30/9) (H 10/4-28/9) J (Q+Z 🕐)
5 **AB**FGIJKLMNOPUZ
6 ACEGHJ**K**(N 0,8km)RT

💬 A quiet, well-maintained campsite with a heated swimming pool with slides and a children's pool. 150m from the beach. Well maintained sanitary facilities. A site in the centre of Marseillan-Plage with good shopping. A large supermarket, greengrocer and various places to eat are next to the site. 1 hour free wifi by the swimming pool.

🚗 A9 exit Agde, from here towards Sète. Right at first roundabout (Ranch la Camargue) then left at second roundabout. Follow signs.

CC € **17** 1/4-4/7 27/8-29/9   🧭 N 43°18'41'' E 3°32'40''

Marseillan-Plage, F-34340 / Languedoc-Roussillon (Hérault)   👫 ♿ 📶 iD (2484)

🔺 Les Méditerranées - Beach Garden*****
📧 avenue des Campings
☎ +33 (0)4-67219283
🕐 7/4 - 1/10
@ info@ beach-garden-camping.com

15ha 370T(80-100m²) 6-10A CEE

1 ACD**G**IJKLMOPST
2 AEFGRSTVWXY
3 B**F**GJKNRUWY
4 (C+F+H 🕐) IJK**LMN** (Q+S+T+U+V+Y+Z 🕐)
5 **AB**EFGJLNOPUW
6 ACEGHJ**K**(N 0,2km)ORTV

💬 Shaded campsite by a nature reserve and the Mediterranean. Marseillan-Plage is in walking distance. Spacious touring pitches, two new restaurants, supermarket and good toilets. Swimming pool with 1000 m² of fun in the water! Free wifi at the bar.

🚗 A9 exit Agde and via the D112 to the roundabout, turn right here (Plage de Rieu). Turn right at junction with the main road of Marseillan-Plage. Beach Garden campsite is located at the end of the street (dead end road).

CC € **19** 7/4-30/6 2/9-30/9   🧭 N 43°18'21'' E 3°32'16''

Marseillan-Plage, F-34340 / Languedoc-Roussillon (Hérault)

👫 ♿ 📶 **iD** (2485)

🏕 Les Méditerranées -
  Charlemagne*****
🏘 avenue des Campings
☎ +33 (0)4-67219249
📠 +33 (0)4-67218611
⏱ 7/4 - 1/10
@ info@charlemagne-camping.com

7ha 170T(70-100m²) 10A CEE

1 ACD**G**IJKLMPST
2 AEFGRSVWXY
3 B**F**JRWY
4 (C+F+H 🌙) IJKP
  (Q+S+T+U+V+Y+Z 🌙)
5 **AB**EFGIJKLMNOPUVWXYZ
6 AEGH**JK**M(N 0,1km)ORT

💬 A comfortable campsite with spacious and
well-maintained pitches. Lovely flowers and plants.
Connected directly to Camping Nouvelle Floride,
through which you can get to the sandy beach.
All facilities at both campsites are available to
campers, from the day it opens to the day it closes!

🚗 From Agde via D112, right at first roundabout,
Plage de Rieu. Campsite on right after last roundabout
in Marseillan-Plage.

CC € **19** 7/4-7/7 2/9-30/9   🔼 N 43°18'37'' E 3°32'36''

Maureillas-las-Illas, F-66480 / Languedoc-Roussillon (Pyrénées-Orientales)

♿ 📶 **iD** (2486)

🏕 Les Bruyères***
🏘 route de Céret
☎ +33 (0)4-68832664
📠 +33 (0)4-68831475
⏱ 10/3 - 18/11
@ campinglesbruyeres@live.fr

4ha 95T(80-180m²) 6A CEE

1 A**G**IJKLPST
2 BFIRTVY
3 AGGQRU
4 (B+G 1/5-30/9)
  (Q+T+Z 1/5-30/10)
5 AGJLNPUVXZ
6 EGIJ**K**(N 0,3km)O**P**TV

💬 A quiet campsite in the lower Pyrenees. The area
is ideal for making trips out to the Mediterranean or
Argelès Sur Mer. Beautiful view of the south side of
the Pic du Canigou.

🚗 A9 exit 43. Follow Gerona (D900). Then D618.
Through Maureillas. Campsite signposted.

CC € **15** 10/3-6/7 25/8-17/11   🔼 N 42°29'32'' E 2°47'42''

Maureillas-las-Illas, F-66480 / Languedoc-Roussillon (Pyrénées-Orientales)

♿ 📶 **iD** (2487)

🏕 Val Roma Park***
🏘 RD900
☎ +33 (0)4-68398813
⏱ 5/5 - 21/9
@ valromapark@wanadoo.fr

2,5ha 65T(80-100m²) 6A CEE

1 A**G**HIJKLOPS
2 BCFGRVXY
3 ANRU
4 (B 🌙) (G 20/6-30/9)
  (Q+R 1/7-30/8)
  (T+U+X+Z 🌙)
5 **A**FIJKLMNPUWZ
6 ABEGJ**K**(N 3km)TV

💬 It's great to be a guest at the basic, but
welcoming campsite Val Roma Park, located in a
wood and by a little river. 100 metres from the Le
Boulou spas, close to the Spanish border, the sea and
the Pyrenees. Many outings are possible.

🚗 Follow A9 motorway from Perpignan as far as
exit 43 direction Le Boulou. Follow RD900 towards
Le Perthus, Les Thermes du Boulou. Campsite 500m
after Les Thermes.

CC € **17** 5/5-14/7 1/9-20/9   🔼 N 42°30'23'' E 2°49'22''

Méjannes-le-Clap, F-30430 / Languedoc-Roussillon (Gard)

2488

La Genèse***
route de la Genèse
☎ +33 (0)5-33092092
FAX +33 (0)4-66245038
⊙ 31/3 - 29/9
@ reservations@socnat.fr

50ha 458T(90-130m²) 6-10A CEE

1 ABCGIJKL**P**ST
2 BCJKNORSTVXY
3 ABGHIMNQRUWX
4 (A 1/7-30/8) (C+G ⊙) JMN
(Q+S+T+U+V+X+Y+Z ⊙)
5 **AB**EGIJKMNOPQRUVWZ
6 AEGH**IJ**(N 7km)OQTV

💬 Located in the Gorges de la Cèze this family naturist campsite extends over 26 hectares of lush and rugged countryside. The river at the campsite offers opportunities for swimming and canoeing.

🚗 From the A7 exit Bollène, D994 direction Pont-St-Esprit. From there N86 direction Bagnols-sur-Cèze, then D6 direction Alès. Turn off to Lussan (D979) after 23.5 km. Follow signs in Méjannes.

CC € 17 31/3-6/7 25/8-28/9

N 44°16'3'' E 4°22'13''

Meyrueis, F-48150 / Languedoc-Roussillon (Lozère)

2489

La Cascade/Cevennes***
Salvinsac
☎ +33 (0)4-66454545
⊙ 7/4 - 23/9
@ contact@
camping-la-cascade.com

1,7ha 39T(100-300m²) 10A CEE

1 ACD**G**IJKLMOPST
2 CJKLMNORVWXY
3 BGHIJNPRUV**W**X
4 (Q+R+T+U+V+X+Z ⊙)
5 **A**CDEFGHIJKLMNOPQUWZ
6 ACEGJ(N 3km)ORTV

💬 Far away from the motorway, in a grand and well-maintained natural area. The ideal place to enjoy pure nature. Wonderful views of the surrounding Causse Méjean mountains, the tranquility of a splashing stream and a diversity of flora and fauna. Because of its small size, this is a great campsite.

🚗 This site is located on the Route de Florac, the road connecting Meyrueis and Florac. It is the second campsite after Meyrueis and is signposted.

CC € 15 7/4-6/7 26/8-22/9

N 44°11'43'' E 3°27'20''

Mèze, F-34140 / Languedoc-Roussillon (Hérault)

2490

Beau Rivage****
RD613
☎ +33 (0)4-67438148
FAX +33 (0)4-67436670
⊙ 14/4 - 15/9
@ reception@
camping-beaurivage.fr

3,5ha 92T(80-95m²) 6A

1 ACD**F**IJKL**P**S
2 ADFGRVWX
3 BGJNRUVW
4 (B+G+T+U+X+Z ⊙)
5 **A**EFGIJKLMNOPSTUXZ
6 CEGJ**K**(N 1,5km)

💬 At the entrance to the village, the campsite is on the edge of the beautiful Bassin de Thau. Walking, cycling, local market, supermarkets, shops, harbours, beaches, tourist attractions and Mediterranean cuisine. Warm, family-friendly atmosphere. Sunny and shady pitches. Swimming pool, free wifi at the bar/restaurant.

🚗 Exit Mèze on A9 motorway. Campsite signposted on the RD163.

CC € 17 14/4-6/7 25/8-14/9 14=13, 21=19

N 43°25'50'' E 3°36'38''

Mialet, F-30140 / Languedoc-Roussillon (Gard)

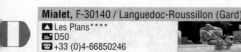

♿ 📶 iD **2491**

⛺ Les Plans****
🚩 D50
☎ +33 (0)4-66850246
📅 13/4 - 9/9
@ info@camping-les-plans.fr

6,5ha 133T(100-120m²) 3-10A CEE

1 ACD**G**IJKLMPST
2 BCGKLNORSTUVWXY
3 BGHJN**P**QRUV**W**X
4 (A 1/7-31/8) (C+G 📅) IJM
(Q 📅) (S 15/5-5/9)
(T+U+V 1/5-8/9)
(X+Y 1/5-9/9) (Z 1/5-8/9)
5 **A**EFGIJKLMNOPQUXZ
6 ACDEGJ**K**(N 5km)OTV

💬 Campsite on the edge of Parc National des Cévennes, in Mialet, in the Gard. Ideal location on a river, with a private beach. Leisure pool, sports grounds, kids club, minigolf, many activities and entertainment. 'La Bambouseraie de Prafance' and the Trabuc caves can be reached by steam train. 9 km from Anduze.

🚗 Route du Soleil, Bollène, Pont Saint Esprit-Bagnols, Alès, Anduze, Generargues, Mialet. Follow signs. The campsite is on the left.

La Grand-Combe N106
D9 D260 CC Alès
D907
D24

CC € **15** 13/4-30/6 27/8-8/9 7=6, 14=12

🏕 N 44°7'30'' E 3°55'7''

Montblanc, F-34290 / Languedoc-Roussillon (Hérault)

♿ 📶 iD **2492**

⛺ Le Rebau***
🚩 rue du Rebau
☎ +33 (0)4-67985078
📅 10/3 - 19/10
@ gilbert@camping-lerebau.fr

3ha 117T(80-120m²) 5-6A

1 A**G**IJKLMPT
2 FGSVXY
3 B**F**GNR
4 (B 1/7-15/9) (Q 1/7-31/8)
(T+Z 10/7-25/8)
5 **A**EFGIJKMNPUV
6 EGHJ(N 0,7km)OV

💬 A very friendly campsite set among vineyards. Within walking distance from the village.
The campsite is shaded without becoming a wood.
A very good base for visiting the area. Perfect as a stopover campsite. Free, efficient wifi

🚗 A75 exit 62 Montblanc. Or A9 exit 34 direction Pézenas via D13. After 4 km D18 direction Montblanc.

D15 D13 D609
A75
D909
N9 CC A9
Béziers Marseillan
D64 D612 **Agde**

CC € **17** 10/3-30/6 1/9-18/10

🏕 N 43°23'54'' E 3°22'24''

Montferrand, F-11320 / Languedoc-Roussillon (Aude)

♿ 📶 iD **2493**

⛺ Domaine St. Laurent***
🚩 Lieu dit Les Touzets
☎ +33 (0)4-68601580
📅 31/3 - 2/11
@ campingdomainesaintlaurent@gmail.com

80ha 35T(70-160m²) 6-10A CEE

1 ACD**G**IJKLMPST
2 BKRVWXY
3 ABDGHJMNR
4 (B 2/6-29/9) **N**
(Q+R+T+U 📅) (V 7/7-1/9)
(Z 📅)
5 **A B**GIJKLMNOPUVZ
6 EGH**J**(N 5km)TV

NEW

💬 Spaciously landscaped campsite with large pitches. Ideal campsite for those who want to get to know the area around the Canal du Midi.

🚗 A61 exit 20 towards Carcassonne (D622A and D6113). Then D43 towards Revel. After 4 km, turn right towards St. Laurent (D218). Left at church. Site is signposted.

D2 D1
D25 D622
Villefranche-de-Lauragais
D813 CC
A61
D91 D625 D6113 D624
D16 **Castelnaudary**

CC € **17** 31/3-1/6 30/6-6/7 25/8-1/11

🏕 N 43°23'14'' E 1°49'54''

Montolieu, F-11170 / Languedoc-Roussillon (Aude)

♿ 🛜 iD (2494)

🏕 Camping de Montolieu
🛣 D629
☎ +33 (0)4-68769501
📅 24/3 - 31/10
@ campingdemontolieu@
gmail.com

1ha 43T(80-120m²) 10A CEE

1 ACGIJKLMPST
2 RTUVWXY
3 AGHMNRUW
4 (A 🚿) (Q 1/7-31/8) (R+Z 🚿)
5 AGIJKLMNPUWZ
6 EGJK(N 1,2km)RT

💬 A campsite marked out by hedges with spacious pitches. Attractive reception building with a lively terrace and recreation room. Modern and well-placed toilet building. Near the literary town of Montolieu. 2 Euros extra payment needed for 10A power.

🚗 From Carcassonne ring road to D6113 direction Castelnaudary. Exit Montolieu D629 until 1 km before the village, indicated on the right.

D103　D73
D629　D118
CC
Bram　D6113
D33
D4　A61
D119　Carcassonne

CC € 13 24/3-30/6 1/9-30/10

📍 N 43°17'52'' E 2°13'20''

Montoulieu, F-34190 / Languedoc-Roussillon (Hérault)

♿ 🛜 iD (2495)

🏕 Le Grillon***
🛣 Place de l'Église
☎ +33 (0)4-67737931
📅 1/1 - 31/12
@ camping@montoulieu.fr

2ha 30T(80-140m²) 10A

1 ACDGIJKLMNOPST
2 JKRVWXY
3 ABHJR
4 (B+G 1/5-20/9)
(Q+R+T+Y 🚿)
5 AEFGJLNPU
6 AEGJ(N 5km)RTV

💬 Montoulieu is a small village between the hills and the Mediterranean, surrounded by vineyards and 'garrigue' scrubland. Quiet but close to fantastic towns: De Grot, Des Demoiselles, Ganges with its weekly market, Montpellier, Cirque de Navacelles, the Mont Aigoual.

🚗 D986 Ganges-Montpellier, take the D108 towards Montoulieu at St. Bauzille-de-Putois. Campsite indicated in the village.

D982
D999　Sauve
Cazilhac　CC
D25
Corconne
D986　D17 E6　D17

CC € 13 1/1-30/6 1/9-31/12

📍 N 43°55'36'' E 3°47'22''

Narbonne, F-11100 / Languedoc-Roussillon (Aude)

👫 ♿ 🛜 iD (2496)

🏕 Camping La Nautique****
🛣 254 avenue des Etangs
☎ +33 (0)4-68904819
📅 1/3 - 31/10
@ info@campinglanautique.com

16ha 250T(130-140m²) 10A

1 ACDGIJKLMPT
2 DFIKLRTVWXY
3 ABGHIJKMNQRUW
4 (A 1/5-30/9) (C+H 1/5-1/10) J
(Q 1/4-1/10) (S 15/4-30/9)
(T 1/7-31/8)
(U+V+Y+Z 1/5-30/9)
5 ABGIJKLSWXYZ
6 ACEGHK(N 4,5km)RTV

💬 Exceptional location on the beautiful Bages bay - lovely panoramic views - and just a few kilometres from the Mediterranean beaches and the historic centre of Narbonne - a friendly welcome, heated swimming pool, private toilet facilities at your camping pitch - most suitable for excursions. Fully equipped for the disabled.

🚗 A9 exit 38 Narbonne-Sud. At the roundabout turn left, follow the signs La Nautique. After about 2.5 km the campsite is on the right hand side.

D607
Coursan
D6113　D1118
Narbonne
D168
A61　D32　D332
CC　D613
D6009
A9

CC € 19 1/3-30/6 1/9-30/10

📍 N 43°8'50'' E 3°0'14''

Narbonne-Plage, F-11100 / Languedoc-Roussillon (Aude)

👫 ⛓ 📶 iD (2497)

▲ Campéole La Côte des Roses***
🏠 route de Gruissan
☎ +33 (0)4-68498365
🗓 30/3 - 30/9
@ cote-des-roses@campeole.com

16ha 410T(80-100m²) 10-16A CEE

1 ACG**I**JKLMOP**S**T
2 ADEFGRSTVWXY
3 BGHJKN**OQ**RUWY
4 (B 15/5-30/9) (H 1/6-7/9) IM
(Q 1/7-31/8) (S 1/6-15/9)
(T+U+V+X+Y+Z 1/7-31/8)
5 **AB**EFGJKLMNOPQRUVZ
6 ACEGHI**J**(N 2km)ORTV

💬 A well-equipped and very spacious campsite close to the beach, 2 km outside the centre of Narbonne-Plage. Ideally located for walking or cycling trips in the La Clape nature reserve. Swimming pool with large slides and a watery playground for young children.

🚗 The campsite is located 2 km south of Narbonne-Plage on the road connecting Narbonne-Plage to Gruissan.

Coursan D31 / A9 / Narbonne / D1118 / D168 / CC / D32

CC € **17** 30/3-6/7 25/8-29/9

📍 N 43°8'37'' E 3°8'39''

Narbonne-Plage, F-11100 / Languedoc-Roussillon (Aude)

👫 ⛓ 📶 iD (2498)

▲ Flower Camping Soleil d'Oc***
🏠 D332 route de Gruissan
☎ +33 (0)4-68498621
📠 +33 (0)4-68493055
🗓 1/4 - 30/9
@ info@soleildoc.fr

3ha 110T(80-120m²) 6-10A

1 ACD**G**IJKLM**P**Q
2 AEGRSTVWXY
3 AGHJNRWY
4 (B 1/5-30/9) (Q+R 🗓)
(T+U+V+X+Z 1/7-31/8)
5 **AB**GIJKLMNP**S**UV
6 ACEG**I**J**K**(N 2km)RV

💬 Welcoming child-friendly family campsite close to Narbonne-Plage with spacious, marked-out pitches. The beach is within walking distance and the campsite has a charming lagoon pool which means great swimming and fun for young and old.

🚗 A9 exit Narbonne-Est direction D168 Narbonne-Plage. Towards Gruissan-Plage from here. Right after about 2 km.

D6009 / D31 / Narbonne / D1118 / Saint-Pierre-la-Mer / D168 / CC / D32

CC € **13** 1/4-9/7 27/8-29/9 7=6, 14=12

📍 N 43°8'42'' E 3°8'32''

Néfiach, F-66170 / Languedoc-Roussillon (Pyrénées-Orientales)

⛓ 📶 iD (2499)

▲ La Garenne***
🏠 D916
☎ +33 (0)4-68571576
📠 +33 (0)4-68573742
🗓 1/3 - 31/10
@ contact@camping-lagarenne.fr

3,5ha 73T(80-130m²) 10A CEE

1 ACGIJKLMOPST
2 FGRTVXY
3 AGHJNR
4 (A 1/7-31/8)
(B+D+G 1/5-31/10) I
(Q 1/7-31/8)
(T+U+V+X+Z 1/5-31/10)
5 **A**DFGIJKMNOPUVZ
6 ACDEG**I**KL(N 2km)TV

💬 Ambiance between orchards and vineyards of Roussillon. Views of the mighty Canigou. Being small is the biggest asset. Peace is guaranteed. Many excursions through the Pyrénées-Orientales with its Cathar castles. The Mediterranean beaches are 30 km away. And the tax haven of Andorra is within 120 km.

🚗 Green signs in Perpignan towards Andorra la Vella/Prades (N116, toll-free road). After 11 km exit Néfiach. D916 at roundabout towards Néfiach.

D614 / Le Soler / Ille-sur-Têt CC / D612 / N116 / Thuir / D618 / D615

CC € **13** 1/3-6/7 25/8-30/10

📍 N 42°41'26'' E 2°39'28''

Palau-del-Vidre, F-66690 / Languedoc-Roussillon (Pyrénées-Orientales)

♿ 📶 **iD** **(2500)**

🏠 Le Haras***
📧 Domaine St. Galdric
☎ +33 (0)4-68221450
🗓 1/4 - 30/9
@ contact@camping-le-haras.com

4ha 99T(80-100m²) 10A CEE

1 ACFIJKLOPST
2 GRTVXY
3 BDGNRU
4 (B 15/4-20/9) (Q 🔑)
   (T+U+X+Z 15/4-20/9)
5 ABGIJKLMNOPUWZ
6 ACEK(N 0,5km)TV

💬 Just before Palau del Vidre is the park-like campsite of Le Haras with its varied flora. The attractive bar next to the swimming pool is surrounded by greenery and beaches of Argeles are 7 km away. Many excursions in the immediate vicinity or to the Pyrenees and Barcelona are possible.

🚗 A9, exit Perpignan-Sud, RD914 direction Argelès-sur-Mer. Exit 9 Palau-del-Vidre. Campsite on the left before the village.

CC € 17 1/4-3/7 28/8-29/9 25=20   📷 N 42°34'33'' E 2°57'53''

Palavas-les-Flots, F-34250 / Languedoc-Roussillon (Hérault)

♿ 📶 **iD** **(2501)**

🏠 Montpellier Plage***
📧 95 av. Saint Maurice
☎ +33 (0)4-67680091
📠 +33 (0)4-67681069
🗓 7/4 - 23/9
@ camping.montpellier.plage@
   wanadoo.fr

10ha 500T(70-120m²) 10A CEE

1 ACDFIJKLMOPST
2 AEFGRSVXY
3 ABGKLNUUW
4 (B+G 1/5-25/9)
   (Q+R+T+U+V+X+Z 🔑)
5 ABEFGIJKLMNPQU
6 ADEGHJK(N 2km)ORTV

💬 Excellent base for Montpellier and the cultural towns in Languedoc. 50 metres from a huge sandy beach. At walking distance from the centre of Palavas-les-Flots.

🚗 Motorway A9 exit 29 Montpellier Est. Direction Les Plages and Palavas-les-Flots. In Palavas-les-Flots direction Rive Gauche. Campsite signposted on avenue St. Maurice.

CC € 17 7/4-7/7 25/8-22/9   📷 N 43°32'4'' E 3°56'56''

Peyremale-sur-Cèze, F-30160 / Languedoc-Roussillon (Gard)

♿ 📶 **iD** **(2502)**

🏔 des Drouilhèdes***
☎ +33 (0)4-66250480
📠 +33 (0)4-66251095
🗓 1/4 - 30/9
@ info@campingcevennes.com

2,5ha 90T(60-100m²) 6A CEE

1 ACGIJKLPS
2 CLNORSVXY
3 BGHJNQRWX
4 (Q+R+U+X+Z 🔑)
5 ACFGIJKMNOPQUWZ
6 AEGHJ(N 4km)OTV

💬 This friendly family campsite, especially suitable for older people and families with children, is located right on the banks of the River Cèze with natural swimming. English, French, Dutch and German are spoken. Enjoy delicious meals at reasonable prices in the friendly bar and restaurant. Plenty of trips out! A relaxing holiday is assured.

🚗 D51 St. Ambroix-Bessèges. In Bessèges take D17 direction Peyremale. Turn right after several kilometres; 3 km west of Bessèges.

CC € 17 1/4-6/7 24/8-29/9   📷 N 44°17'27'' E 4°4'3''

Port-Leucate, F-11370 / Languedoc-Roussillon (Aude)

🐾 🚶 📶 **iD** (2503)

🏔 Rives des Corbières***
📧 avenue du Languedoc
☎ +33 (0)4-68409031
📠 +33 (0)4-68408784
🔑 7/5 - 30/9
@ rivescamping@wanadoo.fr

6ha 192**T**(80-100m²) 6A

1. AC**G**IJKLOPST
2. AESTVWXY
3. AGKNRUWY
4. (B+G+Q+R+T+U+V+Y+Z 🔑)
5. **AB**GIJKLMNPUVZ
6. AEG**K**(N 0,8km)RTV

💬 Situated between the sea and the Étang de Salses, this spacious family campsite offers plenty of watersports opportunities. Equipped with a lovely swimming pool and within walking distance of the sea and the delightful harbour of Leucate.

🚗 A9 direction Perpignan. Exit Leucate. Follow D627 as far as exit Port-Leucate. Then second roundabout right. Campsite after about 700 metres.

CC € **13** 7/5-6/7 27/8-29/9

🗺 N 42°50'57'' E 3°2'26''

Portiragnes-Plage, F-34420 / Languedoc-Roussillon (Hérault)

👫 🚶 📶 **iD** (2504)

🏔 Les Sablons*****
📧 av. des Muriers/Plage Est
☎ +33 (0)4-67909055
📠 +33 (0)4-67908291
🔑 23/3 - 30/9
@ contact@les-sablons.com

15ha 223**T**(85-120m²) 10A CEE

1. ACD**G**IJKLMPRS
2. ADEFGRSTVXY
3. BC**F**GHJKLMN**OP**RUVWY
4. (A+C+E+H 🔑) IJKMP (Q+S+T+U+V+W+X+Y+Z 🔑)
5. **AB**DEFGIJKLMNPRUWYZ
6. ACGH**IJK**M(N 0,2km)ORTV

💬 Large friendly campsite by the sea with swimming pools heated to 26°C from the opening date. Large 200m² indoor swimming pool from 2017. Plenty of entertainment for young and old. There is a lovely sandy beach. Free wifi for ½ hour every 6 hours. The spa is accessible from the age of 18 and open from 1 May.

🚗 A9 exit Béziers-Est, direction Valras-Plage. At the roundabout left direction Portiragnes. Then direction Portiragnes-Plage. Left past the roundabout.

CC € **19** 23/3-30/6 1/9-29/9

🗺 N 43°16'48'' E 3°21'51''

Preixan, F-11250 / Languedoc-Roussillon (Aude)

🚶 📶 **iD** (2505)

🏔 Camping Village Grand Sud***
📧 Le Breil-d'Aude / D118
☎ +33 (0)4-68268818
🔑 31/3 - 15/9
@ accueil@camping-grandsud.com

11ha 65**T**(100-120m²) 6A CEE

1. AC**G**IJKLMPST
2. CDFLRTVXY
3. BGMRUWX
4. (B 1/4-30/9) J(Q 🔑) (R 1/4-30/9) (U 1/7-30/8) (V 🔑) (X+Z 1/7-31/8)
5. **AB**DEFGIJKLMNPU
6. CF**J**(N 10km)RTV

💬 Campsite 10 km from the 'Canal du Midi' and the legendary town of Carcassonne. Just 1 hour from the Mediterranean and 2 hours from the Andorran mountains. In the heart of Catharen country with opportunities for taking lovely walks and visiting picturesque markets. Shaded floral grounds on a lake.

🚗 A61, exit 23 Carcassonne-Ouest, then direction Limoux (7 km) the D118.

CC € **15** 31/3-9/7 27/8-14/9

🗺 N 43°9'31'' E 2°17'36''

Remoulins, F-30210 / Languedoc-Roussillon (Gard)

👫 ♿ 🛜 **iD** **2506**

🏕 La Sousta★★★★
📧 28 avenue du Pont du Gard
☎ +33 (0)4-66371280
🗓 12/3 - 1/11
@ info@lasousta.com

12ha 259**T**(70-120m²) 6A

1 ACDGIJKLMO**P**ST
2 BCFKLNRSVWXY
3 BFGHJKL**M**NRUWX
4 (B+G 1/5-1/11) (Q 🔑)
(S 1/4-1/10)
(T+U+V+Y+Z 🔑)
5 **A**BEFGIJKLMNOPUVWZ
6 CEG**IK**(N 2km)OTUV

💬 Sun and countryside, 800 metres from the Pont du Gard. You will be welcomed to a shaded pine forest of 12 hectares on the Gardon river. The campsite offers sports activities, a bar/restaurant, swimming pool and tennis court.

🚐 Through the centre of Remoulins, turn right after the bridge to the Pont du Gard, on the Rive Droite.

CC € **17** 12/3-7/7 25/8-31/10

🧭 N 43°56'55'' E 4°32'42''

Rennes-les-Bains, F-11190 / Languedoc-Roussillon (Aude)

🛜 **iD** **2507**

🏕 La Bernède★★★
📧 19, chemin de la Bernède
☎ +33 (0)6-37272234
🗓 1/1 - 31/12
@ infos@labernede.fr

1ha 80**T**(80-100m²) 16A CEE

1 ADGIJKLMOPST
2 BCGKTUVX
3 AFGHNUWX
4 (C+**H** 1/5-30/9) (Q+R 🔑)
(T+X+Z 1/5-30/9)
5 **A**ILMNPUVWXYZ
6 DEGIJ(N 0,5km)RTUV

💬 Camping La Bernède is located on the banks of the small River La Sals, close to the picturesque village of Rennes-les-Bains with its thermal spa.

🚐 Carcassonne dir. Quillan D118. In Couiza turn off onto D813. After 5.5 km turn off to Rennes-Bains D14.

CC € **17** 1/1-6/7 25/8-31/12

🧭 N 42°54'54'' E 2°19'5''

Rustiques, F-11800 / Languedoc-Roussillon (Aude)

♿ 🛜 **iD** **2508**

🏕 La Commanderie★★★
📧 6 chemin de l'Eglise
☎ +33 (0)4-68786763
🗓 1/4 - 15/10
@ contact@
campinglacommanderie.com

3,5ha 61**T**(103-247m²) 6A CEE

1 ACD**G**IJKLM**P**ST
2 BFIKTVWXY
3 ABGHJNRU
4 (A 1/7-31/8) (B 1/6-15/10)
(Q 🔑) (X 1/7-31/8)
5 **A**DFGIJKMNPUZ
6 CEGJTV

💬 Campsite located in Aude at 10 minutes from Carcassonne and its citadel and at 2 km from the Canal du Midi. Very quiet and homely with a large pool, playing field, jeu de boule, snack bar. Area rich in history with castles, caves of Limousis and boating on Canal du Midi.

🚐 Exit 24 on A61, Carcassonne-Est, follow Trèbes. Enter Trèbes and then follow Marseillette/Béziers. After Trèbes drive towards Rustiques and follow campsite sign.

CC € **15** 1/5-30/6 1/9-14/10

🧭 N 43°12'53'' E 2°28'13''

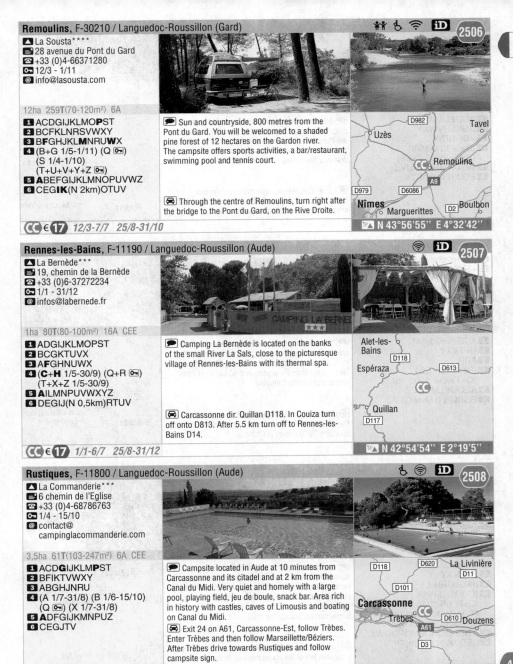

Saissac, F-11310 / Languedoc-Roussillon (Aude)   ♿ 🛜 **iD** (2509)

🏕 La Porte d'Autan
✉ rue Boris Vian
☎ +33 (0)4-68763608
🗓 2/4 - 13/10
@ laportedautan@yahoo.fr

2,3ha 71T(80-150m²) 6A

1 ACD**FIJ**LM**P**
2 BGKLRVWXY
3 ABGHRW
4 (B+G 15/6-15/9)
   (R+T+V+Z 1/7-1/9)
5 **A**GIJKMNPQRUVZ
6 EGJ(N 0,1km)TV

💬 Homely campsite in Saissac, located in the Aude, close to Carcassonne. Beautiful panoramic view of the Pyrenees. Sun, tranquillity, conviviality, walks, enjoyment of nature, visiting Cathar castles. Come discover the beauty of the 'Montagne Noire'.

🚗 Ring Carcassonne direction Castelnaudary D6113, right to Saissac D629. Through village, left after 500m at roundabout. Signposted.

ⒸⒸ € **13** 2/4-6/7 25/8-12/10   ⛰ N 43°21'42'' E 2°9'39''

Saint-Denis — D629 — D103 — D118 — Pexiora — Moussoulens

Salses, F-66600 / Languedoc-Roussillon (Pyrénées-Orientales)   ♿ 🛜 **iD** (2510)

🏕 International du Roussillon**
☎ +33 (0)4-68386072
🗓 1/1 - 31/12
@ camping-roussillon@wanadoo.fr

2,5ha 55T 10A CEE

1 ACDFIJKLMNPT
2 DFTVXY
3 ABR
4 (B+G 1/6-15/9)
   (Q+T+X+Z 1/7-31/8)
5 AEGIJKLMNOPZ
6 EGI**K**(N 0,5km)OTV

💬 In a tourist region where a whole range of activities is at your disposal, this campsite is 500m from the village and castle of Salses, 5 km from a lake, 10 km from Perpignan and 40 km from Spain, where you can go shopping.

🚗 From Montpellier A9, exit 40 direction D900 Fitou/Salses le Château. From L'Espagne A9, exit 41 direction D900 Salses le Château.

ⒸⒸ € **15** 1/1-30/6 25/8-31/12   ⛰ N 42°50'37'' E 2°55'34''

D6009 — D900 — D627 — D12 — A9 — D83 — Saint-Laurent-de-la-Salanque — Rivesaltes

---

Sérignan, F-34410 / Languedoc-Roussillon (Hérault)   🎣 ♿ 🛜 **iD** (2511)

🏕 Le Paradis****
✉ avenue Georges Freche
☎ +33 (0)4-67322403
🗓 1/4 - 30/9
@ paradiscamping34@aol.com

2,2ha 87T(80-115m²) 10A CEE

1 ACDEIJKLOPST
2 FGRVXY
3 BF**GH**JRU
4 (C 10/5-30/9) K
   (Q+R 1/5-30/9)
   (T+U+V+X 20/5-23/9)
   (Z 1/5-30/9)
5 **AB**EFGIJKLMNOPQUWZ
6 CEGJ**K**(N 0,5km)TV

💬 Welcoming family campsite. 3 km from Valras-Plage with its boutiques, pavement cafes and restaurants. Park-like design with its own swimming pool and jacuzzi. Well-maintained restaurant with fresh products every day and a varied menu. Supermarkets across the road.

🚗 A9 exit Béziers Est direction Valras. The campsite is located left of the roundabout at Sérignan.

ⒸⒸ € **17** 1/4-30/6 26/8-29/9   ⛰ N 43°16'9'' E 3°17'6''

Béziers — D612 A — A9 — D609 — D64 — Sérignan — D1118 — Saint-Pierre-la-Mer

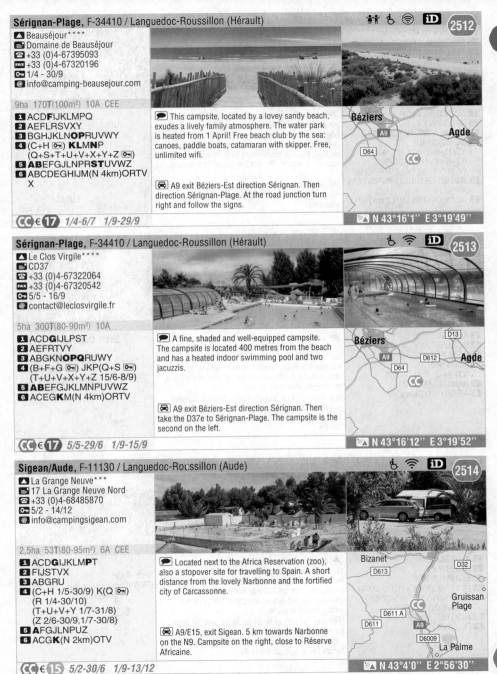

Sérignan-Plage, F-34410 / Languedoc-Roussillon (Hérault) 👫 ♿ 📶 iD (2512)

🏕 Beauséjour★★★★
🏠 Domaine de Beauséjour
☎ +33 (0)4-67395093
📠 +33 (0)4-67320196
🔓 1/4 - 30/9
@ info@camping-beausejour.com

9ha 170T(100m²) 10A CEE

1 ACD**FIJ**KLMPQ
2 AEFLRSVXY
3 BGHJKLN**OP**RUVWY
NP
4 (C+H 🔓) **KL**M**N**P
(Q+S+T+U+V+X+Y+Z 🔓)
5 **AB**EFGJLNPR**ST**UVWZ
6 ABCDEGHIJM(N 4km)ORTV
X

💬 This campsite, located by a lovey sandy beach, exudes a lively family atmosphere. The water park is heated from 1 April! Free beach club by the sea: canoes, paddle boats, catamaran with skipper. Free, unlimited wifi.

🚗 A9 exit Béziers-Est direction Sérignan. Then direction Sérignan-Plage. At the road junction turn right and follow the signs.

Béziers A9 · **Agde** · D64 · CC

CC € **17** 1/4-6/7 1/9-29/9 ⛰ N 43°16'1'' E 3°19'49''

Sérignan-Plage, F-34410 / Languedoc-Roussillon (Hérault) ♿ 📶 iD (2513)

🏕 Le Clos Virgile★★★★
🏠 CD37
☎ +33 (0)4-67322064
📠 +33 (0)4-67320542
🔓 5/5 - 16/9
@ contact@leclosvirgile.fr

5ha 300T(80-90m²) 10A

1 ACD**G**IJLPST
2 AEFRTVY
3 ABGKN**OP**QRUWY
4 (B+F+G 🔓) JKP(Q+S 🔓)
(T+U+V+X+Y+Z 15/6-8/9)
5 **AB**EFGJKLMNPUVWZ
6 ACEG**K**M(N 4km)ORTV

💬 A fine, shaded and well-equipped campsite. The campsite is located 400 metres from the beach and has a heated indoor swimming pool and two jacuzzis.

🚗 A9 exit Béziers-Est direction Sérignan. Then take the D37e to Sérignan-Plage. The campsite is the second on the left.

Béziers D13 · A9 · D612 · **Agde** · D64 · CC

CC € **17** 5/5-29/6 1/9-15/9 ⛰ N 43°16'12'' E 3°19'52''

Sigean/Aude, F-11130 / Languedoc-Roussillon (Aude) ♿ 📶 iD (2514)

🏕 La Grange Neuve★★★
🏠 17 La Grange Neuve Nord
☎ +33 (0)4-68485870
🔓 5/2 - 14/12
@ info@campingsigean.com

2,5ha 53T(80-95m²) 6A CEE

1 ACD**G**IJKLM**P**T
2 FIJSTVX
3 ABGRU
4 (C+H 1/5-30/9) K(Q 🔓)
(R 1/4-30/10)
(T+U+V+Y 1/7-31/8)
(Z 2/6-30/9,1/7-30/8)
5 **A**FGJLNPUZ
6 ACG**K**(N 2km)OTV

💬 Located next to the Africa Reservation (zoo), also a stopover site for travelling to Spain. A short distance from the lovely Narbonne and the fortified city of Carcassonne.

🚗 A9/E15, exit Sigean. 5 km towards Narbonne on the N9. Campsite on the right, close to Réserve Africaine.

Bizanet D613 · D32 · CC · **Gruissan Plage** · D611 A · D611 · A9 · D6009 · **La Palme**

CC € **15** 5/2-30/6 1/9-13/12 ⛰ N 43°4'0'' E 2°56'30''

Sommières, F-30250 / Languedoc-Roussillon (Gard)

🚶 📶 ✿ **iD** **2515**

⛺ Domaine de Massereau＊＊＊＊＊
🏠 1990 route d'Aubais
☎ +33 (0)4-66531120
📅 7/4 - 30/9
@ camping@massereau.com

8ha 90T(100-200m²) 16A CEE

1. ACD**G**IJKLMO**P**S
2. BFLSVWXY
3. ABGHJK**MN**OPQRU**W**
4. (**A** 1/7-31/8)
   (C+E+H 7/4-30/9) J**KLN**
   (Q+S+T+U 7/4-30/9)
   (V 1/7-31/8) (Y+Z 7/4-30/9)
5. **A**BDEFGHIJKLOPQR**S**T**U**W
   XY
6. ACDEGHJ**K**LM(N 2km)RTV

💬 Located in the heart of a wine domain between the Cevennes and the Mediterranean. Quiet and child-friendly. Pitches with plenty of comfort. Heated pool, recreational swimming pool with slide, restaurant, pizzeria, bar, food, adventure park. Private beach, SUP (stand up paddle). Perfect for cycling and walking.

🚗 A9, exit 26 direction Gallargues, then direction Sommières, in Sommières direction Aubais, is indicated.

CC € **19** 7/4-2/6 1/9-29/9

🗺️ N 43°45'58'' E 4°5'50''

(Map showing D999, D35 A, D6110, D40, D34, CC, D610, A9, N113, Valergues, Lunel, Vauvert)

Sorède, F-66690 / Languedoc-Roussillon (Pyrénées-Orientales)

👫👫 🚶 📶 **iD** **2516**

⛺ La Coscolleda＊＊＊
🏠 27 rue de la Coscolleda
☎ +33 (0)4-68891665
📅 1/4 - 1/10
@ camping-la-coscolleda@wanadoo.fr

1,3ha 35T(80-120m²) 10A CEE

1. ACD**G**IJKLOPST
2. BCGJRTVXY
3. AGHJRU
4. (C+H 📅)
   (Q+T+U+Z 1/7-31/8)
5. **A**GIJKLMNOPZ
6. AEGK(N 0,5km)OR

💬 La Coscolleda campsite is located alongside the La Taxo river at the foot of the Pyrenees and 7 km from the Mediterranean Sea. Peace and quiet in the countryside in low season. Heated swimming pool on site, walking, cycling in the area or trips to Collioure, to the Pyrenees or Barcelona.

🚗 A9 exit 43 Le Boulou. Follow Argelès-sur-Mer (D618) as far as St. André/Sorède exit. Direction Sorède (D11) at first roundabout and turn left before Sorède.

CC € **13** 1/4-7/7 25/8-30/9

🗺️ N 42°32'5'' E 2°57'36''

(Map showing Saint-Cyprien, D81, Argelès-sur-Mer, A9, CC, D900, AP-7)

St. Alban-sur-Limagnole, F-48120 / Languedoc-Roussillon (Lozère)

🚶 📶 **iD** **2517**

⛺ Camping Le Galier＊＊
🏠 route de Saint Chély
☎ +33 (0)4-66315880
📅 1/3 - 1/10
@ accueil@campinglegalier.fr

4ha 66T(100-200m²) 6A

1. ABCGIJKLMPS
2. BCLRWXY
3. AGH**M**RU**W**X
4. (A 1/7-30/8) (E+H 1/5-30/9)
   (Q 1/6-31/8) (T 1/5-30/9)
   (V 15/6-30/9) (Z 📅)
5. **A**CGIJKLMNOPUVZ
6. EGJ(N 1km)OT

💬 Not far from the A75 in the Margeride region at the foot of a typical French village. Spacious pitches on the edge of a wood and on both banks of the Limagnole, it is wonderfully healthy. Free bikes for children. Fishing in the Limagnole. Walks with a locally available guide.

🚗 Take the A75 as far as St. Alban, exit 34, then take the N106 in the direction of St. Alban-sur-Limagnole. The campsite is located about 800 metres before the village, on the D987.

CC € **15** 1/3-8/7 26/8-30/9

🗺️ N 44°46'31'' E 3°22'20''

(Map showing D989, D587, Saint-Chély-d'Apcher, Saint-Alban-sur-Limagnole, A75, CC, D809, D806, D987)

St. Cyprien-Plage, F-66750 / Languedoc-Roussillon (Pyrénées-Orientales) 👫 ♿ 🛜 iD (2518)

▲ Cala Gogo★★★★★
📧 Les Capellans, av. Armand Lanoux
☎ +33 (0)4-68210712
📠 +33 (0)4-68210219
🔓 7/4 - 29/9
@ camping@calagogo66.fr

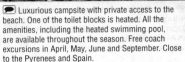

12ha 407T(80-125m²) 10A CEE

1 ACD**G**IJKLMPST
2 AEGRTVX
3 BF**G**K**M**NRUWY
4 (C+H+Q+S+T+U+V+X+Y+Z 🔑)
5 **AB**DEFGIJKLMNOPUVWXYZ
6 ACEGHI**K**M(N 2km)ORTV

💬 Luxurious campsite with private access to the beach. One of the toilet blocks is heated. All the amenities, including the heated swimming pool, are available throughout the season. Free coach excursions in April, May, June and September. Close to the Pyrenees and Spain.

🚗 A9 exit 42 Perpignan-Sud, dir. Argelès-sur-Mer. Follow D914 as far as exit 7 dir St. Cyprien and Elne. Via Latour-Bas-Elne follow St. Cyprien-Plage. Then follow 'Grand Stade' and camping signs.

Saint-Cyprien — D11, D81 A, CC, D914

CC € **19** 7/4-6/7 25/8-28/9   🧭 N 42°35'58'' E 3°2'18''

St. Jean-du-Gard, F-30270 / Languedoc-Roussillon (Gard) ♿ 🛜 ✿ iD (2519)

▲ Les Sources★★★
📧 route de Mialet
☎ +33 (0)4-66853803
📠 +33 (0)4-66851609
🔓 1/4 - 23/9
@ camping-des-sources@wanadoo.fr

2,4ha 68T(80-120m²) 6-10A CEE

1 ACD**G**IJKLM**P**ST
2 BGJKLRSVWXY
3 BGHIJRU
4 (**A** 17/5-30/9)
     (C+H+Q+S+T+U 🔑)
     (V 1/7-31/8) (X+Y+Z 🔑)
5 **AB**DEFGIJKLMNOPSTUVWXYZ
6 ACDEGIJ(N 1,3km)OTV

💬 Magnificent campsite, quiet and family-friendly, in the heart of the southern Cévennes. 1300m from the village and very close to a river with crystal-clear water. In the surroundings there is a well-known bamboo forest, steam train to Anduze, Nimes, Pont du Gard, Uzès. Heated swimming pool and heated toilet facilities.

🚗 A7 Bollène - Pont-St-Esprit - Bagnols-sur-Cèze - Alès - Anduze - St. Jean-du-Gard. After traffic lights right 1.3 km.

La Grand-Combe, L'Habitarelle — D9, D260, CC, D907

CC € **13** 1/4-30/6 1/9-22/9 10=7   🧭 N 44°6'48'' E 3°53'31''

St. Jean-du-Gard, F-30270 / Languedoc-Roussillon (Gard) 👫 ♿ 🛜 iD (2520)

▲ Mas de la Cam★★★★
📧 route de St. André-de-Valborgne
☎ +33 (0)4-66851202
📠 +33 (0)4-66853207
🔓 28/4 - 20/9
@ camping@masdelacam.fr

8ha 200T(80-140m²) 6-10A CEE

1 ACD**F**IJKLOPST
2 BCKLMNRVWXY
3 BGHIJ**M**N**P**RUW**X**
4 (C+H 15/5-10/9) IMP(Q 🔑)
     (S 1/6-5/9) (T+U 1/6-10/9)
     (V 1/7-31/8) (X+Y 1/6-10/9)
     (Z 16/5-10/9)
5 **AB**CEFGIJKLMNOPUVWXZ
6 AEGJ(N 3km)OTV

💬 Peaceful floral campsite located on the river. Beautiful views of the Cevennes mountains. Heated swimming pool (500 m²), free tennis (low season), ideal starting point for cycling and walking. Plenty of entertainment in spring: pétanque and bridge. Maximum 20 pitches available for dog owners. 10A power 1 Euro extra.

🚗 A7 Bollène, Pont-St-Esprit, Bagnols-sur-Cèze, Alès, direction Montpellier, St. Christol, Anduze, St. Jean-du-Gard direction St. André-de-Valbogne.

La Grand-Combe — D9, D260, CC, D907, Anduze, D982

CC € **17** 28/4-5/7 24/8-19/9   🧭 N 44°6'45'' E 3°51'16''

St. Jean-Pla-de-Corts, F-66490 / Languedoc-Roussillon (Pyrénées-Orientales)

2521

de la Vallée***
route de Maureillas
☎ +33 (0)4-68832320
FAX +33 (0)4-68830794
⌚ 1/4 - 31/10
@ campingdelavallee@yahoo.fr

10ha 100T 6A CEE

1 AC**F**IJLMOPST
2 ACFLMQRTVY
3 ABNRU**W**
4 (C ⌚) (G 5/5-9/9) (Q ⌚)
(R+T+U+V+Z 15/6-30/9)
5 **A**EFGJLNPTUVZ
6 CEG**K**(N 0,1km)OTV

💬 At the foot of the Pyrenees, an excellent area for walking with an abundance of marked out routes. Opportunities also for off-road trips in the mountains: les Albères, le Vallespir and the Massif du Canigou (2784m). Heated swimmingpool.

🚗 Le Boulou dir. Céret D115. At the roundabout in St. Jean-Pla-de-Corts go towards village centre left over the bridge. Campsite signposted.

Saint-Génis-des-Fontaines
Le Boulou
D615
D618 / Céret / A9 / D900
AP-7

CC € **15** 1/4-6/7 25/8-30/10

N 42°30'24'' E 2°47'40''

St. Jean-Pla-de-Corts, F-66490 / Languedoc-Roussillon (Pyrénées-Orientales)

2522

Les Casteillets***
☎ +33 (0)4-68832683
FAX +33 (0)4-68833967
⌚ 1/1 - 31/12
@ jc@campinglescasteillets.com

5ha 134T(95-100m²) 10-6A CEE

1 ABC**F**IJKLMPST
2 FKLRTVX
3 ABGMNQR
4 (C+G 1/4-15/10)
(Q+R 1/7-31/8) (U+V+X ⌚)
(Y 1/7-31/8) (Z ⌚)
5 AEGIJKLNPUW
6 CEG**K**(N 2km)OTV

💬 Campsite situated close to mountains and the sea. Ideal spot for relaxation. The area offers many opportunities for a day out, such as Céret, Perpignan and Spain.

🚗 A9 exit 43. Towards Céret via D115. Campsite is signposted.

Montescot
D615
D618 / Le Boulou
D115 / A9
Céret / D900
AP-7

CC € **13** 1/1-6/7 25/8-31/12

N 42°30'37'' E 2°47'0''

St. Pons-de-Thomières, F-34220 / Languedoc-Roussillon (Hérault)

2523

Les Cerisiers du Jaur***
route de Bédarieux
☎ +33 (0)4-67953033
⌚ 7/4 - 14/10
@ info@cerisierdujaur.com

4,8ha 106T(100-170m²) 16A CEE

1 ACD**G**IJKLMPST
2 ACGIJLRTVWXY
3 ABGHJKNRW
4 (C+H+Q+R ⌚) (T 1/7-30/8)
(U+V ⌚)
5 **A**CEFGIJKLMNOPQR**ST**UW
XYZ
6 CDEGK(N 1km)V

💬 The campsite is in an old cherry orchard, alongside which the River Jaur flows. Peaceful climate, plenty of greenery in the area and excellent cycling and walking routes. Free wifi for CampingCard ACSI guests.

🚗 Exit at Beziers on A9 motorway. Continue towards St. Pons-de-Thomières on the N112 or D612. At St. Pons D908 direction Bédarieux. 500 metres on the right.

Labastide-Rouairoux
D908
D612
D920
D907
Saint-Chinian

CC € **17** 7/4-6/7 25/8-13/10 7=6, 14=11, 30=20

N 43°29'25'' E 2°47'6''

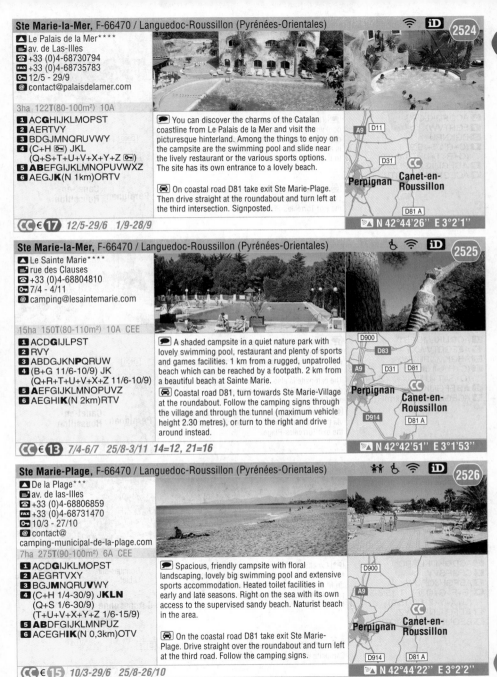

Ste Marie-la-Mer, F-66470 / Languedoc-Roussillon (Pyrénées-Orientales) 🛜 iD (2524)

Le Palais de la Mer****
av. de Las-Illes
☎ +33 (0)4-68730794
FAX +33 (0)4-68735783
⊙ 12/5 - 29/9
@ contact@palaisdelamer.com

3ha 122T(80-100m²) 10A

1 ACG**H**IJKLMOPST
2 AERTVY
3 BDGJMNQRUVWY
4 (C+H ⊙) JKL
   (Q+S+T+U+V+X+Y+Z ⊙)
5 **AB**EFGIJKLMNOPUVWXZ
6 AEGJ**K**(N 1km)ORTV

💬 You can discover the charms of the Catalan coastline from Le Palais de la Mer and visit the picturesque hinterland. Among the things to enjoy on the campsite are the swimming pool and slide near the lively restaurant or the various sports options. The site has its own entrance to a lovely beach.

🚗 On coastal road D81 take exit Ste Marie-Plage. Then drive straight at the roundabout and turn left at the third intersection. Signposted.

Perpignan Canet-en-Roussillon

CC € **17** 12/5-29/6 1/9-28/9   N 42°44'26'' E 3°2'1''

Ste Marie-la-Mer, F-66470 / Languedoc-Roussillon (Pyrénées-Orientales) ♿ 🛜 iD (2525)

Le Sainte Marie****
rue des Clauses
☎ +33 (0)4-68804810
⊙ 7/4 - 4/11
@ camping@lesaintemarie.com

15ha 150T(80-110m²) 10A CEE

1 ACD**G**IJLPST
2 RVY
3 ABDGJKN**P**QRUW
4 (B+G 11/6-10/9) JK
   (Q+R+T+U+V+X+Z 11/6-10/9)
5 **A**EFGIJKLMNOPUVZ
6 AEGHI**K**(N 2km)RTV

💬 A shaded campsite in a quiet nature park with lovely swimming pool, restaurant and plenty of sports and games facilities. 1 km from a rugged, unpatrolled beach which can be reached by a footpath. 2 km from a beautiful beach at Sainte Marie.

🚗 Coastal road D81, turn towards Ste Marie-Village at the roundabout. Follow the camping signs through the village and through the tunnel (maximum vehicle height 2.30 metres), or turn to the right and drive around instead.

Perpignan Canet-en-Roussillon

CC € **13** 7/4-6/7 25/8-3/11 14=12, 21=16   N 42°42'51'' E 3°1'53''

Ste Marie-Plage, F-66470 / Languedoc-Roussillon (Pyrénées-Orientales) 👫 ♿ 🛜 iD (2526)

De la Plage***
av. de las-Illes
☎ +33 (0)4-68806859
FAX +33 (0)4-68731470
⊙ 10/3 - 27/10
@ contact@
camping-municipal-de-la-plage.com

7ha 275T(90-100m²) 6A CEE

1 ACD**G**IJKLMOPST
2 AEGRTVXY
3 BGJ**M**NQRU**V**WY
4 (C+H 1/4-30/9) J**KLN**
   (Q+S 1/6-30/9)
   (T+U+V+X+Y+Z 1/6-15/9)
5 **AB**DFGIJKLMNPUZ
6 ACEGHI**K**(N 0,3km)OTV

💬 Spacious, friendly campsite with floral landscaping, lovely big swimming pool and extensive sports accommodation. Heated toilet facilities in early and late seasons. Right on the sea with its own access to the supervised sandy beach. Naturist beach in the area.

🚗 On the coastal road D81 take exit Ste Marie-Plage. Drive straight over the roundabout and turn left at the third road. Follow the camping signs.

Perpignan Canet-en-Roussillon

CC € **15** 10/3-29/6 25/8-26/10   N 42°44'22'' E 3°2'2''

Torreilles-Plage, F-66440 / Languedoc-Roussillon (Pyrénées-Orientales)   ♿ 🛜 **iD** (2527)

🏕 Le Trivoly****
📧 boulevard des Plages
☎ +33 (0)2-51330505
🔓 30/3 - 29/9
@ info@chadotel.com

5ha 51T(80-120m²) 16A CEE

1 ACD**F**IJKLOPS
2 FGRTVWX
3 BGKNRU
4 (C+G 1/5-15/9) J
   (Q+R+T+U+Z 1/6-8/9)
5 **AB**FGIJKLMNPUZ
6 ACEG**K**(N 3km)RTV

💬 This campsite, equipped with a heated swimming pool with slides, is located 800m from a patrolled clean beach and close to a shopping centre. The site is an ideal location for lovely day trips along the coast to the Pyrenees or Spain.

🚗 A9 exit Perpignan-Centre. Direction Le Barcarès via the D83, then direction Canet/St. Cyprien as far as the exit Torreilles-Plage.

CC € **15**   30/3-7/7   26/8-28/9

📡 N 42°45'57'' E 3°1'37''

Torreilles-Plage, F-66440 / Languedoc-Roussillon (Pyrénées-Orientales)   👫 ♿ 🛜 ✿ **iD** (2528)

🏕 Les Tropiques****
📧 boulevard de la Plage
☎ +33 (0)4-68280509
📠 +33 (0)4-68284890
🔓 1/5 - 15/9
@ contact@lestropiques.fr

8ha 88T(100-115m²) 10A CEE

1 AC**G**IJKLMOPST
2 AEFGRTVWXY
3 ABGKMNRUVWY
4 (C+H 🅾) J**KLP**
   (Q+S+T+U+V+X+Y+Z 🅾)
5 **AB**EFGIJKLMNPUWZ
6 ACEGHJ**K**M(N 3km)RTV

💬 This friendly family campsite is located 400m from the lovely Torreilles Plage beach, where you can enjoy the heated swimming pool, the various wellness facilities or a delicious meal in the restaurent. The campsite is also a perfect starting point for many day trips possible along the coast to the Pyrenees and Spain.

🚗 A9 exit Perpignan-Centre. Direction Le Barcarès via the D83, then direction Canet/St. Cyprien as far as the exit Torreilles-Plage.

CC € **17**   1/5-7/7   27/8-13/9   7=6

📡 N 42°46'3'' E 3°1'47''

Trèbes, F-11800 / Languedoc-Roussillon (Aude)   ♿ 🛜 **iD** (2529)

🏕 A l'Ombre des Micocouliers****
📧 chemin de la Lande
☎ +33 (0)4-68786175
📠 +33 (0)4-68788877
🔓 1/4 - 30/9
@ infos@campingmicocouliers.com

2ha 70T(90-120m²) 16A CEE

1 ACD**G**HIJKLMPQ
2 CFGRSVY
3 ABF**G**HJQRUW
4 (E+F+G+Q 🅾) (T 15/6-31/8)
   (U+X+Y+Z 1/6-15/9)
5 **A**EFGJLNPUVYZ
6 BEGIJ**K**(N 0,3km)OTV

💬 Excellent location for visiting nearby Carcassonne from a peaceful campsite. Cycling along the Canal du Midi and all types of sport available. A central point for Cathar country with its typical villages and fortresses.

🚗 A61/E80 exit 24 direction Trèbes via the RN113. Campsite well signposted in village.

CC € **15**   1/4-8/7   26/8-29/9

📡 N 43°12'24'' E 2°26'31''

Uzès, F-30700 / Languedoc-Roussillon (Gard) 👫 ♿ 🛜 iD (2530)

▲ Centre de Vacances Le
  Moulin Neuf***
🏠 St. Quentin-la-Poterie
☎ +33 (0)4-66221721
📠 +33 (0)4-66229182
📅 30/3 - 30/9
@ lemoulinneuf@yahoo.fr
5ha 137T(90-110m²) 2,5-5A

1 ACDGIJL**PQ**
2 LMRVXY
3 ABF**G**HM**NQ**RU
4 (A 4/7-24/8) (C+Q 🅾)
  (R 1/7-30/9) (T+U 15/6-25/8)
  (V 15/7-25/8) (X 20/6-31/8)
5 **A**EFGIJKLMNOPUW
6 EGJ(N 1,5km)OTV

💬 You will have complete rest in the shade of
deciduous trees at this campsite. It has a varied
range of entertainment and recreational possibilities.
The area offers many chances for making excursions:
just think of the Pont du Gard, Avignon, Nîmes etc.

🚗 From the D982 take Uzes-Bagnols D5, direction
St. Quentin. Then D405.

Connaux
D979
CC
D982 · Uzès
D6086
Remoulins

CC € **15** 30/3-6/7 24/8-29/9   🏖 N 44°1'56'' E 4°27'20''

Vallabrègues/Beaucaire/Tarasc., F-30300 / Languedoc-Roussillon (Gard) 👫 🛜 iD (2531)

▲ Lou Vincen***
☎ +33 (0)4-66592129
📅 1/4 - 1/11
@ contact@campinglouvincen.fr

1,4ha 69T(< 100m²) 6-8A

1 ACD**G**HIJKLPST
2 CDGRSTVXY
3 AGHJKLMNR**W**
4 (B 1/6-30/9) (Q+R 🅾)
  (T+Z 15/6-30/9)
5 **A**GIJKLMNPUVXY
6 AEGH**K**(N 0,3km)OT

💬 A basic, clean, shaded and attractively planted
campsite. Wonderful for walking and cycling. Located
by the Rhône between Beaucaire, Avignon, St. Rémy
and the Camargue.

🚗 From Beaucaire-Tarascon to Vallabrègues.
The campsite is signposted in the village next to the
Rhône.

D6086
A9
D2
CC
D999
D35 D570 N
Beaucaire
Bellegarde
D15

CC € **17** 1/4-30/6 20/8-31/10 7=6, 14=12, 21=18   🏖 N 43°51'18'' E 4°37'32''

Valras-Plage, F-34350 / Languedoc-Roussillon (Hérault) 👫 ♿ 🛜 iD (2532)

▲ Lou Village****
🏠 chemin des Montilles
☎ +33 (0)4-67373379
📠 +33 (0)4-67375356
📅 28/4 - 9/9
@ info@louvillage.com

7ha 100T(80-100m²) 10A CEE

1 ACDGIJKLOPQ
2 AEFGLRTVXY
3 BGKL**M**N**OP**RUWY
4 (C+H 🅾) IJK
  (Q+S+T+U+V+X+Y+Z 🅾)
5 **AB**EFGIJKLMNPUZ
6 ACFGJM(N 1km)ORTVWX

💬 A good, friendly campsite with plenty of fun on
the beach and also in the fabulous leisure pool with
its heated pool and jacuzzi. The owners do all they
can to satisfy everyone. The centre of lively Valras-
Plage and the delightful harbour at Port-Vendres are
merely 2½ km away.

🚗 From Valras the campsite is located by the sea
just before La Yole, path on your left, about 200
metres left. Follow signs campsite Valras Plage Ouest.

Vias
D609 Sérignan
A9 Valras-Plage
CC
D1118
D168
D332

CC € **15** 28/4-7/7 25/8-8/9   🏖 N 43°14'1'' E 3°15'38''

Valras-Plage, F-34350 / Languedoc-Roussillon (Hérault)

♿ 🛜 **iD** (2533)

🏕 Sandaya Blue Bayou*****
📧 Vendres Plage Ouest
☎ +33 (0)4-67374197
📅 20/4 - 16/9
@ bluebayou@sandaya.fr

6ha 350T(80-100m²) 10A CEE

1 AC**G**IJKLMPST
2 AEFGRSVWXY
3 BGKMN**OP**UVWY
4 (C+H 🖭) IJM
　(Q+S+T+U+V+X+Y+Z 🖭)
5 **AB**DEFGIJKLMNP**ST**UZ
6 AEG**K**(N 2,5km)ORTV

💬 A large campsite with pitches for touring guests. Some have private toilet facilities. Refurbished leisure pool with water playpark for small children. Lovely swimming pool. 300m from a sandy beach in a beautiful nature reserve. Attractive location, close to the sea and 5 km from the centre of Valras-Plage.

🚍 Campsite located on the Valras-Plage Ouest-Vendres-Plage D37E9. Campsite south west of Vendre-Plage.

D609　D64　A9　CC　D1118
Saint-Pierre-la-Mer
D168　D332

CC € **17** 20/4-6/7　1/9-15/9　　📍 N 43°13'38'' E 3°14'38''

Valras-Plage/Vendres-Plage, F-34350 / Languedoc-Roussillon (Hérault)

♿ 🛜 **iD** (2534)

🏕 Palmira Beach***
📧 avenue du port de Vendres
☎ +33 (0)4-67942900
📅 2/4 - 30/10
@ contact@palmirabeach.fr

4ha 50T(> 100m²) 10A CEE

1 ACD**F**IJKLM**P**ST
2 AEFGRSVWX
3 BGHJKN**OP**RUWY
4 (C+H 15/5-15/9) J**KMN**
　(Q+S 🖭)
　(T+U+V+X+Z 1/5-15/9)
5 **AB**EFGJLMNPQ**S**UX
6 ACEG**K**L(N 5km)OTV

💬 Welcome to this agreeable camp site where a 300m footpath links it to a lovely sandy beach. There is a lovely water play park for young children next to the heated swimming pool and toddlers' pool. Spacious touring pitches, some with private toilet facilities and rental caravans separated from each other. The foliage offers some shade and flowering oleanders give the whole site a floral appearance.

🚍 From Valras follow Vendres-Plage signs. Then follow camping signs.

D609　D64　A9　CC　D1118
Saint-Pierre-la-Mer
D168　D332

CC € **15** 2/4-2/7　26/8-29/10　　📍 N 43°13'44'' E 3°14'44''

Vauvert, F-30600 / Languedoc-Roussillon (Gard)

👪 ♿ 🛜 ✿ **iD** (2535)

🏕 Flower Camping Le Mas de Mourgues***
📧 Gallician
☎ +33 (0)4-66733088
📅 15/3 - 15/10
@ info@masdemourgues.com

2ha 57T(50-100m²) 10A CEE

1 ACD**G**IJKLMPST
2 STWXY
3 AGHJKR
4 (C 1/4-1/10) (Q+R 🖭)
　(T+U+V 1/4-30/9) (Z 🖭)
5 AFGIJKLMNPQUWZ
6 ACEG**K**(N 5km)T

💬 Welcome to Camping Le Mas de Mourgues, located in an open area of the Camargue in the Gard between Nîmes and Saintes Maries de la Mer. A family campsite with 58 pitches. La Camargue is also known for the sun, its beaches and for doing nothing. Great for cycling. Nice cycle path to Aigues-Mortes and on the Via Rhona.

🚍 A9, exit 26 direction Gallargues. Then N313 direction Aimargues. Then N572. Campsite on the left just beyond Vauvert, dir. St. Jilles.

A9　D135　A54　D42
Lunel Vauvert　Saint-Gilles
D979　CC　D6572
D58　D570

CC € **15** 15/3-14/7　1/9-14/10　　📍 N 43°39'16'' E 4°17'44''

Vendres, F-34350 / Languedoc-Roussillon (Hérault)

👫 ⊗ ♿ 📶 **iD** (2536)

🏕 La Plage et du Bord de Mer
📧 av. de la Mediterranee
☎ +33 (0)4-67373438
📠 +33 (0)4-67373374
🔓 28/4 - 16/9
@ reservation@
camping-plage-mediterranee.com
13ha 466T(80-100m²) 10A CEE

1 ACDEIJKLMOPST
2 AEFGLRSVWXY
3 ABGHK**MNQ**RUWY
4 (A 1/7-31/8) (C+G 🔓) IJK
(Q+S+T+U+V+X+Y+Z 🔓)
5 **AB**EFGIJKLMNOPUVZ
6 CDEGK(N 0km)ORSTV

💬 A peaceful and spacious campsite with direct access to a lovely sandy beach. Spacious pitches with attractive landscaping. The campsite has an attractive aquapark with swimming pools and a large slide. Excellent toilet facilities. Playground equipment throughout the campsite, including in the lovely children's pool. Free wifi throughout the grounds.

🚗 The campsite is located on the boulevard Valras-Plage Ouest. Follow the signs when entering Valras-Plage.

Map: Vias, D609, Sérignan, Salles-d'Aude, A9, CC, D1118, D168, D332

CC € **17** 28/4-23/6 25/8-15/9 14=13 📷 **N 43°14'7'' E 3°16'8''**

Vendres-Plage/Valras-Plage, F-34350 / Languedoc-Roussillon (Hérault)

♿ 📶 **iD** (2537)

🏕 Sandaya Les Vagues****
📧 chemin de Montilles
☎ +33 (0)4-67373312
📠 +33 (0)4-67375036
🔓 6/4 - 16/9
@ t.hannier@sandaya.fr

8ha 107T(85-100m²) 6A

1 ACD**F**IJKLMOP
2 AEFGLSTVXY
3 ABGKN**OP**QRUVWY
4 (C+H 🔓) IJK
(Q+S+T+U+V+Y+Z 🔓)
5 **AB**EFGIJKLMNOPUVXYZ
6 ACEGJ**K**M(N 5km)ORTUVX

💬 Located 500 metres from the Languedoc beaches. The shaded campsite comprises three separate sections. Lovely heated swimming pool with wave pool and slide. Many sights, activities and watersports opportunities in the area.

🚗 From Valras follow Valras-Plage Ouest signs. Then follow camping signs.

Map: Vias, Sérignan, Nissan-Lez-Enserune, A9, CC, D1118, D168, D332

CC € **17** 6/4-6/7 1/9-15/9 📷 **N 43°13'51'' E 3°15'13''**

Vias, F-34450 / Languedoc-Roussillon (Hérault)

👫 ♿ 📶 🌼 **iD** (2538)

🏕 Sunêlia Domaine de la
Dragonnière*****
📧 RD612
☎ +33 (0)4-67010310
📠 +33 (0)4-67217339
🔓 30/3 - 1/11
@ contact@dragonniere.com
20ha 38T(100-120m²) 10A CEE

1 ACD**F**IJKLM**P**S
2 ADFGRVX
3 BC**F**GJKLNRUZ
4 (C+F+H 🔓) IJ**L**M**NP**
(Q+S+T+U+V+X+Y+Z 🔓)
5 **AB**CDEFGHJLNPSTUXYZ
6 ABEGHJ**K**LM(N 4km)O**P**RT
VWX

💬 Lovely campsite with extensive leisure activities. Leisure pool including an indoor pool, fully heated from the opening date and a beautiful lagoon with sandy beach. Individual heated toilet facilities. All amenities open for entire season. Free bus to the beach. Entertainment in several languages all week.

🚗 From A9 between exits 34 and 36, dir. A75 Beziers-centre. After toll station, exit 64 dir. Beziers/Cap d'Agde. Turn right at crossing near airport. Follow signs.

Map: D13, A75, D18, A9, Marseillan, Béziers, CC, Agde, D64

CC € **19** 30/3-21/6 3/9-31/10 📷 **N 43°18'45'' E 3°21'48''**

Vias-Plage, F-34450 / Languedoc-Roussillon (Hérault) ♿ 📶 ✿ 🆔 (2539)

🔺 Camping Club Californie-Plage****
🏠 Côte Ouest
☎ +33 (0)4-67216469
📠 +33 (0)4-67215462
🔓 1/4 - 30/9
@ info@californie-plage.fr

5,5ha 273T(80-100m²) 10A CEE

1 ACD**G**IJKLM**P**Q
2 AEF**Q**SVWXY
3 **B**F**G**KLNRUWY
4 (C+E+H 🔓) IJKP
  (Q+S+T+U+V+W+X+Y+Z 🔓)
5 **AB**EFGIJKLMNOPUWZ
6 ACEGHJ**K**(N 2,5km)RTVX

💬 A well-equipped campsite with a beautiful leisure pool, positioned by the sea in a poplar wood. The pitches are marked out by hedges including oleanders. The heated indoor swimming pool has a roof that can be opened.

🚗 A9 exit Agde/Pézenas direction Agde, then N112 exit Vias-Plage, then over the Côte Ouest bridge and follow the signs.

CC € **15** 1/4-29/6 1/9-29/9   🏖 N 43°17'26'' E 3°23'55''

Vias-Plage, F-34450 / Languedoc-Roussillon (Hérault) 👫 ♿ 📶 🆔 (2540)

🔺 Camping Club Le Napoléon*****
🏠 1171 av. de la Méditerranée
☎ +33 (0)4-67010780
📠 +33 (0)4-67010785
🔓 28/4 - 23/9
@ reception@camping-napoleon.fr

3,4ha 120T(80-100m²) 10A CEE

1 AC**G**IJKLM**P**ST
2 AEFRSVY
3 AB**F**GJKLMN**OPQ**RUVWY
4 (C+H 🔓) IJ**KL**NP
  (Q+S+T+U+V+W+X+Y+Z 🔓)
5 **AB**FGIJKLMNOPUVWXYZ
6 CEG**IK**M(N 1,5km)OQRTVX

💬 A fine campsite with extensive amenities and entertainment for all ages. Tall poplars offer plenty of shade. 150m from the sea and a lovely beach with fine sand. Many boutiques, terraces, restaurants and shops next to the campsite. The new leisure pool is heated from the opening day. You can relax in the wellness and body fitness.

🚗 D612 exit Vias-Plage, then campings Sud, at the end of the road to the right.

CC € **19** 28/4-8/7 26/8-22/9   🏖 N 43°17'31'' E 3°24'58''

Vias-Plage, F-34450 / Languedoc-Roussillon (Hérault) ♿ 📶 🆔 (2541)

🔺 Helios****
🏠 avenue des Pêcheurs
☎ 📠 +33 (0)4-67216366
🔓 21/4 - 30/9
@ contact@camping-helios.com

3ha 108T(80-90m²) 4-6A CEE

1 ACD**G**IJKLMPS
2 ACEFSVY
3 BGNRUWY
4 (C+E+H 🔓) J**KLN**P
  (Q+S+T+U+X+Z 🔓)
5 **A**FGIJKLMNOPSUVZ
6 AEGH**K**(N 4km)OTV

💬 A quiet, natural campsite with a homely ambiance. 200 metres from the beach on the small River Libron and within walking distance from the lively centre of Vias-Plage. The toilet facilities have been renovated and there is a new wellness amenity. From 2015 there is a beautiful new heated leisure pool, partly covered.

🚗 A9 exit Agde/Pézenas. D612 direction Agde; exit Vias-Plage. Then 'campings Sud' and follow the signs at the roundabout.

CC € **15** 21/4-6/7 25/8-29/9   🏖 N 43°17'33'' E 3°24'26''

Vias-Plage, F-34450 / Languedoc-Roussillon (Hérault) ⚹ 🛜 iD (2542)

🔺 L'Air Marin****
☎ +33 (0)4-67216490
📠 +33 (0)4-67217679
🕐 7/4 - 15/9
@ info@camping-air-marin.fr

8ha 150T(70-120m²) 6A

1 AGIJLMPS
2 ACFRTVXY
3 ABGJMNRUVW
4 (C+F+G 🔒) JKP(Q+S 🔒)
   (T+U 1/7-31/8)
   (V+X+Y+Z 🔒)
5 ABFGIJKLMOPUVWX
6 CEGK(N 1km)ORTV

💬 A large, peaceful campsite in the shade of plane trees on the Canal du Midi, 10 minute walk from the sandy beach of Vias-Plage. Free indoor heated swimming pool. All buildings are in Mexican style.

🚗 A9 exit Agde/Pézenas direction Agde, then N112 direction Vias-Plage, then campsites Côte Est and follow signs.

CC €19 7/4-29/6 25/8-14/9   N 43°18'8'' E 3°25'19''

Vias-Plage, F-34450 / Languedoc-Roussillon (Hérault) ⚹ 🛜 iD (2543)

🔺 Le Méditerranée Plage****
🚏 D137
☎ +33 (0)4-67909907
📠 +33 (0)4-67909917
🕐 24/3 - 29/9
@ contact@
   mediterranee-plage.com

7ha 100T(80-90m²) 6-10A CEE

1 ACDGIJKLMPQ
2 AEFRSTVXY
3 ABDGJKMNOPQRUWY
4 (A+C+H 🔒) J
   (Q+S+T+U+V+X+Y+Z 🔒)
5 ABDEFGIJKLMNPUVWZ
6 ABCEGHIJM(N 5km)ORTV

💬 A well-run four-star campsite by a nice sandy beach. The swimming pools are heated from the opening date. Free wifi.

🚗 A9/A75 exit 63 Béziers-centre, dir. Agde/Sète. After 3.5 km to Agde/Sète at roundabout. Right after 1.5 km dir. Portiragnes-Plage. Over the Canal du Midi bridge, turn left and follow signs.

CC €17 24/3-30/6 25/8-28/9   N 43°16'55'' E 3°22'15''

Vias-Plage, F-34450 / Languedoc-Roussillon (Hérault) 🛜 iD (2544)

🔺 Le Roucan West***
🚏 Côte Ouest
☎ +33 (0)4-67216464
🕐 31/3 - 29/9
@ info@campingleroucan.com

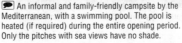

3ha 70T(75-100m²) 10A CEE

1 ACDGIJKLMPS
2 AEFSUVWXY
3 BGJPRWY
4 (C+G 🔒)
   (Q+R+T+U+V 15/6-15/9)
   (Y 15/6-30/8) (Z 15/6-15/9)
5 AFGJLNPUX
6 EGK(N 6km)RTV

💬 An informal and family-friendly campsite by the Mediterranean, with a swimming pool. The pool is heated (if required) during the entire opening period. Only the pitches with sea views have no shade.

🚗 A9 exit Agde/Pézenas direction Agde. Then N112 Vias-Plage, over the bridge Côte Ouest. Then follow signs.

CC €13 31/3-6/7 1/9-28/9   N 43°17'13'' E 3°23'30''

Vic-la-Gardiole, F-34110 / Languedoc-Roussillon (Hérault)

👪 ♿ 📶 **iD** (2545)

🏕 Flower Camping Altea★★★
✉ 1 route des Aresquières
☎ +33 (0)4-67781409
🔓 1/1 - 31/12
@ contact@alteacamping.com

2,5ha 68T(80-100m²) 6A CEE

1 ACD**G**IJKLM**P**S
2 AGNRTVXY
3 AGIRUW
4 (B+G 1/6-30/9)
(Q+T+U+V+Z 1/7-31/8)
5 **A**EFGJLNPUZ
6 EG**K**(N 3km)

💬 Camping Altea is open all year, has a lovely swimming pool, spacious pitches and is easily accessible. The campsite is ideally located: halfway between Montpellier and Sète, close to lakes and the Mediterranean.

🚗 A9 exit Sète. Towards Vic-la-Gardiole at roundabout. Campsite on the D612.

Montpellier — Lattes — D986 — D2 — D613 — A9 — CC — D612 — Sète — Frontignan

CC € **15** *1/1-7/7 25/8-31/12*

🗺 N 43°30'2'' E 3°47'15''

Villegly-en-Minervois, F-11600 / Languedoc-Roussillon (Aude)

♿ 📶 **iD** (2546)

🏕 Sites & Paysages Le
Moulin de Ste Anne★★★★
✉ chemin de Ste Anne
☎ +33 (0)4-68722080
🔓 1/4 - 31/10
@ contact@
moulindesainteanne.com

1,6ha 43T(< 120m²) 10A CEE

1 AC**F**IJLPST
2 CGIJRTVX
3 ABHJNRU
4 (C 1/5-30/9) (G 1/6-30/9) K
(Q+T+U+V+X 15/6-25/8)
5 **A**DGIJKLMNOPUXYZ
6 CEGK(N 0,2km)

💬 This small, peacefully situated campsite is positioned on the edge of the village of Villegly in the Minervois region. Trips out to Carcassonne are possible. Walking routes are conducted in July and August which take you past archaeological discoveries.

🚗 A61 exit 23 direction Mazamet. At the roundabout direction Villegly (signposted).

D73 — D118 — CC — D11 — D620 — Carcassonne — Trèbes — D610 — A61

CC € **17** *1/4-30/6 1/9-30/10*

🗺 N 43°16'59'' E 2°26'29''

Villemoustaussou, F-11620 / Languedoc-Roussillon (Aude)

♿ 📶 **iD** (2547)

🏕 Das Pinhiers★★★
✉ ch. du Pont Neuf
☎ +33 (0)4-68478190
📠 +33 (0)4-68714349
🔓 30/3 - 5/11
@ campindaspinhiers@wanadoo.fr

2ha 56T(80m²) 10A CEE

1 AC**G**HIJL**P**ST
2 FIRTVWXY
3 B**F**GHJKQRU**W**
4 (B 10/6-30/9)
(Q+R+T 1/6-30/9)
(Z 15/6-15/9)
5 **A**EFGIJKLMNPUVZ
6 CEGJ(N 1km)RTV

NEW

💬 Very peacefully located campsite perfect for various days out such as Minervoirs and Carcassone.

🚗 The campsite is located 800 metres outside Villemoustaussou. The town is located north of Carcassonne.

D103 — D620 — D629 — CC — D101 — D33 — D119 — Carcassonne — Trèbes — D118 — A61 — D3 — D610

CC € **13** *30/3-6/7 1/9-4/11*

🗺 N 43°15'35'' E 2°21'58''

Villeneuve-lès-Béziers, F-34420 / Languedoc-Roussillon (Hérault) 👫 ♿ 🛜 (2548)

🏕 Les Berges du Canal***
✉ promenade des Vernets
☎ +33 (0)4-67393609
🔒 10/3 - 20/10
@ contact@campinglbdc.com

1,5ha 30**T**(80-90m²) 16A CEE

1 BCD**G**IJKLM**P**ST
2 CFG**R**TVY
3 ABCGJKLNRUW
4 (B+G 15/5-15/9) **N**
　(Q 16/4-30/9)
　(T+U+V+X+Y+Z 1/5-30/9)
5 **AB**DEFGIJLNPRSUVWZ
6 CDEG**K**L(N 0,1km)ORTV

💬 A quiet, well located, friendly family campsite next to the Canal du Midi. Just a few minutes' walk from Villeneuve-lès-Béziers. Ideally suited as a base for exploring the region. Good place for starting cycle tours. 7 km from the beach. Good, well maintained toilet facilities.

🚗 The campsite is located in the village on the Canal du Midi. When approaching from Béziers: before the bridge to the left.

Béziers — D909, A75, D13, A9, Vias, D609, Sérignan

CC € **17** 10/3-6/7 25/8-19/10 7=6, 14=12, 21=18 　　🏕 N 43°19'0'' E 3°17'4''

Villeneuve-lez-Avignon/Avignon, F-30400 / Languedoc-Roussillon (Gard) 👫 ♿ 🛜 **iD** (2549)

🏕 Campéole L'Île des Papes****
✉ 1497 RD 780
☎ +33 (0)4-90151590
📠 +33 (0)4-90151591
🔒 30/3 - 4/11
@ ile-des-papes@campeole.com

20ha 183**T**(100m²) 6-10A CEE

1 ACD**G**IJKLMO**P**ST
2 CFGKLRSTVW**X**Y
3 B**F**GHJKN**Q**RU**W**
4 (B+G 1/5-30/9) I(Q+R 🔒)
　(T 1/6-31/8) (U 🔒)
　(V+Y+Z 1/4-30/9)
5 **AB**EFGIJLMNPUWZ
6 ACDEGH**J**(N 5km)RTV

💬 Spaciously appointed, luxurious campsite with very many amenities, located on an island in the Rhône. 6 km from Avignon.

🚗 A9, exit Roquemaure, direction Roquemaure-centre, then direction Sauveterre, and Barrage-de-Villeneuve. Campsite signposted.

N580, D907, A9, A7, Villeneuve-lès-Avignon, D976, Avignon, D2, D6

CC € **17** 30/3-6/7 25/8-3/11 　　🏕 N 43°59'37'' E 4°49'4''

Agay/St. Raphaël, F-83530 / Provence-Alpes-Côte d'Azur (Var) ♿ 🛜 **iD** (2550)

🏕 Estérel Caravaning*****
✉ 4481 avenue des Golfs
☎ +33 (0)4-94820328
📠 +33 (0)4-94828737
🔒 24/3 - 29/9
@ contact@esterel-caravaning.fr

15ha 164**T**(100-280m²) 10-16A

1 ACGJKLMOPT
2 JK**R**TVWXY
3 B**F**GHJLMNQRSUV
4 (C+F+H 🔒) IKMN
　(Q+R+T+U+V+X+Z 🔒)
5 **AB**CDEFGHIJKLMNOPQRST
　UWXY
6 ABCDEGIKLMOPRTV

💬 Fantastic facilities when it comes to swimming pools and wellness. Very professional, often very spectacular varied entertainment. Campsite is exceptionally well-maintained and organised.

🚗 From the centre of Agay under the viaduct. The campsite is located to the right after about 3 km.

A8, D4, N7, D6007, D6098, Fréjus, D559, D7, Saint-Raphaël

CC € **19** 24/3-7/7 2/9-17/9 　　🏕 N 43°27'15'' E 6°49'58''

Aiguines, F-83630 / Provence-Alpes-Côte d'Azur (Var)   ♿ 📶 iD (2551)

🔺 L'Aigle***
✉ Quartier Saint Pierre
☎ +33 (0)4-94842375
🔓 28/4 - 17/9
@ aigle@campasun.eu

5ha 70T(80-120m²) 6A CEE

1 ACDG**IJ**KL**P**
2 BIJKRVWXY
3 BHJRT
4 K(Q+U+V+X+Y+Z 🔓)
5 **A**CFGHIJKLMNPUVZ
6 ACDEGJ(N 0,4km)TV

💬 A very nicely located campsite with breathtaking panoramas of Lac Sainte Croix. Relatively modest amenities but very well maintained. A few minutes' walk from the picturesque village of Aiguines.

🚗 Campsite located 600m east of Aiguines (D19).

Moustiers-Sainte-Marie · Roumoules · Riez · D953 · D11 · CC · D957 · D952 · D71

CC € 15 28/4-9/7 27/8-16/9   📡 N 43°46'35'' E 6°14'43''

Albaron/Arles, F-13123 / Provence-Alpes-Côte d'Azur (Bouches-du-Rhône)   ♿ 📶 iD (2552)

🔺 Le Domaine du Crin Blanc***
✉ CD37 - Hameau de Saliers
☎ +33 (0)4-66874878
🔓 30/3 - 30/9
@ camping-crin.blanc@wanadoo.fr

4,5ha 50T(90-160m²) 10A CEE

1 ACD**G**HIJKLMPST
2 KRSTVX
3 B**F**GHJMN**OP**R**U**W
4 (C+H 1/4-30/9) J(Q+R 🔓)
  (T+U+V+Y+Z 1/4-15/9)
5 **AB**EFGIJKLNPUVZ
6 ACEGHJ**K**(N 3km)TV

💬 Spacious campsite located in the Carmargue National Park, with three heated swimming pools and a water slide. 20 km from Arles, Provence and the Mediterranean Sea.

🚗 From Arles D570 direction Stes Maries-de-la-Mer. In Albaron turn right onto CD37 direction St. Gilles. After 7 km on the left.

D15 · D42 · A54 · D38 · D6113 · Saint-Gilles · Arles · D6572 · CC · D36 · D570 · D37

CC € 17 30/3-7/7 26/8-29/9 7=5, 21=14   📡 N 43°39'44'' E 4°28'26''

Annot, F-04240 / Provence-Alpes-Côte d'Azur (Alpes-de-Haute-Prov)   ♿ 📶 iD (2553)

🔺 La Ribière**
✉ route du Fugeret
☎ +33 (0)4-92832144
🔓 24/3 - 1/11
@ info@la-ribiere.com

1ha 65T(70-100m²) 10A CEE

1 ACD**G**IJKLM**P**ST
2 CKORTVWXY
3 AGHJN**OP**R**U**W
4 (Q+T+V+Z 🔓)
5 **A**DEFGIJKLMNOPUZ
6 ACEGJ(N 1km)TV

💬 La Ribière is situated at an altitude of 700 metres between Mercantour, Verdon and the Mediterranean. It is located on the edge of the picturesque village of Annot. Whether you are a sports or nature lover, you will be charmed by 'Le pays d'Annot'.

🚗 Campsite 700 metres north of Annot (D908).

D908 · Saint-André-les-Alpes · D2202 · N202 · CC · Annot · D4202 · D955

CC € 15 24/3-14/7 1/9-31/10   📡 N 43°58'18'' E 6°39'28''

Apt, F-84400 / Provence-Alpes-Côte d'Azur (Vaucluse) 🛜 iD 2554

🏕 Le Luberon***
✉ avenue de Saignon
☎ +33 (0)4-90048540
🗓 30/3 - 29/9
@ leluberon@wanadoo.fr

4ha 75**T**(80-150m²) 6A

1 ACD**F**HIJL**P**S
2 JRTVY
3 AFGHRU
4 (C+H+Q+R 🅿) (T 1/5-30/8) (X 4/7-25/8) (Z 21/5-30/8)
5 **AB**DEFGIJKLNOPRUZ
6 CDEGJ**K**(N 1,5km)TV

💬 A campsite in Apt, the perfect starting point for visiting Lubéron and the typical villages of Roussillon, Gordes, Saignon and Bonnieux. A quiet location in a wood with lovely views of the Saignon cliffs. Heated swimming pool.

🚗 Take the N100. At the roundabout on the east side of Apt take the D48 direction Saignon 'village'.

CC € **19** 30/3-1/7 1/9-28/9 ▨ N 43°51'58'' E 5°24'47''

Apt, F-84400 / Provence-Alpes-Côte d'Azur (Vaucluse) ♿ 🛜 iD 2555

🏕 Les Cèdres**
✉ 63 Impasse de la Fantaisie
☎ FAX +33 (0)4-90741461
🗓 1/3 - 31/10
@ campinglescedres@orange.fr

1,8ha 110**T** 10-16A CEE

1 ACD**G**IJL**P**S
2 CGLRTVWXY
3 AGJLR
4 (Q+R+T+V+Z 🅿)
5 **A**DGIJKLMNOPUWZ
6 EGK(N 0,2km)TV

💬 Located close to Apt (300 metres), in the heart of Natural Park Du Luberon. Enjoy a peaceful stay in natural surroundings and enjoy being near many tourist towns. The grounds (1.8 ha) have pitches with electricity, motorhome service points, security (24/7), two toilet blocks, a bar, a grocer's, climbing wall, jeu-de-boules court, swimming pool (at 800 metres) and much more.
🚗 A7 take Cavaillon exit(25). Then D900 to Apt. Follow the signs in centre of village.

CC € **15** 1/3-30/6 28/8-30/10 ▨ N 43°52'39'' E 5°24'11''

Arles/Pont-de-Crau, F-13200 / Provence-Alpes-Côte d'Azur (Bouches-du-Rhône) 👫 ♿ 🛜 iD 2556

🏕 L'Arlesienne***
✉ 145 Draille Marseillaise
☎ +33 (0)4-90960212
🗓 1/4 - 1/11
@ camping@larlesienne.com

2,2ha 74**T**(80-90m²) 6-10A CEE

1 ABCD**G**HIJKLMOPST
2 FGRSTVWX
3 AFGHJKRU**W**
4 (C+H 15/5-15/9) JK (Q+T+U+X+Z 1/4-30/9)
5 **A**EFGIJKLMNPUZ
6 ACDEGJ**K**(N 0,5km)V

💬 A campsite located 3 km from the old centre of Arles. Attractive pitches, the campsite has lovely modernised swimming pools. There is a bus stop 200m from the site. Many activities in the vicinity, famous for Van Gogh and the Romans, among others.

🚗 The campsite is located in Pont-de-Crau on the south-eastern edge of Arles, direction St. Martin-de-Crau. Signposted.

CC € **17** 1/4-6/7 24/8-31/10 7=6 ▨ N 43°39'34'' E 4°39'15''

Aups, F-83630 / Provence-Alpes-Côte d'Azur (Var) ♿ 🛜 iD (2557)

🔺 L'Oasis du Verdon***
📧 181, Carraire n°1, rte de Tourtour
☎ +33 (0)4-94700093
FAX +33 (0)4-94701441
☷ 1/4 - 14/10
@ contact@oasis-verdon.com

2ha 77T(70-137m²) 6-10A

1 ACD**G**IJKL**P**S
2 GKRVWXY
3 BGHJ**M**RU
4 (C ☷) (G 15/5-14/10) (Q ☷) (T+U+V 15/6-15/9) (Z ☷)
5 **A**DFGIJKLMNOPUZ
6 ADEG**K**(N 0,3km)ORTV

💬 The campsite is located a few minutes' walk from the lively Provençale village of Aups. An ideal campsite for a relaxing stay. Heated swimming pool from 1/4 to 13/10. Central location in a very interesting region: Lac du Verdon, Gorges du Verdon, Salernes, Ampus, Tourtour, etc. Very friendly welcome.

🚗 Campsite located 300m from Aups centre. From centre direction Tourtour. Campsite signposted. Final 150m on a private (gravel) road.

Régusse · Salernes · Flayosc
D957 D30 D9 CC D560 D22 D557 D13

CC € **19** 1/4-29/6 27/8-13/10 · 🧭 N 43°37'26'' E 6°13'44''

Avignon, F-84000 / Provence-Alpes-Côte d'Azur (Vaucluse) 🚻 ♿ 🛜 iD (2558)

🔺 Bagatelle***
📧 Île de la Barthelasse
☎ +33 (0)4-90863039
☷ 1/1 - 31/12
@ camping.bagatelle@wanadoo.fr

4ha 227T(80-130m²) 6-16A CEE

1 ACD**F**IJKLMOPST
2 CFGKLMSTVWXY
3 A**F**GHJKNU**W**
4 (Q+S+T+U+V+Y+Z ☷)
5 **A**BDFGIJKLMNOPRUVWXYZ
6 ACDGH**I**J**K**(N 1km)RTV

💬 Camping Bagatelle is located close to the old centre of Avignon, just a 7 minute walk over the bridge. Lovely views of the Palais des Papes from the terraces.

🚗 From the A9 to Avignon. Campsite located on l'Île de la Barthelasse, opposite the Papal Palace. Campsite indicated on the bridge.

Villeneuve-lès-Avignon · Avignon
A9 D907 A7 D2 D28 D7N D6 CC

CC € **17** 1/1-30/6 18/8-30/12 7=6, 14=11, 28=21 · 🧭 N 43°57'10'' E 4°47'59''

Avignon, F-84000 / Provence-Alpes-Côte d'Azur (Vaucluse) ♿ 🛜 iD (2559)

🔺 Camping du Pont d'Avignon****
📧 10 chemin de la Barthelasse
☎ +33 (0)4-90806350
☷ 1/3 - 18/11
@ camping.lepontdavignon@orange.fr

7,6ha 276T(60-100m²) 10A

1 ACD**G**IJKLMO**P**Q
2 CFGKRSTVXY
3 AB**F**GHJKLMNRU**W**
4 (B+G 10/5-1/10) (Q+S+T+U+V+X+Z ☷)
5 **AB**EFGIJKLMNOPUWZ
6 ACFGI**K**(N 2km)RTUV

💬 A campsite in an attractive parkland setting, located opposite the Pont d'Avignon with views of the Palais des Papes.

🚗 From Remoulins and A9 turn right beyond the bridge. Follow 'Île de la Barthelasse' signs.

Sorgues · Avignon · Caumont-sur-Durance
N580 D907 A9 D976 D980 D942 CC D35 A7 D6 D2 D28 D7 N

CC € **15** 1/3-7/7 25/8-17/11 7=6, 14=11 · 🧭 N 43°57'24'' E 4°48'7''

Banon, F-04150 / Provence-Alpes-Côte d'Azur (Alpes-de-Haute-Prov)

👫 ♿ 🛜 **iD** 2560

🏕 Flower Camping L'Epi Bleu***
📧 Les Gravières
☎ +33 (0)4-92733030
🗓 1/4 - 15/10
@ contact@campingepibleu.com

2ha 40T(65-130m²) 10A CEE

1 ACFIJKLM**P**ST
2 BJKTUVWXY
3 ABGHJ**OP**RU
4 (**A** 1/7-31/8)
(C+H 15/5-15/9) J
(Q 1/5-30/9) (R 1/7-31/8)
(T 15/5-31/8) (U+V 1/7-31/8)
(X 15/5-31/8) (Z 1/5-30/9)
5 **A**DFGIJKLMNOPUVWZ
6 AEGH**K**(N 1km)TV

💬 A hospitable and quiet family campsite close to Banon with views of fields of lavender and sage. Alternating touring pitches and mobile homes. Heated swimming pool from mid-May to mid-September and children's entertainment increased by the pool and playground.

🚗 A7, exit Avignon-Sud. Drive in the direction of Apt, then Banon. In Banon follow the signs.

D950 · Saint-Étienne-les-Orgues · D951 · D5 · D13 · D30 · D51 · Forcalquier · D14 · D22

€ 15 1/4-7/7 25/8-14/10 7=6, 14=12

📍 N 44°1'36'' E 5°37'52''

Baratier, F-05200 / Provence-Alpes-Côte d'Azur (Hautes-Alpes)

♿ 🛜 🌸 **iD** 2561

🏕 Sites & Paysages Le Petit Liou***
📧 ancienne route de Baratier
☎ +33 (0)4-92431910
🗓 1/5 - 22/9
@ info@camping-lepetitliou.com

4,5ha 280T(100-120m²) 3-10A CEE

1 ACD**F**IJKLMPQ
2 BGKRTVWXY
3 BGHJLRU
4 (C+H 1/6-15/9) (Q 1/6-21/9)
(R 1/7-31/8)
(T+U+V+X+Z 20/6-26/8)
5 **A**EFGHIJKLMNOPUVWZ
6 ACEGIJ**K**(N 0,5km)V

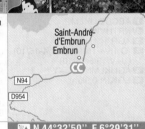

💬 A family campsite in rural surroundings and with spacious shaded pitches. Located between Embrun and Barratier.

🚗 On the N94 from Gap to Briançon, right at the first roundabout just before Embrun. First left after 150m then first right. Clearly signposted.

Saint-André-d'Embrun · Embrun · N94 · D954

€ 15 1/5-8/7 26/8-21/9

📍 N 44°32'50'' E 6°29'31''

Baratier/Embrun, F-05200 / Provence-Alpes-Côte d'Azur (Hautes-Alpes)

🛜 **iD** 2562

🏕 Les 2 Bois***
📧 route de Pra Fouran
☎ +33 (0)4-92435414
🗓 12/5 - 23/9
@ info@camping-les2bois.com

2,5ha 104T(70-110m²) 4-10A CEE

1 ACD**G**IJLPQ
2 CGJKLRTVWXY
3 BGHJRU**W**
4 (B+G 22/5-24/9) (Q 🗓)
(T+U+V 30/5-31/8)
(X 28/5-9/9) (Z 30/5-31/8)
5 **A**BEFGIJKLMNOPUVWZ
6 EGJ(N 0,2km)RT

💬 Homely atmosphere in rural surroundings. Well marked-out, shady pitches. Good bar and restaurant. Nice toilet blocks and swimming pool.

🚗 Turn off the N94 at the Crots-Embrun roundabout to Baratier.

Risoul Station · Embrun · N94 · D954

€ 15 12/5-8/7 26/8-22/9

📍 N 44°32'18'' E 6°29'32''

Beaurecueil, F-13100 / Provence-Alpes-Côte d'Azur (Bouches-du-Rhône) 2563

▲ Sainte Victoire**
◳ Quartier Paradou, 613 av J. Gautier
☎ +33 (0)4-42669131
FAX +33 (0)4-42669643
⌇ 5/3 - 30/11
@ campingstevictoire@orange.fr

2ha 85T(80-170m²) 6A CEE

1 **AG**IJKLMPST
2 BCFGKLMTVWXY
3 AR
4 (Q+R+V+Z ⌫)
5 **A**DGIJKLMNOPRUVZ
6 ACE**IK**(N 7km)OV

💬 A modest campsite, picturesquely located at the foot of Sainte Victoire. Marked out, shaded pitches, an oasis of peace. Starting point for lovely walks or for visiting Aix-en-Provence just 8 km away. Bus to Aix-en-Provence 13 times a day.

🚗 In Aix follow the A8 towards Nice/Toulon. Exit 31. Then 2x right towards Palette/Beaurecueil. Then follow arrows.

CC € **17** 1/4-6/7 25/8-14/10   🧭 N 43°31'2'' E 5°32'26''

Bédoin, F-84410 / Provence-Alpes-Côte d'Azur (Vaucluse) 2564

▲ Camping Le Pastory**
◳ 1105 route de Malaucène
☎ +33 (0)4-90128583
⌇ 1/4 - 16/10
@ info@camping-le-pastory.com

1,6ha 90T(100-130m²) 10A CEE

1 ABCD**G**IJKLM**P**
2 KRTUVWXY
3 AGR
4 (Q 15/4-15/10) (R 1/4-15/10)
(U+V 15/5-15/10)
5 AGIJKLMNOPUXY
6 EG**K**(N 0,9km)

💬 Ideal location at the foot of Mont Ventoux, at 900 metres from the Provence village of Bédoin. Le Pastory offers spacious, shaded pitches with a breathtaking view of Mont Ventaux. There is nature all around. Typical Provence market in Bédoin on Monday mornings. Swimming is possible in the surrounding lakes and the local swimming pool near the campsite.

🚗 A7 exit Orange-Sud to Carpentras direction Bédoin. In centre of Bédoin follow signs.

CC € **15** 1/4-30/6 1/9-15/10 14=12, 30=26   🧭 N 44°7'54'' E 5°10'15''

Belgentier, F-83210 / Provence-Alpes-Côte d'Azur (Var) 2565

▲ Les Tomasses***
◳ chemin du Maoupas
☎ +33 (0)4-94489270
⌇ 1/4 - 30/9
@ info@camping-var-tomasses.fr

2,5ha 86T(80-200m²) 10A

1 ACDGIJKLMPS
2 BCFGRTVWXY
3 BDGNRU
4 (B 1/5-30/9) G(Q 1/7-31/8)
(T+U+V+X+Y+Z ⌫)
5 **A**FGHIJKLMNPUVXYZ
6 ABEGJ(N 2km)TV

NEW

💬 A peaceful campsite by a small river with an abundance of natural beauty. Large pitches with plenty of privacy.

🚗 A57, exit 7 direction Solliès-Toucas (D554). Drive through town, follow D554. Campsite on left before town of Belgentier.

CC € **13** 1/4-6/7 25/8-29/9 7=6, 14=11   🧭 N 43°13'55'' E 6°0'29''

Bollène, F-84500 / Provence-Alpes-Côte d'Azur (Vaucluse) 🔥 🤿 iD (2566)

🏔 La Simioune***
✉ route de l'embisque
☎ +33 (0)4-90631791
📅 1/3 - 25/10
@ camping@la-simioune.fr

3ha 80T(100-200m²) 10A CEE

1 ACD**G**IJKLMOPS
2 BFJKSTUVWXY
3 BDGHINPRU
4 (B+G 1/5-10/10) (Q 1/4-30/9)
(R 📅) (T 1/6-31/8) (U 📅)
(V 1/4-30/9) (X+Z 1/6-31/8)
5 AEFGIJKLMNOPUXZ
6 EGKOQTV

💬 A typically French, hospitable and natural campsite with spacious pitches. Located just outside the town of Bollène in a wood with tall pine trees. Close to Parcours Aventure (clambering and climbing). Wifi free at the campsite.

🚗 Leave A7 at Bollène. To roundabout direction Carpentras and follow signs from there (direction Suze la Rousse).

Pierrelatte   Saint-Paul-Trois-Châteaux

D86
D59
D63
A7
D94
N7
D576
N86
D976
D8

CC € 15 1/3-6/7 24/8-24/10 15=13, 30=25   📍 N 44°17'50'' E 4°47'15''

Callas, F-83830 / Provence-Alpes-Côte d'Azur (Var) 🤿 iD (2567)

🏔 Les Blimouses**
✉ Quartier Les Blimouses, RD225
☎ FAX +33 (0)4-94478341
📅 12/3 - 7/10
@ camping.les.blimouses@orange.fr

6ha 68T(70-150m²) 10A CEE

1 ACD**G**HIJKLMPST
2 BGJRVWXY
3 BGHN**O**PRU
4 (B 1/5-30/9) (G 15/4-30/9) JK
P(Q 📅) (T+U+V 1/6-15/9)
(X 1/4-15/9) (Z 1/6-15/9)
5 AFGIJKMNOPUXZ
6 ACDEGJ(N 3km)OTV

💬 Ideal location in the heart of the Haut Var. Near Callas, the Pennafort gorges and the Provence countryside. You can take a walk, go mountainbiking, enjoy the water activities in the Gorges du Verdon or relax on the beautiful French Riviera beaches. Large pool with slides, toddlers' pool, sun loungers and parasols. Spacious, well marked-out pitches.

🚗 A8 exit Le Muy, direction Callas and follow route RD562, then route RD225.

D955
D563
D25
D19
D54
D562
D4

Draguignan

Lorgues

CC € 15 12/3-30/6 1/9-6/10   📍 N 43°34'28'' E 6°31'55''

Carpentras, F-84200 / Provence-Alpes-Côte d'Azur (Vaucluse) 👫 🔥 🤿 iD (2568)

🏔 Flower Camping Lou Comtadou***
✉ 881 av. Pierre de Coubertin
☎ +33 (0)4-90670316
FAX +33 (0)4-90460181
📅 15/3 - 15/10
@ info@campingloucomtadou.com

2ha 97T(100-110m²) 6A CEE

1 AC**G**IJKLMPST
2 LRVXY
3 ABGU
4 (C+**G** 7/6-30/8) **J**
(Q 15/5-30/9)
(R+T+U+X 15/6-15/9)
(Z 15/5-30/9)
5 AFGIJKLMNPUX
6 CEGK(N 1,2km)TV

💬 A campsite with lovely marked-out pitches and plenty of sun and shade. Good amenities and simple restaurant. Bus stop next to the site. Close to town centre with a large market on Fridays. Good paved roads.

🚗 Follow ring road before Carpentras, then dir. St. Didier. Right at second lights and follow signs. Left at sports complex on leaving the town.

D19
D977
D974
Carpentras
D942
D49
D4
Vedène
A7
D938

CC € 15 15/3-7/7 25/8-14/10 7=6, 14=11   📍 N 44°2'39'' E 5°3'16''

Carqueiranne, F-83320 / Provence-Alpes-Côte d'Azur (Var)

👪 ⎈ 📶 iD 2569

🔺 Le Beau Vezé****
🏠 route de la Moutonne
☎ +33 (0)4-94576530
🔓 1/5 - 15/9
@ info@camping-beauveze.com

5ha 118T(80-130m²) 10A

1 ACDGIJKL**P**ST
2 BFIJKRTVXY
3 BFGMQR
4 (**A** 1/7-31/8) (B+G 🔓) J
(Q 🔓)
(R+T+U+V+X+Y+Z 1/7-31/8)
5 **A**EFGHIJKLMNOPQRUV
6 AEGH**IK**(N 2km)RT

💬 A peacefully located campsite in a wood with mostly pine and olive trees. The beaches at Hyères are about 3.5 km away. Trips to Giens, Hyères and Le Pradet among others are recommended. Really pleasant ambiance.

🚗 Campsite signposted on the RD559.

Toulon | A57
CC
Hyères
D559

CC € **19** 1/5-7/7 25/8-14/9 7=6, 14=11, 21=16

📡 N 43°6'52'' E 6°3'22''

Castellane, F-04120 / Provence-Alpes-Côte d'Azur (Alpes-de-Haute-Prov)

⎈ 📶 iD 2570

🔺 Domaine Chasteuil Provence***
🏠 route des Gorges du Verdon
☎ +33 (0)4-92836121
📠 +33 (0)4-83075229
🔓 4/5 - 15/9
@ contact@chasteuil-provence.com

6ha 210T(90-120m²) 3-10A CEE

1 ACDGIJKLMP
2 CKOTVY
3 BHJNR**W**
4 (C 1/6-15/9) (Q+S 🔓)
(T+U 1/7-31/8) (V 1/7-31/7)
(X 1/7-31/8) (Z 1/7-31/7)
5 **AB**FIJKLMNPU
6 ACEGHJ(N 6km)O

💬 This campsite, run by a family, is located right at the start of the Gorges du Verdon. Recommended for campers who love tranquillity and the countryside.

🚗 D952 from Castellane towards Gorges du Verdon. After 10 km campsite on the left.

Majastres | **Vergons**
CC
D4085
D952
D71 | D955
Bargème

CC € **15** 4/5-6/7 26/8-14/9

📡 N 43°49'49'' E 6°25'40''

Castellane, F-04120 / Provence-Alpes-Côte d'Azur (Alpes-de-Haute-Prov)

⎈ 📶 iD 2571

🔺 International****
🏠 Route Napoléon
☎ +33 (0)4-92836667
🔓 13/4 - 1/10
@ info@campinginternational.fr

6ha 150T(100-120m²) 10A CEE

1 ACD**G**IJKLMP**S**T
2 KRVXY
3 BGHJKRU
4 (**A** 1/7-31/8) (C 1/5-30/9)
(Q+S+T+U+X+Y+Z 🔓)
5 **AB**EFGIJKLMNP**ST**VW
6 CEGHJ**K**(N 1,5km)OQTV

💬 Spacious campsite with shaded, marked-out pitches. The campsite was completely re-developed in 2016. Recommended for its large swimming pool, own restaurant and Castellane nearby.

🚗 D4085. Campsite on right of road 2 km after leaving Castellane, direction Digne.

Barrême | N202
Soleilhas
CC
Castellane | D4085
D952
La Palud-sur-Verdon | N85
D955

CC € **17** 13/4-6/7 26/8-30/9

📡 N 43°51'32'' E 6°29'53''

Castellane, F-04120 / Provence-Alpes-Côte d'Azur (Alpes-de-Haute-Prov) 👫 ♿ 📶 iD (2572)

🏕️ La Ferme de Castellane***
📧 Quartier La Lagne, route de Grasse
☎ +33 (0)4-92836777
🔓 22/3 - 8/10
@ accueil@camping-la-ferme.com

1,3ha 34T(80-100m²) 6A CEE

1 ACD**G**IJKLMOPST
2 CIJKRVWXY
3 BGHJ**OP**RU
4 (Q+R 🔌)
5 **A**BCEFGHIJKLMNOPUVWZ
6 ACDEGHIJ(N 2,3km)TV

💬 An ideal campsite for relaxing, situated among natural beauty. An agreeable, well-kept and well-maintained site. Highly recommended. Special attention on arrival. The main building is a restored 18th century water mill. Site is easily accessible via an asphalted road, 1500 metres from the main road: peace and quiet guaranteed!

🚐 From Castellane centre continue towards Grasse. Campsite signposted, on the right, 1 km further.

Vergons N202
D4085
Castellane CC
D952
Soleils N85 D2
D955 D6085
D71 D21

🅲🅲 € **13** 22/3-12/7 30/8-7/10 · N 43°50'18'' E 6°32'31''

Castellane/La Garde, F-04120 / Provence-Alpes-Côte d'Azur (Alpes-de-Haute-Prov) ♿ 📶 iD (2573)

🏕️ Camping RCN Les Collines de Castellane****
📧 route de Grasse
☎ +31 034-3745090
📠 +33 (0)4-92837540
🔓 27/4 - 24/9
@ reserveringen@rcn.nl

10ha 158T(80-150m²) 8-12A

1 ACD**F**IJKLOPST
2 BIJKLRSTVWXY
3 BGHJ**M**NRU
4 (A 1/5-31/8) (C+H 🔌) J (Q+R+T+U+V+X+Y+Z 🔌)
5 **A**BCEFGHIJKLMNPUWXYZ
6 AEGJ(N 6km)TV

💬 A lovely terraced campsite in unspoilt, breathtaking natural scenery. Located at an altitude of 1000m in the Haute Provence which is characterised by the clean air and the strong sun. Views of the hills and mountains. Informally laid out swimming pool. Characteristic old villages and historic towns in beautiful countryside with purple lavender fields and olive trees.

🚐 The campsite is located on the N85 direction Grasse, 6 km south-east of Castellane.

N202
D4085
Castellane
D952 CC La Foux
La Batie N85 D2
D6085
D955 D563
D71 D21

🅲🅲 € **17** 27/4-30/6 25/8-23/9 7=6, 14=11 · N 43°49'27'' E 6°34'12''

Cavaillon, F-84300 / Provence-Alpes-Côte d'Azur (Vaucluse) ♿ 📶 iD (2574)

🏕️ de la Durance***
📧 495 avenue Boscodomini
☎ +33 (0)4-90711178
📠 +33 (0)4-90719877
🔓 1/4 - 30/9
@ contact@camping-durance.com

4ha 79T(80-120m²) 4-12A CEE

1 ACD**G**IJKLMPQ
2 FRSTVWXY
3 AMNR
4 (Q+T 1/7-30/8)
5 **AB**CDFGIJKLMNPUVXYZ
6 ACGJ**K**(N 0,8km)T

💬 A campsite on the edge of the village of Cavaillon in the heart of Provence, between Alpilles and Luberon. In a park with plane trees. You will also be welcomed in English, German or Dutch.

🚐 Take exit 25 to Cavaillon on the A7. Cross the River Durance. Right at the roundabout. Then follow camping signs.

L'Isle-sur-la-Sorgue D901 D2
D900
A7
Cavaillon
CC
D99 D7 N D973
D569

🅲🅲 € **15** 1/4-7/7 25/8-29/9 · N 43°49'18'' E 5°2'12''

Cavalaire-sur-Mer, F-83240 / Provence-Alpes-Côte d'Azur (Var)

♿ 🛜 iD (2575)

🏕 Bonporteau****
📧 208 chemin Train des Pignes
☎ +33 (0)4-94640324
📠 +33 (0)4-94641862
📅 15/3 - 15/10
@ contact@bonporteau.fr

3ha 110T(80-120m²) 10A CEE

1 A**G**IJKLPST
2 AEGIJKQRSVWXY
3 BGRUWY
4 (C+H 📅) K
(Q+S+T+U+V+X+Y+Z 1/4-30/9)
5 **A**CDEFGHIJKLMNOPUVWX YZ
6 DEG**IK**(N 0,3km)RTV

💬 A really lovely location, a well-maintained campsite with good facilities and a genuine Mediterranean landscape. 200 metres from the beach and 800 metres from the centre of the popular seaside resort of Cavalaire-sur-Mer.

🚗 The campsite is clearly signposted in the centre of Cavalaire.

Cogolin D98
Cavalaire-sur-Mer D93
D559 CC

CC € 19 15/3-7/7 1/9-14/10

N 43°10'2'' E 6°31'9''

Cavalaire-sur-Mer, F-83240 / Provence-Alpes-Côte d'Azur (Var)

♿ 🛜 iD (2576)

🏕 Camping Cros de Mouton****
📧 chemin du Cros de Mouton
☎ +33 (0)4-94641087
📠 +33 (0)4-94646312
📅 22/3 - 28/10
@ campingcrosdemouton@ wanadoo.fr

6ha 117T(60-200m²) 10A

1 ACDGIJKLMOPST
2 ABGIJKQRSVWXY
3 BGKLNRU
4 (A 1/7-31/8) (C+H 📅) K
(Q+R+T+U+V+X+Y+Z 1/4-30/9)
5 **A**CDEFGHIJKLMNOPUWXY Z
6 ABEGH**IK**(N 1,5km)ORTV

💬 A very attractive campsite with plenty of shade and fantastic views of the Mediterranean Sea and a beautiful nature reserve in the distant surroundings. 1.5 km from a lively seaside resort with beautiful sandy beaches. Restaurant and swimming pool with panoramic views.

🚗 A8, exit Le Muy direction Ste Maxime. Direction St. Tropez then direction Cavalaire. Follow signs.

Cogolin
D98 D93
CC
D559
La Favière

CC € 19 22/3-30/6 27/8-27/10

N 43°10'56'' E 6°31'0''

Cavalaire-sur-Mer, F-83240 / Provence-Alpes-Côte d'Azur (Var)

♿ 🛜 iD (2577)

🏕 de la Baie****
📧 bd Pasteur
☎ +33 (0)4-94640815
📠 +33 (0)4-94646610
📅 15/3 - 15/11
@ contact@camping-baie.com

6,5ha 150T(80-120m²) 10A CEE

1 ACDGIJKLPST
2 AEGIJKRSVWXY
3 BGKL**MNOP**RUWY
4 (C+H 📅) K
(Q+S+T+U+V+X+Y+Z 📅)
5 **AB**CDEFGHIJKLMNOPUWZ
6 CEGHIJ**K**(N 0,1km)ORTVWX

💬 Close to the centre of a lively resort, yet still quiet. 400 metres from wonderful sandy beaches. A campsite with an excellent atmosphere.

🚗 A8, exit Le Muy, direction Ste Maxime. From there to La Croix Valmer. Cavalaire centre (harbour). Follow the arrows in the centre.

Cogolin
D98
Cavalaire-sur-Mer D93
CC
D559

CC € 19 15/3-29/6 25/8-14/11

N 43°10'10'' E 6°31'47''

Chasteuil/Castellane, F-04120 / Provence-Alpes-Côte d'Azur (Alpes-de-Haute-Prov) 👫🦽🛜 🆔 (2578)

🔺 Huttopia Gorges du Verdon★★★★
🏕 Clos d'Arémus
☎ +33 (0)4-92836364
📠 +33 (0)4-92837472
🗓 4/5 - 30/9
@ gorgesduverdon@huttopia.com

7ha 188T(80-120m²) 6A

1 AGIJKLO**P**ST
2 CGKORVXY
3 BHNRU**W**
4 (A 1/7-26/8)
   (C+Q+S+T+U+V 🔒)
   (X+Y 8/5-15/9) (Z 🔒)
5 **AB**CEFGHIJKLMNOPUVZ
6 CEGHIJ(N 10km)OQRTV

💬 Very pleasant campsite, located along the Verdon. Very impressive scenery: among other things the famous Gorges du Verdon and the Lac Ste Croix. Great family campsite.

🚗 The campsite is located about 10 km south of Castellane, on road D952 to Draguignan.

(map: D4085, Castellane, La Batie, CC Soleils, D952, D71, D955)

CC €17 4/5-28/6 2/9-29/9 　　📳 N 43°49'22'' E 6°25'53''

Châteauneuf-de-Gadagne, F-84470 / Provence-Alpes-Côte d'Azur (Vaucluse) 👫🦽🛜 🆔 (2579)

🔺 Fontisson★★★
🏕 1125 route d'Avignon
☎ +33 (0)4-90225977
🗓 1/4 - 4/11
@ info@campingfontisson.com

2ha 32T(80-100m²) 10A CEE

1 ACD**G**IJKLPST
2 FISTWX
3 AF**G**HJMN**O**QRTV**W**
4 (C+G 1/5-15/9) (Q+R 🔒)
   (T+U+X+Z 15/6-15/9)
5 A**F**GIJKLMNOPUWZ
6 AEGJ**K**(N 5km)RTV

💬 15 minutes from Avignon and l'Isle-sur-la-Sorgue. An ideally located campsite for visiting Provence, choosing the villages of Lubéron, spending a day by the sea, walking up Mont Ventoux or sauntering through the Provençal markets. The campsite is surrounded by vineyards.

🚗 In Avignon exit Nord, direction Carpentras. Then via Vedène, direction Saint-Saturnin. In Châteauneuf take the RN100 to Avignon.

(map: D980, D49, D938, Avignon, D31, A7, D6, D901, D28, D973, D900, D7N, Cavaillon, CC)

CC €15 1/4-6/7 26/8-3/11 　　📳 N 43°55'44'' E 4°56'1''

Châteauneuf-du-Pape, F-84230 / Provence-Alpes-Côte d'Azur (Vaucluse) 🦽🛜 🆔 (2580)

🔺 Camping L'Art de Vivre★★★
🏕 960 chemin de l'Islon Saint Luc
☎ +33 (0)4-90026543
🗓 14/4 - 30/9
@ contact@
   camping-artdevivre.com

3,5ha 82T(80-120m²) 10A

1 AC**G**IJKLMPST
2 BCFGRTUVXY
3 BGHJK**M**RU
4 (B 15/5-30/9) (G 1/7-31/8)
   (Q+R 🔒)
   (T+U+V+X 1/6-31/8)
   (Z 1/5-2/10)
5 **AB**EGIJKLMNPUZ
6 EGIJ**K**(N 1,5km)T

💬 Tastefully-refurbished site in open wood containing ancient trees, 1.5 km from Châteauneuf-du-Pape. In a wine growing region with quality wines. Lively covered terrace with restaurant and bar. Close to Orange, Avignon and Mont Ventoux. Very rural, quiet place to relax.

🚗 From the north take exit 22 on the A7 or A9. Then dir. Courthézon/Châteauneuf-du-Pape and follow cp signs in the centre. From the south exit Roquemaure/Châteauneuf-du-Pape. Follow arrows.

(map: Orange, D977, D950, N580, A7, A9, CC, D907, D976, D980, Avignon)

CC €17 14/4-4/7 22/8-29/9 　　📳 N 44°2'29'' E 4°49'28''

Châteaurenard, F-13160 / Provence-Alpes-Côte d'Azur (Bouches-du-Rhône)

👫 ♿ 📶 **iD** (2581)

🔺 La Roquette***
📧 745 ave Jean Mermoz
☎ +33 (0)4-90944681
🔑 31/3 - 27/10
@ contact@
camping-la-roquette.com

1,4ha 50T(85-100m²) 10A

1 ACD**G**IJKLMOPST
2 FRSTVWXY
3 A**F**GHJKLM**N**RU**W**
4 (C+H+Q+T+U+V+X+Z 🔑)
5 **A**FGIJKLNPUVWZ
6 ABEGK(N 1,5km)V

💬 A modest, hospitable campsite where a friendly French couple create a pleasant ambiance. Centrally located for lovely trips in Provence. Pitches under the mulberry trees, mostly without fruit. Nice for cycling and walking. The campsite displays the 'Camping Qualité' logo. The swimming pool is heated and wifi is free throughout the camp site.

🚗 A7, exit Avignon-Sud, direction Châteaurenard. The campsite is signposted.

Avignon — D31, D6, D900, D28, D7N, A7, D570 N, D5, D26, D99

CC € **17** 31/3-6/7 25/8-26/10 7=6

📐 N 43°53'2'' E 4°52'13''

Cogolin, F-83310 / Provence-Alpes-Côte d'Azur (Var)

👫 ♿ 📶 ⚙ **iD** (2582)

🔺 L'Argentière****
📧 avenue Saint Maur
☎ +33 (0)4-94546363
📠 +33 (0)4-94540615
🔑 1/4 - 8/10
@ contact@
camping-argentiere.com

5ha 100T(80-120m²) 6-10A

1 A**F**IJKLP
2 BKRTVWXY
3 B**F**GKM**N**RU
4 (C+G 15/4-7/10) JK
(Q 15/6-15/9)
(R+T+U+V+X+Y+Z 1/7-31/8)
5 **AB**EFGIJKLMNOPUZ
6 AEGHJ**K**(N 1km)OTV

💬 Lovely, comfortable campsite with an excellent ambiance. Very central location for trips, e.g. to St. Tropez, Sainte Maxime, Port Grimaud, the world-famous beaches of Pampelonne and Ramatuelle, Grimaud, Gassin. Campsite is located in a nature reserve.

🚗 In Cogolin keep dir. Collobrières. Campsite entrance is next to Château Saint Maur.

D25, D558, Sainte-Maxime, Grimaud, CC, D559, D98, D93, Cavalaire-sur-Mer

CC € **15** 1/4-7/7 25/8-7/10

📐 N 43°15'27'' E 6°31'5''

Cotignac, F-83570 / Provence-Alpes-Côte d'Azur (Var)

♿ 📶 **iD** (2583)

🔺 Camping des Pouverels
📧 3070 chemin des Pouverels
☎ +33 (0)4-94047191
🔑 1/4 - 31/10
@ campingcotignac@orange.fr

3ha 40T(60-100m²) 13A

1 ACD**G**HIJKLM**P**ST
2 BJVWXY
3 AHJ
4 (Q 🔑)
5 **A**EJKMNPU
6 J(N 2km)T

💬 The campsite is small and charming and is located in the countryside. Being a small campsite (40 pitches) it has a peaceful and friendly character. Its location in the heart of the Var makes this campsite an ideal starting point for many excursions and walks.

🚗 D22, campsite located 2 km outside Cotignac.

Aups, Tavernes, D22, D557, D560, D554, D13, CC, D562, Le Val

CC € **15** 1/4-8/7 26/8-30/10

📐 N 43°32'16'' E 6°8'55''

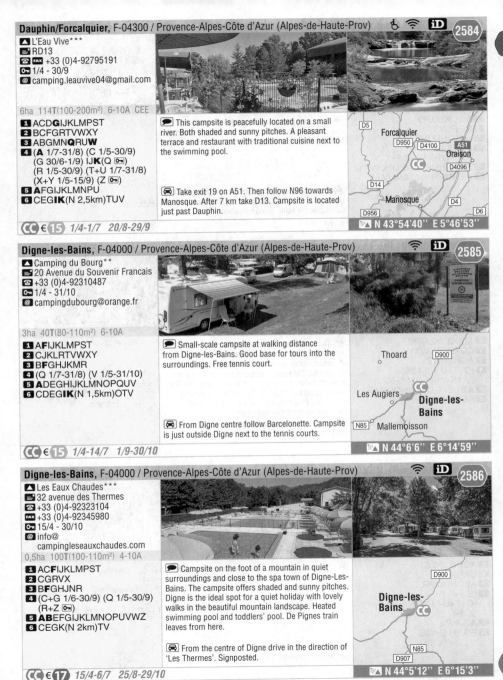

Dauphin/Forcalquier, F-04300 / Provence-Alpes-Côte d'Azur (Alpes-de-Haute-Prov) ♿ 🛜 iD (2584)

L'Eau Vive***
RD13
☎ FAX +33 (0)4-92795191
⌚ 1/4 - 30/9
@ camping.leauvive04@gmail.com

6ha 114T(100-200m²) 6-10A CEE

1 ACD**G**IJKLMPST
2 BCFGRTVWXY
3 ABGMN**Q**RU**W**
4 (A 1/7-31/8) (C 1/5-30/9)
(G 30/6-1/9) IJ**K**(Q ⌚)
(R 1/5-30/9) (T+U 1/7-31/8)
(X+Y 1/5-15/9) (Z ⌚)
5 **A**FGIJKLMNPU
6 CEG**IK**(N 2,5km)TUV

💬 This campsite is peacefully located on a small river. Both shaded and sunny pitches. A pleasant terrace and restaurant with traditional cuisine next to the swimming pool.

🚗 Take exit 19 on A51. Then follow N96 towards Manosque. After 7 km take D13. Campsite is located just past Dauphin.

CC € 15 1/4-1/7 20/8-29/9
📍 N 43°54'40'' E 5°46'53''

Digne-les-Bains, F-04000 / Provence-Alpes-Côte d'Azur (Alpes-de-Haute-Prov) 🛜 iD (2585)

Camping du Bourg**
20 Avenue du Souvenir Francais
☎ +33 (0)4-92310487
⌚ 1/4 - 31/10
@ campingdubourg@orange.fr

3ha 40T(80-110m²) 6-10A

1 A**F**IJKLMPST
2 CJKLRTVWXY
3 B**F**GHJKMR
4 (Q 1/7-31/8) (V 1/5-31/10)
5 **A**DEGHIJKLMNOPQUV
6 CDEG**IK**(N 1,5km)OTV

💬 Small-scale campsite at walking distance from Digne-les-Bains. Good base for tours into the surroundings. Free tennis court.

🚗 From Digne centre follow Barcelonette. Campsite is just outside Digne next to the tennis courts.

CC € 15 1/4-14/7 1/9-30/10
📍 N 44°6'6'' E 6°14'59''

Digne-les-Bains, F-04000 / Provence-Alpes-Côte d'Azur (Alpes-de-Haute-Prov) 🛜 iD (2586)

Les Eaux Chaudes***
32 avenue des Thermes
☎ +33 (0)4-92323104
FAX +33 (0)4-92345980
⌚ 15/4 - 30/10
@ info@
campingleseauxchaudes.com

0,5ha 100T(100-110m²) 4-10A

1 AC**F**IJKLMPST
2 CGRVX
3 B**F**GHJNR
4 (C+G 1/6-30/9) (Q 1/5-30/9)
(R+Z ⌚)
5 **AB**EFGIJKLMNOPUVWZ
6 CEGK(N 2km)TV

💬 Campsite on the foot of a mountain in quiet surroundings and close to the spa town of Digne-Les-Bains. The campsite offers shaded and sunny pitches. Digne is the ideal spot for a quiet holiday with lovely walks in the beautiful mountain landscape. Heated swimming pool and toddlers' pool. De Pignes train leaves from here.

🚗 From the centre of Digne drive in the direction of 'Les Thermes'. Signposted.

CC € 17 15/4-6/7 25/8-29/10
📍 N 44°5'12'' E 6°15'3''

Embrun, F-05200 / Provence-Alpes-Côte d'Azur (Hautes-Alpes)

♿ 🛜 iD (2587)

🏕 La Vieille Ferme★★★★
✉ 6 chemin sous le Roc
☎ +33 (0)4-92430408
🗓 1/5 - 1/10
@ info@campingembrun.com

2,6ha 100T(112-210m²) 6-10A CEE

1 **AG**IJKLMPQ
2 CGRSVY
3 AGHJNRU**W**
4 (A 1/6-30/9)
 (Q+T+U+V+X+Z 🗓)
5 **A**EFGHIJKLMNPQRUWXYZ
6 AEG**IK**(N 1km)QTUV

💬 You will camp on level wooded grounds near a lake and close to Embrun, with an inviting Provençal terrace. Perfect for sportive campers. Dutch owner.

🚗 N94 from Gap to Briançon. At the roundabout go towards Embrun, then over the bridge and first turning on the right, then immediately left.

Embrun
N94
D954

CC € **19** 1/5-7/7 25/8-30/9 21=19

N 44°33'15'' E 6°29'10''

Entrevaux, F-04320 / Provence-Alpes-Côte d'Azur (Alpes-de-Haute-Prov)

♿ 🛜 iD (2588)

🏕 du Brec★★
☎ +33 (0)4-93054245
🗓 15/3 - 15/10
@ info@camping-dubrec.com

3,8ha 76T(80-140m²) 10A CEE

1 ACD**G**IJKLM**P**ST
2 CDKNRTVWXY
3 AGHNRWZ
4 (Q+T+U 1/6-15/9)
 (V 1/7-31/8) (Z 1/6-30/9)
5 **AB**DEFGIJKLMNOPUWZ
6 AEGHI**K**(N 2km)TV

💬 The campsite is fairly basic, but good. Perfect for the active camper who feels at home in an area of natural beauty which has not yet been discovered by tourists. The nearby medieval town of Entrevaux is worth a visit. Set next to a 4-hectare lake with free use of canoes and kayaks. Top quality swimming water. Perfectly suited to families with children. No entertainment, therefore quiet.

🚗 N202, 2.5 miles (4 km) west of Entrevaux. Follow the signs.

D2202
D908
D6202
CC Puget-Théniers
N202
Entrevaux

CC € **15** 15/3-6/7 24/8-14/10

N 43°57'42'' E 6°47'56''

Esparron-de-Verdon, F-04800 / Provence-Alpes-Côte d'Azur (Alpes-de-Haute-Prov)

♿ 🛜 iD (2589)

🏕 Flower Camping La Beaume★★★
✉ route d'Albiosc
☎ +33 (0)4-92771528
🗓 31/3 - 28/10
@ camping.labeaume@free.fr

6ha 34T 6-10A CEE

1 ACD**G**IJKLST
2 CKRX
3 ABGHN**OP**R
4 (E 🗓)
 (Q+T+U+V+X 20/6-31/8)
 (Z 🗓)
5 **A**DJNPZ
6 EGJ(N 2km)O

💬 Very peacefully located campsite in the middle of the countryside, a few kilometres from the lake of Esparron-de-Verdon.

🚗 On A51 take exit Gréoux-les-Bains dir. Esparron-de-Verdon. In village follow arrows.

A51
Valensole
D6
D953
D4
Gréoux-les-Bains
D11
D952
CC
D23 D554
D13
D30

CC € **17** 31/3-4/7 22/8-27/10

N 43°44'36'' E 5°59'41''

Fontvieille, F-13990 / Provence-Alpes-Côte d'Azur (Bouches-du-Rhône) 📶 **iD** (2590)

🏕 Huttopia Fontvieille***
✉ rue Michelet
☎ +33 (0)4-90547869
📅 30/3 - 14/10
@ fontvieille@huttopia.com

4ha 150**T**(70-100m²) 6A

1 ACD**G**IJKLMOPST
2 BIRSTVWX
3 A**F**GHJNRU
4 (Q 1/7-31/8)
5 A**B**FGIJKLMNOPUVWYZ
6 EGK(N 2km)TV

💬 Natural, quiet, basic campsite at walking distance from a lovely Provence village which is well-known for Alphonse Daudet's mill, with nice restaurants.

🚗 D33 from Avignon direction Arles. Campsite signposted in Fontvieille.

Beaucaire — D571 — D90 — D99 — D15 — D33 — D5 — D570 N 〔CC〕 — D17 — Arles — Mouriès — D570 — A54

CC € **17** 30/3-28/6 2/9-13/10 · 🧭 N 43°43'25'' E 4°43'7''

Forcalquier, F-04300 / Provence-Alpes-Côte d'Azur (Alpes-de-Haute-Prov) ♿ 📶 **iD** (2591)

🏕 Camping Forcalquier***
✉ route de Sigonce
☎ +33 (0)4-92752794
📅 1/4 - 15/10

4ha 80**T**(80-110m²) 10A CEE

1 ACD**F**HIJKL**P**S
2 RTVWXY
3 AGHJNRU
4 (A 1/7-31/8) (C+H+Q 📅)
  (R 4/5-26/9)
  (T+U+V+X 1/7-31/8) (Z 📅)
5 A DEFGIJKLMNOPRUWXYZ
6 CEGIJ(N 0,5km)PTV

💬 A small, intimate campsite close to the centre of the village. Quality amenities such as a heated swimming pool, recreational facilities and cafe-restaurant. CampingCard ACSI is only valid for standard pitches.

🚗 A51 Sisteron - Aix-en-Provence to exit 19. Then take the N100 in the direction of Forcalquier. In the centre follow the arrows 'Indigo Camping'.

D951 — D5 — D950 — D4096 — D4 — 〔CC〕 — D12 A51 — D14 — D13 — Oraison — Villeneuve — D4100 — Volx — D907

CC € **15** 1/4-6/7 26/8-14/10 · 🧭 N 43°57'43'' E 5°47'14''

Forcalquier, F-04300 / Provence-Alpes-Côte d'Azur (Alpes-de-Haute-Prov) 🏊 ♿ 📶 **iD** (2592)

🏕 Flower Domaine Naturiste
  des Lauzons****
✉ Limans
☎ +33 (0)4-92730060
📅 14/4 - 13/10
@ leslauzons@wanadoo.fr

60ha 163**T**(40-250m²) 10A CEE

1 ACD**G**IJKLNPST
2 BCIJKLRTVWXY
3 ABGHNRUW
4 (**A** 1/6-20/9) (C+G 1/5-30/9)
  JN(Q+R+U+V+X 1/5-30/9)
  (Z 📅)
5 A DEFGIJKLMNOPUVWXZ
6 EG**J**(N 6km)OV

💬 Very attractive naturist campsite positioned up in the hills. Both shaded and sunny pitches. Heated swimming pool and toilet facilities. Snacks, take-away meals and bread from 1 May.

🚗 A51 Sisteron - Aix-en-Provence, exit 19. Then follow N100 till past Forcalquier. Follow D950 at roundabout direction Limans.

D950 — D951 — D5 — D51 — 〔CC〕 Forcalquier — D12 — A51 — D13 — Villeneuve — D14 — Volx — D4100

CC € **19** 14/4-7/7 25/8-12/10 · 🧭 N 43°58'22'' E 5°44'15''

Freissinières, F-05310 / Provence-Alpes-Côte d'Azur (Hautes-Alpes)

♿ 🛜 **iD** (2593)

🏕 Les Allouviers*
☎ +33 (0)4-92209324
🔓 1/5 - 30/9
@ info@camping-freissinieres.fr

3,9ha 155T(60-130m²) 10A CEE

1 ACDFIJKLMOP**Q**
2 BCDGKLMRTVWXY
3 BGHIJLMNRUW
4 (Q 1/7-31/8) (R 🔓)
  (T+U+V+Z 1/7-31/8)
5 **AB**EFGIJKLMNPUVZ
6 EGHJ(N 5km)RTV

💬 Campsite on 1000 metres altitude with pine trees and bordering on a little lake in the heart of amazing mountain scenery. Plenty of options for walking and water recreation.

🚗 From Gap to Briançon over N94, just past La Roche-de-Rame, take left D38. Steep incline. Campsite is well signposted.

L'Argentière-la-Bessée

N94
CC

Guillestre

D902

CC € **15** 1/5-30/6 20/8-29/9

🗻 N 44°44'30'' E 6°33'42''

Fréjus, F-83600 / Provence-Alpes-Côte d'Azur (Var)

👫 ♿ 🛜 **iD** (2594)

🏕 Flower Camping
  Caravaning Le Fréjus***
📧 3401 rue des Combatt.
  d'Afr.du Nord
☎ +33 (0)4-94199460
🔓 1/1 - 31/12
@ contact@lefrejus.com

8ha 90T(80-100m²) 6A CEE

1 ACD**G**IJKLMPST
2 FGKRVXY
3 BGKLMNRU
4 (A 15/4-15/9) (C 15/4-15/10)
  (E+F 🔓) (H 15/4-15/10) JK
  (Q+R+T+U+V+X+Y+Z
  15/4-15/10)
5 **AB**CDEFGHIJKLMNOPUVXZ
6 ABCEGHJ**K**(N 4km)RTV

💬 Pleasant, child-friendly family campsite with many amenities. The site was originally a farm campsite and it has kept many of these characteristics.

🚗 Leave motorway A8 at Fréjus, exit 38. Then turn to the right twice. Campsite is on the left side of the road.

D4   N7
A8
CC **Fréjus
Saint-
Raphaël**
D7
D25
D559

CC € **15** 1/1-7/7 25/8-31/12 7=6, 12=10

🗻 N 43°27'50'' E 6°43'28''

Fréjus, F-83618 / Provence-Alpes-Côte d'Azur (Var)

♿ 🛜 **iD** (2595)

🏕 La Baume/La Palmeraie*****
📧 3775 rue des Comb. d'Afr. du Nord
☎ +33 (0)4-94198888
📠 +33 (0)4-94198350
🔓 31/3 - 28/9
@ reception@
  labaume-lapalmeraie.com

27ha 230T(90-130m²) 6-10A

1 ACD**G**IJKLMP
2 BFGKRTVWXY
3 BFGKMNRUV
4 (**A**+C+F+H 🔓) IJKL
  (Q+S+T+U+V+X+Y+Z 🔓)
5 **AB**CDEFGHIJKLMNOPUVW
  XYZ
6 AEGH**IJK**(N 3km)ORTV

💬 A lovely campsite with fantastic swimming facilities and very professionally organised entertainment.

🚗 A8, exit 38 Fréjus. Then twice right, campsite is on the left.

D4   N7
A8
CC **Fréjus
Saint-
Raphaël**
D7
D25

CC € **19** 31/3-22/6 8/9-27/9

🗻 N 43°27'59'' E 6°43'23''

Fréjus, F-83600 / Provence-Alpes-Côte d'Azur (Var)

♿ 🛜 ✿ iD (2596)

▲ La Pierre Verte★★★★
🏠 1880 route Départementale 4
☎ +33 (0)4-94408830
📠 +33 (0)4-94407541
🕐 7/4 - 29/9
@ info@campinglapierreverte.com

28ha 150T(80-120m²) 6-10A CEE

1 ACD**G**IJKLPST
2 BFGJKPRVWXY
3 BGHKMN**P**RU
4 (C+H 🕐) JK
  (Q+S+T+U+V+X+Y+Z 🕐)
5 **AB**CEFGHIJKLMNOPUVXYZ
6 ACEGHI**K**(N 6km)OTV

💬 A campsite set in extensive woodland and natural parkland. The site gets its name from the natural green stone which can be seen everywhere.

🚗 Leave autoroute A8 at exit 38 Fréjus. Then direction Bagnols-en-Forêt. Campsite located about 3 km on the right.

CC € **19** 7/4-6/7 26/8-28/9

🏕️ N 43°29'3'' E 6°43'13''

Fréjus, F-83600 / Provence-Alpes-Côte d'Azur (Var)

♿ 🛜 iD (2597)

▲ Les Pins Parasols
🏠 3360 rue des Combatt. d'Afr.du Nord
☎ +33 (0)4-94408843
📠 +33 (0)4-94408199
🕐 21/4 - 30/9
@ lespinsparasols@wanadoo.fr

4,5ha 38T(80-200m²) 10A

1 AC**G**IJLP
2 FGJKLRVXY
3 B**F**GKMNRU
4 (B+G 🕐) J
5 **A**DEFGIJKLMNOPUZ
6 ABEGH**J**(N 0,5km)RTV

💬 A campsite with fairly basic comfort. Centrally located for the Côte d'Azur and Provençal interior.

🚗 A8, exit 38 Fréjus. Then turn to the right twice and the campsite is on the right of the road.

CC € **17** 21/4-6/7 25/8-29/9

🏕️ N 43°27'50'' E 6°43'32''

Gap, F-05000 / Provence-Alpes-Côte d'Azur (Hautes-Alpes)

♿ 🛜 iD (2598)

▲ Alpes Dauphiné★★★★
🏠 route Napoléon / N85
☎ +33 (0)4-92512995
📠 +33 (0)4-92535842
🕐 15/4 - 20/10
@ info@alpesdauphine.com

10ha 150T(70-120m²) 6A CEE

1 ACD**G**IJKLMPQ
2 BGIJKRVWXY
3 AB**F**GHJNRU
4 (A 1/7-31/8) (C 1/6-16/9)
  (G 22/6-15/9) **J**K
  (Q+R 1/5-20/9)
  (T+U 10/5-15/9) (V 1/7-30/8)
  (X+Y 10/5-16/9) (Z 10/5-25/9)
5 **AB**DEFGIJKLMNOPQUZ
6 ACDEGJ(N 3km)ORTV

💬 Right next to the 'Route Napoléon' on the N85. Shaded pitches. Good restaurant. Heated swimming pool with waterslide from 1/6 to 16/9. Panoramic views.

🚗 Located 3 km north of Gap on 'Route Napoléon', direction Grenoble. Clearly signposted.

CC € **17** 15/4-4/7 26/8-14/10

🏕️ N 44°34'49'' E 6°4'57''

Giens/Hyères, F-83400 / Provence-Alpes-Côte d'Azur (Var)

🛜 iD (2599)

▲ La Tour Fondue
🏠 1700 avenue des Arbanais
☎ +33 (0)4-94582359
FAX +33 (0)4-94581163
⏳ 16/3 - 4/11
@ info@camping-latourfondue.com

2,3ha 119T(50-120m²) 16A

1 ACD**G**IJKLPT
2 AEGIKNQRTVWX
3 HKLRWY
4 (Q+R+T+U+V+X+Z 🔒)
5 **A**FGIJKLMNOPU
6 CEG**I**K(N 2km)RTV

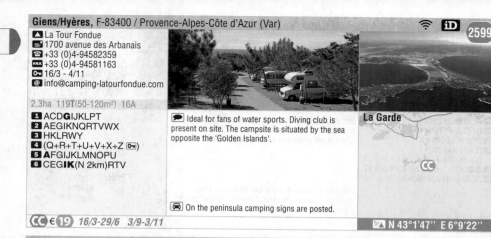

💬 Ideal for fans of water sports. Diving club is present on site. The campsite is situated by the sea opposite the 'Golden Islands'.

La Garde

CC

🚗 On the peninsula camping signs are posted.

CC €**19** 16/3-29/6 3/9-3/11

🗺 N 43°1'47'' E 6°9'22''

Giens/Hyères, F-83400 / Provence-Alpes-Côte d'Azur (Var)

♿ 🛜 iD (2600)

▲ Olbia***
🏠 545 ave René de Knyff, La Madrague
☎ +33 (0)4-94582196
FAX +33 (0)4-94581163
⏳ 31/3 - 7/10
@ info@camping-olbia.com

110T 15A CEE

1 ACD**F**IJLPT
2 ABEGIJQRTVXY
3 BHKLRWY
4 (Q+R+T+U+V+X+Z 🔒)
5 **A**CEFGHIJKLMNOPUV
6 ACEG**I**K(N 5km)ORTV

💬 Grounds set in an attractive park in one of the loveliest parts of the Giens headland, rich in natural beauty. Trips to the Golden Islands and especially Porquerolles, to picturesque Giens and historically interesting Hyères are all highly recommended.

La Garde A570
D559

CC

🚗 Campsite located ± 500m east of the harbour at Madrague on the Giens headland.

CC €**19** 31/3-29/6 3/9-6/10

🗺 N 43°2'23'' E 6°6'12''

Gordes, F-84220 / Provence-Alpes-Côte d'Azur (Vaucluse)

🛜 ✿ iD (2601)

▲ Camping des Sources***
🏠 route de Murs
☎ +33 (0)4-90721248
⏳ 30/3 - 30/9
@ campingdessources@wanadoo.fr

3,5ha 45T(80-120m²) 6-16A CEE

1 ABCD**G**HIJKL**P**S
2 JKTVWXY
3 AGHJLN**Q**RUV
4 (C 🔒) (H 1/6-31/8) (Q+R 🔒) (U 1/7-31/8) (Z 🔒)
5 **A**DFGIJKLMNPUZ
6 ACEGJ(N 1,8km)TV

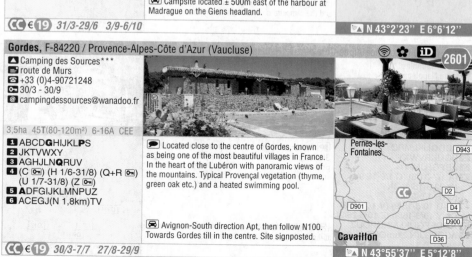

💬 Located close to the centre of Gordes, known as being one of the most beautiful villages in France. In the heart of the Lubéron with panoramic views of the mountains. Typical Provençal vegetation (thyme, green oak etc.) and a heated swimming pool.

Pernes-les-Fontaines
D943

CC
D2
D901
D4
D900

Cavaillon
D36

🚗 Avignon-South direction Apt, then follow N100. Towards Gordes till in the centre. Site signposted.

CC €**19** 30/3-7/7 27/8-29/9

🗺 N 43°55'37'' E 5°12'8''

Graveson, F-13690 / Provence-Alpes-Côte d'Azur (Bouches-du-Rhône) 🛁 📶 iD 2602

🏕 Les Micocouliers***
📧 445 rte de Cassoulen / D5
☎ +33 (0)4-90958149
🗓 15/3 - 15/10
@ micocou@orange.fr

2ha 115T(100m²) 6-8A CEE

1 ACD**G**IJKLMOPST
2 FLRTVWXY
3 A**F**GHJKL**OP**RV
4 (B 15/5-15/9) (G 1/7-30/9)
  (Q+R ⊙)
5 **AB**CEGIJKLPUVZ
6 ACEG**J**(N 1km)

💬 The campsite is in a rural setting. In the middle of Provence, very quiet and natural with large camping pitches. 12 km from Avignon and 7 km from St. Rémy-de-Provence. The centre of Graveson is 1 km from the campsite. Great for cycling.

🚗 A7, exit Avignon-sud, direction Châteaurenard (D28), direction Graveson, between Graveson and Maillane.

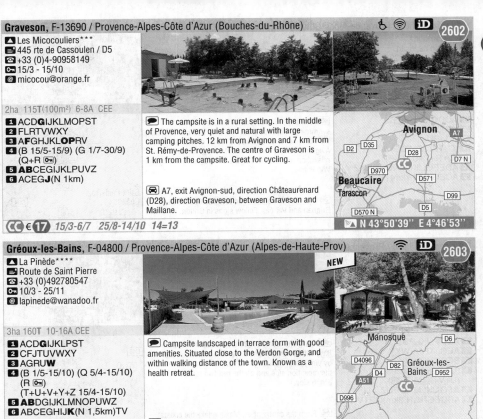

CC € 17 15/3-6/7 25/8-14/10 14=13   📍 N 43°50'39'' E 4°46'53''

Gréoux-les-Bains, F-04800 / Provence-Alpes-Côte d'Azur (Alpes-de-Haute-Prov) 📶 iD 2603

🏕 La Pinède****
📧 Route de Saint Pierre
☎ +33 (0)492780547
🗓 10/3 - 25/11
@ lapinede@wanadoo.fr

NEW

3ha 160T 10-16A CEE

1 ACD**G**IJKLPST
2 CFJTUVWXY
3 AGR**U**W
4 (B 1/5-15/10) (Q 5/4-15/10)
  (R ⊙)
  (T+U+V+Y+Z 15/4-15/10)
5 **AB**DGIJKLMNOPUWZ
6 ABCEGHIJ**K**(N 1,5km)TV

💬 Campsite landscaped in terrace form with good amenities. Situated close to the Verdon Gorge, and within walking distance of the town. Known as a health retreat.

🚗 In Gréoux-les-Bains at roundabout head towards Varages on the D8. Just by the river turn right.

CC € 15 10/3-11/6 1/9-24/11   📍 N 43°44'54'' E 5°52'58''

Gréoux-les-Bains, F-04800 / Provence-Alpes-Côte d'Azur (Alpes-de-Haute-Prov) 🛁 📶 iD 2604

🏕 Verdon Parc****
📧 Domaine de la Paludette
☎ +33 (0)492707086
🗓 30/3 - 4/11
@ info@campingverdonparc.fr

19ha 202T(80-180m²) 16A CEE

1 ACD**F**IJKLPST
2 ACFNRTUVX
3 BGHJKLMNRU**W**X
4 (B 10/4-1/11) (F+G ⊙) IJ
  (Q+R+T+U+V+X+Z ⊙)
5 **AB**DFGIJKLMNOPRUVXYZ
6 CFGH**IJK**(N 1km)RTV

💬 A shaded 11-hectare park in the Haute Provence. Located on the River Verdon the campsite offers you a peaceful and relaxing stay. Close to Lake Esparron (8 km). A spacious campsite with extensive facilities.

🚗 In Gréoux-les-Bains follow the road to Varages (D8) at the roundabout. Campsite well signposted.

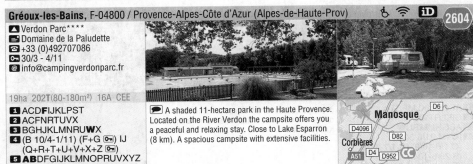

CC € 17 30/3-6/7 25/8-3/11   📍 N 43°45'6'' E 5°53'39''

Grillon, F-84600 / Provence-Alpes-Côte d'Azur (Vaucluse)

🅰 Le Garrigon****
✉ chemin de Visan
☎ +33 (0)4-90287294
🔓 12/3 - 11/11
@ contact@camping-garrigon.com

📶 🛜 iD **2605**

1,4ha 120T(80-160m²) 16A CEE

1 ACD**G**IJKLM**P**T
2 KRTVWX
3 AGJRU
4 (C+H 13/5-20/9) J
    (Q+R+T+U+Z 🔓)
5 ADEFGIJKLMNOPRXYZ
6 ACEGIK(N 1km)TV

💬 Campsite with fine toilet facilities and a swimming pool with slide. In a wine and truffle area. Visit Grignan chateau and the towns of Orange, Avignon, Valréas and Nyons. Here you will find relaxation in the sun or shade in rural surroundings. Wifi is free.

🚗 A7 exit Montelimar-Sud towards Gap between Grignan and Valréas. Follow signs in Grillon.

D9
D24
D541
D10
D538
CC
D976
Saint-Paul-Trois-Châteaux
D59
D576
D94

CC € 15 12/3-8/7 26/8-10/11

🧭 N 44°22'59'' E 4°55'51''

Grimaud, F-83310 / Provence-Alpes-Côte d'Azur (Var)

🅰 Les Mûres****
✉ 2721 route du Littoral
☎ +33 (0)4-94561697
🔓 24/3 - 6/10
@ info@camping-des-mures.com

👫 ♿ 🛜 iD **2606**

7ha 589T(80-130m²) 6A CEE

1 ACD**F**IJKLPST
2 AEGJKRSVWXY
3 BFGKNRUWY
4 (Q+S 🔓) (T 1/6-30/9)
    (U+V+X+Y+Z 🔓)
5 **A**FGIJKLMNOPUZ
6 ABCEG**IK**(N 3km)ORTV

💬 Campsite located right on the sea (St.Tropez Bay) with a friendly ambiance. Site is surrounded by vineyards. CampingCard ACSI is only valid on the reception side and on the last two rows on the beach side.

🚗 From the centre of St. Maxime take the coastal road in the direction of St. Tropez. The entrance to the campsite is located to the right after about 5 km.

D48
D25
D558
Sainte-Maxime
CC
Cogolin
D559
D98
D93

CC € 19 24/3-30/6 1/9-5/10

🧭 N 43°17'2'' E 6°35'30''

Guillestre, F-05600 / Provence-Alpes-Côte d'Azur (Hautes-Alpes)

🅰 Mun. La Rochette***
✉ route des Campings
☎ +33 (0)4-92450215
🔓 5/5 - 24/10
@ guillestre@aol.com

♿ 🛜 iD **2607**

4,4ha 190T(70-130m²) 4-10A CEE

1 ACD**G**IJKLMPST
2 CIKLRTVX
3 ABGHIJ**M**R**U**W
4 (C+H 21/6-30/8)
    (Q 1/6-10/9) (R 1/7-31/8)
    (S 25/6-10/9)
    (T+U+V+X+Z 21/6-30/8)
5 **A**B**F**GIJKLMNOPUVZ
6 ACEGHIJ**K**(N 0,8km)TV

💬 A peaceful, informal campsite within walking distance of Guillestre and at the entrance to the 'Queyras' nature reserve.

🚗 Via the N94 about 30 km south of Briançon take the D902a to Guillestre. Turn right after about 1 km. Follow the camping signs to the end of the road.

CC
N94
D902
Saint-André-d'Embrun
Embrun

CC € 15 5/5-7/7 25/8-23/10

🧭 N 44°39'30'' E 6°38'17''

Istres, F-13800 / Provence-Alpes-Côte d'Azur (Bouches-du-Rhône)

2608

Le Vallon des Cigales***
31 route de St. Chamas
+33 (0)4-42565157
1/1 - 31/12
levallondescigales-camping@orange.fr

6ha 43T(100-120m²) 16A CEE

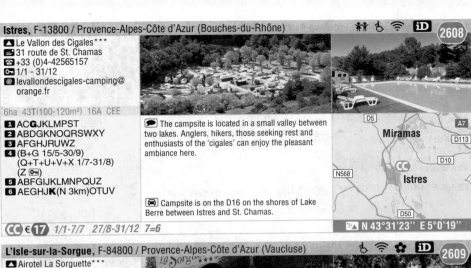

1 AC**G**JKLMPST
2 ABDGKNOQRSWXY
3 AFGHJRUWZ
4 (B+G 15/5-30/9) (Q+T+U+V+X 1/7-31/8) (Z)
5 ABFGIJKLMNPQUZ
6 AEGHJ**K**(N 3km)OTUV

The campsite is located in a small valley between two lakes. Anglers, hikers, those seeking rest and enthusiasts of the 'cigales' can enjoy the pleasant ambiance here.

Campsite is on the D16 on the shores of Lake Berre between Istres and St. Chamas.

D5
A7
Miramas
D113
D10
N568
Istres
D50

N 43°31'23'' E 5°0'19''

CC € 17 *1/1-7/7 27/8-31/12 7=6*

L'Isle-sur-la-Sorgue, F-84800 / Provence-Alpes-Côte d'Azur (Vaucluse)

2609

Airotel La Sorguette***
route d'Apt
+33 (0)4-90380571
FAX +33 (0)4-90208461
15/3 - 15/10
info@camping-sorguette.com

5ha 116T(100-110m²) 10A CEE

1 ACD**G**IJKLPQ
2 CFLRVX
3 A**F**GKNRU**W**X
4 (Q) (R 1/7-28/8) (T+U+Z)
5 **AB**EFGIJKLMNOPUVW
6 ACEGJ**K**(N 1,5km)OQTUV

Quiet campsite located along the Sorgues.
A pleasant and refreshing stay on the river.
The campsite is divided in small fields of 4 pitches surrounded by growth. Large accommodation.

A7 exit Avignon Sud - l'Isle-sur-la-Sorge. Follow N100 at the southeast of l'Isle-sur-la-Sorge.

D4
D31
L'Isle-sur-la-Sorgue
D2
D901
A7
D938
D900
D7N
Cavaillon

N 43°54'52'' E 5°4'17''

CC € 19 *15/3-6/7 25/8-14/10*

La Couronne, F-13500 / Provence-Alpes-Côte d'Azur (Bouches-du-Rhône)

2610

Pascalounet**
route de la Saulce
+33 (0)4-13680285
1/4 - 30/10
contact@camping-pascalounet.com

2ha 41T(70-80m²) 6A CEE

1 ABCD**G**HIJLPST
2 AEFGQTVWXY
3 AGHJRWY
4 (Q) (T 1/7-30/8) Z
5 **A**IJKNPUWX
6 AEGJ**K**(N 3km)OT

A small, friendly campsite within walking distance of a sandy beach. Level marked out pitches. Attention: reception closes in early afternoon (from 12:00 to 15:00).

Take the A7 towards Marseille to the intersection to Fos-sur-Mer (A55). Take exit 8 then the D9 as far as La Couronne.

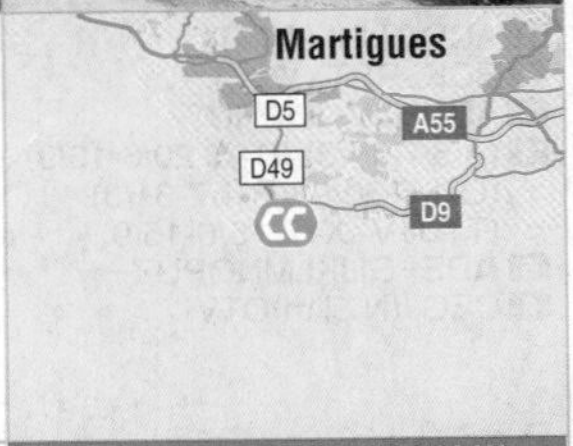
Martigues
D5
A55
D49
D9

N 43°20'4'' E 5°4'11''

CC € 17 *1/4-6/7 25/8-29/10 7=6, 14=11*

La Croix-Valmer, F-83420 / Provence-Alpes-Côte d'Azur (Var)

♿ 📶 **iD** (2611)

🏕 Sélection Camping****
✉ 310 boulevard de la Mer
☎ +33 (0)4-94551030
📠 +33 (0)4-94551039
🗓 15/3 - 15/10
@ camping-selection@wanadoo.fr

4ha 117**T**(65-80m²) 10A

1 ACD**G**IJKLPST
2 AEGIJKRSVXY
3 B**F**GHJKLNQRUWY
4 (C+H 1/4-15/10) K
(Q+S+T+U+V+X+Y+Z 1/4-15/10)
5 **AB**CDEFGHIJKLMNOPUVW
Z
6 ABCEGI**K**(N 3km)ORTV

💬 The campsite has a magnificent location in an extensive Provençal park (pines, mimosa, etc.). Very good atmosphere. A few minutes walk to beach.

🚗 In La Croix-Valmer drive in the direction of Le Lavandou. Signposted at the roundabout 2 km down the road.

D558
Cogolin
D559
D98   D93
Cavalaire-sur-Mer

CC € **19** 15/3-7/7 25/8-14/10

N 43°11'40'' E 6°33'18''

La Roche-de-Rame, F-05310 / Provence-Alpes-Côte d'Azur (Hautes-Alpes)

♿ 📶 **iD** (2612)

🏕 Camping du Lac**
✉ N94
☎ +33 (0)4-92209031
🗓 1/5 - 30/9
@ campingdulacrochederame@
orange.fr

1,3ha 74**T**(70-120m²) 3-10A CEE

1 AGIJKLM**PQ**
2 ACD**G**KLRTVWXY
3 AGHIJNRWZ
4 (Q 1/7-31/8) (T+U 🔑)
(V 1/7-31/8) (X+Y 🔑)
5 **A**FGIJKMNPUZ
6 CEIJ(N 0,3km)T

💬 A peaceful and friendly campsite by a lovely natural lake. Located in the wide Durance valley. Very clean toilet facilities.

🚗 Via the N94, 20 km south of Briançon in the centre of La Roche-de-Rame, left at the lake. From Gap on the right of N94.

L'Argentière-la-   D902
Bessée
CC
Guillestre
N94

CC € **15** 1/5-1/7 25/8-29/9

N 44°44'49'' E 6°34'53''

La Roche-des-Arnauds, F-05400 / Provence-Alpes-Côte d'Azur (Hautes-Alpes)

📶 **iD** (2613)

🏕 Le Parc des Sérigons***
☎ +33 (0)4-92578177
🗓 31/3 - 28/10
@ contact@camping-serigons.com

15ha 130**T**(130-200m²) 10A CEE

1 ACD**G**IJKLMPST
2 B**CK**LRSTXY
3 ABGHJMN**OP**RU
4 (A 5/7-17/8) (B+G 20/6-15/9)
(Q 1/6-30/9) (R 1/7-31/8)
(T+U+V+X+Z 15/6-15/9)
5 **A**DEFGIJKLMNOPUZ
6 CEGJ(N 3km)OTV

💬 You will be enjoying the peace and quiet of nature from a large pitch. Camp in the forest with a lot of privacy. The trees aren't high so there is plenty of light. Mountains surround the site. Family campsite. Friendly welcome. There are European plugs and large electricity cables.

🚗 N75 Grenoble-Sisteron, dir. Veynes. In Veynes dir. Gap - La Roche-des-Arnands. Big campsite signs on left. For safety reasons bear right and then cross road.

D937
La Roche-des-
D320 **CC** Arnauds **Gap**
Veynes
D900 B
D994   N85

CC € **13** 31/3-6/7 25/8-27/10

N 44°33'52'' E 5°55'3''

Lagnes, F-84800 / Provence-Alpes-Côte d'Azur (Vaucluse) ♿ 🛜 ✿ 2614

🏕 La Coutelière****
📧 2765 route de Fontaine de Vaucluse
☎ +33 (0)4-90203397
📅 23/3 - 5/10
@ info@camping-lacouteliere.com

2,8ha 82T(80-142m²) 10A CEE

1 BC**G**IJKL**P**ST
2 CGLMRVXY
3 A**F**GHJMNRU**W**X
4 (C+H 10/4-30/9) (Q 📅)
(R+T 1/5-30/9)
(U+V 7/5-20/9) (Z 📅)
5 **A**DEFGIJKLMNOPQUWYZ
6 ACEGJ**K**(N 4km)ORU

💬 A quiet campsite with level, shaded pitches. Located between Fontaine de Vaucluse and Isle sur la Sorgue. Heated swimming pool with children's pool and tennis. Modern toilet facilities, spacious and heated in the low season.

🚗 Follow A7 motorway as far as exit 24. Take turning towards Apt via the D973 and the D22. Turn left after about 12 km onto the D24 direction Lagnes and Fontaine de Vaucluse. Campsite signposted from here.

Pernes-les-Fontaines
D31 · D4
D6 · CC · D2
· D901
A7 · D938 · D900
Cavaillon
D7N

CC €**17** 23/3-29/6 27/8-4/10 📷 N 43°54'39'' E 5°6'24''

Lambesc, F-13410 / Provence-Alpes-Côte d'Azur (Bouches-du-Rhône) ♿ 🛜 iD 2615

🏕 Flower Provence Camping - Lou Paradou***
📧 avenue d'Aix
☎ +33 (0)4-42570578
📅 31/3 - 30/9
@ provence.camping@wanadoo.fr

2,3ha 44T(80-143m²) 10A CEE

1 ACD**G**HIJL**P**ST
2 BIJTUVXY
3 BGNRU
4 (B 1/5-30/9)
(Q+R+T 1/6-30/9)
(U 1/7-31/8) (X+Z 1/7-30/8)
5 ABFGJLMNOPUZ
6 AEG**K**(N 1,4km)T

💬 Campsite located 2½ km from the town in natural surroundings. Central location for visiting places such as the Salon-de-Provence and Aix-en-Provence. Take note: reception closed from 12:00 to 15:00.

🚗 From Aix-en-Provence follow D7n towards Salon-de-Provence. Left past St-Cannat after entering Lambesc (D917).

○ Mallemort
D943
D561
Lambesc
Pélissanne · CC
D572
A7
D113 · D7 N
A8 · D543

CC €**15** 31/3-7/7 25/8-29/9 📷 N 43°38'23'' E 5°16'31''

Le Cannet-des-Maures, F-83340 / Provence-Alpes-Côte d'Azur (Var) ♿ 🛜 ✿ iD 2616

🏕 Domaine de la Cigalière***
📧 4345 route du Thoronet
☎ +33 (0)4-94738106
📅 1/4 - 1/11
@ contact@domaine-lacigaliere.com

NEW

25T(100-140m²) 10A

1 AC**F**IJKLPST
2 BFIJKRTVWXY
3 AGKRU
4 (C+H 1/5-30/9) (Q 📅)
(T+Z 1/6-30/9)
5 **A**CFGIJKLMNOPUZ
6 ACEGHIJ**K**L(N 4km)TV

💬 A campsite with an authentic Provençale ambiance. Nature and ecology play an important role. Lovely large pitches.

🚗 A8 exit Le Luc. Campsite signposted from Le Cannet-des-Maures.

Lorgues
D562 · D555
D13 · D10
Cabasse · Vidauban
CC
A8
D48
D97 · A57 · D558

CC €**17** 1/4-6/7 25/8-31/10 📷 N 43°25'17'' E 6°20'13''

Le Lavandou, F-83980 / Provence-Alpes-Côte d'Azur (Var)

♿ 🛜 **iD** (2617)

🏕 Beau Séjour***
🏠 route de Bénat, D298
☎ +33 (0)4-94712530
🖥 14/4 - 1/10
@ caravaning.beau.sejour@
gmail.com

1,8ha 135**T**(70-85m²) 10A

1 A**G**IJKLPST
2 GRTVXY
3 A**F**GR
4 (V+X ⊙)
5 A CGIJKLMNOPUVZ
6 AEGJT

💬 Very correct, well-maintained campsite at walking distance from the Mediterranean Sea. Le Lavandou is a very lively bathing resort. Ideal base for all kinds of outings.

🚗 A8, exit 35 direction Brignoles/Le Val D43. Then follow D14, D12 and D98 to D298 in Bormes-les-Mimosas. 2nd exit at roundabout.

CC € **17** 14/4-30/6 20/8-30/9

🏖 N 43°8'7'' E 6°21'6''

Le Lavandou, F-83980 / Provence-Alpes-Côte d'Azur (Var)

♿ 🛜 **iD** (2618)

🏕 Parc Camping de
Pramousquier**
🏠 chemin de la Faverolle
☎ +33 (0)4-94058395
🖷 +33 (0)4-94057504
🖥 14/4 - 30/9
@ camping-lavandou@wanadoo.fr

4,5ha 146**T**(70-100m²) 4-10A

1 ACD**G**IJLPST
2 AEGIJKRTVWXY
3 B**F**GJR**W**Y
4 (Q ⊙) (R 1/5-30/9)
(T+U+V+X+Y+Z 1/6-15/9)
5 A**B**GHIJKLMNOPUVZ
6 CFGHI**K**(N 1,5km)ORTV

💬 A pleasant terraced campsite close to the Mediterranean and a few kilometres from the popular seaside resort of Le Lavandou. Very central location with regard to tourist attractions such as the Golden Islands and St. Tropez. Naturist beach close by.

🚗 The campsite is located on the coastal road, right at the front of the town Pramousquier (east side).

CC € **19** 14/4-6/7 1/9-29/9

🏖 N 43°9'23'' E 6°26'53''

Le Muy, F-83490 / Provence-Alpes-Côte d'Azur (Var)

♿ 🛜 **iD** (2619)

🏕 Camping RCN Domaine de
la Noguière***
🏠 DN7, 1617 route de Fréjus
☎ +33 31034-3745095
🖷 +33 (0)4-94459295
🖥 23/3 - 8/10
@ reserveringen@rcn.nl

14ha 173**T**(50-120m²) 6A

1 ACD**G**IJKLPST
2 FGKLRTVWXY
3 B**F**G**M**NRUW
4 (A+B+G ⊙) J
(Q+R+T+U+V+X+Y+Z ⊙)
5 A**B**CEFGHIJKLMNOPQUWZ
6 AEGHI**J**K**L**(N 1km)ORTV

💬 A lovely well-maintained campsite in beautiful natural surroundings. The campsite offers two magnificent swimming pools with slides. There are views of the Roquebrune from the campsite. The Mediterranean beaches are 20 minutes away. Close to the seaside resorts of St. Raphael, Fréjus and St Tropez.

🚗 Campsite is located by the N7, about 1 km to the east of Le Muy.

CC € **17** 23/3-30/6 25/8-7/10 7=6, 14=11

🏖 N 43°28'5'' E 6°35'31''

Le Pradet, F-83220 / Provence-Alpes-Côte d'Azur (Var)

♿ 🛜 **iD** **2620**

▲ L'Artaudois***
✉ 529 chemin de l'Artaude
☎ +33 (0)4-94217261
📠 +33 (0)4-94217594
📅 31/3 - 14/10
@ info@artaudois.fr

3,5ha 51T(80-100m²) 10A

1 ACD**G**IJL**P**T
2 ABJKNRTVXY
3 B**F**GN**O**P**R**UW
4 (**A** 1/4-30/9)
  (C+H 15/4-30/9)
  (Q 1/4-15/10)
  (T+V+Z 1/7-31/8)
5 **AB**CEFGHIJKLMNOPUXZ
6 CEG**I**K(N 1,2km)T

💬 A terraced campsite in a mediterranean wood with beautiful panoramas. Just over 1 km from the Mediterranean Sea and very central for many places including Toulon, Hyères, Les Îles d'Or and Le Lavandou. Well organised, friendly atmosphere.

🚗 From centre of Le Pradet follow orange arrows with name of campsite.

Toulon — A57 — A570 — CC — D559 — La Seyne-sur-Mer

CC € **15** 31/3-6/7 27/8-13/10   🏖 N 43°5'58'' E 6°1'51''

Le Vernet, F-04140 / Provence-Alpes-Côte d'Azur (Alpes-de-Haute-Prov)

🛜 **iD** **2621**

▲ Lou Passavous***
☎ +33 (0)4-92351467
📅 1/5 - 15/9
@ loupassavous@orange.fr

1,5ha 55T(80-120m²) 6A CEE

1 A**G**IJKLNPST
2 GKRTVX
3 AGHJMNRU**W**
4 (A 📷) (C 15/6-31/8)
  (Q+T+U+V+X+Y+Z 15/5-15/9)
5 **A**EFGIJKLMNPUZ
6 AEGJ**K**(N 8km)TV

💬 Beautifully located campsite with stunning views of the mountains. A good base for mountain walks and car trips through magnificent countryside. Good amenities and a Dutch owner.

🚗 From Gap towards Barcelonette, then the D900 towards Digne-les-Bains. Signposted at Le Vernet. Do not take the D900c from Gap.

Seyne — Barles — CC — Le Vernet — D900 — Beaujeu

CC € **17** 1/5-6/7 26/8-14/9   🏖 N 44°16'55'' E 6°23'29''

Les Adrets-de-l'Estérel, F-83600 / Provence-Alpes-Côte d'Azur (Var)

🛜 **iD** **2622**

▲ Les Philippons***
✉ D237, 378 route de l'Argentière
☎ +33 (0)4-94409067
📠 +33 (0)4-94193592
📅 1/4 - 30/9
@ info@lesphilippons.com

5,2ha 101T(80-160m²) 6-10A CEE

1 ACD**G**IJKLMPST
2 B**F**JKRSTVWXY
3 B**F**GR
4 (B 11/4-3/10)
  (G+Q+R+T+U+V+X+Z 📷)
5 **A**CGHIJKMNPUVZ
6 AEG**K**(N 3km)ORTV

💬 A beautifully located, quiet family campsite. Well cared for and well supervised. Recommended. Favourable location with regard to the Mediterranean Sea and the Provençal hinterland.

🚗 A8 exit 39, direction Les Adrets-de-l'Estérel, campsite signposted on roundabout.

D562 — D37 — A8 — CC — Cannes — Mandelieu-la-Napoule — D4 — Fréjus — D559

CC € **17** 1/4-6/7 25/8-29/9   🏖 N 43°31'44'' E 6°50'23''

Les Issambres, F-83380 / Provence-Alpes-Côte d'Azur (Var)

♿ 🛜 **iD** (2623)

🏕 Au Paradis des Campeurs****
📧 La Gaillarde-Plage
☎ +33 (0)4-94969355
FAX +33 (0)4-94496299
🔓 1/4 - 1/10
@ campingauparadisdescampeurs@
gmail.com

2,7ha 180T(60-120m²) 6A CEE

1 ACDGIJKLM**P**ST
2 AEGIJKQRVWXY
3 B**E**FGHJKNRUWY
4 (Q+S+T+U+V+X+Y+Z 🔓)
5 **AB**CEFGHIJKLMNOPUXYZ
6 CEG**IK**(N 2km)ORTUV

💬 Direct access to the sandy beach from the campsite. A congenial family campsite. CampingCard ACSI is only valid for standard pitches. The discount card is not valid for comfort pitches.

🚗 On the N98 between St. Aygulf and Les Issambres.

Saint-Raphaël
D7
D25
CC
D559

CC € **17** 1/4-7/7 25/8-30/9

📍 N 43°21'58'' E 6°42'43''

Les Vigneaux, F-05120 / Provence-Alpes-Côte d'Azur (Hautes-Alpes)

👫 ♿ 🛜 **iD** (2624)

🏕 Campéole Le Courounba***
📧 Le Pont Du Rif
☎ +33 (0)4-92230209
🔓 11/5 - 16/9
@ courounba@campeole.com

12ha 250T(70-130m²) 6-10A CEE

1 ABCDG**I**JKLM**P**R
2 BCKLMRTVWXY
3 ABGHJMNR**W**
4 (C+H 15/6-17/9) J**KN**
   (Q 1/7-30/8) (R 1/7-31/8)
   (T+U+V 13/6-13/9)
   (X 15/6-13/9) (Z 13/6-13/9)
5 **AB**DEFGIJKLMNOPRUZ
6 ACEGHJ**K**(N 4km)RTV

💬 A peaceful family campsite in the countryside, at the foot of Mont Brison. Spacious shaded pitches. A completely refurbished ecological swimming pool with a slide and toddlers' pool, BMX area, sauna, jacuzzi, multisports field, tennis.

🚗 In L'Argentière-la-Bessée N94 follow the signs to Les Vigneaux, then turn right over the bridge.

Briançon
CC Les Vigneaux
L'Argentière-la-Bessée
N94

CC € **15** 11/5-6/7 25/8-15/9

📍 N 44°49'30'' E 6°31'33''

Lourmarin, F-84160 / Provence-Alpes-Côte d'Azur (Vaucluse)

♿ 🛜 **iD** (2625)

🏕 Les Hautes Prairies***
📧 28 route de Vaugines
☎ +33 (0)4-90680289
🔓 1/4 - 30/9
@ leshautesprairies@campasun.eu

5ha 108T(80-120m²) 10A CEE

1 ACD**G**HIJKLMOPT
2 RTVXY
3 AGNRU
4 (C 15/4-1/10) J(Q+R 🔓)
   (T+U 5/4-18/9) (V 1/7-18/9)
   (X 5/4-18/9) (Z 5/4-30/9)
5 **A**DEFGJLNPQUWXYZ
6 CEGH**K**(N 0,7km)OTV

💬 A campsite located on the south side of the Luberon within walking distance of the historic town of Lourmarin. Quiet location. New luxurious toilet facilities. Reasonably level, marked-out pitches. Privacy. Large swimmingpool.

🚗 A7, exit 25 as far as Cavaillon. Then D973 in the direction of Pertuis. Follow the signs in Lourmarin.

D36
D900
CC
D973
Cadenet
La Roque-
d'Anthéron
D943
D561
Pertuis
D543

CC € **17** 1/4-7/7 25/8-29/9

📍 N 43°46'4'' E 5°22'23''

Malemort-du-Comtat, F-84570 / Provence-Alpes-Côte d'Azur (Vaucluse) 🚶 🛜 iD (2626)

🏕 Font Neuve***
📧 660 chemin de l'Annonciade
☎ +33 (0)4-90699000
🔓 14/4 - 30/9
@ campingfontneuve@orange.fr

1,5ha 66T(80-120m²) 10A CEE

1 AGIJKLMPS
2 IJRTVWXY
3 BGHJMRU
4 (A 1/7-31/8) (B 1/5-30/9)
 (Q 🔌) (U+X+Z 1/5-30/9)
5 AEFGIJKLMNOPUVWXY
6 EGJ(N 1km)RTV

💬 Pleasant, quiet surroundings with fruit and wine fields. Walking distance from village and 20 km from the Mont Ventoux. Welcoming restaurant with a bar by the swimming pool.

🚗 From Carpentras dir. Mazan D4 and D5 dir. Malemort. Follow arrows.

CC €19 14/4-7/7 25/8-29/9   📷 N 44°0'50'' E 5°10'16''

Mallemort, F-13370 / Provence-Alpes-Côte d'Azur (Bouches-du-Rhône) 🚶 🛜 iD (2627)

🏕 Durance Luberon****
📧 Domaine du Vergon
☎ +33 (0)4-90591336
🔓 1/4 - 30/9
@ duranceluberon@orange.fr

4ha 135T(100-150m²) 6-10A CEE

1 AGIJKLMPST
2 FLRVWXY
3 BFGNOPR
4 (B 1/5-30/9) (Q 14/4-30/9)
 (T 1/7-23/8) (Z 1/7-28/8)
5 ADEFGIJKLMNOPRUZ
6 AEGJK(N 2km)T

💬 Lovely campsite with large marked-out pitches on level grounds, located in the Durance valley. Large swimming pool and modern toilet facilities. Quiet location. Ideal for tents and caravans.

🚗 Leave the A7 at exit 26. Then take the N7 in the direction of Aix-en-Provence. After 6 km turn in the direction of Mallemort. The campsite is located just before Charleval, on the D561.

CC €17 1/4-30/6 18/8-29/9   📷 N 43°43'16'' E 5°12'18''

Manosque, F-04100 / Provence-Alpes-Côte d'Azur (Alpes-de-Haute-Prov) 🛜 iD (2628)

🏕 Flower Camping Provence Vallée***
📧 1138 avenue de la Repasse
☎ +33 (0)4-92722808
🔓 30/3 - 31/10
@ contact@provence-vallee.fr

3,2ha 67T(80-110m²) 10A

1 ACDGHIJKLPST
2 FGRVWXY
3 AFGR
4 (B+G 15/5-15/9) (Q 1/6-30/9)
 (R 🔌) (T 15/6-15/9)
 (U+V 1/7-31/8) (Z 15/6-15/9)
5 ABGJLMNPUVWYZ
6 CFGHJK(N 2km)RV

💬 Spacious marked-out pitches on sloping ground. A varied selection of trees provide plenty of shade. Large new swimming pool. At a few kilometres from Manosque, accessible via public transport.

🚗 A51, exit 18 direction Manosque. Follow Apt before town centre. Campsite well signposted.

CC €13 30/3-6/7 25/8-30/10   📷 N 43°49'48'' E 5°45'49''

Maussane-les-Alpilles, F-13520 / Provence-Alpes-Côte d'Azur (Bouches-du-Rhône) ♿ 📶 **iD** (2629)

🏕 Les Romarins***
☎ +33 (0)4-90543360
🕐 15/3 - 3/11
@ camping-municipal-maussane@
wanadoo.fr

3ha 145T(70-100m²) 10A CEE

1 ACD**G**IJKLOPQ
2 RTVWXY
3 A**F**GHJKLMRU**W**
4 (B+G 3/6-3/9) (Q+R 🔒)
5 **AB**DEFGIJKLMNOPUWXYZ
6 AEGHK(N 0,3km)TV

💬 Quiet, green campsite at 200 metres from the centre of a beautiful, authentic Provence village with a lovely shaded church square in the south of Les Alpilles. Heated indoor pool, open from 15 April to 15 October. Several bakers and restaurants in the village.

🚗 The campsite is located on the D5. From Maussane via D17 direction Arles, then the D5. Located near the centre on the St. Rémy side.

Tarascon D99
D33 D5
D570 N
CC
Arles Raphèle-
les-Arles
A54 D113

ⓒⓒ € **17** 3/4-30/4 14/5-30/6 1/9-2/11 | N 43°43'16'' E 4°48'34''

Mazan, F-84380 / Provence-Alpes-Côte d'Azur (Vaucluse) ♿ 📶 **iD** (2630)

🏕 Le Ventoux***
📧 1348 chemin de la Combe
☎ +33 (0)4-90697094
🕐 15/3 - 1/11
@ info@camping-le-ventoux.com

1,5ha 46T(90-120m²) 10A CEE

1 ACD**G**IJKLM**P**Q
2 KSTUVWXY
3 BGHJNRU
4 (B 1/5-31/10) (G 1/5-15/10) (Q+R+U 1/4-31/10) (X+Y 🔒) (Z 1/4-31/10)
5 **AB**DEFGIJKLMNOPRUZ
6 AEGJ**K**(N 3km)TV

💬 A campsite located amid the vineyards with lovely views mostly of Mont Ventoux. A modernised swimming pool in Roman style. Satisfied guests who come back again and again. 3 km from Mazan. Good toilet facilities and a surprisingly good restaurant. There are 46 pitches, 38 of which are CampingCard ACSI pitches.

🚗 A7, exit Orange-Sud, D974 direction Carpentras. After Carpentras direction Bédoin/Mont Ventoux, then follow signs towards campsite.

D8
D7 D938 D19
D974
CC D1
Carpentras D942
Pernes-les-
Fontaines D4

ⓒⓒ € **17** 15/3-7/7 25/8-31/10 | N 44°4'50'' E 5°6'50''

Méolans-Revel, F-04340 / Provence-Alpes-Côte d'Azur (Alpes-de-Haute-Prov) 📶 **iD** (2631)

🏕 Camping River***
☎ +33 (0)4-92855713
📠 +33 (0)6-37360909
🕐 28/4 - 16/9
@ info@camping-river.eu

1ha 40T(80-130m²) 6A CEE

1 ACDGIJKLMNOPST
2 ACDGNRTVXY
3 B**F**GHJRU**W**Z
4 (**A** 1/7-31/8) (C 1/6-30/9) (Q+R 1/5-30/9) (T+U+V+X+Y+Z 🔒)
5 ACFGHJLMNPQRUZ
6 ADEGIJ(N 8km)OTV

💬 A small friendly campsite, situated right by the river. In particular a campsite for nature lovers, walkers and cyclists. Almost all sports activities are possible here.

🚗 Located on the D900 Gap-Barcelonnette. In Le Martinet turn right at the bridge. Campsite signposted.

D954
Saint-Pons
CC
Barcelonnette
Seyne
D908 D902
D900

ⓒⓒ € **17** 28/4-6/7 24/8-15/9 | N 44°23'47'' E 6°29'20''

Méolans-Revel, F-04340 / Provence-Alpes-Côte d'Azur (Alpes-de-Haute-Prov) 📶 iD (2632)

🏕 Domaine de l'Ubaye****
🛣 D900
☎ +33 (0)4-92810196
📅 1/6 - 30/9
@ info@loisirsubaye.com

10ha 268T(100-120m²) 6A

1 ACD**G**IJKLO**P**ST
2 CIJLORTVXY
3 BDGHJKLMNRUV**WX**
4 (A 1/7-30/8) (C+H 📅)
(Q+S+T 1/7-10/9) (U 📅)
(V 1/7-15/9) (X 15/6-15/9)
(Y 📅) (Z 1/7-15/9)
5 **AB**EFGHIJKLMNPQRUWYZ
6 ACEGJ**K**(N 2km)ORTUV

💬 The only four-star campsite in the region. Located by the river in Vallée de l'Ubaye. A spacious campsite with a tennis court and swimming pool. Dutch-run with plenty of activities and entertainment and a homely atmosphere bringing back many campers year after year.

🚐 At the side of the main road Gap-Barcelonnette. 8 km west of Barcelonnette, at the right side of the road, you'll find the camping signs.

CC Barcelonnette
Saint-Pons
D900 | D908 | D902

CC € **17** 1/6-4/7 22/8-29/9 🗺 N 44°23'49'' E 6°32'44''

Mondragon, F-84430 / Provence-Alpes-Côte d'Azur (Vaucluse) ♿ 📶 iD (2633)

🏕 Camping La Pinède en Provence***
🛣 202 chemin de la Maresque
☎ +33 (0)4-90408298
📅 1/1 - 31/12
@ contact@
camping-pinede-provence.com

3,5ha 109T 13A CEE

1 ACDGIJKLM**P**ST
2 BFIJRSTXY
3 ABGHJNRU
4 (C+H 30/4-30/9) J
(Q 1/5-30/9) (R 📅)
(S 1/3-15/11)
(T+U+V+X 1/7-15/9)
(Z 1/3-15/11)
5 ABDFGIJKLMNOPUXYZ
6 ACEGIK(N 2km)TV

💬 A charming campsite in the middle of pine forests in the heart of Provence. There is a new swimming pool and a reception area with bar. Close to the motorway and near Orange and Avignon.

🚐 Exit 19 Bollène, towards town centre at roundabout then direction Mondragon. Follow camping signs.

D86
D901 | D63 | D59 | D94
D8
N86 | A7
CC | N7 | D976
Bagnols-sur-Cèze N580

CC € **17** 1/1-29/6 24/8-31/12 🗺 N 44°14'37'' E 4°43'45''

Moustiers-Ste-Marie, F-04360 / Provence-Alpes-Côte d'Azur (Alpes-de-Haute-Prov) ♿ 📶 iD (2634)

🏕 Le Vieux Colombier***
🛣 Quartier St. Michel
☎ +33 (0)7-85538282
📅 28/4 - 23/9
@ contact@lvcm.fr

2,7ha 55T 6-10A CEE

1 ACD**F**IJKLMP
2 GJKRTVXY
3 AGHIJNRU
4 (Q+T+Z 📅)
5 **AB**GIJKLMNO**P**UVX
6 CEG**K**OV

NEW

💬 Simple but well-maintained campsite 300m from Moustiers. The pitches at this campsite are surprisingly large.

🚐 D592. Campsite is on the right hand side of the road after the roundabout driving around Moustiers (towards Lac Ste Croix).

D907
D953
D6 | CC Moustiers-Sainte-Marie
D957
D11 | D19 | D952

CC € **17** 28/4-5/7 23/8-22/9 🗺 N 43°50'22'' E 6°13'17''

Moustiers-Ste-Marie, F-04360 / Provence-Alpes-Côte d'Azur (Alpes-de-Haute-Prov) ♿ 🛜 iD (2635)

🏕 Manaysse**
📧 rue Frédéric Mistral
☎ +33 (0)4-92746671
📠 +33 (0)4-92746228
🗓 1/4 - 21/10
@ manaysse@orange.fr

1,5ha 100T(60-120m²) 6-10A CEE

1 A**F**IJKLMP
2 IJKRSVX
3 AGHJLNRU
4 (Q+Z ⊙)
5 A**G**IJKLMNP
6 CEG**K**(N 2km)

💬 Basic but well-maintained campsite at 900 metres from Moustiers. About half of the pitches have a view of Moustiers-Ste-Marie. Ste. Croix lake is 4 km away.

🚗 Campsite located on roundabout just outside Moustiers direction Riez (D952).

CC €**15** 1/4-2/7 27/8-20/10   N 43°50'42'' E 6°12'55''

Moustiers-Ste-Marie, F-04360 / Provence-Alpes-Côte d'Azur (Alpes-de-Haute-Prov) ♿ 🛜 iD (2636)

🏕 Saint Clair***
📧 D952
☎ +33 (0)4-92746715
📠 +33 (0)4-84508074
🗓 27/4 - 15/9
@ direction@camping-st-clair.com

3ha 93T(88-136m²) 6A CEE

1 ACDGIJKLPST
2 BCGJKRVWXY
3 BGHR
4 (Q+R ⊙) (T+U+V 1/7-31/8)
5 **A**CDEFGHIJKLMNOPUV
6 ACEGK(N 3km)ORT

💬 A congenial, shaded campsite, located on a river with magnificent panoramas of the very impressive scenery. The very touristy village of Moustiers Ste Marie, with its numerous china shops is just 3 km away. A few minutes drive from Lac Ste Croix.

🚗 Campsite entrance on roundabout 3km south of Moustiers-Ste-Marie (D957).

CC €**17** 27/4-7/7 25/8-14/9   N 43°49'41'' E 6°13'28''

Moustiers-Ste-Marie, F-04360 / Provence-Alpes-Côte d'Azur (Alpes-de-Haute-Prov) 👫 ♿ 🛜 iD (2637)

🏕 Saint Jean***
📧 Quartier Saint Jean
☎ 📠 +33 (0)4-92746685
🗓 1/4 - 9/10
@ contact@camping-st-jean.fr

1,7ha 108T(80-150m²) 6-10A

1 ACD**G**IJKLMPST
2 CGKRVWXY
3 BGHJKNQR**W**
4 (Q+R ⊙)
 (T+U+V+Z 11/5-15/9)
5 **A**CDEFGHIJKLMNOPUVWYZ
6 ACEG**I**K(N 0,7km)ORTV

💬 Exceptionally nicely situated campsite in the heart of the impressive Gorges du Verdon region and 700 metres away from the famous porcelain town of Moustiers Ste. Marie. A lovely, well-maintained campsite with considerate reception. Beautiful view over Moustiers from the campsite.

🚗 D592, campsite located on left of road past the roundabout towards Riez.

CC €**17** 1/4-8/7 26/8-8/10 7=6   N 43°50'37'' E 6°12'54''

Niozelles, F-04300 / Provence-Alpes-Côte d'Azur (Alpes-de-Haute-Prov) 🛜 📱iD ②⑥③⑧

▲ L'Oasis de Provence****
📧 N100
☎ +33 (0)4-92786331
📅 30/3 - 15/10
@ contact@oasisdeprovence.com

28ha 104T(100m²) 6-10A CEE

1 ACGIJKLPS
2 CDFGLMNRTVX
3 ABFGHJNRUWXZ
4 (B+G 1/5-30/9) (Q 📅)
(R 1/7-31/8)
(T+U+V+X+Z 📅)
5 ABDEFGJLNPUWXYZ
6 ACEGHJ(N 2,5km)OTUV

💬 A pleasant family campsite in the heart of nature, peacefully located between two streams on a 1.5 hectare lake. Peaceful, cool nights. Campsite has been renewed and has a restaurant with a charming garden which serves local dishes.

🚗 On the A51 exit Brillane. In Brillane take the N100. The campsite is located on the N100. The campsite is 2.5 km further on, to the left.

Les Mées
Forcalquier — A51
D950 D12
D4100 D13 D4096
Volx D907
D4

CC € ⑲ 30/3-6/7 24/8-14/10 📐 N 43°56'1'' E 5°52'4''

Oraison, F-04700 / Provence-Alpes-Côte d'Azur (Alpes-de-Haute-Prov) ♿ 🛜 📱iD ②⑥③⑨

▲ Les Oliviers****
📧 chemin St. Sauveur
☎ +33 (0)4-92782000
📅 1/3 - 31/12
@ camping-oraison@wanadoo.fr

2ha 33T(25-110m²) 10A CEE

1 AGHIJKLNPST
2 FGKRTVWXY
3 ACGHJNRU
4 (B 15/4-30/9) (Q 1/4-30/9)
(R 15/4-30/9)
(T+U+X+Z 1/7-31/8)
5 AFGJLMNPUXZ
6 ACEGJ(N 2km)TV

💬 A lovely, agreeable campsite with sweeping views of the Lubéron oriental and the 'Montagne de Lurs'. The campsite is set among olive groves. A 5 minute walk to the village and close to the Gorges du Verdon, Lubéron, Forcalquier and Manosque.

🚗 On the A51 take exit 19. Then take the N96 towards Oraison. Follow signs in the centre.

Forcalquier D4096
D12
Oraison CC
D13 A51
D907
D4
Manosque D6

CC € ⑮ 1/3-29/6 25/8-30/12 📐 N 43°55'23'' E 5°55'25''

Orange, F-84100 / Provence-Alpes-Côte d'Azur (Vaucluse) ♿ 🛜 📱iD ②⑥④⓪

▲ Manon
📧 1321, rue Alexis Carrel
☎ +33 (0)4-32819496
📅 20/3 - 31/10
@ campingmanon@yahoo.fr

1,7ha 50T(65-110m²) 10A CEE

1 ACDGIJKLMP
2 FRSTVWXY
3 ABGMR
4 (B 1/6-30/9) (Q 1/5-30/9)
(R 📅) (T 1/6-30/9) (V 📅)
(X+Z 1/6-30/9)
5 AEFGIJKLMNOPUVWZ
6 BDEGK(N 1km)ORTV

💬 Patrick will give you a warm welcome at this small, quiet campsite close to the Arc de Triomphe and the centre of Orange with, among other things, an ancient Roman theatre. Sun 300 days a year, set nicely in the shade of pine trees and cypresses.

🚗 From A7 exit Orange-Centre. Left at the roundabout by McDonald's and left after the school. Then follow camping signs towards Le Jonquier.

Sainte-Cécile-les-Vignes
N7 D8
D976 D975
N580 Orange D977
L'Ardoise A7 D950
A9 Sarrians
D980 D907

CC € ⑰ 20/3-7/7 25/8-30/10 10=9 📐 N 44°8'48'' E 4°47'42''

Orgon, F-13660 / Provence-Alpes-Côte d'Azur (Bouches-du-Rhône) ♿ 🛜 iD 2641

△ La Vallée Heureuse***
🏕 Impasse Lavau
☎ +33 (0)4-84800171
📅 1/4 - 30/10
@ contact@valleeheureuse.com

9ha 180T(70-200m²) 10A CEE

1 ACD**G**HIJKLPST
2 DFJKLRTUVXY
3 AGHKQRUW
4 (B+G+Q+R+V+Z 🖭)
5 **AB**EFGHJLNPUWZ
6 AEGI**K**(N 1km)QUV

💬 The campsite is situated in natural surroundings by a lake in a valley encircled by high cliffs. Well known to mountaineers (Massif des Alpilles). Located close to Cavaillon, but still wonderfully peaceful. Dutch owners.

🚗 Take A7 as far as Cavaillon exit 25. Direction St. Rémy-de-Provence. Direction Sénas as far as Orgon. Campsite signposted.

D938 D900
Cavaillon
A7
D99 CC
D7N D973
Mallemort
D17 D569 D538

CC € **17** 1/4-6/7 25/8-29/10 7=6, 14=11 📷 N 43°46'55'' E 5°2'22''

Orpierre, F-05700 / Provence-Alpes-Côte d'Azur (Hautes-Alpes) 🛜 iD 2642

△ Les Princes d'Orange****
🏕 Flonsaine
☎ +33 (0)4-92662253
📠 +33 (0)4-92663108
📅 30/3 - 4/11
@ campingorpierre@wanadoo.fr

20ha 89T(80-110m²) 10A CEE

1 A**G**IJKLM**P**ST
2 DJKRTVXY
3 BGN**Q**RU**W**
4 (A 1/7-31/8) (C+H 15/6-15/9) J(Q 1/7-31/8) (T+U+V 🖭) (X+Z 15/6-15/9)
5 **AB**EFGIJKLMNPUW
6 AEG**K**(N 0,5km)TV

💬 A very hospitable and personal welcome awaits you at this smart family campsite with stunning views of the charming village of Orpierre. Lovely swimming pool. Renovated toilet facilities and playground. Plenty of activities in the mountains including climbing and walking. Indoor climbing wall at the campsite.

🚗 N75 Serres-Sisteron. Turn off at Eyquians. Campsite in the town of Orpierre.

D1075
CC **Laragne-Montéglin**
D124
D542 D942 **Ribiers**

CC € **19** 30/3-4/6 17/6-7/7 25/8-3/11 📷 N 44°18'39'' E 5°41'41''

Pernes-les-Fontaines, F-84210 / Provence-Alpes-Côte d'Azur (Vaucluse) ♿ 🛜 iD 2643

△ Les Fontaines*****
🏕 125 chemin de la Chapelette
☎ +33 (0)4-90468255
📠 +33 (0)4-90634291
📅 30/3 - 7/10
@ contact@campingfontaines.com

2,1ha 91T(100-115m²) 6-16A CEE

1 ACD**F**HIJKLMO**P**ST
2 RVX
3 ABGRU
4 (C 15/5-30/9) (G 15/5-15/9) IJKM(Q 🖭) (R 1/7-31/8) (T 1/5-15/9) (U 1/4-31/10) (V 1/5-15/9) (Y 1/5-30/9) (Z 🖭)
5 **AB**DEFGIJKLMNPUWXYZ
6 BCEGHK(N 1,3km)RTV

💬 Campsite among fields located 1 km from the village. Marked-out pitches located around a central brand new toilet block. Overlooking Mont Ventoux. New: pitches with extra comfort at additional fee. New aquapark with heated swimming pool.

🚗 On the A7 exit Le Pontet (Avignon Nord). Direction Carpentras. Follow signs in Pernes-les-Fontaines.

D950 D7 D974
D907 **Carpentras** D942
A7 CC
D942 D4
D938
L'Isle-sur-la-Sorgue

CC € **19** 30/3-6/7 27/8-6/10 📷 N 44°0'23'' E 5°2'18''

Peynier, F-13790 / Provence-Alpes-Côte d'Azur (Bouches-du-Rhône) ⚓ 🤚 ◉ (2644)

▲ Le Devançon***
🗐 451, chemin de Pourrachon
☎ +33 (0)4-42531006
🔓 1/3 - 10/11
@ reservation@ledevancon.fr

1,4ha 53T(85-150m²) 6-10A

1 ACD**G**IJKLMP
2 BJTUVXY
3 BGHRU
4 (B 1/5-30/9) (G 10/6-15/9)
　(Q+Z 1/4-1/10)
5 **AB**DFGIJKLMNOPZ
6 ACDEJ(N 0,5km)RTV

💬 A quiet campsite with spacious pitches, close to the village. Excellent toilet facilities and a lovely pool. Excellent starting point for a visit to Aix-en-Provence, Marseille and the Camargue.

🚗 Follow A7, then A8 dir. Nice. Exit 32. Follow D6 dir. Trets. At crossing with D56b, right towards Peynier. In village dir. 'centre-ville'. Then D908 dir. Marseille. Right after bridge and follow Chemin de Pourrachon to the campsite.

ⒸⒸ € ⑰ 1/3-7/7　25/8-9/11　　🏕 N 43°26'32'' E 5°37'46''

Prunières, F-05230 / Provence-Alpes-Côte d'Azur (Hautes-Alpes) ⚓ 🤚 ◉ (2645)

▲ Le Nautic***
🗐 N94
☎ +33 (0)4-92506249
FAX +33 (0)4-92535842
🔓 14/5 - 15/9
@ campinglenautic@wanadoo.fr

3ha 100T(60-120m²) 6-10A CEE

1 ACDGIJKLMP**Q**
2 DJKLMOQTUVWXY
3 AGHJRU**WZ**
4 (C+H 15/6-15/9) K(Q 🔓)
　(R 1/6-15/9)
　(T+U+V 1/7-30/8)
　(Z 1/6-15/9)
5 **A**FGIJLMNOPUZ
6 ABCEG**JL**(N 5km)ORTV

💬 A panoramic setting by the lake. Heated swimming pool from 15/6 to 15/9. Landing stage for boats.

🚗 About 22 km east of Gap on the N94. Just before bridge over the road turn right immediately. Campsite well signposted.

ⒸⒸ € ⑰ 14/5-5/7　25/8-14/9　　🏕 N 44°31'39'' E 6°21'31''

Prunières, F-05230 / Provence-Alpes-Côte d'Azur (Hautes-Alpes) ⚓ 🤚 ◉ (2646)

▲ Le Roustou***
🗐 RN94
☎ +33 (0)4-92506263
🔓 12/5 - 23/9
@ info@campingleroustou.com

9ha 227T(80-150m²) 6A

1 AC**G**IJKLMPQ
2 DJKLMRTVX
3 BG**M**NRU**WZ**
4 (B+G+Q+T+U+V+X+Z 15/6-15/9)
5 **A**FGIJKLMNPUVXZ
6 EGK(N 4km)RTV

💬 Located on a peninsula on the lake. Private beach and landing stage. Pitches marked out by trees and bushes.

🚗 Campsite is located on Serre-Ponçon Lake, halfway between Chorges and Savines-le-Lac. Stay on the N94.

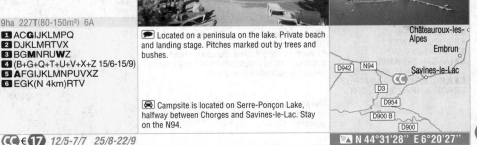

ⒸⒸ € ⑰ 12/5-7/7　25/8-22/9　　🏕 N 44°31'28'' E 6°20'27''

Puget-sur-Argens, F-83480 / Provence-Alpes-Côte d'Azur (Var)

👫 ⛷ 📶 iD 2647

▲ La Bastiane★★★★★
✉ 1056 chemin des Suvières
☎ +33 (0)4-94555594
FAX +33 (0)4-94555593
🔓 12/4 - 8/10
@ info@labastiane.com

3,5ha 40T(80-100m²) 10A

1 ACD**F**IJKL**P**T
2 BFLRTVWXY
3 BFGK**M**NOP**R**U
4 (**A** 1/7-31/8) (C+H 🔓) K
(Q+S+T+U+V+X+Y+Z 🔓)
5 **AB**CDEFGHIJKLMNOPUWZ
6 ABDEGHI**K**(N 2km)RTV

💬 Nice, well-cared-for, well-managed campsite. Beautifully located in the wide Provençal forest and park. Only a few minutes by car from the beaches of Fréjus. It's certainly worth taking a day trip inland and going for a drive along the well-known wine route.

🚗 Signs are posted on the N7, west of Puget-sur-Argens.

D54 · D4 · N7 · A8 · **Fréjus** · **Saint-Raphaël** · D7 · D25 · CC

CC € **17** 12/4-2/6 16/6-30/6 2/9-6/10

🧭 N 43°28'11'' E 6°40'44''

Roquebrune-sur-Argens, F-83520 / Provence-Alpes-Côte d'Azur (Var)

⛷ 📶 iD 2648

▲ Domaine de la Bergerie★★★★★
✉ route du Col du Bougnon
☎ +33 (0)4-98114545
FAX +33 (0)4-98114546
🔓 21/4 - 10/10
@ info@domainelabergerie.com

60ha 200T(80-200m²) 6-10A CEE

1 ACD**G**IJKLMPS
2 BCDFGIJKRTVWXY
3 BD**F**GHIJKLMNP**Q**RUVW
4 (**A** 21/4-15/9) (B+F+G 🔓) IJ
KL**MN**
(Q+S+T+U+V+W+X+Y+Z 🔓)
5 **AB**CDEFGHIJKLMNOPUVW
XYZ
6 AFGHI**K**(N 7km)OPRTV

💬 Well positioned campsite set in a 60-hectare wood full of oak, fir and mimosa trees. Green hedges separate the pitches. Excellent (swimming) facilities including an indoor pool with jacuzzi, sauna and Turkish bath.

🚗 From St. Aygulf to Roquebrune-sur-Argens. After about 3 miles (5 km) there's a roundabout. Turn left to Col du Bougnon. After 1 km follow the signs.

A8 · **Fréjus** · **Saint-Raphaël** · D7 · D25 · CC · D559

CC € **19** 21/4-3/7 26/8-9/10

🧭 N 43°23'55'' E 6°40'30''

Roquebrune-sur-Argens, F-83520 / Provence-Alpes-Côte d'Azur (Var)

👫 ⛷ 📶 iD 2649

▲ Flower Camping Les
Pêcheurs★★★★
☎ +33 (0)4-94457125
FAX +33 (0)4-94816513
🔓 1/4 - 8/10
@ info@camping-les-pecheurs.com

5ha 123T(80-100m²) 10A CEE

1 ACD**G**IJKLPS
2 CDFGKRVWXY
3 BFGKNQRUWZ
4 (A+C+H 🔓) **KNP**
(Q+R+T+U+V+X+Y+Z 🔓)
5 **AB**CDEFGHIJKLMNOPUZ
6 ACEGHI**K**(N 0,7km)ORTV

💬 A lovely, well-run campsite located by a river, 10 km from the sandy beaches of Fréjus and St. Raphaël. There is a lake opposite the hotel offering countless watersports opportunities. Lovely swimming pool with wellness facilities.

🚗 A8, exit Le Muy, direction Roquebrune. The campsite is located just before the village, opposite the lake.

D562 · D4 · D54 · A8 · D125 · CC · **Saint-Raphaël** · D25 · D7 · D559

CC € **17** 1/4-1/7 26/8-7/10

🧭 N 43°27'4'' E 6°38'2''

Roquebrune-sur-Argens, F-83520 / Provence-Alpes-Côte d'Azur (Var)

👪 ♿ 📶 **iD** (2650)

🏕 Le Vaudois***
🏢 D7, 169 rte Hypert Ollivier
☎ +33 (0)4-94813770
📠 +33 (0)9-72431189
🔓 21/4 - 30/9
@ camping.vaudois@wanadoo.fr

3ha 44**T**(80-110m²) 10-16A CEE

1 ACDGIJKL**P**ST
2 FGRTVWXY
3 B**F**GRU**W**
4 (B+G 15/5-30/9)
　(Q+R+T+V 15/5-15/9)
5 **A**CFGHIJKLMNOPUZ
6 AEGJ(N 4km)TV

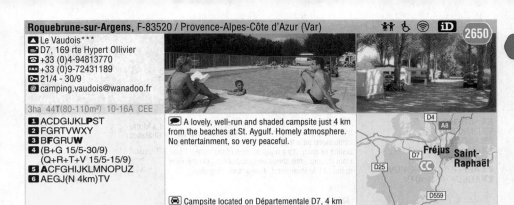

💬 A lovely, well-run and shaded campsite just 4 km from the beaches at St. Aygulf. Homely atmosphere. No entertainment, so very peaceful.

🚗 Campsite located on Départementale D7, 4 km north of St. Aygulf.

©© € **13** 21/4-4/7 25/8-29/9　　　📐 N 43°24'39'' E 6°41'31''

Roquebrune-sur-Argens, F-83520 / Provence-Alpes-Côte d'Azur (Var)

♿ 📶 **iD** (2651)

🏕 Leï Suves****
🏢 rte de Marchand.,bd Ric Hochet 1770
☎ +33 (0)4-94454395
📠 +33 (0)4-94816313
🔓 31/3 - 13/10
@ camping.lei.suves@wanadoo.fr

7,5ha 160**T**(80-120m²) 6A CEE

1 ACD**G**IJKLPS
2 BFGJKRTVWXY
3 B**F**GHJMN**OP**RU**W**
4 (A+C+H+Q+S+T+U+V+X+
　Y+Z 🔓)
5 **AB**CDEFGHIJKLMNOPQUXY
　Z
6 ACEG**IK**(N 4km)ORTV

💬 In every respect an excellently maintained and well organised campsite in the middle of the Provençal landscape. The site has a very appropriate name: 'Leï Suves', this means cork trees. The campsite was once a cork plantation.

🚗 A8, exit Le Muy, direction Fréjus via the N7. Turn left at the roundabout at Roquebrune-sur-Argens, direction La Bouverie.

©© € **17** 31/3-30/6 27/8-12/10　　　📐 N 43°28'40'' E 6°38'19''

Roquebrune-sur-Argens, F-83520 / Provence-Alpes-Côte d'Azur (Var)

♿ 📶 **iD** (2652)

🏕 Moulin des Iscles***
🏢 690 chemin du Moulin des Iscles
☎ +33 (0)4-94457074
📠 +33 (0)4-94454609
🔓 1/4 - 30/9
@ moulin.iscles@wanadoo.fr

1,3ha 79**T**(70-100m²) 6A

1 ACD**G**IJLPST
2 CFKRVWXY
3 B**F**GKNQRU**W**
4 (Q+S 🔓)
　(T+U+V+X 5/4-24/9)
5 **AB**CDEFGHIJKLMNOPUVXY
　Z
6 ABEGHI**K**(N 3km)ORTV

NEW

💬 A pleasant, quiet campsite on the banks of the Argens. The owner takes up her position at the stove and cooks superbly!

🚗 A8 exit Le Muy, then N7 direction Fréjus. After about 10 km right, Roquebrune. Campsite is located just to the south of the village, direction St. Aygulf.

©© € **17** 1/4-7/7 25/8-29/9 7=6　　　📐 N 43°26'43'' E 6°39'28''

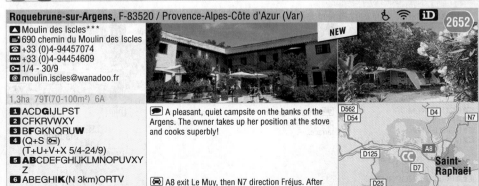

Rosans, F-05150 / Provence-Alpes-Côte d'Azur (Hautes-Alpes)

👥 📶 **iD** (2653)

🔺 Les Hauts de Rosans****
📧 rte du Col de Pomerol
☎ +33 (0)4-92666155
🔓 30/4 - 30/9
@ contact@
camping-hautsderosans.com

7ha 57T(80-140m²) 10A CEE

1 ACD**G**IJKLMPT
2 DIJKRTVWXY
3 ABGHJU
4 (C+Q 1/5-30/9) (T 🔲)
(V+X+Z 1/5-30/9)
5 **A**EFGHIJKLMNOPUWZ
6 ABEGK(N 1km)TV

💬 Chantal and Henri offer a hospitable welcome to their campsite. You can appreciate the beauty of this landscaped park from every terrace, and this gives a feeling of calm. It's a magical view of the valley. 1 km from Rosans with shops and restaurants. On the road to the Col de Pommerol, a unique walking area.

🚗 Nyons-Gap D94, left in Rosans centre. Follow 'Col de Pommerol' signs.

La Motte-Chalancon · D61
Rémuzat
D94 · D994
CC
Rosans

CC € **17** 30/4-7/7 26/8-29/9 7=6, 14=11

🧭 N 44°23'44'' E 5°27'40''

Rousset/Serre-Ponçon, F-05190 / Provence-Alpes-Côte d'Azur (Hautes-Alpes)

📶 **iD** (2654)

🔺 La Viste****
📧 Serre-Ponçon
☎ +33 (0)4-92544339
🔓 15/5 - 1/10
@ camping@laviste.fr

6ha 160T(90-120m²) 5A CEE

1 ACD**F**IJLPST
2 JKRVXY
3 BGHNRU**W**
4 (C+G 15/5-15/9) J(Q 🔲)
(R 15/5-15/9)
(T+U 15/6-15/9) (V 1/6-31/8)
(X 15/5-15/9) (Y 1/6-31/8)
5 **AB**FGIJKLNPRUV
6 CEGIJ(N 4km)TV

💬 A high-altitude campsite with good toilet facilities and spacious pitches. Lovely views from the terrace and from several of the pitches. The restaurant is certainly worth a visit.

🚗 D900 Gap-Barcelonette, exit D3. Then take the route to Rousset, or N94 Gap-Briançon exit D3 for caravans.

Chorges · Savines-le-Lac
D942 · D3
D900 B · CC · D954
D900

CC € **19** 15/5-29/6 1/9-30/9

🧭 N 44°28'33'' E 6°15'48''

Salignac/Sisteron, F-04290 / Provence-Alpes-Côte d'Azur (Alpes-de-Haute-Prov)

📶 **iD** (2655)

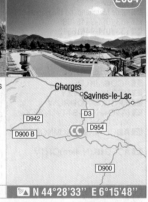

NEW

🔺 Le Jas du Moine***
☎ +33 (0)4-92614043
🔓 10/3 - 20/10
@ contact@
camping-jasdumoine.com

4,5ha 109T(80-100m²) 10A CEE

1 BCD**G**IJKLMOS
2 BFGTVXY
3 BGKNRU**W**
4 (**A** 1/7-30/8) (C 15/6-15/9)
(Q 15/4-15/10)
(R+T 1/7-31/8) (U 🔲)
(V+X 1/7-31/8) Z
5 **A**FGIJKLMNOPRUZ
6 CDEGJ(N 3km)ORTV

💬 Beautiful terrain with plenty of shade. Some pitches have stunning views. Nice pool and lively terrace.

🚗 On the D4 4 km south of Sisteron. Campsite is well signposted in Volonne and in Sisteron.

D4075
A51
Sisteron
D946
CC
D4
Château-Arnoux
D951 · N85

CC € **13** 10/3-30/6 25/8-19/10

🧭 N 44°9'27'' E 5°58'16''

Salon-de-Provence, F-13300 / Provence-Alpes-Côte d'Azur (Bouches-du-Rhône) ♿ 🛜 iD 2656

🔺 Nostradamus***
✉ 2837 route d'Eyguières, RD 17
☎ +33 (0)4-90560836
⌚ 1/3 - 31/10
@ camping.nostradamus@gmail.com

2,7ha 70T(80-120m²) 6A CEE

1 ACGIJKLPRS
2 CFGRVXY
3 AFGJNQRUWX
4 (A 10/7-20/8)
(B+G 15/5-20/9) (Q ⌚)
(R+T+U+V+X 1/5-30/9)
(Z ⌚)
5 ABEFGIJKNPRUZ
6 CEGJ(N 3km)TV

💬 The campsite is located in a 40-hectare farm, hidden away in an orchard. In a rural location on level grounds. Located in the heart of Provence. Excellent starting point for walks, bike rides and trips out and for visiting places such as Les Baux de Provence, Saint Rémy, Lubéron, Arles, Marseille, Aix-en-Provence and Avignon.

🚗 Stay on A7 as far as exit 27 Salon-de-Provence. Continue towards Eyguières (D17) from Salon-de-Provence. Signposted after a few kilometres.

CC €**17** 1/3-8/7 26/8-30/10 ◻ N 43°40'41'' E 5°3'52''

Sanary-sur-Mer, F-83110 / Provence-Alpes-Côte d'Azur (Var) ♿ 🛜 iD 2657

🔺 Campasun Mas de Pierredon****
✉ 652 chemin Raoul Coletta
☎ +33 (0)4-94742502
📠 +33 (0)4-94746142
⌚ 7/4 - 30/9
@ pierredon@campasun.eu

4ha 52T(80-100m²) 10A CEE

1 ACDGHIJKLPS
2 FIJRTVX
3 AFGKMNQRU
4 (C+G ⌚) JK
(Q+R+T+U+V 29/4-25/9) (Z ⌚)
5 ADEFGIJKLMNOPRSUW
6 ACGHJK(N 1km)RTV

💬 Lovely campsite 3 km from the beaches at Sanary and Bandol. Renovated, heated pool with slides, aquapark. Multi sports grounds and excellent restaurant with traditional cuisine. Comfort pitches (100 m²) with private toilet facilities (extra fee: EUR 19). Refurbished toilet block with self-cleaning toilets.

🚗 A50 exit 12 Sanary direction Jardin Exotique. Direction Ollioules after the Mercedes garage, then follow signs.

CC €**17** 7/4-7/7 25/8-29/9 ◻ N 43°7'54'' E 5°48'53''

Sanary-sur-Mer, F-83110 / Provence-Alpes-Côte d'Azur (Var) ♿ 🛜 iD 2658

🔺 Campasun Parc Mogador****
✉ 167 chemin de Beaucours
☎ +33 (0)4-94745316
📠 +33 (0)4-94741058
⌚ 1/3 - 31/12
@ mogador@campasun.eu

3ha 75T(80-100m²) 10A CEE

1 ACDGHIJKLPST
2 BFGNRTVX
3 ABFGKRTU
4 (C+G 1/4-30/9) K
(Q+R+T+U+V+Z 1/4-30/9)
5 ABDEFGIJKLMNOPRUWXYZ
6 ACDEGHJK(N 0,8km)ORTV

💬 A quiet campsite located 800 metres from the sea. Very conveniently located a few kilometres from Sanary and Bandol. Pitches with sufficient shade. Restaurant and toilet block with self-cleaning toilets.

🚗 A50, exit 12 Bandol. Follow D559 direction Sanary. Then take second right.

CC €**19** 1/3-7/7 25/8-31/12 ◻ N 43°7'26'' E 5°47'16''

Serres, F-05700 / Provence-Alpes-Côte d'Azur (Hautes-Alpes) 🛜 iD (2659)

🅰 Flower Camping Domaine
des 2 Soleils★★★★
🔁 D1075
☎ +33 (0)4-92670133
🔓 7/4 - 30/9
@ dom.2.soleils@orange.fr

12ha 114T(80-200m²) 6A CEE

1 ACDGIJKLMOPS
2 BIJKRTUVWXY
3 BGHNPRU
4 (B+G 15/6-15/9) J
(Q+T+U+X+Z 1/7-31/8)
5 AFIJKLMNOPQUVZ
6 DEGKORV

💬 Family campsite with many terraces and a beautiful view from the pitches. Many options for cycling, walking, horse riding, canyoning and swimming. Caravans are brought to the pitch by tractor if necessary.

🚗 N75, from Serres direction Sisteron, after 1.5 km turn left.

Aspres-sur-Buëch
Aspremont
D994 CC
D1075
D942

CC €15 7/4-7/7 25/8-29/9 7=6 ⛺ N 44°25'21'' E 5°43'46''

Seyne-les-Alpes, F-04140 / Provence-Alpes-Côte d'Azur (Alpes-de-Haute-Prov) ♿ 🛜 iD (2660)

🅰 Sites & Paysages Les Prairies★★★
🔁 Haute Greyere
☎ +33 (0)4-92351021
🔓 8/5 - 8/9
@ info@campinglesprairies.com

3,9ha 100T(100-140m²) 10A CEE

1 ACDFIJLPS
2 CLRTVXY
3 ABGHJRUW
4 (C 1/6-9/9) (Q 🔓)
(R 1/6-1/9) (T+U 10/6-30/8)
(V 1/7-30/8) (X 10/6-30/8)
(Z 🔓)
5 ABDEFGIJLMNPUVWXYZ
6 CEGJ(N 0,8km)RTV

💬 This exceptionally beautiful campsite offers peace, comfort and relaxation. Besides good sanitary facilities this site has the advantage of being within walking distance of a typical Montagnard (mountain) village. The friendly owners will always have time for you.

🚗 From Gap direction Barcelonette. Then D900 direction Digne. Signposted at Seyne.

Saint-Martin-lès-Seyne
Seyne
CC
D900

CC €17 8/5-2/7 25/8-7/9 8=7, 16=14 ⛺ N 44°20'34'' E 6°21'37''

Sillans-la-Cascade, F-83690 / Provence-Alpes-Côte d'Azur (Var) ♿ 🛜 iD (2661)

🅰 Flower Camping Le Relais
de la Bresque★★★
🔁 15 chemin de la Piscine
☎ +33 (0)4-94046489
📠 +33 (0)4-94771954
🔓 1/4 - 30/9
@ info@lerelaisdelabresque.net

3ha 44T(100-140m²) 10A CEE

1 ACDGIJKLPST
2 BKRSVXY
3 AGHJNR
4 (C 1/5-15/9) (H 🔓)
(Q 1/6-30/9) (R 🔓)
(T+U+V 1/7-31/8)
(X+Z 1/6-30/9)
5 AEFGIJKLMNPUW
6 CEGIKOTV

💬 Campsite with marked-out, shaded pitches, a stone's throw from Sillans-La-Cascade. Easy-going Provence atmosphere and a large swimming pool mean this campsite comes recommended.

🚗 D22 Aups - Sillans-la-Cascade. Campsite about 1 km before Sillans on the left. Signposted.

D30 D957
D9 Aups
Tavernes D22
CC D557
D560
D13 Cotignac
D562 D10

CC €17 1/4-7/7 27/8-29/9 ⛺ N 43°34'24'' E 6°11'13''

Six-Fours-les-Plages, F-83140 / Provence-Alpes-Côte d'Azur (Var) ♿ 🛜 iD (2662)

🏕 Hôtellerie de Plein Air
Les Playes****
✉ 419 rue Grand
☎ +33 (0)4-94255757
📅 1/1 - 31/12
@ camplayes@wanadoo.fr

1,5ha 19T(50-80m²) 10A CEE

1 ACD**G**HIJKLPT
2 BFGJTVWXY
3 R
4 (C+H 28/3-1/11)
　　(Q+R+T+U+Z 1/7-31/8)
5 **A**DFGIJKLMNPRUWXYZ
6 ACDEGJ**K**(N 1,5km)V

💬 Peacefully located campsite on the edge of a wood, 1.5 km from the sea and characteristic harbour in Sanary-sur-Mer. Lovely heated swimming pool. A warm welcome throughout the year.

🚗 Follow the signs in Six-Fours-les-Plages to Les Playes. Campsite signposted.

CC € **17** 1/1-6/7 26/8-31/12

🏕 N 43°6'47'' E 5°49'50''

Sorgues, F-84700 / Provence-Alpes-Côte d'Azur (Vaucluse) ♿ 🛜 iD (2663)

🏕 La Montagne***
✉ 944 chemin de la Montagne
☎ +33 (0)4-90833666
📅 1/1 - 31/12
@ camping.lamontagne@
　wanadoo.fr

1,8ha 31T(70-90m²) 16A CEE

1 ACD**G**IJKLO**P**ST
2 BFISTVXY
3 AGHJKLNRU**W**
4 (C+H 2/4-30/9) JK
　　(Q 1/6-31/8) (R 1/6-30/9)
　　(T+U+V+X 1/7-31/8)
　　(Z 1/5-30/9)
5 **AB**DFGIJKLMNPUXY
6 ACDEGK(N 3,5km)RTUV

💬 Located at a 10-minute drive from Avignon in 2 hectares of pine woods and with a lovely (heated) swimming pool and pleasant catering facilities. Free wifi on entire site.

🚗 On the A7 take exit 23 Avignon Nord, direction Carpentras, right after 800m direction Sorgues. Campsite signposted from there.

CC € **15** 1/1-13/7 31/8-30/12 7=6

🏕 N 44°1'15'' E 4°53'30''

St. Apollinaire, F-05160 / Provence-Alpes-Côte d'Azur (Hautes-Alpes) 🏕🏕 ♿ 🛜 ❁ iD (2664)

🏕 Campéole Le Clos du Lac***
✉ route des Lacs
☎ +33 (0)4-92442743
📅 15/5 - 16/9
@ clos-du-lac@campeole.com

2ha 49T(50-100m²) 6-16A CEE

1 ACD**G**IJKLM**P**S
2 CDHIJKLORVWX
3 BGHJQRUWZ
4 (Q 🖼) (R 1/7-31/8)
　　(T+V+Z 🖼)
5 **A**CFGIJKLMNOPUZ
6 EGHJ(N 10km)T

💬 An exceptional campsite surrounded by a magnificent mountain range and situated not far from an extensive 5 hectare lake. Angles and swimmers can live life to the full here.

🚗 Via N94 between Gap and Embrun at Chorges follow D9 to Reallon. At shrine St. Apollinaire drive up the steep little road, 2.5 km.

CC € **15** 15/5-6/7 25/8-15/9

🏕 N 44°33'42'' E 6°20'46''

St. Aygulf, F-83370 / Provence-Alpes-Côte d'Azur (Var)

👪 ♿ 📶 iD (2665)

🔺 La Barque****
📧 3055 Quartier les Fougerettes, D8
☎ +33 (0)4-94813186
📠 +33 (0)4-94814922
📅 31/3 - 29/10
@ lecamping-labarque@
club-internet.fr

3ha 42T(100-150m²) 8-16A CEE

1 ACD**G**IJKLM**P**ST
2 CFGRSVWXY
3 B**F**GHJKNRW
4 (C+H 📅) K
(Q+T+U+V+X+Y+Z 📅)
5 **AB**CEFGHIJKLMNPUXZ
6 ABCEGH**IK**(N 0,5km)OTV

💬 A friendly, quietly located family campsite with plenty of shade and a really good atmosphere. The seaside resorts of Fréjus and St. Raphael are just a few kilometres away. New in 2015: beautiful swimming pool and whirlpool, located next to a very attractive terrace and restaurant.

🚗 From the centre of St. Aygulf towards Roquebrune. Right at roundabout after 4 km. 500m to campsite.

CC € **17** 31/3-4/7 25/8-28/10 🏖 N 43°25'3'' E 6°42'12''

St. Aygulf, F-83370 / Provence-Alpes-Côte d'Azur (Var)

♿ 📶 iD (2666)

🔺 La Plage d'Argens***
📧 541, RD559
☎ +33 (0)4-94511497
📠 +33 (0)4-94512944
📅 1/4 - 20/10
@ info@laplagedargens.fr

7ha 154T(80-100m²) 5A CEE

1 ACD**G**IJL**P**S
2 ACEFG**L**RTVXY
3 BDF**G**KLNRUWY
4 (**A**+C+H 📅) K
(Q+S+T+U+V+X+Y+Z 📅)
5 **AB**CEFGHIJKLMNOPRUWZ
6 BCEGH**IJK**(N 2,5km)ORTV

💬 A new team, new recreational facilities and beautiful touring pitches. Shaded grounds in a privileged location, on the banks of the Argens, in the heart of the protected coastal area. Easy access to the beaches (500m walk). Leisurely atmosphere. A campsite to discover and rediscover.

🚗 On N98, 3 km east of St. Aygulf.

CC € **19** 1/4-6/7 27/8-7/10 🏖 N 43°24'32'' E 6°43'30''

St. Aygulf, F-83370 / Provence-Alpes-Côte d'Azur (Var)

👪 ♿ 📶 iD (2667)

🔺 Les Jardins du Maï Taï***
📧 99 route de Roquebrune
☎ +33 (0)4-94454893
📅 31/3 - 15/10
@ lesjardinsdumaitai@gmail.com

1,5ha 34T(90-120m²) 16A

1 ACD**GH**IJL**P**ST
2 AFGRWXY
3 B**F**GKNRU
4 (A 1/7-31/8) (C 📅) K
(T+U+V+X+Z 15/5-15/9)
5 ACEFGHIJKLMNOPUXYZ
6 AEG**IK**(N 0,1km)OTV

💬 A recently fully-renovated campsite with well-maintained amenities and an excellent ambiance. About 2 km to the sandy beaches of the lively seaside resort of Saint-Aygulf.

🚗 Towards Roquebrune-sur-Argens from the centre of St. Aygulf. Just over 2 km, campsite on the right.

CC € **17** 31/3-7/7 25/8-14/10 14=13, 21=19, 28=25 🏖 N 43°24'37'' E 6°42'29''

St. Aygulf, F-83370 / Provence-Alpes-Côte d'Azur (Var)

♟ 📶 iD (2668)

🔺 Sandaya Riviera d'Azur★★★★★
📧 189 Les Grands Chât.de Villepey/RD7
☎ +33 (0)4-94810159
📠 +33 (0)4-94810164
🕐 13/4 - 7/10
@ riv@sandaya.fr

10ha 104T(100m²) 10A CEE

1 ACD**G**IJKLM**P**ST
2 ACFGLRTVWXY
3 BFGHJKL**MN**QRUW
4 (**A** 1/7-31/8) (C+H 🕐) J
(Q+S+T+U+V+X+Y+Z 🕐)
5 **AB**CEGHIJKLMNOPSUXYZ
6 AEGH**IK**(N 2,5km)ORTVWX

💬 Be charmed by the natural resources of the Var and the Mediterranean. Become acquainted with our Provencal villages, our characteristic markets, our festivals and local events. 2.5 km from beaches with fine sand and watersports activities.

🚘 The campsite is located on the RD7, 2 km north of St. Aygulf.

Fréjus — Saint-Raphaël

CC € **17** 13/4-6/7 1/9-6/10

N 43°24'33'' E 6°42'32''

St. Crépin, F-05600 / Provence-Alpes-Côte d'Azur (Hautes-Alpes)

♟ 📶 iD (2669)

🔺 Camping de L'Ile★★★
☎ +33 (0)9-67496790
🕐 1/5 - 1/10
@ camping@saintcrepin.com

5ha 94T(100-200m²) 10A CEE

1 ACDGIJKLMO**P**ST
2 CDGKLRTVWXY
3 ABGHIJMQR**W**
4 (C 1/6-30/9)
(H+Q+T+U 1/7-31/8)
(Z 1/7-30/8)
5 **A**GIJKLMNOPUVWZ
6 EGHIJ(N 0,5km)V

NEW

💬 Campsite situated on the banks of a river with activities including wild water rafting. Also ideally located for those who enjoy gliding, with the possibility of gliding in the Écrins National Park with its beautiful panorama.

🚘 Campsite is on N94 and well signposted. Between Briançon and Guillestre on N94. At St. Crepin follow signs to Aerodrome. Cross railway tracks. Campsite is directly left.

L'argentière-la-Bessée

CC € **15** 1/5-6/7 27/8-30/9

N 44°42'18'' E 6°36'9''

St. Cyr-sur-Mer, F-83270 / Provence-Alpes-Côte d'Azur (Var)

♟ 📶 iD (2670)

🔺 Le Clos Ste. Thérèse★★★★
📧 route de Bandol
☎ +33 (0)4-94321221
🕐 2/4 - 30/9
@ camping@clos-therese.com

4ha 80T(65-150m²) 6-10A CEE

1 ACD**F**IJL**P**T
2 FGJKTVX
3 A**F**GHNRU
4 (B 4/4-30/9) (G 1/7-1/10) K
(Q 🕐)
(T+U+V+X+Z 15/6-15/9)
5 **A**DFGIJKLMNPUVWZ
6 CDFGHJ(N 1km)RTUV

💬 A small, well-shaded family campsite protruding high above the sea and the Gulf of Frégate 4 km from a sandy beach. Two swimming pools, one of which is heated. 15 km from the medieval village of Castellet and 25 km from Cassis and its magnificent bays.

🚘 Follow A50 as far as St. Cyr-sur-Mer exit, then continue towards Bandol. Site is located 3.5 km from the village, on the left.

La Seyne-sur-Mer

CC € **17** 2/4-6/7 27/8-29/9

N 43°9'35'' E 5°43'46''

St. Laurent-du-Verdon, F-04500 / Provence-Alpes-Côte d'Azur (Alpes-de-Haute-Prov) ♿ 📶 iD (2671)

🏕 La Farigoulette★★★★★
✉ 1029, route de Montpezat
☎ +33 (0)4-92744162
📠 +33 (0)9-70067678
🔓 13/4 - 1/10
@ lafarigoulette@cielavillage.com

14ha 113T(90-110m²) 4A

1 ACDGIJKLMP ST
2 ABDNRSVY
3 BGHJLNQRUVZ
4 (A 🔓) (C 1/5-2/9)
(H 1/5-30/9)
(Q+S+T+U+V+X+Y+Z 🔓)
5 ABEFGIJKLMNPUWZ
6 ACEGHKOTV

💬 Large, spacious campsite with lots of shade. Campsite has many facilities, its own beach and offers access to the Verdon.

🚗 D11 coming from Riez. Left D311 direction St. Laurent-du-Verdon. Well signposted.

D6 — Allemagne-en-Provence — Aiguines
D952 — D11
D957
D13
La Verdière — D30 — D9

CC € 17 13/4-6/7 26/8-30/9 ⛰ N 43°44'3'' E 6°4'40''

St. Maime, F-04300 / Provence-Alpes-Côte d'Azur (Alpes-de-Haute-Prov) ♿ 📶 iD (2672)

🏕 Flower Camping La Rivière★★★
✉ Lieu-dit 'Les Côtes'
☎ +33 (0)4-92795466
📠 +33 (0)4-92795103
🔓 15/4 - 30/9
@ camping-lariviere@orange.fr

3,5ha 44T(50-100m²) 10A

1 ACDGIJKLPS
2 CDFKLOPRTVX
3 AFGNRUW
4 (A 1/7-31/8) (B+G 1/6-15/9)
(Q 🔓) (R+T 6/6-31/8)
(U+V+X 1/7-31/8) (Z 🔓)
5 ABDFGIJKLMNOPU
6 EGHJK(N 10km)RUV

💬 A peacefully located campsite in a valley by a stream and a small lake, with the chance to go fishing. One section of the toilet facilities is heated in low season. Ideal starting point for walks and for visiting i.a. the Gorges du Verdon, Valensole and its lavender fields.

🚗 A51, exit 19 La Brillanne. Then N96 towards Manosque. After 7 km take the D13. Campsite on the right of the road.

D5
D950 — D12 — A51
D13 — Oraison
D4100 — CC — D4096
D14 — Volx
Manosque — D4
D956 — D6

CC € 13 15/4-6/7 24/8-29/9 ⛰ N 43°53'52'' E 5°48'23''

St. Martin-de-Brômes, F-04800 / Provence-Alpes-Côte d'Azur (Alpes-de-Haute-Prov) 📶 iD (2673)

🏕 Le Bleu Lavande★★
✉ 31 chemin de Pauron
☎ +33 (0)4-92776489
📠 +33 (0)4-92776032
🔓 1/5 - 31/10
@ info@camping-bleu-lavande.fr

3ha 32T 6A

1 ADGIJKLOP
2 GJKTVX
3 AGHIJNRU
4 (Q 15/5-30/9) (R 🔓)
(T 1/6-15/9) (U 1/7-31/8)
(Z 1/6-15/9)
5 AFGJLNPUXYZ
6 ACDEGJTV

💬 Campsite in terrace formation with a view of the 'Gorges du Verdon' massive and the picturesque village of St. Martin-de-Brômes.

🚗 On the A51 take exit 19 or 18 to Greoux-les-Bains. Then D952 to just before the village. Campsite is signposted.

Manosque — Valensole
D6
A51
D4 — D82 — CC — D952
D554
D11

CC € 15 1/5-7/7 25/8-30/10 ⛰ N 43°46'14'' E 5°56'7''

St. Martin-de-Crau, F-13310 / Provence-Alpes-Côte d'Azur (Bouches-du-Rhône) ♟ ♿ 🛜 iD (2674)

🏕 De La Crau**
✉ ave de Saint Roch
☎ +33 (0)4-90471709
🔓 24/3 - 30/9
@ contact@campingdelacrau.com

3ha 35T(> 80m²) 6-10A CEE

1 ACDGIJKLMPST
2 FGRSTVWXY
3 AFGJNRU**W**
4 (B 1/6-15/9)
(Q+S+U+X+Y+Z 🔓)
5 **A**EFGIJKLMNOPRUZ
6 ACDEGKM(N 0km)V

💬 A natural campsite located behind a hotel-café-restaurant in the centre of a Provençe village. An ideal starting point for visiting towns in Provence, such as Les Beaux, St. Rémy and Arles, as well as the Camargue, Avignon and Nîmes.

🚗 Take D27 from St. Rèmy-de-Provence to the centre of St. Martin. Then N113 direction Arles. The campsite is on your right.

Mouriès — D17
Saint-Martin-de-Crau — CC — D113 — A54
D10
D5
D36 — D35 — N568

CC € **17** 7/4-7/7 25/8-29/9 🏖 N 43°38'16'' E 4°48'21''

St. Maurice-en-Valgodemard, F-05800 / Provence-Alpes-Côte d'Azur (Hautes-Alpes) 🛜 iD (2675)

🏕 Le Bocage**
✉ Hameau le Roux
☎ +33 (0)4-92218648
🔓 21/4 - 8/10
@ campinglebocage@orange.fr

1,3ha 41T(70-150m²) 3-10A CEE

1 ACD**G**IJKLPST
2 BCGKRTVWXY
3 AGHR**W**
4 (C 25/6-5/9) (Q+R+Z 🔓)
5 **AB**EFGIJKMNPUV
6 BCEG**K**(N 8km)T

💬 A lovely, well-maintained and friendly campsite with a swimming pool. Located on the River Séveraisse. If you are following the 'Route Napoleon' this is the perfect stopover campsite. Unique 300 m² miniature train network.

🚗 From Grenoble to Gap via the N85. Take D985a in Saint-Firmin. Campsite 8 km from St. Maurice in the hamlet of Le Roux on the D985B.

Entraigues
Gragnolet
CC
N85

CC € **15** 21/4-8/7 27/8-7/10 🏖 N 44°48'43'' E 6°6'47''

St. Maximin-la-Ste-Baume, F-83470 / Provence-Alpes-Côte d'Azur (Var) 🛜 iD (2676)

🏕 Camping Le Provençal Flower***
✉ 1866 route de Mazaugues
☎ +33 (0)4-94781697
🔓 1/4 - 30/9
@ camping.provencal@wanadoo.fr

4,5ha 58T 10A

1 ACDGHIJKLP
2 BFIJKRUVXY
3 AGNR
4 (C+G 15/6-15/9)
(Q+R 9/7-24/8)
(U+V+X+Z 1/7-31/8)
5 **A**DGJLMNPQ
6 ACDEGJ(N 3km)R

💬 Campsite 2 km from the centre, located amongst the vineyards. Montagne Sainte-Victoire and the St. Baume massif nearby. Landscaped in terraces, in a quiet location, and with plenty of greenery.

🚗 Autoroute A8 exit St Maximin drive through centre and follow the signs.

NEW

Pourrières
D3 — D560
D6 — A8
CC
D1 — D205
D5
La Roquebrussanne

CC € **17** 1/4-28/6 27/8-29/9 🏖 N 43°25'44'' E 5°51'52''

St. Mitre-les-Remparts, F-13920 / Provence-Alpes-Côte d'Azur (Bouches-du-Rhône) ♿ 📶 iD (2677)

🏕 Félix de la Bastide***
📧 Massane Est
☎ +33 (0)4-42809935
📅 15/4 - 15/10
@ info@campingfelix.com

4,5ha 88T(100-200m²) 10A CEE

1 ABCD**G**IJKLOPST
2 ADGRWX
3 AHJRWZ
4 (B+G 1/5-30/9)
(Q+T+V+X+Z 🔲)
5 **AB**GIJKLMNOPU
6 CEHI**K**(N 0,2km)V

💬 Quiet, homely campsite located between the hills on the shore of l'Etang de Berre, a salty lake with open access to the sea. Two beaches at walking distance. Warm welcome at campsite. Level grounds, protected by woods and reeds.

🚗 In Istres take the D5 Martigues, St. Mitre-les-Remparts. At the end of Istres, after about 2 km, exit D52: Varage, Massane (Les plages). Drive past the campsite Neptune and turn left towards the campsite.

CC €**17** 15/4-6/7 24/8-14/10

🧭 N 43°28'8'' E 5°1'20''

St. Mitre-les-Remparts, F-13920 / Provence-Alpes-Côte d'Azur (Bouches-du-Rhône) ♿ 📶 iD (2678)

🏕 Le Neptune***
📧 4 allée Gustave Eiffel
☎ +33 (0)4-42440660
📅 1/1 - 31/12
@ campingneptune@wanadoo.fr

3,2ha 60T(100m²) 16A CEE

1 ACD**G**HIJKLMOPST
2 DFGKLRUVWXY
3 AGHJRWZ
4 (B+G 1/6-30/9) (Q 🔲)
5 **AB**DGIJKLMNOPUVXYZ
6 EGI**K**(N 7km)

💬 The campsite has lovely views of l'étang de Berre, good for plenty of water activities. Large marked-out pitches. Ideal for people seeking some peace and quiet in the low season. 10% discount from 8th night, 15% discount from 15th night. Take note: reception closed from 12:00 to 15:00.

🚗 In Istres follow D5 towards Martigues. At end of town towards Varage Massane (les plages) at roundabout.

CC €**17** 1/1-6/7 24/8-31/12

🧭 N 43°28'6'' E 5°1'6''

St. Paul-en-Forêt, F-83440 / Provence-Alpes-Côte d'Azur (Var) 📶 iD (2679)

🏕 Camping Le Parc****
📧 408 Quartier Trestaure
☎ +33 (0)4-94761535
📅 1/4 - 30/9
@ contact@campingleparc.com

3,5ha 55T(80-110m²) 10A CEE

1 AF**IJKLMPST
2 BGIRTVXY
3 BFGMNQRUV
4 (C+G 1/5-15/9) K(Q+R 🔲)
(T+U+V+Y 1/7-31/8)
(Z 1/6-30/9)
5 **AB**DEFGIJKLMNOPUZ
6 ACEG**K**(N 4km)OTV

💬 Campsite with spacious, shaded pitches in the heart of Provence. Many authentic and charming towns and villages to visit. Swimming pool and (heated) spa are open from early May.

🚗 A8, exit 39 direction Fayence/Les Adrets. Campsite 4 km south of Fayence direction St. Paul-en-Forêt. Signposted.

CC €**13** 1/4-7/7 25/8-29/9

🧭 N 43°35'4'' E 6°41'23''

St. Raphaël, F-83700 / Provence-Alpes-Côte d'Azur (Var)

🏕 Sandaya Douce Quiétude*****
📧 3435, bd Jacques Baudino
☎ +33 (0)4-94443000
📠 +33 (0)4-94443030
🔑 13/4 - 16/9
@ dou@sandaya.fr

10ha 84T(60-100m²) 16A CEE

1 ACD**G**IJKLPST
2 BGRVWXY
3 B**F**GKLM**N**QR**U**V
4 (C+H 🔑) IJK
　(Q+S+T+U+V+W+Y+Z 🔑)
5 **AB**DEFGIJKLMNOPSUWXYZ
6 ABEGH**K**(N 3km)RSTVX

💬 Five-star campsite close to the Mediterranean coast in wooded surroundings on the edge of the Esterel volcanic massive. The Var area is a dream location for many for a successful holiday. Relaxation, sports and discovery are the keywords for a holiday in the Provence.

🚗 A8, exit Fréjus-Ouest exit 38. On all roundabouts follow direction St. Raphaël, then direction Boulouris/Agay. Turn left after the second roundabout at the Valescure stadium: Boulevard Baudino.

CC € ⑰ 13/4-6/7 1/9-15/9

📍 N 43°26'52'' E 6°48'20''

St. Rémy-de-Provence, F-13210 / Provence-Alpes-Côte d'Azur (Bouches-du-Rhône) 👫 ♿ 🛜 iD 2681

🏕 Le Parc de la Bastide***
📧 12 avenue Jean Moulin
☎ +33 (0)4-32619486
🔑 3/3 - 3/11
@ auberthonore@orange.fr

4ha 70T(80-140m²) 6-10A CEE

1 AGIJKLMOPST
2 RTVWX
3 **F**GHJN
4 (B 15/4-10/10) (Q 15/4-30/9)
　(R 🔑)
5 ADEFGIJKLOPUZ
6 ACEGK(N 0,5km)OTUV

💬 A campsite in Provence, in the heart of the Alpilles. A campsite landscaped with bamboo and mediterranean varieties of trees. 15 minutes walk from the centre of Saint Rémy de Provence. The pitches are easily accessible, level, shaded and bordered by bamboo hedges. Wonderful cycling.

🚗 A7 exit 5 Avignon-Sud, from Noves D30 to St. Rémy. In St. Rémy second roundabout left towards town centre. Campsite 50m further on the left.

CC € ⑰ 3/3-9/7 27/8-2/11 14=13

📍 N 43°47'24'' E 4°50'39''

St. Saturnin-les-Apt, F-84490 / Provence-Alpes-Côte d'Azur (Vaucluse)

🏕 Domaine des Chênes Blancs***
📧 chemin des Lombards
☎ +33 (0)4-88700007
🔑 1/4 - 15/10
@ contact@leschenesblancs.com

4ha 114T(80-100m²) 10A CEE

1 ACD**G**IJKL**P**T
2 BTVWXY
3 BGJNR
4 (C+G+Q+R+T+U+V 🔑)
　(X 1/7-31/8) (Z 🔑)
5 **A**EFGIJKLMNOPUZ
6 ACDEGI**K**(N 3km)O

💬 A shaded campsite peacefully located in an oak forest. Basic toilet facilities but all amenities are available. Spacious pitches on level ground. Restaurant open: May (weekend), June (Wednesday to Saturday). Heated swimming pool.

🚗 From A7 exit 24 continue towards Apt (D900). Just before Apt take the D943 then the D2.

CC € ⑰ 1/4-6/7 25/8-14/10 7=6, 14=11

📍 N 43°55'15'' E 5°20'28''

St. Vincent-les-Forts, F-04340 / Provence-Alpes-Côte d'Azur (Alpes-de-Haute-Prov) 👫 🤶 iD (2683)

▲ Campéole Le Lac***
✉ Le Fein
☎ +33 (0)4-92855157
FAX +33 (0)4-92855763
📅 15/5 - 16/9
@ lac@campeole.com

14ha 300T(100-110m²) 6A CEE

1 ACG**I**JLPS
2 DIJLMRTVWXY
3 ABGHNRU**W**Z
4 (B+G 1/6-31/8) (Q 📅)
   (S+T+U+V 15/6-10/9)
   (X 1/6-10/9) (Z 15/6-10/9)
5 **AB**FGIJKLMNOPUZ
6 AEGH**IJ**(N 5km)T

💬 A spacious campsite adjoining a lake with beautiful views and a quiet location.

🚗 D900 Gap-Barcelonnette, signposted between La Bréole and Le Lauzet-Ubaye.

Savines-le-Lac
D3
Espinasses D954
D900 B CC
D900

CC € 17 15/5-6/7 25/8-15/9   🧭 N 44°27'25'' E 6°21'49''

Ste Maxime, F-83120 / Provence-Alpes-Côte d'Azur (Var) 👫 ♿ 🤶 iD (2684)

▲ Les Cigalons**
✉ 34 ave du Croiseur Léger Le Malin
☎ +33 (0)4-94960551
FAX +33 (0)4-94967962
📅 1/4 - 15/10
@ campingcigalon@wanadoo.fr

30T(70-100m²) 10A CEE

1 ACD**G**IJKLPST
2 AEGJKRSVWXY
3 A**F**GWY
4 (Q+T+V+Z 📅)
5 **A**CGHIJKLMNOPUVZ
6 ABEG**K**(N 0,2km)TV

💬 Pleasant, quiet, well-maintained terraced campsite in a park with centuries-old trees. There is a magnificent sandy beach 50 metres away. Sainte Maxime is just 5 km away and is a very animated resort with countless facilities for sport and recreation.

🚗 A8, exit 36 to Le Muy. Once on the coast turn left towards Fréjus. Campsite about 5 km on the left.

Saint-Raphaël
D25
D559
CC
D93

CC € 17 1/4-7/7 1/9-14/10   🧭 N 43°19'50'' E 6°40'1''

Stes Maries-de-la-Mer, F-13460 / Provence-Alpes-Côte d'Azur (Bouches-du-Rhône) 👫 ♿ 🤶 iD (2685)

▲ Le Clos du Rhône****
✉ route d'Aigues-Mortes, CD38
☎ +33 (0)4-90978599
📅 6/4 - 11/11
@ info@camping-leclos.fr

7ha 248T(60-100m²) 16A CEE

1 ACD**G**IJKLO**P**ST
2 AEGKSVWXY
3 BGHJKLNOPRUVWY
4 (C+H 📅) JK**L**P
   (Q+S+T+U+V+X+Z 📅)
5 **AB**DEFGIJKLMNPQRUWXYZ
6 ACEGHI**K**(N 2km)QRTV

💬 A spacious campsite in traditional Camargue style. Positioned directly on a fine sandy beach 800m from Saintes Maries de la Mer. Views of the Camargue opposite the campsite.

🚗 From Arles beyond Chateau d'Avignon right onto D38c. Left after a few km on D38. Turn right before Stes Maries-de-la-Mer. Campsite signposted.

D570
Saintes-Maries-de-la-Mer
CC

CC € 17 6/4-8/7 26/8-10/11   🧭 N 43°27'0'' E 4°24'6''

Tallard, F-05130 / Provence-Alpes-Côte d'Azur (Hautes-Alpes) 📶 iD (2686)

🏔 Le Chêne
📧 Quartier le Chêne
☎ +33 (0)4-92541331
🗓 6/4 - 14/10
@ contact@camping-lechene.com

1ha 45T(60-80m²) 6A CEE

1️⃣ ACGIJLP
2️⃣ FJKUVX
3️⃣ GMN
4️⃣ (C 1/7-31/8)
5️⃣ ADEIJKLMNPU
6️⃣ JT

💬 Relaxing, welcoming campsite in the heart of the Hautes-Alpes. Shaded pitches with a view on Mount Céüse. Ideal for hikers. 800 m from Tallard airport, known worldwide for unique aeronautics. Dutch, German and English spoken at reception.

🚗 From Valance take D93 dir. Gap, then D993 to Aspres-sur-Buëch. Then towards Veynes and Gap on D994. Follow signs to Marseille then signs to Tallard.

CC €11 6/4-6/7 25/8-13/10 ⛰ N 44°27'21'' E 6°2'58''

Tarascon-en-Provence, F-13150 / Provence-Alpes-Côte d'Azur (Bouches-du-Rhône) ♿ 📶 iD (2687)

🏔 Saint Gabriel***
📧 route de Fontvieille
☎ +33 (0)4-90911983
🗓 19/3 - 12/11
@ contact@
   campingsaintgabriel.com

1,4ha 45T(70-110m²) 6A

1️⃣ ACDGIJKLOPQ
2️⃣ LRTVXY
3️⃣ AFGHJRUVW
4️⃣ (C+H 15/4-1/10)
   (Q 16/4-20/10) (R 🗓)
   (U+V+X 1/6-10/9) (Z 🗓)
5️⃣ ADEFGIJKLMNOPUWXYZ
6️⃣ ABEGK(N 3km)TV

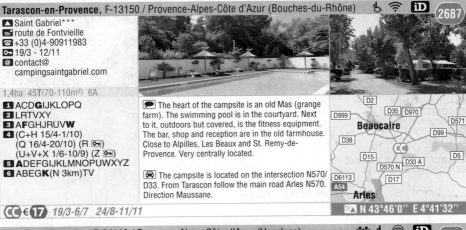

💬 The heart of the campsite is an old Mas (grange farm). The swimming pool is in the courtyard. Next to it, outdoors but covered, is the fitness equipment. The bar, shop and reception are in the old farmhouse. Close to Alpilles, Les Beaux and St. Remy-de-Provence. Very centrally located.

🚗 The campsite is located on the intersection N570/D33. From Tarascon follow the main road Arles N570. Direction Maussane.

CC €17 19/3-6/7 24/8-11/11 ⛰ N 43°46'0'' E 4°41'32''

Vaison-la-Romaine, F-84110 / Provence-Alpes-Côte d'Azur (Vaucluse) 🚻 ♿ 📶 iD (2688)

🏔 Le Voconce***
📧 route de St. Marcellin
☎ +33 (0)4-90362810
🗓 1/4 - 15/10
@ contact@camping-voconce.com

96T(70-100m²) 10A

1️⃣ ACGIJLMPST
2️⃣ COTVXY
3️⃣ ABGNRUWX
4️⃣ (B+G 15/5-15/9) (Q+R 🗓)
   (T 15/5-15/9) (Z 🗓)
5️⃣ AFGIJKLMOPU
6️⃣ EGJ(N 2,5km)OTV

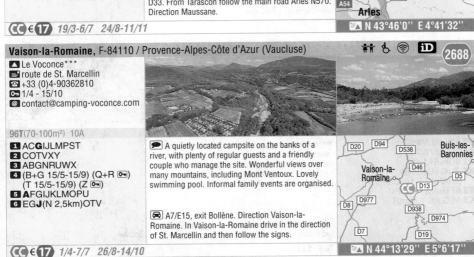

💬 A quietly located campsite on the banks of a river, with plenty of regular guests and a friendly couple who manage the site. Wonderful views over many mountains, including Mont Ventoux. Lovely swimming pool. Informal family events are organised.

🚗 A7/E15, exit Bollène. Direction Vaison-la-Romaine. In Vaison-la-Romaine drive in the direction of St. Marcellin and then follow the signs.

CC €17 1/4-7/7 26/8-14/10 ⛰ N 44°13'29'' E 5°6'17''

Vaison-la-Romaine/Faucon, F-84110 / Provence-Alpes-Côte d'Azur (Vaucluse) 2689

🏕 de l'Ayguette***
✉ Quartier de l'Ayguette, CD86
☎ +33 (0)4-90464035
📠 +33 (0)4-90464617
🕐 14/4 - 30/9
@ info@ayguette.com

3ha 75T(80-200m²) 10A

1 ACGIJLPST
2 JRTVXY
3 ABGNRU
4 (C+Q+R 🔒)
  (T+U+V+X 2/6-30/8) (Z 🔒)
5 AFGJKLNPUV
6 CEGJ(N 1km)OTV

💬 A well-kept terraced campsite in a changing landscape of mountains, woods and vineyards close to Vaison-la-Romaine.

🚌 Follow Vaison-la-Romaine - Nyons - Gap road. After a few km north follow signs to Faucon from the Intermarché intersection. From the north from Nyons-Vaison-la-Romaine to Mirabel. Left at crossroads to Faucon. Right before Faucon. Look for camping signs.

CC € 15 14/4-1/7 19/8-29/9 — N 44°15'44'' E 5°7'45''

Vallouise, F-05290 / Provence-Alpes-Côte d'Azur (Hautes-Alpes) 2690

🏕 Huttopia Vallouise***
✉ chemin des Chambonnettes
☎ +33 (0)4-92233026
📠 +33 (0)4-92223403
🕐 18/5 - 30/9
@ vallouise@huttopia.com

6,5ha 111T(80-100m²) 10A CEE

1 ACDGIJKLPST
2 CGKRTVWXY
3 BGHIMNRUW
4 (A 9/7-30/8)
  (C+Q+R 19/5-2/10)
  (T+V+Z 1/7-31/8)
5 ABDFGIJKLMNOPQUWZ
6 ACEGIJ(N 0,2km)OTV

💬 A campsite with lovely views of 'Les Ecrins' mountains. Spacious pitches in sun or shade. Parapente landing area!

🚌 Take the D994 in L'Argentière-la-Bessée. Left over the river in Vallouise.

CC € 15 18/5-5/7 26/8-29/9 — N 44°50'39'' E 6°29'25''

Valréas, F-84600 / Provence-Alpes-Côte d'Azur (Vaucluse) 2691

🏕 La Coronne***
✉ route du Pegue
☎ +33 (0)4-88700013
🕐 1/4 - 15/10
@ contact@lacoronne.com

2ha 50T(80-130m²) 10A CEE

1 AGIJKLMPST
2 CRTUVWXY
3 BGHJRU
4 (B+G+Q+T 🔒)
  (U+V+X+Z 1/6-30/9)
5 AFGIJKLMNOPU
6 AEGJ(N 1,5km)T

💬 A family campsite with plenty of pitches in the shade or in the sun. Lovely swimming pool and many fun activities in the town. Good opportunities for cycling and walking. Many facilities in the town of Valréas and close by in Vaison, Orange and Avignon.

🚌 Exit Montélimar south. Direction Nyons. Turn left just before Valréas and follow the signs.

CC € 15 1/4-6/7 25/8-14/10 7=6, 14=11 — N 44°23'34'' E 4°59'32''

Vedène, F-84270 / Provence-Alpes-Côte d'Azur (Vaucluse) ♙♙ ♿ 📶 ✿ **iD** (2692)

▲ Yelloh! Village Avignon Parc★★★
▤ 385 route d'Entraigues
☎ +33 (0)4-90310051
🔓 12/4 - 16/9
@ contact@avignonparc.com

6,5ha 138T(80-200m²) 10A

1 ACD**G**IJKLM**P**S
2 FIKRSVWXY
3 A**F**GHJKNOPRU**W**
4 (C+E+H 🔓) JK(Q+R 🔓)
   (T+X+Z 1/7-31/8)
5 **AB**EFGIJKLMNPUVWZ
6 ACEGK(N 2km)OTV

💬 Yelloh! Village family campsite located 10 km from Avignon. Wooded park of 6.5 hectares west of Mont Ventoux. Indoor heated swimming pool and jacuzzi, 2 outdoor lagoons, slide. Many towns to discover nearby, such as Avignon, Isle-sur-la-Sorgue, St. Rémy-de-Provence.

🚗 A7, 3 km from the Avignon Nord exit, direction Carpentras, follow the second sign to Vedène (right).

CC € **17** 12/4-6/7 25/8-15/9   🏔 N 43°59'25'' E 4°54'49''

Veynes, F-05400 / Provence-Alpes-Côte d'Azur (Hautes-Alpes) ♿ 📶 **iD** (2693)

▲ Camping Solaire★★★★
▤ Quartier des Iscles
☎ FAX +33 (0)4-92581234
🔓 1/1 - 31/12
@ info@camping-solaire.com

6,5ha 158T(150-200m²) 6A CEE

1 AC**F**IJKLMPST
2 KLRVWXY
3 BGHIJKLN**OPQ**RU**W**
4 (B+G 15/6-30/9) K
   (Q+R+T+U+V+X+Z 1/7-31/8)
5 **AB**DEFGIJKLMNOPUVWZ
6 EGH**IK**L(N 2km)OQTV

💬 A family campsite with a swimming pool, restaurant with terrace and views of the mountains. It has a shaded section but you can also choose a sunny pitch. Pitches of 150 m² or even more. Well-maintained grass.

🚗 From Grenoble N75 direction Sisteron. Then D994 towards Veynes. Follow Plan d'Eau and camping signs.

CC € **17** 1/4-1/7 19/8-30/9 8=7   🏔 N 44°31'14'' E 5°48'15''

Veynes, F-05400 / Provence-Alpes-Côte d'Azur (Hautes-Alpes) ♿ 📶 ✿ **iD** (2694)

▲ Les Rives du Lac★★★
▤ Plan d'eau Les Iscles
☎ +33 (0)4-92572090
🔓 28/4 - 30/9
@ booking@camping-lac.com

2,7ha 224T(80-190m²) 10-16A CEE

1 ACD**G**IJKLMOPST
2 CDKMNRVWXY
3 ABCGHIJKLN**OPQ**RU**W**XZ
4 (**A** 1/7-30/8)
   (E+G 15/6-15/9) K
   (Q 1/5-20/9) (S 1/7-31/8)
   (T+U+V 15/6-31/8) (X+Z 🔓)
5 **A**DEFGIJKLMNPQRUXYZ
6 AEGIJ**K**(N 2km)TV

💬 A lovely family campsite with a swimming pool, by a lake where you can swim from May to September. Countless opportunities for walking, cycling and mountain biking from the site up into the surrounding mountains. Fishing in the lake or river. Sports and sports ground for the children. Restaurant with terrace.

🚗 From Grenoble N75 direction Sisteron. Then D994 direction Veynes. Follow Plan d'Eau and camping signs.

CC € **15** 28/4-7/7 25/8-29/9 14=12   🏔 N 44°31'8'' E 5°47'56''

Villes-sur-Auzon, F-84570 / Provence-Alpes-Côte d'Azur (Vaucluse) ♿ 🛜 **iD** (2695)

🏕 Camping Municipal de
Villes-sur-Auzon
🏠 30 chemin du Stade
☎ +33 (0)6-10489115
🔑 30/3 - 31/10
@ camping@villes-sur-auzon.fr

1ha 60T(80-100m²) 10A CEE

1 ACD**G**IJKLMOPST
2 RTWXY
3 ABGH**J**M**U**
4 (B 1/7-31/8)
5 GIJKLMNOPUZ
6 BCEGHJ(N 0,5km)T

💬 French campsite with well-maintained toilet facilities, under pine trees, sunny or shaded pitches, close to a centre with restaurants, bakery and shops. Excursions to Mont Ventoux, Orange, Avignon and to Sault via the Route de La Nesque and the Lavender route.

🚗 Follow signs in Villes-sur-Auzon.

CC € **17** 30/3-30/6 18/8-30/10   🏕 N 44°3'19'' E 5°14'13''

Villes-sur-Auzon, F-84570 / Provence-Alpes-Côte d'Azur (Vaucluse) ♿ 🛜 ✿ **iD** (2696)

🏕 Les Verguettes★★★★
🏠 119 bis route de Carpentras
☎ +33 (0)4-90618818
🔑 31/3 - 1/10
@ verguettes@
provence-camping.com

2ha 67T(80-110m²) 10A CEE

1 AC**G**IJKLPST
2 JKRTVWXY
3 BGHJN**Q**RU
4 (C+G 1/5-1/10) (Q 1/6-30/9) (U 1/6-15/9) (X 15/6-15/9) (Z 🔑)
5 **A**DFGIJKLMNPQUYZ
6 ACEG**I**J**K**(N 0km)QTV

💬 The campsite is located near the village centre with its cafes and restaurants and wonderful views of Mont Ventoux. A lovely swimming pool blends in with the bar and reception area. Good base for walking and cycling tours, also through lavender fields. Romantic mountain villages and the Gorges de la Nesque close by.

🚗 Campsite on the D942 Carpentras-Mazan- Villes-sur-Auzon - Sault. Follow the signs in the town.

CC € **19** 31/3-7/7 25/8-30/9   🏕 N 44°3'26'' E 5°13'42''

Visan, F-84820 / Provence-Alpes-Côte d'Azur (Vaucluse) ♟ ♿ 🛜 **iD** (2697)

🏕 Camping de L'Hérein★★★
🏠 879 route de Bouchet
☎ +33 (0)4-90419599
🔑 6/4 - 14/10
@ accueil@campingvisan.com

3ha 75T(80-300m²) 6-16A CEE

1 ACGIJKLM**P**ST
2 LRTVXY
3 BGNU
4 (A 1/7-31/8) (B+G 1/5-14/10) (Q 15/5-30/9) (R 🔑) (T+U+V+X+Y 1/5-30/9) (Z 🔑)
5 **A**EFGIJKLMNPUV
6 EGK(N 1km)TV

💬 A quiet family campsite with new toilet facilities, a large swimming pool, bar and new restaurant. Wifi on the entire site is free. Small shop selling fresh fruit from the site's orchard. Plenty of cycling opportunities, close to Nyons, Vaison-la-Romaine and the Mont Ventoux.

🚗 Leave the A7 at Bollène, direction Suze-la-Rousse. At Tulette to Visan, then via signposts to Valreas, direction Bouchet on the route Visan-Bouche on the D161.

CC € **15** 6/4-5/7 23/8-13/10 21=18   🏕 N 44°18'44'' E 4°56'9''

Volonne, F-04290 / Provence-Alpes-Côte d'Azur (Alpes-de-Haute-Prov)   ♿ 🛜 iD (2698)

🏕 Sunêlia l'Hippocampe*****
📧 route Napoleon
☎ +33 (0)4-92335000
📠 +33 (0)4-92335049
🗓 21/4 - 16/9
@ camping@l-hippocampe.com

11ha 447T(100-130m²) 10A CEE

1 ACD**F**IJKLMP**S**T
2 D**F**LMRTV**X**
3 B**F**GHJKMN**OP**RU**W**
4 (**A**+C+H 🗓) IJKM(Q 🗓)
   (R 1/7-31/8)
   (T+U+V+Y+Z 🗓)
5 **AB**FGHJLNPUWXYZ
6 ACDEGH**JK**L(N 0,6km)TV

💬 Five-star campsite under the sun in the centre of Provence, in quiet surroundings on the banks of a river. With swimming pools with slides, jacuzzi and toddler pool, restaurant, snacks and take-away meals.

🚗 From Sisteron take the N85, southerly direction. Then exit Volonne. The campsite is located south of Volonne.

Sisteron
D4
D951 CC
Château-Arnoux-
Saint-Auban   N85
Les Mées
A51

CC € **17**   21/4-7/7   25/8-15/9   🗺 N 44°6'16'' E 6°1'1''

Antibes, F-06600 / Rivièra-Côte d'Azur (Alpes-Maritimes)   ♿ 🛜 iD (2699)

🏕 Le Rossignol***
📧 2074 av. M. Pellissier/av. J. Grec
☎ +33 (0)4-93335698
📠 +33 (0)4-92919899
🗓 1/4 - 29/9
@ campinglerossignol@wanadoo.fr

1,8ha 111T(90-110m²) 10A CEE

1 AC**F**IJKL**P**ST
2 FGJNRTV**Y**
3 A**F**GRU
4 (C 20/4-26/9) (G 1/6-26/9)
   (Q+R 1/7-31/8) (Z 🗓)
5 **AB**EFGIJKLMNOPUWXYZ
6 ACEG**IK**(N 0,3km)RTV

💬 1200 metres from the beach, close to Atibes and the Picasso and Léger museums, in natural and pleasant surroundings, Le Rossignol offers pitches marked out by small hedges. Satellite TV connection. Heated swimming pool. Reception open between 09:30 and 19:00.

🚗 A8, exit Antibes; direction Marineland. Campsite is signposted.

D3   **Nice**
A8
CC
Antibes

CC € **19**   1/4-12/7   30/8-28/9   🗺 N 43°36'23'' E 7°6'43''

Cagnes-sur-Mer, F-06800 / Rivièra-Côte d'Azur (Alpes-Maritimes)   🛜 iD (2700)

🏕 Le Colombier***
📧 35 chemin Sainte Colombe
☎ 📠 +33 (0)4-93731277
🗓 1/4 - 1/10
@ campinglecolombier06@
   gmail.com

1,1ha 34T(80-110m²) 6A CEE

1 A**F**IJKL**P**ST
2 FGTVXY
3 ABCGR
4 (B 20/5-30/9) (T 1/6-20/9)
5 **AB**DEGIJKLMNOPUVZ
6 CEG**J**(N 0,5km)QTV

💬 Small, homely campsite, peaceful location in green surroundings. Level and shaded grounds. Swimming pool and solarium. Wifi on entire campsite, table football, mini-billiards. 10 minutes to sea, 15 minutes to medieval village, 400 metres to shops and 1 km to town centre.

🚗 On the A8 take exit 47. Continue towards Cagnes-sur-Mer centre, follow Colline de la Route de Vence as far as the Durante roundabout. Follow camping signs then Le Colombier campsite sign.

D3   D2
D6
D2210   **Nice**
CC
Cagnes-sur-Mer
A8
Antibes

CC € **19**   1/4-10/7   1/9-30/9   🗺 N 43°40'17'' E 7°8'20''

Cagnes-sur-Mer, F-06800 / Rivièra-Côte d'Azur (Alpes-Maritimes)

🛜 iD (2701)

🔺 Le Val Fleuri***
📧 139 chemin Vallon des Vaux
☎ FAX +33 (0)4-93312174
🔓 1/4 - 30/9
@ valfleur2@wanadoo.fr

1,5ha 86T(80-100m²) 6A CEE

1 ACFIJKLMPST
2 FGJLNRTVXY
3 ABGR
4 (C+H 15/4-26/9) (Q 🔓)
   (R+T 1/5-30/9)
5 ADGHIJKLMNOPUZ
6 AFGK(N 3,5km)TV

💬 The campsite comprises two sections. The part on the right side of the road has lovely shaded pitches. Away from the bustle of the coast. A very friendly lady owner. Bread ordered in advance is delivered to your caravan in the early and late seasons. Reception closed between 12:00 and 14:00.

🚗 A8 exit Cagnes-sur-Mer. Then N7 direction Nice. Signposted through Cagnes-sur-Mer.

D6202 | D19
D2
D6 | D6202 BIS | A8 | **Nice**
D2210 | CC
Cagnes-sur-Mer
D6007

CC € **17** 1/4-7/7 25/8-29/9 | 📍 N 43°41'14'' E 7°9'21''

La Colle-sur-Loup, F-06480 / Rivièra-Côte d'Azur (Alpes-Maritimes)

❌ 🛜 iD (2702)

🔺 Flower Camping Le Vallon Rouge***
📧 route de Roquefort / D6
☎ +33 (0)4-93328612
FAX +33 (0)4-93328009
🔓 9/4 - 29/9
@ info@auvallonrouge.com

3ha 80T(70-100m²) 10A

1 ACDEIJKLMPST
2 BCFGLNRTVY
3 ABGHNOQRUWX
4 (B+G+Q 🔓)
   (R+T+U+V+X+Y 1/7-31/8)
   (Z 1/7-30/8)
5 ABEFGIJKLMNPUWZ
6 AEGIJ(N 3km)OQRTV

💬 Set in lush and shaded surroundings, bordered by a river, you will be welcomed in an oasis of tranquillity.

🚗 A8, exit 47 direction Villeneuve-Loubet, after that D6 direction Grasse. Signposted.

D2
D6
D3 | D2210
CC
Grasse Cagnes-sur-Mer
A8

CC € **17** 9/4-30/6 1/9-28/9 7=6 | 📍 N 43°41'4'' E 7°4'24''

La Colle-sur-Loup, F-06480 / Rivièra-Côte d'Azur (Alpes-Maritimes)

🛜 iD (2703)

🔺 Sites & Paysages Les Pinèdes****
📧 route du Pont de Pierre
☎ +33 (0)4-93329894
FAX +33 (0)4-93325020
🔓 1/4 - 30/9
@ info@lespinedes.com

4ha 106T(80-110m²) 10A

1 ACFIJKLPST
2 BCFGJRUVXY
3 BFGHNORUVWX
4 (C+H 7/4-30/9) (Q 1/5-30/9)
   (S 15/5-30/9)
   (T+U+V+X+Y+Z 🔓)
5 ABDEFGIJKLMNPUVWXYZ
6 ACEGIK(N 1km)QRTV

💬 Close to the sea (7 km) and St. Paul de Vence, ideally located in the centre of the Rivièra/Côte d'Azur. This lovely quiet terraced campsite offers campers spacious pitches, good toilet facilities and a restaurant for culinary indulgence. Heated swimming pool with space for sunbathing open from 11 April.

🚗 A8, exit 47 direction Villeneuve-Loubet. Exit La Colle and take route D6 in the direction of Grasse.

D2
D6 | D6202
D3 | D2210
CC
Saint-Laurent-du-Var
A8
Antibes

CC € **17** 1/4-6/7 25/8-29/9 | 📍 N 43°40'54'' E 7°5'0''

Le Bar-sur-Loup, F-06620 / Rivièra-Côte d'Azur (Alpes-Maritimes) ♿ 📶 iD (2704)

🔺 Les Gorges du Loup****
✉ 965 chemin des Vergers
☎ FAX +33 (0)4-93424506
🗓 14/4 - 22/9
@ info@lesgorgesduloup.com

1,6ha 65T(80-160m²) 6-10A CEE

1 **AG**HIJKL**P**ST
2 GJKRTVXY
3 B**F**GNRU
4 (C+Q+R 🅿)
  (T+U+V+X 1/5-15/9) (Z 🅿)
5 **A**CEGHIJKLMNOPUVZ
6 AEG**I**K(N 1km)ORTV

💬 Ideally located for discovering this part of France in low season. A convenient location for Cannes, Nice and the perfume city of Grasse. Attentive welcome. Pleasant ambiance. A visit to the Gorges du Loup is highly recommended.

🚗 A8 exit 47, dir. Roquefort-les-Pins, Le Rouret, Châteauneuf and finally towards Bar-sur-Loup. Campsite signposted just outside village (about 1.5 km). Do not follow GPS in village. You can turn back 2km after Le Bar-sur-Loup.

CC € **17** 14/4-6/7 25/8-21/9   🗺 N 43°42'6'' E 6°59'43''

Le Cannet/Cannes, F-06110 / Rivièra-Côte d'Azur (Alpes-Maritimes) ♿ 📶 iD (2705)

🔺 Le Ranch***
✉ 275 chemin Saint Joseph, l'Aubarède
☎ +33 (0)4-93460011
FAX +33 (0)4-93464430
🗓 15/4 - 15/9
@ aubarede06110camping@gmail.com

2ha 71T(80-150m²) 6A CEE

1 ACD**G**IJKLMOST
2 AGIJKTVXY
3 ABF**G**HJNRUV
4 (E+Q+R+T+U+V+Z 🅿)
5 **AB**EFGIJKLMNPQUXZ
6 ACE**K**(N 1km)RV

💬 Located on a wooded hillside with views of Grasse and Mandelieu. Plenty of shade and a swimming pool (open from 15/4-15/9) with a sliding roof are a big advantage. 2 km from Cannes beach (inexpensive bus connection).

🚗 A8 exit Le Cannet. Follow direction La Bocca D809. Campsite well signposted.

CC € **19** 15/4-30/6 1/9-14/9   🗺 N 43°33'52'' E 6°58'40''

Mandelieu-la-Napoule, F-06210 / Rivièra-Côte d'Azur (Alpes-Maritimes) ♿ 📶 iD (2706)

🔺 Les Cigales****
✉ 505 av. de la Mer
☎ +33 (0)4-93492353
FAX +33 (0)4-93493045
🗓 1/1 - 29/12
@ campingcigales@wanadoo.fr

2ha 43T(60-120m²) 6A

1 ACD**G**IJKLM**P**ST
2 ACFGKRSVWXY
3 B**F**GRUW
4 (B+G 1/5-30/9)
  (Q+T+U+Z 🅿)
5 **AB**CDEFGHIJKLMNOPRUXY
  Z
6 CDEGIJ(N 0,25km)TV

💬 A small, well-kept campsite in a rural setting but close to the centre. In addition to a swimming pool the site has its own small harbour. Ideal for exploring the azure coast by train or bus (no stress or expensive parking). Call ahead for free pitches (English, French, German and Dutch spoken).

🚗 A8, exit 40. Then first road right, second traffic lights left. Or N98, between La Napoule and Cannes follow in the direction of Mandelieu-Centre.

CC € **19** 1/1-29/6 22/9-28/12   🗺 N 43°32'20'' E 6°56'33''

Puget-Théniers, F-06260 / Rivièra-Côte d'Azur (Alpes-Maritimes) 🏕 ♿ 🛜 iD (2707)

🏠 Origan****
☎ +33 (0)4-93050600
📠 +33 (0)4-93050934
🗓 14/4 - 14/10
@ origan@orange.fr

35ha 60T(50-100m²) 6A

1 ACD**G**IJKLPST
2 BC**I**JKLTVWY
3 BHMNRV**W**
4 (A 1/7-31/8) (C+G 🔒) JK**L**N
(Q+R+T+U+V+X+Y+Z 🔒)
5 **A**EFGIJKLMNOPUVWZ
6 ADEGHIJ(N 3km)ORV

💬 A very well-maintained, beautifully situated naturist campsite in impressive surroundings. Nestling on a hillside near a typical village in Haute Provence. 60 km from the Mediterranean Sea.

🚗 About 500 metres west of the village Puget-Théniers (by the level crossing) an arrow shows the way.

D2202 D28
N202 D4202 CC Touët-sur-Var
Roquesteron

CC € **17** 14/4-7/7 25/8-13/10   ⛰ N 43°57'26'' E 6°51'35''

Vence, F-06140 / Rivièra-Côte d'Azur (Alpes-Maritimes) ♿ 🛜 iD (2708)

🏠 La Bergerie***
🏤 1330 chemin de la Sine
☎ +33 (0)4-93580936
📠 +33 (0)4-93598044
🗓 25/3 - 16/10
@ info@
camping-domainedelabergerie.com
13ha 450T(80-160m²) 5A

NEW

1 ABCDGIJKLMPST
2 BFGLRTVY
3 BGHJMR
4 (B 1/5-30/9) (Q 🔒)
(S+T+U+X+Y+Z 1/5-30/9)
5 **A**EFGIJKLMNOPTUVWYZ
6 CEG**J**(N 3km)OT

💬 An ideal and quiet family campsite, suitable for campers with small children, and located in a nature reserve. The toilet facilities in Provençale style are well maintained. Those who appreciate space are well catered for by the remarkably large pitches.

🚗 Follow Vence from motorway. Only use GPS after Vence. From Vence centre continue 2 km towards Tourrettes-sur-Loup/Grasse. Left at roundabout after 2 km. Follow signs for 1 km.

D2
D3
D6
D2210 A8
Grasse Cagnes-sur-Mer
D6007

CC € **17** 25/3-30/6 1/9-15/10   ⛰ N 43°42'44'' E 7°5'24''

Aléria, F-20270 / Corse ♿ 🛜 iD (2709)

🏠 Marina d'Aléria****
🏤 route de la Mer
☎ +33 (0)4-95570142
📠 +33 (0)4-95570429
🗓 28/4 - 6/10
@ info@marina-aleria.com

9ha 130T(80-120m²) 9A CEE

1 ACD**F**IJKLPQ
2 ABEKRSVXY
3 BGHK**M**RUVWY
4 (C+H 🔒) K
(Q+S+T+U+V+Y+Z 🔒)
5 **AB**EFGIJKLMNOPU
6 AEGHK(N 3km)OQTV

💬 A lovely family campsite on a long sandy beach. Plenty of comfort and shaded pitches.

🚗 Located in Aléria itself, on the intersection in the direction of the coast. Clearly signposted. Coastal road about 3 km.

N200
Aléria
CC
Aghione
N198

CC € **19** 28/4-17/6 1/9-5/10   ⛰ N 42°6'41'' E 9°33'5''

Aléria, F-20270 / Corse

🔺 Riva Bella Thalasso &
  Spa Resort****
✉ B.P. 21
☎ +33 (0)4-95388110
📠 +33 (0)4-95389129
🔓 1/1 - 31/12
@ riva-bella@orange.fr

78ha 200T(100-120m²) 10A CEE

1 ACD**F**IJKLMNOPST
2 ABDEIKSTXY
3 BDGKLMNRUVWY
4 (**A** 1/7-31/8) **KL**N**OP**
  (Q+S 1/5-30/9) (T 🔓)
  (U 1/6-15/9) (V+Y+Z 🔓)
5 **AB**EFGIJKLMNOPUWZ
6 AEGH**I**K(N 7km)OQRTVX

💬 Four-star campsite, with 'Clé Verte' label, located on the coast and open all year round. Open for naturists from 01/04 to 05/11. A large terrain (79 ha) in the middle of the countryside and fine sandy beach as far as the eye can see. Extensive thalassic centre, fitness trail, sports pitch, gym, paddle tennis, Nordic Walking and cycle paths.

🚗 Located near the N198, 9 km north of Aléria, then 3 km on a private country road to the coast.

ⒸⒸ €**19** 1/1-12/6 10/9-31/12   📍 N 42°10'24'' E 9°31'44''

2710

Bonifacio, F-20169 / Corse

🔺 Pian del Fosse***
✉ route de Santa Manza
☎ +33 (0)4-95731634
🔓 20/4 - 15/10
@ pian.del.fosse@wanadoo.fr

5ha 100T(40-80m²) 10A CEE

1 ACD**G**IJLP
2 JRVY
3 B**F**G**O**P**R**V
4 (Q 1/6-30/9) (R+T 1/7-31/8)
  (Z 1/7-30/9)
5 **AB**EFGIJKLMNOPUVZ
6 ACDEG**J**L(N 3,5km)OTV

💬 Very well-maintained campsite with a friendly welcome and plenty of shade. The perfect starting point for visiting bays, beaches and towns. A quiet campsite. Cycle or walk inland from the campsite to Bonifacio along marked out paths.

🚗 From Porto Vecchio N198 dir. Bonifacio. Left at white Sant' Amanza (D60) sign close to Bonifacio. Right at end of road (D58). Follow camping sign. For Satnav enter: Pian del Fosse/Bonifacio or coordinates.

ⒸⒸ €**17** 20/4-14/7 1/9-14/10   📍 N 41°23'59'' E 9°12'4''

2711

Bravone, F-20230 / Corse

🔺 Bagheera****
✉ N198
☎ +33 (0)4-95388030
📠 +33 (0)4-95388347
🔓 15/1 - 16/12
@ bagheera@bagheera.fr

100ha 250T(80-120m²) 10A

1 ABCD**G**IJKLMO**P**S
2 ABEKLRSTXY
3 BDGHJK**M**NRUWY
4 (**A** 1/7-31/8) N
  (Q+S 1/5-30/9)
  (T+U+V 15/5-15/9)
  (Y+Z 15/5-30/9)
5 **AB**DFGIJKLMNOPQUZ
6 ACEGIJ(N 6km)O**P**QRTV

💬 Site with modern heated toilet facilities, restaurants and mini-market. In a eucalyptus forest by the sea with clear water. Many sports: swimming, aqua-gym, yoga, diving, fishing, pedalos, cycling or windsurfing. Or relax in a chaise longue in the shade of the eucalyptus trees. Naturist campsite.

🚗 The campsite is located on the San Nicolao/ Bravone N198, about 18 km south of San Moriani-Plage, and about 12 km north of Aléria, about 3 km from the N198.

ⒸⒸ €**19** 15/1-2/6 1/9-15/12   📍 N 42°12'53'' E 9°33'19''

2712

Calvi, F-20260 / Corse

🏕 Dolce Vita★★★
📧 route de Bastia, N197
☎ +33 (0)4-95650599
📠 +33 (0)4-95653125
📅 27/4 - 30/9
@ dolce-vita.office@orange.fr

 🚿 🛜 iD (2713)

6ha 161T(80-100m²) 10A CEE

1 ACDFIJKLMOPST
2 ABCEGSVWXY
3 BCGMNOPRWY
4 N(Q+R+T+V+Y+Z 1/5-30/9)
5 ABDEFGJLMNOPQUVWZ
6 CEGHK(N 4km)ORTV

💬 Quiet family campsite, located directly on the coast only 3 km from Calvi. Shaded pitches. Fully renovated toilet facilities.

🚐 Located on the N197, l'Île Rousse-Calvi, ca. 4 km north of Calvi.

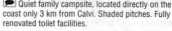

Monticello
Calvi
N197
CC
D151
D81

CC € 15 27/4-30/6 1/9-29/9 7=6, 14=11   🧭 N 42°33'15'' E 8°47'19''

Calvi, F-20260 / Corse

🏕 La Pinède★★★★
📧 route de la Pinède
☎ +33 (0)4-95651780
📠 +33 (0)4-95651960
📅 31/3 - 10/11
@ info@camping-calvi.com

 🚿 🛜 iD (2714)

5ha 123T(80-100m²) 12A CEE

1 ACDFIJKLMPS
2 AEGSTVXY
3 BGMNOPQRUVWY
4 (A 1/7-31/8) (C+H 🔑) IJKLM
  N(Q+S+T+U+V+Y+Z 🔑)
5 ABFGIJKLMNOPUVZ
6 CEGHJK(N 1km)OQRTV

💬 Situated at one of the most beautiful fine sandy beaches in Europe. Campsite La Pinède welcomes you in a forest of pine and eucalyptus trees. A 20 minute walk from the centre of Calvi. Experience an unforgettable holiday under the Corsican sun in this oasis of 5 hectare full of flowers and greenery.

🚐 N197 from l'Île Rousse direction Calvi. At Calvi (after the place name sign) turn right after 200 metres. Follow camping signs. Campsite situated in La Pinède woods.

L'Île-Rousse
Calvi
N197
CC
D71
D151
D81

CC € 19 31/3-30/6 1/9-9/11 7=6, 14=11   🧭 N 42°33'13'' E 8°46'7''

Ghisonaccia, F-20240 / Corse

🏕 Arinella Bianca★★★★★
📧 route de la Mer
☎ +33 (0)4-95560478
📠 +33 (0)4-95561254
📅 28/4 - 13/10
@ arinella@arinellabianca.com

 🚿 🛜 iD (2715)

10ha 100T(80-100m²) 10A CEE

1 ACDFIJKLMPST
2 ACEGKRSVY
3 BGMNOPRUWY
4 (A 15/6-31/8)
  (C+G 1/5-7/10) KP
  (Q+S 15/5-7/10)
  (T+U 15/5-10/9)
  (V+X+Y+Z 15/5-7/10)
5 ABFGIJKLMNOPUWZ
6 ACEGHK(N 1km)ORTU

💬 A beautiful family campsite on the beach with a swimming pool and plenty of entertainment. Separated, well shaded pitches. Charges for the spa and pool.

🚐 From the N198 roundabout after Ghisonaccia centre, take route de la Mer 5 km, and turn right at the roundabout. Follow camping signs.

D344 D343
Ghisonaccia
Prunelli-di-Fiumorbo
CC
N198

CC € 19 28/4-6/7 1/9-12/10   🧭 N 41°59'56'' E 9°26'32''

Ghisonaccia, F-20240 / Corse

🛖 Marina d'Erba Rossa★★★★
✉ route de la Mer
☎ +33 (0)4-95562514
📠 +33 (0)4-95562723
🗓 1/4 - 15/10
@ erbarossa@wanadoo.fr

20ha 70T(80-120m²) 10A CEE

1 ACD**F**IJKLMPRS
2 ABEKRSTVWXY
3 ABDGJKMNQRUWY
4 (B 🅾) **KNP**(Q 8/4-30/9)
　(S 🅾)
　(T+U+V+Y+Z 15/5-30/9)
5 **AB**FGIJKLMNOPUW
6 AEGHJ**K**(N 1km)QRTV

💬 A beautiful family campsite located on the beach, with every comfort, shady pitches and lots of entertainment.

🚗 From N198 at roundabout after Ghisonaccia centre. Route de la Mer 5 km.

ⓒ€ **17** 7/4-7/7 2/9-13/10

🏕 N 42°0'2'' E 9°26'49''

Ghisonaccia, F-20240 / Corse

🛖 U Casone
✉ route de la Mer
☎ +33 (0)4-95560241
📠 +33 (0)4-95561295
🗓 1/5 - 1/10
@ info@ucasone.net

4ha 100T(100-160m²) 4-16A CEE

1 ACD**G**IJKLMPST
2 ACKSTVXY
3 AKR**W**
4 (**A** 1/7-30/8) (B 1/5-30/9)
　(Q 15/6-15/9) (R 1/7-31/8)
　(V+X 15/6-15/9) (Z 🅾)
5 **A**FGIJKLMNOPUWXZ
6 CEGJ(N 1km)TVW

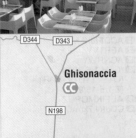

💬 Very quiet campsite with friendly welcome. Basic toilet facilities. Shaded and sunny marked-out pitches. Swimming pool and cocktail bar. Beach at 700 metres, accessible via a path.

🚗 From N198, after centre at roundabout take route de la Mer. Turn right after about 4 km and follow campsite signs.

ⓒ€ **17** 1/5-30/6 1/9-30/9

🏕 N 41°59'58'' E 9°26'10''

Lecci, F-20137 / Corse

🛖 Mulinacciu★★★
☎ +33 (0)4-95714748
🗓 20/5 - 30/9
@ infos@mulinacciu.com

14ha 160T(40-100m²) 6A CEE

1 A**G**IJKLOP
2 BCSTXY
3 BG**M**NRTUWX
4 (C+H 1/6-30/9) J
　(Q 15/6-31/8)
　(T+U+V+X+Z 1/6-31/8)
5 **A**FGIJLMNPU
6 CEG**K**(N 1km)QV

💬 A quiet campsite next to a river in the woods. The campsite has a heated swimming pool and there is also a bowling alley. Unmarked pitches. Good starting point for walking, 5 km from the sea.

🚗 From Lecci N198 towards Porto Vecchio, indicated beyond the village with large signs. On the right of the road.

ⓒ€ **17** 20/5-29/6 1/9-29/9

🏕 N 41°39'59'' E 9°18'29''

Lumio, F-20260 / Corse

♿ 📶 **iD** (2719)

🏔 Le Panoramic***
🛏 route de Lavatoggio
☎ +33 (0)4-95607313
🗓 1/5 - 30/9
@ info@le-panoramic.com

100T 6A CEE

1 **A**GIJKL**P**S
2 IJKSTVXY
3 AGHJR
4 (B 🖥) (Q 15/5-30/9) (R 🖥)
   (T+U+V+X+Z 1/6-30/9)
5 **A**FGIJKLMNPQUZ
6 AEGJ(N 1,5km)OTV

💬 Camping Panoramic is located 1,5 km from Lumio between Calvi and L'Ile Rousse and just 5 minutes from the beaches. The campsite has lovely views of Sant'Ambroggio bay. Its hallmarks are the friendly atmosphere, relaxation and shade. The campsite has a swimming pool and shaded pitches which are marked out by eucalyptus and mimosa trees.

🚌 Follow the N197 and take the D71 towards Lavatoggio. Campsite 1500m north of Lumio.

(CC) € **17** 1/5-4/7 24/8-29/9   🏖 N 42°35'24'' E 8°50'55''

Olmeto, F-20113 / Corse

♿ 📶 **iD** (2720)

🏔 Ras l'Bol***
🛏 Olmeto-Plage
☎ +33 (0)4-95740425
📠 +33 (0)4-95740130
🗓 1/4 - 15/10
@ infos@raslbol.com

5ha 150T(60-120m²) 6-10A CEE

1 ACD**F**IJKLMO**P**
2 AERTVY
3 AGNRWY
4 (C+H 1/5-30/9)
   (Q+S+T+U+V+X 🖥)
   (Z 1/5-15/9)
5 **A**EFIKMOPUZ
6 CGJ(N 7km)OTV

💬 Spacious campsite with free choice of pitches. Long, wide sandy beach close to Filitosa. Good toilet facilities and motorhome service, two heated swimming pools, one of which is a children's pool.

🚌 Leave the T40 between Olmeto and Propriano via the D157. The campsite is located close to the beach after ca. 6 km.

(CC) € **17** 1/4-30/6 1/9-14/10   🏖 N 41°42'11'' E 8°50'9''

Olmeto, F-20113 / Corse

♿ 📶 **iD** (2721)

🏔 Vigna Maggiore***
🛏 T40/D157
☎ +33 (0)4-95746202
📠 +33 (0)685930106
🗓 1/4 - 30/10
@ vignamaggiore@gmail.com

5,5ha 140T(70-180m²) 6A CEE

1 **A**F**I**JKLMO**PRS**
2 IKLSTWXY
3 ABGHR
4 (C 🖥) (Q+R+S 15/5-20/9)
   (T+U+V 1/7-15/9)
   (X+Z 1/6-30/9)
5 **A**EIJKLMNOPUZ
6 CEGIJ(N 3km)OT

💬 A peaceful campsite on the southwest coast close to Olmeto and about 5 km from Propriano. Beach 5 minutes towards Porto Pollo. Lovely swimming pools, the smallest of which is heated, with bar, patio and sea views.

🚌 From Propriano direction Olmeto, campsite on a bend on the left just after the D157 intersection. From Ajaccio on T40, campsite on a bend after Olmeto, 2nd entrance on the right. After bend take D157 exit, campsite on the right after the filling station.

(CC) € **15** 1/4-7/7 25/8-29/10   🏖 N 41°41'53'' E 8°53'47''

Pietracorbara, F-20233 / Corse ⚲ 🕪 iD `2722`

🔺 Domaine LP****
✉ Marine de Pietracorbara
☎ +33 (0)4-95352749
📠 +33 (0)4-95352857
⌚ 20/3 - 4/11
@ lapietra@wanadoo.fr

5ha 170T(95-120m²) 10A CEE

1 ACD**G**IJKLMOPST
2 AGKLQSVWXY
3 BGRU
4 (B 1/6-15/9) K(Q 🔑)
　(R 15/6-30/9)
　(T+X 15/6-15/9) (Z 🔑)
5 **A**FGIJKLMNOPUVW
6 CDEGHJ(N 3km)TV

💬 Quietly located campsite with excellent sanitary facilities on Cap Corse, a unique part of Corsica. New swimming pool. There is a lovely beach 600 metres away via a footpath.

🚗 On the D80 from Bastia to Cap Corse, turn left after 20 km, well signposted.

CC € **17** 20/3-30/6 10/9-3/11 　　⛰ N 42°50'20'' E 9°28'25''

Porticcio, F-20166 / Corse 👫 🕪 🛜 iD `2723`

🔺 Benista****
✉ Pisciatello / D55
☎ +33 (0)4-95251930
📠 +33 (0)4-95259370
⌚ 1/4 - 1/10
@ camping.benista@orange.fr

5ha 170T(90-110m²) 5A CEE

1 ACD**G**IJKLMO**P**ST
2 CGRSTVY
3 AB**EF**G**M**N**Q**RU
4 (B+G 15/5-15/9)
　(Q+R+S+T+U 🔑)
　(V 1/7-31/8) (X 1/6-31/8)
　(Z 15/5-15/9)
5 **AB**EFGIJKLMNPUW
6 ACGK(N 0,1km)OQRTV

💬 A friendly, shaded family campsite with a lovely swimming pool. 6 hole golf course next to the site, as well as shops and a restaurant. Lovely sandy beaches 1.5 km away. 10 km from Ajaccio.

🚗 Coming from the T40 drive up the D55. The campsite is on the right, after about 600 metres.

CC € **19** 1/4-29/6 1/9-30/9 　　⛰ N 41°54'25'' E 8°49'21''

Porto Vecchio, F-20137 / Corse 🕪 🛜 iD `2724`

🔺 Les Ilots d'Or***
✉ Pezza Cardo - La Trinité
☎ +33 (0)4-95700130
⌚ 2/5 - 30/9
@ campinglesilotsdor@sfr.fr

4ha 180T(20-110m²) 6A CEE

1 ACFIJLM**P**S
2 ABEJKLMRSTUVXY
3 ABGRWY
4 (Q+S+T+U+V+X 1/6-15/9)
　(Z 10/5-10/9)
5 **A**FGIJKLMNOPSUV
6 CEGJ(N 0,2km)OTV

💬 Beautiful campsite close to Porto Vecchio. Spacious, well-maintained beach campsite with asphalted road by a small bay. Sandy beach inclines only slightly. Suitable for families with children. Watersports options.

🚗 5 km north of Porto Vecchio (N198) at Ste Trinité, exit in direction of ocean (D468), take D568 when road splits. Second campsite on left.

CC € **17** 2/5-29/6 1/9-29/9 　　⛰ N 41°37'21'' E 9°17'59''

Sagone, F-20118 / Corse

⚲ 📶 iD (2725)

🏕 Le Sagone Camping****
🛣 route de Vico
☎ +33 (0)4-13594417
📠 +33 (0)4-95280828
📅 1/4 - 4/11
@ contact@camping-sagone.fr

9ha 270T(80-120m²) 10A

1 ACD**F**IJKLM**P**S
2 ABCGRSVY
3 BGJL**M**NRU**V**W
4 (C+E+G+Q+S+T+U+V+Y+Z 📅)
5 **AB**EFGIJKLMNPUWZ
6 ABCEGHJ**K**(N 0,1km)OQTU VW

💬 Le Sagone is surrounded by miracles: white sandy beaches, the 'Greek' Cargèse, the Piana Calanques, the Scandola nature reserve, the tower of Porto and Genoese Ajaccio. The coast is home to seabirds that nest here peacefully. Le Sagone is also a wild water paradise. Spectacular waterfalls and natural pools give the countryside a special appeal.

🚗 Located on the D70, 2 km along the Sagone-Vico road. Signposted in Sagone.

Cargèse — D70 — D81 — Sagone — Plein Soleil

CC € **17** 1/4-30/6 1/9-3/11

🏔 N 42°7'51'' E 8°42'18''

Sartène, F-20100 / Corse

👫 ⚲ 📶 iD (2726)

🏕 Campéole L'Avena***
🛣 route de Tizzano
☎ +33 (0)4-95770218
📠 +33 (0)4-95772447
📅 15/5 - 16/9
@ avena@campeole.com

6,5ha 80T(50-90m²) 6A

1 ABCD**G**IJL**P**
2 AEHKQRVWXY
3 ABGNRWY
4 (Q+S+T+V+X+Z 15/6-15/9)
5 **A**GIJKLMNOPUX
6 EHJORT

💬 This shaded family campsite is located 15 km south-west of Sartène, with a pleasant sea breeze, at the end of a long valley. Beach at 400 metres.

🚗 Bonifacio direction Sartène N196. Then D48 to Tizzano. Left before the village, follow signs. 1 km to campsite, steep access road.

Sartène — N196 — CC — Monacia-o d'Aullène

CC € **17** 15/5-6/7 25/8-15/9

🏔 N 41°32'6'' E 8°52'1''

Solaro, F-20240 / Corse

👫 ⚲ 📶 iD (2727)

🏕 Les Eucalyptus**
🛣 N198
☎ +33 (0)6-86810371
📅 1/5 - 15/10
@ camping.eucalyptus@orange.fr

3ha 60T(100m²) 15A

1 ABGIJKLMOPQ
2 ACEKTWX
3 RY
4 (Q+Z 1/5-30/9)
5 **A**GIJKLMNOPU
6 GJ(N 1,5km)

💬 A beautiful campsite situated on the beach. Shaded pitches under eucalyptus trees. Pick your own pitch.

🚗 Campsite is on N198, 2 km north of Solenzara.

Ventiseri — N198 — CC — Solenzara — D268 — N198

CC € **17** 1/5-30/6 1/9-14/10

🏔 N 41°52'38'' E 9°23'47''

Spain

Map labels:
- A Coruña
- Galicia **595**
- Vigo
- Asturias **598**
- Gijón
- Oviedo
- León
- Cantabria **593**
- Santander
- Bilbao
- San Sebastián
- País Vasco **591**
- Pamplona
- Navarra **589**
- Burgos
- La Rioja **588**
- Logroño
- Castilla y Leon **600**
- Valladolid
- Salamanca
- Zaragoza
- Aragón **582**
- Cataluña **533**
- Lérida
- Barcelona
- Tarragona
- Madrid **603**
- MADRID
- Toledo
- Extremadura **605**
- Badajoz
- Castilla-La Mancha **605**
- Albacete
- Castelló de la Plana
- Valencia
- Comunidad Valenciana **564**
- Palma
- Córdoba
- Jaén
- Murcia **620**
- Elche
- Alicante
- Murcia
- Huelva
- Sevilla
- Andalucía **607**
- Granada
- Cartagena
- Jerez de la Frontera
- Cádiz
- Málaga
- Almería
- P
- F

General
Spain is a member of the EU.

Time
The time in Spain is the same as Amsterdam, Paris and Rome and one hour ahead of London. Time on the Canary Islands is the same as London.

Languages
Spanish.

Border formalities
Many formalities and agreements about matters such as necessary travel documents, car papers, requirements relating to your means of transport and accommodation, medical expenses and taking pets with you do not only

depend on the country you are travelling to but also on your departure point and nationality. The length of your stay can also play a role here. It is not possible within the confines of this guide to guarantee the correct and most up to date information with regard to these matters.

We advise you to consult the relevant authorities before your departure about:
- which travel documents you will need for yourself and your fellow passengers
- which documents you need for your car
- which regulations your caravan must meet
- which goods you may import and export
- how medical treatment will be arranged and paid for in your holiday destination in cases of accident or illness
- whether you can take pets. Contact your vets well in advance. They can give you information about the necessary vaccinations, proof thereof and obligations on return. It would also make sense to enquire whether any special regulations apply to your pet in public places at your holiday destination. In some countries for example dogs must always be muzzled or transported in a cage.

You will find plenty of general information on ▸ *www.europa.eu* ◂ but make certain you select information that is relevant to your specific situation.

For the most recent customs regulations you should get in contact with the authorities of your holiday destination in your country of residence.

Currency
The currency in Spain is the euro. Approximate exchange rates September 2017: £1 = € 1.09.

Credit cards
Credit cards can be used in most places, including toll roads.

Opening times /Public holidays
Banks
Banks are open Monday to Friday until 14:00, Saturday until 13:00. Banks are closed on Saturdays in June, July and August.

Shops
Most shops are open from Monday to Friday until 13:30 and from 16:30 to 20:00, on Saturdays

from 9:30 to 13:30. Department stores and shopping centres in big towns are open all day from 10:00 to 21:00 or 22:00. During the tourist season shops in the coastal areas are often open until after 22:00.

Chemists
Spanish chemists, which can be recognised by a green cross, are open from Monday to Friday until 13:30 and from 16:30 to 20:00.

Public holidays
New Year's Day, 6 January (Epiphany), Maundy Thursday, Good Friday, Easter, 1 May (Labour Day), Whitsunday, 31 May (Corpus Christi), 15 August (The Assumption), 12 October (National Day), All Saints Day, 6 December (Constitution Day), 8 December (Immaculate Conception), Christmas Day.

In the week before Easter (the 'Semana Santa') the shops open for half the day.

Communication

(Mobile) phones
The mobile network works well throughout Spain. There is a 4G network for mobile internet.

Wifi, internet
You can make use of a wifi network at more and more public locations, often for free.

Post
In general post offices are open on weekdays until 14:30 and from 17:00 to 20:00, on Saturdays until 13:00.

Roads and traffic

Road network
You are not advised to drive in the dark except on main roads. If you break down you can contact the Spanish motoring organisation RACE (in Catalonia the RACC) using the emergency phones.

Traffic regulations
Remember, all traffic in Spain drives on the right and overtakes on the left! Headlight deflectors are advisable to prevent annoying oncoming drivers. Spain uses the metric system, so distances are measured in kilometres (km) and speeds in kilometres per hour (km/h). You must give way to traffic from the right, except on priority routes. This also applies to slow traffic. When driving on a roundabout you have priority over drivers entering it. Trams always have priority.

Maximum speed

The maximum permitted alcohol level is 0.5‰. Dipped headlights are compulsory in tunnels. Phones may only be used hands-free. Drivers who wear spectacles must carry a spare pair. Use of the horn is compulsory on blind corners in mountain areas. Carrying a spare set of lamps is mandatory. Radios and mobile phones must be switched off when refuelling your vehicle. Use of a head set in cars is not permitted. Winter tyres are not compulsory in winter conditions but are very much advised, especially in areas such as the Pyrenees and the Sierra Nevada.

Caravans, motorhomes

If your caravan is longer than 12 metres, the so called ECE 70 is mandatory. You must then have two small or one large, yellow and red reflective sticker on the back of your caravan.

If your caravan is longer than 12 metres you must keep a distance of at least 50 metres from another vehicle outside built up areas.

Maximum allowed measurements of combined length

Height 4 metres, width 2.55 metres and maximum length 18.75 metres (of which the trailer maximum 12 metres).

Fuel

Lead-free petrol and diesel are easily available everywhere. LPG is reasonably well available.

Filling stations

Most filling stations along motorways are open between 06:00 and 24:00. Elsewhere they are open between 07:00 and 22:00. Pay attention when filling up: 'gasolina' means petrol and 'gasoleo' means diesel! You can pay by credit card at all service stations on motorways.

Tolls

Most motorways in Spain charge a toll. You can pay in cash, by credit card or automatically with an electronic (ETC) box.

Toll roads are indicated by the letters AP, while toll free motorways are indicated by the letter A. More information: ▶ *www.autopistas.com* ◀

Mountain passes with caravans

The Bonaigua Pass: is not prohibited for caravans but snow chains must be used in the winter months when there is snow on the ground, and the pass may sometimes be closed. The Portillón Pass: is not prohibited for caravans but the road is not very wide and going in the direction of France is even narrower; driving with a large(r) caravan may then be difficult.

Emergency number

112: the national emergency number for fire, police or ambulance.

Camping

Spain has more than 1000 campsites, of which the sites on the northern Mediterranean coast are the busiest. Reservations here are recommended! Trees, bushes and flowers ensure beautiful campsites, and also provide marked out pitches which increases privacy.

Campsites in Spain are classified by category. Category 1 is the most luxurious. Free camping is not allowed. If you still want to camp where there is no campsite, permission from the landowner must be sought.

Practical

- The Spanish are renowned for eating late; quite often people eat at home and in catering establishments between 20:30 and 22:30.
- Blue camping gas bottles cannot be refilled in Spain. You are advised to buy a Spanish container which can be returned when you leave the country.
- Make sure you have a world adaptor for electrical appliances.
- You are advised to drink bottled (mineral) water in preference to mains water.

Albanyà, E-17733 / Cataluña

🚹 📶 **iD** (2728)

🏕 Bassegoda Park Cat. 1
📧 Camí de Bassegoda S/N
☎ +34 972-542020
📠 +34 972-542021
🔓 16/3 - 9/12
@ info@bassegodapark.com

4,5ha 126T(70-110m²) 10-16A

1 ACD**G**IJKLM**P**
2 BCILTVXY
3 ABCGHIJKN**OPQ**RUWX
4 (**A** 1/7-31/8) (B 1/6-30/9) P
(Q+R+T+U+V+Y+Z 🔓)
5 **AB**DEFGIJKLMNOPUWXY
6 EG**IK**(N 0,5km)ORTV

💬 A campsite in wooded hilly surroundings with amenities that will surprise you. Only open at weekends from March to May and from October to December. Open every day from June to September.

🚗 From France exit 3, from Spain exit 4 direction Llers, then Terrades and Sant Llorenç de la Muga and finally Albanyà, keep straight ahead; the road is a dead end.

Castellfollit De La Roca — A-26 — Navata — N-260

🆑 € **17** 16/3-8/7 12/9-8/12 7=6, 14=10 — 🏔 N 42°18'25'' E 2°42'31''

Amposta, E-43870 / Cataluña

🚹 📶 (2729)

🏕 Eucaliptus Cat.2
📧 Platja Eucaliptus
☎ 📠 +34 977-479046
🔓 16/3 - 23/9
@ eucaliptus@ campingeucaliptus.com

4,5ha 240T(60-90m²) 6A

1 BCDGIJKLM**P**RS
2 AEGLRVXY
3 BHJKNRVWY
4 (B+G 1/5-23/9)
(Q+S+T+U+X+Y 🔓)
(Z 1/5-23/9)
5 **AB**EFGIJKLMNOPUWX
6 ACEGJ**K**(N 2km)ORTUV

💬 A campsite located in the Ebro delta with excellent toilet facilities, outdoor swimming pool from the beginning of May. Good opportunities for windsurfing and cycle trips in the 'Delta del Ebre' nature reserve. A paradise for bird enthusiasts.

🚗 On the A7 take exit 41 to Amposta and Deltebre. On the N340 take the Amposta exit, turn right at Amposta. Take the TV3405 to Platja dels Eucaliptus, then follow the camping signs.

Deltebre Sant Jaume D'Enveja

🆑 € **17** 16/3-28/3 2/4-26/4 1/5-5/7 24/8-6/9 11/9-22/9 7=6, 14=12, 21=18 — 🏔 N 40°39'24'' E 0°46'47''

Arnes, E-43597 / Cataluña

🚹 📶 **iD** (2730)

🏕 Els Ports Cat. 2
📧 Carretera T-330, km 12
☎ +34 977-435560
🔓 1/1 - 31/12
@ info@camping-elsports.com

3,5ha 81T(40-85m²) 6-10A

1 ACDGIJKLMPQ
2 LRTXY
3 ABHJKNR
4 (B+G 15/6-30/9)
(Q+R+T+V+X+Z 🔓)
5 **A**DGIJKLMNOPUWX
6 AEGJ(N 1km)TV

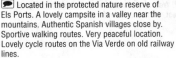

💬 Located in the protected nature reserve of Els Ports. A lovely campsite in a valley near the mountains. Authentic Spanish villages close by. Sportive walking routes. Very peaceful location. Lovely cycle routes on the Via Verde on old railway lines.

🚗 AP7 Barcelona-Valencia, exit 40 direction Tortosa, continue towards Lleida as far as Horta/Sant Joan exit. Then left towards Arnes T330 (40 km from AP7) After 3 km on the right.

N-420 T-333 T-330 Valderrobres Alfara De Carles

🆑 € **19** 1/1-27/3 2/4-30/6 1/9-31/12 7=6, 14=11, 30=22 — 🏔 N 40°55'10'' E 0°16'6''

Berga, E-08600 / Cataluña

🏔 Berga Resort Cat.1
🛣 E-9/C-16 km 96,3, Exit 95
☎ +34 938-211250
📠 +34 938-222388
📅 1/1 - 31/12
@ bergaresort@bergaresort.com

5,5ha 345T(70-90m²) 10A CEE

1 BCDFIJKLMNOPQ
2 FJKLRUVY
3 BCGHIJKNRUV
4 (A 🅿) (B 1/5-12/10) (F 🅿) (H 1/5-12/10) JKLMNP (Q 🅿) (S 24/6-11/9) (T+U+V+Y+Z 🅿)
5 ABDGIJKLMNOPSTUWX
6 CEGHK(N 1km)PQSTUV

💬 A shaded terraced campsite with extensive amenities for fitness and health, such as hydro massage, sauna, Turkish Bath, hot water pools, ice fountain etc. Located on the edge of the Pyrenees. CampingCard ACSI guests who stay at least 2 nights can get a pitch with private toilet facilities for 10 Euros extra per night.

🚗 Campsite is located on the E9/C16 from Puigcerdà to Barcelona. 1 km south of Berga.

La Rodonella

Berga C-16

CC

C-26   C-16Z
                    C-154
Casserres C-1411A   C-62

2731

CC € 19 2/1-22/3 2/4-26/4 1/5-21/6 20/9-10/10 14/10-30/10 4/11-4/12 7=6, 10=8, 14=10, 30=22   📍 N 42°5'29'' E 1°51'22''

Blanes, E-17300 / Cataluña

🏔 Bella Terra
🛣 Av. Villa de Madrid 35-40
☎ +34 972-348017
📠 +34 972-348275
📅 24/3 - 30/9
@ info@campingbellaterra.com

12ha 644T(70-90m²) 6A

1 ACDGIJKLMOPQ
2 AEGLSTVXY
3 AGKMNRUY
4 (B+G 1/5-30/9) IJ(Q+R 🅿) (T 1/5-1/10) (U+X+Y 🅿) (Z 1/5-30/9)
5 ABEFGIJKLMNOPUWXYZ
6 GHIKM(N 0,1km)ORTUVX

💬 Family campsite with excellent amenities for children and adults. The campsite is located in a pine forest along a beach and boulevard. Water park for children and a fantastic sports centre.

🚗 Exit 10 in Blanes, follow the camping signs. Bella Terra is located at the end of the campsite road.

AP-7   C-63
N-II   Lloret De Mar

CC   Blanes

2732

CC € 19 2/4-22/6 24/6-30/6 1/9-29/9   📍 N 41°39'31'' E 2°46'44''

Blanes, E-17300 / Cataluña

🏔 Camping El Pinar
🛣 Av. Villa de Madrid, 39
☎ +34 972-331083
📠 +34 972-331100
📅 30/3 - 30/9
@ camping@elpinarbeach.com

6,8ha 449T(60-80m²) 6-10A

1 ACDGIJKLOPQ
2 AEGLRSVWXY
3 ADKNRUVY
4 (B+G 1/5-15/9) (Q+S+T+U+X+Z 🅿)
5 ABFGIJKLMNOPUW
6 EGHK(N 0km)ORTVW

💬 Welcoming beach campsite half under a pine forest, with basic toilet facilities.

🚗 Follow the camping signs from the outskirts of Blanes. This brings you to Av. Villa de Madrid. El Pinar is the very last campsite.

AP-7   C-63
N-II   Lloret de Mar

CC   Blanes

C-32

2733

CC € 19 30/3-22/6 1/9-29/9   📍 N 41°39'18'' E 2°46'44''

Blanes, E-17300 / Cataluña 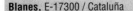 📶 iD 2734

🏕 Solmar
✉ Colom 48
☎ +34 626072640
📠 +34 972-348283
🔓 24/3 - 14/10
@ campingsolmar@
   campingsolmar.com

6ha 200T(65-85m²) 6A

1 ACDGIJKLO**P**RS
2 AEGRTVXY
3 BG**M**NRY
4 (B+G 1/5-30/9) (Q+S 🔓)
   (T+U+V 1/5-1/10) (X+Z 🔓)
5 **AB**FIJKLMNOP
6 AG**K**(N 0km)ORTV

💬 Campsite in the centre of the nightlife area with reasonably good sanitary facilities and plenty of shade.

🚗 From the edge of Blanes follow signs 'camping'. Arrive in Av. Villa de Madrid. Sign to the right 'Solmar'.

Ap-7 · N-ii · C-63
Tordera
Blanes
CC

CC € **17** 1/4-22/6 1/9-13/10   📷 N 41°39'43'' E 2°46'50''

Calella, E-08370 / Cataluña 📶 iD 2735

🏕 Roca Grossa Cat.2
✉ Ctra NII km 665
☎ +34 93-7691297
📠 +34 93-7661556
🔓 23/3 - 3/10
@ rocagrossa@rocagrossa.com

7ha 280T(60-90m²) 6-10A

1 ACD**G**IJKLMOPQ
2 AEFIJKSVY
3 BFGKL**M**NRUV**W**Y
4 (B+G 1/5-1/10)
   (Q+S+T+U+X+Z 🔓)
5 **A**FGIJKMNOPUWZ
6 AEGH**I**J**K**M(N 0,5km)OQRV
   WX

💬 A terraced campsite with beautiful sea views. A little 'train' takes you to the swimming pool.

🚗 Coastal road NII Malgrat-Barcelona. Between Calella and Sant Pol, 300 metres after 'el Faro' (lighthouse) turn right. Take care! Turn right directly after the bend. Caravan will be placed.

Ap-7
Blanes
C-61
Malgrat De Mar
CC

CC € **19** 23/3-30/6 1/9-2/10 7=6, 21=16, 31=25   📷 N 41°36'23'' E 2°38'19''

Calonge, E-17251 / Cataluña 📶 iD 2736

🏕 Senia Cala Gogo Cat.1
✉ Av. Andorra 13
☎ +34 972-651564
📠 +34 972-650553
🔓 21/4 - 24/9
@ calagogo@calagogo.es

20ha 670T(60-115m²) 6-10A

1 ACD**G**IJKLMOPQ
2 AEGIJKRSTVWXY
3 BFHKLMNRUWY
4 (C+H 🔓) IJ
   (Q+S+T+U+X+Y+Z 🔓)
5 **AB**EFGIJKLMNOP**ST**UWXY
   Z
6 ACEGHJ**K**M(N 1km)ORTVW
   X

💬 A friendly family campsite backing onto a hillside with plenty of shade. Designer toilet facilities, a lively swimming pool and plenty of free entertainment.

🚗 Exit 6 Palafrugell-Palamós. Direction San Feliu, then Palamós-est. Then Platja d'Aro. Campsite on the right side of the road. Campsite clearly signposted.

Sant Feliu De
Guíxols
CC

CC € **19** 21/4-29/6 1/9-23/9   📷 N 41°49'49'' E 3°5'2''

Cambrils, E-43850 / Cataluña

♿ 🛜 **(2737)**

📐 Joan Cat.2
🚏 N340, km 1141 /
　　Passeig Marítim 88
☎ +34 977-364604
📠 +34 977-794214
🔓 15/1 - 16/12
@ info@campingjoan.com
4,5ha 218T(< 90m²) 5A

1 BCG IJKLMOPQ
2 AEFGRSTVY
3 ABFGKRUVWY
4 (B+G 15/4-30/9) (Q+R 🔓)
　　(S+T+U+X+Y+Z 1/3-15/10)
5 AB DFGIJKLMNOPUWX
6 BCEGH IK M(N 2km)ORTVW
　　X

💬 A peacefully located site, not all that big, right by the beach. Close to a holiday homes development on the southern edge of Cambrils.

🚗 Motorway AP7, exit 37, dir. Cambrils. At traffic lights right N340 dir. Hospitalet. Directly after Shell service station right and take flyover over the N340. Follow camping signs.

Reus

T-310
Cambrils　Salou
CC
A-7
Ap-7

CC € **19** 15/1-28/3 2/4-21/6 9/9-15/12 7=6, 15=12, 30=23, 60=45 　 📍 N 41°3'28'' E 1°1'36''

Cambrils, E-43850 / Cataluña

♿ 🛜 **(2738)**

📐 La Llosa Cat.3
🚏 C/ Camí de les Lloses 1
☎ +34 977-362615
📠 +34 977-362604
🔓 1/1 - 31/12
@ info@camping-lallosa.com

4,5ha 400T(40-75m²) 6A

1 BCG IJKLMPQ
2 AEFSVY
3 ABFGKNRUWY
4 (B+G 15/5-8/10)
　　(Q+S 1/6-30/9)
　　(T+U+X+Y 15/5-30/9)
5 A EGIJKLMNOPUWXYZ
6 ACDEG IK M(N 0,5km)ORTX

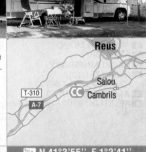

💬 Small shaded campsite 500 metres from the friendly town of Cambrils and within walking distance of the beach. The site works jointly with Club Nautico.

🚗 Toll motorway A7, exit 37, follow direction Cambrils. Right at traffic lights (N340) direction Hospitalet. Then bear left and turn left at the blue Camping & Bungalows sign. Follow the signs from here.

Reus

T-310
Salou
CC Cambrils
A-7

CC € **19** 1/1-27/3 4/4-21/6 1/9-31/12 7=6, 15=12 　 📍 N 41°3'55'' E 1°2'41''

Cambrils, E-43850 / Cataluña

👫 ♿ 🛜 **(2739)**

📐 Platja Cambrils Cat.2
🚏 Av. Oleastrum 12
☎ +34 977-361490
📠 +34 977-364988
🔓 15/3 - 16/10
@ info@playacambrils.com

8ha 400T(45-70m²) 5A CEE

1 BCG IJKLMO PQ
2 AEFGSTVY
3 BFGHKM NRUWY
4 (B+G 🔓) (Q 15/6-15/9)
　　(S+T+U 🔓) V(W+X+Y+Z 🔓)
5 AB CFGHIJKMNOPUWXY
6 GH IJ(N 0km)OQRTUV

💬 This campsite is located on the outskirts of Cambrils near Salou at 250 metres from the beach. There is a large swimming pool and a solarium. Shaded but small pitches. Close to railway line.

🚗 Toll motorway AP7, exit 35 Salou. N340 or AP7 to Cambrils. At the roundabout in the direction of Vilafortuny, at the end of the road at traffic lights to the right. Then follow signs to the campsite.

Reus AP-7
T-310 Vila-Seca
A-7 Salou
CC

CC € **17** 15/3-23/3 3/4-22/6 25/8-15/10 7=6 　 📍 N 41°4'1'' E 1°4'59''

Campdevànol, E-17530 / Cataluña

♢ 📶 iD **2740**

- ▲ Moli Serradell
- 🗁 Ctra Campdevanol a Gomb.
- ☎ 📠 +34 972-730927
- 🏭 2/5 - 16/10
- @ info@campingmoliserradell.com

1,2ha 40T(60-80m²) 6-12A

1 **AGIJKLMPQ**
2 **BCJKLRTVY**
3 **ABHJKR**
4 **(B+G 20/6-30/8)**
 (Q+R+T+U+X+Z 🔒)
5 **AB**DGIJKLMNOPUW
6 **AEGIJ(N 4km)OTV**

🗪 A small but idyllic campsite with shaded pitches under tall trees. It has a swimming pool and a restaurant where you can enjoy locally butchered meat and home baked bread. Impressive sanitary facilities.

🚗 Route N152 Puigcerdà-Barcelona.
In Campdevànol route GI-401 direction Gombren.
Campsite about 4.5 km on the left (take note; it is the 2nd campsite).

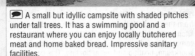

Ribes De Freser

N-152

Ripoll

N-260

C-26

CC € **19** 2/5-22/6 1/9-15/10 7=6, 14=11 🏝 N 42°14'8'' E 2°7'7''

Canet de Mar, E-08360 / Cataluña

♢ 📶 iD **2741**

- ▲ Globo Rojo Cat. 1
- 🗁 Ctra Nac. II km 660,9
- ☎ 📠 +34 93-7941143
- 🏭 7/4 - 30/9
- @ camping@globo-rojo.com

2ha 155T(60-90m²) 10A

1 **AGIJKLOPQ**
2 **AERVXY**
3 **AF**GHJKLMNRY
4 **(C+G 7/4-29/9)**
 (Q+R+U+X+Y+Z 🔒)
5 **AFGIJKMNOPUWZ**
6 **GHK(N 0,5km)OQRTVW**

🗪 A family campsite close to the beach with good facilities and plenty of shade. Ideally located for visiting Barcelona by bus, train or car. 5 minutes' walk from Canet de Mar. It also has three lovely swimming pools, one of them with jacuzzi. Free wifi provided.

🚗 Coast road 11 Malgrat-Barcelona on the right after Sant Pol.

C-61

Arenys De Mar CC
C-32
Mataró

CC € **19** 7/4-30/6 1/9-29/9 14=13 🏝 N 41°35'27'' E 2°35'31''

Capmany, E-17750 / Cataluña

📶 iD **2742**

- ▲ Camping l'Albera
- 🗁 C/ Ventador s/n
- ☎ +34 972-549192
- 🏭 1/1 - 31/12
- @ info@campingalbera.com

7,5ha 150T(100m²) 6-10A CEE

1 **ACFIJKLMOP**ST
2 **FKLRSVWXY**
3 **F**GHJRU
4 **(B 15/5-15/9) (Q 1/7-31/8)**
 (Z 1/7-10/9)
5 **A**DGIJKLMNOPUX
6 **CEGJK(N 0,5km)V**

🗪 The views are a 'delight' to the eye. Highly recommended for a 'relaxing' holiday. Dutch-Spanish management. A combination of 'modern' and the peace and quiet of an old-fashioned campsite.

🚗 Exit 2 after Jonquera; direction Figueres; exit Capmany. Follow the camping signs. Coming from Barcelona (A7) exit 4 (salida) to the NII, direction Francia. Turn right before the border towards Capmany.

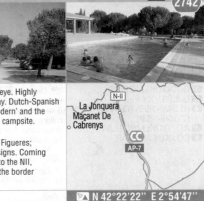

N-II

La Jonquera
Maçanet De
Cabrenys

CC
AP-7

CC € **17** 1/1-9/7 27/8-31/12 🏝 N 42°22'22'' E 2°54'47''

Colera, E-17496 / Cataluña

(2743)

NEW

△ Sant Miquel
🏠 Urb. Sant Miquel s/n
☎ +34 972-389018
📠 +34 972-389180
🔓 24/3 - 30/9
@ info@campingsantmiquel.com

5ha 120**T**(60m²) 10A CEE

1 BCDFIJKLMOPQ
2 AEGLNRVWXY
3 AHJKR**W**Y
4 (B+G 🔓) K
(Q+S+T+U+V+X+Y+Z 🔓)
5 **AB**EFGIJKLMNOPUWX
6 CEGHJ**K**(N 0,5km)RTV

💬 Quiet, family-friendly campsite 5 minutes from the beach. With a restaurant with a traditional kitchen. Ideal base for walks. Water sports at the campsite include: diving, kayaking, paddle boarding, snorkeling, boating and pedal boating. This campsite is in the unspoiled part of the Costa Brava.

🚗 Exit 3 after the border, N260 towards Llançá. After 5 km to Colera, then follow signs.

D914

Port de
Llançà

N-260

Peralada

CC € **17** 24/3-30/6 2/9-29/9 7=6 | N 42°24'11'' E 3°8'56''

Coma-Ruga/El Vendrell, E-43880 / Cataluña

👫 ♿ 🛜 **(2744)**

△ Vendrell Platja Cat.1
🏠 Av. Sanatori, s/n
☎ +34 977-694009
📠 +34 977-694106
🔓 23/3 - 14/10
@ vendrell@
camping-vendrellplatja.com

7ha 421**T**(70-105m²) 6A

1 BCDGIJKLMOP**Q**
2 AEFGLSTVX
3 AB**F**GKNRUWY
4 (B 27/3-1/11) (G 🔓) J
(Q+R+S+T+U+X+Y+Z 🔓)
5 **AB**EFGIJKLMNOP**T**UW
6 CEG**K**(N 0,5km)QRTUV

💬 The campsite is 50 metres from the beach and has various swimming pools and lawns. Make trips out to Barcelona (70 km), Tarragona (30 km) or to the Port Aventura theme park. Entertainment at weekends in low season. Shaded pitches. Additional facilities on the campsite: modern toilet facilities, bar, restaurant and supermarket. Close to railway line.

🚗 Toll motorway sortida (exit) 31. Then take direction Coma-Ruga. Continue to the coast, turn left and follow the signs.

N-340

El Vendrell
Calafell C-32

CC

CC € **17** 23/3-29/6 27/8-13/10 7=6, 14=12, 21=18 | N 41°11'8'' E 1°33'19''

El Pont de Suert (Lérida), E-25520 / Cataluña

🛜 **(2745)**

△ Alta Ribagorça
🏠 Ctra Les Bordes s/n km 131
☎ +34 973-690521
🔓 26/3 - 31/10
@ ana.uma@hotmail.com

3ha 50**T**(100m²) 5-10A

1 BCD**G**IJKLMO**P**RS
2 GJLRTVXY
4 (B 24/6-15/9) (Q+R 1/7-31/8)
(Z 15/6-15/9)
5 **A**DFGIJKLMNOPUW
6 EGJ**K**(N 3km)TV

💬 Campsite is close to the beautiful countryside in the valleys of Isabena, Fosca, Aran, Boi and Benasque, for discovering the national parks, the culture and the tradition. More information available at reception. A free meal is offered for paid stays of ten nights.

🚗 Coming from Vielha N230 in the direction of Pont de Suert. About 4 km past the town of Vilaller, the campsite is on the left side of the road.

Montanuy

CC

El Pont De
Suert

N-230 N-260

CC € **13** 26/3-14/7 1/9-30/10 4=3 | N 42°26'54'' E 0°42'38''

Esponellà (Girona), E-17832 / Cataluña ⛺⛺ 📶 (2746)

🔺 Esponellà Cat.2
📧 Ctra de Banyoles a Figueres, km 8
☎ +34 972-597074
📅 1/1 - 31/12
@ informa@campingesponella.com

4,5ha 130T(60m²) 5-10A

1 BCD**F**IJKLOPR
2 CRSTVXY
3 B**F**GHJMN**Q**RU**W**
4 (C+E+G+Q+R+T+U+X+Y+Z 📵)
5 **A**DGIJKLMNOPUX
6 ACEGH**K**(N 8km)OTV

💬 Located in hinterland of Figueres on River Fluviá. Marked-out walks and mountain bike routes. Trips out in the area, e.g. Nuria (cog railway to an altitude of 2 km). River close to the campsite for fishing, canoeing or kayaking. Special birds for spotting. Covered heated swimming pool.

🚗 A7 exit 3, dir. Figueres N260 Figueres-Besalu. After Navata past service station turn left dir. Banyoles. At hairpin bend after bridge over Fluvia turn right. Signposted.

Figueres
A-26 · N-260 · CC · AP-7 · C-66 · N-II · Banyoles

(C)C € **19** 1/1-30/6 1/9-31/12 7=6, 14=11 📍 N 42°10'54'' E 2°47'42''

Fornells de la Selva, E-17458 / Cataluña ♿ 📶 🆔 (2747)

🔺 Girona Can Toni Manescal Cat.3
📧 Forn. a Llambil, km 2 (B9)
☎ +34 647-714654
📅 15/3 - 30/9
@ campinggirona@campinggirona.com

1,1ha 45T(200m²) 5A

1 A**G**IJKLMO**P**
2 RVWX
3 AD**F**J
4 (B 15/6-30/9) (Q 1/7-15/8) (Z 📵)
5 AGIJKMOPUW
6 EJ(N 2km)

💬 A rustic cosy campsite, where rest, relaxation and 'slow camping' are important. Large pitches (200 m²), basic toilet facilities. Beautiful surroundings, lovely pool and within cycling distance of Girona (10 km) and 13 km from the airport.

🚗 Toll road A7, exit 7 Girona Sud. Dir. San Feliu. Follow until Llambilles (7 km). Turn right after leaving village. When using SatNav, from that point (traffic lights) it's 2 more km and follow campsite signs.

Sant Gregori · **Girona**
N-141 · Salt · A-2 · C-25 · AP-7 · C-65 · C-63 · N-II · CC

(C)C € **13** 15/3-8/7 27/8-29/9 📍 N 41°55'20'' E 2°49'42''

Garriguella, E-17780 / Cataluña 📶 (2748)

🔺 Vell Empordà Cat.2
📧 Ctra Roses-La Jonquera s/n
☎ +34 972-530200
📅 24/3 - 28/10
@ vellemporda@vellemporda.com

7ha 230T(80-100m²) 6-10A

1 BCDFIJLPQ
2 JLRTVXY
3 ABHJKNRU
4 (**A** 📵) (B+G 18/5-23/9) (Q 📵) (S+T 18/5-23/9) (U+X+Y 1/6-23/9) (Z 18/5-23/9)
5 **AB**FGIJKLMOPUWX
6 CEGJ**K**(N 0,5km)ORTUV

💬 A quiet campsite not quite on the coast. You can visit it close by. In just 10 km you can be on the beach or in the mountains. A family business where mother takes care of the kitchen. Spanish, friendly atmosphere. Beautiful large swimming pool with a separate children's pool.

🚗 A7, exit 3, N260 Figueres Llançà. After 9 km, the campsite is signposted. Turn right, C252, turn left under the viaduct direction La Jonquera. Then another 2 km.

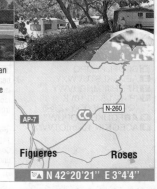

Figueres · **Roses**
N-260 · AP-7 · CC

(C)C € **17** 24/3-21/6 1/9-27/10 7=6, 14=11 📍 N 42°20'21'' E 3°4'4''

Gavà (Barcelona), E-08850 / Cataluña ♿ 📶 iD (2749)

- 🔺 3 Estrellas Cat.1
- 🚏 C-31, km 186,2/
  Aptdo de Correos 238
- ☎ +34 936-330637
- 📠 +34 936-331525
- 🔓 12/1 - 16/12
- @ ICIA@camping3estrellas.com

8ha 240T(70-100m²) 5A

L'Hospitalet
de Llobregat

1. ABCD**G**IJKLMPQ
2. ABEFGLRSVWXY
3. AGMNR**W**Y
4. (B+G 15/6-30/9)
   (Q+S+T+U+W+X+Y+Z 🔓)
5. **AB**DFGIJKLMNOPUWXYZ
6. ACFGKM(N 4km)ORTUV

💬 A perfect campsite for visiting Barcelona, bus stop at the site, a lovely swimming pool and good toilet facilities. Right by a sandy beach. 25% discount from 23/6 to 15/7 to CampingCard ACSI holders. CampingCard ACSI discount only for standard pitches.

🚗 In Barcelona follow 'Ronda de Dalt' (B20), dir airport. C-31 dir Castelldefels, exit Gavà Mar (on the left along the beach), with viaduct over C-31, then 3 times to the right and back dir Barcelona to campsite.

CC € 19 12/1-22/6 1/9-15/12   📐 N 41°16'21'' E 2°2'35''

Guardiola de Berguedà, E-08694 / Cataluña ♿ 📶 iD (2750)

- 🔺 El Berguedà
- 🚏 Ctra B400 a Saldes, km 3,5
- ☎ +34 938-227432
- 🔓 1/4 - 1/11
- @ info@campingbergueda.com

2ha 40T(70-110m²) 6A CEE

Bagà
La Pobla De
Lillet

C-16

C-26

1. ACDGIJKLMP
2. BCIJKLRTVWXY
3. ABGHJNR
4. (**A** 1/7-31/8) (B+G 24/6-1/9)
   (Q 🔓) (R+S+T+Z 8/7-31/8)
5. **AB**DFGIJKLMNOPUWZ
6. BEGJ**K**(N 5km)OTV

💬 A campsite with spacious pitches separated by trees and bushes. Simple meals available out of season at weekends or on special occasions. Nice area for mountain walks. The reception staff gladly provide you with maps of the area.

🚗 From Berga C16 in the direction of Cadi Tunnel. Just before Guardiola de Berguedà turn left (Saldes). After about 3.5 km you'll reach the campsite.

CC € 17 3/4-26/4 2/5-6/7 27/8-6/9 12/9-10/10 15/10-30/10   📐 N 42°12'59'' E 1°50'13''

Hospitalet del Infante, E-43890 / Cataluña ♿ 📶 (2751)

- 🔺 La Masia***
- 🚏 Ctra N340, km 1121
- ☎ +34 977-820588
- 📠 +34 977-823354
- 🔓 1/2 - 30/11
- @ admon@camping-lamasia.com

2,6ha 264T(60-90m²) 6A

C-44 T-318

A-7

El Perelló L'Ametlla De Mar

Ap-7

1. BCDFIJKLMPQ
2. AEFGKLSTUVWXY
3. B**F**GHJKMNRUVWY
4. (B+G 1/5-30/10) K
   (Q+R+T+V+X+Y+Z 🔓)
5. **AB**FGIJKLMNOPUWZ
6. ACEG**K**(N 10km)OTVWX

💬 A campsite on the Playa de l'Almadrava, a beautiful sandy beach. New swimming pool and jacuzzi, lawn and tennis court. Very good toilet facilities. Very peaceful location. Free Spa and wifi from 01/02 to 31/05 and from 01/09 to 30/11.

🚗 On the N340 (Tarragona-Valencia) at the 1120,5 km post direction Platja de l'Almadrava. Coming via Autopista Salida 38. Take note: new road under construction.

CC € 19 1/2-28/3 2/4-8/7 1/9-29/11   📐 N 40°56'25'' E 0°51'25''

L'Ametlla de Mar, E-43860 / Cataluña

☢ 📶 (2752)

🔺 Camping Ametlla Cat.1
📧 Paratje de Santes Creus
☎ +34 977-267784
📠 +34 977-267868
🔑 1/1 - 31/12
@ info@campingametlla.com

8ha 294T(70-120m²) 5-10A

1 BCDGIJLMPQ
2 EFLNTVXY
3 BGHMNRUVWY
4 (B+G 1/4-30/9) (Q 🔑)
    (R 1/1-31/3,1/10-31/12)
    (S+T+U+V+X+Y+Z 1/4-30/9)
5 ABEFGIJKLMNOPRUWXZ
6 ACEGIK(N 2km)ORTV

💬 Attractive campsite. Set in a nature reserve 100 metres from the beach, excellent for walking. Lovely, new swimming pools and a very good restaurant. Pitches separated by hedges. Sports options: football, basketball, volleyball, padel

🚗 A7/E15, exit 39. Take the N340 and turn at km-marker 1113 to L'Ametlla de Mar. Follow the signs, just before reaching the town turn right. After 2.5 km you reach the campsite.

El Perelló

CC

Ap-7

L'Ampolla

N-340

(CC) € **15** 1/1-29/3 2/4-30/6 27/8-31/12 7=6, 14=11, 30=21   📷 N 40°51'54'' E 0°46'44''

L'Ametlla de Mar, E-43860 / Cataluña

☢ 📶 (2753)

🔺 Nautic Cat.1
📧 Calle Llibertat s/n
☎ 📠 +34 977-456110
🔑 24/3 - 4/11
@ info@campingnautic.com

6ha 215T(60-75m²) 10A

1 BCDGIJKLMPQ
2 AEFGJLNTUVXY
3 BGHKMRUWY
4 (A 1/7-31/8)
    (B+G+Q+R+X+Y+Z 🔑)
5 AGIJKMNOPUXZ
6 CEGK(N 0,2km)ORTV

💬 A lovely peaceful site right on the beach in a bay and near an attractive fishing village. Excellent toilet facilities. Pitches in the sun or shade. Lovely outdoor pools, tennis and a good restaurant. Free wifi. Reception closed from 14:00-17:15, in that period press the button opposite reception.

🚗 Take exit 39 on the A7, cross the railway bridge then follow signs in L'Ametlla. On N340 at the 1113 km marker to L'Ametlla then follow camping signs.

A-7

El Perelló N-340 CC

AP-7

(CC) € **17** 24/3-9/7 27/8-3/11 14=11, 30=23   📷 N 40°53'12'' E 0°48'17''

L'Ampolla, E-43895 / Cataluña

☢ 📶 (2754)

🔺 Camping Ampolla Playa Cat. 2
📧 Playa Arenal s/n
☎ 📠 +34 977-460535
🔑 16/3 - 4/11
@ reservas@campingampolla.es

5ha 85T(60-80m²) 10A

1 BCDGIJKLMPQ
2 AEFGLNRSVWXY
3 ABFGHJKLNOPQRUVWY
4 (A 🔑) (B 15/6-30/9)
    (Q+R+S+T+U+V+X+Y+Z 🔑)
5 AEFGHIJKLMNOPQRUWXZ
6 ADEGHJK(N 1km)ORSTUV
    WX

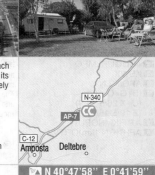

💬 A campsite on a bay right next to a sandy beach near a fishing village. Close to the Ebro delta with its unusual flora and fauna, including flamingos. Lovely cycle routes. Watersports. Close to the N340 so suitable as a stopover site.

🚗 On A7 exit 39a. From N340 1096 km marker. Keep south in L'Ampolla. Follow camping signs on beach road.

N-340

AP-7 CC

C-12

Amposta Deltebre

(CC) € **17** 16/3-28/3 2/4-10/7 28/8-3/11 7=6, 14=11, 30=20   📷 N 40°47'58'' E 0°41'59''

L'Escala, E-17130 / Cataluña

2755

🏔 Cala Montgó Cat.1
✉ Av. de Montgó s/n
☎ +34 972-770866
📠 +34 972-774340
🕐 16/3 - 30/9
@ calamontgo@betsa.es

12ha 525T(80m²) 5-10A

1 BCDFIJKLMO**P**Q
2 AEGJLQSVXY
3 BGLN**Q**RU**W**Y
4 (B+G 1/5-11/9) **L**
(Q+S+T+U+V+X+Y+Z 🔒)
5 **AB**FGIJKLMNOPUWX
6 CEGH**I**K(N 2,5km)ORTV

💬 Situated on the road that goes to Montgó Bay, there are three campsites which offer the necessary rest and relaxation at the beach. Swimming, snorkelling, and various water sports are all possible. The surroundings offer various day trips, for example Figueres Dalí museum, Barcelona. The lively beach town of L'Escala is accessible by car.

🚗 Toll road exit 5 towards L'Escala. Before L'Escala 'sector sud'. In L'Escala towards Montgó until the campsite. Well signposted.

L'escala
C-31
Torroella de Montgrí
C-252

CC € **19** 16/3-29/3 3/4-26/4 2/5-20/6 27/8-29/9   N 42°6'37'' E 3°9'38''

L'Escala, E-17130 / Cataluña

2756

🏔 Illa Mateua Cat.1
✉ Avda. de Montgó, 260
☎ +34 972-770200
📠 +34 972-772031
🕐 24/3 - 21/10
@ info@campingillamateua.com

6,4ha 318T(80-90m²) 6A

1 ABF**I**JLPQ
2 ABEGJLORSVY
3 BGHJ**M**NRUWY
4 (C+H+Q+S+T+U+X+Y+Z 🔒)
5 **AB**DFGIJKLMNOPUW
6 EG**I**KM(N 3km)ORTV

💬 A family site, spectacularly located on the sandy beach at Montgó and bordering the Montgrí nature park and the rocky beach at Illa Mateua which has excellent snorkelling. Breathtaking views of Roses Bay. Picturesque villages inland. A friendly welcome in various languages.

🚗 Toll road exit 5 direction L'Escala. Before L'Escala direction Escala Riells. Then follow camping signs and Montgó. Clearly signposted.

C-31
L'Escala
Torroella De Montgrí

CC € **19** 24/3-30/6 30/8-20/10 7=6, 15=12, 28=22   N 42°6'37'' E 3°9'56''

L'Estartit, E-17258 / Cataluña

2757

🏔 Emporda
✉ Ctra Torroella-l'Estartit, km 4,8
☎ +34 972-750649
🕐 24/3 - 7/10
@ info@campingemporda.com

3,5ha 230T(70-100m²) 6A

1 ACD**G**IJKLMPQ
2 KSWX
3 AFGJKLN
4 (B+G+Q+R 🔒)
(U+X 26/5-16/9)
(Z 19/5-16/9)
5 **AB**FIKMNOPUW
6 AFH**I**K(N 1km)ORTVW

💬 A small, peaceful campsite. Close to the beach and the village of Estartit and next to the Montgri nature reserve, the Medes islands and the Baix Ter. The area around River Ter is perfect for cycle rides and there are fantastic walking routes in the Montgri mountains.

🚗 Exit direction Torroella de Montgri, to L'Estartit, right.

L'Escala
Torroella De Montgrí

CC € **17** 24/3-17/6 1/9-6/10   N 42°3'0'' E 3°11'1''

L'Estartit, E-17258 / Cataluña — 2758

🏕 La Sirena
✉ C/ La Platera s/n
☎ 🅵🅰🆇 +34 972-751542
🕐 8/4 - 7/10
@ info@camping-lasirena.com

4,4ha 279T(70-100m²) 6A CEE

1 B**G**IJKLOPQ
2 AFRSVWXY
3 A**F**
4 (B+G 🅾) (X+Z 1/5-30/9)
5 **A**FGIJKLMOPU
6 FG**K**(N 0,1km)RT

💬 Located in the heart of the Costa Brava: L'Estartit. Close to natural parks 'Parque Natural Montgri' and 'Islas Medes'. Sandy beach, including a part for disabled people, signaled by a blue flag. Small homely campsite with 279 pitches, sunny as well as shaded. Playground, large and small pool, canteen, bar, restaurant and mini club. Beach and centre within walking distance. Car can remain parked.

🚗 Before Jocs turn right into L'Estartit.

CC € ⑰ 8/4-30/6 1/9-6/10

L'Escala
C-31
CC
Torroella de Montgrí

🧭 N 42°2'54'' E 3°11'16''

L'Estartit, E-17258 / Cataluña — 2759

🏕 Les Medes Cat.1
✉ Paratge Camp de l'Arbre
☎ +34 972-751805
🅵🅰🆇 +34 972-750413
🕐 1/1 - 31/12
@ info@campinglesmedes.com

2,6ha 170T(70-80m²) 6-16A CEE

1 CD**G**IJKLMPQ
2 GLRVXY
3 B**F**GHJKL**M**NRU
4 (B 1/5-15/9)
 (F 1/1-15/6,15/9-31/12)
 (G 1/5-15/9) **N**
 (Q+S+T+U 🅾) (Y 1/4-1/11)
 (Z 🅾)
5 ABDEFGIJKLMNOPUWXYZ
6 ACEGH**IK**L(N 2km)ORTVWX

💬 A top class campsite, open all year. Indoor swimming pool in early and late seasons. An excellent campsite for overwintering.

🚗 A7, exit 5. On the road from Torroella de Montgri to Estartit turn right before 'Jocs' and follow signs. Another 2 km to the campsite.

CC € ⑲ 1/1-28/3 2/4-27/4 1/5-30/6 1/9-8/9 11/9-31/12

C-31
L'Escala
Torroella De Montgrí CC
C-66

🧭 N 42°2'33'' E 3°11'0''

L'Estartit, E-17258 / Cataluña — 2760

🏕 Ter Cat. 2
✉ Ctra Torroella-l'Estartit km 4,3
☎ +34 972-751110
🕐 26/3 - 16/9
@ ter@campinger.com

2,2ha 191T(60-80m²) 6-10A

1 ACD**G**IJKLMOPST
2 GRVWXY
3 A**F**HJKLR
4 (B+G 1/5-16/9) (R 🅾)
 (T+Z 15/6-31/8)
5 **AB**GIJKMNOPU
6 AFG**IK**(N 0,8km)QRTWX

💬 A small campsite near a pleasant village with sunny and shaded pitches. Good toilet facilities. Bar and swimming pool. Near a Lidl supermarket and a restaurant.

🚗 Salida (exit) 6 direction Torroella de Montgri, towards L'Estartit. Turn right past Lidl.

CC € ⑰ 26/3-3/7 21/8-15/9

Torroella De Montgrí CC

Pals
Begur

🧭 N 42°2'55'' E 3°10'45''

La Guingueta d'Àneu, E-25597 / Cataluña

👬 🎿 📶 🆔 **2761**

🔺 Nou Camping S.L.
🚩 C13, km 156
☎ +34 973-626261
📠 +34 973-626706
🔓 1/1 - 31/10, 1/12 - 31/12
@ noucamping@noucamping.com

1,5ha 150T(75m²) 6-10A

1 ACD**G**IJKLM**P**
2 CDGIJLRVWXY
3 ABHJNRU**W**
4 (A 1/7-31/8) (C 🔓)
　(H 15/6-15/9)
　(Q+R+T+U+V+W+X+Y+Z 🔓)
5 **AB**DFGIJKLMNOPUWZ
6 EG**I**K(N 0,1km)OTV

💬 Easily accessible luxury campsite close to the Aigüestortes national park and the Saint Maurice lake. Also suitable as a base for sports: cycling, walking and rafting.

🚗 From France take N125 as far as Viella. There the C13 direction Sort. Campsite is located first thing in the village, on the right.

C-28

La Guingueta D'Àneu CC

C-13

Llavorsí

(CC) € **19** 1/3-27/3 2/4-21/6 25/6-30/6 1/9-30/10 7=6, 14=11, 30=23　　📍 N 42°35'33'' E 1°7'54''

Les Cases d'Alcanar, E-43569 / Cataluña

♿ 📶 **2762**

🔺 Estanyet
🚩 Paseig del Marjal s/n
☎ 📠 +34 977-737268
🔓 1/3 - 5/11
@ info@estanyet.com

1,5ha 120T(55-100m²) 5-10A

1 BCDGIJKLMOPQ
2 AEFNRTUVWXY
3 B**F**GHJKUWY
4 (B+G 1/4-31/10)
　(Q+R+T+U+V+X+Y+Z 🔓)
5 **AB**DEFGIJKLMNOPUWZ
6 ADEGHIK(N 1km)OPRTV

💬 An attractive, quietly situated campsite with excellent toilet facilities located right on the beach. Lovely new swimming pool and very good restaurant. Close to the Ebro and Els Ports nature reserves.

🚗 From the north A7 take exit 41, from the south take exit 43, then on N340 past the petrol station (there is a campsite sign on the right), turn right and after ±300 metres is campsite Estanyet.

Sant Carles De La Ràpita

T-331

AP-7　CC
N-238 N-340
N-232

(CC) € **19** 1/3-28/3 3/4-20/6 10/9-4/11　　📍 N 40°32'25'' E 0°31'11''

Llagostera, E-17240 / Cataluña

👬 ⊗ ♿ 📶 🆔 **2763**

🔺 Ridaura
🚩 Ctra Girona-Platja d'Aro
　C65 km 6,5
☎ +34 639-434557
🔓 2/3 - 14/10
@ info@campingridaura.com

4ha 202T(60-110m²) 10A CEE

1 ACDEIJKLMOPST
2 BITXY
3 B**EF**HJKN
4 (B+G 15/5-15/9)
　(Q+R+T+V+X+Z 🔓)
5 **A**FGIJKLMNOPUX
6 AFGJ**K**(N 3km)ORTV

💬 A campsite located in woods alongside the C65. Close to Sant Feliu and Playa d'Aro. It has good toilet facilities and a very attractive swimming pool with a chair hoist. Located next to natural woodland paths and walking and cycling routes from Girona (Voies Vertes, i Ruta Pirinexus).

🚗 AP7 exit 9 direction Playa d'Aro (25 km). Ridaura campsite is on the left.

C-65

C-253A　CC

Sant Felìu De Guíxols

C-63

(CC) € **17** 27/4-14/7 1/9-16/9　　📍 N 41°49'40'' E 2°57'29''

Lloret de Mar, E-17310 / Cataluña 📶 iD (2764)

🏕 Lloret Blau
✉ C/ Aiguaviva s/n
☎ +34 972-365483
🕐 22/4 - 30/9
@ info@campinglloretblau.com

2,4ha 300T(50-90m²) 5-10A

1 ACDGIJKLMOPQ
2 XY
4 (B 🔑) (Q 24/6-30/8)
(R 1/7-30/8) (T 24/6-30/8)
(U 🔑) (X+Z 24/6-30/8)
5 IJKMOP
6 ADHIJK(N 0km)RTV

💬 Located in the heart of the Costa Brava. In the proximity you will find beautiful sandy beaches and lovely bays. The campsite has a swimming pool and basic toilet facilities. You will find a variety of shops a short distance from the campsite in Lloret de Mar.

🚗 E15, exit 9 to Lloret. Left at lights past 'Water World'. Straight on, campsite on left after traffic lights.

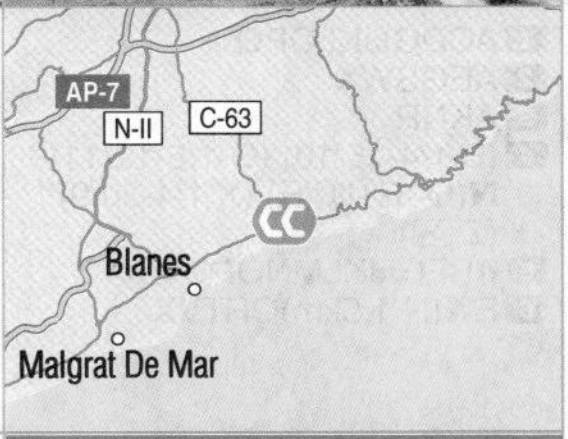

CC € 19 22/4-5/7 24/8-29/9 7=6

N 41°42'20'' E 2°50'35''

Lloret de Mar, E-17310 / Cataluña 📶 iD (2765)

🏕 Sènia Cala Canyelles Cat.2
✉ Cala Canyelles
☎ +34 972-364504
📠 +34 972-368506
🕐 24/3 - 30/9
@ info@ccanyelles.com

10ha 301T(60-80m²) 6A

NEW

1 ACDGIJKLMOPQ
2 AEGHJKTVXY
3 AY
4 (B+G+Q+R 🔑)
(T+U+X+Z 15/6-31/8)
5 AGIJKLMNOPUW
6 CEGIJM(N 2km)ORTV

💬 Terraced campsite with pitches with panoramic views, basic toilet facilities and a beautiful swimming pool. Within walking distance of the Cala.

🚗 Toll road E15 exit 9 Lloret towards Tossa. 2 km outside of Lloret turn right and then immediately left (well signposted).

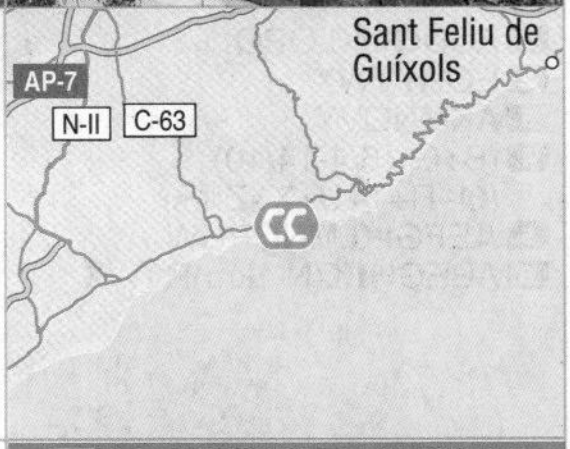

CC € 19 24/3-30/6 1/9-20/9

N 41°42'26'' E 2°52'50''

Lloret de Mar, E-17310 / Cataluña ♿ 📶 iD (2766)

🏕 Sènia Tucan**
✉ Ctra de Blanes a Lloret
☎ +34 972-369965
📠 +34 972-360079
🕐 20/4 - 24/9
@ info@campingtucan.com

4,2ha 324T(65-100m²) 3-10A

1 ACDFIJKLMOPQ
2 AGJLSVXY
3 ADFGKNQRU
4 (A 1/7-31/8) (B+G 🔑) JM
(Q 🔑) (R 20/6-15/9)
(T+U+X+Y+Z 🔑)
5 AFGIJKLMNOPUXYZ
6 AFGHKM(N 0km)OQRTV

💬 Campsite with excellent amenities on the southern outskirts of Lloret de Mar.

🚗 The last campsite on the right from Lloret de Mar to Blanes.

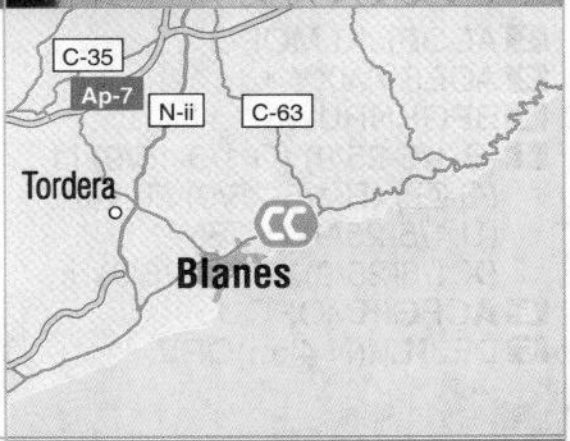

CC € 19 20/4-30/6 1/9-23/9

N 41°41'50'' E 2°49'19''

Malgrat de Mar, E-08380 / Cataluña 📶 🆔 (2767)

🏕 Camping Resort Els Pins
✉ Avda Pomareda s/n
☎ +34 937-653173
📠 +34 937-653280
🗓 1/4 - 31/10
@ pinsresort@campingelspins.es

3,2ha 220T(70-110m²) 6A CEE

1 ACDGIJKLOPQ
2 AEGSWX
3 AKNR
4 (B 1/4-15/10) (G 1/6-12/11)
  N(Q+R+U 🅿) (X 1/4-30/9)
  (Z 🅿)
5 ABFGIJKLMNO**P**UWXYZ
6 E**K**(N 1,5km)ORTVX

💬 Malgrat de Mar is a town with more than 5 km of paradisiacal beaches. 1.5 km from the market, shopping and touristic areas. Nearby the Tordera river with its natural diversity of animals and nature. 40 km from Gerona and 60 km from Barcelona. 50 metres from the beaches. Pitches (± 80 m²) limited by trees. Good toilet facilities.

🚗 Past Blanes-sud towards centre of Malgrat de Mar. Cross river, left at roundabout, left again at beach. Campsite on the left.

AP-7 · N-II · C-63 · **Lloret De Mar** · **Blanes** · CC

CC € **19** 1/4-19/6 25/6-30/6 1/9-30/10 7=6   🏖 N 41°38'54'' E 2°46'12''

Malgrat de Mar, E-08380 / Cataluña ♿ 📶 🆔 (2768)

🏕 del Mar
✉ Camí de la Pomareda s/n
☎ +34 937-653767
📠 +34 937-619121
🗓 23/3 - 14/10
@ info@campingdelmar.com

3ha 124T(20-64m²) 6A

1 ACD**G**IJKLOPQ
2 EORTVWX
3 AKMNQVY
4 (B+G 15/4-14/10)
  (Q+R+T+U+X+Z 🅿)
5 **A**EFGIKLMNOPUW
6 ABEGH**I K**(N 1km)RVWX

💬 A lovely pre-season beach campsite with good facilities and within walking distance of the beach.

🚗 Exit Blanes-Sud, then direction Malgrat de Mar, over the bridge, left at roundabout, as far as the sea, then right after ± 100 metres.

AP-7 · N-II · C-63 · **Tordera** · **Blanes** · CC

CC € **19** 23/3-29/6 18/8-13/10 7=6   🏖 N 41°38'51'' E 2°45'50''

Malgrat de Mar, E-08380 / Cataluña 👪 ♿ 📶 🆔 (2769)

🏕 La Tordera
✉ Camí de la Tordera, sn-Ap. 58
☎ +34 937-612778
📠 +34 937-655551
🗓 3/3 - 3/11
@ camping@latordera.com

2,2ha 400T(60-80m²) 10A CEE

1 ACD**F**IJKLMOPQ
2 ACESVWXY
3 B**F**GKNRUWY
4 (B 1/6-25/9) (G 1/6-15/9) IJ
  (Q 🅿) (R 1/5-25/9) (T 🅿)
  (U 1/5-25/9) (V 🅿)
  (X 1/6-25/9) (Z 1/5-25/9)
5 **A**CFGIKMOPQU
6 DEJ**K**M(N 4km)QRV

💬 Beautiful beach campsite with large pitches close to the sea, good toilet facilities and parking next to your caravan. Until 1 May and after 25 September only open at weekends.

🚗 Blanes-Sud exit, then towards Malgrat de Mar. Over bridge, immediate left. Campsite at end of road, signposted.

AP-7 · N-II · C-63 · **Lloret De Mar** · **Malgrat De Mar** · CC

CC € **17** 3/3-21/6 1/9-2/11   🏖 N 41°38'57'' E 2°46'39''

Mataró, E-08304 / Cataluña 2770

♿ 📶 iD

- 🏔 Barcelona Cat.1
- 🛣 Ctra N-II, km 650
- ☎ +34 93-7904720
- 📠 +34 93-7410282
- 🔑 1/3 - 1/11
- @ info@campingbarcelona.com

7ha 320T(60-120m²) 10-16A CEE

1 ACDGIJKLMOPQ
2 AEFGKLQRVWXY
3 ADFGHJKNRU**W**
4 (B+G+Q+S 🅾) (T 17/5-28/9)
(U+V+X+Y+Z 🅾)
5 **AB**FGIJKLMNOPUWXY
6 ACFGH**I**K(N 2km)ORSTV

💬 The campsite is located on the coast. Free bus service to the beach, the beach club, Mataró, the train and swimming pool complex. The campsite also offers a free bus service to Barcelona (take note: the bus service to Barcelona is not free 1/6 - 30/9, 2.90 Euros per person). Free activities in the pre-season. Swimming pool always open.

🚗 C32, exits 103 or 104. Or via AP-7 at km 12B exit to Mataró via C60.

CC € 19 1/3-30/6 1/9-31/10

🏖 N 41°33'2'' E 2°29'0''

Miami-Platja (Tarragona), E-43892 / Cataluña 2771

♿ 📶

- 🏔 Els Prats Village Cat.1
- 🛣 Ctra N340, km 1137
- ☎ +34 977-810027
- 📠 +34 977-170901
- 🔑 16/3 - 4/11
- @ info@campingelsprats.com

8,5ha 391T(80-115m²) 5-10A

1 BC**G**IJKLMOPQ
2 AEFGLRTVY
3 BFGHJKM**N**QRUVWY
4 (B+G 1/4-20/10) IJ**KLN**
(Q+S+T+U+V+W+X+Y+Z 🅾)
5 **AB**EFGIJKLMNOPQRUWXY
Z
6 ABDEGH**I**KM(N 5km)OPQR
TUVWX

💬 A really friendly family campsite with spacious pitches right by the sea. Most suitable for swimming enthusiasts, both in the sea and in the modern swimming pool.

🚗 AP7, exit 37 Cambrils. Follow Cambrils as far as roundabout, then right onto N340 towards Hospitalet. Follow camping signs after km 1137.

CC € 19 16/3-27/3 2/4-21/6 26/8-3/11 21=20, 28=25

🏖 N 41°2'24'' E 0°58'50''

Mont-roig (Tarragona), E-43300 / Cataluña 2772

✈ ♿ 📶

- 🏔 Playa Montroig Camping Resort Cat.1
- 🛣 Apartado de Correos 3
- ☎ +34 977-810637
- 📠 +34 977-811411
- 🔑 23/3 - 28/10
- @ info@playamontroig.com

35ha 1200T(80-110m²) 10A CEE

1 BCDEIJKLMOPQ
2 AEFGLRTVY
3 BFGHJKLM**N**QRUVWY
4 (A 17/6-17/8) (C+H 🅾) IJ**KL**
MNOP
(Q+S+T+U+V+Y+Z 🅾)
5 **AB**DEFGIJKLMNOPUWXYZ
6 CEGH**IJK**M(N 3km)ORTVW

💬 A luxuriously laid out, well maintained campsite with a lovely swimming pool. On the Costa Dorada with beaches of fine golden sand and an ideal climate for most of the year. Partly between the N340 and a railway line. Salt water swimming pool with 6 slides and a new toddlers' play pool.

🚗 AP7, exit 37 Cambrils. Follow direction Cambrils as far as roundabout then right onto N340 direction Hospitalet. Right after km 1137 sign and follow signs under the N340.

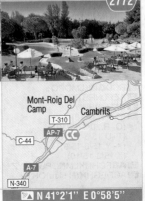

CC € 19 23/3-27/3 2/4-21/6 2/9-27/10 21=20, 30=27, 45=36

🏖 N 41°2'1'' E 0°58'5''

547

Mont-roig del Camp, E-43300 / Cataluña

2773

🖐 ⚐ 📶

🔺 La Torre del Sol Cat.1
📧 Ctra N340 km 1136
☎ +34 977-810486
📠 +34 977-811306
📅 15/3 - 30/10
@ info@latorredelsol.com

24ha 600T(70-100m²) 6-10A

1 BCDEIJKLO**P**Q
2 AEFGLRTVWXY
3 AB**F**GJK**MN**Q**RS**UVWY
4 (A+C+H 📅) K**LNO**
　(Q+S+T+U+V+X+Y+Z 📅)
5 **AB**EFGIJKLMNOPQRUWXY
6 CEGH**IK**LM(N 6km)PRTVW

💬 This campsite is located on the Costa Dorada with a long, beautiful white sandy beach, in a heavenly park with palm trees and mulberry trees. Excellent amenities for all ages. Swimming pool decorated as a tropical lagoon.

🚗 AP7 exit 37 Cambrils direction Cambrils as far as roundabout, then right onto N340 dir. Hospitalet. Right after km 1137 sign and follow signs under the N3.

Mont-Roig Del Camp — Cambrils — Salou — T-310 — C-44 — Ap-7 — A-7 — N-340

€ **19** 15/3-29/3 2/4-22/6 27/8-29/10 21=20, 28=25

📍 N 41°2'15'' E 0°58'29''

Mont-roig del Camp, E-43892 / Cataluña

2774

📶

🔺 Miramar Cat.2
📧 Ctra N340, km 1134
☎📠 +34 977-811203
📅 15/1 - 1/12
@ recepcio@camping-miramar.com

3,7ha 50T(80-100m²) 6-10A

1 BCGIJKLMOPRS
2 AEFGSVX
3 AGHJKWY
4 (Q+R+T+U+X+Z 15/6-10/9)
5 **A**CEFGHJLMNPUW
6 ABDEGH**K**(N 2km)TV

💬 Rural location on the Costa Daurada with spacious touring pitches right by the sea, and close to the lively town of Miami Platja with many Spanish guests.

🚗 AP7, exit 37 Cambrils. Follow direction Cambrils as far as roundabout then right onto N340 direction Hospitalet. Left after km 1137 sign to the campsite.

Mont-Roig Del Camp — T-310 — AP-7 — C-44 — A-7 — N-340

€ **13** 15/1-30/6 1/9-30/11 7=6, 14=12, 30=21

📍 N 41°1'31'' E 0°57'33''

Mont-roig del Camp, E-43300 / Cataluña

2775

⚐ 📶

🔺 Oasis Mar Cat.2
📧 Ctra N340, km 1139
☎ +34 977-179595
📠 +34 977-179516
📅 1/3 - 31/10
@ info@oasismar.com

2,5ha 252T(60-80m²) 5-10A CEE

1 BCD**G**IJKLMOPQ
2 AEFLNRSTVWXY
3 B**F**HJNRWY
4 (B 1/4-31/10)
　(Q+R 20/3-15/10)
　(T+U 15/3-15/10)
　(X+Y 15/6-15/9)
　(Z 15/3-15/10)
5 **AB**FGHIJKLMNOPUWXYZ
6 ACDEGH**K**(N 5km)ORTV

💬 This campsite is right by the sea and has many Spanish guests, pitches with or without shade and a swimming pool. Located between Cambrils and Miami Platja.

🚗 AP7 exit 37, A7 exit 1138. Then N340 direction Hospitalet. At Montroig/Falset crossroads, 3rd exit right on roundabout. From A7 2nd right. Follow 'platja' and 'camping' signs.

Vila-Seca — Mont-Roig Del Camp — T-310 — AP-7 — T-318 — C-44 — A-7

€ **17** 1/3-6/7 1/9-30/10

📍 N 41°2'49'' E 1°0'15''

Montagut, E-17855 / Cataluña

🦽 📶 iD (2776)

🏕 Montagut
🛣 Ctra Montagut a Sadernes km 2
☎ +34 972-287202
📅 14/4 - 14/10
@ info@campingmontagut.com

2ha 93T(65-110m²) 6A

1 ACDFIJKLM**P**Q
2 JKLRTVXY
3 BGNRU
4 (B+G 1/5-30/9) (Q+R 📅)
(T+U+V+X+Y+Z 1/7-31/8)
5 **AB**DFGIJKLMNOPUW
6 CEGJK(N 2km)OTV

💬 A beautiful swimming pool, carefully maintained grounds with camping pitches varying from sunny to shaded. Suitable for fascinating walking and cycle trips in the surroundings. The restaurant is only open at the weekend in early and late season.

🚗 A7, exit Figueras-Norte. C260 direction Besalú. From Besalú A26 exit 75 to Montagut. Then follow the signs.

CC € 17 14/4-7/7 26/8-13/10

🧭 N 42°14'43'' E 2°35'58''

Montferrer, E-25711 / Cataluña

📶 iD (2777)

🏕 Gran Sol
🛣 N260, km 230
☎ +34 973-351332
📅 23/3 - 14/10
@ info@campinggransol.com

1,7ha 160T(70-140m²) 3-10A

1 ABCD**G**IJKLMPQ
2 LRVWXY
3 ABC**F**HJNRUW
4 (B+G 20/6-11/9)
(Q+R+T+U+X+Y+Z 📅)
5 **A**DFGIJKLMNOPUWZ
6 EGK(N 1km)OTV

💬 A level campsite with spacious pitches between trees. Lovely swimming pool, good restaurant. Most suitable as a starting point for visiting Seu d'Urgell/ Seo de Urgel, Puigcerdá and Andorra. Also excellent for visiting the mountains.

🚗 Coming from Bourg Madame (F) until 3 km beyond La Seu d'Urgell on the N260.

CC € 19 3/4-8/7 27/8-11/10 7=6, 14=11

🧭 N 42°20'52'' E 1°25'51''

Olot, E-17800 / Cataluña

🧒 🦽 📶 iD (2778)

🏕 La Fageda
🛣 Ctra Olot-Sta Pau, km 3,8
☎ +34 972-271239
📅 1/1 - 31/12
@ info@campinglafageda.com

7ha 109T(70-120m²) 10A

1 ACGIJKLM**P**R
2 BJLRVY
3 ABHJNR
4 (A 1/7-31/8) (B 24/6-9/9)
(Q+R+T+U+X 1/3-31/12)
(Z 📅)
5 **A**BDEFGIJKLMNOPUW
6 CEGK(N 4km)TV

💬 The campsite is located in a volcanic region including the Croscat and the Santa Margarida, 4 km from Olot, capital of Garrotxa. Close to the beech woods at La Fageda d'en Jorda. Caravans and tents each have their own level field.

🚗 From Olot direction Santa Pau. Campsite on left of road at 3.8km sign.

CC € 17 1/1-23/3 3/4-22/6 12/9-31/12 7=6

🧭 N 42°9'27'' E 2°31'0''

Palamós, E-17230 / Cataluña

🛜 iD (2779)

- 🔺 Benelux
- ✉ Apt. de Correos 270
- ☎ +34 972-315575
- 📠 +34 972-601901
- 🔓 30/3 - 30/9
- @ cbenelux@cbenelux.com

4,6ha 250T(50-80m²) 6A

1 ACDGIJLMPQ
2 AILSTVY
3 AGKL
4 (B+G 1/6-15/9)
    (Q+R+X+Z 🔓)
5 AFGIJKLMNOPUW
6 AEGHIJ(N 2,5km)OQRTVX

💬 An attractive campsite, located in a protected nature reserve in one of the loveliest locations on the Costa Brava. Perfect walking and cycling opportunities. Within walking distance of the sea: Platja Castell. Lovely swimming pool, shop, bar, good restaurant and free wifi. Diving school.

🚗 C31 Palafrugell-Palamós take exit 328. Then follow camping signs.

C-66

Palafrugell

CC

CC € **19** 30/3-10/7 28/8-29/9

🏕 N 41°52'21'' E 3°9'4''

Palamós, E-17230 / Cataluña

♿ 🛜 (2780)

- 🔺 Internacional Palamós Cat.1
- ✉ Camí Cap de Planes s/n
- ☎ +34 972-314736
- 📠 +34 972-317626
- 🔓 24/3 - 30/9
- @ info@internacionalpalamos.com

5,2ha 398T(60-80m²) 6-10A

1 BGIJKLMOPQ
2 ERSVXY
3 AFKY
4 (B+G 1/6-23/9)
    (Q+R+T+U+X+Z 🔓)
5 AFGIJKLMNOPUWXYZ
6 ACEGHIKM(N 1,3km)RTVW

💬 Family campsite on undulating grounds with many trees and good toilet facilities, with CampingCard ACSI you will be given a gran-confort pitch.

🚗 Palafrugell-Palamós exit Palamós-La Fosca. Direction La Fosca. Turn right before King's campsite. Then follow signs.

Begur ○

CC

Palamós
Sant Feliu De Guíxols

CC € **17** 24/3-6/7 28/8-29/9

🏕 N 41°51'26'' E 3°8'17''

Pals, E-17256 / Cataluña

♿ 🛜 iD (2781)

- 🔺 Mas Patoxas Cat.1
- ✉ Ctra de Palafrugell a Pals, km 339
- ☎ +34 972-636928
- 📠 +34 972-667349
- 🔓 12/1 - 16/12
- @ info@campingmaspatoxas.com

11ha 400T(72-100m²) 6-10A

1 ACDGIJKLMOPQ
2 JLRVWXY
3 BDFGHJKLMNRUV
4 (B+G 1/5-1/10) J(Q 🔓)
    (S+T+U+Y+Z 1/4-1/10)
5 ABDEFGIJKLMNOPUWXYZ
6 AEGHKM(N 1,5km)ORTUV WX

💬 A family campsite around a large swimming pool on a hilly grounds with trees.

🚗 Motorway exit 6 direction Bisbal. From Pals follow direction Begur/Palamos. At roundabout direction Begur. About 1 km after, Pals campsite is located on the left of the road.

C-252
C-66

CC Begur
        Palafrugell
Mont-Ras

CC € **17** 12/1-9/7 27/8-15/12 7=6, 14=10

🏕 N 41°57'19'' E 3°9'26''

Pineda de Mar, E-08397 / Cataluña

🔺 Bellsol Cat.2
✉ Passeig Marítim 46
☎ +34 937-671778
📠 +34 937-655551
📅 1/1 - 31/12
@ info@campingbellsol.com

3ha 240T(60m²) 5A

1 ABCD**F**IJKLOPRS
2 AEFGSVXY
3 A**F**GKRY
4 (B+G 1/6-15/9) (Q 23/6-11/9)
  (R+T 🔒) (U+Y+Z 23/6-11/9)
5 **A**FGIJKMNOPUW
6 AGJ**K**(N 0,2km)ORTV

💬 A small family campsite with good toilet facilities, close to a beach and plenty of greenery.

🚗 Toll E15, exit 9 Malgrat. Take the NII to Barcelona. On the southern outskirts of Pineda de Mar, on the NII, take the 1st road to the left (after sign indicating end of built-up area). Continue as far as the Boulev. Turn right towards the campsite.

Blanes
C-61 · C-32 Malgrat De Mar
CC

🏕 CC € **17** 1/1-30/6 1/9-31/12

📍 N 41°37'6'' E 2°40'44''

Pineda de Mar, E-08397 / Cataluña

🔺 Enmar Cat.2
✉ Av. de la Mercè s/n
☎ +34 937-671730
📠 +34 937-670763
📅 6/3 - 31/10
@ info@campingenmar.com

2,4ha 240T(75-90m²) 6-10A

1 ACDGIJKLMOPQ
2 AEFGSTVXY
3 AKNRUY
4 (B+G 1/4-31/10) IJ
  (Q+R+T+U+X+Z 🔒)
5 **A**BFGIJKLMNOPU
6 ABCEGHJ**K**(N 0km)ORTVW
  X

💬 Small, friendly campsite with plenty of palm trees, new toilet facilities and close to the beach and a small town.

🚗 Follow campsite signs on the Promenada in Pineda de Mar.

Tordera
Blanes
C-32
CC

🏕 CC € **17** 6/3-6/7 27/8-30/10

📍 N 41°37'19'' E 2°41'10''

Pineda de Mar, E-08397 / Cataluña

🔺 Sènia Caballo de Mar
✉ Passeig Marítim,
  s/n Apdo Correos 3
☎ +34 937-671706
📠 +34 937-671615
📅 20/3 - 30/9
@ info@caballodemar.com

3ha 310T(60-70m²) 6A

1 ACD**F**IJL**P**R
2 AEF**T**VXY
3 AGKNR**V**WY
4 (B+G 🔒) IJK(Q 🔒)
  (R 1/6-30/9) (T+U+X+Z 🔒)
5 **A**EFGIJKLMNOPRSUXYZ
6 ABFG**I**KM(N 0,1km)ORTV

💬 A family campsite with sufficient shade and within walking distance of Calella. The site is located by the beach. The toilet facilities include individual shower cabins, baby baths and disabled toilets. Located 50 km north of Barcelona. Good train connections.

🚗 Take the NII in the direction of Calella, south of Pineda de Mar. Follow the camping signs.

Blanes
C-61 · C-32 Malgrat De Mar
CC

🏕 CC € **19** 20/3-30/6 1/9-29/9

📍 N 41°37'2'' E 2°40'39''

Platja d'Aro, E-17250 / Cataluña

  ♿ 🛜 (2785)

🔺 Riembau Cat.1
🏠 Santiago Rusiñol s/n
☎ +34 972-817123
📠 +34 972-825210
🔓 24/3 - 30/9
@ camping@riembau.com

19,7ha 1114T(96m²) 5A

1 CDGIJKLMOPQ
2 LRVXY
3 BFGKMNQRUV
4 (B 🔓) (F 31/7-1/9) (G 🔓) K
  LN(Q+S+T+U+X+Y+Z 🔓)
5 ABFGIJKLMNOPUWZ
6 CEGHJK(N 2km)ORTVW

💬 A large level campsite located in natural surroundings close to golden sandy beaches. Culture, gastronomy, relaxation, countryside and fun at your fingertips. The campsite is located on the Costa Brava, in Platja d'Aro.

🚐 Exit 6 direction Palamós, then centre of Playa d'Aro. Drive straight over the roundabout. The campsite is located on the right 600 metres down the road.

Sant Feliu De Guíxols

CC € 19   24/3-8/7   27/8-29/9   🗺 N 41°48'35'' E 3°2'48''

Platja d'Aro, E-17250 / Cataluña

  ♿ 🛜 ✿ iD (2786)

🔺 Valldaro Camping &
  Bungalows Resort Cat.1
🏠 Cami Vell 63
☎ +34 972-817515
📠 +34 972-816662
🔓 23/3 - 24/9
@ info@valldaro.com

18,3ha 600T(70-90m²) 10A

1 ACGIJKLMOPQ
2 ALRVXY
3 BFGHJKMNQRUV
4 (B+G 🔓) IK
  (Q+S+T+U+X+Y+Z 🔓)
5 ABDEFGIJKLMNOPUWZ
6 ABCEGHIJKM(N 0,5km)OQ
  RTUVW

💬 A campsite with a jacuzzi, plenty of greenery and trees, located on the edge of a town with plenty of opportunties for going out. For stays longer than a week: one week's free wifi, after that it must be paid for.

🚐 Exit 7 Palafrugell/Palamós direction San Feliu. On C31 exit 314 Castell d'Aro, three quarters round first roundabout direction Platja d'Aro. The campsite is 200m on the right.

Mont-Ras

Palamós
C-31

CC

CC € 17   23/3-8/7   27/8-23/9   🗺 N 41°48'54'' E 3°2'42''

Platja d'Aro/Calonge, E-17251 / Cataluña

  🛜 iD (2787)

🔺 Internacional de Calonge Cat.1
🏠 Avda Andorra 9
☎ +34 972-651233
📠 +34 972-652507
🔓 1/1 - 31/12
@ info@intercalonge.com

15ha 771T(60-90m²) 5-10A

1 ACDGIJKLMOPQ
2 AEGIJRSTVXY
3 BFGHJKLMNRUWY
4 (A 1/4-30/9) (B+G 1/4-15/10)
  (Q+S 1/4-1/11)
  (T+U 1/4-15/10) (X+Y+Z 🔓)
5 ABDEFGIJKLMNOPRUWXY
  Z
6 DEGHIJKM(N 1km)ORTUV
  WX

💬 Campsite with everything a camper could wish for. Situated against a hill with lots of trees.

🚐 Exit 6 Palafrugell-Palamós. Drive in the direction of San Feliu, then Palamós-est and then Platja d'Aro. The campsite is located on the right side of the road. Clearly signposted.

Palafrugell
C-31

CC

Platja D'Aro

CC € 19   1/1-29/3   2/4-8/7   26/8-31/12   🗺 N 41°50'0'' E 3°5'4''

Platja de Pals, E-17256 / Cataluña  2788

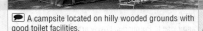

- ⏏ Camping Interpals
- ✉ C/Mediterrani. S/N
- ☎ +34 972-636179
- FAX +34 972-667476
- 🔓 20/4 - 23/9
- @ info@interpals.com

7ha 560T(60-200m²) 5A

1 ACD**G**IJKLMPQ
2 ABHIJLSVY
3 A**FK**M**N**R
4 (B+G 🔓) K
　(Q+S+T+U+X+Z 🔓)
5 **AB**FGIJKLMNOPUW
6 AEGH**I**K(N 5km)ORTUVW
　X

💬 A campsite located on hilly wooded grounds with good toilet facilities.

🚌 Motorway, exit 6 direction La Bisbal. From Pals direction Platja de Pals. At roundabout after 'Aparthotel Golf Beach' straight ahead. After a few hundred metres campsite on the right.

Begur
Mont-Ras

CC € 17 20/4-8/7　27/8-22/9　　N 41°58'52'' E 3°12'4''

Platja de Pals, E-17256 / Cataluña　2789

NEW

- ⏏ Neptuno
- ✉ C/Rodors, n. 23
- ☎ +34 972-636731
- FAX +34 972-667951
- 🔓 1/5 - 16/9
- @ info@campingneptuno.com

6,5ha 262T(80-120m²) 6-10A

1 AEIJKLMOPS
2 BLTY
3 B**F**GKLM**N**R
4 (B 1/6-15/9) (G 15/6-15/9) IJ
　K(Q 🔓) (R 1/6-15/9)
　(T 1/5-15/9) (Z 🔓)
5 **A**FGIJKMNOPUW
6 BEG**I**K(N 1km)ORTWX

💬 Located in a quiet area, this family campsite has a slide. The campsite is in the woods, and is accessible via a dirt road.

🚌 Towards Platja de Pals signs on left. After signs take side road for 1 km to the campsite.

C-31　Torroella de Montgrí
C-66　Palafrugell

CC € 17 1/5-30/6　1/9-15/9　　N 41°59'7'' E 3°11'26''

Pont d'Arros, E-25537 / Cataluña　2790

- ⏏ Verneda Camping Mountain Resort
- ✉ N230, km 171
- ☎ +34 973-641024
- 🔓 2/4 - 14/10
- @ info@campingverneda.com

180T(40-80m²) 5A

1 BCD**G**IJKLMOPS
2 CGLRVWXY
3 ABHJLNPRU**W**
4 (A 23/6-10/9)
　(C+H+Q 22/6-10/9) (R 🔓)
　(T+U+V+X+Y+Z 22/6-10/9)
5 **AB**EFGIJKLMNPUWZ
6 AEGJ**K**(N 7km)OTV

💬 A lovely, well-maintained campsite by the river. Ideal area for walking and cycling. Wild-water activities, canoeing and rafting. Free wifi during opening times at the bar. Val d'Aran offers unforgettable locations with challenges and activities for the whole family. Also great as stopover campsite.

🚌 From Bossost (N230) the campsite is clearly signposted on the right.

Bagnères-de-Luchon
D618　N-141
N-230

CC € 17 2/4-30/6　1/9-13/10　　N 42°44'12'' E 0°44'47''

Porqueres/Banyoles, E-17834 / Cataluña

🏕 El Llac Cat. 2
✉ Ctra Circumal.lació de l'Estany
☎ +34 972-570305
🔓 16/1 - 14/12
@ info@campingllac.com

6ha 300T(70-100m²) 6-10A

1 BCD**F**IJKLMO**P**ST
2 BDMRTVWXY
3 ABGHJNRU**W**Z
4 (B+H 15/6-15/9)
   (Q 15/6-11/9) (R 1/6-31/8)
   (T+U+X+Y+Z 1/6-15/9)
5 **AB**DFGIJKLMNOPWZ
6 ACEG**K**OTV

💬 Camping El Llac is situated by Banyoles Lake and close to Porqueres. Lovely area for walking and cycling around the lake.

🚗 From Figueres exit 6 towards Banyoles/Porqueres.

2791

CC € **17** 16/1-25/3 2/4-15/6 11/9-13/12 7=6, 14=11   📷 N 42°7'14'' E 2°44'51''

Prades (Tarragona), E-43364 / Cataluña

🏕 Prades Park
✉ Ctra T-701, km 6.850
☎ +34 977-868270
🔓 1/1 - 31/12
@ camping@campingprades.com

3ha 70T(70-100m²) 8-13A CEE

1 BCD**G**IJKLMOPQ
2 BCGKLRWXY
3 ABGHJKLN**O**RU
4 (**A** 🔓) (C+H 15/6-15/9)
   (Q+R+T+U+V+X+Y+Z 🔓)
5 **A**DEFGIJKLMNOPQRUWZ
6 ACEGH**K**(N 0,5km)OTV

💬 Located in the heart of the Prades mountains, quiet surroundings, ideal for adventurous sports and hikes. Pitches with shade and lovely views, good sports amenities. Restaurant.

🚗 From motorway AP-2 (Lleida-Barcelona): exit 9 Montblanc, follow N-240 dir. Lleida past Espluga de Francoli, Vimbodí, Vallclara, Vilanova de Prades and Prades. From motorway AP-7: exit 34 Reus, follow N-240 dir. Falset past Les Borges del Camp, Alforja, Cornudella and Prades.

2792

CC € **19** 1/1-27/3 3/4-26/4 2/5-21/6 25/6-13/7 3/9-6/9 12/9-31/12 7=6, 14=11   📷 N 41°18'44'' E 0°58'47''

Ribera de Cardós, E-25570 / Cataluña

🏕 Del Cardós Cat.2
✉ Av/Hug Roger III s/n
☎ +34 973-623112
📠 +34 973-623183
🔓 23/3 - 20/9
@ info@campingdelcardos.com

3ha 190T(60-100m²) 4-6A

1 AGIJKLMPQ
2 BCKLRVXY
3 ABGHJNR**W**
4 (C+H 15/6-15/9) J
   (Q+R+T+V+Z 🔓)
5 **AB**EFGIJKLMNOPUWZ
6 AEGK(N 0,5km)OTV

💬 Located right in the centre of Cardos valley. You camp under huge trees on separated pitches, on the banks of a small river. Sanitary facilities of excellent quality. Swimming pool. The snackbar/kiosk offers freshly baked bread each morning.

🚗 Take the exit at the electricity works in Llavorsí on the road C13 Sort-Esterri d'Àneu. Then follow this road for about 9 km. The campsite is located just before the village.

2793

CC € **19** 23/3-14/7 1/9-19/9   📷 N 42°33'35'' E 1°13'46''

Ribera de Cardós, E-25570 / Cataluña

🏔 La Borda del Pubill Cat.2
📧 Ctra Tavascan, km 9,5
☎ +34 973-623088-28
🔄 1/1 - 31/10, 1/12 - 31/12
@ info@
   campinglabordadelpubill.com

4ha 154**T**(70m²) 6-10A

1 ABCDGIJKLMPQ
2 BCKLRVXY
3 ABHJMN**OQ**RU**VW**
4 (C+H 1/6-30/9) **KN**
   (Q+R+T+U+V+X+Y+Z ⌂)
5 **AB**DFGIJKLMNOPUWZ
6 EGK(N 0,5km)OQTV

💬 A level campsite with shady, marked out pitches, close to a river. It has everything you need for a comfortable stay, as well as a pool and mini golf course. Good base for mountain trips and mountain biking. Restaurant at the campsite, and day trips possible by both bike and car.

🚗 At the power plant in Llavorsi on the C13 Sort-Esterri d'Àneu, exit to Ribera de Cardós. Campsite is 300m after the village.

Esterri d'àneu C-28
CC
C-13 Tírvia

CC € **17** 1/1-14/7 1/9-30/10 1/12-31/12   🧭 N 42°34'8'' E 1°13'51''

(2794) NEW 📶 iD

Roses, E-17480 / Cataluña

🏔 Rodas Cat.2
📧 C/ Punta Falconera 62
☎ +34 972-257617
🔄 27/4 - 15/10
@ info@campingrodas.com

3,2ha 279**T**(70-80m²) 6A

1 BCD**F**IJKLMO**P**ST
2 EGLRVWXY
3 AGHJKR**W**
4 (B+G+Q+T+U+X+Z ⌂)
5 **AB**FGIJKLMNOPUWZ
6 CEG**K**(N 0,05km)ORTV

💬 Campsite Rodas is a family campsite located in quiet surroundings with comfortable pitches, marked-out by trees. The perfect spot to relax and enjoy the landscape, the culture, the cuisine and the leisure opportunities in an area as special and unique as Bahía de Roses.

🚗 A7, exit 3, C260 Figueres-Roses, cross roundabout at Empuriabrava. Well signposted from the roundabout before Roses.

N-260
Castelló D'Empúries CC **Rosas**
Empuriabrava
C-31

CC € **19** 27/4-21/6 3/9-14/10   🧭 N 42°16'8'' E 3°9'9''

(2795) 👫 ♿ 📶

Roses, E-17480 / Cataluña

🏔 Salatà
📧 C/ Port Reig 44
☎ +34 972-256086
🔄 9/3 - 11/11
@ info@campingsalata.com

4ha 180**T**(70-180m²) 6-10A

1 BCD**F**IJKLMOPS
2 AERSV**W**XY
3 ABHJK**M**NR**W**Y
4 (C+G ⌂) **KN**
   (Q+S+T+U+V+X+Y+Z ⌂)
5 **AB**DEFGIJKLMNOPUWXY
6 BCEGH**IJK**(N 1km)ORTVW

💬 Situated in the old fishing village of Roses which has a very old centre. You can spend a lovely time in the beautiful bays. Swimming, snorkeling, water skiing.

🚗 A7, exit 3. C260 Figures-Roses, straight on on roundabout B4 Empuriabrava. From roundabout, before Roses well-signposted.

N-260
Roses
CC
Castelló D'Empúries
C-31

CC € **19** 9/3-28/3 2/4-27/4 1/5-30/6 11/9-10/11   🧭 N 42°15'59'' E 3°9'22''

(2796) 👫 ♿ 📶

Saldes, E-08697 / Cataluña

2797

🛉 ♿ 📶 **iD**

▲ Repòs del Pedraforca Cat.1
🚏 B400, km 13,5
☎ +34 938-258044
🕐 1/1 - 31/12
@ pedra@campingpedraforca.com

4ha 70T(70-100m²) 5-16A

1 ABC**G**IJKLM**P**Q
2 BIJKLRTUV**Y**
3 ABGHIJNRU**V**
4 (A 1/7-31/8) (B 15/5-15/9)
  (F 🕐) (G 15/5-15/9) **KNP**
  (Q+S 1/4-30/11)
  (T+U+Y 24/6-11/9) (Z 🕐)
5 **AB**DEFGIJKLMNOPUWXZ
6 CDEGK(N 2km)OTV

💬 A real mountain campsite with marked-out pitches under spruce trees. The campsite has a sauna, gym and indoor swimming pool. The campsite also has a bar and a restaurant. Area on right is less steep with terraces, coming from Guardiola de Berguedà.

🚗 From the C16 to the south of the Caditunnel at Guardiola de Bergueda take the B400 to Salades. The campsite is located on the left after 13.5 km.

Guardiola De Berguedà — *Saldes* CC — B-400 — C-16

CC € **17** *3/4-21/6 25/6-6/7 24/9-4/10 5/11-5/12 21/12-31/12 7=6, 14=11* 🏕 N 42°13'45'' E 1°45'33''

Sant Antoni de Calonge, E-17252 / Cataluña

2798

♿ 📶 **iD**

▲ Eurocamping
🚏 Avinguda Catalunya 15
☎ +34 972-650879
🕐 27/4 - 16/9
@ info@euro-camping.com

13ha 682T(60-100m²) 5-10A

1 ACD**G**IJKLMOPQ
2 AEGLRTVX**Y**
3 B**F**G**M**N**Q**UVY
4 (B+G 🕐) IKMP(Q+S 🕐)
  (T 15/6-1/9) (U+X+Y 🕐)
  (Z 15/6-1/9)
5 **AB**FGIJKLMNOPQRUWXYZ
6 ACEGH**K**M(N 0km)RTUV

💬 First-class campsite on the edge of a pretty little town with an attractive boulevard. All within walking distance. Free wifi. Campers who stay for 14 nights or longer within the CampingCard validity period, can also stay for the CampingCard ACSI rate during the Spanish holiday of 21/6-25/6.

🚗 Exit 6, Palafrugell-Palamós, direction San Feliu, then Palamós-est and then Platja d'Aro. The campsite is located on the right side of the road at Sant Antoni. Clearly signposted.

Sant Feliu De Guíxols

CC € **19** *27/4-21/6 25/6-1/7 31/8-15/9* 🏕 N 41°50'49'' E 3°5'55''

Sant Antoni de Calonge, E-E17251 / Cataluña

NEW

2799

📶 **iD**

▲ Pla de la Torre
🚏 Cl Pinedes S/N
☎ +34 972-650149
📠 +34 972-317626
🕐 15/5 - 16/9
@ pladelatorre@
  internationalpalamos.com

1ha 140T(60-75m²) 6A

1 AGIJLMOPQ
2 ABFGSVY
3 **F**K
4 (Q+R+Z 🕐)
5 **A**CGIJKLMNOPU
6 CEG**IJK**(N 0,3km)TW

💬 Level town campsite on the edge of the Calonge. In the woods, with modern toilet facilities. Free bikes for the beach. Free swimming at the campsite. International Palamos.

🚗 Exit 6 Palafrugell-Palamos towards San Feliu de Guíxols until exit Calonge towards St. Antoni. Campsite on the right.

Palafrugell — CC — *Sant Feliu de Guíxols*

CC € **13** *15/5-14/7 1/9-15/9* 🏕 N 41°50'59'' E 3°5'15''

Sant Carles de la Ràpita, E-43530 / Cataluña

2800

🔼 Alfacs Cat.2
📧 Ctra Alcanar Platja
☎ +34 977-740561
📠 +34 977-742595
🕐 23/3 - 14/10
@ info@alfacs.com

2,5ha 155**T**(45-70m²) 7-10A

1 BCD**G**IJKL**P**RS
2 BEFGOQTVXY
3 AGJMNRWY
4 (**B**+**G** 22/6-11/9)
(Q+S+T+U+X+Y+Z 🔒)
5 **A**GIJKMNOPUZ
6 ACEGK(N 2km)OTV

💬 Right by the Mediterranean coast. 6 km from Ebro Delta nature reserve past the rice fields with unusual flora and fauna. Excellent walking, cycling and fishing in the Delta.

🚗 North: on the A7 exit 41 dir. Sant Carles de la Ràpita. N340 at the 1072 km marker, exit to Sant Carles de la Ràpita. Turn right at 2nd roundabout to Calle Sant/Sidre. South: exit 43 on A7, N340 between 1066 and 1065 km markers dir. Sant Carles de la Ràpita. Campsite 2 km on the right.

T-331
Sant Carles De La Ràpita
Ap-7
N-340
N-238

CC € **17** 23/3-28/3 3/4-22/6 11/9-13/10 7=6 | 〰 N 40°35'43'' E 0°34'13''

Sant Llorenc de Montgai, E-25613 / Cataluña

2801

🔼 La Noguera
📧 Partida La Solana s/n
☎ +34 973-420334
🕐 2/1 - 7/1, 26/1 - 31/12
@ info@campinglanoguera.com

2,5ha 220**T** 10A

1 BCD**G**IJKLMO**P**Q
2 JKLRTVWXY
3 B**C**GHIJNRUV**W**
4 (B 24/6-11/9) (**F** 🔒)
(G 24/6-11/9) M
(Q+R+T+U+V+X+Y+Z 🔒)
5 **AB**DEFGIJKLMNOPUWZ
6 ACFGJ**K**(N 9km)OTUV

💬 Modern terraced campsite in the nature reserve around the lake of Sant Llorenç de Montgai. Many facilities for sports and leisure activities at the site and in the area. Restaurant with local products.

🚗 C13 from Lleida via Balaguer to Sant Llorenc de Montgai.

Alòs de Balaguer
C-13
C-26 **Balaguer**
C-53

CC € **19** 26/1-28/3 2/4-26/4 1/5-21/6 11/9-10/10 14/10-30/10 4/11-5/12 7=6 | 〰 N 41°51'37'' E 0°49'57''

Sant Pere Pescador, E-17470 / Cataluña

2802

🔼 Aquarius Cat.2
📧 Camino de la Playa S/N
☎ +34 972-520101
📠 +34 972-550216
🕐 15/3 - 31/10
@ reservas@aquarius.es

8ha 450**T**(80-100m²) 6-16A CEE

1 B**G**IJKLMOPQ
2 AERVWXY
3 ABGHJKNQRU**W**Y
4 (G 🔒) M
(Q+S+T+U+V+X+Y+Z 🔒)
5 **AB**DEFGIJKLMNOPQRUW
6 ACEGH**IK**M(N 2,5km)OPRT
VWX

💬 Located on the beach where the sea water provides the ultimate relaxation. Many trips out are possible in the area. This is a peaceful campsite. Top of the range toilet facilities. The campsite only offers standard pitches in the 'B' zone. For an extra car in addition to your motorhome there's a surcharge.

🚗 Exit 3, after 12 km dir. Sant Pere Pescador, or exit 5 dir. L'Escala at St. Marti-Empuries via coast road to Sant Pere Pescador.

Figueres   Roses

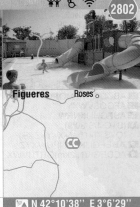

CC € **19** 15/3-28/3 2/4-18/5 23/5-19/6 14/9-30/10 | 〰 N 42°10'38'' E 3°6'29''

Sant Pere Pescador, E-17470 / Cataluña ♿ 🛜 iD (2803)

🏕 La Gaviota
📧 Ctra Platja s/n
☎ +34 972-520569
📠 +34 972-550348
🔓 24/3 - 24/10
@ info@lagaviota.com

2ha 153T(70m²) 5-8A CEE

1 ABG**I**JLPQ
2 ACEKLRVWXY
3 ABHJKNR**W**XY
4 (C+G+Q+S+T+U+V+X+Y+Z
🔓)
5 **AB**DEFGIJKLMNOPRUW
6 EGH**I**J**K**(N 2km)ORTV

💬 This campsite is positioned by the beach. The surroundings offer opportunities for various trips out. A quiet campsite with friendly, attentive staff and lovely landscaping. This site has added value as it is actually connected to the beach.

🚐 Exit 3 after La Jonquera, direction Roses, after 12 km direction Sant Pere Pescador. After the bridge follow signs.

Figueres   **Roses**

C-31   CC

CC €19 2/4-18/5 23/5-17/6 12/9-23/10   📍 N 42°11'21'' E 3°6'30''

Sant Pere Pescador, E-17470 / Cataluña 🛜 (2804)

🏕 Riu**
📧 Ctra de la Platja s/n
☎ +34 972-520216
🔓 29/3 - 23/9
@ info@campingriu.com

4ha 159T(100m²) 5-10A CEE

1 BCD**F**IJKLMOPQ
2 ACGLRVWXY
3 ABHJK**M**NR**VW**
4 (B+G 🔓) KP(Q 🔓)
(R 1/7-31/8)
(T+U+V+X+Y+Z 🔓)
5 **AB**FGIJKLMNOPUWXY
6 CEGHJ**K**M(N 0,2km)ORTV

💬 A family campsite 2 km from the beach set in a pine forest. Tourist attractions such as Figueres, the Dalí Museum and Barcelona. The open pitches ensure a continuous welcome cool breeze. The site is located directly next to a connecting channel to the sea with landing stages. 200m from the centre.

🚐 Take exit 3 towards Rosas. After 12 km direction Sant Pere Pescador. Signposted after the bridge. Or exit 5 direction L'Escala then direction Sant Pere Pescador.

Figueres   Roses

Ap-7   CC   C-31

CC €19 1/4-30/6 1/9-22/9   📍 N 42°11'15'' E 3°5'21''

Sitges, E-08870 / Cataluña ♿ 🛜 iD (2805)

🏕 El Garrofer Cat.2
📧 Ctra C246a, km 39
☎ +34 93-8941780
📠 +34 93-8110623
🔓 23/2 - 16/12
@ info@garroferpark.com

8ha 526T(70-90m²) 6-20A CEE

1 ABCD**G**IJKLMO**P**Q
2 AFGOSVWXY
3 ABF**G**HIJKNRW
4 (B+G 1/5-30/9)
(Q+S+T+U+V+X+Y+Z 🔓)
5 **AB**EFGIJKLMNPUWXYZ
6 ACDEGK(N 2km)ORTUVWX

💬 A campsite 2 km south of Sitges. 900 metres by footpath to the beach. You will pitch on gravel under the pine trees. Bus service to Barcelona. 1 dog is included in the rate.

🚐 Road C32, exit 26 direction Sitges, road C246a.

Vilanova I La Geltrú   C-31   CC

CC €19 23/2-13/7 1/9-15/12 7=6, 14=12, 21=18, 28=24   📍 N 41°14'2'' E 1°46'51''

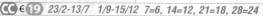

Solsona (Lleida), E-25280 / Cataluña

🛩 ⛷ ♿ 📶 ✿ **iD** **2806**

🔺 El Solsonès Cat.1
✉ Ctra St. Llorenç km 2
☎ +34 973-482861
📠 +34 973-481300
🔑 12/1 - 9/12
@ info@campingsolsones.com

6,3ha 268T(70-100m²) 6-10A

1 ABCDEIJKLMOPQ
2 JKLRUVXY
3 AFGHJM**NOQR**SU
4 (A 🔑)
   (B+G+Q+S+T 17/6-10/9)
   (U+V+X+Y+Z 22/6-10/9)
5 AB DEFGIJKLMNOPUWZ
6 ACEGK(N 2km)ORTV

💬 A shaded campsite with a separate area for touring pitches. Various walks from the campsite. 2 km from the town of Solsona with its medieval centre. Many sports facilities. Excellent toilet facilities. Ecological restaurant and shop which are also open every weekend outside the stated periods.

🚗 From La Seo de Urgel follow the C1313. Turn left at Basella. In Solsona direction S. Llorenç de Morunys via Coll de Jou, follow signs.

CC € 19 12/1-24/3 3/4-14/7 1/9-11/10 15/10-8/12 7=6

📡 N 42°0'43'' E 1°31'0''

Tamarit/Tarragona, E-43008 / Cataluña

👫 ♿ 📶 **2807**

🔺 Tamarit Beach Resort Cat.1
✉ Platja de Tamarit, N340a km 1172
☎ +34 977-650128
📠 +34 977-650451
🔑 21/3 - 4/11
@ resort@tamarit.com

17ha 476T(66-200m²) 10-16A CEE

1 BCD**G**IJKLMO**P**Q
2 ABCEFGKLQSTVWXY
3 ABF**G**HJK**M**NQRU**V**WY
4 (B 27/3-12/10) (G 🔑) JM
   (Q+S+T+U+V+X+Y+Z 🔑)
5 ABDEFGIJKLMNOPQRS**T**U
   WXYZ
6 ACDEGHJKM(N 1km)OQRS
   TUVW

💬 The campsite is beautifully located at the foot of Tamarit castle, right on the beach and some distance from the coast road and railway line. Lively restaurant/bar with roof garden and sea views where the sandy beach meets the rocky coast.

🚗 AP7 exit 32, dir. Altafulla/Torredembarra/Tamarit. N340a dir. Tarragona, 1st exit at roundabout, 4th exit next roundabout dir. Tamarit/Altafulla. Right after 250m, follow green and yellow 'Tamarit Park' signs. Campsite on the left.

CC € 19 21/3-21/6 11/9-3/11

📡 N 41°7'57'' E 1°21'37''

Taradell/Osona, E-08552 / Cataluña

♿ 📶 **iD** **2808**

🔺 La Vall Cat.1
✉ Camí de la Vallmitjana s/n
☎ +34 93-8126336
📠 +34 93-8126027
🔑 7/1 - 13/12
@ lavallpark@campinglavallpark.cat

9ha 119T(80-100m²) 5-10A

1 ABCDGIJKLMOPQ
2 BIJKLRUVXY
3 AFGHJMNRU
4 (B+G 22/6-11/9) (Q 🔑)
   (R 7/1-23/6,11/9-13/12)
   (S 22/6-11/9) (T 23/6-10/9)
   (U+V+X+Z 22/6-11/9)
5 AB DEFGHIJLMNPUWXYZ
6 CEGK(N 1km)OTUV

💬 Located in a lovely valley where the natural surroundings have remained unspoilt. Ideal area for walking, mountain biking and participating in other sports activities. Not far from the town of Vic with many cultural events on offer. Campsite is close to 'Parc Naturel del Montseny'.

🚗 C17 Vic-Barcelona, exit Taradell, continue to T junction in Taradell, turn right then follow signs. Attention!! On SatNav choose Urbanització de Goitallops. Then follow signs.

CC € 19 7/1-28/3 2/4-14/7 1/9-12/12 16=14

📡 N 41°51'54'' E 2°17'42''

Tarragona, E-43080 / Cataluña

♿ 📶 **2809**

🏕 Las Palmeras Cat.1
🛣 Ctra N340, km 1168
☎ +34 977-208081
📠 +34 977-207817
🔑 24/3 - 14/10
@ laspalmeras@laspalmeras.com

17ha 140T(70-110m²) 5-10A

1 BC**F**IJKLMOPQ
2 AEFGKLRSTVWXY
3 BF**G**KM**N**RUWY
4 (B+G 1/6-25/9)
(Q+S+T+U 🔑) (V 1/7-31/8)
(W+X+Y 🔑) (Z 24/7-11/9)
5 **AB**EFGIJKLMNOPUWX
6 ACFGH**K**M(N 4,5km)ORTUV

💬 Paradise for the beach lover. You can camp beside or up to 50m from the beautiful sandy beach. At the end of the campsite is the Punta de la Mora walking area. 4 km from the historic city of Tarragona. All this compensates for the sound of the railway.

🚗 Toll road A7, exit 32, roundabout direction Tarragona N340. After a few kilometres on the left restaurant 'El Trull'. Then beyond km-marker 1168 turn left through the tunnel under the railway track to the campsite.

CC € **17** 3/4-14/6 12/9-13/10
🧭 N 41°7'49'' E 1°18'43''

Tarragona, E-43008 / Cataluña

♿ 📶 **2810**

🏕 Torre de la Mora S.A. Cat.1
🛣 Ctra N340 km 1171
☎ +34 977-650277
📠 +34 977-652858
🔑 23/3 - 14/10
@ info@torredelamora.com

16ha 319T(50-70m²) 7A

1 BC**G**IJLMST
2 ABEFGIJQSTVY
3 BF**G**N**Q**RUWY
4 (B+G 1/5-30/9)
(Q+S+T+U+X+Y+Z 🔑)
5 **AB**EFGIJKLMNOPUW
6 EGH**IJ**M(N 2km)ORTV

💬 A terraced campsite with a lovely beach. Enormous water park. Terrace with free wifi. 2 km from the N340 and railway line.

🚗 Toll road A7 exit 32 Torredembarra/Altafulla, on roundabout direction N340 Tarragona, at the next roundabout direction La Mora and follow signs to campsite further on.

CC € **17** 23/3-21/6 3/9-13/10
🧭 N 41°7'44'' E 1°20'39''

Torredembarra, E-43830 / Cataluña

♿ 📶 **2811**

🏕 Clara Cat.2
🛣 Passeig Miramar, 276
☎ +34 977-643480
📠 +34 977-646076
🔑 16/3 - 16/10
@ info@campingclara.es

1,4ha 125T(60-90m²) 6-10A

1 BCDGIJKLMOPQ
2 AEFGSTVWXY
3 ABGHKNRWY
4 (Q+S+T+U+V+X+Y+Z 🔑)
5 ABCEFGHIJKLMNOPUWZ
6 ACDEGK(N 0,5km)OQRTUV

💬 Not such a big campsite, near the village and 150 metres from the beach. Naturist recreation allowed on the left side of the beach. Free wifi. Close to railway line.

🚗 AP7 exit 31 or 32 to N340 direction Torredembarra. Exit Torredembarra Est. 2nd exit at roundabout. On the left after 500m.

CC € **15** 16/3-5/7 27/8-15/10 7=6, 15=12, 30=23
🧭 N 41°8'58'' E 1°25'11''

Torredembarra, E-43830 / Cataluña

👫 ♿ 📶 (2812)

🔺 La Noria Cat.2
📧 Passeig Miramar 278
☎ +34 977-640453
📠 +34 977-645272
🔓 24/3 - 1/10
@ info@camping-lanoria.com

5ha 440T(50-60m²) 6A

1 BCDGIJKLOPQ
2 AEFGRSTVXY
3 ABGHJKNRWY
4 (Q+S+T+U+V+X+Y+Z 🅿)
5 ABEFGIJKLMNOPUWZ
6 CEGHIK(N 0,5km)ORTV

💬 A well maintained campsite. Close to a village and beach. Naturist recreation is permitted on the left side of the beach. Free wifi. Attractive terrace and a good restaurant. There is a railway track next to the campsite.

🚗 AP7 exit 31 or 32 to N340 direction Torredembarra Est. 2nd exit on roundabout and campsite 400m on the left of the road.

El Vendrell

CC € 15 24/3-5/7 27/8-29/9 7=6, 14=12, 21=18, 30=23   📍 N 41°9'1'' E 1°25'16''

Torredembarra, E-43830 / Cataluña

👫 ♿ 📶 (2813)

🔺 Relax-Sol Cat.2
📧 Passeig Miramar 246
☎ +34 977-646271
📠 +34 977-646034
🔓 15/2 - 31/10
@ info@campingrelaxsol.com

2,5ha 51T(70-110m²) 10A CEE

1 BCFIJKLMOPQ
2 AEFGTVXY
3 ABHLRUWY
4 (Q+R+S+T+U+V 🅿)
  (W+X+Y 1/3-15/10)
  (Z 1/5-30/9)
5 ACEFGHIJKLMNOPUWXZ
6 BCDEGHIK(N 0,04km)ORTV

💬 Campsite close to Torredembarra. 150m from the beach, bordering on a protected natural area, where guests can enjoy the flora and fauna. Naturist recreation possible on the left beach. Free wifi.

🚗 AP7 exit El Vendrell/Coma-Ruga. Exit 32 Torredembarra. Follow N340 dir. Tarragona at 1177,8 km marker, roundabout dir. Torredembarra-Est (2nd exit right). After viaduct 3rd exit on roundabout dir. Barcelona, site 100m on right.

Torredembarra
Tarragona

CC € 15 15/2-10/7 28/8-30/10 7=6, 14=12, 30=23   📍 N 41°8'56'' E 1°25'7''

Torroella de Montgri, E-17257 / Cataluña

♿ 📶 iD (2814)

🔺 El Delfin Verde Cat.1
📧 C/ Rossinyol 1
☎ +34 972-758454
📠 +34 972-760070
🔓 18/5 - 26/9
@ info@eldelfinverde.com

45ha 1100T(100-120m²) 6-20A

1 ACGIJKLMOPQ
2 AELRSVWXY
3 BFGHJKLMNQRUVY
4 (B+G+Q+S+T+U+V+X 🅿)
  (Y 15/6-1/9) (Z 🅿)
5 ABEFGIJKLMNOPUWXYZ
6 ACEGHIJKM(N 8km)ORTV
  WX

💬 Large, level campsite with spacious pitches and excellent amenities. Many trees in the middle of the site. And a lovely "glamping" area.

🚗 Motorway exit 5. About 2 km to the south of Torroella de Montgri turn left direction Pals (signposted). 4 km to the campsite.

Torroella de Montgrí

C-66

Palafrugell

CC € 19 18/5-30/6 30/8-25/9   📍 N 42°0'43'' E 3°11'17''

Tossa de Mar, E-17320 / Cataluña

⌂ Cala Llevadó Cat.1
☷ Ctra GI-682
  Lloret a Tossa km 18,9
☎ +34 972-340314
FAX +34 972-341187
☷ 26/3 - 26/9
@ info@calallevado.com

17ha 612T(40-100m²) 10A CEE

1 ACD**G**IJLPST
2 ABE**G**HIJKOQSTVXY
3 BHJNRUWY
4 (A 1/7-30/8)
  (B+G+Q+S+T ☷)
  (U 1/5-29/9) (V+X+Y+Z ☷)
5 **AB**FGIJKLMNOPUWXYZ
6 ACEGH**IJK**M(N 3km)OQRTV

💬 A fantastic location in the loveliest part of the Costa Brava. Quiet, four beaches, swimming pool, bar, restaurant, supermarket and excellent toilet facilities.

🚗 Toll road E15 exit 9. In Lloret drive in the direction of Tossa. Turn to the right after 8 km (clearly signposted). Then continue another 800 metres to the campsite on the private road.

2815

C-35
N-II   C-63
Lloret De Mar   CC
Blanes

CC € **19** 26/3-6/7 27/8-25/9

📷 N 41°42'47'' E 2°54'23''

Vall-Llòbrega/Palamós, E-17253 / Cataluña

⌂ Castell Park Cat.1
☷ Ctra Palamós-Palafrugell, km 328
☎ FAX +34 972-315263
☷ 24/3 - 11/9
@ info@campingcastellpark.com

4,2ha 195T(70-90m²) 3-5A

1 AGIJLMOPQ
2 GRTVY
3 AGKN
4 (B+G 15/6-11/9)
  (Q+S+T+U+X+Z ☷)
5 **A**GIJKMNOPUW
6 CFG**IK**(N 2,5km)OQRTV

NEW

💬 Lively, level, family-run campsite with a Dutch owner. Good toilet block and beautiful swimming pool. Lots of greenery and shade.

🚗 The campsite is located on the right of the C31 between Palafrugell en Palamós. Clearly signposted with flags.

2816

C-66
Palafrugell
CC
Sant Feliu de Guíxols

CC € **13** 1/5-21/6 1/9-10/9

📷 N 41°52'55'' E 3°8'27''

Vilallonga de Ter, E-17869 / Cataluña

⌂ Conca de Ter Cat.1
☷ Ctra Setcases s/n, km 5,4
☎ +34 972-740629
FAX +34 972-130171
☷ 1/1 - 31/12
@ concater@concater.com

2ha 100T(70-110m²) 5-11A CEE

1 BCD**G**IJKLMOPRT
2 BCGKLRTVY
3 ABCD**EF**GHJLMN**O**RU**V**WX
4 (B+G 20/6-1/9) **K**
  (Q+R+T+U+V+X+Z ☷)
5 **AB**DFGHIJKLMNOPQRUW
  XZ
6 ABEGK(N 0,5km)ORSTV

💬 Set among the colourful mountains, the campsite itself has even grounds. Remarkable because of its many sports options, including cycling and walking.

🚗 Route N260 from Ripoll to Camprodon, 4th exit on roundabout to Vilallonga de Ter. From Figueres N26, then A26 to Camprodon and then to Vilallonga de Ter.

2817

Setcases
C-38
CC
N-260   Camprodon
Campdevànol

CC € **17** 2/4-14/7 1/9-9/12 7=6, 14=11

📷 N 42°20'2'' E 2°18'27''

Vilanova de Prades, E-43439 / Cataluña

2818

🛖 Serra de Prades Resort Cat.1
📧 Sant Antonio s/n
☎ 📠 +34 977-869050
🔓 1/1 - 31/12
@ info@serradeprades.com

5ha 215**T**(92-100m²) 6A

1 BCD**G**IJKLMOPQ
2 JKLRSTVWXY
3 BCDGHJKL**MN**P**R**U**V**
4 (**A** 🌧) (C+H 15/6-15/9) **KN**
(Q+S+T+U+V+X+Y+Z 🌧)
5 **AB**DFGIJKMNOPUWZ
6 ACEG**I**J**K**O**P**TV

💬 Campsite with beautiful and quiet location with heated pool, own wine productions, wellness and restaurant. Surroundings: museums, wine cellars, walking, sports activities. Organised theme options such as photography, plants, nature, animals etc.
🚗 From Barcelona AP-7 to Tarragona, AP-2 to Lleida, exit 9 Montblanc, N240 Lleida, Vimbodi, Vilanova de Prades. From Lleida N240, Vimbodi, Vilanova de Prades. From Vimbodi dir. Vallclara. Don't use SatNav but follow directions.

AP-2 · Vimbodi i Poblet
CC
C-242 · Prades

CC € **17** 1/1-26/4 2/5-21/6 25/6-14/7 7/9-26/10 5/11-31/12 7=6, 14=11 📶🛖 N 41°20'59'' E 0°57'30''

Vilanova i la Geltrú, E-08800 / Cataluña

👤 🛜 **iD** **2819**

🛖 Vilanova Park Cat.1
📧 Carretera Arboç km 2,5
☎ +34 93-8933402
📠 +34 93-8935528
🔓 1/1 - 31/12
@ info@vilanovapark.com

40ha 348**T**(70-100m²) 10A

1 ABCD**F**IJKLM**P**RS
2 FG**J**LSTUVXY
3 BC**F**GHJK**M**NQRU**V**
4 (**A** 1/7-31/8) (B 24/3-4/11)
(F 🌧) (G 24/3-4/11) J**KLNP**
(Q+S+T+U+V+W+X+Y+Z 🌧)
5 **AB**DFGIJKLMNOPUWXY
6 ACDEGH**I**J**K**M(N 2,5km)OQ
RSTVWX

💬 On a hillside, 2 km from Vilanova i la Geltrú and 3.5 km from the beach. Enjoyable stays in early and late season with adapted facilities including an indoor pool, sauna, jacuzzi and fitness. Bus stop at the entrance for the beach, village and station. Daily bus to Barcelona.
🚗 Toll road A7, exit 29 direction Vilanova. Before Vilanova turn right on roundabout direction Cubelles C31. After km-marker 153 exit right direction Arboç. Then follow signs.

Ap-7 · N-340
C-15
CC
Vilanova I La Geltrú

CC € **19** 3/1-22/6 25/6-1/7 27/8-31/12 14=12 📶🛖 N 41°13'54'' E 1°41'28''

Vinyols i Els Arcs, E-43391 / Cataluña

👫👫 👤 🛜 **2820**

🛖 Eco-camp Vinyols
📧 Camí de Barenys, 13
☎ +34 977-850409
🔓 2/3 - 9/12
@ hola@ecocampvinyols.cat

3,8ha 56**T** 6A

1 BCD**G**IJLPQ
2 FGRSXY
3 BDJKLRU
4 (B 1/5-30/10) (Q 23/6-11/9)
(R 1/3-8/12)
(T+U+X+Z 23/6-11/9)
5 **A**JKNPUW
6 EG**J**(N 0,5km)T

NEW

💬 300m from the village, amidst the fruit and olive trees, this campsite is in quiet surroundings. Suitable for bike rides, for instance to Reus. You can pick fruit here and go on wagon tours nearby. There's a swimming pool to help you cool down.

🚗 Toll road AP7 exit 37 towards Montbrio del Camp. After 2.5 km towards Vinyols i Els Arcs. In Vinyols at roundabout 1st exit right. Campsite is 300m further on the left.

C-242
N-420 · **Reus**
T-310 · CC
A-7 · Salou
AP-7 · Miami Platja

CC € **17** 2/3-23/3 2/4-22/6 11/9-8/12 7=6, 14=11 📶🛖 N 41°6'44'' E 1°2'52''

Alcossebre (Castellón), E-12579 / Comunidad Valenciana

2821

🔺 Playa Tropicana Cat.1
✉ Camino de l'Atall s/n
☎ +34 964-412463
FAX +34 964-412805
⊙ 1/1 - 31/12
@ info@playatropicana.com

3ha 380T(50-100m²) 10A

1 BCDGIJKLOPQ
2 AEFGNTUVXY
3 BGKMRUWY
4 (B ⊙) (E 1/1-1/6,15/9-31/12)
(G ⊙) JK
(Q+S+T+U+V+X+Y+Z ⊙)
5 ABDEFGIJKLMNOPUWZ
6 ACEGIK(N 2,5km)ORTVW

💬 A large campsite on a sandy beach. New toilet facilities. Pitches separated by hedges. Lovely swimming pool, covered and heated in winter and a good restaurant and large supermarket. 4 km from Alcossebre. Good cycling and challenging walks.

🚗 On A7 take exit 44; on N340 at km-marker 1018 to Alcossebre. Follow signs. Take 1st exit at roundabout. Enter village, turn right at 2nd traffic lights. Right at the T junction, then follow signs on coast road to the campsite.

Alcalà De Xivert

CC € ⑲ 1/1-28/3 3/4-21/6 1/9-31/12 14=12, 21=18, 28=24

📍 N 40°13'13'' E 0°16'6''

Alcossebre (Castellón), E-12579 / Comunidad Valenciana

2822

🔺 Ribamar Cat.1
✉ Partida Ribamar s/n
☎ +34 964-761601
FAX +34 964-994085
⊙ 1/1 - 31/12
@ info@campingribamar.com

2,2ha 71T(40-100m²) 6-10A CEE

1 BCDGIJKLMPST
2 EINOQTUVX
3 BGHJMNRUWY
4 (B+G+Q+R ⊙) (Y 1/6-31/10)
(Z ⊙)
5 ABDEFGIJKLMNOPUWXYZ
6 AEGIK(N 2,5km)ORTV

💬 Excellent amenities. Very quiet and 150m from the beach in the 'Sierra de Irta' nature reserve with excellent walking and cycling. Lovely swimming pool, tennis and basketball. Pitches with water tap. Heated toilet facilities. Campsite only accessible along a 1 km unsurfaced road, but worth the effort to stay at this lovely site!

🚗 A7, exit 44. Via the N340 to Alcoceber at the 1018 km sign along Las Fuentes. Follow camping signs. The final km is unsurfaced road.

Alcalà De Xivert

CC € ⑲ 1/1-28/3 2/4-21/6 9/9-31/12

📍 N 40°16'13'' E 0°18'24''

Altea/Alicante, E-03590 / Comunidad Valenciana

2823

🔺 Cap-Blanch
✉ Playa de Cap-Blanch 25
☎ +34 96-5845946
FAX +34 96-5844556
⊙ 1/1 - 31/12
@ info@camping-capblanch.com

4ha 288T(80-120m²) 5-10A

1 ABCDFIJKLMOPQ
2 EFGKNOSTUVWXY
3 BFGKMNRUVWY
4 (Y+Z ⊙)
5 ABDEFGHIJKLMNOPUZ
6 CGK(N 2km)ORT

💬 Attractive grounds with plenty of palms and plants. Located in a bay with a lovely white pebble beach. A lively boulevard with views of Altea. Free wifi and webcam. Heated toilet facilities.

🚗 AP7, exit 64 dir. Altea. Then N332 Valencia-Alicante south of Altea take exit Port Plaja at the traffic lights. Down to the sea. Turn right on boulevard. Campsite at the end of boulevard on the right.

L'Alfàs Del Pi

Benidorm

CC € ⑲ 1/1-25/3 3/4-14/7 1/9-31/12

📍 N 38°34'40'' W 0°3'54''

Benicarlo, E-12580 / Comunidad Valenciana

♿ 📶 **2824**

🏕 Alegria del Mar Cat.2
📧 Ctra Nacional 340a km 1046
☎ +34 964-470871
🗓 1/1 - 31/12
@ info@campingalegria.com

0,8ha 145T(60-135m²) 6-10A

1 BCDGIJKLMOPQ
2 AEFNTUVWX
3 BGWY
4 (B+G 1/4-31/10)
(Q+S+T+U+V+X+Y+Z 🔑)
5 **AB**DFGIJKLMNOPUWXZ
6 CDEG**K**(N 2km)OSTVW

💬 A medium sized campsite right by the sea, good facilities, swimming pool, restaurant. Very peaceful location, close to Benicarlo. Good walking and cycling opportunities.

🚗 Take exit 42 on the A7. On the N340 (Tarragona-Valencia) follow signs to N340a. Take exit on N340a at km 1046 towards the sea. Then about 1 km on a minor road.

N-232   N-238

Vinaròs

AP-7   N-340

CC

Benicarló

CC € **17** 1/1-1/7 20/8-31/12   🧭 N 40°25'36'' E 0°26'17''

Benicasim, E-12560 / Comunidad Valenciana

♿ 📶 **2825**

🏕 Azahar Cat.1
📧 Partida Vilarroig s/n
☎ +34 964-303196
🗓 1/1 - 31/12
@ info@campingazahar.es

4ha 130T(70-95m²) 6A

1 BCD**G**IJLPQ
2 AEFRTVWXY
3 B**F**GHJKL**M**UWY
4 (B+G+Q 🔑) (S 1/7-31/8)
(T 🔑) (U+X+Y 1/7-31/8)
(Z 🔑)
5 **AB**DEFGIJKLMNOPUWZ
6 EGHJ**K**(N 1km)ORTV

💬 A campsite in a pleasant little town with a good restaurant 100m from a lovely boulevard and beach. The inland area lends itself to trips out; excellent cycling and walking opportunities on 'Via Verde', north and south on an old railway track through the lovely countryside to the town of Castellón.

🚗 A7, exit 45 or 46. Take exit Benicasim on N340 at km-marker 987 or 989. Follow signs in Benicasim.

N-340

Ap-7

CC

Castellón De La Plana

CC € **19** 1/1-27/3 3/4-30/6 1/9-31/12 7=6, 14=12   🧭 N 40°3'32'' E 0°5'7''

Benicasim, E-12560 / Comunidad Valenciana

♿ 📶 **2826**

🏕 Bonterra Park Cat.1
📧 Avinguda de Barcelona 47
☎ +34 964-300007
📠 +34 964-100669
🗓 1/1 - 31/12
@ info@bonterrapark.com

5ha 334T(65-102m²) 6-10A CEE

1 BCD**G**IJKLMPQ
2 AEFGTUVXY
3 B**F**GKNRU**VW**Y
4 (**A**+B+E+G+Q+R+T+U+X+Y +Z 🔑)
5 **AB**DEFGHIJKLMNOPQRU WXYZ
6 BCEGHI**K**(N 0,1km)ORTUV

💬 Beautiful, spacious campsite 300m from a sandy beach and a small town. Excellent heated toilet facilities. Swimming pools, one of which is covered and heated. Fitness room, Spanish lessons. Sunny marked out pitches. Cycling and walking opportunities on 'Via Verde' from north to south on an old railway track. Suitable for longer stays in the low season.

🚗 A7, exit 46, take the N340. At km-marker 987 or 989 turn to Benicasim. Follow the signs.

N-340

Ap-7

CC

Castellón De La Plana

CC € **19** 1/1-28/3 2/4-30/6 1/9-31/12   🧭 N 40°3'25'' E 0°4'28''

Benicasim, E-12560 / Comunidad Valenciana ♿ 📶 (2827)

🏕 Tauro***
✉ Avenida Jaume I, 295
☎ +34 964-392967
🗓 1/1 - 31/12
@ info@campingtauro.com

80T(50-100m²) 10A CEE

1 BCDGIJKLMOPQ
2 AEFGTUVWXY
3 BFGHJKRUWY
4 (B+G+Q+R+T+U 🔒)
(X+Y 1/4-30/9) (Z 🔒)
5 **AB**DFGIJKLMNOPUWXZ
6 AEGIK(N 1km)OTV

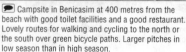

💬 Campsite in Benicasim at 400 metres from the beach with good toilet facilities and a good restaurant. Lovely routes for walking and cycling to the north or the south over green bicycle paths. Larger pitches in low season than in high season.

🚗 On N340 from Barcelona take exit Benicasim-south to Avenida Jaume I, no. 295. From Valencia take exit Benicasim-south to Avenida Jaume I, no. 295.

CC € **15** 1/1-30/6 1/9-31/12 7=6, 14=12   📡 N 40°2'15'' E 0°2'28''

Benidorm, E-03503 / Comunidad Valenciana ⊗ ♿ 📶 iD (2828)

🏕 Villasol
✉ Avda Bernat de Sarriá 13
☎ +34 965-850422
📠 +34 966-806420
🗓 1/1 - 31/12
@ info@camping-villasol.com

7ha 506T(70-90m²) 16A

1 ABCDEIJKLMO**PQ**
2 FGJLSUVWXY
3 A**F**GNU
4 (B 🔒) (F 1/1-30/6,1/9-31/12)
(G+Q+S+T+U+X+Z 🔒)
5 **AB**DFGIJKLMNOPUWZ
6 ABG**IK**M(N 4,0km)RSTV

💬 Large campsite, spaciously appointed with all amenities, open all year. Varied foliage and many flowering plants. Terrace with a view of the pool and the Benidorm skyline.

🚗 On N332 between 151 and 152 km markers, take Benidorm/Playa de Levante exit. Then follow camping signs.

CC € **19** 7/1-22/3 2/4-12/7 2/9-20/12   📡 N 38°32'51'' W 0°6'37''

Benidorm/Alicante, E-03503 / Comunidad Valenciana ♿ 📶 ✿ iD (2829)

🏕 Arena Blanca****
✉ Avda Doctor Severa Ochoa 44
☎ +34 96-5861889
📠 +34 96-5861107
🗓 1/1 - 31/12
@ info@camping-arenablanca.es

2,5ha 95T(60-80m²) 16A

1 ABCDGIJLO**P**ST
2 FGJLSTUVWXY
3 A**F**G
4 (B 1/5-15/10)
(E 1/1-1/5,15/10-31/12)
(Q+R+T+U+V+X+Z 🔒)
5 **AB**DFGHIJKLMNOPUWXY
6 ABCFG**I**K(N 0,8km)ORSTV

💬 A charming campsite. Small-scale. Swimming all year. Wonderful sunbathing on real lawns when the weather is nice. Pool covered and heated in winter. Very clean toilet facilities. Free wifi.

🚗 On the N332 Valencia-Alicante take Benidorm/Playa de Levante exit between 151 and 152 km markers. Then follow camping signs.

CC € **17** 1/1-25/3 3/4-8/7 10/9-31/12   📡 N 38°33'4'' W 0°5'47''

Benidorm/Alicante, E-03503 / Comunidad Valenciana

♿ 📶 ✿ iD (2830)

🏕 Armanello***
📧 Avda Com. Valenciana
☎ +34 96-5853190
📠 +34 96-5853100
📅 1/1 - 31/12
@ info@campingarmanello.com

2,2ha 100T(60-100m²) 10-16A CEE

1 ABCDGIJKLMOPQ
2 FGLSUVWXY
3 BFKRU
4 (B+G+Q+R+T+U+V+X+Z 🔌)
5 **AB**DFGIJKLMNOPUWXYZ
6 ABCGHIK(N 1,5km)ORSTUV

💬 A lovely new rear part of the campsite with views of Benidorm and of the mountains in the background. New heated toilet facilities. Pleasant ambiance. Many interesting trips out into the hinterland. Free wifi.

🚗 AP7, exit 65 to the N332. Straight on at 1st roundabout. 3rd exit at 2nd roundabout. Then follow camping signs.

N-332
Ap-7
Benidorm CC
Villajoyosa

CC € **17** 1/1-25/3 3/4-8/7 10/9-31/12 7=6

📍 N 38°32'52'' W 0°6'39''

Benidorm/Alicante, E-03503 / Comunidad Valenciana

♿ 📶 iD (2831)

🏕 Benisol
📧 Av. Com. Valenciana s/n
☎ +34 96-5851673
📠 +34 96-5863616
📅 1/1 - 31/12
@ info@campingbenisol.com

7ha 100T(60-80m²) 6-10A CEE

1 ABCDGIJLOP**Q**
2 FGJSTUVWXY
3 F**G**MRU
4 (B 1/6-31/10)
   (F 1/1-31/5,1/11-31/12)
   (G 1/6-31/10) JK
   (Q+R+T+U+V+X+Y+Z 🔌)
5 **AB**DFGIJKLMNOPUVXY
6 ABDEG**I**KM(N 3km)ORSTV

💬 A campsite with very friendly reception. Ideal for visiting Benidorm and its beautiful surroundings. Heated swimming pool in the winter and a large outdoor pool in summer, with bar and terrace by the pool.

🚗 AP7, exit 65. Turn right twice after toll booth. Then keep right again(= exit). The campsite is located on the left a few hundred metres down the road.

N-332
Ap-7
Benidorm CC

CC € **17** 1/1-28/3 2/4-10/7 1/9-31/12 7=6

📍 N 38°33'36'' W 0°5'54''

Bétera, E-46117 / Comunidad Valenciana

♿ 📶 (2832)

🏕 Valencia Camper Park***
📧 Calle Universo s/n
☎ +34 960-718095
📅 1/1 - 31/12
@ valcampark@gmail.com

1,4ha 64T(40-80m²) 4-6A CEE

1 BCDGIJKLMOPQ
2 FGLSTUVWX
3 BF**G**HJR
4 (B+G 15/5-15/11)
   (Q+R+T+U+Y+Z 🔌)
5 **A**DFGHIJKLMNOPQUW
6 CEGK(N 2km)TV

💬 Campsite with good amenities for motorhomes but also for caravans, situated on the north-west side. If you arrive with your caravan, you can park your car on the car park not far from the touring pitch. The campsite is also very suitable as a stopover campsite for people headed to the south of Spain. Ask reception about the extra discounts for a longer stay.

🚗 On A7 exit Bétera, then follow signs.

Rafelbunyol
CC
A-7
Paterna

CC € **15** 15/5-30/6 15/9-30/9

📍 N 39°34'46'' W 0°26'44''

Bigastro/Alicante, E-03380 / Comunidad Valenciana

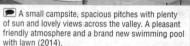

2833

🛖 La Pedrera*
📧 Cañada de Andrea 100
☎ +34 966-183020
📅 1/1 - 31/12
@ info@campinglapedrera.com

4,4ha 46T(50-185m²) 16A

1 ABCDGIJKLMOPST
2 BJKLSUVWX
3 AB**F**GHJNR
4 (B+G 1/5-31/10) KP
(Q+R+T+U+V+X+Y+Z 🔲)
5 **AB**DFGIJKLMNOPUWXY
6 ABCDEGJK(N 2km)OPTV

💬 A small campsite, spacious pitches with plenty of sun and lovely views across the valley. A pleasant friendly atmosphere and a brand new swimming pool with lawn (2014).

🚗 AP7, exit 740. 1st roundabout dir. Orihuela (CV921). 2nd roundabout dir. Benejúzar. 3rd roundabout dir. Jacarilla. In Jacarilla dir. Bigastro. Follow camping signs in Biagastro.

Cox
A-7 N-340
Orihuela
El Raal CC
AP-7

CC € **17** 1/1-24/3 2/4-5/7 27/8-31/12 7=6

📍 N 38°3'4'' W 0°53'54''

Càlig/Castellon, E-12589 / Comunidad Valenciana

♿ 🛜

2834

🛖 L'Orangeraie Cat. 2
📧 Camino Peñiscola-Calig
☎ +34 964-765059
📅 1/3 - 31/10
@ info@camping-lorangeraie.es

1,8ha 62T(70-140m²) 6-16A CEE

1 BCDFIJKLMPST
2 FJKLRVX
3 BFGR
4 (B+G 🔲) J
(Q+R+T+U+Z 28/3-15/10)
5 **AB**FGIJKLMNOPUZ
6 AEGK(N 1km)T

💬 A top-quality campsite in a lovely setting 10 km from the beach. Perfect amenities. Set among orange and olive groves in a botanical garden. Free wifi, lovely swimming pool/jacuzzi. Run by Patricia and Laurent, a hospitable French couple. Wonderfully peaceful.

🚗 AP7 take exit 43 Benicarlo-Peñiscola. 1st right at roundabout to Càlig, then follow signs. From N340 St. Mateu-Calig exit and follow the signs.

N-232 N-238
Vinaròs
CC AP-7 N-340
Benicarló

CC € **17** 1/3-6/7 27/8-30/10 10=9, 30=24

📍 N 40°27'7'' E 0°21'8''

Calpe/Alicante, E-03710 / Comunidad Valenciana

♿ 🛜 iD

2835

🛖 CalpeMar Cat. 1
📧 C/ Eslovenia, 3
📠 +34 965-875576
📅 1/1 - 31/12
@ info@campingcalpemar.com

1ha 107T(54-125m²) 10A CEE

1 ABCDGIJKLMO**PQ**
2 AEFGSUVWXY
3 AFGNRUWY
4 (A 1/1-30/4,1/10-31/12)
(B+Q+T+X+Z 🔲)
5 **AB**DFGIJKLMNOPUWXY
6 ABEG**IK**(N 0,45km)OTV

💬 A modern, small-scale campsite on the edge of Calpe within walking distance of the sea, beaches, restaurants and supermarket. Perfect for sun worshippers. Views of Calpe and the famous (Peñon Ifach) rocks.

🚗 AP7, exit 64 to N332 dir. Calpe. Exit Calpe Norte 800m. Straight on. Turn left at Mercadona to large roundabout with artwork. Then straight on through 2nd roundabout with artwork. Then left and follow camping signs.

Benitachell
Calp
Ap-7 CC
Altea
N-332

CC € **19** 1/1-30/6 1/9-31/12

📍 N 38°38'42'' E 0°3'22''

Crevillente/Alicante, E-03330 / Comunidad Valenciana   ♿ 🛜 iD   2836

🏕 Camping Internacional
Las Palmeras****
✉ Partida Deula 75
☎ +34 96-6680630
📅 1/1 - 31/12
@ laspalmeras@
laspalmeras-sl.com

1ha 51T(70-120m²) 10A CEE

1 ABCGIJLOQ
2 FSUVWXY
4 (B+G+Q+T+X+Y+Z ⊙)
5 ABDFGIJKLMNOPUWXYZ
6 ABEGIK(N 0,3km)ORTV

💬 Small campsite behind a hotel, lots of flowers. Excellent and very clean toilet facilities. Beautiful pool with sun loungers under palms. Bar and restaurant are good and affordable. Also ideal as a stopover campsite. Register at hotel reception.

🚐 AP7, exit 77 direction Crevillente. Then towards N340. Campsite on this road at 708 km marker. Behind hotel Las Palmeras.

CC € 17   1/1-28/3   3/4-7/7   25/8-31/12   7=6   📷 N 38°14'26'' W 0°48'42''

Crevillente/Alicante, E-03330 / Comunidad Valenciana   ♿ 🛜 iD   2837

🏕 Marjal Costa Blanca
Camping & Resort*****
✉ Partida de las Casicas, 5
☎ +34 965-484945
📅 1/1 - 31/12
@ reservas@marjal.com

35ha 1202T(90-180m²) 16A

1 ABCD**G**IJKLMOPQ
2 FGLSTUVWX
3 BCF**G**HJKL**MN**QR**UV**
4 (A+B+**F**+H ⊙) IJ**KLNOP**
(Q+S+T+U+V ⊙)
(W 24/6-3/9) (X+Y+Z ⊙)
5 **AB**CDEFGHIJKLMNOPQRU
WXYZ
6 ABCDGH**IJ**K**M**(N 1km)ORS
TUVWX

💬 A very complete, luxurious campsite for long or short stays. Comfortable pitches with all amenities. The most important towns are not far away. Friendly ambiance in the main square with terraces and fountains. Seeing is believing. You will come again.

🚐 AP-7 Alicante-Cartagena, exit 730. Follow camping signs.

CC € 19   1/1-28/3   2/4-28/6   9/9-31/10   4/11-27/12   📷 N 38°10'44'' W 0°48'30''

Cullera/Valencia, E-46400 / Comunidad Valenciana   ♿ 🛜 iD   2838

🏕 Santa Marta****
✉ Avinguda Raço, 25
☎ +34 96-1721440
📅 15/1 - 15/12
@ info@santamartacamping.com

4ha 146T(25-80m²) 10A

1 ABCD**G**IJLP
2 ABEGIJLTUVWXY
3 AKNRUY
4 (B+G 10/6-10/9)
(Q+R 28/3-9/4,15/6-9/9)
(T+V+X+Z 15/6-9/9)
5 **AB**DFGIJKLMNOPUWXYZ
6 AEG**K**(N 1km)RTV

💬 An attractive campsite at the foot of a mountain slope with the scent of pine trees. The beach is 300 metres away. There are sunny pitches for those staying through the winter. Campsite is close to the town.

🚐 AP7, exit 59 N332 after km post 252 towards Cullera. Follow Cullera platges far signs, then far or faro (lighthouse) signs. Campsite on small roundabout on the right.

CC € 15   15/1-28/3   3/4-15/6   10/9-14/12   📷 N 39°10'37'' W 0°14'31''

Daimús/Valencia, E-46710 / Comunidad Valenciana

👪 ♿ 🛜 🆔 (2839)

🔺 L'Aventura
📧 Ctra Playa Daimús s/n
☎ +34 962-818330
🔓 1/1 - 31/12
@ info@campinglaventuraplaya.com

1,8ha 130T(60-65m²) 6-10A

1 ABCDGIJLQ
2 BFSVXY
3 AFKU
4 (B+G 1/6-15/9)
   (Q+T+X+Z 🔒)
5 ABFGIJKLMNOPUWZ
6 ABFGK(N 0,1km)OTV

💬 Campsite is 600 metres from the beach. Deciduous trees offer plenty of shade in summer and sufficient sun in winter. Brand-new toilet block (2016).

🚗 Route A7 Salida 60 to Gandía on the N332. Continue to Grao de Gandía. Then towards Daimús. In Daimús left at 2nd roundabout. Campsite about 300 metres on the right.

Simat de la Valldigna

Gandia
CC
AP-7
Oliva

CC € ⑮ 1/1-28/3 3/4-15/6 1/9-31/12 15=10   🧭 N 38°58'25'' W 0°9'3''

El Campello/Alicante, E-03560 / Comunidad Valenciana

♿ 🛜 🆔 (2840)

🔺 Costa Blanca***
📧 C./Convento 143, N332 km 120,5
☎ +34 965-630670
🔓 1/1 - 31/12
@ info@campingcostablanca.com

1,1ha 66T(40-80m²) 6-25A CEE

1 ABCDGIJLOP
2 FGUVXY
3 AFGUV
4 (B+Q+T+U+V+X+Y+Z 🔒)
5 ABDFGIJKLMNOPUWXY
6 ACEGK(N 1,2km)ORTV

💬 Small-scale campsite. Spotlessly clean toilets, very tidy grounds. Agreeable ambiance and friendly staff who will be happy to help you get your caravan onto the pitch (can be difficult for larger caravans). Conveniently located between Benidorm and Alicante. Close to beach (800 metres), swimming in lovely pool (open all year).

🚗 AP7 exit 67. Right at 1st roundabout after toll booths, 2nd right, 3rd roundabout straight on, right at 4th roundabout. Follow camping signs.

Ap-7
CC
San Vicente Del Raspeig
Alicante

CC € ⑰ 1/1-25/3 1/4-13/7 31/8-31/12   🧭 N 38°26'10'' W 0°23'17''

El Campello/Alicante, E-03560 / Comunidad Valenciana

👪 ♿ 🛜 🆔 (2841)

🔺 El Jardin
📧 Doctor Severo Ochoa 39
☎ +34 965-657580
🔓 1/1 - 31/12
@ info@campingeljardin.com

1ha 120T(70-80m²) 10-16A

1 ABCDGIJKLMOPST
2 FGSUVX
3 AFG
4 (B+G 20/3-31/10) (Q 🔒)
   (T 12/4-23/4,1/7-31/8)
   (X+Z 🔒)
5 ABFGIJKLMNOPUWXY
6 ABCDEGJK(N 0,6km)OSTV

💬 A small-scale campsite in a pretty and quiet village close to the sea (600 metres). Located on the Costa Blanca. The very friendly wardens are at the service of campers throughout the year. Very clean toilet facilities.

🚗 A7, then A70 exit 67 to N332 dir. San Joan. Dir. playas/platges at first roundabout to the beach. Then left. Left again at camping sign and straight on. Campsite on dead end road.

N-332
A-7 AP-7
San Vicente Del Raspeig
CC
A-70
Alicante

CC € ⑰ 1/1-27/3 3/4-18/6 25/6-8/7 27/8-31/12 10=9   🧭 N 38°23'35'' W 0°24'55''

El Saler/Valencia, E-46012 / Comunidad Valenciana   ♿ 🛜 (2842)

🏕 Camping Valencia el Saler
✉ Carrera del Riu 552
☎ +34 961-830212
🗓 1/1 - 31/12
@ campingvalencia1981@
  hotmail.com

50T(50-74m²) 10A CEE

1 BCDGIJKLMOPQ
2 ABEFGLTVX
3 ABFGHJKNRY
4 (A+B+G 🔒) P
  (Q+R+T+U+X+Y+Z 🔒)
5 ABEFGIJKLMNOPUWXZ
6 EGK(N 0,4km)RTV

💬 Campsite with 50 camping pitches, reasonably quiet location at 7 km from Valencia centre, which is easily accessible by bus or bike. About 200 metres from the sea and near nature park Albufera.

🚗 From north A7 and V21 to Valencia, in town take dir El Saler. On CV500 left on roundabout to CV5010, campsite on left after 300 metres. From south A7 before Valencia to Albufera and El Saler on CV500, take exit on El Saler roundabout. Site after 200 metres.

Valencia
Torrent

CC
A-7

CC € ⑮ 1/1-8/7   26/8-31/12   📍 N 39°23'16'' W 0°19'55''

El Saler/Valencia, E-46012 / Comunidad Valenciana   ♿ 🛜 iD (2843)

🏕 Devesa Gardens Resort
✉ Ctra de El Saler km 13
☎ FAX +34 961-611136
🗓 1/1 - 31/12
@ info@devesagardens.com

6,9ha 87T(84-96m²) 16A

1 ABCDGIJLOPQ
2 CDGLSUVWXY
3 BCDFGKMNORU
4 (B+G 19/3-12/10) IJ
  (Q+S+T+V+X+Y+Z 🔒)
5 ABDFGIKMNOPUW
6 ABEGK(N 5km)OTV

💬 Very well-maintained grounds with two completely renovated toilet blocks. Surprisingly large meadows for relaxing by a beautiful pool with little groups of trees. Very suitable for a visit to Valencia. Bus stop in front of the campsite with a bus every half hour. Renovated bar and restaurant.

🚗 From north: A7 and V21 to Valencia. Direction El Saler (CV500) in town. Campsite south of El Saler on the CV500 at kilometre sign 13.

Albal

A-7
AP-7   A-38

CC
El Perellonet

CC € ⑲ 1/1-14/3   19/3-27/3   2/4-25/4   2/5-21/6   2/9-30/12   7=6, 14=11   📍 N 39°19'23'' W 0°18'35''

Grau de Gandía, E-46730 / Comunidad Valenciana   ♿ 🛜 iD (2844)

🏕 L'Alquería
✉ Avda del Grau, 142
☎ +34 96-2840470
FAX +34 96-2841063
🗓 1/1 - 31/12
@ lalqueria@lalqueria.com

4,4ha 123T(70-80m²) 10A

1 ABCDGIJKLOPQ
2 AFGSUVXY
3 ARV
4 (B 1/6-30/9)
  (D 1/1-31/5,1/10-31/12)
  (G 1/6-30/9) KLNP
  (Q+R+S 🔒)
  (T+V+X+Z 16/3-9/10)
5 ABEFGIJKLMNOPUWXYZ
6 AGK(N 0,3km)ORTV

💬 Campsite under various types of trees. Lovely swimming pool with plenty of deck chairs, covered and heated out of season. Cycle routes to the beach, the town and the surroundings and also guided cycle tours in the winter months. No dogs on the dangerous breeds list and no dogs weighing more than 10 kg.

🚗 AP7, exit 60 to N332. After 3.1 km turn onto N337. Then take the first right on each of the four roundabouts. Campsite 300m on the left.

Tavernes De La Valldigna
N-332

Ap-7 CC
Gandía
Oliva

CC € ⑲ 1/1-28/3   3/4-30/6   1/9-20/12   7=6, 14=11   📍 N 38°59'10'' W 0°9'49''

Guardamar del Segura/Alicante, E-03140 / Comunidad Valenciana

🚻 📶 ⚙ **iD** (2845)

🏕 Marjal Guardamar Camping & Resort*****
📍 Ctra N332 km 73,4
☎ +34 96-5484945
📠 +34 96-6726695
🔓 1/1 - 31/12
@ reservas@marjal.com
4ha 120T(90m²) 16A

1 ABCD**G**IJKLMOP
2 CFLSTUVWX
3 B**CF**GHJKM**N**QRUV
4 (**A**+B+E 🔓) IJKMNP
(Q+S+T+U+V 🔓)
(W 18/6-4/9) (X+Y+Z 🔓)
5 **AB**CDFGHIJKLMNOPUWXYZ
6 ABGH**IJK**M(N 2km)ORSTUVW

💬 A spacious campsite with large pitches. Sunny in winter and in the early and late seasons. Large outdoor swimming pool and heated indoor pool. Lovely sunny terrace. Wifi and fitness included in the price. Excursions to Elche (palm gardens), Alicante and Guardamar.

🚗 A70, exit 72. From the N332 turn off at roundabout between the villages of La Marina and Guardamar. Campsite clearly signposted.

Santa Pola · Almoradí

CC € ⑲ 1/1-28/3 2/4-14/6 9/9-31/10 4/11-27/12 · N 38°6'33'' W 0°39'18''

Jávea/Alicante, E-03730 / Comunidad Valenciana

🚻 📶 **iD** (2846)

🏕 El Naranjal
📍 Cami dels Morers 15
☎ +34 96-5792989
📠 +34 96-6460256
🔓 1/1 - 31/12
@ info@campingelnaranjal.com

2,3ha 164T(30-60m²) 10A

1 ACDGIJKLOPQ
2 SUVXY
3 A**FGMQ**RUV
4 (B 15/5-30/9) (Q 1/4-11/9)
(T 24/3-16/9) (U 1/4-11/9)
(V+X+Z 24/3-16/9)
5 **AB**DFGIJKLMNOPUZ
6 ACEG**K**(N 1km)ORTV

💬 Very-well maintained campsite with excellent and clean toilet facilities. 3 km from the centre of Jávea, but just 600 metres from a shopping area with small restaurants, bars, beach and promenade. Modern amenities for campers.

🚗 AP7, exit 62 to the N332. Exit Jávea. Enter Jávea. Drive straight on at roundabout. At Arenal-Platges and Cap de la Nao signs turn right. Then follow signs.

Dénia · Jávea

CC € ⑲ 1/1-26/3 3/4-8/7 27/8-31/12 · N 38°46'14'' E 0°10'55''

Jávea/Alicante, E-03730 / Comunidad Valenciana

🚻 📶 **iD** (2847)

🏕 Jávea Cat.1
📍 Camino de la Fontana, 10
☎ +34 96-5791070
🔓 1/1 - 31/12
@ info@campingjavea.es

2,5ha 193T(40-80m²) 8-16A

1 ABCDGIJKLMOPQ
2 LSTUVWXY
3 A**FGM**NRU
4 (B+G 15/4-15/10) (Q 🔓)
(R+T+U+V+X+Z 9/1-31/8,
11/9-31/12)
5 **AB**DEFGIJKLMNOPUWXYZ
6 ABEGH**K**(N 0,8km)ORTV

💬 Situated next to an orange tree plantation. View of the Montgo Mountain and the historic town centre of Jávea. Cycling to the local supermarket, village or beach (El Arenal about 2.5 km).

🚗 AP7, exit 62 naar N332. Exit Jávea. Drive into Jávea. Straight on at roundabout. Follow signs Arenal/Platges and Cap de la Nao. After McDonalds, Euromarkt take bridge across (dried up) river. Sharp right onto side road. Follow camping signs.

Dénia · Gata De Gorgos · Jávea

CC € ⑲ 1/1-27/3 2/4-6/7 27/8-31/12 · N 38°47'1'' E 0°10'20''

La Vall de Laguar/Alicante, E-03791 / Comunidad Valenciana

🔼 Vall de Laguar
📧 Carrer Sant Antoni, 24
☎ 🖶 +34 96-5584590
📅 1/1 - 31/12
@ info@campinglaguar.com

📶 iD (2848)

1,7ha 39T(50-120m²) 6A

1 ABCD**G**IJKLNOPQ
2 GJKSTUVX
3 H
4 (B+G 15/5-31/10)
(X+Z 1/7-31/8)
5 **AB**DFGJLMNOPUWXYZ
6 ABEGK(N 0,3km)ORTV

💬 A small, peacefully located terraced campsite with lovely views of the village, the Montgo mountain and the sea (about 10 km as the crow flies). A place to relax and stay for a long time. A good base for walking in the mountains. Very friendly, helpful management.

🚗 AP7, exit 62 direction Ondara/Valencia (N332). On Ondara bypass find CV731 towards Orba-Benidoleig-Vall de Laguar. In Campell follow camping signs.

Pego · El Verger · Pedreguer · CC · AP-7

CC € **⑲** 1/1-15/3 9/4-14/7 1/9-4/10 15/10-31/12

📍 N 38°46'36'' W 0°6'19''

Mareny de Barraquetes/Sueca, E-46410 / Comunidad Valenciana

♿ 📶 iD (2849)

🔼 Barraquetes
📧 Ctra Nazaret-Oliva km 25
☎ +34 961-760723
🖶 +34 961-760130
📅 15/1 - 15/12
@ info@barraquetes.com

3,7ha 113T(40-65m²) 20A

1 ABCD**G**IJKLMOPR
2 BGSVXY
3 AMNU
4 (B 14/6-1/9) (G 24/6-1/9) J
(Q+R+V+X+Z 23/6-1/9)
5 **AB**FGIKMOPUVXZ
6 CDEG**K**(N 0,4km)OTV

💬 Relaxation and space. For nature lovers: the beach and Albufera nature reserve with a wide variety of native trees and plants. Rice fields and picturesque villages in the area.

🚗 A7 exit Sueca N332. Then exit to Perelló/Mareny de Barraquetes. Then follow camping signs.

Benifaió · A-38 · CC · Sueca · AP-7 · Cullera

CC € **⑮** 15/1-15/6 8/9-14/12 7=5, 14=10

📍 N 39°14'31'' W 0°15'50''

Moncofa, E-12593 / Comunidad Valenciana

📶 (2850)

🔼 Los Naranjos****
📧 Cami de Cabres
☎ +34 964-580337
📅 1/1 - 31/12
@ info@campinglosnaranjos.com

185T(60-130m²) 10A CEE

1 BCDGIJKLMOPST
2 AEFNTUVY
3 BCGHJKNRWY
4 (B+G 18/6-11/9)
(Q+R+T+U+V+X+Y+Z 📅)
5 **AB**DEFGIJKLMNOPRSTUX
YZ
6 DEGJ**K**(N 2km)OQRTV

💬 Medium-sized campsite, 300 metres from a sandy and pebble beach. 2 km from Moncofa.

🚗 N340 exit Moncofa. AP-7 exit 49 Moncofa, A7 exit Vall d'Uxo and then Moncofa, in Moncofa right onto ring road and follow signs.

La Vall d'Uixó · AP-7 · CC · A-7 · Sagunto

CC € **⑮** 1/1-28/3 10/4-24/6 10/9-31/12 11=10, 21=19, 30=27

📍 N 39°46'53'' W 0°8'56''

Moncofa/Castellón, E-12593 / Comunidad Valenciana

2851

- ⛺ Camping Mon Mar Cat.2
- ✉ Camino Serratelles s/n
- ☎ FAX +34 964-588592
- 🔓 1/1 - 31/12
- @ monmarcamping@gmail.com

2ha 110T(70m²) 6-10A

1 BCDEIJKLMPQ
2 AEFGNUVXY
3 BCGJMNRUWY
4 (B+G 🔓) IM
(Q+R+T+U+X+Y+Z 🔓)
5 ABDFGIJKLMNOPUWXYZ
6 ACDEGJK(N 0,3km)ORTV

💬 Ideal for Valencia (45 km) with monuments, science park, modern architecture, aquarium, museums, botanical garden, festivals, opera! Cycling. Orange plantations and vineyards. Visit the underwater caves at San Josep.

🚗 A7 exit 49 dir. Moncofa. In Moncofa follow 'Camping Mon Mar' signs. A7 exit 283 Moncofa. Then follow 'Camping Mon Mar' signs. On the N340 exit Moncofa between 950 and 953 km markers. In Moncofa follow 'Camping Mon Mar' signs.

Borriana — La Vall D'Uixó — Ap-7 — A-7

CC € 17 1/1-27/3 9/4-29/6 3/9-31/12 7=6, 10=8, 20=15, 30=22 | 📍 N 39°48'31'' W 0°7'40''

Moraira/Alicante, E-03724 / Comunidad Valenciana

iD 2852

- ⛺ Moraira Cat.1
- ✉ Camíno Paellero 50, Teulada
- ☎ +34 96-5745249
- 🔓 1/3 - 31/10
- @ campingmoraira.info@gmail.com

1,1ha 105T(50-90m²) 10A

1 ABCDGIJLP
2 EFJKSTUVXY
3 FU
4 (B+Q+T+V+X+Z 🔓)
5 ABDFGIJKLMNOPUWXYZ
6 AEGK(N 1,2km)ORT

💬 Small, terraced campsite with a pleasant ambiance by a hill under fir trees. Lovely views of the swimming pool and sea from some of the pitches, certainly from the terrace. Close to town (shops) and beach. Possibility for trips out into the area.

🚗 From the N332 exit towards Moraira. In Moraira turn right at the roundabout. Follow the camping signs. Clearly signposted. Take care: turn right towards the campsite immediately after passing the restaurant, not before.

Benitachell — Benissa — Ap-7 — N-332 — Calp

CC € 17 8/3-22/3 3/4-29/6 3/9-28/10 7=6 | 📍 N 38°41'9'' E 0°7'10''

Navajas (Castellón), E-12470 / Comunidad Valenciana

2853

- ⛺ Altomira Cat.1
- ✉ CV-213 Navajas, km 1
- ☎ +34 964-713211
- 🔓 1/1 - 31/12
- @ reservas@campingaltomira.com

2,5ha 50T(70-80m²) 6A

1 BCDGIJKLMOPQ
2 FGJKTUVWX
3 BGHJLMNRUW
4 (A 1/7-31/8)
(B+G 15/6-15/9)
(Q+R+U+X+Y+Z 🔓)
5 ABDFGIJKLMNOPUWXYZ
6 AEGJK(N 0,3km)PTV

💬 A beautiful campsite located in the hills with panoramic views. Just 20 km from the Mediterranean. Good for walking and cycling. A direct train connection to the beautiful city of Valencia. Natural, mineral springs with health-giving water in the area. Good swimming pool and restaurant. Lovely cycling opportunities along a former narrow-gauge railway line.

🚗 On the A23 Sagunto-Teruel, at the exit 33 Navajas. Then follow the campingsigns.

A-23 — Vall De Almonacid — CC — Segorbe — Altura

CC € 17 1/1-25/3 10/4-30/6 1/9-31/12 7=6, 14=12, 30=21 | 📍 N 39°52'29'' W 0°30'38''

Oliva/Valencia, E-46780 / Comunidad Valenciana ♿ 🛜 iD (2854)

△ Azul
▤ Playa Rabdells
☎ +34 96-2854106
FAX +34 96-2854096
⌕ 1/3 - 31/10
@ info@campingazul.com

2,5ha 109T(60-100m²) 10A

1 ABCDGIJKLPQ
2 AEFKSUVWXY
3 AFGKRWY
4 (Q+R+T+U+V+X+Z ⌕)
5 **AB**DFGIJKLMNOPUWZ
6 CEGI**K**(N 5km)ORT

💬 Among flowering oleanders, next to a beach. Homely, natural campsite with a chance to cycle through orange groves. Friendly atmosphere. Lovely new showers and washbasins (2016).

🚗 North: on the N332, exit at the 213 km marker. Left under viaduct at 1st roundabout. Right at 2nd roundabout then 3rd road on left (Playa Rabdells). South: on the N332 at the 209 km marker exit at service station (go under viaduct). Keep right after the service station and follow camping signs.

Map: Gandia, Oliva, Ap-7 CC, N-332, Pego

CC € **17** 1/3-28/3 2/4-30/6 1/9-30/10   🏕 N 38°54'27'' W 0°4'4''

Oliva/Valencia, E-46780 / Comunidad Valenciana ♿ 🛜 iD (2855)

△ Eurocamping
▤ Partida Rabdells s/n
☎ +34 96-2854098
FAX +34 96-2851753
⌕ 1/1 - 31/12
@ info@eurocamping-es.com

4,5ha 299T(70-120m²) 6-10A

1 ABCDG IJKLMPQ
2 ACEFKSTUVWXY
3 AFGWY
4 (Q+R+T+U+X+Y+Z ⌕)
5 **AB**DFGIJKLMNOPUWZ
6 ABEG**K**(N 5km)ORTV

💬 A campsite right on sandy beach. Ideal for beach lovers. Very clean grounds and excellent toilet facilities. Very accessible for caravans and motorhomes. Reception closed between 14:00 and 16:00. Normal camping rate applies to pitches in the dunes.

🚗 From the north: on the N332, at the km-marker 210, turn towards the sea (across the viaduct). From the south: on the N332, at the km-marker 209, turn right. Signposted before and at the roundabout. Follow camping signs.

Map: Gandia, Oliva, AP-7 CC, N-332, Els Poblets

CC € **17** 1/1-28/3 9/4-30/6 1/9-31/12   🏕 N 38°54'22'' W 0°4'2''

Oliva/Valencia, E-46780 / Comunidad Valenciana ♿ 🛜 iD (2856)

△ Kiko Park Cat.1
▤ C/. Assagador de Carro, 2
☎ +34 96-2850905
FAX +34 96-2854320
⌕ 1/1 - 31/12
@ kikopark@kikopark.com

2,9ha 170T(60-110m²) 16A CEE

1 ACDG IJKLMOPQ
2 AEFGSTUVWXY
3 FKVWY
4 (C+H ⌕) **KLNP**
  (Q+S+U+V+Y+Z ⌕)
5 **AB**DFGIJKLMNOPUWXYZ
6 ABCEGI**K**M(N 0,5km)ORTV

💬 An international, floral campsite situated right next to the sea with a lovely sandy beach, perfect restaurant, large terrace and a tropical bar with sea views. Cycling and walking opportunities in the area. Enlarged with a lovely swimming pool and wellness centre. Also take away meals.

🚗 Motorway AP7, exit 61. Take the N332 to Oliva. Turn left at the first roundabout/traffic lights. Then follow 'Platges' and campsite signs.

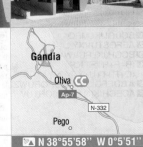

Map: Gandia, Oliva CC, Ap-7, N-332, Pego

CC € **19** 1/1-27/3 3/4-14/6 1/9-31/12   🏕 N 38°55'58'' W 0°5'51''

Oliva/Valencia, E-46780 / Comunidad Valenciana ♿ 📶 **iD** (2857)

Olé★★★★
Pda. Aigua Morta s/n
☎ +34 96-2857517
FAX +34 96-2857516
☀ 1/1 - 31/12
@ camping-ole@camping-ole.com

4,2ha 314T(50-90m²) 6A

1 ACD**G**IJKLMOP**Q**
2 AEKSUVWXY
3 A**F**GNUWY
4 (B 1/7-31/8) (Q ☀)
(S 29/3-2/4,1/7-31/8)
(U+V+X+Y+Z 15/3-15/12)
5 **AB**DFGIJKLMNOPUWXYZ
6 ABCEG**K**(N 5km)ORTV

A campsite right on the beach with fine white sand. Extensive views of the sea and beach. Great for beach walkers. Cycling opportunities. Excursions to Denia and inland. CampingCard ACSI not accepted for pitches on the beach.

When approaching from the north: on the N332 at km-marker 210 turn towards the sea (over the viaduct). When approaching from the south: on the N332 at the km-marker 209 turn right. Signposted before and at the roundabout. Follow camping signs.

Gandia
Oliva
AP-7 CC
Els Poblets
N-332

CC € **19** 1/1-28/3 3/4-30/6 1/9-31/12 | N 38°53'40'' W 0°3'13''

Oliva/Valencia, E-46780 / Comunidad Valenciana ♿ 📶 **iD** (2858)

Rio-Mar★★★
N332 km 207
☎ +34 96-2854097
FAX +34 96-2839132
☀ 1/1 - 31/12
@ riomar@campingriomar.com

0,8ha 64T(50-80m²) 6-10A

1 ABCD**G**IJKLPQ
2 ACEFKSUVWXY
3 **F**WY
4 (Q+S ☀)
(T+U+X+Z 5/1-5/12)
5 **AB**DFGIJKLMNOPUWZ
6 EGK(N 7km)ORTV

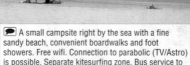

A small campsite right by the sea with a fine sandy beach, convenient boardwalks and foot showers. Free wifi. Connection to parabolic (TV/Astro) is possible. Separate kitesurfing zone. Bus service to Denia six times a day and once a week to the market in Oliva. Also easy to cycle there.

AP7, exit 61 direction Oliva or N332 Valencia-Alicante at km marker 207 direction beach and sea, follow signs to the campsite.

Gandia
Oliva
Ap-7
CC
N-332 Dénia

CC € **17** 1/1-8/7 26/8-31/12 | N 38°53'10'' W 0°2'20''

Oropesa del Mar (Castellón), E-12594 / Comunidad Valenciana ♿ 📶 (2859)

Didota S.L. Cat.1
Avda Barcelona /
Vereda Didota s/n
☎ +34 964-319551
FAX +34 964-319847
☀ 1/1 - 31/12
@ info@campingdidota.es

1,6ha 144T(90-120m²) 6-10A

1 BCDGIJKLMPQ
2 AEFGSTUVXY
3 BCGHJKLRUVWY
4 (B+F+H ☀) **K**P
(Q+R+T+U+X+Y ☀)
5 **AB**DEFGIJKLMNOPQRUWZ
6 ACEGHIK(N 0,5km)ORTUV

A beautiful campsite by the beach. Lovely outdoor swimming pools, heated indoor pool with bubble bath and jacuzzi. Pitches with plenty of sun, pitches in summer with shade. Good restaurant and renovated toilet facilities. Plenty of opportunities in low season for dance evenings with live music, flamenco, Spanish lessons, bingo and tennis.

A7, exit 45. Or on the N340 Tarragona-Valencia turn off at 999,2 km sign towards the sea. Follow camping signs (about 1 km).

N-340
CC
Oropesa Del Mar
Ap-7
Benicàssim

CC € **15** 1/1-9/7 27/8-31/12 7=6, 15=12, 30=22, 45=30 | N 40°7'16'' E 0°9'30''

Peñíscola, E-12598 / Comunidad Valenciana   ♿ 🛜 (2860)

- 🏔 El Edén Cat.1
- 📧 Calle Madrid 6
- ☎ +34 964-480562
- 📠 +34 964-489828
- 🔓 1/1 - 31/12
- @ camping@camping-eden.com

3,3ha 254T(60-100m²) 10A

1 BCD**G**IJKLMPQ
2 AEFGLSTVXY
3 BGHJKRUWY
4 (B+G 20/3-15/10) JK(Q 🔌)
  (T+U+X+Y+Z 20/1-31/12)
5 **AB**DEFGIJKLMNOPUWXYZ
6 ABCEGJ**K**M(N 0,8km)OQRT
  V

💬 An attractive large campsite 50 metres from the boulevard and Peñiscola beach with a lovely swimming pool and a good restaurant. Good walking, cycling and watersports opportunities.

🚗 A7 exit 43 to Peñiscola. Campsite signposted on the boulevard. Take Peñiscola exit on the N340. Continue on boulevard to Benicarlo. Campsite located 6 km on Avenida Papa Luna. There is a sign before the El Edén restaurant/campsite.

Vinaròs
Benicarló
AP-7 CC
N-340

CC €19 1/1-28/3 2/4-22/6 9/9-31/12 8=7, 16=14, 24=21   📍 N 40°22'16'' E 0°24'10''

Peñíscola, E-12598 / Comunidad Valenciana   ♿ 🛜 iD (2861)

- 🏔 Los Pinos SL Cat.1
- 📧 Camino Abellers, s/n
- ☎ 📠 +34 964-480379
- 🔓 1/1 - 31/12
- @ campinglospinos@hotmail.com

1,2ha 120T(80-120m²) 10A

1 ACGIJKLMOPST
2 FSTVY
3 ABF GHJNRU
4 (B+G 🔌) K
  (Q+R+T+U+X+Y+Z 🔌)
5 **AB**DEFGHIJKLMNOPQRU
  WXYZ
6 ACDEGK(N 1,5km)ORTV

💬 A medium sized family campsite with a nice swimming pool, jacuzzi, good restaurant and free wifi. 1.5 km from Peñiscola with a lovely long promenade and a beautiful sandy beach. The former castle of pope 'Papa Luna' can also be viewed here.

🚗 A7, exit 43 Peñiscola, drive for 4 km towards Peñiscola then the campsite is signposted.

Benicarló
AP-7 CC
N-340

CC €13 1/1-27/3 3/4-20/6 1/9-31/12   📍 N 40°22'45'' E 0°23'18''

Peñíscola, E-12598 / Comunidad Valenciana   🛜 (2862)

- 🏔 Sol d'Or
- 📧 Avenida de la Estación, 137
- ☎ +34 964-480653
- 📠 +34 964-467583
- 🔓 1/1 - 31/12
- @ info@campingsoldor.com

1ha 164T(60-100m²) 10A

1 BCDGIJKLMOPQ
2 AFGRVWXY
3 B**F**GNRUW
4 (B+G 1/5-30/9)
  (Q+T+U+V+X+Y+Z 🔌)
5 **AB**DFGHIJKLMNOPUZ
6 EGJK(N 1km)ORTVWX

💬 Campsite Sol d'Or is 1.5 km from the sandy beach of Peñiscola, has good toilet facilities, spacious camping pitches and a good restaurant.

🚗 AP1 exit 43 to N340 dir. Peñiscola, campsite located on right of this road before town.

Benicarló
AP-7 CC
N-340

CC €13 1/1-28/3 2/4-15/6 15/9-31/12   📍 N 40°22'50'' E 0°23'9''

Peñíscola, E-12598 / Comunidad Valenciana

⚐ Vizmar Cat. 2
✉ Ctra Vieja Peñíscola-Benicarló s/n
☎ FAX +34 964-473439
⌚ 1/1 - 31/12
@ campingvizmar@hotmail.com

1,6ha 138T(60-70m²) 6A

1 BCDGIJLMPQ
2 EFGTUVXY
3 BGRWY
4 (B+G 1/6-30/9) (Q+R+T ⌂)
(U+X+Y 1/7-31/8)
(Z 1/6-30/9)
5 ABFGIJKLMNOPUZ
6 ACEGJK(N 1km)OTV

💬 A campsite with reasonable toilet facilities. Plenty of shaded pitches, but sunny pitches also available. Campsite about 400m from the lovely beach and boulevard at Peñíscola, famous for the Papa Luna castle.

🚗 On N340 exit at Peñíscola sign. Towards Benicarlo at roundabout. Campsite ± 2 km on the left.

🏕 N 40°23'32'' E 0°24'25''

♿ 📶 **2863**

Vinaròs
N-340
Benicarló
AP-7 CC

CC €**11** 1/1-27/3 2/4-30/6 1/9-31/12

Pilar de la Horadada/Alicante, E-03191 / Comunidad Valenciana

⚐ Lo Monte****
✉ Avda Comunidad Valenciana, 157
☎ +34 966-766782
FAX +34 966-746536
⌚ 1/1 - 31/12
@ info@campinglomonte.com

7,2ha 205T(60-125m²) 16A CEE

1 ABCDGIJKLMOP
2 FGLTUVW
3 AFGHJKUV
4 (B 1/6-30/9) (F ⌂)
(G 1/6-30/9) KP
(Q+R+T+U+V+X+Y+Z ⌂)
5 ABDFGIJKLMNOPUWXY
6 ABCEGJK(N 0,5km)ORTUV

💬 Spaciously appointed campsite. Beautiful, stylish building including a spa and fitness. Attractive terrace overlooking the swimming pools. Recommended for the whole year. Indoor and outdoor pools are also suitable for people with a disability as there is a plastic wheelchair.

🚗 AP7, exit 770 to N332 direction Pilar de la Horadada. Towards Pueblo Latino at 2nd roundabout. Left at 1st traffic lights.

♿ 📶 iD **2864**

Torrevieja
CC
AP-7

🏕 N 37°52'45'' W 0°45'56''

CC €**17** 3/4-26/4 3/5-28/6 3/9-4/10 15/10-30/10

Playa de Puçol, E-46530 / Comunidad Valenciana

⚐ Camping Valencia***
✉ c/ Rio Turia 1
☎ +34 961-465806
⌚ 15/3 - 9/12
@ info@campingvalencia.com

6ha 320T(70-80m²) 10A

1 BCGIJKLMOPR
2 AEFGTUVXY
3 BGKMRY
4 (B+G 18/5-15/9) J
(Q+R+T+X+Y+Z ⌂)
5 ABFGIJKLMNOPUWXY
6 CEGIJK(N 3km)ORTV

📶 **2865**

NEW

💬 Large and very clean campsite 20km from Valencia. New motorhome area with all amenities. Swimming pool is open from 18 May. The campsite is just a few metres from the beautiful beach of Puzol, certified with the international environmental award 'Blue Flag'. Family-friendly and in a quiet area. Cycling and walking routes. Free wifi on the whole campsite.

🚗 From the north: A7 exit Puçol in Puçol follow the signs. From Valencia: V21 exit Puçol then follow the signs.

Sagunto
AP-7
A-7 CC
Benimàmet

🏕 N 39°36'4'' W 0°16'15''

CC €**15** 15/3-15/6 10/9-8/12 7=6, 14=12, 30=20

Puçol/Valencia, E-46530 / Comunidad Valenciana

♿ 🛜 iD (2866)

🔺 Puzol Cat.2
🏖 Playa de Puçol
☎ +34 961-421527
📠 +34 961-465586
🕐 15/1 - 16/12
@ campingpuzol@gmail.com

3ha 70T(60-70m²) 10A

1 ACDGIJKLMPQ
2 AEFGLTVWXY
3 BGHJRSUW
4 (B+G 15/6-30/9) J
   (Q+R+X 🅿)
5 **AB**DFGIJKLMNOPUWXYZ
6 CDEG**IK**(N 4km)TV

💬 A campsite 20 km from Valencia; little by little being reorganised and renovated for touring campers. There is a separate section with adequate amenities for these tourists. Lovely swimming pool from mid June. About 150m from the Mediterranean with a fine sandy beach.

🚘 On the A7 exit Puçol; on N340 exit Puçol then follow signs to Playa and campsite.

Sagunto

A-7

CC

Burjassot

CC € 15 15/1-1/7 1/9-15/12 7=6, 14=12, 30=21   🧭 N 39°36'20'' W 0°16'8''

Ribera de Cabanes, E-12595 / Comunidad Valenciana

🚫 ♿ 🛜 (2867)

🔺 Torre La Sal Cat.1
🏖 Avenida Camí l'Atall, 19
☎ +34 964-319596
📠 +34 964-319629
🕐 1/1 - 31/12
@ info@campingtorrelasal.com

2ha 177T(60-120m²) 15A

1 BCDEIJKLMNOPQ
2 AEFTUVWY
3 BCGHIJNRUWY
4 (A 1/1-1/5,1/10-31/12)
   (E+H+Q+S+T 🅿)
5 **AB**DEFGIJKLMNOPUWZ
6 AEGHK(N 1km)OQRTVW

💬 A peaceful family campsite right on a sandy beach. With a heated, covered swimming pool and recreation room. Pitches with plenty of shade and sunny pitches in winter. Library with books in Dutch, English, German and French. Free wifi!

🚘 E15 exit 44 or 45. Leave N340 Tarragona-Valencia at 1000 km marker. Then follow signs. Campsite beyond Torre La Sal 2 campsite.

AP-7
N-340
CC
Oropesa Del Mar
Benicàssim

CC € 15 1/1-27/3 3/4-30/6 1/9-31/12 15=14, 30=27   🧭 N 40°7'42'' E 0°9'34''

Ribera de Cabanes, E-12595 / Comunidad Valenciana

♿ 🛜 (2868)

🔺 Torre la Sal 2 Cat.1
🏖 Avda Camí l'Atall 44
☎ +34 964-319567
📠 +34 964-319744
🕐 1/1 - 31/12
@ camping@torrelasal2.com

9ha 517T(60-140m²) 10A

1 BCDGIJKLMPQ
2 AEFNTUVXY
3 BC**F**GHJLMN**Q**R**S**TU**V**WY
4 (B 1/4-31/10) (E+F+H 🅿) IJK
   M**N**(Q+S 🅿) (T 1/3-15/10)
   (U+V+X+Y+Z 🅿)
5 **AB**DEFGIJKLMNOPRUWXZ
6 ABEGHK(N 3km)OTUVW

💬 A large residential campsite with beautiful, new toilet facilities and many other amenities: indoor and outdoor swimming pools, heated in winter. Covered car park, tennis and multisports grounds. Fitness, sauna and jacuzzi. Good cycling opportunities. Free wifi. Also well-equipped for people with a disability.

🚘 On the A7 Barcelona-Valencia take exit 45. On the N340 km-marker 998 or 1000. Signposted.

N-340
AP-7
CC
Oropesa Del Mar
Benicàssim

CC € 19 1/1-27/3 2/4-21/6 1/9-31/12 15=13, 30=26   🧭 N 40°7'40'' E 0°9'32''

Santa Pola/Alicante, E-03130 / Comunidad Valenciana

♿ 🛜 iD (2869)

⛺ Bahia de Santa Pola Cat.2
🏠 Ctra Elche-Snta Pola km 11
☎ +34 96-5411012
📠 +34 96-5416790
🔓 1/1 - 31/12
@ campingbahia@gmail.com

6ha 455T(65-90m²) 10A

1 ABCDGIJKLMOPQ
2 IJTUVXY
3 AG
4 (B+G 15/6-15/9) (Q 🔓)
   (R 1/7-31/8) (Z 🔓)
5 **AB**DFGIJKLMNOPUXYZ
6 ACGJ**K**(N 1km)ORTV

💬 Rather large terraced site with artificial shade in summer. On the slopes of a hill, with a nice cooling breeze on hot days and a great view of the city.

🚗 A70, exit 72 Santa Pola. On the N332 turn right at the roundabout to Elche after the 88 km marker. Campsite 100m on the right.

Elx

N-332
CC
Santa Pola

San Fulgencio

CC € **17** 1/1-7/7 25/8-31/12
📐 N 38°12'3'' W 0°34'13''

Valencia, E-46012 / Comunidad Valenciana

♿ 🛜 iD (2870)

⛺ Coll Vert Cat. 2
🏠 Ctra del Riu, nr. 486 Pinedo
☎ +34 96-1830036
📠 +34 96-1830040
🔓 16/1 - 15/12
@ info@collvertcamping.com

2,4ha 80T(40-80m²) 10A

1 ACDGIJKLMPQ
2 AEFGRTVXY
3 B**F**GHJNRWY
4 (B+G 1/6-30/9) J(Q+R 🔓)
   (T+U+V+X+Z 1/4-30/9)
5 **AB**DFGIJKLMNOPUWZ
6 ACDGI**JK**(N 1km)STV

💬 6 km from Valencia and 300m from a wide sandy beach and l'Albufera nature park. You can get to Valencia by cycle path or by bus. If you don't mind some surrounding noise you will not be disappointed.

🚗 N: A7 and V21 dir. Valencia, follow El Saler signs in town. On CV500 1. roundabout go 3/4 of the way roundabout exit on CV5010. Campsite 300m on le.
S: A7 before Valencia dir. Albufera and El Saler on the CV500, turn off at El Saler roundabout, campsite 200m on le.

Valencia
Torrent

CC

A-7

CC € **15** 16/1-14/7 1/9-14/12 7=6, 14=12, 30=21
📐 N 39°23'47'' W 0°19'58''

Villajoyosa/Alicante, E-03570 / Comunidad Valenciana

♿ 🛜 iD (2871)

⛺ Camping Alicante Imperium
🏠 CV-759, km 1
☎ +34 96-5063232
🔓 1/1 - 31/12
@ ave@
   campingalicanteimperium.com

2,5ha 159T(75-130m²) 16A CEE

1 ABCD**G**IJKLMOPST
2 FGJKUVWY
4 (B+G 1/3-1/10)
   (Q+R+X+Z 🔓)
5 **AB**DFGIJKLMNOPUWXY
6 ABCEK(N 0,5km)STV

💬 Brand-new campsite (2016). Large pitches with views of the mountains. Sunny all year round. Well-maintained grounds and toilet facilities. Free wifi.

🚗 From north: on the N332 direction Alicante take Villajoyosa (Hospital) exit. Follow CV 759 on 5th roundabout. Campsite on the right.

L'Albir

CC
AP-7   **Benidorm**

CC € **17** 1/1-25/3 3/4-8/7 10/9-31/12 7=6
📐 N 38°31'5'' W 0°13'23''

Villajoyosa/Alicante, E-03570 / Comunidad Valenciana ♿ 📶 iD (2872)

🔺 Camping El Torres
📧 Calle Ilici 29, Playa El Torres
☎ +34 965-995077
🔓 1/1 - 31/12
@ info@campingeltorres.com

2ha 114T(55-115m²) 10-16A

1 ABCD**G**IJKLMO**P**ST
2 AEFIKLUVWXY
3 A**F**GU**W**Y
4 (B+G+Q+R+T+U+X+Y+Z 🔧)
5 **AB**DFGIJKLMNOPUWXY
6 ABEG**K**(N 3km)OTV

💬 New campsite (2014), right on the beach. Lots of sun in winter, artificial shade in summer. From every pitch and from the welcoming terrace there is a lovely view of the sea, and from the other side there is a view of the mountains.

🚗 From the N: N332 exit Villajoyosa (Hospital). Left at 3rd roundabout. Follow camping signs.

CC €**19** 9/4-17/6 16/9-30/9 | 📡 N 38°30'57'' W 0°12'1''

Villajoyosa/Alicante, E-03570 / Comunidad Valenciana ♿ 📶 iD (2873)

🔺 Playa Paraíso Cat.2
📧 Paraíso, 66
☎ +34 966-851838
📠 +34 966-298700
🔓 1/1 - 31/12
@ info@campingplayaparaiso.com

NEW

1,3ha 100T(40-60m²) 6-10A

1 ABCDGIJLOQ
2 ENSUVWXY
3 RUY
4 (B+Q+R+T+U+V+X+Z 🔧)
5 **AB**FGIJKLMNOPUWZ
6 BEGK(N 1km)OTV

💬 Small, family-run campsite right on the sea. Close to the colourful town of Villajoyosa. Spacious and lively terrace.

🚗 Campsite is on the old N332 go through the town,and don't take new bypass around the town. So on N332 exit Villajoyosa. Campsite is at kilometre marker 136 on the seaward side of the road.

CC €**17** 1/1-28/3 2/4-8/7 26/8-31/12 | 📡 N 38°29'59'' W 0°14'57''

Villargordo del Cabriel, E-46317 / Comunidad Valenciana ♿ 📶 (2874)

🔺 Kikopark Rural
📧 Ctra Embalse de Contreras km 3
☎ +34 96-2139082
📠 +34 96-2139337
🔓 1/1 - 31/12
@ rural@kikopark.com

2ha 76T(70-90m²) 10A CEE

1 BCD**G**IJKLMOPQ
2 DFJLSTUVXY
3 BGHJUW
4 (**A** 1/7-31/8)
  (B+G 15/5-30/9)
  (Q+R+T+U+X+Y+Z 🔧)
5 **AB**DFGIJKLMNOPUWXYZ
6 AEGK(N 3km)TV

💬 A campsite for peace and quiet. Views of the mountains and close to a large reservoir. Situated in a nature area with opportunities for walking, water sports, rafting, fishing, canoeing, hiking and mountain biking.

🚗 A3, exit 255 towards Villargordo. Enter the village, turn right at T junction, campsite clearly signposted there. Another 3 km towards campsite.

CC €**19** 1/1-27/3 3/4-14/6 1/9-31/12 | 📡 N 39°33'8'' W 1°28'28''

Xeraco, E-46770 / Comunidad Valenciana 🛜 iD (2875)

🏔 San Vicente
📧 Avenida de la Mota 24
☎ +34 962-888188
📠 +34 962-888147
🕐 1/1 - 31/12
@ info@campingsanvicente.com

0,5ha 42T(50-60m²) 5-10A

1 ABCDFIJLR
2 AEHSUVXY
3 UY
4 (Q+R+T 🅿) (U 1/5-30/9)
(V+X+Z 🅿)
5 **AB**GIJKLMNOPUWZ
6 ABEGKOTV

💬 Small campsite with small fields. Only suitable for tents, small caravans and small motorhomes. Right by the beach. Very easy-going atmosphere.

🚐 AP7, exit 59 Favara to N332 dir. Tavernes. On roundabout take CV603 and then CV605. Left after the bridge. Right on roundabout. Campsite is on left.

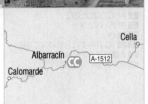

N-332 · AP-7 · Xeraco CC · A-38 · **Gandia**

CC € **15** 1/1-27/3 2/4-20/6 3/9-31/12 7=6, 14=11 📷 N 39°3'12'' W 0°11'53''

Albarracín/Teruel, E-44100 / Aragón ♿ 🛜 (2876)

🏔 Ciudad de Albarracín**
📧 Camino de Gea s/n
☎📠 +34 978-710197
🕐 9/3 - 25/11
@ campingalbarracin5@hotmail.com

1,5ha 100T(70m²) 10A

1 BCDGIJKLMOPST
2 RVWXY
3 AHJN
4 (Q+R+T+X+Z 🅿)
5 **A**FGIJKLMNOPUW
6 AEGK(N 0,8km)OTV

💬 A quiet campsite on the edge of the 'most beautiful city in Spain' (classified historical heritage including Islam) and near an area with prehistoric rock paintings. Abundant fauna and flora. In July and August you pay 1 Euros per person per day in the municipal open air swimming pool.

🚐 From Teruel to Albarracín. Follow camping signs in Albarracín .

Cella · Albarracín CC A-1512 · Calomarde

CC € **17** 9/3-24/3 1/4-10/7 28/8-24/11 📷 N 40°24'43'' W 1°25'39''

Alquézar, E-22145 / Aragón 🛜 (2877)

🏔 Alquézar
📧 Ctra Barbastro s/n
☎ +34 974-318300
📠 +34 974-318434
🕐 1/1 - 31/12
@ camping@alquezar.com

1,5ha 120T(70-100m²) 10A

1 BCDG**I**JKLMO**P**
2 JKLRTVWXY
3 BHJRU
4 (**A** 🅿) (B+G 1/4-30/9)
(Q+R 🅿)
(T+U+X+Y+Z 1/1-1/11,
1/12-31/12)
5 **AB**CFGIJKLMNOPUWZ
6 CDEGKOQTV

💬 A campsite for families and those who love walking, rafting, canyoning, escalade (rock climbing), etc. Located in the beautiful Sierra de Guara. ± 1 km from the medieval town of Alquézar with its castle (Christian and Moorish influences). UNESCO World Heritage Site (century-old rock drawings) and typical fauna.

🚐 A22 Huesca-Barbastro. Take N240 west of Barbastro direction Barbastro. Then A1232 and A1233 to Alquézar. Follow camping signs.

Alberuela de la Liena · CC · Abiego · A-22

CC € **17** 1/1-30/6 1/9-31/12 📷 N 42°9'53'' E 0°0'55''

Alquézar, E-22145 / Aragón

2878

🏔 Rio Vero
✉ Puente de Colungo s/n
☎ +34 974-318350
⊙ 15/3 - 31/10
@ info@campingriovero.com

3ha 187T(70-100m²) 5A

1 BCD**G**IJKLMO**P**
2 CJORVWXY
3 AHJR**W**X
4 (Q+S+T+U+V+X+Y+Z ⊙)
5 **A**GIJKLMNOPUZ
6 ACEGJOTV

💬 A campsite in a wooded area of the Sierra de Guara national park and close to nearby canyons. Canyoning equipment can be hired at the campsite. The campsite is situated beside the Rio Vero river with opportunities for swimming. Guides for canyoning, escalade, via ferrata, ornitology, VTT (all terrain bikes) and trekking.

🚗 From Barbastro A1233 direction Alquézar. Right A2205 direction Colungo. Follow camping signs.

Alquézar
Abiego
N-240 Castillazuelo

ⒸⒸ €**17** 15/3-30/6 1/9-30/10 7=6 📍 N 42°9'7'' E 0°1'45''

Benasque (Huesca), E-22440 / Aragón

🚶 🎿 📶 **2879**

🏔 Aneto Cat.1
✉ Ctra Barbastro Francia, km 100
☎ +34 974-551141
⊙ 1/1 - 31/10, 1/12 - 31/12
@ info@campinganeto.com

6ha 200T(40-100m²) 10A

1 BCD**F**IJKLMO**P**
2 CJKLRVWXY
3 BHJU**W**X
4 (A ⊙) (C+H 15/6-15/9)
   (Q ⊙)
   (S+T+U+X+Y+Z 15/6-15/9)
5 **AB**DFGIJKLMNOPUW
6 AEGIJ(N 3,5km)OTV

💬 This family campsite offers relaxation, tranquillity and fresh mountain air. Starting point for various (mountain) walks, also in the rugged countryside. It has a swimming pool. The restaurant is open in the week before Easter and during Holy Week.

🚗 From Castejón take the Sos A139 direction Benasque. The campsite is on the left 3 km beyond Benasque.

Benasque

ⒸⒸ €**19** 1/1-1/7 31/8-30/10 1/12-31/12 📍 N 42°37'27'' E 0°32'39''

Boltaña (Huesca), E-22349 / Aragón

📶 **2880**

🏔 Boltaña
✉ Ctra N260,km 442/
   Ctra de Margudgued
☎ +34 974-502347
⊙ 1/1 - 31/12
@ raquel@campingboltana.com

6ha 204T(75-130m²) 10A CEE

1 BCD**F**IJKLMO**P**ST
2 JLRTVWXY
3 BGHJNRU**W**
4 (A 22/6-31/8)
   (B+G 1/6-30/9) (Q+R ⊙)
   (T+U+V+X+Y+Z 28/3-13/10)
5 **AB**DEFGIJKLMNOPUWZ
6 ACEGJ(N 1km)OTUV

💬 This quiet family campsite is located in an area with an agreeable climate in all seasons. An excellent base for trips out to the various National Nature Parks and historic centres in the Pyrenees. It offers a wide variety of activities including the Guara canyons and rock climbing. Excellent restaurant. There is a thermal bath within walking distance of the site.

🚗 From Ainsa continue to Boltaña. After ± 7 km take Boltaña exit. Then follow camping signs.

Laspuña
N-260
Boltaña
Aínsa-
Sobrarbe

ⒸⒸ €**17** 2/4-26/4 2/5-21/6 25/6-8/7 27/8-10/10 14/10-30/10 4/11-27/12 📍 N 42°25'49'' E 0°4'44''

Bonansa (Huesca), E-22486 / Aragón

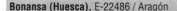

🏕 Camping Baliera Cat.2
🛣 N260, km 355,5
☎ +34 974-554016
📠 +34 974-554099
🔴 30/11 - 9/12, 26/12 - 28/10
@ info@baliera.com

5ha 173T(80-130m²) 5-10A

1 BCD**G**IJKLMO**P**ST
2 CLRVWXY
3 ABGHJNRUV**W**X
4 (B+G 15/6-25/9) (Q 🔴)
  (R+V 1/7-31/8)
5 **AB**CDEFGHIJKLMNOPUWZ
6 CEGIK(N 4km)OTUV

💬 Camping Baliera is located in the centre of the Isabena, Benasque, Aran and Boi valleys. It offers access to unusual and beautiful landscapes. Sample a mix of tradition and culture. Various activities all year: mountain sports, fishing, mushroom collecting in the autumn, skiing.

🚗 From Viella N230 direction Pont de Suert. After about 3 km from Vilaller turn right direction Castejón de Sos. After 2.5 km turn left at the forked road. Campsite immediately on the left.

Taüll
La Vall De Boí
N-230
Bonansa CC
El Pont De Suert
N-260

2881

CC € 19 1/1-14/7 1/9-27/10 30/11-8/12 26/12-31/12 7=6, 10=8, 15=12, 18=14 🏕 N 42°26'22'' E 0°41'56''

Bronchales/Teruel, E-44367 / Aragón

🏕 Las Corralizas 1727M***
🛣 Ctra Fuente del Canto, km 1,5
☎ +34 978-721050
🔴 16/3 - 1/11
@ reservas@lascorralizas.com

8,5ha 112T(70-100m²) 6-16A

1 BCD**G**IJKLMOPST
2 BIKRVWXY
3 ABGHJRU
4 (Q 🔴) (T+U+X+Z 1/7-31/8)
5 **AB**DFGIJKLMNOPRUW
6 ACEGK(N 1,5km)OSTV

💬 Nice countryside campsite in a pine forest within walking distance of the village via a path. Some pitches are not marked out. Fresh bread and restaurant open to order. Free wifi. Albarracin 30 km away.

🚗 Motorway A23 Zaragoza-Teruel: exit 144 (Santa Eulalia) or exit 131 (Cella) dir. Bronchales. Drive through centre and then turn right into the forest and follow signs.

Bronchales   A-23
Santa Eulalia
A-1511
CC
Cella
A-1512

2882

CC € 17 16/3-28/3 9/4-26/4 1/5-11/7 29/8-4/10 14/10-31/10 7=6, 14=11, 21=18, 30=24 🏕 N 40°30'0'' W 1°35'42''

Caspe, E-50700 / Aragón

🏕 Lake Caspe Camping***
🛣 Ctra N211 km 286,7
☎ +34 976-634174
📠 +34 976-634187
🔴 3/3 - 4/11
@ lakecaspe@lakecaspe.com

10ha 140T(70-140m²) 5-10A

1 BCD**G**IJKLMOPST
2 DKLNPRTVXY
3 BHJR**W**Z
4 (**A** 1/8-31/8) (B+G 1/5-30/9)
  (Q+S+T+U+Y+Z 🔴)
5 **A**EFGIJKLMNOPUW
6 ACEGJOTUV

💬 Campsite on the Mequinenza Reservoir, ideal for nature and watersports lovers. Kayaks, fishing boats, archery, mountain bikes for rent. Excursions: with guide, kayak and motor boat. Water skiing, windsurfing and sailing courses. Located in lovely Aragón with an agreeable climate. Zaragoza, Lleida and Barcelona are easy to reach.

🚗 A2 Lleida-Fraga. After Fraga exit 433, take N211 as far as Caspe. Campsite on right (286,7 km marker).

A-230
CC
N-211
Caspe
A-221

2883

CC € 17 3/3-24/3 2/4-14/7 3/9-16/9 24/9-3/11 7=6, 14=12, 21=18, 28=24 🏕 N 41°17'38'' E 0°3'45''

Gavín, E-22639 / Aragón

2884

- Camping Gavín S.L. Cat.1
- Ctra N260 km 503
- +34 974-485090
- FAX +34 974-485017
- 1/1 - 31/12
- @ info@campinggavin.com

7ha 150T(80m²) 10A

1. BCD**G**IJKLMO**P**
2. CJKLRVWX
3. ABCHJ**M**RU
4. (B+G 5/6-15/9) (Q+S ☾)
   (T+U+X+Y+Z 1/1-31/10,
   1/12-31/12)
5. **AB**DEFGIJKLMNOPRUWX
6. ACEGJ(N 2km)OTV

💬 An attractive terraced campsite, modernly appointed with an excellent restaurant. Beautiful natural surroundings, close to walking and skiing areas and national parks. From a relaxing stroll to a tour lasting several days, wild water recreation, mountain and adventure sports, trips out with cultural and historical flavour.

🚗 From France at Col de Portalet A136 direction Biescas. At Biescas N260 direction Broto (left at the service station). Campsite 3 km on the right.

A-136 / Biescas / CC / N-260 / N-330 / Sabiñánigo

CC € **17** 1/1-6/7 1/9-31/12 7=6

📍 N 42°37'10'' W 0°18'12''

La Puebla de Castro, E-22435 / Aragón

2885

- Lago Barasona Cat. 1
- Ctra Barbastro-Graus/N123a, km 25
- +34 974-545148
- 1/3 - 31/10
- @ info@lagobarasona.com

30ha 180T(70-120m²) 6A CEE

1. BCDGIJKLMOP**ST**
2. DJKLMORVWXY
3. ABHJKMN**Q**R**VW**Z
4. (B+G 1/5-30/9) **KLN**
   (Q 1/4-30/10) (R 1/6-30/9)
   (T 1/6-30/8)
   (U+V+Y+Z 1/4-30/9)
5. **AB**DEFGIJKLMNOPRUWX
6. ACEGHJ(N 6km)OTV

💬 A friendly family campsite on several levels. Good base for interesting sights with remnants of several cultures. Located on a lake with a beach and a meadow. Set in the foothills of the Pyrenees with many natural parks. Various watersports options.

🚗 From Aínsa A138 direction Barbastro. About 8 km before Barbastro turn left towards N123 Benabara/Graus. Take the 123a to Graus at intersection. Campsite 2.4 km on the left. Follow the loop.

Graus / El Grado / N-123A / CC / N-123 / Estadilla

CC € **17** 1/3-30/6 1/9-30/10

📍 N 42°8'32'' E 0°18'51''

La Puebla de Castro (Huesca), E-22435 / Aragón

2886

- Bellavista & Subenuix Cat.1
- Ctra Barbastro en Benasque
- +34 974-545113
- 2/1 - 24/9, 2/10 - 31/12
- @ info@
  hotelcampingbellavista.com

22,5ha 133T(80-100m²) 7.5A

1. BCD**G**IJKLO**P**RS
2. DJKLMRVXY
3. ABHJNRU**W**Z
4. (B+G 15/6-1/9)
   (Q+R+T+U+V+X+Y+Z ☾)
5. **A**DFGIJKLMNOPUWZ
6. EGJ(N 6km)OTV

💬 Friendly campsite with lawns by the lake. The best restaurant in the area (according to the Tourist Office). Boats, pedal boats and water skis can be rented. Only at weekends during May and June. Daily in July and August. The area is fascinating with churches, chapels and monasteries next to vineyards. Fishing licence applications only by mail.

🚗 From Barbastro to Benasque, campsite on left 6 km before Graus. Take note: take the right hand loop to the site.

Graus / CC / Barbastro / N-230 / A-22 / N-240

CC € **17** 2/1-1/7 1/9-23/9 2/10-31/12

📍 N 42°7'48'' E 0°18'36''

La Puebla de Roda, E-22482 / Aragón

▲ Isábena
🚌 Ctra Graus a Viella km 27
☎ +34 974-544530
🔓 25/3 - 15/11
@ info@isabena.eu

👫 📶 **(2887)**

3ha 135T(100m²) 6A CEE

1 BCDGIJKLMO**PS**
2 CGLRVWXY
3 BHJNRU**W**
4 (**A** 🔓) (B 15/5-15/10) **KLN**
(Q+T+U+X+Z 🔓)
5 **AB**DFGIJKLMNOPUWZ
6 ACEGJ(N 2km)OTV

💬 Welcoming campsite, located in a rough and beautiful mountain area. Walking enthusiasts can enjoy peaceful signposted walks.

🚗 From Veilla N230 dir. Lerida, exit Graus (A1605). After 28 km campsite is on right. Or from Graus on the A1605. Site is on left after 28 km.

La Puebla de Roda
La Puebla de Fantova

CC € **17** 25/3-14/7 1/9-14/11

📍 N 42°18'27'' E 0°32'43''

Labuerda/Ainsa (Huesca), E-22360 / Aragón

▲ Peña Montañesa
🚌 Ctra Ainsa-Francia, km 2
☎ +34 974-500032
FAX +34 974-500991
🔓 1/1 - 31/12
@ info@penamontanesa.com

⛷ 📶 **(2888)**

10ha 330T(64-100m²) 6-10A

1 BCD**G**IJKLMO**PST**
2 CRVWXY
3 ABGHJMNRU**WX**
4 (**A** 🔓) (B 1/4-30/9) (F 🔓)
(G 1/4-30/9) **K**N**P**
(Q+S+T+U+V+X+Y+Z 🔓)
5 **AB**DFGIJKMNOPSUWZ
6 ACDEGJ(N 2km)OTV

💬 Something for everyone, including an outdoor swimming pool, heated indoor pool, sauna, jacuzzi, playground, supermarket, bar, restaurant with democratic pricing, multifunctional sportsground, horse riding, squash, canyoning, rafting, good toilet facilities. Close to the National Parks of Ordesa and Monte Perdido.

🚗 Ainsa direction French border (Escalona). The campsite is 2 km beyond Ainsa indicated by flags.

Laspuña
A-1604   CC   Ainsa   N-260
La Fueva
A-138

CC € **19** 1/1-30/6 1/9-31/12

📍 N 42°26'6'' E 0°8'7''

Ligüerre de Cinca (Huesca), E-22393 / Aragón

▲ Ligüerre de Cinca
🚌 Ctra A138, km 28
de Barbastro a Aín
☎ +34 974-500800
🔓 1/3 - 31/12
@ info@liguerredecinca.com

👫 📶 **(2889)**

NEW

8ha 150T(70-80m²) 10A

1 BCD**F**IJKLMOP
2 DJPRTVWXY
3 ABGHJMNRU**W**
4 (**A** 🔓) (B+G 15/6-15/9)
(Q+S+T+U+X+Y+Z 🔓)
5 **AB**DFGIJKLMNOPSUWZ
6 CEGJRTUV

💬 Campsite next to the El Grado reservoir with all types of water recreation opportunities. The campsite has plenty of sports facilities.

🚗 A138 from Ainsa direction Barbastro. The campsite is on the left side of the road at km-marker 28.

La Fueva
Urriales
CC
Naval   A-138   Graus

CC € **17** 1/3-7/7 25/8-30/12

📍 N 42°16'52'' E 0°11'47''

Morillo de Tou/Ainsa, E-22395 / Aragón
👫 🛜 **2890**

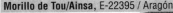

🔺 Morillo de Tou
🚏 Ctra A138 Barbastro-Ainsa, km 41,8
☎ +34 974-500793
🔓 1/3 - 31/12
@ info@morillodetou.com

54T(60-70m²) 10A

1️⃣ BCD**G**IJKLMOPS
2️⃣ DGJRTVWXY
3️⃣ BDGHJNRU**W**
4️⃣ (**A** 🔲) (B 24/6-7/9) (Q 🔲) (R 1/7-31/8) (T+U+X+Y+Z 🔲)
5️⃣ **A**GIJKLMNOPUWX
6️⃣ CDEGK(N 4km)TV

💬 The campsite is located in the Morillo de Tou holiday centre, a reconstructed village in the Aragon Pyrenees and close to national parks and centres full of art, culture and history.

🚗 Campsite on the A138 between Barbastro and Ainsa in Morillo de Tou.

Boltaña
N-260
Ainsa-Sobrarbe
CC

(CC) € **17** 1/3-5/7 24/8-31/12 7=6, 14=11   📷 N 42°22'31'' E 0°9'11''

Nuévalos (Zaragoza), E-50210 / Aragón
🛜 **2891**

🔺 Lago Resort***
🚏 Ctra Alhama de Aragón-Nuevalos,s/n
☎ +34 976-849038
🔓 10/2 - 9/12
@ lagoresort@gmail.com

10ha 120T(70-90m²) 6A

1️⃣ BCDGIJKLMOP
2️⃣ JLTVXY
3️⃣ ABCHJKRU
4️⃣ (**A** 🔲) (B 15/6-10/9) (Q+R+T+U+V+X+Z 🔲)
5️⃣ **A**FGIJKLMNOPUWZ
6️⃣ ACEGJ(N 0,4km)OTV

💬 A terraced campsite close to the Monasterio de Piedra (1194) and the nature park and thermal baths of Jaraba and Alhama. Near the Tranquera reservoir (water sports recreation).

🚗 From Calatayud to Nuévalos. Follow camping signs in Nuévalos. Campsite on the left of the road to Alhama opposite the lake.

Alhama de Aragón   A-2   **Calatayud**
N-234
CC
Nuévalos

(CC) € **17** 10/2-23/3 2/4-9/7 27/8-5/12   📷 N 41°13'5'' W 1°47'32''

Valderrobres, E-44580 / Aragón
♿ 🛜 **2892**

NEW

🔺 El Roble
🚏 Ctra A231, km 18
☎ +34 608-318481
🔓 1/1 - 31/12
@ campingelroble@gmail.com

1ha 45T(70-100m²) 6-10A

1️⃣ BCDGIJKLMOPQ
2️⃣ BCSUVWX
3️⃣ HJKUWX
4️⃣ (**A** 🔲) (B 1/5-30/9) (Q+T+U+Z 🔲)
5️⃣ **AB**DFGIJKLMNOPUWX
6️⃣ AEK(N 2km)OTV

💬 Small new campsite, located in the beautiful quiet area of Terra Alta (a good wine region) and near the Els Ports National Park. Very good walking and cycling on the special Cami Verde cycling routes.
🚗 From the south: AP-7 or N340 to Vinaros then N232 towards Morella to Monyoro then A1414 to Valderrobres then A321. After 2 km campsite is signposted on left. From Tortosa C12 via N2306, T333 to Valderrobres and turn right A321. After 3 km campsite is on the left.

N-232
CC
Arnes
Fuentespalda

(CC) € **15** 1/1-28/3 2/4-10/7 28/8-31/12 7=6, 15=12, 30=23, 60=45   📷 N 40°52'56'' E 0°7'30''

Vera de Moncayo, E-50580 / Aragón ⛺ 👫 📶 **(2893)**

🏔 Veruela Moncayo
🛣 Ctra Vera a Veruela s/n
☎ +34 609-783365
📅 1/1 - 31/12
@ campingveruelamoncayo@gmail.com

1,8ha 80T(60-100m²) 6A

1 BCD**G**IJKLMOP
2 RVWX
3 AHJR
4 (Q+R+T+U+X+Y+Z 🔌)
5 **A**GIKMNOPUW
6 EGJ(N 0,15km)TUV

💬 Basic campsite with a good restaurant on the edge of the village and at 500m from the Monasterio de Veruela (13th century). Located on the Parque Natural de Moncayo and at 150m from the centre (shops, municipal outdoor swimming pool). Nature reserve for cycling and walking. Zaragoza is an hour's drive away.

�’ Take the AP68 or the N232 between Zaragoza and Tudela. Then follow the N122 to Vera de Moncayo (direction Tarazona). Then follow the signs.

Tarazona
N-122
Borja
CC
Añón De Moncayo

CC € **15** 1/1-7/7 25/8-31/12 | 📷 N 41°49'9'' W 1°41'32''

Haro, E-26200 / La Rioja ♿ 📶 **iD** **(2894)**

🏔 De Haro Cat.2
🛣 Avenida de Miranda 1
☎ +34 941-312737
📅 27/1 - 9/12
@ campingdeharo@fer.es

5ha 125T(72-80m²) 6-10A

1 ABCD**G**IJKLMOP
2 CFKLRTVWXY
3 BHJNRU**W**
4 (B+G 3/6-15/9) (Q 🔌)
   (T+X+Z 3/6-15/9)
5 **AB**DFGIJKLMNOPUWZ
6 ACEGJ**K**(N 0,6km)OTV

💬 The lovely small town of Haro (capital of the Rioja Alta wine region) is within walking distance. Also within walking distance is the bus stop and railway station. The annual Haro wine festival (end of June) is famous throughout the whole of Spain.

�’ N232 Logroño-Miranda de Ebro. Follow the camping signs in Haro.

Ap-68
CC
N-232a
Haro
San Vicente De La Sonsierra
N-232

CC € **19** 27/1-21/6 1/9-8/12 7=6, 14=11 | 📷 N 42°34'41'' W 2°51'16''

Navarrete, E-26370 / La Rioja ♿ 📶 **iD** **(2895)**

🏔 Navarrete Cat.1
🛣 Ctra de Entrena s/n
☎ +34 941-440169
📅 12/1 - 12/12
@ campingnavarrete@fer.es

3ha 50T(30-70m²) 6A

1 ABCD**G**IJKLMOPST
2 FKLRVWXY
3 B**F**MNRU
4 (**A** 1/7-31/8)
   (B+G 15/6-15/9)
   (Q+R+T+U+X+Z 🔌)
5 **AB**DFGIJKLMNOPUWZ
6 ACEGJ(N 1,5km)ORTV

💬 A good campsite in the Rioja region, 10 km from Logroño. A base for trips out in the area, but also suitable as a stopover campsite. Naturally a visit to one of the many Rioja bodegas is 'compulsory'. A very well maintained campsite with top class toilet facilities.

�’ Exit 11 on motorway AP68 (Logroño-Bilbao) to Navarrete. Campsite is signposted and is outside the village on the LR137.

N-232
N-232A
AP-68
Logroño
Navarrete
Lardero
A-12
CC
N-111

CC € **17** 12/1-24/3 3/4-29/6 1/9-11/12 7=6, 14=11 | 📷 N 42°24'58'' W 2°33'6''

Santo Domingo de la Calzada, E-26257 / La Rioja

⚓ ♿ 📶 **iD** (2896)

🔺 Bañares****
🏠 Ctra N120, km 42,2
☎ +34 941-340131
🔓 1/1 - 31/12
@ info@campingbanares.es

20ha 250T(70m²) 5-10A

1 ABCDGIJKLMNO**P**S
2 FKLRTVWXY
3 B**F**GJ**M**NRU
4 (**A** 1/7-31/8)
(B+G 23/6-13/9)
(Q+S+T+U+X+Y+Z 🔓)
5 **AB**DFGIJKLMNOPUWXYZ
6 ACDEGH**I**K(N 3km)ORTV

💬 A large campsite with many permanent pitches, a lovely swimming pool and plenty of play equipment. Located near the beautiful village of Santo Domingo de la Calzada on the pilgrims route to Santiago.

🚗 Campsite located on N120/A12 at 42.2 km marker near Santo Domingo de la Calzada.

CC € (19) 1/1-29/6 1/9-30/12 7=6   📍 N 42°26'28'' W 2°54'55''

Etxarri Aranatz, E-31820 / Navarra

♿ 📶 **iD** (2897)

🔺 Camping Etxarri S.L.
☎ +34 948-460537
📠 +34 948-461509
🔓 31/3 - 8/10
@ info@campingetxarri.com

2,3ha 100T(50-80m²) 6A

1 ABC**G**IJKLMOPQ
2 BCFLRSVWXY
3 BHJMNRSU
4 (B+G 1/6-15/9)
(Q+R+T+U+V+X+Y+Z 🔓)
5 **A**EFGIJKLMNOPUWXYZ
6 ACEGIK(N 2km)OTV

💬 A lovely campsite located in the natural area of the Urbasa and Aralar ranges. It has a good swimming pool (open from June). A perfect starting point for visiting the towns of Pamplona, Logroño, Vitoria, San Sebastián and other historical places. Campsite is only open at weekends in March.

🚗 AP10 Pamplona-Victoria, exit Etxarri/Aranatz. Campsite signposted in the village.

CC € (19) 31/3-29/6 1/9-7/10 7=6, 14=11   📍 N 42°54'46'' W 2°4'46''

Eusa/Oricain/Pamplona, E-31194 / Navarra

📶 **iD** (2898)

🔺 Ezcaba Cat.1
🏠 Ctra a Francia, km 2,5
☎ +34 948-330315
📠 +34 948-331316
🔓 1/1 - 31/12
@ info@campingezcaba.com

4ha 539T(40-70m²) 10A

1 ABC**G**IJKLMOPQ
2 CFKLRTVWXY
3 B**F**HJR**W**
4 (B+G 18/6-15/9) (Q 🔓)
(R+T+U+X+Z 24/3-12/10)
5 **AB**EFGIJKLMNOPUWXZ
6 CDEG**I**K(N 3km)OTV

💬 Peacefully located campsite with a swimming pool. Mountain bikes can be rented on the campsite for visiting Pamplona (9 km away) among other places. Positioned on the pilgrimage route to Santiago de Compostela.

🚗 N121A from Irua to Pamplona. Turn right before Oricain. Campsite signposted.

CC € (19) 1/1-29/6 1/9-30/12 7=6, 14=12, 21=8, 30=25   📍 N 42°51'26'' W 1°37'25''

Mendigorria, E-31150 / Navarra ♿ 🛜 ✿ iD 2899

🏕 Errota - El Molino Cat.1
✉ Ctra Larraga s/n
☎ +34 948-340604
📠 +34 948-340082
📅 1/2 - 15/12
@ info@campingelmolino.com

10ha 150T(60-80m²) 6-22A

1 ACDGIJKLMOPQ
2 CKLRVWXY
3 BGHJK**M**N**Q**RSUW
4 (**A** 1/7-31/8) (B 1/6-15/9)
(**E** 🔲)(G 1/6-15/9) JKN (Q 🔲)
(R 28/3-30/9)(T+U+V+X+Y
15/3-15/11)(Z 26/3-9/4,15/6-15/9)
5 **AB**DEFGIJKLMNOPQRSTU
WYZ
6 ACEGH**I**KM(N 5km)OTUV

💬 A lovely campsite about 25 km from Pamplona. Conveniently located for visits to Logrono and San Sebastian. The pilgrims' route to Santiago passes nearby through the lovely village of Puente La Reina. Indoor heated winter pool and squash and tennis on the campsite. The area invites you to go walking, mountain biking or canoeing and to take cultural trips out.

🚗 A12 Pamplona-Logroño, exit 23 Mendigorria, west of the city centre (ca. 0,5 km). Signposted from the A12.

Obanos — A-12

CC

Larraga

Berbinzana

CC € ⑲ 1/2-30/6 1/9-14/12 7=6, 14=11   N 42°37'28'' W 1°50'35''

Olite, E-31390 / Navarra ♿ 🛜 iD 2900

🏕 Camping de Olite
✉ Ctra N115, km 2,3
☎📠 +34 948-741014
📅 1/1 - 31/12
@ info@campingdeolite.com

10ha 90T(75-120m²) 16A

1 ABCD**G**IJKLMOPR
2 FLSW
3 BMNRU
4 (B+G 15/6-15/9) (Q 🔲)
(R 1/7-31/8)
(T+U+X+Y+Z 🔲)
5 **AB**FGIJKLMNOPUWZ
6 CEGK(N 3km)OTV

NEW

💬 Particularly suited for a visit to the imposing natural park 'Bardenas Reales' and the historic town of Olite with its medieval streets and a beautiful Parador (stately hotel).

🚗 The campsite is on the NA115 (Tafalla-Peralta-Ricon de Soto) at kilometre marker 2.3 about 4 km from Olite.

Tafalla

Miranda de Arga

CC

N-121

AP-15

CC € ⑲ 1/1-27/3 3/4-29/6 3/9-30/12 7=6   N 42°28'49'' W 1°40'41''

Villafranca, E-31330 / Navarra 👫 ♿ 🛜 iD 2901

🏕 Bardenas
✉ Ctra NA-660 PK 13.4
☎ +34 948-846191
📅 10/1 - 21/12
@ info@campingbardenas.com

3ha 50T(70-105m²) 12A

1 ABCD**G**IJKLMOPR
2 FKLRVWXY
3 BGHJMNRUV
4 (**A** 🔲) (B 15/6-15/9) (Q 🔲)
(R 1/4-31/10)
(T+U+X+Y+Z 🔲)
5 **A**BFGIJKLMNOPUWXYZ
6 ACEGHJ(N 1,5km)OTV

💬 Campsite located on a main road with excellent toilet facilities. Bardenas nature reserve (walking, cycling) is 18 km away. Bodegas, gastronomy and plenty of culture in the area, including the castles of Olite and Marcilla.

🚗 From AP15 Pamplona-Zaragoza, take exit 29. Then towards Villafranca, campsite 1500m south of Villafranca.

Azagra

AP-15

Rincón De Soto

CC N-121

AP-68 N-232

Alfaro

CC € ⑲ 10/1-27/3 2/4-13/7 1/9-20/12 7=6, 14=12   N 42°15'48'' W 1°44'19''

Itziar, E-20829 / Pais Vasco

🚫 🛜 iD (2902)

- 🔼 Itxaspe Cat.1
- 📧 CN634, km 38,2
- ☎ +34 943-199377
- 📅 23/3 - 16/9
- @ info@campingitxaspe.com

1,9ha 110T(35-100m²) 6A

1. ABCD**G**IJLPQ
2. FJKLOQRTVWXY
3. BHJNRUW
4. (B 10/6-15/9)
   (Q+S+T+U+X+Y+Z 🔑)
5. **AB**EFGIJKLMNOPUWXYZ
6. ACEGK(N 2km)OTV

💬 Situated in beautiful surroundings with lovely views of the sea in a protected geo-nature park of great ecological and biological value. About 8 km from the magnificent beaches at Deba and Zumaia. Bilbao (Guggenheim museum) is 50 min. by car, San Sebastian 30 min. Plenty of opportunities for walking and trips out.

🚗 N634 Zumia direction Deba. At km 37,5 marker, campsite signposted on the right. Via A8 exit 54, then direction Zumaia, left after 100m, site signposted.

Ondarroa

Zarautz

CC € ⑲ 23/3-30/6 3/9-15/9

N 43°16'42'' W 2°19'46''

Nuvilla, E-01428 / Pais Vasco

🛜 iD (2903)

- 🔼 El Roble Verde
- 📧 Nuvilla 99
- ☎ +34 945-063350
- 📅 15/3 - 9/12
- @ info@campingelrobleverde.com

NEW

4ha 76T(35-90m²) 6-10A CEE

1. ABCD**G**IJKLMO**P**Q
2. FGKLRVWX
3. ABIJNRU
4. (E 1/4-30/10) (Q 15/6-15/9)
   (R 🔑) (T 15/6-15/9) (U 🔑)
   (X+Y+Z 15/6-15/9)
5. **AB**FGIJKLMNOPUWXZ
6. ACEGK(N 6km)OTV

💬 A quiet family campsite in an area of natural beauty, and just 5 km from the AP68 Bilbao-Logroño (exit Pobes). Very well situated for a visit to the Basque and Rioja regions. Campsite has spacious grassy pitches and an indoor pool (open from Easter until 1 November). The bar and restaurant are only open at weekends in the low season.

🚗 On the A3322 between Pobes and Puebla de Arganzon. At kilometre marker 24 towards Nuvilla, campsite is at the entrance to the village.

Nanclares de La Oca

Rivabellosa

CC € ⑲ 15/3-27/3 2/4-26/4 1/5-14/6 31/8-10/10 14/10-30/10 4/11-8/12 11=10

N 42°47'43'' W 2°52'45''

Orio, E-20810 / Pais Vasco

🚫 🛜 iD (2904)

- 🔼 Camping Orio/Orio Kanpina Cat. 1
- 📧 Hondartza Bidea S/N
- ☎ +34 943-834801
- 📅 1/3 - 11/11
- @ info@oriokanpina.com

3,2ha 122T(60-80m²) 10A

1. ABCDEIJKLMOPQ
2. AEFKLMRVWX
3. BFHRUWY
4. (B+G 15/6-15/9)
   (Q+S+T+U+V+X+Y+Z 🔑)
5. **AB**EFGIJKLMNOPUWZ
6. CEGHK(N 1km)ORTV

💬 A family campsite 200m from the sea. It has a sandy beach and you can swim in the sea. There is a harbour for pleasure craft 50m from the campsite. The site has a swimming pool and a good restaurant. Located 20 km from San Sebastián.

🚗 A8 from San Sebastián exit Orio, then direction beach/campsite. A8 from Bilbao: exit Zarautz, then dir. Orio. Follow N634 beyond river bridge, left at 1st roundabout then dir. beach/campsite.

San Sebastián

CC € ⑰ 1/3-29/6 1/9-10/11

N 43°16'56'' W 2°6'44''

San Sebastián, E-20018 / Pais Vasco   2905

🏕 Camping Igara de San Sebastián
✉ Camino de Igara 195
☎ +34 943-374287
⌨ 1/3 - 10/12
@ info@campingigara.com

3,5ha 75T(40-80m²) 16A

1 ABCDGIJLOPQ
2 BFHJKLRSVWX
3 HJRU**V**
4 (B+G 1/5-1/10)
   (Q+R+T+U+V+X+Y+Z 🅿)
5 **AB**FGIJKLMNOPUWXZ
6 ACEGK(N 3km)ORTV

📝 A campsite with plenty of new amenities and a fantastic restaurant. From the campsite it's possible to take the bus to San Sebastián. The access road to the campsite is not suitable for larger caravans and large motorhomes.

🚗 On AP8 motorway take exit Ondarreta then towards Polygono Igara and campsite is signposted.

San Sebastián

(CC) € 15 1/3-29/6 1/9-9/12   N 43°17'48'' W 2°2'15''

San Sebastián, E-20008 / Pais Vasco   2906

🏕 Igueldo Cat.1
✉ P. Padre Orkolaga 69
☎ +34 943-214502
📠 +34 943-280411
⌨ 1/1 - 31/12
@ info@campingigueldo.com

5ha 316T(20-70m²) 6-10A

1 ABCD**G**IJKLMO**P**Q
2 FGJKLRTVWXY
3 B**F**HJR
4 (B+G 15/6-15/9)
   (Q+R+T+U+X+Y+Z 🅿)
5 **AB**EFGIJKLMNOPUWXYZ
6 ACDEGH**I**K(N 1,5km)ORTV

📝 Large, well-maintained campsite, excellent toilet facilities. Bus to San Sebastián stops in front of the campsite. Campsite has a welcoming bar and an excellent restaurant. Beautiful view of the surroundings and a new swimming pool since 2016.

🚗 From border follow A8. Exit Ondarreta, dir. San Sebastián centre. On coast follow Monte Igueldo to campsite. Attention: SatNav chooses route unsuitable for caravans and motorhomes. Ignore this route and follow campsite signs.

San Sebastián

(CC) € 19 1/1-29/6 1/9-30/12 7=6   N 43°18'48'' W 2°1'45''

Villanañe, E-01425 / Pais Vasco   2907

🏕 Angosto
☎ +34 945-353271
⌨ 23/2 - 9/12
@ info@camping-angosto.com

1,8ha 68T(70-80m²) 6A

1 ABCDGIJKLOPQ
2 CGLRWXY
3 AHIJRU**W**X
4 (E 1/4-1/11) N
   (Q+R+T+U+V+X+Y+Z 🅿)
5 **AB**DFGIJKLMNOPQRUWZ
6 BCDEGHIJ(N 3km)OTV

📝 Quiet family campsite close to two natural parks, ideal for walkers and mountain bikers. There is a good restaurant. Bilbao, Vitoria and the Rioja are close by.

🚗 From Bilbao follow N625 to exit Villanañe. From Miranda de Ebro on the A68 take exit Puentelarrá, then the N625. Site is then signposted.

Villanueva de Valdegovía

Herrán

(CC) € 19 3/4-20/6 10/9-30/10   N 42°50'9'' W 3°3'43''

Zarautz, E-20800 / Pais Vasco

△ Gran Camping Zarautz Cat.2
🏠 Monte Talai-Mendi
☎ +34 943-831238
🔓 1/1 - 31/12
@ info@grancampingzarautz.com

2908

5ha 440T(60-90m²) 6-10A

1️⃣ ABCDGIJKLMOPQ
2️⃣ FJKLRTVWXY
3️⃣ ABFH
4️⃣ (Q+S+T+U+V+X+Y+Z 🅿)
5️⃣ ABDFGIJKLMNOPUWZ
6️⃣ ACDEGHIJM(N 1,5km)ORTV

💬 A beautifully located campsite with lovely views of Zarautz Bay. An ideal starting point for trips out to San Sebastián, Bilbao and Pamplona. Many opportunities for walking and mountain biking in the area.

🚗 Coming from France take A8 San Sebastián-Bilbao, exit 38 Zarautz. Straight ahead at first roundabout, campsite signposted.

San Sebastián
N-634 · AP-8 CC AP-1

CC €19 1/1-29/6 16/9-30/12 7=6

🏴 N 43°17'22'' W 2°8'45''

Zumaia, E-20750 / Pais Vasco

△ Camping & Bungalows
   Zumaia Cat.1
🏠 Basusta bidea, 16
☎ +34 943-860475
🔓 19/1 - 16/12
@ info@campingzumaia.com

2909

2,2ha 109T(35-70m²) 10A

1️⃣ ABCDGIJKLMOPQ
2️⃣ FGJKLRSUVW
3️⃣ ABHJRU
4️⃣ (B+G 24/6-10/9)
   (Q+R+T+U+X+Y+Z 🅿)
5️⃣ ABEFGIJKLMNOPUWXZ
6️⃣ ACEGJKM(N 1,5km)RTV

💬 New campsite on the edge of the beautiful coastal town of Zumaia. Many options for walking nearby, good connection by bus and train to Zarautz and San Sebastián.

🚗 From N634, on edge of Zumaia, follow dir. station. Site is then signposted.

AP-8 CC **Zarautz**
N-634 AP-1 Orio
Zestoa

CC €19 19/1-5/7 27/8-15/12

🏴 N 43°17'23'' W 2°14'51''

Islares, E-39798 / Cantabria

△ Playa Arenillas Cat.2
🏠 Cu 634 km 156
☎ +34 942-863152
🔓 23/3 - 30/9
@ luis.cueva62@gmail.com

2910

1,7ha 120T(50-70m²) 6A

1️⃣ BCDEIJKLMOPQ
2️⃣ AEFGKLRVWX
3️⃣ BHJKNRWY
4️⃣ (Q+R+T+U+X+Y+Z 🅿)
5️⃣ ABFGIJKLMOPUWZ
6️⃣ AEGK(N 7km)OTV

💬 A friendly and appropriate welcome. Close to a sandy beach. 100m from the bus to Bilbao. Watersports opportunities. Ideal for enjoyable trips out into the surroundings. All information about Bilbao (35 km away) is available at the campsite.

🚗 A8 Bilbao to Santander exit 156 in the direction of Islares. Signposted here.

N-634 CC
A-8
N-629 **Castro-Urdiales**

CC €19 23/3-5/7 24/8-29/9

🏴 N 43°24'13'' W 3°18'37''

Laredo, E-39770 / Cantabria

⊗ ♿ 🛜 iD **2911**

🏕 Camping Laredo Cat.2
✉ Camino el Regaton 2
☎ +34 942-605035
📠 +34 942-613180
📅 1/5 - 14/9
@ info@campinglaredo.com

5,5ha 315T(60-90m²) 6-10A

1 ABCDEIJKLMOPQ
2 AEFGLRVWXY
3 ABH**OP**R**UW**
4 (B+G 1/7-31/8) (Q+S 📷)
  (X 15/6-14/9) (Z 📷)
5 **AB**FGIJKLMNOPUWZ
6 ACEGJ(N 3km)ORTV

💬 A large campsite with good clean toilet facilities. 400m from a sandy beach. Opportunities for horse riding within 100m. Bilbao and Santander are both about 50 km from the campsite.

🚗 A8 from Bilbao to Santander. Second exit direction Laredo towards hospital. Signposted after 1 km. Ignore Satnav. Follow yellow signs to campsite.

Santoña
Cicero Laredo
A-8
N-629

CC € **17** 1/5-29/6 1/9-13/9

📍 N 43°25'3'' W 3°26'43''

Potes, E-39570 / Cantabria

♿ 🛜 iD **2912**

🏕 La Viorna Cat.1
✉ Car. Santo Toribio
☎ +34 942-732021
📅 24/3 - 1/11
@ info@campinglaviorna.com

1,9ha 110T(70m²) 6A

1 ABCDFIJKLO**P**Q
2 JKRVXY
3 ABGHJ
4 (A 1/7-15/9)
  (B+G 25/5-15/10)
  (Q+R+X 📷) (Y 1/7-20/9)
  (Z 📷)
5 **AB**EFGIJKLMNOPUW
6 ACEGJ(N 1km)ORTV

💬 Lovely campsite with excellent amenities. The pitches at this terraced campsite have grass and shade. Large swimming pool. Most suitable as starting point for various walks and excursions. Plenty of information about the region available at the reception. Excellent restaurant, appetizing menus of the day. You can be assured of a pleasant stay. Magnificent views of the mountain peaks of the Picos.

🚗 1 km past Potes, direction Fuente Dé, turn left to Santo Toribio.

Cillorigo De
Liébana
Camaleño Potes
N-621

CC € **19** 24/3-29/6 1/9-31/10

📍 N 43°9'16'' W 4°38'37''

Potes/Turieno, E-39570 / Cantabria

🛜 iD **2913**

🏕 La Isla-Picos de Europa Cat.2
✉ Ctra Potes-Fuente Dé km 2
☎ 📠 +34 942-730896
📅 26/3 - 15/10
@ campinglaislapicosdeeuropa@
  gmail.com

1,5ha 140T(60-70m²) 3-6A

1 ABCDGIJKLMO**P**ST
2 CGRVXY
3 BHJN**P**RX
4 (A 📷) (B 1/6-30/9)
  (Q+R+T+U+X+Z 📷)
5 **AB**GIJKLMOPUWZ
6 AEGK(N 2km)OTV

💬 This beautiful campsite 2500m from Potes is located on the Rio de Deva River. The grassy field has plenty of shade from the countless fruit trees. Lively restaurant and terrace. Excellent climate at the foot of the majestic Picos de Europa. Departure point for various excursions, walks and mountain sports. Plenty of information at the reception. Excellent toilet facilities. You are most welcome here.

🚗 Past Potes direction Fuente Dé. Turn right after about 2.5 km.

Cillorigo De
Liébana
Camaleño Potes
N-621

CC € **15** 26/3-14/7 1/9-14/10

📍 N 43°9'27'' W 4°39'22''

Ruiloba, E-39527 / Cantabria  (2914)

- 🏕 Camping El Helguero
- 📧 Barrio de la Iglesia
- ☎ +34 942-722124
- 📠 +34 942-721020
- 🔑 23/3 - 30/9
- @ reservas@
  campingelhelguero.com

6,5ha 240T(70-120m²) 6A

1 BCDGIJKLMO**P**Q
2 FGJRVWXY
3 BHJR
4 (B 1/4-30/9)
  (G+Q+S+T+U+X+Y+Z 🔑)
5 **AB**DFGIJKLMNOPUW
6 EG**K**(N 3km)OTV

💬 Friendly campsite with Spanish ambiance. Good restaurant with pavement cafe. 3 km from lovely little town Comillas with culture (Gaudí), beaches and boulevards. Possible daytrips: a visit to the imposing Picos de Europa, the historic town of Santillana del Mar or the caves of Altamira.

🚗 E70/A8, exit 249 dir. Comillas. After 7 km take the CA 359 dir. Ruiloba. Through La Iglesia village and turn right onto CA 358. Campsite 300 metres on the right.

San Vicente De La Barquera

CC € **17** 23/3-8/7 26/8-29/9

📍 N 43°22'59'' W 4°14'47''

S. Vicente de la Barquera, E-39540 / Cantabria ♿ 🛜 iD (2915)

- 🏕 Caravaning Oyambre Cat.1
- 📧 Finca Peña Gerra
- ☎ +34 942-711461
- 📠 +34 942-711530
- 🔑 3/3 - 21/10
- @ camping@oyambre.com

4ha 128T(20-120m²) 10A

1 ABCDGIJKLMOPQ
2 AGJLRVWX
3 B**F**N
4 (B+G 1/4-28/9)
  (Q+R+T+U+X+Y 🔑)
5 **AB**FGIJKMNOPUWZ
6 EGK(N 5km)OTV

💬 A luxury campsite in one of the nature parks of Cantabria. You can go on lovely excursions from the campsite in all weather conditions. Culture (Gaudi in Comillas), nature (dunes, sea, Picos de Europa), history (caves of Altamira in Santillana del Mar). Fine campsite restaurant.

🚗 E70/A8 Santander-Oviedo, exit km post 264 S. Vicente de la Barquera, then N634 for 3 km to Comillas exit on the Ctra La Revilla-Comillas (CA 131) between km posts 27 and 28.

San Vicente De La Barquera

CC € **19** 3/3-29/6 1/9-20/10

📍 N 43°23'42'' W 4°20'17''

Foz, E-27780 / Galicia ♿ 🛜 iD (2916)

- 🏕 San Rafael
- 📧 Playa de Peizas
- ☎ 📠 +34 982-132218
- 🔑 27/4 - 1/10
- @ info@campingsanrafael.com

1,2ha 100T(60-80m²) 6A

1 ACDFIJLPQ
2 AEFRVWXY
3 BHWY
4 (A 1/7-31/8) (Q 1/4-30/9)
  (R 20/6-30/9) (X 27/4-27/9)
  (Z 🔑)
5 **A**GIJKMOPUWX
6 CEGJK(N 2km)TV

NEW

💬 Located in Playa de Peizás, close to Foz in the centre of Losta de Lugo, an area full of recreation with many opportunities for fishing, (water)sports, walking and more. 3 km from San Martin de Mondoñedo, 2 km from the ruins of Castro de Fazouro and 15 km from Playa de las Catedrales.

🚗 Coming from Foz, in the direction of Ferrol N642, turn right to Playa de Peizas. From Ferrol towards Foz roundabout. Campsite signposted.

Burela / Foz / Barreiros

CC € **13** 27/4-9/7 27/8-30/9

📍 N 43°35'16'' W 7°16'56''

Louro, E-15291 / Galicia

A' Vouga
Ctra Muros-Finisterre, km 3
☎ 📠 +34 981-826115
⌚ 16/3 - 15/10
@ avouga@hotmail.es

👫 ♿ 📶 **iD** (2917)

1,5ha 70T 10A

1 ACDGIJLMPST
2 AEGOQRVWX
3 HWY
4 (Q+U+X+Y+Z 🔒)
5 **AB**IJKLMNOPUWX
6 CEGIK(N 0,5km)OTV

💬 A small level campsite on the beach. Easily accessed 500m from the village centre of Louro. 3 km from Muros. Bus stop in front of the campsite, which gets you to Santiago in 1 hour and 45 minutes. Very spacious, excellent and pleasant restaurant with typical Galician dishes and panoramic views of the sea. Dolphins can be seen from the terrace. Motorbike riders welcome.

🚌 Campsite on the Santiago-Noia-Muros-Louro road. 3 km beyond Muros. Well signposted.

AC-550 Muros
CC
Porto Do Son

CC € **17** 16/3-30/6 18/8-14/10 10=8

🏕 N 42°45'39'' W 9°3'44''

Louro/Muros, E-15291 / Galicia

San Francisco Cat.1
☎ +34 981-826148
⌚ 23/3 - 16/9
@ info@campingsanfrancisco.com

♿ 📶 **iD** (2918)

NEW

74T(60-80m²) 10A CEE

1 ABCDGIJKLMPST
2 AEOQR
3 AMNUY
4 (Q+R+S+U+X+Y+Z 🔒)
5 **AB**CGHIJKMNOPUWX
6 EGJ(N 0,2km)TV

💬 San Francisco campsite is located in the small village of Louro, in a beautiful area with trees, sea and mountains. With walking paths, architectural sights, petroglyphs, and just 200m from the beach. The campsite has all the facilities you could need on holiday. You can exercise and relax in a peaceful, pleasant atmosphere in direct contact with nature.

🚌 Campsite is on the road Santiago-Noia-Muros-Louro.

Muros
CC
Porto Do Son

CC € **19** 23/3-30/6 2/7-8/7 26/8-15/9

🏕 N 42°45'44'' W 9°4'20''

Mougas/Oia, E-36309 / Galicia

O Muiño Cat.1
C550 km 158
☎ +34 986-361600
⌚ 23/3 - 14/10
@ info@campingmuino.com

📶 **iD** (2919)

2,2ha 65T(50-80m²) 6-10A CEE

1 ACDFIJKLOPQ
2 EFGJKLQRVWX
3 ABGHJKMNUW
4 (A 1/7-31/8) (B+G 15/6-30/9)
   (Q 🔒) (S 20/6-15/9)
   (T+U+X+Z 🔒)
5 **AB**EFGIJKMNPUWX
6 CGK(N 10km)RTV

💬 A really beautiful, well run, level campsite by the sea with a lovely swimming pool. Every comfort is provided. The campsite is only open at the weekend (including Friday) from October up to and including March.

🚌 C550 Baiona-La Guardia as far as km-marker 26. Motorway Vigo-Baiona-a, Guardia. Campsite well signposted.

Nigrán
CC
Tomiño

CC € **19** 23/3-9/7 1/9-13/10 7=6

🏕 N 42°3'50'' W 8°53'29''

Muros/Louro, E-15250 / Galicia ✈ 📶 (2920)

🔼 Camping Ancoradoiro
📧 Ancoradoiro N6
☎ +34 981-878897
📅 25/4 - 16/9
@ wolfgangh@hotmail.es

1,5ha 50T(50-80m²) 20A

1 BCDEIJKN**P**
2 AEIJKLQRTVWXY
3 AWY
4 (Q 🍴) (Y+Z 1/7-31/8)
5 **A**GIJKMNOPUW
6 EGJ(N 3km)T

💬 Located in a natural area, quiet campsite with lots of greenery. Pitches offer privacy and the experience of nature, with a view of the sea from almost all pitches.

🚗 From Noia follow AC550 to Muros/Louro. Site is on right of road about 3 km after Louro. Site is well signposted.

AC-550
Muros
Porto do Son

CC € **15** 25/4-30/6 1/9-15/9 📍 N 42°45'27'' W 9°6'44''

Portonovo/Sanxenxo, E-36970 / Galicia ♿ 📶 🆔 (2921)

🔼 Paxariñas Cat.2
📧 Paxariñas - 34
☎ +34 986-723055
📠 +34 986-721356
📅 15/3 - 15/10
@ info@campingpaxarinas.com

2ha 205T(60-80m²) 10A

1 ACDFIJKLMOPQ
2 AEFGIJQRVX
3 ABKRWY
4 (Q 🍴) (S 19/6-30/9)
(T 1/7-30/8)
(U+Y+Z 1/7-15/10)
5 **AB**FGIJKLMNOPUX
6 CDEGK(N 1,5km)RTV

💬 A beautifully located campsite on two large bays with beautiful sandy beaches, easily accessible for motorhomes. Reaches down to the sea with all amenities at the hotel complex. A convenient starting point for visits in the area and the special bathing resort Sanxenxo.

🚗 Hotel and campsite complex face the sea. (C550). The entrance is on the bend. Clearly signposted.

Marín
Bueu

CC € **17** 15/3-1/7 1/9-14/10 8=7, 15=12 📍 N 42°23'32'' W 8°50'39''

Ribeira, E-15993 / Galicia ♿ 📶 ✿ 🆔 (2922)

🔼 Ria de Arosa 2 Rural
📧 Balteiro-Oleiros
☎ +34 981-865911
📠 +34 981-865555
📅 1/1 - 31/12
@ rural@campingriadearosa.com

10ha 245T(60-90m²) 10A

1 ABCD**G**IJLMPQ
2 BCFJRVWXY
3 BHJKMNRU
4 (B+H 15/5-30/9) (Q 🍴)
(S 15/6-15/9)
(T+U+X+Y+Z 🍴)
5 **AB**FGIJKLMNOPUWX
6 ACDEGK(N 2km)OTV

💬 A lovely campsite in a natural area. Peaceful location with plenty of space. Ideal for walkers and sportive people. Quads also for rent. Two swimming pools with terraces by the restaurant. Adapted for the disabled. 8 km from the motorway, and just 35 minutes from Santiago de Compostela.

🚗 Motorway Santiago-Padrón. Freeway Padrón-Ribeira, exit Ribeira. Well signposted.

Boiro
Ribeira

CC € **19** 1/1-30/6 1/9-31/12 7=4 📍 N 42°37'15'' W 8°59'14''

Valdoviño, E-15552 / Galicia

▲ Valdoviño Cat.1
🚏 Ferrol-Cedeira km 13
☎ +34 981-487076
🔑 26/3 - 2/4, 15/4 - 15/10
@ campingvaldovino@yahoo.es

🚻 📶 **iD** (2923)

1,7ha 80T(60-80m²) 15A

1 AFIJLPQ
2 AEGJRVWXY
3 AKNRWY
4 (Q 1/6-30/9) (S 1/7-31/8)
(U+V 🔑) (X+Y+Z 1/5-14/10)
5 **AB**FGIJKLMNOPUWZ
6 EG**K**(N 0,3km)ORTV

💬 This quiet campsite has well maintained toilet facilities and is within walking distance of a beautiful bay; surfers are quite in their element here. Restaurant serves traditional, tasty dishes. Special menu for ACSI customers.

🚗 A9, exit 34 (8 km). Valdoviño is located on the C646 Ferrol-Ortiguera coast road. The site is well signposted.

Cedeira

CC

N-655 **Narón**

CC € **17** 26/3-1/4 15/4-30/6 1/9-14/10

🔻 N 43°36'43'' W 8°9'0''

Avin, E-33556 / Asturias

▲ Picos de Europa Cat.2
🚏 Carratera Cangas, km 16
☎ +34 985-844070
🔑 1/1 - 31/12
@ info@picos-europa.com

🚻 📶 (2924)

4ha 150T(30-100m²) 6A

1 BCDFIJKLMO**PQ**
2 CGJRVWXY
3 AHJ
4 (A+B+G 1/7-31/8)
(Q+S+U+X+Y+Z 🔑)
5 **AB**FGIJKMOPUWZ
6 EGJ(N 2km)ORTV

💬 You will feel very welcome at this well-maintained family campsite in the heart of the Picos de Europa! Imposing natural scenery during all seasons. Campsite has a lot of tourist information for various (guided) excursions. Free wifi. Campsite and restaurant open all year. History, nature and culture.

🚗 A8-E70 exit 306 direction Naves. Then A263 direction Posada. Then A5-115 to end. Then follow camping signs.

N-634

A-8

Onís CC La Salce

Cabrales

CC € **17** 1/1-14/7 1/9-30/12

🔻 N 43°20'5'' W 4°56'47''

Caravia/Prado, E-33344 / Asturias

▲ Arenal de Morís Cat.1
🚏 El Pontón
☎ +34 985-853097
🔑 4/5-6/5,11/5-13/5,18/5-20/5
@ camoris@desdeasturias.com

📶 **iD** (2925)

6ha 260T(50-150m²) 10A

1 ABCD**G**IJKLMO**PQ**
2 AEFIJORTVW
3 BMR**W**Y
4 (B+Q+S+T+U+W 4/6-15/9)
(X 1/6-15/9) (Z 🔑)
5 **AB**GIKMOPUWXY
6 DEGJ(N 6km)OTV

💬 Attractive, spacious campsite 200m from the sea. The restaurant is also open in June and September. This coast is known for its many fossil discoveries and original dinosaur tracks. Go back in time millions of years in the new Jurassic Museum in Colunga (10 km). In April and May, opening and acceptance only at the weekends.

🚗 E70/A8 Santander-Oviedo. Exit 330. Direction Caravia, then N632 between 16 and 15 km posts direction Playa.

A-8 CC

Ribadesella

Parres N-634

CC € **19** 4/5-5/5 11/5-12/5 18/5-19/5 23/5-29/6 31/8-14/9

🔻 N 43°28'22'' W 5°10'59''

Cudillero, E-33154 / Asturias

🛖 Cudillero Cat.2
🏖 Playa de Aguilar
☎ +34 985-590663
🗓 23/3 - 2/4, 1/5 - 16/9
@ info@campingcudillero.com

📶 iD **2926**

2ha 141T(30-80m²) 3-6A CEE

1 ABFIJKLMO**P**RS
2 FRVWXY
3 BR
4 (B+G 1/6-16/9)
(Q+R 1/5-7/9) (X 26/6-28/8)
(Z 1/6-10/9)
5 **AB**EFGIJKLMNOPUW
6 CEGK(N 2km)OTV

💬 This well cared for and flower filled campsite is located 1 km from the sea. Lovely sandy beach, and a picturesque fishing village renowned for its authentic fish restaurants. Well worth a visit. The campsite has a lovely swimming pool with deckchairs. Nice level pitches. Excellent toilet facilities.

🚗 Don't take exit 431 Cudillero but exit 425 on A8 Oviédo-Coruña. Then N632 El Pito-Cudillero and follow campsite signs on AS-317.

A-8 CC **Castrillón**
Soto Del Barco

CC € **17** 23/3-1/4 1/5-7/7 27/8-15/9   📷 N 43°33'15'' W 6°7'45''

Llanes/Vidiago, E-33597 / Asturias

🛖 La Paz Cat.1
🏖 Playa de Vidiago
☎ +34 985 411235
🗓 23/4 - 14/10
@ delfin@campinglapaz.com

📶 **2927**

1,1ha 432T(40-90m²) 10-16A

1 BCD**G**IJKLOPQ
2 AEFGHJKQRVWXY
3 A**F**GHJ**W**Y
4 (Q+S+T+U+X+Y 🗓)
5 **AB**FGIJKLMNOPUWZ
6 ACEGJ(N 7km)ORTV

💬 A terraced site with fine views of the sea. Picos de Europa (30 min). Caravans towed to and from the pitch. Not much shade on the side facing the sea. Enjoy a beautiful sunset in the campsite restaurant. Due to big differences in high and low tides you have wonderful wide beaches. Good renovated toilet facilities.

🚗 Motorway A8 exit 285, then from Ovieda roundabout dir. N634 Unguera, 2nd roundabout Playa de Vidiago from Santander, exit Playa de Vidiago, cp.

Llanes
N-634 CC
Val De San Vicente
N-621

CC € **19** 23/4-29/6 1/9-13/10   📷 N 43°23'59'' W 4°39'11''

Ribadedeva, E-33590 / Asturias

🛖 Camping Colombres Cat.1
🏖 Ctra El Peral a Noriega, km 1
☎ +34 985-412244
🗓 26/3 - 16/9
@ info@campingcolombres.com

♿ 📶 iD **2928**

22ha 89T(86-100m²) 6-10A

1 ABCDGIJKLMOPST
2 FKLRVWX
3 AHJNR
4 (B+G+Q+R 🗓)
(U 29/3-1/4,22/6-16/9)
(X+Y 22/6-16/9) (Z 🗓)
5 **AB**FGIJKLMNOPUWX
6 CEGJ(N 3km)OTV

💬 A campsite with completely renovated amenities. Panoramic views of the Picos de Europa mountain range. Spacious pitches with plenty of vegetation. The enthusiastic owners will do all they can to make your holiday a success. Beautiful, new swimming pool. Also new: special room for children to play and be creative.

🚗 E70/A8 Santander-Oviédo exit 277 direction El Peral N634. Right at petrol station towards Noriéga. Follow campsite signs.

N-634
CC
San Vicente De La Barquera
N-621

CC € **19** 26/3-7/7 25/8-15/9   📷 N 43°22'31'' W 4°33'51''

Ribadesella, E-33560 / Asturias

2929

🔼 Ribadesella Cat.1
🏠 Ctra de C. Sebreño
☎ +34 985-857721
📠 +34 985-858293
🔓 23/3 - 23/9
@ info@camping-ribadesella.com

4ha 200T(40-120m²) 10A CEE

1 BCDGIJKLMOPQ
2 FJKLRVXY
3 BGHJMNOQRV
4 (B 1/6-16/9) (E 🔓)
   (G 15/5-16/9) KP
   (Q 23/3-16/9) (S 🔓)
   (T+X+Y+Z 19/3-27/3,
   18/6-18/9)
5 ABEFGIJKMNOPUWZ
6 ACEGHIK(N 0,5km)ORTV

💬 High above the charming town of Ribadesella. A natural campsite with a pleasant restaurant and a large covered terrace offering views of the Picos de Europa mountains. New indoor swimming pool. Enjoy a snack and a drink in the stylish new lounge with TV and panoramic views.

🚗 From E70/A8 Santander-Oviedo, exit 326 direction Pando. Turn left past Pando on the AS341. Campsite signposted 1.5 km further on. Key in ctra de Sebreño into SatNav.

N-632 — Ribadesella — A-8 — Parres — N-634 — N-625

CC € 19 23/3-27/3 2/4-29/6 1/9-22/9 · N 43°27'42'' W 5°5'13''

Abejar, E-42146 / Castilla y León

2930

🔼 Urbion
🏠 Ctra Soria-Burgos, N234
☎ +34 646-243349
📠 +34 975-090330
🔓 23/3 - 1/11
@ info@campingurbion.com

15ha 500T(120m²) 10A

1 ACDGIJKLMOP
2 BDIKLMRWXY
3 BHJMNRUW
4 (B+G 23/6-31/8)
   (Q+R+T+U 22/6-9/9)
   (X+Y+Z 8/6-2/9)
5 ADFGIJKLMNOPUWZ
6 CEGJ(N 4km)OTV

💬 A spacious campsite for a wonderful, relaxing stay in beautiful natural surroundings. The campsite has good amenities: bar-restaurant, tennis court, football pitch, swimming pool, supermarket etc. The campsite is located close to a recreational area where you can sunbathe or enjoy watersports. The surroundings are rich in art, history, flora and fauna.

🚗 From Soria take the N234 direction Burgos, in Abejar towards Molinos on the CL117, campsite 4 km on the right.

Vinuesa — Molinos De Duero — CC — N-234 — Abejar — N-122

CC € 19 9/4-7/7 1/9-31/10 7=6 · N 41°50'8'' W 2°47'13''

Burgos, E-09193 / Castilla y León

2931

🔼 Fuentes Blancas Cat.1
🏠 Cartuja Miraflores
☎ 📠 +34 947-486016
🔓 1/1 - 31/12
@ info@campingburgos.com

4,6ha 300T(50-70m²) 6A

1 ABCDGIJKLMOPQ
2 FGRVXY
3 AFGJKNQRU
4 (B+G 30/6-31/8) (Q 🔓)
   (R 1/5-30/9)
   (T+U+X+Y+Z 🔓)
5 ABDFGIJKLMNOPUWZ
6 CEGIK(N 3km)ORTV

💬 Ideally located for visiting Burgos. The bus to the town stops in front of the campsite and the centre is only 15 minutes away by bike. Burgos cathedral is world-famous and is a must for any visitor to the city. Free wifi on entire campsite.

🚗 A1 Madrid-Burgos. At Burgos follow N623 to Santander. Campsite then signposted.

N-627 — N-623 — AP-1 — N-I — A-231 — **Burgos** — CC — Ibeas De Juarros — A-62 — A-1 — N-234

CC € 19 1/1-27/3 3/4-9/7 27/8-30/12 7=6 · N 42°20'30'' W 3°39'28''

Cabrerizos/Salamanca, E-37193 / Castilla y León 👫 ♿ 📶 iD (2932)

🏕 Don Quijote***
📧 Ctra Aldealengua km 1,930
☎ +34 923-209052
🗓 1/3 - 31/10
@ info@campingdonquijote.com

6ha 86T(70-100m²) 10A CEE

1 ABCDFIJKLMO**P**
2 ACRSTVXY
3 BJWX
4 (B+G 1/6-30/9)
   (Q+R+S+T+U+X+Y+Z 🔲)
5 **AB**GIJKLMNOPQRUW
6 ACEGK(N 2km)RTV

💬 Campsite close to the river and Salamanca, a town with plenty of sights. Friendly family campsite with different types of pitches available. A beautiful cycling/walking path runs along the river to the town. Renewed sanitary facilities (2016).

🚗 When entering Salamanca from any direction: follow the signs to Plaza de España, then follow the signs to Aldealengua village. The campsite is 4 km on the right from Plaza de España.

CC € **17** 1/3-11/7 29/8-30/10 7=6, 14=11 | 🗺 N 40°58'30'' W 5°36'11''

Castrojeriz, E-09110 / Castilla y León 📶 iD (2933)

🏕 Camino de Santiago
📧 Virgen del Manzano s/n
☎ +34 947-377255
🗓 15/3 - 11/11
@ info@campingcamino.com

2ha 40T(30-60m²) 10A CEE

1 ACD**F**IJKLO**P**RS
2 KRVXY
3 HJK
4 (Q+R+U+X+Z 🔲)
5 **AB**GIJKLMOPUW
6 AEGJ(N 1km)ORTV

💬 Family campsite on the Santiago de Compostela pilgrim route, 20 min. from Burgos. Panoramic views of a Templars' Castle. History, walking and cycling. Birds of prey excursion. Traditional dishes from outdoor oven. Free wifi at restaurant.

🚗 A231 Leon-Burgos, exit 132, on BU 404 9 km or A62/E80 Valladolid-Burgos, exit 32 on BU 400 16 km to Castrojeriz. Right past petrol station on roundabout. Campsite signposted.

CC € **19** 15/3-14/7 1/9-10/11 | 🗺 N 42°17'23'' W 4°8'0''

Figueruela de Arriba, E-49520 / Castilla y León 📶 iD (2934)

🏕 Sierra de la Culebra Cat.1
📧 Carretera de Riomanzanas s/n
☎ +34 980-683020
🗓 10/3 - 4/11
@ info@
   campingsierradelaculebra.com

4,2ha 64T(< 110m²) 10A CEE

1 ABCDGIJKLMO**PQ**
2 BKLRVWXY
3 JM
4 (B+G 24/6-3/9) **N**(T+X 🔲)
   (Z 1/7-31/8)
5 **A**FGIKMNOPUW
6 ADEGJTV

💬 You will be given a warm welcome on this site surrounded by nature. Especially in spring there is an abundance of wild flowers. Peace and quiet. Spacious pitches. The Iberian wolf lives here and may be observed. Restaurant with home-made traditional specialities. Pool open 24/6 - 3/9.

🚗 A52 Benavente-Ourense exit 49 N631. After 4 km ZA912 dir. Alcañices 20 km after Mahide ZAP2438 dir. Figueruela, site after 3 km. Or E82 Zamora-Bragana at Alcañices N631.

CC € **19** 10/3-23/6 9/9-3/11 | 🗺 N 41°51'52'' W 6°24'52''

Galende/Zamora/Castilla y Leon, E-49361 / Castilla y León

⛺ El Folgoso Cat.2
🚏 Ctra Puebl. de Sanabr- S.M.de Castan
☎ +34 980-626774
⌚ 1/3 - 30/9
@ info@campingelfolgoso.com

🏕⛺ ♿ 📶 iD (2935)

13ha 500T 6A

1 ABCGIJKLMOP
2 ABDGIJORSTY
3 AHWZ
4 (Q 🔒)
  (R+T+U+X+Y+Z 1/7-31/8)
5 AGHIJKLMNOPUWZ
6 CEGJ(N 1,5km)TV

💬 A campsite located in the woods of a nature park and beside the Lago de Sanabria. The campsite has good quality clean toilet facilities, a beach for sunbathing and a lake for non motorised water recreation.

🚍 Via A52 exit Benavente/Puebla 79. Towards Ribadelago via ZA104. Follow arrows to El Folgoso.

Rosinos De La Requejada
N-525 A-52 CC

CC € ⑰ *1/3-14/7 1/9-29/9* **🏕 N 42°7'52'' W 6°42'7''**

Riaza/Segovia, E-40500 / Castilla y León

⛺ Riaza
🚏 Ctra de la Estación s/n
☎ +34 921-550580
⌚ 1/1 - 31/12
@ info@camping-riaza.com

📶 iD (2936)

12ha 185T(96-144m²) 12A

1 ABCDGIJKLMOPQ
2 BFLRSVWX
3 AGHMNRSU
4 (B+G 1/7-31/8)
  (Q+R+T+U+V+X+Z 🔒)
5 ABDFGIJKLMNOPUWXY
6 AEGJK(N 2km)OTV

💬 Campsite close to the delightful village of Riaza. The villages offer many possibilities for trips out. The province of Segovia is renowned for its excellent food and wine. Restaurant on the campsite is closed on Tuesdays. Wintersports possible in La Pinilla (9 km) from December to March.

🚍 From Burgos A1, exit 104. From Madrid A1, exit 103, N110 direction Riaza and Soria. Right at roundabout after 12 km. Campsite on the left, next to the 'Campo de Futbol'.

Bocéguillas   Urbanización Prado Pínilla
A-1   Riaza
N-110 CC

CC € ⑲ *1/1-29/6 31/8-31/12 7=6* **🏕 N 41°16'10'' W 3°29'50''**

Sta Marta de Tormes/Salamanca, E-37900 / Castilla y León

⛺ Regio Cat.1
🚏 Ctra Salamanca-Madrid, km 4
☎ +34 923-138888
📠 +34 923-138044
⌚ 1/1 - 31/12
@ recepcion@campingregio.com

♿ 📶 iD (2937)

3ha 129T(50-80m²) 10-12A

1 ABCDFIJLMOPQ
2 FGLRTVXY
3 BKMN
4 (B+G 1/6-15/9)
  (Q+S+T+U+V+X+Y+Z 🔒)
5 ABCEFGHIJKLMNOPUWXY Z
6 ACDEGHIK(N 1km)ORTVW

💬 Spacious, shaded site with large swimming pool. Direct bus to central Salamanca, which can also be reached by foot or bike along level back roads. Adjacent hotel has an excellent restaurant.

🚍 Campsite about 4 km outside Salamanca, on N501 to Avila. First drive through Sta Marta de Tormes, hotel on right with same name. Campsite behind hotel. From Salamanca: drive to roundabout and continue to Santa Marta de Tormes, site on the right. From Madrid: site on the left.

N-620
Villamayor A-62
Salamanca
CC   N-501
A-50
A-66

CC € ⑰ *1/1-14/7 1/9-31/12* **🏕 N 40°56'53'' W 5°36'53''**

Villares de la Reina/Salamanca, E-37184 / Castilla y León

🏕 Ruta de la Plata Cat.2
📧 Cam. Alto de Villamayor
☎ +34 923-289574
🔓 1/1 - 31/12
@ recepcion@
campingrutadelaplata.com

1,2ha 60T(60-80m²) 5A

1 ABCFIJKLMO**PQ**
2 FGIRTVXY
3 **F**
4 (B 1/6-15/9) (Q+R 🔓)
(Z 1/7-30/8)
5 **A**DGIJKLMNOPUW
6 AEJ(N 2km)OT

💬 The campsite is excellently located on the route to Southern Spain, Portugal and the city of Salamanca. The bus to Salamanca stops at the entrance.

🚗 On the N620 exit to Salamanca/Zamora at 238 km marker. Direction Salamanca then right immediately before 1st hotel restaurant under viaduct. Campsite on right. From Portugal exit 240 dir. Villamayor.

CC € **17** 1/1-5/7 23/8-31/12 7=6 — N 40°59'58'' W 5°40'44''

Aranjuez (Madrid), E-28300 / Madrid

🏕 Camping Internacional
Aranjuez Cat.1
📧 C/ Soto del Rebollo s/n
☎ +34 91-8911395
📠 +34 91-8920406
🔓 1/1 - 31/12
@ info@campingaranjuez.com

3ha 147T(35-110m²) 16A CEE

1 ABCDGIJKLMO**P**ST
2 CFRSVWXY
3 BFG**NORW**
4 (B+G 1/5-30/9) I
(Q+S+T+U+V+X+Y+Z 🔓)
5 **AB**DFGIJKLMNOPUWXYZ
6 ABCEGI**J**K(N 2km)ORSTV

💬 Friendly, helpful staff. Site is located on the River Tajo. Plenty of vegetation. 42 km from Madrid, 40 km from Toledo. A lovely palace at Aranjuez. Gardens, avenues, fountains, flowers and plenty of walks. Trains to the heart of Madrid.

🚗 From Madrid A4 exit 37 Aranjuez Norte. Turn left after 8 km before Aranjuez and follow camping signs. From the south exit 52, then straight through the town. On the left next to 'La Rana Verde'. Follow camping signs.

CC € **19** 1/1-27/3 2/4-25/4 2/5-27/6 2/9-31/12 7=6, 14=11 — N 40°2'32'' W 3°35'58''

El Escorial/Madrid, E-28280 / Madrid

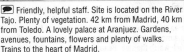

🏕 Camping El Escorial Cat.1
📧 M-600 km 3,5
☎ +34 918-902412
🔓 1/1 - 31/12
@ escorial@capfun.com

30ha 693T(90-120m²) 5-10A

1 ABCDFIJKLMO**P**ST
2 FLSTUVWXY
3 BF**G**HJKLMNRSU
4 (C+H 16/6-10/9) (Q+S 🔓)
(T+U+V+X+Y+Z 7/4-1/10)
5 **AB**DFGIJKLMNOPUWXZ
6 CGJ(N 4km)ORTV

💬 A large, spaciously laid out and well patrolled campsite. Large pitches with shade provided by many old trees and artificial sails. Also many sunny pitches. Plenty of opportunities for trips out close by (El Escorial, San Lorenzo) and further afield (Guadarama, Segovia). Madrid is easily reached by bus or train.

🚗 Located on the M600, km-marker 3.5 close by El Valle de Los Caidos. When approaching from Madrid take A6, exit 47 El Escorial/Guadarama.

CC € **19** 1/1-22/3 2/4-27/4 2/5-24/6 3/9-30/12 7=6 — N 40°37'37'' W 4°6'0''

Gargantilla del Lozoya/Madrid, E-28739 / Madrid

♿ 📶 ⚙ **iD** **2941**

🔺 Monte Holiday Cat.1
🅿 C604-km 9
☎ 🖷 +34 918-695278
🔓 1/1 - 31/12
@ monteholiday@monteholiday.com

30ha 125T(60-200m²) 7A CEE

1 **ABCD**GIJKLMO**P**
2 **B**FIJKLSTUVWXY
3 **B**GHJ**M**NRU
4 (**A** 🔓) (C+H 2/6-17/9)
   (Q+R 🔓)
   (T+U+V+X+Y+Z 13/3-1/4,
   15/6-16/9)
5 **AB**DFGIJKLMNOPUWZ
6 ACEGHIK(N 2km)ORTUV

💬 Lovely, eco-conscious campsite with a view of the mountain (Sierra de Guadarama). Quiet, clean, good restaurant and pool. Pitches with real green grass all year (for an extra fee). Suitable for visiting Segovia and Madrid.

🚗 From the A1 at the 69 km-marker exit towards Rascafria/Lozoya (M604). Turn off at the 8.8 km-marker (just after the tunnel) to the campsite (800 metres).

ℂℂ € **19** 1/1-27/3 2/4-26/4 2/5-21/6 24/6-28/6 1/7-5/7 26/8-31/12 7=6   🏕 N 40°57'0'' W 3°43'46''

La Cabrera (Madrid), E-28751 / Madrid

♿ 📶 **iD** **2942**

🔺 Pico de la Miel Cat.1
🅿 Autovia A1, salida 57
☎ +34 918-688082
🔓 1/1 - 31/12
@ info@picodelamiel.com

30ha 75T(50-90m²) 10A CEE

1 **ABCD**GIJLOP
2 FGSTUVWXY
3 **BFGHMNS**U
4 (B+G 9/6-16/9)
   (Q+S 15/5-30/9) (T 🔓)
   (U 1/5-15/9) (X+Y+Z 🔓)
5 **AB**DGIJKLMNOPUWXYZ
6 AEG**K**(N 0,2km)ORTV

💬 A campsite with a wide variety of trees, set at the foot of a beautiful mountain range, with a separate area for campers and swimming pools. A trip out to the mountain villages and a tour along the valley are well worth the visit. Beautiful panoramic views in rural nature. Ideal also as an overnight stop on your way to Portugal and the south of Spain.

🚗 Campsite located about 1 km from the A1. From Burgos and Madrid exit 57. Follow campsite signs.

ℂℂ € **19** 1/1-29/6 31/8-31/12 7=6   🏕 N 40°51'30'' W 3°36'59''

Villaviciosa de Odón/Madrid, E-28670 / Madrid

♿ 📶 ⚙ **iD** **2943**

🔺 Camping Madrid Arco Iris
🅿 M501 km 7,100
☎ +34 916-160387
🔓 17/1 - 31/12
@ madrid@bungalowsarcoiris.com

5ha 133T(70-207m²) 6-10A

1 **ABCD**F**IJ**KLOP**ST**
2 FGIJLSTUVWXY
3 **B**F**G**MRU
4 (B+G 1/6-15/9) **KN**
   (Q+S+T+U+V+X+Y+Z 🔓)
5 **AB**DFGIJKLMNOP**S**UWXYZ
6 ACEG**IK**(N 2km)ORTV

💬 A deceptively small campsite. Easy to find using the Madrid ring road. Ideal for a visit to Madrid (go to Boadilla by car, free parking, then by metro to the centre). Or go by car to Villaviciosa then take the bus. Very good restaurant.

🚗 Take exit 36 on the M40 ring road around Madrid. Take M501 direction Boadilla. Then direction Villaviciosa, take exit 7. The campsite is located on the right. Coming on the M50, exit 69, M501 direction Villaviciosa. Exit 7.

ℂℂ € **19** 17/1-25/3 2/4-30/6 1/9-31/12 6=5   🏕 N 40°22'52'' W 3°54'26''

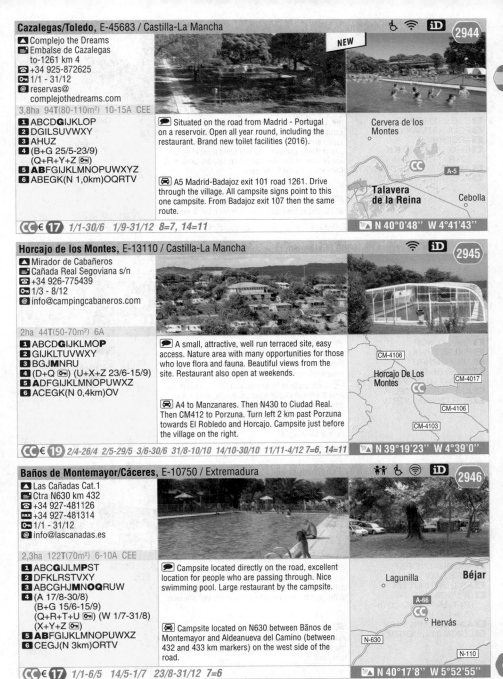

Cazalegas/Toledo, E-45683 / Castilla-La Mancha ♿ 📶 iD (2944)

🏕 Complejo the Dreams
📧 Embalse de Cazalegas
to-1261 km 4
☎ +34 925-872625
🕐 1/1 - 31/12
@ reservas@
complejothedreams.com

3,8ha 94T(80-110m²) 10-15A CEE

NEW

1 ABCD**G**IJKLOP
2 DGILSUVWXY
3 AHUZ
4 (B+G 25/5-23/9)
(Q+R+Y+Z 🕐)
5 **AB**FGIJKLMNOPUWXYZ
6 ABEGK(N 1,0km)OQRTV

💬 Situated on the road from Madrid - Portugal on a reservoir. Open all year round, including the restaurant. Brand new toilet facilities (2016).

🚗 A5 Madrid-Badajoz exit 101 road 1261. Drive through the village. All campsite signs point to this one campsite. From Badajoz exit 107 then the same route.

Cervera de los Montes

Talavera de la Reina   Cebolla

CC € 17 1/1-30/6 1/9-31/12 8=7, 14=11   📐 N 40°0'48'' W 4°41'43''

Horcajo de los Montes, E-13110 / Castilla-La Mancha 📶 iD (2945)

🏕 Mirador de Cabañeros
📧 Cañada Real Segoviana s/n
☎ +34 926-775439
🕐 1/3 - 8/12
@ info@campingcabaneros.com

2ha 44T(50-70m²) 6A

1 ABCD**G**IJKLMO**P**
2 GIJKLTUVWXY
3 BG**J**MNRU
4 (D+Q 🕐) (U+X+Z 23/6-15/9)
5 **A**DFGIJKLMNOPUWXZ
6 ACEGK(N 0,4km)OV

💬 A small, attractive, well run terraced site, easy access. Nature area with many opportunities for those who love flora and fauna. Beautiful views from the site. Restaurant also open at weekends.

🚗 A4 to Manzanares. Then N430 to Ciudad Real. Then CM412 to Porzuna. Turn left 2 km past Porzuna towards El Robledo and Horcajo. Campsite just before the village on the right.

CM-4106

Horcajo De Los Montes   CM-4017
CC
CM-4106
CM-4103

CC € 19 2/4-26/4 2/5-29/5 3/6-30/6 31/8-10/10 14/10-30/10 11/11-4/12 7=6, 14=11   📐 N 39°19'23'' W 4°39'0''

Baños de Montemayor/Cáceres, E-10750 / Extremadura 🚹🚺 ♿ 📶 iD (2946)

🏕 Las Cañadas Cat.1
📧 Ctra N630 km 432
☎ +34 927-481126
📠 +34 927-481314
🕐 1/1 - 31/12
@ info@lascanadas.es

2,3ha 122T(70m²) 6-10A CEE

1 ABC**G**IJLM**P**ST
2 DFKLRSTVXY
3 ABCGHJ**MN**O**Q**RUW
4 (A 17/8-30/8)
(B+G 15/6-15/9)
(Q+R+T+U 🕐) (W 1/7-31/8)
(X+Y+Z 🕐)
5 **AB**FGIJKLMNOPUWXZ
6 CEGJ(N 3km)ORTV

💬 Campsite located directly on the road, excellent location for people who are passing through. Nice swimming pool. Large restaurant by the campsite.

🚗 Campsite located on N630 between Baños de Montemayor and Aldeanueva del Camino (between 432 and 433 km markers) on the west side of the road.

Lagunilla   **Béjar**

A-66
CC   Hervás
N-630
N-110

CC € 17 1/1-6/5 14/5-1/7 23/8-31/12 7=6   📐 N 40°17'8'' W 5°52'55''

Cáceres, E-10005 / Extremadura   ♿ 🛜 (2947)

🏕 Cáceres Camping Cat.1
🛣 Ctra N630, km 549,5
☎ +34 927-233100
📅 1/1 - 31/12
@ reservas@campingcaceres.com

5,5ha 129T(90-110m²) 10-15A

1 BCGIJKLMO**P**ST
2 FGIJKLRSTVWXY
3 ABCFHRV
4 (B+G 15/6-15/9) **KN**
  (Q+R+T+U+V+X+Y+Z 🔌)
5 **AB**FGIJKLMNOPSTUWXYZ
6 ACEGK(N 3km)ORTV

💬 Unusually well-equipped and quiet, terraced campsite (with your own shower, washbasin and toilet) and a lovely large swimming pool. Spa and sauna (free). Excellent starting point for visiting the lovely town of Cáceres and the Natural Malpertida de Cácenes monument (10 min).

🚗 Campsite located 4 km north of the town on the N630 next to the football stadium with tall floodlights.

CC € ⑰ 1/1-15/3   3/4-28/6   2/9-31/12   4=3, 8=6, 12=9, 16=12   📷 N 39°29'19'' W 6°24'46''

Malpartida de Plasencia, E-10680 / Extremadura   ♿ 🛜 iD (2948)

🏕 Camping Parque Nacional
  de Monfragüe
🛣 C. Plasencia-Trujillo K10
☎ FAX +34 927-459233
📅 1/1 - 31/12
@ campingmonfrague@
  hotmail.com

4,8ha 128T(45-100m²) 10A

1 ABFIJKLMO**P**
2 FIKLRSTVWXY
3 ABGHJ**M**NRU
4 (A 🔌) (B+G 15/6-15/9)
  (Q+R+T+U+X+Y+Z 🔌)
5 **AB**FGIJKLMNOPUWZ
6 EGHJ(N 6km)OQRTV

💬 Quiet site under holm trees close to Parque Nacional de Monfragüe. 10 km from the town of Plasencia. Facilities: swimming pool with lawn, good restaurant, horse riding, guided tours, bike hire.

🚗 6 km south of Plasencia, exit EX108 Navalmoral. After 5 km exit EX208 towards Trujillo. After 4 km drive under the small viaduct. Site is located on the left directly after the viaduct. From Madrid EX-A1 exit 46, roundabout 3/4 round, follow signs of Nat. Park of Monfragüe.

CC € ⑰ 1/1-25/3   2/4-14/7   1/9-31/12   📷 N 39°56'38'' W 6°5'5''

Navaconcejo/Cáceres, E-10613 / Extremadura   👪 ♿ 🛜 iD (2949)

🏕 Cp Bungalows Rio Jerte
  (Las Veguillas) Cat.2
🛣 Ctra N110 km 375.800
☎ FAX +34 927-173006
📅 15/1 - 15/12
@ info@campingriojerte.com

1,5ha 25T(70m²) 5-10A

1 ABC**G**IJKLMO**P**ST
2 CLRSTVXY
3 ABGHJ**M**NRUVWX
4 (B 1/6-30/9) (Q 🔌)
  (R+T+U+X+Y 1/3-30/9)
  (Z 🔌)
5 **AB**FGIJKLMNOPUW
6 EGK(N 0,6km)ORTV

💬 Campsite with excellent location among the mountains, directly on the Rio Jerte river with a natural pond for swimming. Ideal for visiting the Jerte Valley and the natural area Garganta de los Infiernos.

🚗 From Plasencia via N630 and N110 towards Avila. After 26 km Navaconcejo. Left just before the village, over small bridge to campsite, clearly indicated.

CC € ⑰ 15/1-22/3   2/4-30/6   1/9-14/12   7=6, 14=11   📷 N 40°10'13'' W 5°50'39''

Plasencia/Cáceres, E-10600 / Extremadura ♿ 🛜 **iD** (2950)

🏕 La Chopera Cat.2
🛣 Ctra Nat.110 km 401,300
☎ +34 927-416660
📅 1/1 - 31/12
@ lachopera@
   campinglachopera.com

6ha 150**T**(65-80m²) 5-10A CEE

1 ABCGIJKLM
2 CLRTXY
3 ABGRU**W**X
4 (B 1/6-10/9) (G 1/6-15/9)
   (Q 📅) (R 1/7-31/8)
   (T+U+X+Y+Z 📅)
5 **A**FGIJKLMNOPUW
6 EGK(N 3km)ORTV

💬 Campsite on level ground with spacious pitches and abundant plants on the banks of a river. In the Jerte Valley, close to the Monfragüe National Park. Just 3 km from the historical town of Plasencia, the geographical centre of northern Extremadura. Access via a foot and cycle path beside the river.

🚐 From the N630 drive into the town of Plasencia. Then via the N110 in direction Avila. The campsite is about 3 km to the left of the road in the valley. Clearly signposted.

CC € **17** 1/1-14/7 1/9-31/12 7=6, 15=13   🏔 N 40°2'43'' W 6°3'31''

Alcalá de los Gazules, E-11180 / Andalucia ♿ 🛜 **iD** (2951)

🏕 Los Gazules Cat.2
🛣 Ctra de Patrite, km 4
☎ +34 956-420486
📠 +34 956-420388
📅 1/1 - 31/12
@ info@campinglosgazules.com

40ha 140**T**(40-80m²) 10A

1 ABCD**G**IJKLMPST
2 CFLRSVWX
3 ABGHN**O**
4 (B+G 15/5-30/9)
   (Q+R+T+U+X+Z 📅)
5 **AB**GIJKLMNOPUW
6 AEG**J**(N 5km)OV

💬 Set in beautiful countryside in the heart of the Los Alcornocales nature park. Perfectly suited to all types of outdoor activities and walks. No traffic disturbance. Well equipped campsite with as much shade as you want. Advantageous menus.

🚐 Between Jerez de la Frontera and Los Barrios via Ctra 381 to Alcalá de los Gazules. Exit 45 on the A381. Enter village. Follow road (not SatNav) into centre. Campsite signposted at end of road outside the town. Another 4 km.

CC € **19** 1/1-24/3 1/4-14/7 1/9-31/12 7=6, 14=12   🏔 N 36°27'49'' W 5°39'53''

Almayate (Málaga), E-29749 / Andalucia 🚫 ♿ 🛜 (2952)

🏕 Almayate Costa Cat.1
🛣 Ctra N340a km 267
☎ +34 952-556289
📅 19/1 - 15/10
@ info@campingalmayatecosta.com

3ha 234**T**(40-90m²) 10A

1 BCDEIJKLMO**P**ST
2 AEFGLTVWY
3 B**F**MNRUWY
4 (B 20/4-30/9)
   (Q+S+T+U+X+Y+Z 📅)
5 **AB**FGIJKLMNOPUWZ
6 EGJK(N 1km)ORSTV

💬 Well maintained beachside campsite with excellent sanitation. Plenty of shade from trees. The campsite has a beautiful swimming pool.

🚐 Located on the (old) coastal road N340a at km-marker 267. On Autovia A7 Málaga-Almería from Almería exit 272 to Torre del Mar. Continue direction Málaga. From Málaga exit Benejarafe/Chilches; continue towards Almería.

CC € **19** 19/1-28/3 1/4-22/6 1/9-14/10   🏔 N 36°43'28'' W 4°8'5''

Almayate (Málaga), E-29749 / Andalucia

△ FKK Camping Naturista Almanat
🖂 Ctra N340, km 269
☎ +34 952-556462
☷ 1/1 - 31/12
@ info@almanat.es

2953

2ha 240T(50-115m²) 8-20A

1 BGIJKLMOPQ
2 AEFGLNTVWXY
3 BFGKNOQRUWY
4 (A+B ☷)
(F 1/1-14/6,15/9-31/12) N
(Q+R+T+X+Y+Z ☷)
5 ABGIJKMNOPUWXZ
6 ACEGK(N 2km)ORTV

💬 Attractive naturist campsite located right by the sea with indoor and outdoor swimming pool. Restaurant by the beach.

🚗 A7 Málaga-Motril and vice versa, exit 272 Torre del Mar. In Torre del Mar keep in direction Málaga. Located on the N340a, at km-marker 269, just outside Torre del Mar, on the seaward side of the road. Signposted.

A-356
Vélez-Málaga Sayalonga
A-7
CC

CC €19 1/1-5/7 27/8-31/12   📷 N 36°43'58'' W 4°6'52''

Almería, E-04002 / Andalucia

△ La Garrofa
🖂 Ctra N340a, km 435,4
☎ +34 950-235770
☷ 1/1 - 31/12
@ info@lagarrofa.com

2954

2ha 100T(10-65m²) 6-10A

1 BCGIJKLMOPST
2 EFGJKNTVXY
3 AFHNWY
4 (Q+R+U+X+Z ☷)
5 AGIJKLMNOPUWZ
6 EGK(N 4km)OTV

💬 Small and friendly campsite; lovely location, right by the sea. Well shaded in parts. The bus to Almería stops outside the campsite.

🚗 N340 Almería-Málaga v.v. At Almería towards 'Puerto'. Turn around at roundabout. Keep to the left (left hand tunnel towards Aguadulce). Turn left after about 3 km. Campsite signposted.

A-92
Almería
A-7 CC
Roquetas De Mar

CC €17 1/1-30/6 15/9-31/12   📷 N 36°49'35'' W 2°30'59''

Balerma/Almería, E-04712 / Andalucia

△ Mar Azul Balerma Cat.2
🖂 Ctra de Guardias Viejas, s/n
☎ +34 950-937637
FAX +34 950-912126
☷ 1/1 - 31/12
@ info@campingbalerma.com

2955

5ha 220T(70-100m²) 16A

1 BCDGIJKLMOPQ
2 AEFNUVWX
3 BFGHJNRUWY
4 (A+B+G+Q+R+T+U+V+Y+Z ☷)
5 ABDFGIJKLMNOPUWXY
6 ABCDEGK(N 0,5km)OTUV

💬 Modern, new campsite at about 100 metres from the beach. Shade limited for now. Pitches with water and drainage. Excellent toilet facilities.

🚗 A7 Almería/Motril, from both directions, take exit 400 or 403, dir. Balerma. Follow signs instead of Satnav.

El Ejido
Adra A-7
CC

608 CC €17 1/1-30/6 1/9-31/12   📷 N 36°43'20'' W 2°52'40''

Beas de Granada, E-18184 / Andalucia

                           ♿ 🛜 (2956)

🅰 Alto de Viñuelas Cat. 2
✉ Ctra Beas de Granada s/n
☎ +34 958-546023
🗓 1/1 - 31/12
@ info@
    campingaltodevinuelas.com

1ha 48T(30-60m²) 10A

1 BCDGIJKLMOPQ
2 FGJKRTVWXY
3 GHJR
4 (B 1/5-30/9) (G 1/7-31/8)
    (Q+T+U+X+Y+Z 🔲)
5 **AB**FGIJKLMNOPUWZ
6 ACEG**K**(N 1km)RTV

💬 An unpretentious and peaceful campsite. Attractively laid out terraces. Lovely views of the Sierra Nevada. Good local cuisine. The bus to Granada stops outside the campsite. 2 Euros are charged for a trailer. From a second pet 1 Euros extra is charged.

🚗 A92 Granada-Almería/Murcia and vice versa, exit 256 direction Beas de Granada. Follow the signs.

A-92

CC

Granada

La Zubia

CC €19 1/1-14/7 1/9-31/12 7=6, 15=13   🗺 N 37°13'29'' W 3°29'19''

Cabo de Gata (Almería), E-04150 / Andalucia

                           ♿ 🛜 **iD** (2957)

🅰 Cabo de Gata Cat. 2
✉ Ctra Cabo de Gata s/n
☎ +34 950-160443
📠 +34 950-916821
🗓 1/1 - 31/12
@ info@campingcabodegata.com

3,6ha 228T(30-130m²) 6-16A

1 ABCD**G**IJKLMOPQ
2 AFTVWX
3 B**F**GHJ**M**RU
4 (B+Q+R+T+U+X+Y+Z 🔲)
5 **AB**EFGIJKMNOPUWXZ
6 EG**K**(N 2km)ORTV

💬 A very well maintained and equipped campsite. A lovely spot on the edge of a desert-like nature park, about 1 km from a long sandy beach.

🚗 A7 (N340) Almería-Murcia, exit 460; Murcia-Almería, exit 467. Follow San José signs, then Cabo de Gata, 1 km on the right.

A-7 ° Las Cuevas De Los Medinas

CC

CC €19 1/1-30/6 1/9-31/12 14=11   🗺 N 36°48'29'' W 2°13'55''

Caños de Meca/Barbate, E-11159 / Andalucia

                           ♿ 🛜 **iD** (2958)

🅰 Pinar San José
✉ Zahora 17
☎ +34 956-437030
📠 +34 956-437174
🗓 1/1 - 31/12
@ info@campingpinarsanjose.com

3,7ha 150T(25-150m²) 16A

1 ABCD**G**IJKLMP
2 BFGJLRSVWXY
3 BK**MN**S
4 (B+G 25/5-15/10)
    (Q+S+T+U+X+Y+Z 🔲)
5 **AB**GIJKMNOPUWXYZ
6 ACEGIK(N 0km)STV

💬 Located in a large pine forest next to Breña nature park, with predominantly comfort pitches on fresh grass, this campsite offers plenty of natural recreation and is close to spacious beaches.

🚗 On N340/E5 Cadiz-Algeciras take the Vejer/Caños de Meca exit. Left at the roundabout and the campsite is 10 km further left on, just past the bend. 1 km from the sea. Via A48, exit 36 to Los Caños de Meca and continue as above.

Conil De La Frontera **A-48**

N-340

CC

CC €19 1/1-28/3 2/4-14/6 9/9-31/12   🗺 N 36°12'3'' W 6°2'5''

Carchuna/Motril (Granada), E-18730 / Andalucia

⚀ 📶 **2959**

- ▲ Don Cactus Cat.1
- 🕛 CN340, km 343
- ☏ +34 958-623109
- 🕒 1/1 - 31/12
- @ info@doncactus.com

4ha 254T(60-70m²) 5-12A CEE

1. BCD**G**IJKLMOPST
2. AEGLNTVXY
3. BGK**M**NRUV**W**Y
4. (**A** 1/11-31/12, 1/1-31/3)
   (**B**+G 🔑) IJ
   (Q+S+T+U+X+Y+Z 🔑)
5. **AB**EFGIJKLMNOPUWXYZ
6. CEG**IK**M(N 0,5km)OSTV

🗪 A well maintained and organised campsite. Plenty of trees. The campsite is located by the beach. The large swimming pool with water slide and bubble bath is open all year round. All pitches with water and drainage.

🚙 A7 Motril-Almería, exit Carchuna. Follow signs Carchuna exit 342. Here, follow campsite signs.

Motril
Salobreña
N-340
A-7
CC

CC € **19** 1/1-22/3 1/4-26/4 1/5-30/5 3/6-21/6 9/9-31/12 7=6, 14=11 | 🏔 N 36°41'45'' W 3°26'36''

Conil de la Frontera, E-11149 / Andalucia

⚀ 📶 **iD** **2960**

- ▲ Camping Los Eucaliptos Cat.2
- 🕛 Crta del Pradillo km 0200 c.p.
- ☏ +34 956-441272
- 🕒 23/3 - 30/9
- @ eucaliptos@hotmail.es

2ha 133T(50-100m²) 10A

1. AB**G**IJL**P**
2. ABFSVXY
3. U
4. (B 1/6-30/9)
   (Q+R+T+U+X+Z 🔑)
5. **AB**GIKMOPUVW
6. EGIK(N 0,1km)QRTV

🗪 A very shaded campsite under eucalyptus trees, close to the centre. A friendly bar and restaurant with views of the swimming pool.

🚙 Take the N340/E5 between Cadiz and Tarifa to Conil. Campsite and playas well signposted in town, follow signs on ring road just before the town.

CC
Conil De La Frontera
A-48

CC € **17** 23/3-14/7 1/9-29/9 | 🏔 N 36°17'14'' W 6°5'26''

Conil de la Frontera, E-11140 / Andalucia

⚀ 📶 **iD** **2961**

- ▲ Camping Roche Cat.2
- 🕛 Carril de Pilahito s/n
- ☏ +34 956-442216
- 📧 +34 956-442624
- 🕒 1/1 - 31/12
- @ info@campingroche.com

6ha 300T(60-90m²) 10A CEE

1. ABCD**G**IJKLMO**P**ST
2. ABFGLRSVWX
3. AF**H**JM**R**SVW
4. (B+G 10/5-30/10)
   (Q+S+T+U+X+Y+Z 🔑)
5. **AB**GIJKLMNOPUWX
6. AEGK(N 3km)ORTV

🗪 Site with spacious pitches. Ideal for winter. Older section newly laid out with comfort pitches. On grass, with a lovely swimming pool in the middle and plenty of deckchairs. Barbecues permitted in winter.

🚙 N340/E5 between Cadiz and Tarifa to Conil (2 km). Follow the 'playas' and/or 'camping' signs on the ring road, then campsite's own sign. Also accessible along the N340, 2 km before the Conil exit to Cadiz. From A48/E5 exit 15 dir. N340, right at km-marker 19.

A-48
CC
Conil De La Frontera

CC € **15** 1/1-30/6 1/9-31/12 | 🏔 N 36°18'38'' W 6°6'46''

Conil de la Frontera, E-11140 / Andalucia

♿ 🛜 **iD** (2962)

🏠 La Rosaleda Cat. 1
📧 Ctra del Pradillo km 1,3
☎ +34 956-443327
📠 +34 956-443385
📅 1/1 - 31/12
@ info@campinglarosaleda.com

6ha 335T(72-150m²) 10A

1 ABGIJKLMO**P**ST
2 AJLRTVWXY
3 B**F**GHJKL**M**NR**V**
4 (**A** 🔒) (B 1/6-30/9) **N**
(Q+S 🔒)(T+U+X+Y+Z
1/1-30/9,1/11-31/12)
5 **AB**EFGHIJKLMNOPUWXYZ
6 ABEGIK(N 0,5km)ORTVW

💬 Terraced campsite with spacious pitches screened by various types of tree. Beautifully landscaped with wide avenues and borders. Variety of winter entertainment. Barbecues permitted in low season. Sauna and fitness room.

🚐 Take the N340/E5 between Cadiz and Tarifa to Conil (2 km). On the right the 'playas' and/or 'campsite' signs are clearly indicated. Follow signs. Campsite about 1 km on the right.

Conil De La Frontera
A-48

CC € **17** 1/1-21/6 10/9-31/12

📐 N 36°17'36'' W 6°5'44''

El Puerto de Santa Maria, E-11500 / Andalucia

👫 ♿ 🛜 **iD** (2963)

🏠 Playa Las Dunas Cat.1
📧 P.M. Playa La Puntilla s/n
☎ +34 956-872210
📠 +34 956-860117
📅 1/1 - 31/12
@ info@lasdunascamping.com

13ha 300T(50-80m²) 10A

1 ABCDGIJKLM**P**
2 AEGJLSVWXY
3 B**F**G**M**N**W**Y
4 (**B**+**G** 15/6-30/8)
(Q+T+U+Y+Z 🔒)
5 **AB**FGIJKLMNOPUV
6 EGI**K**(N 1,5km)OTV

💬 Situated in pine woods with three excellent toilet blocks, this campsite offers excellent possibilities for families with children; large children's pool, huge sandy beach. Larger caravans can pitch in the newer section but there is not much shade there. Barbecues not accepted from 15/5 to 15/10. Swimming pool free during weekdays.

🚐 Follow signs from El Puerto de Santa Maria. Well signposted throughout the town. (Do not drive to the centre.)

El Puerto De Santa María
CC A-4

Cádiz
AP-4

CC € **17** 1/1-29/6 16/9-31/12

📐 N 36°35'15'' W 6°14'26''

El Rocío, E-21750 / Andalucia

♿ 🛜 ✿ **iD** (2964)

🏠 La Aldea Cat.1
📧 Ctra del Rocío, km 25
☎ +34 959-442677
📠 +34 959-442582
📅 1/1 - 31/12
@ info@campinglaaldea.com

6ha 200T(27-90m²) 10A

1 ABCD**G**IJKLPQ
2 **G**LRVWXY
3 B**G**JN**OU**
4 (B 23/3-2/10)
(Q+S+T+U+Y+Z 🔒)
5 **AB**GIJKLMNOPUWXZ
6 EGK(N 1km)ORTV

💬 Extremely well-maintained site with large grassy pitches surrounded by hedges with shade. Swimming pool, attractive restaurant and air-conditioned recreational bar. Special seaside town near the famous Doñana natural area. CampingCard ACSI not accepted from 16/05 to 22/05 (La Romería de El Rocío).

🚐 E1/A49 Sevilla-Portugal. Exit 60 Almonte A483, this road becomes the A484 (new road). Follow El Rocio signs.

Los Cabezudos

CC
El Rocío
A-483

A-494

CC € **19** 1/1-15/5 23/5-6/7 24/8-31/12 7=6, 14=11

📐 N 37°8'29'' W 6°29'27''

Estepona (Malaga), E-29680 / Andalucia

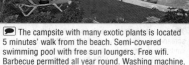

🏕 Parque Tropical Cat.2
🛏 Ctra N340, km 162
☎ +34 95-2793618
🗓 1/1 - 31/12
@ parquetropicalcamping@hotmail.com

〰 📶 iD 2965

1,2ha 71T(60-100m²) 10A CEE

1 ABCD**G**IJKLMNO**P**Q
2 AEFGJSTVWXY
3 B**F**JVWY
4 (E+G+Q+R+T+U+X+Y+Z ⊙)
5 **AB**GHIJKLMNOPUW
6 ABEGK(N 3km)ORTW

💬 The campsite with many exotic plants is located 5 minutes' walk from the beach. Semi-covered swimming pool with free sun loungers. Free wifi. Barbecue permitted all year round. Washing machine. Chemical toilet.

🚐 Via A7 (not the motorway) between Marbella and Estepona (6 km) between 163 and 162 km markers. Well signposted.

Estepona — AP-7 Nueva Andalucía A-7 CC

CC € 17 1/1-14/7 1/9-31/12 · 🗺 N 36°27'15'' W 5°4'51''

Granada/La Zubia, E-18140 / Andalucia

🏕 Reina Isabel Cat.2
🛏 Laurel de la Reina 15
☎ +34 958-590041
📠 +34 958-591191
🗓 1/1 - 31/12
@ info@campingreinaisabel.com

♿ 📶 2966

0,6ha 57T(30-70m²) 6A

1 BDGIJKLMO**P**Q
2 FGTVXY
3 **F**HJ
4 (**A** ⊙) (B 5/5-30/9) (Q+R+T+U+V+Y+Z ⊙)
5 **AB**DFGIJKLMNOPUWZ
6 ABCEG**K**(N 0,5km)R

💬 A well equipped campsite with stylish buildings. The site is mainly used for visiting Granada and its sights. The pitches are well marked out and offer sufficient shade. The site is well located for visiting Granada and the bus to Granada stops in front of the campsite.

🚐 Located on the edge of the village of La Zubia, south of Granada. When approaching from any direction: via Circunvalación/Autovia Granada. Exit Ronda Sur, then exit 2 La Zubia. Follow the signs.

Santa Fé — **Granada** A-338 CC A-44

CC € 19 1/1-28/2 29/5-30/6 1/9-31/12 · 🗺 N 37°7'28'' W 3°35'12''

Granada/Otura, E-18630 / Andalucia

🏕 Suspiro del Moro Cat.2
🛏 Autovia A44, exit 139
☎ 📠 +34 958-555411
🗓 1/1 - 31/12
@ campingsuspirodelmoro@yahoo.es

📶 2967

1ha 59T(60m²) 5A

1 BCDGIJKLMO**P**Q
2 FGKRTVXY
3 B**F**R
4 (B+G 24/6-4/9) (Q+R+T+Z ⊙)
5 **A**DFGIJKMNOPUWZ
6 ACEGI**K**(N 3km)OTV

💬 A peaceful, unpretentious campsite with plenty of trees and shaded pitches. Suitable as a stopover campsite and as a base for visiting Granada and surroundings. Campsite will book for Alhambra palace. Bus service to Granada from the campsite.

🚐 A44, Granada-Motril, exit 139 Otura. Follow signs to Padul, Suspiro del Moro and camping signs. Take note: after leaving roundabout on the west of the A44, turn left after ± 20m to Padul. After a few km keep right.

Granada A-338 CC A-44 N-323A Dúrcal

CC € 17 1/1-7/4 17/4-1/7 5/9-11/10 16/10-5/12 11/12-31/12 · 🗺 N 37°4'6'' W 3°39'9''

Güejar Sierra (Granada), E-18160 / Andalucia

2968

◢ Camp. & Carav. Las Lomas Cat.1
✉ Ctra Güejar Sierra km 6
☎ +34 958-484742
📠 +34 958-484000
🗓 1/1 - 31/12
@ info@campinglaslomas.com

1,6ha 100T(40-110m²) 10A

1 BCDGIJKLMO**PQ**
2 GIJKLRTVWXY
3 BGH**Q**RU
4 (A 🔌) (B 15/4-31/10)
  (G 1/6-15/9) **N**
  (Q+S+T+U+Y+Z 🔌)
5 **AB**DFGIJKLMNOP**RST**UW
  XYZ
6 CEG**IK**(N 2km)RTV

💬 Comfortable campsite with lots of facilities and spacious, marked out pitches in the shade. Altitude: 1100 metres, about 200 metres above storage reservoir. Beautiful view of the mountains of the Sierra Nevada. Only 30 km away from a skiing area.
🚗 Circunvalación (Motril-Jaén v.v.) then exit 132 to Ronda Sur. Follow Sierra Nevada. Take right hand lane 3 km past the tunnel then turn left. Follow signs 'Güejar Sierra' and 'Las Lomas'. Ignore small camping signs.

N-342 A-92
Granada
La Zubia CC

CC € **19** 1/1-28/3 2/4-6/7 1/9-5/12 9/12-27/12 **21=20, 30=27** | 📍 N 37°9'36'' W 3°27'14''

Hinojos, E-21740 / Andalucia

🛜 ✿ **iD** **2969**

◣ Yelloh! Village Doñarrayan Park
✉ Ctra Hinojos a El Rocío 7 km
☎ +34 959-027502
🗓 1/1 - 4/11, 5/12 - 31/12
@ info@donarrayan-park.com

7ha 48T(100-120m²) 16A

1 ABCDGIJKLMOPST
2 BKLSVWXY
3 ABGHJKN
4 (A 🔌) (B 15/6-15/9)
  (Q+R+T+U+V+Y+Z 🔌)
5 **AB**GIJKLMNPUWXYZ
6 CDEG**K**(N 5km)QRTUVW

💬 Beautiful campsite located in the woods in the heart of the Doñana National Park. Ideal for people seeking some peace and quiet, nature lovers, walkers and families with young children. Excellent amenities, swimming pool with lawn, restaurant and a small shop.
🚗 Follow E1/A49 Sevilla-Huelva. Take exit 34 Chucena/Hinojos. Via A481 to Hinojos. Take ring road A474 dir. Almonte. After ± 500m left to Almoradux and ± 5 km to campsite.

Almonte
CC
Villamanrique de La Condesa
A-483

CC € **17** 1/1-22/3 7/4-2/6 16/6-30/6 1/9-3/11 5/12-31/12 | 📍 N 37°14'30'' W 6°22'58''

Humilladero, E-29531 / Andalucia

🛜 **2970**

◣ La Sierrecilla
✉ Avda de Blas Infante
☎ +34 951-199090
🗓 1/1 - 31/12
@ info@lasierrecilla.com

4ha 120T(60-90m²) 10A

1 BCD**G**IJKLMOPST
2 FIJKLSTUVWXY
3 AGHJ**NOP**U
4 (B+G 1/6-5/9) **N**
  (Q+T+U+X+Y+Z 🔌)
5 **A**DFGIJKLMNOPUWZ
6 CEGJ(N 2km)V

💬 A relatively new campsite in which the planting has not yet matured. High quality toilet facilities, luxuriously designed, attractive hinterland.

🚗 Autovia A92 (Antequera-Sevilla), exit 138, direction Humilladero. Left at roundabout after ±2km. Follow signs. SatNav not reliable here.

Fuente De
Piedra ○ Mollina
CC A-92
A-45
N-331

CC € **17** 1/1-22/3 1/4-21/6 10/9-11/10 15/10-5/12 9/12-31/12 | 📍 N 37°6'28'' W 4°41'47''

Isla Cristina, E-21410 / Andalucia

2971

🔼 Giralda Cat.1
🛏 Ctra la Antilla, km 1,5
☎ +34 959-343318
📠 +34 959-343284
📅 1/1 - 31/12
@ recepcion@campinggiralda.com

15ha 450T(40-80m²) 10A

1 ABCD**G**IJKLMPST
2 ABCEJSWXY
3 A**F**GJNRU**W**Y
4 (B+G+Q+S+T 📅)
   (U 31/3-8/4,1/7-31/8)
   (W 31/3-7/4,1/7-31/8)
   (Z 1/6-30/9)
5 **AB**FGIJKLMNOPUW
6 EGIJ**K**(N 1,5km)ORTV

💬 Small squares under the pine trees, separated by roads and slopes divide up this extensive campsite. Located close to a sandy beach and next to the Rio Carreras swamp area which can be visited by pedal boat. All types of meals, including pizza and paella are available in the snack bar. Campsite with ISO Certificate.

🚗 From the direction of Huelva towards Portugal, take exit to Isla Cristina. Then in direction La Antilla. Campsite about 1.5 km on the left.

CC € ⑲ 1/1-30/6 1/9-31/12 12=10, 30=20   📡 N 37°12'0'' W 7°18'3''

La Mamola, E-18750 / Andalucia

2972

🔼 Castillo de Baños Cat.2
🛏 CN340, km 360
☎ +34 958-829528
📅 1/1 - 31/12
@ info@campingcastillo.com

3ha 234T(30-70m²) 5-12A

1 BCD**G**IJKLMOPST
2 EFGNORTVWXY
3 G**W**Y
4 (B+Q+S+T+U+Y+Z 📅)
5 **AB**GIJKLMNOPUWXYZ
6 EG**K**(N 0,2km)ORTV

💬 The campsite has marked out pitches with plenty of trees for good, natural shade. The campsite is located right by a narrow beach.

🚗 A7, exit 359 between Motril and Almeria. Look out for camping signs. Do not use SatNav.

CC € ⑲ 1/1-30/6 1/9-31/12 7=6, 14=11   📡 N 36°44'27'' W 3°18'4''

La Redondela, E-21430 / Andalucia

NEW

2973

🔼 Camping Playa Taray
🛏 Ctra. La Antilla-Isla Cristina km 4
☎ +34 959-341102
📅 1/1 - 31/12
@ info@campingplayataray.es

165T(72-90m²) 6-10A

1 ABCD**G**IJKLMNO**P**T
2 ABCEGKSTVWXY
3 BHKNWY
4 (B 15/5-15/10)
   (Q+R+T+U+X+Y+Z 📅)
5 **AB**CGHIKMNOPU
6 ABDFGK(N 1km)TV

💬 This renovated campsite exudes a fresh new look. With the beautiful beach on the other side of the road, the nearby harbour, resorts (Isla Christina and La Antilla), the nature reserve and Portugal just a stone's throw away, this is one place you won't get bored.

🚗 A49 exit 117 then left N445 towards Lepe (West). Follow the signs La Redondela Isla Christina to A5054. At roundabout Playa Taray campsite is on the left.

CC € ⑪ 1/1-30/6 1/9-31/12   📡 N 37°12'21'' W 7°15'56''

Los Escullos/Nijar (Almería), E-04118 / Andalucia    ♿ 🛜 **iD** (2974)

🔺 Los Escullos Cat.1
🏕 Parque Natural Cabo de Gata
☎ +34 950-389811
📠 +34 950-106400
🔓 1/1 - 31/12
@ info@losescullossanjose.com

4,5ha 216**T**(40-80m²) 16A

1 ABCD**G**IJKLMO**P**ST
2 AJNOQTVWXY
3 BGHIJK**M**NRU**V**W
4 (**A**+B 🔓) **K**N(Q+S 🔓)
  (T 1/6-15/9)
  (U+V+X+Y+Z 🔓)
5 **AB**FGIJKLMNOPUWZ
6 ABCEGHK(N 5km)TV

💬 A campsite with pitches shaded by trees or (in summer) by sun screens. About 1 km from the sea with beautiful bays. Situated in the very dry, desert-like park Cabo de Gata. The campsite has extras such as a sauna, fitness, etc.

🚗 Located in the Parque Natural Cabo de Gata. On the Autovia A7, exit 479 direction San José (AL 3108). Follow camping signs.

A-7
El Barranquete
CC
San José

CC € **19**   1/1-30/6   1/9-31/12   7=6   🏔 **N 36°48'24'' W 2°4'53''**

Marbella, E-29604 / Andalucia   ♿ 🛜 (2975)

🔺 Cabopino
🏕 Ctra N340, km 194,7
☎ +34 952-850106
📠 +34 951120263
🔓 1/1 - 31/12
@ info@campingcabopino.com

5ha 280**T**(50-80m²) 10A

1 BCD**G**IJKLMO**P**ST
2 AEFGIJLSTVXY
3 BFGKLNRUVWY
4 (A 🔓) (B 11/4-30/9) (E 🔓) **N**
  (Q+R+T+U+V+X+Y+Z 🔓)
5 **AB**EFGIJKMNOP**S**UWZ
6 FGJ**K**M(N 1km)RTUVWX

💬 A large, well-equipped campsite with spacious pitches. Some with minimal shade, others with plenty. The campsite is just a few hundred metres from the beach. Bus connections to Marbella.

🚗 The campsite is located close to the N340. From Fuengirola, at km 194,7, exit Cabopino. Site located on the right. From Marbella, at km 194,7, exit Cabopino. At the roundabout take the motorway. Campsite in front of you.

Marbella   Fuengirola
AP-7
CC A-7

CC € **19**   1/1-22/3   1/4-26/4   2/5-21/6   10/9-11/10   15/10-5/12   9/12-31/12   🏔 **N 36°29'21'' W 4°44'35''**

Marbella/Málaga, E-29600 / Andalucia   ♿ 🛜 (2976)

🔺 La Buganvilla Cat.2
🏕 Ctra N340, km 188.8
☎ +34 95-2831973
📠 +34 95-2835621
🔓 1/1 - 31/12
@ info@campingbuganvilla.com

4,3ha 304**T**(60-80m²) 16A

1 BCD**G**IJKLMO**P**Q
2 AFGIJKLTVWXY
3 BF**G**H**M**RUW
4 (B 🔓) (G 15/6-15/9)
  (Q+R+T+U+V+X+Y+Z 🔓)
5 **AB**FGIJKLMNOPUWXYZ
6 CEGJ(N 0,3km)ORTV

💬 A large, spacious camping, some pitches have limited shade, others have plenty of shade. Camping pitches for tents are completely shaded by old pine trees. The campsite is close to the N340.

🚗 Campsite on the N340 between Fuengirola (25 km) and Marbella (6 km), on the landward side of the road near 189 km marker. Short exit and sharp right.

Marbella   AP-7
CC Calahonda   A-7

CC € **17**   1/1-24/3   2/4-30/6   1/9-31/12   🏔 **N 36°30'11'' W 4°48'12''**

María/Almería, E-04838 / Andalucia

👪 ♿ 📶 **iD** (2977)

🏔 Sierra María
🏠 Ctra María a Orce
　(AL-9101), km 7
☎ +34 620-232223
🗓 1/1 - 31/12
@ info@campingsierramaria.com

7ha 100T(65-200m²) 16A CEE

1 ABCD**G**IJKLMOP
2 BKSTUVWXY
3 ABHJRU
4 (B+G 15/6-31/8)
　(Q+R+T+V+X+Y+Z 🅿)
5 **AB**DGIJKMNOPUWZ
6 ACDEGJ(N 6km)OTV

💬 The campsite is located in a nature park and is perfectly suitable for nature lovers, considering its many opportunities. You will find two beautiful Andalusian white villages close to the campsite. An ideal resting place en route to Granada.

🚗 A91 direction Granada becomes A92N. Take exit 112. Then take A317 until 5 km past María, keep left onto AL9101, then follow camping signs.

Vélez-Blanco
Vélez-Rubio
A-92N

CC € ⑰ 1/1-22/3 1/4-14/7 1/9-30/11 10/12-31/12 7=6, 14=11, 21=17   📍 N 37°42'33'' W 2°14'10''

Motril/Granada, E-18600 / Andalucia

♿ 📶 (2978)

🏔 Playa de Poniente S.L. Cat.2
🏠 Playa de Poniente s/n
☎ +34 958-820303
📠 +34 958-604191
🗓 1/1 - 31/12
@ info@
　campingplayadeponiente.com

3ha 202T(60-100m²) 6-10A

1 BCDGIJKLMOPST
2 AEFGLNRSTVWXY
3 BF**GH**JK**MNO**RVWY
4 (A 🅿) (B 1/5-30/9)
　(Q+R+T+U+X+Y+Z 🅿)
5 **AB**DEFGIJKLMNOPUWZ
6 ACEGIK(N 0,5km)ORTV

💬 A good campsite for stopovers or as a base for visiting Granada, the Sierra Nevada and its southern edge (Alpujarras). Good toilet facilities. The campsite has a quiet location and is close to the beach. Plenty of shade.

🚗 A7 exit Salobreña (325), then direction Puerto Motril. Follow the signs. After a few kilometres at sign turn right; then at T-junction turn right again. Campsite after about 500 metres.

A-44
A-7
Almuñécar   Motril
CC
N-340

CC € ⑰ 1/1-27/3 1/4-30/6 1/9-31/12   📍 N 36°43'6'' W 3°32'46''

Olvera, E-11690 / Andalucia

♿ 📶 **iD** (2979)

🏔 Pueblo Blanco Cat.1
🏠 Ctra N384, km 69
☎ +34 956-130033
📠 +34 952-834373
🗓 1/1 - 31/12
@ info@campingpuebloblanco.com

14ha 220T(100m²) 16A

1 ABCD**G**IJKLMOPST
2 JKLSTVWX
3 ABHNU
4 (B 14/5-31/10)
　(Q+R+T+U+V+X+Y+Z 🅿)
5 **A**CGHIJKLMNOPUWXYZ
6 ACEG**K**(N 3km)ORTV

💬 A campsite established in 2011. On the top of a hill in the immense Los Gredales grounds with views out over the Olvera and the nearby Sierras. Here you will find spacious pitches, all modern amenities and several toilet blocks.

🚗 Between Antequera and Jerez de la Frontera, on the A384, at 69 km marker. About 3 km before Olvera on the right. Wide driveway 600 metres to the top.

Olvera
CC
Alcalá Del Valle

CC € ⑰ 1/1-25/3 1/4-29/6 1/9-11/10 15/10-5/12 10/12-31/12 7=6, 14=11, 30=22   📍 N 36°56'14'' W 5°13'18''

Palomares, E-04617 / Andalucia

2980

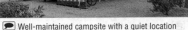

🔺 Cuevas Mar Cat.2
🏕 Ctra Villaricos-Garrucha s/n
☎ FAX +34 950-467382
📅 1/1 - 31/12
@ cuevasmar@arrakis.es

3ha 180T(40-100m²) 10A

1 BC**G**IJKLMOP**Q**
2 AEFLNTVWXY
3 **F**G**U**W
4 (B 1/5-15/10) K(Q+Z 📅)
5 **AB**EFGIJKLMNOPUW
6 EGI**K**(N 0,5km)OQTV

💬 Well-maintained campsite with a quiet location with little natural shade at 400 metres from the beach.

🚗 On the Costa de Almería. On Autovia A7 (E15) Alicante-Almería exit 537 Cuevas de Almanzora. After a few kilometres, a short drive to Vera at the T-junction, then direction Palomares; located on the Villaricos road.

Cuevas del Almanzora
AP-7
Vera
A-7 CC

CC € **17** 1/1-30/6 1/9-31/12

🧭 N 37°14'16'' W 1°47'57''

Roquetas de Mar (Almería), E-04740 / Andalucia

2981 🆔

🔺 Roquetas Cat.2
🏕 Ctra Los Parrales 90
☎ +34 950-343809
FAX +34 950-342525
📅 1/1 - 31/12
@ info@campingroquetas.com

8ha 600T(60-100m²) 10-16A

1 ABCD**G**IJKLMOP**Q**
2 AEFJLNOTVWX
3 B**F**GKMNUV**W**Y
4 (B+G 1/5-30/9)
(Q+S+T+U+X+Y+Z 📅)
5 **AB**EFGIKLMNOPUWXY
6 CEG(N 0,7km)ORTUV

💬 A well equipped campsite, partially shaded, partially sun-drenched for the many winter visitors. The beach is accessible from the campsite via a footpath. Roquetas is about 3 km away.

🚗 Located on the Costa Almería. On motorway A7, take exit 429. In the village of El Parador turn left at the roundabout, follow signs to the campsite.

Almería
A-7
CC
Roquetas De Mar

CC € **19** 1/1-1/7 27/8-31/12

🧭 N 36°47'51'' W 2°35'28''

Santa Elena (Jaén), E-23213 / Andalucia

2982

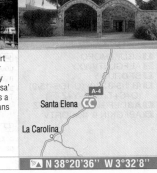

🔺 Despeñaperros Cat.1
🏕 Infanta Elena s/n
☎ FAX +34 953-664192
📅 1/1 - 23/12, 25/12 - 30/12
@ info@
campingdespenaperros.com

4ha 112T(70-100m²) 10A

1 BCD**G**IJKLMOPST
2 BFGLTVXY
3 AHJN**O**U
4 (**A** 📅) (B+G 20/6-15/9)
(Q+R 📅) (T 15/6-15/10)
(U+X+Y 20/6-15/10) (Z 📅)
5 **A**FGIJKLMNOPUWXYZ
6 CEG**I**K(N 0,1km)ORSTV

💬 Quiet wooded site conveniently located a short distance from the N IV/E5. Suitable for staying for some time to relax. Level grounds with sufficiently shaded pitches. The 'Batalla de Las Navas de Tolosa' museum in Sta Elena is most interesting. It shows a scene from a historical battle between the Christians and the Moors in 1212.

🚗 A4 Sevilla-Madrid, exit 259; Madrid-Sevilla, exit 257 or 258. Follow signs.

Santa Elena CC
A-4
La Carolina

CC € **17** 1/1-24/3 2/4-15/6 15/9-22/12 25/12-29/12

🧭 N 38°20'36'' W 3°32'8''

Tarifa, E-11380 / Andalucia   ♿ 🛜 **iD** 2983

🔺 Paloma Cat.2
🚩 Ctra N340 Cadiz-Malaga, km 74
☎ +34 956-684203
📠 +34 956-684233
🔑 27/2 - 30/10
@ campingpaloma@yahoo.es

4,9ha 297**T**(40-120m²) 10A

1 ABCDGIJKLMPQ
2 AELRSVWXY
3 BHN**O**RWY
4 (B 15/6-15/9) (Q+S+T 🔑)
  (X+Y 16/4-30/9) (Z 🔑)
5 **AB**FGIKMNOPU
6 EGJ(N 10km)ORTV

💬 Located near to the famous Valdevaqueros sandy beach and close to the Necropolis de los Algarbes from the bronze age, this campsite offers many possibilities. The campsite is divided by hedges, and is mostly shaded. Barbecues in low season.

🚗 Located next to N340 Tarifa-Cadiz. At 10 km from Tarifa campsite indicated by signs along the road (sea at 500m with big beach).

Zahara De Los Atunes

Tarifa

CC € **15** 27/2-23/3 3/4-15/6 10/9-29/10 6=5   N 36°4'35'' W 5°41'37''

Tarifa/Cádiz, E-11380 / Andalucia   ♿ 🛜 **iD** 2984

🔺 Valdevaqueros Cat.2
🚩 Ctra N340, km 75,5
☎ +34 956-684174
📠 +34 956-681898
🔑 1/1 - 31/12
@ info@
  campingvaldevaqueros.com

5ha 324**T**(50-100m²) 6A CEE

1 ABCDG**I**JKLM**P**ST
2 AELRVWXY
3 BHJK**M**S**W**Y
4 (**A** 🔑) (B+G 1/4-30/9)
  (Q+S+T+U+V+X+Y+Z 🔑)
5 **AB**GIJKMNOPSTUWXYZ
6 CDEGIJ(N 9km)ORTUV

💬 A campsite with individual connections and spacious, marked out pitches. Shade for caravans and tents. Barbecues permitted outside the summer months.

🚗 Located by the N340 Tarifa-Cadiz. Campsite is signposted 9 km from Tarifa towards Cadiz on the right.

Urbanización Atlanterra

Tarifa

CC € **17** 1/1-3/4 8/4-30/6 1/9-31/12 7=6, 14=12, 21=18, 28=24   N 36°4'9'' W 5°40'49''

Torre del Mar (Málaga), E-29740 / Andalucia   ♿ 🛜 2985

🔺 Camping Caravaning
  Laguna-Playa Cat.1
🚩 Prol. Paseo Marítimo Poniente s/n
☎ +34 95-2540631
🔑 1/1 - 31/12
@ info@lagunaplaya.com

2ha 141**T**(70-75m²) 10A

1 BGIJKLMOPQ
2 AEFGLNTVWXY
3 B**FO**RUWY
4 (B 1/5-31/10) (G 15/6-15/9)
  (Q+S+T+U+X+Y+Z 🔑)
5 **AB**DEFGIJKLMNOPUWZ
6 ABFGK(N 0,4km)ORTV

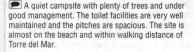

💬 A quiet campsite with plenty of trees and under good management. The toilet facilities are very well maintained and the pitches are spacious. The site is almost on the beach and within walking distance of Torre del Mar.

🚗 A7 (E15, N340), exit 272 Torre del Mar. To old coast road 340a. Then Torre del Mar-West (ouest), past bus station. Follow signs.

Vélez-Málaga

Torrox

CC € **19** 1/1-22/6 10/9-31/12   N 36°43'46'' W 4°6'9''

Torrox-Costa (Málaga), E-29793 / Andalucia ♿ 📶 (2986)

🏕 El Pino
🏠 Urb. Torrox-Park s/n
☎ +34 952-530006
📠 +34 952-532578
🔓 1/1 - 31/12
@ info@campingelpino.com

5ha 290T(20-100m²) 10A

1 BGIJKLMO**P**ST
2 AFGJLNSTVWXY
3 B**F**GHRVW
4 (B+G 1/6-15/9)
　　(Q+R+T+U+V+X+Y+Z 🔓)
5 **AB**GIJKMNOP**RST**UWZ
6 EGKM(N 2km)ORTV

💬 A large but quietly located campsite with many (avocado) trees. The campsite is about 1 km from the beach.

🚗 A7 Motril-Malaga, exit 285 direction Torrox-Costa, follow the signs.

Vélez-Málaga
A-7　Nerja

CC € ⑮ 1/1-30/6 1/9-31/12 　📍 N 36°44'22'' W 3°56'59''

Valle Niza/Málaga, E-29792 / Andalucia ♿ 📶 (2987)

🏕 Camping Valle Niza Playa Cat. 2
🏠 Ctra N340, km 264,1
☎ +34 952-513181
📠 +34 952-513476
🔓 1/1 - 31/12
@ info@campingvalleniza.es

2,5ha 150T(40-120m²) 6-10A

1 BCD**G**IJKLMOPQ
2 AEFGLNRTVWXY
3 B**F**GHJKRVWY
4 (B+Q+R+T+U+X+Y+Z 🔓)
5 A**F**GHIJKLMNOPUWZ
6 ACDEG**K**(N 3km)OTVWX

💬 The campsite is positioned by the sea, separated from it only by the old coast road 340. The toilet facilities were recently renovated. The lovely swimming pool is open year round and is surrounded by a beautiful lawn.

🚗 A7 Málaga-Motril, exit 265 Cajiz Costa. Campsite located between Benajarafe and Motril on the N340. Follow signs.

Vélez-Málaga
A-7
CC

CC € ⑲ 1/1-8/7 26/8-31/12 　📍 N 36°43'10'' W 4°9'53''

Villafranca de Córdoba, E-14420 / Andalucia ♿ 📶 (2988)

🏕 La Albolafia Cat.2
🏠 Camino de la Vega s/n
☎ +34 957-190835
🔓 15/2 - 9/12
@ informacion@
　campingalbolafia.com

3ha 88T(60-85m²) 10A CEE

1 BCD**G**IJKLMOPQ
2 FGLTVXY
3 BGJ
4 (**A** 🔓) (B 15/5-15/9)
　　(Q+R 🔓)
5 **A**GIKMNOPUWZ
6 CEGJ(N 0,5km)RT

💬 A lovely open plan campsite with spacious pitches and plenty of trees. Close to the Madrid-Cordóba-Seville motorway. Ideally located for visiting Cordóba, also for a few days of relaxation and for visiting the authentic hinterland.

🚗 The village is located on route N IV/E5 Madrid-Córdoba. Exit 377. Follow the signs.

Adamuz
Pedro Abad
CC
A-4　A-306

CC € ⑲ 15/2-30/6 1/9-8/12 　📍 N 37°57'13'' W 4°33'15''

Viñuela, E-29712 / Andalucia

▲ Presa La Viñuela Cat. 2
🚏 Ctra A356, km 30
☎ +34 952-554562
FAX +34 952-554570
🔓 1/1 - 31/12
@ campingpresalavinuela@
   hotmail.com

1ha 39T(60-70m²) 10A

1 BCD**G**IJKLMOPST
2 JKLTVXY
3 RW
4 (B+Q+R+X+Y 🔓)
5 **AB**GIJKLMNOPUWXY
6 ACEGK(N 7km)STV

💬 Small, peaceful campsite with good amenities and an excellent restaurant. Beautiful view of the lake and mountains.

🚐 N340, A7, exit 272 (e.g. Vélez-Malaga-La Viñuela). Follow A356 past La Viñuela. Campsite just past km 30. Indicated.

Zafarraya
Colmenar
CC
Moclinejo

2989 📶

CC €**17** 1/1-14/7 1/9-31/12 7=6

📶▲ N 36°52'26'' W 4°11'10''

Águilas, E-30880 / Murcia

▲ Bellavista*
🚏 Ctra de Vera, km 3
☎ FAX +34 968-449151
🔓 1/1 - 31/12
@ info@campingbellavista.com

1ha 65T(50-80m²) 10A CEE

1 ABCD**G**IJKLMO**P**
2 AEFGTVWXY
3 AGHRUWY
4 (B 12/4-1/11) K(Q+R 🔓)
   (T+V 1/4-1/11) (Y+Z 🔓)
5 **AB**FGIJKLMNOPUWXYZ
6 ABDEGIK(N 1km)OTUV

💬 Small campsite with an eye for detail. Situated quite high up, giving some of the pitches wonderful sea views (250 metres). Many small bays in the area. Good restaurant next to the campsite. No credit cards or debit cards in low season.

🚐 Located on route N332 from Águilas to Vera, km post 3.

Pulpí [AP-7] **Águilas**
CC

♿ 📶 **iD** **2990**

CC €**17** 1/1-15/2 26/2-28/3 2/4-30/6 1/9-31/12

📶▲ N 37°23'31'' W 1°36'34''

Águilas (Murcia), E-30889 / Murcia

▲ La Quinta Bella
🚏 Finca El Charcon 31
☎ +34 968-438535
🔓 1/1 - 31/12
@ jonathan@quintabella.com

14ha 43T(125-225m²) 10-16A CEE

1 ABCDGHIJKLMOPQ
2 CFTUVWX
3 FG
4 (B+Q+R+T+U+V+X+Z 🔓)
5 **AB**GJKLMNOPUWXYZ
6 ABCDEG**K**(N 2,5km)OTU

💬 New campsite (2015), small-scale, large pitches. Rural location. Lots of sun. Very friendly, helpful management.

🚐 AP7, exit 878. On 1st roundabout dir. Los Arejos RM-D24. Right at campsite sign after 2.9 km. Campsite is on right after 1.9 km.

CC
[AP-7] Calabardina

Águilas

📶 **iD** **2991**

CC €**17** 1/1-14/7 1/9-31/12

📶▲ N 37°27'14'' W 1°38'43''

Baños de Fortuna (Murcia), E-30626 / Murcia

♿ 📶 iD (2992)

🏔 La Fuente
✉ Camino de la Bocamina s/n
☎ +34 968-685017
📠 +34 968-685125
🔓 1/1 - 31/12
@ info@campingfuente.com

2ha 105T(60-70m²) 10-16A CEE

1 ABCD**G**IJKLMO
2 GKTUVWX
3 BGHJMNU
4 (C+E 🔓) **KO**
  (Q+R+U+X+Y+Z 🔓)
5 **AB**DGIJKLMNOP**RST**UWX YZ
6 ABCFGIJ**K**(N 3km)OTV

💬 A jewel in the hinterland of Alicante (province of Murcia). A small, good and charming site. Reservations between 15 December and 15 February are absolutely necessary. There is a spa heated to 36°C. Open all year.

🚗 A7, exit 559AB. Then 559A dir Fortuna. Towards Yecla RM423 at 1st roundabout, then A21 direction Baños de Fortuna. Campsite just before village on the left.

CC € **15** 1/1-14/7 1/9-31/12

📡 N 38°12'24'' W 1°6'26''

Bolnuevo/Mazarrón, E-30877 / Murcia

♿ 📶 iD (2993)

🏔 Playa de Mazarrón
✉ Avda Pedro Lopéz Meca s/n
☎ +34 968-150660
📠 +34 968-150837
🔓 1/1 - 31/12
@ camping@playamazarron.com

8ha 500T(60-80m²) 11A

1 ABCDGIJKLOPQ
2 AEFGSTVXY
3 BG**M**N**S**UWY
4 (B+G 1/4-15/10) **N**
  (Q 1/7-10/9)
  (S 12/4-17/4,1/7-10/9)
  (U+X+Y 1/7-10/9) (Z 🔓)
5 **AB**FGIJKLMNOPUWXY
6 ABCEG**I**KM(N 0,1km)ORTV

💬 Flower-filled campsite right by the sea. Plenty of winter sun. Plenty of shade from May onwards. On one side you can walk into a lively village, on the other side you can go straight to the beach. Two very spacious, new (2016) disabled toilet facilities.

🚗 A7, exit 627B, via MU603 direction Mazarrón. At the end of the motorway left towards Cartagena. Right at first roundabout towards Bolnuevo (D6). Right at next roundabout. Campsite about 300 metres on the left.

CC € **17** 1/1-28/3 2/4-30/6 17/9-31/12

📡 N 37°33'47'' W 1°18'14''

El Berro/Alhama de Murcia, E-30848 / Murcia

📶 iD (2994)

🏔 Sierra Espuña
✉ C/Juan Bautista s/n
☎ +34 968-668038
📠 +34 968-668079
🔓 1/1 - 31/12
@ camping@ campingsierraespuna.com

2ha 47T(45-80m²) 6A

1 ABCD**G**IJLMOP
2 IJKTUVWXY
3 ABGHJ**M**NQR
4 (B 1/6-31/8) (T+Z 🔓)
5 **AB**DFGIJKMNOPUWXZ
6 ABCDEGHK(N 0,2km)OTV

💬 A small, good campsite. Village and campsite are located in an area of natural beauty. A swimming pool with a lawn, the terrace for a drink, a small restaurant. You won't want to leave!

🚗 A7 Murcia-Granada, exit 627 Alhama de Murcia. Dir. Mula on C3315. 2nd exit El Berro C25 (1st exit unsuitable). Follow signs at beginning of village. Don't go through village. Assistance available if required. Call in advance!

CC € **17** 1/1-23/3 3/4-14/7 1/9-31/12 7=6

📡 N 37°53'17'' W 1°29'35''

El Portús/Cartagena, E-30393 / Murcia

🎿 ♿ 📶 **iD** (2995)

🔺 Naturista 'El Portús'*
📧 Ctra Canteras-El Portús s/n
☎ +34 968-553052
📠 +34 968-553053
🔑 1/1 - 31/12
@ elportus@elportus.com

10ha 350T(60-120m²) 6A

1 ABCD**G**IJKLMO**PQ**
2 AEFGIJKLNQSTUVWX
3 AGH**MR**VY
4 (C 15/6-15/9) (F 🔑)
　(H 15/6-15/9) **KNP**
　(Q+S+T+V+X+Y+Z 🔑)
5 **AB**DFGIJKLMNOPUWXY
6 ABCEGH**IK**(N 1km)OTV

💬 Naturist campsite. Located on a bay with its own beach, surrounded by beautiful countryside. The restaurant, bar and supermarket are located higher up, from where there are stunning views. Indoor and outdoor swimming pool, spa and wellness.

🚗 Located on the bay of El Portús, south-west of Cartagena. In Cartagena follow the signs Mazarrón N332 as far as Canteras/El Portús exit. After Canteras turn left towards El Portús. Follow the camping signs.

La Azohía CC **Cartagena** Ap-7

CC € **19** 1/1-22/6 11/9-31/12　　📡 N 37°35'11'' W 1°4'4''

Isla Plana/Cartagena, E-30868 / Murcia

🚫 ♿ 📶 **iD** (2996)

🔺 Los Madriles
📧 Ctra a la Azohia km 4,5
☎ +34 968-152151
📠 +34 968-152092
🔑 1/1 - 31/12
@ camplosmadriles@forodigital.es

6,5ha 311T(80-100m²) 10A CEE

1 ABEIJKLOPQ
2 GJKLSTUVWXY
3 BGH**M**NRU
4 (C+E 🔑) (H 15/6-15/9) K
　(Q+S+T+V+Z 🔑)
5 **A**DFGIJKLMNOP**RST**UXYZ
6 ABCEGHJ**K**(N 1,5km)ORTV

💬 Lovely terraced campsite with beautiful sea views. Attractive pitches screened by trees and bushes. You can swim all year round in warm water taken straight from the sea. The pools are emptied, cleaned and refilled every night. Dogs not permitted.

🚗 A7, exit 627B, via MU603 direction Mazzarón. Left at the end of the MU603 onto the N332 and after this keep on direction Cartagena until Isla Plana is signposted (E22). Then follow camping signs.

Mazarrón CC Isla Plana Ap-7

CC € **19** 1/1-7/7 25/8-31/12　　📡 N 37°34'47'' W 1°11'42''

La Manga del Mar Menor, E-30385 / Murcia

📶 **iD** (2997)

🔺 Caravaning La Manga
📧 Autovía de La Manga, salida 11
☎ +34 968-563019
📠 +34 968-563426
🔑 1/1 - 31/12
@ lamanga@caravaning.es

32ha 950T(84-110m²) 10A CEE

1 ABCD**G**IJKLMO**PQ**
2 AEFGISUVWX
3 B**F**GMNQRSU**V**WY
4 (B 1/4-30/9)
　(**F** 1/4-31/3,1/10-31/12)
　(G 1/4-30/9) **N**
　(Q+S+T+U 🔑) (V 1/7-31/8)
　(X+Y+Z 🔑)
5 **AB**DFGIJKLMNOPUWXYZ
6 ABCFG**IK**M(N 3km)OQRTV

💬 A good, extended campsite with pitches separated by hedges. Restaurant, bar and terrace by the sea with a beach and palms. In winter there's swimming in a heated indoor pool.

🚗 AP7, exit 800 to La Manga MU-312, exit 11. Across the viaduct and drive 500 metres back via the parallel road. Clearly signposted.

La Unión CC Portman AP-7

CC € **17** 1/1-30/6 1/9-31/12　　📡 N 37°37'30'' W 0°44'37''

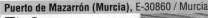

Puerto de Mazarrón (Murcia), E-30860 / Murcia

 ♿ 📶 **iD** (2998)

🔺 Las Torres
🚏 Ctra N332 km 26
☎ 📠 +34 968-595225
🗓 1/1 - 31/12
@ info@campinglastorres.com

5ha 210**T**(70m²) 16A

1 ABCD**G**IJLOQ
2 GLSTUVWXY
3 AMRU
4 (B 1/5-30/9)
   (E 1/1-31/3,1/10-31/12)
   (Q+R+T+U+X+Z 🖳)
5 **A**GIJKLMNOPUWZ
6 ABEG**J**K(N 2km)OTV

💬 The region has a favourable climate, especially in winter. Very helpful managers. Attractive bar and restaurant run by 2 charming Spanish ladies. Spanish cuisine. Entertainment programme is adapted in winter and indoor swimming in a heated pool.

🚗 A7 exit 627B via MU603 direction Mazarrón. Left at end of MU603 onto N332 and continue driving until 26 km marker.

Mazarrón   AP-7
CC
Puerto De Mazarrón

📍 N 37°35'23'' W 1°13'45''

CC € **17** 1/1-15/6   15/9-31/12

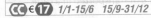

623

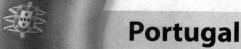

Portugal

General
Portugal is a member of the EU.

Time
The time in Portugal is one hour behind Amsterdam, Paris and Rome and the same as London.

Language
Portuguese, but you will usually get by in English or French.

Border formalities
Many formalities and agreements about matters such as necessary travel documents, car papers, requirements relating to your means of transport and accommodation, medical expenses and taking pets with you do not only depend on the country you are travelling to but also on your departure point and nationality. The length of your stay can also play a role here. It is not possible within the confines of this guide to guarantee the correct and most up to date information with regard to these matters.

We advise you to consult the relevant authorities before your departure about:
- which travel documents you will need for yourself and your fellow passengers
- which documents you need for your car
- which regulations your caravan must meet
- which goods you may import and export
- how medical treatment will be arranged and paid for in your holiday destination in cases of accident or illness
- whether you can take pets. Contact your vets well in advance. They can give you

information about the necessary vaccinations, proof thereof and obligations on return. It would also make sense to enquire whether any special regulations apply to your pet in public places at your holiday destination. In some countries for example dogs must always be muzzled or transported in a cage.

You will find plenty of general information on ▸ *www.europa.eu* ◂ but make certain you select information that is relevant to your specific situation.

For the most recent customs regulations you should get in contact with the authorities of your holiday destination in your country of residence.

Currency
The currency in Portugal is the euro. Approximate exchange rates September 2017: £1 = € 1.09. You can recognise cash machines by the sign 'MB'.

Credit cards
You can pay by credit card in many places.

Opening times/Public holidays
Banks
Banks are open Monday to Friday until 15:00.

Shops
Generally open until 19:00 on weekdays. Many shops have a siesta from 13:00 to 15:00. On saturdays shops are open until 13:00.

Chemists, doctors

You can get medical assistance at the local health centre (centro de saúde). Chemists are open on weekdays until 19:00, often with an afternoon break from 13:00 to 15:00. Chemists are open on Saturdays until 13:00.

Public holidays

New Year's Day, 13 February (Mardi Gras), Good Friday, Easter Sunday, 25 April (Revolution Remembrance Day), 1 May (Labour Day), 31 May (Corpus Christi), 10 June (Portugal Day), 15 August (The Assumption), 5 October (Republic Day), All Saints, 1 December (Independence Day), 8 December (Immaculate Conception) and Christmas Day.

Communication

(Mobile) phones

The mobile network works well throughout Portugal except in remote areas. There is a 4G network for mobile internet.

Wifi, internet

You can make use of a wifi network at more and more public locations, often for free.

Post

Post offices (correios) are normally open weekdays until 18:00.

Roads and traffic

Road network

You are advised not to drive outside the towns during darkness. The ACP operates a breakdown service on all roads. To receive help you must have breakdown insurance. Emergency phones are located every 4 km on main roads. On other roads you should call 707509510.

Traffic regulations

Remember, all traffic in Portugal drives on

the right and overtakes on the left! Headlight deflectors are advisable to prevent annoying oncoming drivers. Traffic coming from the right has priority. On roundabouts you have priority over approaching traffic. On narrow roads, the car that can move over most easily has to give way.

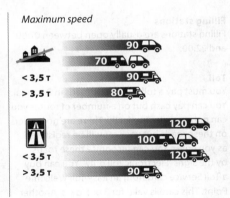

Maximum speed

Maximum permitted alcohol level is 0.5‰. You must use a phone hands-free. In built up areas stopping and parking is only permitted where indicated or partly on the pavement in the direction of the traffic. You may not stop on bridges and in tunnels. Winter tyres are not compulsory in winter conditions but are certainly recommended.

Take note: transporting bikes on a bicycle carrier on the back of a car is not forbidden, but the Portuguese government advises against it. You are permitted to carry them on a roof rack on the car, or on a bike rack on the back of your caravan or motorhome. The bike must not protrude on the sides and must not protrude for more than 45 cm at the back.

Maximum allowed measurements of combined length

Height 4 metres, width 2.55 metres and maximum length 18.75 metres (of which the trailer maximum 12 metres).

Fuel

Unleaded petrol, LPG and diesel are available almost everywhere. You can often pay by credit card.

Filling stations

Filling stations are usually open between 07:00 and 22:00.

Toll

You must pay a toll on various roads in Portugal. You can pay cash but on a number of routes you can only pay electronically. There are no barriers on these roads but your car will be registered as you enter. You can recognise these roads by the signs 'Electronic toll only'. You can buy a Toll Service card from an Easy Toll Welcome Point. This card is valid for 3 or 5 days. Another possibility is Easytoll. This is an automatic payment via credit card (MasterCard or Visa) which is registered together with your car number plate. You will need to register (free) at the border. You will receive a ticket that is valid for 30 days. You can also buy a pre-paid card (Toll card). You can purchase this at post offices, tourist offices and Easy Toll sales points.

You will find more information on ▶ www.visitportugal.com ◀ and search for 'electronic tolls'.

Emergency number

112: the national emergency number for fire, police and ambulance.

Camping

Portugal has its own classification system for campsites. Campsites are categorised by 1 to 4 stars in proportion to their infrastructure and services, or simply as 'rural'. In this last category the campsite is part of a farm. You are recommended to reserve in high season.

Practical

- Make sure you have a world adaptor for electrical equipment.
- Tap water is of good quality. If in doubt you can drink bottled (mineral) water.

Aboboreiras/Tomar, P-2300-093 / Santarém 🛜 iD (2999)

- 🏕 Camping Pelinos-Tomar
- 📧 Pelinos 77
- ☎ +351 249301814
- 📅 15/3 - 1/10
- @ info@campingpelinos.com

1ha 30T(75-120m²) 6A

1. **AB**G**IJKLP**ST
2. BFG**IJ**RSTWXY
3. HR
4. (B+Q+T+X+Z 🔑)
5. **AB**FG**IJ**KMOP**QU**WZ
6. ABE**K**(N 4km)V

💬 Cosy terraced campsite with lively bar and pavement cafe. Easy-going, small and hospitable. Idyllic surroundings. Portuguese restaurant within walking distance. Extensive information folder for days out. Enthusiastic Dutch owners. Limited number of places.

🚐 IC9/IC3/A13, exit Tomar Norte. Left after 200m direction Aboboreiras. This is just before the petrol station. Follow camping signs from here.

CC €17 15/3-2/6 1/9-30/9   N 39°38'18'' W 8°20'12''

Alvor Portimão, P-8500-053 / Faro ♿ 🛜 iD (3000)

- 🏕 Alvor***
- 📧 Estrada dos Montes
- ☎ FAX +351 282459178
- 📅 1/1 - 31/12
- @ info@campingalvor.com

4,5ha 400T 6-16A

1. **AG**IJKLMOP**RS**
2. AFG**IJ**LQSTWXY
3. AFG**J**KRU
4. (**B**+**G** 1/3-30/10) (Q+R+T+U+X+Z 🔑)
5. **AG**IJKMNOP**UV**Z
6. CEG**K**(N 0,05km)RTV

💬 By being divided into small terraces with plenty of shade, this large campsite always has a relaxed ambiance. Varied landscaping. Swimming pool with deckchairs close to the bar. Extra discount if staying 7 nights or more.

🚐 Over two roundabouts by the white church on the N125 to Alvor (between Portimão-Lagos) then 1st exit. Campsite on the left, quite a way past the airport.

CC €15 1/1-1/7 1/9-31/12   N 37°8'6'' W 8°35'26''

Arco de Baúlhe, P-4860-067 / Braga 🛜 iD (3001)

- 🏕 Campismo Arco Unipessoal, LDA
- 📧 Lugar das Cruzes
- ☎ +351 968176246
- 📅 5/4 - 3/10
- @ campismoarco@hotmail.com

2ha 30T 6A

1. **AG**IJKL**PRS**
2. CFGH**J**KL**R**SWXY
3. **JW**X
4. (B+G 28/5-30/9) (T+U+X+Z 5/4-30/9)
5. **A**G**IJ**KLMOP**U**Z
6. E**J**(N 0,15km)V

💬 Geert & Martine, a couple with 20 years experience in the region welcome you to this new, small, quiet site with swimming pool 100m from the centre. Centrally located near historic towns and nature parks. Plenty of documentation. Restaurant with cataplana (fish stew) and casserole. 300m from a cycle route.

🚐 A7 exit 12 Mondim/Cabeceiras. 2nd right at roundabout direction Arco de Baúlhe. Call 00351968176246 and you will be picked up.

CC €17 5/4-30/6 1/9-2/10 10=9, 20=18, 30=27, 40=36   N 41°29'11'' W 7°57'31''

Budens/Vila do Bispo, P-8650-196 / Faro

🎿 ♿ 📶 **iD** 3002

🏕 Salema Eco-camp Surf & Nature**
✉ Praia da Salema
☎ +351 282695201
📠 +351 282695122
📅 1/1 - 31/12
@ info@salemaecocamp.com

20ha 360T(60-150m²) 6-12A

1 ACD**G**IJKLO**P**ST
2 BGIJKQSTWXY
3 FHJK
4 (Q+R 📅) (U+Y 1/4-31/10) (Z 📅)
5 A**G**IK**L**MO**P**RUYZ
6 EGIJ(N 1km)ORT

💬 The many small terraces against the slope mean that there is peace and calm everywhere. Everyone will find the perfect (even shaded) spot among the rich and varied plant life. The well-maintained toilet facilities are not far off. Separate part for naturists. The sea is 1 km away. Extra discount if staying 7 nights or more.
🚗 On N125 Lagos-Sagres left to Praia da Salema after 17 km. The campsite is located on the right of the road.

CC € **13** 1/1-1/7 1/9-31/12

📷 **N 37°4'31'' W 8°49'53''**

Casfreires/Sátão, P-3560-043 / Viseu

♿ 📶 **iD** 3003

🏕 Quinta Chave Grande
✉ Rua do Barreiro 462
☎ +351 232665552
📅 15/3 - 31/10
@ info@chavegrande.com

9,5ha 180T(100-150m²) 6A CEE

1 ACD**G**IJKL**P**RS
2 CGIJRSTWXY
3 AGHJ**M**RU**W**
4 (A 📅) (B+G 15/5-15/9) (Q+U+Z 📅)
5 **AB**GHIJKMNOPU
6 CEJK(N 4km)OUV

💬 Located in the evergreen and sunny inlands sun of Central Portugal. Beautiful campsite in a green valley with magnificent views. Very spacious pitches and a lovely big swimming pool which uses salt instead of chlorine. 40 km from golf course.
🚗 A25 dir. Viseu, exit 19 dir. Sátão. Then IP5 exit 17 Sátão. Stay on N229 to Sátão (Ferreira de Aves), when nearing Sátão follow arrow 'Campismo 12 km', from here switch off SatNav but follow arrows 'Campismo' to campsite.

CC € **17** 15/3-14/7 1/9-30/10 10=9

📷 **N 40°49'22'' W 7°41'46''**

Coimbra, P-3030-011 / Coimbra

♿ 📶 **iD** 3004

🏕 AR Puro Camping Coimbra****
✉ Rua da Escola
☎ 📠 +351 239-086902
📅 1/1 - 31/12
@ coimbra@cacampings.com

7ha 750T(40-100m²) 12A

NEW

1 ABCD**G**IJKLMO**P**Q
2 FGIJRWX
3 A**F**QUV
4 (A 📅) (B+G 1/5-30/9) **N** (Q+T+U+X+Z 📅)
5 **AB**CGHIKMNOPUWZ
6 CFGIJ(N 0,5km)ORV

💬 City campsite in Coimbra. Good facilities. Bus 38 stops close to the campsite for a visit to the city. Discount from 1/1 - 31/5 and from 1/9 to 31/12, 7 days for price of 6, 14 days for price of 11.

🚗 A1 exit 13 take IP3 to Coimbra-Viseu to exit 8, take IC2 towards Coimbra-Lisboa (not towards centre). Follow IC2, A31 signs to Campismo past Coimbrashopping and Leroy to Rua de Escola.

CC € **17** 1/1-14/7 1/9-31/12

📷 **N 40°11'20'' W 8°23'59''**

Entre Ambos-os-Rios/P. da Barc, P-4980-312 / Viana do Castelo

♿ 📶 **3005**

🔺 Lima Escape
📧 Lugar de Igreja
☎ +351 258588361
🔓 1/1 - 31/12
@ info@lima-escape.pt

5ha 80T 6-12A

1 BCD**G**IJKLNO**P**
2 BCDFGISUXY
3 AGHJK**W**XZ
4 (Q+R+T+U+Y+Z 🅿)
5 **A**GIKMOPUZ
6 CDEG**J**(N 1km)OTV

💬 This campsite is a fine base for the expansive national park Peneda Geres. Lots of information at reception. Campsite is located in natural surroundings on the Rio Lima. Restaurant open all year. Basic and clean toilet facilities. Free wifi.

🚗 A3 exit 12 IC28 to Ponte da Barca. After bridge over the Lima 2nd exit dir. Lindoso. After 10 km left site at Ambos-os-Rios. From Spain A52 Xinzo de Limia or Ourense dir. Portugal. After Lindoso right after 15 km.

CC €**15** *1/1-14/7 1/9-11/11 1/12-31/12 7=6, 14=12, 21=18, 28=24*

🗺 N 41°49'26'' W 8°19'3''

Gondesende/Bragança, P-5300-561 / Bragança

♿ 📶 ✿ **iD** **3006**

🔺 Cepo Verde***
📧 Lugar da Vinha do Santo
☎ FAX +351 273-999371
🔓 1/3 - 31/10
@ cepoverde@montesinho.com

3ha 50T(15-60m²) 6A

1 ABCD**G**IJKLMO**P**RS
2 BFGIJKLRSVY
3 AHR
4 (**A** 1/3-30/6,1/9-31/10)
　(**B** 1/6-30/9) (Q+T+U+Y 🅿)
5 **AB**FGIJKMNOPUZ
6 DEG**J**(N 9km)OTUV

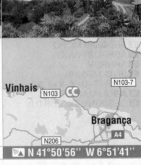

💬 In this wooded terraced campsite in the Montesinho nature park you can enjoy a relaxed atmosphere. Birdsong will help you to enjoy the beautiful panorama. Nearby you will discover typical villages such as Gimonde, Babe, Guadramil. Minor roads traverse the Montesinho Nature Park.

🚗 A4 exit Vinhais/Bragança (N103). 2nd exit at roundabout to Bragança/Vinhais via IP4. After 7 km exit right to N103 Bragança Oeste/Vinhais and Campismo. Follow signs.

CC €**13** *1/3-7/7 25/8-30/10 7=6, 14=12, 21=18, 28=24*

🗺 N 41°50'56'' W 6°51'41''

Luz/Lagos, P-8600-109 / Faro

♿ 📶 **iD** **3007**

🔺 Turiscampo****
📧 E-N 125, km 17 - Espiche
☎ +351 282789265
FAX +351 282788578
🔓 1/1 - 31/12
@ info@turiscampo.com

7ha 258T(60-110m²) 6-10A

1 ACD**G**IJKLMO**P**Q
2 FGIJLTVWXY
3 AFGKNR
4 (B+G 🅿) KLN
　(Q+R+T+U+V+Y+Z 🅿)
5 **AB**DEFGIJKLMNOPUWZ
6 CEGHI**K**(N 4km)ORTVW

💬 Turiscampo campsite with a Californian swimming pool. Luxurious toilet facilities. Individual toilet facilities available. Mild Algarve climate. Welcome all year round on a campsite with plenty of luxurious amenities. Pitches of 60-100 m² available for CCA-holders.

🚗 Drive via the IP1/E1 or the N125 to Lagos and continue in the direction of Sagres. After exit Luz, continue on the N125. The campsite is located along this road, on the right, just after the traffic lights.

CC €**17** *1/1-23/6 16/9-31/12*

🗺 N 37°6'5'' W 8°43'56''

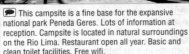

Meruge/Oliveira do Hospital, P-3405-351 / Coimbra

🏔 Toca da Raposa
🍽 Quinta do Ameal
☎ +351 238601547
⌚ 15/3 - 15/10
@ campingtocadaraposa@
gmail.com

1ha 30T(75-150m²) 6A

1 ABG**G**IJKL**P**S
2 BIJKRSTWXY
3 AHJNRU
4 (B+G+Q+T+X+Z 🔑)
5 GIJKMOPUWZ
6 CEGJ(N 2,5km)

💬 Friendly campsite at the foot of Serra da Estrela in central Portugal. Exotic terrace and swimming pool, good sanitary facilities, bar, wifi, restaurant. An ideal base for exploring the beautiful region. Footpaths from the campsite. You can also go cycling.

🚗 On N17 at Oliveira Do Hospital exit industrial zone, follow campsite sign, dir. Lagares da Beira/Viseu via N230. Right 6 km at roundabout Meruge via EM504. Left to campsite after about 2 km.

📶 iD **3008**

CC € **17** 15/3-14/7 1/9-14/10 8=7   ▲ N 40°23'57'' W 7°49'34''

Nazaré, P-2450-138 / Leiria

🏔 Vale Paraíso Natur Park***
🍽 Estrada Nac. 242
☎ +351 262561800
📠 +351 262561900
⌚ 1/1 - 16/12, 27/12 - 31/12
@ info@valeparaiso-naturpark.com

8ha 500T(50-120m²) 6-16A CEE

1 ABD**G**IJKLMOPQ
2 ABFGIJSTVWXY
3 AHNRU**V**
4 (B+G 1/5-30/9)
  (Q+R+T+U+X+Y+Z 🔑)
5 **AB**GIJKLMNOPUVZ
6 CEGIK(N 0,5km)ORTUV

💬 Campsite Vale Paraíso is a fine campsite with an excellent restaurant and swimming pool. There is always a pleasant climate here. A short distance from the attractive fishing villages of Nazaré and Praia do Norte, ideal for surfing and bodyboarding. The lovely beaches there are among the most beautiful in Portugal.

🚗 Located on the N242 from Lieiria to Nazaré, 2 km before Nazaré, on the west side of the road. Can also be reached via the new motorway A8.

🏃 👶 🚿 📶 ❀ iD **3009**

CC € **17** 1/1-14/7 1/9-15/12 27/12-31/12 7=6, 15=12, 30=25   ▲ N 39°37'14'' W 9°3'23''

Odemira, P-7630-592 / Faro

🏔 Campismo S. Miguel****
🍽 EN 120
☎ +351 926680611
📠 +351 282947245
⌚ 1/1 - 31/12
@ camping.sao.miguel@
mail.telepac.pt

7,5ha 460T 6A

1 ACDEIJKLM**P**Q
2 ABILQSWX
3 A**M**U
4 (**B**+G 31/3-30/9)
  (Q+R+T+U+V+W+X+Z
  15/3-5/10)
5 **AB**GIJKLMNOPUZ
6 EG**IK**M(N 1,5km)TV

💬 Campsite where the pitches are not marked out, with excellent amenities and recreational options. Swimming pool. Many places with shade under the spruce or eucalyptus trees. Sandy grounds.

🚗 Campsite is 1.5 km before Odeceixe on EN120 (IC4) from Odemira to Lagos, on left. Campsite is well-signposted.

🐕 📶 iD **3010**

CC € **17** 1/1-1/7 1/9-31/12   ▲ N 37°26'18'' W 8°45'20''

Outeiro do Louriçal, P-3105-158 / Leiria

3011

🅰 O Tamanco (Lda.)***
🏠 Casas Brancas 11
☎ 📠 +351 236952551
📅 1/3 - 31/10
@ tamanco@me.com

1,5ha 40T(80-120m²) 6-16A CEE

1 ABGIJKLMOPQ
2 FRSVWXY
3 DHJKRU
4 (B+G 1/4-1/10) (Q 📅)
(T 1/7-31/8) (X 1/4-31/10)
(Y 1/7-31/8) (Z 📅)
5 ABCGHIJKLMNOPUWZ
6 EGJ(N 2km)V

💬 A forged gate swings open, and you arrive in a green oasis where you will spend a lovely time in the old orchard or among the bamboo. With clucking chickens and honking geese in the background you can dream of the rural life. Enjoy the honest and delicious food in the welcoming cantina. End the day by the campfire under the stars.

🚐 Pombal IC8 exit Outeiro do Louriçal. Take the N109 exit roundabout IC8-A1. Follow signs.

CC € ⑲ 1/3-29/6 1/9-30/10

N 39°59'29'' W 8°47'20''

Ponte das Três Entradas, P-3400-591 / Coimbra

3012

🅰 Ponte das Três Entradas**
🏠 Rua Principal nr. 1
☎ +351 238670050
📠 +351 238670055
📅 9/2 - 31/12
@ ponte3entradas@sapo.pt

2ha 75T(60-90m²) 4-6A

1 ABCDFIJKLPS
2 CGIJRTWXY
3 AHJKNRUX
4 (A 📅) (B+T 1/5-1/10) (Z 📅)
5 ADGIJKLMNPUVWZ
6 CDEGIJ(N 0,1km)V

💬 Peaceful, rural setting by the River Alva. Plenty of shade. Bar with a terrace, swimming pool and sports field. Sights such as Sierra da Estrela with its granite formations, lakes and imposing glacial valley. Wifi zone.

🚐 At end of IC6 take exit N17, dir. Oliveira do Hospital/Covilhã. In Vendas Galizes N230 dir. Covilhã Vide (switch off SatNav) until Ponte das Três Entradas. For campsite take sharp right down before bridge.

CC € ⑮ 9/2-29/6 1/9-31/12

N 40°18'25'' W 7°52'18''

Praia da Barra, P-3830-772 / Aveiro

3013

🅰 Praia da Barra Campismo***
🏠 Rua Diogo Cão 125
☎ +351 234369425
📅 1/1 - 31/12
@ info@campingbarra.com

5ha 75T 10A

1 ACDGIJKLNPQ
2 ACEFGRSTVW
3 AHJNQWY
4 (Q+R+T+U+V+X+Z 15/6-7/9)
5 ABEFGIJKMOPUZ
6 CDEGIJ(N 0,05km)ORTV

💬 The campsite is located in an urban area of seaside resort Barra, close to beautiful beaches. There are not many pitches with shade. Toilet facilities are basic. Good amenities for motorhomes. 10 km from the city of Aveiro, known as the Venice of Portugal. Plenty of water sports options. Discount from 1/1 to 31/5 and 1/9 to 31/12. 7=6 days and 14=11 days.

🚐 From the A25 Aveiro East direction Barra. Over the bridge and 1st right at the roundabout. Follow camping signs.

CC € ⑮ 1/1-14/7 1/9-31/12

N 40°38'19'' W 8°44'42''

S. Martinho do Porto, P-2460-697 / Leiria

🅰 Colina do Sol***
✉ Serra dos Mangues
☎ +351 262989764
📅 1/1 - 24/12, 26/12 - 31/12
@ geral@colinadosol.org

♿ 🛜 iD 3014

NEW

9,5ha 400T(30-70m²) 6A

1 ABCD**G**IJKLO**P**RS
2 AFIJKSTVWX
3 AKQR
4 (B+G 1/6-30/9) (Q 📅)
  (R 1/7-30/9) (T 📅)
  (U+X 1/7-30/9) (Z 📅)
5 **AB**GIJKMNOPUZ
6 CEGJ(N 1km)OV

💬 Via a central road with tidy and organised permanent pitches, touring campers are welcome on the upper part of this campsite in the dunes, with both level and sloping pitches.

🚗 Motorway A8 take exit 21 S. Martinho do Porto N242 towards S. Martinho do Porto. Avoid centre. Follow Nazare to Intermarché direction Nazare and camping sign. Campsite on the left after 500m.

[map: N242 Alcobaça, A8, N8, Foz do Arelho, N8-6]

CC € **15** 1/1-30/6 1/9-23/12 26/12-31/12 7=6, 14=11 📍 N 39°31'21'' W 9°7'23''

Terras de Bouro, P-4840-030 / Braga

🅰 Parque de Cerdeira***
✉ Rua de Cerdeira 400
☎ +351 253351005
📠 +351 253353315
📅 1/1 - 31/12
@ info@parquecerdeira.com

♿ 🛜 iD 3015

NEW

6ha 200T(100m²) 5-10A

1 ABCD**G**IJKLMO**PQ**
2 BGIJLRSTVY
3 AHIJLMNQU**W**
4 (**A** 📅) (**B+G** 15/6-15/9)
  (Q+R+T+U 📅)
  (Y 1/1-1/11,1/12-31/12)
  (Z 📅)
5 **AB**DEFGIJKMNOPUZ
6 CEGJL(N 0,5km)OTV

💬 Wooded campsite located high up in the Parque National Penedal-Gerets. Ideal campsite for those who enjoy sports.

🚗 Route 205-3 from Terras de Bouro to Campo do Gerês. Follow the signs to the campsite.

[map: N203, Vila de Terras de Bouro, N308-1, N308]

CC € **15** 1/1-30/6 1/9-31/12 📍 N 41°45'47'' W 8°11'27''

Torreira, P-3870-340 / Aveiro

🅰 Torreira
✉ Rua da Saudade
☎ 📠 +351 234838397
📅 1/1 - 31/12
@ info@torreiracamping.com

♿ 🛜 ✿ iD 3016

NEW

200T(64m²) 12A

1 AC**G**IJKLMNO**P**RS
2 AERSVWX
3 AHJKUY
4 (Q+R 15/6-15/9) (T 📅)
5 ABFGIKMNOPXZ
6 CDEGJ(N 0,2km)OTV

💬 Campsite is located in the residential part of Torreira, a village on a peninsula between the sea and Ria de Aveiro. Sandy beach nearby. Good toilet block. Limited number of shady pitches. From 1/1 - 31/5 and from 1/9 - 31/12 discount 7 days for 6 and 14 days for 11.

🚗 From the A29 exit towards Ovar, then towards Furadouro, then road along river to Torreira. On entering Torreira on roundabout turn right. Campsite is signposted. Campsite is next to the water tower.

[map: Ovar, N109, CC, São Jacinto]

CC € **15** 1/1-14/7 1/9-31/12 📍 N 40°45'44'' W 8°42'10''

Vila do Conde, P-4485-722 / Porto   ♿ 📶 iD (3017)

🏕 Parque de Campismo Sol de Vila Chã***
🏠 Rua do Sol, 150 Vila Chã
☎ +351 229283163
📠 +351 229280632
🗓 1/1 - 31/12
@ info@campingvilacha.pt

3ha 50T(80m²) 10A

1 **ACD**G**IJKLM**P**RS**
2 AEFGRWXY
3 AMNRUWY
4 (Q+S+T+Z ⊕)
5 **AB**EGHIJKMNOPUVZ
6 ACEGJ(N 2km)ORTV

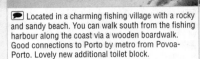

💬 Located in a charming fishing village with a rocky and sandy beach. You can walk south from the fishing harbour along the coast via a wooden boardwalk. Good connections to Porto by metro from Povoa-Porto. Lovely new additional toilet block.

🚗 A28 exit Mindelo, then continue towards Vila Chã past Brico Outlet. At T-junction right to Vila Chã. Then immediately left. (Don't follow GPS and turn left, very narrow roads). Follow camping signs.

Póvoa De Varzim

CC

CC €**15** 1/1-7/7 1/9-31/12 7=6, 14=12, 21=18, 28=21   🏔 N 41°17'53'' W 8°43'58''

Vila Nova de Cerveira, P-4920-042 / Viana do Castelo   ♿ 📶 iD (3018)

🏕 Camp Covas ITR (Inic. Tur. Rural)
🏠 Calçada da Torre 437, Covas
☎📠 +351 251941555
🗓 1/1 - 31/12
@ p.campismo.covas@gmail.com

2,5ha 80T(45-70m²) 4A

1 **AG**IJKLMN**P**RS
2 FGRSVXY
3 AHKN**O**RU
4 (**A** 1/6-30/9) (B+G ⊕) (Q+R+T+X+Z 1/4-30/9)
5 **A**FGIJKLMNOPUZ
6 CEG**I**K(N 0,3km)OTV

💬 The campsite is located in the beautiful countryside of the Minho valley near the village of Covas. It is a good base for walks and outings to beautiful little towns in the area such as Caminha, Viana do Castelo and Valença. The campsite has a swimming pool. The restaurant also serves regional dishes.

🚗 From A3 Porto-Valenca-Spain, exit 13 Vila Nova Cerveira. N303 Candemil. Then N302 Covas. Follow campsite signs. Don't use SatNav.

A Calle   Passos
N302
N13   A3   N303
Caminha   CC
N301
A28   N201

CC €**11** 1/1-30/6 1/9-31/12 7=6   🏔 N 41°53'19'' W 8°41'43''

Vila Praia de Âncora, P-4910-024 / Viana do Castelo   📶 iD (3019)

🏕 Parque de Campismo do Paço***
🏠 Rua do Paço
☎ +351 258912697
🗓 15/4 - 30/9
@ geral@campingpaco.com

4ha 250T 6A

1 AC**F**IJKLM**P**RS
2 ABCFGQRWXY
3 ARUX
4 (Q+R+T+Z ⊕)
5 **AB**GIJKLMNOPUWZ
6 CEGK(N 0,5km)OTV

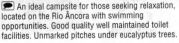

💬 An ideal campsite for those seeking relaxation, located on the Rio Âncora with swimming opportunities. Good quality well maintained toilet facilities. Unmarked pitches under eucalyptus trees.

🚗 A28, exit Moledo/VP Âncora. Approach campsite via coastal road N13 Caminha-Viana do Castelo. At traffic lights turn inland and follow signs. Don't use SatNav.

N13   A28   N301
Vila Praia De Âncora
CC
N305

CC €**13** 15/4-14/7 1/9-29/9   🏔 N 41°48'10'' W 8°50'53''

Zambujeira do Mar, Beja

▲ Camping Villa Park Zambujeira
✉ Estrada Municipal
da Zambujeira 2
☎ 📠 +351 283958407
🗓 1/1 - 31/12
@ info@campingzambujeira.com

3,5ha 750T(70-100m²) 6-16A

1 ACDFIJKLMOQ
2 AEGJKLTUWX
3 AMNSU
4 (B+G 🅟) K(Q+R+T+Z 🅟)
5 **AB**EIKMOP
6 DEIKM(N 0,4km)OTV

♿ 📶 🆔 (3020)

💬 Beautiful, very well-maintained campsite with shaded pitches. Swimming pool and whirlpool filled with sea water and without chemicals. Within walking distance of the beach and a small historic town.

🚗 Campsite is on left on route N393-1 directly after sign to Zambujeira do Mar, by a water tower.

N393
Odemira

CC São Teotónio

N120

CC € 15 1/1-15/6 13/9-31/12

🗺 N 37°31'33" W 8°46'32"

Valle
d'Aosta
640

Piemonte
641

Torino

Novara

Bergamo

Milano

CH

AT

Trentino-
Alto Adige
657

Trento

Friuli-
Venezia Giulia
679

LJUBLJANA

Trieste

SLO

ZAGREB

HR

Lago di Garda
664

Verona

Veneto
671

Venezia

Lombardia
653

Emilia Romagna
681

Bologna

Ferrara

Ravenna

Genova

FR

Liguria
647

Pisa

Prato

Firenze

Livorno

Forlì

Rimini

SARAJEVO

Toscana
686

Perugia

Umbria
704

Marche
708

Ancona

Pescara

FR

Abruzzo
716

ROMA

Lazio
711

Molise

Foggia

Bari

Campania
718

Napoli

Salerno

Basilicata

Puglia
722

Lecce

Taranto

Sassari

Calabria
727

Catanzaro

Sardegna
731

Cagliari

Messina

Palermo

Reggio di Calabria

Sicilia
736

Catania

Siracusa

Tunis

General

Italy is a member of the EU.

Time

The time in Italy is the same as Amsterdam, Paris and Rome and one hour ahead of London.

Languages

Italian is the main language in Italy but you can also get by with English, French or German.

Border formalities

Many formalities and agreements about matters such as necessary travel documents, car papers, requirements relating to your means of transport and accommodation, medical expenses and taking pets with you do not only depend on the country you are travelling to but also on your departure point and nationality. The length of your stay can also play a role here. It is not possible within the confines of this guide to guarantee the correct and most up to date information with regard to these matters.

We advise you to consult the relevant authorities before your departure about:
- which travel documents you will need for yourself and your fellow passengers
- which documents you need for your car
- which regulations your caravan must meet
- which goods you may import and export
- how medical treatment will be arranged and paid for in your holiday destination in cases of accident or illness
- whether you can take pets. Contact your vets well in advance. They can give you information about the necessary vaccinations, proof thereof and obligations on return. It would also make sense to enquire whether any special regulations apply to your pet in public places at your holiday destination. In some countries for example dogs must always be muzzled or transported in a cage.

You will find plenty of general information on ▶ www.europa.eu ◀ but make certain you select information that is relevant to your specific situation.

For the most recent customs regulations you should get in contact with the authorities of your holiday destination in your country of residence.

Currency

The currency in Italy is the euro. Approximate exchange rates September 2017: £1 = € 1.09. If travelling to Sicily and arriving at the weekend it is advisable to take sufficient cash with you as the cash machines are often empty.

Credit cards

You can pay by credit card in many places.

Opening times/Public holidays

Banks

Banks are in general open from Monday to Friday from 08:30 to 13:30 and from 15:00 to 16:00. In tourist areas banks are open without a break until 16:00.

Shops

Shops are open from 09:00 to 13:00 and from 16:00 to 20:00. Many shops in tourist areas are open all day and on Sundays.
In Northern Italy (Milan, Venice) shops open earlier in the afternoon and they also close earlier than in the south.

Chemists

Chemists ('farmacia') are generally open from Monday to Friday between 08:30 and 12:30 and between 15:00 and 19:30. In larger towns many chemists are open without a break from 08:30 to 19:30.

Public holidays

New Year's Day, 6 January (Epiphany), Easter, 25 April (Liberation Day), 1 May (Labour Day), 2 June (National holiday), 15 August (The Assumption), All Saints Day, 8 December (Immaculate Conception), Christmas.

Communication

(Mobile) phones

The mobile network works well throughout Italy. There is a 4G network for mobile internet.

Wifi, internet

You can make use of a wifi network at more and more public locations, often for free.

Post

Most post offices are open from Monday to Friday until 14:00 and on Saturdays until 12:00.

Roads and traffic

Road network

In general, the further south you drive, the poorer the quality of the roads. You need to watch out for traffic overtaking you on the right in Italy. You should also look out for scooters and mopeds. You are not advised to drive on country roads after dark. The Italian automobile association (ACI) offers breakdown assistance on many roads. Foreigners can request free help (if they have breakdown insurance) from this service by using the emergency phones located every 2 km along the motorway: tel. 803116.

Traffic regulations

Remember, all traffic in Italy drives on the right and overtakes on the left! Headlight deflectors are advisable to prevent annoying oncoming

drivers. Italy uses the metric system, so distances are measured in kilometres (km) and speeds in kilometres per hour (km/h). Traffic from the right has priority. Trams always have priority. Traffic that is on the roundabout has priority over traffic that is entering the roundabout, unless traffic signs indicate otherwise. Police and emergency vehicles always take priority when their flashing blue lights are on, even if their siren is not on. On narrow roads a heavier vehicle has priority over a lighter vehicle. Uphill traffic on mountain roads has priority over downhill traffic. The use of winter tyres and/or snow chains is mandatory between 15 November and 15 April anywhere in Italy where this is indicated.

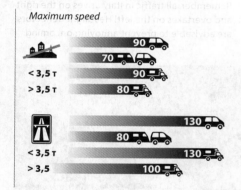

Maximum speed

Maximum permitted alcohol level is 0.5‰. Dipped headlights must always be used during the day outside built-up areas and also in all tunnels. Phones may only be used hands-free. Nothing may protrude from a car or trailer. This means that bikes on a bike rack may not stick out at the side!

Caravans, motorhomes
The SS163 south of Naples is currently closed to caravans and motorhomes between Vietri sul Mare and Positano (a distance of 40 km) due to increasing traffic congestion.

Maximum allowed measurements of combined length
Height 4 metres, width 2.55 metres and maximum length 18.75 metres (of which the trailer maximum 12 metres).

Zona traffico limitato (ZTL)
In a number of cities, such as Rome and Florence, a 'zona traffico limitato' (ZTL) has been introduced. This zone prohibits entry to the city centre to protect it from air pollution. Signs which denote a ZTL vary from city to city and are not always easily recognisable. Take care, as the police enforce this strictly and cameras register cars that drive into the ZTL.

Fuel
Lead free petrol and diesel are widely available. LPG is easily available in northern and central Italy, less so in southern Italy.

Filling stations
Filling stations are open between 07:00 and 19:30 with a break from 12:30 to 15:30. You can usually pay by credit card. Outside opening times you can pay at unmanned filling stations at card terminals. Filling stations alongside motorways are open day and night.

Mountain passes
The following mountain passes are prohibited for caravans:
The mountain pass between Domodossola and Locarno, Col de St. Bernard between Martigny and Aosta, Timmelsjoch (Passo del Rombo) between Sölden and Moso, Staller Sattel between Anterselve and Erlsbach, Passo di Selva between Selva and Canazei, Passo di Garden between Selva and Corvera, Passo di Costalonga between Merano and Vipiteno, Passo di Penzes between Vipiteno and Bolzano.

Tolls
Nearly all motorways are toll roads. You must also pay a toll in the following tunnels: Mont Blanc Tunnel, Fréjus Tunnel and the Great St Bernard Tunnel. You can pay in cash or by credit card or with a prepaid card (Viacard) which contains a credit amount for toll roads. More information ▶ *www.autostrade.it* ◀ (in English).

Emergency number
112: the national emergency number for fire, police and ambulance.

Camping
Northern Italy (South Tyrol, Trentino, Lake Garda and Tuscany) has campsites which are among the best in Europe. Reserve in plenty of time. Campsites in Southern Italy, with a few exceptions, offer a lower level of quality than in the north of Italy. The islands of Sicily and Sardinia are becoming increasingly popular and campsites here are full in high season. The north of Sardinia is popular with divers and surfers. You must be able to identify yourself with an identity document at all Italian campsites. Your identity document will be kept at the campsite reception for the period of your stay.
Free camping is allowed with permission from the landowner.

Crossing to Sardinia
You can reach Sardinia by various routes. Several ferry services make the crossing to Sardinia directly or via Corsica, from France or Italy.

Practical
- Tourist tax is levied in Italy. Take into account surcharges for amenities and entertainment.
- Many swimming pools only open at the end of May and a swimming cap is often compulsory. Swimming shorts are often prohibited and you will need to wear traditional swimming costumes.
- You should always take a world adaptor with you.
- You can usually drink tap water. If in doubt, buy bottled water.

Etroubles, I-11014 / Valle d'Aosta

🏔 Tunnel**
✉ Str. Chevrieres 4
☎ 📠 +39 0165-78292
🕐 1/1-8/1,24/1-1/5,25/5-14/10
@ info@campingtunnel.it

3021

1,6ha 45T(60-80m²) 6A CEE

1 ACD**G**IJKLMNOPQ
2 GJKLRVWX
3 A**F**HIM**N**RU**W**
4 (B+G 1/6-15/9) K
(T+U 1/6-15/9,27/12-6/1)
(X 1/6-10/9,26/12-6/1)
(Z 1/6-15/9,27/12-6/1)
5 A**B**DGIJKLMNPUVXY
6 ACDEG**K**(N 0,4km)TV

💬 Not far from the St Bernard Tunnel, a well-maintained terraced campsite with lovely panoramic views. German and English speaking owner. Lovely walks in the high mountains possible from the campsite. Also a good stopover campsite. Grocery shopping within walking distance.

🚗 Turn right from the St. Bernhard past the bridge in Etroubles. Form here the campsite is signposted.

CC € **19** 24/1-30/4 25/5-14/7 1/9-13/10 6/12-20/12

SS27

Aosta
Gressan Charvensod

📷 N 45°49'8'' E 7°13'45''

Morgex, I-11017 / Valle d'Aosta

🏔 Arc en Ciel*
✉ Strada Feysoulles 9
☎ 📠 +39 0165-809257
🕐 1/1 - 3/11, 5/12 - 31/12
@ info@campingarceciel.it

3022

1,3ha 85T(70m²) 2-6A

1 ACD**G**IJKLMNOPQ
2 FJKLRWXY
3 ARU
4 (B 1/7-31/8) (Q+V 🕐)
(X 1/7-31/8) (Z 🕐)
5 **A**GIJKLMNOPUVWZ
6 CDEGJ(N 2km)OV

💬 This peaceful, natural terraced campsite with renovated toilet facilities is located between Courmayeur and Morgex. Supermarket and thermal baths 2 km. Excellent base for exploring the beautiful surroundings: Val Veny, Val Ferret (Mont Blanc) and the valleys of the Gran Paradiso. Pizzeria at weekends.

🚗 Mont Blanc tunnel direction Aosta (SS26). In Morgex first roundabout third exit behind petrol station towards Dailly (see brown campsite sign).

CC € **17** 10/1-30/6 1/9-31/10

D1205

Courmayeur

CC La Salle

SS26

D1090

📷 N 45°45'47'' E 7°0'37''

Sarre, I-11010 / Valle d'Aosta

🏔 Monte Bianco**
✉ Fraz. St. Maurice 15
☎ 📠 +39 0165-258514
🕐 15/5 - 30/9
@ info@campingmontebianco.it

3023

0,7ha 60T(80-100m²) 6A CEE

1 AGIJKLMPQ
2 CFGJRVWXY
3 AMRS**W**
5 **A**GIJKMNO**P**UV
6 ACEGK(N 0,5km)O

💬 Well-maintained, small and green campsite under deciduous trees. Situated in the beautiful, busy Aosta Valley on the Italian side of Europe's highest mountain. Close to the high valleys of the Gran Paradiso, Val Ferret and Valpelline.

🚗 Follow the road Aosta-Courmayeur SS26. Entering Sarre it is the second openend campsite on the left.

SS27

Aosta
Saint-Pierre **CC**
A5

CC € **17** 15/5-30/6 20/8-29/9

📷 N 45°43'0'' E 7°15'42''

Agliano Terme, I-14041 / Piemonte

♿ 🛜 **3024**

🏔 Camping International Le Fonti★★★★
📧 Via alle Fontane 54
☎ +39 0141-954820
🔑 31/3 - 28/10
@ info@campinglefonti.eu

54**T**(20-50m²) 6A

1 BCDGIJKLMNO**PQ**
2 AJKLMRSUWXY
3 BHJKRU
4 (**A** 🔒) (B+G 19/5-16/9) K
　 (Q 🔒) (T+U+X+Z 19/5-16/9)
5 **A**FGIJKLMNOPUVWXZ
6 ACEGHJ(N 3km)QTVX

💬 The campsite is located in a beautiful nature reserve. Terraces with spacious pitches. Also suitable for the whole family. Guided excursions in this wine-producing area. Friendly and helpful staff. Suitable for cycling and walking trips. Lovely swimming pool.

🚗 From A21 Torino-Alessandria, exit Asti-Est, dir. Alba. Then exit Turchino, route 456, then right dir. Agliano Terme. Keep right, campsite is clearly signposted. Don't use SatNav.

CC € **19** 31/3-8/6　3/9-27/10

🧭 N 44°47'49'' E 8°14'31''

Baveno, I-28831 / Piemonte

🛜 **iD** **3025**

🏔 Camping Village Parisi★★
📧 Via Piave 50
☎ FAX +39 0323-924160
🔑 25/3 - 30/9
@ info@campingparisi.it

0,6ha 51**T**(60-80m²) 6A CEE

1 AGIJLPR
2 DFGKLNRTXY
3 **A**FWZ
4 (Q 15/7-15/8) (R 🔒)
5 **AB**GIJKMNOPUV
6 EIJ(N 0,2km)T

💬 A small, friendly campsite in the centre of Baveno. Located directly on Lago Maggiore.

🚗 Baveno is located between Verbania and Stresa. Follow camping signs in the centre of Baveno.

CC € **19** 3/4-27/4　1/5-9/5　13/5-17/5　21/5-30/5　3/6-16/6　6/9-29/9

🧭 N 45°54'39'' E 8°30'21''

Baveno/Oltrefiume, I-28831 / Piemonte

👫 ♿ 🛜 **iD** **3026**

🏔 Tranquilla
📧 Via Cave Oltrefiume, 2
☎ FAX +39 0323-923452
🔑 24/3 - 7/10
@ info@campingtranquilla.it

1,8ha 60**T**(70-80m²) 6A CEE

1 AG**I**JKLOPQ
2 FJKRVXY
3 **A**FGR
4 (B+G 1/6-15/9) (Q+R 🔒)
5 **AB**FGIJKLMNOPUV
6 EGJ**K**(N 1,5km)OQTV

💬 A very well-maintained campsite with basic amenities, quietly located 1 km from Lago Maggiore.

🚗 In the centre of Baveno drive in the direction of Verbania. After about 1 km turn to the left in the direction of Oltrefiume. Signposted along the road.

CC € **17** 24/3-15/6　1/9-6/10

🧭 N 45°54'44'' E 8°29'21''

Cannobio, I-28822 / Piemonte

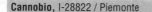

🔥 📶 **iD** (3027)

🔺 Del Sole**
📧 Via Sotto i Chiosi 81/a
☎ +39 0323-70732
📠 +39 0323-72387
🔓 1/3 - 4/11
@ info@campingsole.it

1ha 100T(32-64m²) 6A CEE

1 ABCD**G**IJKLMPQ
2 CLORTVY
3 BHJK**M**NQRWX
4 (**A** 1/6-30/8) (B 20/5-20/9)
  (Q+R+T+U+V+Y+Z 🔓)
5 **AB**FGIJKLMNPUWXYZ
6 CEG**K**(N 0km)TVWX

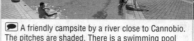

💬 A friendly campsite by a river close to Cannobio. The pitches are shaded. There is a swimming pool and an excellent restaurant.

🚗 E35, exit Locarno direction Brissago. In Cannobio the campsite is signposted to the left. Turn left after the first bridge, then directly right.

Ascona
SS337
SS394
CC
Luino
SS34
Germignaga

CC € **19** 1/3-28/3 2/4-9/5 3/6-5/7 3/9-3/11 | 🏕 N 46°4'0'' E 8°41'42''

Castelletto Ticino, I-28053 / Piemonte

📶 **iD** (3028)

🔺 Lido Verbano
📧 Via Sempione, 100
☎ 📠 +39 0331-923542
🔓 15/3 - 15/10
@ info@campinglidoverbano.com

6,7ha 64T(80-110m²) 6A CEE

1 ACD**G**HIJLMOQ
2 ADFGKLRTVXY
3 AGHJ**M**NRUWZ
4 (Q+T+U 🔓) (X 1/4-30/9)
  (Z 🔓)
5 **AB**EFGIJKLMNO**P**V
6 BDEGJ(N 0,1km)OTUV

NEW

💬 A well maintained campsite with plenty of permanent accommodation and moorings. Very spacious and well kept touring pitches close to the lake. A beach bar makes the lawns and the beach very pleasant. The 'wakeboard school' is unique.

🚗 Via E62 motorway exit 'Castelletto Sodra Ticino' direction 'Arona'. Campsite on the right after about 3 km.

Armeno
SS33
SS629
A26
CC
A8DIR
SS336
Suno
SS32
Gallarate

CC € **17** 15/3-29/3 3/4-29/6 1/9-14/10 | 🏕 N 45°43'12'' E 8°37'4''

Castelletto Ticino/Novara, I-28053 / Piemonte

👫 📶 (3029)

🔺 Italia Lido**
📧 Via Cicognola 104
☎ 📠 +39 0331-923032
🔓 10/3 - 14/10
@ info@campingitalialido.it

2ha 50T(50-70m²) 6A CEE

1 B**G**IJLNO**P**Q
2 ADFJKLRTVWX
3 AGKNRWZ
4 (Q+R+T+V+W+X+Z 🔓)
5 **AB**GIJKLMNOPUV
6 CEGJ(N 2km)OQTV

💬 Quiet campsite with a beautiful sandy beach on Lake Maggiore. From 2017 the campsite will feature a floating swimming pool on the lake (unique in Europe).

🚗 The campsite is located directly on Lago Maggiore on the left of the road from Dormelletto to Sesto Calende.

Ispra
SS33
SS629
A26
CC
A8DIR
Cardano al
SS32
Campo

CC € **19** 10/3-30/3 3/4-9/5 22/5-30/6 26/8-13/10 | 🏕 N 45°43'28'' E 8°36'33''

Chiusa di Pesio, I-12013 / Piemonte 🐂 ♿ 📶 iD (3030)

🏠 Pian Bosco
✉ Loc. Pian Bosco 12
☎ +39 347-3332630
🗓 1/1 - 31/12
@ info@campeggiopianbosco.com

NEW

2,7ha 31T(45-60m²) CEE

1 ABGIJKLMOQ
2 BIJKLRTY
3 ABGHJN
4 (B+G 1/7-31/8)
(U+V+X+Y+Z 🍴)
5 DEGIJKLMNOPUVXZ
6 EJ(N 1,6km)OTU

💬 Small, very quiet campsite with excellent restaurant/pizzeria. Large, green pitches, outdoor pool, solarium. Green, forested surroundings within walking distance.

🚗 The campsite is located on the Chiusa to Villanova road, about 1 km from Chiusa.

Cuneo Mondovi
SS28
CC
SS20

CC € **11** 1/5-14/7 1/9-15/9 🏕 N 44°18'50'' E 7°41'40''

Dormelletto, I-28040 / Piemonte 📶 (3031)

🏠 Eden
✉ Corso Cavour 59
☎📠 +39 0322-497524
🗓 15/3 - 31/10
@ info@campingeden.it

3ha 50T 6A CEE

1 BCDFHIJKLMNOP
2 ADFGKLMRXY
3 BGKNRWZ
4 (B 20/5-17/9)
(Q+R+T+U+V+Y+Z 🍴)
5 ABGIJKMNPQUVXZ
6 EIJ(N 1km)OTV

💬 A small and peaceful campsite with good swimming opportunities on Lake Maggiore. From 20 September to 31 October the snack bar, take-away meals, pizzeria and restaurant are only open at the weekends.

🚗 From Arona direction Sesto Calende. Campsite is on the left and is clearly signposted.

SS33 SS629
A26 CC
Borgomanero A8DIR
SS32
Casorate
Sempione

CC € **17** 15/3-29/6 1/9-30/10 🏕 N 45°43'53'' E 8°34'35''

Dormelletto, I-28040 / Piemonte ♿ 📶 (3032)

🏠 Lago Maggiore***
✉ Via Salvador Dalí
☎ +39 0322-497193
📠 +39 0322-498600
🗓 30/3 - 30/9
@ info@lagomag.com

5ha 110T(60-90m²) 6A CEE

1 BGIJKLMOPQ
2 ADFRVY
3 BGHMNRUWZ
4 (B+G 9/5-9/9)
(Q+R+T+U+V+W+X+Y+Z 🍴)
5 AEFGIJKLMNOPUVW
6 ACEGJ(N 1km)ORTV

💬 Located directly on the beautiful Lago Maggiore. Large, well-maintained beach pitches, restaurants, two beaches with lounge bar, several sports fields and swimming pools: all this means campers can enjoy all comforts.

🚗 From Arona direction Sesto Calende. Campsite is clearly marked on the left of the road.

SS33 SS629
CC Vergiate
Borgomanero
SS336
A26

CC € **19** 30/3-22/6 3/9-29/9 🏕 N 45°44'7'' E 8°34'31''

Entracque, I-12010 / Piemonte

3033

🅰 Campeggio Valle Gesso**
📧 Strada Provinciale per Valdieri 3
☎ +39 0171-978247
📠 +39 0171-978858
⊙ 1/1-8/1,10/2-25/2,24/3-7/10
@ info@campingvallegesso.com

4,9ha 145T(60-115m²) 6A CEE

1 BCD**G**HIJKLNOS
2 BCGKLRXY
3 ABGJKLNRU**W**
4 (**A** 14/4-1/11) (B 1/7-31/8)
MP(Q 20/6-15/9)
(R 1/1-7/3,14/4-31/12) (U 1/7-31/8)
(V 1/1-7/3,14/4-31/12) (Z ⊙)
5 **AB**DEFGIJKLMNO**P**RUVWX
YZ
6 BCDEGK(N 1km)OTV

💬 Peacefully located campsite on a river. Wonderful nature park close by. Lovely swimming pool. Well maintained toilet facilities. Climbing wall for beginners close by (Via Ferrata).

🚗 Campsite already signposted on route 20 at the T junction to the south of Bargo San Dalmazzo. Via Valdieri-Entracque. The campsite is situated 1 km before Entracque, and is clearly signposted.

Boyes
Borgo San
SS21 Dalmazzo
CC

CC € **17** 28/4-22/6 3/9-30/9

🗺 N 44°15'3'' E 7°23'25''

Feriolo di Baveno, I-28831 / Piemonte

3034

🅰 Camping Village Conca d'Oro***
📧 Via 42 Martiri 26
☎ +39 0323-28116
📠 +39 0323-28538
⊙ 29/3 - 24/9
@ info@concadoro.it

7ha 250T(70-100m²) 6A CEE

1 B**F**IJKLMPQ
2 ADF**K**LRVXY
3 A**F**HJKN**O**RUWZ
4 (Q+S+T+U+V+W+X+Y+Z ⊙)
5 **A**EFGIJKMNOPUVW
6 CEG**K**(N 1km)OSTVWX

💬 A campsite with plenty of excellent facilities. Peacefully located. Private sandy beach by the picturesque Lago Maggiore.

🚗 The campsite is located in between of the roundabout in the village of Fondotoce di Verbania and the village of Feriolo, on the shores of Lago Maggiore.

SS34
Gravellona CC Verbania
Toce A26
SS33

CC € **19** 29/3-18/5 2/6-30/6 1/9-23/9

🗺 N 45°56'11'' E 8°29'11''

Feriolo di Baveno, I-28831 / Piemonte

iD **3035**

🅰 Orchidea***
📧 Via 42 Martiri, 20
☎ +39 0323-28257
📠 +39 0323-28573
⊙ 22/3 - 8/10
@ info@campingorchidea.it

3ha 234T(60-73m²) 6A CEE

1 A**G**IJKLMPQ
2 ADF**G**JKLRVXY
3 B**F**GHJNWZ
4 (**C** 1/5-23/9)
(Q+S+T+U+V+X+Z ⊙)
5 **A**FGIJKMNOPUV
6 CFGIK(N 1km)ORTV

💬 Very well-maintained campsite with a beautiful beach on the shores of Lago Maggiore, and within walking distance of the village of Feriolo. Great sports grounds for teens and special play equipment for kids. New swimming pool opened in 2017.

🚗 Campsite located on road between Verbania-Fondotoce and Feriolo, just before the centre of Feriolo by the side of the lake. Signposted on the left of the road.

SS34
Gravellona CC Verbania
Toce A26
SS33

CC € **19** 22/3-29/6 2/9-7/10

🗺 N 45°56'1'' E 8°28'52''

Fondotoce/Verbania, I-28924 / Piemonte

‼ 📶 **3036**

🏕 La Quiete**
📧 Via Turati 72
☎ +39 0323-496013
📠 +39 0323-496139
🔓 21/3 - 8/10
@ info@campinglaquiete.it

2,8ha 180T(60-70m²) 6A CEE

1 BGIJKLPQ
2 ACDFKLRVXY
3 BFGHJNRWZ
4 (Q+R+T+V+X+Y+Z 🔓)
5 AGIJKMOPUV
6 EGJK(N 1,5km)TV

💬 Campsite with basic amenities located directly on the clean, peaceful lake of Mergozzo. Beautiful view of the lake, you can even see the Alps.

🚗 Campsite is located between Mergozzo and Fondotoce, on the lakeside (SS34). It is about 2 km from Mergozzo centre.

CC € **17** 21/3-17/5 4/6-29/6 1/9-7/10

🧭 N 45°57'13'' E 8°28'37''

Garbagna, I-15050 / Piemonte

♿ 📶 **3037**

🏕 Piccolo Camping E Maieu**
📧 Strada per Ramero 10
☎ +39 339-1466287
🔓 26/3 - 30/9
@ emaieu@camping.it

6ha 45T(30-70m²) 3-10A CEE

1 BGIJKLPQ
2 GJKLRTUVWXYQ
3 FHJRU
4 (B 1/6-30/9)
5 AFGIJKLMNOPQUVX
6 AEGJ(N 0,5km)

💬 A very peaceful, small terraced campsite in a hilly area, with a natural atmosphere. Clean toilet facilities. Terraces. Suitable as a stopover campsite. Walking routes available. One hour's drive from the Mediterranean. 30 minutes from outlet with all the big fashion labels.

🚗 A7 Milano-Genova, exit Vignole B. Right after toll booth direction Garbagna. Follow road to the left after 7 km (direction Garbagna). 3 km beyond tunnel. In the village follow 'E Maieu' and 'camping' signs.

CC € **17** 26/3-30/6 1/9-29/9

🧭 N 44°46'56'' E 8°59'19''

Ghiffa, I-28823 / Piemonte

‼ 📶 **iD** **3038**

🏕 La Sierra**
📧 Belvedere 337
☎ +39 333-7815534
🔓 1/3 - 31/10
@ info@campinglasierra.it

8ha 42T(55-70m²) 6A CEE

1 ABCDGIJKLOPQ
2 DJKNOUVX
3 AHKRWZ
4 (Q+R+T+U+V+X+Z 🔓)
5 AGIKMOPUWXZ
6 AEGK(N 5km)OT

💬 Small friendly terraced campsite situated right on Lago Maggiore. The views over the lake are breathtaking. The lively town of Verbania is close by.

🚗 Campsite located on the Verbania and Cannobio road beside Lago Maggiore. Site clearly indicated in Ghiffa.

CC € **15** 1/3-5/7 24/8-30/10 14=11

🧭 N 45°58'36'' E 8°38'2''

Orta San Giulio, I-28016 / Piemonte 📶 3039

🔼 Cusio Lyons Edda
✉️ Via Don Bosco 5
☎️ 📠 +39 0322-90290
🔓 1/4 - 30/11
@ info@campingcusio.it

45T(42-49m²) 6A

1 BCDGIJKLN**P**Q
2 GKLRXY
3 AH**M**R
4 (B 15/6-15/9) (X 1/7-31/8) (Z 🔓)
5 **AB**DGIJKMNO**P**UV
6 EGJ(N 3km)T

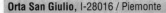

NEW

💬 A peacefully located campsite with an attractive swimming pool within walking distance of Orta Lake.

🚐 From 'Gravellona Toce' follow 'Omenia'. Then via tunnel towards 'Orta' beside the lake to the roundabout. Exit left and campsite is indicated. Follow signs, campsite is on the left.

Stresa
SS33
CC · A26
Dormelletto
Borgosesia

CC € ⑰ 9/4-11/6 10/9-29/11   📐 N 45°47'51'' E 8°25'15''

Orta San Giulio, I-28016 / Piemonte 👫 📶 3040

🔼 Orta**
✉️ Via Domodossola 28
☎️ 📠 +39 0322-90267
🔓 1/3 - 30/12
@ info@campingorta.it

3,6ha 80T(70-80m²) 6A CEE

1 B**G**IJKLOPQ
2 DFJKLMORTVXY
3 AHKRUWZ
4 (Q+R 🔓) (T+X+Z 15/3-4/11)
5 **AB**FGIJKLMNO**P**UV
6 AFG**IJ**(N 2km)OTW

💬 Small, well-maintained campsite in natural surroundings on the shores of Lake Orta. Pitches on the lake for an extra fee.

🚐 You'll find the campsite between Gozzano and Omegna 229. About 2 km past the crossing which leads to Orta San Giulio. Situated on the shores of the lake.

Omegna
SS33
A26
SS299
CC
Borgomanero

CC € ⑰ 1/3-29/6 1/9-29/12 7=6, 14=12   📐 N 45°48'4'' E 8°25'16''

Pettenasco, I-28028 / Piemonte ♿ 📶 iD 3041

🔼 Camping Royal**
✉️ Via Pratolungo 32
☎️ +39 0323-888945
📠 +39 0323-888100
🔓 1/3 - 30/10
@ info@campingroyal.com

1,8ha 30T 5A CEE

1 ACD**F**HIJKLO**P**Q
2 JKRTVXY
3 ABGHKNR
4 (B 1/6-15/9) (Q+Z 🔓)
5 **A**DGJKMNPUVW
6 CDEG**IJ**(N 3km)ORTVX

💬 A very peacefully located and well kept campsite with beautiful views of Lake Orta below.

🚐 Pettenasco is half way between 'Gravellona Toce' and Borgomanero. Follow camping signs in centre of Pettenasco.

Omegna
SS33
A26
Varallo
CC
SS299
Arona

CC € ⑰ 1/3-9/7 27/8-29/10   📐 N 45°49'25'' E 8°24'51''

Peveragno, I-12016 / Piemonte

3042

△ Il Melo**
≡ Via dello Sport 1
☎ 📠 +39 0171-383599
🕐 15/1 - 15/12
@ info@campingilmelo.it

1,3ha 40T(60-70m²) 6A CEE

1 ABGHIJKLOQ
2 CIJKLRWXY
3 AFGHJMNR
4 (A 1/5-30/9) (B 1/6-31/8)
   (Q 1/7-31/8)
   (T+U+V+X+Z 🕐)
5 ABDEGIJKLMNOPUVZ
6 ACEGIJ(N 1km)T

💬 The campsite is located 800 metres from the village in the middle of typical mountainous countryside. Situated at a sunny, panoramic elevation at the foot of a 2400 metre high mountain. An oasis of calm for those who love nature, walking and a lovely swimming pool.

🚗 From Cuneo and from Mondovi in Peveragno village opposite gas station go uphill towards San Giovenale, then follow campsite signs. If SatNav will not find new address, use old address: Via don G. Peirone 57.

Cuneo
Boves
Borgo San
Dalmazzo

CC € **17** 15/1-2/2 19/3-30/6 1/9-26/10 12/11-14/12   N 44°19'39'' E 7°36'19''

Solcio di Lesa, I-28040 / Piemonte

3043

△ Solcio**
≡ Via al Campeggio
☎ +39 0322-7497
📠 +39 0322-7566
🕐 8/3 - 22/10
@ info@campingsolcio.com

1,5ha 100T(60-80m²) 6A CEE

1 ABGIJKLMOPQ
2 ADFGKMRVXY
3 AGKORUWZ
4 (Q+R+T+V+X+Y+Z 🕐)
5 ABEFGIKLMNOPUVW
6 AEGK(N 0,5km)OTUV

💬 Peaceful campsite with good amenities within walking distance of the small church at Solcio, situated right on Lake Maggiore. The restaurant is of very good quality.

🚗 Solcio di Lesa is located between Stresa and Arona. Turn into the street directly opposite the church, direction 'Lago'. Entrance to the campsite is 50 metres further on.

SS33
A26
CC
Arona
SS629
Sesto Vergiate
Calende

CC € **19** 8/3-7/7 25/8-21/10   N 45°48'57'' E 8°33'0''

Albenga, I-17031 / Liguria

3044

△ Bella Vista***
≡ Via Campore 23
☎ +39 329-5923683
🕐 20/3 - 13/11, 15/12 - 15/1
@ campingbellavista@hotmail.com

1,2ha 58T(50-80m²) 6A CEE

1 BCDGIJKLMOPRS
2 FJRTVWXY
3 BFJR
4 (A+B+G+Q+R+U+X+Z
   1/5-30/9)
5 ABDFGIJKMOPUVWXYZ
6 ACGK(N 1,5km)T

💬 Colourful, natural, Dutch run campsite. 1½ km from the sea. Large swimming pool. Clean toilet facilities. Activities: walking and eating out.

🚗 A10, exit Borghetto SS to Ceriale. In Ceriale take a right on the oval roundabout. Right at traffic lights. Follow signs (not SatNav).

Loano
CC
Albenga
A10
SS1BIS

CC € **17** 1/1-14/1 20/3-6/7 25/8-12/11 15/12-31/12   N 44°5'3'' E 8°12'35''

Albenga, I-17031 / Liguria

🏕 Delfino
✉ Strada Comunale Villaggio Iris 23
☎ +39 0182-591066
📠 +39 0182-51998
🔓 29/3 - 30/9
@ info@campingdelfino.it

1,7ha 145T(52m²) 6A CEE

1 BCDGHIJKLMOPST
2 AEFGNRVWXY
3 ABFGRUWY
4 (B+G 1/5-28/9) KP
(Q+R+T+U+V+Y+Z 🔌)
5 AGHIKMOPUVZ
6 ACDFGJ(N 0,5km)OTV

💬 Campsite located by the sea. Plenty of shade from natural vegetation and overhead cover. Plenty of pitches for short stops. Good toilet facilities. The campsite has a shop and a bar/restaurant, pizzeria, swimming pool and a fitness room.

🚗 A10, exit Albenga direction Alassio/Imperia (Strada Panoramica). Left 150m after tunnel. Campsite clearly signposted.

CC € ⑰ *3/4-20/4 25/4-27/4 2/5-1/6 4/6-8/7 26/8-29/9*

N 44°2'9'' E 8°12'28''

Ameglia, I-19031 / Liguria

🏕 River***
✉ Località Armezzone
☎ +39 0187-65920
📠 +39 0187-65183
🔓 1/4 - 30/9
@ info@campingriver.it

4ha 190T(60-100m²) 3-10A CEE

1 ABCDGHIJKLMNOPRS
2 CFGLRTVY
3 BFKMNOPRUW
4 (A 1/8-31/8) (B+G 1/5-30/9)
(Q 12/4-30/9)
(S+T+U+V+W+X+Z 🔌)
5 ABFGIJKLMNOPUVZ
6 CDEGJ(N 0,7km)QRTV

NEW

💬 Peaceful campsite located on a river and close to the sea. Lovely level pitches with ample shade. The campsite has its own large swimming pool. A good base for visiting Pisa, Lucca and other places of interest. A helicopter base is located nearby the campsite.

🚗 A12 Genua-Livorno, exit Sarzana, direction Lerici. 3 km further on follow signs to Bocca di Magra (S432). Campsite clearly marked after Ameglia sign. Small entry to the campsite.

CC € ⑰ *1/4-30/6 26/8-29/9*

N 44°4'33'' E 9°58'12''

Arenzano/Genova, I-16158 / Liguria

🏕 Caravan Park La Vesima
✉ Via Rubens 50R
☎ +39 010-6199672
📠 +39 010-6199686
🔓 1/3 - 15/10
@ info@caravanparklavesima.it

2ha 70T(37-60m²) 3-10A CEE

1 ACDEIJKLMNOP
2 EFGNOQTUVWXY
3 ABEFHJRWY
4 (Q 🔌)
(R+T+U+V+X+Z 1/5-30/9)
5 ABDGIKMOPUVZ
6 GK(N 1km)RT

💬 Campsite located right by the sea, 800m from Arenzano fishing village and 17 km from Genoa. Ideal for visiting Genoa aquarium. The site has 2 restaurants, 2 bars, a pizzeria and motorhome service. Most suitable for an overnight stop before taking the ferry to Corsica/Sardinia/Sicily.

🚗 From the A10 exit Arenzano direction Genova. Campsite about 500m beyond the tunnel on the right of the road.

CC € ⑲ *1/3-29/3 3/4-30/5 4/6-30/6 10/9-14/10*

N 44°24'51'' E 8°42'17''

Ceriale/Savona, I-17023 / Liguria

🛆 Bungalow Camping Baciccia***
🏠 Via Torino 19
☎ +39 0182-990743
📅 23/3 - 16/10, 21/12 - 7/1
@ info@campingbaciccia.it

🛜 iD (3048)

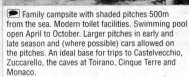

1,5ha 110T(45-70m²) 6A CEE

1 ABCD**G**IJKLMNOPQ
2 AEFGLNORTWXY
3 AB**F**GHJKMNRUWY
4 (B+G+Q+R+T+U+V+X+Z 📅)
5 **AB**GIJKLMNOPUVWXYZ
6 ACEG**K**(N 0,2km)RTV

💬 Family campsite with shaded pitches 500m from the sea. Modern toilet facilities. Swimming pool open April to October. Larger pitches in early and late season and (where possible) cars allowed on the pitches. An ideal base for trips to Castelvecchio, Zuccarello, the caves at Toirano, Cinque Terre and Monaco.

🚗 A10, exit Borghetto Santo/Spirito, then SS1 'Via Aurelia' direction Ceriale. At Ceriale follow signs. Right at roundabout with Lidl. 200m to campsite.

Loano
CC
Albenga
A10
SS1BIS

CC € **19** 1/1-6/1 23/3-29/3 4/4-21/6 5/9-15/10 21/12-31/12 | 🏔 N 44°4'54'' E 8°13'4''

Déiva Marina, I-19013 / Liguria

🛆 La Sfinge
🏠 Località Gea
☎ 📠 +39 0187-825464
📅 15/3 - 2/11
@ lasfinge@camping.it

♿ 🛜 iD (3049)

1,8ha 100T(20-90m²) 3A CEE

1 ACD**G**IJKLMOPRS
2 FGJRTVXY
3 BH
5 **AB**GIJKLMNPUVW
6 ACEGK(N 0,1km)OT

💬 Friendly attractive campsite with plenty of shaded pitches for tents on terraces under the trees. Excellent sanitary facilities. Ideal location for trips out, for example to Cirque Terre. Déiva has a railway station with plenty of opportunity for visiting local attractions by public transport.

🚗 A12 Genova-La Spezia, exit Déiva Marina. About 4 km in the direction of Déiva Marina. Follow the signs. Cp on the right.

Sestri
Levante
SS523
Moneglia
CC

CC € **17** 15/3-30/6 1/9-1/11 | 🏔 N 44°13'35'' E 9°33'0''

Déiva Marina, I-19013 / Liguria

🛆 Valdeiva**
🏠 Località Ronco
☎ +39 0187-824174
📠 +39 0187-825352
📅 5/2 - 15/11, 3/12 - 7/1
@ camping@valdeiva.it

♿ 🛜 iD (3050)

4ha 65T(15-56m²) 3A CEE

1 ACD**G**IJKLMNOPS
2 FGJRTVWXY
3 AHR
4 (B 15/6-15/9) (Q 📅)
    (R+T+U+V+X+Z 20/5-20/9)
5 **AB**GIJKLMNOPUV
6 CEGIJ(N 0,3km)OQRT

💬 A family campsite with plenty of shade-giving vegetation. It has a camp shop and restaurant. There is also a swimming pool. Free transport to the coast/ station. Ideal for a visit to Cinque Terre.

🚗 A12 Genova-La Spezia, exit Déiva Marina. About 4 km direction Déiva Marina. Signposted to the left of the road, across new bridge.

Sestri
Levante
SS523
A12
CC

CC € **17** 1/1-6/1 5/2-30/6 1/9-4/11 3/12-31/12 | 🏔 N 44°13'31'' E 9°33'2''

Déiva Marina, I-19013 / Liguria

 ♿ 🛜 **iD** (3051)

- 🏕 Villaggio Turistico Arenella
- 📧 Loc. Arenella
- ☎ +39 0187-825259
- 📠 +39 0187-826884
- 🔓 1/3 - 31/10
- @ info@campingarenella.it

1,8ha 75T(20-60m²) 3A CEE

1. ACDGIJKLMOPRS
2. FJRTVWXY
3. AB
4. (Q+U+V+X+Y+Z 1/6-15/9)
5. **AB**GIJKLMNOPUVZ
6. CEG**J**(N 0,2km)RTV

💬 A terraced camp in a rustic location which is perfect for tourist trips to Genoa and Cinque Terre. Deiva has a (railway) station, so you can make excellent use of public transport.

🚗 A12 Genova-Livorno, exit Déiva Marina, about 5 km. Signposted to the right of the road beyond petrol station.

Sestri Levante
A12
Moneglia
CC

CC € **17** 1/3-30/6 1/9-30/10　　　　N 44°13'44'' E 9°32'6''

Imperia, I-18100 / Liguria

 ♿ 🛜 **iD** (3052)

- 🏕 De Wijnstok
- 📧 Via Poggi 2
- ☎ +39 0183-64986
- 📠 +39 0183-660323
- 🔓 1/1 - 31/12
- @ info@campingdewijnstok.com

0,8ha 40T(30-40m²) 6A CEE

1. ABCDGIJKLPQ
2. EFGNOQSTVWXY
4. (T+U+V+X+Z 1/6-15/9)
5. **A**GIJKLMNOP**UV**
6. ACFG**K**(N 0,3km)ORT

💬 Typical Italian campsite in the centre of the Italian Riviera. Close to the sea. Campsite under Italian management. Open all year.

🚗 Signposted about 1.5 km west of Imperia (San Remo side) on the SS1 'Via Aurelia'. The campsite is located on the northern side of the road. Or when approaching on the A10: exit Imperia Ovest.

SS28
Imperia
Taggia
A10
CC

CC € **19** 1/1-29/3 3/4-27/4 2/5-31/5 4/6-14/7 1/9-31/12　　　N 43°52'10'' E 7°59'52''

Isolabona, I-18035 / Liguria

 🛜 (3053)

- 🏕 Delle Rose
- 📧 Regione Prati Gonter 4
- ☎ +39 0184-208130
- 🔓 31/3 - 4/11
- @ info@campingdellerose.eu

1ha 46T(30-80m²) 3-6A CEE

1. BCD**G**IJKLMNO**P**RS
2. BCGJKRTVWXY
3. ABRUW
4. (**A** 1/7-31/8) (B+G 1/6-30/9) (Q+R 🔓) (T+U+V+X+Z 1/6-30/9)
5. **A**EFGIJKLMNOPUV
6. ADEGJL(N 2km)R

💬 A friendly family campsite set in countryside. Excellent toilet facilities. Swimming pool and children's pool. The campsite is located close to the sea and is a good base for trips out to mountain villages and coastal resorts.

🚗 A10, exit Ventimiglia towards main street in Aurelia. Drive through Ventimiglia, left at Nervia roundabout and follow Strada Provinciale 64 in Val Nervia. Campsite on the right 2 km past Isolabona village. Follow the signs and not SatNav!

D6204
D93
SS20
Camporosso
A10
Sanremo
CC

CC € **15** 31/3-7/7 25/8-3/11　　　　N 43°53'40'' E 7°38'51''

Pietra Ligure, I-17027 / Liguria

▲ Dei Fiori**
▼ Viale Riviera 17
☎ +39 019-625636
⎘ 31/3 - 22/10, 27/12 - 31/12
@ info@campingdeifiori.it

2,5ha 130T(35-70m²) 6A CEE

1 ACD**G**HIJKLNPS
2 FJKRTUVWXY
3 BGHRU
4 (B+G 20/5-20/9)
   (Q+R+T+U+V+X 15/6-15/9)
   (Z 1/5-15/9)
5 **A**GIJKMNOPUV
6 CEGK(N 0,6km)OQRT

🗨 The campsite is located in a quiet and tranquil country estate with century-old olive trees. It is 600 metres from the village and the sea. The campsite has a lovely swimming pool and a good restaurant. Walking, trekking and mountain bike excursions are organised. Campsite has new, modern toilet facilities and free wifi.

🚗 On A10, exit Pietra Ligure. Right immediately after toll booth. Campsite about 1500m on the right.

3054 ♿ € **17** 3/4-23/4 25/4-27/4 2/5-31/5 4/6-30/6 3/9-21/10   ▲ N 44°8'52'' E 8°16'4''

Pietra Ligure, I-17027 / Liguria

▲ Pian dei Boschi***
▼ Via Ponti 1
☎ +39 019-626881
📧 +39 019-625425
⎘ 24/3 - 4/11
@ info@piandeiboschi.it

4ha 215T(30-80m²) 6A CEE

1 BCD**G**HIJKLMNPQ
2 AFJLTVY
3 B**M**R
4 (B+G 12/5-7/10)
   (Q+S+T+U+V+X+Y+Z 🔑)
5 **A**GIJKLMNOPUV
6 ABCEG**J**(N 1km)ORTV

🗨 Campsite 700m from the sea. Most shaded pitches by 'Pietra Ligure' (A10) exit. Pool, shop, restaurant, Wifi zone. Starting point for walks, biking, mountain biking. Pietra Ligure: lively resort, nice boulevard. English spoken. Ideal for mountain villages inland.

🚗 A10, exit Pietra Ligure. Turn right after toll booth. Campsite about 1500m on the left.

3055 ♿ € **19** 24/3-29/3 3/4-20/4 2/5-31/5 3/6-29/6 27/8-31/10   ▲ N 44°8'57'' E 8°16'7''

Sarzana (SP), I-19038 / Liguria

▲ Iron Gate Marina 3B
▼ Viale XXV Aprile 54
☎ +39 0187-676370
📧 +39 0187-670094
⎘ 15/3 - 30/9
@ info@marina3b.it

12ha 540T(40m²) 3-6A CEE

1 ACDGHIJKLMNOPRS
2 CFLMRUVY
3 BKRW
4 (B+G 1/5-15/9)
   (Q+R 1/5-30/9) (T 1/6-30/9)
   (V+Y+Z 🔑)
5 **AB**EFGIJKLMNOPUVXZ
6 ACDEGJM(N 2km)OTW

🗨 A large, very modern campsite by the River Magra with a restaurant, swimming pool and lawns by the river. A lovely starting point for boating enthusiasts. Suitable for visiting The Cinque Terre.

🚗 A12 Genova-Livorno, exit Sarzana direction Sarzana. Right at 4th roundabout towards Carrare/Marinella. Campsite about 3 km before motorway bridge through a small tunnel.

3056 ♿ € **17** 15/3-2/7 20/8-29/9   ▲ N 44°4'36'' E 9°58'52''

Sestri Levante, I-16039 / Liguria
♿ 📶 **iD** (3057)

🏕 Fossa Lupara**
🏠 Via Villa Costa 31
☎ +39 0185-1873287
📠 +39 0185-1871719
🗓 1/2 - 31/10
@ info@campingfossalupara.it

1,5ha 30T(30-50m²) 6A CEE

1 AGIJKLMOPST
2 FGRSVWXY
3 BG**M**R
4 (Q+R+T+U+V+X+Z 1/4-30/9)
5 **A**GIJKLMNPUVWXZ
6 CDEGK(N 0,3km)ORST

💬 This basic campsite is located right by the A12. Not far from the lively centre and beach resort. Good train connections to Genoa and the Cinque Terre, all of which are worth a visit. Free transport to train station in July; in low season for a fee.

🚗 A12 Genova-Livorno, take Sestri Levante exit. The campsite is well signposted from there (about 500m) close to the motorway. Warning: do not use SatNav but follow signs because of low tunnel (avoids damage).

Chiavari
Sestri Levante · CC · A12

CC € **17** 1/2-30/3 3/4-27/4 2/5-31/5 4/6-14/7 1/9-30/10
📶 N 44°16'26'' E 9°25'22''

Sestri Levante, I-16039 / Liguria
♿ 📶 **iD** (3058)

🏕 Mare Monti
🏠 Via Aurelia km 469
☎ +39 0185-44348
📠 +39 0185-482327
🗓 18/3 - 14/10
@ info@campingmaremonti.com

2ha 50T(20-70m²) 6A CEE

1 ACDGIJKLMOPS
2 FJKRTVX
3 BHR
4 (B+G 1/6-30/9)
    (Q 15/4-14/10)
    (R 15/4-15/10) (Z 🗓)
5 **AB**EGIJKLMNOPUVXZ
6 CFGJK(N 2km)RT

💬 An attractive and friendly family campsite with stunning panoramic views over the surroundings. The campsite is equipped with a swimming pool for both caravan and tent campers. Starting point for trips out to Cinque Terre, Portofino and Genua. Shuttle bus to the station (on request).

🚗 SS1 Aurelia, exit Sestri Levante A12, dir. La Spezia. 3rd campsite on the left past Trigoso. Steep access road. SatNav cannot always be trusted, choose SS1 dir. Trigoso.

Chiavari
Sestri Levante · CC · A12

CC € **17** 18/3-30/6 1/9-13/10
📶 N 44°15'49'' E 9°26'31''

Vallecrosia, I-18019 / Liguria
♿ 📶 (3059)

🏕 Vallecrosia
🏠 Lungomare Marconi, 149
☎ 📠 +39 0184-295591
🗓 23/3 - 7/10
@ info@campingvallecrosia.com

0,4ha 65T(35-70m²) 6A CEE

1 BCD**G**IJKLMPST
2 EFGKNRSVWXY
3 AKRUWY
5 **AB**GIJKLMNOPUVXZ
6 CFGK(N 0,5km)RTV

💬 Small, quiet campsite with pitches marked out by wooden fences and very neat toilet facilities. Located on the sea. Most of the campsite is set under beautiful old trees. There is a separate place on the beach for walking your dog.

🚗 A10, exit Ventimiglia towards San Remo/Bordighera. In Vallecrosia follow campsite signs. Do not use SatNav. Due to small gate one street further.

SS20
Sanremo
A10
Menton · CC

CC € **19** 23/3-30/6 8/9-6/10
📶 N 43°47'3'' E 7°38'1''

Idro, I-25074 / Lombardia

 ♿ 🛜 **iD** (3060)

▲ AZUR Sportcamping Rio Vantone★★★★
🏠 Via Vantone 45
☎ +39 0365-83125
📠 +39 0365-823663
🕐 20/4 - 3/10
@ idro@azur-camping.de

4,5ha 203**T**(60-100m²) 6A CEE

1 ABG HIJKLMPRS
2 DIKLNRVX
3 BHLRU**W**Z
4 (A 1/7-31/8)
  (C+H+Q 1/5-30/9) (S 🕐)
  (T 1/7-10/9)
  (U+Y+Z 15/5-30/9)
5 AB DEFGIJKLMNOPUWXYZ
6 CDEGK(N 2km)OPRTV

💬 Lovely campsite with marked-out pitches. Sloping beach. Entertainment in English, German and Dutch. Lovely swimming pool, surf school and good restaurant. Good facilities.

🚗 From the A22 drive towards Riva. In Sarche take the SS237 towards Tione Brescia. At the end of the lake drive towards Crone-Vantone. The campsite is located by the lake.

Storo — CC — Vestone — Sabbio Chiese

CC €**19** 20/4-18/5 3/6-22/6 26/8-2/10   📐 N 45°45'16'' E 10°29'52''

Idro, I-25074 / Lombardia

 ♿ 🛜 **iD** (3061)

▲ Venus★★
🏠 Via Trento 94
☎ 📠 +39 0365-83190
🕐 20/4 - 20/9
@ info@campingvenus.it

1,8ha 98**T**(30-100m²) 3-6A CEE

1 ABC GIJKLMPQ
2 DKLNRTVXY
3 BHNR**W**Z
4 (B 1/5-15/9)
  (Q+S+U+Y+Z 🕐)
5 AB FGIJKLMNOPUVZ
6 CEGK(N 1km)V

💬 Located on the shores of Lake Idro with unspoiled natural surroundings. Plenty of relaxing walks in the woods near the campsite possible. The ambiance at the camp is fun and casual. There is a small swimming pool with sunbathing area. The beach slopes down gently

🚗 A22, exit Trento. In Trento exit Riva. In Sarche direction Tione Brescia. After Anfo the campsite is situated at the left side of the road.

SS237 — Vestone — CC — Sabbio Chiese — Sant' Apollonio

CC €**17** 20/4-6/7 24/8-19/9   📐 N 45°44'24'' E 10°28'2''

Iseo, I-25049 / Lombardia

 ♿ 🛜 (3062)

▲ Covelo★★★
🏠 Via Covelo 18
☎ 📠 +39 030-9821305
🕐 29/3 - 4/11
@ info@campingcovelo.it

1ha 96**T**(50m²) 6A CEE

1 BCD GIJKLMNOPRS
2 DGKLRTVWXY
3 AKR**W**Z
4 (Q+R+T+V+Y+Z 🕐)
5 AB GIJKLMNOPUVWZ
6 ACEGK(N 1km)RTV

💬 A small and friendly campsite on Lake Iseo. Pitches right by the lake with panoramic views. Restaurant with local dishes.

🚗 From the A4 exit Rovato, follow signs to Lago d'Iseo. In Iseo continue for 1 km past the supermarket, direction Pisogne at the roundabout. Campsite just after the turning on the left of the road.

SS469 — Gardone Val Trompia — CC — Erbusco

CC €**19** 29/3-30/6 3/9-3/11   📐 N 45°40'1'' E 10°4'4''

Iseo, I-25049 / Lombardia ✈ ♿ 🛜 iD (3063)

🏠 Del Sole****
✉ Via per Rovato 26
☎ +39 030-980288
📠 +39 030-9821721
🗓 20/4 - 30/9
@ franconulli1@libero.it

6,5ha 153T(60-80m²) 3-6A CEE

1 ABCDEIJKLMNOPRS
2 DFGLRVWXY
3 BK**M**NRU**W**Z
4 (A 🔌) (B+G 19/5-16/9)
(Q+S+T+U+V+Y+Z 🔌)
5 **AB**EFGIJKLMNOPU
6 CEGK(N 0,4km)ORTV

💬 A well-equipped campsite located directly on Lake Iseo, with shaded pitches and many options for sports and recreation. The historic towns of Brescia and Bergamo are easily accessible by car. A few kilometres from the campsite, among the hills, you will find the Franciacorta vineyards.

🚗 A4, exit Rovato, direction Iseo. Follow the signs in Iseo.

SS42 — Gardone Val Trompia — CC — Palazzolo Sull' Oglio — A4 — **Brescia**

CC € 19 20/4-30/6 25/8-29/9 7=6, 14=11 ⛺ N 45°39'25'' E 10°2'15''

Iseo, I-25049 / Lombardia ♿ 🛜 iD (3064)

🏠 Quai***
✉ Via Ipp. Antonioli 73
☎ 📠 +39 030-9821610
🗓 24/4 - 26/9
@ info@campingquai.it

1,3ha 83T(40-80m²) 6A CEE

1 ABCD**G**IJKLMOPRS
2 DFKLOPRVWXY
3 AGKR**W**Z
4 (Q+T+U+V+X+Z 🔌)
5 **A**GIJKLMNOPUVZ
6 CEGK(N 0,7km)RTV

💬 A shaded family campsite right by Lake Iseo with beautiful views. Boat ramp. Good toilet facilities. Restaurant with terrace and view of the lake. With car-free pitches, parking on a central car park. CampingCard ACSI is not valid for pitches right on the lake. Dogs allowed (one per pitch). Not possible to reserve without CampingCard ACSI.

🚗 A4 Milan-Brescia, exit Rovato direction Iseo. Follow the signs in Iseo.

SS469 — Gardone Val Trompia — CC — Erbusco

CC € 19 24/4-30/6 1/9-25/9 ⛺ N 45°39'58'' E 10°3'47''

Ispra, I-21027 / Lombardia 👫 🛜 iD (3065)

🏠 International Camping Ispra****
✉ Via Carducci, 943
☎ +39 0332-780458
📠 +39 0332-784882
🗓 17/3 - 21/10
@ info@
internationalcampingispra.it

2,5ha 106T 6A CEE

1 ABC**G**HIJKLMO**PQ**
2 DKLMRTVY
3 BGHKMRU**W**
4 (B 15/6-15/9)
(Q+R+T+U+V+X+Z 🔌)
5 **A**GIKMN**P**VZ
6 EG**K**(N 1km)TV

💬 A campsite with a lovely swimming pool, located on the shores of Lago Maggiore in a peaceful and natural setting. Flyboarding possible.

🚗 From Sesto Calende continue towards Laveno. Campsite clearly indicated on the left of the road in Ispra.

Verbania — SS33 — A26 — CC — Arona — SS629 — Vergiate

CC € 19 17/3-1/7 20/8-20/10 7=6 ⛺ N 45°49'38'' E 8°37'38''

Lavena Ponte Tresa, I-21037 / Lombardia

▲ International Camping***
✉ Via Marconi 18
☎ +39 0332-550117
📠 +39 0332-551600
🗓 1/1 - 31/12
@ info@internationalcamping.com

3066

2ha 80T(60-90m²) 2-6A CEE

1 CDEIJKLOPQ
2 ADLPRVY
3 AHRUWZ
4 (Q+V+Z 🔒)
5 **A**FGIJKLMNOPUV
6 ACEGJ(N 1km)R

💬 A beautifully located, tranquil campsite next to Lake Lugano. Within walking distance of the village of Ponte Tresa. Electricity supply 2-6 amps. Dogs not allowed.

🚗 A2/E35, at Lugano exit Ponte Tresa/Varese. Direction Ponte Tresa/Varese as far as Customs. Immediately after border continue towards Porto Ceresio. Campsite 800 metres on the left.

SS394 SS34 | Lugano | A2 | CC | Mendrisio | SS233

🏔 N 45°57'35'' E 8°51'48''

CC € **19** 1/1-6/7 25/8-31/12

Maccagno con Pino e Veddasca, I-21010 / Lombardia

▲ Lido
✉ Via Pietraperzia 13
☎ +39 0332-560250
📠 +39 0332-359863
🗓 30/3 - 7/10
@ lido@boschettoholiday.it

3067

0,8ha 50T(36-60m²) 4-6A CEE

1 ABC**G**HIJKL**P**RS
2 DGKLMNRTVWXY
3 AWZ
4 (Q 1/7-30/8) (R+U+Z 🔒)
5 **A**FGIJKMOPUZ
6 CEGJ(N 0,5km)V

💬 A small, quiet and basic campsite directly on the Lago Maggiore at walking distance from the village of Maccagno, with mostly shaded pitches. Campsite has sun all day.

🚗 From Bellinzona drive on the eastern side of Lago Maggiore towards Luino, right just before Maccagno, follow signs.

13 | 405 | SS394 | CC | SS34 | Luino | Lavena Ponte Tresa

🏔 N 46°2'27'' E 8°43'58''

CC € **17** 7/4-18/5 4/6-7/7 2/9-6/10

Marone (Lago di Iseo), I-25054 / Lombardia

▲ Riva di San Pietro***
✉ Via Cristini 5
☎ 📠 +39 030-9827129
🗓 1/5 - 30/9
@ info@rivasanpietro.it

3068

2ha 116T(45-64m²) 6A CEE

1 ABCD**G**IJKLMNOPRS
2 DGKLRVWXY
3 A**F**HJKRV**W**Z
4 (A 15/7-15/8)
   (B+G 15/5-15/9)
   (Q+R+T+U+V+Y+Z 🔒)
5 **AB**EFGIJKLMNOPUWZ
6 ACEGK(N 0,3km)OQTUV

💬 Situated at the foot of the San Pietro mountain with extensive shores directly on Lake Iseo. The site has lovely landscaping and lawns and excellent views of the lake. New sanitary facilities.

🚗 A4, exit Rovato direction Iseo, follow lakeside road towards Pisogne. Campsite just before Marone on the lake.

Marone | CC | SS469 | Iseo

🏔 N 45°43'56'' E 10°5'35''

CC € **19** 1/5-30/6 1/9-29/9

Monvalle, I-21020 / Lombardia

♀♂ 📶 **iD** **3069**

⛺ Lido di Monvalle***
🏠 Via Montenero 63
☎ FAX +39 0332-799359
🔑 24/3 - 8/10
@ campinglidomonvalle@libero.it

1,5ha 80T(60-80m²) 6A CEE

1. AB**G**IJKLO**P**Q
2. ADKLMRVXY
3. ARUWZ
4. (Q+R+T+U+V+X+Z 🔑)
5. **A**GIJKMNO**P**UV
6. CEG**J**(N 4km)ORTV

💬 Basic, peaceful campsite with ideal swimming in Lago Maggiore. The restaurant on the lake shore is very attractive and has a beautiful view over the lake.

�car From Laveno drive in direction Ispra.
The campsite is located to the right of the road, about 10 km.

Verbania

SS33
A26 CC Gavirate
Arona
SS629

CC €**19** 3/4-7/7 25/8-7/10 7=6, 14=11

▨▲ N 45°50'51'' E 8°37'13''

Piano di Porlezza, I-22010 / Lombardia

♿ 📶 **iD** **3070**

⛺ Ranocchio**
🏠 Via Al Lago 139A
☎ FAX +39 0344-70385
🔑 29/3 - 29/9
@ campeggioranocchio@gmail.com

3,5ha 200T(50-90m²) 3-6A CEE

1. AC**G**IJKLPRS
2. DG**J**KLNRTVXY
3. AHJRWZ
4. (**B**+**G** 15/6-15/9) (U 🔑)
   (Z 1/5-15/9)
5. **AB**FGIJKMNO**P**U
6. CEG**J**(N 0,15km)RTV

💬 A family campsite with a swimming pool and good modern toilet facilities. The campsite is on Lake Piano, and surrounded by countryside with lovely walking and cycling.

🚗 N2, exit Lugano Nord dir. St. Moritz/Gandria. From Porlezza dir. Mennachio. In Piano Porlezza turn right. Alternative route via Como. New tunnel open between Gandria and Porlezza since 2013. Recommended to use coordinates.

SS340 DIR
Lanzo
D'Intelvi CC
SS340
Lezzeno

CC €**17** 9/4-7/5 4/6-7/7 1/9-28/9

▨▲ N 46°2'26'' E 9°10'6''

Porlezza, I-22018 / Lombardia

♿ 📶 **iD** **3071**

⛺ Darna***
🏠 Via Osteno 50
☎ +39 0344-61597
🔑 24/3 - 31/10
@ campingdarna@hotmail.it

6ha 300T(50-80m²) 3A CEE

1. ABCD**G**IJKLM**P**RS
2. DKNRVY
3. ABGHJK**M**NRUWZ
4. (A 1/7-31/8) (**B**+**G** 1/5-31/8)
   (Q 1/4-30/9)
   (S+T+U+V+Y 🔑)
   (Z 16/4-15/9)
5. **AB**CDFGIJKLMNOPUV
6. CEGH**K**(N 2km)OT

💬 Located on the southern shore of Lake Lugano. The campsite has shaded pitches, 3 Amp electricity, mini-market, restaurant, swimming pool, beach, playground, tennis courts and volleyball pitch. An ideal starting point for cycling and walking tours.

🚗 N2, exit Lugano Nord direction St. Moritz. New tunnel between Gandria and Porlezza now operational. In Porlezza direction Osteno. The campsite is signposted on the right (last campsite).

Pregassona CC
Lugano
2
SS340
E35

CC €**17** 24/3-22/6 1/9-30/10

▨▲ N 46°1'31'' E 9°7'33''

Ranzanico al Lago di Endine, I-24060 / Lombardia ♿ 🛜 iD 3072

▲ La Tartufaia***
✉ Via Nazionale 2519
☎ FAX +39 035-819259
🗓 1/5 - 23/9
@ info@latartufaia.com

1,7ha 75T(40-90m²) 4A CEE

1 ABCD**G**HIJKLMOPS
2 DGJKLMNRTVWXY
3 AHJKLMNRU**W**Z
4 (B+H 1/6-1/9) **P**
(Q+R+T+U+V+X+Z 🔒)
5 **AB**GIJKLMNOPUVZ
6 ABCDFG**K**(N 4km)OTV

💬 A beautifully laid-out terraced campsite with views of Lake Endine 50 metre further on. Restaurant with produce from the campsite's own farm. Very helpful owners. Boats without motors permitted.

🚗 A4 Milan-Venice, exit Seriate. SS42 direction Lovere, campsite on the left past Ranzanico exit.

Nembro
Trescore
Balneario

🅿📶 N 45°47'19'' E 9°56'49''

CC € **17** 1/5-30/6 24/8-22/9

Sesto Calende, I-21018 / Lombardia 👫 🛜 iD 3073

▲ Lido Okay****
✉ Via per Angera 115
☎ FAX +39 0331-974235
🗓 24/3 - 14/10
@ campingokay@
camping-okay.com

1,5ha 80T(60-100m²) 6A CEE

1 AB**G**IJLOPQ
2 DFGJLMORTVWX
3 ABGKLRUZ
4 (B+G 1/6-31/8)
(Q+T+V+Z 🔒)
5 FGIKMNO**P**UZ
6 AEG**K**(N 2km)OQRTV

💬 A campsite with modern toilet facilities and a lovely swimming pool. Situated right on Lake Maggiore.

🚗 Take direction Angera from Sesto Calende. Campsite on the left of the road in Lisanza.

Borgomanero
Somma
Lombardo

🅿📶 N 45°44'56'' E 8°35'48''

CC € **19** 24/3-30/6 26/8-13/10 7=6

Bellamonte/Predazzo, I-38037 / Trentino-Alto Adige ⛷♿ 🛜 iD 3074

▲ Fiemme Village***
✉ Via Cece 16
☎ +39 0462-576119
🗓 21/5 - 24/9
@ info@fiemmevillage.it

6ha 275T(50-170m²) 6-10A CEE

1 ABCDGIJKLMOPQ
2 GIJKLRVXY
3 ABHJKLMNRU**W**
4 (A 1/7-31/8) (C 🔒) **KL**
(Q+R+T+U+V+X+Z 🔒)
5 **AB**DFGIJKLMNOP**QR**STUV
WXYZ
6 CEGJ(N 0,4km)OTV

💬 Bellamonte Campsite stands for nature and relaxation: a heated pool, a traditional restaurant, entertainment in the evenings, a playground and a spa. Perfect for a camping holiday in the mountains.

🚗 From Predazzo dir. Bellamonte (Passe Rolle). Follow signs in village.

Soraga
Predazzo

🅿📶 N 46°18'36'' E 11°39'39''

CC € **15** 21/5-7/7 1/9-23/9

Calceranica al Lago, I-38050 / Trentino-Alto Adige

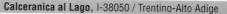

3075

△ Al Pescatore**
🏠 Via dei Pescatori 1
☎ +39 0461-723062
📠 +39 0461-724212
🗓 5/5 - 9/9
@ trentino@campingpescatore.it

3ha 248T(70-100m²) 6A CEE

1 ABCD**G**IJKLMOPQ
2 DLNRTVY
3 BHJNRW**Z**
4 (B+G 16/5-9/9) P
(R+T+U+V+X+Y+Z 🗓)
5 **AB**EFGIJKLMNPUVXZ
6 EGIK(N 1km)OT

💬 Hospitable, attractive campsite. Natural shaded pitches. New modern swimming pool with hydro massage. Located on Lake Caldonazzo. With CampingCard ACSI wifi is free and you can occupy a larger pitch with 6A in early and late season.

🚗 A22, exit Trento. Via SS47 direction Padova. After Pergine direction Caldonazzo. After S. Cristoforo continue direction Calceranica. Campsite well signposted.

Trento — Pergine Valsugana
A22 / SS12 / SS47 / SS349 / SS350

CC €**17** 5/5-10/7 28/8-8/9

N 46°0'7'' E 11°15'19''

Calceranica al Lago, I-38050 / Trentino-Alto Adige

3076

△ Belvedere**
🏠 Viale Venezia 6
☎📠 +39 0461-723239
🗓 20/4 - 23/9
@ info@campingbelvedere.it

1ha 95T(65-120m²) 3-6A CEE

1 ABCD**F**IJKLMOPQ
2 DMNRWXY
3 ABJRU**WZ**
4 (Q+R+T+Z 🗓)
5 **AB**DEFGIJKLMNOP**ST**UVZ
6 ABCEG**IJK**(N 1,5km)TV

💬 A very friendly small campsite near the lake (on the other side of the road) close to pavement cafes and places to eat.

🚗 A22, exit Trento. Via the SS47 direction Padova. After passing Pergine drive in the direction of Caldonazzo. After passing S. Cristoforo drive in the direction of Calceranica, where the campsite is signposted.

Trento — Pergine Valsugana
A22 / SS12 / SS47 / SS349 / SS350

CC €**17** 20/4-1/7 19/8-22/9

N 46°0'12'' E 11°15'29''

Calceranica al Lago, I-38050 / Trentino-Alto Adige

3077

△ Fleiola**
🏠 Viale Trento 42
☎ +39 0461-723153
📠 +39 0461-724386
🗓 21/4 - 3/10
@ info@campingfleiola.it

1,2ha 107T(65-80m²) 3-6A CEE

1 ABCD**G**HIJKLMOPQ
2 DGLNORTVX
3 ABJKRU**WZ**
4 **K**(R+T+Z 15/5-20/9)
5 **AB**DEFGIJKLMNOP**S**UWXYZ
6 ACEGK(N 0,1km)OTV

💬 Pleasant campsite on the shore of Lake Caldonazzo. Several pitches right by the lake. Lovely views of the Trentino mountains. CampingCard ACSI is valid only for standard pitches.

🚗 A22, exit Trento. Take the SS47 to Padova. Past Pergine take the direction of Caldonazzo. Beyond S. Cristoforo you can just follow the signs leading to the campsite, on the left side of the road.

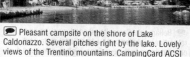

Trento — Pergine Valsugana
A22 / SS12 / SS47 / SS349 / SS350

CC €**17** 21/4-19/5 3/6-6/7 3/9-2/10

N 46°0'23'' E 11°14'44''

Calceranica al Lago, I-38050 / Trentino-Alto Adige ♿ 🛜 iD (3078)

▲ Penisola Verde**
🏠 V. Penisola Verde 5
☎ +39 0461-723272
📠 +39 0461-1820746
⊙ 5/5 - 16/9
@ info@penisolaverde.it

3ha 129T(60-80m²) 4-6A CEE

1 ABCD**F**IJKLMO**P**Q
2 CDLNRVXY
3 BHJRU**W**Z
4 (A 8/7-26/8) (R+T+Z ⊙)
5 **A**BDEFGIJKLMNOPUW
6 BCEG**K**(N 0,4km)ST

NEW

💬 A peaceful campsite right by the lake. Private beach with plenty of shade. The toilet facilities were recently renovated. Wifi. Bar with terrace and views of the lake. Swimming water and playground. 400 metres from the village, and pizzerias and restaurants within 200 metres.

🚗 A22, exit Trento. Via the SS47 direction Padova. After Pergine direction Caldonazzo. Left after the bridge in Calceranica al Lago.

Trento — Pergine Valsugana / A22 / SS47 / SS12 / CC / SS349 / SS350

CC € **17** 5/5-7/7 26/8-15/9   📡 N 46°0'20'' E 11°14'50''

Calceranica al Lago, I-38050 / Trentino-Alto Adige 🛜 iD (3079)

▲ Riviera**
🏠 Viale Venezia 10
☎ +39 0461-724464
📠 +39 0461-718689
⊙ 14/4 - 23/9
@ info@camping-riviera.net

2ha 137T(75-100m²) 6A CEE

1 ABCD**F**IJKLMO**P**Q
2 DMNRVY
3 BKLR**W**Z
4 (Q ⊙)
   (T+U+V+X+Y 23/4-16/9)
   (Z ⊙)
5 **AB**GIJKLMNOPU
6 ABEG**K**(N 1,5km)RTUV

💬 Located on the southern shore of Lake Caldonazzo, 10 metres from the lake and the beach. Camping Riviera awaits you for a wonderful holiday, surrounded by countryside and in a quiet location. Many opportunities for walks and excursions in the surrounding mountains.

🚗 A22, exit Trento. Via SS47 direction Padova. After Pergine direction Caldonazzo. After S. Cristoforo direction Calceranica. Campsite well signposted.

Trento — Pergine Valsugana / A22 / SS47 / SS12 / CC / SS349 / SS350

CC € **17** 14/4-5/7 23/8-22/9   📡 N 46°0'13'' E 11°15'31''

Calceranica al Lago, I-38050 / Trentino-Alto Adige ♿ 🛜 iD (3080)

▲ Spiaggia
🏠 Viale Venezia 14
☎ 📠 +39 0461-723037
⊙ 13/4 - 22/9
@ info@campingspiaggia.net

1,3ha 110T(80-120m²) 6A CEE

1 ACDGIJKLMO**P**Q
2 DLNRTVWXY
3 ABKLR**VW**Z
4 (A 1/6-15/9) **KNP**
   (Q+R+Z ⊙)
5 **AB**DFGIJKLMNOP**S**TUWXZ
6 ABEG**K**(N 1,5km)OTV

💬 A hospitable campsite with its own beach on Lake Caldonazzo. Ideal base for mountain walks, excursions and bike trips. Spacious pitches (80-100 m²), 6 Amp. CCA-holders have a choice of all pitches except those with private toilet facilities. Modern toilet facilities. Wifi 100%.

🚗 A22, exit Trento-Nord, direction Padova via the SS47. Beyond Pergine take exit towards Calceranica and Caldonazzo (lake). Follow Spiaggia campsite signs beyond Caldonazzo.

Trento — Pergine Valsugana / A22 / SS12 / CC / SS47 / SS349 / SS350

CC € **17** 13/4-4/7 24/8-21/9   📡 N 46°0'15'' E 11°15'34''

Caldonazzo, I-38056 / Trentino-Alto Adige

♿ 📶 iD **3081**

🔺 Camping Mario Village★★★★
✉️ Via Lungolago 4
☎ +39 0461-723341
📠 +39 0461-723106
🔑 20/4 - 23/9
@ info@campingmario.com

3,5ha 160T(70-150m²) 6-10A CEE

1 ABCDGIJKLMOPQ
2 DKLMNRTVWXY
3 AB**F**KLNRU**W**Z
4 (C 🔑) **P**
  (Q+R+T+U+V+X+Z 🔑)
5 **AB**DEFGIJKLMNOP**ST**UWX YZ
6 BCEGIK(N 1,5km)TVW

💬 Use CampingCard ACSI in a four-star campsite just a few metres from Caldonazzo Lake. Shaded pitches 70-80m², 6A electricity, modern toilet facilities, heated swimming pool up to 28°C, and free wifi throughout the campsite.

🚗 A22, exit Trento. Via the SS47 towards Padova. Past Pergine take direction Caldonazzo. After S. Cristoforo direction Calceranica. Then follow 'Mario' camping signs.

Trento Pergine Valsugana
A22 SS12 CC SS47
SS349
SS350

CC € **17** 20/4-6/7 26/8-22/9

📶 N 46°0'16'' E 11°15'37''

Carbonare di Folgaria, I-38044 / Trentino-Alto Adige

🚶 ⛷ ♿ 📶 iD **3082**

🔺 Sole Neve
✉️ Via Carducci 120
☎ +39 0464-765257
🔑 1/1 - 15/10, 5/12 - 31/12
@ camping.soleneve@libero.it

42ha 70T(50-120m²) 4-6A CEE

1 ABFIJKLMOPRS
2 BJKLRTVWX
3 BD**F**HJ**O**R
4 (Q+R+V+Y+Z 🔑)
5 **AB**DEFGIJKLMNPUVWXZ
6 DEGJ(N 1km)OTV

💬 Campsite is located on the edge of a forest with a lovely view of the peaks of the southern Dolomites. Ideal campsite for a relaxing stay and outings on foot, by bike, motorbike or car.

🚗 A22 Bolzano-Verona, exit Trento Sud direction SS349. Follow road towards Passo del Sommo. Campsite on the right after about 23 km.

Ravina
SS47
Caldonazzo
A22 SS12 SS349
Folgaria CC
SS350
SS46

CC € **15** 1/4-14/7 1/9-14/10

📶 N 45°56'31'' E 11°14'11''

Ledro/Pieve, I-38067 / Trentino-Alto Adige

♿ 📶 iD **3083**

🔺 Al Lago
✉️ Via Alzer 7
☎ +39 0464-591250
📠 +39 0464-905467
🔑 30/3 - 6/10
@ info@camping-al-lago.it

1ha 90T(56-80m²) 6A CEE

1 ABCD**G**IJKLMOPRS
2 DGKNRTVWXY
3 BGHJKLR**W**Z
4 (**A** 1/7-31/8)
  (T+U+V+Y+Z 🔑)
5 **AB**GIJKLMNOPUVW
6 ACEGK(N 0,2km)RTV

💬 Beautiful, peaceful campsite on the lovely Lake Ledro. Swimming, surfing, mountain biking, and afterwards a fine meal in the restaurant. English, Dutch and German speaking staff. Free wifi. CampingCard ACSI is valid on 'Piazzole classic'.

🚗 In Riva del Garda towards Val di Ledro. Through a newly built tunnel N240 you will reach the pass. Beyond Molina drive along the lake on the SS240 and turn left in the town of Pieve di Ledro.

SS237
Arco
Riva del Garda
Storo CC
SS45BIS

CC € **17** 30/3-29/6 2/9-5/10

📶 N 45°53'1'' E 10°43'54''

Levico Terme, I-38056 / Trentino-Alto Adige

♿ 🛜 **iD** (3084)

🔺 2 Laghi****
🏠 Località Costa 3
☎ +39 0461-706290
📠 +39 0461-707381
🗓 28/4 - 9/9
@ info@campingclub.it

11ha 426T(80-120m²) 6-10A CEE

1. ABCD**G**IJKLMOPQ
2. LMRVXY
3. BGJKLMNRU**W**
4. (A+C+G+R+T+U+V+W+Y 🅾)
5. **AB**FGIJKLMNOP**S**TUVXYZ
6. CDEGJ(N 1km)ORTUV

💬 A campsite located between the Levico and Caldonazzo lakes. The site has tennis courts, a swimming pool and very good toilet facilities. Pitches with plenty of shade and a very quiet campsite in early and late seasons.

🚗 A22, exit Trento. Drive via the SS47 towards Padova. Take the first exit towards Levico. Turn left after 300m opposite petrol station. Campsite on the left at slip road.

Trento · **Pergine Valsugana**
SS47
CC
SS349
SS350

CC € 19 28/4-7/7 1/9-8/9

📍 N 46°0'16'' E 11°17'21''

Meran, I-39012 / Trentino-Alto Adige

♿ 🛜 (3085)

🔺 Camping Hermitage****
🏠 Via Val di Nova 29
☎ +39 0473-232191
📠 +39 0473-256407
🗓 8/4 - 5/11
@ info@einsiedler.com

1,5ha 71T(60-90m²) 10-15A

1. BCDGIJLMQ
2. GRST
3. AB
4. (B 15/5-15/9) (**F** 🅾) M**N** (Q+U+X+Y+Z 🅾)
5. **A**IJLMNOP**ST**U
6. K(N 1km)

💬 Quiet, modern campsite with a view of the town of Meran and the surrounding mountains. There is a bus connection to Meran, 3 km. There is an outdoor swimming pool and covered pool. Free wifi.

🚗 From the Brenner Pass, direction Bolzano south. Motorway Bolzano/Merano south, 4 km towards Meran 2000.

SS44   SS508
Merano CC
Lana
SS38
SS238

CC € 19 8/4-10/5 13/5-18/5 21/5-31/5 3/6-6/7 9/9-16/9 14/10-4/11

📍 N 46°40'18'' E 11°12'11''

Pergine, I-38057 / Trentino-Alto Adige

♿ 🛜 **iD** (3086)

🔺 Punta Indiani
🏠 Valcanover
☎ +39 0461-548062
📠 +39 0461-548607
🗓 29/4 - 30/9
@ info@campingpuntaindiani.it

1,5ha 115T(60-100m²) 6A CEE

1. ABCD**G**IJKLMOPQ
2. ADGJKLMNRVWXY
3. ABJKRW**Z**
4. (Q+T+U+V+Y+Z 🅾)
5. **AB**GIJKLMNPUVWZ
6. AEGK(N 0,1km)TU

💬 A family campsite right by Lake Caldonazzo with a private beach. Spacious, grassy and leafy pitches. Supermarket, bank, restaurant and bus all within 100m. Cycle track close to the campsite, an ideal starting point for excursions and walks. CampingCard ACSI is valid on pitches in Zone Relax.

🚗 A22, exit Trento Nord. Via SS47 dir. Padova. Exit S. Cristoforo (Lago di Caldonazzo). Follow camping signs, campsite is located at lake 1.5 km after S. Cristoforo.

Trento · Pergine Valsugana
SS47
A22 CC
SS12
SS349

CC € 17 29/4-5/7 28/8-29/9

📍 N 46°1'39'' E 11°13'54''

Pergine Valsugana, I-38057 / Trentino-Alto Adige 🦽 🛜 iD 3087

△ S. Cristoforo**
🏕 Loc. Cristoforo
☎ 📠 +39 0461-512707
📅 18/5 - 23/9
@ info@campingclub.it

2,5ha 157T(80-120m²) 6A CEE

1 ABCDGIJKLO**P**RS
2 ADGLMRVXY
3 BFJKLRU**W**
4 (A+B+Q+R+T+U+V+Y+Z 📅)
5 **AB**CFGHIJKLMNOPUWXZ
6 ACEGJ(N 0,8km)ORTV

💬 San Cristoforo campsite has the perfect location for a family holiday in Valsugana, Trentino... Magical surroundings to discover all that the area has to offer.

🚗 A22, exit Trento. Via the SS47 direction Padova. Take exit S. Cristoforo (Lago di Caldonazzo). Follow camp signs in the village.

SS12 **Trento** Pergine Valsugana
A22 CC SS47
SS349

CC € **15** 18/5-30/6 1/9-22/9

📍 N 46°2'19'' E 11°14'12''

Predazzo, I-38037 / Trentino-Alto Adige 🦽 🛜 iD 3088

△ Valle Verde***
🏕 Loc. Ischia 2, Sotto Sassa
☎ 📠 +39 0462-502394
📅 28/4 - 30/9
@ camping.valleverde@tin.it

1,4ha 117T(60-110m²) 6A CEE

1 ABCD**G**HIJKLMOPQ
2 CGRVWXY
3 ABDHKLNR**W**X
4 **LP**(Q 📅) (R 15/6-15/9)
  (T+U+V+Y+Z 📅)
5 **AB**DEFGJLNP**S**UVWXYZ
6 ACEGIK(N 2km)ORSV

💬 An ideal campsite for those who like walks in the middle of mountains, lakes, streams, flora and fauna. 2 km from Predazzo. The Guest Card is included in the extra tax.

🚗 A22, exit Ora, N48 direction Cavalese/Predazzo. In Predazzo exit S. Martino di Castrozza. Follow campsite signs.

SS241
SS346
SS48
SS620 Predazzo CC SS50
Cavalese

CC € **19** 28/4-7/7 25/8-29/9

📍 N 46°18'38'' E 11°37'54''

Racines/Casateia, I-39040 / Trentino-Alto Adige 🎿 🦽 🛜 iD 3089

△ Gilfenklamm*
🏕 Jaufenstraße 2
☎ +39 0472-779132
📅 1/1-7/1,10/2-25/2,24/3-8/4
@ info@camping-gilfenklamm.com

4ha 135T(50-90m²) 8A

1 ABC**G**IJKLMNO**P**Q
2 BFGRTUWXY
3 A**C**GRU**W**
4 (Q+R 1/7-31/8)
  (T+U+V+X+Y+Z 📅)
5 **AB**DFGIJKLMNO**P**UVW
6 BCGJ(N 0,3km)S

💬 The first campsite after the Brenner Pass. The site is located just 3 km from the motorway. The unmarked pitches are located in several small lawns surrounded by lawns with seasonal pitches. Starting point for mountain walks or ski trips.

🚗 Take the Vipiteno-Sterzing exit from the Brenner pass. Another 2 km towards Racines/Casateia.

SS12
CC A22
SS44
San Leonardo In Passiria SS508

CC € **17** 24/3-7/4 28/4-30/6 1/9-13/10

📍 N 46°52'58'' E 11°24'29''

Rasen/Rasun, I-39030 / Trentino-Alto Adige

3090

△ Corones★★★★
🏠 Gepaiden 13
☎ +39 0474-496490
📠 +39 0474-498250
🔓 10/5 - 21/10, 7/12 - 8/4
@ info@corones.com

2,5ha 135T(70-110m²) 10A CEE

1 ACD**F**IJKLMPST
2 CLRTUVWX
3 B**F**HJ**NOPQ**RU**VW**
4 (A 1/7-31/8)
(B+G 24/5-25/10) **N**
(Q+R+T+U+X+Y+Z 🔓)
5 **AB**DEFGIJKLMNOPR**ST**UW
Z
6 CDEG**IK**(N 1km)O**P**RSTV

💬 A comfortable and luxuriously equipped campsite on the edge of a large nature and ski area in the Dolomites ('Der Kronplatz'). The perfect base for all summer and winter sports including mountain climbing, cycling, walking, and both downhill and cross country skiing. Back at the campsite there is a swimming pool, a restaurant and a sauna.

🚗 From Bruneck (Brunico) continue towards Toblach. Past Olang 600m, left to Rasen. Follow camping signs from here.

CC € 19 10/5-5/7 16/9-20/10

🧭 N 46°46'33'' E 12°2'13''

Terlago, I-38096 / Trentino-Alto Adige

3091

△ Laghi di Lamar★★★
🏠 Via alla Selva Faeda 15
☎ +39 0461-860423
📠 +39 02-700538636
🔓 25/3 - 30/9
@ campeggio@laghidilamar.com

2ha 113T(80-100m²) 3-10A CEE

1 ABCD**G**IJKLMNOPQ
2 B**G**HJKLMRTVVX
3 ABCHIJ**Q**RU
4 (C 1/6-15/9) (Q+R+V+Z 🔓)
5 **AB**DEFGIJKLMNOP**ST**UXY
Z
6 ACEGK(N 4km)ORTV

💬 Campsite located in the wonderful setting of the Dolomites, in the Valle de Laghi. An oasis combining nature and hospitality. The grounds offer total peace and quiet and make an excellent starting point for walks, mountain bike trips and visits to Trento. New facilities.

🚗 Exit Trento Nord or Trento Sud. Follow SS45B and take exit 6 dir. Riva del Garda. Continue dir. Valle dei Laghi and follow signs. Route is through Terlago. Less suitable for caravans. Alternative via Vezzano.

CC € 19 25/3-30/6 1/9-29/9

🧭 N 46°6'38'' E 11°2'52''

Toblach/Dobbiaco, I-39034 / Trentino-Alto Adige

3092

△ Toblacher See★★★
🏠 Toblacher See 3
☎ +39 0474-973138
📠 +39 0474-976647
🔓 1/1 - 31/10, 25/12 - 31/12
@ camping@toblachersee.com

2,5ha 132T(80-130m²) 6A CEE

1 ABCD**G**HIJKLM**P**Q
2 BDGIJLMRTVWX
3 AHJKNR**W**
4 (Q+T+U+V+Y+Z 🔓)
5 **AB**DEFGIJKLMNOPR**ST**UW
XYZ
6 BCEG**IJ**(N 2km)OSTU

💬 A lovely comfortable summer and winter campsite located on the Toblacher lake. The site is an excellent base for summer and winter sports. Back at the campsite you can take advantage of the restaurant. Very easily accessible, located beside the N51 Toblach to Cortina d'Ampezzo road.

🚗 From the Pustertal take the exit towards Cortina via the SS51. Campsite on the right 2 km further on.

CC € 19 8/1-28/3 3/4-15/6 10/9-30/10

🧭 N 46°42'23'' E 12°13'5''

Bardolino, I-37011 / Lago di Garda

▲ La Rocca Camping Village***
✉ Via Gardesana dell' Acqua 37
☏ +39 045-7211111
FAX +39 045-7211300
⚷ 30/3 - 28/10
@ info@campinglarocca.com

8ha 262T(20-120m²) 6-16A CEE

1 ABCD**G**IJKLMOPRT
2 DFGJKLMNRVWXY
3 BCKLNRUV**WZ**
4 (A 15/5-15/9)
(C+H 1/4-14/10) J**K**M
(Q+S+T+U+V+Y+Z ⚷)
5 **AB**EFGIJKLMNOPRUVWZ
6 CEGH**IK**(N 1km)QRSTUV

(3093)

SS45BIS
Salò
SS12
A22
Bussolengo

💬 A lovely well-equipped campsite with swimming pool and sports facilities, located directly on Lake Garda. Within walking distance of Garda and Bardolino. CampingCard ACSI pitches are in the lower section, only in the first four rows from the campsite entrance.

🚗 A22, exit Lago di Garda Sud, then direction Bardolino/Lago di Garda. In Bardolino turn right in the direction of Garda, via the N249. Clearly signposted. Located at the lake.

CC € **17** 9/4-22/4 1/5-8/5 13/5-17/5 3/6-1/7 9/9-30/9 8/10-27/10 ▲ N 45°33'52'' E 10°42'46''

Bardolino, I-37011 / Lago di Garda

▲ Serenella***
✉ Località Mezzariva 19
☏ +39 045-7211333
FAX +39 045-7211552
⚷ 17/3 - 21/10
@ serenella@camping-serenella.it

5ha 272T(65-100m²) 6-16A CEE

1 ABCDEIJKLOPRS
2 DFGILMNRVWXY
3 BKRV**WZ**
4 (B+H ⚷) MP
(Q+S+T+U+V+Y+Z ⚷)
5 **AB**EGIJKLMNOPR**S**TUVWX
YZ
6 ACEG**K**(N 2km)OSTV

(3094)

SS45BIS
SS12
CC
A22
Desenzano del Garda

💬 A well maintained campsite on the shores of Lake Garda, just 1 km from both Garda and Bardolino. Modern facilities and water sports opportunities. The first three rows of pitches on the campsite (as seen from the lake) are not available to CampingCard ACSI holders.

🚗 A22, exit Lago di Garda-Sud, then direction Bardolino/Lago di Garda. Turn right in Bardolino direction Garda via de N249. Campsite located by the lake beyond Bardolino.

CC € **17** 17/3-30/6 1/9-20/10 ▲ N 45°33'33'' E 10°42'59''

Cisano di Bardolino, I-37010 / Lago di Garda

▲ Cisano/San Vito*****
✉ Via Peschiera 48
☏ +39 045-6229098
FAX +39 045-6229059
⚷ 17/3 - 8/10
@ cisano@camping-cisano.it

15ha 460T(50-110m²) 6-16A CEE

1 ABCDEIJKLMOPQ
2 ADGIJKLRTVWXY
3 BKLMNQRUV**WZ**
4 (B+G 30/4-15/9) JP
(Q+S+T+U+V+Y+Z ⚷)
5 **AB**EFGIJKLMNOP**QRST**UV
WXYZ
6 ACEG**JM**(N 0,3km)QRTV

(3095)

SS12
A22
CC
Bussolengo
Castelnuovo del Garda
A4

💬 Cisano campsite with its narrow sandy beach on Lake Garda has an area on the other side of the road where you will find the swimming pool and the restaurant. The two parts are connected by an underpass.

🚗 A22, exit Lago di Garda Sud, then direction Bardolino/Lago di Garda. At Bardolino turn left in the direction of Lazise via the N249. The campsite is located just after Cisano, by the lake.

CC € **17** 17/3-30/6 25/8-7/10 ▲ N 45°31'32'' E 10°43'43''

Desenzano del Garda, I-25015 / Lago di Garda

🔺 Camping Village San Francesco****
📧 Str.Vic.S.Francesco
☎ +39 030-9110245
🔑 20/4 - 30/9
@ booking@ campingsanfrancesco.com
10,4ha 348T(60-96m²) 6-10A CEE

1 ABCD**G**IJKLMOPQ
2 DFGKLMNRTVWXY
3 B**FKMN**RUWZ
4 (B+G 25/4-16/9) M
(Q+S+T+U+V+Y+Z 🔑)
5 **AB**EFGIJKLMNOPUWXY
6 ABCDEGH**IK**(N 2km)OTUV
W

💬 This site has its own 300-metre beach on the south side of Lake Garda and is located close to the village of Sirmione. The site boasts luxurious modern facilities. Excellent (water)sports activities. The modern swimming complex with spray park is surrounded by terraces and landscaping. The CampingCard ACSI rate is valid for the standard pitches and the equipped pitches. Extra fee applies for 'superior' pitches.

🚗 A4 Milano-Venezia, exit Sirmione. Campsite signposted.

(3096)

Desenzano del Garda

CC

CC€ **19** 20/4-13/7 31/8-29/9

N 45°27'56'' E 10°35'41''

Lazise sul Garda, I-37017 / Lago di Garda

🔺 Belvedere***
📧 Strada del Roccolo 11
☎ +39 045-7590228
FAX +39 045-6499084
🔑 23/3 - 7/10
@ info@campingbelvedere.com

6ha 262T(70-90m²) 6A CEE

1 ABCD**G**IJKLMOPQ
2 ADFGIJKLNRVWXY
3 BC**F**KMNR**W**Z
4 (B+G 1/5-22/9) JK
(Q+S+T+U+V+Y+Z 🔑)
5 **AB**DEFGIJKLMNOP**ST**UVX
YZ
6 ACEGH**J**M(N 2km)QTV

💬 A campsite with a swimming pool and stony beach by a lake, behind the Acquasplash Caneva sports centre. A good restaurant with lovely views over the lake. The first two rows by the lakeside (pitches 1 to 28) are not for CampingCard ACSI. 10% discount in the restaurant in low season with CampingCard ACSI.

🚗 A22, exit Lago di Garda Sud, then dir. Lazise/ Lago di Garda via N249. Follow signs beyond Lazise. The campsite is located before Caneva Sport, by the lake.

(3097)

Bussolengo

CC

Sommacampagna

CC€ **17** 23/3-30/6 26/8-6/10

N 45°28'47'' E 10°43'22''

Lazise sul Garda, I-37017 / Lago di Garda

🔺 Fossalta***
📧 Loc. Fossalta
Str. del Roccolino 22
☎ +39 045-7590231
FAX +39 045-7590999
🔑 23/3 - 8/10
@ info@fossalta.com
6ha 272T(60-135m²) 6A CEE

1 BCD**G**IJKLMOPRS
2 ADFGIJKLNRVWXY
3 B**F**MNR**W**Z
4 (B+G 1/5-30/9)
(Q+S+T+Z 🔑)
5 **A**DEFGIJKLMNOPUVZ
6 CEGHKM(N 2km)ORTV

💬 A quiet, well-maintained campsite right next to Lake Garda. Spacious shaded pitches with plenty of greenery and flowers. The first two rows from the lake (0-29) are not available with CampingCard ACSI. 10% discount at the bar during CampingCard ACSI acceptance period.

🚗 A22, exit Lago di Garda Sud, then direction Bardolino/Lago di Garda. At Bardolino turn left in the direction of Peschiera. Clearly signposted after Lazise.

(3098)

Bussolengo

CC

Sommacampagna

CC€ **17** 23/3-29/6 25/8-7/10

N 45°28'49'' E 10°43'21''

Limone, I-25010 / Lago di Garda

3099

△ Campingpark Garda***
✉ Via IV Novembre 10
☎ 📠 +39 0365-954550
🕐 24/3 - 20/10
@ info@hghotels.com

2,3ha 200T(40-60m²) 3-6A CEE

1 BGIJKLMOP**RS**
2 DJLNRTVXY
3 MW**Z**
4 (B+G 1/4-16/10) (Q 🔒)
   (S 15/6-30/9) (U+V+Y+Z 🔒)
5 AGIJKLMOPUVZ
6 CFGJ(N 1km)OQRTV

💬 Natural area, old town nearby, view of lake and private beach. Sunbathing by two new pools. Restaurant, bar, pizzeria, supermarket, barbecue on beach. Sailing and surfing lessons. Mooring for motor and sailing boats. Beauty of lake and mountains, for outdoor and sports enthusiasts. CampingCard ACSI only for pitches.

🚗 From Riva del Garda take SS45bis dir. Salò. After many tunnels you reach Limone. After Limone at Tamoil service station, site is left of the road.

Riva del Garda
Limone sul Garda SS249
Malcesine
SS45BIS
A22

© €19 24/3-9/5 2/6-30/6 1/9-19/10

📍 N 45°48'20'' E 10°47'16''

Manerba del Garda, I-25080 / Lago di Garda

3100

△ Baia Verde****
✉ Via dell'Edera, 19
☎ +39 0365-651753
📠 +39 0365-651809
🕐 31/3 - 6/10
@ info@campingbaiaverde.com

4,8ha 225T(72-90m²) 4-16A CEE

1 ABC**G**IJKLMOPQ
2 CGLRVXY
3 BNRW
4 (A 1/6-26/9) (B 7/4-3/10) KP
   (Q+S+T+U+V+X+Z 🔒)
5 AB**C**DEFGIJKLMNOPR**ST**U
   VWXYZ
6 DEGKQRTV

💬 This lovely campsite with 2 swimming pools, whirlpools, hydro massage, roof solarium and much more is located right by Lake Garda. All this is situated in an oasis of greenery and peace in the breathtaking surroundings of Lago di Garda. Lovely spacious pitches. 80 new pitches with electricity.

🚗 A4 exit Desenzano, then direction Salò via the SS572. Follow camping signs at Manerba del Garda.

SS45BIS
Desenzano del Garda

© €19 31/3-29/6 1/9-5/10

📍 N 45°33'41'' E 10°33'13''

Manerba del Garda, I-25080 / Lago di Garda

3101

△ Sivino's Resort
✉ Via Gramsci, 78
☎ +39 0365-552767
🕐 30/3 - 30/9
@ info@sivinos.it

3ha 75T(60-105m²) 6-12A CEE

1 BCDGIJKLMOPQ
2 DJKLNORTX
3 Z
4 (Q+T 🔒)
5 AGIJKLMNPUVX
6 BEGJ(N 1km)TV

NEW

💬 A beautiful and peaceful campsite in the countryside close to Moniga del Garda. Lovely beach and undisturbed views of the lake. Free wifi, bread service, (snack)bar open in the evening and at weekends in low season.

🚗 A4, exit Desenzano direction Salò. At Moniga del Garda follow the Via San Sivino. Follow brown camping signs and drive to the end of the road (±300m incl. 3 or 4 bends).

SS45BIS
Desenzano del Garda
A4

© €15 30/3-10/6 3/9-29/9

📍 N 45°31'55'' E 10°33'25''

Manerba del Garda, I-25080 / Lago di Garda ♿ 📶 iD **3102**

🔺 Zocco★★★
✉ Via del Zocco 43
☎ +39 0365-551605
🔑 21/4 - 7/10
@ info@campingzocco.it

5ha 209T(60-80m²) 6A CEE

1 ABC**F**HIJKLMOPQ
2 DG**J**KNRTVWXY
3 B**F**GKL**M**NRUW**Z**
4 (B 🔑) P(Q+S+U+V+X+Z 🔑)
5 **AB**EFGIJKLMNOPUV
6 CEGK(N 2km)QRTV

💬 This lovely, well-kept campsite is close to Lake Garda. Lovely views. Partly terraced under olive trees. The staff, the central bar, the pizzeria and the small shop ensure a relaxing atmosphere. The lovely swimming pool will tempt you.

🚗 A4, exit Desenzano, then towards Salò via the SS572. Leave this road at Manerba del Garda. Follow the brown camping signs. The campsite is located by the lake.

CC € **17** *21/4-18/5 3/6-1/7 8/9-6/10*   📍 N 45°32'24'' E 10°33'22''

Moniga del Garda, I-25080 / Lago di Garda ♿ 📶 iD **3103**

🔺 Piantelle★★★★
✉ Via San Cassiano 1a
☎ +39 0365-502013
📠 +39 0365-502637
🔑 24/3 - 17/10
@ info@piantelle.com

8,5ha 121T(60-100m²) 6A CEE

1 ABC**G**IJKLMOPQ
2 DFJKLNRWXY
3 BGKLNRWZ
4 (B 10/5-2/10) **N**
(Q+R+U+V+Y+Z 🔑)
5 **AB**GJLNPUVWXYZ
6 CDEGK(N 0,5km)RT

💬 A lovely campsite on Lake Garda with its own 250m beach and private slipway. Modern swimming pool. Well-maintained marked-out pitches. Delicious food in the restaurant. Nine free wifi points. Pitches by the lake are not available for CampingCard ACSI.

🚗 A4, exit Dezenzano. Then towards Salò via the SS572. Leave the road at Moniga del Garda. Follow brown camping signs.

CC € **19** *24/3-29/6 17/9-16/10*   📍 N 45°31'12'' E 10°31'48''

Moniga del Garda, I-25080 / Lago di Garda ♿ 📶 iD **3104**

🔺 Sereno Camping Holiday★★★
✉ Via San Sivino 72
☎ +39 0365-502080
📠 +39 0365-503893
🔑 24/3 - 8/10
@ info@campingsereno.it

4ha 32T(50-90m²) 6A CEE

1 ABCGHIJKL**P**Q
2 DKLNRTVWXY
3 B**EF**G**M**NQRUW**Z**
4 (B 1/5-26/9)
(Q+S+U+V+Y+Z 🔑)
5 **A**GIJKLMNOPUVX
6 CEGJ(N 2km)TV

💬 A campsite with a large swimming pool and an extensive entertainment team. Good toilet facilities. Peacefully located touring pitches. Good restaurant.

🚗 A4, exit Desenzano, then direction Salò via the SS572. Follow the brown camping signs at Moniga del Garda. Campsite located by the lake.

CC € **17** *24/3-29/3 3/4-23/4 2/5-20/5 4/6-17/6 25/8-7/10*   📍 N 45°31'48'' E 10°33'12''

Pacengo di Lazise, I-37017 / Lago di Garda

♿ 🛜 **iD** (3105)

🏕 Camping Le Palme***
✉ Via del Tronchetto 2
☎ +39 045-7590019
FAX +39 045-7590554
🔑 22/3 - 22/10
@ info@lepalmecamping.it

2,5ha 112T(50-100m²) 6-10A CEE

1 ABCD**F**IJKLMOPQ
2 ADFGJLNRVXY
3 B**F**GKNRV**W**Z
4 (C+H 🔑) JKP
 (Q+S+T+U+V+X+Z 🔑)
5 **AB**DFGIJKLMNOP**S**TUWXY
 Z
6 CEG**K**M(N 0,5km)RSTV

💬 Campsite with excellent toilet facilities and where all pitches have electricity, water and drainage connections. The site has two swimming pools with hydro massage and a slide. One third of the pitches are available for CampingCard ACSI holders.

🚗 A22, exit Lago di Garda Sud. Follow SR450 direction Lago di Garda Sud/Peschiera. After 7 km head towards Lazise. S249 direction Pacengo. Campsite signposted in Pacengo.

Desenzano
del Garda CC A22

Peschiera del Garda A4

CC € **17** 22/3-29/3 5/4-18/5 3/6-25/6 9/9-21/10

📷 N 45°27'54'' E 10°42'52''

Pacengo di Lazise, I-37017 / Lago di Garda

♿ 🛜 **iD** (3106)

🏕 Lido***
✉ Via Peschiera 2
☎ +39 045-7590030
🔑 23/3 - 14/10
@ info@campinglido.it

12ha 523T(60-100m²) 6-10A CEE

1 ABCD**G**IJKLMOPRS
2 DFGIJLNRVWXY
3 B**F**GK**M**NR**VW**Z
4 (C 14/4-7/10) (G 10/5-30/9) J
 P(Q+S+U+V+Y+Z 🔑)
5 **AB**DEFGIJKLMNOP**ST**UVX
 YZ
6 CEG**HJ**(N 0,1km)RTV

💬 Spacious, shaded campsite with marked out pitches. New toilet facilities, lovely new swimming pools with waterslide, children's pool and fitness centre. Located on Lake Garda. Dogs are welcome. 10% discount in the restaurant in low season with CampingCard ACSI. One third of the pitches are available with CampingCard ACSI.

🚗 A22, exit Lago di Garda Sud, then take SR450 dir. Peschiera. After 7 km exit Lazise. In Lazise dir. Pacengo. Campsite is south of Movieland.

Sirmione SS12

CC

Desenzano
del Garda A4

CC € **17** 23/3-30/6 3/9-13/10

📷 N 45°28'12'' E 10°43'15''

Padenghe sul Garda, I-25080 / Lago di Garda

♿ 🛜 **iD** (3107)

🏕 La Ca'****
✉ Via della Colombaia 6
☎ +39 030-9907006
FAX +39 030-9907693
🔑 17/2 - 10/11
@ info@campinglaca.it

4ha 136T(60m²) 6A CEE

1 AB**G**IJKLOP
2 DFGHJKNRTVX
3 AFNR**W**Z
4 (B 1/3-31/10) P
 (Q+U+V+Y+Z 1/3-5/11)
5 **A**GIJKLMNOPR**ST**UWZ
6 EGK(N 0,2km)QT

💬 A beautifully maintained terraced campsite. Beautiful view of Lake Garda, also from the swimming pool and the welcoming restaurant. 13 euros in February, March, April and October. Possible to have the caravan towed up.

🚗 A4, exit Desenzano, then towards Salò via the SS572. Follow the brown camping signs at Padenghe sul Garda. Enter 'Via San Cassiano' at roundabout. Campsite located by the lake.

SS45BIS

CC

Desenzano del
A4 Garda

CC € **15** 17/2-6/7 27/8-9/11

📷 N 45°30'45'' E 10°31'27''

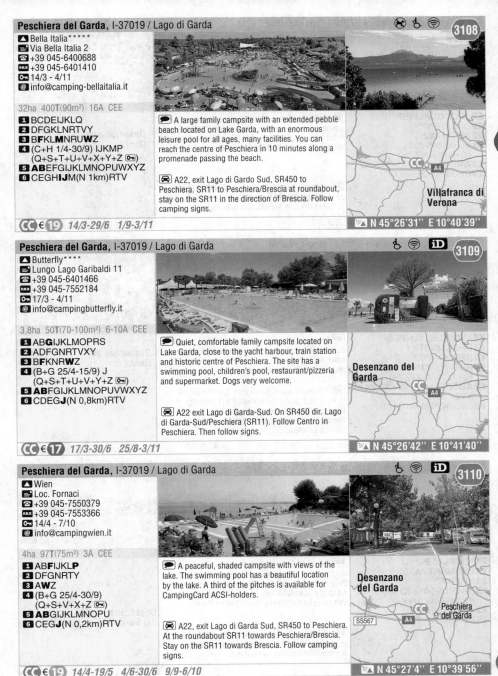

Peschiera del Garda, I-37019 / Lago di Garda ✈ ♿ 📶 3108

🏕 Bella Italia✷✷✷✷✷
📧 Via Bella Italia 2
☎ +39 045-6400688
📠 +39 045-6401410
🔑 14/3 - 4/11
@ info@camping-bellaitalia.it

32ha 400T(90m²) 16A CEE

1 BCDEIJKLQ
2 DFGKLNRTVY
3 BFKLMNRUWZ
4 (C+H 1/4-30/9) IJKMP
　(Q+S+T+U+V+X+Y+Z 🔑)
5 ABEFGIJKLMNOPUWXYZ
6 CEGHIJM(N 1km)RTV

💬 A large family campsite with an extended pebble beach located on Lake Garda, with an enormous leisure pool for all ages, many facilities. You can reach the centre of Peschiera in 10 minutes along a promenade passing the beach.

🚗 A22, exit Lago di Gardo Sud, SR450 to Peschiera. SR11 to Peschiera/Brescia at roundabout, stay on the SR11 in the direction of Brescia. Follow camping signs.

Villafranca di Verona

CC €19 14/3-29/6 1/9-3/11   🧭 N 45°26'31'' E 10°40'39''

Peschiera del Garda, I-37019 / Lago di Garda ♿ 📶 iD 3109

🏕 Butterfly✷✷✷✷
📧 Lungo Lago Garibaldi 11
☎ +39 045-6401466
📠 +39 045-7552184
🔑 17/3 - 4/11
@ info@campingbutterfly.it

3,8ha 50T(70-100m²) 6-10A CEE

1 ABGIJKLMOPRS
2 ADFGNRTVY
3 BFKNRWZ
4 (B+G 25/4-15/9) J
　(Q+S+T+U+V+Y+Z 🔑)
5 ABFGIJKLMNOPUVWXYZ
6 CDEGJ(N 0,8km)RTV

💬 Quiet, comfortable family campsite located on Lake Garda, close to the yacht harbour, train station and historic centre of Peschiera. The site has a swimming pool, children's pool, restaurant/pizzeria and supermarket. Dogs very welcome.

🚗 A22 exit Lago di Garda-Sud. On SR450 dir. Lago di Garda-Sud/Peschiera (SR11). Follow Centro in Peschiera. Then follow signs.

Desenzano del Garda

CC €17 17/3-30/6 25/8-3/11   🧭 N 45°26'42'' E 10°41'40''

Peschiera del Garda, I-37019 / Lago di Garda ♿ 📶 iD 3110

🏕 Wien
📧 Loc. Fornaci
☎ +39 045-7550379
📠 +39 045-7553366
🔑 14/4 - 7/10
@ info@campingwien.it

4ha 97T(75m²) 3A CEE

1 ABFIJKLP
2 DFGNRTY
3 AWZ
4 (B+G 25/4-30/9)
　(Q+S+V+X+Z 🔑)
5 ABGIJKLMNOPU
6 CEGJ(N 0,2km)RTV

💬 A peaceful, shaded campsite with views of the lake. The swimming pool has a beautiful location by the lake. A third of the pitches is available for CampingCard ACSI-holders.

🚗 A22, exit Lago di Garda Sud, SR450 to Peschiera. At the roundabout SR11 towards Peschiera/Brescia. Stay on the SR11 towards Brescia. Follow camping signs.

Desenzano del Garda

Peschiera del Garda

CC €19 14/4-19/5 4/6-30/6 9/9-6/10   🧭 N 45°27'4'' E 10°39'56''

San Benedetto/Peschiera, I-37010 / Lago di Garda ♿ 🛜 🆔 3111

🏕 Bergamini***
🏠 Strada Bergamini 51
☎ 🄵🄰🄷 +39 045-7550283
🗓 21/3 - 7/10
@ info@campingbergamini.it

1,5ha 70T(60-80m²) 6A CEE

1 ABCD**G**IJKLPRS
2 DFGKNRVY
3 B**F**GK**RW****Z**
4 (B+G 15/5-20/9)
　 (Q+R+T+U+Z 🔑)
5 **AB**EFGIJKLMNOP**T**UWZ
6 CEGJ(N 0,3km)RTV

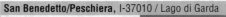

💬 Quiet, shaded campsite. Suitable for families with young children as well as the over-50s. Modern, new toilet facilities. Directly on the lake and at walking distance from the fortified town of Peschiera.

🚗 A22, exit Lago di Garda Sud, SR450 to Peschiera. At roundabout SR11 towards Peschiera/Brescia. Stay on SR11 towards Brescia. Campsite signposted.

Desenzano del Garda

Peschiera del Garda

CC € ⑲ 3/4-10/5 27/5-30/6 2/9-6/10 ⚑ N 45°27'2'' E 10°40'14''

San Benedetto/Peschiera, I-37019 / Lago di Garda ♿ 🛜 🆔 3112

🏕 Village San Benedetto
　 Vecchio Mulino****
🏠 Strada Bergamini 14
☎ +39 045-7550544
🄵🄰🄷 +39 045-7551512
🗓 24/3 - 21/10
@ info@villaggiosanbenedetto.it

6,6ha 72T(40-100m²) 3-10A CEE

1 ABCD**G**HIJKLM**P**RS
2 DFGILMNRTVY
3 B**F**GJKNR**W****Z**
4 (B+G 1/5-30/9)
　 (Q+T+U+V+Y+Z 🔑)
5 **AB**CEFGHIJKLMNOPQRUW
　 XYZ
6 CEG**IK**(N 2km)RTUV

💬 Located directly on Lake Garda next to a small marina. Atmospheric family campsite with many amenities, including a pool, entertainment and restaurant with specialities.

🚗 A22, exit Lago di Garda Sud. Take the SR450 to Peschiera, at the roundabout SR11 direction Peschiera/Brescia. Continue on the SR11 towards Brescia. Turn right in San Benedetto towards the lake. Campsite signposted.

Desenzano del Garda

CC € ⑰ 24/3-30/3 3/4-28/4 2/5-18/5 22/5-1/6 4/6-7/7 25/8-20/10 ⚑ N 45°26'53'' E 10°40'11''

Sirmione, I-25019 / Lago di Garda ♿ 🛜 🆔 3113

🏕 Tiglio
🏠 Loc. Punta Grò
☎ 🄵🄰🄷 +39 030-9904009
🗓 24/3 - 30/9
@ info@campingtiglio.it

3ha 168T(60-80m²) 4A CEE

1 ABC**F**IJKL**P**Q
2 DFGMNRTVWXY
3 BFJR**W****Z**
4 (B+G 1/5-30/9) (Q 🔑)
　 (S 1/4-27/9) (U+V+Y+Z 🔑)
5 **A**GIJKLMNOPUZ
6 EG**K**(N 3km)RSTV

💬 The campsite, a family business, is located on the shores of Lake Garda in a quiet setting between the picturesque villages of Sirmione and Peschiera. An ideal campsite for city trips to Verona, Milan and Venice. Extra fee applies for pitches on the lake.

🚗 A4 Milano-Venezia, exit Sirmione. On the SPBS11 roundabout direction Peschiera-Verona. Campsite signposted 4 km after roundabout.

Sirmione

Desenzano del Garda

SS567

CC € ⑲ 24/3-14/7 1/9-29/9 ⚑ N 45°27'26'' E 10°38'26''

Toscolano Maderno, I-25080 / Lago di Garda 🛜 iD (3114)

🏕 Riviera***
📧 Via Promontorio 59
☎ 📠 +39 0365-643039
📅 29/3 - 30/9
@ info@camping-riviera.com

3,8ha 160T(64-100m²) 3A CEE

1 ABGIJKLMOPQ
2 DGKNRTVWXY
3 BFRWZ
4 (B+Q+R+V 15/6-31/8)
  (Z 1/4-30/9)
5 AEGIJKLMNOPUV
6 CEGJ(N 0,2km)OT

💬 Campsite right by a lake in a peaceful area with plenty of greenery. Centre can be reached within minutes via a promenade along the water. Water is very clear and clean and suitable for divers, anglers and windsurfers. Free wifi. Beach bar. In low season: swimming pool open in the afternoons during the week, whole day during the weekend.

🚐 From Riva del Garda towards Salò via the SS45Bis. After Gargnano drive towards Toscolano. Campsite well indicated. Site by a lake.

SS45BIS

Gavardo Raffa Garda Cavaion Veronese

CC € 17 29/3-28/6 1/9-29/9   ⛺ N 45°38'4'' E 10°36'47''

Toscolano Maderno, I-25088 / Lago di Garda ♿ 🛜 iD (3115)

🏕 Toscolano***
📧 Via Religione 88
☎ +39 0365-641584
📠 +39 0365-642519
📅 24/3 - 1/11
@ campeggiotoscolano@virgilio.it

5ha 350T(80m²) 3A CEE

1 ABGIJKLMPQ
2 ADGNRTVWXY
3 BFMNWZ
4 (B 1/4-30/9) K(Q 30/5-25/9)
  (S 1/5-20/9) (U 📅)
  (V 29/4-30/9) (X+Y 1/4-30/9)
  (Z 📅)
5 ABGIJKLMNOPUVZ
6 CFGJ(N 0,3km)TV

💬 Located within the walls of a 14th-century monastery. Surrounded by a flower garden. Private beach, spacious pitches, shop, fish restaurant, bar and pizzeria. Pools, tennis courts and football field. Horseback excursions bookable. CampingCard ACSI only valid on standard pitches.

🚐 From Riva del Garda dir. Salò via SS45bis. After Gargnano dir. Toscolano. Site is well signposted from here. Site is on a lake.

SS45BIS

Toscolano-Maderno
CC
Salò
San Felice del Benaco Garda

CC € 19 24/3-9/5 2/6-30/6 1/9-31/10   ⛺ N 45°38'15'' E 10°36'46''

Arsiè, I-32030 / Veneto ♿ 🛜 iD (3116)

🏕 Camping Village Lago Arsiè***
📧 Via Campagna 14
☎ +39 0439-58540
📠 +39 0439-58471
📅 20/4 - 23/9
@ info@campinglago.info

2ha 168T(60-100m²) 4-6A CEE

1 ABCDGIJKLMOPRS
2 BCDGKLMRTUVWXY
3 ABHJKLNRUWXZ
4 (A 10/7-20/8)
  (Q+R+T+U+V+Y+Z 📅)
5 ABEGIJKLMNOPUWXYZ
6 ABCDEGK(N 3km)OTV

💬 A peaceful, small campsite located on Lake Corlo. Come to visit a very natural place, surrounded by the breathtaking Belluno Dolomites. This 'off the beaten track spot' is perfect for those who love to relax and doing activities such as walking and fishing. Dogs are welcome.

🚐 From Trento follow the SS47 direction Padova as far as the Feltre exit onto the SS50bis. Take Rocca exit after the tunnel. Campsite is then signposted.

Lamon
Fonzaso Feltre
SS50BIS
CC
SS47

CC € 17 20/4-5/7 23/8-22/9   ⛺ N 45°57'52'' E 11°45'33''

Arsiè, I-32030 / Veneto

♿ 🛜 iD (3117)

🏕 Gajole
📧 Loc. Gajole
☎ 📠 +39 0439-58505
📅 1/4 - 30/9
@ info@campinggajole.it

1,7ha 100T(50-90m²) 6A CEE

1 ABG**H**IJKLMNO**P**RS
2 DIJKLMRTUVX
3 AHJKLMR**W**Z
4 (A 1/4-31/5,1/9-30/9)
   (R+T+U+X 1/5-30/9) (Z 📅)
5 **AB**DFGIJKLMNOP**T**UVXYZ
6 CDEG**K**(N 3km)TVW

💬 Gajole campsite is probably the most peaceful campsite in the world. Gajole campsite was started in 1975 by the Turra family which still runs it. The site is located on the shores of Lake Corlo (including the pitches), a strategic starting point for trips out to various coastal towns and the Dolomites.

🚗 From Trento take the SS47 dir. Padova, exit Feltre. Take the SS50B. After tunnel exit Rocca. Campsite then signposted with big, clear signs.

Fonzaso — Feltre
Seren del Grappa
SS47 ©©

©© € **17** 1/4-5/7 23/8-29/9 | 🧭 N 45°58'4'' E 11°45'58''

Campalto/Venezia, I-30173 / Veneto

🛜 iD (3118)

🏕 Rialto
📧 Via Orlanda 16
☎ 📠 +39 041-5420295
📅 22/3 - 31/10
@ info@campingrialto.com

2ha 150T(20-80m²) 6A CEE

1 ABCGIJKLMP
2 FGRWXY
4 (Q 📅) (R+V+Z 1/5-30/9)
5 **A**GIJKLMOPUV
6 CEG**J**(N 0,3km)T

💬 A small, attractive and modest campsite with grass and deciduous trees. Near the approach road to Venice. By bus (7 minutes away) just a 15 minute ride to the centre of Venice (Piazzale Roma).

🚗 A4 continue towards Venice. Immediate right after bus stop and car park on SS14 towards Trieste. Over viaduct, follow Trieste-Aeroporto road. Campsite another 1 km on the right.

A4 SS13 SS14
Mestre
©©
Mira **Venezia**
SS309

©© € **17** 1/5-9/5 29/5-30/6 10/9-30/9 | 🧭 N 45°29'4'' E 12°17'0''

Caorle, I-30021 / Veneto

♿ 🛜 iD (3119)

🏕 Laguna Village***
📧 Via dei Cacciatori 5
☎ +39 0421-210165
📠 +39 0421-217085
📅 5/5 - 16/9
@ info@campinglagunavillage.com

10ha 500T(60-90m²) 6-10A CEE

1 ABCDGHIJKLMPQ
2 AEGRVY
3 AB**F**JKNRY
4 (B 📅) JK
   (Q+S+U+V+Y+Z 📅)
5 **AB**FGIJKLMNOPUVWXYZ
6 EG**K**M(N 0km)QRT

💬 A lovely, quiet campsite with a pleasant ambiance, partly in pine woods. Excellent toilet facilities. The campsite is located by the sea with a wide beach. The picturesque town of Caorle nearby is worth a visit. CampingCard ACSI is only valid on the 'Laguna' pitches.

🚗 When entering Caorle follow signs left 'Spiaggia di Levante' (corso Chiggiato-Viale Falconera). Then follow camping signs.

Bibione
Caorle ©©

©© € **17** 5/5-28/6 31/8-15/9 | 🧭 N 45°36'59'' E 12°54'25''

Caorle, I-30020 / Veneto

♿ 🛜 **iD** (3120)

🔺 San Francesco*****
📧 Via Selva Rosata
☎ +39 0421-2982
📠 +39 0421-299284
🔑 19/4 - 30/9
@ agency@villaggiosfrancesco.com

32ha 898T(70-100m²) 10-16A CEE

1 ABCD**F**HIJKLMOPQ
2 AEGLRSVXY
3 B**F**GJK**MNQ**RUVY
4 (B+H 🔑) **JK**M
(Q+S+T+U+V+W+X+Y+Z 🔑)
5 **AB**EFGIJKLMNOPR**ST**UWX
YZ
6 CEG**IJK**M(N 0km)ORTV

💬 A lively holiday village in a pine forest, close to the sea. The campsite has a private beach more than 500m in length. The campsite is an ideal base for exploring the area, including the small town of Caorle, a traditional fishing village.

🚗 In Caorle drive first in the direction of Porto S. Margherita, then Duna Verde. The campsite is signposted and is located on the left side of the road.

Caorle / Eraclea / Jesolo

CC € **17** 19/4-15/6 25/8-29/9   **N 45°33'59'' E 12°47'40''**

Cavallino, I-30013 / Veneto

🛜 ♿ (3121)

🔺 Italy****
📧 Via Fausta 272
☎ +39 041-968090
📠 +39 041-5370076
🔑 20/4 - 23/9
@ giuliano.castelli@campingitaly.it

3,9ha 220T(60-100m²) 10A CEE

1 BCDEHIJKLPST
2 AEGRSVY
3 ABJK**MOPQ**RUVY
4 (C+H 1/5-20/9) JP
(Q+S+T+U+V+Y+Z 🔑)
5 **A**BEFGIJKLMNOP**ST**UWXY
Z
6 ACEGK(N 2km)ORTV

💬 A small campsite with deciduous trees and plenty of attention to the environment, close to the sea. The guests can make use of the many sports facilities at the Union Lido campsite. All pets are prohibited (not just dogs!). Luxurious toilet facilities with a separate, nicely decorated space for children.

🚗 Campsite located in Cavallino, on the main road (Via Fausta). Campsite signposted.

SS14 / Jesolo / Lido di Venezia

CC € **15** 20/4-18/5 1/6-30/6 8/9-22/9   **N 45°28'6'' E 12°31'59''**

Cavallino, I-30013 / Veneto

♿ 🛜 **iD** (3122)

🔺 Villa Al Mare***
📧 Via del Faro 12
☎ +39 041-968066
📠 +39 041-5370576
🔑 21/4 - 13/10
@ info@villaalmare.com

2ha 100T(60-100m²) 6A CEE

1 ABCDEHIJKLMOPQ
2 AEGLRSVY
3 B**E**F**G**HJKLRV**W**Y
4 (H 4/5-14/9) **KP**
(Q+S+T+U+V+Y+Z 🔑)
5 **A**FGIJKLMNOPUVWXYZ
6 CDEGH**K**L(N 2,5km)OQRST
V

💬 A peaceful campsite located on the beach next to the marina and fishing harbour. Shaded pitches, all with electricity, water supply and drainage and satellite TV socket. Direct connection to St. Mark's Square in Venice. Excellent cuisine with fresh vegetables and fish at a very reasonable prices and local Italian dishes. Wifi available.

🚗 From the Jesolo roundabout choose direction Cavallino. Campsite close to the lighthouse (Faro) and is signposted

SS14 / Jesolo / Burano

CC € **17** 21/4-25/5 4/6-23/6 13/9-12/10   **N 45°28'45'' E 12°34'52''**

673

Cavallino, I-30013 / Veneto ♿ 📶 **iD** (3123)

🏠 Village Cavallino****
📧 Via delle Batterie 164
☎ +39 041-966133
📠 +39 041-5300827
🔑 22/3 - 5/11
@ info@campingcavallino.com

11ha 560T(64-120m²) 6A CEE

1 ABC**F**IJKLMO**P**Q
2 ABEGRSVWXY
3 ABK**Q**R**V**Y
4 (C+G 1/5-15/9) JKP
　(Q+S+T+U+V+Y+Z 🔑)
5 **AB**DFGIJKLMNOP**QRS**UXY
6 CEGH**K**M(N 2km)RTV

💬 A family campsite with lovely, modern toilet facilities set close to the sea in a pine forest. The abundant flowers add a splash of colour to the site. You cannot pitch by the sea if using CampingCard ACSI. New toilet facilities (2014).

🚗 From Cavallino direction Punta Sabbioni on the Via Fausta, turn left just after Ca'Ballerin. Follow the campsite signs.

Jesolo
SS14
CC
Venezia

CC € **19**　22/3-18/5　4/6-27/6　10/9-4/11　　📍 N 45°27'24'' E 12°30'3''

Cavallino/Treporti, I-30013 / Veneto 🚫 📶 **iD** (3124)

🏠 Ca'Savio***
📧 Via di Ca'Savio 77
☎ +39 041-966017
📠 +39 041-5300707
🔑 28/4 - 6/10
@ info@casavio.it

27ha 800T(80-100m²) 10A CEE

1 ABCDEHIJKLM
2 AELRSVXY
3 BJK**Q**RY
4 (B 🔑) (G 1/5-27/9) (Q+S 🔑)
　(T 1/5-27/9) (U 8/5-25/9)
　(V 1/5-27/9) (W 8/5-25/9)
　(Y+Z 🔑)
5 **AB**FGIJKLMNOPU
6 CEG**K**LM(N 1km)ORTV

NEW

💬 A large, busy campsite with lots of entertainment, close to the sea in a pine forest. Suitable for families. Children can enjoy their time here fully.

🚗 In Cavallino drive onto main road to Punta Sabbioni (Via Fausta). In Ca'Savio at the crossroads turn left onto the Via di Ca'Savio. Then follow signs.

Lido di
Jesolo
SS14
CC
Venezia

CC € **17**　28/4-18/5　2/6-23/6　8/9-5/10　　📍 N 45°26'44'' E 12°27'41''

Cavallino/Treporti, I-30013 / Veneto ♿ 📶 ✿ **iD** (3125)

🏠 Scarpiland***
📧 Via Poerio 14
☎ 📠 +39 041-966488
🔑 28/4 - 30/9
@ info@scarpiland.com

3ha 204T(70-90m²) 6A CEE

1 ABCD**F**HIJKLMPS
2 AEGRSVY
3 AKRY
4 (Q+R+S+T+U+V+Y+Z 🔑)
5 **AB**FGIJKLMNOPUVWXYZ
6 ACEG**K**M(N 2km)OQRSTV

💬 A small but very neat campsite by the sea with separated pitches as well as open ones. It is cosy and peaceful to camp here between the pine trees.

🚗 From Cavallino via Fausta to Punta Sabbioni. Past Ca'Ballarin turn left at first traffic lights, then right at first intersection and follow the camping signs.

Jesolo
SS14
CC
Venezia

CC € **17**　28/4-6/7　24/8-29/9　10=9　　📍 N 45°27'19'' E 12°29'20''

Fusina/Venezia, I-30030 / Veneto

👫 ♿ 🛜 **iD** 3126

🏕 Fusina***
📧 Via Moranzani 93
☎ +39 041-5470055
📠 +39 041-5470050
🔓 1/1 - 31/12
@ info@campingfusina.com

5,5ha 275T 6A CEE

1. ABCDGIJKLMNOPST
2. CFGKLRXY
3. ABJK**VW**
4. (Q+R+T+U+V+X 1/4-30/10)
   (Y 1/4-31/10) (Z 1/4-30/10)
5. **AB**DEFGIJKLMNOPUW
6. CG**J**M(N 5km)ORTV

💬 A peacefully located campsite on the lagoon with a landing stage close by. Plenty of deciduous trees on the site. Views of Venice. Perfect for visiting the town.

🚗 Signposted on the SS309 Ravenna-Venice, direction Malcontenta/Fusina. The campsite is at the end of the road next to the Fusina-Venice landing stage.

SS14 — Venezia — Mira — CC — SS309

CC € 19 1/1-23/3 4/4-13/5 4/6-30/6 7/9-31/12

🏕 N 45°25'10'' E 12°15'22''

Lido di Jesolo, I-30016 / Veneto

♿ 🛜 **iD** 3127

🏕 Camping Park dei Dogi
📧 Viale Oriente 13
☎ +39 0421-1885626
📠 +39 0421-1885619
🔓 1/3 - 31/10, 22/12 - 6/1
@ info@campingparkdeidogi.com

2,8ha 250T(60-80m²) 6A CEE

1. ABCDGHIJKLMOPQ
2. AEGRTVX
3. BJY
5. **AB**EFGJKN**PRT**UWXZ
6. DE**K**(N 0,3km)TU

💬 A basic campsite with an excellent toilet block. Washing machines available. The pathways are separated by trees and conifers, giving both shade and sun. Very suitable for motorhomes and caravans. At walking distance from the sea.

🚗 Campsite on the Viale Oriente. Well signposted, use of coordinates recommended.

San Donà di Piave — CC

CC € 13 1/1-5/1 1/3-15/6 1/9-30/10 22/12-31/12

🏕 N 45°31'18'' E 12°41'17''

Lido di Jesolo, I-30016 / Veneto

♿ 🛜 **iD** 3128

🏕 Parco Capraro***
📧 Via Corer 2° ramo, 4
☎ +39 0421-961073
📠 +39 0421-362994
🔓 30/3 - 23/9
@ info@parcocapraro.it

5,7ha 400T(60-90m²) 6-8A CEE

1. ABCDGHIJKLMO**PS**
2. AEGRUVXY
3. BF**G**NRVWY
4. (B+G 21/4-23/9) (Q 🔓)
   (S+U+V+Y 21/4-16/9)
   (Z 21/4-23/9)
5. **AB**GIJK**L**MNO**P**RUVWXYZ
6. ACDEG**K**(N 1km)ORTV

💬 Staying on this shaded campsite with its large swimming pool is the guarantee of a good holiday. During the day you can walk along a wide woodland path and be on the beach in 5 minutes, while in the evenings you can have a delicious Italian meal in the large restaurant. Special site for plenty of motorhomes. A combined bus and boat ticket to Venice can be purchased at reception.

🚗 In Jesolo turn off the Viale Oriente. Follow brown camping signs. Campsite clearly indicated.

San Donà di Piave — Jesolo — CC

CC € 15 30/3-21/6 21/8-22/9

🏕 N 45°31'37'' E 12°41'49''

Malcontenta/Venezia, I-30176 / Veneto

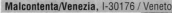

▲ Serenissima***
📧 Via Padana 334a
☎ +39 041-921850
📠 +39 041-920286
🔑 26/3 - 5/11
@ info@campingserenissima.it

2ha 120T 10A CEE

1 ABCGIJKLMOPT
2 CFRY
3 AKR**W**
4 (B 1/6-15/9) (Q+S 🔑)
   (U+V+X 10/6-30/9) (Z 🔑)
5 **AB**GIJKLMNOPUVW
6 CEGI**K**(N 2km)ORV

💬 A shaded and very peaceful family campsite with well maintained toilet facilities. Bus (3 Euros) to Venice centre 100m from the entrance. Lovely level cycle path along the Brenta River. The centre of Malcontenta with its Renaissance villas is very pleasant. A peaceful retreat after a busy day in Venice.

🚗 A4 exit Oriago/Mira. Follow signs at the first roundabout to Ravenna and Venezia and at the second roundabout to Padova / Riviera del Brenta (SR11).

CC € **19** 26/3-28/3 3/4-17/5 23/5-30/6 27/8-4/11   N 45°27'14'' E 12°11'0''

3129

Mestre/Venezia, I-30170 / Veneto

▲ Venezia**
📧 Via Orlanda 8/C
☎ +39 041-5312828
📠 +39 041-5327618
🔑 8/2 - 31/12
@ info@veneziavillage.it

2ha 200T(50-80m²) 6A CEE

1 ABCDGIJKLMOPQ
2 FGLRSVXY
3 AB
4 (F 🔑) **KNP**
   (Q+R+U+V+X+Y+Z 🔑)
5 **AB**DEFGIJKLMNOPUWXZ
6 CEG**K**(N 3km)O

💬 A quiet family campsite with a heated indoor pool, sauna and jacuzzis, charges apply. New modern toilet facilities. Good cuisine with local specialities. 8 minutes by city bus to Piazzale Roma. Then 20 minutes by boat on the Grand Canal to San Marco.

🚗 Stay on the A4 at first towards Venezia. Keep right after bus stop and car park towards Trieste (SS14). Drive over the viaduct, follow Trieste-Aeroporto road. The campsite is on the right after a few hundred metres.

CC € **19** 8/2-29/3 4/4-16/5 22/5-6/7 27/8-28/12   N 45°28'51'' E 12°16'31''

3130

Rosolina Mare/Rovigo, I-45010 / Veneto

▲ Rosapineta Camping Village***
📧 Strada Nord 24
☎ +39 0426-68033
📠 +39 0426-68105
🔑 14/5 - 16/9
@ info@rosapineta.it

46ha 1151T(60-70m²) 10A CEE

1 ABCD**G**IJKLMP
2 ABEGIKRSTWXY
3 ABHJKM**O**QRT**VW**Y
4 (B+G 🔑) J**KP**
   (Q+S+T+U+V+W+X+Y+Z 🔑)
5 **AB**GIJKLMNOPUVXYZ
6 EGK(N 1km)ORT

💬 46 hectares to enjoy the flora in peaceful surroundings near the beach. Good cuisine and a romantic terrace. Visit Venice with own transport. Relax at the site. Two swimming pools, one with a whirlpool. Shopping facilities near the village centre. 7=6 or 14=11 from 2/6 - 30/6 and 1/9 - 15/9.

🚗 A4 Milano-Venezia, exit Padova Interporto. SS Romea direction Chioggia/Ravenna. Turn right 14 km beyond Chioggia and 200m past bridge over the Adige and follow signs to Rosolina Mare.

CC € **17** 14/5-30/6 1/9-15/9   N 45°8'20'' E 12°19'25''

3131

Sappada, I-32047 / Veneto

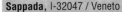

🏂 📶 **iD** (3132)

🏕 Alpin Park Sappada
🏤 Borgata Cima, Località Eirl
☎ +39 340-6353354
🗓 1/1 - 11/3, 26/5 - 30/9
@ info@alpinpark.it

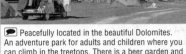

2ha 44**T**(> 80m²) 4A

1 ACDGIJKLMPQ
2 BCGJKLRTVX
3 AB**EFHJMN**OP**Q**
4 (A+Q+Z ⌾)
5 FXYZ
6 CHJ(N 0,7km)Q

💬 Peacefully located in the beautiful Dolomites. An adventure park for adults and children where you can climb in the treetops. There is a beer garden and a good restaurant. Free wifi at reception.

🚍 From Brenner direction Brixen-Bruneck-Dobbiaco (Toblach)-Sexten-San Stefano di Cadore-Sappada.

Santo Stefano di Cadore **CC**

CC € **19** 8/1-31/1 1/3-10/3 27/5-7/7 3/9-29/9 📷 N 46°34'16'' E 12°43'6''

Sottomarina, I-30015 / Veneto

🪂 📶 **iD** (3133)

🏕 Atlanta***
🏤 Viale Barbarigo 73
☎ +39 041-491311
📠 +39 041-4967198
🗓 20/4 - 23/9
@ info@campeggioatlanta.com

4ha 220**T**(50-70m²) 6A CEE

1 ABCEHIJLMOPQ
2 AELRSVWXY
3 AGRY
4 (B+G 29/5-11/9)
    (Q+R+S+T+U+V+X+Y+Z ⌾)
5 **A**GIJKLMNOPUVXYZ
6 CEG**K**(N 0,5km)OV

💬 Spacious campsite with level grass pitches. Direct access to beach. Swimming pools, bar, restaurant and mini market. Modern toilet block. Medium sized trees, satellite reception, water faucet at the pitch. The level beach is very suitable for children.

🚍 Clearly signposted on the SS309 Ravenna-Venice. In Sottomarina turn right before the beach, follow country road. Campsite is signposted.

Chioggia
CC
SS309

CC € **17** 20/4-30/6 26/8-22/9 14=12, 21=18 📷 N 45°11'34'' E 12°18'7''

Sottomarina, I-30015 / Veneto

📶 **iD** (3134)

🏕 Camping Village Adriatico***
🏤 Lungomare Adriatico 82
☎ +39 041-492907
📠 +39 041-5548567
🗓 28/3 - 30/9
@ info@campingadriatico.com

1,7ha 121**T**(45-80m²) 5A CEE

1 ABCDFHIJKLOPRS
2 AEGLRSVY
3 BGKRVY
4 (B+G 14/5-30/9)
    (Q+R+S+T+U+X+Z ⌾)
5 **A**FGIJKLMNOPUVXYZ
6 CEG**K**(N 0km)ORV

💬 Small, friendly campsite by the boulevard near the beach. Close to the town centre. Ferry to Venice is within walking distance. A family-run business for more than 50 years. New: motorhome service area next to the site with toilet facilities, shower and all amenities. Noise barriers around the campsite.

🚍 Clearly signposted on the SS309. In Sottomarina follow the boulevard. Campsite is located on the landside, near the middle of the boulevard.

Chioggia
CC
SS309

CC € **17** 3/4-23/4 2/5-30/5 5/6-21/6 26/8-29/9 14=12 📷 N 45°12'17'' E 12°17'55''

Sottomarina, I-30015 / Veneto

3135

⊠ Internazionale***
📧 Via A. Barbarigo 117
☎ +39 041-491444
📠 +39 041-5543373
🗓 22/4 - 17/9
@ info@campinginternazionale.net

7ha 300T(60-90m²) 6A CEE

1 ABCEHIJKLMNOS
2 AERSVWX
3 AGKY
4 (B+G 1/6-31/8)
(Q+S+T+U+V+X+Y+Z 🔌)
5 AGIJKLMNOPUVXYZ
6 EGIK(N 1km)OV

💬 This campsite is located right by the beach and has modern toilet blocks. There is a supermarket, bar, pizzeria and bazaar. Wifi right down to and on the beach. In the middle of the site there is a lovely swimming pool next to an enchanting castle that certainly adds to the atmosphere.

🚗 Clearly signposted from the SS309 Ravenna-Venice. In Sottomarina-Lido turn right before the beach on the the country road. The campsite is located left on the seaward side.

Chioggia

CC
SS309

CC €⑰ 22/4-30/6 26/8-16/9 7=6, 14=12, 21=18   N 45°11'19'' E 12°18'16''

Sottomarina, I-30015 / Veneto

3136

⊠ Miramare***
📧 Via A. Barbarigo 103
☎📠 +39 041-490610
🗓 19/4 - 24/9
@ info@miramarecamping.com

5,5ha 350T(60-100m²) 6A CEE

1 ABCGHIJKLMOPQ
2 AERSVWXY
3 BGKNRY
4 (B+G 13/5-24/9)
(Q+S+T+U+V+X+Y+Z 🔌)
5 AFGIJKLMNOPUVXYZ
6 CEGK(N 1km)ORV

💬 This campsite run by the Boscolo family is located right by the sea and offers modern toilet buildings, a bar, restaurant, minimarket and swimming pool. There is a wide beach with many facilities. The modern comforts will bring even more pleasure to your holiday.

🚗 Clearly signposted on the SS309 Ravenna-Venice. In Sottomarina turn right before the beach, follow country road.

Chioggia   ○ Sottomarina

CC
SS309

CC €⑰ 19/4-30/6 22/8-23/9 7=6, 14=12, 21=18   N 45°11'25'' E 12°18'12''

Sottomarina, I-30015 / Veneto

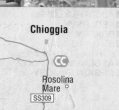

3137

⊠ Oasi***
📧 Via A. Barbarigo 147
☎ +39 041-5541145
📠 +39 041-490801
🗓 30/3 - 1/10
@ info@campingoasi.com

2,5ha 150T(56-100m²) 6A CEE

1 ACGHIJKLMNOPST
2 ACELRSVXY
3 AGKMNOPRUWY
4 (B+G 15/5-15/9) KP
(Q+R+S+T+U 🔌)
(V 27/5-10/9) (W 30/5-30/9)
(X+Y 1/5-30/9) (Z 🔌)
5 ABFGIJKLMNOPTUVXYZ
6 CEGK(N 2km)QRV

💬 Small, neat and very quiet family campsite on the sea with well-maintained toilet facilities and an own marina on the mouth of the Brenta. Very neat fish restaurant.

🚗 Clearly signposted on the SS309 Ravenna-Venice. In Sottomarina follow the signs. Turn right before the beach, then follow the country road as far as the end.

Chioggia

CC

Rosolina
Mare ○
SS309

CC €⑰ 30/3-6/7 27/8-30/9 7=6, 14=12, 21=17   N 45°10'54'' E 12°18'28''

Tarzo, I-31020 / Veneto

&♿ 🛜 **iD** (3138)

🏕 Camping al Lago di Lago
📧 Località Fratta 89
☎ +39 0438-586891
🔑 24/3 - 13/10
@ info@campingallagodilago.it

2,2ha 83T(60-120m²) 6-8A CEE

1 ABGIJKLMO**P**RS
2 DFKLMRY
3 ABJ**Q**RWZ
4 (B+G 1/6-15/9)
   (Q+V+X+Z 🅿)
5 **AB**GJLNPQRUWXYZ
6 AEGJ(N 1,4km)OQT

💬 In the foothills of the Alps you will find this campsite in a national park on a beautiful small lake. The surroundings are perfect for active and cultural outings, such as a visit to Venice, Vicenza or other historic locations.

🚐 From A27 9 km Bellum-Treviso exit Vittorio Venero Nord. From SSS1 to SP35 dir. Tarzo, via SP153 or SP635 follow road. Follow campsite signs.

SS51
Vittorio Veneto
CC
A27
Conegliano

CC € **17** 24/3-6/7 25/8-12/10

🗺🏕 N 45°58'57'' E 12°13'40''

Alesso/Trasaghis, I-33010 / Friuli-Venezia Giulia

&♿ 🛜 **iD** (3139)

🏕 Lago 3 Comuni**
📧 Via Tolmezzo 52
☎ 🅵🅰🆇 +39 0432-979464
🔑 1/4 - 30/9
@ camping@lago3comuni.com

1,2ha 54T(64-84m²) 6A CEE

1 ABCD**G**IJKLMOPQ
2 CDFKLMNRVWXY
3 AHJKWZ
4 (Q+T+X+Z 🅿)
5 **A**DGHIKMNOPUZ
6 AEGHJ(N 1,5km)OT

💬 Set in a lovely countryside by a lake, located about 8 km from the autostrada. Also suitable as stopover campsite. Groceries on sale 1500m from the site. Of the two adjacent campsites this site, coming from the north is the second site on the left. Entrance is round the bend in the road.

🚐 From Villach on the A23 direction Udine. Exit at Gemona-Osoppo. Take the SS13 towards Trasaghis and continue on the SR512 until Alesso. Campsite signposted.

Tolmezzo
A23
CC
SS13
Gemona del Friuli

CC € **17** 1/4-18/5 3/6-7/7 2/9-29/9

🗺🏕 N 46°19'31'' E 13°3'53''

Aquileia, I-33051 / Friuli-Venezia Giulia

&♿ 🛜 **iD** (3140)

🏕 Aquileia**
📧 Via Gemina 10
☎ +39 0431-91042
🅵🅰🆇 +39 0431-30804
🔑 1/4 - 30/9
@ info@campingaquileia.it

3,2ha 115T(70-140m²) 6A CEE

1 ACD**G**IJKLMOPQ
2 CGLRVWXY
3 AJKR
4 (C+G+Q+S+U+Y+Z 🅿)
5 **A**GIJKLMNOPUV
6 ACDEGK(N 0,2km)OQTV

💬 A peaceful campsite with a swimming pool, located 10 km from Grado and about 7 km from the sea. Plenty of grass and lovely shaded pitches. There is a supermarket opposite the campsite. There is a large culture park right next to the site with Roman excavations.

🚐 Coming from the north in Aquileia turn left at the first traffic lights. After about 450 metres you will see the campsite entrance.

A4
San Giorgio di Nogaro
SS305
Monfalcone
CC
SS352

CC € **19** 1/4-30/6 21/8-29/9

🗺🏕 N 45°46'34'' E 13°22'15''

Belvedere/Grado, I-33051 / Friuli-Venezia Giulia

♿ 🛜 **iD** (3141)

🔺 Belvedere Pineta Camping Village****
📧 Via Martin Luther King
☎ +39 0431-91007
📠 +39 0431-918641
🔓 28/4 - 16/9
@ info@belvederepineta.it

50ha 2686T(100-120m²) 6-10A CEE

1️⃣ ACDG**I**JKLMOPQ
2️⃣ ABE**I**KLRSTVWXY
3️⃣ AB**F**GK**M**N**Q**RWY
4️⃣ (B+G+Q+S+T+U+V+X+Y+Z 🔒)
5️⃣ **AB**EGJKLMNPU
6️⃣ DE**J**(N 5km)TV

💬 Large, quiet campsite located at a bay, 5 km from Grado. Many possibilities for sport. Large pitches in the site. Lovely swimming pool. Pitches with and without shade. Lovely bicycle routes in the surroundings.

🚗 On the A23 exit Palmanova, then take the direction Grado. Go past Aquilea. Just before the dyke to Grado turn left. Follow the signs.

Cervignano del Friuli · **Monfalcone**
CC
Grado

CC € **17** 28/4-6/7 27/8-15/9   📷 N 45°43'35'' E 13°23'59''

Grado, I-34073 / Friuli-Venezia Giulia

⊗ ♿ 🛜 (3142)

🔺 Tenuta Primero****
📧 Via Monfalcone 14
☎ +39 0431-896900
📠 +39 0431-896901
🔓 21/4 - 22/9
@ info@tenuta-primero.com

22ha 672T(60-110m²) 6-10A CEE

1️⃣ BCDE**I**JKLMOPQ
2️⃣ AEGLRSTVXY
3️⃣ AB**E**GHJKLMNRUWY
4️⃣ (B+G 1/5-16/9) KM(Q+S 🔒) (T+U+V 15/5-16/9) (X 🔒) (Y 15/5-16/9) (Z 🔒)
5️⃣ **AB**FGIJKLMNOPRUVWXYZ
6️⃣ ACDEGHIJ(N 5km)OQRTV

💬 This well-maintained campsite is located 8 km from Grado village. Pine trees provide shade and you can enjoy the sun on the beach. A very good swimming pool and all the facilities available ensure carefree holiday pleasure. There is a golf course next to the campsite which can be used (for a payment) by campers.

🚗 Exit the A23 towards Palmanove, and then drive in the direction of Monfalcone. Follow the camping signs in Grado. The campsite is the fourth on the right.

Terzo D'Aquileia
SS352
CC
Grado

CC € **17** 21/4-18/5 4/6-30/6 3/9-11/9 16/9-21/9   📷 N 45°42'19'' E 13°27'51''

Sistiana, I-34019 / Friuli-Venezia Giulia

♿ 🛜 **iD** (3143)

🔺 Mare Pineta Baia Sistiana****
📧 Via Sistiana 60/D
☎ +39 040-299264
📠 +39 040-299265
🔓 29/3 - 5/11
@ info@marepineta.com

107ha 500T(80-100m²) 6A CEE

1️⃣ ABCD**F**IJKLMN**P**Q
2️⃣ BEFGJKLMNQRTVWXY
3️⃣ ABH**J**MNRUVW
4️⃣ (B+G 1/6-10/9) (Q+S+T+U 🔒) (V 1/6-15/9) (X 1/4-30/9) (Y 15/4-15/9) (Z 🔒)
5️⃣ **AB**EFGIJKLMNOP**S**UVXZ
6️⃣ CEG**K**(N 1km)ORTV

💬 Lovely well-kept site located right by the A4 motorway. Views of the sea and 1500m from the beach. Marked out pitches. The site is also suitable as a stopover site, for example on the way to Croatia. In June, July and August a small train rides between the campsite and the beach lower down from 10:00 to 18:00 (free for campsite guests).

🚗 Take A4 direction Trieste, exit Duino. Direction Trieste via the coast road. Campsite located on the right beyond Duino.

A4 · SS55 · Komen
Monfalcone
CC
SS14

CC € **19** 29/3-18/5 28/5-29/6 3/9-4/11   📷 N 45°46'19'' E 13°37'27''

Casal Borsetti, I-48010 / Emilia Romagna
♿ 🛜 ✿ **iD** (3144)

🏔 Adria***
✉ Spallazzi 30
☎ +39 0544-445217
📠 +39 0544-442014
⌚ 21/4 - 16/9
@ info@villaggiocampingadria.it

3,4ha 528T(60-120m²) 10A CEE

1 ABC**F**HIJKLMPQ
2 AEGLRSVWXY
3 BGHJK**M**NRUWY
4 (B+G 15/5-14/9)
(Q+R+T+U+V+X+Y+Z ⌂)
5 **AB**EFGIJKLMNOPRUVWXY
Z
6 CDG**IJK**(N 0,2km)ORSTV

💬 A good campsite close to the sea. A regular and a new swimming pool up to 1m in depth and a large bubble bath. Lovely trips out from here to Venice, Rimini, etc.

🚗 Take A14 to Ravenna. Then via the SS309 direction Venice. You will shortly see signs to 'Casal Borsetti' and campsite 'Adria'.

Lido di Spina

CC

SS309

CC € **17** 21/4-29/6 25/8-15/9 7=6, 14=12 🏔 N 44°33'32'' E 12°16'47''

Lido degli Scacchi, I-44020 / Emilia Romagna
♿ 🛜 **iD** (3145)

🏔 Florenz****
✉ Viale Alpi Centrali 199
☎ +39 0533-380193
📠 +39 0533-381456
⌚ 24/3 - 4/11
@ info@holidayvillageflorenz.com

8ha 300T(50-70m²) 6A CEE

1 ABC**F**HIJLPST
2 AEGRSVX
3 ABGHJK**M**NRUWY
4 (**B**+**G** 20/5-10/9) **LP**
(Q+S+T+U+V+X+Y+Z ⌂)
5 **AB**EFGIJKMOPUVXYZ
6 EGHKM(N 0,5km)OQRTUV

💬 Campsite with a private sandy beach located on the Adriatic sea. You can reserve parasols and sun loungers at reception. There is also a separate beach for dogs. All kinds of activities organised at the campsite.

🚗 Take the A14 as far as Bologna, then take the A13 in the direction of Padova as far as Ferrara Sud. Continue 49 km to Lidi di Comacchio. Clearly signposted.

Lido delle Nazioni

CC

Comacchio

SS309

CC € **19** 24/3-3/6 25/8-31/10 14=12 🏔 N 44°42'4'' E 12°14'18''

Lido di Dante, I-48100 / Emilia Romagna
🈲 ♿ 🛜 **iD** (3146)

🏔 Classe***
✉ Via Catone 1
☎ +39 0544-492005
📠 +39 0544-492058
⌚ 29/3 - 7/10
@ info@campingclasse.it

70ha 400T(60-80m²) 4-10A CEE

1 ABC**F**HIJKLMPQ
2 AEGLRSVXY
3 BGHKNRUVWY
4 (B+G 21/5-8/10)
(Q+S+T+U+V+X+Y+Z ⌂)
5 **A**EFGIJKLMNOPSUVXYZ
6 CEG**K**(N 0,5km)ORTV

💬 Partly naturist campsite. A peaceful site by the sea with its own swimming pool and reasonably sized pitches. Perfect for sea and sun worshippers.

🚗 Follow signs to Lido Sud from the Ravenna area, then to Lido di Dante. Then follow Porto Fuori. Follow signs if in the village, it's closer.

SS309

Punta Marina Terme

Ravenna

CC

SS3BIS

CC € **19** 29/3-9/7 1/9-6/10 🏔 N 44°23'5'' E 12°18'57''

Lido di Dante, I-48122 / Emilia Romagna

♿ 📶 **iD** **3147**

🔺 Ramazzotti***
🏠 Via Paolo e Francesca
☎ +39 0544-492250
📠 +39 0544-492009
🔓 21/4 - 9/9
@ info@campingramazzotti.it

2,8ha 300T(60-80m²) 3-10A CEE

1 ABC**G**HIJKLMPQ
2 AEGRSV
3 BGJ**M**NRWY
4 (Q+T+U+V+W+X+Y+Z 🔓)
5 **AB**EFGIJK**L**MNOPUV
6 CEGIJ(N 0,5km)OQRTV

💬 Located by the sea in a small village. A basic campsite with adequate amenities. An excellent base for visiting Ravenna and the famous church at Lido di Dante.

🚐 From surroundings of Ravenna follow the Lido Sud signs, then follow signs to Lido di Dante.

SS309 — Punta Marina Terme — **Ravenna** — CC — SS67 SS16

CC € **17** 21/4-14/7 1/9-8/9 7=6

🔼 N 44°23'6'' E 12°19'8''

Lido di Spina, I-44024 / Emilia Romagna

♿ 📶 **iD** **3148**

🔺 Spina Camping Village****
🏠 Via del Campeggio 99
☎ +39 0533-330179
📠 +39 0533-333566
🔓 20/4 - 16/9
@ spinacampingvillage@
   clubdelsole.com

24ha 1450T(50-80m²) 6A CEE

1 ABC**G**HIJKLMPST
2 ABELNRSVY
3 BDGHJK**M**NRUWY
4 (B+G 15/5-10/9) **N**
   (Q+S+T 🔓) (U 1/6-31/8)
   (V+X+Y+Z 🔓)
5 **AB**EFGIJKLMOP**S**UVZ
6 CEGH**J**M(N 2km)ORTUV

NEW

💬 A campsite with plenty of space, a beautiful private beach, and lots of lovely, new amenities.

🚐 A14 to Bologna, then A13 direction Padova. Exit at Ferrara Sud. 49 km further to Lidi di Comacchio. Clearly signposted from here.

A13 — **Comacchio** — CC — SS309

CC € **15** 20/4-30/6 25/8-15/9

🔼 N 44°37'40'' E 12°15'19''

Marina di Ravenna, I-48122 / Emilia Romagna

♿ 📶 **iD** **3149**

🔺 Piomboni Camping Village***
🏠 Viale della Pace 421
☎ +39 0544-530230
📠 +39 0544-538618
🔓 20/4 - 10/9
@ info@campingpiomboni.it

5ha 400T(60-90m²) 10A CEE

1 ABC**G**HIJKLMPST
2 ABEGRSVY
3 BGHJKNRUWY
4 (G 1/6-31/8)
   (Q+S+T+U+V+X+Y+Z 🔓)
5 **AB**FGHIJKLMNOPUV
6 CEGJ(N 2km)OQRTV

💬 A very friendly and well-maintained family campsite 100 metres from the beach, part of which is freely accessible. Here you are really a guest. Located in a 50,000 m² park with majestic, centuries-old pine trees. New in 2018: swimming pool.

🚐 A14 from Bologna to Ravenna. Follow signs to Marina di Ravena (campsite signposted) as far as the SS309 Romea. Then right and follow camping signs.

Sant' Alberto — SS309 — CC — Punta Marina — SS16 — **Ravenna**

CC € **19** 20/4-23/6 26/8-9/9

🔼 N 44°27'59'' E 12°17'7''

Misano Adriatico/Cattolica, I-47843 / Emilia Romagna

🛜 iD **3150**

🏕 Camping Village Misano***
✉ Via Litoranea Sud 60
☎ +39 0541-614330
📠 +39 0541-613502
⌚ 1/4 - 1/10
@ info@campingmisano.com

7ha 600**T**(43-80m²) 6A CEE

1 ABCD**F**IJKLMNPRS
2 AEFGVXY
3 BJK**M**RU**W**Y
4 (C 3/6-24/9) KP
(Q+R+S+T+U+V+X+Z 🔓)
5 **AB**GIJKLMNOPQR**S**TUV
6 ACEGIKM(N 0,5km)ORTV

💬 The campsite is located on the Adriatic coast with its own sandy beach. Ideal for a relaxing holiday. The campsite is equipped with all comforts. Modern toilet facilities, also private. The surroundings are perfect for cultural day trips or lovely bicycle and walking tours along the coast or boulevard. CampingCard ACSI not valid during WDW and Motor G.P.

🚗 A14, exit Cattolica, stay on SS16, follow campsite signs. Direction of Cattolica.

Rimini

Riccione

SS16

A14

CC € **19** 1/5-18/6 14/9-30/9

📍 N 43°58'29'' E 12°42'39''

Novafeltria, I-47863 / Emilia Romagna

🐕 🛜 iD **3151**

🏕 Camping Perticara***
✉ Via Serra Masini 10/d
☎ +39 335-7062260
⌚ 1/5 - 23/9
@ info@campingperticara.com

8ha 77**T**(100-120m²) 10A CEE

1 AE**I**JKLPQ
2 GJKLRVWX
3 BHIJNRU
4 (C+Q+R+T+U+X+Z 🔓)
5 **A**FGIJKLMNOPRUWXYZ
6 ADEGH**K**L(N 1km)TV

💬 A very well-equipped campsite. You will be warmly welcomed by the owners. Excellent service. The panoramic views of the picture postcard hills are a bonus (also from the lovely swimming pool). Very well-maintained toilet facilities. No mosquitoes. An excellent base for excursions.

🚗 Exit Rimini Nord, direction San Leo-Montefeltro. Right onto SP258 towards Novafeltria, turn off Satnav. Turn right to Perticara in Novafeltria 400m past traffic lights. Follow camping signs.

Cesena

Rimini

SS3BIS

San Marino

SS310

CC Novafeltria

SS71

SP258

SS73BIS

CC € **19** 1/5-29/6 1/9-22/9

📍 N 43°53'43'' E 12°14'32''

Pinarella di Cervia, I-48015 / Emilia Romagna

♿ 🛜 ✿ iD **3152**

🏕 Adriatico***
✉ Via Pinarella 90
☎ +39 0544-71537
📠 +39 0544-974411
⌚ 19/4 - 16/9
@ info@campingadriatico.net

3,4ha 280**T**(60m²) 6A CEE

1 ABC**G**HIJKLMPQ
2 AEGRTVY
3 BF**H**IJKRU**W**
4 (B+**G** 15/5-15/9)
(Q+R+T+U+V+X+Z 🔓)
5 **AB**FGIJKLMNOPUVWZ
6 CDEG**J**(N 0,8km)ORTUV

💬 A friendly, well-kept family campsite with attractive amenities. This campsite is well worth a visit in the early season.

🚗 Follow the SS16 between Rimini and Ravenna. Exit at Cervia and follow signs.

Cervia

CC

SS71

A14

Bellaria-Igea Marina

CC € **17** 1/5-29/6 23/8-15/9

📍 N 44°14'51'' E 12°21'32''

Ponte Messa di Pennabilli (RN), I-47864 / Emilia Romagna

⬆ Marecchia 'Da Quinto'*****
📧 Via Mulino Schieti 22
☎ +39 338-7226690
📠 +39 0541-928936
🔑 1/5 - 9/9
@ info@campingmarecchia.it

0,8ha 30T(20-80m²) 6A CEE

1 BCDGIJKLNOP
2 CGLRVWXY
3 AHN
4 (B+G 1/6-9/9) **K**
   (T+U+X 1/6-9/9) (Z 1/6-10/9)
5 ACGIJKMNO**P**UWZ
6 EGHKL(N 0,8km)UV

🛝 🛜 ⚙ (3153)

💬 A unique campsite decorated with art and culture in Emilia Romagna on the River Marecchia and close to the town of Pennabilli. A large natural site paying attention to the environment. Lovely swimming pool and excellent restaurant. Nature walks and cultural centres close by.

🚗 A14, exit Rimini Nord, direction Sanleo-Montefeltro (SP258). Novafeltria-Pennabilli at roundabout direction Ponte Messa (follow camping signs). The campsite is on the right before the village.

San Leo
Novafeltria
Carpegna

CC € **19** 1/5-29/6 1/9-8/9   📷 N 43°49'32'' E 12°15'1''

Repubblica San Marino, I-47893 / San Marino

⬆ Centro Vacanze San Marino****
📧 Strada S. Michele 50
☎ +39 0549-903964
📠 +39 0549-907120
🔑 1/1 - 31/12
@ info@
   centrovacanzesanmarino.com
10ha 200T(50-80m²) 5-10A CEE

1 ABCD**F**IJKLMOPRS
2 GJLRUVXY
3 ABDGMNRU
4 (B 1/6-31/8) K(Q 🔑)
   (R 15/4-30/9)
   (T+U+V+Y+Z 1/1-15/1,
   1/3-31/12)
5 **AB**DEFGHIJKLMNOPW
6 CEGIKL(N 3km)OTUV

🛝 🛜 **iD** (3154)

💬 Large, well-equipped terraced campsite at an altitude of 250m in San Marino. Swimming pool and good sports fields. Spacious marked out pitches. Bus service to Rimini beach. Well placed for cultural trips out. CampingCard ACSI not valid for groups.

🚗 Exit Rimini Sud, direction San Marino, follow the SS72. On entering the Republic follow the main road and you will see the camping sign high up on the right 3 km further on. Turn right at the Brico ID Shop. Look out for signs.

A14
SS72
Verucchio
San Marino

CC € **17** 2/1-29/3 3/4-8/7 26/8-4/10 23/10-27/12 7=6, 14=11   📷 N 43°57'33'' E 12°27'41''

Riccione, I-47838 / Emilia Romagna

⬆ Adria***
📧 Via Torino 40
☎ +39 0541-601003
📠 +39 0541-602256
🔑 29/3 - 30/9
@ info@campingadria.com

10ha 516T(60-70m²) 6A CEE

1 BCD**G**IJKLMOPST
2 AEFGRVY
3 ABD**F**RUWY
4 (Q+S+T+U+V+X+Y+Z 🔑)
5 **AB**EFGIJKLMNOPUVYZ
6 ACDEGHKM(N 1km)ORTUV

🛝 🛜 (3155)

💬 A family campsite right next to the sea. Within walking distance of the resort of Riccione. Lovely excursions possible in the area. Wifi is free for CampingCard ACSI holders.

🚗 Take A14 as far as Riccione. Then the SS16 for about 500 metres then follow the large signs.

Rimini
Riccione
A14

CC € **19** 29/3-14/7 1/9-29/9   📷 N 43°59'28'' E 12°40'43''

Riccione, I-47838 / Emilia Romagna ⚒ 📶 iD (3156)

🏠 Riccione****
✉ Via Marsala 10
☎ +39 0541-690160
📠 +39 0541-690044
🗓 20/4 - 23/9
@ info@campingriccione.it

6,5ha 450T(65-100m²) 5-10A CEE

1 ABCFIJKLMPQ
2 AEFGLRSTVY
3 BFGKMNQRUVY
4 (B+G 🗓) JP
　(Q+S+T+U+V+W+X+Y+Z 🗓)
5 **AB**EFGIJKLMNOPUVWX
6 ACFGKM(N 1km)ORTV

💬 A friendly campsite with lovely swimming pools. The toilet facilities are very well maintained. Shuttle train to the centre. The surroundings invite you to go out for enjoyable trips. CampingCard ACSI users must pay their bill in cash.

🚗 On the motorway take exit Riccione. Follow the signs.

Rimini
Riccione
CC
A14

CC € **19** 20/4-10/6 1/9-22/9 7=6　　📐 N 43°59'7'' E 12°40'45''

Riccione, I-47838 / Emilia Romagna ⚒ 📶 iD (3157)

🏠 Romagna Camping Village***
✉ Via Torino 56
☎ +39 0541-615449
🗓 20/4 - 16/9
@ romagnacampingvillage@
　clubdelsole.com

NEW

5,8ha 500T(60-90m²) 6A CEE

1 ABCGIJKLMNOPST
2 AEFGRVY
3 ABDFJWY
4 (Q+S+U+V+X+Y+Z 🗓)
5 **AB**EFGIJKLMNOPUVXYZ
6 BCDEGKM(N 1,5km)TU

💬 Well-situated, clean family campsite right on the coast. Plenty of opportunities for days out in the area. Lots to see.

🚗 Take the A14 as far as exit Riccione, then the SS16, signposted from there.

Rimini
SS16　Riccione
SS72　CC
A14

CC € **17** 20/4-30/6 25/8-15/9　　📐 N 43°59'21'' E 12°40'54''

Rioveggio, I-40040 / Emilia Romagna ⚒ 📶 iD (3158)

🏠 Riva del Setta****
✉ Ginepri 65
☎ 📠 +39 051-6777749
🗓 1/4 - 30/9
@ info@rivadelsetta.com

3,5ha 86T(70-80m²) 3A CEE

1 ACGHIJKLMOPRS
2 CFRVXY
3 AMRW
4 (B 15/6-31/8)
　(Q+R+T+V+Y+Z 🗓)
5 AGIJKLMNOPUV
6 CFGJ(N 0,5km)

💬 The campsite is situated in the Setta valley between Bologna and Florence. Close to the autostrada. It has a pizzeria and swimming pool. Good base for cultural visits to Bologna and Florence. Reception closed for lunch 12:30 - 15:00.

🚗 Before Rioveggio, follow 'old A1' (left), so do not follow dir. Badia, and then exit Rioveggio, right and follow campsite signs. (A1 Bologna-Firenze.)

A1
Vergato　CC　Loiano
SS64　San Benedetto Val
　di Sambro

CC € **17** 1/4-14/7 1/9-29/9　　📐 N 44°17'29'' E 11°13'5''

San Mauro Mare, I-47030 / Emilia Romagna

👫 📶 **iD** **3159**

🔺 Camping Green**
📧 Via Amerigo Vespucci 6
☎ FAX +39 0541-1743047
🔓 6/4 - 30/9
@ info@campinggreen.it

100T(36-80m²) 6A CEE

1 ABC**G**HIJKLMPQ
2 AEGRY
3 B**F**GKRWY
4 (T+U+Z 16/6-9/9)
5 **A**FGIJKMNOPUV
6 AEK(N 0,3km)OT

💬 Not by the sea, but in a village. Everything easily accessible, including the beach. The surroundings are very attractive. Lovely villages and good cycling opportunities. A modest site with plenty of relaxation.

🚗 A14, exit Rimini Nord. Follow SS16 towards Ravenna as far as San Mauro Mare. Enter village and turn left at the 'Green' sign.

SS16
Cesenatico
A14
SS9
Rimini

CC €**17** 6/4-30/6 1/9-29/9   🧭 N 44°9'45'' E 12°26'32''

Arezzo, I-52100 / Toscana

♿ 📶 **iD** **3160**

🔺 Villaggio Le Ginestre***
📧 Loc. Ruscello 100
☎ +39 0575-363566
FAX +39 0575-366949
🔓 1/3 - 5/11
@ info@campingleginestre.it

2,2ha 40T(81m²) 6A CEE

1 ABCGIJKLO**P**Q
2 FGJLRVWXY
3 BJ**M**NRU
4 (B 15/5-15/9)
     (T+U+V+Y+Z 🔓)
5 **AB**DEGJLMNPUVZ
6 ACEGIK(N 0,3km)RTV

💬 A peaceful rural campsite. Very convenient for visiting Arezzo and surroundings. Also suitable as a stopover campsite. Great restaurant with Tuscan cooking.

🚗 A1 Firenze-Roma, exit Arezzo. Direction Battifolle. Then direction Ruscello. Follow the camping signs, 2 km from the motorway.

A1
Arezzo
SS73
Castiglion
Fiorentino

CC €**19** 1/3-29/6 1/9-4/11   🧭 N 43°26'59'' E 11°47'25''

Barberino di Mugello, I-50030 / Toscana

👫 ♿ 📶 ✿ **iD** **3161**

🔺 Il Sergente***
📧 SS 65 Monte di Fo
☎ +39 055-8423018
FAX +39 055-8423907
🔓 1/1 - 31/12
@ info@campingilsergente.it

3ha 25T(40-80m²) 10A CEE

1 ACDGIJLMO**P**Q
2 GIJRTVXY
3 BGMNR
4 (C 15/5-30/9) (Q+R 🔓)
     (T+U+V+Y+Z 1/1-30/12)
5 **AB**DEFGIJKLMNOPUVWZ
6 CEGIK(N 7km)OQRTV

💬 A modern family campsite with a swimming pool and restaurant located in the Mugello area of Tuscany. The campsite is close to the Futa pass. It is a good base for visiting Florence or Siena and other historic Tuscan towns.

🚗 A1 Bologna-Firenze (A1 Direttissing), exit Firenzuola-Mugello. Take road towards Futapas 3 km on the left.

A1
Barberino di   Scarperia
Mugello

CC €**19** 1/1-14/7 1/9-31/12   🧭 N 44°4'39'' E 11°16'53''

Barberino Val D'Elsa, I-50021 / Toscana

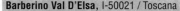

3162

- ▲ Semifonte**
- ✉ Via Ugo Foscolo 4
- ☎ 📠 +39 055-8075454
- ⌚ 16/3 - 4/11
- @ semifonte@semifonte.it

1,6ha 120**T**(45-70m²) 4-6A CEE

1 BCGHIJKLMPQ
2 FGJLRTVXY
3 AR
4 (B 1/6-10/9) (Q+R 16/4-30/9)
5 **AB**GJLNOPU
6 CEGK(N 0,3km)TV

💬 Terraced campsite next to the village, against a slope. A few pitches have a lovely view over the surrounding countryside. Great base for numerous sights.

🚗 From motorway Firenze-Siena, exit Poggibonsi coming from south. Exit Tavernelle from north. Then follow campsite signs.

Poggibonsi · Castellina In Chianti

CC € **17** 16/3-6/7 27/8-3/11   ◪ N 43°32'47'' E 11°10'42''

Bibbona, I-57020 / Toscana

3163

- ▲ Le Capanne***
- ✉ Via Aurelia km 273
- ☎ +39 0586-600064
- 📠 +39 0586-600198
- ⌚ 14/4 - 16/9
- @ info@campinglecapanne.it

9ha 324**T**(60-130m²) 10A CEE

1 ABCD**G**IJKLMOPST
2 BGLRVXY
3 B**F**JKL**M**N**Q**RU
4 (B+G 🔑) IJKP (Q+S+T+U+V+W+Y+Z 🔑)
5 **AB**EFGIJKLMNOPQRUWXYZ
6 CDEGHKM(N 2km)OPRSTUV

💬 The campsite is situated in a park with olive, pine and eucalyptus trees. Excellent toilet facilities. Lovely swimming pool with large sunbathing area, children's pool, water slide and hydro massage. Attractive restaurant with terrace and extensive menu.

🚗 A12, exit towards Rosignano Marittimo, and take the SS1 Livorno-Grosseto in the direction of Grosseto. Then exit towards La California and take the SP39 and drive south. Campsite entrance after ± 3 km.

Cecina
SS1
Castagneto Carducci

CC € **17** 14/4-17/6 1/9-15/9   ◪ N 43°15'13'' E 10°33'10''

Casale Marittimo, I-56040 / Toscana

3164

- ▲ Valle Gaia****
- ✉ Via Cecinese 87
- ☎ +39 0586-681236
- 📠 +39 0586-683551
- ⌚ 24/3 - 6/10
- @ info@vallegaia.it

4,3ha 240**T**(80-120m²) 6A CEE

1 AB**G**HIJKLMOPST
2 FJRTVXY
3 BGHJ**K**M**N**RU
4 (B+G+Q+S+T+U+V+Y+Z 🔑)
5 **A**DEFGIJKLMNOPUV
6 CEG**IK**M(N 3,5km)RTV

💬 Valle Gaia campsite, with its good toilet facilities, various swimming pools, restaurant and pizzeria is located on the edge of the Tuscan hills 9 km from the sea. Ideally positioned for trips out to the Tuscan art cities.

🚗 A12, exit Rosignano Marittimo, SS1 direction Roma, exit Cecina-Centro (NOT Cecina-Nord). At the roundabout direction Casale Marittimo; turn left at the intersection in the direction of Casale Marittimo. Campsite located 3 km down the road.

Rosignano Marittimo
Cecina
SS1

CC € **15** 24/3-7/7 1/9-5/10   ◪ N 43°18'2'' E 10°34'54''

Casciano di Murlo/Siena, I-53016 / Toscana

♿ 📶 **iD** **3165**

△ Le Soline***
✉ Via delle Soline 51
☎ +39 0577-817410
FAX +39 0577-817415
� 1/1 - 31/12
@ camping@lesoline.it

6,5ha 170**T**(24-90m²) 6A CEE

1 ABC**G**I**J**KLOPQ
2 JKRTWXY
3 A**F**JN**OP**R
4 (A 1/7-31/8)
(B+G 31/3-10/10) KP
(Q+R 1/4-30/9)
(U+V+Y 26/3-15/10)
(Z 1/4-30/9)
5 **AB**DFGIJKMNO**PS**UVWZ
6 CEGK(N 1km)ORTV

💬 The campsite is made up of terraces set into the hillside. Both the pitches and the large swimming pool have lovely views of the surrounding countryside.

🚗 SS223 Siena-Grosseto. Exit Fontazzi/Cassiano. Follow campsite signs.

Monteroni D'Arbia ○

Monticiano

CC

SS223

CC € **19** 1/1-30/6 31/8-31/12   🏔 N 43°9'18'' E 11°19'55''

Castagneto Carducci, I-57022 / Toscana

♿ 📶 **iD** **3166**

△ Le Pianacce***
✉ Località Le Pianacce
☎ +39 0565-763667
FAX +39 0565-766085
� 28/4 - 16/9
@ info@campinglepianacce.it

9ha 156**T**(60-80m²) 6-10A CEE

1 ABCD**G**IJKLMPST
2 BJKRUVXY
3 BHJKL**M**NQR
4 (B+G �) M
(Q+S+T+U+V+W+Y+Z �)
5 **AB**EFGIJKLMNOPUWXYZ
6 ACDEGHKM(N 2km)ORTU

💬 A peaceful campsite 6 km from the sea and beach. Laid out in terraces with accessible pitches of different sizes. Unusual swimming pool and lovely playground. Ideal for small children. Restaurant/bar with extensive menu. Good toilet facilities.

🚗 SS1 Aurelia exit Donoratico, direction Castagneto Carducci. Before Castagneto Carducci turn left in the direction of Bolgheri. The campsite is located on the right.

Castagneto Carducci **CC**

SS1

San Vincenzo

CC € **17** 28/4-24/6 1/9-15/9   🏔 N 43°9'57'' E 10°36'49''

Castiglione della Pescaia, I-58043 / Toscana

📶 **iD** **3167**

△ Maremma Sans Souci***
✉ Località Casa Mora
☎ +39 0564-933765
FAX +39 0564-935759
� 29/3 - 3/11
@ info@maremmasanssouci.it

30ha 372**T**(30-100m²) 3-6A CEE

1 ABCD**F**HIJKLNOPST
2 ABEGSVY
3 B**F**JKLUWY
4 (Q+R+S+T+U+V+W �)
(Y 28/3-15/10) (Z �)
5 **AB**FGIJKMNOPQUVZ
6 CEGHKM(N 2,5km)RSTV

💬 Atmospheric campsite with private marked-out pitches of various sizes, in a pine forest, located directly on on the sea with a sandy beach. Centrally-located restaurant/pizzeria/bar with large terrace. Simple toilet facilities.

🚗 In Grosseto or in Follonica, take route SS322 direction Castiglione della Pescaia. The campsite is 2 km north of Castiglione della Pescaia, sea side.

CC ○

Castiglione della Pescaia

Marina di Grosseto ○

CC € **15** 29/3-13/7 1/9-2/11 7=6   🏔 N 42°46'25'' E 10°50'39''

Castiglione della Pescaia, I-58043 / Toscana

🏔 Santapomata
📧 S.P. 62 delle Rocchette
☎ +39 0564-941037
📠 +39 0564-941221
🗓 29/3 - 20/10
@ info@campingsantapomata.it

6ha 342T(50-80m²) 3A CEE

1 BCG**H**IJKLMN**P**RS
2 ABEGRSVXY
3 WY
4 (Q+S+T+U+V+Y+Z 🔑)
5 **AB**GIJKMNOPUV
6 AEGHKM(N 5km)OTV

💬 This campsite with plenty of shade and good toilet facilities is located directly on a gently sloping beach. There is a bar on the beach.

🚗 From Follonica take the SS322. A few kilometres before Castiglione della Pescaia turn right towards Le Rocchette. Signposted.

3168

Castiglione della Pescaia

Marina di Grosseto

(C€ 15 29/3-13/7 1/9-19/10 7=6 | ⛰ N 42°46'36'' E 10°48'34''

Castiglione della Pescaia, I-58043 / Toscana

🏔 Stella del Mare★★★★
📧 Strada Provinciale delle Rocchette
☎ 📠 +39 0564-947100
🗓 21/4 - 14/10
@ info@stelladelmarecamping.it

7ha 150T(30-90m²) 3A CEE

1 ABCG**H**IJKLMNOPST
2 AEGJQRTVXY
3 BG**M**NRWY
4 (B+G+Q+S+T+U+V+Y+Z 🔑)
5 **A**BEFGIJKLMNOPUW
6 ACEGJ(N 7km)ORT

💬 Stella del Mare campsite with its lovely swimming pools and children's pool, lawns and deckchairs is positioned on the Mediterranean coast of Maremma opposite the island of Elba. It is partly level and partly laid out in terraces. Sandy beach and a rocky coastline close to the site. Castiglione delle Pescaia is within cycling distance.

🚗 From Fallonica the SS322 southwards direction Castiglione della Prescaia. Take exit Le Rocchette. Campsite at the end of the road.

3169

Castiglione della Pescaia

(C€ 17 21/4-30/6 1/9-13/10 | ⛰ N 42°46'38'' E 10°47'34''

Cavriglia, I-52022 / Toscana

🏔 Camping Orlando in Chianti
📧 Località Cafaggiolo
☎ 📠 +39 055-967422
🗓 21/4 - 14/10
@ info@campingorlandoinchianti.it

6ha 50T(70-120m²) 6-10A CEE

1 ABCDGIJKLNO**P**ST
2 BIJKSTVXY
3 ABHJR
4 (A+C+H 🔑) JK
　　(Q+S+T+U+V+Y+Z 🔑)
5 **AB**GIJKLMNPUVWX
6 ACEGHK(N 7km)OTVX

💬 Situated in a nature reserve in the Chianti region, in the middle of a forest. The campsite provides a good restaurant, pizzeria with wood oven, minimarket, three swimming pools (heated) and a jacuzzi. Perfect location for hiking, mountain biking, visits to wine castle and for trips to Florence, Siena, Arezzo.

🚗 Leave the A1 at Incisa, direction Figline Valdarno, then direction Greve in Chianti. Follow camping signs towards Lucolena and Park Cavriglia. Don't follow SatNav.

3170

A1
San Giovanni Valdarno

CC **Montevarchi**

(C€ 17 21/4-6/7 25/8-13/10 7=6, 14=12 | ⛰ N 43°32'18'' E 11°24'50''

Cecina Mare, I-57023 / Toscana

&♿ 🛜 iD (3171)

🔺 Delle Gorette****
📧 Via dei Campilunghi
☎ +39 0586-622460
📠 +39 0586-620045
📅 30/3 - 30/9
@ info@gorette.it

8ha 150T(50-80m²) 6A CEE

1 ABCDFIJKLOPST
2 AEFGNRVXY
3 BGK**M**NRUY
4 (B+G 1/5-30/9) JKP
    (Q+S+T+U+V+W+Y+Z ⊙)
5 **AB**GIJKLMNOPUVWZ
6 CEGJKM(N 1,5km)OQTV

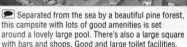

💬 Separated from the sea by a beautiful pine forest, this campsite with lots of good amenities is set around a lovely large pool. There's also a large square with bars and shops. Good and large toilet facilities.

🚗 A12, exit Rosignano-Marittimo, then SS1 (Aurelia) direction Roma, exit Vada. In Vada direction Mazzanta, then straight ahead direction Cecina Mare. The campsite is located on the same side of the road as the sea, before the roundabout.

°Rosignano Marittimo

CC

CC € **15** 30/3-17/6 27/8-29/9 7=6, 14=11   🏖 N 43°18'45'' E 10°29'2''

Cecina Mare/Livorno, I-57023 / Toscana

&♿ 🛜 iD (3172)

🔺 Mareblu S.R.L.***
📧 Via del Campilunghi
☎ +39 0586-629191
📠 +39 0586-629192
📅 24/3 - 20/10
@ info@campingmareblu.com

10ha 280T(50-105m²) 6A CEE

1 ABCGHIJKLMNOPS
2 ABEFGLNRSTVWXY
3 BGK**M**NRUW**Y**
4 (B+G 15/4-10/10)
    (Q+S+T+U+V+W+Y+Z ⊙)
5 **AB**FGIJKLMNOPUVZ
6 CEG**IK**M(N 2km)ORTV

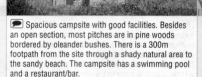

💬 Spacious campsite with good facilities. Besides an open section, most pitches are in pine woods bordered by oleander bushes. There is a 300m footpath from the site through a shady natural area to the sandy beach. The campsite has a swimming pool and a restaurant/bar.

🚗 A12, exit Rosignano-Marittimo. Then take the SS1 'Aurelia' to Roma, exit Vada. In Vada take the direction of Mazzanta (Vada-Cecina-Mare). Follow the signs. Campsite is on the seaward side of the road.

°Rosignano Marittimo

CC

CC € **17** 24/3-30/6 1/9-19/10 14=12   🏖 N 43°19'6'' E 10°28'28''

Cecina Mare/Livorno, I-57023 / Toscana

&♿ 🛜 iD (3173)

🔺 New Camping Le Tamerici SRL ***
📧 Via della Cecinella 5
☎ +39 0586-620629
📠 +39 0586-687811
📅 13/4 - 30/9
@ info@letamerici.it

8ha 130T(50-80m²) 6A CEE

1 ABCD**F**HIJKLMNO**P**
2 AEFGNRSTUVXY
3 BGK**M**NRUW**Y**
4 (B ⊙) (G 1/5-7/10)
    (Q+S+T+U+V+Y+Z ⊙)
5 **AB**GJKMNOPUV
6 DFGJM(N 1km)ORT

💬 This campsite is separated from the sea and the beach by a lovely walking area (pine forest) 600m from the sea and a short distance from Cecina and Cecina Mare. Swimming and children's pools, sports fields, shops and a good restaurant. Special camping pitches.

🚗 A12, exit Rosignano Marittimo, then the SS1 (Aurelia) direction Roma, exit Cecina Nord direction Cecina Mare. Straight on at traffic lights, campsite signposted.

Rosignano Solvay

Cecina

CC

SS1

CC € **17** 13/4-14/6 3/9-29/9   🏖 N 43°17'31'' E 10°30'38''

Certaldo/Marcialla, I-50020 / Toscana

🛰 iD (3174)

⛺ Camping Panorama Del Chianti**
✉ Via Marcialla 349
☎ 📠 +39 0571-669334
📅 15/3 - 5/11
@ campingchianti@outlook.com

2,1ha 61T(60-80m²) 3-6A CEE

1 ABCD**G**IJKLOPQ
2 JKLRTVWXY
3 HIJ
4 (B 25/5-30/9)
    (Q+R+T+U+V+Z 🔌)
5 **AB**GIKMNOPUVWZ
6 ACEGJ(N 1,6km)T

💬 A rural terraced campsite. From the campsite you can see the Tuscan countryside in the distance. Peacefully located on the green hills of Tuscany and close to cultural cities such as Florence, Siena, San Gimignano, Certaldo and Volterra.

🚗 From motorway Florence-Siena, take exit Tavarnelle. In Tavarnelle direction Marcialla/Certaldo. In Marcialla direction Fiano and follow campsite signs.

Castelfiorentino   Tavarnelle Val di
CC   Pesa

CC € 17 15/3-3/7 21/8-4/11

🗺 N 43°34'55'' E 11°8'19''

Coltano, I-56121 / Toscana

♿ 🛰 iD (3175)

⛺ Camping Lago Le Tamerici
✉ Via della Sofina 6
☎ +39 050-989007
📠 +39 050-989935
📅 26/3 - 14/10
@ info@lagoletamerici.it

18ha 44T(100-120m²) 6A CEE

1 ABCDGIJKLMPRS
2 DFLRTUVWXY
3 AGN**OPW**
4 (B 1/6-15/9)
    (Q+R+U+V+X+Z 🔌)
5 **AB**GIJKLMNOPUWXZ
6 ACFGJ(N 2km)

💬 Campsite located in a nature reserve between Livorno and Pisa. Spacious pitches with grass, by a lake. View of the Pisan mountains. Organic meats and regional dishes in the pizzeria/restaurant with wood-burning oven. Bikes and kayaks available for use for free. Also motorhome pitches.

🚗 Firenze-Pisa-Livorno exit Darsena Pisna, to SS1 direction Coltano, right after ± 3 km dir. Caltano, then follow camping signs, or use coordinates with SatNav (do not use address).

Pisa   Calci

SS1
CC   SS67BIS
A12

Livorno

CC € 17 26/3-14/7 1/9-13/10 7=6

🗺 N 43°38'14'' E 10°22'3''

Elba/Lacona/Capolíveri, I-57037 / Toscana

♿ 🛰 iD (3176)

⛺ Lacona***
✉ C.P. 65
☎ +39 0565-964161
📠 +39 0565-964330
📅 20/4 - 17/10
@ info@camping-lacona.it

2,6ha 158T(40-80m²) 4-6A CEE

1 ABCD**G**HIJKLMNOPS
2 ABEGJLNQTVXY
3 B**F**HJKRUVWY
4 (B+Q+R+T+U+V+X+Z 🔌)
5 **AB**FGIJKLMNOPUVW
6 ACEGJK(N 8km)OQRTVX

💬 This shady campsite, set among eucalyptus trees, is laid out in easily accessible terraces on a narrow headland with a pebble beach, marker buoys and a boat winch close by on one side, and a long sandy beach on the other. Scooter rental. Bikes, safe and kayaks free.

🚗 Follow 'tutti direzioni' in Portoferraio. Direction Porto Azzurro at 3rd roundabout. Straight on at traffic lights. Take next exit to Lacona. Campsite after the bend on the left.

Portoferraio   Rio Marina

CC

CC € 17 20/4-20/6 1/9-16/10

🗺 N 42°45'37'' E 10°18'56''

Elba/Lacona/Capolíveri, I-57031 / Toscana ♿ 📶 (3177)

🏕 Lacona Pineta
📧 Viale dei Golfi 249
☎ +39 0565-964322
📠 +39 0565-964087
📅 15/4 - 15/10
@ info@campinglaconapineta.com

4ha 179T(50-80m²) 3-5A CEE

1 BCD**G**HIJKLMNOPQ
2 AEGJLNOQUVY
3 ABCWY
4 (A 📅) (B 30/5-20/10) KP (Q+R+S+T+U+V+X+Y+Z 📅)
5 ABFGIJKLMNOPUVWZ
6 ABEGH**IK**M(N 2km)OQRSTU

💬 Terraced campsite with a lovely swimming pool. Located in a pine forest at 50 metres from the beach. Excellent toilet facilities, centrally-located bar/restaurant.

Portoferraio

🚌 In Portoferraio, dir. Porto Azzurro. Then dir. Lacona. Campsite is located on right after the bend.

CC € 19 15/4-18/6 5/9-14/10   🏔 N 42°45'33'' E 10°18'49''

Elba/Marina di Campo, I-57034 / Toscana ♿ 📶 iD (3178)

🏕 Ville degli Ulivi***
📧 Via della Foce 89
☎ +39 0565-976098
📠 +39 0565-976048
📅 21/4 - 20/10
@ info@villedegliulivi.it

7ha 285T(40-95m²) 6A CEE

1 ACD**F**HIJKLMNO**P**ST
2 ABEQSTVXY
3 BHJK**M**NQR**V**WY
4 (**B** 1/5-30/9) (G 10/5-30/9) **I KLNP**(Q+S+T+U+V+Y+Z 📅)
5 **AB**EFGIJKLMNOP**ST**UVWXY
6 CDEGJ**K**M(N 1km)ORTUVWX

💬 Luxury family campsite with beautiful swimming pools and playground, 200m from a long sandy beach. This well-maintained site is on the edge of the lively resort of Marino di Campo. Excellent toilet facilities. Also a wellness centre and a restaurant with an extensive menu.

Portoferraio
Marciana

🚌 From Portoferraio follow 'tutti direzioni'. At the third roundabout direction Procchio. In Procchio direction Marino di Campo. Before the town direction Lacona. Over the bridge on the sea side.

CC € 19 21/4-9/6 1/9-19/10   🏔 N 42°45'7'' E 10°14'42''

Figline Valdarno, I-50063 / Toscana 🚻 ♿ 📶 iD (3179)

🏕 Norcenni Girasole Club****
📧 Via Norcenni 7
☎ +39 055-915141
📠 +39 055-9151402
📅 19/4 - 12/10
@ girasole@ecvacanze.it

11ha 154T(40-100m²) 10-16A CEE

1 ABCDGIJKLMOPQ
2 FGJKLSTVWXY
3 BCHJK**M**NOQRUV
4 (A 21/4-22/9) (C 22/4-15/10) (E 📅) (G 22/4-30/9) **JKLNP** (Q+S+T+U+V+Y+Z 📅)
5 **AB**DEFGIJKLMNPR**ST**UWXYZ
6 CFGHIKM(N 3km)ORTUVWX

💬 Large, luxury campsite, partly even grounds, partly terraced. Very many amenities: swimming pools, fitness, shopping and entertainment. Own excursions to e.g. Florence and Rome. Since 2015: game park with adventure trail and a new game room.

Reggello

🚌 A1 Firenze-Roma, exit Incisa. SS69 direction Figline Valdarno. Follow camping signs 'Girasole Club'. Located about 8 km from the autostrada exit. From Figline follow camping signs, don't use SatNav.

CC A1

Montevarchi

CC € 19 19/4-14/6 25/8-11/10   🏔 N 43°36'48'' E 11°26'58''

Marina di Bibbona, I-57020 / Toscana   🛗 📱 **iD** (3180)

🏕 Camping I Melograni
📧 Via dei Cipressi 11
☎ +39 0586-600222
📠 +39 0586-602717
🔑 1/4 - 30/9
@ info@campeggioimelograni.it

4,5ha 100**T**(55-90m²) 4A CEE

1 ACD**G**HIJKLNOP
2 AFGUVXY
3 BJK**Q**R
4 (**A** 15/6-31/8)
  (Q+S+U+V+Y+Z 🔑)
5 **A**EFGIKMNPUVXY
6 ACDEG(N 0,2km)OT

💬 A simple campsite located at walking distance from the seaside resort of Marina di Bibbona. Restaurant next door. Large, simple toilet facilities.

🚗 SS1, exit Cecina Sud dir. Marina di Bibbona, straight on on roundabout. Right on mini-roundabout. Site is located on left of road.

Cecina

CC

Castagneto
Carducci

CC € **15** 1/4-30/6 1/9-29/9 7=6, 14=11   📍 **N 43°14'58'' E 10°31'59''**

Marina di Bibbona, I-57020 / Toscana   📶 (3181)

🏕 Free Beach***
📧 Via Cavalleggeri Nord 88
☎ +39 0586-699066
📠 +39 0586-696041
🔑 29/3 - 23/9
@ info@campingfreebeach.it

9ha 150**T**(75-80m²) 3A CEE

1 BCD**G**HIJKLMNOPS
2 AEGRSVXY
3 BGKNRU**W**Y
4 (B+Q+S+T+U+V+X+Z 🔑)
5 **AB**GIJKMNOPUW
6 AEG**J**(N 0,3km)PTV

💬 A family campsite located in Marina di Bibbona within walking distance of the beach. Centrally located square with swimming pool and bar/restaurant/pizzeria. Basic toilet facilities.

🚗 A12, exit Rosignano Marittimo, then SS1 'Aurelia' towards Roma. Exit La California/Cecina Sud towards Marina di Bibbona. Straight ahead at roundabout; straight ahead at mini-roundabout. Right after small bend. Follow the signs. Campsite at the end of the road around the corner on the right.

Cecina
SS1

CC

Castagneto
Carducci

CC € **17** 29/3-30/6 1/9-22/9   📍 **N 43°15'6'' E 10°31'41''**

Marina di Bibbona, I-57020 / Toscana   🛗 📶 **iD** (3182)

🏕 Free Time***
📧 Via dei Cipressi
☎ +39 0586-600934
📠 +39 0586-602682
🔑 21/4 - 23/9
@ info@freetimecamping.it

4ha 100**T**(80-105m²) 6A CEE

1 ACDGHIJKLMN**PRS**
2 AEGRVWXY
3 BKNRV**W**
4 (B+G 🔑) JN
  (Q+S+U+V+Y+Z 🔑)
5 **AB**EFGIJKLMNOP**S**TUWXY
  Z
6 ACDEG**J**(N 0,5km)RTV

💬 Close to town of Marina di Bibbona with many modern amenities: fitness centre, massage and internet point. Large pool. Plenty of sunny or lightly shaded pitches. 800 metres from sea and a sandy beach, accessible through a pine forest. Fishing lake. Pitches with private toilet facilities for 5 Euros extra.

🚗 A12, exit Rosignano Marittimo, then SS1 Aurelia to Roma, exit La California/Cecina Sud. Dir. Marina di Bibbona. Right 'Via dei Cipressi', site just before the bend.

Cecina
SS1

CC

Castagneto
Carducci

CC € **17** 21/4-30/6 1/9-22/9   📍 **N 43°15'9'' E 10°31'51''**

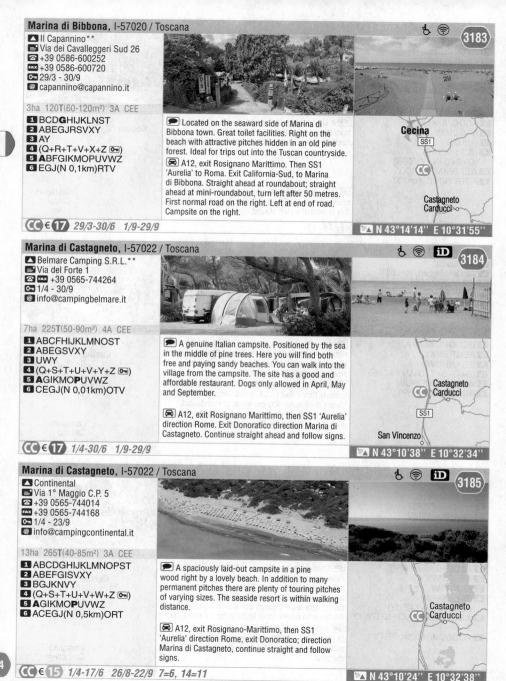

Marina di Bibbona, I-57020 / Toscana

Il Capannino**
Via dei Cavalleggeri Sud 26
☎ +39 0586-600252
FAX +39 0586-600720
⌾ 29/3 - 30/9
@ capannino@capannino.it

3ha 120T(60-120m²) 3A CEE

1 BCD**G**HIJKLNST
2 ABEGJRSVXY
3 AY
4 (Q+R+T+V+X+Z ⌾)
5 **A**BFGIKMOPUVWZ
6 EGJ(N 0,1km)RTV

💬 Located on the seaward side of Marina di Bibbona town. Great toilet facilities. Right on the beach with attractive pitches hidden in an old pine forest. Ideal for trips out into the Tuscan countryside.

🚗 A12, exit Rosignano Marittimo. Then SS1 'Aurelia' to Roma. Exit California-Sud, to Marina di Bibbona. Straight ahead at roundabout; straight ahead at mini-roundabout, turn left after 50 metres. First normal road on the right. Left at end of road. Campsite on the right.

Cecina
SS1

CC

Castagneto Carducci

3183

CC € **17** 29/3-30/6 1/9-29/9 N 43°14'14'' E 10°31'55''

Marina di Castagneto, I-57022 / Toscana

Belmare Camping S.R.L.**
Via del Forte 1
☎ FAX +39 0565-744264
⌾ 1/4 - 30/9
@ info@campingbelmare.it

7ha 225T(50-90m²) 4A CEE

1 ABCFHIJKLMNOST
2 ABEGSVXY
3 UWY
4 (Q+S+T+U+V+Y+Z ⌾)
5 **A**GIKMOPUVWZ
6 CEGJ(N 0,01km)OTV

💬 A genuine Italian campsite. Positioned by the sea in the middle of pine trees. Here you will find both free and paying sandy beaches. You can walk into the village from the campsite. The site has a good and affordable restaurant. Dogs only allowed in April, May and September.

🚗 A12, exit Rosignano Marittimo, then SS1 'Aurelia' direction Rome. Exit Donoratico direction Marina di Castagneto. Continue straight ahead and follow signs.

Castagneto Carducci
SS1

CC

San Vincenzo

3184

CC € **17** 1/4-30/6 1/9-29/9 N 43°10'38'' E 10°32'34''

Marina di Castagneto, I-57022 / Toscana

Continental
Via 1° Maggio C.P. 5
☎ +39 0565-744014
FAX +39 0565-744168
⌾ 1/4 - 23/9
@ info@campingcontinental.it

13ha 265T(40-85m²) 3A CEE

1 ABCD**G**HIJKLMNOPST
2 ABEFGISVXY
3 BGJKNVY
4 (Q+S+T+U+V+W+Z ⌾)
5 **A**GIKMOPUVWZ
6 ACEGJ(N 0,5km)ORT

💬 A spaciously laid-out campsite in a pine wood right by a lovely beach. In addition to many permanent pitches there are plenty of touring pitches of varying sizes. The seaside resort is within walking distance.

🚗 A12, exit Rosignano-Marittimo, then SS1 'Aurelia' direction Rome, exit Donoratico; direction Marina di Castagneto, continue straight and follow signs.

Castagneto Carducci

CC

3185

694

CC € **15** 1/4-17/6 26/8-22/9 7=6, 14=11 N 43°10'24'' E 10°32'38''

Marina di Castagneto, I-57022 / Toscana

♿ 🛜 iD **(3186)**

🔺 Int. Camping Etruria**
📧 Via della Pineta
☎ +39 0565-744254
📠 +39 0565-744494
🔓 20/4 - 14/10
@ info@campingetruria.it

14ha 234T(60-100m²) 6A CEE

1 ABCD**G**IJKLMOPS
2 ABEGSVXY
3 BKLRWY
4 (Q+S+T+U+V+W+Z 🔓)
5 **AB**FGIKMNO**P**U
6 CEGHKM(N 1km)ORT

💬 A family campsite located in a pine forest. Right by the sea with a spacious sandy beach. Modern toilet facilities. Centrally positioned restaurant/bar with a large terrace and shops.

🚗 A12 Genova-Rosignano. Then SS1 'Aurelia', direction Roma, exit Donoratico, direction Marina di Castagneto. Follow the camping signs.

CC Castagneto Carducci

CC € **17** 20/4-17/6 9/9-13/10 14=12   🏖 N 43°11'16'' E 10°32'30''

Marina di Grosseto, I-58100 / Toscana

♿ 🛜 🌼 iD **(3187)**

🔺 Cieloverde****
📧 Via della Trappola 181
☎ +39 0564-321611
📠 +39 0564-30178
🔓 12/5 - 16/9
@ info@cieloverde.it

60ha 1260T(80-100m²) 3-6A CEE

1 ABCDGHIJKLMNOPS
2 ABEGRSVXY
3 BGHJKNRUWY
4 (A+**B**+**G**+Q+S+T+U+V+W+Y +Z 🔓)
5 **AB**FGHIJKLMNOP**S**UV
6 EGHJM(N 2km)ORTUV

💬 Very nicely appointed campsite in park with e.g. many play options for children. The site is 1km from the beach, but a campsite train will get you there, from where there is a walking/cycle path to the sea. Large, first-rate toilet blocks.

🚗 In Grosseto drive in the direction of Marina di Grosseto (mare). In Marina di Grosseto drive in the direction of Principina a Mare. The campsite is located on the right side of the road, before the exit towards Principina a Mare.

Castiglione della Pescaia   **Grosseto**

CC

SS1

CC € **17** 12/5-30/6 1/9-15/9   🏖 N 42°42'47'' E 11°0'27''

Marina di Grosseto, I-58046 / Toscana

♿ 🛜 iD **(3188)**

🔺 Le Marze**
📧 S.P. 158 km 30.200
☎ +39 0564-35501
📠 +39 0564-744503
🔓 20/4 - 23/9
@ info@lemarze.it

20ha 452T(50-110m²) 3-6A CEE

1 ABCD**G**HIJKLMN**P**RT
2 ABEGRSUVWXY
3 BJKR**W**Y
4 (B 15/6-15/9) (Q+S+T+U+V+W+Y+Z 🔓)
5 **AB**EFGIJKLMNOP**ST**UV
6 CEGJM(N 5km)OTX

💬 Located in a beautiful pine forest with pitches of varying dimensions. Several toilet blocks including private and children's toilets. Large built-up swimming pool 6 x 24 metres with supervision. A lovely walking and cycle path takes you to the sandy beach.

🚗 From Follonica take the SS322 south direction Castiglione della Pescaia. In the town cross the bridge towards Marina di Grosseto. The campsite is on the left after about 5 km.

SS1

Castiglione della Pescaia   **Grosseto**

CC

CC € **17** 20/4-23/6 1/9-22/9   🏖 N 42°44'42'' E 10°56'44''

Marina di Massa, I-54100 / Toscana

⛺ Camping Giardino
✉ Via delle Pinete 382
☎ +39 0585-869291
📠 +39 0585-240781
🔑 31/3 - 30/9
@ info@campinggiardino.com

3189

3,8ha 140T(40-60m²) 3A CEE

1 BCDGHIJKLMOPQ
2 AEFGLORVXY
3 BFKRVWY
4 (B 19/5-15/9)
  (Q+S+U+V+X 1/6-15/9)
5 ABGIJKMOPUVZ
6 ACEGHK(N 0,1km)ORTV

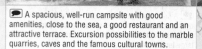

💬 A spacious, well-run campsite with good amenities, close to the sea, a good restaurant and an attractive terrace. Excursion possibilities to the marble quarries, caves and the famous cultural towns.

🚗 A12 exit Massa, 1st roundabout right to Massa, 2nd roundabout right, 3rd roundabout right ± 2 km straight ahead. Campsite on the right.

Carrara
Massa
CC A12

CC € 17 31/3-11/7 1/9-29/9

N 44°1'30'' E 10°4'27''

Marina di Massa, I-54037 / Toscana

⛺ Luna***
✉ Via delle Pinete 392
☎ +39 0585-780460
📠 +39 0585-784058
🔑 14/5 - 15/9
@ info@campingluna.it

iD 3190

6,5ha 36T(50-60m²) 6A CEE

1 ABCDFHIJKLMPS
2 AEFGRSTVWXY
3 FRWY
4 (Z 22/5-30/9)
5 AGIJKMOPUVX
6 AEGIK(N 0,1km)TV

💬 A friendly, peaceful and presentable campsite close to the beach. Ideal for those seeking relaxation. A good base for trips to the Cinque Terre, the marble quarries and the Tuscan art towns.

🚗 A12 exit Massa. Immediate right on roundabout over viaduct A12. To next roundabout, campsite about 2 km on the right. (Route differs from most navigation systems).

Carrara
Massa
CC A12

CC € 19 14/5-6/7 1/9-14/9

N 44°1'38'' E 10°4'14''

Marina di Massa, I-54037 / Toscana

⛺ Partaccia 1***
✉ Via delle Pinete 394
☎ +39 0585-780133
📠 +39 0585-784728
🔑 21/4 - 7/10
@ info@partaccia.it

3191

4,3ha 80T(20-50m²) 5A CEE

1 BCGIJLPS
2 ABEFGSVWXY
3 AY
4 (Q 🔑) (S+U 1/5-15/9)
  (V+Y 🔑) (Z 1/5-19/9)
5 AIKMOPUV
6 CEGK(N 0,5km)ORTV

💬 A park-like established campsite, a natural oasis with shady trees and colourful flowers, well maintained, 65m from a free beach. The campsite is situated on lively vibrant coastal road. Many opportunities for excursions.

🚗 A12 La Spezia-Livorno, exit Massa, left after toll booth. Follow road to intersection bar/café 'La Dolce Vita'. Turn left and follow camping signs.

Carrara
Massa
CC A12

CC € 17 21/4-7/7 1/9-6/10

N 44°1'37'' E 10°4'11''

Marina di Massa, I-54100 / Toscana

🛏 Taimì****
✉ Via del Cacciatore, 30
☎ +39 0585-789262
📠 +39 0585-632504
📅 19/4 - 15/9
@ info@campingtaimi.it

2ha 60T(< 90m²) 6A CEE

1 ABCDFIJKLMOPS
2 AEFGLSVXY
3 AFRY
4 (B 16/5-15/9) (Q+U+X+Z 🔑)
5 **AB**EFGIJKLMNOPUWXY
6 ABCEGK(N 0,1km)OSTV

💬 Spaciously appointed, luxury campsite with spacious pitches (lots of shade). Relaxation is valued at this campsite. The beach is a short cycle away, shops within walking distance. You can choose your own pitch at this campsite.

🚗 A12 exit Massa. Left dir. Carara. Left at 1st traffic light. 5th exit turn right. Campsite on right after 500 metres.

🆔 3192

Carrara
Massa

CC € 19 19/4-6/7 27/8-14/9

📡 N 44°1'49'' E 10°4'24''

Montecatini Terme, I-51016 / Toscana

🛏 Belsito***
✉ Via delle Vigne 1/a
☎ +39 0572-67373
📠 +39 0572-549100
📅 1/4 - 30/9
@ info@campingbelsito.it

3,7ha 250T(50-100m²) 15A CEE

1 ABCD**G**HIJKLMOPST
2 FGIJKLRTVWXY
3 AHNRU
4 (B 🔑) (G 16/5-16/9) KP (Q+S+T+U+V+X+Z 🔑)
5 **AB**EFGIJKLMNOPQR**S**UVX YZ
6 ACDEG**K**(N 3km)OTV

💬 A peaceful shaded campsite, many of the camping pitches have lovely views of the Tuscan countryside. There are two lovely swimming pools where you can cool off after a trip of discovery through Tuscany.

🚗 A11 Firenze-Pisa, exit Montecatini Terme. Straight ahead after toll booths direction Montecatini Terme. Follow camping signs and Montecatini Alto signs. Do not use SatNav.

🆔 3193

SS64

Pistoia

CC A11

Ponte Buggianese
Altopascio

CC € 19 1/4-7/7 1/9-29/9

📡 N 43°54'19'' E 10°47'17''

Passo de la Futa/Firenzuola, I-50033 / Toscana

🛏 La Futa**
✉ Via Bruscoli, 889/H
☎ +39 055-815297
📅 15/4 - 30/9
@ info@campinglafuta.it

10ha 80T(60-80m²) 10A CEE

1 ABCD**G**HIJKLMOPQ
2 BFJKRTWXY
3 AHJR
4 (B 15/5-16/9) (Q+R+V+Z 🔑)
5 **AB**FGIJKLMNOPUWZ
6 CEGJ(N 3km)OTV

💬 This lovely campsite with stunning panoramic views is located in the Futa Pass (about 900 metres). The campsite is equipped with a swimming pool. Starting point for walks in the mountain areas. Florence, Siena and other historic towns are within easy reach of this Tuscan campsite.

🚗 A1 Bologna-Firenze, exit Roncobilaccio (from Firenze: Firenzuola-Mugello). SS65 to Passo della Futa. Campsite close to the Futa Pass (war cemetery).

🆔 3194

CC

A1

Barberino di Mugello   Scarperia

CC € 19 15/4-30/6 25/8-29/9

📡 N 44°5'52'' E 11°16'7''

Principina a Mare, I-58100 / Toscana

⌂ Campeggio Principina**
✉ Via del Dentice 10
☎ +39 0564-31347
🗓 20/4 - 30/9
@ info@principinacampeggio.it

10ha 400T(50-140m²) 3A CEE

1 ABCD**G**HIJKLMNOP
2 ABGRSTVWXY
3 BGJK**M**N**Q**R
4 (Q ☕) (R 15/4-1/6)
(S 1/6-1/10) (U+V+Y+Z ☕)
5 **AB**EGIJKLMOPUVZ
6 ADEGIJ(N 1,5km)OT

💬 Camping Principina is located at walking distance from a wide sandy beach on the Mediterranean Coast. The campsite offers spacious pitches under the pine trees and is an ideal destination for people looking for that typical Italian atmosphere. Has good toilet facilities.

🚗 SS1 Aurelia, exit Grosseto Sud. Then follow direction 'Mare'/Principina a Mare. After 10 km follow camping signs in Principana a Mare.

Castiglione della Pescaia

Grosseto

ⓒⓒ € **13** 20/4-30/6 1/9-29/9 7=6, 14=12, 21=17   📷 N 42°42'16'' E 11°0'20''

Punta Ala, I-58040 / Toscana

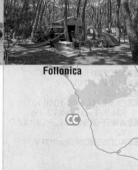

⌂ Baia Verde***
✉ Loc. Casetta Civinini
☎ +39 0564-922298
📠 +39 0564-923044
🗓 23/4 - 13/10
@ info@baiaverde.com

20ha 1138T(60-100m²) 3A CEE

1 ABC**G**HIJKLMNOPRS
2 ABEGRSVY
3 B**F**GJKN**OP**RTUWY
4 (Q+S+T+U+V+W+X+Y+Z ☕)
5 **AB**FGIKMOPUV
6 CEGH**IJ**M(N 6km)ORTV

💬 The campsite is located right on an extensive sandy beach inviting you to take long beach walks. The site has spacious pitches and many amenities including several shops.

🚗 From Follonica take the SS322 in the direction of Castiglione della Pescaia. At Pian d'Alma drive in the direction of Punta Ala. The campsite is located on the right.

Follonica

ⓒⓒ € **19** 23/4-17/6 15/9-12/10   📷 N 42°50'2'' E 10°46'46''

Riotorto, I-57025 / Toscana

⌂ Pappasole****
✉ Loc. Carbonifera 14
☎ +39 0565-20414
📠 +39 0565-20346
🗓 21/4 - 20/10
@ info@pappasole.it

20ha 476T(90-100m²) 6-10A CEE

1 ABCD**G**HIJKLMNOPQ
2 AEFGLRTUVXY
3 BGK**M**N**Q**RUWY
4 (B+G 16/4-13/10) IKP
(Q+S+T+U+V+Y+Z ☕)
5 **AB**EFGIJKLMNOP**ST**UWXY
Z
6 ACEGH**IK**M(N 7km)OQRTU
V

💬 Luxurious campsite, a 4 minute walk from a long sandy beach with separate new area with a modern toilet block for CampingCard ACSI holders. The 90-100 m² marked out pitches are covered with a light gauze sail providing shade. Beach accessible by wheelchair and the minigolf is also suitable for the disabled.

🚗 SS1 Aurelia exit Riotorto direction Folllonica/Grossetto. Take the flyover over the motorway about 5 km before Follonica, then turn right and follow the signs.

SS398
SS1
Piombino   **Follonica**

ⓒⓒ € **19** 21/4-24/5 28/5-30/5 3/6-7/6 11/6-13/6 2/9-19/10   📷 N 42°57'3'' E 10°41'14''

San Baronto/Lamporecchio, I-51035 / Toscana

🔥 📶 **iD** **3198**

🏔 Barco Reale****
🏠 Via Nardini 11
☎ +39 0573-88332
📠 +39 0573-856003
🗓 30/3 - 30/9
@ info@barcoreale.com

10ha 253T(60-110m²) 10A CEE

1 ABCDFHIJKLMPQ
2 BHIJKLRTVWXY
3 BFGHJKNRU
4 (A 🗓) (C+H 1/4-30/9)
   (Q+S+T+U+V+Y+Z 🗓)
5 ABDEFGIJKLMNOPUWXYZ
6 ACEGK(N 1km)OTV

💬 This family campsite is located in a wooded, hilly area with panoramic views. Extensive sports, entertainment and excursion programme for all ages. Centrally located between Pisa-Florence-Lucca-Vinci-Pistoia. Attractive restaurant, bar and terrace.

🚗 Motorway A11 Firenze-Pisa, exit Pistoia. Take the direction of San Baronto/Lamporecchio/Vinci. Follow the signs.

Pistoia
A11
Iolo San Pietro
CC
SS67

CC € **19** 30/3-30/6 1/9-29/9

🏔 **N 43°50'30'' E 10°54'38''**

San Vincenzo, I-57027 / Toscana

♿ 📶 **3199**

🏔 Park Albatros****
🏠 Pineta di Torre Nuova 2
☎ +39 0565-701018
📠 +39 0565-701400
🗓 20/4 - 16/9
@ parkalbatros@ecvacanze.it

23ha 200T(80-100m²) 10A CEE

1 BCDGIJKLMOPST
2 ABRSVWXY
3 BKNQR
4 (E+F+H 🗓) IJP
   (Q+S+T+U+V 🗓)
   (W 1/6-31/8) (Y+Z 🗓)
5 ABEFGIJKLMNOPUWXYZ
6 FGIJM(N 6km)ORTV

💬 The moment you enter Park Albatros you won't help noticing the swimming pools with 3000 m² of lagoons encircled by deckchairs. Keep going and you will find the very modern toilet facilities, a large supermarket, an excellent restaurant and large touring pitches in sunny surroundings with gentle shade.

🚗 SS1 'Aurelia', exit San Vincenzo Nord, follow the SP23 direction Piombino through the town. Entrance to campsite on the left near 7.0 km-marker.

Campiglia Marittima
Venturina
CC

CC € **19** 20/4-17/6 25/8-15/9

🏔 **N 43°1'40'' E 10°32'1''**

Scarlino, I-58020 / Toscana

♿ 📶 **iD** **3200**

🏔 Vallicella
🏠 Loc. Vallicella
☎ +39 0566-37229
📠 +39 0566-37232
🗓 21/4 - 15/9
@ info@vallicellavillage.com

10ha 242T(60-100m²) 6A CEE

1 ABCGHIJKLMNPST
2 FGIJKRTVWXY
3 BFGHMNPRU
4 (B+G 🗓) P(Q 🗓)
   (R 1/5-31/8) (T+U+V 🗓)
   (Y+Z 1/5-31/8)
5 ABIJKLMNOPTUV
6 ACEGIJ(N 4km)ORTV

💬 An well-run terraced campsite in a mediterranean setting. A romantic atmosphere is created by the illuminated terraces, the castle and the village of Scarlino. The site has two swimming pools. Basic toilet facilities. A bar/restaurant is centrally located next to the pool.

🚗 SS1 Aurelia exit Scarlino/Scalo, direction Scarlino/Punta Ala (Sp.84). Continue straight ahead at the crossroads and straight ahead at the next crossroads. The campsite is in the bend of the road.

Gavorrano SS1
Follonica
CC

CC € **13** 21/4-7/7 25/8-14/9 7=6, 14=11

🏔 **N 42°54'46'' E 10°51'10''**

Scarperia e San Piero, I-50037 / Toscana ⊚ 3201

🏕 Camping Village Mugello Verde***
🏠 Via Massorondinaio 39
☎ +39 055-848511
⊙ 16/3 - 4/11
@ mugelloverde@florencevillage.com

12ha 250T 6A CEE

1 BCGIJKLMO**PQ**
2 BIJRSTWXY
3 A**F**HJMR
4 (B 1/6-15/9)
  (Q+R+T+U+V+X+Z ⊙)
5 **AB**GIJKLMNOPUVW
6 CEGHJ(N 1km)ORTV

💬 A quietly located, basic campsite in natural, wooded surroundings with pitches next to a hillside. 3 children up to 11 years are included.

🚗 A1 Bologna-Firenze, exit Barberino. Direction Borgo San Lorenzo. Follow the signs and turn to the right at the service station.

Barberino di Mugello Scarperia A1

CC € ⑲ 16/3-25/5 9/6-3/7 21/8-3/11   ⛰ N 43°57'40'' E 11°18'37''

Sovicille, I-53018 / Toscana 🛜 iD 3202

🏕 La Montagnola
🏠 S.P. 52 della Montagnola
☎ FAX +39 0577-314473
⊙ 29/3 - 30/9
@ montagnolacamping@libero.it

2,5ha 66T(80m²) 5A CEE

1 ABCGIJKLMOPQ
2 BGJRSTUVY
3 AKR
4 (Q+R+Z ⊙)
5 **AB**GJKMNOPUVW
6 CEG**K**(N 1km)ORTV

💬 A quiet campsite in wooded rural surroundings, with level marked-out pitches. Good opportunities for walking. The bus to Siena stops at the campsite.

🚗 Left at the Ovest exit on the Florence-Siena motorway towards Sovicille and follow camping signs.

SS408 Siena Sovicille Radicondoli CC SS223

CC € ⑲ 29/3-8/7 26/8-29/9   ⛰ N 43°16'51'' E 11°13'8''

Torre del Lago Puccini, I-55049 / Toscana ♿ 🛜 3203

🏕 Bosco Verde Camping
🏠 Viale John Fitzgerald Kennedy 5
☎ +39 0584-359343
FAX +39 0584-341981
⊙ 20/4 - 19/9
@ info@campeggioboscoverde.com

6,5ha 135T(48-90m²) 4-10A CEE

1 BCD**G**HIJKLMOPRS
2 ABFGRSVWXY
3 AKNU**W**
4 (**A** 1/7-30/8) (B 1/6-10/9)
  (Q 1/5-15/9)
  (R+U+V+Y+Z ⊙)
5 **AB**FGIJKLMOPUVWX
6 CEGK(N 0,9km)OTU

NEW

💬 This campsite is located in a stunning forested area of the Migliarino-San Rossore nature reserve where a path leads to the beach. Free swimming pool and good restaurant.

🚗 A12 exit Viareggio to Torre del Lago Puccini. Follow 'Mare' signs. Then follow camping signs.

Viareggio A11 CC A12 San Giuliano Terme SS1 Pisa

CC € ⑲ 20/4-12/6 1/9-18/9 7=6   ⛰ N 43°49'20'' E 10°16'25''

Torre del Lago Puccini, I-55049 / Toscana

3204

🚹🚻 ♿ 📶 ✿ **iD**

▲ Europa*
🏠 Viale dei Tigli, 51
☎ +39 0584-350707
📠 +39 0584-342592
🔑 7/4 - 5/10
@ info@europacamp.it

5,3ha 200T(54-70m²) 6A CEE

1 ABCD**G**IJKLMOPRS
2 AFGRSVXY
3 BGHJKMNRU
4 (A 🔑) (B 13/5-24/9)
 (Q+S+T+U+V+Y+Z 🔑)
5 **AB**GIJKMO**P**UVWZ
6 ACFGHK(N 2km)ORTUV

💬 Well-maintained campsite close to the free beach. Trips to Tuscan cultural cities. Cash payment required for CampingCard ACSI. Free bottle of Chianti when staying at least a week. Attention: dogs allowed entire season. Free wifi.

🚗 A12 La Spezia-Livorno, exit Viareggio, along the dual-carriageway Aurelia road to Torre del Lago, exit Marina di Lago, follow the 'Mare' signs. Follow camping signs.

Viareggio Massarosa

CC €**17** 7/4-8/7 26/8-4/10 7=6, 14=12, 21=18

📐 N 43°49'52'' E 10°16'14''

Torre del Lago Puccini, I-55049 / Toscana

3205

♿ 📶 **iD**

▲ Italia
🏠 Viale dei Tigli 52
☎ +39 0584-359828
📠 +39 0584-341504
🔑 18/4 - 28/9
@ info@campingitalia.net

10ha 150T(50-80m²) 6A CEE

1 ABCD**G**IJKLMOPQ
2 ABF**G**RSWXY
3 BGHJKM**M**NRU
4 (B 1/6-28/9)
 (Q+S+T+U+V+Y+Z 🔑)
5 **AB**EFGIJKMNO**P**UVWZ
6 CEG**K**(N 2km)ORTV

💬 If you appreciate art, nature and endless beaches you should visit Versilia in the heart of Tuscany with the Alpi Apugne in the background. Here you will find the Italia campsite in Torre del Lago Puccini, a shady campsite with good facilities. Dogs permitted 12/4-31/5 and from 1/9-29/9. CampingCard ACSI holders can swim free.

🚗 A12 La Spezia-Livorno exit Viareggio, then SS1 direction Pisa. Take Marina di Torre del Lago exit, then follow camping signs.

Viareggio Massarosa

CC €**17** 18/4-30/6 20/8-27/9 7=6

📐 N 43°49'45'' E 10°16'14''

Troghi/Firenze, I-50067 / Toscana

3206

♿ 📶 **iD**

▲ Camp. Village Il Poggetto
🏠 Strada Provinciale 1
 Aretina km 14
☎ 📠 +39 055-8307323
🔑 24/3 - 14/10
@ info@campingilpoggetto.com

4,5ha 110T(60-85m²) 6-10A CEE

1 ABCD**G**IJKLMNO**P**Q
2 FGJKLRTVWXY
3 BF**G**HJKN**OP**RUV
4 (A 15/6-15/9) (B+G 1/5-30/9)
 (Q+S+T+U+V+Y+Z 🔑)
5 **AB**EFGIJKLMNOP**S**UVW
6 CEGH**K**(N 0,5km)ORTV

💬 Campsite is situated on wide terraces against a mountainside. The bus to Florence stops by the entrance. Beautiful swimming pool and well-maintained toilet facilities.

🚗 A1 Firenze-Roma, exit Incisa. Turn right, after about 4 km turn left. After the bridge crossing the Arno river left. Then follow the camping signs.

Firenze Pontassieve

Reggello

CC €**19** 24/3-29/6 27/8-13/10

📐 N 43°42'6'' E 11°24'19''

Vada/Livorno, I-57016 / Toscana

♿ 📶 ⚙ **iD** **3207**

🏕 Baia del Marinaio***
✉ Via dei Cavalleggeri 177
☎ FAX +39 0586-770164
📅 21/4 - 8/10
@ info@baiadelmarinaio.it

6ha 286T(40-85m²) 6A CEE

1 ABCD**G**HIJKLNOQ
2 AEFG**R**TUVWXY
3 BDJK**M**NR**W**Y
4 (B 25/4-27/9) (G 📅) IJP
   (Q+S+T+U+V+X+Y+Z 📅)
5 **A**BGIJKLMNOPUVW
6 EGJ(N 1km)ORTV

💬 A family campsite 300 metres from the sea with a sandy beach. Plenty of entertainment for children and adults. Large toilet building. Restaurant-pizzeria with large terrace.

🚗 A12, exit Rosignano Marittimo. Then take the SS1 Aurelia to Roma, exit Vada. In Vada take the direction of Mazzanta. Campsite is on the landward side of the road.

Rosignano Marittimo

CC SS1

Cecina

€ **17** 21/4-30/6 1/9-7/10   🧭 N 43°20'5'' E 10°27'41''

Vada/Livorno, I-57018 / Toscana

♿ 📶 **iD** **3208**

🏕 Campo dei Fiori**
✉ Via Cavalleggeri
☎ +39 0586-770096
FAX +39 0586-770323
📅 3/4 - 22/10
@ info@campingcampodeifiori.it

15ha 500T(60-120m²) 3-6A CEE

1 ACD**G**IJKLMO**P**RS
2 BFG**R**TVWXY
3 ABDGK**M**NRU
4 (C 1/5-30/9) KP
   (Q+S+T+U+V+W+Y+Z 📅)
5 **A**BDEFGIJKLMNOPUVXYZ
6 AEJ**K**(N 1km)ORTV

💬 A large family campsite with shaded pitches. Modern new swimming pool. Centrally located square with restaurant, pizzeria, bar and shops. Separate area for entertainment for all ages. Excellent modern toilet facilities. Plenty of opportunities for sport.

🚗 A12, exit Rosignano, then take the SS1 Aurelia in the direction of Roma, exit Vada. In Vada drive in the direction of Mazzanta (Vada-Celina-Mare). After about 1 km turn left and follow the signs.

Rosignano Marittimo

SS1

CC **Cecina**

€ **15** 3/4-23/4 25/4-27/4 2/5-31/5 4/6-30/6 3/9-21/10 14=12   🧭 N 43°20'8'' E 10°27'56''

Vada/Livorno, I-57018 / Toscana

♿ 📶 ✿ **iD** **3209**

🏕 Molino a Fuoco***
✉ Via Cavalleggeri 32
☎ +39 0586-770150
FAX +39 0586-770031
📅 20/4 - 13/10
@ info@campingmolinoafuoco.com

5ha 120T(40-75m²) 4-10A CEE

1 ABCD**G**HIJKLMNPS
2 AEFGLNRVXY
3 BHJK**M**NR**T**UVWY
4 (**B**+G+Q+S+T+U+V+Y+Z 📅)
5 **A**BEFGIJKLMNOPUZ
6 ACDEG**IJK**M(N 2km)ORTUV

💬 Lovely surroundings with various places to visit; Vada, Volterra and Cecina. A day trip to the island of Elba is worth the visit. Cyclist will love it here (bikes for hire). In the evening enjoy an excellent meal in the restaurant. Larger pitches for a surcharge. Now with new swimming pool.

🚗 A12, exit Rosignano-Marittimo then the SS1 Aurelia direction Rome, exit Vada. In Vada direction Mazzanta, the campsite is on the seaward side 2 km further on.

Rosignano Marittimo

SS1

CC **Cecina**

€ **17** 20/4-30/6 9/9-12/10   🧭 N 43°19'55'' E 10°27'37''

Vada/Livorno, I-57016 / Toscana

♿ 🛜 **iD** (3210)

🏕 Toscana Bella
📧 Loc. I. Mozzi
☎ +39 0586-770091
📠 +39 0586-770268
🔓 13/4 - 16/9
@ direzione@
 campingtoscanabella.com

6ha 100T(40-80m²) 6A CEE

1 ABCD**G**HIJKLMNOP
2 AFGLRVXY
3 BGKNU
4 (B 🔓) (G 30/5-11/9)
 (Q+S+T+U+V+X+Z 🔓)
5 **AB**GIJKMNOPUVZ
6 CDEGJ(N 0,6km)OTV

💬 'Rifugio del Mare' located 600 metres from the beach extends over a natural area of 60,000 m². It offers a new swimming pool for children, playground, bar, supermarket, bazaar and restaurant. Marked out pitches. A good base for making excursions to the art towns in Tuscany.

🚗 A12, exit Rosignano Marittimo. Then SS1 Aurelia to Roma, exit Vada. In Vada take the direction of Mazzanta. You'll reach the campsite after about 2 km. It is on the landward side.

Rosignano Marittimo

SS1

CC **Cecina**

CC € **13** 13/4-30/6 18/8-15/9

〰 N 43°19'50'' E 10°27'50''

Viareggio, I-55049 / Toscana

♿ 🛜 ✿ **iD** (3211)

🏕 La Pineta**
📧 Via dei Lecci 105
☎ 📠 +39 0584-383397
🔓 29/3 - 23/9
@ campinglapineta@interfree.it

3,2ha 85T(35-70m²) 5A CEE

1 ABCD**G**HIJKLMOPQ
2 AFGRSVXY
3 AKRU
4 (B+G 15/5-23/9) **N**
 (Q+R+T+U+X+Z 🔓)
5 **A**GIKMOPUVWZ
6 AG**K**(N 0,3km)OTV

💬 A very peaceful campsite with shaded pitches; 1300 metres from the sea with a large, free beach. 2 km from the centre of Viareggio, 3 km from Torre del Lago Puccini; 20 km from Lucca and Pisa; Florence 90 km. 1 hour free wifi with CampingCard ACSI. Free swimming pool.

🚗 A12, exit Viareggio and follow 'campings' signs towards Torre del Lago Puccini.

Lido di Camaiore

Viareggio A11

CC

A12

SS1

CC € **17** 29/3-30/6 26/8-22/9 7=6

〰 N 43°51'2'' E 10°15'56''

Viareggio, I-55049 / Toscana

♿ 🛜 **iD** (3212)

🏕 Viareggio
📧 Via Comparini 1
☎ 📠 +39 0584-391012
🔓 1/4 - 30/9
@ info@campingviareggio.it

3ha 250T(36-80m²) 4A CEE

1 ABCD**G**HIJKLMOPQ
2 BFGRSVY
3 BHJKNRU
4 (B 1/6-30/8)
 (Q+S+T+U+V+Y+Z 🔓)
5 **AB**EFG**I**JKMO**P**UWZ
6 FG**IK**(N 0,2km)ORTV

💬 The campsite is located about 1.5 km from the town. The beach is accessible from the campsite through a wood (800m distance). Hospitable and friendly atmosphere. Outstanding toilet facilities. The campsite offers many facilities such as a restaurant and a supermarket. Countless opportunities for trips out.

🚗 Take direction Torre del Lago from the centre of Viareggio and then follow the signs to the campsite.

Viareggio Massarosa

CC

A12 A11

CC € **17** 1/4-30/6 27/8-29/9 7=6

〰 N 43°51'5'' E 10°15'35''

Vignale Riotorto, I-57020 / Toscana

🔼 Campo Al Fico
✉️ Loc. Campo al Fico 15
☎️ +39 0565-21008
📠 +39 0565-21118
⏱️ 21/4 - 23/9
@ info@campingcampoalfico.com

3213

4,5ha 80**T**(42-60m²) 3A CEE

1 BC**F**HIJKLNR
2 FGLRVY
3 BJK**M**R
4 (B+G 1/6-29/9)
(Q+R+T+U+V+Y+Z 🔑)
5 **A**BGIKMOPUVZ
6 CEGJ(N 7km)OTV

💬 A family campsite with shady pitches. A 1 km cycle route takes you to the sandy beach. A square with a pool, bar and supermarket is centrally located. Simple toilet facilities. Ideally situated for a trip to Elba.

🚗 SS1 Aurelia, exit Vignale/Riotorto. On the roundabout Piombino. The campsite is located on the left hand side of the road.

Piombino   **Follonica**

ⒸⒸ € **17** 21/4-29/6 21/7-3/8 1/9-22/9

📐 N 42°58'0'' E 10°39'0''

Assisi/Perugia, I-06081 / Umbria

♿ 🛜 iD 3214

🔼 Green Village Assisi***
✉️ Via S.G. in Campiglione 110
☎️ +39 075-816816
📠 +39 075-812335
⏱️ 26/3 - 4/11
@ info@greenvillageassisi.it

3ha 95**T**(50-120m²) 6A CEE

1 ABCDGIJKLMO**P**ST
2 BLRVY
3 ABHJKLNRUV
4 (**B+G** 1/6-1/9) **K**
(Q+R+T+U+V+Y+Z 🔑)
5 **AB**CGHIJKLMNOPUVWZ
6 ACDEGIK(N 2km)OQTUV

💬 A fairly large campsite with spacious, shaded pitches. Suitable for campers who want to spend some time in Assisi. The campsite is right on the road to Assisi and has its own shuttle bus. Good restaurant. Assisi campsite is a good base for visiting other towns: Spello, Perugia, Gubbio and Lake Trasimeno.

🚗 A1/E6, take exit Perugia (SS75). After Perugia take the Ospedalicchio-Sud exit, under the motorway and right at the roundabout. Follow signs to Assisi (SS147).

SS298   SS444
SS3BIS   SS318
ⒸⒸ **Assisi**
SS147
SS75
Spello
Deruta

ⒸⒸ € **19** 26/3-30/6 1/9-3/11

📐 N 43°4'33'' E 12°34'24''

Bevagna, I-06031 / Umbria

♿ 🛜 iD 3215

🔼 Pian di Boccio***
✉️ Via Pian di Boccio 10
☎️ +39 0742-360164
📠 +39 0742-360391
⏱️ 30/3 - 30/9
@ info@piandiboccio.com

8ha 70**T** 6A CEE

1 ABCDGHIJKLMO**PQ**
2 BFJRTWXY
3 BGHJK**M**NQRU
4 (B 15/5-30/9) (G 1/7-31/8) P
(Q+R 🔑) (U+V 1/7-31/8)
(Y+Z 🔑)
5 **A**EGIJKLMNO**P**UV
6 CEGK(N 3,5km)ORV

💬 This campsite is situated on hilly grounds in a mixed forest. There are no marked out pitches, which means campers are free to chose their own space. An ideal base for visiting Umbria.

🚗 In Foligno exit Foligno Nord dir. Bevagna. Without caravan: just past Bevagna first road on the right past the bridge. With caravan straight on S316 and after 3 km turn right. Follow the signs.

SS75
Foligno
Gualdo ⒸⒸ   SS3
Cattaneo

ⒸⒸ € **17** 30/3-30/6 1/9-29/9

📐 N 42°54'44'' E 12°35'10''

Castiglione del Lago, I-06061 / Umbria

♿ 📶 **iD** **3216**

🏕 Badiaccia Camping Village****
🏠 Via Pratovecchio 1
☎ +39 075-8230103
📠 +39 075-9659019
🗓 1/4 - 30/9
@ info@badiaccia.com

5,5ha 260T(55-110m²) 4-10A CEE

1. ABCD**G**HIJKLMNOPQ
2. ADKLRSTVXY
3. ABGHJKMNQRU**V**WZ
4. (A 1/7-31/8) (B 15/5-30/9)
   (G 1/5-30/9) KP
   (Q+R+S+T+U+V+X+Y+Z 🗓)
5. **AB**EFGJKLMNOPSTUVWX
   YZ
6. ACDEGIJL(N 0,8km)OQRTV

💬 A large campsite with many shaded pitches, its own harbour, swimming pool and hydro massage baths. The campsite is located on the lake between Tuscany and Umbria. Close to the towns of Florence, Siena and Perugia.

🚗 A1/E6, via Val di Chiana SS75 exit to Castiglione del Lago exit. Then via route 71 southwards, turn off towards Borghetto.

Cortona

SS416

CC SS71
Castiglione del Lago
A1

CC € **19** 1/4-6/7 24/8-29/9 🏔 N 43°10'52'' E 12°0'59''

Castiglione del Lago, I-06061 / Umbria

♿ 📶 **3217**

🏕 Listro**
🏠 Via Lungolago
☎ 📠 +39 075-951193
🗓 1/4 - 30/9
@ listro@listro.it

1ha 100T(40-85m²) 3A CEE

1. BCD**G**HIJKLMOPQ
2. ADKLRTXY
3. A**F**HJKM**R**WZ
4. (Q+R+T+U+Z 🗓)
5. **A**CEFGHIJKLMNOPQRUV
6. CEGI**J**(N 0,8km)OTV

💬 Small, shaded and hospitable campsite right by the lake and close to the town centre. This site is part of the Trasimeno National Park.

🚗 A1/E6, exit Val di Chiana, take the Perugia SS75. Then take exit Castiglione del Lago (SS71) to the south. In Castiglione second street left. Follow the signs.

SS416

SS71 **Magione**

CC Castiglione del Lago
SS454
A1 SS599
SS326

CC € **17** 1/4-30/6 1/9-29/9 🏔 N 43°8'4'' E 12°2'39''

Costacciaro, I-06021 / Umbria

♿ 📶 **iD** **3218**

🏕 Rio Verde***
🏠 Loc. Fornace 1
☎ 📠 +39 075-9170181
🗓 29/3 - 30/9
@ campingrioverde@gmail.com

3ha 50T(50-100m²) 6A CEE

1. ABCDGHIJKLMO**P**RS
2. BRWXY
3. ABGN**O**P**R**
4. (A 🗓) (B 15/5-30/9)
   (Q+R+T+U+V+X+Z 🗓)
5. **A**GIJKMOPUV
6. EGJ(N 8km)T

💬 Peaceful and quiet campsite with a beautiful location in a green valley. Free pitches with plenty of shade. Ideal base for delta flying and mountain biking. A well-maintained, hospitable campsite with a familial atmosphere. Many options for outdoor sports in Park Monte Cucco.

🚗 SS3 Flaminia, from Fano or Rome. 2 km from the SS3 in Costacciaro. Follow the signs at km-marker 206,5 on the Via Flaminia SS3 (Fano-Folligno). The campsite is located on a slightly steep winding road.

Sassoferrato

SS452

Gubbio **CC**

SS298 SS219 SS76
SS3

CC € **17** 29/3-14/7 1/9-29/9 🏔 N 43°21'2'' E 12°41'5''

Narni/Borgheria, I-05035 / Umbria ♿ 📶 **3219**

🔼 Monti del Sole**
🏠 Strada di Borgaria 22
☎ 📠 +39 0744-796336
🔑 29/3 - 8/9
@ info@campingmontidelsole.it

8ha 80T(45-80m²) 6A CEE

1 CFHIJKLMOPRS
2 BGJLRTVWXY
3 ABGHMNR
4 (B+G 31/5-31/8) (Q 🔑)
   (U+V+X+Z 1/6-8/9)
5 AGIJKLMNOPUVZ
6 ACEGJ(N 3km)R

💬 A peaceful, friendly family campsite with spacious shaded touring pitches and very well maintained sanitary facilities. Swimming pools, tennis, bar, restaurant, little stone cottages. An ideal base for excursions to Umbria and Lazio. Rome can be reached by train in 40 minutes.

🚗 A1 between Siena and Rome. Take Magliano Sabina exit towards Narni. SS3 km 80.800. From the SS3/E45 Perugia-Cesena, take Narni/Scalo exit. Direction Narni, then follow camping signs.

Terni
Amelia
Narni
SS675
Orte
A1
SS3
CC

CC € **17** 29/3-14/7 1/9-7/9 ⛰ N 42°29'5'' E 12°30'55''

Passignano sul Trasimeno, I-06065 / Umbria ♿ 📶 iD **3220**

🔼 Camping Trasimeno
🏠 Via Tancredo Marchini
☎ +39 075-828321
🔑 1/5 - 1/10
@ info@camping-trasimeno.it

3ha 100T(30-70m²) 6-10A CEE

1 ABCDGHIJKLMOPRS
2 ADFKLMRVWX
3 JMNWZ
4 (B+G 🔑) K
   (Q+R+U+V+X+Z 🔑)
5 ABCFGHIJKLMNOPQRSU
   WXYZ
6 AEGJKSV

💬 Campsite located directly on the lake with an exotic beach and beautiful view. All facilities were renovated in 2016, every comfort has been taken care of.

🚗 A1/E6, exit Val di Chiana. Direction Perugia SS75. Exit Passignano Est. Then left and after 500m under railway, immediate left.

SS416
Magione
Corciano
CC
Castiglione del Lago
SS71
SS599

CC € **19** 1/5-8/7 26/8-30/9 ⛰ N 43°10'55'' E 12°9'56''

Passignano sul Trasimeno, I-06065 / Umbria ♿ 📶 iD **3221**

🔼 Kursaal***
🏠 Viale Europa 24
☎ +39 075-828085
🔑 24/3 - 4/11
@ info@campingkursaal.it

2,5ha 60T(40-70m²) 6A CEE

1 ABCDGHIJKLMNOPRS
2 ADGKLMNRSVY
3 AGHJKNRWZ
4 (B+G 1/5-15/10) JK(Q
   (R 10/5-30/9) (U+Y+Z 🔑)
5 ABFGIJKLMNOPUW
6 ACEGIKL(N 0,8km)RTV

💬 A small campsite by the lake set in the exotic gardens of a stylish villa hotel with an excellent restaurant. The fact that camping guests may use the same outdoor facilities as the hotel guests is a sign of the kind-heartedness of the owners.

🚗 A1/E6, exit Val di Chiana, SS75 direction Perugia. Then exit Passignano Est. Drive in the direction of Passignano. The campsite is located on the left after the tracks.

Cortona
SS416
CC
SS71
Castiglione del Lago
SS599

CC € **19** 24/3-9/7 27/8-3/11 ⛰ N 43°11'2'' E 12°9'2''

Passignano sul Trasimeno, I-06065 / Umbria

♻ 📶 iD **3222**

🔺 La Spiaggia★★★
📧 Via Europa 22
☎ +39 075-827246
📠 +39 075-827276
🔓 29/3 - 16/10
@ info@campinglaspiaggia.it

1,8ha 50T(50-100m²) 10A CEE

1 ABCD**G**IJKLMO**P**RS
2 ADGKLMNRWXY
3 ABGHJKRWZ
4 (A 1/4-15/9) (B 20/5-16/9)
(Q+R+T+U+V+X+Y+Z 🔓)
5 **AB**EFGIJKLMNOPU
6 AEGK(N 0,7km)OTUV

💬 A quiet lakeside campsite with its own beach. Large, often shaded pitches, a number with a view of the lake. Swimming pool, supermarket, bar and restaurant. Completely renovated toilet facilities (2016) with free showers (also for dogs), facilities for the disabled and a baby room. Free wifi, new playground and dog beach.

🚗 A1/E6, Val di Chiana exit, direction Perugia SS75. Exit Passignano Est. Keep right direction Passignano. Second campsite over the railway line.

Cortona

SS416

CC

SS71

Castiglione del Lago

SS599

CC € **19** 29/3-8/7 27/8-15/10

📡 N 43°11'2'' E 12°9'3''

Piediluco, I-05100 / Umbria

♻ 📶 iD **3223**

🔺 Lago di Piediluco★★
📧 Via dell'Ara Marina 2
☎ +39 328-1099396
🔓 1/3 - 4/11
@ campinglagodipiediluco@
gmail.com

3,3ha 150T(60-80m²) 6A CEE

1 ABC**G**IJKLMNOPQ
2 DGKLMRVXY
3 BGH**M**NRVWZ
4 (**C** 10/6-31/8) (Q 1/4-30/9)
(R+V 1/6-31/8) (Z 1/4-30/9)
5 GIJKLMOPUVZ
6 CEGK(N 0,6km)OTV

💬 This campsite has everything you need for a successful holiday. Located on the shores of Lake Piediluco. Quiet pitches among greenery. Extensive sports facilities including an Olympic size swimming pool. An ideal location for visiting Rome and Assisi.

🚗 A1 exit Orte direction Terni. Exit Terni Est, follow dir. Rieti. After 2 tunnels exit Marmore. In Marmore dir. Piediluco. In Piediluco follow ('piscina') signs.

Ferentillo

Terni SS3

SS209

CC

Stroncone

CC € **15** 1/3-7/7 25/8-3/11

📡 N 42°32'6'' E 12°46'20''

Preci, I-06047 / Umbria

♻ ♿ 📶 iD **3224**

🔺 Il Collaccio★★★★
📧 Fraz. Castelvecchio
☎ +39 0743-939084
📠 +39 0743-939094
🔓 1/4 - 30/9
@ info@ilcollaccio.com

10ha 120T(25-80m²) 6A CEE

1 ACDFIJKL**P**Q
2 JKLRTVXY
3 BGK**M**NRU
4 (**A** 1/6-15/9)
(B+G 20/5-20/9)
(Q+S+U+V+Y+Z 🔓)
5 **A**EGIJKMNOPUV
6 ACEG**I**K(N 2km)OTV

💬 A beautifully situated terraced campsite with fine panoramic views of the Umbrian hills. The site makes a really well-maintained impression. The renewed toilet facilities and the shop with its own bread oven will make your stay complete.

🚗 SS3 from Foligno to Spoleto. Turn left towards Norcia. Then S209 direction Visso. Before Preci exit left towards Castelvecchio. Then follow camping signs. (Do not use SatNav!)

CC

SS209

Cerreto di Spoleto **Norcia**

SS320

CC € **17** 1/4-14/7 1/9-29/9

📡 N 42°53'18'' E 13°0'53''

Tuoro sul Trasimeno, I-06069 / Umbria

⛑ 📶 ❀ **iD** **3225**

🏕 Village Punta Navaccia***
✉ Via Navaccia 4
☎ +39 075-826357
📠 +39 075-8258147
🔑 17/3 - 21/10
@ info@puntanavaccia.it

6,5ha 120T(75-100m²) 6A CEE

1 ABCDGIJKLMO**P**Q
2 ADFKRUVY
3 B**F**HJKMNRUVWZ
4 (A 1/7-30/8) (B+G 1/5-30/9)
KP(Q+R+T+U+V+Y+Z 🔑)
5 **AB**EFGIJKLMNOPUWXZ
6 ACDEGK(N 1km)ORTVX

💬 A large, friendly campsite by the lake. Also suitable for young children and teenagers. Shaded pitches by Lake Trasimeno with panoramic views. Touring pitches by a private harbour with free boat trips. Sandy beach, bars and adult disco close by.

🚗 A1/E6, exit Val di Chiana. Take the SS75 to Perugia. Exit Tuoro, then left under the bridge. At the end of the road on the shore of the lake you will find the campsite.

Cortona
SS416
CC
SS71
Castiglione del Lago

CC € ⑲ 17/3-30/6 1/9-20/10   🧭 N 43°11'30'' E 12°4'35''

Cupra Marittima, I-63012 / Marche

⛑ 📶 **iD** **3226**

🏕 Calypso***
✉ Contrada Boccabianca 7
☎ +39 0735-778686
📠 +39 0735-778106
🔑 1/4 - 30/9
@ info@campingcalypso.it

2,6ha 220T(50-80m²) 6A CEE

1 ACDFHIJKLQ
2 AEFGRVXY
3 ABKMNRUWY
4 (B 15/5-30/9) J(Q 🔑)
(S+T+U+V+W+Y 5/5-15/9)
(Z 🔑)
5 **AB**GIJKLMNOPUV
6 GHKLM(N 1km)ORSTV

💬 Well-maintained, large campsite. Private beach, swimming pool and sports facilities.

🚗 From the north, the campsite is accessible via the A14, exit Pedaso. A further 6 km southwards. Follow camping signs. From the south via the A14 exit Grottammare; direction Ancona; 5 km northwards then follow signs.

CC
A14
SS16
San Benedetto del Tronto

CC € ⑰ 1/4-10/6 28/8-29/9   🧭 N 43°2'39'' E 13°51'12''

Fiorenzuola di Focara/Pesaro, I-61121 / Marche

📶 **iD** **3227**

🏕 Panorama***
✉ Strada Panoramica
☎ +39 0721-208145
📠 +39 0721-209799
🔑 15/4 - 30/9
@ info@campingpanorama.it

2,5ha 140T(45-100m²) 6A CEE

1 ABCD**F**IJKLMNOPRS
2 EFJRUVXY
3 ABF**H**JNRUWY
4 (B 20/5-14/9) (G 20/5-13/9)
(Q+S+T+U+V+X+Z 🔑)
5 **A**GIJKMNOPUVZ
6 CEGK(N 3km)OQRTV

💬 Camping Panorama is located in the region of La Marche in the green heart of the San Bartolo Nature Park, 100m above sea level on the scenic Strada Panoramica route. An ideal place for rest and recreation. The campsite includes a swimming pool, bar, pizzeria and free wifi. Activities in the area include golf, fishing and diving. Nearest beach 10 to 15 minutes by car.

🚗 A14 exit Pesaro. SS16 direction Gabicce Mare. In Cattabrighe follow camping signs.

Cattolica
SS16 CC **Pesaro**
A14

CC € ⑲ 15/4-29/6 1/9-29/9   🧭 N 43°56'30'' E 12°50'45''

Monteciccardo, I-61020 / Marche

🚶 ♿ 📶 **iD** (3228)

🏕 Podere Sei Poorte
✉ Via Petricci 14
☎ +39 333-1406043
📠 +39 0721-910286
🔓 20/4 - 29/9
@ info@podereseipoorte.it

6ha 110T(100-200m²) 6-10A CEE

1 ACD**G**IJKLMNOPQ
2 CIJKLRTVWX
3 AGHJNRU
4 (B+Q+R+Y+Z 🔓)
5 **AB**CGHIJKLMNOPRUVWXZ
6 ACEGHJL(N 7km)OV

💬 Picturesque area. Swimming pool with panoramic views, hospitable atmosphere, spacious pitches. Authentic farm, Italian cuisine, communal brunch on Sundays. Charming olive/wine tastings. Dutch couple.

🚗 A14, exit Pesaro/Urbino towards Urbino, then S. Angelo in Lizzola, then follow SP26 (brown signs Camping P6P). Located between Monteciccardo and Mombaroccio in Villa Ugolini, take Via Petricci, after 1.4 km P6P.

Tavullia • · A14 · SS16
Sant'Angelo In Lizzola
CC
SS73BIS

CC € **19** 20/4-6/7 24/8-28/9 🛰 N 43°48'4'' E 12°49'18''

Numana, I-60026 / Marche

♿ 📶 (3229)

🏕 Camping Village Numana Blu****
✉ Via Costaverde 37
☎ +39 071-7390993
📠 +39 071-7391793
🔓 19/4 - 30/9
@ info@numanablu.it

8,6ha 330T(60-80m²) 6A CEE

1 BCD**G**HIJKLOPQ
2 AEFGLRTVXY
3 B**F**JK**M**NOPRUVWY
4 (A 1/6-14/9) (B+G 20/5-20/9) KP(Q+S+T+U+V+W+Y+Z 🔓)
5 **AB**CEFGHIJKLMNOPRUVWZ
6 ACDEGHK(N 2km)OQRTUV

💬 Palm trees and beautiful flowers welcome you to this well-maintained 4-star campsite. At walking distance there is a private beach (no trains nearby), close to Sirolo, Connero nature reserve, the Loreto pilgrimage site, and much more culture and countryside. Cycling options.

🚗 A14, in the direction of Loreto, and then drive in the direction of Porto Recanati. When the coastal road is in sight drive in the direction of Sirolo/Numana. Turn left at the sign 'Numana Blu'.

Osimo **CC**
° Castelfidardo
A14
SS16

CC € **19** 19/4-16/6 1/9-29/9 🛰 N 43°28'35'' E 13°38'4''

Porto Recanati, I-62017 / Marche

⊗ ♿ 📶 **iD** (3230)

🏕 Bellamare***
✉ Lungomare Scarfiotti 13
☎ +39 071-976628
📠 +39 071-977586
🔓 29/3 - 7/10
@ info@bellamare.it

5ha 360T(30-60m²) 6A CEE

1 ACDEHIJKLMOPQ
2 AEFGNRVWX
3 ABF**G**JKLN**O**RUWY
4 (B+G 1/5-20/9) (Q+R 🔓) (T 1/5-30/9) (U 🔓) (V+Y 1/5-30/9) (Z 🔓)
5 **AB**FGIJKMOP**U**V
6 ABCDEG**K**(N 3km)OTVX

💬 Well-maintained campsite with pool (open depending on weather), located directly on beach. Comfortable amenities. Lovely view of 'Rivièra de Conero', close to Ancona and many villages offering culture and history. Lovely interior with villages, hills and nature.

🚗 A14. take exit Porto Recanati. After the toll booth turn directly right at the sign 'P.Rec'. Turn left (centre). Follow Numana. Follow the road over the hill along the beach (about 6 km in total).

Osimo **CC**
° Castelfidardo
A14
SS16

CC € **17** 29/3-6/7 25/8-6/10 🛰 N 43°28'17'' E 13°38'29''

Porto Recanati, I-62017 / Marche

♿ 🛜 **iD** 3231

▲ La Medusa***
✉ Lungomare Scarfiotti
☎ +39 071-7500725
📠 +39 071-7500801
🕙 27/4 - 23/9
@ info@campinglamedusa.it

5,5ha 100T(25-36m²) 5A CEE

1 ACD**G**HIJKLMNP
2 AEFNRSTVWXY
3 B**F**GHJKLRUWY
4 (**A** 10/6-7/9) (B 1/6-7/9)
(Q+R+T+U+V 🔑)
(W 15/6-15/9) (Y 🔑)
5 **A**FGIJKLMNOPUVZ
6 GJ(N 2km)OQRTUV

💬 Campsite with swimming pool (1/6 - 7/9) located on a boulevard. Facilities for dogs such as a beach. Close to Ancona and many villages with culture and history. A beautiful interior with villages, hills and plenty of countryside to enjoy.

🚗 A14, take exit Porto Recanati. After toll booth right directly after sign 'P.Rec.'. Left (centre). Follow Numana. Follow road over hill along beach (5 km in total).

CC € **17** 27/4-10/6 1/9-22/9

🧭 N 43°27'59'' E 13°38'44''

Sarnano, I-62028 / Marche

♿ 🛜 **iD** 3232

▲ Quattro Stagioni***
✉ Contrada Brilli
☎ +39 0733-651147
📠 +39 0733-651104
🕙 1/1 - 31/12
@ quattrostagioni@camping.it

4,5ha 50T(80-100m²) 6A CEE

1 ACDFHIJKLPQ
2 CGIJKLRVXY
3 BG**J**M**NO**RU
4 (B+G 1/6-10/9)
(Q+R 1/7-31/8)
(T+U+V+Y+Z 1/6-30/9)
5 **A**EGIJKLMNOPUV
6 ACEGI**J**(N 3km)OTV

💬 A terraced campsite near the Sibillini National Park. Lovely views of the mountains. Spacious pitches with plenty of shade. A perfect spot for lovers of peace and the countryside. This campsite is ideal for people of a sportive nature.

🚗 A14, exit Civitanova Marche. Motorway to Macerata as far as Sarnano exit. In Sarnano turn right at square (follow main road). Campsite a few km outside Sarnano.

Sant'Angelo In Pontano
SS78

CC € **17** 1/5-10/7 1/9-30/9

🧭 N 43°1'4'' E 13°16'55''

Stacciola/San Costanzo, I-61039 / Marche

🛜 3233

▲ Camping Village Mar y Sierra***
✉ Strada San Gervasio, 3
☎ 📠 +39 0721-930044
🕙 1/5 - 17/9
@ info@marysierra.it

4ha 58T(45-60m²) 6A CEE

1 BCDFIJKLPRS
2 FJKLRTUWXY
3 ABMNRU
4 (B+G 1/6-17/9) P
(Q+R+U+V+Y+Z 🔑)
5 **A**GIJKLMNOPUVXYZ
6 EGJ(N 3km)ORTV

💬 Friendly hospitable terraced campsite with swimming pool and restaurant. Beautifully situated with panoramic views. Renewed toilet block. Asphalted road to the terraces. Ideal stop to/from Greece. Ferry at Ancona 45 min drive.

🚗 Leave A14 from Rimini-Ancona at Marotta Mondolfo. At the exit turn right. Follow this route (SS424) for about 4 km. In Ponte Rio turn right towards Stacciola (SP154). The campsite is at the top of the hill. Follow Mar y Sierra signs.

CC € **19** 1/5-8/7 27/8-16/9

🧭 N 43°44'44'' E 13°4'56''

Bolsena, I-01023 / Lazio

♿ 📶 **3234**

🔺 BLU International Camping***
📧 Via Cassia km 111,650
☎ 📠 +39 0761-798855
📅 20/4 - 5/10
@ info@blucamping.it

3ha 230T(50-70m²) 8A CEE

1 BCD**G**IJKLMNOPQ
2 ADKLRTVXY
3 ARWZ
4 (B 19/5-15/9) (Q 📅)
(S 26/5-28/9)
(U+V+Y+Z 20/4-28/9)
5 **AB**GIJKMOPUZ
6 CEG**K**(N 1,5km)OTV

💬 All pitches are clearly marked-out and shaded. The campsite is located directly on the lake and has a neat and excellent restaurant.

🚗 From A1/E6 via SS71 to Bolsena. In the centre at the traffic lights direction Montefiascone/Viterbo. The campsite is located 1.4 km past Bolsena alongside the lake.

Orvieto
SS74 | SS71
SS489
SS2
Montefiascone

CC € **17** 20/4-30/6 1/9-4/10

📍 N 42°37'53'' E 11°59'41''

Bolsena, I-01023 / Lazio

♿ 📶 **3235**

🔺 Lido Camping Village****
📧 Via Cassia km 111
☎ +39 0761-799258
📠 +39 0761-796105
📅 19/4 - 30/9
@ info@lidocampingvillage.it

10ha 600T(49-70m²) 3A CEE

1 CD**F**HIJKLMNOPQ
2 ADGKLRSVXY
3 AGHJK**M**NRWZ
4 (**B**+**G** 15/6-31/8)
(Q+S+T+U+V+W+Z 📅)
5 **AB**EFGIJ**K**MNO**P**SU
6 CFG**K**(N 2km)ORTV

💬 An extensive campsite with shaded pitches right by Lake Bolsena. Every amenity and excellent toilet facilities.

🚗 From the A1/E6 via route SS71 (past Orvieto) to Bolsena. In the centre, at the traffic lights, turn in the direction of Montefiasone/Viterbo. The campsite is located at the lake, 1.5 km past Bolsena.

Orvieto
SS74 | SS71
SS2
SS489
CC
Montefiascone

CC € **17** 19/4-30/6 1/9-29/9

📍 N 42°37'39'' E 11°59'39''

Bolsena, I-01023 / Lazio

♿ 📶 **3236**

🔺 Val di Sole****
📧 Via Cassia km 117,8
☎ +39 334-9952575
📅 1/5 - 30/9
@ info@campingvaldisole.it

10ha 350T(50-85m²) 6A CEE

1 CD**F**HIJKLMOPQ
2 ADGKRVXY
3 BHNRUWZ
4 (Q+S+T+V+X+Y+Z 📅)
5 **A**GIKMNOPUVW
6 EG**K**(N 4km)TUV

💬 Directly on Bolsena Lake in a 10 hectare forest. Campsite offers all facilities for an untroubled holiday.

🚗 A1/E6, exit Orvieto. Then via SS71 to Bolsena. In Bolsena turn right to S. Lorenzo (Via Cassia Rd). Campsite 5 km on the left.

Acquapendente
Castel Giorgio
SS74 | CC | SS71
SS312

CC € **17** 1/5-30/6 3/9-29/9

📍 N 42°39'13'' E 11°55'52''

Bracciano, I-00062 / Lazio

3237

🔺 Porticciolo
📧 Via Porticciolo 2
☎ +39 06-99803060
FAX +39 06-97240136
🔓 1/4 - 30/9
@ info@porticciolo.it

3,3ha 170T(40-80m²) 4-6A CEE

1 ABCD**F**IJKLMNOPRS
2 ABDGKLMORVY
3 AKNRWZ
4 (Q+R+T+U+V+X+Z 🔓)
5 **A**EFG**IJKL**MNOP**U**VZ
6 ACEG**I**K(N 2km)ORTUVW

💬 Enjoy the lake and Rome, good food and a relaxed atmosphere on the terrace, sailing and excursions, also by bike and ferry. Private bus to train station; maps and tickets at the reception. Free wifi on 80% of the site.

🚗 SS2 Viterbo-Roma, at Sutri right towards Trevignano. At lake dir. Bracciano and at 2nd crossing dir. Anguillara. See campsite signs. Or A1 exit Maglino towards Nepi, SS2 towards Sutri. Before Sutri to lake follow Bracciano and 1st crossing dir. Anguillar.

Anguillara Sabazia
Bracciano
SS493

CC € **17** 1/4-30/6 1/9-29/9

N 42°6'21'' E 12°11'11''

Bracciano, I-00062 / Lazio

3238

🔺 Roma Flash***
📧 Via Settevene Palo km 19,800
☎ FAX +39 06-99805458
🔓 1/4 - 30/9
@ info@romaflash.it

7ha 175T(50-120m²) 6A CEE

1 ABCD**G**HIJKLMNO**P**Q
2 ABDGKLMRVWXY
3 BG**KM**NRWZ
4 (B+G 1/6-31/8) (Q+R 🔓)
   (T 15/4-20/9) (U+V+X 🔓)
   (Z 15/4-20/9)
5 **AB**EFG**IJ**KLNPUVX
6 ACEGHJ(N 4km)RTUVW

💬 The campsite is located 35 km from Rome and has a good restaurant/pizzeria. The bus to Bracciano station stops at the campsite 12 times a day. Excursion to Pompeii once a week on Sunday. Wifi is available for a payment and covers the entire site.

🚗 SS2 Viterbo-Roma, head right towards Trevignano at Sutri. On reaching the shore of the lake take direction Bracciano, campsite clearly signposted on the left.

SS2
SS493
CC
Bracciano
Anguillara Sabazia

CC € **15** 1/4-7/7 25/8-29/9

N 42°7'48'' E 12°10'25''

Fiano Romano/Roma, I-00065 / Lazio

3239

🔺 I Pini Family Park****
📧 Viale delle Sassete 28
☎ +39 0765-453349
FAX +39 0765-1890941
🔓 30/3 - 30/9
@ ipini@ecvacanze.it

5ha 30T(60-90m²) 6-10A CEE

1 ABCD**F**IJKLMOPQ
2 B**F**ILRVWXY
3 BC**J**K**M**NQRU
4 (B 15/4-30/9) (G 🔓) M
   (Q+S+T+U+V+Y+Z 🔓)
5 **AB**EFG**IJ**KLMNOPUWXZ
6 CEGH**I**JLM(N 2,5km)ORTUV
   WX

💬 A rural campsite north of Rome. Campsite is very friendly and suitable for families with young children. Good restaurant. Dietary considerations are taken into account.

🚗 A1 Roma Nord. After the toll booth exit Roma Nord-Fiano Romano. After the Holiday Inn at roundabout right. Drive 2 kilometres, 2nd roundabout straight on to crossing, then turn left. The campsite is signposted after 2 km.

Fiano Romano
CC
SS3
SS4
A1
A1DIR
Monterotondo

CC € **17** 30/3-30/6 25/8-29/9

N 42°9'20'' E 12°34'23''

Marina di Montalto di Castro, I-01014 / Lazio

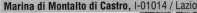

⊗ ♿ **3240**

🏕 Pionier Etrusco***
📧 Via Vulsinia 2
☎ +39 0766-802807
📠 +39 0766-801214
⚙ 24/3 - 30/9
@ info@campingpe.it

6,5ha 250T(50-100m²) 3A CEE

1 BCDEHIJKLMNO**P**
2 ABEGSTY
3 BG**M**RWY
4 (A 1/7-30/8) (B 1/6-30/9)
(Q+R+T+U+V+W+X+Z 🚗)
5 **A**GIJKMNOPRUV
6 EG(N 0,1km)TV

💬 This shaded campsite located by the Tyrrhenean Sea is an ideal base for visiting the countless historical and cultural sites in the area.

🚗 A1, exit Firenze, then SS1 direction Grosseto/Rome. Turn right at the 108 km-marker and follow the campsite signs.

SS312
Montalto di Castro
CC
SS1

CC € **17** 24/3-30/6 26/8-29/9 | 🌐 N 42°19'38'' E 11°34'54''

Pescia Romana, I-01010 / Lazio

♿ 📶 **3241**

🏕 Club degli Amici**
📧 Loc. Cavallaro
☎ +39 0766-830250
📠 +39 0766-831749
⚙ 20/4 - 16/9
@ info@
clubdegliamicicampingvillage.com

4ha 175T(20-56m²) 6A CEE

1 BCDGHIJKLMNOS
2 AELRSVWXY
3 ABM**N**O**R**WY
4 (A 1/6-31/8)
(Q+S+T+U+V+Y+Z 🚗)
5 **A**GIKMP**S**UVZ
6 DEG**J**(N 5km)ORT

NEW

💬 This is a fairly quiet, shaded and secluded campsite a short distance from the sea. This campsite is recommended for water sports enthusiasts.

🚗 SS1 'Via Aurelia' Grosseto-Roma. Exit Pescia Romana at 120 km marker. Follow camping signs in centre of village.

CC
Montalto di Castro
SS1

CC € **15** 20/4-15/6 1/9-15/9 | 🌐 N 42°22'3'' E 11°29'18''

Roma, I-00125 / Lazio

👫 ♿ 📶 **iD** **3242**

🏕 Camping Village Fabulous
📧 Via di Malafede 205
☎ +39 06-5259354
📠 +39 06-25496193
⚙ 31/3 - 28/10
@ fabulous@ecvacanze.it

30ha 70T(< 100m²) 6A CEE

1 ABCD**G**IJKLMOP**Q**
2 BFGKLSTUVY
3 BG**M**N**Q**RU**V**
4 (B 1/5-30/9) (G 28/4-30/9) K
M(Q 14/4-31/10)
(U 1/4-31/10) (V 🚗)
(Y 1/4-31/10) (Z 🚗)
5 **AB**EFGIJKLMNOPU
6 CEGH**I**J**M**(N 3km)OTUV

💬 Camping Fabulous is located in a 30 hectare pine forest between Rome and Lido di Ostia. It has every comfort and large swimming pools. There is an aqua park. It has a disco for teenagers and an inline skate track. A good, friendly restaurant. Excursions are organised regularly.

🚗 Follow direction Aeroporto Fiumicino on the G.R.A. ring road. Take exit 27 via Colombo towards Ostia. Turn right at the traffic lights by 18 km marker. Campsite on the right.

A12 A91
A90
Fiumicino CC
Casal
Palocco

CC € **17** 31/3-30/6 25/8-27/10 | 🌐 N 41°46'38'' E 12°23'46''

Roma, I-00189 / Lazio

♿ 🛜 **iD** (3243)

🏕 Flaminio Village Camping & Bungalow Park★★★★
📧 Via Flaminia Nuova, 821
☎ +39 06-3332604
📠 +39 06-3330653
🅾 1/1 - 31/12
@ info@villageflaminio.com

8,6ha 260T 6A CEE

1 ABCD**G**IJKLMO**PQ**
2 FGIJLRTY
3 A**F**HJK
4 (B 15/5-30/8)
(Q+R+T+V+Y+Z 🔌)
5 **AB**DEFGIJK**L**MNOPUW
6 CEGIJ(N 0,3km)ORTUVW

💬 Well-shaded, numbered or free choice pitches, this site is perfect for visiting Rome. Bus stop outside the entrance and metro station just across the road. Good restaurant. An unusual feature is the classical music in the toilet blocks. Wifi free. Discount 14 days = 11 days from 1/1 - 15/3.

🚗 On G.R.A. (Rome ring road) exit 6 Via Flaminia, and towards Flaminio/Centro. At fork in road: left towards Flaminio. Take note: campsite entrance is immediately on right.

| SS3 | SS4 |
| A1DIR |
| SS2 |
| A90 |
CC
Città del Vaticano **Roma**

CC € **19** 8/1-28/3 2/4-26/4 2/5-31/5 4/6-30/6 18/8-30/8 23/9-31/10

📍 N 41°57'23'' E 12°28'56''

Roma, I-00123 / Lazio

🛜 ✿ **iD** (3244)

🏕 Happy Village & Camping★★★
📧 Via del Prato della Corte 1915
☎ +39 06-33626401
📠 +39 06-33613800
🅾 1/3 - 18/12, 27/12 - 31/12
@ info@happycamping.net

4ha 220T(30-75m²) 6A CEE

1 ABCD**G**IJKLMO**PQ**
2 FGIJKLRTVY
3 A
4 (B+G 15/5-30/9)
(Q+R+T+U+V)
(Y 1/3-2/11) (Z 🔌)
5 **AB**DEFGIJKLMNOPU
6 CEG**K**(N 3km)RTUV

💬 Ideal campsite for a visit to Rome. Free bus to Prima Porta metro station from where you can be in the centre of Rome in 20 minutes. Well laid-out campsite with good toilet facilities (plenty of hot water). 2 fantastic swimming pools, new restaurant and an excellent, inexpensive pizzeria. Wifi free for first half hour.

🚗 GRA (Rome Ring Road), exit Cassia Veientana/Viterbo. Then 1st exit, 10 m. on the right, then left uphill. Look out for signs; it is well indicated.

| SS3 |
| SS493 | SS2BIS | A1DIR |
| SS2 | SS4 |
CC
Città del Vaticano **Roma**

CC € **17** 1/3-30/6 20/8-17/12

📍 N 42°0'2'' E 12°27'12''

Roma, I-00165 / Lazio

♿ 🛜 ✿ (3245)

🏕 Real Village Roma
📧 Via Licio Giorgieri, 50
☎ +39 06-66411585
📠 +39 06-66411580
🅾 1/1 - 31/12
@ realbooking1@gmail.com

40T 3A

1 BCFIJKLOPR
2 BFGITWXY
3 **F**MV
4 (C 1/6-30/9) (F 🔌)
(**G** 1/6-30/9) KLN**P**
(Q+U+V+Y+Z 🔌)
5 **A**BEGIJKLMNOPSUWXYZ
6 DEGH**J**(N 0,3km)ORTV

💬 Only 1 metro stop from the Vatican, Real Village Roma is the ideal campsite for guests who wish to enjoy some sports and relaxation after a day of visiting Rome. The swimming pool is free, but there is a charge for the wellness facilities.

🚗 From A1 motorway exit Roma Nord continue towards Civitavecchia. From G.R.A. follow centre Vatican City, then signs to Real Sporting Village after 500 m.

| A90 |
CC **Roma**
| A12 |
| A91 |

CC € **19** 3/1-14/7 1/9-22/12

📍 N 41°53'7'' E 12°23'15''

Roma, I-00132 / Lazio

- ▲ Roma Capitol****
- 🏠 Via di Castelfusano 195
- ☎ +39 0620190700
- 🗓 22/3 - 5/11
- @ info@romacapitol.com

27ha 700T(50-100m²) 16A

1. ABCD**G**IJKLMOPR
2. ABLRSXY
3. AB**JM**NQ
4. (C+H 1/4-15/10) KP
   (Q+R+T+U+W+X+Z 🔒)
5. **AB**DEFGIJKLMNOPU
6. AEGJL(N 1km)STU

💬 Large, brand-new 27-hectare four-star campsite. Located close to Rome and the 'Lido di Ostia' coast, which makes it suitable for both cultural and beach outings. Campsite is located in a protected nature reserve.

ⒸⒸ € **19** 22/3-13/7 3/9-4/11   🏕 N 41°44'28'' E 12°18'50''

Roma, I-00189 / Lazio

ⓘⒹ 3247

- ▲ Seven Hills Village
- 🏠 Via Vittorio Trucchi 10
- ☎ +39 06-30362751
- 🗓 1/3 - 31/10
- @ sevenhillscamping@gmail.com

NEW

41ha 70T CEE

1. BCGIJLNOP
2. BFUY
3. RV
4. (**B** 1/5-30/9) QSTVXYZ
5. **AB**GJKLMNOPUXYZ
6. A

💬 Instead of camping in a city like Rome, stay in a beautifully landscaped sub-tropical garden. Hot water available all day. Camping bus to La Giustiniana metro station. In 'Parco di Veio' you're in the middle of the countryside.

🚗 The Seven Hills campsite is signposted on the G.R.A. (Rome ring road), exit 3 via Cassia; direction Bracciano-Viterbo. Look for the signs!

ⒸⒸ € **17** 1/3-30/6 25/8-30/10 7=6, 14=11   🏕 N 41°59'51'' E 12°25'25''

Roma, I-00188 / Lazio

ⓘⒹ 3248

- ▲ Tiber Camping Village***
- 🏠 Via Tiberina km 156
- ☎ +39 06-33610733
- 📠 +39 06-33612314
- 🗓 14/4 - 31/10
- @ campingtiber@ecvacanze.it

6ha 200T 6A CEE

1. ABCD**G**IJKLMOQ
2. CFGRTXY
3. AR
4. (B 1/5-30/9)
   (Q+R+T+U+V+Y+Z 🔒)
5. **AB**EFGIJKLMNOPUWZ
6. CEGH**I**J(N 1,5km)RTU

💬 Tiber campsite is situated on the River Tiber and offers shade and rest. The shuttle bus will take you to Prima Porta station for one euro every half hour. Tiber campsite offers a swimming pool, wifi, bar, a restaurant and a shop. The site also has relatively new toilet facilities. New: Tiber dog park.

🚗 On the G.R.A. (Rome ring road) exit 6, direction Flaminia-Prima Porta, after 2 km turn right on the Via Tiberina. Campsite clearly signposted.

ⒸⒸ € **17** 14/4-7/7 25/8-30/10   🏕 N 42°0'36'' E 12°30'13''

Tarquinia, I-01016 / Lazio

⊞ Europing 2000 srl****
✉ Via Aurelia km 102
☎ +39 0766-814010
FAX +39 0766-814075
⌚ 28/4 - 16/9
@ europing@europing.it

25ha 700T(60-90m²) 3A CEE

1 BCDEHIJKLMNOPQ
2 AELRSVXY
3 BKMNORUVWY
4 (B 31/5-15/9) (G 15/5-15/9)
　　(Q+S+T+U+V+W+X+Y+Z ⌂)
5 AGIKMOPUVWXY
6 CEGK(N 5km)OPRTV

💬 An extended campsite located in pine woods. The private beach is 200 metres from the site. Various Etruscan archaeological sites in the immediate vicinity.

🚗 SS1 'Via Aurelia' Grosseto-Roma. At the 102 km-marker turn right exit Riva dei Tarquini. Immediately after the railway bridge turn right. Follow the camping signs.

Montalto di Castro

CC €**17** 28/4-6/7 24/8-15/9　　　🧭 N 42°17'53'' E 11°38'12''

Trevignano Romano, I-00069 / Lazio

⊞ Camping Internazionale
　Lago di Bracciano***
✉ Via Settevene Palo km 7.400
☎ +39 06-9985032
FAX +39 06-99826770
⌚ 1/4 - 30/9
@ camping.village@gmail.com

2ha 100T(60-80m²) 4A CEE

1 ABCDGHIJKLMOPRS
2 ADGKLRVXY
3 ABHJKNRUWZ
4 (B+G 1/6-31/8)
　　(Q+R+U+V+X+Z ⌂)
5 ABCEGIJKLMNOPUV
6 CEGHK(N 3,5km)TUVW

💬 A quiet, friendly and well maintained campsite with a swimming pool, bar and restaurant. Close to Rome. Private beach on Lake Bracciano. Nice children's toilet facilities and a disabled toilet with shower. Private bus service to Anguillara station.

🚗 SS2 'Via Cassia' exit Lago Bracciano. At the lakeside take the direction of Trevignano, then Anquillara. A sudden turn to the right to a small country road that leads to the camping.

Manziana
Anguillara
Sabazia

CC €**13** 1/4-6/7 27/8-29/9 7=6　　　🧭 N 42°8'48'' E 12°16'9''

Giulianova Lido, I-64022 / Abruzzo

⊞ Camping & Village Don Antonio
✉ Via Padova
☎ +39 085-8008928
FAX +39 085-8006172
⌚ 18/5 - 20/9
@ info@campingdonantonio.it

5ha 222T(50-140m²) 6A CEE

1 ABCDFHIJKLMNOPST
2 AEFGLRSTVWXY
3 ABGHJKWY
4 (B+G ⌂) JKP
　　(Q+R+U+V+W+Z ⌂)
5 ABFGIJKLMNOPSTUVXYZ
6 ACDEGHJKM(N 1km)ORTV

💬 A campsite by the sea with sandy beaches. Large and small pitches. Lovely swimming pool with two slides and hydro massage. Cycle route (42 km). 2 km from the centre. Bus from site to centre, 2 bars, free wifi.

🚗 E2/A14, exit Val Vibrata. Via the SS259 dir. Alba Adriatica on the intersection of SS259 and SS16 to Giulianova. Follow indications. From the south, take Teramo exit on E2/A14, follow SS80 to the intersection with SS16, then follow the signs Via Padova.

Giulianova

CC €**19** 18/5-30/6 1/9-19/9　　　🧭 N 42°46'39'' E 13°57'10''

Giulianova Lido, I-64022 / Abruzzo ♿ 📶 ✿

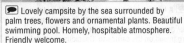

▲ Holiday
✉ Via Padova
☎ +39 085-8000053
📠 +39 085-8004420
🗓 12/5 - 13/9
@ info@villaggioholiday.it

2ha 70T(> 50m²) 6A CEE

1 BCFHIJKLNPQ
2 AEFGRSVXY
3 ABGJNRU**W**Y
4 (B 7/5-12/9) (G+Q 🗝)
(S 20/5-12/9) (T+U+V+W 🗝)
(Y 7/5-12/9) (Z 🗝)
5 **A**GIJKLMNOPUV
6 CFG**K**M(N 3km)OTV

💬 Lovely campsite by the sea surrounded by palm trees, flowers and ornamental plants. Beautiful swimming pool. Homely, hospitable atmosphere. Friendly welcome.

🚗 From north to south: E2/A14 exit Val Vibrata and follow the SS259 to intersection SS16, direction Pescara. Via SS16 to Giulianova. Turn left directly after the Salinello bridge. Under the railway tunnel and turn left immediately Via Padova.

(3252)

SS16 / A14 / Giulianova

CC € **17** 12/5-30/6 1/9-12/9 ⛰ N 42°46'39'' E 13°57'13''

Opi, I-67030 / Abruzzo ♿ 📶 iD

▲ Il Vecchio Mulino
✉ SS83 Marsicana km 52
☎ +39 0863-912232
🗓 1/1 - 31/12
@ ilvecchiomulino@tiscali.it

6ha 300T(100-120m²) 6A CEE

1 ACD**F**IJKLMOPRS
2 BCGLRTVWXY
3 ADHIJR
4 (Q+R+U+V+Y+Z 🗝)
5 **AB**DGIJKLMNOPUVZ
6 CEJ(N 2km)OV

💬 After a cultural visit to hectic cities such as Rome and Naples, this campsite is in a fantastic setting in the Abruzzen national park. You can enjoy the beautiful countryside, footpaths and even spot bears and wolves here.

🚗 The campsite is located on the SS83 from Opi direction Barrea/Alfedena. Clearly signposted.

(3253)

Pescasseroli CC

CC € **19** 1/1-14/7 1/9-31/12 ⛰ N 41°46'45'' E 13°51'46''

Pineto, I-64025 / Abruzzo 🧍‍♀️🧍 ♿ 📶 iD

▲ Pineto Beach Village & Camping***
✉ SS16 Adriat. km 425
☎ +39 085-9492724
📠 +39 085-9492796
🗓 19/4 - 22/9
@ info@pinetobeach.it

5ha 288T(21-105m²) 6A CEE

1 ACDGHIJKLMNOQ
2 AEFGNRUVY
3 ABDGIJKNRUVWY
4 (B+G 15/5-24/9) P
(Q+R+S+T+U+V+W+X+Y+Z 🗝)
5 **AB**GHIJLMNOP**ST**UVXYZ
6 ACDEGIJ(N 0,8km)ORTUV

💬 A campsite by the sea with plenty of amenities. New restaurant, pizzeria and bar suitable for all types of weather. Wifi and a solarium.

🚗 Motorway E2/A14 to Bari, exit Pineto (SatNav off). Follow 'Pineto Beach' signs on the SS16. Tunnel (4m20 headroom).

(3254)

A14 CC / Montesilvano

CC € **17** 19/4-24/6 1/9-21/9 ⛰ N 42°37'26'' E 14°3'21''

Roseto degli Abruzzi, I-64026 / Abruzzo

♻ 🔢 **iD** **(3255)**

🔺 Eurcamping***
📧 Lungomare Trieste 90
☎ +39 085-8993179
FAX +39 085-8930552
⊙ 1/5 - 15/10
@ info@eurcamping.it

5ha 265T(50-100m²) 6A CEE

1 **AG**HIJKLMNPQ
2 AEFQRVWXY
3 **AB**GK**M**NRUW**Y**
4 (B+G 20/5-15/9)
   (Q+R+T+U+V+X+Z 15/5-30/9)
5 **AB**FGIJKLNPUVZ
6 EGI**K**(N 2km)OTV

💬 A lovely campsite positioned right by the sea. It has its own private beach and service. Large playground and jogging track. Many things are organised on the campsite. Spacious grounds! The site has a wonderful swimming pool.

🚗 E2/A14, exit Roseto. Roseto degli Abruzzi. In Roseto direction Pineto SS16. For gas station left and follow signs. Tunnel height 5 m.

SS80 **Roseto degli Abruzzi**
CC
A14 SS16

CC € **19** 1/5-6/7 25/8-14/10   📷 N 42°39'28'' E 14°2'7''

Baia Domizia, I-81030 / Campania

⊗ ♻ 🔢 **iD** **(3256)**

🔺 Baia Domizia Camping Village****
📧 SP 272 Garigliano Monte Massico
☎ +39 0823-930126
FAX +39 0823-930375
⊙ 19/4 - 23/9
@ info@baiadomizia.it

30ha 900T(60-100m²) 10A CEE

1 ABCDEHIJL**PRS**
2 ABEGLRSVWXY
3 BK**M**NRUVY
4 (B+G ⊙) K
   (Q+S+T+U+V+W+X+Y+Z ⊙)
5 **AB**GIJKLMNOPUVXYZ
6 CEG**K**L(N 6km)ORTV

💬 Beautiful campsite with all possible amenities. Large grounds nonetheless offer plenty of peace and quiet. The swimming pools and the sea mean you are sure to have a wonderful holiday.

🚗 A1, exit Cassino, direction Formia. Then the SS Domitiana IV direction Naples. Exit at km 3 and then 2 km further. Clearly signposted.

SS630 Minturno SS430
SS7
CC
SS7QUATER
Mondragone

CC € **19** 19/4-11/5 26/5-29/6 1/9-22/9   📷 N 41°12'26'' E 13°47'30''

Capaccio/Paestum, I-84047 / Campania

🔢 ✧ **iD** **(3257)**

🔺 La Foce dei Tramonti***
📧 Via Foce Sele 2
☎ FAX +39 0828-861220
⊙ 1/4 - 31/10
@ info@lafocedeitramonti.com

1,2ha 30T(75m²) 4-10A CEE

1 ACDGHIJKLMNOPQ
2 ACEGKLRTUVWY
3 BGKNRWY
4 (Q+S 15/6-15/9)
   (T+U+V+X 2/6-15/9)
   (Z 15/5-15/9)
5 **A**GIKMOPUVXYZ
6 CDEGJ(N 5km)OT

💬 A beautifully located campsite at the mouth of a river. The ideal place to relax next to the sea, with views of the sunset every evening.

🚗 Along the coast road about 7 km north of Paestum direction Salerno, at the mouth of the Sele.

CC SS166
Capaccio
SS18

CC € **17** 1/4-10/7 28/8-30/10 14=12   📷 N 40°28'51'' E 14°56'41''

Massalubrense/Marina d.Cantone, I-80061 / Campania

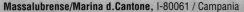  3258

🏕 Villaggio Nettuno Srl
✉ Via A. Vespucci 39
☎ +39 081-8081051
📠 +39 081-8081706
🗓 20/3 - 31/10
@ info@villaggionettuno.it

0,5ha 60T(10-40m²) 4A CEE

1 ABDFIJLN**P**RS
2 EGHIJKNQSTWXY
3 H**M**RUWY
4 (**A**+R+T+U+V+Y+Z ⊙)
5 GIJKLMNOPU
6 EG**J**(N 2km)OPRV

💬 Between Positano, Sorrento and Capri, on Marina del Cantone Bay on the gorgeous Amalfi coast. Direct access to crystal clear sea with private beach access. Ideal spot for relaxing, peaceful holiday. Diving centre. Small pitches (40 m²).

🚗 Coastal road to Sorrento. In Meta di Sor. dir. Positano. Then dir. San Agata and Marina del Cantone. (At site keep going, turn around). Difficult road for cars with caravans and motorhomes longer than 6m.

Vico Equense
SS163
CC

CC € 19 20/3-12/5 27/5-30/6 15/9-30/10 · N 40°35'0'' E 14°21'15''

Paestum, I-84063 / Campania

♿ 🛜 iD 3259

🏕 Villaggio dei Pini***
✉ Via Torre di Mare/Via Urano
☎ +39 0828-811030
📠 +39 0828-811025
🗓 1/1 - 31/12
@ info@
campingvillaggiodeipini.com

3ha 158T(40-100m²) 6A CEE

1 ACD**G**HIJKLMOPQ
2 ABEGLRTUVXY
3 ABGJKMN**Q**RWY
4 (**A** ⊙) M(Q+R ⊙)
(U+V+Y 1/3-31/10) (Z ⊙)
5 **AB**EGHIJKLMNOPUV
6 ABCDEGIJ(N 0,3km)ORTUV

💬 Beach campsite with plenty of greenery and excellent location. Enclosed touring pitches. Beautiful private beach with play equipment for children. Good restaurant with fresh local dishes, including buffalo mozzarella. Close to the Paestum archeological site with the flawless remains of Greek temples.

🚗 In Paestum centre follow signs to campsite. Campsite is located directly on sea.

SS18
SS166
CC Capaccio
Agropoli
SS267

CC € 17 1/1-20/6 19/9-31/12 · N 40°24'46'' E 14°59'28''

Pompei, I-80045 / Campania

🛜 iD 3260

🏕 Fortuna Village Pompei
✉ Via Plinio 115
☎ 📠 +39 081-8508439
🗓 1/1 - 31/12
@ info@fortunavillagepompei.it

0,5ha 50T(30-60m²) 6A CEE

1 ACDGIJKLO**P**ST
2 FGKRVWX
4 (Q+T+U+V+Y+Z 19/3-10/11)
5 **A**GIJKLMNOPUW
6 CEGJ(N 1km)R

💬 Campsite is located at 100 metres from the entrance to the Pompei ruins and is also an excellent base for visits to Napels, Sorrento and the Vesuvius crater.

🚗 From A3 Napoli-Salerno, exit Pompeï Ovest left. Site is on right after 300 metres.

A30
Torre del Greco
CC A3
SS145 SS366
SS373

CC € 17 8/1-29/3 4/4-28/4 3/5-31/5 4/6-14/7 1/9-31/12 · N 40°44'48'' E 14°29'3''

Pompei, I-80045 / Campania

♿ 📶 **iD** **3261**

△ Spartacus***
🏕 Via Plinio 127
☎ FAX +39 081-8624078
🔓 1/1 - 31/12
@ staff@campingspartacus.it

1ha 80T(25-32m²) 8A CEE

1 ABCDFIJKLPRS
2 FGRVWXY
3 U
4 (B 1/6-15/9)
(Q+U+V+Z 1/5-31/10)
5 **AB**GIJKMNOPUVX
6 CGK(N 0,5km)RV

💬 A shaded, small-scale campsite close to the Pompei excavations.

Torre del Greco

🚗 A3 Napoli-Salerno, exit Pompei Ovest, then left. Campsite about 250 metres on the right.

A30 / A3 / SS145 / SS366 / SS373

CC €**19** 4/1-29/3 2/5-30/6 28/8-28/12   📍 N 40°44'44'' E 14°29'2''

Pompei, I-80045 / Campania

📶 **iD** **3262**

△ Zeus
🏕 Villa dei Misteri
☎ +39 081-8615320
FAX +39 081-8617536
🔓 1/1 - 31/12
@ info@campingzeus.it

2ha 80T(40-100m²) 10A CEE

1 ABCDFIJL**PQ**
2 FGRSTVWXY
4 (Q 🔓) (R 1/4-31/10)
(T+U+V+X+Y 1/4-30/10)
(Z 1/4-15/11)
5 **AB**GIJKMOPU
6 CEG**IK**(N 1km)ORT

💬 Zeus campsite is located near the famous archaeological excavations at Pompei; evening visits are possible until 19:30. In a lovely park with tropical plants at the foot of Vesuvius. Many facilities: bar/restaurant, souvenir shop and internet point. Good location for excursions by public transport to Naples, Sorrento, Amalfi, Positano and Capri.

Torre del Greco

🚗 A3 from Napoli or Salerno: exit Pompeï Ovest, left. After 200 metres left again, then left uphill.

A30 / A3 / SS145 / SS366

CC €**19** 8/1-28/3 3/4-24/4 2/5-30/5 4/6-14/7 1/9-22/12   📍 N 40°44'57'' E 14°28'51''

Pontecagnano Faiano, I-84098 / Campania

♿ 📶 **iD** **3263**

△ Lido di Salerno
🏕 Via Lago Trasimeno 1
☎ +39 327-3669705
FAX +39 089-200270
🔓 1/1 - 31/12
@ campingsalerno@gmail.com

1,1ha 70T(36-50m²) 6-16A CEE

1 ABCD**G**IJKLMOPQ
2 AEFGKRTVY
3 A**F**RUWY
4 (Q 🔓)
(R+U+V+X 30/4-31/10)
(Z 🔓)
5 **AB**EGIJMO**P**UVXY
6 DEGK(N 5km)OTUV

💬 Lovely campsite, located directly on the sea with a sandy beach. Near Salerno, Paestum and Pompei, close to the Amalfi coast, very friendly and helpful staff.

Salerno A3 **Battipaglia**

🚗 From the Tangenziale di Salerno to coast road SP175 towards the south (about 12 km). This coast road is then called Via Lago Trasimeno.

SS18

CC €**17** 7/1-14/7 1/9-21/12   📍 N 40°35'44'' E 14°52'16''

Pozzuoli, I-80078 / Campania

3264

▲ Int. Vulcano Solfatara***
✉ Via Solfatara 161
☎ +39 081-5267413
📠 +39 081-5263482
🗓 1/1 - 31/12
@ camping@solfatara.it

3ha 160T(40-70m²) 4A CEE

1. ABCDFIJKLMOPRS
2. BFGRSWXY
3. AGR
4. (B+G 1/6-30/9) N
   (Q+S+T+U 1/4-31/10) (Z 🔒)
5. AB GIKMNOPUVW
6. CEGHJ(N 1km)ORT

💬 The campsite is located in the Solfatara volcanic crater. Basic toilet facilities. An ideal place for visiting Naples, Pompeii etc.

🚗 Located just outside Pozzuoli direction Napoli. ('Tangenziale' exit 11 Agnano). The campsite is clearly signposted. Gate at entrance 2m 70 wide and 3m 40 high.

Casoria

Napoli

CC € 19 5/1-25/3 3/4-26/4 2/5-3/7 26/8-23/12   N 40°49'43'' E 14°8'12''

Sorrento, I-80067 / Campania

3265

▲ Santa Fortunata/Campogaio****
✉ Via Capo 39
☎ +39 081-8073579
📠 +39 081-8073590
🗓 25/3 - 7/10
@ info@santafortunata.eu

30ha 350T(80-120m²) 6A CEE

1. AFIJKLMOPQ
2. EGIJKOQRSTVWXY
3. ABDGRUVY
4. (A 🔒) (B+G 1/6-27/10)
   (Q+S+U+V+Y+Z 🔒)
5. AB GIJKLMNOPUVW
6. CEGJ(N 1km)ORTVWX

💬 Campsite with wonderful view over the bay of Sorrento. Excursions to Pompeii, Vesuvius, Naples and by boat to the Amalfi Coast and Capri from the campsite. Lots of facilities: swimming pool, beach, campsite shop, playground, and a bar. The excellent restaurant is another advantage.

🚗 A3, exit Castellammare towards Sorrento. 1 km from Sorrento towards Massalubrense. After Sorrento follow the signs.

Castellammare
di Stabia

SS145VAR

SS163

CC € 19 2/4-18/5 3/6-6/7 27/8-6/10   N 40°37'39'' E 14°21'27''

Vico Equense, I-80069 / Campania

3266

▲ Sant'Antonio****
✉ Via Marina d'Equa 21
☎📠 +39 081-8028570
🗓 15/3 - 31/10
@ info@campingsantantonio.it

1ha 60T 5A CEE

1. ACDFHIJKLPRS
2. AEGHNRWXY
3. WY
4. (Q+S+Y+Z 🔒)
5. AGIKMOPU
6. EGJ(N 1km)OR

💬 A peaceful campsite under lemon, olive and walnut trees by a picturesque harbour. The restaurant serves typical Italian home cooking. Basic toilet facilities. Boat trips to Capri. The campsite has wifi.

🚗 A3, exit Castellammare direction Sorrento. Take tunnel left dir. Sorrento. After tunnel and bridge turn right and drive slowly.

Castellammare
di Stabia SS366

A3

SS163

CC € 19 1/5-14/7 1/9-30/9   N 40°39'34'' E 14°25'8''

Bisceglie, I-76011 / Puglia

♿ 🛜 iD **3267**

🏕 La Batteria
📧 Panoramica Umb.
   Paternostro 16/18
☎ +39 340-7584019
🔓 1/1 - 31/1, 1/3 - 31/12
@ labatteriacamping@gmail.com

160**T**(50-110m²) 6A CEE

1 ABCDFHIJKLMNO**P**RS
2 EFGKOQTUWXY
3 BGKRUWY
4 (B 1/6-15/9) (Q+R+T+Z 🔓)
5 GIKMNOPXYZ
6 EGJ(N 2km)OT

💬 Welcoming, busy campsite on a boulevard. Plenty of opportunities to reach and discover the little town on foot.

🚐 From the north on the A14 exit Trani to the SS16, then dir. Bisceglie. Follow the signs in Bisceglie, amphitheatre, continue to the boulevard, left at T junction. Campsite 1500 m on the right.

Trani
CC
Bisceglie
Molfetta
A14

CC € **17** 1/1-30/1 1/3-30/6 1/9-31/12 7=6 📡 N 41°15'19'' E 16°28'51''

Borgagne, I-73026 / Puglia

🛜 iD **3268**

🏕 Agriturismo Malapezza
📧 Masseria Malapezza Prov.
   (S.Andrea)
☎ +39 333-2525219
📠 +39 083-2811402
🔓 1/1 - 31/12
@ malapezza@yahoo.it

6ha 80**T**(25-40m²) 16A CEE

1 ABCDGIJKLMOPRS
2 ABGKLQRTUWXY
3 **F**HJKR
4 (Q+T+X+Y 1/6-31/8)
   (Z 1/4-30/10)
5 **A**GIKMOPUZ
6 EGJ(N 3km)TV

💬 Cosy campsite with restaurant with local products, tastings possible.

🚐 From Lecce dir. Melendogno-Borgagne a Sant'Andrea. Campsite 2 km on the left.

San Foca
SP366
CC
Martano
Zollino
Otranto

CC € **15** 1/1-14/7 1/9-31/12 7=6 📡 N 40°15'8'' E 18°25'2''

Foce Varano (Isola Varano), I-71010 / Puglia

🛜 iD **3269**

🏕 Camping 5 Stelle***
📧 SP41 Località Isola Varano
☎ +39 0884-917583
📠 +39 0884-917561
🔓 1/5 - 23/9
@ info@camping5stelle.it

4ha 150**T**(80-100m²) 4A CEE

1 ABGIJKLMPRS
2 ABDEGSY
3 ABKMNRY
4 (A+**B** 1/5-21/9)
   (**G** 26/5-10/9) (Q 1/5-21/9)
   (S 29/5-15/9) (T 15/5-15/9)
   (U+V 1/6-15/9) (X 15/5-15/9)
   (Z 🔓)
5 **A**FGIKMOPR**ST**UVXY
6 CDEG**IJ**(N 5km)OTV

💬 Located between the sea and the lake. Large pitches encircled by the Parco Nazionale del Gargano. A beach several kilometres long slopes down gently to the clear blue sea. Swimming pool, supermarket, restaurant/pizzeria. Trips out include Pater Pio and Foresta Umbra.

🚐 A14, exit Poggio Imperiale towards Vieste Strada as far as Sannicandro Garganico (SS693). 20 km Litoranea SP41 Isola Varano dir. Torre Mileto (provincial road 14). Campsite on the right.

CC
San Nicandro
Garganico

CC € **17** 1/5-1/7 26/8-22/9 📡 N 41°54'45'' E 15°43'56''

Gagliano del Capo (LE), I-73034 / Puglia

&♿ 🛜 **iD** **3270**

🏕 S. Maria di Leuca***
🚌 SS 275, km 35.700
☎ +39 0833-548157
📠 +39 0833-548485
🗓 1/1 - 31/12
@ info@campingsmleuca.com

3ha 200T 3-5A CEE

1 ABC**G**HIJKLMNO**P**RS
2 BGTUXY
3 ABHKMNRW
4 (**A** 1/6-30/9) (B 31/5-15/9) P
(Q 🅿) (R+T+U 1/6-31/8)
(V 1/7-31/8) (W+Z 31/5-15/9)
5 **A**GIJKLMNO**PT**U
6 EG**I**KM(N 2km)OQRTV

💬 Surrounded by green trees on 3 hectares.
3 km from the crystal clear sea of Santa Maria
di Leuca. The campsite has its own shuttle bus.
The pitches are comfortable with plenty of shade
and electricity. 3 bath houses with hot showers and
motorhome service. The 2 swimming pools and
sports field are central. Bar, restaurant, shop open
from end of May to mid September.

🚗 From S. Maria di Leuca follow the SS275 till past
Gagliano del Capo. Well marked by signs.

Alessano
Presicce *Presicce*
SS274 CC

CC € **17** 1/1-14/7 1/9-31/12 7=6 📶 N 39°49'28'' E 18°22'7''

Gallipoli, I-73014 / Puglia

&♿ 🛜 **iD** **3271**

🏕 Agricampeggio & Glamping
"Torre Sabea"
🚌 Litoranea per Santa Maria
al Bagno
☎ +39 0833-298273
🗓 1/1 - 31/12
@ info@torresabea.it

30T(80-120m²) 3-6A CEE

1 ABGIJKLPRS
2 EGQTXY
3 AKWY
4 (Q+Z 🅿)
5 **A**GIKMOPUZ
6 DEK(N 0,2km)OT

💬 Very friendly family campsite with local
specialities in most interesting surroundings.

Parabita

CC

Melissano

🚗 SS101 Lecce-Gallipoli. Follow signs.

CC € **15** 1/1-14/7 1/9-30/12 📶 N 40°4'22'' E 18°0'23''

Gallipoli, I-73014 / Puglia

🛜 **iD** **3272**

🏕 Baia di Gallipoli
Camping Resort****
🚌 S.P. 215 km 0,100
☎ +39 0833-273210
📠 +39 0833-275405
🗓 1/4 - 31/10
@ info@baiadigallipoli.com

11ha 600T(40-120m²) 6A CEE

1 ABCD**G**HIJKLMN**P**S
2 AGKORSY
3 ABGHJK**MN**O**R**UW
4 (A+B 1/5-15/9) (Q 🅿)
(R 1/4-9/6) (S 10/6-15/9)
(T+U+V+W+Y+Z 🅿)
5 **AB**FGIKMNOPUV
6 EGJ**K**(N 4km)TUVWX

💬 A quiet, rural campsite with large shaded pitches
set on a hill. When staying for 7 or more nights you
will receive a regional product as a gift.

🚗 From the south take the SS101 Lecce-Gallipoli.
Keep left before Gallipoli on the SS274 to S. Maria di
Leuca. Lido Pizzo exit about 2 km further on. After
about 5 km turn left at end of road. Campsite on the
left.

SS101
Gallipoli
Casarano

CC

SS274

CC € **19** 1/4-22/6 27/8-30/10 📶 N 39°59'54'' E 18°1'34''

Lecce/Loc. Torre Rinalda, I-73100 / Puglia

♿ 📶 iD **3273**

🏔 Torre Rinalda Camping Village
✉ Via Simeone D'Antona 1
☎ +39 0832-382161
📠 +39 0832-382165
🔓 19/5 - 21/9
@ info@torrerinalda.it

15,5ha 730T(81m²) 6A CEE

1 ACD**G**HIJKLMNOP
2 AEFGRTVXY
3 BGMNRY
4 (B 28/5-11/9)
 (Q+R+S+T+U+V+W+Y+Z 🔓)
5 **A**FGIKMOPUVZ
6 DEGIJ(N 7km)ORT

💬 Beautiful seaside, with lots of sports opportunities, combined with an interesting arty town. A wonderful place to visit.

🚗 SS16 exit Trepuzzi towards Squinzano/Trapuzzi. After 200 m, left onto SS100. On to SP133 San Cataldo/Casalabate. Follow signs.

CC € **17** *19/5-30/6 1/9-20/9*

⛰ N 40°28'51'' E 18°8'48''

Manfredonia, I-71043 / Puglia

🧑‍🤝‍🧑 ♿ 📶 iD **3274**

🏔 Lido Salpi
✉ SS159, km 6,2
☎ 📠 +39 0884-571160
🔓 1/1 - 31/12
@ lidosalpi@alice.it

1ha 52T(50-70m²) 6-16A CEE

1 ABCGHIJKLMPRS
2 AEGKTVY
3 ABGRUWY
4 (Q+R+T+V+X+Z 🔓)
5 **A**GHIJKMNO**P**UVYZ
6 CDEGHIJK(N 7km)ORTV

💬 Campsite is open all year and is located on a sandy beach. Ideal for long beach walks and right by the sea. There are new toilet facilities and limited provisions are always available. A good bar with delicious food. Excursions to Gargano, S. Giovanni Rotondo, Foresto Umbra, Monte S. Angelo, Vieste. An ideal stopover site from the A14.

🚗 A14, exit Foggia, direction Monfredonia. SS89 exit Monfredonia Sud. Southwards on the SS159 to the campsite sign on the left.

CC € **13** *1/1-14/7 1/9-31/12*

⛰ N 41°33'18'' E 15°53'45''

Ostuni, I-72017 / Puglia

📶 iD **3275**

🏔 Cala dei Ginepri***
✉ Contrada Montanaro, SS379, km 23,5
☎ 📠 +39 0831-330402
🔓 13/5 - 17/9
@ info@caladeiginepri.com

10ha 400T(< 80m²) 5A CEE

1 ACFHIJKLMNP
2 AEQTUVXY
3 ACM**O**P**R
4 (B 1/7-10/9) (Q 15/6-10/9)
 (S+T+U+V+Y+Z 1/6-10/9)
5 **A**IMPXZ
6 EIKT

💬 Good campsite for sporty campers. Each pitch has its own toilet, which of course you'll need to keep clean during your stay.

🚗 On SS379 to km marker 23.5. Well signposted.

CC € **19** *13/5-30/6 1/9-16/9 7=6*

⛰ N 40°45'52'' E 17°39'1''

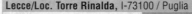

Peschici (FG), I-71010 / Puglia

♿ 🛜 **iD** (3276)

🏕 Camping Internazionale Manacore★★★★
📍 Lit. Pes.-Vieste
☎ +39 0884-911020
📠 +39 0884-911049
📅 12/5 - 30/9
@ manacore@gruppoaccia.it

22ha 700T(40-60m²) 3-6A CEE

1 ABC**F**HIJKLMN**P**RS
2 AEGJKRSVY
3 BGK**M**NRWY
4 (B 16/5-26/9)
   (Q+S+T+U+V+W+X+Y 🔑)
   (Z 7/5-23/9)
5 **A**GIJKLMNOPUVZ
6 CFG**IJ**(N 10km)OQT

💬 This site is a village by itself. Right by the sea and with a lovely swimming pool. This is a good area for surfing and snorkelling. A beautiful coastline near Gargano and just 10 minutes from Peschici. Excursions possible to Monte S. Angelo, Padre Pio and Foresta Umbra. XL pitch by the sea for a supplement

🚗 A14, exit Poggio Imperiale, SS89 direction Vieste as far as Peschici. Then take coast road towards Vieste (Litoranea) as far as service station. Then onto campsite road.

SS89 CC — Vico del Gargano / Vieste

CC € **19** 12/5-15/6 31/8-29/9 📐 N 41°56'14'' E 16°4'12''

Peschici (FG), I-71010 / Puglia

🛜 **iD** (3277)

🏕 Parco Degli Ulivi★★★
📍 Località Padula
☎ +39 0884-962299
📅 13/5 - 16/9
@ contatti@parcodegliulivi.it

16ha 300T(50-90m²) 5A

1 ABF H IJKLMN**P**RS
2 AEG K QRY
3 AGK**M**NRWY
4 (A 1/6-13/9) (B+G 21/5-13/9)
   J(Q+S 🔑)
   (T+U+V+Y 1/6-8/9) (Z 🔑)
5 **A**GIKMOPUVZ
6 CEG**J**(N 1,5km)OQRT

💬 The 'Park of Olives' is near the bay in the picturesque village of Peschici, 150m from the sea, surrounded by olive groves and forests. Not far from the marina, private beach, 140,000 m² and well equipped for a good holiday. The sports and leisure facilities: swimming pool, tennis, volleyball, children's playground, bowling, disco and entertainment with shows and games.

🚗 A14, exit Poggio Imperiale, SS89 direction Vieste as far as Peschici. Then follow camping signs.

CC — Vico del Gargano

CC € **15** 13/5-1/7 26/8-15/9 7=6 📐 N 41°56'35'' E 16°0'23''

Specchiolla di Carovigno, I-72012 / Puglia

♿ 🛜 **iD** (3278)

🏕 Pineta al Mare★★★
📍 Via di Tamerici
☎ +39 0831-987803
📠 +39 0831-994057
📅 12/5 - 24/9
@ info@campingpinetamare.com

5,5ha 135T(49-80m²) 4A CEE

1 ABCD**F**IJKLMN**P**RS
2 ABEGLORVY
3 ABJKNRUWY
4 (B 1/5-20/9) (G 🔑) JKP
   (Q+S+T+U+V+Y+Z 🔑)
5 **A**EGIKMOPUV
6 CEG**IJ**(N 0km)ORTV

💬 Family campsite located by the sea and within walking distance of Specchiolla. Shaded, marked out pitches. Separate section specially equipped for motorhomes. Free wifi, also for CampingCard ACSI holders.

🚗 On the SS379 coast road take at km-marker 32.5 the exit to Specchiolla. Follow the camping signs.

SS379 CC / SS16 — San Vito dei Normanni

CC € **19** 12/5-30/6 27/8-23/9 📐 N 40°44'27'' E 17°44'10''

Vieste del Gargano, I-71019 / Puglia ⚙ 🔌 🛰 **iD** 3279

▲ Baia e Cala Campi★★★
🚏 Litoranea Vieste-Mattinata,
km 11,sp
☎ +39 0884-700000
FAX +39 0884-700003
⌚ 1/4 - 30/9
@ info@baiadicampi.it
11ha 416T(80-100m²) 16A CEE

1 ABC**F**HIJKLMPQ
2 EGKNTY
3 BMW
4 (Q+S+V+Y+Z 13/5-16/9)
5 **AB**GIKMPUVZ
6 EGJ**J**(N 10km)RTV

💬 Village Baia di Campi is a perfect destination for campers who want to spend their holiday in contact with nature. The pitches are positioned among the dense vegetation of Aleppo pine trees and olive trees, guaranteeing coolness and shade. Free wifi in early season.

🚗 Exit Poggio Imperiale A14, then main road to Vico del Gargano. Then towards Rodi Garganico, Peschici, Vieste. From Vieste follow coast road south for about 10 km.

Vieste

CC

SS89

CC € **17** 1/4-30/6 26/8-29/9   🏔 N 41°48'53'' E 16°11'24''

Vieste del Gargano, I-71019 / Puglia 🎯 🛰 **iD** 3280

▲ Vill. Baia degli Aranci★★★
🚏 Lungomare Europa 48
☎ +39 0884-706591
FAX +39 0884-705064
⌚ 21/4 - 14/10
@ info@baiadegliaranci.it

11ha 400T(30-40m²) 6A CEE

1 ABEHIJKLMNPRS
2 AEGJKRTVXY
3 BGNRU**V**WY
4 (B+G 1/5-22/10) P
(Q+S 15/5-10/10)
(T+U 20/5-14/10)
(V 1/6-15/9) (Y 22/4-22/10)
(Z ⌚)
5 **A**GIJKMOPUVZ
6 CFGIJ(N 0,7km)ORTV

💬 A camping village with hotels, within walking distance of the town of Vieste. Situated by the beach, accessible through an underpass, views of Vieste, the rocky coast, the beach and the yacht harbour from the higher pitches on the site.

🚗 A14, exit Poggio Imperiale, SS89 direction Vieste inner road. Go as far as Vieste, there turn left and drive to the coast road. Campsite located on the road before the village.

CC
Vieste

CC € **17** 21/4-30/6 1/9-13/10   🏔 N 41°53'13'' E 16°9'59''

Vieste del Gargano (Fg), I-71019 / Puglia 🚹 🛰 **iD** 3281

▲ Camping Village
Molinella Vacanze★★★
🚏 Località Molinella nr. 72
☎ +39 0884-707530
FAX +39 0884-704399
⌚ 1/4 - 30/10
@ info@molinellavacanze.com
2ha 100T(30-60m²) 6-10A CEE

1 ABCGIJKLMNPQ
2 AEJKQSVX
3 AGKRUVWY
4 (Q+R+S+T+V+X+Z ⌚)
5 **A**CFGIJKLMNOPUVZ
6 ACDEGH**IJK**(N 3km)OQRS
TVW

💬 Quiet campsite. Ideally located for excursions in the surrounding area. The campsite is directly on the beach, 3 km from Vieste. Bar, restaurant and pizzeria on the beach. Modern toilet facilities. Dog washing area and baby room. Free wifi, gym, and bus service to Vieste.

🚗 A14 exit Poggio Imperiale, SS89 dir. Vieste. Side road after Peschici (not Littoranea) past Foresta Umbra exit, 1st road left, right at T-junction as far as traffic lights, then left, see signs.

SS89

CC Vieste

CC € **17** 1/4-23/6 25/8-29/10   🏔 N 41°54'28'' E 16°9'2''

Cirò Marina, I-88811 / Calabria ♿ 📶 iD (3282)

🔺 Punta Alice★★★
📧 Via Punta Alice
☎ +39 0962-31160
📠 +39 0962-373823
📅 1/1 - 31/12
@ info@puntalice.it

5,5ha 280T 3-6A CEE

1 ABC**F**HIJKLM**P**R**S**
2 AENSTVY
3 BK**MN**RUWY
4 (B 30/5-15/9) (**G** 20/5-30/9)
P(Q 📅) (R 20/6-15/9)
(T 1/4-30/9)
(U+V+W+Y 1/6-30/9) (Z 📅)
5 **AB**GIJKLMNO**P**UVXYZ
6 CDEG**IK**(N 0,1km)ORTV

There is plenty of opportunity to enjoy the beautiful surroundings among the vineyards of the famous 'Ciro' wines. The campsite is right by the sea. The beach has Blue Flag status. You will find a real mediterranean ambiance on the site.

🚗 From the SS106, at the Ciro Marma exit km-marker 279 enter the town below on the left. From the north at km-marker 280 right. Then follow signs.

SS106 · CC · **Cirò Marina**

CC € 15 1/1-30/6 9/9-31/12 · 📷 N 39°23'6'' E 17°8'34''

Corigliano/Calabro, I-87060 / Calabria ♿ 📶 iD (3283)

🔺 Thurium★★★★
📧 Contrada Ricota Grande
☎ 📠 +39 0983-851101
📅 1/1 - 31/12
@ info@campingthurium.com

10ha 500T(60-80m²) 6A CEE

1 ABC**F**HIJKLM**P**
2 AER**S**Y
3 AB**F**GJKMNRUWY
4 (A 1/6-15/9) (**B**+G 1/6-30/9)
(S+T+U+V+W+Y+Z
1/5-10/10)
5 **AB**DEFGIJKLMNO**P**UV
6 CEG**IJ**(N 7km)ORTV

A beautiful, well-kept campsite located in the middle of countryside. Peace and privacy on spacious pitches. The Calabria region offers many opportunities for trips out. Visit the mountains of Sila and Pollino or historical cities such as Corigliano, Rossano or Altomonte. Extensive sports facilities and an attractive swimming pool on the campsite.

🚗 Turn off the SS106-Bis coast road towards the sea at 21 km post. Campsite then signposted.

SS106 · SS534 · CC · SS106RADD. · SS106BIS · **Corigliano Calabro**

CC € 13 1/1-14/7 1/9-31/12 · 📷 N 39°41'29'' E 16°31'20''

Cropani Marina, I-88050 / Calabria 📶 iD (3284)

🔺 Camping Case Vacanza Lungomare★★★
📧 Viale Venezia 46
☎ +39 0961-961167
📠 +39 0961-961600
📅 30/3 - 3/11
@ info@campinglungomare.com

2,1ha 100T(20-42m²) 6A CEE

1 ABC**F**HIJKLMN**P**R**S**
2 AEUVXY
3 BNY
4 (T+U+V+W 1/4-30/10)
(Y 1/7-15/9) (Z 1/4-30/10)
5 **A**IKMOPUV
6 EGK(N 0,5km)TV

A family campsite with modest but attractive facilities right in the village. Only separated from the fine sandy beach by a boulevard. Very good restaurant/pizzeria. Open from April to October. Close to National Park Sila.

🚗 From Catanzaro coast road SS106 to the north direction Crotone. Follow signs in Cropani Marina village.

Andali · SS106VS · SS180 · **Sellia Marina** · CC · SS106

CC € 15 30/3-14/7 1/9-2/11 · 📷 N 38°54'32'' E 16°48'34''

Marina di Nicotera, I-89844 / Calabria

🛜 iD **3285**

🔺 Maris Villaggio Camping***
📧 Località Mortelletto
☎ +39 0963-887834
🔑 1/5 - 30/9
@ info@mariscalabria.it

2ha 45T(60-120m²) 10A CEE

1 ABCDGIJKLMNOPRS
2 AEFKTUXY
3 ABGKM**OP**RWY
4 (B 1/6-30/9) (G 🔑) P
(Q+R+T+X+Z 🔑)
5 A**G**IKMO**PST**UV
6 EGJ(N 2,5km)OTV

💬 Quiet campsite, located by a beautiful sandy beach, with spacious pitches. Very many amenities and a beautiful pool.

🚗 A3 Salerno-Reggio Calabria. Exit Rosarno dir. San Ferdinando Porto. On SP50 follow campsite signs for ± another 7 km.

CC **Rosarno**
Gioia Tauro SS18 SS682 A3

CC € **17** 1/5-14/7 1/9-29/9

📍 N 38°30'37'' E 15°55'22''

Marina di Nicotera, I-89844 / Calabria

🛜 iD **3286**

🔺 Villaggio Camping Mimosa***
📧 Loc. Mortelletto
☎ +39 0963-81397
FAX +39 0963-81933
🔑 1/1 - 31/12
@ info@villaggiomimosa.com

3ha 50T 12A CEE

1 ABCGHIJKLMNO**P**RS
2 AEFLRTUXY
3 B**F**GJKNRWY
4 (B+G 1/5-20/10) (Q 🔑)
(R+U 15/4-30/10)
(V 15/4-15/9) (Y 15/4-30/10)
(Z 15/4-31/10)
5 A**G**HIKMOPR**ST**VXZ
6 CEG**I**K(N 2km)ORTWX

💬 Right by the sea with a long beach of white sand. An oasis of peace surrounded by a lovely pine forest. Market, pizzeria, bar-restaurant, swimming pool. Excursions directly from Tropea (15/3-15/10) to the Aeolian Islands.

🚗 A3 Salerno-Reggio Calabria, exit Rosarno direction San Ferdinando Porto. Follow camping signs on the Strada Communale S.Ferdinando-Nicotera. Another ±7 km.

CC A3
Gioia Tauro SS18 SS682

CC € **17** 1/1-14/7 1/9-31/12

📍 N 38°30'27'' E 15°55'36''

Marina di Zambrone, I-89868 / Calabria

🚫 🦽 🛜 iD **3287**

🔺 Il Calabriano***
📧 Via del Mare snc
☎ FAX +39 0963-392096
🔑 15/5 - 15/10
@ direzione@ilcalabriano.it

2ha 110T 3-6A CEE

1 ABCDEHIJKP
2 AEGKNTUVWXY
3 BGRY
4 (Q+R 1/7-31/8)
(T+U+V 25/6-15/10)
(Y 1/7-31/8) (Z 🔑)
5 A**G**IKMOPUVZ
6 EGJ(N 1km)ORTV

NEW

💬 This campsite is run by the whole family. Good atmosphere and in the middle of a stunning coastal area.

🚗 From the north A3 Salerno-Reggio Calabria exit Pizzo Calabro, then to SS522 direction Tropea. Exit Zambrone Marina (±20 km). Follow camping signs.

CC **Vibo Valentia**
SS522 SS18

CC € **17** 15/5-14/7 1/9-14/10

📍 N 38°42'32'' E 15°58'14''

Marina di Zambrone, I-89868 / Calabria
♿ 🛜 iD (3288)

▲ Villaggio Camping Sambalon★★★★
🏠 SS 522 per Tropea
☎ +39 0963-392828
📠 +39 0963-392836
🕐 20/5 - 23/9
@ info@sambalon.com

1,5ha 110T(35-80m²) 6-10A

1️⃣ ACDF HIJKLM**P**RS
2️⃣ AEGKTUVY
3️⃣ ABGR**W**Y
4️⃣ (Q+R 1/7-30/8)
　 (T+U+V+W+X+Y 20/6-30/8)
5️⃣ AGIJKLMNOPQRSTUVXYZ
6️⃣ DEGIJ(N 4km)ORT

💬 A large, hospitable campsite in fantastic surroundings on the so-called 'coast of the gods', the Tyrrhenian Sea. The sea really is blue here. Culinary delights at affordable prices. Trips out to the nearby Tropea and Capo Vaticano. Motorhomes longer than 7 m cannot use standard pitches, there's a Euro 3 fee.

🚗 From the north A3 Salerno-Reggio Calabria exit Pizzo Calabro, then to the SS522 direction Tropea. Exit Zambrone Marina (± 20 km). Follow campsite signs.

Vibo Valentia
SS18

CC € **17** 20/5-14/7 1/9-22/9　　🏖 N 38°42'23'' E 15°58'12''

Praia a Mare, I-87028 / Calabria
🛜 iD (3289)

▲ International Camping Village★★★
🏠 Lungomare F. Sirimarco
☎ 📠 +39 0985-72211
🕐 1/5 - 26/9
@ reception@
　 campinginternational.it

5,7ha 360T(30-45m²) 4A CEE

1️⃣ ACGHIJKLMNQ
2️⃣ EKNQRTVY
3️⃣ ABGMNRWY
4️⃣ (G 1/7-20/9)
　 (Q+S+U+V+Y 1/5-21/9)
　 (Z 🔌)
5️⃣ **A**GIKMOPUVZ
6️⃣ CDEGJ(N 0,5km)OT

💬 A campsite for the camper in search of a Mediterranean atmosphere and 100% chance of sun, sea and beach. For the culinary traveler ristorante 'L'Isola' on this campsite is a must!

🚗 In Praia a Mare follow signs to 'Lungomare'. Campsite located on the Isola di Dino.

SS585　A3
Praia a Mare
CC
Scalea
SS18

CC € **13** 1/5-1/7 27/8-20/9 7=6, 14=11　　🏖 N 39°52'55'' E 15°47'8''

Praia a Mare, I-87028 / Calabria
♿ 🛜 iD (3290)

▲ La Mantinera★★★★
🏠 C. da Mantinera
☎ +39 0985-779023
📠 +39 0985-779009
🕐 14/4 - 30/9
@ lamantinera@tiscali.it

12ha 350T(30-50m²) 3-6A CEE

1️⃣ ACG HIJKLMPQ
2️⃣ EGLNRTVY
3️⃣ ABGK**M**NUW**Y**
4️⃣ (**A** 22/4-30/9) (**B** 18/4-30/9)
　 (**G**+Q 🔌) (S 1/6-15/9)
　 (T+U+V 15/6-15/9)
　 (W+Y+Z 🔌)
5️⃣ **AB**GIKMNOPUVXZ
6️⃣ CEGJ(N 2km)ORTVW

💬 Beautifully landscaped campsite with a luxurious reception and plenty of facilities. Swimming pool on the site, free until 27 June and from 29 August. The beach is 300 metres away by an azure blue sea and will make your stay complete.

🚗 Take the Praia a Mare exit on the SS18 and then follow the camping signs. The campsite is located just south of Praia a Mare.

SS585
Praia a Mare
CC
Scalea
SS18

CC € **15** 24/4-30/6 1/9-29/9 7=6　　🏖 N 39°52'36'' E 15°47'19''

Sibari/Cosenza, I-87011 / Calabria ♿ 📶 iD **3291**

⛺ Camping-Village Pineta di Sibari***
📧 Contrada Fuscolara
☎ FAX +39 0981-74135
🔓 30/3 - 23/9
@ info@pinetadisibari.it

17ha 500**T**(100-120m²) 5A CEE

1 ACFHIJKLMPRS
2 ABEKNRSUWXY
3 ABGJMNRWY
4 (Q 🔓) (S 1/6-10/9)
(U 15/5-15/9) (V+Y 1/6-10/9)
(Z 15/5-15/9)
5 AGIKMOPUVZ
6 EGJ(N 2km)RTV

💬 A large and very peaceful campsite by the sea. Tall pine trees provide shaded pitches.

🚗 Coast road SS106 dir.Reggio di C. Villapiana Scalo exit. Right in village dir. Sibari. Past village cross over the railway. Left at sign. Dirt road. Keep right. Follow camping signs. Beware 2.7m high tunnel. Use other entrance over railway track ± 300m towards village.

Trebisacce
SS106
Cassano Allo Ionio CC
SS534
SS106RADD.

CC € **17** 31/3-14/7 1/9-22/9 7=6   📍 N 39°46'47'' E 16°28'46''

Tropea, I-89861 / Calabria ♿ 📶 **3292**

⛺ Camping Marina dell'Isola
📧 Lungomare Sorrentino
☎ +39 0963-61970
🔓 29/3 - 31/10
@ info@campingmarinaisola.it

1,1ha 100**T**(40-60m²) 16A CEE

1 BCDGHIJKLMOPRS
2 AEGKQSTUVXY
3 Y
4 (Q 🔓)
(T+U+V+Y+Z 1/6-30/9)
5 AGIKMOPUXZ
6 EGJ(N 0,3km)OTV

💬 Campsite well-equipped for every camping vehicle, on the edge of the lovely town of Tropea; only one flight of stairs separates the campsite from the centre. Welcoming, familial and with a fine restaurant.

🚗 From the North, A3 exit Pizzo Calabro. SS522 dir. Tropea. Take beach/port exit. Avoid centre coming from South! Follow port signs after Tropea.

Pannaconi
CC Parghelia

CC € **13** 29/3-14/7 1/9-30/10   📍 N 38°40'43'' E 15°53'41''

Tropea, I-89861 / Calabria ♿ 📶 iD **3293**

⛺ Marina del Convento***
📧 Via Marina del Convento
☎ FAX +39 0963-62501
🔓 18/5 - 28/10
@ info@marinadelconvento.it

1,3ha 130**T**(36m²) 6A CEE

1 AFIJKLMN**P**Q
2 EGKNQRVXY
3 AH**W**
4 (Q+R 15/6-30/9) (T 1/8-31/8)
(U+Z 1/6-1/9)
5 AGIKMO**P**UVZ
6 EGK(N 0,03km)TV

💬 A campsite located at the foot of a rocky cliff with the old town of Tropea at the top. The tourist village looks out over a lovely white sandy beach and a calm, clear sea.

🚗 A3 exit Pizzo Calabro. SS522 direction Tropea. Follow Beach/Porto (harbour) signs. Avoid centre coming from south. After Tropea follow Porto signs. Then follow camping signs.

Pannaconi
SS522
CC Zaccanopoli

CC € **17** 18/5-30/6 1/9-27/10   📍 N 38°40'30'' E 15°53'23''

Aglientu, I-07020 / Sardegna

♿ 🛜 **iD** (3294)

🏕 Camping Village Baia Blu
La Tortuga****
🏖 Pineta di Vignola Mare
☎ +39 079-602060
📠 +39 079-602040
🗓 29/3 - 15/10
@ info@campinglatortuga.com
17ha 700T(40-120m²) 3-6A CEE

1 ACD**G**HIJKLMOPST
2 ABEGJRSTVWXY
3 BGK**M**NRUVWY
4 (Q+S+T+U+V+W+Y+Z 🗓)
5 **AB**EFGIJKLMNOP**ST**UVXZ
6 CDEG**IJ**M(N 9km)ORTVWX

💬 Extensive campsite mostly located in pine forests with plenty of shade. Close to the sea and with a private beach. The spacious pitches are marked out by small trees. First class comfort. Numerous water sports opportunities.

🚗 SP90 at exit to Aglientu and Vignola Mare. Entrance to the campsite direction Vignola Mare.

Luogosanto

SS133

CC € ⑲ 29/3-18/5 26/5-18/6 10/9-14/10

📡 N 41°7'28'' E 9°4'3''

Alghero, I-07041 / Sardegna

♿ 🛜 **iD** (3295)

🏕 Camping Village Laguna
Blu (Calik)****
🏖 SS 127 bis km 41 Fertilia
☎ +39 079-930111
📠 +39 079-930595
🗓 22/3 - 5/11
@ info@campinglagunablu.com
11ha 450T 8-10A CEE

1 ABCD**G**IJKLMOPQ
2 ABDEGKRSUVWXY
3 B**EF**HJKNRUVWY
4 (A 1/4-31/10) (Q+S+U+V 🗓) (W 20/4-31/10) (Y+Z 🗓)
5 **AB**CEFGIJKLMNOPUXYZ
6 ACDEG**K**(N 0,5km)ORSTUV WX

A large open campsite offering all amenities. One section is in pine woods and one section is open. Modern toilet facilities. 20 metres from the sea.

🚗 From Alghero direction Fertilia on the SS127bis at km 41 marker.

SS291
Olmedo

SS127BIS

Alghero

SS292

CC € ⑲ 22/3-6/7 3/9-4/11

📡 N 40°35'41'' E 8°17'29''

Alghero, I-07041 / Sardegna

🛜 **iD** (3296)

🏕 La Mariposa***
🏖 Via Lido 22
☎ +39 079-950480
📠 +39 079-984489
🗓 28/4 - 7/10
@ info@lamariposa.it

4ha 256T(80-90m²) 6A CEE

1 ABCDFIJKLMNOP
2 AEGIRSTVXY
3 KUWY
4 (A 15/7-31/8) (Q+S 🗓) (T 15/7-31/8) (V 1/6-30/9) (W 1/8-31/8) (Z 🗓)
5 AGIKMO**P**UW
6 CEGIJ(N 1,5km)OQRTV

💬 A city campsite located in a slightly hilly area with fields for tents. There are flat, open pitches for caravans and motorhomes. Some of them are located in the shade of the trees, others lie in the sun on the beach. You will find the toilets in a pleasant square. There are a lot of opportunities for water sports. Old excavations and Alghero are worth visiting.

🚗 The campsite is located on the seaward side of the road Alghero Centro-Fertilia. Follow the signs.

Olmedo

SS127BIS

Alghero

SS292

CC € ⑲ 28/4-29/6 1/9-6/10

📡 N 40°34'46'' E 8°18'45''

Cannigione di Arzachena, I-07021 / Sardegna ♿ 🛜 (3297)

🏕 Centro Vacanze Isuledda★★★★
✉ Loc. Isuledda
☎ +39 0789-86003
📠 +39 0789-86089
🔑 22/3 - 5/11
@ info@isuledda.it

15ha 650T(25-90m²) 4A CEE

1 BCDFHIJKLMNO**P**Q
2 AEGIJKLMNOQSTUVXY
3 ABKNRU**V**WY
4 (Q 26/3-30/11)
   (S+T+U+V+W+Y+Z 🔒)
5 **AB**GIJKLMNOPUV
6 EG**IJ**M(N 2km)OQRTV

💬 A beautiful campsite (15 hectares) on a bay with a private beach. Shaded pitches on gently sloping grounds. Restaurant, bar, shop, diving and sailing school and many watersports opportunities. Boat trips to La Maddalena Archipelago. Archaeological sights in the neighbourhood. A visit to Porto Cervo is most fascinating.

🚗 Route 125 from Olbia to Paula-Arzachena for 20 km, continue towards Cannigione. The campsite is located about 3 km past Cannigione.

La Maddalena

SS133 ㏄

Arzachena

SS125

㏄ € **19** 22/3-18/5 26/5-18/6 10/9-4/11   🧭 N 41°7'54'' E 9°26'26''

Cuglieri, I-09073 / Sardegna 🛜 (3298)

🏕 Camping Village Bella Sardinia★★★
✉ Torre del Pozzo
☎ +39 0785-38058
📠 +39 0785-389218
🔑 27/4 - 15/10
@ info@camping-bellasardinia.it

33ha 275T(40-100m²) 6A CEE

1 BCDFIJKLMO**P**
2 ABEGRSY
3 AB**F**GKMNQRUWY
4 (A+B+G+Q+S+V+W+Y+Z 🔒)
5 **AB**EFGIJKLMNOPUZ
6 CEGH**I**J(N 7km)OTVWX

💬 A very large campsite on sloping grounds, sufficiently shaded. Several sunny pitches. Free choice on unmarked pitches. Wide sandy beach and watersports opportunities. There is a bar/restaurant with a large terrace and a swimming pool. A visit to the excavations is highly recommended.

🚗 Route 292 between Cuglieri and Riola Sardo. Campsite signposted at exit post 109. Follow Bella Sardinia.

Santu Lussurgiu

SS292

㏄

㏄ € **17** 27/4-7/7 25/8-14/10   🧭 N 40°4'15'' E 8°29'40''

Is Aruttas/Cabras, I-09072 / Sardegna ♿ 🛜 🆔 (3299)

🏕 Is Aruttas★★★
☎ 📠 +39 0783-1925461
🔑 1/4 - 30/9
@ info@campingisaruttas.it

12ha 200T(60-100m²) 6A CEE

1 ABCD**G**IJKLMNOPQ
2 AEGJNTUVXY
3 BJKRY
4 (B+G 15/6-30/9)
   (Q 25/4-30/9) (R+T 🔒)
   (V 1/6-30/9) (Y 20/4-30/9)
   (Z 🔒)
5 **A**GIKMNOPUV
6 CEGJ(N 15km)O

NEW

💬 A very large terraced campsite about 200 metres from the sea. The spacious pitches are sheltered from the sun by straw screens. Large restaurant, pizzeria, bar and shop. An ideal starting point for visiting the famous excavations at Tharros.

🚗 Oristano-Cabras road. Continue west after Cabras. Campsite signposted.

SS292

Riola Sardo

㏄

Cabras

㏄ € **17** 1/4-29/6 1/9-29/9   🧭 N 39°56'57'' E 8°24'30''

Muravera, I-09043 / Sardegna

♦ ♿ 🛜 **iD** **3300**

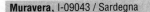

🔺 Torre Salinas***
📧 Loc. Torre Salinas
☎ +39 070-999032
🔑 1/4 - 31/10
@ info@
campingvillagetorresalinas.it

NEW

1,5ha 100T(90-100m²) 4A CEE

1 ACD**G**IJKLMO**P**Q
2 ABE**Q**RSUVY
3 ABGKL**M**RY
4 (Q+R+T+U+V+Y+Z ⌖)
5 **A**EGIJKLMNOPUVWZ
6 EG**I**J(N 7km)RU

💬 A campsite on slightly sloping grounds, with spacious, shady pitches marked out by trees. About 200 m from the sea with a wide sandy beach. The campsite offers all the comfort you could want.

San Vito Villaputzu

CC

SS125

🚐 SS125var, exit San Priamo. Then follow the signs.

CC € **17** 1/4-13/7 1/9-30/10

🧭 N 39°22'1'' E 9°35'47''

Palau, I-07020 / Sardegna

♿ 🛜 **iD** **3301**

🔺 Capo d'Orso****
📧 Loc. Le Saline
☎ +39 0789-702007
📠 +39 0789-702006
🔑 23/4 - 30/9
@ info@capodorso.it

13ha 450T(40-80m²) 3A CEE

1 ABCDFHIJKLMNOPQ
2 AEGJKOSTVXY
3 ABMNUWY
4 (A 1/7-31/8) (Q ⌖)
(S 15/5-15/9) (T ⌖)
(U 15/7-20/8) (V 30/5-15/9)
(W 15/7-20/8) (X 20/5-25/9)
(Y+Z ⌖)
5 **A**GIKMOPUV
6 CEGH**J**(N 5km)ORT

💬 A big campsite with a series of partially shaded terraces by the sea with a private beach. Ideal for practicing or taking various water sports lessons (surfing, diving). The facilities on the site are luxurious. Palau and the Maddalena Archipelago are well worth visiting. Only small dogs allowed.

La Maddalena

SS133BIS

CC

SS133   SS125

Arzachena

🚐 From Sta Teresa follow the panoramic road around Palau (is indicated!). From Cannigione follow Palau, site is signposted on the roundabout.

CC € **19** 23/4-6/7 3/9-29/9

🧭 N 41°9'41'' E 9°24'10''

Piscina Rei/Costa Rei, I-09043 / Sardegna

♿ 🛜 **iD** **3302**

🔺 Le Dune***
☎ +39 070-9919057
🔑 12/5 - 30/9
@ info@campingledune.it

6ha 180T(80m²) 3A CEE

1 ABCD**F**HIJKLMNO**P**Q
2 AEGRSUVWXY
3 BHK**M**NOU**W**Y
4 (**A** 15/6-30/9)
(**B**+**G**+Q+S+T+U+V+W+Y+Z
⌖)
5 **A**GIKMNOPUZ
6 CDEGH**J**(N 2km)RTV

💬 A level campsite with pitches marked out by poplar and plane trees. A footpath leading through a lagoon with water birds takes you to the beach.

SS125

CC

Castiadas

🚐 New road SS125var direction Muravera/Villasimius/Costa Rei, dir. Costa Rei (see brown sign). Follow signs to Le Dune.

CC € **19** 12/5-16/6 1/9-29/9

🧭 N 39°16'36'' E 9°34'56''

Porto San Paolo, I-07020 / Sardegna

♿ 🛜 **iD** **3303**

🔺 Tavolara***
✉ Soc. Ariel S.r.l. SS125 km 300
☎ +39 0789-40166
📠 +39 0789-480778
📅 28/4 - 15/10
@ info@camping-tavolara.it

5ha 260T(9-60m²) 3-10A CEE

1 ABCD**G**HIJKLMNOPS
2 AEIKLORSTUVWXY
3 ABK**M**NRW
4 (**A**+Q 🖦) (S 15/5-15/9)
(T+U+V+Y 1/5-30/9) (Z 🖦)
5 **A**GIJKMOPUVW
6 ACDEGJ(N 2km)ORTVWX

💬 A natural campsite, particularly in spring with many flowers and birds. Enclosed pitches with excellent views provided by many bushes and flowers. The beach with its views of the Tavolara rock is highly recommended. A 500 metre walk.

🚗 Located on the SS125 close to 300 km-marker.

Olbia

SS131D.C.N. CC

San Teodoro

CC € **19** 28/4-5/7 30/8-14/10   📐 N 40°51'33'' E 9°38'34''

Pula, I-09010 / Sardegna

🛜 **iD** **3304**

🔺 Flumendosa
✉ Flumendosa 12
☎ +39 070-4615332
📅 1/3 - 13/11
@ info@campingflumendosa.com

6ha 99T(40-60m²) 8A CEE

1 ABCDFHIJKLMO**P**R
2 ABEGLSTWXY
3 BGHJKVWY
4 (**A**+B+G 🖦) (Q 1/5-30/9)
(R+T+U+V+X+Z 🖦)
5 **A**GIJKLMNOPUZ
6 ABCEGJK(N 3km)OTW

💬 On the beach of Santa Margherita di Pula, a short distance from Chia, 5 minutes from the Phoenician town of Nora and only 30 km from Cagliari. Campsite Flumendosa is surrounded by unspoilt nature and the typical smells and colours of the Mediterranean Sea. An oasis of peace and relaxation. Enjoy the crystal clear sea a few metres from the campsite. All necessary amenities.

🚗 Campsite clearly signposted on the SS195, km-marker 33,8.

Domus de Maria CC

SS195

CC € **17** 1/3-29/6 1/9-12/11   📐 N 38°58'4'' E 8°58'41''

Santa Lucia/Siniscola, I-08020 / Sardegna

♿ 🛜 **iD** **3305**

🔺 Selema Camping***
✉ Thiria Soliana
☎ 📠 +39 0784-819068
📅 15/4 - 15/10
@ info@selemacamping.com

7,5ha 350T(30-120m²) 6A CEE

1 ABCDGHIJKLMNO**P**Q
2 ABCEGJKOSUY
3 ABK**M**NRWY
4 (B+G 15/6-15/10) **KP**
(Q+R+T+U+V 15/5-15/10)
(X 15/5-10/10) (Z 🖦)
5 **A**FGIJKMNOPUVWZ
6 ADEGIJ(N 0,3km)OTVWX

💬 A large campsite, partly level, partly sloping, partly terraced, in a pine forest by the sea. There are even trees halfway down the beach! The pitches are numbered. The campsite offers every comfort. There is a small village within walking distance. The sandy beach is ideal for families with (small) children.

🚗 From the SS125 take the S. Lucia exit at the 252 VIII km marker. Campsite signposted.

Posada

Siniscola CC

SS131D.C.N.

SS125

CC € **19** 15/4-29/6 1/9-14/10   📐 N 40°34'43'' E 9°46'23''

Torre Grande, I-09170 / Sardegna

△ Spinnaker****
▲ Strada per il Pontile
☎ +39 0783-22074
FAX +39 0783-22071
⏰ 1/5 - 30/9
@ info@spinnakervacanze.com

3,5ha 120T(40-90m²) 6A CEE

1 ABCD**G**HIJLMNO**P**
2 ABEGISTVUY
3 ABGNQRWY
4 (B+G+Q+S+U+V+Y+Z ⏰)
5 **A**EGIKMNOPUZ
6 ABCDEGJ(N 1,5km)OTV

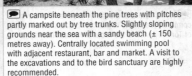

🗨 A campsite beneath the pine trees with pitches partly marked out by tree trunks. Slightly sloping grounds near the sea with a sandy beach (± 150 metres away). Centrally located swimming pool with adjacent restaurant, bar and market. A visit to the excavations and to the bird sanctuary are highly recommended.

🚕 SS131, exit Oristano N. Follow Tharros (brown sign on the big blue one). Then follow signs to Torre Grande. The campsite is signposted before Torre Grande.

3306

Cabras
SS131
CC **Oristano**

CC € **19** 1/5-29/6 1/9-29/9

⚘ N 39°54'14'' E 8°31'51''

Tortolì/Arbatax, I-08048 / Sardegna

△ Camping Village Orrì***
▲ Loc. Orrì
☎ +39 0782-624695
FAX +39 0782-624685
⏰ 1/5 - 30/9
@ orricamping@tiscali.it

3ha 100T(80m²) 4A CEE

1 ABCDFHIJKLNOP
2 AEGRSTUVXY
3 ABKLNRWY
4 (B+G 14/5-20/9) (Q ⏰)
   (S+U+V+X 1/6-10/9)
   (Z 20/5-15/9)
5 **A**FGIJKLMNOPUV
6 ACEGK(N 3km)TVX

🗨 The campsite is located 4 km from Arbatax harbour on the east coast of Sardinia on a large sandy beach, right next to the crystal clear sea. The campsite has a bar, mini-market, restaurant, pizzeria and swimming pool.

🚕 SS125 exit Tortolì/Lido di Orri; take Lido di Orri (turn right after 500 metres); follow the camping signs.

3307

Arzana **Tortolì**
CC
SS125

CC € **17** 1/5-29/6 1/9-29/9

⚘ N 39°54'24'' E 9°40'52''

Tortolì/Arbatax, I-08048 / Sardegna

△ Cigno Bianco***
▲ Loc. Orri
☎ +39 0782-624927
FAX +39 0782-624565
⏰ 25/4 - 25/10
@ info@cignobianco.it

4ha 100T(60-80m²) 6A CEE

1 ABCDFIJKLMOP
2 AEGSTUVWXY
3 ABK**M**RUWY
4 (Q+S+T+U 1/5-30/9)
   (V 1/6-30/9) (Y 1/5-1/10)
   (Z ⏰)
5 **A**GIJKMNOPUVZ
6 CEGJ(N 3km)OQRTV

🗨 A rectangular level campsite 300 metres long and 80 metres wide, shaded by tall trees with numbered but unmarked pitches. Washing facilities are centrally located. The site is right by the sea with a lovely sandy beach.

🚕 SS125 exit Tortolì/Lido di Orri; Follow Lido di Orri (right after 500 metres); follow camping signs.

3308

Arzana **Tortolì**
CC
SS125

CC € **15** 25/4-29/6 5/9-24/10

⚘ N 39°54'28'' E 9°40'45''

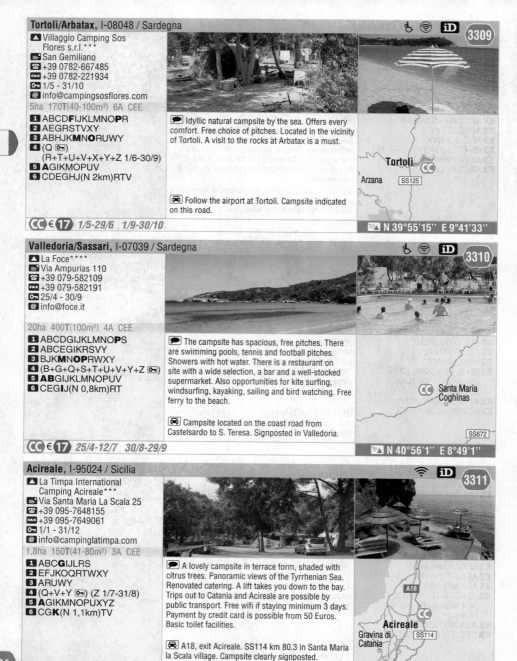

Tortolì/Arbatax, I-08048 / Sardegna

♿ 📶 iD (3309)

Villaggio Camping Sos
 Flores s.r.l.***
San Gemiliano
☎ +39 0782-667485
📠 +39 0782-221934
🗓 1/5 - 31/10
@ info@campingsosflores.com
5ha 170T(40-100m²) 6A CEE

1 ABCD**F**IJKLMNO**P**R
2 AEGRSTVXY
3 ABHJK**M**NO**R**UWY
4 (Q 🅿)
  (R+T+U+V+X+Y+Z 1/6-30/9)
5 **A**GIKMOPUV
6 CDEGHJ(N 2km)RTV

💬 Idyllic natural campsite by the sea. Offers every comfort. Free choice of pitches. Located in the vicinity of Tortolì. A visit to the rocks at Arbatax is a must.

🚗 Follow the airport at Tortolì. Campsite indicated on this road.

Tortolì
Arzana SS125

CC € **17** 1/5-29/6 1/9-30/10

📍 N 39°55'15'' E 9°41'33''

Valledoria/Sassari, I-07039 / Sardegna

♿ 📶 iD (3310)

La Foce****
Via Ampurias 110
☎ +39 079-582109
📠 +39 079-582191
🗓 25/4 - 30/9
@ info@foce.it

20ha 400T(100m²) 4A CEE

1 ABCDGIJKLMNO**P**S
2 ABCEGIKRSVY
3 BJK**M**NO**P**RWXY
4 (B+G+Q+S+T+U+V+Y+Z 🅿)
5 **AB**GIJKLMNOPUV
6 CEG**I**J(N 0,8km)RT

💬 The campsite has spacious, free pitches. There are swimming pools, tennis and football pitches. Showers with hot water. There is a restaurant on site with a wide selection, a bar and a well-stocked supermarket. Also opportunities for kite surfing, windsurfing, kayaking, sailing and bird watching. Free ferry to the beach.

🚗 Campsite located on the coast road from Castelsardo to S. Teresa. Signposted in Valledoria.

Santa Maria
Coghinas
SS672

CC € **17** 25/4-12/7 30/8-29/9

📍 N 40°56'1'' E 8°49'1''

Acireale, I-95024 / Sicilia

📶 iD (3311)

La Timpa International
 Camping Acireale***
Via Santa Maria La Scala 25
☎ +39 095-7648155
📠 +39 095-7649061
🗓 1/1 - 31/12
@ info@campinglatimpa.com
1,8ha 150T(41-80m²) 3A CEE

1 ABC**G**IJLRS
2 EFJKOQRTWXY
3 ARUWY
4 (Q+V+Y 🅿) (Z 1/7-31/8)
5 **A**GIKMNOPUXYZ
6 CG**K**(N 1,1km)TV

💬 A lovely campsite in terrace form, shaded with citrus trees. Panoramic views of the Tyrrhenian Sea. Renovated catering. A lift takes you down to the bay. Trips out to Catania and Acireale are possible by public transport. Free wifi if staying minimum 3 days. Payment by credit card is possible from 50 Euros. Basic toilet facilities.

🚗 A18, exit Acireale. SS114 km 80.3 in Santa Maria la Scala village. Campsite clearly signposted.

A18
Acireale
Gravina di SS114
Catania

CC € **17** 1/1-8/7 17/9-31/12 7=6, 14=12, 30=23

📍 N 37°37'12'' E 15°10'23''

Agrigento (San Leone), I-92100 / Sicilia   ♿ 🛜 🆔 3312

- 🏔 Valle dei Templi internaz. S.L.
- 🏠 Viale Emporium 192
- ☎ 📠 +39 0922-411115
- 🔓 1/1 - 31/12
- @ info@campingvalledeitempli.com

2ha 180T 6A CEE

1. ABCGIJKLMRS
2. AGJRTVWXY
3. K
4. (B 1/6-15/9) (X 1/4-30/10) (Z 1/5-30/9)
5. AGIKMOPUZ
6. CFGIK(N 0km)T

NEW

💬 A lovely campsite close to the Temple Valley. Simple pool. Enthusiastic management. Guided excursions on request, discount for ACSI guide users. Self-service bar with hot and cold drinks. Grounds with olive trees.

🚗 Around Agrigento head towards San Leone. Campsite is well signposted there (tip: it's also possible to follow signs to 'Valle dei Templi').

SS118   SS640   SS122

Agrigento

CC

SS115

CC € 19   1/1-14/7   1/9-31/12   🏕 N 37°16'10'' E 13°34'59''

Avola, I-96012 / Sicilia   ♿ 🛜 🆔 3313

- 🏔 Sabbiadoro
- 🏠 Via Chiusa di Carlo 45
- ☎ 📠 +39 0931-822415
- 🔓 1/1 - 31/12
- @ info@campeggiosabbiadoro.it

2,2ha 150T 10A CEE

1. ABGHIJKLNRS
2. AEFIJUY
3. KWY
4. (Q+R 🔓) (T 1/5-30/9) (V 15/5-30/9) (X 1/5-30/9) (Z 🔓)
5. AGIKMNOPUVZ
6. CFGK(N 4km)TW

💬 A gem of a campsite, situated in a tropical botanical garden on a beautiful sandy bay. Ideal for a visit to Siracusa, Noto, Cava Grande. Modern toilet facilities. Access can be difficult for caravans and motorhomes because of the narrow road.

🚗 New E45/A18 autostrada Catania-Gela exit Avola. About 700m left on the SS115. 500m narrow access road.

Canicattini Bagni

SS115

A18

CC

SS287   Avola

Noto

CC € 19   1/1-14/7   11/9-31/12   🏕 N 36°56'11'' E 15°10'29''

Catania/Ognina, I-95126 / Sicilia   ♿ 🛜 🆔 3314

- 🏔 Jonio***
- 🏠 Via Villini a Mare 2
- ☎ +39 095-491139
- 📠 +39 095-492277
- 🔓 1/1 - 31/12
- @ info@campingjonio.com

1,2ha 80T 6A CEE

1. ABCGIJKLNRS
2. EFGJKLOTWXY
3. BRUWY
4. (Q+R+T 🔓) (U 1/6-30/9) (V+Y+Z 🔓)
5. ABGIJKMNOPU
6. ACEGIK(N 3km)ORTV

💬 Beautifully located above the Ionian Sea. Wonderful swimming among the lava islands. Trips out to Catania, Etna, Syracuse and Taormina.

🚗 SS114 north of Catania, exit Ognina. From the Catania ring road, take exit Catania centro (San Gregorio) and then Catania Est. Campsite clearly signposted. On SatNav enter via Salvatare Quasimodo.

Acireale

A18

SS114

CC

Catania

CC € 17   1/1-14/7   1/9-31/12   7=6, 14=12, 30=20   🏕 N 37°31'58'' E 15°7'12''

Falconara/Sicula, I-92027 / Sicilia

🛜 iD (3315)

🔺 Eurocamping Due Rocche***
🚩 SS115 km 241,800
☎ +39 0934-349006
📠 +39 0934-349007
🔓 1/4 - 30/11
@ duerocche@duerocche.it

2,8ha 50T(40-75m²) 3A CEE

1 ABCGHIJKLMNRS
2 AEOWXY
3 ABGNRUWY
4 (Q+R 🔒) (T+U 1/7-31/8)
(V+Y 1/6-31/8) (Z 🔒)
5 AGIJKMNOPUV
6 AEG**K**(N 8km)ORTV

💬 A campsite by the sea with its own sandy beach. It has many loyal Italian guests who create a lively Sicilian atmosphere. The toilet facilities are outdated but well-maintained. Trips out to Agrigento (60 km) and Piazza Armerina (50 km) possible.

🚗 SS115 Gela direction Agrigento. The campsite is signposted with a large yellow sign on the SS115 at the km-marker 241.8.

Butera
SS644
Licata SS115 CC

CC € 17 1/4-14/7 1/9-29/11
📐 N 37°6'35'' E 14°2'19''

Fondachello/Mascali, I-95016 / Sicilia

♿ 🛜 iD (3316)

🔺 Mokambo**
🚩 Via Spiaggia 211
☎ +39 095-938731
📠 +39 095-7799243
🔓 1/4 - 30/9
@ mokambo@camping.it

2,8ha 180T(40-75m²) 3-6A CEE

1 ABCGHIJKLMNORS
2 EFGKNRSVWXY
3 BNRUWY
4 (Q+R 🔒) (T+U 1/7-31/8)
(V+Y+Z 🔒)
5 AGIKMOPUV
6 ACEG**K**(N 1km)ORTV

💬 An attractive unpretentious campsite right by the sea with wifi zone. Lovely pebble beach. Unique views of Etna. Good bar, restaurant and pizzeria. The campsite is located on the coast road.

🚗 A20, take exit Giarre, up to Riposto. Road parallel to sea became one-way in June 2016. You must come from Riposto and follow Via Torrente Vallonazzo in Carrabba and then Via Spiaggia in Sant' Anna.

A18
CC
Giarre
Zafferana
Etnea

CC € 17 1/4-30/6 1/9-29/9 7=6, 14=11
📐 N 37°44'58'' E 15°12'27''

Isola delle Femmine, I-90040 / Sicilia

🛜 iD (3317)

🔺 La Playa SRL**
🚩 Viale Marino 55
☎ 📠 +39 091-8677001
🔓 21/3 - 15/10
@ campinglaplaya@virgilio.it

2,2ha 80T(40-70m²) 6A CEE

1 ABGHIJKLMO**P**Q
2 AEFGKOSTVWXY
3 BWY
4 (Q+R+Z 1/4-30/9)
5 **AB**GIJKLMNO**P**UVZ
6 ACG**K**(N 0km)QRT

💬 A shaded, medium-sized campsite. Situated by the sea with well-maintained toilet facilities. Sometimes there is noise disturbance in the summer from the nearby disco. Payment by credit card is not possible under 100 Euros. Metro station to Palermo is close by.

🚗 A29, exit Isola delle Femmine. Better not use SatNav (too many one-way streets). Follow signs to campsite.

A29
CC
Palermo

CC € 17 21/3-30/6 1/9-14/10
📐 N 38°11'49'' E 13°14'39''

Letojanni, I-98037 / Sicilia ♿ 📶 iD (3318)

🏕 Paradise
🛏 SS114 km 41
☎ 📠 +39 0942-36306
🗓 1/4 - 15/10
@ campingparadise@
campingparadise.it

1,5ha 350T 6A CEE

1 ABCGHIJKLNRS
2 AEFGJSUVWXY
3 AGM NR V WY
4 (**B** 1/5-30/9)
(Q+S+T+U+V 1/4-30/9)
(W+X+Z 🔒)
5 AGIJKLMNOPUVXY
6 CEGJ(N 3km)TV

💬 Well maintained, modern campsite with wide private beach. Excellent toilet facilities. Located in an olive grove close to Taormina. Great for trips to Etna, Alcantara Gorges, Taormina, Catania, Acireale and much more.

🚗 A18 take exit Taormina (very busy). On SS114 after about 3km turn towards Messina. Campsite is on the SS114 at kilometre marker 41.

NEW

Antillo
SS114
CC
A18
SS185
Calatabiano

CC € **17** 1/4-29/6 3/9-14/10 | 🏔 N 37°53'51'' E 15°19'31''

Marsala, I-91025 / Sicilia ♿ 📶 iD (3319)

🏕 Camping Lilybeo Village
🛏 Contrada Bambina 131 Bbis
☎ +39 0923-998357
📠 +39 0923-986648
🗓 1/1 - 31/12
@ info@campinglilybeovillage.it

1ha 40T(50m²) 3A CEE

1 ABCD**F**IJKLMORS
2 GTVWXY
3 AGKNU
4 (B+Q 🔒)
5 AGIJKLMNOPUVW
6 E I K(N 0,3km)TV

💬 Small campsite with a quiet location outside the town of Marsala. Tripani airport is 20 km away. Great base for visiting many islands. Charming swimming pool was installed in 2016. Plants and trees ensure that the campsite is shaded and green.

🚗 On the SS115 (Mazara-Trapani) exit at km 38.5 by traffic lights, right coming from Mazara, left coming from Trapani. Beyond roundabout, 200 m on left.

Marsala
SS188
CC
SS115
A29

CC € **17** 1/1-14/7 1/9-31/12 | 🏔 N 37°44'52'' E 12°29'46''

Mazara del Vallo, I-91026 / Sicilia ♿ 📶 iD (3320)

🏕 Sporting Club Village &
Camping***
🛏 C. da Bocca Arena
☎ +39 0923-947230
📠 +39 0923-909569
🗓 15/3 - 15/10
@ info@sportingclubvillage.com

60ha 300T(80-110m²) 6A CEE

1 ABC**G**HIJKLMORS
2 AEFGRWX
3 BKMNQRUWY
4 (B+Q 1/6-30/9) (R 1/6-10/9)
(T 1/6-15/9) (V+Y 🔒)
(Z 1/4-30/9)
5 AGIKMNOPUVXZ
6 ACEG**K**(N 2km)ORTV

💬 Large campsite with lots of facilities and entertainment programme. Ideal for families with children and singles. Also for those who enjoy nature, sports, good food and everything else this region offers. A meeting place for different nationalities and cultures.

🚗 From Palermo: End of motorway A29, exit Mazara del Vallo. From Marsala: the SS115 becomes the A29 motorway. Take the Mazara exit where the roads change number. Campsite signposted after about 1 km.

SS115
Mazara del
Vallo
CC
A29

CC € **17** 15/3-7/7 25/8-14/10 14=11 | 🏔 N 37°38'11'' E 12°37'2''

Oliveri/Marinello, I-98060 / Sicilia

♿ 🛜 **iD** **3321**

🏕 Villaggio Marinello★★★★
📧 Località Marinello
☎ +39 0941-313000
📠 +39 0941-313702
🗓 1/3 - 15/11
@ villaggiomarinello@gmail.com

3,2ha 250**T**(40-75m²) 6A CEE

1 ABCGHIJKLMNORS
2 AEFKSVY
3 ABGKM**R**WY
4 (Q+S 1/3-31/10)
  (T+U+V+Y+Z 20/3-15/9)
5 **A**GIKMNOPUW
6 ACEGIK(N 1km)OQRTV

💬 Well run 4-star campsite with a pebble beach. Attractive marked out pitches among the trees. Sophisticated Sicilian gastronomy. Internet point and wireless internet available. Tyndaris and the Aeolian islands are close by.

🚗 A20, exit Falcone, then SS113 direction Palermo. Then follow the campsite signs and/or 'Laghetti Martinello'.

Barcellona Pozzo di Gotto

SS113 · A20 · SS185 · **CC**

CC € **19** 1/3-14/7 1/9-14/11 7=6 · 🏕 N 38°7'56'' E 15°3'16''

Punta Braccetto/S. Croce Cam., I-97017 / Sicilia

♿ 🛜 **iD** **3322**

🏕 Camping Luminoso★★★
📧 Viale dei Canalotti
☎ +39 0932-918401
📠 +39 0932-918455
🗓 1/1 - 31/12
@ info@campingluminoso.com

1,5ha 50**T**(< 65m²) 6A CEE

1 ABCDGHIJKLMNOR
2 AEUVY
3 ABHKRUVWY
4 (Q+S+Z 🗓)
5 **AB**GIJKLMNOP**S**UXZ
6 AEG**K**(N 5km)TUVW

💬 A campsite with private beach, fully renovated and reopened in 2009. Spacious and offering every comfort. Ideal for families and those seeking relaxation. Many sights in the area. Very attentive management.

🚗 Take the SS194 from Catania to Ragusa. Then take the SS514 to Ragusa. From Ragusa take exit towards S.Croce Camerina SP60. From S. Croce Camerina continue via the SP85 then SR25 to Punta Bracetto.

Scoglitti

CC

CC € **17** 1/1-5/7 1/9-31/12 7=6, 14=11 · 🏕 N 36°49'2'' E 14°27'57''

Punta Braccetto/S. Croce Cam., I-97017 / Sicilia

♿ 🛜 **iD** **3323**

🏕 Scarabeo Camping★★
📧 Via dei Canalotti
☎ +39 0932-918096
🗓 1/1 - 31/12
@ info@scarabeocamping.it

12ha 50**T**(50-70m²) 6A CEE

1 AB**G**HIJKLMNORS
2 AESUVY
3 ARUWY
4 (Q+R 🗓)
5 **AB**GIJKLMNO**P**STXYZ
6 ACEG**K**(N 3km)**P**QTUV

💬 Small, well-kept quiet campsite with lots of flowers and greenery. Spacious, marked-out pitches. Lovely sandy beach on the site. Private toilet facilities for every pitch. Atmospheric lighting. From 1 October to 31 March extra discounts with longer stays.

🚗 Coming from Comiso to Santa Croce. From there follow the signs 'Punta Braccetto' (4 km).

Santa Croce Camerina

CC

CC € **17** 1/1-30/6 1/9-31/12 · 🏕 N 36°49'2'' E 14°28'2''

Punta Secca/Santa Croce Camer., I-97010 / Sicilia

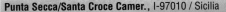

🔼 Capo Scalambri
📧 Via Torre di Mezzo,
   C.da Punta Secc
☎ +39 0932-915600
📠 +39 0932-616359
🔓 1/1 - 31/12
@ info@caposcalambri.com

5ha 150T(50-100m²) 6A CEE

1 ABGIJKLMOPRS
2 AESTUVY
3 BGKWY
4 (Q 1/6-31/8)
5 AGIKMOPUZ
6 CDEGJ(N 0,8km)T

3324

💬 This very modest campsite is set in natural surroundings. Free beach, shaded by trees. The site has limited and outdated toilet facilities. There is plenty of space and no noise.

🚗 From Comiso to Santa Croce Camerina, then continue to Punta Secca. Campsite is well signposted.

Scoglitti
Marina di Ragusa

CC €11 1/1-30/6 1/9-31/12   N 36°47'37'' E 14°29'24''

Ribera/Seccagrande, I-92016 / Sicilia

🔼 Kamemi Camping Village**
📧 Contrada Cam. Sup.
☎ 📠 +39 0925-69212
🔓 1/1 - 31/12
@ info@kamemivillage.com

4,8ha 50T(40-75m²) 6A CEE

1 ABCGHIJKLMNORS
2 RTVXY
3 ABGMNU
4 (B 15/5-10/9) (Q 🔓)
   (S 1/3-31/10)
   (T+U+V+W+Y 21/6-10/9)
   (Z 🔓)
5 AGIKMOPSTU
6 CEGJ(N 5km)QTV

3325

💬 A well-organised campsite with a large swimming pool. Enthusiastic campsite managers. Located close to the sea. Agrigento, Scala dei Turchi, Eraclea Minoa and Selinunte are all within easy reach. Substantial discounts if you stay longer.

🚗 From the SS115 (south coast) turn off at 142 km marker (follow signs).

Ribera
Montallegro
SS115

CC €17 1/1-14/7 1/9-31/12   N 37°26'21'' E 13°14'29''

San Giórgio, I-98063 / Sicilia

🔼 Il Cicero
📧 Lungomare Annarita Sidoti, 129
☎ +39 0941-39551
📠 +39 0941-39295
🔓 1/5 - 15/10
@ villaggiocicero@tin.it

2,5ha 144T(20-50m²) 8A CEE

1 ABCGHIJKLMNPRS
2 AEFKLSUXY
3 BRWY
4 (B+Q 🔓) (V 1/6-9/9)
   (Y 15/5-15/9) (Z 🔓)
5 AGIKMOPU
6 CEGJ(N 0,4km)T

3326

💬 The campsite stretches out along the blue Tirreno Sea opposite the Aeolian islands. The bungalow park in the tropical botanical gardens is separated from the friendly campsite. The village of San Giorgio is within walking distance.

🚗 A20 Messina-Palermo, exit Patti, 5 km direction Palermo on the SS113.

Gioiosa Marea
SS113 A20
Patti

CC €19 1/5-14/7 1/9-14/10 7=6, 14=11, 30=17   N 38°10'9'' E 14°56'56''

San Vito Lo Capo, I-91010 / Sicilia

♿ 📶 ✿ iD **3327**

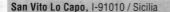

▲ El Bahira****
▤ Contrada Salinella
☎ +39 0923-972577
FAX +39 0923-972552
⌚ 1/1 - 31/12
@ info@elbahira.it

8ha 400**T**(25-65m²) 6A CEE

1 ABCGHIJKLMNOPQ
2 EGLNOQSTUVXY
3 ABGHJKMNUY
4 (A 🔌)
   (B+G+Q+S+T+U 1/4-10/10)
   (V 1/7-30/8) (W 1/4-30/9)
   (Y+Z 1/4-10/10)
5 **A**GIKLMNO**P**UVXYZ
6 AEGH**I**J(N 4km)OQRTV

💬 Large site with many amenities e.g. wonderful seawater pool. Beautiful location on north-west cape of Sicily, near 'Lo Zingaro' nature reserve and resort San Vito Lo Capo. Much attention given to landscaping and cosy little areas. Cyclists are very welcome (repairs done). Entertainment and folklore in summer.

🚐 From Palermo A29 dir. Trapani. Exit Castellammare del Golfo. Follow SS187. Follow San Vito Lo Capo between km-markers 18 and 17. Follow sign after km-marker 18.

San Vito Lo Capo
CC

CC € **17** 1/4-14/7 1/9-31/12 7=6, 15=12   📷 N 38°9'1'' E 12°43'54''

San Vito Lo Capo, I-91010 / Sicilia

📶 iD **3328**

▲ La Pineta****
▤ Via del Secco 90
☎ +39 0923-972818
FAX +39 0923-621382
⌚ 1/1 - 4/11, 1/12 - 31/12
@ lapineta@camping.it

3,2ha 200**T**(56m²) 10A CEE

1 ABCGIJKLMO**P**RS
2 AETUVY
3 BGHK**M**NRWY
4 (B 1/4-4/11) (G 5/4-1/10)
   (Q 🔌) (S 15/5-1/10)
   (V 1/6-30/9) (Y 1/4-15/10)
   (Z 🔌)
5 **A**GIJKLMNO**P**UXYZ
6 EGJSTV

💬 A very ambient and shaded campsite with two lovely swimming pools right by the sea. The restaurant is a culinary experience. This small campsite has many facilities and gained its fourth star in 2006. Free wifi.

🚐 A29 Palermo direction Trapani. Follow exit Castellammare del Golfo. Follow SS187 between km 18-17 San Vito Lo Capo.

San Vito Lo Capo
CC

CC € **17** 1/1-13/7 3/9-3/11 1/12-31/12 7=6   📷 N 38°10'26'' E 12°44'53''

Sant'Alessio Siculo/Taormina, I-98030 / Sicilia

♿ 📶 iD **3329**

▲ La Focetta Sicula**
▤ Contrada Siena 40
☎ +39 0942-751657
FAX +39 0942-756708
⌚ 1/1 - 31/12
@ info@lafocetta.it

1,2ha 120**T** 6A CEE

1 ABCGHIJLMNORS
2 AEFGKNRSXY
3 ANUWY
4 (A 9/8-23/8) (T 1/7-31/8)
   (Z 🔌)
5 **AB**GIJKMO**P**UV
6 CEGI**K**(N 0,002km)ORT

💬 A small, peaceful campsite, beautifully located on the Ionian Sea with a fine, black shingle beach. Basic accommodation located close to Taormina.

🚐 SS114, km 34 exit Sant'Alessio Siculo. The first campsite south of Messina. A18, exit Roccalumera.

Sant'Alessio Siculo
CC
A18
SS114
Taormina

CC € **17** 1/1-13/7 10/9-31/12 7=6, 14=11, 30=20   📷 N 37°55'54'' E 15°21'20''

Triscina di Selinunte/Castelv., I-91022 / Sicilia   🔌 📶 **iD** (3330)

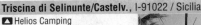

🏕 Helios Camping
🏠 Strada 1 n.271
☎ FAX +39 0924-84301
🔓 15/3 - 30/11
@ info@campinghelios.it

1,2ha 76**T**(35-50m²) 5A

1 ABG**I**JKL**P**RS
2 AEFLSUVXY
3 BGKRUWY
4 (B 15/6-15/9) (V 1/6-30/9)
   (X+Z 🔓)
5 A**I**JKLMNO**P**UV
6 CDEG**K**(N 1km)TV

💬 Camping Helios is located right by the sea and has a large sandy beach. It is 5 km from the archaeological site at Selinunte and 120 km from Palermo harbour. Check-in 24 hours a day is possible. Call 0924 84301/338 7322131 on arrival.

🚗 A29, exit Castelvetrano direction Selinunte (±3 km) and continue to Campobello di Mazara. Follow signs to Triscina. Campsite signposted from there.

NEW

Castelvetrano
A29   SS115
CC

CC € **17** 15/3-14/7   1/9-29/11   ▨▲ N 37°34'57'' E 12°46'10''

Place name index

745

Naturist camp sites

In this CampingCard guide you will find the following naturist camp sites or camp sites with a naturist section. Be aware that on most of these sites you will need to be a member of a naturist association.

🧖 Naturist camp sites

France